W9-BSI-583

HANDBOOK OF LATIN AMERICAN STUDIES No. 42

A Selective and Annotated Guide to Recent Publications in Art, Folklore, History, Language, Literature, Music, and Philosophy

VOLUME 43 WILL BE DEVOTED TO THE SOCIAL SCIENCES: ANTHROPOLOGY, ECONOMICS, EDUCATION, GEOGRAPHY, GOVERNMENT AND POLITICS, INTERNATIONAL RELATIONS, AND SOCIOLOGY

EDITORIAL NOTE: Comments concerning the *Handbook of Latin American Studies* should be sent directly to the Editor, *Handbook of Latin American Studies*, Hispanic Division, Library of Congress, Washington, D.C. 20540.

HANDBOOK OF LATIN AMERICAN STUDIES: NO. 42

HUMANITIES

Prepared by a Number of Scholars for the Hispanic Division of The Library of Congress

Edited by DOLORES MOYANO MARTIN

1980

UNIVERSITY OF TEXAS PRESS *AUSTIN*

International Standard Book Number 0-292-73016-0
Library of Congress Catalog Card Number 36-32633

Printed in the United States of America

First Edition, 1981

CONTRIBUTING EDITORS

HUMANITIES

Earl M. Aldrich, Jr., *University of Wisconsin, Madison*, LITERATURE
Jean A. Barman, *University of British Columbia*, HISTORY
Roderick J. Barman, *University of British Columbia*, HISTORY
Bruce-Novoa, *Yale University*, LITERATURE
David Bushnell, *University of Florida*, HISTORY
Edward E. Calnek, *University of Rochester*, HISTORY
D. Lincoln Canfield, *Southern Illinois University at Carbondale*, LANGUAGES
Carlos J. Cano, *University of South Florida*, LITERATURE
Donald E. Chipman, *North Texas State University, Denton*, HISTORY
Don M. Coerver, *Texas Christian University*, HISTORY
Michael L. Conniff, *University of New Mexico, Albuquerque*, HISTORY
Edith B. Couturier, *Chevy Chase, Md.*, HISTORY
Lisa E. Davis, *York College*, LITERATURE
Maria Angélica Guimarães Lopes Dean, *University of Wisconsin, Parkside*, LITERATURE
Ralph E. Dimmick, *General Secretariat, Organization of American States*, LITERATURE
Rubén A. Gamboa, *Mills College*, LITERATURE
Naomi M. Garrett, *West Virginia State College*, LITERATURE
Cedomil Goić, *The University of Michigan*, LITERATURE
Roberto González Echevarría, *Yale University*, LITERATURE
Richard E. Greenleaf, *Tulane University*, HISTORY
Oscar Hahn, *University of Iowa*, LITERATURE
Michael T. Hamerly, *Hebrew University, Jerusalem*, HISTORY
John R. Hébert, *Library of Congress*, BIBLIOGRAPHY AND GENERAL WORKS
Carlos R. Hortas, *Yale University*, LITERATURE
Ann Hagerman Johnson, *University of California, Davis*, HISTORY
Djelal Kadir, *Purdue University*, LITERATURE
Franklin W. Knight, *Johns Hopkins University*, HISTORY
David Lagmanovich, *Universidad Nacional de La Plata*, LITERATURE
Pedro Lastra, *State University of New York at Stony Brook*, LITERATURE
Asunción Lavrin, *Howard University*, HISTORY
James B. Lynch, Jr., *University of Maryland, College Park*, ART
Murdo J. MacLeod, *University of Arizona*, HSTORY
Wilson Martins, *New York University*, LITERATURE
Carolyn Morrow, *University of Utah*, LITERATURE
Gerald M. Moser, *Pennsylvania State University*, LITERATURE
Robert J. Mullen, *University of Texas, San Antonio*, ART
John V. Murra, *Cornell University*, HISTORY
José Neistein, *Brazilian American Cultural Institute, Washington*, ART
Betty T. Osiek, *Southern Illinois University at Edwardsville*, LITERATURE
José Miguel Oviedo, *University of California, Los Angeles*, LITERATURE
Margaret S. Peden, *University of Missouri*, LITERATURE
Vincent C. Peloso, *Howard University*, HISTORY

Humberto M. Rasi, *Inter-American Publications, Pacific Press*, LITERATURE
Daniel R. Reedy, *University of Kentucky*, LITERATURE
James D. Riley, *The Catholic University of America*, HISTORY
Eliana Rivero, *The University of Arizona*, LITERATURE
Alexandrino E. Severino, *Vanderbilt University*, LITERATURE
Nicolas Shumway, *Yale University*, LITERATURE
Merle E. Simmons, *Indiana University*, LITERATURE
Saúl Sosnowski, *University of Maryland, College Park*, LITERATURE
Hobart A. Spalding, Jr., *Brooklyn College*, HISTORY
Robert Stevenson, *University of California, Los Angeles*, MUSIC
Juan Carlos Torchia-Estrada, *General Secretariat, Organization of American States*, PHILOSOPHY
John Hoyt Williams, *Indiana State University*, HISTORY
Benjamin M. Woodbridge, Jr., *University of California, Berkeley*, LITERATURE
George Woodyard, *University of Kansas*, LITERATURE
Thomas C. Wright, *University of Nevada*, HISTORY
Winthrop R. Wright, *University of Maryland, College Park*, HISTORY

SOCIAL SCIENCES

Fuat Andic, *University of Puerto Rico, Río Piedras*, ECONOMICS
Suphan Andic, *University of Puerto Rico, Río Piedras*, ECONOMICS
R. Albert Berry, *University of Toronto*, ECONOMICS
William E. Carter, *Library of Congress*, ANTHROPOLOGY
Manuel J. Carvajal, *Nova University*, ECONOMICS
Lambros Comitas, *Columbia University*, ANTHROPOLOGY
Michael L. Cook, *Texas A&M University*, ECONOMICS
David Denslow, *University of Florida*, ECONOMICS
David W. Dent, *Towson State College*, GOVERNMENT AND POLITICS
Clinton R. Edwards, *University of Wisconsin, Milwaukee*, GEOGRAPHY
Everett Egginton, *U.S. Department of Health and Human Services*, EDUCATION
Robert C. Eidt, *University of Wisconsin, Milwaukee*, GEOGRAPHY
Gary S. Elbow, *Texas Tech University*, GEOGRAPHY
Clifford Evans, *Smithsonian Institution*, ANTHROPOLOGY
Yale H. Ferguson, *Rutgers University, Newark*, INTERNATIONAL RELATIONS
Kathleen B. Fischer, *University of California, Los Angeles*, EDUCATION
William R. Garner, *Southern Illinois University*, GOVERNMENT AND POLITICS
R. A. Halberstein, *University of Miami*, ANTHROPOLOGY
Norman Hammond, *Rutgers University*, ANTHROPOLOGY
Shirley Harkess, *University of Kansas*, SOCIOLOGY
Margaret Daly Hayes, *U.S. Senate Committee on Foreign Relations*, GOVERNMENT AND POLITICS
John R. Hébert, *Library of Congress*, BIBLIOGRAPHY AND GENERAL WORKS
Mario Hiraoka, *Millersville State College*, GEOGRAPHY
John M. Hunter, *Michigan State University*, ECONOMICS
John M. Ingham, *University of Minnesota*, ANTHROPOLOGY
Quentin Jenkins, *Louisiana State University*, SOCIOLOGY
W. Jerald Kennedy, *Florida Atlantic University*, ANTHROPOLOGY
Waud H. Kracke, *University of Illinois at Chicago Circle*, ANTHROPOLOGY
Dennis J. Mahar, *World Bank*, ECONOMICS
Markos Mamalakis, *University of Wisconsin, Milwaukee*, ECONOMICS
Tom L. Martinson, *Ball State University*, GEOGRAPHY
Betty J. Meggers, *Smithsonian Institution*, ANTHROPOLOGY
Andrew M. Modelski, *Library of Congress*, GEOGRAPHY
Lisandro Pérez, *Louisiana State University*, SOCIOLOGY

Foreign Corresponding Editors

Special Contributing Editors

CONTENTS

EDITOR'S NOTE

I. GENERAL TRENDS

In previous volumes, we noted the growing interest of European and other extrahemispheric scholars in Latin American studies, a trend exemplified by the 1978 meeting of SALALM in London where Europeans reviewed Latin American studies at their universities, and by the 1979 first interdisciplinary meeting of Latin Americanists held in Japan at Tsukuba University. The latest evidence of this interest is found in the prestigious French journal *Annales: Economies, Sociétés, Civilisations* which dedicated a double issue to the ethnohistory of the Andes. The 17 articles by French, British, US, Argentine, Chilean and Peruvian scholars will be published in English by Cambridge University Press and in Spanish by Editorial Crítica of Barcelona. Such French interest in ethnohistory notwithstanding, the lack of collaboration between anthropologists and historians of the Andes is lamented by one ethnohistorian (p. 135), while another attributes the decline of such collaboration in Mesoamerican studies, "a notably broad and open field until now," to the development of an unprecedented tendency towards specialization (see p. 127).

Social themes continue to dominate much of the history of this volume, with some commanding more interest than others. The decline in studies of European immigration and slavery, dominant in recent years, has coincided with the rise of interest in the study of women. In this volume women appear often, not only as the subjects of scholarship and literary works but as the authors of both. A historian regards as "noteworthy" the fact that out of three fine studies of the independence period, two were written by women (see p. 318). The role of the colonial woman in Mexico and Brazil is examined by a number of female scholars. Finally, several contributors to the literature section remark on the number of women writers and poets who have emerged in places such as Mexico, Costa Rica and Haiti.

There has also been an upsurge of interest in the role of the Catholic Church as a social force, one such history having been written with the avowed purpose of inspiring "a popular readership to social action" (see p. 405). The social theme to command the *least* attention from historians is the military in this century, a fact openly deplored by one contributor as inconsistent with the Latin American military's "central role in the polity" (see p. 407). The exploration of regional themes continues. One historian praises the growing sophistication and caliber of regional studies for colonial South America (see p. 279), another attributes the emergence of regional themes in the republican history of Peru to the opening of provincial archives (see p. 345), and a third asserts that the light shed on economic developments by studies of pre-industrial societies more than justifies the time needed for digging into such provincial archives (see p. 283). All of this would seem consistent with the emergence of historical demography as a separate discipline (see p. 283).

In folklore, the application of innovative methodologies to research, common in the US, is still fairly rare in Latin America. Examples of new approaches in folklore research by Latin Americans are found in the use of statistical methods to study Puerto Rican songs and in the examination of the social context of Peruvian riddles (see p. 75).

It is interesting to note how the urbanization process, one of the leading topics in the social sciences volume—Latin American cities being among the fastest growing in the world (see *HLAS 41*, p. xiii)—is perceived in the literature section of this volume. Many young poets and other writers regard urbanization as one of the chief evils of the age and a leading cause of the "de-Latinization" of Latin America, a prospect anticipated and lamented by the Uruguayan José Enrique Rodó at the turn of the century (see p. 520). The sense of loss of the uniqueness and pluralism of Latin American culture permeates much of the poetry and fiction of this volume and to an extent explains the sort of "cultural quest" exemplified by so many works of fiction devoted to the exploration of identities other than the indigenous ones (e.g., blacks, Jews, women, homosexuals, etc.).

The coming of age of Latin American criticism is noted in both the art and literature sections of this volume. In the past, the patronizing attitude of foreigners towards the modern art of Latin America provoked defensive and nationalistic responses among its artists and critics. Secure nowadays about world recognition of the region's art, critics and artists express their views more freely, including negative ones (see p. 49). The universal acclaim received by the literature of Latin America has exceeded the recognition granted to its art. Thanks to numerous and able translations into most European and other languages during the last 20 years (see p. 679 and *HLAS 40*, p. 517–518), Latin American writers have moved far beyond the Spanish-speaking orbit and become part of modern literature. No longer are their works perceived as marginal, exotic, or dependent on European models (see p. 469). Some criticis welcome this development noting that Latin American criticism, following in the wake of literature, has gained by having to compete with older and more established literary traditions (see p. 469). Other critics, however, deplore the concomitant overexposure and underresistance of Latin American criticism to the international winds of ideology and fashion that have resulted in interpretations that are often reductionist of or irrelevant to the region's literature (see p. 655). Indeed, the best works of literary criticism annotated in this volume follow the classical model of the traditional interpretative essay rather than fashionable trends exemplified by the theoretical (often linguistic) *crítica textual* or the ideological (often politicized) *crítica sociológica*. It is emphasized in this volume that the best results in criticism of Latin American literature are achieved in inverse proportion to the predominance of theoretical or ideological considerations (see p. 519 and p. 655).

II. REGIONAL TRENDS

Mexico

Mexico's leadership in the social sciences, noted in *HLAS 41* (see p. xiv), is also apparent in the humanities. In modern art, Mexican publications and scholarship surpass those of other countries, in both quality and quantity (see p. 49). Mexico also leads in the number of literary prizes and writing workshops, most of them government sponsored, that encourage publications by many young writers and poets (see p. 495). The nation is also noted for the application of innovative methodologies to the writing of social history (see p. 188). And finally, Mexico is the first country to publish the vocal score of an entire opera composed by a Latin American, the Mexican José Pablo Moncayo's *La mulata de Córdoba* (see p. 697).

Caribbean and Central America

In the Caribbean, Cuba continues to command the greatest interest and a crossdisciplinary study, *Cuba: order and revolution* by Jorge I. Domínguez, praised by the economist in the social sciences volume (see *HLAS 41:3058*), is hailed by the historian in this volume as among "the best" books "ever written" on the country (see item **2598**). In literature, it is observed that Cuba leads in the way of reprinting scarce 19th-century works and in interpreting the heritage of that period (see p. 489). According to one contributor, Cuba's concentration on its literary past could help explain "the lack of more vigorous works by young writers who must eventually replace Carpentier and Lezama Lima" (see p. 513).

The political turbulence and warfare of Central America have inhibited publishing, especially in El Salvador and Guatemala and, to an extent, in Nicaragua where two topics, the Sandinista victory and the overthrow of the Somoza dynasty, monopolize the publishing industry. Exceptions to this trend are Panama and Costa Rica. In Panama, the Canal question continues to generate the most interest, although the flood of publications noted in *HLAS 41* (see p. xiv) has abated. In Costa Rica, historians continue to lead as the most sophisticated in Central America, combining archival research with imaginative manipulations of data (see p. 245). Moreover, the number of Costa Rican women who have achieved recognition as poets and other writers in recent years is a further indication of the freedom and vigor of the nation's intellectual life (see p. 508).

Andean Countries

In *HLAS 41* we noted that Venezuela had made notable progress in economic research but that the country lagged behind in other fields of the social sciences. This lag is also apparent in the humanities. For example, very little of consequence has appeared on the country's contemporary history (1830–present) despite exhortations by the National Academy of History and specific allocations of petroleum revenues. This deficiency is attributed to the lack of training in modern methodology of most young historians, to the relative inaccessibility of archival materials, and to the fact that there are no major publishing houses in the country that stimulate and promote the writing of modern history (see p. 331). Likewise in literature, contributors deplore the lack of good anthologies of contemporary Venezuelan poetry and the scarcity of scholarship on the subject (see p. 566). Some good works of fiction have appeared, chiefly political novels on the archetypal figure of the *caudillo* and on the question of oil (see p. 520). In contrast, Colombia, a research mecca in the social sciences, also leads in the humanities. The outstanding work of modern history published in this biennium is Marco Palacio's *Coffee in Colombia: 1850–1970* (see item **2989**). Like the above-mentioned book on Cuba by Domínguez, Palacio's work sets high standards in interdisciplinary study and constitutes an "extraordinary account of the impact of coffee upon merchants, landowners, laborers and politicians" (see p. 333). There is also much praise in this volume for the quality of Colombian poetry, fiction and literary scholarship (see p. 519). In Ecuador, there has been a remarkable increase in the publication of poetry, largely sponsored by the Casa de la Cultura Ecuatoriana. A similar institution in Bolivia, the Casa Municipal de la Cultura Franz Tamayo, also plays a leading role in the publishing and promotion of Bolivian poetry. With regard to the modern history of Bolivia, this volume records an astonishing increase of 60 percent more works on the subject than did *HLAS 38* and *HLAS 40* (see p. 361).

In the three previous volumes (*HLAS 38*, *HLAS 39* and *HLAS 40*) historians, literary critics, and social scientists remarked on the notable improvement in the quality and quantity of publications issuing from Peru. Especially apparent in modern history, this trend is attributed to historical anniversaries and political events of the last two years (e.g., the Centennial of the War of the Pacific; the end of military rule; the election of a constitutional government; the death of the grand old man of Peruvian politics, Haya de la Torre; etc.) that have stimulated a number of important studies (see p. 344). In literature, it is also noted that "some of the most interesting and varied work has come out of Peru during these two years" (see p. 520). With regard to Chile, the flood of works on the history of Allende years, the 1973 coup and its aftermath, continues but at a diminished rate and in a more reflective vein. Although there is a similar decline of interest in the rise and fall of Allende as a topic in Chilean literature, the most important novel published in the last two years, José Donoso's *Casa de campo*, says much about the social and political context of Chilean life (see item **5462**). Nevertheless, both contributors to the Chilean fiction and poetry sections of this volume lament the depression of the Chilean publishing industry, once among the liveliest in Latin America (see p. 539 and p. 564).

The River Plate Countries

The marked decline in the number of works on Argentina's two perennial historical controversies—19th-century Rosas and 20th-century Perón—has been offset by rising interest in several new topics (e.g., the yellow fever epidemic of 1871, the Welsh settlement of Patagonia, Tucumán's sugar industry, the fate of Buenos Aires' Afro-Argentines, etc.). Recent literary works continue to manifest the concern of Argentine writers with "fiction as pure language, pure texture" (see p. 545) and, not surprisingly, Borges is the commanding topic in literary criticism (see p. 545 and p. 564). With regard to Paraguay, three major monographs have appeared on the country's history but all three written in English by Americans. In Uruguay, historical research remains "at a virtual standstill" (see p. 381) and the country's foremost poet, Mario Benedetti, continues to write from exile (see p. 564).

Brazil

Together with Mexico, Brazil leads in the humanities and social sciences. The relaxation of censorship, sanctioned by Brazil's military rulers, has encouraged a new climate of openness and free discussion which favors the public examination of issues as well as the portrayal of controversial themes in the arts. The latter is especially apparent in Brazilian literature. Topics such as political repression and the politically-committed character have reappeared in fiction (see p. 626). In Brazil, where verse has always been produced in what one contributor describes as "industrial quantities" (see p. 639), the poetry of social protest is now much in vogue. Manifestations of the latter range from the amateur to the sophisticated to the unexpected as in the protest poetry of an immigrant bishop (see item **6234**). Concern about possible censorship in Brazilian history is, in the words of one historian, "not warranted simply because of the multiplicity and diversity of government organizations" (see p. 405). The latter fact is exemplified by the active publication program of the Brazilian Congress which has stimulated interest in congressional history and demonstrated the value of the Brazilian House and Senate as "political institutions and their independence from the Executive" (see p. 405). Indeed, the vigor of Brazilian historical studies is evident in the rising volume of graduate theses of "high quality and originality" (see p. 405). Likewise, a number of outstanding works have appeared on the nation's contemporary art (see p. 60), and Brazil is the first Latin American country to produce the most complete lexicography of its music in an excellent two-volume encyclopedia on the subject (see item **7048**).

III. SPECIAL DEVELOPMENTS

Established in April 1978, the Hispanic Acquisitions Project of the Library of Congress has become an invaluable asset to the *Handbook of Latin American Studies* (see *HLAS 41*, p. xvi). It continues to add important new research publications from Latin America to the Library's collections. In 1980–81, there was a notable increase in receipts from Mexico, where both the federal and state governments have greatly expanded their publishing programs. In the Caribbean basin, over 100 monographs were acquired from Surinam, a country that was not well covered in previous *HLAS*. In 1981–82, the Project will intensify its efforts in the French- and Dutch-speaking Caribbean, Panama and the River Plate countries.

IV. CHANGES IN VOLUME 42

Film and/or Folklore

In *HLAS 40* (see p. xii) we noted that space limitations had prompted us to alternate the sections on Film and Folklore in the Humanities volume so that each would appear every four instead of every two years. *HLAS 40* carried the last section on Film (see p. 57–68). This volume, *HLAS 42*, includes a section on Folklore prepared by Merle E. Simmons. The next Film section will appear in *HLAS 44*, scheduled for publication in the fall of 1983.

History

James D. Riley (The Catholic University of America) collaborated with Donald E. Chipman in the General section. Michael L. Conniff (University of New Mexico, Albuquerque) joined Roderick J. and Jean A. Barman in preparing the section on Brazil. As of this volume 42, all materials on the Spanish Borderlands of Florida and Louisiana will appear in The Caribbean and the Guianas section instead of in the one devoted to Mexico: Colonial Period which was the case until *HLAS 40*. The reasons for the change are set forth in the introduction to the latter section (see p. 188). Also, works on 19th- and 20th-century Ecuador will be annotated together with Colombia and Venezuela (see p. 331) instead of with Peru as in *HLAS 40*.

Literature

The growing volume and sophistication in the criticism of contemporary Latin American literature and the new interest in the novel and other prose writings of the 19th century have prompted the reorganization of the literature section of this volume. Instead of one general subsection for both the 19th and 20th centuries, there are now four subsections organized as follows: 1) *General*; 2) *Colonial*; 3) *Prose Fiction of the 19th Century*; and 4) *Prose Fiction of the 20th Century*. The first or *General* section precedes all of Literature and offers a broad perspective. Prepared by Roberto González-Echevarría (Yale University), it will note new trends in criticism, identify individuals, schools or journals that affect or reflect these trends, and discuss the emergence, disappearance or permanence of certain values and concepts. The second or *Colonial* section which was formerly first, has not changed in content, only in order of precedence. It will continue to cover all colonial works (fiction, prose, poetry, drama, criticism and history), as has been customary in *HLAS*. The third section or *Prose Fiction and other Prose Writings of the 19th Century*, prepared by Nicolas Shumway (Yale University), will note the reissue of significant 19th-century prose works and cover the growing volume of criticism and history of the prose fiction and other prose writings of this period. The poetry and drama of the 19th century will continue to appear in the respective Poetry and Drama subsections, as has been customary in *HLAS*. Likewise, the third and largest section, *Prose Fiction of the 20th Century*, will continue to be subdivided according to geographic region, as in previous volumes.

The following new editors worked on *Prose Fiction of the 20th Century*: Lisa Davis (York College) was responsible for Central America; Carlos J. Cano (University of South Florida) collaborated by preparing Cuba and the Dominican Republic for the Hispanic Caribbean; and Saúl Sosnowski (University of Maryland, College Park) reviewed all critical writings for Argentina, Paraguay and Uruguay. David Lagmanovich (Universidad de La Plata, Argentina) annotated all of the poetry of the River Plate countries for the Poetry section. George Woodyard (University of Kansas) assumed responsibility for the Drama section.

Subject Index

The policy of the *HLAS* Subject Index is to use the Library of Congress Subject Headings as much as possible, but, when necessary, to adapt them to terms that predominate in the literature as familiar and useful ones to Latin Americanists. In this volume, geographic index terms have been expanded to include not only regions and countries as customary in the past but provinces and cities as well. Geographic terms are cross-referenced to smaller and larger geographic entities (e.g., PERU. *See also* the cities of Arequipa, Cuzco, Lima; the departments of Chancay, Junín, Puno; the regions of Amazonia, Andean Region; South America). The geographic terms are broken down according to the disciplines covered by this volume. It is hoped that increased cross-referencing of subject and geographic terms will facilitate the use of this index for beginner and specialist alike.

Numbering

The numbering system adopted in *HLAS 40* (see p. xii) has been changed. As of *HLAS 42*, the block numbers for the humanities are:

Bibliography and General Works	1–250
Art	251–950
Folklore	951–1500
History	1501–4500
Language	4501–5000
Literature	5001–7000
Music	7001–7500
Philosophy	7501–8000

Other Changes

Changes in the editorial staff of the *Handbook*, the administrative officers of the Library of Congress, and membership of the Advisory Board are reflected in the title page of the present volume.

Dolores Moyano Martin

Washington, December 1980

HANDBOOK OF LATIN AMERICAN STUDIES No. 42

BIBLIOGRAPHY AND GENERAL WORKS

JOHN R. HÉBERT, *Hispanic Division, Library of Congress*

DURING THE PAST YEAR, an endless stream of wide-ranging publications of interest to this section were received at the Library of Congress. Materials such as national, subject, and collective bibliographies, works of reference as well as on library science and general topics, collection and acquisition studies, and many new serial titles were canvassed for review. There were a number of fine contributions and impressive works among them that were selected for annotation. And of the latter, items encompassing broad themes, facilitating the study of Latin America, and describing collections, materials and depositories are specifically mentioned in this essay.

National bibliographies that are useful to the researcher in Latin American studies are noted for their infrequent and tardy publication. Usually, accessions lists or partial bibliographies from a National Library or a major research center may appear but timely information on recent publications is rarely available in a single compendium and more likely scattered throughout unrelated sources. Noteworthy exceptions to this phenomenon are the national bibliographies of several nations: the *Anuario Bibliográfico Uruguayo, 1978* (item **13**); *The National Bibliography of Barbados, 1978* (item **23**); *Trinidad and Tobago: National Bibliography, 1978* and *1979* (items **25–27**); and the *Anuario Bibliográfico Ecuatoriano, 1976* and *1977* (item **12**). The effort of the Cuban National Library to compile a national bibliography for the years 1921–36, reported in *HLAS 41* (see p. 3) was completed with the publication in 1979 of the bibliography for the years 1933–36 (item **15**).

The publication of research aids that further the understanding of Latin American subjects is of importance to this section of *HLAS*. Of even greater importance, however, are extra-hemispheric publications which reflect the interest of other areas of the world in the region. This is exemplified by the increasing number of Japanese studies on Latin America such as the *Bibliografía de publicaciones japonesas sobre América Latina en 1978* (item **36**) which lists nearly 400 books and articles. The sophistication and extent of Latin American studies in Europe is evident in the fine review and guide to nearly 100 programs prepared by Carmelo Mesa Lago (item **153**). Insofar as Latin American studies in the US are concerned, Donald Shea and Maureen Smith offer an edited account of the comments and discussion of the program directors who met in Feb. 1979 in Racine, Wisconsin for the Wingspread Conference (item **189**).

A number of well conceived guides to historical research appeared in the past three years. Lyman DePlatt's *Genealogical historical guide to Latin America* (item **133**) and Thomas Barnes *et al.*, *Northern New Spain: a research guide* (item **121**) provide assistance to those beginning or currently engaged in researching the social history of the colonial period. The Barnes guide provides basic information on the US Spanish Southwest and is intended to facilitate research in the Documentary Relations of the Southwest Project File at the Arizona State Museum. The latter work is complemented by Henry P. Beers' *Spanish and Mexican Records of the American Southwest* (item **122**) which describes materials on Arizona, California, New Mexico, and Texas in US institutions. Jane Garner's *Archives and manuscripts on microfilm in the Nettie Lee Benson Latin American Collection: a checklist* notes holdings of over 5300 reels, mainly from US, Mexican and British archival sources and primarily related to Mexico (item **91**).

A fine group of varied subject bibliographies and reference works have also been published. The most noteworthy are the following: the first two volumes of Nicólas Matijevic's planned six of a *Bibliografía patagónica y de las tierras australes* (item **53**); William Davidson's *Geographical research in Latin America* which identifies over 800 master and doctoral theses in geography completed at US universities (item **42**); William Sullivan's *El petróleo en Venezuela* which consists of an extensive bibliography on the technical, economic, judicial, sociological, historical, and polemical aspects of the subject (item **66**); Jorge Morales Gómez' bibliography on Colombian folklore which covers publications prior to 1974 (item **54**); Bolivar Lamounier and Maria D'Alva Gil Kinzo's list of works on Brazilian politics, party organizations and recruitment, electoral strategies, and party attitudes entitled *Partidos políticos, representação e processo eleitoral no Brasil: 1945–1978* (item **48**); Reece Bothwell González' *Puerto Rico: cien años de lucha política*, which contains copies of political party documents for Puerto Rico since 1869 (item **124**); Roger Cunniff's bibliography *Popular culture in Latin America* (item **59**); and Michael Meyer's completed *Supplement to a bibliography of United States-Latin American relations since 1810* (item **67**) which provides 3500 additional citations to the 1968 work by Meyer, Trask, and Trask, *A Bibliography of United States-Latin American relations since 1810*.

Bertie Cohen Stuart's *Women in the Caribbean* (item **39**) and Donald Herdeck's *Caribbean Writers* (item **127**) provide specific coverage of the region. The latter contribution is a bibliographical encyclopedia on 2000 English, French, Spanish and Dutch Caribbean writers. Complementing Herdeck's study is Richard L. Jackson's annotated *The Afro-Spanish American author: an annotated bibliography of criticism* (item **46**) which identifies the works and published criticism of them for 25 major Afro-Spanish American writers. The identification of African influence in Latin America is further noted in Benjamín Núñez' valuable *Dictionary of Afro-Latin American civilization* (item **157**).

The publication of a guide to collections or an index to periodicals is always a welcome event for the researcher. This body of literature was enriched by the appearance of the following: the Organization of American State's *Index to Latin American Periodical Literature, 1966–1970* (item **158**) which continues the eight-volume compilation of the publication for 1929–65; the *HAPI: Hispanic American Periodical Index, 1977* edited by Barbara C. Valk (item **140**); and Beatriz Martínez de Cartay's *Catálogo de publicaciones oficiales; 1840–1977* which covers over 3850 Venezuelan governmental official publications in the Venezuelan National Library (item **117**). The Mexican Archivo General de la Nación has produced a multi-volume *Catálogo de ilustraciones* (item **105**) which contains descriptions and photographic reproductions of maps, plans, and drawings in the archive; we have reviewed two volumes in this section and have seen references to four or five additional ones of this important work. The effort of the Costa Rican National University and the Organization of American States' Library Development Program to establish a centralized cataloguing center in Central America is reported in the papers and minutes of a meeting on the subject held in San José in Dec. 1979 (item

86). The continuing body of collection literature has been enhanced by the appearance of the Institute of Jamaica's six-volume *Catalogue of the West India Reference Library* which identifies books, pamphlets, and periodicals catalogued by the Institute before 1976 (item **104**); and the seven-volume *Bibliografía argentina: catálogo de materiales argentinos en las bibliotecas de la Universidad de Buenos Aires* (item **95**) which comprises approximately 110,000 author cards for books and pamphlets found in 17 central and 56 departmental libraries of the University of Buenos Aires' faculties, school, and institutes for works published from the oldest work to the last items received in 1979.

We continue in this volume the practice, instituted in *HLAS 41:158–171*, of devoting one subsection to a "List of New Serial Titles." While it is impossible to provide a complete list of all new titles that have appeared or have been received, we have included the most significant ones we found.

GENERAL BIBLIOGRAPHIES

1 **Bibliografía:** obras de autores nacionales. Asunción: Ministerio de Educación y Cultura, Instituto Superior de Educación, 1980. 21 p.

Alphabetical listing of 335 contemporary monographs by Paraguayan authors. Subjects of works vary widely.

2 *Bibliographie d'Articles des Revues: Novembre 1979–Juillet 1980.* Institut des Hautes Études de l'Amérique Latine. Centre de Documentation. No. 9, nov. 1980– . Paris.

Contains citations from 201 journals related to Latin American studies; specific sections are devoted to each Latin American nation and special sections appear for citations on developing countries, and general Latin America, Central America and the Caribbean.

3 *Bibliography of the English-Speaking Caribbean.* Books, articles and reviews in English from the arts, humanities, and social sciences. Vol. 1, Nos. 1/2, 1979– . Iowa City, Iowa.

An ongoing serial (edited by Robert J. Neymeyer) which will list published works in English from North America, Europe, and the Caribbean that relate to the arts, humanities, and social sciences. It does not list travel guides, cookbooks, school textbooks, juvenile literature or popular fiction, or works not relating to the region by Caribbean authors. Future issues promise a list of papers on Caribbean subjects presented at scholarly conferences; information on future conferences; bibliographical essays and short reviews of new books from the Caribbean. This issue is limited to material published in 1978; future issues will be even more current. Publications are indexed by country. Subscriptions are available through Robert Neymeyer, Editor, Box 1833, Iowa City, Iowa 52244.

4 **Jones, David Lewis.** Paraguay: a bibliography. New York: Garland Publishing, 1979. 499 p. (Garland reference library of social sciences; 51)

This selectively annotated listing of more than 4500 articles and monographs related to Paraguay is divided into 15 subjects. Works appear in alphabetical order in each subject except for literature in which works and criticism appear under each author. Scientific works are generally excluded. Articles from more than 300 journals appear. Includes author/subject index.

5 **Lovera de Sola, R.J.** Guía de fuentes generales sobre Venezuela: pt. 1 (Libros al Día [Caracas] 4:52, dic. 1979, p. 31–41)

This initial listing of general bibliographies and reference works on Venezuela is the basis for Lovera de Sola's future *Manual para la investigación venezolana.* Contains citations of monographs, articles, and pamphlets, with selected annotations, through letter B. Future issues of the publication will appear in *Libros al día.*

6 **Medellín,** *Colombia.* Universidad de Antioquia. Departamento de Bibliotecas. Centro de Documentación. Indice latinoamericano de ciencias sociales y humanidades, 1970–1973. Bogotá: División de Documentación e Información, Banco Nacional de Analíticas, 1978. 3 v. (876 p.)

Presents 5789 journal citations, in subject arrangement, from issues of 460 journal titles issued between 1970–73. Includes author index and list of articles published in Latin American journals related to non-Latin American topics.

7 **Nagelkerke, Gerard A.** Suriname: a bibliography, 1940–1980. Leiden, The Netherlands: Royal Institute of Linguistics and Anthropology, Department of Caribbean Studies, 1980. 336 p.

This selected bibliography lists 2600 titles, monographs and articles, of the nearly 5080 titles on the subject in the Royal Institute's collection. Publications appear in alphabetical order by author. A list of periodicals consulted and a subject/personal names index are included. Dutch language entries are translated into English.

8 **Oltheten, Theo M.P.** Inventory of Caribbean studies: an overview of social scientific publications on the Caribbean by Antillean, Dutch and Surinamese authors in the period 1945–1978/79. Leiden, The Netherlands: Royal Institute of Linguistics and Anthropology, Department of Caribbean Studies, 1979. 280 p.

Attention of bibliography is focused on French Guiana, Surinam, Guyana, coastal regions of South and Central America, Belize and the Caribbean. Majority of publications are in sociology, psychology and education. Includes English translations of Dutch titles. Entries are arranged in alphabetical order with access provided through separate subject indexes for Netherland Antilles, Surinam, Antilleans and Surinamese in The Netherlands, and general Caribbean topics. Lists of authors and periodicals appear.

9 **Piedracueva, Haydée.** Annual report on Latin American and Caribbean bibliographic activities, 1980. Madison, Wis.: SALALM Secretariat, 1980. 49 p. (XXV SALALM working paper; A-2) (mimeo)

Presented at the 25th meeting of the Seminar on the Acquisition of Latin American Library Materials in Albuquerque, this work lists 426 publications related to the theme of Latin American bibliographies, e.g., national, trade, personal, general and subject, and catalogs and bulletins of libraries and archives, issued in the past year. Contains a list of works in progress and includes subject and author indexes.

10 **Robinson, Barbara J.** and **J. Cordell.** The Mexican American: a critical guide to research aids. Greenwich, Conn.: JAI Press, 1980. 287 p. (Foundations in library and information science; 1)

Lists 668 annotated citations to articles, monographs, and other publications that serve as bibliographies and research aids related to the study of the Mexican American. This selected listing contains chapters devoted to general works and to specific subjects, e.g., education, folklore, history, labor, linguistics, literature, social and behavioral sciences and women. Includes separate author, title, and subject indexes. Each chapter is preceded by an introductory essay.

11 **Woods, Richard D.** Reference materials on Latin America in English: the humanities. Metuchen, N.J.: The Scarecrow Press, 1980. 639 p.

A selected list of 1252 annotated items in English that serve as reference works on Latin America. Items are presented in alphabetical order by author with access through subject, author, and title indices provided. Includes bibliographies, dictionaries, guidebooks, handbooks, directories, collective biographies, catalogs, indexes, encyclopedias, etc. Excludes references to items on British and Dutch cultures or non-Latin colonies in the New World. The Latin American reference collection at the University of Texas was primary source for data.

NATIONAL BIBLIOGRAPHIES

12 *Anuario Bibliográfico Ecuatoriano 1976 y 1977 y Bibliografía Ecuatoriana.* Universidad Central del Ecuador, Biblioteca General, Editorial Universitaria. Nos. 8/9, 1978– . Quito.

Records separate Ecuadorian titles for 1976 and 1977. Includes monographic and periodical titles and indexes for titles, subjects, institutions, and general categories. More than 800 citations appear; selected titles are abstracted. A valuable bibliographic and acquisition tool.

13 *Anuario Bibliográfico Uruguayo de 1978.* Biblioteca Nacional. 1979– Montevideo.

Lists over 1000 monographs and 600 serial titles published in Uruguay during the year. Monographs are arranged by subject. Includes author index (for monographs), subject index to periodicals, books of foreign authors published in Uruguay, and periodical publications published in Uruguay edited by foreign and international institutions.

14 **Bibliografía cubana,** 1921–1936: 1929–1932. La Habana: Biblioteca Nacional José Martí [and] Editorial Orbe, 1979. 212 p.

In its continuing effort to complete the gap from 1917–36 existing in the Cuban national bibliography, this new installment for the period 1929–32 has been produced. An analytical index to the 2025 entries enhances the use of the volume.

15 **Bibliografía cubana,** 1921–1936: 1933–1936. La Habana: Biblioteca Nacional José Martí [and] Editorial Orbe, 1979. 167 p.

A list of 1689 titles appear in this final volume in the effort to provide bibliographic record of Cuban publications from 1917–36. Analytical index provides access to the material in the volume.

16 *Bibliografía cubana: 1975*. La Habana: Biblioteca Nacional José Martí, 1976. 391 p.

Identifies 2476 books, pamphlets, posters, exhibit catalogs, cinema, recordings, stamps, and new serials appearing in 1975. Varied format material appear in separate chapters with each including title, author/subject, and series indexes.

17 *Bibliografía cubana: 1977*. La Habana: Biblioteca Nacional José Martí, 1979. 431 p.

Lists various materials published in Cuba during 1976 and 1977. In addition to the usual listing of books, pamphlets, journals, posters, exhibit catalogs, cinema, recordings and postage stamps, a list of cartographic materials for the period 1959–1977 appears.

18 **Bibliografía nacional** en curso, 1977 (PEBN/B, 21/22:73/76, 1975/1976, p. 63–87)

Lists mainly current (i.e., 1977) publications, monographs and articles, on Peru or by Peruvians. Citations are presented in Dewey Decimal classification order.

19 **A bibliography of books** on Belize in the National Collection. 4. ed. Belize City: Central Library, Bliss Institute, 1977. 102 p.

A listing in classified arrangement of material on Belize or works written by Belizeans. Separate author and title indexes supplied.

20 **A bibliography of books** on Belize in the National Collection: supplement to the fourth edition. Belize City: Central Library, Bliss Institute, 1979. 12 p.

Includes nearly 50 additional titles not given in item **19**.

21 *Boletim Bibliográfico da Biblioteca Nacional.* Biblioteca Nacional. Vol. 24, No. 1 [1. trimestre] 1979– . Rio de Janeiro.

Lists recent monographs by subject, maps, posters and music received during 1978. A separate record of the more than 1750 Brazilian periodical titles received in 1978 is also given. Includes author index to monographs and publisher/printer addresses.

22 *Ecuador, Bibliografía Analítica.* Banco Central del Ecuador. Centro de Investigación y Cultura. Vol. 1, No. 1, julio 1979– Cuenca, Ecuador.

This list of national and foreign publications on Ecuador published in 1978 includes separate sections for monographs and periodical articles arranged in Dewey Decimal classification. Personal names and subject indexes are included. This new publication will provide information on current publications (this issue and the next to cover 1978 and number 3 to cover 1979). The final issue of the year will contain a cumulative index; each five years a cumulative bibliography is contemplated. Three issues were planned for 1979. A valuable complement to the *Bibliografía ecuatoriana* produced by the Central University's Library. For subscription information write to: Centro de Investigación y Cultura, Banco Central de Ecuador, P.O. Box 1505, Cuenca, Ecuador.

23 *The National Bibliography of Barbados.* Public Library. Jan./Dec. 1978– Bridgetown, Barbados.

Lists works published in Barbados or by Barbadians abroad. Periodicals, except for first issues, have been excluded. Titles are arranged by subject. Includes author/title/series index and list of legislation.

24 ———. ———. Jan./Dec. 1979– Bridgetown, Barbados.

Lists new works published in Barbados as well as those works of Barbadian authorship published abroad. Entries are arranged in a classified subject section. Author/title/series index included. Separate lists of statutory instruments, bills, acts, and debates appear in chronological order.

25 *Trinidad and Tobago National Bibliography.* Central Library of Trinidad and Tobago [and] The University of the West Indies Library. Vol. 4, No. 4, 1978– . Port of Spain.

This cumulated issue provides a listing of all works published in Trinidad and Tobago and deposited in the Central Library and the University of the West Indies, St. Augustine. Periodicals, except for first issues and annual reports, and certain government publications (e.g., acts, bills, gazettes) are excluded. Items appear in a classified section and in an author-title-series index in alphabetical order. A list of publishers and printers and their addresses is provided. Essential work on current national publishing.

26 ———. ———. Vol. 5, No. 2, April/June 1979– . Port of Spain.

Second quarter (1979) issuance of national bibliography. Contains listings of recent works deposited in the Central Library or the University of West Indies Library at St. Augustine, Trinidad, and works acquired by each. Author-title-series index and a list of publishers and printers (with addresses) are included.

27 ———. ———. Vol. 5, No. 4 [Cumulative issue] 1979– . Port of Spain.

Contains listings of recent works deposited in the Central Library or the University of West Indies Library at St. Augustine, Trinidad, and works acquired by each. Lists works in classification order. Author-title-series index and list of publishers and printers are included.

COLLECTIVE AND PERSONAL BIBLIOGRAPHIES

Antuña, María Luisa and **Josefina García-Carranza.** Bibliografía de Nicolás Guillén: suplemento 1972–1977. See item **5928**.

28 **Arze, José Roberto.** Apuntes preliminares para una bibliografía biográfica boliviana (*in* Estudios bolivianos en homenaje a Gunnar Mendoza L. [see item **2638**] p. 283–326)

Lists 367 biographic studies of Bolivians, published as separates. Arranged by authors and indexed by biographies. [M.T. Hamerly]

Becco, Horacio Jorge. Leopoldo Lugones, bibliografía en su centenario: 1874–1974. See item **5929**.

29 **Bibliografía** sobre Juan Tomás Roig y Mesa. Compilada por Luiz Berta Marín *et al.* La Habana: Biblioteca Nacional, Departamento de Hemeroteca e Información de Humanidades, 1977. 20 p.

Compiled in honor of the centenary of the birth of the noted Cuban scientist. Includes works by and about Juan Tomás Roig located in various Cuban libraries. Includes subject and onomastic indexes.

Caracas. Universidad Católica Andrés Bello. Centro de Investigaciones Literarias. Contribución a la bibliografía de Teresa de la Parra, 1895–1936. See item **5447**.

Cohen, Howard R. Eduardo Mallea: a selective annotated bibliography of criticism. See item **5569**.

30 **Epple, Juan Armando.** Bibliografía de Manuel Puig y sobre él (RIB, 28:2, abril/junio 1978, p. 165–168)

This brief bibliography provides citations to this contemporary Argentine writer's works and articles of criticism of them by other writers. For literary critic's comment, see item **5577**.

31 **Felker, William.** Flavio Herrera: a bibliography (RIB, 28:3, julio/sept. 1978, p. 291–304)

This article contains a bibliography of Flavio Herrera's works, divided into novels, short stories, nonfiction, essays, poetry and criticism of his works by others. A bio-bibliographical essay on this noted 20th-century Guatemalan author (1894–1968) precedes the list.

32 **Foster, David William.** Bibliography of writings by and about Victoria Ocampo: 1890–1979 (RIB, 30:1, 1980, p. 51–58)

Lists all Ocampo's known imprints (excluding her translations of other authors' writings) and all known criticism published in monographs, collections of essays, scholarly journals, and cultural and intellectual reviews. Includes review articles of her works. Does not include Ocampo's essays in journals, magazines, and newspapers not gathered in her collections of essays. Arranged in two main groups: works by Victoria Ocampo and criticism about Ocampo. Useful listing of the noted Argentine writer and publisher.

María Eugenia Vaz Ferreira, 1875–1975: bibliografía. See item **5936**.

33 **Mendoza L., Gunnar.** Bibliografía de Gunnar Mendoza L., 1938–1977 (*in* Estudios bolivianos en homenaje a Gunnar Mendoza L. [see item **2638**] p. 9–19)

This chronological list of Mendoza's archival, historical and other works as of 1977 (unpublished as well as published) is especially useful because many of his publications have eluded notice in this country. Mendoza, a major Bolivian scholar, has been Director of the National Archive and Library in Sucre since 1944. [M.T. Hamerly]

Rodríguez, René and **Antonio Acevedo.** Augusto C. Sandino: bibliografía. See item **2476**.

34 **Smith, Janet Lynne.** An annotated bibliography of and about Ernesto Cardenal. Tempe: Center for Latin American Studies, Arizona State University, 1979. 61 p.; index (Special studies. Arizona State University, Center for Latin American Studies; 21)

A selective annotated bibliography on the Nicaraguan priest, poet, and political activist. Book length works, journal or anthology contributions, edited works, English translations of works, translations of the works of others by Cardenal, and literary criticism appear in this timely publication.

Victoria Ocampo: la viajera y una de sus sombras. See item **5618**.

SUBJECT BIBLIOGRAPHIES

Arellano, Jorge Eduardo. Bibliografía fundamental del español en Nicaragua. See item **4517**.

35 **Becco, Horacio Jorge.** Bibliografía general de las artes del espectáculo en América Latina. Paris: UNESCO, 1977. 118 p. (América Latina en su cultura)

This general bibliography contains separate chapters on bibliographies of bibliographies, essays on theater and art, regional studies and specialized journals. Includes a general names index.

——. La historia de las ideas en América Latina: contribución a su bibliografía. See item **7622**.

Bibliografía de la Guerra Chiquita: 1879–1880. See item **2554**.

36 **Bibliografía de publicaciones** japonesas sobre América Latina en 1978. Tokyo: Sofia University, Instituto Iberoamericano, 1979. 56 p.

Lists, in Japanese, nearly 400 books and articles published in Japan on Latin American topics.

37 **Boils Morales, Guillermo.** Bibliografía sobre ciencias sociales en América Latina (UNAM/RMS, 40, 1978, p. 349–378)

Selected bibliography of 263 works on the social sciences with particular emphasis on sociology. Materials are presented in two groupings of books, theses and documents and of articles and chapters. Mainly 20th-century publications.

38 **Cerqueira, Eli Diniz** and **Renato Raul Boschi.** Estado e sociedade no Brasil: uma revisão crítica (Boletim Informativo e Bibliográfico de Ciências Sociais [Associação Nacional de Pós-Graduação e Pesquisa em Ciências Sociais, Rio de Janeiro] 1, 1977, p. 12–31)

Bibliographical essay on the theme in Brazil. A selected listing of key works is divided into sections on social actors, authoritarianism and corporatism and recent changes in the state, electoral process and parties. Useful introductory work.

Cerutti Guldberg, Horacio. Aproximación a la historiografía del pensamiento. See item **7557**.

39 **Cohen Stuart, Bertie A.** Women in the Caribbean: a bibliography. Leiden, The Netherlands, Department of Caribbean Studies, Royal Institute of Linguistics and Anthropology, 1979. 167 p.; index.

This annotated bibliography includes works on women of the Caribbean and the Guianas. In addition to a listing of general works, works on individual women and a directory of women's organizations, the bibliography is divided into sections on family and household, cultural factors, education, economic factors and politics and law. Author and subject indexes are included.

Costa de la Torre, Auturo. Bibliografía de la Revolución del 16 de Julio de 1809: año del protomártir Pedro Domingo Murillo. See item **3147**.

40 Duviols, Jean-Paul. Voyageurs français en Amérique: colonies espagnoles et portugaises. Paris: Bordas, 1978. 272 p.

An analytical and critical bibliography of material by French travellers in the Spanish and Portuguese colonies of America. Describes 140 key items related to the voyages of discovery, missionaries, piracy and contraband, scientific voyages, and political and commercial voyages. Selected portions of key writings are reproduced. A useful reference work. See also item **2636**.

41 Ferguson, Stephen. Recently identified Braziliana (RIB, 28:3, 1978, p. 247–258)

Describes 34 books and pamphlets published prior to 1830 that had not been identified before as containing textual material of Brazilian interest. A record of the known copies in the US has been added.

42 Geographical research on Latin America: a cartographic guide and bibliography of theses and dissertations, 1909–1978. Compiled by William V. Davidson. Baton Rouge, La.: The Author, 1980. 52 p.

Locates over 800 masters and doctoral theses on the geography of Latin America completed in US universities before 1978. Items have been arranged in lists according to political units. An appended table reveals that 25 percent of the theses and dissertations concentrated on Mexican themes. After Mexico, dissertations on Puerto Rican geography were most populous followed closely by Brazilian topics. The greatest output of theses and dissertations occurred between 1965 and 1975.

43 Graber, Eric S. An annotated bibliography of rural development, urbanization, and levels of living in Peru. Washington: Agency for International Development, Bureau of Latin America and the Caribbean, Rural Development Division, 1979. 109 p. (Peru, general working documents; 1)

This listing of nearly 750 publications and reports on the general development, social conditions and levels of living; agriculture; rural life and organization; and small farm development, technology and marketing published since 1950 includes works from the fields of economics, sociology, anthropology, political science, agriculture, nutrition and history. This partially annotated bibliography lists works in alphabetical order with subject matter noted. Contains no index.

44 Grupo de Trabalho em Ciências Sociais e Humanas de Minas Gerais. Bibliografia de D. Pedro II [i.e. Segundo] e sua época, 1840–1889: levantamento realizado em Minas Gerais por ocasião das comemorações do sesquicentenário de nascimento do Imperador. Belo Horizonte: O Grupo, 1977. 162 p.; ill.; index.

Compiled from a survey of pertinent materials in 31 libraries in the state of Minas Gerais; locations of materials are indicated. Lists over 1175 titles arranged by subjects. Includes author index. For historian's comment, see item **3666**.

45 Guimarães, Alba Zaluar. Os movimentos "messiânicos" brasileiros: uma leitura (Boletim Informativo e Bibliográfico de Ciências Sociais [Associação Nacional de Pós Graduação e Pesquisa em Ciências Sociais, Rio de Janeiro] 6, 1979, p. 9–21)

Bibliographic essay describes various examples of the phenomenon in Brazil. A selected listing of works appears.

Hardoy, Jorge Enrique. Urbanización en América Latina: una bibliografía sobre su historia. See item **1782**.

Instituto de Direito Público e Ciências Política, *Rio de Janeiro.* **Centro de Pesquisa e Documentação e História Contemporânea do Brasil.** Tenentismo: bibliografía. See item **3677**.

46 Jackson, Richard L. The Afro-Spanish American author: an annotated bibliography of criticism. New York: Garland Pub., 1980. 129 p.; index (Garland reference library of the humanities; 194)

A listing of the works and their criticism of 25 Afro-Spanish American authors; publication relates primarily to Cuban writers, to Nicólas Guillen, and black poetry. Restricted to Spanish authors only.

47 Jiménez, Roberto and **P. Zeballos.** América Latina y el mundo desarrollado: bibliografía comentada sobre relaciones de dependencia. Bogotá: CEDIAL, 1977. 315 p.; bibl.; index.

This partially annotated bibliography

on dependency theory presents works in separate chapters on imperialism, Latin American relations, dependency theory and criticism. The bibliography is introduced by an essay on the genesis of the dependency theory and its criticism. Author and journal title indexes are given. Contains over 1000 references.

48 **Lamounier, Bolivar** and **Maria D'Alva Gil Kinzo.** Partidos políticos, representação e processo eleitoral no Brasil, 1945–1978 (Boletim Informativo e Bibliográfico de Ciências Sociais [Associação Nacional de Pós Graduação e Pesquisa em Ciências Sociais, Rio de Janeiro] 5, 1978, p. 11–32)

Excellent bibliographical essay of basic works on Brazilian politics, party organization and recruitment, electoral strategies, and party attitudes. Listing of key works is included.

49 **Laraia, Roque de Barros.** Relações entre negros e brancos no Brasil (Boletim Informativo e Bibliográfico de Ciências Sociais [Associação Nacional de Pós-Graduação e Pesquisa em Ciências Sociais, Rio de Janeiro] 7, 1979, p. 11–21)

Bibliographic essay describes the efforts of key writers on racial relations in Brazil. A selected listing of works is given.

50 **Lidmilová, Pavla.** Bibliografia seleta: 1945–1978 (ASB/PP, 23:1, 1980, p. 13–20)

Lists publications by Czechoslovakian writers on Luso-Brazilian literary themes. List is divided into sections on general works, linguistics, and literature.

51 **Luzuriaga C., Carlos** and **Clarence Zuvekas, Jr.** An annotated bibliography of income, income distribution, and levels of living in rural Ecuador. Washington: Agency for International Development, Bureau for Latin America and Caribbean, Rural Development Division, 1979. 97 p. (Ecuador, general working document; 1)

Annotated listing of nearly 700 works written since 1950 that are directly or indirectly related to the subjects given in title. Includes glossary of acronyms, library location of materials, and a subject index.

52 **Marino Fores, Anselmo.** Bibliografía de antropología americana: temas generales; antropología social y aplicada; arqueología; arte y prehistoria; etnología y etnohistoria; antropología física; lingüística; varios (BBAA, 34:48, 1977, p. 163–250)

Provides citations for 960 articles and monographs presented in alphabetical order in one of eight themes.

53 **Matijevic, Nicolás** and **Olga H. de Matijevic.** Bibliografía patagónica y de las tierras australes. v. 1, Historia; v. 2, Geografía. Bahía Blanca, Argentina: Centro de Documentación Patagónica, Universidad Nacional del Sur Dr. Miguel López Francés, 1973/1978. 2 v. (266, 383 p.); index.

Consists of more than four centuries of writings on Patagonia. These are vols. 1/2 of a six-volume work which will provide information on 15,000 works covering the fields of history, geography, Indians, botany and zoology, geology and paleontology, natural resources and development. Vol. 1 on history includes sections on archaeology, chroniclers, mythology, history, and the question of the border between Argentina and Chile; v. 2 on geography has sections on bibliographic notes, exploration, physical and human geography, transportation and Antarctic. Both volumes contain author indexes.

Mörner, Magnus. Recent research on Negro slavery and abolition in Latin America. See item **1799**.

54 **Morales Gómez, Jorge.** Contribución a la bibliografía del folclor colombiano: listado hasta 1973. Bogotá: s.n., 1978. 130 p.; index.

Lists 1431 titles on various subjects related to Colombian folklore (e.g., art/techniques, ethnobiology/zoology, medicine, magical/religious practices and ideas, literary and musical expressions, and recreation). Only works published before 1974 appear. Includes author, subject, and geographic indexes.

55 **Movimiento de países** no alienados: bibliografía. La Habana: Ministerio de Relaciones Exteriores, Dirección de Documentación, 1979. 214 p.

Prepared in response to the VI Conference of the Non-Aligned Nations Movement held in 1979 in Havana, this bibliography contains references to previous meetings of these nations, texts of principal speeches, and distinct themes discussed in the meetings and conferences. Nearly 1500 citations appear; an onomastic index is included.

Mulher brasileira: bibliografia anotada. See item **3541**.

56 **Musso Ambrosi, Luis Alberto.** Anotaciones de bibliografía uruguaya sobre historia argentina en el período, 1831–1852. s.l.: s.n., between 1974 and 1980. 41 p.

Selective annotated list of books and pamphlets on the Rosas period of Argentina. Primary and secondary source materials appear. Pertinent chapters and/or pages of certain general works are given.

Norris, Robert E. Guía bibliográfica para el estudio de la historia ecuatoriana. See item **2650**.

57 **Oberbeck, Charles D.** An annotated bibliography of income distribution in Paraguay. Washington: Agency for International Development, Bureau for Latin America and the Caribbean, Rural Development Division, 1979. 22 p. (Paraguay, general working document; 1)

Annotated listing of 69 items of information available in Paraguay and the US relating to income distribution and to socio-economic characteristics of low-income groups. Works appear in alphabetical order; author index is provided.

58 **Oliveira, Lucia Lippi.** Revolução de 1930: uma bibliografia comentada (Boletim Informativo e Bibliográfico de Ciências Sociais [Associação Nacional de Pós-Graduação e Pesquisa em Ciências Sociais, Rio de Janeiro] 4, 1978, p. 8–18)

Brief bibliographical essay of key works for the study of the 1930 revolution; particular themes studied include the Liberal Alliance, the states and the revolution, tenentismo and the military, political parties, and the new government structure. Key works from the 1930s appear in the selected bibliography following the essay.

59 **Popular culture** in Latin America: an introductory bibliography. Edited by Roger Cunniff (PCCLAS/P, 5, 1976, p. 147–191)

Annotated selected listing of 264 works on popular culture. Separate sections on general, Afro-Latin culture, Brazil's *literatura de cordel*, social protest music, popular culture and Latin American cinema, and graphics appear. Offers a variety of viewpoints and definitions to illustrate the facets of popular culture studies as they apply to Latin America.

60 **Reátegui G., Mirca.** Bibliografía sobre antropología y arqueología de la selva del Perú (PEBN/B, 73/76, 1978, p. 5–58)

Contains 57 annotated citations on the subject divided into two main themes, archaeology and anthropology. The presentation is further refined to include separate listings on anthropology, forest tribes, linguistics, economy, living conditions, myths and legends, archaeology-remains and excavations.

61 **Reynal, Susana Mallo.** Bibliografía sobre movimiento obrero latinoamericano (UNAM/RMCPS, 23:89, julio/sept. 1977, p. 223–233)

This is a non-annotated listing of selected, primarily current, works on 20th-century labor movements and organizations in individual Latin American countries; works are arranged by country. [H.A. Spalding, Jr.]

62 **São Paulo** (city). **Museu de Arte.** Historia da tipografia no Brasil. São Paulo: 1979. 277 p.

An exhibit catalog that serves as an illustrated bibliography of Brazilian imprints, presented by state. A brief introductory essay on the history of printing in Brazil precedes the illustrated guide.

63 **Seeger, Anthony** and **Eduardo Viveiros de Castro.** Pontos de vista sobre os índios brasileiros: um ensaio bibliográfico (Boletim Informativo e Bibliográfico de Ciências Sociais [Associação Nacional de Pós-Graduação e Pesquisa em Ciências Sociais, Rio de Janeiro] 2, 1977, p. 11–35)

A useful introductory essay on the state of research followed by a selected bibliography.

64 **A select bibliography** on economic development: with annotations. Compiled by John P. Powelson. Boulder, Colo.: Westview Press, 1979. 450 p.

An annotated, selected, basic list for students and researchers interested in economic development in Asia, Africa, and Latin America. Most items listed are less than eight years old. The Latin American section is divided by country (p. 354–456).

65 **Strum, Fred** and **Robert J. Goodland.** The ecology of Guyana: a bibliography of environmental resources. Monticello, Ill.: Vance Bibliographies, 1978. 44 p. (Public administration series: Bibliography; P-61)

This unannotated bibliography is divided into sections on bibliographies, general works, history, health-disease, economics-industry engineering, tribal people, agriculture-pests, livestock, solid-geology, forests-timber, flora-vegetation-biology, insects, fauna, and fish-ocean-water.

66 **Sullivan, William M.** and **Winfield J. Burggraaff.** El petróleo en Venezuela: una bibliografía. Caracas: Ediciones Centauro, 1977. 229 p. (Colección Manuel Segundo Sánchez)

The vital interest of Venezuela in petroleum is demonstrated by this bibliography of nearly 2200 works on the technical, economic, juridical, sociological, historical, and polemical aspects of the subject. Works are grouped into sections on theses, official publications (US and Venezuelan), books and pamphlets, journal titles and articles.

67 **Supplement to a bibliography** of United States-Latin American relations since 1810. Compiled and edited by Michael C. Meyer. Lincoln: University of Nebraska Press, 1979. 193 p.

A listing of more than 3550 partially annotated citations on various subjects of the general theme of US-Latin American relations. Over three quarters of the works listed appeared since 1965. Includes cross references of complementary items taken from the 1968 work edited by Trask, Trask, and Meyer, *A bibliography of United States-Latin American relations since 1810* (University of Nebraska Press, 1968). Author index included.

68 **Torres Bruno, Ofelia.** Sanidad en el Uruguay: información bibliográfica, 1804–1976. Montevideo: Universidad de la República, Facultad de Medicina, Biblioteca Nacional de Medicina, 1978, cover 1979. 2 v. (512, 30 p.); bibl.; indexes.

An impressive bibliography on the broad themes of public health in Uruguay. Includes sections on treaties and conventions, national health institutions, health services, rehabilitation services, health related conferences and congresses in Uruguay and Latin America, and legislation. Names of professional and technical schools, courses of study, and scientific and documentation centers appear. Includes general and subject indexes.

69 **United States. Department of Housing and Urban Development. Office of International Affairs.** Housing and urban development planning in Mexico: a bibliography. Washington: 1980. 54 p.

This selected, annotated bibliography presents a variety of materials on a broad range of subjects on the current approaches to housing and urban development planning implemented in Mexico. A brief bibliographical essay precedes the list.

70 **Uruguay. Biblioteca Nacional. Departamento de Servicos Públicos. Sección Referencia y Bibliografía.** Bibliografía uruguaya sobre el niño: 1952–1979. Montevideo: 1979. 152 p.

Lists 777 citations on social and legislative assistance, health, education, literature, and music related to the well being and formation of the child written between 1952 and 1979. Includes only works published in Uruguay and by Uruguayans published abroad; translations are excluded. Subject and author indexes appear.

71 **Vianna, Luiz Werneck.** Estudos sobre sindicalismo e movimento operário: resenha de algumas tendências (Boletim Informativo e Bibliográfico de Ciências Sociais [Associação Nacional de Pós-Graduação e Pesquisa em Ciências Sociais, Rio de Janeiro] 3, 1978, p. 9–24)

Excellent selection of recent research on the worker movement in Brazil. Useful bibliographical essay precedes the listing.

Weber, David J. Mexico's far northern frontier, 1821–1845: a critical bibliography. See item **2259**.

LIBRARY SCIENCE & SERVICES

Alzola Zárate, José Daniel. La organización de archivos históricos. See item **3288**.

72 *Bibliografía brasileira de documentação.* Suplemento 1. v. 3/4, 1971/1977. Rio de Janeiro: Instituto Brasileiro de Informação em Ciência e Tecnologia, 1979. 2 v.

Index to more than 1350 articles pertaining to library and information science, archival work, and automation issues between 1971 and 1977 in Brazil. This supplement contains analysis of 58 Brazilian periodicals. Author, subject, and key word indexes are provided.

73 *Boletín Bibliográfico.* Biblioteca del Congreso Nacional. Sección Procesamiento. Año 4, No. 20, mayo/junio 1979– . Santiago.

Lists recent accessions of monographs, indexes journals, provides brief reviews of current publications from Chile and abroad, and contains information notes on library development in the country and in Latin America.

74 **Briquet de Lemos, Antonio A.** UAP and Brazil (UNESCO/JIS, 1:2, April/June 1979, p. 78–81)

Provides information on major sources of inter-library loan in Brazil.

75 **Coba, Arabia Teresa** and **Noehmí de Pérez.** Estado actual de la preparación professional en Venezuela en las áreas de bibliotecología y archivología (Revista de SINASBI [Información Científica y Tecnológica de Archivos y de Estadística e Informática; Comisión Coordinadora del Sistema Nacional de Servicios de Bibliotecos e Información, Caracas] 1, julio/dic. 1978, p. 13–32)

Authors review of the current development of academic library science programs in Venezuela and the future needs of the country in the field of library science. By 1980 between 956 and 1145 new librarians are needed; authors question whether the two library science schools in Venezuela are capable of providing the demand.

76 **Estadísticas de lectura** por oficinas, salas y materias: 1974 (PEBN/B, 21/22:73/76, 1975/1976, p. 88–93, tables)

Readership statistics for the Peruvian National Library for the years 1974–76. Pure and social sciences are the major area of reader interest although collectively the readership in the humanities is quite high.

77 **Figueiredo, Nice.** O ensino de biblioteconomia no Brasil: relatório de equipe de pesquisa sobre o status quo das escolas de biblioteconomia e documentação, com ênfase na situação do pessoal docente. v. 2, Cadastro de entidades; escolas, departamentos e faculdades de biblioteconomia e documentação; v. 3, Análise da literatura recomendada no ensino de biblioteconomia no Brasil. Texto elaborado por Nice Figueiredo, coordenadora de equipe. Membros: Abigail de Oliveira Carvalho, Maria Martha de Carvalho, Antonio Miranda. Brasília: Ministério da Educação e Cultura, Departamento de Assuntos Universitários, Coordenação do Aperfei-coamento de Pessoal de Nível Superior, 1978. 2 v. (277, 216 p.); bibl.; ill.

V. 2: this survey identifies 28 academic programs in library science, arranged by regional groupings. Course offerings, school activities, and brief résumés on faculty members appear. V. 3: Bibliography of literature, 1947 entries, utilized in library science courses in Brazil. This compilation is based on a survey of 29 library science faculties in the country. English language materials, especially US publications, are heavily used in course offerings. Includes subject index.

Fleming, William J. Regional research in Argentina: a critical evaluation of the archives and libraries of Mendoza province. See item **2639**.

78 **Gazzola de Sangster, Mercedes.** Legal deposits and the universal availability of publications (UAP): the case of Peru (UNESCO/JIS, 2:1, Jan./March 1980, p. 29–34, table)

Reports on problems of attaining an accurate record of current publishing in Peru. Cites existing legal measures by which copyright deposit is required for all forms of Peruvian publications.

79 **Kavanagh, Rosemary.** Information management in progressive Jamaica (IJ/JJ, 11:3/4, 1978, p. 44–47, plate)

Author comments on the current state of data gathering and retrieval in Jamaica, lamenting the lack of government document data banks and information systems. Actually the article is a call for more rational development of library and information science services.

80 **Martínez Baeza, Sergio.** Pasado, presente y futuro de la Biblioteca Nacional (EC/M, 26, 1978, p. 109–116)

A brief review of the development and continuation of the National Library concept in Chile. Useful for dates and key figures.

81 **Montevideo. Biblioteca del Poder Legislativo.** Bibliotecas del Uruguay. Selección, textos, y compilación por María Teresa Goicoechea de Linares, con la colabo-

ración de Cristina O. de Pérez Olave y Lilian Fernández Citera. Montevideo: 1978. 252 p.: ill. (Serie de temas nacionales; 5)

A directory of over 200 libraries (city, school, governmental, private) in Uruguay providing information on the date of creation of the library, directorship, services, readership, location, and general history of development.

82 **Moraes, Rubens Borba de.** Livros e bibliotecas no Brasil colonial. Rio de Janeiro: LIC, 1979. 234 p.; bibl.; ill.; index (Biblioteca universitária de literatura brasileira: Série A, Ensaio, crítica, história literária; 6)

Introductory history of book publishing and distribution and libraries in colonial Brazil. The first major libraries were those of the Jesuits and other religious orders. Chapters on the history refer to censorship in Brazil, the establishment of printing presses and printers, and the development of the Royal Library in Rio de Janeiro. An appendix includes the statues of the Royal Library (1821).

83 **Muñoz, Elvira.** La nueva sede de la Biblioteca Nacional (Revista de SINASBI [Información Científica y Tecnológica de Archivos y de Estadística e Informática; Comisión Coordinadora del Sistema Nacional de Servicios de Bibliotecos e Información, Caracas] 1, julio/dic. 1978, p. 57–62)

Brief discussion of the antecedents, plans and stages to the location of the Venezuelan National Library.

84 **Penna, Carlos Víctor.** Estudio preliminar para la organización de un Servicio Nacional de Información Educativa en el Paraguay (Revista de Biblioteconomia de Brasília [Universidade de Brasília, Associação dos Bibliotecários do Distrito Federal e Departamento Biblioteconomia, Brasília] 5:2, julho, dez. 1977, p. 641–662)

This article, from the annals of the 8th Brazilian Congress for Library Science and Documentation, describes a joint UNESCO/PNUD project to assist the Paraguayan government in improving the knowledge of its teachers at the primary and the secondary levels. UNESCO suggested that a national educational information system be built instead of relying on traditional library and pedagogical documentation center support.

85 **Quijano Solis, Alvaro.** La situación de las unidades de información en el campo económico y social. México: Asociación de Bibliotecarios de Instituciones de Enseñanza Superior e Investigación, 1977. 30 leaves (Cuadernos de ABIESI; 5)

Provides information received from 30 libraries with extensive holdings in socioeconomic fields in Mexico. Size of collections, hours of service, location, number of employees and periodical publications are given. An analytical article on the library situation precedes the directory.

86 **Reunión Centroamericana sobre Centros Catalográficos,** *San José, 1979.* Informe final. San José: Organización de Estados Americanos [and] Universidad de Costa Rica, 1980. 206 p.

Reports the activities of the Central American centralized cataloging project, OAS support of centralized cataloging, the possibility of automating Central American cataloging, and on cataloging in Guatemala, Honduras, El Salvador, Nicaragua, Costa Rica and Panamá.

87 **Tanodi, Aurelio.** Archival training in Latin America (UNESCO/JIS, 1:2, April/June 1979, p. 112–123)

Provides an outline of archival training in selected countries of Latin America (i.e., Argentina, Colombia, Brazil, Venezuela, Mexico and Ecuador) with particular emphasis on the role of the Inter-American Centre for Archives Development, Córdoba, Argentina. Tanodi is the director of the archivists' school at the University of Córdoba, Argentina.

88 **Toledo, José Cláudio Fama.** Arquivos (Revista Brasileira de Biblioteconomia e Documentação [Federação Brasileira de Associações de Bibliotecários, São Paulo] 11:3/4, julho/dez. 1978, p. 245–253)

Unannotated listing of selected titles related to data control preservation, organization, and reference of archival material.

89 **Tomé, Martha.** El PREDE y las bibliotecas escolares y universitarias (OAS/LE, 22:78/80, 1978, p. 117–122)

Briefly reviews the efforts of the Regional Program for Educational Development (PREDE) and the multinational project for school and university libraries which are highlighted by the Interamerican School for

Library Science at the University of Antioquia, the Central American Centralized Cataloging Project at the University of Costa Rica and the Institute for the Study and Development of Education in Peru. Continuing needs include the formation of qualified professional librarians, the development of library and documentation networks, and the creation of pilot projects that utilize new communication technologies to disseminate information.

ACQUISITIONS, COLLECTIONS, CATALOGUES

90 **Alanís Boyso, José Luis.** Los archivos municipales del estado de México: proceso de organización y guía descriptiva (CM/HM, 28:4[112], abril/junio 1979, p. 567–595, bibl.)

Describes the types of material maintained in the municipal archives of the state. Describes types of material and dates of coverage for the municipalities of: Tepetloaxtoc; Ogoyoacac; Ixtlahuaca; Malinalco; Papalotla; Atlacomulco; Naucalpan; Chalco; San Bartolo Morelos; Acambay; Tepetlixpa; Villa del Carbón; Toluca; Almoloya del Río; San Felipe del Progreso; Valle de Bravo; Hueypoxtla; El Oro; Texcoco; and Atlautla.

91 **Archives and manuscripts** on microfilm in the Nettie Lee Benson Latin American Collection: a checklist. Compiled by Jane Garner. Austin: The University of Texas, General Libraries, 1980. 48 p.

Lists holdings of over 6300 reels of microfilm from national and foreign repositories in the Nettie Lee Benson Collection at Texas. The bulk of the microfilm (nearly 80 percent) is of material related to Latin America in the US National Archives (Washington), the Archivo General de la Nación (Mexico), and the British Public Record Office (London). Most of the material is historical, largely for Mexico from the colonial period to the early 20th century. Material is arranged in four geographical areas: Mexico, Central America, Caribbean and South America. Includes a list of institutional sources of the microfilm.

92 **Archivo Histórico** del Estado "Lic. Antonio Rocha." San Luis Potosí, S.L.P., México: El Archivo, 1979. 70 p.; bibl.; ill.

Provides brief history and description of the historical archive and the legislation and regulations affecting its establishment. Includes Rafael Montejano y Aguiñaga's "Trayectoria de los Archivos Potosinos."

93 **Arrieta Alvarez, Ada E.** and **César Gutiérrez Muñoz.** Indice analítico de la Colección Maldonado (PUCP/CSH, 11, enero 1973/dic. 1975, p. 22–90)

The Catholic University of Peru acquired in 1975 the historic collection on the chemist-pharmacist Angel Maldonado. That collection is now located in the Archivo Histórico Riva-Agüero. It consists of 338 documents related to the history of medicine and pharmacy in Peru. The index provides a description of each item, its title, date, and location.

94 **Banco Central de Nicaragua. Centro Nicaragüense de Información Tecnología. Departamento de Investigaciones Tecnológicas.** Catálogo colectivo de publicaciones periódicas y fuentes de referencias técnicas: principales bibliotecas de Nicaragua. Managua: 1976. 125 p. (Bibliografía y documentación; 1)

Provides a union list, with holdings, of technical journals and reference works contained in eight governmental and university libraries in Nicaragua.

95 **Bibliografía argentina:** catálogo de materiales argentinos en las bibliotecas de la Universidad de Buenos Aires. Boston: G.K. Hall, 1980. 7 v.

Lists, by author, approximately 110,000 cards for books and pamphlets found in 17 central and 56 departmental libraries of the University of Buenos Aires' faculties, schools, and institutes. Citations cover scientific, technical, and humanistic areas from the oldest works printed in Argentina through 1979. Locations of individual works are given.

96 **Bibliographic guide** to Latin American studies: 1979. v. 1, A–D; v. 2, E–M; v. 3, N–Z. Boston: G.K. Hall, 1980. 3 v. (740, 778, 804 p.)

Lists publications cataloged during 1979 by the Latin American Collection, The University of Texas at Austin, supplemented by Latin American publications cataloged by the Library of Congress. Material is arranged by title, author, and subject.

97 *Boletín Bibliográfico.* Banco Central de Nicaragua. No. 9, abril/oct. 1979– . Managua.

Entire issue devoted to the Bank's library and information services. Includes catalogue record of recent accessions in the bank's library. Most important section lists recent Nicaraguan titles. Useful bibliographical and acquisition source.

98 **Brazil. Arquivo Nacional. Divisão de Publicações. Biblioteca.** Catálogo de jornais brasileiros: 1808–1889. Rio de Janeiro: 1979. 36 p. (Instrumentos de trabalho; 12)

Lists over 330 serials in alphabetical order, located in the National Archives. Gives holdings. Chronological and geographical indexes appear.

Castro Nevares, Federico. El Archivo de la Confederación. See item **3317**.

99 **Documentos atinentes** a la historia colonial hondureña existentes en el Archivo General de Centroamérica en Guatemala: comercio lícito e ilícito. Compilador: Mario Argueta (Boletín del Sistema Bibliotecario de la UNAH [Universidad Nacional Autónoma de Honduras, Tegucigalpa] 7:2, abril/junio 1979, p. 16–25)

Lists 155 documents in chronological order from 1593–1819 found in the Guatemalan archives. Document title, item number and legajo are provided.

100 **Documentos relativos** a la historia colonial hondureña existentes en el Archivo General de Centroamérica en Guatemala. Compilador: Mario Argueta (Boletín del Sistema Bibliotecario de la UNAH [Universidad Nacional Autónoma de Honduras, Tegucigalpa] 7:1, enero/marzo 1979, p. 27–35; 7:3, julio/sept. 1979, p. 14–21; 8:2, abril/mayo 1980, p. 9–15)

The author lists pertinent documents related to mining, the Real de Minas de Tegucigalpa, encomiendas and city councils of Honduras for the colonial period. Item number and legajo are given.

101 **Dominican Republic. Universidad Autónoma de Santo Domingo. Dirección de Publicaciones.** Catálogo de las publicaciones de la Universidad Autónoma de Santo Domingo 1978. Santo Domingo: 1978. 32 p.

Lists monographs and periodicals produced by the university since 1938. Useful guide to academic interests and trends.

Dorn, Georgette M. Luso-Hispanic recordings at the Library of Congress. See item **5931**.

102 **Hilton, Ronald.** A bibliography of Latin America and the Caribbean: the Hilton Library. Metuchen, N.J.: Scarecrow Press, 1980. 675 p.

An alphabetical listing of the more than 11,000 titles in Hilton's personal library. A list of tape recordings of prominent Latin Americans concludes the listing. Includes no index.

103 **Indiana University. Latin American Studies Program.** A supplementary guide to selected Latin American manuscripts in the Lilly Library of Indiana University. Bloomington: 1980. 24 p. (Latin American studies working papers; 10)

This publication supplements the 1974 publication, *A guide to selected Latin American manuscripts in the Lilly Library of Indiana University* by Rebecca Campbell Mirza. This new publication describes materials acquired since the 1974 work and provides an account of over 25,000 items pertaining to Latin America and the Philippines. The rich Mexican and Peruvian collections are described in detail while short summaries are given for the Brazilian, Philippine, Claude Bowers, Orson Welles, and literary manuscript collections.

104 **Institute of Jamaica,** *Kingston.* **West India Reference Library.** The catalogue of the West India Reference Library. pt. 1, Catalogue of authors and titles; pt. 2, Catalogue of subjects. Millwood, New York: Kraus International Publications, 1980. 6 v.

This catalog identifies the books, pamphlet, and periodical holdings of the West India Reference Library of the Institute of Jamaica, now Jamaica's National Library, that were catalogued prior to the end of 1975. Catalogue is arranged into author/title and subject parts. This work brings to the attention of scholars an outstanding collection of printed materials related to the history and culture of the West Indies, with primary emphasis on materials related to Jamaica and the other English-speaking islands and former British colonies in the Caribbean area written in English. The collection is especially noted for listings on history, description and travel, government, economic and social conditions, and literature. Works on scientific and technical subjects are less prevalent.

105 Mexico. Archivo General de la Nación. Centro de Información Gráfica. Catálogo de ilustraciones. México: 1979. 2 v. (200, 219 p.)

Provides catalog descriptions of 1058 manuscript maps, plans, and drawings from the colonial period, 16th to early 19th centuries, located in the Archivo General. Maps and plans comprise the majority of the material listed. General and geographic indexes appear. This is an extremely useful and valuable contribution for a wide range of scholarly endeavors.

106 Millares Carlo, Agustín. Libros del siglo XVI. Mérida, Venezuela: Universidad de los Andes, Consejo de Publicaciones: Biblioteca "Tulio Febres Cordero," 1978. 187 p.; bibl.; 15 leaves of plates: ill.; indexes.

Lists and fully describes 16th-century imprints in the Biblioteca Tulio Febres Cordero. An informative essay on the appearance of 16th-century imprints in the New World precedes the list. A chronological list of titles by imprint, printer/book publisher/editor and names/titles indexes appear.

107 Parada Fortín, Armida. Catálogo de libros y publicaciones periódicas. San Salvador: Universidad de El Salvador, Departamento de Arqueología e Historia, Biblioteca Central, 1974. 521 p.

Inventory of the nearly 6200 monographs and 640 periodicals in the Department of Archaeology and History of the University arranged in alphabetical order by author and title. Separate sections are devoted to books and periodicals. Lacks index and information on holdings of periodicals.

108 Pedrero Nieto, Gloria. Situación general de los Archivos del Estado de Chiapas (MAGN/B, 2:4 [3. serie] oct./dic. 1978, p. 42–44)

Provides a detailed, but brief, description of the state and ecclesiastical archives of the state. Most detail is devoted to the Archivo Histórico de San Cristóbal de las Casas, in Tuxtla Gutiérrez, which contains materials related to the Church from the 17th to the 20th centuries. In addition to the administration and financing of the Church, items provide much information on the situation of the Indians, landowners and government.

109 Romero Frizzi, María de los Angeles. Indice del microfilm del Centro Regional de Oaxaca: serie Teposcolula. Oaxaca, México: Instituto Nacional de Antropología e Historia, Centro Regional de Oaxaca, 1975. 69 p. (Estudios de antropología e historia; 8)

Identifies more than 500 documents of the archive of the Juzgado de Teposcolula (Oaxaca, Mexico). Material contained includes information on livestock raising and other commerce, on the Mixtec caciques, and the system of labor and tribute. Items cover the 16th to the 18th centuries. Microfilm of material is located in the Central Regional de Oaxaca. The publication has no author or subject index.

110 ———. Información sobre el acervo documental de archivos en La Mixteca, Oaxaca. Oaxaca, México: Instituto Nacional de Antropología e Historia, Central Regional de Oaxaca, 1979. 46 p. (Estudios de antropología e historia; 18)

Briefly describes contents of local archives related to the Mixtec. Descriptions for 25 governmental and religious archives are included.

111 St. Juste, Laurore. Recherches haitiennes dans les bibliothèques et archives americaines (IFH/C, 141/142, fév. 1979, p. 65–73)

Briefly describes pertinent materials in the Library of Congress, National Archives, and the New York Public Library, especially the Schomburg Center; passing reference is made to the existence of Haitian materials in other institutions, including those in the Moorland Library at Howard University, Georgetown University, Fisk University and South Carolina Archives.

112 Súarez, Santiago Gerardo. Catálogo 1958–1978. Caracas: Academia Nacional de la Historia, 1978. 1 v. (Serie Fuentes para la historia colonial de Venezuela)

This is an annotated listing of the 180 titles prepared over the past 20 years for the series Fuentes para la Historia Colonial de Venezuela. Publications are given in alphabetical order by author and in numerical order by volume.

Tavares Bastos, A.C. Correspondência e catálogo de documentos da Coleção da Biblioteca Nacional. See item **3761**.

113 Tucumán, Argentine Republic (province). **Archivo Histórico.** Indices documentales: sección Actas Capitulares. v. 5, 1680–1739; v. 6, 1740–1783; v. 7, 1784–1824. Tucumán: 1972. 3 v.; indexes (Publicación del Archivo Histórico de Tucumán; 29. Serie 5:5)

Identifies, in chronological order, the *Actas Capitulares* of the Cabildo of San Miguel de Tucumán from 1680 until its demise in 1824. The archival location of material is indicated. While the actas do not in themselves provide a complete history of Tucumán, city and province, they are indispensable for the information they provide. Fundamental pieces, such as that of the open cabildo of 1810, are found in the actas.

114 Tyson, George F., Jr. A guide to manuscript sources in United States and West Indian depositories relating to the British West Indies during the era of the American Revolution. Wilmington, Delaware: Scholarly Resources, 1978. 96 p.

Provides brief descriptions of pertinent special collections in 72 libraries and archives in the US and the British West Indies. Does not indicate size of individual collections. Includes general index to personal names and geographical locations.

115 Universidad Autónoma del Estado de México. Colección Histórica. Catálogos de documentos sobre el Instituto Literario del Estado. Toluca, México: 1980. 98 p.

This is a calendar of the university archives from 1841–80 and includes references to the papers of the Literary Institute of Toluca (1827–60) in the Mexican National Archives. Box and other arrangement information are provided.

116 Universidad de los Andes. Biblioteca Central Tulio Febres Cordero. Catálogo de tesis de grado y trabajos de ascenso. Suplemento 1. Mérida, Venezuela: 1977. 120 p.

Presents thesis and other qualifying papers, produced between 1971–76, in alphabetical order by faculty. Includes author index.

117 Venezuela. Instituto Autónoma Biblioteca Nacional. Sección de Publicaciones Oficiales. Catálogo de publicaciones oficiales 1840–1977. Compilación de Beatriz Martínez de Cartay. Mérida, Venezuela: Imprenta Oficial, 1978. 445 p.

This important work lists more than 3850 titles of national governmental publications (1840–1977) in the Venezuelan National Library. Issuances of the national government (i.e., of the executive, legislative, and judicial agencies) appear; a list of publications of autonomous agencies and of state governments has been planned. Citations appear in alphabetical order by agency. Brief chronological histories of ministries precede listings for each. Subject and institutional index and national library filing information are provided.

Williams, John Hoyt. The Archivo General de la Nación of Uruguay. See item **2658**.

REFERENCE WORKS AND RESEARCH

Alisky, Marvin. Historical dictionary of Peru. See item **3053**.

118 Aranda Pamplona, Hugo. Biobibliografía de los escritores del Estado de México. México: Universidad Nacional Autónoma de México, Dirección General de Publicaciones, 1978. 105 p.; index (Serie Bibliografías. Instituto de Investigaciones Bibliográficas. Biblioteca Nacional; 5. Biobibliografías)

Provides useful descriptions of 115 writers of the state who flourished from pre-Cortesian to the present date. Among those described are José Antonio Alzate y Ramírez, Isidro Fabelá, Sor Juana, and José Moziño.

119 Asociación Panamericana de Instituciones de Crédito Educativo. Centro de Información y Documentación. Instituciones que ofrecen estudios de archivística y bibliotecología en Latinoamérica y el Caribe: directorio. Bogotá: Fondo Colombiano de Investigaciones Científicas y Proyectos Especiales Francisco José de Caldas, 1978. 32 p.

Lists names and addresses of undergraduate and graduate institutions, by country, with academic programs in archival and library science.

Auza, Néstor Tomás. El periodismo de la Confederación, 1852–1861. See item **3296**.

120 **Barcía, José.** Diccionario hípico: voces y expresiones rioplatenses. Buenos Aires: Editorial Plus Ultra, 1978. 208 p. (Temas argentinos; 1)

Contains about 4500 expressions and terms used currently in the La Plata area, including southern Brazil. Gaucho terms and racetrack language appear.

121 **Barnes, Thomas C.; Thomas H. Naylor;** and **Charles W. Polzer.** Northern New Spain: a research guide. Tucson: The University of Arizona Press, 1981. 147 p.

Provides basic information of use to researchers interested in the history of the US Spanish Southwest. Intended to facilitate the research of those involved in the Documentary Relations of the Southwest Project at the Arizona State Museum. In addition, the guide contains information on the colonial governmental structure, money, weights and measures, racial terminology, colonial officials of the borderlands, and references to manuscript collections and repositories.

122 **Beers, Henry Putney.** Spanish & Mexican records of the American Southwest; a bibliographical guide to archive and manuscript sources. Tucson: University of Arizona Press, 1979. 493 p.; bibl.; index.

Provides descriptive information found in US institutions on Spanish and Mexican records on the US Southwest (i.e., Arizona, California, New Mexico and Texas) from the 1600s to 1850. Based primarily on finding aids published by archival and manuscript repositories containing materials on the region. Divided into sections by state subdivided into chapters on: history and government; provincial records; legislative records; archival reproductions; documentary publications; manuscript collections; land records; records of local jurisdiction; and ecclesiastical records. Appendices list the lost records of California. Classified bibliography is included. Onomastic index facilitates access. An extremely useful work for borderlands researchers. For historian's comment, see item **2110**.

123 **Biblioteca Nacional José Martí,** *La Habana.* Indice general de publicaciones periódicas cubanas 1974. t. 6,/7, Humanidades y ciencias sociales. La Habana: 1978. 2 v. (357, 457 p.)

Tomo 6 indexes 57 Cuban journals. Separate sections consisting of more than 4375 citations are devoted to: social sciences; folklore; linguistics and literature; art; music; ballet; cinema; culture; and sports. Author and subject indexes are given. Tomo 7 offers 5689 citations in 48 Cuban journals to articles on: social sciences; literature; plastic arts; cinema and television; dance and ballet; music; education; culture; and sports. Author and subject indexes appear. A separate segment of each section is devoted to interviews and writings on individuals.

124 **Bothwell González, Reece B.** Puerto Rico: cien años de lucha política. Río Piedras, Puerto Rico: Editorial Universitaria, 1979. 4 v. in 5 (1500, 702, 602, 624 p.)

Contains copies of varied documents (platforms, manifestoes) related to the history of Puerto Rican political parties since 1869. Nearly 750 documents are reproduced in this valuable source book. Includes an introductory essay on the documents as well as a descriptive essay entitled "Síntesis Histórica de la Evolución de los Partidos Políticos en Puerto Rico." A major research and reference tool.

125 **Business International Corporation,** *New York.* Latin American forecasting study 1979–83. New York: Business International Corporation, 1978. 1 v.

In order to anticipate the business climate through 1983, this publication provides insights into the current economic forces, political trends, and social situations of Argentina, Brazil, Chile, Colombia, Dominican Republic, Ecuador, Mexico, Peru, and Venezuela. The political and economic direction of these countries is anticipated for the next five years by providing in-depth studies of their economies, investment problems, key sectors, development, and basic macroeconomic indicators.

126 *Caravelle.* Cahiers du monde hispanique et luso-brésilien. Université de Toulouse, Institut d'Études Hispaniques, Hispano-Americaines et Luso-Brésiliennes. Numéro spécial, 1980– . Toulouse, France.

This issue is entitled "La Recherche Latino-Americaniste en France: 1976–1978." Lists 112 theses on Latin American themes completed in France between 1976–78. A selection of 44 abstracts appear. Historical and literary themes predominate.

127 **Caribbean writers:** a bio-bibliographical-critical encyclopedia. Edited by Donald E. Herdeck *et al.* Washington: Three Continents Press, 1979. 943 p.

Contains biographical data on some 2000 creative writers and bibliographical detail on nearly 15,000 works. Lists of authors by country, by language used, and by social-political entity are provided. Publication is actually four volumes in one with separate volumes on English, French, Spanish and Dutch Caribbean writers. Each volume contains essays on national literature (e.g., Haitian, Cuban) and listings of pertinent literary journals. This is a major work for the study of the literature of the Caribbean. Both current and inactive writers are identified.

Carter, Boyd G. Mexican literary periodicals since 1968. See item **5223**.

128 *CCS Current Awareness Service.* Caribbean Community Secretariat. Information and Documentation Section. Vol. 1/2, Jan./Feb. 1980– . Georgetown, Guyana.

Lists new works, in subject arrangement, relevant to Caribbean studies. List of journals received given. A supplemental listing provides brief descriptions of selected journal articles.

Chacón del Campo, Julio. La prensa del Linares, 1871–1972. See item **3209**.

129 **Chicano scholars** and writers: a bio-bibliographical directory. Edited and compiled by Julio A. Martínez. Metuchen, N.J.: Scarecrow Press, 1979. 579 p.

Provides biobibliographical data on more than 500 living Chicano scholars and writers and non-Chicanos who have written on Chicanos or other Hispanics in the US. Includes index of authors arranged by subject specialization.

130 *Cladindex.* Resúmen de documentos CEPAL/ILPES. Organización de las Naciones Unidas. Comisión Económica para América Latina (CEPAL). Centro Latinoamericano de Documentación Económica y Social (CLADES). Vol. 2, 1979– . Santiago.

Provides abstracts of reports, meeting reports, working papers, studies, books, and articles produced by ECLA and ILPES. Author, title, subject, symbol, and series indexes appear. (UN document number is: E/CEPAL/CLADES/G.1.) For vol. 1, see *HLAS 41:102.*

131 **Committee on Latin America,** *London.* Literature with language, art, and music. Edited by L. Hallewell. London: 1977. 253 p. (Latin American serials; 3)

This third list of serials published by COLA covers serials held in libraries in the British Isles on the linguistics, literature, arts and music of Latin America and the West Indies. Titles and holdings are provided in alphabetical order in separate national sections. An index to titles, sponsors and publishers is given. A most useful list.

132 **Dávila, Mauro.** Arqueo hemerográfico de la ciudad de Mérida: 1900–1950. Mérida, Venezuela: Universidad de Los Andes, Facultad de Humanidades y Educación, Instituto de Investigaciones Literarias Gonzalo Picón Febres, 1977. 161 p.; bibl. (Serie bibliográfica. Instituto de Investigaciones Literarias Gonzalo Picón Febres; 12)

Identifies 259 serials that have appeared in Mérida, Venezuela, between 1900–50. The names of Tulio Febres Cordero, Mariano Picón Salas, Gonzalo Picón Febres, Humberto Tejera, Caracciolo Paria Pérez, among others, appear. The work provides an alphabetical listing of serials with information on editor, date of first appearance, frequency, format included; a chronological list of journals by appearance of the initial issue; listing of printers and typographers; and a list of editors, administrators and founders.

133 **DePlatt, Lyman.** Genealogical historical guide to Latin America. Detroit: Gale Research Co., 1978. 273 p. (Gale genealogy & local history series; 4)

An indispensible introduction and guide to conducting research on genealogical and social topics in Latin America. Introduced by general chapters on research standards, civil registration, ecclesiastical records, paleography, abbreviations, research aids, colonial calendar, ecclesiastical division in Latin America (1492–1912), population movements and political divisions. Listing of frequently encountered abbreviations and a glossary of words used in documents appear. For each of 20 Latin American countries separate chapters provide key facts concerning civil registration; ecclesiastical, census and notarial records; cemeteries, miscellaneous records; and major national archival sources. A general index is provided. Areas never under Spanish or Portuguese dominion are excluded; Haitian records before 1800 are discussed.

134 Di Genio de Carlomagno, Ana M. and **Elis Duarte de Bogadjian.** Repertorio nacional de siglas. Montevideo: Biblioteca Nacional José Artigas, Junta de Vecinos de Montevideo, 1977. 316 p.; bibl.; index.

Provides complete names and addresses to Uruguayan acronyms. Index provides access by subject of organization.

135 Doctoral dissertations in Hispanic American literature: a bibliography of dissertations completed in the United States, 1964–1974. Compiled by Barbara J. Robinson. Austin, Tex.: SALALM Secretariat, 1979. 49 p.; index (Bibliography-Seminar on the Acquisition of Latin American Library Materials; 5)

A record of the more than 300 percent increase in the number of dissertations for the 10-year period. Interest in contemporary fiction and comparative literature most evident. The strong interest in Mexican literature (25 percent of the total) persisted; titles related to Argentina, Chile, and Cuba followed. Production by university, by year, and by country is provided. Includes geographical index. For literary critic's comment, see item **5059**.

Echevarría, Evelio. Panorama y bibliografía de la novela social boliviana. See item **3151**.

136 Elkin, Judith Laikin. Latin American Jewish studies. Cincinnati: American Jewish Archives, 1980. 53 p.

Assesses the history, present state and future development of Latin American Jewish studies. After an introductory essay discusses the evolution of this new area of scholarly inquiry, a survey of published literature available for the study of Latin American Jewry at the undergraduate and general readership levels, an inventory of current research needs in Latin American Jewish studies and a directory of scholars identified by name, institution, research and publications in the field are presented. See also the author's excellent history, *Jews of the Latin American republics* (item **1927a**).

137 Faculty research and publication, the Center for Latin American Studies of Tulane University. Compiled by Arthur Carpenter. New Orleans, Louisiana: Tulane University, 1980. 1 v.

Briefly provides academic information about Latin America oriented professors and lists books and articles authored by each.

138 *Foreign Language Index.* Public Affairs Information Service. Vol. 7, No. 3, 1977– . New York.

A selected index to periodical materials in the fields of economics and public affairs published in French, German, Italian, Portuguese and Spanish. A key to periodical references and a directory of publishers and organizations are provided. Subject and geographical accesses to pertinent Latin American literature provided.

139 A guide to reviews of books from and about Hispanic America 1978 (Guía a las reseñas de libros de y sobre Hispanoamérica 1978). Edited by Antonio Matos. Detroit: Blaine Ethridge-Books, 1980. 1696 p.

Provides reviews of books on Hispanic America which appear in over 570 of the principal periodicals which include reviews. Citations are presented in alphabetical order by author; title, subject, and author of review indexes appear. Annotations appear in Spanish or English. Titles brought to the attention of the author are included from the first issue available from 1972 on.

140 *HAPI: Hispanic American Periodicals Index,* 1977. Edited by Barbara G. Valk. Los Angeles: University of California, Latin American Center, 1980. 719 p.

This annual listing provides separate subject and author access to all articles appearing in more than 200 journals containing contributions on Latin America. Only the pure and technical sciences have been excluded. Issues of journals appearing in this volume were published in 1977, although some bear earlier dates because of delayed or irregular publication schedules. Spanish and Portuguese translations of subject headings are given. This is an important bibliographical tool for access to journal articles.

Hemerografía sobre las huelgas en el siglo XIX. See item **2205**.

Hirst, Mónica. Uma guia para a pesquisa histórica no Rio de Janeiro: os documentos privados nos arquivos públicos. See item **3672**.

141 Hoffman, Herbert H. Cuento mexicano index. Newport Beach, Ca.: Headway Publications, 1978. 599 p.; indexes (A Humanitas book)

Indexes stories in 674 anthologies of Mexican short stories. Separate title/author and author/title indexes appear. Especially useful for identifying short stories by author.

142 **Indice análitico** de autores y temas: tomo 1, no. 1, dic. 1907 a tomo 50, no. 148/150, dic. 1977 de *Revista Histórica* (UMHN/RH, 71[50]: 148/150, 2. época, dic. 1977, p. 197–274)

This work provides analytical indexes by author and by subject of the articles that have appeared in the Uruguayan Museo Histórico Nacional's *Revista Histórica* from issue No. 1 (dic. 1907) to issue No. 150 (dic. 1977).

143 *Indice de Artículos de Publicaciones Periódicas en el Area de Ciencias Sociales y Humanidades.* Instituto Colombiano para el Fomento de la Educación Superior (ICFES). División de Documentación e Información. Vol. 3, No. 6, nov. 1977– . Bogotá.

Indexes issues of 66 journal titles published between 1974–77. Provides listings of articles by journal title, author and subject indexes, and lists of journals used and cooperating libraries. Good coverage of Colombian publications as well as selected titles from throughout the world. Journals beginning with letters A–M alone are indexed in this issue.

144 *Información Documental Costarricense y Centroamericana.* Universidad de Costa Rica. Instituto de Investigaciones Sociales. Centro de Documentación. Serie A, No. 2, Centro América, enero/junio 1980– . San José.

Describes 300 selected items from a base of 1800 records, reports, addresses, and bibliographies, on economic development, Central American economic integration, balance of payments, natural resources, and land tenure in Central America, Latin America and the world in the Documentation Center's files. Additional publications in the series will address the issues of social theory and documental information on Costa Rica and Central America. A series B is contemplated and will contain reproduction of selected research materials. Access to these documents and those in other publications is through personal and corporate author, personal name, key word, and imprint data indexes. Each entry contains a résumé.

145 **Instituto Histórico e Geográfico de Alagoas. Museu.** Catálogo ilustrado da Coleção Arqueológica. Compilação de Napoleão Figueiredo e Maria Helena de Amorim Folha. Maceió: O Instituto, 1976. 55 p.; bibl.; ill.

Provides descriptions of the pieces of the Joaquim Jonas Bezerra Montenegro collection and other artifacts in the museum. An introductory article traces the evolution of archaeological studies of the occupation of the Amazon region and the ceramic traditions existing in the Amazon Basin.

146 **Jackson, William Vernon.** Resources for Brazilian studies at the Bibliothèque Nationale. Austin, Tex.: Jackson, 1980. 57 p.; bibl.

This survey is the result of a five-week survey of the Library's holdings in the Département des Imprimés conducted in 1979. It does not reflect holdings of books and other resources (e.g., manuscripts, maps, music, prints, etc.) in other departments of the Library. Strongest holdings are found in late 19th-century imprints and in the fields of history, description and literature.

147 **Jalisco,** *Mexico* (state). **Secretaría General de Gobierno. Archivo Histórico de Jalisco.** Guía de los archivos históricos de Guadalajara. Guadalajara, México: Unidad Editorial, 1979. 1 v. (Bibliografías y catálogos)

Provides two-three-page descriptions on each of 17 archives in Guadalajara. General information on the contents of collections, location of the archive, hours of service and director is given for each. A bibliography accompanies the work. A very useful introductory tool.

Lapido, Graciela and **Beatriz Spota de Lapieza Elli.** De Rivadavia a Rosas: *The British Packet.* See item **3373**.

148 **Latin American** shipping 1979. Colchester, England: Seatrade Publications, 1979. 168 p.

Contains information and analysis about maritime developments in Latin America. Work is divided into two parts: the Latin American Maritime Scene and the Latin American Countries. Pt. 1 contains a series of short assessments of each sector of the industry and of latest developments in

Latin American maritime transportation; pt. 2 is a country-by-country breakdown which provides basic facts and figures, and lists major shipowners and shipbuilders in: Mexico, Ecuador, Colombia, Venezuela, Peru, Brazil, Bolivia, Chile, Paraguay, Uruguay, and Argentina.

149 Leal, Ildefonso. Libros y bibliotecas en Venezuela colonia, 1633–1767. Caracas: Universidad Central de Venezuela, Facultad de Humanidades y Educación, 1979. 148 p.

A preliminary study to a larger two volume work by the author. Examines, in this bibliographical essay, the history of the book in America and in particular the book in Venezuela from 1633 to the expulsion of the Jesuits in 1767. An excellent study.

Levine, Robert M. Historical dictionary of Brazil. See item **3528**.

150 Lollett C., Carlos Miguel. Bibliografía de *Cultura Venezolana*. Mérida, Venezuela: Universidad de Los Andes, Instituto de Investigaciones Literarias Gonzálo Picón Febres, 1977. 136 p. (Serie bibliográfica; 11)

The first publication of a work completed in 1942 contains a general index to authors and institutions and a subject index to the 117 numbers of the noted journal, *Cultural Venezolana* (1918–32). That publication contained critical essays, short stories, poems, book reviews and notices and was considered the most valuable guide to Venezuelan literature following the demise of *El Cojo Ilustrado*.

151 Major companies of Brazil, Mexico and Venezuela 1979/1980. Edited by S.J. Longrigg. London: Graham & Trotman, 1979. 405 p.

Provides information such as company location, directors, subsidiaries, principal activities, financial value (paid up capital, turnover), principal stockholders and number of employees. Companies are listed in alphabetical order by country. An index classifies companies by activity.

Martins, Ari. Escritores do Rio Grande do Sul. See item **6422**.

152 Medina, Rubens and **Cecilia Medina-Quiroga.** Nomenclature & hierarchy: basic Latin American legal sources. Washington: The Library of Congress, 1979. 123 p.

Identifies for each Latin American nation the hierarchy of its legal authorizations (i.e., constitution, laws/treaties, and decrees) and the current status of each authorization. Provides valuable legal information relevant to each national entity.

Méndez, Mabel. Indice analítico de *Pégaso*. See item **5633**.

Meneses, Raimundo. Dicionário literário brasileiro. See item **6427**.

153 Mesa-Lago, Carmelo. Latin American studies in Europe. Pittsburgh, Pa.: University of Pittsburgh Press, 1979. 190 p.; bibl.; maps; tables (Latin American monographs and document series; 1)

A guide to and an analysis and comparison of Latin American studies programs in Europe. Includes full description of programs in Austria, Czechoslovakia, East and West Germany, France, Italy, The Netherlands, Poland, Portugal, Spain, Sweden, USSR and U.K. and summaries for Belgium, Hungary, Switzerland and Yugoslavia. Nearly 100 programs are identified with information on personnel, students, publications and the history (evolution, status, and future prospects) of each provided. A valuable reference work. For historian's comment, see item **1797**.

154 Mexico. Instituto Nacional de Antropología e Historia. Proyectos Especiales de Investigación. Informe 1979, 5 años de vida: evaluación 1975–1979. México: 1980. 62 p.

Describes the activities of the special research projects group at INAH during the past five years. Monographs and articles completed and in progress as well as conferences and seminars conducted are given.

155 ———. Secretaría de Educación Pública. Dirección General de Publicaciones y Bibliotecas. Directorio de bibliotecas de la República Mexicana. Compilación de Cecilia Culebra y Vives. 6. ed. México: La Dirección, 1979. 2 v. (924 p.)

This sixth edition provides an alphabetical listing of 2532 public, academic, governmental, and private libraries in Mexico, by state. Basic information on location, directorship, size of collection, subject specificity, and hours of service appear. Includes selected general and state statistics on Mexican libraries. Institutional, personal names, geographic and subject indexes are given.

156 *México: Artículos Clasificados.* Universidad Nacional Autónoma de México. Facultad de Ciencias Políticas y Sociales. Centro de Documentación. Vol. 2, No. 5/6, nov./dic. 1979– . México.

This publication appears 12 times per year and contains reference to articles in the fields of political and social science published in Mexico and on Mexico in foreign journals. Access to the material is provided by subject, country/region/organ, and author indexes. Citations are presented in alphabetical order by author. This issue contains articles gleaned from 37 Mexican and 18 foreign journals.

157 **Núñez, Benjamín.** Dictionary of Afro-Latin American civilization. Westport, Conn.: Greenwood Press, 1980. 1 v.; bibl.; index.

Provides a wide selection of terms related to the African experience in the Latin American and Caribbean areas. A useful work for those searching for the precise meaning of origin of terms.

158 **Organization of American States. Columbus Memorial Library.** Index to Latin American periodical literature 1966–1970. v. 1, A–Ins; v. 2, Int–Z. Boston: G.K. Hall, 1980. 2 v. (760, 788 p.)

This listing, containing about 51,000 author, subject, and cross reference entries, covers periodical articles processed in the Columbus Memorial Library during 1966–70 and continues the eight volume compilation of the *Index* (1929–65). Articles in economic, political, social and cultural fields predominate.

Ortega, José and **Adolfo Cáceres Romero.** Diccionario de la literatura boliviana. See item **5383**.

159 *Planindex.* Resúmen de documentos sobre planificación. Organización de las Naciones Unidas. Comisión Económica para América Latina (CEPAL). Centro Latinoamericano de Documentación Económica y Social (CLADES). Vol. 1, 1980– . Santiago.

This listing of 336 works constitutes the initial effort of the Information System for Planning in Latin America and the Caribbean (United Nations Document No. E/CEPAL/CLADES/L.3). It is designed to provide up-to-date information on studies, plans and research produced on development planning in the region. Goal is to become the basic working tool for the planner. Each issue of *Planindex* (a semestral publication) will continue documentation on planning processed and entered in the CLADES (Latin American Center for Economic and Social Documentation) data base during the six months prior to publication of each issue. *Planindex* results from the joint effort of CLADES and the Caribbean Documentation Center of ECLA; summaries appear indiscriminately in Spanish or English. The index consists of two parts: 1) a bibliographical reference section arranged by major subject groups with each entry summarized (general subject areas include models, development plans, information and basic data, and suggestions for policy), and 2) a series of indexes (separate author, subject, geographical, symbol). A valuable tool for the researcher.

160 **Ramos, Dulce Helena Alvares Pessôa.** Um exemplo de pesquisa bibliográfica como elemento da pesquisa pública: as teses americanas sobre o Brasil, 1960–1970. São Paulo: s.n., 1977. 317 p.; ill. (Coleção da Revista de história; 71)

An indication of the output of a decade by US institutions in the fields of history, economics, sociology, literature and political science. Greatest number of dissertations were in economics, followed by history and literature. Abstracts of dissertations appear in an appendix.

161 *Revista de Información Científica y Técnica Cubana.* Academia de Ciencias de Cuba. Instituto de Documentación e Información Científica y Técnica. Año 10, No. 1, marzo 1979– . La Habana.

Indexes 15 Cuban scientific journals issued between 1975 and 1976. Individual articles are abstracted.

162 **Rodríguez Demorizi, Emilio.** Sociedades, cofradías, escuelas, gremios y otras corporaciones dominicanas. Santo Domingo: Editora Educativa Dominicana, 1975. 267 p. (Academia Dominicana de la Historia; 35)

Provides brief descriptions of civic organizations, religious confraternities and sodalities, schools, and baseball clubs existing throughout Dominican history. Index to persons, sites, and subjects appear. Useful publication if one is aware of the town in which a club is located.

163 Román Lagunas, Jorge. La littérature hispano-américaine en *Cahiers du Monde Hispanique et Luso-Brésilien (Caravalle)*, 1963–1979 (UTIEH/C, 35, 1980, p. 59–88)

Provides a list of articles, reviews, and reports classified by country that appeared in the journal during the period. Fully one-third of the journal's issues during the period were devoted to individual countries of Latin America.

164 Sehlinger, Peter J. A select guide to Chilean libraries and archives. Bloomington: Latin American Studies Program, Indiana University, 1979. 35 p. (Latin American studies working papers; 9)

Briefly describes the research materials and facilities found in 22 major libraries and archives in Chile. Sections describing the National Library and National Archives holdings and organization are especially useful. Author suggests that personal contact with Chilean scholars is the most reliable method for effective research in the country.

165 *Síntesis Informativa Iberoamericana.* Instituto de Cultura Hispánica. Centro de Documentación Iberoamericana. 1975– Madrid.

This is a day-to-day synthesis of news on Latin America, in general, and on each country during 1975. A review of Spanish-Latin American relations over the same period appears in the appendix. This publication is a synthesis of the Centro de Documentación Iberoamericana's *Resúmen Mensual Iberoamericano*. The majority of the news is from Agence France Presse.

166 Sonntag, Iliana L.; Shelley E. Phipps; and **Ross W. McLachlan.** Guide to Chicano resources in the University of Arizona Library. 2. ed. Tucson, Ariz.: 1980. 186 p.

Emphasis of the guide is on the Mexican American, his sociological, political and cultural milieu. Selected materials in the arts, economics, education, folklore, health, history, labor and laboring classes, language, literature, politics and government, psychology, religion, sociology, and sports appear. Author, title, and subject indexes are included.

167 Statistical abstract of Latin America. v. 20. Edited by James W. Wilkie and Peter Reich. Los Angeles: University of California, Latin American Center, 1980. 623 p.

Based on statistics generated by UCLA researchers and published for the first time as well as upon data abstracted from published sources. Contains 684 tables emphasizing main social and economic indicators; geographic, social, socioeconomic, economic, and political data; and international statistics. Four articles in the publication use data to measure political conflict in Latin America 1948–67, the rural population of Argentina to 1970, Mexico in the US press 1972–78, and the Mexican leadership since 1935. Much of the data presented provides a review of statistical activity over time (i.e., over a 10–20 year period). Includes subject index.

168 *Statistical Bulletin of the OAS.* Organization of American States. General Secretariat. Vol. 1, No. 1, 1979– . Washington.

This quarterly publication is prepared by the Planning and Statistics Program of the OAS and is available from the OAS Department of Publications, Washington, D.C. 20006, for $12.00 per year. Contains current data on wide ranges of topics related to demography and economy, foreign trade and international reserves, public finances, domestic prices, interest and exchange rates, employment, salaries, and goods and services production. An analytical article appears in each issue. In Vol. 1, no. 4 (1979), Michael Zuntz discussed chronological per capita GDP and growth statistics of Latin America, Caribbean, and industrialized countries; in Vol. 1, no. 2–3 (1979), Karen Stevens considered the Latin American labor force in perspective. Useful current data appears in this publication.

169 United Nations. Economic Commission for Latin America. Latin American Center for Economic and Social Documentation. Directorio del medio ambiente: América Latina y el Caribe, versión definitiva—1977. Santiago: 1979. 576 p.

Provides addresses, basic objectives, activities, and thematic areas of concern of 470 national and international institutions with some emphasis on the environment in the region. Items are arranged in separate national and international lists; thematic, institutional and symbols indexes are provided.

170 United States. Agency for International Development. Directorio de recursos para el desarrollo. Washington: 1980. 1 v.

This directory, available in Spanish, French and English, attempts to identify the available resources in the US and overseas for development planning. It includes information on available data banks, information centers, journals, technical help services and institutions and organizations for development at national, regional and the international level. A description of each service is provided.

171 **Vasco de Escudero, Grecia.** Los archivos quiteños. Quito: n.p., 1977. 184 p.

This guide to the Archives of Quito was presented at the XI Asamblea General del IPGH (Instituto Panamericano de Geografía e Historia) and Reuniones Panamericanas de Consulta Conexas. It provides information on religious and public archives in Quito. A later work, *Directorio ecuatoriano de archivos* (see item **172**) complements this publication. More than 160 archives are described in this work, including those for monasteries, religious orders, ecclesiastical archives, and administrative and permanent public archives.

172 **———.** Directorio ecuatoriano de archivos. Quito: Instituto Panamericano de Geografía e Historia, Sección Nacional del Ecuador, 1979. 163 p.

A guide to the 125 public and private archives in Ecuador. Provides basic data (i.e., name, address, hours of service, brief description of collection, personnel) on each depository. Also includes information on church parish and other ecclesiastical archives. Does not include those archives listed in the author's companion volume, *Los archivos quiteños* (see item **171**).

173 **Werlich, David P.** Research tools for Latin American historians: a select, annotated bibliography. New York: Garland Publishing, 1980. 269 p. (Garland reference library of social science; 60)

A classified, annotated bibliography of nearly 1400 reference works, compendiums of source materials, and periodicals useful to Latin American historians. Reference books, pamphlets, official documents, periodicals, periodical articles and essays in English, Portuguese, Spanish, French, and German, concerning the Latin American nations exclusive of the non-Hispanic Caribbean and Puerto Rico. Work is divided into two parts: one devoted to general Latin American topics and the other to individual countries.

174 **Who's who** in Costa Rica 1979–1980. San José: Lubeck, 1979. 1 v.

This bilingual publication contains a separate business and government institution section in addition to the personal names section. Business section contains information on location, purpose and directors of business. Publication has decidedly business and professional orientation.

GENERAL WORKS

175 **Alegría, Ricardo E.** El Instituto de Cultura Puertorriqueña 1955–1973. 18 años contribuyendo a fortalecer nuestra conciencia nacional. San Juan, Puerto Rico: Instituto de Cultura Puertorriqueña, 1978. 266 p.

An impressive panoramic review of the Institute's broad range of programs and other activities. Briefly describes activities within its archive and library, research, monuments and famous personages, museums and parks, plastic arts, music, theater, printing, films and grant programs.

176 **Arencibia-Huidobro, Yolanda.** The modern concept of Latin America (UNESCO/CU, 5:3, 1978, p. 147–177)

A diversity of definitions is found in this collected set of excerpts from monographs and journal articles that address the idea of Latin America. Provides a very usable starting lecture for an introductory course on Latin America.

177 *Boletín del Archivo General de la Nación.* Archivo General de la Nación. Vol. 1, oct./dic. 1979– . Managua.

Contains a study on the first historian of Nicaragua, Pedro Francisco de la Rocha; a reprint of article regarding Sandino in *Repertorio Americano*; inventories of documents related to Nicaragua in foreign archives and libraries; and reproductions of documents on the Virgen de El Viejo and a trip from Portobelo to Nicaragua. A useful addition to historical literature.

Catálogo do Arquivo Cochrane; edição comemorativa do bicentenário de nascimento do Primeiro-Almirante Lord Thomas Cochrane, Marquês do Maranhão: 1775–1860. See item **3151**.

178 Ciclo de Estudios Históricos de la Provincia de Santander, *2nd, 1977.* Santander y el Nuevo Mundo. Santander, Spain: Institución Cultural de Cantabria, Diputación Provincial, 1979. 661 p.

Contains a wide range of essays, papers, and presentations on the impact of Santander on the New World. Main area of writing concerns the colonial period with emphasis on Argentina, Mexico, Puerto Rico, Cuba, and Colombia.

179 Cordero, Luis Agustín. Incunables peruanos y estudios bibliográficos. Lima: Universidad Nacional Mayor de San Marcos, Dirección Universitaria de Proyección Social, Seminario de Historia Rural Andina, 1979. 136 p.; bibl.; ill.

Records the history of 16th and 17th-century publishing in Peru through the identification of works and the inclusion of brief historico-biographical accounts of the major publishers and printers, including Nicolás Antonio, Antonio de León Pinelo and Antonio Ricardo.

180 Drekonja Kornat, Gerhard. Ecuador: ensayo bibliográfico (*in* Ecuador, hoy. Edición de Gerhard Drekonja *et al.* Apéndice documental de Gustavo Jarrin Ampudia. Bogotá: Siglo Veintiuno Editores, 1978, p. 281–313 [Historia inmediata])

Brief general overview of political development in Ecuador to the present. Contains references to social science contributions in the body of the presentation and in an appended bibliography; the emergence of a national corps of social scientists in the past decade is noted.

181 Enciclopedia yucatanense. 2. ed. Patrocinado por el Gobierno del Estado de Yucatán a cargo del Dr. Francisco Luna Kan. Publicada bajo la dirección de la Comisión Reeditora de la Enciclopedia Yucatanense. Integrada por Luis H. Hoyos Villanueva *et al.* México: Gobierno de Yucatán, 1977 [1945]. 9 v.; bibl.; indexes.

A new edition of the 1945 work, but with little change. Individual volumes are devoted to specific themes and disciplines (e.g., geography, history, publishing, poetry, education, medicine, music, art, biography, local and current history, bibliography). General indexes appear.

182 EPICA Task Force, *Washington.* Jamaica: Caribbean challenge; a people's primer by the EPICA Task Force. Washington: 1979. 119 p.

Provides an opinionated review of the social history and the current economic, political and social conditions in Jamaica. Contains strong views on political party activities and international involvement in the island's economy. The publication is available from the Ecumenical Program for Inter-American Communication and Action (EPICA), 1470 Irving St., N.W., Washington, D.C. 20010.

183 Grases, Pedro. De la imprenta de Venezuela y algunas obras de referencia. Caracas: Universidad Central de Venezuela, Facultad de Humanidades y Educación, Escuela de Bibliotecología y Archivología, 1979. 260 p.

An anthology of works and articles by the author on the themes noted in the title. Both themes are well represented with major emphasis on imprints of the 19th century (e.g., *Gazeta de Caracas, Correo del Orinoco,* and *Leander*) and with brief articles on historical documents, facsimile editions, bibliographies, and informative publications (e.g., *El Cojo Ilustrado, El Nacional*). Contributions by R.A. Humphreys and Carlos Miguel Lollett appear. A general index is included.

184 Knight, Thomas J. Latin America comes of age. Metuchen, N.J.: Scarecrow Press, 1979. 325 p.; index.

General introduction to Latin America utilizing brief sketches on its history, geography, politics and development. Work is divided into sections on South America, Middle America, and international relations. Index and selected sources are given.

185 Latin America 1978. Edited by Grace M. Ferrara. New York: Facts on File, 1979. 186 p.

Provides general coverage of the Latin American region and all countries, except Honduras, during 1978, providing information on political, economic, and social happenings. Includes general index. A useful review.

186 Mass media in/on Cuba and the Caribbean area: the role of the television, radio, and the free press. Edited by Jan Herd.

Erie, PA: Northwestern Pennsylvania Institute for Latin American Studies; Mercyhurst College, 1979. 79 leaves; bibl. (Latin American monograph series; 10)

These papers by John Lent, Judy Milner, Jon Cozean, and Marvin Alisky, originally presented at the 26th annual conference of the South Eastern Council on Latin American Studies in 1979, discuss the mass media (i.e., television, radio, and press) in Trinidad, Barbados, Jamaica, Guyana, Cuba, and Mexico. Jon Cozean's study reviews US press coverage of Cuba prior to the Bay of Pigs invasion.

187 Matijevic, Nicolás. Imprenta bahiense. Bahía Blanca, Argentina: Universidad Nacional del Sur, Departamento de Ciencias Sociales, 1978. 92 p.

In honor of the 150th anniversary of Bahía Blanca's founding, the author has written a brief review of the development of printing in the city (from 1856) and has compiled a bibliography, by printer, of 561 works printed in Bahía Blanca. Author index included. See also item **3389**.

Millones, Luis. Las religiones nativas del Perú: recuento y evaluación de su estudio. See item **1676**.

188 Mohler, Stephen C. Publishing in colonial Spanish America: an overview (RIB, 28:3, julio/sept. 1978, p. 259–273)

This brief introduction to publishing and printing during the colonial period considers mainly the laws affecting publishing and the enforcement of those laws. He suggests that economic limitations, loss of manuscripts, availability of printing presses and supplies, limitations of potential sales, attitudes and tastes also were inhibiting factors to a strong publishing tradition during the colonial period.

189 New directions in language and area studies: priorities for the 1980's. Edited by Donald R. Shea and Maureen J. Smith. Milwaukee: University of Wisconsin, Center for Latin America, Consortium of Latin American Studies Programs, 1979. 153 p. (CLASP publication; 9)

Provides commentary from selected representatives of academic Latin American studies programs in the US regarding future emphasis of developmental assistance programs, institutional development and language and area studies, outreach and citizen education, and problems of research in Latin American studies. Governmental service and congressional perspectives of the future funding and role of Latin American and international studies are suggested by Viron P. Vaky and Dante Fascell respectively. Views of the 1980s from African, Middle Eastern, Slavic and Canadian studies are given. Publication is a record of the conference held on the theme at Wingspread, Racine, Wisconsin, Feb. 18–20, 1979.

190 Uma política integrada do livro para um país em processo de desenvolvimento: preliminares para a definição de uma política nacional do livro. São Paulo: Câmara Brasileira do Livro [and] Sindicato Nacional dos Editores de Livros, Rio de Janeiro, 1976. 2 v.

Discusses the book in Brazil, the publishing and the distributing by national and foreign publishers, and the search for a national policy for the book. Vol. 1 attempts to define a national policy while vol. 2 contains the proposed law. Valuable information on book production and distribution.

191 *Revista Lotería.* Lotería Nacional de Beneficencia. No. 292, julio 1980– . Panamá.

The entire issue of this monthly journal is devoted to theme "Centenario del Canal Francés," honoring the initiation of the construction of the canal in Panama in 1880 by Ferdinand de Lesseps. Articles discuss impact of the French in 19th-century Panama, ecology and mortality in the country during the canal's construction, Carlos de Lesseps, and the Jews of Panama (1876–1903). Also includes series of period photographs.

Rodrigues, José Honório. História da história do Brasil. See item **3603**.

192 *SECOLAS Annals.* Kennesaw College, Southeastern Conference on Latin American Studies. Vol. 10, March 1979– . Marietta, Georgia.

This work contains selected papers from the XXV annual SECOLAS program at Charleston, South Carolina, April 6–8, 1978. The general theme of the conference was "Politics and Political Participation in Latin America." Ten papers from the sessions on politics and policy making, Latin American women, writers and politics, political parties and the formation of the Latin American democracies, and the military appear.

193 ———. ———, ———. Vol. 11, March 1980– . Marietta, Georgia.

A selection of papers from the XXVI annual SECOLAS program held in Tampa, April 19–21, 1979. The general theme of the conference, "Cuba and the Caribbean: Twentieth Century Perspectives," is reflected in the eight contributions of the volume. Four papers are concerned with politics and economics of Castro period Cuba, one paper addresses the theme of pre-revolutionary politics and social classes in Cuba, two papers are on the Dominican Republic's relations with the United States and Haiti and one article presents another view of the Colombian *violencia.*

194 **Servicio de Extensión de Cultural Chilena** (SEREC), *Santiago.* Guía de museos y salas de arte de Chile. Santiago: 1979. 26 p.

This directory provides information on the location, directorship, sponsor, and characteristics of collections of museums and art salons in Chile. An index to facilities by discipline interest is included.

LIST OF NEW SERIAL TITLES

Actualidades. Centro de Estudios Latinoamericanos Rómulo Gallegos. Caracas.

195 *Anuario.* Instituto de Investigaciones Históricos Dr. José Gaspar Rodríguez de Francia. Año 1, No. 1, mayo 1979– . Asunción.

This first issue is entirely devoted to the subject of Francia. However, the editor's preface states that articles on all topics and from all viewpoints concerning Paraguayan history will appear in subsequent issues. Edited by Alfredo Viola, the journal's address is: Teniente Colmán 1281, Asunción, Paraguay.

196 *Boletín.* Academia de Historia del Cauca. Vol. 1, No. 1, Año 1, julio 1980– . Popayán, Colombia.

Articles authored by members of the Academia de Historia del Cauca as well as other institutions throughout Latin America. All professors and researchers in the field of Latin American history are welcome to submit articles. This publication is edited by Edgar Penagos Casas, and the address is: Apartado Aéreo 890, Popayán, Colombia.

197 *Boletín de Antropología Americana.* Instituto Panamericano de Geografía e Historia. Vol. 1 [nueva época] junio 1980– México.

This journal replaces the PAIGH's *Boletín Bibliográfico de Antropología Americana.* It contains a variety of articles touching all areas of Latin American culture. It is available from Servicios Bibliográficos, Instituto Panamericano de Geografía e Historia, Ex-Arzobispado 29, México 18, D.F., México.

198 *Boletín de Ciencias Económicas y Sociales.* Universidad Centroamericana José Simeón Cañas, Departamento de Economía. Año 2, No. 11, abril 1979– . San Salvador.

Monthly publication consists of articles on economic, social, national, international, Central American, and Salvadorean themes. Subscription cost: US $4.00 per year.

199 *Boletín de Coyuntura Socioeconómica.* Universidad del Valle, División de Ciencias Sociales y Económicas, Centro de Investigación y Documentación Socioeconómica. No. 1, mayo 1980– . Cali, Colombia.

Journal intends to publish articles concerning the principal social and economic problems of the region. This publication is available from CIDSE, División de Ciencias Sociales y Económicas, Universidad del Valle, Meléndez, Cali, Colombia (Apartado Aéreo 2188, Cali). Articles in this issue are on social mobility; magic and politics; the labor market in Cali; the 1980 elections in Cali; and transnational companies in the Andean automobile program.

200 *Boletín de Información.* Centro Interamericano de Artesanía y Artes Populares (CIDAP). No. 1, enero/abril 1979– . Cuenca, Ecuador.

Available from CIDAP, Hermano Miguel 2-23, Apartado 557, Cuenca, Ecuador. Contains information on organizations, activities and reports of other groups involved in the subject. Bibliographic citations are included.

201 *Boletín Informativo para Asuntos Migratorios y Fronterizos.* Comité de Servicio de Los Amigos, Centro de Información para Migración y Desarrollo. México.

Discusses US-Mexican relations in terms of border area problems and immigration. Deals with social, political, and economic topics affecting the border regions. Includes a section concerning up-coming lectures, activities, and investigations. Also includes bibliography and notes (for works in Spanish and English). Available from Casa de los Amigos, Ignacio Mariscal 132, México 1, D.F., México. Cost US $5.00 per year (six issues).

202 *Boletín Informativo Trotskysta.* Tendencia Cuartainternacionalista. Organización Trotskysta Revolucionaria. No. 1, abril 1979– . Lima.

Trotskyite journal. Contributing organizations are: Partido Obrero Revolucionario (Bolivia); Política Obrera (Argentina); Comité de Enlace de Militantes Trotskystas Chilenos; Organización Trotskysta Revolucionaria (Perú); Tendencia Trotskysta (Brazil); and Política Proletaria (Venezuela). The first issue contains the declaration approved by the International Conference held in early April 1979.

203 *Britain and Latin America.* An annual review of British-Latin American relations. Latin American Bureau. 1979– . London.

Contains articles on politics, the arms trade, and international relations of Latin America; special emphasis on British interest in Latin America, e.g., regarding immigration, political relations, trade, investment, aid. A listing of British organizations concerned with Latin America and British journals on the subject appears. Copies are available from Latin American Bureau, P.O. Box 134, London NW1/4JY, England.

204 *Bulletin d'Information.* Association des Archivistes, Bibliothecaires, Documentalistes Francophones de la Caraïbe, Section Haiti. Vol. 1, 1980– . Port-au-Prince.

This new serial provides information on the activities of Haitian documentalists. Discusses items of interest on Haiti and the Caribbean. This quarterly publication is available from the Institut Français d'Haiti, Blvd. Harry Truman & Avenue Marie Jeanne, B.P. 131, Port-au-Prince, Haiti.

205 *El Caribe Contemporáneo.* Universidad Nacional Autónoma de México, Facultad de Ciencias Políticas y Sociales, Centro de Estudios Latinoamericanos. México.

Consists of political, social, and cultural essays on present-day Caribbean life. Includes some reprinted articles, lists of new publications, and bibliography. Edited by Suzy Castor, this triennial publication is available from CELA, UNAM, México 20, D.F., México at US $2.25 per issue.

206 *Caricom Perspective.* Caribbean Community Secretariat. No. 1, March 1980– . Georgetown, Guyana.

Provides brief reports on happenings inside the community of nations of CARICOM. Issues are available from the Caribbean Community Secretariat, P.O. Box 607, Bank of Guyana Building, Georgetown, Guyana. Frequency of issues is not indicated.

207 *Casa del Tiempo.* Universidad Autónoma Metropolitana. Dirección de Difusión Cultural. Vol. 1, No. 1, sept. 1980– México.

Monthly journal devoted to literature and the arts. Includes book reviews, art reviews, poetry, and prose. Focus is not on Mexican authors but rather translations (into Spanish) of many other writers and poets throughout the world. The publication, available at US $24.00 per year, is edited by Carlos Montemayor, Medellín 28, Colonia Roma, México 7, D.F., México.

208 *Casas Reales.* Museo de las Casas Reales. Año 1, No. 1, dic. 1976– . Santo Domingo.

Researchers composed of both Spanish and Dominicans work under the auspices of the Museo de las Casas Reales, which is dedicated to the preservation and restoration of monuments in the Dominican Republic. This publication includes information from several historical preservation groups dealing with landmarks, monuments, and cultural treasures. Includes photos and illustrations. Reports on documentation and conferences relating to the preservation of cultural treasures and monuments. Edited by Pedro Santiago, Diógenes Céspedes, Cayo Castillanos and Amadeo Julián. This publication can be obtained from Museo de las Casas Reales, Las Damas 1, Santo Domingo, República Dominicana.

209 *Ciencia y Tecnología.* Editorial Universidad de Costa Rica. Vol. 1, No. 1, 1977– . San José.

Appears every semester and is available through the Oficina de Biblioteca, Documentación, e Información, Universidad de Costa Rica, San José, Costa Rica. Serves as a vehicle for the publication of university conducted research. First number contains articles in the fields of mathematics, geology, physics, and chemistry.

210 *Controversia: Para el Exámen de la Realidad Argentina.* México.

Mexican publication concerning present-day Argentina. Topics include "socialismo," "desaparecidos," feminism, book, journals, and bibliographic information. This monthly publication, edited by Hugo Vargas and Jorge Tula, may be obtained for US $30.00 per year from Apartado Postal 20-619, México 20, D.F., México.

211 *Económico.* Ministerio de Economía y Finanzas. Vol. 1, No. 1, nov. 1978– . Montevideo.

Official publication of the Ministry of Economics and Finance. Discusses Uruguayan economy by divisions or sectors (i.e., public finances, external economies, prices, and production). Includes numerous graphs and charts. Publication available from Asesoría Económico Financiera, Servicio de Información y Biblioteca, Colonia 1013, Piso 8, Montevideo, Uruguay. The publication is distributed free of charge and appears three times a year.

212 *Encuentro: Selecciones para Latinoamérica.* Centro de Proyección Cristiana. No. 1, enero/feb. 1980– . Lima.

Material is all reprints/reproductions from major journals and newspapers in Latin America and Europe. The majority of articles are in sociopolitical and economic areas, but also contains minor sections on culture, communications, and theology. This publication, edited by Eduardo Bastos, S.J., appears 11 times per year at a subscription rate of US $85.00. It can be obtained from the Centro, Jr. Aguarico 586, Breña, Lima, Peru.

Escritos de Filosofía. Academia Nacional de Ciencias, Centro de Estudios Filosóficos. Buenos Aires.

213 *Estudios Contemporáneos.* Universidad Autónoma de Puebla, Instituto de Ciencias, Centro de Estudios Contemporáneos. Año 1, No. 1, enero/feb. 1980– . Puebla, México.

The Centro de Estudios Contemporáneos began in March 1979, as a collective project dealing with contemporary issues in Mexico. The 11 researchers involved discuss the publication as a whole. However, projects are the responsibility of individual researchers. Main fields of interest are economics, history, and sociology. Edited by Enrique Semo and available quarterly from 2 Sur 709, Puebla, México.

214 *Estudios Fiscales.* nov./dic. 1977– . México.

Bimonthly publication deals with the analysis of tax problems both within Mexico and abroad, and includes many different perspectives. The journal is divided into three sections: 1) Sección de Investigación; 2) Sección de Información; and 3) Sección de Documentos. Discusses the legal and economic policies for Mexico and Latin America. Available from *Revista de Estudios Fiscales*, Apartado 28-234, México, D.F., México.

215 *Estudos e Pesquisas em Administração.* Universidade Federal de Paraíba, Curso Mestrado em Administração. Ano 1, No. 1, jan./abril 1979– . João Pessoa, Brazil.

Material included was submitted by professors and researchers, and edited by the Curso de Mestrado em Administração. Geographically, the journal covers only Brazil, with an emphasis on the Northeast (Paraíba area). Attempts to publish specific, original research conducted in Brazil and theoretical studies that deal with administrative problems in Brazilian businesses. Edited by Afrânio de Aragão and Dean Shepard Ellis. Available for Cruzeiros $120 per year from Curso de Mestrado em Administração, Centro de Ciências Sociais Aplicadas, Campus Universitário, CEP 58.000, João Pessoa, Paraíba, Brazil.

216 *Futurable.* Fundación Argentina Año 2000. Año 1, No. 1, mayo 1979– . Buenos Aires.

Attempts to show Argentina's position in the world currently and projected. Publication calls for future of peace based on justice and freedom. Deals with themes of political economic and social strategy. Edited by Ramón Genaro Díaz Bessone and available from

Leandro N. Alem 36, 11° piso, 1003 Buenos Aires, Argentina.

217 *Geosur.* Asociación Sudamericana de Estudios Geopolíticos e Internacionales. Año 1, No. 2, sept. 1979– . Montevideo.

Articles discuss integration of frontiers, Peruvian regionalization, Bolivia's eastward march, and the South Atlantic in Brazilian geopolitics. Appended to the monthly publication every month are essays or bibliographies pertinent to the interest of the organization (e.g., in Sept. 1979, a bibliography on geopolitics; in Oct. 1979, Lewis Tambs "Factores Geopolíticos en América Latina"). Edited by Bernardo Quagliotti de Bellis, the publication can be acquired from the Asociación, Casilla 5006, Montevideo, Uruguay.

218 *Guatemala.* Unión de Guatemaltecos. La Habana.

Bulletin contains information concerning economic, political, and social affairs in Guatemala. Expresses the viewpoints of the Union of Guatemaltecos residing in Cuba, whose objectives are similar to those of Cuba today.

Guías y Catálogos. Archivo General de la Nación. No. 1, 1977– . México.

219 *Historia Crítica.* Revista de la Carrera de Historia. Universidad Nacional Autónoma de Honduras. Etapa 1, No. 1, enero 1980– . Tegucigalpa.

The focus of the journal is on the history of Honduras, but in context with the rest of the world. Includes texts and summaries of publications that are used at the University, translations, bibliographies, and book reviews. In particular, it lists the recent publications of the Universidad Nacional Autónoma de Honduras. Authors are both Hondurans and foreigners who contribute to the journal. Edited by Ramón A. Fletes Díaz.

220 *Históricas.* Universidad Nacional Autónoma de México, Instituto de Investigaciones Históricas. Año 1, No. 1, sept./dic. 1979– . México.

The principal objective of this bulletin is to relate the news and activities of the Instituto de Investigaciones Históricas, including lectures, courses, research projects, conferences, and recent acquisitions of bibliographic materials. Although it deals mainly with events at the Institute, information in the field of history at other Mexican, as well as foreign, institutions will be included. Also covers critical reviews, editorial, and other brief descriptions of historical materials. Edited by Josefina García Quintana and Roberto Moreno de las Arcos; available from the Institute, Torre 1 de Humanidades, 8° piso, Ciudad Universitaria, México, D.F., México.

221 *Indice de Ciências Sociais.* Instituto Universitário de Pesquisas do Rio de Janeiro (IUPERJ). Ano 1, No. 1, julho 1979– . Rio de Janeiro.

This index is published with the assistance of the Instituto de Planejamento Econômico e Social (IPEA). The publication covers academic works in the area of sociology and political science. Available from IUPERJ, Rua da Matriz, 82, Botafogo, Rio de Janeiro, Brazil.

222 *Informaciones.* Universidad Nacional de Asunción, Escuela de Bibliotecología. Asunción.

Contains bibliographies for various fields in the humanities and social sciences pertaining to Paraguay. Also lists recent acquisitions of note in the library at the University.

223 *Labor Information Bulletin.* Organization of American States. Inter-American Commission of Women. Vol. 1, No. 1, sept. 1980– . Washington.

Contains summaries of current news events, including a historical perspective of many issues. Reports on activities beneficial to trade unionism.

224 *Meyibó.* Universidad Nacional Autónoma de México, Centro de Investigaciones Históricas [and] Universidad Autónoma de Baja, Centro de Investigaciones Históricas. Vol. 1, No. 2, sept. 1979– . México.

Historical journal that concerns the area of Baja California. Includes bibliographies and lists of activities of the Centro de Investigaciones Históricas UNAM-UABC.

225 *Modern Language Review.* University of Guyana, Department of Modern Languages. Vol. 1, No. 1, Dec. 1977/Jan. 1978– . Georgetown, Guyana.

Published by the Department of Modern Languages, Faculty of Arts, University of Guyana, Box 841, Georgetown, Guyana.

Planned quarterly issues. Articles by members of the Department appear in Spanish, English, French and Portuguese as well as in the indigenous languages of Guyana.

226 *Nicaráuac.* Revista bimestral del Ministerio de Cultura. Managua.

Includes works by authors not only from Nicaragua but from other Latin American countries. Consists of interviews, reports, prose and poetry dealing with today's Nicaragua. Biobibliographical notes. Editorial council includes Junta member Sergio Ramírez, Bayardo Arce and Daisy Zamora; available for US $18.00 for six issues from Apartado Postal 3269, Managua, Nicaragua.

Nova Americana. Giulio Einaudi Editore. Vols. 1/2, 1978/1979– . Torino, Italy.

Plantation Society. University of New Orleans. Vol. 1, No. 1, Feb. 1979– . New Orleans, La.

Polémica. Universidad de Carabobo, Dirección de Cultura. Valencia, Venezuela.

227 *Relaciones.* Estudios de historia y sociedad. El Colegio de Michoacán. No. 1, invierno 1980– . Zamora, México.

Subsidized by the Secretary for Public Education, this journal publishes scientific works in the fields of social sciences and history of Mexico. Five main sections include articles, documents, essays and notes, book reviews, and new publications in the field. Available from El Colegio de Michoacán, Madero 310 Sur, Zamora, Michoacán, México; quarterly publication at US $15.00 per year.

228 *Revista Argentina de Administración Pública.* Instituto Nacional de la Administración Pública. Año 1, No. 1, oct./dic. 1979– . Buenos Aires.

Irregular serial. Includes a section on the activities of the different sub-groups of the Instituto Nacional de la Administración Pública, commentaries and information on both national and international conferences and symposia, legislation relating to the field, and bibliographic notes. The general articles on public administration discuss international events but the focus is on Argentina.

229 *Revista Centroamericana de Economía.* Universidad Nacional Autónoma de Honduras, Programa de Postgrado Centroamericano en Economía y Planificación del Desarrollo. Año 1, No. 1, sept. 1979– . Tegucigalpa.

This journal serves as an organ for the diffusion of theoretical and practical economic and planning themes discussed in the Post-Graduate Center for Economic and Development Planning of CSUCA located at the National University of Honduras (UNAH). It is dedicated primarily to the study of Central American economic problems and themes. Available from: Programa de Postgrado Centroamericano en Economía y Planificación del Desarrollo, Ap. Postal 1748, Tegucigalpa, Honduras for US $14.00 per year.

230 *Revista de Estadística y Geografía.* Secretaría de Programación y Presupuesto, Coordinación General de los Servicios Nacionales de Estadística, Geografía e Informática, Dirección General de Estadística. Vol. 1, No. 1, junio 1980– . México.

Bimonthly publication which supersedes the *Revista de Estádistica,* whose last issue was enero/marzo 1978. This new journal contains theories, methodologies, and techniques in statistics and geography. Contributing authors for the first issue are all specialists in the Coordinación General de los Servicios Nacionales Estadística. Issues are available from the Subdirección de Integración de Información, Insurgentes Sur 795, 9° piso, México 18, D.F., México.

231 *Revista de la Academia Boliviana de Ciencias Económicas.* No. 1, enero 1980– . Cochabamba, Bolivia.

Both the articles and the notes and commentaries section concern only Bolivian economics, however, the studies are informative and in-depth. Publishes articles by both private and public entities. This publication may be acquired for US $5.50 from Los Amigos del Libro, Casilla 450, Cochabamba, Bolivia.

232 *Revista de SINASBI.* Comisión Coordinadora del Sistema Nacional de Servicios de Bibliotecas e Información Humanística, Información Científica y Tecnología de Archivos y de Estadísticas e Informática. No. 1, julio/dic. 1978– . Caracas.

Useful review of library and information science in Venezuela. Address: Apartado 68350, Altamira, Caracas 106, Venezuela. Annual subscription: US $7.00.

233 *Revista Nacional de Cultura.* Ministerio de Cultura y Educación, Secretaría de Estado de Cultura. Año 1, No. 1, julio/sept. 1978– . Buenos Aires.

With the collaboration of experts in various disciplines of the humanities and the social sciences, this quarterly publication contains articles in the fields of anthropology, political science, natural sciences, history, art, literature, and music. Includes numerous reviews of books written by Argentine authors.

234 *SELA en Acción.* Secretaría Permanente del Sistema Económico Latinoamericano, Oficina de Información. No. 5, feb. 1979– . Caracas.

A monthly economic journal of Latin America. Comments on relations within Latin America and with Europe (i.e., the EEC-European Economic Community). The journal is informative but does not consist of official documents. Publication of the permanent Secretariat of the Sistema Económico Latinoamericano, Apartado de Correo 17035, El Conde, Caracas 101, Venezuela.

Semestre de Filosofía. Universidad Central de Venezuela. Caracas.

235 *Temas Económicos.* Universidad de Antioquia, Facultad de Ciencias Económicas, Departamento de Economía. Medellín, Colombia.

Although this journal is published by the Universidad de Antioquia, articles by authors that are not related to the University are included. The focus is on Colombian economics, however, the area of economics in general is discussed.

236 *Thesis.* Nueva revista de filosofía y letras. Universidad Nacional Autónoma de México, Facultad de Filosofía y Letras. Año 1, No. 2, julio 1979– . México.

Broad interests in philosophy and literature. This issue contains articles on Hobbes, poems by Jibonananda Das, Christian atheism, Macbeth, and revolutionary militancy among intellectuals.

Yucatán: Historia y Economía. Revista de análisis socioeconómico regional. Universidad de Yucatán, Centro de Investigaciones Regionales, Departamento de Estudios Económicos y Sociales. Mérida, México.

JOURNAL ABBREVIATIONS BIBLIOGRAPHY AND GENERAL WORKS

ASB/PP Philologica Pragensia. Academia Scientiarum Bohemoslovenica. Praha.

BBAA B.B.A.A. Boletín Bibliográfico de Antropología Americana. Instituto Panamericano de Geografía e Historia, Comisión de Historia. México.

CM/HM Historia Mexicana. El Colegio de México. México.

EC/M Mapocho. Biblioteca Nacional, Extensión Cultural. Santiago.

IFH/C Conjonction. Institut Français d'Haïti. Port-au-Prince.

IJ/JJ Jamaica Journal. Institute of Jamaica. Kingston.

MAGN/B Boletín del Archivo General de la Nación. Secretaría de Gobernación. México.

OAS/LE La Educación. Organization of American States, Dept. of Educational Affairs. Washington.

PCCLAS/P Proceedings of the Pacific Coast Council on Latin American Studies. Univ. of California. Los Angeles.

PEBN/B Boletín de la Biblioteca Nacional. Lima.

PUCP/CSH Cuadernos del Seminario de Historia. Ponitifica Univ. Católica del Perú, Instituto Riva-Agüero. Lima.

RIB Revista Interamericana de Bibliografía [Inter-American Review of Bibliography]. Organization of American States. Washington.

UMNH/RH Revista Histórica. Museo Histórico Nacional. Montevideo.

UNAM/RMCPS Revista Mexicana de Ciencias Políticas y Sociales. Univ. Nacional Autónoma de México, Facultad de Ciencias Políticas y Sociales. México.

UNAM/RMS Revista Mexicana de Sociología. Univ. Nacional Autónoma de México, Instituto de Investigaciones Sociales. México.

UNESCO/CU Cultures. United Nations Educational, Scientific and Cultural Organization. Paris.

UNESCO/JIS Unesco Journal of Information Science, Librarianship and Archives Administration. United Nations Educational, Scientific and Cultural Organization. Paris.

UTIEH/C Caravelle. Cahiers du monde hispanique et luso-brésilien. Univ. de Toulouse, Institut d'Études Hispaniques, Hispano-Americaines et Luso Brésiliennes. Toulouse, France.

ART

SPANISH AMERICA: Colonial

ROBERT J. MULLEN, *Assistant Professor of Art History, The University of Texas at San Antonio*

A LARGE NUMBER OF BOOKS GAVE wide geographic coverage and a considerable array of categories to the colonial art of Latin America. Several long-awaited monographs have been published on the following subjects: Manuel Samaniego, painter, Ecuador (item **288**); Bitti, Jesuit painter, Peru (item **262**); Domingo Gutiérrez, craftsman, Venezuela (item **330**); 10 sculptors of the Cathedral of Lima, Peru (item **323**); and an iconographic study of the retablos of Tepotzotlán, Mexico (item **304**). Three splendid catalogues of colonial paintings and sculpture from exhibits held in Spain (item **287**), Venezuela (item **265**) and the US (item **292**) have also appeared.

In Mexico, the reexamination of works by an earlier generation has led to the facsimile publication of milestones such as Valle's 1924 account of the Jesuit seminary and church at Tepotzotlán (item **317**) and Peñafiel's 1905 classic history of Tlaxcala (item **309**). Francisco de la Maza's masterpiece on choir screens in convents (women) has appeared in a second edition (item **305**). José Mesa and Teresa Gisbert, that remarkable team, have published a new edition of their definitive work on colonial painting in Bolivia (item **263**). Several outstanding documentaries deserve notice, particularly the one on the missionary work of the Zacatecas' Franciscans in northern Mexico and the Borderlands (item **297**) and the one about the Jesuits and Tarahumaras (item **311**). A primary source of the little known churches of Nayarit now exists (item **290**). A preliminary report on the recently discovered archives in Teposcolula reveals several unknown contracts for retablos by Andrea de Concha in the Mixteca and other significant data on convents in that area (item **312**).

National concerns for preservation are exemplified in the careful inventory of structures in the Departamento de Arica in northern Chile (item **279**); Colombia's effort to alert its citizens to its patrimony (item **285**); the thorough study of two rural and little known templos in Ecuador (item **286**); and a rare and revealing analysis of the colonial architecture of Buenos Aires (item **259**). An outstanding accomplishment is a monumental survey, based on extensive documentary research, of cities and pueblos founded in Chile between 1540 and 1826 (item **281**). An additional study of military fortifications in Venezuela (item **336**) and the most thorough one for the entire Caribbean area (item **257**) have also appeared. Two fine books on textiles cover rural areas of Bolivia (item **338**) and central Mexico, particularly Oaxaca (item **343**). The latter is a superb example of bookmaking.

The journal articles annotated below span as broad a geographic area as the preceding books. What might be called "mini-monographs" concentrate on the Mexican painters Juan de Alfaro y Gamón (item **299**), José Salomé Pina (item **291**), and Basilio de Salazar (item **307**). The very valuable inventory of the Cathedral in Santiago, Chile, has been completed and includes an analysis of the foundations (item **278**). The careful study of five churches in Granada, Nicaragua (item **274**), is exemplary and a most welcome addition to our generally skimpy knowledge of Central America. Another significant contribution is the first general study of religious architecture in the State of Veracruz, Mexico (item **293**). An additional work traces mudéjar influence in Mexico's architecture from the 16th to 19th centuries (item **298**). Imaginative analyses of documents have generated several unusual articles on the following topics: types of building activities in Mexico City between 1780–85 (item **302**); 20 lost lienzos (item **320**); and the change in patronage from encomendero/Crown to wealthy private citizen (item **294**).

After an initial year, the "Association for Latin American Art" (ALAA), was formally invested with working by-laws and elected its first slate of officers on 2 Feb. 1980. Jacinto Quirarte was elected President for a three-year term. The slate includes a Vice-President for each of the major fields: Merle Green Robertson (precolumbian); Donald Robertson (colonial); and Jorge Manrique (modern). The five officers and eight at-large members reflect virtually every region of Latin America. Among the approved purposes of the ALAA are the promotion of scholarship, publishing, professional relations, governmental policies regarding the arts of Latin America, student incentives and awards, and foundation support. Membership is open to all persons interested in Latin American art. Annual meetings are prescribed. The Secretariat is located at the Research Center for the Arts (see *HLAS 40*, p. 24), The University of Texas at San Antonio, Texas 78285.

GENERAL

Alcina, José. L'art précolombien. See *HLAS 41:562.*

251 **Cordy-Collins, Alana** and **Jean Stern** *eds.* Pre-columbian art history: selected readings. Palo Alto, Calif.: Peek Publications, 1977. 519 p., bibl., plates.

Consists of 33 articles deemed "basically art historical and timely" concerning Mesoamerica (18) and Andean area (15). A splendid aid to the art historian pending adequate "survey" of precolumbian art. Adequate illustrations. For archaeologist's comment, see *HLAS 41:252.*

252 **Florida. University, Gainesville. University Gallery.** The University Gallery and the Center for Latin American Studies present a special exhibition of the folk arts and crafts of the Andes from the University Gallery's collection: University Gallery, February 26 through April 30, 1978, College of Fine Arts, University of Florida, Gainesville. Introduction by Robert P. Ebersole. Foreword & photography by Roy C. Craven, Jr. Gainesville: The Gallery, 1978. 52 p., ill. (University Gallery bulletin; 2:1)

Attempts to indicate the continuity of tradition throughout the entire Andean region. Of the 247 items in the exhibit only a few are illustrated. Essentials described in nine categories according to usage, materials, product.

253 **González Galván, Manuel.** El oro en el barroco (IIE/A, 13:45, 1976, p. 73–96, plates)

Exegesis on gold. Symbolic value through the ages. Impact of studies on Solomon's temple; salomonic style. Use of gold during Baroque period in Americas (2½ p.). Somewhat strained.

254 **Kelemen, Pál.** Vanishing art of the Americas. New York: Walker, 1977. 323 p., plates.

Nine vignettes of arts "that lie . . . on the geographical and historical periphery and that are rapidly vanishing." Places range from Lake Titicaca in Peru to the shores of Vancouver, British Columbia. Buildings, sculpture, paintings, weavings, catafalques, ancient customs are portrayed exquisitely in words and pictures. 150 b/w photos, highest quality, are of rarely seen places and objects.

255 Museo Municipal de Arte Precolombino y Colonial. Catálogo descriptivo del Museo Municipal de Arte Precolombino y Colonial. Montevideo: Intendencia Municipal de Arte Precolombino y Colonial, 1976. 105 p., plates.

Catalog of prehispanic and colonial holdings in museum in Montevideo. Objects are from Mexico and Latin America. Quite representative but nothing new.

256 Telesca de Abbondio, Ana María. Arquitectura colonial. Buenos Aires: Centro Editor de América Latina, 1977. 96 p., bibl., ill. (some col.) (Pueblos, hombres y formas en el arte)

Covering the Caribbean, Bolivia, Peru and Argentina in 96 p. is something of a record. Intended as an introductory work but misses because of poor quality of photos. Handy bibliography.

257 Zapatero, Juan Manuel. La fortificación abaluartada en América. San Juan, Puerto Rico: Instituto de Cultura Puertorriqueña, 1978. 323 p., bibl., ill., index.

Perhaps the definitive study on military fortifications in Hispanic America. Precepts, dimensions, schools, index of military engineers, many drawings (good quality, though small) from archives. Unusual, impressively thorough.

ARGENTINA

González, Alberto Rex. Arte precolombino de la Argentina: introducción a su historia cultural. See *HLAS 41:592*.

258 Moyano Aliaga, Alejandro. Candonga, revelaciones históricas. Ilustraciones de Emilio Buteler Ríu. Córdoba, Argentina: 1976. 31 p., bibl., ill.

Documentary. Once a private chapel on an *estancia* in province of Cordoba, Argentina, is now the property of the provincial government. A few drawings give visual evidence of a local style. Popularly known as "la capilla de Candonga" but officially named Nuestra Señora del Rosario.

259 Nadal Mora, Vicente. La arquitectura tradicional de Buenos Aires, 1536–1870. 3. ed. Buenos Aires: Editorial Nadal Mora, 1977. 278 p., bibl., ill., index, plates.

"Buenos Aires is a city which does not care about its past." Author then recreates, in numerous detail, its colonial past through line drawings of religious, private and civil architecture. His role as technical advisor to national preservation organization assures accuracy. General history of architectural developments covers 1536–1870. Includes 157 plates of drawings; thoroughly indexed; extensive bibliography. Exemplary publication.

BOLIVIA

260 Elías, Julio María. Copacauana-Copacabana. La Paz: Santuario de Copacabana, 1978. 197 p., bibl., ill.

History of site on Lake Titicaca (Bolivia) as ceremonial center (prehispanic); as pilgrimage site from colonial times to present. Interspersed with illustrations (fair quality), mostly scenic, though some details of sculpture. A national monument.

261 La Paz: casco urbano central. Editor: Honorable Alcaldía Municipal de La Paz. Prólogo de Mario Mercado Vaca Guzmán [and] Adolfo Navarro Flores. La Paz: Alcaldía Municipal de La Paz, 1977. 303 p., bibl., col. maps, fold. maps, plates, tables.

Urban renewal study for center of La Paz—block by block. Thorough, many charts, some illustrations.

262 Mesa, José de and **Teresa Gisbert.** Bitti: un pintor manierista en Sudamérica. La Paz: División de Extensión Universitaria, Instituto de Estudios Bolivianos, Universidad Mayor de San Andrés, 1974. 116 p., bibl., ill. (Cuadernos de arte y arqueología; 4)

Monograph on very influential Italian painter, a Jesuit, active in Peru in late 16th century whose works have been cataloged. Also includes concise account of religious orders in 16th-century Peru and details of Jesuit church in Lima, started 1569. Many illustrations but of fair quality. Excellent study and major contribution.

263 ——— and ———. Holguín y la pintura virreinal en Bolivia. 2. ed. La Paz: Librería Editorial Juventud, 1977. 358 p., bibl., col. ill., ill., index, plates.

This is the definitive work on colonial

painting in Bolivia. New edition of 1956 original based on intensive investigations which is divided as follows: Pt. 1, Painting in Bolivia prior to Holguín; Pt. 2, Melchior Pérez Holguín (1655–1732); Pt. 3, Bolivian painters, 18th century; and Pt. 4, Mural painting. Includes extensive bibliography, archival material, and 380 small, sharp b/w photos (many originals) divided among the four parts. Another example of a masterful work by this team.

264 Pinacoteca de San Francisco. La Paz: Universidad Mayor de San Andrés, División de Extensión Universitaria, Instituto de Estudios Bolivianos, 1973. 58 p., plates.

Catalog of an exhibition of 99 paintings of the 17th–20th centuries, from a Franciscan convent in La Paz. Next to the National Museum this is the "most important repository of paintings in La Paz." Includes 28 good b/w photos.

265 Pintura colonial boliviana. Catalog of an exhibition held in Caracas, March 1976, consisting of works from the Museo Nacional de Arte, La Paz. La Paz: Municipalidad de La Paz, 1976. 12 p., ill., plates.

Catalog of 1976 exhibition held in Caracas of colonial paintings from Bolivia. Artists include Gamarra, Holguín, de Berrio and Ecoz, but most works are unidentified. Includes 26 large, good quality b/w photos and historical outline.

CARIBBEAN

266 Museo de las Casas Reales. Guía del Museo de las Casas Reales. Texto de la guía de Consuelo Sanz-Pastor Fernández de Piérola. Fotografías, Onorio Montas. Santo Domingo: El Museo, 1976. 76 p., col. ill.

Guide to recently opened museum. Story of restoration. Contents illustrated, color. Model of Santo Domingo in 16th century. Attractive. Quality reproductions.

267 Palm, Erwin Walter. Arquitectura y arte colonial en Santo Domingo. Santo Domingo: Editora de la Universidad Autónoma de Santo Domingo, 1974. 251 p., ill., plates (Colección Historia y sociedad; 8)

Reprint in one volume of nine studies (1941–50) by Palm on colonial art and architecture of Santo Domingo and island. Domestic, civil, religious edifices studied. Paintings, sculpture, silver objects catalogued. Some illustrations of fair quality.

268 Priddy, Anthony. The 17th and 18th century settlement pattern of Port Royal (Jamaica Journal [Institute of Jamaica, Kingston] 9:2/3, 1975, p. 8–17, illus.)

Archaeological investigation of settlement pattern and house design in Port Royal, Jamaica, before 1692.

269 Rubio, Vicente. El título de la Catedral Dominico-politana (ADH/C, 44:132, enero/dic. 1976, p. 17–37)

Lengthy analysis of documents leading to correct vs. popular, title of America's first cathedral—in city of Santo Domingo (1512–15). Strictly historical.

270 Saiz, M.C. García. Dos obras religiosas de Campeche, en Madrid (IGFO/RI, 36:145/146, julio/dic. 1978, p. 301–303)

Describes two paintings by José Campeche of Puerto Rico: *San José* (1780s) and *San Juan Bautista* (1792), which hang in Madrid's Museo de Américas. No illustrations.

271 Taylor, René. Dos cuadros de Miguel Cabrera en Puerto Rico (IIE/A, 46, 1976, p. 59–63, plate)

Careful description and analysis of two paintings by Cabrera, "Santa María Magdalena" and "Santa María Egipciaca," recently acquired by Museo de Arte de Ponce. Illustrated. No dates.

272 Weiss, Joaquín E. Techos coloniales cubanos. La Habana: Editorial Arte y Literatura, 1978. 161 p., plates (Colección Arquitectura cubana)

Brief text (dates by century) accompanies 154 b/w quality photos showing three types of colonial ceilings in Cuba: polygonal (wood, mudejar); flat (wood); and vaulted (stone). Includes many views of interiors as well.

CENTRAL AMERICA

273 Breve bibliografía de la arquitectura en Nicaragua (BNBD, 28, marzo/abril 1979)

Ten works dating from 1947 to 1978.

274 Enríquez de Aldana, María Lourdes and **Carmen Sotomayor de Ocón.** Centro urbano y construcciones religiosas de

Granada (BNBD, 28, marzo/abril 1979, p. 37–113, illus., maps, tables)

Official study directed to preservation. Identifies characteristics of five building periods, from 1524 to present. Identifies five churches: Cathedral, San Francisco, La Merced, Guadalupe, Jalteva (location, chronology, environment, interior, exterior, sculpture/painting, recommendation). A major contribution.

Kendall, Aubyn. The art and archaeology for precolumbian Middle America: an annotated bibliography of works in English. See *HLAS 41:34*.

275 Luján Muñoz, Jorge. Algunos ejemplos de urbanismo en Guatemala en la última parte del Siglo XVIII. San Carlos: Universidad de San Carlos de Guatemala, Sección de Publicaciones, Facultad de Humanidades, 1978. 35 p., bibl., 3 fold. leaves of plates: ill.

Eighteenth-century town planning exemplified in founding of several pueblos and Guatemala City.

276 Monasterio Peralta, Francisco Alberto. Algunos aspectos de historia de la arquitectura de Antigua Guatemala. Guatemala: Universidad de San Carlos de Guatemala, Facultad de Arquitectura, 1970. 61 leaves, bibl., 18 leaves of plates: ill.

Thesis for degree in architecture. Nothing significantly new. Fails to cite S. Markman's classic work on Antigua.

277 Pohl, Bernardo. La Casa La Bermuda: programa de investigación y restauración (MNDJG/A, 50, 1977, p. 67–81)

Meticulous analysis, with graphs, of subsoil of hacienda "La Bermuda" in El Salvador, preparatory to restoration.

Torres de Araúz, Reina. Arte precolombino de Panamá. See *HLAS 41:560*.

CHILE

278 Araneda Bravo, Fidel. La Iglesia Catedral de Santiago (SCHG/R, 142, 1974, p. 95–118, bibl.)

This continued inventory of cathedral in Santiago, Chile, lists tombs (earliest 1564), bells, sacristy (paintings), silver and gold pieces. Includes extensive bibliography and technical analysis of foundations. Very valuable.

279 Benavides C., Juan; Rodrigo Márquez de la Plata Y.; and **León Rodríguez V.** Arquitectura del altiplano: caseríos y villorrios arqueños. Santiago: Facultad de Arquitectura y Urbanismo, Universidad de Chile, 1977. 109 p., bibl., ill.

Cultural assets from 1536 to present of northernmost part of Chile (Dept. of Arica, Province of Tarapacá) are studied in depth. Thorough inventory includes pictures (b/w of high quality), measured drawings, dates, materials, contents. Urban and area maps. Preceded by sharp, concise account of prehispanic Andean cultures. An exemplary work.

280 Dávila Carson, Roberto. Apuntes sobre arquitectura colonial chilena. Selección, presentación y diseño, Oscar Ortega S., Silvia Pirotte M. Santiago: Departamento de Diseño Arquitectónico, Facultad de Arquitectura y Urbanismo, Universidad de Chile, 1978. 273 p., bibl., ill.

Consists of more than 200 of Dávila's drawings (made 1920–26) of Chilean colonial architecture, mostly domestic. Includes descriptions of structures, many details, measures, and excellent reproductions. A unique legacy for both art historian and restoration specialists.

281 Guarda, Gabriel. Historia urbana del Reino de Chile. Santiago: Editorial Andrés Bello, 1978. 509 p., bibl., ill.

Complete account of cities and pueblos founded in Chile between 1540 and 1826. Author's objective is achieved by showing "how the modest settlements constitute a living lesson for architects and urbanists for gaining maximum benefits from minimum means." Seven chapters concern 16th and 19th centuries; remaining four deal with economy, society, education, daily life. Bibliography is so extensive (4648 items), it has 31 divisions. Includes 444 illustrations, mostly archival maps and drawings (good quality) supplemented with well chosen photos (fair quality), mostly street scenes. Arrangement of texts, notes and illustrations is an artistic achievement. Indispensable reference for art historian for founding dates of churches and other significant architecture. Moreover, this is a work of highest quality scholarship and outstanding accomplishment. Deserves a "Book of the Year" award.

282 **Martínez Lemoine, René.** El modelo clásico de ciudad colonial hispanoamericana: ensayo sobre los orígenes del urbanismo en América. Santiago de Chile: Departamento Planificación Urbano Regional F.A.U., Universidad de Chile, 1977. 102 p., bibl., ill.

Urban analysis of founding, growth of Santiago, Chile. A "classic model" of colonial city planning.

COLOMBIA

283 **Bustamante, Francisco de.** Cartagena de Indias: historial de 1533 a 1830. Cartagena, Colombia: Editora Bolívar, 1977. 139 p., bibl., 22 leaves of plates: ill.

Essentially historical. Three sections briefly provide names, dates of religious, civil and military architecture. Some photos, fair quality.

284 **Carvajal Pérez, Gabriel.** Boyacá. Dirección, Dario Arizmendi Posada, Juan Manuel del Corral Suescún. Fotografías, Gabriel Carvajal Pérez. Colaboradores especiales, Eduardo Mendoza Varela, Luis Guillermo Nieto Roa, Hernando Gómez Otálora. Versión al inglés, Rose Smith. Presentación, Guillermo Galán Correa. Plumillas, René Muñoz. Medellín: Interprint, 1977. 160 p., ill. (some col.) (Colección Regiones colombianas)

Pictorial essay on Department of Boyacá, Colombia. Includes excellent color photos of Tunja, capital, and of other villages. Brief history. Spanish/English text.

285 **Instituto Colombiano de Cultura.** Normas mínimas para la conservación de los bienes culturales. Bogotá: Instituto Colombiano de Cultura, 1978. 117 p., bibl., ill., plates.

Purpose is to gain understanding by public of all that is involved in preservation of Colombia's visual patrimony. Good photos and drawings illustrate urban characteristics by periods; architectural by century (16th to 20th). Basic factors in preservations—its do's and don't's. Though didactic, it reveals much of the country. Glossary, good bibliography. A most unusual work, attractively published.

ECUADOR

286 **Quito. Universidad Central. Facultad de Arquitectura y Urbanismo.** Los templos de Pujilí y Salcedo: trabajo de investigación. Autores, Mario Solís and others. Quito: Facultad de Arquitectura y Urbanismo, Universidad Central del Ecuador, 1974. 64 p., 13 leaves of plates: ill.

Professional analysis and scholarly study by faculty of School of Architecture of Univ. Central, Quito, of two colonial churches in Ecuador. Includes plans, elevations, drawings (no photos). Each site has background, cultural, technical historical treatment. A solid work. (Same group completed studies on cathedrals in Riobamba and Latacunga.)

287 **Spain. Instituto de Cultura Hispánica.** Exposición arte colonial quiteño: catálogo general. Madrid: Instituto de Cultura Hispánica, 1965. 45 p., ill.

Although published in 1965, this work was received at the Library of Congress in 1978 and never annotated in *HLAS*. It is the catalog of an exhibition held in Spain and provides a splendid overview of colonial painting. Consists chiefly of polychrome sculpture and paintings from Quito. The 112 small, relatively sharp b/w illustrations with complete details are thematically arranged. Also includes some 19th-century pieces, particularly *costumbristas* (e.g., Pinto).

288 **Vargas, José María.** Manuel Samaniego y su Tratado de pintura. Quito: Editorial Santo Domingo, 1975. 124 p., bibl., ill., 14 leaves of plates.

Monograph on painter active in Ecuador late 18th and early 19th centuries. Thematic analysis. Transcription of his "Tratado de pintura." Glossary. Many illustrations, fair quality.

MEXICO

289 **Aguilera, Carmen.** El arte oficial tenochca: su significación social. México: Universidad Nacional Autónoma de México, 1977. 168 p., bibl., ill. (some col.), 9 leaves of plates (Cuadernos de historia del arte; 5)

After lengthy cultural and historical discussions, author focuses on what functions, especially social ones, art had in Aztec world. Illustrations, fair quality, are of pre- and postconquest.

290 Algunos documentos de Nayarit: los publica el padre Eucario López. Guadalajara: Librería Font, 1978. 129 p., 1 fold. leaf of plates, index, map.

Documents of Diocese of Nayarit reveal conditions in Sierra del Nayarit in 18th and 19th centuries. Particularly valuable is 1884 inspection giving condition, size, inventory of churches. Many in ruins. Primary source on little known area.

291 Báez Macías, Eduardo. La Virgen del Refugio de Salomé Pina (IIE/A, 13:45, 1976, p. 151–155, plates)

This 1851 painting in 19th-century church of Loretto in Tepotzotlán is carefully described and firmly attributed to José Salomé Pina, pupil of Clavé. Author also identifies other works. Includes good illustrations.

292 Bantel, Linda and **Marcus B. Burke.** Spain and New Spain: Mexican colonial arts in their European context. Exhibition held at the Art Museum of South Texas between 15 February and 30 April 1979. Corpus Christi: Art Museum of South Texas, 1979. 134 p., bibl., 2 leaves of plates: ill. (some col.)

Catalog, Mexican colonial paintings from US collections on exhibition (1979) in Corpus Christi, Texas. Historical preface to viceregal Mexico; overview of its colonial painting. Crisp illustrations in b/w and color are grouped by European and Mexican artists. Full particulars of work, artists and subject matter. Among catalogs this deserves highest ranking.

293 Cabral Pérez, Ignacio. Arquitectura religiosa del centro de Veracruz (INAH/A, 6:54, 1976, p. 125–148, bibl., map, plates)

First general study of colonial religious architecture in Veracruz State. History and role of key city, Orizaba. Characteristics of region: plans, dimensions, vaulting, portals, retablos. Description of 23 buildings. Effects of 1973 earthquake. Quality photos. Selected bibliography. A major contribution.

294 Díaz, Marco. El patronazgo en las iglesias de la Nueva España: documentos sobre la Compañía de Jesús en Zacatecas en el siglo XVII (IIE/A, 13:45, 1976, p. 97–105)

Documentary analysis of change in patronage from encomendero/Crown to wealthy private citizen in 17th century. Contractual obligations; extent of donor's role. Excellent.

295 Díaz-Berrio Fernández, Salvador. Zona de monumentos históricos de Real de Catorce, SLP [San Luis Potosí]: estudio para su rehabilitación. México: Instituto Nacional de Antropología e Historia, SEP, Dirección de Monumentos Históricos, 1976. 86 p., bibl., ill. (Colección científica. Instituto Nacional de Antropología e Historia; 49: Catálogos y bibliografías)

Historical, architectural and archaeological study of this late 18th-century mining town in State of San Luis Potosí. Recommendations for rehabilitation. Professional, but illustrations are at best fair quality.

296 ———; Olga Orive; and **Francisco Zamora.** Conservación de monumentos y zonas monumentales. México: Secretaría de Educación Pública, 1976. 222 p., bibl., ill. (SepSetentas; 250)

Historic preservation laws passed in Mexico since 1934 are stated in full, the last being 1972. Preceded by résumé of preservation history and UN declarations.

297 Esparza Sánchez, Cuauhtemoc. Compendio histórico del Colegio Apostólico de Propaganda Fide, de Nuestra Señora de Guadalupe de Zacatecas. 2. ed. Zacatecas, México: Departamento de Investigaciones Históricas, Universidad Autónoma de Zacatecas, 1974. 214 p., bibl., index, 48 leaves of plates: ill. (Serie Historia; 1)

This seminary (colegio) established by Franciscans in Zacatecas (1702) was chiefly devoted to conducting missionary work in the north. Author describes site, building, paintings, contents, and history of activities. Indispensable to understanding vast missionary effort of 18th and 19th century Franciscans into northern Mexico, Baja California and Texas. Includes maps, plans, plates (mostly of friars), many documents.

298 García Barragán, Elisa. Supervivencias mudéjares y presencias orientalistas en la arquitectura mexicana (IIE/A, 13:45, 1976, p. 137–146, plates)

After noting continuous history of mudéjar influence in Mexico since 16th century, author focuses on neo-mudéjar of 19th, especially works by Eduardo Tamariz and Ramón Ibarrola. An extension of Katzman's work on 19th-century architecture. Includes many photos.

299 **García Sáiz, María Concepción.** De la falsa asistencia de un pintor colonial: Juan de Alfaro y Gamón (IGFO/RI, 36: 143/144, enero/junio 1976, p. 269–283, plates)

The shadowy Mexican 17th-century painter Don Juan de Alfaro y Gamón turns out to be the Spanish painter Juan de Alfaro y Gámez who never left the Peninsula. Includes three illustrations. Excellent research.

300 ——— and **Adela Espinosa Díaz.** Modelos italianos en la pintura mexicana de fines del virreinato: el apostolado de José Luis Rodríguez Alconedo (IGFO/RI, 37: 149/150, julio/dic. 1977, p. 707–711, plates)

Eleven quality photos show drawings by Alconedo, late 18th-century artist in Mexico. His "Santiago el Mayor" is traced thematically through several engravings by European artists to the original painting by the Italian, Piazetta, done before 1742.

301 **Heyden, Doris.** Economía y religión de Teotihuacan. México: Departamento de Etnología y Antropología Social, Instituto Nacional de Antropología e Historia, 1977. 48 p., bibl. (Cuadernos. D.E.A.S., I.N.A.H.; 19)

Pre-hispanic. Exactly what its title says.

302 **Lombardo de Ruiz, Sonia.** La construcción y los constructores: metodología en el estudio de los estilos arquitectónicos de la Ciudad de México, 1780–1805 (IIE/A, 46, 1976, p. 71–79, maps, tables)

Using municipal records, author studies kinds of building activities in Mexico, 1780–85. Includes graphs, tables, maps. Preliminary conclusions discuss remodeling, restoration, new construction levels. Essentially an urban analysis but provides some observations of style changes.

303 **López Cervantes, Gonzalo.** Cerámica colonial en la Ciudad de México. México: Instituto Nacional de Antropología e Historia, SEP, Departamento de Prehistoria, 1976. 67 p., bibl., ill. (Colección científica. Instituto Nacional de Antropología e Historia; 38: Arqueología)

Scientific study of ceramic production in Mexico City during colonial times. Markings, types, locations of producers, frequency tables. Only few illustrations, excellent quality. Methodology is archaeological, proving that much ware was produced in the City.

304 **Maquívar, María del Consuelo.** Los retablos de Tepotzotlán. México: Instituto Nacional de Antropología e Historia, SEP, Museo Nacional del Virreinato, 1976. 104 p., bibl., ill. (some col.) (Colección científica; 47. Catálogos y bibliografías)

Formal and iconographic study of the many excellent 18th-century (estipite) retablos in the church and convento at Tepotzotlán. A masterful analysis and interpretation of symbolism, devotions, religious customs. Drawings, b/w and color photos, all high quality. Exemplary presentation.

305 **Maza, Francisco de la.** Arquitectura de los coros de monjas en México. 2. ed. México: UNAM, Instituto de Investigaciones Estéticas, 1973. 126 p., facsim., ill., plates (Estudios y fuentes del arte en México; 6)

Choir screens of female convents in colonial Mexico: 11 in Mexico City; eight in Puebla; three in Querétero; three in Guadalajara; etc. This second ed. has highest quality paper, print, photos (all 103 b/w).

306 **Montejano y Aguiñaga, Rafael.** Tres planos antiguos de la ciudad de San Luis Potosí. San Luis Potosí, México: Academia de Historia Potosina, 1976. 28 p., bibl., 2 fold. leaves of plates: maps (Biblioteca de historia potosina. Serie cuadernos; 41)

Documentary account of founding and growth of SLP, Mexico.

307 **Moyssén, Xavier.** Basilio de Salazar, un pintor del siglo XVII (IIE/A, 46, 1976, p. 49–57, plates)

Six paintings done by Salazar in Mexico (1637–45) are analyzed in terms of style, quality, condition, origin, influences and impact. A substantial addition to our knowledge of colonial painting in Mexico. All six works are illustrated, plus details. Quality photos.

308 **Ortiz Juárez, Dionisio.** Orfebrería mexicana en España: las piezas de Chillón (FJB/BH, 46, enero 1978, p. 73–80)

Description of two 17th-century silver pieces made in Mexico—an altar *frontal* and a door to a sagrario—now located in Chillón, Spain. No illustrations.

309 **Peñafiel, Antonio.** Ciudades coloniales y capitales de la República mexicana. v. 2, Estado de Tlaxcala. Ilustraciones por Carlos Macazaga Ramírez de Arellano. México: Editorial Cosmos, 1978. 216 p., appendix, bibl., 19 leaves of plates: ill.

Reprint of Peñafiel's (1905) classic history of Tlaxcala (State). Chaps. 1–15 concern the prehispanic period; chaps. 20–21 recount story of 16th-century apparition of Virgen de Ocotlán, transformation of place into pilgrimage site, and construction of its wondrous church. Drawings, reproductions (Lienzo de Tlaxcala) and photos enliven text.

310 **Rivera Cambas, Manuel.** La Villa de Guadalupe a través del arte. México: Editorial Cosmos, 1976. 86 p., bibl., ill. (some col.)

Story of this famous shrine, with illustrations drawn from art works dating from the 16th to 19th centuries.

311 **Roca, Paul M.** Spanish Jesuit churches in Mexico's Tarahumara. Tucson: University of Arizona Press, 1979. 369 p., bibl., plates.

Describes some 90 very hard-to-reach, large and small churches built by the Jesuits for the Tarahumara Indians (mostly in western Chihuahua) between 1611 and 1767. Their condition ranges from ruins to restorations. Reference material (pt. 3) has biographical directory of no less than 500 names, mostly Jesuit missionaries. Includes 50 high quality b/w photos. A labor of love resulting from many difficult excursions (1968–76). An incomparable addition to the Northern Mexico/Borderlands story.

312 **Romero Frizzi, María de los Angeles.** Más ha de tener este retablo. México: Instituto Nacional de Antropología, Centro Regional de Oaxaca, 1978. 60 p., bibl., plates (Estudios de antropología e historia, 9)

Selected 16th, 17th-century documents, from recently discovered archives in Teposcolula (e.g., contracts for retablos by Andrés de Concha; 1692 enlargement of church). A significant contribution to our knowledge of Mixteca Alta, Oaxaca.

313 **Sánchez Flores, Ramón.** Localización de la casa de Fray Juan de Zumárraga, donde se veneró la imagen de Nuestra Señora de Guadalupe: nuevas noticias documentales (A, 43:2, 1979, p. 140–164)

Scholarly, imaginative analysis of old and new documents bearing on question of which house (in Mexico City) Zumárraga lived in when Juan Diego showed him the image of Our Lady of Guadalupe.

314 **Sebastián, Santiago.** Grabado inspirador de un Zurbarán de la Academia de San Carlos (IIE/A, 46, 1976, p. 67–70)

Engraving by Jusepe Martínez (1601–82) cited as possible source of Zurbarán's painting "San Pedro Nolasco" in Academia de San Carlos. Illustrated.

315 **———.** El tema de la Virgen de Guadalupe en Juan Correa (IIE/A, 46, 1976, p. 65–66, ill.)

Juan Correa is said to have restored original Virgen de Guadalupe. Includes illustrations of several of his relevant paintings, especially the one owned by Carlos Aguilera, Barcelona.

316 **Los Tlacuilos** de Fray Diego Durán. Prólogo y textos de Gonzalo Obregón. México: Cartón y Papel de México, 1975. 30 leaves, 30 leaves of plates: col. ill.

Fray Durán's *Historia de las Indias* . . . was illustrated by at least three indigenous artists (Nahuatl: *tlacuilo*). This edition faithfully reproduces 30 illustrations from the 18th century copy. Each facing page has quote(s) from Durán (1530–87) and excellent explanatory notes. Superb example of post-conquest painting (manuscript) showing prehispanic vestiges done in European style.

317 **Valle, Rafael Heliodoro.** El Convento de Tepotzotlán, Estado de México. Ed. facsimilar de la de 1924 preparada por Mario Colín. México: Biblioteca Enciclopédica del Estado de México, 1975. 130 p., bibl., 25 leaves of plates: ill. (Biblioteca enciclopédica del Estado de México; 46)

Facsimile of Valle's 1924 study of 17th–18th century Jesuit seminary and church at Tepotzotlán. New introduction cites other works on the subject published since then. Also includes biography of Valle. His thorough documentary account is reprinted as one of more than 50 works being published as an "encyclopeida" on the State of Mexico. Illustrations are only fair but valuable for showing conditions 50 years ago.

318 **Vidal Rivero, Miguel.** Valladolid y su Convento de San Bernardino (UY/R, 20:117/118, mayo/agosto 1978, p. 97–99, plate)

Announces decision to reconstruct abandoned Franciscan convento of San Bernardino, founded 1560 in Sisal, today a suburb of Valladolid, Yucatán. One photo.

PARAGUAY

319 **El Barroco paraguayo:** exposición. Madrid: El Instituto de Cultura Hispánica, Servicio de Publicaciones, 1976. 28 leaves, bibl., ill., plates.

Catalog of exhibition of colonial sculpture from Paraguay held in Spain. Includes brief account of the history of Jesuit *reducciones* among the Guaraní Indians, Baroque architecture, silver work, and 51 sharp b/w photos.

PERU

Donna, Christopher B. Moche art of Peru: precolumbian symbolic communication. See *HLAS 41:788*.

320 **Dorta, Enrique Marco.** Las pinturas que envió y trajo a España don Francisco de Toledo (PMNH/HC, 9, 1975, p. 67–78, illus.)

Documentary citation of some 20 *lienzos*, now lost, commissioned and sent to Spain in the late 16th century by Viceroy Francisco de Toledo. Inventories quoted. Uses 18th-century examples in attempt to show what originals looked like. Masterful and scholarly article.

321 **Durán Montero, María Antonia.** Fundación de ciudades en el Perú durante el siglo XVI: estudio urbanístico. Sevilla: Escuela de Estudios Hispano-Americanos de Sevilla, 1978. 210 p., bibl., 19 leaves of plates (3 fold.): ill., index (Publicaciones de la Escuela de Estudios Hispano-Americanos de Sevilla; 247)

Archival (AGI) research results in plans of 16 cities founded in Peru in 16th century. Divided into three categories, the cities are described in detail with many illustrations. Dates and locations of buildings shown on maps are helpful to art historian.

322 **Fischer-Hollweg, Brigitte.** Zu einem Zusammenhang zwischen Keru-Malerei und Cuzco-Schule (IAI/I, 4, 1977, p. 187–200)

Poses question concerning decorative pattern of Cuzco school of painting: whether its tradition might be traceable to the Kerus Indian of the Inca period. Analyzes six compositional aspects. Includes comparative illustrations of good quality.

Gasparini, Graziano and **Luise Margolies.** Arquitectura doméstica. See *HLAS 41:1299*.

——— and ———. Arquitectura inka. See *HLAS 41:793*.

Guidoni, Enrico and **Roberto Magni.** Monuments to civilization: the Andes. See *HLAS 41:796*.

323 **Harth-Terré, Emilio.** Escultores españoles en el Virreinato del Perú. Lima: Librería-Editorial J. Mejía Baca, 1977. 228 p., bibl., 10 leaves of plates: 20 ill.

Ten 17th-century artists are identified as sculptors of major pieces in Lima's Cathedral. All are from Spain. Author describes his documentary sources, how most of the 1000 artisans and artists who came to colonial Peru remained anonymous, and their dominant use of polychrome over natural stone. Author found only one drawing. Includes chronologically arranged, biographical sketches of: Arrona; Mesa; Noguera; Vargas; Aguilar; Salas; Aguirre; Fray Caballero; Torres; and Oquendo (O.F.M.). Includes 20 illustrations of sculpture, mostly in the Cathedral, and of fair quality. A careful, studious work which lifts the curtain of anonymity but published in paperback and poorly bound.

324 **Macera dall'Orso, Pablo.** Retrato de Tupac Amarú. Lima: Dirección Universitaria de Biblioteca y Publicaciones de la Universidad Nacional Mayor de San Marcos, 1975. 30 p.: ill.

A visage of Tupac Amaru, the Inca "hero without a face," might be that of a late 18th-century painting.

325 **Mariátegui Oliva, Ricardo.** Techumbres y artesonados peruanos: arte peruano de los siglos XVI y XVII. Lima: Mariátegui Oliva, 1975. 39 p., bibl., 18 leaves of plates: 36 ill.

Scholarly, technical study of one of Peru's glories: the *mudéjar* wood ceiling. Includes three classifications; 36 illustrations of fair quality, mostly of churches dating to the 16th century in Lima and Cuzco, but a few elsewhere; glossary; and selected bibliography. Though limited in subject, a much needed work especially as it applies to 16th century.

326 **El Obispado** de Trujillo del Perú (HUMB, 19:66, 1978, p. 47–55, map, plates)

"Costumbres" of life in Peru by unknown artist(s); possibly commissioned by Bishop-designate of Trujillo before arriving from Spain in 1768.

Saco, María Luisa. Fuentes para el estudio del arte peruano precolombino. See *HLAS 41:46*.

327 **Tord, Luis Enrique.** Crónicas del Cuzco. 2. ed. n.p.: Delfos Ediciones, 1977 or 1978. 118 p., 8 leaves of plates: ill.

Good introduction to fascinating area. Author describes colonial buildings of Cuzco and surroundings and provides historical background. Includes eight color and 23 b/w good quality illustrations. No bibliography. Reprint of articles originally published in *La Prensa* (Lima, May/Nov. 1977).

URUGUAY

328 **Montevideo. Intendencia Municipal.** El Cabildo de Montevideo. Montevideo: Servicio de Publicaciones y Prensa, 1977. 63 p., bibl., 21 leaves of plates: ill.

Entirely historical.

VENEZUELA

329 **Duarte, Carlos F.** Los biombos en la Caracas hispana (FJB/BH, 45, sept. 1977, p. 315–326)

Author reveals use of folding screens through an analysis of inventories. Describes major centers of execution, especially Mexico, and the thematic content of screens of which only a few remain. An historical rather than stylistic analysis of a subject rarely treated.

330 ———. Domingo Gutiérrez: el maestro del rococó en Venezuela. Caracas: Ediciones Equinoccio, Universidad Simón Bolívar, 1977. 108 p., bibl., ill.

Monograph on a Venezuelan master craftsman active in the second half of the 18th century, mostly in Caracas. Includes chronologically arranged documents as well as 10 color and 28 b/w high quality illustrations. Masterfully written and superbly published. A delight.

331 ———. Loza hecha en Venezuela durante la dominación española (FJB/BH, 44, mayo 1977, p. 179–186)

Documentary evidence of extent of manufacture of porcelain in Venezuela, especially in the 18th century. No illustrations.

332 **Gómez Canedo, Lino.** De mi fichero: nuevos datos para la historia del arte en Venezuela (FJB/BH, 44, mayo 1977, p. 257–263)

Sundry dates, mostly 18th century, on artists and building activities in Venezuela. Father Canedo, not an art historian, noted them while researching archives on other topics.

333 **Machado Rivero, Eduardo.** La Quinta de Anauco (FJB/BH, 44, mayo 1977, p. 165–178)

History of the colonial mansion and its gardens known as *La Quinta de Anauco* (near Caracas) from its founding in 1796 to its acceptance by Venezuela as part of its national patrimony in 1958. Opened to the public in 1961. No architectural details but a considerable description of its gardens and orchards.

334 **Montenegro, Juan Ernesto.** La Capilla de Santa Rosa de Lima: fragua de la Universidad y de la libertad. Caracas: Consejo Municipal del Distrito Federal, 1977. 333 p., bibl., facsims., 12 leaves of plates: ill.

Extensive account of seminary in Caracas (1640s–1872) whose chapel has been restored. Includes line drawings, extensive citations of documents, facsimiles, and color plates of paintings. No index. A most thorough investigation.

335 **Portillo, Julio.** Gárgolas de Maracaibo. Maracaibo: Litográfica Zulia, 1974. 37 p., bibl., 3 p.: ill.

Thirty color photos and brief text exemplify the fanciful aspects of the rain spouts—hence called gargoyles. All from old Maracaibo.

336 **Suárez, Santiago Gerardo.** Fortificación y defensa. Caracas: Academia Nacional de la Historia, 1978. lxxvii, 510 p., bibl., index (Fuentes para la historia colonial de Venezuela. Biblioteca de la Academia Nacional de la Historia; 131)

Third in a series of four publications on the armed forces in Hispanic America, especially Venezuela. This volume contains an analysis of artillery (canons, ammunition) in incredible detail. Lengthy (465 p.) citations of documents, including inventories. Indexed and cross-indexed. Chronological table. Thorough.

337 **Unceín Tamayo, Luis A.** El Carmen de Maracaibo: una capilla con historia (FJB/BH, 45, sept. 1977, p. 336–346, ill.)

Clarifies origin (1714) and patron (Governor La Rocha Ferrer y Labarcés) of original El Carmen Chapel in Maracaibo, Venezuela, now demolished. Includes illustration of statue moved to present chapel of same name.

Folk Art

338 **Adelson, Laurie** and **Bruce Takami.** Weaving traditions of highland Bolivia: exhibition, December 19, 1978 to February 4, 1979. Los Angeles: Craft and Folk Art Museum, 1978. 65 p., bibl., ill. (some col.)

". . . a highly developed art . . . largely unrecognized outside of Bolivian rural regions . . . they must be the most exquisitely spun and woven objects anywhere." Hard to argue the point. Many details; regional tribes and motifs. Superbly illustrated with many color plates. A visual delight. [R.J. Mullen]

Berrin, Katheleen *ed.* Art of the Huichol Indians. See *HLAS 41:885.*

Cason, Marjorie and **Adele Cahlander.** The art of Bolivian highland weaving. See *HLAS 41:1237.*

339 **Cumper, Pat.** Cecil Baugh, master potter (IJ/JJ, 9:2/3, 1975, p. 18–27, illus.)

Fascinating article on Jamaican potter who began his craft in 1920s from traditional techniques inherited from slavery, studied under the great English master Bernard Teach after World War II, and returned to Jamaica to create and teach. [J.B. Lynch, Jr.]

Higgins, Kitty and **David Kenny.** Bolivian highland weaving of the 18th, 19th and 20th centuries. See *HLAS 41:1242.*

Hirschfeld, Lawrence A. Art in Cunaland: ideology and cultural adaption. See *HLAS 41:926.*

———. Cuna aesthetics: a quantitative analysis. See *HLAS 41:927.*

340 **Millikan, Louise C.** La alegría de crear artesanías del Perú (OAS/AM, 30:11/12, nov./dic. 1978, p. 49–54)

Appealing article which discusses Peruvian folk art in general rather than the illustrated pieces. Based on author's introduction to the catalog of an exhibit held at Washington's Phillips Gallery. [R.J. Mullen]

341 **Romero Giordano, Carlos.** Somera semblanza de las artesanías mexicanas (BBAA, 37:46, 1974/1975, p. 221–223)

Economic impact of folk art. Not relevant to colonial art. [R.J. Mullen]

Scheller, Ulf and others. Artesanía folclórica en el Ecuador. See *HLAS 41:1275.*

342 **Three folk artists from Mexico:** Craft and Folk Art Museum, Los Angeles, California, June 27 to August 20 — Artesanos mexicanos: 27 de junio a 20 de agosto. Guest curator, Judith Bronowski. Los Angeles: The Museum, 1978. 68 p., ill. (some col.)

Simply delightful! The three folk artists are a papier-mache specialist, an embroidery expert, and a wood carver—all three of exceptional talent. A "self-portrait" and a cultural context for each—both engagingly unpretentious—constitute the English and Spanish text. Color reproductions are superb. [J.B. Lynch, Jr.]

343 **Weitlaner-Johnson, Irmgard.** Design motifs on Mexican Indian textiles. Graz, Austria: Akademische Druck- u. Verlagsanstalt, 1976. 2 v., ill. (some col.) (Artes Americanae; 1)

Pt. 2 of vol. 1 of what must be one of the finest books of modern printing. Four color and 198 b/w plates, many containing several designs, beautifully illustrate a host of motifs created by contemporary weavers from central Mexico, particularly Oaxaca. Carefully drawn, each design is identified: origin, people (e.g., Mixtec); type of garment, weave, cloth; size, description of design; date, location. [R.J. Mullen]

19th and 20th Centuries

JAMES B. LYNCH, JR., *Professor of Art, University of Maryland*

AS WE REVIEW THE LITERATURE for this volume of *HLAS*, we detect among Latin American writers a tendency, not widespread yet, to adopt more critical attitudes toward Latin American art. Because so many North American critics have long treated Latin American art—especially its contemporary manifestations—with attitudes ranging from contempt, through condescension, to indifference, self-criticism often appeared somewhat defensive.

Characteristic of this new emergent self-criticism, and not to be confused with romantic soul-searching, are the essays by Roberto Pontual on "The First Latin American Bienal of São Paulo . . ." (item **348**), and by David Kunzle on "Chile's *la firme* versus ITT" (item **398**), in which sexist bias or *machismo* concern the author much more than "Yankee imperialism."

Not surprisingly, Mexico leads in the number and quality of publications. The growing interest in Frida Kahlo is evident in the studies by Breslow (item **351**), Conde (item **356**), and especially the one by Tibol (item **377**) which adds to our knowledge of this Mexican surrealist.

Among other works from this country, one of the most outstanding is Xavier Moyssén's monumental essay on a little investigated period, 1911–20, of Siqueiros' career: "Siqueiros antes de Siqueiros" (item **370**). Donald Robertson and others have contributed a distinguished volume of essays in homage to the late, venerated Justino Fernández (item **374**). Another fine work is the private edition *Egerton en México, 1830–1942*, with superb reproductions of lithographs, watercolors, and drawings (item **357**). Another contribution to the growing bibliography on Julio Ruelas is the monograph by Teresa del Conde (item **355**). Eduardo Báez Macías has authored a much needed history of the Academy of San Carlos (item **349**). Finally, we recommend "La Caricatura Política" (item **353**).

As for the Caribbean area, we may single out especially *Culture et révolution: l'affiche cubaine contemporaine* (item **385**) edited by Hélène Larroche—a more profound and inclusive study than Donald Sterne's *The art of revolution: Castro's Cuba* (see *HLAS 34:459*). A remarkably perceptive review by a graduate student of a book on Wifredo Lam needs to be read (item **388**). One should also note the increasing number of studies on the art history of Jamaica published therein.

Colombia and Venezuela maintain their customary high standards in quality publications: Colombia in works such as Adelaida de Juan's *Medio siglo de arte colombiano* (item **406**); Maria Elvira Iriarte's *La historia inicial del arte abstracto en Colombia* (item **405**); and Lorenzo M. Fonseca's *Aspectos de la arquitectura contemporánea en Colombia* (item **403**); Venezuela in studies such as Alfredo Boulton's of Carlos Cruz-Diez and Soto (items **417** and **418**); and Rafael Pineda's catalog of works of art in the Ministerio de Relaciones Exteriores (item **428**).

Chilean entries, for the most part, are commendable. Besides the above mentioned provocative essay by Kunzle, there is an interesting study on the Argentine-born Jaime Bendersky (item **397**).

In addition to publications, one should note the growing activity of conferences and panels devoted to Latin American art here in the US. Foremost in this regard is the Association of Latin American Art, ALAA, founded on 1 Feb. 1979 at an ad-hoc meeting of Latin Americanists during the annual conference of the College Art Association in Washington. At the 1980 meeting of the latter held in Tulane, a special panel on the colonial art of Latin America was held under the auspices of the ALAA. Other panels on Latin American art, including papers on the contemporary period, were convened in April 1980 at Santa Fe, New Mexico and Newark, Delaware.

In closing we salute the passing of one of the pioneers of the Mexican mural movement, Jean Charlot: artist, writer, teacher, 1898–1979.

GENERAL

344 *Boletín de Artes Visuales*. Anuario. Organización de los Estados Americanos. Secretaría General. No. 20, 1977– Washington.

Good reproduction and informative data enable this publication of the Museo de Arte Contemporáneo de América Latina to keep one abreast of the latest exhibitions at the OAS and at galleries and museums throughout the Americas.

345 **107** [i.e. Ciento siete] **gráficos del AGI, Alliance Graphique Internationale.** Presentada por Olivetti. Buenos Aires: Museo Nacional de Bellas Artes, 1976. 250 p.: chiefly ill.

Sponsored by the Olivetti Corp., this work opts for what it calls "communication graphics." The prints reproduced here are frankly commercial in a literal sense—but no need to blush, for many of them attain a high esthetic level, with designs that are fresh, striking, and artistic. The artists involved in their creation cover a wide geographical spectrum. Short biographical captions comprise the text of numerous b/w illustrations.

346 **Díaz, Marco.** Carta sobre la Bienal de São Paulo, 1975 (IIE/A, 46, 1976, p. 177–185, plates)

Sketchy but informative appraisal. Díaz is particularly interested in "Video Art" (exhibited at the US and Japanese pavilions) and Brazilian as well as other Latin American exhibitions. Nevertheless, he does not ignore European entries.

347 **Juan, Adelaida de.** Las artes plásticas en las Antillas, México y América Central (*in* Africa en América Latina. Edited by Manuel Moreno Fraginals [see *HLAS 39:9035*] p. 304–324)

Although some of the material deals with cultural problems independent of art, there are useful passages on Haitian art and Wifredo Lam.

348 **Pontual, Roberto.** The First Latin American Bienal of São Paulo: scattered myths, shattered magic (REVIEW, 24, 1974, p. 90–94, illus., plate)

Dedicated to the theme of myth and magic, this Bienal was, according to Pontual, seriously flawed. Many important artists were missing, especially from the Mexican and Brazilian contingents. Moreover, the exhibition failed to illuminate the central theme, as did the symposium of scholars complementing it. A penetrating, even devastating, critique.

MEXICO

349 **Báez Macías, Eduardo.** Fundación e historia de la Academia de San Carlos. México: Departamento del Distrito Federal, Secretaría de Obras y Servicios, 1974. 111 p., bibl., ill. (Colección popular Ciudad de México; 7)

This much needed booklet traces the history of Mexico's Academy of San Carlos, which from the late 18th to the early 19th century educated so many Mexican artists. After a brief but knowledgeable chapter on the origin of modern academies in the Renaissance period and their subsequent development, the author moves on to the founding and history of San Carlos. An excellent short study.

350 Bienal Iberoamericana de Pintura, *I, México, 1978.* I [i.e. Primera] Bienal Iberamericana de pintura. México: Instituto Cultural Domecq [and] Instituto Nacional de Bellas Artes, 1978. 92 p., plates (Artes de México; 22:193)

Among the introductory essays one in particular is worth reading: Juan Acha's "Algunos Problemas de la Pintura Iberoamericana." On the whole, the quality of the exhibition—if the reproductions are accurately reproduced—is mediocre.

351 Breslow, Nancy. Frida Kahlo: a cry of joy and pain (OAS/AM, 32:3, marzo 1980, p. 33–39)

This is probably the best study in English to date on Kahlo. Analyses of particular paintings are invaluable, especially those that relate to precolumbian and colonial influences.

352 Las calaveras vivientes de Posada. Selección, prólogo y comentarios de Carlos Macazaga, Ramírez de Arellano y César Macazaga Ordono. México: Editorial Cosmos, 1977. 120 p., illus.

The text traces the use of death motifs in prehispanic México, and identifies the creators of "calaveras vivientes" in the 19th century as the lithographers Santiago Hernández and Manilla. A short essay by Diego Rivera, first to recognize in print (1930) the importance of Posada, is reprinted. The rest of this timely study is given over to excellent reproductions of Posada's works.

353 La caricatura política. Prólogo, estudios y notas de Manuel González Ramírez. México: Fondo de Cultura Económica, 1974. xlii, 143 p., 254 leaves of plates: 501 ill., bibl. (Fuentes para la historia de la Revolución Mexicana; 2)

An indispensable work of scholarship on a subject of increasing interest. The essays offer a vast amount of information about political cartoons during the Díaz and Madero regimes. Indeed, they are particularly valuable as a record of the Mexican Revolution. Although indifferently reproduced, the illustrations offer scholars and students alike a rich pictorial history of an epoch seen through the eyes of contemporaries.

354 Climent, Enrique. Enrique Climent. Diseño y cuidado de la edición: Jordi Boldo. México, Editorial Joaquín Mortiz, 1977. 143 p., illus., plates.

After years of study and work in his native Spain, Climent emigrated to Mexico in 1939. Although not completely severing his ties with Europe, Climent has resided in Mexico since then. Excellent color reproductions reveal an artist of singular talent.

355 Conde, Teresa del. Julio Ruelas. México: UNAM, Instituto de Investigaciones Estéticas, 1976. 1 v. (Various pagings) bibl., illus., plates (Estudios y fuentes del arte de México; 34)

Probably the best work to date on the Mexican disciple of Modernismo and fin-de-siècle decadence. Conde's chapter on Ruelas as illustrator is particularly interesting. Thanks to Conde, Ruelas appears more and more as one of the most important and neglected artists of modern Mexico.

356 ———. La popular en la pintura de Frida Kahlo (IIE/A, 13:45, 1976, p. 195–203, plates)

Deft study of the popular roots of Kahlo's surrealism, with special attention to analogies between her small paintings on metal done in the US in 1931–33 and Mexican ex-votos. Illuminating analyses of individual works.

357 Egerton, Daniel Thomas. Egerton en México, 1830–1842: reproducción de la edición del autor con sus textos originales y otras obras aisladas. Prólogo de Martin Kiek. Traducciones de textos: Marita Martínez del Rio de Redo. México: Cartón y Papel de México, 1976. 77 p.: col. ill.

Egerton, one of the chief *costumbristas* of the 19th century, receives his due in this superb edition, which includes the lithographs published in 1830 plus a number of watercolors and drawings. Kiek's prologue contains a most interesting account of the murders of Egerton and his mistress.

358 Fernández, Justino. José María Velasco. Toluca, México: Gobierno del Estado de México, Dirección de Patrimonio Cultural, 1976. 98 p., plates (Serie José María Velasco. Monografías de arte; 1)

Brief but cogent monograph in which Velasco is seen as the key to 19th century Mexican painting. At the same time Fernández asks and attempts to answer the question: "¿cómo se insierte Velasco en el panorama de la pintura Europea de su tiempo?"

359 ——— and **Diego de Mesa.** Juan Soriano. México: UNAM, Dirección General de Publicaciones, 1976. 161 p.: chiefly ill. (some col.) (Colección de arte; 32)

Born in 1920, Soriano belongs to the second generation of Mexican painters. An important artist, he deserves more critical attention than the sparse texts provided by Justino Fernandez and Diego de Mesa. The illustrations, most of them black and white, offer, on the other hand, a large clear glimpse of Soriano's talent.

360 **Frida Kahlo:** exposición nacional de homenaje, septiembre-noviembre, Sala Nacional, Palacio de Bellas Artes, Instituto Nacional de Bellas Artes, SEP, México, D.F., 1977. Fotografías, Dolores Alvarez Bravo and others. México: Instituto Nacional de Bellas Artes, 1977. 48 p., bibl., ill. (some col.)

Several writers, least of all Diego Rivera, contribute to this important study of Frida Kahlo. They include Alejandro Gómez Arias, who provides an informative biography, and the estimable critic Teresa del Conde. The latter treats expertly critical problems on the development of Kahlo. Xavier Moyssén offers a well chosen anthology of short critical notices regarding the artist.

361 **Gaigneron, Axelle de.** Les fantasmes de José Luis Cuevas (CA, 308, Oct. 1977, p. 94–99, illus., plates)

Skip the text, which offers nothing new about Cuevas. The reproductions, on the other hand, are worth a glance.

362 **García Ascot, Jomí.** Roger von Guten. México: UNAM, Dirección General de Publicaciones, 1978. 81 p., 15 leaves of plates: ill. (Cuadernos de historia del arte; 7)

Born in Switzerland and trained in Europe, von Guten came to Mexico in 1957. A rambling interview discloses significant information about this Expressionist's training, early years in Mexico, artistic likes and dislikes, influences, etc. It adds to the growing body of art historical writings concerning the colony of foreign artists in modern Mexico.

363 **Garcidueñas Castro, Luis.** Viaje mitológico: Galería Universitaria, Independencia y Belén, febrero 2, 8:30 p.m. a marzo 4 de 1977, Guadalajara, Jalisco, México. Guadalajara: Departamento de Relaciones Públicas, Universidad de Guadalajara, 1977. 7 p., 20 leaves of plates: ill.

The work of Garcidueñas belongs to the Surrealist movement, which has deep roots in modern Mexican art. He has his own distinctive idiom.

Garza, Gustavo and **Marta Schteingart.** Mexico City: the emerging megalopolis. See *HLAS 41:9076*.

364 **Gómez-Sicre, José.** El Caso Cuevas (OAS/AM, 30:11/12, nov./dic. 1978, p. 2–8)

Author's thesis: Cuevas has remained independent of passing fads and stylistic fashions. He reminds readers that although Cuevas excells in drawing, he is master of a great variety of media. Gómez-Sicre is able to draw upon many years of friendship with Cuevas in order to illuminate new facets of his artistic personality.

365 **Hammer, Olga.** Continuity and change in the art of Mexico (Apollo [London] 108:198, p. 96–111, plates)

As one might expect, the theme invites oversimplication. Nevertheless, many of the observations are apposite and some of the examples fresh and discerning.

366 **Lynch, James B., Jr.** José María Velasco: images of early genesis (OAS/AM, 31:1, Jan. 1979, p. 4–11)

Traces the development of Velasco as he expands his themes from single motifs to panoramic views and then, near the end of his career, contracts them to tiny—but poetic and Impressionistic—landscapes. The author hails Velasco as "Probably the greatest landscapist of Latin America."

367 **Manrique, Jorge Alberto.** La pintura en la historia mexicana reciente (IIE/A, 46, 1976, p. 127–139)

Although the "Mexican School" is a product of the Mexican Revolution, the forms and theories of that movement are not. After refining this argument, Manrique deals with the "official art" of the "Big Three," which nevertheless maintained a certain independence, contrasting it with the sterility of the minor artists. Finally, he deals with the rebels of the 1950s. Sometimes unclear, but stimulating article.

368 ——— and others. El geometrismo mexicano. México: UNAM, Instituto de Investigaciones Estéticas, 1977. 180 p., bibl., plates (Monografías: Serie mayor; 1)

Well known and respected are the scholars involved. Rodríguez Prampolini contributes a general essay. "La Geometría en las Artes Visuales 1880–1945," which analyzes the international antecedents of the common theme. Acha probes "El Geometrismo Reciente y Latinoamérica." Moyssén deals with the older, more prominent, artists: Mérida, Gerzso, and Goeritz. Manrique is concerned with "Los Geometristas Mexicanos en su Circunstancia." Del Conde presents a study of "Las Jóvenes Generaciones de Geometristas Mexicanos." The reproductions are good, and the bibliographical and other information about the artist is helpful.

369 **El México de Guadalupe Victoria:** 1824–1829. Prólogo de Gonzalo Obregón. Ed. privada de Cartón y Papel de México. México: Empresa Editorial Cuauhtémoc, 1974. 112 p., bibl., col. ill., facsims.

Dedicated to the first President of the Republic, this is a collection of watercolor sketches of typical Mexican costumes of his times. Beautifully reproduced, this publishing venture deserves congratulations and plaudits.

370 **Moyssén, Xavier.** Siqueiros antes de Siqueiros (IIE/A, 13:45, 1976, p. 177–193, plates)

A major work of scholarship. Moyssén has investigated an almost unknown epoch of Siqueiros' career: the period 1911–20. In a variety of techniques including oil, pastel, watercolor, and pen the artist executed a body of work most of which has remained unpublished in our time until now. Siqueiros reflects the influence of Saturnan, the Symbolists, art nouveau, and other currents of art. Moyssén sifts the evidence of his research with extraordinary acumen.

371 **Peniche Barrera, Roldán.** La caricatura en Yucatán (UY/R, 20:119, sept./oct. 1978, p. 97–116)

Inverviews with five cartoonists and caricaturists: Alonso Rejón Montalvo, Humberto Lara y Lara, Arturo Abreu Gómez, Alfredo Barrera Vásquez, and Pedro Vadillo Bojórquez. By and large the interviewer confines himself to bromidic questions; occasionally there is an exception, as in the problem of ancient Maya graffiti.

372 **Plazola Cisneros, Alfredo** and **Alfredo Plazola Anguiano.** Arquitectura habitacional. México, Editorial Limusa, 1977. 560 p., illus., plates.

This is a highly technical volume. After a survey of the history of housing from ancient to modern times, the authors approach their subject from almost every conceivable direction: color theory, techniques of architectural representation, the functions of sleeping, eating, cooking, etc.

Posada's Mexico. See item **1362**.

373 **Quintana, José Miguel.** Francisco Morales Van Den Eynden: un pintor poblano del siglo XX (IIE/A, 46, 1976, p. 123–139, plates)

Judging from an output of nearly 2000 paintings and 200 miniatures, some of which are reproduced here, Morales Van Den Eynden deserves this rehabilitation. Other evidence of his talents can be found in commissions from Spain and from an Augustian church in Boston, US.

374 **Robertson, Donald** and others. Del arte: homenaje a Justino Fernández. México, UNAM, Instituto de Investigaciones Estéticas, 1977. 312 p., facsims., illus., maps, plates.

Homage by 33 scholars to the late eminent art historian. The majority of essays pertain to prehispanic and colonial themes. Modernists will read with interest Clementina de Díaz y de Ovando's "El Palacio de Iturbide" and Xavier Moyssén's "El Valle de México desde Atzacoalco." The latter relates to a little known painting by José María Velasco in a private collection. The last portion of the book contains memorials and testaments to Justino Fernández.

Roza Zaragoza, José Luis. Guadalajara. See *HLAS 41:5364*.

375 **Rufino Tamayo:** myth and magic. Introductory essay by Octavio Paz. New York: Solomon R. Guggenheim Foundation, 1979. 248 p., bibl., plates.

The central idea behind this exhibition of Tamayo's art was, for analogical reasons, to surround the paintings by an ambience of precolumbian artifacts and specimens of popular art. The Guggenheim claims that this is the largest retrospective of Tamayos ever held in this country. An illuminating essay by Octavio Paz precedes the text.

376 Tamayo, Rufino. Rufio Tamayo: fifty years of his painting: [exhibition] the Phillips Collection, October 7 to November 16, 1978, Marion Koogler McNay Art Institute, January 6 to February 17, 1979. With an introd., "Tamayo Revisited," by James B. Lynch, Jr. Washington: Phillips Collection, 1978. 89 p., bibl., ill. (some col.)

Traces the development of Tamayo since the late 1920s, using works from the exhibition to cite relevant influences and crucial milestones. He finds analogies between Tamayo's art—especially late works—and certain ideas in the writings of Octavio Paz and Carlos Fuentes. As it is so often the case with Tamayo, the b/w illustrations are poorly reproduced; for the most part, the color plates are accurate.

377 Tibol, Raquel. Frida Kahlo: crónica, testimonios y aproximaciones. México: Ediciones de Cultura Popular, 1977. 159 p., bibl., 16 leaves of plates: ill. (Filosofía y letras; 34)

Tibol pursues the thesis, now growing in currency, that Frida Kahlo was a surrealist before knowing Andre Breton. The chapter "Frida por Frida" contains interesting, sometimes unfamiliar, biographical information. Other portions of the text illuminate Kahlo's relationship to international surrealism.

378 Vargas Lugo, Elisa. "Los hacendados de Bocas" de Antonio Becerra Díaz (IIE/A, 13:45, 1976, p. 157–163, plates)

Executed in 1896, a fine painting by Becerra Díaz is for the author more than a family portrait; it is a portrait of an epoch: "la del México rural y aristocratizante de fin de siglo." Historical information about the hacienda de Bocas and about the artist are provided. Details of this and of another painting—Cain—enhance the text.

CENTRAL AMERICA

379 Echeverría, Carlos Francisco. Ocho artistas costarricenses y una tradición. San José: Ministerio de Cultura, Juventud y Deportes, Departamento de Publicaciones, 1977. 167 p.: ill. (Serie del creador analizado; 6)

An interesting and provocative thesis: Costa Rican painting of the 20th century can be clearly differentiated not only from Latin America but from Central America as well. The proof of this hypothesis, however, is not overwhelming: Costa Rican emphasis on realistic landscape and on the so-called "casa campesina."

CARIBBEAN (except CUBA)

380 Alegría, Ricardo E. Los dibujos de Puerto Rico del naturalista francés Augusto Plée: 1821–1823 (ICP/R, 68, julio/sept. 1975, p. 20–41, illus.)

Plée produced a valuable historical record: 58 drawings, limited to towns and prominent buildings, ports and bays, with one important exception—the first drawing of an archaeological artifact of Puerto Rico. The author believes that these sketches were done for military purposes.

381 Fernández Méndez, Eugenio. Le primitivisme haïtien (The Haitian Primitivism. El primitivismo haitiano). Edition en trois langues. Illustrations de Dieudonné Cedor. Barcelona: Galerie Georges S. Nader, 1972. 95 p., bibl., plates.

The text adds little to our knowledge of the Haitian "Primitives." On the other hand, the plates contain very completely many works hitherto not reproduced in books and articles on the subject. These illustrations, unfortunately, are not dated. Biographical information is appended.

382 Prasad, Usha. National exhibition of paintings 1975 (IJ/JJ, 9:2/3, 1975, p. 28–35, illus.)

Thoughtful essay by an Indian art critic on an exhibition at the Institute of Jamaica in 1975. His perceptions of individual artists, however, are more compelling than his generalizations about art criticism.

383 The self and each other: exhibition at the National Gallery of Jamaica, June to August 1977, 91 exhibits mounted (IJ/JJ, 11:3/4, 1978, p. 30–34, illus.)

An interesting idea, this: an exhibition of self-portraits. Dedicated to the late Jamaican artist Henry Daley, this show is keyed to the theme: "to what extent one artist sees himself or the other—objectively or interpretively." In some instances self-portraits in sequence throw interesting lights on the development of certain painters.

384 **Squirrú, Rafael.** Francisco Rodón: pintor de Puerto Rico (ICP/R, 67, abril/junio 1975, p. 43–48, illus.)

This witty, delphic, and paradoxical essay repays careful study if one can tread a path through a verbal labyrinth of nuances and associations. Squirrú emphasizes Rodón's relationship to prints—particularly serigraphy—and to art-nouveau and romanticism.

CUBA

385 **Culture et révolution:** l'affiche cubaine contemporaine. Edited by Hélène Larroche. Introduction by Alejo Carpentier. Text by Antonio Saura. Layout by Volume Edouard Maurel. Photographs by Hélène Larroche and Mayito. Paris: Centre National d'Art et de Culture Georges Pompidou, Centre de Création Industrielle, 1977. 1 v. (Unpaged), 49 plates (Expositions Itinérantes CCI; 1)

Both Carpentier and Saura emphasize the transformation of the Cuban poster from its aggressively commercial function under capitalism to its social and political orientation under Castro's socialism. Except for several by outstanding artists the posters are anonymous. The illustrations, confined to b/w reproductions, are adequate. Although by no means definitive, this little volume deserves attention.

Dulzaides, Marta and **Elena Graupera Arango** *comps.* Bibliografía cubana: 1976. See *HLAS 41:9*.

386 **Juan, Adelaida de.** Las artes plásticas en Cuba socialista (CDLA, 19:113, marzo/abril 1979, p. 27–39)

Main theme: involvement of older generation of artists—Portocarrero, Mariano, Feijóo, Acosta León, Torriente, etc.—and their adjustment to post-Revolutionary art. There is an interesting section on architectural achievements and problems, as well as significant information on graphics, films, and posters. Well worth reading.

387 **Lynch, James B., Jr.** Cuban architecture since the Revolution (Art Journal [College Art Association of America, New York] 39:2, Winter 1979/1980, p. 100–106, bibl., plates)

Published some six years after acceptance, this study, though dated, has valuable material on post-Revolution architecture. It contains a brief survey of pre-Castro architecture, an analysis of building and urban planning since the Revolution, and an evaluation of certain significant structures of the new regime.

388 **Pau-Llosa, Ricardo.** Wifredo Lam: Max-Pol Fouchet's book on the famed Cuban painter (FIU/CR, 7:4, oct./dec. 1978, p. 54–56, illus.)

A line of criticism that was part of my annotation of Fouchet's book on Lam (see *HLAS 40:338*) was omitted because of printer's error. The line referred to the unscholarly character of Fouchet's bibliography. This very perceptive review—by a graduate student, incidentally—leaves one with the uncomfortable sensation that Fouchet's beautiful reproductions and rich anecdotal material blinded one to other basic weaknesses in his monograph. This critical evaluation is recommended for all those interested in Lam.

389 **Venegas Delgado, Hernán.** Historia, caricaturas y dibujos del Sancti Spíritus colonial (UCLV/I, 55/56, sept. 1976/abril 1977, p. 65–116, plates)

A scholarly, not too tendentious, and indeed delightful study of genre—treated from the viewpoint of folklore and caricature—in the 19th-century, centrally located, Cuban town. Much valuable material here.

SOUTH AMERICA
ARGENTINA

390 **Alonso, Carlos** and others. Principium. Buenos Aires: Palatina, 1976. 137 p.: ill. (some col.)

Eleven Argentine artists (Carlos Alonso; Luis Barragán; Horacio Blas Mazza; Santiago Cogorno; Carlos de la Mota; Jorge Dellepaine; Teresio José Fara; Jorge Mario Ludueña; Leopoldo Presas; Raúl Soldi; and Miguel Angel Vidal) are examined by seven critics and a fellow artist. Their comments are too brief and general to throw much light on the 11. Good reproductions, on the other hand, allow the reader to form his own opinion about the quality—rather high, incidentally—of the art in question.

391 Arean, Carlos. El primer encuentro con el cubismo y con la abstracción en la pintura argentina (CH, 349, julio 1979, p. 48–62, plates)

An assessment of the contributions of three key figures: 1) Emilio Pettoruti, who the author claims was one of less than a dozen pioneers of Western abstraction; 2) Ramón Gómez Cornet, who introduced Cubism to Argentina (although Pettoruti later was to carry it to greater development); and 3) Juan del Prete, an Italian immigrant, who passed swiftly from one stage of abstraction to another.

392 El Gaucho: documentación, iconografía. Horacio Jorge Becco, documentación; Carlos Dellepaine Cálcena, iconografía. Buenos Aires: Editorial Plus Ultra, 1978. 371 p., bibl., 20 leaves of plates: ill. (Grandes obras de la literatura gauchesca)

An anthology of writings about the gaucho from the early 18th to the late 19th century. As a type of symbol, the gaucho is defined in terms of many categories, which serve to render him far more complex than the romantic and mystical stereotypes described in the brief introduction. Illustrations are of high esthetic as well as historical value.

393 Pérez, Daniel E. Valor y el desarrollo de las artes plásticas en Tandil. Tandil, Argentina: Grafitan, 1976. 101 p., plates.

A competent addition to the growing number of regional studies on Argentine art. Judging from the plates, one cannot place Ernesto Valor, "father" of art in Tandil, in the first rank of modern Argentine painters.

394 Rivera, Jorge B. Madí y la vanguardia argentina. Buenos Aires: Paidós, 1976. 86 p., illus.

A most interesting account of the formation of Madí—a name invented by Gyulo Kosice, leader of a movement of artists, writers, sculptors, and musicians—from its inception in 1946 to its demise in the early 1960s. Madí painting was non-figurative, *arte concreto*, but romantic and expressive.

395 Steimberg, Oscar. Leyendo historietas: estilos y sentidos en un "arte menor." Buenos Aires: Ediciones Nueva Visión, 1977. 154 p., bibl., ill. (Colección Lenguajes)

A serious, fascinating addition to the growing literature on the *historieta* (comic strips). Of special interest is the chapter, "1936–1937 en la Vida de un Superhéroe de las Pampas (Patoruzú)."

396 Vega, Jorge de la. Jorge de la Vega, 1930–1971: catalog of an exhibition, Museo Nacional de Bellas Artes, Aug. 26, 1976. Buenos Aires: Museo Nacional de Bellas Artes, 1976. 74 p., bibl., chiefly ill.

Vega was related to the "nueva figuración" of Argentine painting of the 1950s and 1960s. His images, poorly reproduced here in b/w, tend to polarize uneasily between a Goyesque expressiveness, and pop art. The texts, fragmentary and discursive, are disappointing.

CHILE

397 Bendersky, Jaime. Exposición de pinturas. Relato curricular de Jaime Bendersky. Santiago: Instituto Cultural de las Condes, 1976. 29 p., plates.

Born in Argentina, Bendersky has lived and worked in Chile since the age of 11. His paintings of doorways, locked doors, shabby old cars are executed with an almost photographic realism infused with a magical, haunting quality.

398 Kunzle, David. Chile's *la firme* versus ITT (LAP, 5:1, Winter 1978, p. 119–133, plates)

Deals with two issues of a comics magazine devoted to exploitation of Chile's telephonic system by ITT. However, author is less concerned with "Yankee imperialism" and the magazine's response to it than with the sexist bias ("machismo") of the two issues. Provocative.

399 Museo Nacional de Bellas Artes. Pintura chilena. Santiago: Editorial Universitaria, 1977. 86 p., plates.

Too brief to serve as a definitive or even adequate survey of Chilean painting, this work contains factual information on 19th- and early 20th-century artists. Lists the first directors of the Academia de Pintura. Thus, it may be of some use to students.

400 Pinturas y esculturas de hoy. Santiago: Instituto Cultural de las Condes, 1976. 77 p., plates.

The painters are: Carmen Aldunate, Gonzalo Cienfuegos, and Benjamín Lara; the sculptors: Francisco Gazitúa, Mario Irarrázabal, and Hernán Puelma.

401 Valdivieso, Raúl. Exposición de esculturas. Santiago: Instituto Cultural de las Condes, 1976. 30 p., plates.

Valdivieso's works have been widely exhibited in Europe and the Americas. Categorically minimal, they now and then evoke images of precolumbian techniques and even precolumbian themes.

COLOMBIA

402 Aldor, Peter. Caricaturas y dibujos. Bogotá: Futura-Grupo Editorial, 1977. 153 p.: chiefly ill.

Aldor was a Hungarian cartoonist who came to Colombia with impeccable anti-Fascist credentials and worked for the daily *El Tiempo* from 1949 to his death in 1976. Nothing totalitarian and nothing absurd escaped his satirical pen, guided by and large by contact with European cartoonists such as the fame Low of England. Explanatory captions that accompany the cartoons are terse and pungent.

403 Aspectos de la arquitectura contemporánea en Colombia. Proyecto y coordinación general, Eric P. Witzler. Bogotá: Centro Colombo Americano, 1977. 349 p., bibl., ill.

Third major work on this subject in the past quarter of a century. Comprehensive and thorough, indispensable for the student and useful for the specialist. After a historical survey, the editors deal with such themes as "arquitectura como artefacto," "arquitectura como símbolo," "paisaje arquitectónico," etc.

404 Botero, Fernando. Botero. Text by Klaus Gallwitz. Stuttgart: G. Hatje, 1976. 87 p., bibl., chiefly ill. (some col.) (Kunst heute; 25)

After a brief excursion through Botero's hierarchy of themes, Gallwitz pursues his career, beginning with the exhibitions of his first works in Europe in the middle 1950s. The author's level of perception and acumen can be gauged by this solemn observation: "Toda la obra de Botero se adhiere a un precepto básico: la transformación de la realidad en arte." Nevertheless, this study can be read with some profit.

405 Iriarte, María Elvira. La historia inicial del arte abstracto en Colombia, 1949–1960 (*in* El nuevo pensamiento colombiano. Bogotá: FEDELCO, 1977, p. 9–33)

Important study not only for the development of abstract art—the first movement of 20th-century art in which Colombia drew abreast of the international avant-garde—but also for the stages leading to it.

406 Juan, Adelaida de. Medio siglo de arte colombiano (CDLA, 18:104, sept./oct. 1977, p. 114–121, plates)

Cuba's Casa de las Américas, so hospitable a showcase for modern Latin American art, herein exhibits some 60 Colombian artists: painters, sculptors, printmakers, and potters. They include such luminaries of the past half century as Obregón, Negret, Rayo, Grau, Botero, etc. The author is a well informed and professionally competent art historian.

407 McCabe, Cynthia Jaffee. Fernando Botero: Hirshhorn Museum and Sculpture Garden, Smithsonian Institution. Washington: Smithsonian Institution Press: *for sale by the* Supt. of Docs., U.S. Govt. Print. Off., 1979. 118 p., bibl., illus., plates (some col.)

This is a fine retrospective, worthy of a distinguished artist. The introductory essay is informative, biographical—with quotations from Botero himself—but not really critical. Reproductions are excellent especially those in color.

408 Moreno Clavijo, Jorge. 85 [Ochenta y cinco] Colombianos en el lápiz de Moreno Clavijo. Bogotá: Programas Editoriales, 1977. 85 leaves: chiefly ill.

Pungent cartoons of prominent Colombians by Moreno Clavijo who reduces each subject to its quintessence. Seemingly incomplete in structure, the forms fill in as a very clever artist stimulates the viewer's imaginative eye.

409 Traba, Marta. Los grabados de Roda. Fotografías de Oscar Monsalve. Bogotá: Museo de Arte Moderno, 1977. 81 p.: ill.

Traba devotes a sensitively written essay to the brilliant printmaker Roda, beginning with his enigmatic series "El Escorial" and enlarging upon it until she encompasses his figural studies. She then provides a chapter to Roda's "Retratos de un Desconocido," which itself becomes a prelude for still another series: "Risa." Most significant of all, however, is the series "Delirio de las Monjas Muertas," which Traba rightly considers his masterpiece. As always she brings an extremely intelligent judgment to bear upon a complex and rich artistic problem.

PERU

410 **Gálvez, Cristina** and **José Ruiz Rosas.** Arakne. Dibujos de Cristina Gálvez. Sonetos de José Ruiz Rosas. Lima: Perugraph Editores, 1978. 22 leaves: ill.

Good quality drawings of spidery lines manipulated by disjointed hands explain the mythological title of *Arakne.* The sonnets by Ruiz Rosas were written when the drawings were first exhibited in Lima's gallery Sala Pancho Fierra, April 1972.

411 **Pintura contemporánea.** v. 1, 1820–1920; v. 2, 1920–1960. Text: Teodoro Núñez Ureta. Artistic consultant: Sara de Lavalle. Photography: Werner Lang. Layout: José Bracamonte. Lima: Banco de Crédito del Perú, 1975. 2 v. (196, 193 p.) bibl., chiefly ill. (some col.) (Colección Artes y Tesoros del Perú)

Presents a wealth of 19th- and early 20th-century painting. Includes well-known artists like Daniel Hernández, Carlos Baca Flor, and Francisco Laso as well as lesser-known painters such as Ignacio Merino (e.g., see his *Obsequies of Atahualpa*) and José Effio, with his quaint but charming genre scenes. The introduction by Núñez Ureta is much too brief and cursory to serve adequately this otherwise valuable and much needed survey. Good reproductions, most of them in color, are supplemented by biographical information.

URUGUAY

412 **Arena.** Punta del Este, Uruguay: Centro de Artes y Letras de Punta del Este, 1978. 48 p.: ill. (some col.)

Capriciously chosen, the title refers to the theme of an exhibition of avant-garde paintings, sculptures, graphic arts, literature, etc., held in 1977.

413 **Kalenberg, Angel.** Germán Cabrera: reencuentro y recuperación de lo monstruoso (Colóquio [Fundação Calouste Gulbenkian, Lisboa] 19:33, junho 1977, p. 14–23)

Since 1964, a pivotal year in the career of this Uruguayan sculptor, Cabrera's art has become polarized between what Kalenberg defines as "tectonic" and "biomorphic." The author divides Cabrera's huge output into four basic categories: *disecciones, desencajonados, tectones,* and *permutables.* A well informed, thoughtful essay, only slightly flawed by jargon.

414 **Montevideo. Biblioteca del Poder Legislativo.** Plásticos uruguayos. Compilado hasta el año 1970 por la Biblioteca del Poder Legislativo. Montevideo: La Biblioteca, 1975. 2 v. (457, xli p.) bibl., ill.

This is a kind of dictionary of Uruguayan artists, with a long informative introduction. Highly useful for research in this area. On the other hand, poor typography and reproductions.

415 **Torres García:** exposición Museo Nacional de Bellas Artes, Buenos Aires, Argentina, septiembre 1974. Buenos Aires: Museo Nacional de Bellas Artes, 1974. 42 p., 13 leaves of plates: ill. (some col.)

As a result of the devastating destruction of so much of the artist's work not long ago in Rio de Janeiro, every item of information about Torres García (1874–1949) is precious. The text consists of 1) an essay which clarifies with diagrams and exposition the artist's immensely difficult and complex concepts of Universal Constructivism; 2) a biographical chapter; and 3) an anthology; useful for researchers.

VENEZUELA

416 **Arte de Venezuela.** Text by Alfredo Boulton and others. Caracas: Consejo Municipal del Distrito Federal, 1977. 159 p.: ill. (some col.)

Essays by 11 writers, including Boulton. Among them are Juan Calzadilla's analysis of the collaboration between artists and architects at Caracas, University City; a survey by Clara Diament Sujo of Venezuelan art since Independence; the unpublished diary of Emilio Boggio (July/Sept. 1919); "Un Siglo de Crítica de Arte en Venezuela;" and "La Escultura de Marisol." The last three essays by Rafael Pineda are highly recommended.

417 **Boulton, Alfredo.** Cruz-Diez. Caracas: E. Armitano Editor, 1975. 230 p.: ill. (some col.), bibl. and filmography: p. 229.

A fascinating study of the work of Carlos Cruz-Diez, whose experiments with color belong to the general category of "Op Art." His scientific studies have propelled Cruz-Diez into a vanguard of this movement known as "kinetic" art. The latter involves transformations of the work of art itself because of the spectator's changing viewpoints and differentiations of light.

418 ———. Soto. Caracas: E. Armitano, 1973. 220 p.: ill. (some col.) (Serie Pintores venezolanos)

With his profound knowledge of contemporary European art, Boulton is able to trace brilliantly the development of Soto's first days in the European avant-garde (1950), and his subsequent pursuit of artistic independence. Excellent reproductions enhance the text.

419 **Calzadilla, Juan** and **Pedro Briceño.** Escultura, escultores: un libro sobre la escultura en Venezuela. Caracas: Maraven, 1977. 233 p., bibl., ill. (some col.)

Calzadilla writes on Venezuelan sculpture of the 19th century and the first half of the 20th, Briceño on the contemporary. Broad historical and stylistic problems are probed; important artists are analyzed. On the whole, this work is indispensable for students of Venezuelan sculpture. Reproductions, however, are of uneven quality.

420 **Carnevali, Gloria.** Plástica: trayectoria de Francisco Narváez (CONAC/RNC, 228/231, enero/junio 1977, p. 113–128, plates)

Venezuela's grand old man of sculpture was honored in 1976 by a retrospective of nearly 150 works. This essay is an evaluation of his career, from his early reliance on Rodin and Bourdelle to his emergence in late years into the mainstream of abstraction.

421 **Center for Inter-American Relations.** A century of Venezuelan landscape painting: la Escuela de Caracas; exhibition held at the Center, Feb. 20–April 15, 1979. New York: Center for Inter-American Relations, 1979. 48 p.: ill. (some col.)

A short sketch of the subject by the distinguished artist Alejandro Otero includes perceptive evaluations of Armando Reverón, Antonio Edmundo Montsanto, Rafael Monasterios, Federico Brandt, and others. Good color reproductions.

422 **Hernández, Hugolino.** Andrés Pérez Mujica: la voluntad hacia la gloria; vida y obra de un artista venezolano. Caracas?: n.p., between 1971 and 1977. 184 p.: ill. (some col.)

Active in the first two decades of our century, painter-sculptor Pérez Mujica (1873–1920) was a transitional figure caught between the dominant academic art of the 19th century and the genesis of modern art. His sculpture can be ignored, but his early paintings reflect an uncompromising integrity of vision.

423 **La Plaza, Ramón de.** Ensayos sobre el arte en Venezuela. Caracas: Presidencia de la República, Imprenta Nacional, 1977. 262 p., 56 p. of music: ill. (Colección Clásicos venezolanos; 6. Serie Historia)

Ramón de la Plaza was the first director of the Instituto Nacional de Bellas Artes after it was founded in 1877. As Alfredo Boulton points out in one of the three prologues, *Ensayos* (published originally in 1885) represents a summing up of significant cultural factors toward the end of the last century. Luis García Morales and José Antonio Calcaño contribute the other two short introductory essays. This edition of *Ensayos*, incidentally, is a commemorative facsimile.

424 **Lynch, James B., Jr.** Reveron: the hermit of Macuto (OAS/AM, 32:2, feb. 1980, p. 18–25)

Increasingly, the author maintains, critics are discovering that Reveron, long regarded as an eccentric or buffoon, has made lasting contributions to modern art and is in fact Venezuela's most distinguished painter of this century.

425 **Museo de Bellas Artes.** Héctor Poleo: retrospectiva, Caracas, julio–septiembre 1974. Caracas: 1974. l v. (Unpaged) plates.

Of the two essays introducing this retrospective, Boulton's is the better by far.

Brief but pithy, it cuts through to the essence of Poleo's art. A few full-page color reproductions delight the eye, but the illustrated catalog in general consists of scores of black-and-white of postage stamp size.

426 Narváez, Francisco. Francisco Narváez, el maestrazo. Editor: Rafael Pineda. Caracas: Gráficas Armitano, 1976. 36, 27 p.: ill.

Painter as well as sculptor, Narváez is considered to be the father of modern sculpture in Venezuela. Certain of his works were civic enterprises which embellish Caracas; others beautify the campus of the Univ. Central de Venezuela. Rather good photographs of major works.

427 Las obras de arte del Salón Arturo Michelena, 1943/1976. Caracas: C.A. Tabacalera Nacional, 1977. 136 p.: ill. (some col.)

Of the four salons established during World War II, only the one founded in 1943 by Arturo Michelena exists today. A history of this salon comprises the text, followed by a list of prize winners, biographical notes, and representative works. In brief, one is presented with the development of "Official Art" in Venezuela since the War.

428 Venezuela. Ministerio de Relaciones Exteriores. Catálogo de las obras de arte del Ministerio de Relaciones Exteriores. Text by Rafael Pineda. Caracas: El Ministerio, 1977. 180 p.: bibl., ill., index.

One would expect a far more expensive and elegant format than this for a work of comparable distinction. A large number of male portraits, seldom published before, by Martín Tovar y Tovar are reproduced along with an explanatory and critical text. The well-known Venezuelan painters Cristóbal Rojas, Antonio Herrera Toro, and Arturo Michelena are among other artists treated here. Highly recommended.

BRAZIL

JOSÉ NEISTEIN, *Director, Brazilian-American Cultural Institute, Washington*

CURRENT SUBDIVISIONS OF THIS SECTION on Brazilian art are the same as in *HLAS 40* except for the subheading "Cartoons and Comic Strips" eliminated because the only relevant publication received did not justify it and appears under "Miscellaneous."

A notable trend in recent years is the growing number of reference and theoretical works worthy of annotation. This increase is evident in the size of this subsection, now the second most voluminous after the one on 20th-century Brazilian art. Among valuable reference works, one should note *História da tipografia no Brasil* (item **444**), the *Dicionário de artistas e artífices dos séculos XVIII e XIX em Minas Gerais* (item **432**), and the *Dicionário de artistas e artífices na Bahia* (item **429**), all three model works in their fields because of the volume and quality of information provided. Among the theoretical studies, one should mention *Da cor à cor inexistente* (item **441**) because of its original contribution to the theory of color, and *O corpo significa* (item **436**) because of its exploration of the anthropological aspects of aesthetics.

As far as the colonial period is concerned, *Rio Barroco* (item **459**) gathers quality material never published before in one book. *Vida e obra de Antônio Francisco Lisboa, o Aleijadinho* (item **460**) is not only a model of research but provides the most complete chronology on the artist.

Rio Neoclássico (item **466**) constitutes the most important study of the 19th century, largely because of the range and quality of the iconographical material that is gathered and analyzed. Finally, and not surprisingly, the dominant topic is Brazilian art of the 20th century, the commanding interest of most critics and historians. Outstanding among recommended publications are: the overall view of Portinari's drawings (item **489**); the Castilian version of essays compiled by Aracy Amaral concerning Brazilian modernism in art and architecture (item **468**); *Visão da terra,* an examination of representative works of several artists made by important critics (item **497**); and *Projeto construtivo brasileiro na arte* (item **490**), a required reference work on this topic.

Roberto Burle Marx: homenagem à natureza (item **485**) is a collection of essays on the artist and landscape architect on the occasion of his 70th birthday. *Artesanato brasileiro* (item **504**) provides a great variety of information on artisans whereas *Arte popular e dominação* (item **501**) records the polemics generated by this explosive subject. *Sete brasileiros e seu universo* is a fascinating book about seven great popular artists (item **503**). *Abstração na arte dos indios brasileiros* (item **507**) draws very interesting parallels. And finally, *Xingu* (item **510**) is probably the finest color photography portfolio ever published on Brazilian Indians.

REFERENCE AND THEORETICAL WORKS

429 **Alves, Marieta.** Dicionário de artistas e artífices na Bahia. Salvador: Universidade Federal da Bahia, 1976. 210 p., index.

Author's research brought together virtually all the artists and craftsmen who worked in Bahia from the 16th to the 19th century. Concise information, mostly documented, make it a valuable dictionary. Unfortunately, no illustrations.

430 **Andrés, Maria Helena.** Os caminhos da arte. Prefácio de Pierre Weil. Petrópolis: Editora Vozes, 1977. 143 p., bibl., 19 leaves of plates: ill. (Coleção Psicologia transpessoal; 3)

An artist herself, the author reflects on the universality of paths leading to the unity of an universal Being. Fifty essays are gathered under the following topics: Modern Art, Art and the Integration of Cultures, and Art and Man. West meets East through a myriad of suggestions. Stimulating reading. Notes and bibliography cover wide international range.

431 **Arte brasileira.** English. Brazilian art. Translated by Dagmar Lagnado. Brasília: Ministry of External Relations, 1976. 128 p., bibl., ill. (some col.)

Great variety of photographs and reproductions of the many aspects of visual arts in Brazil. Survey covers from early colonial times to the 20th century. Introductory essay, comments accompanying each reproduction and bibliography make this book a useful source of general information on the field. Quality of the reproduction and of the printing acceptable.

Barbosa, Ana Mae Tavares Bastos. Teoria e prática da educação artística. See *HLAS 41:4603*.

432 **Diccionário de artistas** e artífices dos séculos XVIII e XIX em Minas Gerais. Organizado por Judith Martins. Rio de Janeiro: Instituto do Patrimônio Histórico e Artístico Nacional, 1974. 2 v., bibl. (Publicações do Instituto do Patrimônio Histórico e Artístico Nacional; 27)

Probably the best reference of its kind, this dictionary gives minute information about the lives and works of artists and craftsmen of the period, and whenever possible quoting from original documents. Illustrations would have added much to this volume.

433 **Franca, Rubem.** Monumentos do Recife: estátuas e bustos, igrejas e prédios, lápides, placas e inscrições históricas do Recife. Recife: Governo do Estado de Pernambuco, Secretaria de Educação e Cultura, 1977. 382 p., bibl., ill., indexes.

To commemorate the 150th anniversary of Recife as the Capital of Pernambuco, this book presents and describes the major monuments both religious and civilian of Arrecife and Maurícia—the old names for Portuguese Colonial and Dutch Recife—as well as the 19th-century sections of Boa Vista, Guararapes and other surroundings.

The author consulted many archives for this edition.

434 **Klintowitz, Jacob.** Arte e comunicação. 2. ed. São Paulo: Editora Shalom, 1979. 94 p.

This is the first book of an art critic whose writings for the last 12 years have consisted of articles and essays in newspapers, magazines, and show catalogues. The essays in this polemical and provocative book revolve around three basic themes: art and communication, the structure of the contemporary work of art, and the museum and cultural politics, with several subsidiary topics.

435 ———. A cor inexistente e o aprendiz do novo. São Paulo: Editora Odisséia, 1979. 93 p., ill.

Book gathers essays written over a 10-year period, about painter Israel Pedrosa, who for 28 years painted "with light itself." This book on the theory of color also discusses related topics such as: color and emotion, color and thinking, color and light, painting with light, the theory of Chevreul, Israel Pedrosa and a new humanism, and a glossary of concepts not yet consecrated in dictionaries. Color reproductions of excellent quality.

436 **Lima, Sérgio Cláudio F.** O corpo significa. São Paulo: EDART, 1976. 231 p., bibl., index.

Anthropological and aesthetic essay on the meaning of the body—primarily the female's—in art. The experience of the body, its many implications, its symbolic presence in art, the ultimately amorous posture of art itself. An original and speculative contribution. Rich bibliography of universal range.

437 **Monterado, Lucas de.** História da arte. Com um apêndice sobre as artes no Brasil. 2. ed., rev. e aumentada. Rio de Janeiro: Livros Técnicos e Científicos Editora, 1978. 331 p., bibl., ill., index.

Second and revised edition of a Brazilian original contribution to the universal history of art, especially of the Western Hemisphere. Of particular interest to this section is the chapter devoted to art in Brazil, a succinct, general survey. Reproductions in b/w only. No bibliography.

438 **Ostrower, Fayga.** Algunas consideraciones acerca del grabado en el Brasil (Revista de Cultura Brasileña [Madrid] June 1978, p. 17–31, ill.)

Introduction to Brazil's contemporary printmaking, its historical background, main influences, artistic trends, major names and specific techniques Brazilian artists work with. Eight reproductions. Author is a major printmaker herself.

439 **Panorama de Arte Atual Brasileira.** São Paulo: Museu de Arte Moderna de São Paulo, 1978. 72 p., ill.

Volume devoted to sculpture and objects. Every artist who participated in the exhibit showed three works, of which only one per artist is reproduced on the catalogue. An article by Mario Schenberg introduces 58 artists. Four major prizes were given. Reproductions in b/w.

440 **Panorama de Arte Atual Brasileira.** São Paulo: Museu de Arte Moderna de São Paulo, 1979. 80 p., ill.

Devoted to painting, this show assembled works by 67 artists, with three works each, of which only one per artist is reproduced. Introductory article by Francisco Luiz de Almeida Salles celebrates the 30th Anniversary of the Museu de Arte Moderna de São Paulo's first location, and the 10th of its second and current one. Reproductions in b/w.

441 **Pedrosa, Israel.** Da cor à cor inexistente. Rio de Janeiro: L. Christiano Editorial, 1977. 219 p., bibl., ill.

Original contribution to the theory of color by an artist who for many years has been reflecting and experimenting on both a scientific and artistic level. Traditional theories such as Leonardo da Vinci's and Newton's are discussed, along with a new psychic, symbolic and mystical approach. Excellent color reproductions.

442 **Pereira, Wilson.** Sobre a Bienal de Número XII (Trans/Form/Ação [Faculdade de Filosofia, Ciência e Letras de Assis, Assis, Brazil] 2, 1975, p. 181–194)

Discusses polemical issues concerning the São Paulo Biennial after the Francisco Matarazzo Sobrinho era: the Avant-Garde and the unmotivated public, "Latinoamericanidad," video art, etc.

Pereira Júnior, José Anthero. Pesquisas arqueológicas no "Pátio do Colégio." See *HLAS 41:673*.

443 **Saia, Luis.** Roteiro dos monumentos históricos e artísticos de São Paulo (IHGGB/R, 20:11, 1978, p. 71–100, ill.)

Panoramic view of the historical and artistic monuments of the state of São Paulo, both religious and civilian, from the first half of the 16th century to our days. Very useful reference in the form of an essay.

444 **São Paulo, Brazil** (city). **Museu de Arte.** História da tipografia no Brasil. Coordenação geral, Cláudia Marino Semeraro e Christiane Ayrosa. Colaboração, Alice A. de Barros Fontes. Fotografias, Romulo Fialdini. Fotografia de capa, Paulo Muniz. Capa, Prensa Aguia. São Paulo: Museu de Arte de São Paulo, Secretaria de Cultura, Ciência e Tecnologia do Governo do Estado de São Paulo, 1979. 277 p., bibl., ill. (some col.), index.

Catalogue of a major exhibition which became the standard reference book on the subject. Includes a relevant essay by Cláudia Marino Semeraro; scholarly information on each item; bibliography; index; and b/w and color reproductions of virtually all important Brazilian incunabula. A very valuable and well printed book.

445 **2a.** [i.e. Segunda] **Trienal de Tapeçaria.** São Paulo: Museu de Arte Moderna de São Paulo, 1979. 70 p., ill.

Catalogue of this major exhibition includes b/w reproductions of works by almost 70 Brazilian fiber artists. Unfortunately, no introductory essay, biographies or bibliography.

446 **36°** [i.e. Trigésima Sexta] **Salão Paranaense.** Curitiba, Brazil: n.p., 1979. 60 p., ill.

Catalogue of an important survey of Brazil's current output of drawings. Includes articles by Aline Figueiredo, Rubens Cabral, and Eduardo Rocha Virmond and b/w reproductions of most of the drawings selected for the Salon.

447 **Valladares, Clarival do Prado.** Memória do Brasil: um estudo da epigrafia erudita e popular. Rio: Universidade Federal do Rio de Janeiro, 1976. 44 p., bibl., plates.

Essay on the value and interpretative methods used in the epigraphy of tombs, paintings and other art documents of Brazil's 18th and 19th centuries. Original contribution to the subject.

COLONIAL PERIOD

448 **Brancante, María Helena.** Cerámica no Brasil antiguo (IHGGB/R, 20:11, 1978, p. 139–153)

Comments on the use of china in Brazil's colonial society. Inventories of old families show consistent imports of late Ming sets from Canton, Peking and Shanghai as well as china from Portugal, the Netherlands and Spain.

449 ———. Subsídio para a história da prata e seus artífices na vila de São Paulo nos séculos XVII et XVIII (Boletim [Seminários do Museu da Casa Brasileira, Secretaria de Cultura, Esportes e Turismo, São Paulo] 2, fev. 1975, p. 30–39)

Documented essay on the main silversmiths of São Paulo during the colonial period. Includes technical data and bibliography.

450 **Calmon, Pedro.** A arte no Brasil e suas origens (IHGGB/R, 20:11, 1978, p. 9–23)

The departure point of this essay is that 16th-century Brazilian art is a chapter in the history of Portuguese art. The method adopted for the study of both religions and secular art consists of comparisons of structures and architectural details.

451 **Chaves, Maria Paula Ramos.** O Convento de Santo Antônio e as Dorotéias. Belém: AAD, 1977. 89 p., bibl., ill.

This brief history of the Dorotéias Order in Belém, Pará, devoted a chapter to the 18th-century building itself. Only few illustrations.

452 **Gomes Machado, Lourival.** Características do barroco no Brasil (IHGGB/R, 20:11, 1978, p. 45–58)

Essay discusses the concept of Baroque and its stylistic implications, as well as the basic characteristics of the style in Brazil, mainly in architecture, sculpture and painting.

453 **Maurício, Augusto.** Igrejas históricas do Rio de Janeiro. Nova ed., atualizada. Rio de Janeiro: Livraria Kosmos Editora, 1978? 286 p.: ill. (Coleção Estado do Rio de Janeiro)

This book provides historical and subsidiary information on 18th and 19th-century Rio's churches but lacks technical discussions. It does, however, place Rio's religious monuments in the broader context of the city's past.

454 Moraes, Geraldo Dutra de. O Aleijadinho de Vila Rica: edição comemorativa do IV Congresso Paulista de Farmacêuticos. Prefácio, Renato Baruffaldi. São Paulo: Conselho Regional de Farmácia do Estado de S. Paulo, 1977. 80 p.: ill.

Consists of quotes from travelers' accounts including Wilhelm Ludwig von Eschwege's 1811 visit to Minas and his description of Aleijadinho's work. Although the book's approach is rather superficial, it includes a useful chapter on the location of Aleijadinho's works.

455 Rabello, Elizabeth Darwiche. Os ofícios mecânicos e artesanias em São Paulo na segunda metade do século XVII (USP/RH, 56:112, out./nov. 1977, p. 575–588, tables)

Agriculture was the main activity in the Captaincy of São Paulo; urban life was minimal, and yet the crafts thrived long before the industrial revolution. Essay includes documents, statistics and bibliography.

456 Ribeiro Neto, Pedro de Oliveira. Imagens paulistas no século SVII (IHGGB/R, 20:11, 1978, p. 25–42, illus.)

Clay santos from 17th-century São Paulo are the focus of this essay. Their origins in the works of Jesuit artists—who arrived in 16th-century São Paulo from Portugal, Spain, Italy and France—are emphasized.

457 Salgado, Cesar. O Pátio do Colégio: história de uma igreja e de uma escola. São Paulo: n.p., 1976. 279 p., bibl., ill.

This monograph covers the origins, foundation and history of the founders of São Paulo, through the ending of the Society of Jesus, their College and Church in the colonial period, through the Empire and the Republic to the final reconstruction of these monuments in the 20th century on the same site where the city of São Paulo was established in 1554. Includes many documents but few photographs.

458 Seraphico, Luiz. Arte colonial, mobilíario/Art colonial, mobilier. Texto, Luiz Seraphico. Indicações e pesquisa, João Carlos Martel. Fotos, Horst Merkel. Versão, Annette Worms. Direção de arte e acompanhamento, MPM-Casabranca Propaganda São Paulo Ltda. São Paulo: Editora das Américas, 1977. 111 p., bibl., ill. (some col.)

Author concentrates on the 17th and 18th centuries when Portuguese influence was strongest and avoids the 19th century and post-colonial period which were influenced by various currents of which strongest was French. A wide variety of examples is included, discussed and reproduced. Lists of institutions and private collectors are given. Covers main colonial areas of Brazil. More technical and stylistic information would have enhanced this elegant edition.

459 Valladares, Clarival do Prado. Rio Barroco. Rio de Janeiro: Bloch Editores, 1978. 1 v. (Unpaged) ill.

Vol. 1 of a set of two provides chronological analysis of Rio's Baroque architecture. Includes introductory text, color photographs and commentaries for 591 illustrations. Standard work. High quality reproductions. Deluxe edition.

460 Vasconcellos, Sylvio de. Vida e obra de Antônio Francisco Lisboa, O Aleijadinho. São Paulo: Companhia Editora Nacional, 1979. 156 p., illus.

Designed for the informed layman and not the specialist, this essay is now regarded as the standard work on the subject. In many ways, it sums up the researches of a lifetime and is the most accurate chronology ever set together on Aleijadinho's output, according to year, location and individual item. In this manner, the author discusses the man and his milieu, provides critical analysis, the characteristics of the oeuvre, and basic conclusions all of which are formulated with lapidary simplicity. Clear and objective, the essay is complemented with drawings by the author. No bibliography appears because the author has already included many in his other works on this subject.

461 ———. Vida e arte do Aleijadinho (IHGGB/R, 20:11, 1978, p. 119–136)

Overall view of Aleijadinho's creative itinerary. The author's basic ideas of this subject are developed in depth in his book *Vida e obra de Antônio Francisco Lisboa, O Aleijadinho* (see item **460**).

19TH CENTURY

462 **Coustet, Robert.** Le Palais Impérial de Pétropolis: le néo-classicisme sous les tropiques (OEIL, 275, juin 1978, p. 32–37, plates)

Author analyzes the Brazilian blend of French neoclassical ideals with tropical landscaping during the reign of Dom Pedro II, as a technical development and from a social and historical perspective.

463 **Guillobel, Joaquim Cândido.** Usos e costumes do Rio de Janeiro nas figurinhas de Guillobel / Life and manners in Rio de Janiero as seen in Guillobel's small drawings. Curitiba?: C. Guinle de Paula Machado, 1978. 19 p., bibl., 25 leaves of plates: col. ill.

Born in Lisbon of a French father and Portuguese mother, Guillobel arrived in Brazil in 1808. Although he pursued a military career, he also became an architect and draftsman, creating many miniature paintings and watercolors, some of them in postcard form. Many of these are beautifully reproduced in this book. An important contribution to 19th-century Braziliana.

464 **Mello Júnior, Donato.** Grandjean de Montigny: bicentenário do nascimento do grande arquiteto de Rio de Janeiro imperial (IHBG/R, 317, out./dez. 1977, p. 17–26)

One of the pioneers of neoclassical art in Brazil, Montigny arrived in Rio with the French Artistic Mission of 1816. He developed many Brazilian disciples.

465 **Schaeffer, Enrico.** A Missão Artística Holandesa (IHGGB/R, 20:11, 1978, p. 103–115, bibl.)

Many artists brought to Brazil by Count Johann Maurits van Nassau, such as Frans Post and Albert Eckhout, are examined in this article. Their output in Brazil is referred to as "The Dutch Artistic Mission."

466 **Valladares, Clarival do Prado.** Rio Neoclássico. Rio de Janeiro: Bloch Editores, 1978. 1 v. (Unpaged) ill.

Vol. 2 of a set of two provides a chronological analysis of neoclassical architecture in Rio. Includes introductory text, color photographs and commentaries for 454 illustrations. Standard work and deluxe edition with high quality reproductions.

20TH CENTURY

467 **Almeida, Paulo Mendes de.** Ianelli: do figurativo ao abstrato. São Paulo: Laborgraf, 1978. 176 p., bibl., ill. (some col.)

Deluxe edition covers the trajectory of this artist from the mid 1940s to late 1970s with texts by Aracy Amaral, Juan Acha, Jacob Klintowitz and Marc Berkowitz in addition to those by Mendes de Almeida himself. Current period is emphasized. Excellent quality of color reproductions, minute chronology, extensive bibliography, and biographic data.

468 **Amaral, Aracy.** Arte y arquitectura del modernismo brasileño: 1917–1930. Traducción de Marta Traba. Caracas: Biblioteca Ayacucho, 1978. 244 p., illus.

This book (translated from the original Portuguese by Marta Traba) is the most complete study of the subject, chiefly because of the volume of information, the essays by seminal authors assembled by Aracy Amaral and the chronology established by José Carlos Serroni. Comprehensive set of illustrations and reproductions in color and b/w. Bibliography rather incomplete.

469 **Araújo, Emanoel.** Relevos: esculturas e gravuras. Salvador, Brazil: Museu de Arte da Bahia, Fundação Cultural do Estado da Bahia, 1979/1980. 26 p., bibl., ill.

Catalogue of the artist's most important show in the past decade includes articles by José Pedreira, Jaime Maurício, Roberto Pontual, Clarival do Prado Valladares and Jacob Klintowitz. Bibliography. Excellent quality of b/w and color reproductions.

470 **Ayala, Walmir.** Acervo do Grupo Sul América de Seguros: artistas brasileiros. Textos de Walmir Ayala. Rio de Janeiro: Colorama, 1975. 68 p.: col. ill.

This collection consists of paintings by Volpi, Di Cavalcanti, Portinari, Teruz, Pancetti, Djanira, Marcier, Dacosta, Iberê Camargo, Fukushima, Krajcberg, Arcangelo Ianelli, Zaluar, Mabe, Toyota, Wakabayashi, Maria Polo, Marcia Barroso do Amaral, Carybé, Newton Resende, Enrico Bianco, Inimá, Scliar, Reynaldo Fonseca, Raimundo de Oliveira, José Maria, Heitor dos Prazeres, Danilo di Prete, Rosina Becker do Valle and Ivan Morais. Good quality color reproductions.

471 ———. Rubem Valentim: fiz do fazer minha Salvação (MEC/C, 29, 1978, p. 49–59, ill.)

Essay on the constructivist artist, with emblematic characteristics drawn from the Afro-Brazilian symbology of Bahia. Good color reproductions of Valentim's paintings and reliefs. No bibliography.

472 **Bardi, P M.** O modernismo no Brasil. São Paulo: Gráficos Brunner, 1978. 186 p., ill.

Essay, photographs, illustrations and reproductions cover essentially the 1920s and early 1930s in São Paulo. All possible expressions are discussed: painting, sculpture, architecture, printmaking, drawings, decorative arts, commercial art. Excellent quality reproductions.

473 **Camargo Júnior, Geraldo A.** and **Marcos A. Osello.** O arquiteto, o desenvolvimento e a qualidade de vida. São Paulo: Instituto Roberto Simonsen, 1978. 47 p., bibl., 1 leaf of plates: ill.

Leading theme is the relation between architecture and the improvement of the quality of life. Chapters discuss: the architect and the large public, industrial language, industrial metropolis, and speculation and styles. Conclusion emphasizes how the architect's role takes place in a social dynamics beyond his control.

474 **Campiglia, Oscar.** Aspectos artísticos das velhas cidades do Brasil (IHGGB/R, 20:11, p. 61–69)

Essay concentrates on the period from 1540 to 1660 in Pernambuco, Bahia and São Paulo. Also includes few references to the 18th and 19th centuries.

475 **Chazan, Daniel; Juvenil Longo de Souza;** and **Wilson Duarte de Almeida.** Arquitetura contemporânea brasileira: criatividade e inventividade. São Paulo: Instituto Roberto Simonsen, 1977. 118 p., bibl., ill.

Provides social and cultural history of Brazilian contemporary architecture. Some of the main topics are the quality of city living, space and social process, creativity, leisure. Insufficient space is devoted to the problems of contemporary Brazilian architecture and the bibliography is poor.

476 **Coelho, Fernando.** Fernando Coelho: desenhos da série Zanini, S.A. Text by Clarival do Prado Valladares. n.p.: n.p., 1977/1979. 60 p., ill.

Consists of the best of the artist's output in 1977, preceded by Valladares' theoretical essay and aesthetic evaluation. Fine quality reproductions, elegant edition.

477 **Coutinho, Evaldo.** O espaço da arquitetura. São Paulo: Editora Perspectiva, 1977. 239 p. (Coleção Estudos; 59)

Philosophical essay on the nature of architecture, the autonomy and plenitude of created space, the counterpoint of specific values which aim at balance, and, finally, how all of architecture is related to man, his behaviour, his needs and responses. A valuable theoretical contribution.

478 **Cunha, Euclydes da.** Os Sertões. Selections. O episódio de Canudos. Pinturas de Grover Chapman. Introdução e seleção de textos por Luís Viana Filho. Rio de Janeiro: Salamandra, 1978. 56 p.: ill.

Euclydes de Cunha's version of the episode of *Canudos* is visualized by Grover Chapman. Expressionistic paintings, predominantly in dark ochres and browns, of portraits, battle scenes, religious topics. Good selection of texts and fair quality reproductions.

479 **Di Cavalcanti, Emiliano.** Emiliano Di Cavalcanti. Introdução, Luis Martins. Legendas, Paulo Mendes de Almeida. São Paulo: Gráficos Brunner, 1976. 144 p.: chiefly col. ill.

Deluxe edition of artist's output (1922–76). Introductory essay points to Di Cavalcanti's sensuous and romantic approach to life and art, as the reason why he chose figurativism instead of the abstractionism of his contemporaries. Each painting is preceded by an appropriate text by critic Paulo Mendes de Almeida. Excellent quality color reproductions.

480 **Evenson, Norma.** Two Brazilian capitals; arquitecture and urbanism in Rio de Janeiro and Brasília. New Haven: Yale University Press, 1973. 225 p., bibl., 100 p.: ill.

Arbitrary monograph brings together two capitals with nothing in common, opposites of one another, in fact. Nevertheless, certain discussions of each city have intrinsic merit by drawing together various strings of history, politics, economics and art. B/w photos of city planning, architectural samples, plans, projects provide a wealth of information.

481 Guimarães, Lais de Barros Monteiro. Luz. São Paulo: Prefeitura do Município de São Paulo, Secretaria Municipal de Cultura, Departamento do Patrimônio Histórico, Divisão do Arquivo Histórico, 1977. 118 p., bibl., ill. (part fold.) (História dos bairros de São Paulo; 12)

Monograph in a series devoted to São Paulo neighborhoods. This one, on Luz, discusses the origins, development, expansion, residential and commercial functions of the area in the context of São Paulo, from the last days of the Empire through the first decades of the Republic. Examines artistic monuments, cultural institutions, gardens of the Belle Epoque, and the old station building of the "São Paulo Railway Company" founded by the British and now nationalized. Includes photographs, maps and bibliography.

482 Jaime, Maurício. 50 [i.e. Cinqüenta] anos de escultura brasileira no espaço urbano (MEC/C, 29, 1978, p. 90–100, ill.)

This essay was written for a special show organized by Rio's newspaper *O Globo* in order to discuss problems posed by 20th-century outdoors sculpture in general, but especially in Brazil. Only a few b/w reproductions. No bibliography.

483 Jardim, Evandro Carlos. Evandro Carlos Jardim: Museu de Arte de São Paulo Assis Chateaubriand: exposição patrocinada pela editora Livraria e Galeria Seta. São Paulo: Editora Livraria e Galeria Seta, 1973/1976. 90 p., bibl., ill.

Catalogue of a retrospective show held at São Paulo's Art Museum of a living Brazilian printmaker considered most representative and introduced by P.M. Bardi. Notebooks, preliminary drawings, watercolors, objects and prints at various stages, interrelated the many moments of Evandro Carlos Jardim's creative process. Evocations, Antonio Maluf's brief essay and extensive curriculum cast further light on the subject. Good quality printing.

484 Maia, Tom. Recife & [i.e. e] Olinda. Text by Gilberto Freyre. Legends by Thereza Regina de Camargo Maia. São Paulo: Companhia Editora Nacional *com a colaboração da* Editora da Universidade de São Paulo, 1978. 178 p., 70 leaves of plates: ill. (Série Documentos Instituto Joaquim Nabuco de Pesquisas Sociais; 7)

Fine pen and ink drawings by Tom Maia, 71 altogether, evoke beautifully, along with texts, the colonial architecture of Recife and Olinda.

485 Marx, Roberto Burle. Roberto Burle Marx: homenagem à natureza. Coordenadores: Paulo Queiroz, Lucia Victoria Peltier de Queiroz, Leonardo Boff. Petrópolis, Brazil: Editora Vozes, 1979. 126 p., ill.

Publication in homage to the artist on the occasion of his 70th birthday. Includes essays on many aspects and implications of his work by: Lúcio Costa, Leonardo Boff, O.F.M., Claude Vincint, S. Giédion, Bruno Sevi, F. Clerici, L.V. Peltier de Queiroz, Gastão de Holanda, Artur da Távola, C.P. Valladares, A.H. Teixeira, Marcos Tamoyo and by Roberto Burle Marx himself. Biography, curriculum and bibliography.

486 Mendonça, Mario. Via-Sacra da justiça. Pinturas de Mario Mendonça. Texto de Leonardo Boff. Petrópolis, Brazil: Vozes, 1978. 95 p.: col. ill.

Contemporary version of the Stations of the Cross, with expressionistic orientation. Elaborate text based on the Gospels accompanies each Station and the corresponding image. The original paintings are in the Santa Mônica Church, Leblon, Rio de Janeiro. Very good quality reproductions.

487 Ohtake, Tomie. Tomie Ohtake. São Paulo: Grifo Galeria de Arte, 1979. 22 p., ill.

Catalogue of artist's major show in the 1970s. Essay by José Neistein points out characteristics of Ohtake's current state of creativity and how it integrates her main aesthetic views from the past decades. Nine reproductions in color of generally good quality. Ohtake is one of Brazil's most representative living painters.

488 Pontual, Roberto. 5 [i.e. Cinco] mestres brasileiros: pintores construtivistas, Tarsila, Volpi, Dacosta, Ferrari, Valentim. Texto de Roberto Pontual. Organização, Ladi Biezus. Rio de Janeiro: Livraria Kosmos Editora, 1977. 174 p.: ill. (some col.)

Author studies these five constructivist painters in the context of Brazil's visual traditions as well as in relation to one another, noting their common denominators and differences. Excellent quality color reproductions.

489 Portinari: desenhista. Edited by Ralph Camargo. Rio de Janeiro: Museu Nacional de Belas Artes [and] Museu de Arte de São Paulo, 1977? 264 p., bibl., ill., plates.

Possibly the most comprehensive survey of Portinari's drawings to date. Conceptualized and edited by Ralph Camargo, it includes many statements, photographs, documents and chronology. Excellent quality reproductions.

490 Projeto construtivo brasileiro na arte: 1950–1962. Supervisão, coordenação geral e pesquisa, Aracy A. Amaral. Rio de Janeiro: Museu de Arte Moderna do Rio de Janeiro [and] São Paulo: Secretaria da Cultura, Ciência e Tecnologia do Estado de São Paulo, Pinacoteca do Estado, 1977. 357 p., bibl., ill. (some col.)

Publication generated by and devoted to the exhibition of constructivist art in Brazil in the 1950s. Consists of Brazilian and international documents, manifestoes, original texts and poems, essays on concrete and neoconcrete artists as well as on other constructivists, and recent critical texts. Vast bibliography, great variety of appropriate illustrations. Standard reference book on the subject.

491 Scaldaferri, Sante. A cultura popular na pintura de Sante Scaldaferri, de 30/9 a 16/10/77, Museu de Arte Moderna da Bahia. Colaboração, Tereza Galeria de Arte. Salvador: Artes Gráficas, 1977. 69 p., ill. (some col.)

Scaldaferri already had a background in abstract painting when he decided to recreate some of the traditions of Brazilian folk art. This work gathers statements by artists, critics, historians, novelists and poets on Scaldaferri's trajectory. His principal works (1957–77) are reproduced in color and b/w.

492 Silva, José Antonio da. José Antonio da Silva: English and Portuguese text. Introdução e comentários, Theon Spanudis. Organização, Ladi Biezus. Düsseldorf: H. Krüger, 1976. 160 p.: col. ill.

Monograph on one of the most representative naif painters of Brazil. Introduction first discusses the very concept of primitive painting, the characteristics and principal four stages of Silva's style, then provides some insights into the artist as a product but also synthesis of his environment, and concludes with a statement by Silva himself. Excellent reproductions of the canvases discussed, each preceded by a description and critical assessment.

493 Souza, Abelardo de. Arquitetura no Brasil: depoimentos. São Paulo: Livraria Diadorim Editora, 1978. 130 p., bibl., 18 leaves of plates: ill.

Statements by and about Lucio Costa, Gregori Warchavchik, Oscar Niemeyer, Rino Levi, Luiz Nunes, Marcelo Roberto, Affonso Eduardo Reidy, and Flavio de Carvalho concerning their approaches, main projects, historical perspectives, controversies, accomplishments.

494 Valladares, Clarival do Prado. Análise iconográfica da pintura monumental de Portinari nos Estados Unidos. n.p.: n.p., 1975. 60 p., bibl., ill.

Includes the four large frescoes in the Hispanic Division of the Library of Congress, in Washington, D.C. (i.e., Descobrimento da Terra, Catequese, Bandeirantes, Descoberta do Ouro), and the two murals at the UN, in New York. Discusses stylistic and technical features, related to Portinari's previous periods and further accomplishments. Well documented. Unfortunately, reproductions in b/w.

495 ———. Djanira. n.p.: n.p., 1978. 24 p., ill.

Essay on the painter, for the catalogue of her Vienna exhibition. Text in Portuguese and German.

496 ———. Lula Cardoso Ayres: revisão crítica e atualidade. 2. ed. Rio: Construtora Norberto Odebrecht, 1978. 200 p., 83 ill.

A facsimile of first ed., this one includes a preface by Gilberto Freyre. This critical reevaluation of the 20th-century painter from Pernambuco casts further light on his work.

497 Visão da terra: arte agora, Antonio Henrique Amaral, Antonio Maia, Emanoel Araújo, Francisco Brennand, Frans Krajcberg, Gilvan Samico, Glauco Rodrigues, Humberto Espíndola, Ione Saldanha, Márcio Sampaio, Millôr Fernandes, Rubem Valentim. Coordenação, Roberto Pontual. Rio de Janeiro: Atelier de Arte Edições, 1977. 153 p.: ill.

These artists, representative of Brazilian art, are presented and evaluated by Roberto Pontual, Ferreira Gullar, Olívio Tavares de Araújo, Clarival do Prado Valladares, César Leal, Sheila Leirner, Ariano Suassuna, Aline Figueiredo, Jayme Maurício, Angelo Oswaldo de Araújo Santos, Antonio Houaiss and Frederico Morais. Includes b/w reproductions and portraits of the artists.

498 **Vital, Marcia Maria de Paiva.** O espaço urbano como manifestação cultural de nossa cidade. São Paulo: Instituto Roberto Simonsen, 1977. 75 p., bibl., ill.

Speculation on the nature of space and the relation of man and the urban space he creates organized as follows: the individual between past and present; his commitment to heritage and to nature; the contradictions of new patterns in modern Brazil. The author does not delve into the role and contribution of architects themselves.

FOLK ART

499 **Cedran, Lourdes.** Cerâmica de Apiaí. São Paulo: Secretaria de Cultura do Estado de São Paulo, Paço das Artes, n.d. 43 p., ill.

Catalogue of an exhibition of folk pottery from Apiaí, Ribeira Valley, State of São Paulo, a very little known area of Brazilian folk art. Excellent b/w photographs by José Colucci Júnior show the environment, craftswomen, and ceramics themselves.

500 **Macedo, Nertan.** Cancioneiro de Lampião. Gravuras, Jô Oliveira. n.p.: n.p., 1976. 26 p.: 7 ill. (inserted)

For Nertan Macêdo's set of 73 short poems, Jô Oliveira created a set of seven large and striking woodcuts, inspired by the folk tradition of woodcuts from the Northeast, all of them depicting Lampião/Lampeão's prowess in imaginary situations.

501 **Maurício, Ivan; Marcos Cirano;** and **Ricardo de Almeida.** Arte popular e dominição. Recife: Alternativa, 1978. 106 p.: ill.

Record of discussions of folk art held in Pernambuco, Nov. 1975–March 1978. Sections of the book are devoted to: Debate, Research, Testimonies, Documentation. Mass media is perceived not merely as competitor but mostly as instrument for the oppression of the lower classes. Claims revindications. Politically slanted, polemical study.

502 **Scheuer, Herta Loëll.** Estudo da cerâmica popular do Estado de São Paulo. São Paulo: Secretaria da Cultura, Ciência e Tecnologia, Conselho Estadual de Cultura, 1976. 131 p., bibl., 4 p.: ill. (Coleção Folclore; 3)

Discusses research and notes classification of folk ceramics, their different styles and methods in the state of São Paulo. Includes many drawings and technical data, some photographs, accurate description of the methods and processes but no evaluation. General and specific bibliography, both Brazilian and international.

503 7 [i.e. Sete] **Brasileiros e seu universo:** artes, ofícios, origens, permanências. Realização do Programa de Ação Cultural do Departamento de Assuntos Culturais do Ministério da Educação e Cultura. Projeto e execuçao, Equipe Artesanato e Artes Populares do Programa de Ação Cultural. Organização da exposição e coordenação do catálogo, Gisela Magalhães e Irma Aretizábal. Brasília: Departamento de Documentação e Divulgação, 1974. 215 p., bibl., ill.

Short but relevant essays by Clarival do Prado Valladares, Lélia Coelho Frota, Luís da Câmara Cascudo, Luiz Felipe Baêta Neves, Luís Saia, Márcio Sampaio, Napoleão Figueiredo and Veríssimo de Melo on the strong folk art statements of Benedito, Dezinho de Valença, G.T.O., Louco, Maria de Beni, Nhozim, Nô Caboclo. Biographies, bibliography and b/w photographs enhance this publication.

504 **Valladares, Clarival do Prado.** Artesanato brasileiro. Rio de Janeiro: Funarte, 1978. 165 p., ill.

Various essays by scholars, assembled by C.P. Valladares, on folk art as expressed in pottery, wood, fabrics, laces, metal, etc. Many reproductions in color and b/w. Short but comprehensive view.

505 **Vives, Vera de.** O homem fluminense. Fotografias, Zalmir Gonçalves and others. Niterói: Governo do Estado do Rio de

Janeiro, Secretaria Estadual de Educação e Cultura, Fundação Estadual de Museus do Rio de Janeiro, Museu de Artes e Tradições Populares, 1977. 107 p., bibl., ill.

Survey of crafts created in State of Rio for generations, many of them still alive. Also includes description of traditional games and celebrations, along with techniques for crafts involving wood, clay, cloth, fibers, leather, iron and many more. Author regards folk tradition not only as the counterpoint but also as the complement to mass culture.

506 Xilógrafos nordestinos: Jerônimo Soares, Abraão Bezerra Batista, Ciro Fernandes, Franklin de Cerqueira Machado, Franklin Jorge do Nascimento Roque, João de Barros, Arlindo Marques da Silva, José Cavalcanti e Ferreira, José Costa Leite, José Francisco Borges, José Stênio Silva Dinis, Marcelo Alves Soares. Text by Lourival Gomes Machado, Salvador Monteiro and Homero Senna. Rio de Janeiro: Fundação Casa de Rui Barbosa, 1977. 218 p.: ill.

The brief introductory texts by Homero Senna and Salvador Monteiro discuss basic aspects of the folk woodcuts from Brazil's Northeast such as affiliation of local living artists to the old and learned European traditions they stem from. Anonymous artists are also included. Three important articles by Lourival Gomes Machado, originally published in 1960 in the newspaper *O Estado de S. Paulo,* are reprinted at the end. Very good lay-out and printing.

AFRO-BRAZILIAN AND INDIAN TRADITIONS

507 Bento, Antonio. Abstração na arte dos indios brasileiros. Rio de Janeiro: Spala Editora, 1979. 176 p., ill.

Predecessors of this extremely interesting book are chiefly 18th and 19th-century scholars and artists from Portugal, France, Germany and Austria. Among the topics discussed, some of the most stimulating are: "Uma Visualidade Brasileira;" "O Pioneirismo dos Cubistas;" "A Geometria dos Brasilíndios;" "Dos Auetôs aos Cadiveus;" "A Plumária;" "Pinturas Corporais;" "Cerâmicas Carajás;" "Carrancas Indígenas;" "Cores da Pintura;" and "O Mistério dos Indios." Great wealth of excellent color photographs. Vast bibliography. Deluxe edition.

508 Valladares, Clarival do Prado. The impact of African culture on Brazil = L'impact de la culture africaine au Brésil = O impacto da cultura africana no Brasil: Brazilian exhibition, II FESTAC, Lagos, Nigeria. Brasília: Ministério das Relações Exteriores: Ministério da Educação e Cultura, 1976 or 1977. 296 p.: ill. (some col.)

Author discusses the christianization of the African black in Brazil, his attachment to the religious art of the colonial era, the rediscovery of his African roots in the 20th century, the black as creator and the black as theme, and last but not least, the black as a vivid component of Brazilian culture in sculpture, painting, printmaking, dance, music, jewelry and the crafts. Biographies of the participant artists and reproductions of their works both in color and b/w.

PHOTOGRAPHY

509 Barreto, Eduardo. Pau de arara. n.p.: n.p., 1977. 25 p.: ill.

Provocative and humorous avant-garde photographs with verbal commentaries in the same vein.

510 Bisilliat, Maureen. Xingu: tribal territory. Photos by Maureen Bisilliat. Text by Orlando Villas-Bôas and Cláudio Villas-Bôas. London: Collins, 1979. 31 p., 80 leaves of plates: chiefly col. ill.

The photographs, taken 1974–77, were part of a documentary record of Xingú National Park but inadvertedly turned out as the subject's best artistic portrayal in photography to date. Album includes a selection of 20 originals in color. Introductory essay by the Villas-Bôas brothers provides appropriate insight into the different Indian tribes of the state of Mato Grosso.

511 Moraes, Pedro de. Vi vendo. Fotografia de Pedro de Moraes. Texto de Hélio Pellegrino. Capa de Roberto Magalhães. Rio de Janeiro: Atelier de Arte, 1976. 40 p.: ill.

Photographs of high artistic quality made during 1954–75 of various striking, sometimes pathetic aspects of life in Rio. Book also includes views of other areas of Brazil. Sharp introduction by Hélio Pellegrino.

512 Perez, Mazda. Missa do Vaqueiro. Text by Haroldo and Flavia de Faria Castro. São Paulo: n.p., 1979. 1 v. (Unpaged) ill.

Private and limited edition of great interest consisting of seven original b/w photographs covering aspects of the Eighth Mass of the Cowboy in Serrita, Pernambuco. Photos by Mazda Perez of high artistic quality. Curriculum of photographs included.

513 Pires, Jack and **Paulo Leminski.** Quarenta clics em Curitiba. n.p.: n.p., 1976. 1 portfolio: chiefly ill.

Photographic images of life in Curitiba are accompanied by comments in form of short poems. Range of outdoors life shown somewhat limited.

MISCELLANEOUS

514 Aquino, Flávio de. Aspectos da pintura primitiva brasileira = Aspects of Brazilian primitive painting. Rio de Janeiro: Spala Editora, 1978. 195 p., bibl., col. ill.

Plush edition on contemporary naif painters of Brazil. Consists of excellent reproductions and essays on the most representative ones including account of their national and foreign precursors.

515 Barata, Mario. Rodrigo M.F. de Andrade e a preservação dos monumentos arquitetônicos e da paisagem no Brasil (CFC/RBC, 19, jan./março 1974, p. 139–146)

Article focuses on the unique personality and contribution of R.M.F. de Andrade who founded Brazil's agency for the Preservation of the Artistic, Historical and National Patrimony.

516 Brandão, Jacyntho José Lins. Velhas histórias em quadrinhos: subsídios para uma pré-história dos quadrinhos (VOZES, 71:2, março 1977, p. 41–50, plates)

Author goes back to the Middle Ages to search for the roots of comic strips and compares them to contemporary creations. Scholarly essay.

517 Brazil. Instituto Joaquim Nabuco de Pesquisas Sociais. Subsídios para implantação de uma política museológica brasileira. Recife: Ministério da Educação e Cultura, Departamento de Assuntos Culturais, Instituto Joaquim Nabuco de Pesquisas Sociais, 1976. 58 leaves (Série Documentos — Instituto Joaquim Nabuco de Pesquisas Sociais; 5)

This publication discusses propositions which would enhance the effectiveness and performance of Brazilian museums such as the scientific training of curators, the establishment of research programs and the formulation of a consistent policy of cooperation between museums and other federal or state institutions.

518 Draeger, Alain. Fascinating Brazil. Rio de Janeiro: Gráfica Editor Primor, 1977. 196 p.: ill. (some col.)

Discusses the wide range of Brazilian culture with emphasis on the visually striking aspects of the country portrayed in excellent color photographs. Includes synthesis of Brazil.

519 Golyscheff, Jef. Exposição Jef Golyscheff, 22 de maio a 22 de junho de 1975, Museu de Arte Contemporânea da Universidade de São Paulo. São Paulo: MAC, 1975. 28 p., bibl., ill. (some col.)

Ex-member of the Dada Club in Berlin, Golyscheff died in Paris but lived several years in São Paulo where he painted dozens of canvases, in 1963 and 1964. Many of them recreated from memory paintings of his that were destroyed by the Nazis in Germany in the 1930s and 1940s. This catalogue of Golyscheff's show includes several reproductions, documents and bibliography.

Molotnik, J.R. Politics and popular culture in Brazil. See *HLAS 41:7561*.

520 O que é arte?: São Paulo responde. Compiladora, Regina Vater. Arte da capa e foto, Regina Vater. São Paulo: Massão Ohno, 1978. 78 p.: ill.

In 1978, artist Regina Vater organized an inquest to explore the nature and formulate a definition of art. The respondents were a cross-section of São Paulo's population including well-known artists and critics. Their replies are introduced in their original handwritten form.

521 Pacello, Julio. Julio Pacello e sua obra editorial. São Paulo: Museu de Arte de São Paulo, 1979. 32 p., ill.

Catalogue of the retrospective show of Julio Pacello's exceptional career as an art publisher in Brazil. The books he produced, with originals by some of Brazil's major 20th-century artists are outstanding examples of the kind. José Mindlin's introductory essay captures the personality and accomplishments of J. Pacello with perception and breadth. B/w reproductions of his major editions.

522 **Rio de Janeiro. Museu Nacional de Belas Artes.** Aquisições do Museu Nacional de Belas Artes, 1970–1976. Rio de Janeiro: MNBA, 1977. 71 p.: ill.

The acquisitions of Brazil's National Museum of Fine Arts cover Brazilian learned and naif paintings, graphics, ceramics, sculpture, and folk art. These holdings date from the 19th and 20th centuries but also include some 18th-century colonial pieces. There are very few items from other countries. The book includes minute descriptions of each work, short biographies of the artists and introductions to the folk traditions of several pieces.

523 **———. ———.** Peça do mês. Rio de Janeiro: O Museu, 1975/1977. 200 p.: ill.

"Peça do mês" or "Art-Work of the Month" is an advertising device launched by Brazil's National Museum of Fine Arts aimed at promoting its collection, especially the Brazilian holdings, among a wider audience. This catalogue shows the chronology of works promoted since 1971, when the "Art-Work of the Month" program was initiated.

524 **São Francisco:** o rio da unidade = a river for unity. 2. ed. Brasília: Companhia de Desenvolvimento do Vale do São Francisco, 1978. 163 p.: ill., map (1 fold. in pocket)

The destiny and history of Brazil's São Francisco River is told with a wealth of documents and a great variety of high-quality, color photographs. Tasteful edition.

525 **Telles, Leandro Silva.** Manual do patrimônio histórico. Arte, Vera Gonzatto e Diva Guizzo. Porto Alegre: Universidade de Caxias do Sul, 1977. 121 p., bibl., ill. (Coleção Temas gauchos; 2)

The main topics of this book are: the concept of historical patrimony; its relation to a country's historical heritage and environment; the destruction of patrimony throughout the centuries; protection laws and preservation methods; international societies for the preservation of monuments; and Brazilian examples. Basic bibliography and a few photographs complete the edition.

526 **Wiesenthal, Mauricio.** Brazil. New York: Crescent Books, 1978. 92 p.: col. ill.

Known and lesser-known aspects of Brazilian cities, landscape, life and traditions. Although the quality of color photographs is average they offer glimpses of city planning and architectural details. Text consists of basic information.

JOURNAL ABBREVIATIONS ART

A Abside. Revista de cultura mexicana. México.

ADH/C Clio. Académia Dominicana de la Historia. Santo Domingo.

BBAA B.B.A.A. Boletín Bibliográfico de Antropología Americana. Instituto Panamericano de Geografía e Historia, Comisión de Historia. México.

BNBD Boletín Nicaragüense de Bibliografía y Documentación. Banco Central de Nicaragua, Biblioteca. Managua.

CA Critica d'Arte. Studio Italiano de Storia dell'Arte. Vallecchi Editore. Firenze, Italy.

CDLA Casa de las Américas. Instituto Cubano del Libro. La Habana.

CFC/RBC Revista Brasileira de Cultura. Ministério da Educação e Cultura, Conselho Federal de Cultura. Rio.

CH Cuadernos Hispanoamericanos. Instituto de Cultura Hispánica. Madrid.

CONAC/RNC Revista Nacional de Cultura. Consejo Nacional de Cultura. Caracas.

FIU/CR Caribbean Review. Florida International Univ., Office of Academic Affairs. Miami.

FJB/BH Boletín Histórico. Fundación John Boulton. Caracas.

HUMB Humboldt. Revista para o mundo ibérico. Ubersee-Verlag. Hamburg, FRG.

IAI/I Indiana. Beiträge zur Völker-und Sprachenkunde, Archäologie und Anthropologie des Indianischen Amerika. Ibero-Amerikanisches Institut. Berlin, FRG.

ICP/R Revista del Instituto de Cultura Puertorriqueña. San Juan.

IGFO/RI Revista de Indias. Instituto Gonzalo Fernández de Oviedo [and] Consejo Superior de Investigaciones Científicas. Madrid.

IHGB/R Revista do Instituto Histórico e Geográfico Brasileiro. Rio.

IHGGB/R Revista do Instituto Histórico e Geográfico Guarujá/Bertioga. São Paulo.

IIE/A Anales del Instituto de Investigaciones Estéticas. Univ. Nacional Autónoma de México. México.

IJ/JJ Jamaica Journal. Instituto of Jamaica. Kingston.

INAH/A Anales del Instituto Nacional de Antropología e Historia. Secretaría de Educación Pública. México.

LAP Latin American Perspectives. Univ. of California. Riverside.

MEC/C Cultura. Ministério da Educação e Cultura, Diretoria de Documentação e Divulgação. Brasília.

MNDJG/A Anales del Museo Nacional David J. Guzmán. San Salvador.

OAS/AM Américas. Organization of American States. Washington.

OEIL L'Oeil. Revue d'art mensuelle. Nouvelle Sedo. Lausanne, Switzerland.

PMNH/HC Historia y Cultura. Museo Nacional de Historia. Lima.

REVIEW Review. Center for Inter-American Relations. New York.

SCHG/R Revista Chilena de Historia y Geografía. Sociedad Chilena de Historia y Geografía. Santiago.

UCLV/I Islas. Univ. Central de las Villas. Santa Clara, Cuba.

USP/RH Revista de História. Univ. de São Paulo, Faculdade de Filosofia, Ciências e Letras, Depto. de Histórica [and] Sociedade de Estudos Históricos. São Paulo.

UY/R Revista de la Universidad de Yucatán. Mérida, Mex.

VOZES Vozes. Revista de cultura. Editora Vozes. Petrópolis, Brazil.

FOLKLORE

MERLE E. SIMMONS, *Professor of Spanish, Indiana University*

APPROXIMATELY FOUR YEARS HAVE PASSED since the last folklore bibliography appeared in *HLAS 38*. For this reason this current listing is much longer than the earlier bibliographies that were compiled at two-year intervals.

One of the most interesting developments in the field of Latin American folklore is the sustained appearance of a new scholarly serial of high quality, the *Journal of Latin American Lore,* edited by James Wilkie and published at the Univ. of California, Los Angeles. It began publication in the summer of 1975 and has since that time become one of the best serial publications dealing with folklore of the Americas. Vol. 5 of the *Journal* appeared in 1979. Another long-running review, *Folklore Americano,* still published by the Instituto Panamericano de Geografía e Historia but now printed in Mexico, has been given new life under the vigorous editorship of the Guatemalan folklorist, Celso A. Lara. No longer appearing in desultory fashion, six large issues of this important journal, Nos. 20–25 inclusive, saw the light between 1975 and 1978. Although characterized by an unusually large number of articles that reflect the Marxist orientation of Lara and his close collaborators, *Folklore Americano* remains overall the best specialized folklore journal published in Latin America.

For sheer quantity of publications on folklore, Brazil has in recent years ranked first among Latin American countries, and some of the studies published there are of excellent quality. Particularly worthy of note is the series of over a dozen attractively printed volumes in the *Coleção Folclore* that between 1976 and 1979 were published by the Conselho Estadual de Artes e Ciências Humanas of the state of São Paulo.

Following the death of the eminent Argentine scholar Augusto Raúl Cortazar in 1976, and since the distinguished Brazilian folklorist Paulo de Carvalho Neto settled in the US some years ago, Manuel Dannemann of Chile has become the most active folklorist working in Latin America. Scholarly in his approach and methodology, widely traveled in Europe and the US, and possessing the linguistic competence to work in most of the major European languages as well as his native Spanish, Dannemann is today one of the most competent folklorists at work on the world scene. Eight of his contributions listed here testify to the breadth of his interests, which encompass such diverse topics as folklore theory, the creation of a folklore atlas for Chile, studies of various genres of folklore, and folklore bibliography.

Latin America has over the years not customarily been in the forefront of theoretical or methodological advances in the field of folklore research, though there have been occasional exceptional theoreticians like Cortazar and Dannemann. However, Pedro and Elsa Escabí's *La décima: vista parcial del folklore* (item **1265**) stands as an interesting example of the application of statistical methods to the analysis of some 3700 popular songs and verses from Puerto Rico. This type of approach has seldom been used in Latin America. Also interesting for its methodology, though in this case the work in question was done under the direction of a North American scholar, is a study of Peruvian riddles in their *social context* by Billie Jean Isbell and Freddy Amílcar Roncalla Fernández: "The Ontogenesis of Metaphor: Riddle Games among Quechua Speakers seen as Cognitive Discovery Procedures" (item **1406**). This study employs a performance-oriented approach of the kind that has become so prevalent in recent years in the US, though rarely employed by Latin American folklorists. More traditional in its analytical methods, but an important work among literary studies of Hispanic folksongs, is the recently published second of five proposed volumes in the series called *Cancionero folklórico de México*. Vol. 2, *Coplas de amor desdichado y otras coplas de amor* (item **1311**), was published in 1977 by a team of scholars from the Colegio de México working under the direction of Margit Frenk Alatorre. The volume adds about 3000 carefully annotated *copla* texts to the collection begun in *Coplas del amor feliz* published in 1975.

One final development worthy of note is the ever increasing activity of scholars working in the field of Chicano folklore and Puerto Rican folklore found in New York City and other large urban centers of the US. Because the folklore of Chicanos is related in so many ways to that of Mexico, and Puerto Rican folklore in the US derives directly from that of the island of Puerto Rico, I have in this bibliography pragmatically included the folklore of these two large minority groups in the US under the broad geographical heading of "Mexico" and "Greater Antilles" respectively. This implies no inclination on my part to downgrade the uniqueness, richness, and importance of the folklore of Hispanic groups in the continental US, only a belief that it can best be studied in close association with the Mexican or Puerto Rican cultural traditions that have nurtured it.

GENERAL

951 Andrews, David H. Flirtation walk—*piropos* in Latin America (Journal of Popular Culture [Bowling Green, Ohio] 11:1, Summer 1977, p. 49–61)

An entertaining article on the *piropo* in Latin America that gives a few examples and discusses the context in which *piropos* are used.

952 Angeles Caballero, César. La folklorología (UIA/C, 11:57, agosto 1976, p. 446–455, illus.)

Seeks to synthesize in a brief article certain concepts about folklore and the study of folklore. Draws upon ideas expressed by various scholars in Spain and Spanish America.

953 Aretz, Isabel and **Luis Felipe Ramón y Rivera.** Areas musicales de tradición oral en América Latina: una crítica y tentativa de reestructuración de los "cancioneros" establecidos por Carlos Vega (UCIEM/R, 30:134, abril/sept. 1976, p. 9–55, bibl., maps, music)

Using strictly musical criteria, the authors attempt to refine Vega's earlier division of Latin American traditional music into various groupings known as "cancioneros." Offers 45 illustrative musical examples gathered from most of the countries of Central and South America, Mexico, and the Antilles.

954 Bascom, William. Oba's ear: a Yoruba myth in Cuba and Brazil (Research in African Literatures [University of Texas Press, Austin] 7:2, Fall 1976, p. 149–165, illus.)

Studies numerous Cuban and Brazilian versions of a myth that had its origins in Africa. Includes in Yoruba with English translations some poetic versions that were collected in the field.

955 Becco, Horacio Jorge. Bibliografía de Augusto Raúl Cortazar (ANH/B, 47, 1974, p. 377–391)

A compilation of the recently deceased folklorist's personal bibliography, 226 items in all.

956 Bozzoli de Wille, María E. Bibliografía antropológica de Costa Rica (Boletín de Antropología Americana [México] 38:47, 1976, p. 63–82)

Lists several hundred works, most of them published between 1969–1975. Some deal with folklore. For earlier years a bibliography of bibliographies is appended.

957 **Brednich, Rolf W.** *ed.* Internationale Volkskundliche Bibliographie (International Folklore and Folklife Bibliography, Bibliografie Internationale des Arts et Traditions Populaires) für die Jahre 1975 und 1976 mit Nachträgen für die vorausgehenden Jahre. Bonn, FRG: Rudolf Habelt Verlag BmbH, 1979. 727 p.

A huge bibliography of world folklore that contains 8637 entries divided into 21 sections according to genre. Manuel Dannemann is the collaborator for South America. Unfortunately, because of the arrangement of items by genre, it is difficult to search out entries by regions. Includes indexes.

958 **Cáceres, Abraham.** Preliminary comments on the marimba in the Americas (*in* Discourse in ethnomusicology: essays in honor of George List. Bloomington: Ethnomusicology Publications Group, Indiana University, 1978, p. 225–250)

Describes and categorizes marimbas in the two regions of the Americas where they are found: i.e., from southern Mexico to Costa Rica and in the Colombo-Ecuadorian area. Studies comparatively such matters as the instruments themselves, performance styles, social contexts in which marimbas and xylophones are played, etc.

959 **Carvalho-Neto, Paulo de.** Concepto y realidad del teatro folklórico latinoamericano (IPGH/FA, 23, junio 1977, p. 101–115)

Treats folk theatre as a genre and gives a very complete historical and analytical view of folk theatre in Latin America, specifically in Ecuador. Discusses masks, scenery, and dance associated with this folk genre.

960 ———. Diccionario de teoría folklórica. Guatemala: Editorial Universitaria, Universidad de San Carlos, 1977. 230 p.

Defines in alphabetical order several hundred technical terms, names of types or genres of folklore, etc. All are very personal definitions that draw upon the author's own theories of folklore and his approaches for studying it. Of great value for clarifying many concepts, or at least stimulating thought about them.

961 **Childers, James Wesley.** Tales from Spanish picaresque novels: a motif-index. Albany: State University of New York Press, 1977. 262 p., bibl.

A motif index of tales from 30 Spanish picaresque novels with an introductory discussion of the picaresque genre, its influence on Spanish and other literatures, etc. Not about Latin America, but invaluable to any scholar working in Hispanic folklore the world over. Includes index.

962 **Coluccio, Félix.** Aproximación a la raíz folklórica en la novelística latinoamericana (IPGH/FA, 20, junio/dic. 1975, p. 167–170)

Calls attention to 15 of the most outstanding Latin American novelists whose works are based to a significant degree upon folkloric elements. Analyzes briefly the work of the Venezuelan Rómulo Gallegos by way of proving the point.

963 ———. En torno al problema de los calendarios folklóricos (IPGH/FA, 24, dic. 1977, p. 7–20)

Reports on research that has been done on folklore calendars for some Latin American countries. Discusses data gathering techniques and future goals for this kind of investigation.

963a **Congreso Internacional de Folklorología,** *1st, Guararé, Panamá, 1973.* Actas del I [i.e., Primer] Congreso Internacional de Folklorología en Panamá, Guararé, Provincia de Los Santos, Panamá, 1973. Panamá: Instituto Nacional de Cultura, Dirección Nacional de Patrimonio Histórico, 1976. 351 p., bibl., illus.

Contains 14 papers presented by the following scholars: Ida Bremmé de Santos (see item **1146**); Julián Cáceres Freyre (see item **1015**); Ernesto J. Castillero R.; Lila Cheville; Augusto Raúl Cortazar (see item **1019**); Armando Fortune (see item **1158**); Roberto de la Guardia (see item **1162**); Nieves de Hoyos S.; Coralia H. de Llorente (see item **1174**); Silvano Lora (see item **1175**); Mildred Merino de Zela (see item **991**); Gabriel Moedano (see item **1349**); Emilia Prieto (see item **1183**); and Reina Torres de Araúz (see item **1191**).

964 **Cortazar, Augusto Raúl.** Ciencia folklórica aplicada: reseña teórica y experiencia argentina. Buenos Aires: Fondo Nacional de las Artes, 1976. 118 p., bibl., illus.

The renowned Argentine folklorist's last work, published posthumously. Sums up many theoretical and practical ideas about how folklore can be applied, particularly to the production of arts and crafts but to other ends as well. Includes a comprehensive bibliography on this subject and also Cortazar's personal bibliography, which spans his career (1930–75).

965 **Courlander, Harold.** A treasury of Afro-American folklore: the oral literature, traditions, recollections, legends, tales, songs, religious beliefs, customs, sayings, and humor of peoples of African descent in the Americas. New York: Crown Publishers, 1976. 618 p., bibl., illus., music, plates.

A huge anthology of materials on black folklore taken from many sources and covering practically all aspects of the subject except material lore. Geographical coverage includes all parts of North, South, and Central America where black culture is found. The author ties all of this together with a general introduction and running commentary. The contents are too vast to be summarized here in detail, but students of black folklore will find this to be a valuable collection of readings and texts on the subject.

966 **Craven, Roy C.** Andean art: an endangered tradition (OAS/AM, 30:1, Jan. 1978, p. 41–47, plates)

Comments upon an exhibition of traditional arts and crafts from Bolivia, Peru, Ecuador, and Colombia that was gathered from fieldwork and presented at the Univ. of Florida. Includes excellent photographs of representative pieces. Discusses the effects of modern life upon such popular art.

967 **DeCosta, Miriam.** The use of African folklore in Hispanic literature (UWI/CQ, 23:1, March 1977, p. 22–30)

Traces the introduction of African folk elements into American tradition in three different historical periods and lists such contributions, though without explanations, by genres and by countries. Also considers various writers who have used African folk elements in art literature of different kinds.

968 **Díaz Castillo, Roberto.** El folklore y la investigación folklórica: un problema ideológico (IPGH/FA, 22, dic. 1976, p. 131–142)

Discourses on the relationship and interplay between Marxist materialism and its teachings and folklore's place in society and tradition. Focuses primarily on Guatemala and Cuba. The same article also appeared in: *La Tradición Popular* (Guatemala, 7, 1976, p. 2–19) and in *Casa de las Américas* (La Habana, 19:110, sept./oct. 1978, p. 19–28).

969 **Domínguez, Luis Arturo.** El folklore (*in* Enciclopedia de Venezuela. Edited by Lucas Morán Arce. Caracas?: A. Bello, 1974?, v. 12, p. 1–36, plates)

An encyclopedia article designed to inform the general reader about three types of folklore: 1) *folklore material* (recipes of regional dishes and popular crafts); 2) *folklore social* (language, customs, fiestas, dances, etc.); and 3) *folklore espiritual-mental* (music and song, tales and legends, beliefs and superstitions, etc.).

970 **Dorson, Richard M.** The African connection: comments on "African Folklore in the New World" (Research in African Literatures [Univ. of Texas Press, Austin] 8:2, Fall 1977, p. 260–265)

In continuing polemics with several folklorists of different persuasion, Dorson sustains his point of view that most Negro folktales collected in the US are not of African origin.

971 **Dowdall, Roberto C.** Trabajando de a caballo. Buenos Aires: Editorial Hemisferio Sur, 1977. 119 p., illus.

About the way of life of men who work on horseback. Focuses primarily upon Argentina, but also touches on other areas such as Venezuela, Mexico, and the US. Deals at times with folklore: e.g., material objects such as lariats and saddles, work customs, specialized vocabulary, etc. Contains appendix.

972 **Fortún de Ponce, Julia Elena.** Actual problemática del folklore en Latino América. La Paz: Dirección Nacional de Antropología, 197–. 14 p.

Discusses the present state of folklore in Latin America. Expresses concern about preserving it and suggests means of achieving this goal.

973 **García-Prada, Carlos** *ed.* Baladas y romances de ayer y hoy. Bogotá: Instituto Caro y Cuervo, 1974. 241 p.

Intended for the student or the general reader. Contains 60 old *romances* from before 1600 and 50 by known authors dating from about 1600 to the present time. The editor provides a good introduction that treats the history of *romances* and of ballad studies in both Spain and Spanish America.

974 **Garrido, Pablo.** Meditaciones en torno al folklore (UC/AT, 436, 1977, p. 153–167)

Prints a complete Spanish translation of William J. Thom's letter of 1846 where he proposes the use of the term *folk-lore* and discusses what it is. Garrido uses this as a point of departure for pondering once again various problems of defining folklore, and in so doing he summarizes and discusses many theoretical questions old and new.

975 **Goodman, Frances Schaill.** The embroidery of Mexico and Guatemala. New York: Scribner, 1976. 81 p., plates.

Studies by commentary, excellent photographs (many in color), and drawings of the traditional embroidery work of Mexico and Guatemala. Touches on the history of the craft, materials, techniques, designs, etc.

976 **Granda, Germán de.** Elementos lingüísticos afroamericanos en el área hispánica; nuevos materiales para su estudio sociohistórico: pt. 1, América (ICC/T, 31:3, sept./dic. 1976, p. 481–501)

Surveys briefly some socio-historical aspects of the Negro's presence in Spanish America over the centuries, but documents this commentary with copious footnotes containing hundreds of bibliographical leads. Touches on folklore, popular speech, Afro-American religions, music, etc. For linguist's comment, see *HLAS 40:6046*.

977 **Grebe, María Ester.** Objeto, métodos y técnicas de investigación en etnomusicología: algunos problemas básicos (UCIEM/R, 30:133, enero/marzo 1976, p. 5–27, bibl.)

An interesting essay that seeks to define ethnomusicology and to examine its relationship to other disciplines, including folklore. Also assesses various methodological approaches to research in the field and notes the kind of training needed by professional ethnomusicologists. Good bibliography.

978 **Guerra, Francisco.** La medicina popular en Hispanoamérica y Filipinas (CSIC/A, 25, 1973, p. 323–330)

A cursory but fairly informative overview of the elements that entered into the popular medicine of Spanish America and the Philippine Islands from Spanish and Indian sources.

979 **Guevara, Darío.** Breve ojeada sobre la teoría del folklore (IPGH/FA, 22, dic. 1976, p. 11–51, bibl., music)

Summarizes the history of folklore studies and discusses various theoretical problems, questions of definition of terms, etc. Concludes with a detailed discussion of the use and connotations of the term "folklore" in the Spanish language.

980 **Harrison, Ira E.** and **Sheila Cosminsky.** Traditional medicine: implications for ethnomedicine, ethnopharmacology, maternal and child health, mental health, and public health: an annotated bibliography of Africa, Latin America, and the Caribbean. New York: Garland Publishing, 1976. 229 p.

Covers the literature on traditional medicine in Africa, Latin America, and the Caribbean from 1950–75. Includes indexes.

981 **Ibérico Mas, Luis.** El mito en el folklore (IPGH/FA, 24, dic. 1977, p. 21–27)

Addresses the question of whether myth should be considered as part of literary or philosophical folklore.

982 **Lara F., Celso A.** Algunas consideraciones metodológicas sobre la aplicación del folklore a los estudios históricos (Sarance [Otavalo, Ecuador] 3:1, junio 1977, p. 28–45)

Comments upon the contribution that a study of folklore can make toward historical research and cites the opinions of many scholars who concur in this view. Gives methodological suggestions for using folklore in this way.

983 ———. Aproximación científica al estudio del folklore (IPGH/FA, 22, dic. 1976, p. 53–79, bibl.)

Defines folklore as a social phenomenon, a patrimony of the exploited classes of society. Reviews concepts of folklore in capitalist and socialist countries. Introduces various theories about folklore and its origins, and finally discusses the scientific validity of the discipline.

984 ———. En torno al problema de la proyección folklórica (CIF/FA, 20, junio/dic. 1975, p. 35–48, bibl.)

Elaborates on what is meant by a "projection" of folklore as the term has been understood by such Spanish American theorists as Carlos Vega and Augusto Raúl Cortazar; then seeks to differentiate between the proper and improper use of the term.

985 ———. Implicaciones del folklore como fuente histórica (IPGH/FA, 21, junio 1976, p. 159–176, bibl.)

Discusses the way in which folklore provides a very important source for historical research. Includes a summary of studies that show the permanence of history in oral tradition and proposes a research method for studying folklore and history.

986 ——— and **J. Gonzalo Mejía Ruiz.** XXV [i.e. Vigésimo quinto] aniversario de fundación de *Folklore Americano*: 1953–1978 (IPGH/FA, 25, junio 1978, p. 9–15)

Reviews the history of the journal *Folklore Americano* and its sponsoring committee, the Folklore Committee of the Panamerican Institute of Geography and History (IPGH).

987 **Lemos, Néstor.** Folklore y filosofía: la literatura paremiológica o refranesca, fuente primigenia de la filosofía. Buenos Aires: Editorial Axioma, 1976. 79 p.

A theoretical statement by a professor of philosophy who seeks to show that the roots of his discipline are to be found in paroemiology, and that the modern philosophic orientation known as "materialist dialectic" developed from these origins in folklore. However, the author's knowledge of worldwide paroemiological studies and of folklore research in general is obviously deficient.

988 **List, George.** Musical concepts in traditional cultures (*in* Folklore today: a festschrift for Richard M. Dorson. Edited by Linda Dégh, Henry Glassie, and Felix J. Oinas. Bloomington: Research Center for Language and Semiotic Studies, Indiana University, 1976, p. 335–346)

Relates the emic concepts of two cultures (the Hopi Indians and the Colombian Costeños) about their own musical traditions. Contrasts them with the etic concepts developed by outside scholars.

989 **Litto, Gertrude.** South American folk pottery: traditional techniques from Peru, Ecuador, Bolivia, Venezuela, Chile, Colombia. New York: Watson-Guptill Publications, 1976. 224 p., illus., plates.

The author and her husband, who contributed photographs and drawings, survey traditional techniques used by potters along the west coast of South America.

990 **Melgar Vásquez, Alejandro.** Algunas consideraciones sobre la epistemología de la folklorología (IPGH/FA, 22, dic. 1976, p. 81–109)

Discusses the limitations of idealistic epistemology and emphasizes the need for the study of folklore to be based on a historical and materialistic framework, which in the Marxist view is the only acceptable scientific theory and method for social research.

991 **Merino de Zela, Mildred.** El folklore como técnica educativa (*in* Actas del I Congreso Internacional de Folklorología en Panamá [see item **963a**] p. 55–67)

A brief essay on the application of folklore to teaching in the classroom.

992 **Mundkur, Balaji.** The alleged diffusion of Hindu divine symbols into precolumbian Mesoamerica: a critique (UC/CA, 19:3, Sept. 1978, p. 541–583, illus.)

Criticizes parallels drawn between certain religious symbols in Hindu and Mesoamerican cultures. Useful to students interested in the history of astronomical-astrological beliefs in Mesoamerican tradition.

993 ———. The cult of the serpent in the Americas: its Asian background (UC/CA, 17:3, Sept. 1976, p. 429–455)

Attempts to establish the prehistoric origins of serpent myths and cults among American Indians. Describes many of the ceremonies, narratives, and art forms dealing with the venerated serpent.

994 **Muriel, Inés.** Comentario sobre la aplicación de métodos cuantitativos al estudio de las culturas tradicionales (IPGH/FA, 20, junio/dic. 1975, p. 161–165)

Examines critically the methodological bases of statistical and computerized studies in the social sciences, including folklore, and ultimately warns Latin Americans against the misuse of such studies by the US and its military groups in order to dominate or destroy traditional cultures.

Neglia, Erminio. The teaching of Latin American culture: a Spanish teacher's view and suggestions. See *HLAS 41:4331.*

Palarea, Alvaro Fernaud. Comportamiento musical, educación musical y folklore en América Latina. See *HLAS 40:9014.*

995 **Pollak-Eltz, Angelina.** Cultos afroamericanos: vudú y hechicería en las Américas. Caracas: Universidad Católica Andrés Bello, 1977. 344 p., bibl. (Colección Manoa, 8)

A sympathetic study of black religions in Africa and America. Surveys the history of blacks and aspects of their life as slaves; then treats their religions, practices, beliefs, etc., area by area. A great deal of folklore in the discussion of superstitions, rites, beliefs in magic, etc. Includes index.

996 **Ramos Pérez, Demetrio.** El mito del Dorado: su génesis y proceso. Con el *Discovery* de Walter Raleigh (traducción de Betty Moore) y otros papeles doradistas. Caracas: Academia Nacional de la Historia, 1973. 718 p., map.

A detailed historical study of the myth of El Dorado and other myths and legends that were important at the time of the conquest of America. Folklorists will find here many topics of interest, although they are not studied with a folklorist's perspective.

997 **Sadie, Stanley.** Latinoamérica en el nuevo *Grove* (UCIEM/R, 30:134, abril/sept. 1976, p. 69–74)

Discusses the treatment given Latin American music in the fifth ed. of the British *Grove's Dictionary of Music and Musicians.* Stresses the attention paid to musical folklore and ethnomusicology in this newest edition of the work. For musicologist's comment, see *HLAS 38:9018.*

998 **Salgado Herrera, Antonio.** La brujería en Hispanoamérica. México: B. Costa-Amic Editor, 1977. 204 p., illus.

A popularized hodgepodge of short pieces about many aspects of witchcraft in Spanish America. Very unscholarly, but parts of it might be of value if used cautiously by a trained folklorist.

999 **Segato, Rita.** Folklore y relaciones sociales en América Latina: un intento de definir el campo del folklore a partir del nivel modo de producción (IPGH/FA, 22, dic. 1976, p. 111–120)

Seeks to define folklore in terms of tracing its origins to pre-capitalistic societies. A corollary is that capitalism destroys folklore because the former alters the conditions that produce the latter.

1000 **Sharon, Douglas.** Distribution of the *mesa* in Latin America (UCLA/JLAL, 2:1, 1976, p. 71–95, bibl.)

Surveys information available at present about the distribution of the use of a *mesa* (i.e., an altarlike arrangement of power objects used by shamans from Mexico through Central America and the Andean region to Chile). Good bibliography on indigenous medicine, folk healing, etc.

1001 **Simmons, Merle E.** Folklore bibliography for 1974. Bloomington: *published for the* Folklore Institute *by the* Research Center for Language and Semiotic Studies, Indiana University, 1977. 159 p. (Indiana University Folklore Institute monograph series, 29)

An annotated bibliography of the folklore of the New World plus Spain and Portugal. Contains 1151 items grouped according to genre. Also includes index.

1002 ———. Folklore bibliography for 1975. Philadelphia: Institute for the Study of Human Issues, 1979. 186 p. (Indiana University Folklore Institute monograph series, 31)

An annotated bibliography of the folklore of the New World plus Spain and Portugal. Contains 1235 items grouped according to genre. Includes index.

1003 ———. Literary folklore in the *Historia verdadera* of Bernal Díaz del Castillo (*in* Folklore today, a festschrift for Richard M. Dorson. Edited by Linda Dégh, Henry Glassie, and Felix J. Oinas. Bloomington: Research Center for Language and Semiotic Studies, Indiana University, 1976, p. 451–462)

Extracts from a 16th-century chronicle about the conquest of Mexico some songs and proverbs that were part of the folklore brought to America by Spanish soldiers.

1004 Swetnam, John. Class-based and community-based ritual organization in Latin America (UP/E, 17:4, Oct. 1978. p. 425–438)

Studies Ladino religious organizations (*hermandades*) which the author considers "class-based" and compares them to "community-based" Indian *cofradías*. Describes and analyzes their similarities and differences.

1005 Teorías del folklore en América Latina. Caracas: CONAC, Talleres Italgráfica, 1975. 290 p. (Biblioteca INIDEF, 1)

Collection of essays on the theoretical aspects of the study of folklore by some of the most outstanding folklorists in Latin America: Guillermo Abadía Morales, Renato Almeida, Isabel Aretz, Luis da Câmara Cascudo, Augusto Raúl Cortazar, Manuel Dannemann, Darío Guevara, Ildefonso Pereda Valdés, and Dora P. de Zárate.

1006 Valenzuela de Garay, Carmen. Indices de los veinticuatro volúmenes de la revista *Folklore Americano*, por autor y por título (IPGH/FA, 25, junio 1978, p. 17–42)

A complete index by author and title of articles published in the first 24 volumes of *Folklore Americano*.

1007 Vigneras, Louis-André. La búsqueda del paraíso y las legendarias Islas del Atlántico. Valladolid, Spain: Casa-Museo de Colón, 1976. 71 p. (Cuadernos Colombinos, 6)

A historical and universal survey of legendary voyages and searches for ideal islands where death does not exist.

1008 Wilkie, James W. and **Edna Monzón de Wilkie** *eds.* Elitelore as a new field of inquiry: influences of the novel, film, and oral history on national policy decisions in Latin America. Los Angeles: Pacific Basin Economic Study Center, Graduate School of Management, UCLA, 1979. 1 v. (Various pagings)

A collection of offprints (with their original pagination, p. 79–101, 183–224, 221–238, 239–256 and 257–263) of five articles from the *Journal of Latin American Lore* here reprinted in book form. They explain the concept of "elitelore" first developed in 1967 by James W. Wilkie to refer to the lore of leaders on all levels of society. "Elitelore" interacts with folklore to influence political and other decisions.

1009 ———; ———; and **María Herrera-Sobek.** Elitelore and folklore: theory and a test case in *One hundred years of solitude* (*in* Elitelore as a new field of inquiry [see item **1008**] p. 183–224)

Applies Wilkie's theory of "elitelore" (i.e., lore of leaders on all levels of society) to one of Latin America's most important novels, *One hundred years of solitude* by the Colombian writer Gabriel García Márquez. Posits a thesis that elitelore-cum-folklore influences decisions about national development.

1010 Williams, Lance A. Theoretical problem in New World folklore: a need for standardization of terminology (IPGH/FA, 25, junio 1978, p. 111–117)

Laments the lack of uniformity in the use of folklore terminology and recommends as a valuable work for helping solve this problem Paulo de Carvalho Neto's *Diccionario de teoría folklórica*, a work annotated in this section (see item **960**).

Zapata Olivella, Manuel. Opresión y explotación del africano en la colonización de América Latina. See *HLAS 40:2342*.

ARGENTINA

1011 Agüero Blanch, Vicente Orlando. La artesanía del cuero en el departamento Malargüe-Mendoza (UNC/AAE, 27/28, 1972/1973, p. 147–159, illus.)

Describes various kinds of gaucho equipment made of leather, tells how they are made, and explains their use.

1012 Ambrosetti, Juan B. El diablo indígena: supersticiones y leyendas en la Argentina. Buenos Aires: Editorial Convergencia, 1976. 145 p.

New edition of an early study of evil spirits known to different Indian groups in Argentina, superstitions of the Misiones region, phantoms, legends, customs and legends of the Calchaquí Valley, popular cures, Carnival customs, gaucho superstitions, etc.

1013 ———. Supersticiones y leyendas. Buenos Aires: Ediciones Siglo XX, 1976. 140 p.

New edition of one of Argentina's pioneer studies, but it includes no new material or even an introductory note to caution readers that the book first appeared many decades ago. Describes and comments upon the superstitions of three areas: Misiones; the Calchaquí Valley, province of Salta; and the pampa area. Includes a few legends from Misiones only, and occasionally treats other types of folklore.

1014 Ayala Guana, B. Velmiro. Perurimá: andanzas y malandanzas de un Bertoldo guaraní. Introducción, notas y vocabulario de Luján Carranza. Buenos Aires: Editorial Huemul, 1975. 102 p.

Literarily retold version of 13 orally collected folktales about Perurimá, who is the Corrientes, Arg., folk hero who corresponds to Pedro de Urdemalas, the trickster of general Hispanic tradition. Includes data about informants, comparative notes, and a good introduction by Carranza.

1015 Cáceres Freyre, Julián. Los museos folklóricos al aire libre y su importancia educativa y científica para la República Argentina (*in* Actas del I Congreso Internacional de Folklorología en Panamá [see item **963a**] p. 175–194, bibl.)

Discusses open-air museums and notes that efforts to form them have met with very limited success in Argentina. Points out the need for such museums, especially folklore museums.

1016 Carrizo, Juan Alfonso. Historia del folklore argentino. 2. ed. Buenos Aires: Ediciones Dictio, 1977. 194 p.

Second ed. of work first published in 1953. No changes have been made to up-date the book, but it is a basic source of information about folklorists and folklore research in Argentina through the first half of the 20th century.

1017 Chertudi, Susana. Cuentos populares de la Cordillera de Neuquén, Argentina (IPGH/FA, 26, dic. 1978, p. 23–36, bibl.)

Texts of four orally collected folktales from a single informant with Aarne-Thompson tale-type numbers and a short bibliography. Previously published in the *Boletín del Colegio de Graduados en Antropología de Argentina* (No. 4).

1018 ———. La leyenda folklórica en la Argentina (SAA/R, 1:9, 1975, p. 69–75)

Explains the international classification of legends adopted in Budapest in 1963 by the International Society for Folk-Narrative Research and places the corpus of Argentina legends in this framework. Comments upon some Argentine legends.

1019 Cortazar, Augusto Raúl. Folklore aplicado en la Argentina: fundamentos y prácticas en el campo de las artesanías (*in* Actas del I Congreso Internacional de Folklorología en Panamá [see item **963a**] p. 285–333, bibl., map)

Offers some theoretical and practical comments about the study of folklore in general, then directs attention to the application of knowledge about folklore to arts and crafts and the revitalization of these in modern Argentine life.

1020 Cruz Varela, Juan. Fábulas inéditas. Edited by María Luisa Olsen de Serrano Redonnet and Antonio E. Serrano Redonnet. Buenos Aires: Ediciones Culturales Argentinas, 1978. 111 p., bibl., illus.

Offers the texts of 11 unpublished literary fables by Cruz Varela, the Argentine poet, probably written in 1816. Includes good bibliography, notes, and an introductory essay about Cruz Varela and his fables. Not folklore but interesting as an adaptation of the fable genre to literary uses. Includes index.

1021 *Folklore Americano* rinde homenaje a Susana Chertudi: 1925–1977; Curriculum Vitae de Susana Chertudi (IPGH/FA, 26, dic. 1978, p. 9–20)

Celso A. Lara, editor of *Folklore Americano,* writes an introduction to a special number of the journal dedicated to the memory of the recently deceased Argentine folklorist. A curriculum vitae is added that lists the main events in Chertudi's personal and professional life and offers a bibliography of her works.

1022 García, Silvia Perla. Una leyenda de creencia en el oeste de la provincia de Buenos Aires: Las Luces Malas (*in* Informes del Instituto Nacional de Antropología: formas culturales tradicionales en el área pampeana. Buenos Aires: Instituto Nacional de Antropología, 1978, v. 1, p. 9–22, map)

Offers texts of 28 legends or tales about the appearance of lights or apparitions usually having to do with hidden treasures or the dead. They were orally collected in the province of Buenos Aires. Includes an introductory commentary and Thompson motif numbers.

Golbert de Goodbar, Perla. Epu Peñiwen (los dos hermanos): cuento tradicional araucano. See *HLAS 41:1365*.

1023 Jofre Barroso, Haydée M. Los hijos del miedo: reportaje a las supersticiones y creencias del porteño. Buenos Aires: Emecé Editores, 1975. 256 p.

A general discussion of popular cults or religions such as spiritism, occultism, witchcraft, and belief in such things as magic, astrology, etc. as found in B.A. and elsewhere. There is considerable folklore in all of this, but the folklorist will have to identify and extract it for himself since the author's focus is not on folklore as such.

1024 Lázaro, Orlando. Los estudios folklóricos en Tucumán, 1900–1968: datos para una historia (UNTIA/R, 2, 1975, p. 131–146)

Surveys the history of folklore studies in the state of Tucumán, Arg., from colonial times, with particular stress on the period since 1900.

1025 Moreno Cha, Ercilia. El *Cancionero de los Pagos de Cañada de la Cruz* de Jesús María Pereyra y Emilia Altomare de Pereyra. Presentación y estudio crítico de Ercilia Moreno Cha (*in* Informe del Instituto Nacional de Antropología: formas culturales tradicionales en el área pampeana. Buenos Aires: Instituto Nacional de Antropología, 1978, v. 1, p. 41–209, bibl.)

Moreno Cha edits and presents here an unpublished *cancionero* of 100 Argentine songs, mostly *décimas*, collected orally by Jesús María Pereyra and his wife in the province of Buenos Aires between 1927–52. Texts are grouped according to themes.

1026 Newberry, Sara Josefina. Vigencia de las antiguas formas de curar en tres partidos de la provincia de Buenos Aires: Ayacucho, Madariaga y Rauch (*in* Informe del Instituto Nacional de Antropología: formas culturales tradicionales en el área pampeana. Buenos Aires: Instituto Nacional de Antropología, 1978, v. 1, p. 23–40)

Deals with present-day popular cures. Based upon fieldwork in the areas indicated. Studies different traditional concepts about the causes of illnesses and differing kinds of treatment used by *curanderos* to treat them. Considers the attitude of official medicine toward *curanderos*.

1027 Pasteknik, Elsa Leonor. Misiones y sus leyendas. Buenos Aires: Editorial Plus Ultra, 1977. 95 p., illus.

Consists of 35 Tupi-Guaraní legends and myths from Misiones, Arg. The author's approach is literary and non-scholarly, but they are written in a simple and unpretentious style that preserves something of the flavor of their folk origins.

1028 Rapela, Enrique José. Conozcamos lo nuestro. v. 1. Buenos Aires: Cielosur Editora, 1977. 106 p., illus.

A fascinating book about Argentine gauchos. Treats their clothing, knives, *boleadoras*, saddles, stirrups, and other objects of daily use; also their horses, social life, dwellings, ways of breaking horses and caring for them, methods of branding cattle, etc. The descriptive material is accompanied by innumerable line drawings.

1029 Salmon, Russell O. The tango: its origins and meaning (Journal of Popular Culture [Bowling Green, Ohio] 10:4, Spring 1977, p. 859–866)

A historical survey of the tango since its modest origins in the 1880s. Discusses the dance, the lyrics, and the social values it portrays, mentioning both the "myth" of Carlos Gardel and Bertolucci's film "Last Tango in Paris."

1030 Segovia de Giuliano, Sixta. El cuervo blanco: cuentos y leyendas. Santa Fe, Argentina: Librería y Editorial Colmegna, 1976. 106 p.

A collection of tales and legends retold in literary style. Some are based on authentic folklore.

1031 Taylor, Julie M. Tango: theme of class and nation (Ethnomusicology [Ann Arbor, Michigan] 20:2, May 1976, p. 273–291)

Analyzes the folklore, song, and dance elements of the Argentine tango, focusing on the recurrent themes found in the lore surrounding it, in the lyrics of the song, and in the dance choreography. Considers the social significance of the tango in Argentina. For musicologist's comment, see *HLAS 40:9032*.

1032 Teruggi, Mario E. Panorama del lunfardo: génesis y esencia de las hablas coloquiales urbanas. Buenos Aires: Ediciones Cabargón, 1974. 228 p., illus.

Examines the formation, the distribution, and the sociological implications of *lunfardo*, an urban argot that originated in Buenos Aires in the second half of the 19th century.

1033 Vázquez, Juan Adolfo. Nacimiento e infancia de Elal: mitoanálisis de un texto tehuelche meridional (IILI/RI, 42:95, abril/junio 1976, p. 201–216)

Literary analysis of a myth text collected from the Tehuelches of Tierra del Fuego. Although the analysis is carefully done, folklorists will find that there is no reference whatsoever to the standard motif indexes and other research tools of the folklorist's trade.

1034 Vece, José Antonio. Sumamao y un interrogante (CER/C, 5:5, julio/dic. 1977, p. 25–28)

Describes briefly the fiesta of San Esteban in the village of Sumamao, near Santiago del Estero, Arg. Then speculates on its possible relationship with an ancient Indian fiesta of the same region.

1035 Vidal de Battini, Berta Elena. Motivos del *Roman de Renard* en la narrativa popular argentina (*in* Homenaje al Instituto de Filología y Literaturas Hispánicas Dr. Amado Alonso en su cincuentenario, 1923–1973. Buenos Aires: Editorial Fernando García Cambeiro, 1975, p. 410–423)

Points out many motifs of the French medieval *Roman de Renard* that are alive in Argentine oral tradition, though frequently adapted to fit the New World setting.

1036 Visconti Vallejos, Ricardo R. Leyendas del litoral. Buenos Aires: Ediciones Litoral, 1977. 102 p., illus.

Short narrative pieces based mostly on Guaraní legends from the north of Argentina. Of interest to folklorists but of limited value because the author's approach is primarily literary.

1037 Wilbert, Johannes *ed.* Folk literature of the Selknam Indians: Martin Gusinde's collection of Selknam narratives. Los Angeles: UCLA Latin American Center Publications, 1975. 266 p., bibl., maps.

An English translation of folk narratives collected by Gusinde in Tierra del Fuego. Contains texts of 59 myths and legends along with summaries, motif-index numbers, and explanatory annotations. Includes glossary and indexes. For anthropologist's comment see *HLAS 39:1779*.

BOLIVIA

1038 Anibarro de Halushka, Delina. La tradición oral en Bolivia. La Paz: Instituto Boliviano de Cultura, 1976. 458 p., bibl., map.

100-tale texts orally collected in the Sucre, Potosí, and Cochabamba areas of Bolivia, some in Spanish and some in Quechua. Includes Aarne-Thompson tale-type numbers and excellent comparative notes and informant data; also, an introduction that explains procedures. The best book on Bolivian folktales available. Includes appendix.

1039 Beltrán Heredia, Augusto and others. Carnaval de Oruro: Tarabuco y Fiesta del Gran Poder. La Paz: Editorial Los Amigos del Libro, 1977. 133 p., plates.

Three descriptions of festivals in Bolivia: Augusto Beltrán Heredia's "Carnaval de Oruro" (p. 17–70); Blanco Thórrez Martines and Marcelo Thórrez López's "El Carnaval en Tarabuco" (p. 73–100); and Carlos Urquizo Sossa's "Grandiosa Festividad del Gran Poder" (p. 103–130). Excellent colored plates. Includes index.

1040 Cason, Marjorie and **Adele Cahlander.** The art of Bolivian highland weaving. New York: Watson-Guptill Publications, 1976. 216 p., bibl., illus.

A comprehensive study of Bolivian hand-weaving, techniques, patterns, and designs. Includes appendix, glossary and index.

1041 Cuevas Acevedo, Huberto. Tierra sin tiempo: Patagonia india: cuentos, leyendas y relatos. n.p.: n.p., n.d. 120 p.

Narratives in literary style that are sometimes based, though not very directly, upon legends and other traditions of the Tehuelche Indians of Patagonia. Written by a doctor who spent several years among the Tehuelches.

1042 Feria exposición de Alasita del 24 al 31 de enero: Sesquicentenario de la República. La Paz: Ediciones de la Casa Municipal de la Cultura Franz Tamayo, 1975. 31 p., map.

The Municipality of La Paz issued this booklet on the occasion of restructuring the Feria de Alasita to restore its traditional character. Includes a map of the fair grounds and five brief articles about the festival: Manuel Rigoberto Paredes' "El Mito del Ekeko" (Ekeko is an Indian god who is the fair's patron); Maks Portugal Zamora's "El Mundo Mágico del Ekeko;" Félix Eguino Zaballa's "Breve Relación de la Feria de Alasita;" Yolanda Bedregal de Conitzer's "Noticia sobre el Ekeko y su Fiesta;" and Carlos Urquizo Sossa's "El Periodismo en Alasita."

1043 Fortún, Julia Elena. Folklore y artesanía. La Paz: Editorial e Imprenta Crítica, 1976. 62 p., bibl.

Consists of two separate studies: "El Folklore en el Mundo Contemporáneo" (p. 7–37) which seeks to define folklore and folklore research and place them in the modern world; and "Política Artesanal" (p. 39–62) which considers the status of traditional arts and crafts in Bolivia.

1044 Olsen, Dale A. Música vesperal mojo en San Miguel de Isidoro (UCIEM/R, 30:133, enero/marzo 1976, p. 28–46, bibl., music, plates)

Studies the music and dance associated with a syncretistic fiesta in San Miguel de Isiboro, Bolivia. It combines shamanism and Christianity. Includes descriptions of the dance of the *macheteros*, musical transcriptions, etc. For musicologist's comment see *HLAS 40:9039*.

1045 Paniagua Chávez, Freddy. Manual práctico de plantas medicinales en Bolivia. Cochabamba, Bolivia: Imprenta Visión, 1975? 65 p., illus.

A practitioner of vegetarianism and natural medicine publishes here a guide to the use of medicinal plants that exist in Bolivia. Lists the plants and tells how to use them in the treatment of specific illnesses. There is probably a considerable amount of folklore here.

1046 Paredes, M. Rigoberto. Mitos, supersticiones y supervivencias populares de Bolivia. 4. ed. La Paz: Biblioteca del Sesquicentenario de la República, 1976. 329 p., bibl., illus.

New ed., actually the fourth, of a work first published in 1920. Deals broadly with Bolivian folklore with stress on ethnography (e.g., customs, ceremonies, superstitions, fiestas, popular medicine, myths, etc.). Includes a bibliography of Paredes' works and index.

1047 Paredes Candia, Antonio. Adivinanzas de doble sentido: folklore secreto. La Paz: Ediciones Isla, 1976. 70 p., illus.

A collection of 30 riddles that suggest obscene answers. However, as part of the riddling game, the actual answer given by the riddler turns out to be quite inoffensive.

1048 ———. Fiestas populares de Bolivia. La Paz: Librería-Editorial Popular, 1976–1977. 2 v., illus.

A series of short chapters that describe various types of fiestas of different places in Bolivia. Paredes Candia wrote many of these and also did the introduction, but numerous other writers also contribute chapters. Includes words without music of many songs.

1049 ———. El sexo en el folklore boliviano. La Paz: Ediciones Isla, 1977. 138 p., illus.

Offers examples of sexually oriented and other obscene folklore with explanations, though without informant data. Includes popular speech and sayings, riddles, verses, tales and anecdotes, beliefs and superstitions, toys and games, double-entendre letters, fiestas, etc.

1050 ———. Tradiciones de Bolivia. La Paz: Editorial Los Amigos del Libro, 1976. 266 p.

Consists of 43 literary pieces based on historical and legendary materials from Bolivian tradition. Similar to the famous *Tradiciones* written by the Peruvian author, Ricardo Palma.

1051 ———. Voces de trabajo: pregones, juramentos e invocaciones; folklore de Bolivia. La Paz: Editorial Isla, 1976. 28 p.

Gives 24 cries and onomatopoeiac sounds used by country people in Bolivia; then offers some traditional city cries. A few oaths and invocations of various kinds complete the small collection.

1052 Peñaranda de Guillén Pinto, Natty. Espíritu eterno, *Pacha Ajayu*: mitos, poemas, cuentos, leyendas, tradiciones, narraciones, anotaciones, supersticiones, curiosidades, apodos aymaras, símbolos aymaras. La Paz: Empresa Editora Universo, 1974. 235 p., illus.

A book about Aymara life and culture that sometimes discusses in a non-scholarly way interesting aspects of musical folklore, *coplas* (includes some texts without music), superstitions, customs, dances, etc. Gives a fair number of retold literary versions of folktales, myths, and legends.

1053 Zalles Ballivián, Elías. Tradiciones y anécdotas bolivianas. 2. ed. La Paz: Ediciones Isla, 1977. 134 p.

Second ed. of a work first published, apparently, in 1930. Contains short literary pieces that relate tales and legends associated with places in Bolivia. Most are based on historical or religious traditions, and some are of interest to folklorists.

1054 Zeballos Miranda, Luis. Artesanía boliviana. La Paz: Talleres-Escuela de Artes Gráficas Don Bosco, 1975. 92 p., illus., plates, tables.

Defines the whole field of arts and crafts, their study, the promotion of such activity and its commercialization, etc. Then surveys in text, drawings, and photographs Bolivian arts and crafts: e.g., weaving, ceramics, leather-work, basketry, objects made of wood, dyeing, etc.

BRAZIL

1055 Almeida, Renato. Candomblé em cordel. Salvador, Brazil: Departamento de Assuntos Culturais, Secretaria Municipal da Educação e Cultura, 1978. 1 v. (Unpaged) illus.

Almeida, the well known folklorist, writes a poem that explains in detail many of the beliefs of the popular religion Candomblé and also sings the praises of Bahia. The form he chooses is that of *literatura de cordel.*

1056 ———. Folclore. Rio: Ministério da Educação e Cultura, Departamento de Assuntos Culturais, Programa de Ação Cultural, 1976. 21 p., bibl. (Cadernos de Folclore. Nova série, 3)

A very brief introduction to the study of folklore.

1057 Alves, Luiz Antônio. O Círio de Nazaré (MEC/C, 6:22, julho/set. 1976, p. 16–23, plates)

Describes a festival in honor of Nossa Senhora de Nazaré as observed in Belem de Pará, Brazil. Traces its history in Portugal and Brazil.

1058 Amaral, Amadeu. Tradições populares. Com um estudo de Paulo Duarte. 2. ed. São Paulo: Editora Hucitec *com a* Secretaria de Cultura, Ciência e Tecnologia do Estado de São Paulo, 1976. 418 p.

Facsimile of the 1948 ed. Duarte's introductory study provides a biography and appreciation of the work of Amaral, a Brazilian journalist and man of letters (1875–1929). The book itself is a collection of brief articles or longer studies that deal with folklore theory, *romances* and other popular songs, proverbs, riddles, tales, religious folklore, etc. Dated, but still of value.

1059 Baden, Nancy T. Popular poetry in the novels of Jorge Amado (UCLA/JLAL, 2:1, 1976, p. 3–22)

Studies the way Jorge Amado, the Brazilian novelist, incorporates various kinds of popular and oral verse forms into his novels (e.g., *literatura de cordel*, religious songs, work songs, children's songs and rounds, songs of blind beggars, recreation songs, etc.). Includes some representative texts.

1060 Barros, Leandro Gomes de. Antologia. t. 3, v. 2, Leandro Gomes de Barros. João Pessoa, Brazil: Universidade Federal de Paraíba, 1977. 338 p., illus. (Literatura popular em verso)

Offers facsimile reproductions of 13 *folhetos* of poetry by Barros, an outstanding *literatura de cordel* poet of the early 20th century. Homero Senna, Ariano Suassuna, and Idellete Muzart Fonseca dos Santos provide introductory essays. This is vol. 2 on Barros but vol. 3 of the *Antologia* that is being published in the series "Literatura popular em verso."

1061 Bastos, Wilson de Lima. Folclore no setor religião em Juiz de Fora. Juiz de Fora, Brazil: Edições Paraibuna, 1973. 46 p., plates.

Surveys religious folklore and practices of many kinds, mostly beliefs and customs associated with various saints in the city of Juiz de Fora, Minas Gerais, Brazil.

1062 **Benjamin, Roberto.** Congos da Paraíba. Rio: Ministério da Educação e Cultura, Departamento de Assuntos Culturais, Fundação Nacional de Arte (FUNARTE), Campanha de Defesa de Folclore Brasileiro, 1977. 23 p., bibl., music, plates (Cadernos de Folclore. Nova Série; 18)

Describes the dance-dramas that are part of a religious festival in the city of Pombal. Includes words and music of some songs, choreographic charts, etc.

1063 **Brandão, Adelino.** Amadeu Amaral e o folclore brasileiro. São Paulo: Ministério da Educação e Cultura, Campanha de Defesa do Folclore Brasileiro, 1977. 190 p., bibl.

Studies the scholarly work of Amaral (1875–1929) as a folklorist. In assessing his contributions in the field and dealing with his theoretical orientation, the study touches on the whole history of folklore research in Brazil.

1064 **Cacciatore, Olga Gudolle.** Dicionário de cultos afro-brasileiros com origem das palavras. Rio: Forense Universitária, 1977. 279 p., bibl.

A comprehensive dictionary of Brazilian cults preceded by an introduction with useful theoretical comments. Many entries contain material of interest to folklorists.

1065 **Camargo, Maria Thereza L. de Arruda.** Medicina popular. Rio: Ministério da Educação e Cultura, Departamento de Assuntos Culturais, Fundação Nacional de Arte, 1976. 40 p., bibl. (Cadernos de Folclore. Nova Série; 8)

An informative basic discussion of popular medicine in Brazil in its multiple aspects (e.g., African elements, Indian elements, material medicine, spiritual medicine, various kinds of illnesses, etc.)

1066 ———. Verdades terapêuticas da medicina popular (CDFB/RBF, 14:41, maio/agôsto 1976, p. 37–44, bibl.)

Offers some thoughts on popular medicine, its importance among different social classes, its scientific validity, methodology for studying it, etc.

1067 **Campina, Júlio.** Subsidio ao folclore brasileiro: anedotas sobre caboclos e portugueses, lendas, contos e canções populares, etc. 2. ed. Posfacio de Théo Brandão. Maceió, Brazil: Museo Théo Brandão, Universidade Federal de Alagoas (UFAL), 1977. 82 p. (Biblioteca Alagoana de Folclore; 1)

A new ed. of a work published in 1897. Contains tales and anecdotes, words without music of popular songs, etc., from the Pernambuco and Alagoas region. Théo Brandão's *posfacio* provides a useful overview of the early history of folklore studies in Brazil.

1068 **Campos, Renato Carneiro.** Ideologia dos poetas populares do Nordeste. 2. ed. Recife, Brazil: Instituto Joaquim Nabuco de Pesquisas Sociais, Campanha de Defesa do Folclore Brasileiro, Fundação Nacional de Arte (FUNARTE), 1977. 75 p., plates (Série Estudos e pesquisas; 5)

First published in 1959, the work surveys and comments upon the content of many *folhetos* and *literatura de cordel* from Northeastern Brazil. Contains chapters on themes such as animals, religion, political ideology, Pedro Malasartes, etc.

1069 **Cascudo, Luís de Câmara.** História dos nossos gestos: uma pesquisa na mímica do Brasil. São Paulo: Edições Melhoramentos, 1976. 248 p., illus.

Surveys 332 gestures, facial expressions, body movements, etc. used to convey meaning as the author has observed them in Brazil. Offers lengthy comments based not only on his own interpretation but on extensive knowledge of literature in the field from many countries. Contains a good index.

1070 ———. Imagens de Espanha no popular do Brasil (CEEP/RD, 32:1/4, 1976, p. 73–81)

An essay about the presence in Brazilian folklore of many tales, proverbs, and other kinds of verbal lore that have their origins in Spanish tradition, both folkloric and literary.

1071 ———. Mitos brasileiros. Rio: Ministério da Educação e Cultura, Departamento de Assuntos Culturais, Fundação Nacional de Arte, 1976. 23 p. (Cadernos de Folclore. Nova Série; 6)

A brief basic introduction to the study of myths in Brazil. Discusses nine representative examples.

Centro Rural Universitário de Treinamento de Ação Comunitária de Pernambuco

(CRUTAC-Pe), *Recife, Brazil.* Presença da universidade no interior. See *HLAS 39:4594.*

Costa, Joaquim Ribeiro. Conceição do Mato Dentro: fonte da saudade. See *HLAS 40:3970.*

1072 Curran, Mark J. Rodolfo Coelho Cavalcante: Brazilian popular poet and propagandist of the *literatura de cordel* (PCCLAS/P, 5, 1976, p. 11–24)

Characterizes the popular poet Coelho Cavalcante as writer, salesman, and public relations man for his own works and for *literatura de cordel* in general over the past 35 years. Gives examples of his work.

1073 A dança do Lélé na cidade de Rosário, no Maranhão. São Luís, Brazil: Fundação Cultural do Maranhão, Campanha de Defesa do Folclore Brasileiro, 1977. 72 p., bibl., illus., map, music (mimeo)

Describes and analyzes through text, diagrams, and photos a regional dance of Maranhão. Includes some musical transcriptions.

1074 Dantas, Beatriz G. Dança de São Gonçalo. Rio: Ministério da Educação e Cultura, Departamento de Assuntos Culturais, Fundação Nactional de Arte, 1976. 20 p., bibl., charts, music, photos (Cadernos de Folclore. Nova Série; 9)

Describes the Dança de São Gonçalo as performed in two towns in the state of Sergipe, Brazil. Discusses costumes, music and musical instruments, choreography, etc.

1075 ———. Taieira. Rio: Ministério da Educação e Cultura, Departamento de Assuntos Culturais, Fundação Nacional de Arte, 1976. 20 p., bibl., music, plates (Cadernos de Folclore. Nova Série; 4)

Describes a traditional dance as observed in the town of Larangeiras, state of Sergipe, Brazil. Traces its history to the 18th century, gives words and music of some songs that accompany it, provides some diagrams of dance movements, etc.

1076 Fernandes, Ciro. Capas de cordel de Ciro Fernandes. n.p.: n.p., 1976. 1 v. (Unpaged)

Contains merely eight outside covers for the booklets of popular poetry or prose known as *literatura de cordel.* All are the work of a single artist, Ciro Fernandes.

1077 Fernandes, Waldemar Iglésias. 52 [i.e. Cinqüenta e dois] estorias populares: sul de São Paulo e sul de Minas. São Paulo: Editora Franciscana, 1971 [i.e., 1977]. 135 p., bibl.

Orally collected folktale texts, 40 from São Paulo and 12 from Minas Gerais, along with informant data. Those from São Paulo are sub-divided according to themes (e.g., tales of magic, saints, devils, animals, etc.).

1078 Freitas, Affonso A. de. Tradições e reminiscências paulistanas. 3. ed. São Paulo: Governo do Estado de São Paulo, 1978. 228 p., illus., maps, music (Coleção Paulística; 9)

New ed. of a book first published in 1921. Frequent attention to festivals, songs and dances (very little music), regional speech and popular sayings, customs, games, etc. Of value despite its lack of organization and scholarly rigor.

1079 Gonçalves, David. Para uma teoria literaria dos ditados e provérbios (Letras de Hoje [Pontifícia Universidade Católica do Rio Grande do Sul, Centro de Estudos da Lingua Portuguesa, Porto Alegre] 27, março 1977, p. 72–80)

Studies the role of proverbs and popular sayings in some literary short stories using the analytical techniques of linguistic and semiotic science.

1080 Guimarães, Reginaldo. O folclore na ficção brasileira: roteiro das *Memórias de um sargento de milícias.* Rio: Livraria Editora Cátedra *em convenio com o* Instituto Nacional do Livro, Ministério da Educação e Cultura, 1977. 118 p., bibl.

Studies folkloric elements in Manuel Antônio de Almeida's famous *Memórias de um sargento de milícias* (1854). Contains chapters on festivals, folk medicine, popular types, traditional expressions and sayings, etc.

1081 Hampl, Zdeněk. A literatura de cordel brasileira como manifestação de participação social e política (ASB/PP, 17:1, 1974, p. 5–17)

Seeks to show how the *literatura de cordel* of Northwestern Brazil reflects political and other events. Quotes many representative texts of the past 30 or 40 years.

1082 Husseini, Maria Marta Guerra. Literatura de cordel enquanto meio de comunicação no Nordeste brasileiro (AM/R, 188, jan./dez. 1976, p. 117–293, bibl.)

An excellent monographic study of Brazilian *literatura de cordel.* Chap. 1 of two long chapters deals with origins, the genre's importance on many levels, its influence, and many other *external* features. Chap. 2 contains an interesting line-by-line *internal* analysis of the content of 10 *folhetos* selected from a corpus of 245 compositions.

Ibiapina, João Nonon de Moura Fontes. Passarela de marmotas. See *HLAS 41:9331.*

1083 Jardim, Mára Públio de Souza Veiga. Aspectos folclóricos da Semana Santa em Macatuba. São Paulo: Conselho Estadual de Artes e Ciências Humanas, 1978. 80 p., plates (Coleção Folclore; 9)

Gives historical and other information about the town of Macatuba, São Paulo, and then describes in detail its observance of Holy Week with particular attention to traditional plays that are presented.

1084 Jordão, M.F. Embu, terra das artes e berço de tradições. n.p.: Serviço Gráfico da Secretaria de Cultura, Esportes e Turismo, n.d. 150 p., illus.

About the municipality of Embu, São Paulo, Brazil. Includes a chapter on folklore that contains a few tales and legends and describes some festivals and dances.

1085 Kopte, Johanna Martha and **Ana Louro.** Um estudo de olaria no contexto do folclore. São Paulo: Conselho Estadual de Artes e Ciências Humanas, 1979. 106 p., bibl., illus (Coleção Folclore; 17)

Studies the making of tiles and bricks in various areas of Brazil, particularly in the São Paulo region. Based on fieldwork.

1086 Lago, Mário. Chico Nunes das Alagoas. Rio: Civilização Brasileira, 1975. 167 p.

A biography and appreciation of the life and works of Francisco Nunes de Oliveira (d. 1953), a *repentista* poet of Alagoas, Brazil. Includes numerous textual samples of some of his poems.

1087 Lenko, Karol and **Nelson Papavero.** Insetos no folclore. São Paulo: Conselho Estadual de Artes e Ciências Humanas, 1979. 518 p., bibl. (Coleção Folclore; 18)

Lenko, an entomologist, was the principal author of 28 separate chapters on a like number of different subjects having to do with insects and their relationship to many kinds of Brazilian folklore. After Lenko's death in 1975, Papavero completed and organized the work for publication. Each chapter has its own separate bibliography and these are frequently quite extensive.

1088 Lima, Jackson da Silva. O folclore em Sergipe. v. 1, Romanceiro. Rio: Livraria Editôra Cátedra [and] Instituto Nacional do Livro, Ministério da Educação e Cultura, Brasília, 1977. 595 p., bibl., illus., music.

A large scholarly collection of *romances* and *xácaras* orally collected from 58 informants. Excellent comparative notes and music for many of the songs along with indexes, data about informants, etc. Includes appendix.

1089 Lima, José Ossian. Patativa do Assaré: a comunicação na poesia popular (Revista de Comunicação Social [Ceará, Brazil] 4:1, 1974, p. 50–60)

Discusses the work of a popular poet, Patativa do Assaré, whose compositions lie somewhere between art poetry, folk poetry, and *literatura de cordel.* Examples of his work presented and analyzed show the strong influence of genuine folklore.

Lima, Vivaldo da Costa. O conceito de Nação nos candomblés da Bahia. See *HLAS 41:9338.*

1090 Limeira, Eudenise de Albuquerque. A comunicação gestual: analise semiótica de danças folclóricas nordestinas. Rio: Editora Rio, 1977. 102 p., bibl., illus., tables.

Defines semiology, semiotics, and folklore and then analyzes gestures and body movements of some traditional dances of Northeastern Brazil using structural and semiotic methods.

1091 Literatura de cordel. Antologia. v. 1/2. São Paulo: Global Editora e Distribuidora, 1976. 2 v. (168, 189 p.) bibl., illus.

Vol. 1 contains recently written poems by José Soares, José Pacheco, José Costa Leite, and Manuel Florentino Duarte, preceded by an essay on *literatura de cordel* by Mário Souto Maior. Vol. 2 has similar compositions, all by Abraão Batista. Engraved illustrations accompany the texts. Batista's poems have illustrations by the poet himself.

1092 Lody, Raul Giovanni. Afoxé. Rio: Ministério da Educação e Cultura, Departamento de Assuntos Culturais, Fundação Nacional de Arte, 1976. 36 p., bibl., plates (Cadernos de Folclore. Nova Série; 7)

Describes a street procession known as *afoxé*, or *candomblé de rua*, that is part of the Carnival celebrations in Salvador, Fortaleza, and Rio. Of African origin, it is related to religious practices, particularly the cult of *orixás*. Includes glossary.

1093 ———. Alimentação ritual (Ciência & Trópico [Recife, Brazil] 5:1, jan./junho, 1977, p. 37–47, bibl.)

Studies ritual foods offered to gods in their function as socio-religious links between members of Afro-Brazilian cults. Includes glossary.

———. O som do Adjá. See item **7057**.

1094 Lona, Fernando. O romance desastroso de Josiano e Mariana ou A gesta do boi menino. São Paulo: Editora McGraw-Hill do Brasil, 1977. 93 p., illus.

An interesting art poem written in the style of the *literatura de cordel*. Joseph M. Luyten provides an introduction entitled "Literatura de Cordel: Tradição e Atualidade."

1095 Machado, Cristina de Miranda Mata. Contribuição ao estudo das rodas infantis em Minas, Brasil (IPGH/FA, 20, julio/dic. 1975, p. 83–101, bibl., music)

Presents and analyzes comparatively words and music of several children's dance-games in their Portuguese and Brazilian versions.

1096 Maia, Thereza Regina de Camargo. Paraty, religião & folclore. 2. ed. revista e ampliada. Rio: Arte e Cultura, 1976. 165 p., bibl., illus., music.

Studies folkloric aspects of religious practices, fiestas, brotherhoods, ceremonies, etc. in the Paraty region of Brazil. Gives texts of several songs and music for some songs and dances.

1097 Marconi, Marina de Andrade. Folclore do café. São Paulo: Secretaria de Cultura, Ciência e Tecnologia, Conselho Estadual de Cultura, 1976. 134 p., bibl., illus., music.

Traces briefly the history of coffee in the world and the growing of coffee in Brazil; then offers a miscellany of folklore having to do with coffee (e.g., recipes, cures, superstitions, games, prayers, words and music of songs, tales and anecdotes, etc.). For musicologist's comment, see item **7058**.

1098 ———. Garimpos e garimpeiros. São Paulo: Conselho Estadual de Artes e Ciências, 1978. 152 p., bibl., illus., maps, tables (Coleção Folclore; 11)

A sociological study of the diamond mining area of the northeastern part of the state of São Paulo, Brazil. In studying the miners' (i.e., *garimpeiros*) way of life, attention is directed toward certain fiestas, customs, superstitions, regional speech, etc. Contains glossary.

1099 Martins, Saul. Arte e artesanato folclóricos. Rio: Ministério da Educação e Cultura, Departamento de Assuntos Culturais, Fundação Nacional de Arte, 1976. 22 p., bibl., illus., table (Cadernos de Folclore. Nova Série; 10)

Seeks to differentiate between art and handcrafts (i.e., *arte* and *artesanato*) and then describes and analyzes some of the more important characteristics of the latter. Useful bibliography.

1100 Melo, José Maria de. Enigmas populares. Rio: Ministério da Educação e Cultura, Departamento de Assuntos Culturais, Fundação Nacional de Arte, 1976. 29 p., bibl. (Cadernos de Folclore. Nova Série; 13)

A general discussion of riddles in Brazil and elsewhere with mention of some of the scholars who have studied them. Proposes a new system of classification and then groups together some sample riddles from Brazil using this classification.

1101 Melo, Veríssimo de. O conto folclórico no Brasil. Rio: Ministério da Educação e Cultura, Departamento de Assuntos Culturais, Fundação Nacional de Arte, 1976. 15 p., bibl. (Cadernos de Folclore. Nova Série; 11)

A brief introductory discussion of the folktale in Brazil. Touches on theoretical problems, methods of study, the history of folktale scholarship, problems of classification, etc.

1102 Monica, Laura della. Manual de folclore. São Paulo: Produções Audiovisuais Brasileiras Ltda., 1976. 201 p., bibl., illus., music.

A manual designed as a textbook to be used in teaching folklore. Gives some history of folkloristic studies, defines terms, explains the different folklore genres, etc. All this is basic information oriented toward Brazil and Brazilian education.

1103 **Monteiro, Mário Ypiranga.** Roteiro do folclore amazônica. t. 1/2. Manaus, Brazil: Editora Sergio Cardoso [and] Edições Cultural do Amazonas, 1964/1974. 2 v. (228, 564 p.) bibl., illus. (Etnografia Amazônica; 1)

Discusses the theoretical and methodological bases of the work and then in approximately 30 chapters offers what amounts to a detailed catalogue of literary folklore: myths, legends, tales, fables, popular poetry, songs (some with music), proverbs, etc. Many texts are given along with good bibliography. A useful compilation with good commentary.

Montero, Paula and **Renato Ortiz.** Contribuição para um estudo quantitativo da religião umbandista. See *HLAS 41:9360.*

1104 **Moraes, Wilson Rodrigues de.** Escolas de samba de São Paulo—capital. São Paulo: Conselho Estadual de Artes e Ciências Humanas, 1978. 167 p., bibl., map, music, plates (Coleção Folclore; 14)

As a scholar and as an active participant, the author studies the groups that dance sambas in São Paulo at Carnival time. Surveys their history, their organization, and the way they take part in Carnival celebrations. Includes excellent drawings and photographs, words and music of many songs, good bibliography, etc.

1105 **Mota, Atico Vilas Boas da.** Rezas, benzeduras et cetera: medicina popular em Goiás. Goiâna, Brazil: Oriente, 1977. 105 p., bibl.

Contains mostly field collected conjurations and prayers used in Brazil, primarily in Goiâs, to cure illnesses or deal with other misfortune. Also offers some discussion of omens and a few texts of folktales. Includes good bibliography and index.

1106 **Mota, Leandro.** Cantadores. 4. ed. Rio: Livraria Editora Cátedra *em convênio com o* Instituto Nacional do Livro, Ministério da Educação e Cultura, 1976. 308 p., illus.

New ed. of a work first published in 1921. A pioneer study of the traveling popular poets-singers of Ceará. Sections on individual singers with representative texts of their works. Also includes chapters on topics related to the general subject and a glossary of popular speech.

1107 ———. Sertão alegre. 4. ed. Rio: Livraria Editora Cátedra *em convênio com o* Instituto Nacional do Livro, Ministério da Educação e Cultura, 1976. 245 p.

New ed. of a useful but unorganized miscellany of brief sketches of popular life and culture in the Sertão of Brazil. Includes poetry and song (many texts) as well as stories and anecdotes, beliefs, sayings, etc. Contains a whole section on "Linguagem Popular."

1108 **Moura, Clóvis.** O preconceito de cor na literatura de cordel. São Paulo: Editora Resenha Universitaria, 1976. 87 p., tables.

Studies stereotypes and prejudice against Negroes found in 25 *folhetos* of *literatura de cordel* (i.e., popular poetry) collected in Paraíba and Bahia, Brazil. Includes appendix.

1109 **Mucci, Alfredo.** Acauã: alguns aspectos morfocromáticos do medo e ansiedade no fabulário popular brasileiro. São Paulo: Editora Morumbi Ltda., 1977. 76 p., bibl., plates.

Inventories in brief sections many fantastic beings or imaginary monsters found in Brazilian myths, legends, and other folkloric sources. Includes drawings of some of these as presumably seen by people who suffer from anxieties and fears.

1110 **Nascimento, Haydée.** Aspectos folclóricos do Carnaval de Santana de Parnaíba. São Paulo: Conselho Estadual de Artes e Ciências Humanas, 1977. 158 p., bibl., map, plates (Coleção Folclore; 8)

Describes (p. 5–36) the Carnival customs of Parnaíba, São Paulo, drawing upon materials gathered in fieldwork. Most of the volume, however, is made up of transcriptions of taped interviews with informants. Information found here is often interesting but quite diffuse.

1111 **Negrão, Maria José da Trinidade.** Introdução à literatura de cordel (UFP/RL, 23, 1975, p. 135–152, bibl.)

Characterizes *literatura de cordel* in a

general way and gives some textual examples. Discusses their themes, form, style, etc.

1112 Neves, Guilherme Santos. Ticumbi. Rio: Ministério da Educação e Cultura, Departamento de Assuntos Culturais, Fundação Nacional de Arte, 1976. 1 v. (Unpaged) bibl., illus. (Cadernos de Folclore. Nova Série; 12)

Differentiates between the dance-drama known as *Tucumbi* in the state of Espírito Santo and similar *autos* from other regions. Describes this particular dance and gives words only of some passages from it.

1113 ———. Variações sobre o Tangolomango (CDFB/RBF, 14:41, maio/agôsto 1976, p. 13–35, bibl., music)

Documents the existence of the Tangolomango, a kind of devil or destructive force that appears in both Portuguese and Brazilian tradition. It is frequently associated with verses or songs that revolve around an inverted kind of game based on a progressive decreasing of the "magic" number from nine to zero. Gives words and music of some examples.

1114 Oliveira, José Zula de. Trilha folclórica de Guaraqueçaba (UFP/EB, 1:1, 1976, p. 137–153, music, plates)

A miscellany of field-collected folklore of various kinds from Guaraqueçaba, Brazil. Includes beliefs, popular medicine, words and music of some songs, poetry, etc. For musicologist's comment, see item **7062**.

Ortiz, Renato. Reflexões sobre o Carnaval. See *HLAS 41:9368.*

1115 Pacheco, Renato José Costa. Cerámica popular em Vitória. Casa de farinha em São Mateus. Os presépios de Maestre Pedro. Primeira notícia sobre tropas e tropeiros. Vitória, Brazil: Comissão Espírito-Santense de Folclore, 1975. 20 p., plates (Cadernos de Etnografia e Folclore; 5)

Four separate brief contributions. The first is about pottery-making in Vitória; the second deals with the making of manioc flour in a town of the state of Espíritu Santo; the third characterizes a wood-carver who specializes in Christmas nativity scenes; and the last gives information about mule trains as carriers of cargo in Brazil in the not too distant past.

1116 Paula, Zuleika de. Festa de Anhembi: encontro e amortalhados. São Paulo: Conselho Estadual de Artes e Ciências Humanas, 1978. 150 p., bibl., illus., map, music, plates (Coleção Folclore; 15)

A very detailed description of the festival of the Divino Espírito Santo in Anhembi, São Paulo. Based on fieldwork, it touches on practically every aspect of the festival: e.g., history, organization, processions, prayers, songs (many texts and some music), etc.

1117 Pellegrini Filho, Américo. Calendário e documentário de folclore paulista. São Paulo: Instituto Musical de São Paulo, 1975. 209 p., illus., map, music, tables.

The first section seeks to establish the folklore areas of the state of São Paulo. A second section offers a calendar of festivals and ceremonies for the entire state. The third and longest section (p. 49–185) comments upon each event in chronological order and documents observations with texts of songs, musical transcriptions, photographs, etc. Includes appendix and index.

1118 ———. Literatura oral no Estado de São Paulo (AM/R, 36:185, jan./dez. 1973, p. 175–324, bibl.)

An important collection of orally collected texts of folktales, ballads and other popular songs (no music), and a few riddles. Includes good data about informants, Aarne-Thompson tale-type numbers, etc.

1119 Pereira, Niomar de Souza and **Mára Público de Souza Veiga Jardim.** Uma festa religiosa brasileira: Festa do Divino em Goiás e Pirenópolis. São Paulo: Conselho Estadual de Artes e Ciências Humanas, 1978. 125 p., bibl., map, music, plates (Coleção Folclore; 13)

Traces the history of the Festival of the Divino Spírito Santo in Luso-Brazilian tradition, then describes the Festival as it takes place today in the cities of Goiás and Pirenópolis. Includes words of some songs and musical transcriptions. Based on fieldwork.

1120 Pescatello, Ann M. Music *festas* and their social role in Brazil: *Carnaval* in Rio (Journal of Popular Culture [Bowling Green, Ohio] 9:4, Spring 1976, p. 833–839)

Discusses the structural organization, the role of participants, and the music of the Brazilian *Carnaval.*

1121 **Piauí, Francelino S.** Sarapatel: um poco da sabedoria e humor do sertão nordestino. Campinas, Brazil: Edição do Autor, 1978. 124 p.

Contains mainly items of popular speech from the Piauí region of northeastern Brazil along with some proverbs and humorous or satirical names given to people because of their physical or personal attributes. Provides explanations of all items listed.

1122 **Pino-Saavedra, Yolando.** As narrativas brasileiras de Aluísio de Almeida (AM/R, 188, jan./dez, 1976, p. 79–89, bibl.)

Sketches briefly the biography and bibliography of Aluísio de Almeida, pseudonym of Monsignor Luiz Castanho de Almeida, who published important but little known collections containing 235 folktales in Portuguese; then surveys the texts themselves by titles and assigns Aarne-Thompson tale-type numbers to them.

1123 **Proença, Ivan Cavalcanti.** A ideologia do cordel. Rio: Imago Editora Ltda., 1976. 109 p.

Considers some of the salient characteristics of *literatura de cordel* and then makes an effort to analyze some texts in order to prove that the genre's alleged lack of ideology (i.e., *não-ideologia*) is actually itself a form of ideology.

1124 **Rabaçal, Alfredo João.** As congadas no Brasil. São Paulo: Secretaria da Cultura, Ciência e Tecnologia, Conselho Estadual de Cultura, 1976. 294 p., bibl., plates.

A detailed study of the genre of dance-drama-fiesta known as *congos, congados,* and *congadas.* Traces their history and describes their current status in innumerable locales. Includes many photographs, some texts of plays presented, good bibliography, and brief summaries of the study's main findings in Portuguese, English, and French.

1125 **Renier, Victor.** Sens et signification dans un conte oral brésilien (UCL/LR, 33:1, fév. 1979, p. 13–31)

Uses structural and semiotic methods in order to analyze a Brazilian saint's tale.

1126 **Ribeiro, Joaquim.** Folclore do açucar. Rio: Ministério da Educação e Cultura, Campanha de Defesa do Folclore Brasileiro, 1977. 227 p., bibl., music.

A lengthy study of Brazilian folklore having to do with sugar. Includes sections on stories, myths, games, dances, riddles, festivals, sugar's role in the country's economic life as reflected in folklore, superstitions, songs (words of many are included, a few with music), regional foods, proverbs, etc.

1127 **Ribeiro, M. de Lourdes Borges.** O folclore na escola. Rio: Ministério da Educação e Cultura, Departamento de Assuntos Culturais, Fundação Nacional de Arte, 1976. 30 p., bibl. (Cadernos de Folclore; 5)

Seeks to define what folklore is and the role it should play in education. Treats its importance in training teachers, how it serves in the classroom, and its relationship to teaching such things as recreation, social studies, mathematics, physical sciences, art, and other subjects.

1128 **Rocha, José Maria Tenório.** Folclore brasileiro: Alagoas. Rio: Ministério da Educação e Cultura, 1977. 79 p., bibl., illus., music.

A general introductory survey of the folklore of Alagoas. Includes brief sections on history, geography and culture, oral literature, popular speech, dances, popular religion, arts and crafts, regional dishes, festivals, etc.

1129 **Scheuer, Herta Loëll.** Estudo da cerâmica popular do estado de São Paulo. São Paulo: Conselho Estadual de Cultura, 1976. 131 p., bibl., illus., map, plates, tables.

In successive sections describes and classifies the ceramics produced in different towns in the state of São Paulo. Also describes manufacturing techniques. Profusely illustrated.

1130 **Sergipe, Brazil** (State). **Departamento de Cultura e Patrimônio Histórico.** Manifestações da lúdica folclórica em Sergipe. Equipe de trabalho, Terezinha Alves de Oliva. Coordenação, Maria Lúcia Ramos de Carvalho. José Valfran de Brito, auxiliar de Pesquisas. Aracaju: O Departamento, 1975. 40 l., tables.

Reports on the results of a survey of fiestas, dances, dramas, and other traditional group activities found in the state of Sergipe, Brazil. Lists activities by the towns where they take place, then indicates the names and addresses of persons responsible for organizing them, the number of participants, musical instruments used, etc.

1131 Silva, Francisco Pereira da. O desafio calangueado: monografia folclórica. São Paulo: Conselho Estadual de Artes e Ciências Humanas, 1978. 78 p., illus. (Coleção Folclore; 10)

Describes and comments upon a type of song-duel called Calango where two singers vie with each other. The genre seems to exist in several areas of Brazil. Includes words without music of many representative songs that were orally collected.

1132 Simpósio de Pesquisas de Folclore, *1st, São Paulo, 1976.* Anais: São Paulo, 4 a 8 de outubro de 1976. Coordenador, Alfredo João Rabaçal. São Paulo: Secretaria de Cultura, Ciência e Tecnologia, Conselho Estadual de Artes e Ciências Humanas, 1977. 189 p., plates (Coleção Folclore; 7)

A report on the introductory session and six other sessions plus a round-table discussion that made up the Symposium. Contains transcriptions of most of the speeches and discussions that took place. Most are fairly general statements about folklore in Brazil and suggestions for studying it.

1133 Slater, Candace. The stone in *A pedra do reino*: folk symbolism in literature (UCLA/JLAL, 2:1, 1976, p. 23–61, illus.)

Deals perceptively with Ariano Suassuna's use of folk tradition in his novel *A pedra do reino* (1971). Themes treated are the stone, the sun, and the mountain lion. Includes appendixes.

1134 Souza, Liédo M. de. Classificação da literatura de cordel: em texto integral de 23 folhetos. Petropolis, Brazil: Editora Vozes, 1976. 104 p.

An interesting and useful attempt to classify *literatura de cordel* using the terminology employed by poets, publishers, and salesmen of this kind of popular literature and songs (e.g., *Folhetos de Conselhos, Folhetos de Profecias, Folhetos de Política*). Based upon fieldwork in northeastern Brazil. Gives texts of examples of each type and includes index.

1135 Thiéblot, Marcel Jules. Os homens do sal no Brasil. São Paulo: Conselho Estadual de Artes e Ciências Humanas, 1979. 139 p., bibl., illus., maps, plates.

A study of a "folkloric profession," that of the Brazilian *salineiros* (i.e., men who extract salt from the sea). Based on fieldwork in two main areas, the states of Rio de Janeiro and Rio Grande do Norte. Treats the saltmakers' way of life, customs, beliefs, tools, clothing etc. Includes appendixes.

1136 ———. Rondônia: um folclore de luta. São Paulo: Secretaria da Cultura, Ciência e Tecnologia, Conselho Estadual de Artes e Ciências Humanas, 1977. 122 p., bibl., illus., maps.

Surveys the geography, history, and social conditions of the territory of Rondônia in the interior of Brazil on the Bolivian frontier, and then devotes the bulk of the book to a study of folklore, mostly ethnographic and material aspects of life in the region. Includes attention to *literatura de cordel*, folk cures, etc.

1137 Vendramini, Maria do Carmo. A dança de São Gonçalo em Ibiúna (CDFB/RBF, 14:41, maio/agôsto 1976, p. 45–78, bibl., maps, music, plates, tables)

A detailed description, accompanied by photographs and charts, of a dance that the author observed and studied in the town of Ibiúna, São Paulo, Brazil, in 1975. Also includes words and music of some songs associated with the dance.

1138 Vidigal, Alba Carneiro. Folclore em Campinas: artesanato. São Paulo: Conselho Estadual de Artes e Ciências Humanas, 1978. 185 p., maps, plates (Coleção Folclore; 12)

Reports the results of field study of the handcrafts of the city of Campinas, São Paulo. Surveys the history of the city and describes some of the conditions of life in it; then offers sections on different crafts arranged according to materials used (e.g., tin, wood, leather, paper, etc.). Includes many photographs, data about the artisans who were informants, maps, etc.

1139 Vieira Filho, Domingos. Folclore do Maranhão: la. série. São Luis, Brazil: Sioge, 1976. 74 p., bibl.

Surveys several types of folklore from Maranhão. Touches on dances, prayers, ritual baths, legends, myths, customs, regional dishes, children's folklore, etc.

1140 Weitzel, Antônio Henrique. Literatura e linguagem folclórica. Juiz de Fora, Brazil: Centro de Estudos Sociológicos de

Juiz de Fora, 1976. 19 p. (Coleção Arquivos de Folclore; 3)

A basic little manual for beginning students of folklore. Defines some theoretical concepts and terms used by folklorists and gives a few texts of tales, songs, proverbs, riddles, sayings, tongue-twisters, etc., as illustrative examples.

CENTRAL AMERICA

1141 **Agerkop, Terry.** Música de los mískitos de Honduras (IPGH/FA, 23, junio 1977, p. 7–37)

Analyzes the music of the Miskito Indian group of Honduras and considers its role and function in the community. Provides a preliminary socio-historical panorama of the group and concludes with examples of musical transcriptions. For musicologist's comment, see *HLAS 40:9070*.

1142 **Alonso de Rodríguez, Josefina.** El exvoto y el arte de la platería en Guatemala (Tradiciones de Guatemala [Guatemala] 5, 1976, p. 47–130, plates)

Offers numerous photos and a brief explanation of votive offerings commonly found in Hispanic Catholic churches. The devotional images described are small silver replicas of parts of the body that have been cured or material objects that have been received through the intercession of a saint.

1143 **Alvarez, Rosa María.** Cerámica de Rabinal (Tradiciones de Guatemala [Guatemala] 5, 1976, p. 31–46)

Describes the types of pottery made and used in the town of Rabinal, Guatemala, distinguishing between items used for domestic and religious purposes.

1144 **Arosemena Moreno, Julio.** Aportes a la clasificación del folklore panameño (IPGH/FA, 23, junio 1977, p. 39–62)

Reviews the contributions made by several individuals to the creation of a folklore index for Panama. Offers a classification of folklore items in a listing devised by the author.

1145 **———.** Danza de Grandiablos en la Villa de los Santos. Panamá: Impresora Panamá, n.d. 28 p., music, plates.

Describes and studies in a comparative way the Dance of the Devils in Villa de los Santos, Panama, and its relationship to similar dances in the Old World and the New. Includes music, choreographic data, a transcription of the text that accompanies the dance, etc. For musicologist's comment, see *HLAS 40:9083*.

1146 **Bremmé de Santos, Ida.** Artesanías de Guatemala (*in* Actas del I Congreso Internacional de Folklorología en Panamá [see item **963a**] p. 87–174, plates)

Surveys arts and crafts all over the world and notes efforts in many countries to study and promote them as local industries. Then directs attention to specific kinds of crafts such as ceramics, weaving, wax products, basketry, leather-working, the manufacture of musical instruments, etc., with most emphasis on Guatemala.

1147 **Bullard, M. Kenyon.** Marbles: an investigation of the relationship between marble games and other aspects of life in Belize (AFS/JAF, 88:350, Oct./Dec. 1975, p. 393–400)

Discourses on the social and psychological implications of various marble games as played by both children and adults in Belize.

1148 **Castillero R., Ernesto J.** El folklore en la literatura panameña (*In* Actas del I Congreso Internacional de Folklorología en Panamá [see item **963a**] p. 77–85)

A bibliographical essay that surveys the main works on Panamanian folklore written over the years. Also notes folklore festivals or other celebrations where folklore played a role.

1149 **Castillo, Félix** and others. La alfarería de Santa Apolonia (Tradiciones de Guatemala [Guatemala] 5, 1976, p. 245–263)

Describes the process of making ceramic jugs and vessels in a Guatemalan town.

1150 **Cheville, Lila R.** and **Richard A. Cheville.** Festivals and dances of Panama. Panamá: Litho-Impresora Panamá, 1977. 187 p., bibl., illus., music.

Describes Panamanian fiestas and dances of many kinds. Chap. 4 is specifically about folkloric dances. Also contains a chapter on Panamanian dress and a calendar of fiestas and dances.

1151 Collins Lazo, J. Roberto and **María Antonieta Puente de Collins.** Creencias en torno a la piedra imán (Tradiciones de Guatemala [Guatemala] 5, 1976, p. 293–298)

Notes popular beliefs associated with magnetic stones, focusing on the powers attributed to them and the prayers or practices used to make them effective.

1152 Consejos sanos de medicinas en botánica (Tradiciones de Guatemala [Guatemala] 5, 1976, p. 191–210)

An interesting reproduction of a pamphlet listing some Guatemalan folk medical beliefs. The author of the work is listed simply as J.G., and there is no indication of date or place of publication.

1153 Díaz Castillo, Roberto. Los exvotos pintados de San Felipe (USCG/TP, 9, 1976, p. 2–19, plates)

Offers a short description and numerous photos of devotional images painted by the parishioners of San Felipe de Jesús in Guatemala.

1154 ———. Nuestras artes industriales (USCG/TP, 8, 1976, p. 2–19, plates)

Offers five notes on traditional skills or crafts written by Ignacio Solís (1838–1912) but never published. They deal with carpentry and furniture-making, construction of houses, the making of candy boxes, the production of woven mats, etc. Includes excellent photos.

1155 Díaz Panigua, Aída and **José Fernando Rodríguez.** Cerámica vidriada de Jalapa (Tradiciones de Guatemala [Guatemala] 5, 1976, p. 215–233)

Describes the materials, equipment, and process of production employed in a pottery workshop in Jalapa, Guatemala. Includes photos of the craftsmen at work.

1156 Espino, Miguel Angel. Mitología de Cuscatlán. 2. ed. San Salvador: Ministerior de Educación, Dirección de Publicaciones, 1976. 96 p.

A new ed. of a book first published in 1919. A long introduction plays up the Indian past of Mexico and exalts the values of Indian culture. Somc litcrary retellings of a few Indian myths follow.

1157 Exploración etnográfica: Departamento de Sonsonate. San Salvador: Ministerio de Educación, 1975. 415 p., illus., maps, plates, tables (Colección Estudios y documentos; 4)

An ethnographic survey done by a team of investigators from the Museo Nacional "David J. Guzmán." Touches on many aspects of folklore: e.g., legends, beliefs, traditional customs and practices, dances such as the Moors and Christians dance, etc.

1158 Fortune, Armando. Presencia africana en la música panameña (*in* Actas del I Congreso Internacional de Folklorología en Panamá [see item **963a**] p. 335–348)

Stresses the importance of the Negro to the culture and especially to the music of Panama.

1159 Gamboa Alvarado, Gerardo. Del folklore costarricense: relatos de La Bajura y de La Serranía. San José, Editorial Fernández-Arce, 1975. 205 p., illus. (Serie Francisco Fernández B.; 3)

A literary evocation of small-town and rural life that touches on many folkloric subjects. Folkloristic subjects are seldom in very usable form for folklorists, but students of Costa Rican traditions, legends, folk speech, popular songs, etc. will find the book occasionally useful.

1160 García Añoveros, Jesús María. El cuatasinc k'ekchi (Tradiciones de Guatemala [Guatemala] 5, 1976, p. 157–164)

Describes a Guatemalan Holy Week ceremony witnessed by the author in 1975. The ritual forms part of the *cuatasinc* tradition: i.e., a series of religious rites of inauguration or blessing for new buildings or special objects.

1161 Golley, Frank B. Bus names in Costa Rica (CFS/WF, 37:1, Jan. 1978, p. 58–60)

Lists 175 names of buses observed in Costa Rica and comments upon the tradition of naming buses and the nature of the names chosen.

1162 Guardia, Roberto de la. Las ánimas (*in* Actas del I Congreso Internacional de Folklorología en Panamá [see item **963a**] p. 243–284)

Surveys field-collected Panamanian beliefs about the souls of the dead, principally *almas en pena* who intervene in affairs of the living. Informants are not identified except by geographical location.

Guatemala Indígena. See *HLAS 41:1653.*

1163 Gudeman, Stephen. Saints, symbols, and ceremonies (AAA/AE, 3:4, Nov. 1976, p. 709–729, bibl., table)

Discusses Roman Catholic saints as folk symbols in a Panamanian village and shows how the system of saints reflects the people's world view.

1164 Guevara, Concepción Clará de. El baile de San Benito en El Salvador (IPGH/FA, 20, julio/dic, 1975, p. 103–105)

Describes a dance that is part of a fiesta that takes place in Uluazapa, El Salvador, on Pentecostal Sunday. Gives words without music of the song that accompanies the dance.

1165 ———. Los bailes de historiantes o historias de moros y cristianos (MNDJG/A, 50, 1977, p. 83–102)

Discusses the history of the introduction of the "Moors and Christian" dance-drama into the New World, and then describes some of the features of the 33 versions of the dance that exist in El Salvador.

1166 ———. La Fiesta del Día de la Cruz (MNDJG/A, 42/48, 1968/1975, p. 69–81, plates)

Describes the Salvadorean Day of the Cross festival and interprets it as a syncretistic fiesta with prehispanic origins.

1167 Hadel, Richard. Black Carib folk music (UWI/CQ, 22:2/3, June/Sept. 1976, p. 84–96)

Describes various types of dance and non-dance folk music popular among the Black Caribs of Honduras, Guatemala and British Honduras. For musicologist's comment, see *HLAS 40:9072.*

1168 Helms, Mary W. Iguanas and crocodilians in tropical American mythology and iconography with special reference to Panama (UCLA/JLAL, 3:1, Summer 1977, p. 51–132, bibl., illus., tables)

Interprets certain iconographic themes from ancient Panama through analysis of myths and chants of the contemporary Cuna people. Reinterprets the "crested dragon" and the "crocodile god" as varieties of lizards, most notably iguanas, and reviews the role of the iguana in classic Maya cosmology.

1169 Herrera Porras, Tomás. Cuna cosmology: legends from Panama. Washington: Continents Press, 1978. 105 p., bibl., illus.

Herrera Porras, of Cuna origin, collects and translates into Spanish some traditional legends of the Indians of San Blas, Panama. These are then translated into English and edited by Anita G. McAndrews, who also provides a commentary on the history and traditions of the Cuna or Tulé people.

1170 Herrera Vega, Adolfo. Expresión literaria de nuestra vieja raza: folklore. 2. ed. San Salvador: Ministerior de Educación, Dirección de Publicaciones, 1975. 344 p., illus.

A valuable compendium of information about fiestas and popular theatre, beliefs, etc. Lacks scholarly rigor, so important data about informants, sources, and the like are missing, but the texts of several dance-dramas, songs, etc. are of great interest.

1171 Juárez Toledo, Manuel. El baile de las flores (Tradiciones de Guatemala [Guatemala] 5, 1976, p. 167–189, music)

Presents the music, text, and basic choreography for the *Baile de las flores,* a popular Guatemalan dance.

1172 Lara F., Celso A. Cuentos y cuenteros populares de Guatemala (USCG/TP, 11, 1977, p. 2–19, bibl., illus., maps, plates)

Defines the nature of folktales in general and discusses the tale tradition in Guatemala. Gives an example of an orally collected text that also contains some portions that are sung. Then provides personal data about several of the best Guatemalan *cuenteros* who have served the author as informants. For musicologist's comment, see item **7088**.

1173 ———. Los rosarios de tusa y azúcar de San Martín Jilotepeque (USCG/TP, 10, 1976, p. 2–15)

A description of a traditional Guatemalan rosary made from pieces of sugar and dried corn leaves. Briefly explains the function, production, and distribution of the rosary and includes photos of rosary makers and their wares.

1174 Llorente, Coralia Hassán C. de. La Festividad de Jesús Triunfante el Domingo de Ramos en la población de Chepo (*in* Actas del I Congreso Internacional de Folklorología en Panamá [see item **963a**] p. 195–223, plates)

Describes in considerable detail through text and photographs a fiesta that takes place in the town of Chepo, Panama.

1175 Lora, Silvano. La pintura popular en Panamá (*in* Actas del I Congreso Internacional de Folklorología en Panamá [see item **963a**] p. 21–31)

Characterizes in general terms "popular" painting as found in restaurants, bars, barber shops, buses, etc. Finds in it a kind of affirmation of the soul of Panama. Dora P. de Zárate offers a comment on the article.

1176 Montenegro, Jorge. Cuentos y leyendas de Honduras. Tegucigalpa: Empresa de Transportes El Rey, 1975? 200 p., illus.

An anthology of tales, stories, anecdotes, etc., gathered from many sources, mostly literary ones, with no critical acumen or knowledge of folklore. Nevertheless, the collection contains some narratives of interest to folklorists. The work is annotated here chiefly because of the scarcity of Honduran materials.

1177 Moore, Alexander. Initiation rites in a Mesoamerican cargo system: men and boys, Judas and the bull (UCLA/JLAL, 5:1, Summer 1979, p. 55–81, bibl., map)

Studies the first year of *cargo* service (i.e., initiation of young men into public life) in Atchalán, Guatemala, as a male initiation rite. Done as an ethnographic study, the article treats many folkloric subjects in dealing with fiestas, processions, beliefs, etc.

1178 Navas, María Guadalupe and others. La alfarería de Chinautla y su transformación (Tradiciones de Guatemala [Guatemala] 5, 1976, p. 265–292)

Examines the modeling of ceramic figures in Chinautla, Guatemala, considering the influence of the town's historical, geographical, and socioeconomic conditions on the craft. Concludes that traditional ceramics are disappearing, and suggests several possible reasons for their demise. Includes numerous photos of finished objects.

1179 Núñez Meléndez, Esteban. Plantas medicinales de Costa Rica y su folclore. San José: Oficina de Publicaciones de la Universidad de Costa Rica, 1975. 278 p., bibl.

A professor of pharmacy surveys the flora of Costa Rica and the history of the folklore of medicine in that country. Then offers an exhaustive dictionary of plants with an explanation of their medicinal uses. There are useful bibliographies, a glossary, and an index.

1180 O'Brien, Linda Lee. La música folklórica de Guatemala (Tradiciones de Guatemala [Guatemala] 5, 1976, p. 7–17)

Identifies traditional characteristics of Spanish and Indian folk music in Guatemala.

1181 Payne, Arvilla C. Whistle language (OAS/AM, 30:4, April 1978, p. 17–19, illus.)

A brief but interesting discussion of the whistled language found in certain areas of Central America. It apparently is derived from Mayan origins.

1182 Pino Saavedra, Yolando. Los cuentos populares españoles entre los indígenas de Guatemala y Honduras (IPGH/FA, 25, junio 1978, p. 73–78)

A motif and tale-type analysis of the tales collected by the Summer Institute of Linguistics in Guatemala and Honduras and published under the title, *Según nuestros antepasados . . . Textos folklóricos de Guatemala y Honduras* (Guatemala, 1972).

1183 Prieto, Emilia. Breve reseña del folklore en Costa Rica (*in* Actas del I Congreso Internacional de Folklorología en Panamá [see item **963a**] p. 69–75)

Some observations about folklore and its systematic study in Costa Rica.

1184 Ramírez M., María A. Bibliografía del folklore guatemalteco (Tradiciones de Guatemala [Guatemala] 6, 1976, p. 15–68)

An unannotated bibliography of Guatemalan folklore. Entries are arranged under such headings as material culture, social customs, beliefs, genres, folkloristics, and applied folklore.

1185 Sherzer, Joel F. Cuna ikala: literature in San Blas (*in* Verbal art as performance. Edited by Richard Bauman. Rowley, Mass., Newbury House Publishers, 1977, p. 133–149 [Series in sociolinguistics])

Studies the speaking and chanting tradition of the Cuna Indians in San Blas, Panama, viewing it as a verbal art and analyzing its texture, content, classification, and social role.

1186 ———. Strategies in text and context: *Cuna kaa kwento* (AFS/JAF, 92:364, April/June 1979, p. 145–163)

Gives an English translation of "The Story of the Hot Pepper," a tale-text orally collected among the Cuna Indians of Panama. Interprets and analyzes the text from various perspectives.

1187 Smith, Kenneth W. *Todos los Santos*: spirits, kites, and courtship in the Guatemalan Maya highlands (IPGH/FA, 26, dic. 1978, p. 49–58, plates)

Describes customs associated with All-Saints' Day in Santiago Sacatepéquez, Guatemala, with particular emphasis on description and analysis of the practice of flying huge kites in the cemetery. Describes how the kites are constructed.

1188 Smith, Mary C. Esquipulas (OAS/AM, 21:1, Jan. 1979, p. 26–31)

About a pilgrimage to the town of Esquipulas, Guatemala, that attracts thousands of people. Tells something of its past and present. The main attraction is a black Christ.

1189 Tejeira Jaén, Bertilda. Los congos de Chepo (INC/PH, 1:3, 1974, p. 129–148, bibl., plates)

Describes the traditional dance of the Congos as observed in the town of Chepo. Ties the dance to the history of rebellious slaves. Includes some words of songs and photographs.

1190 Termer, Franz. Los bailes de culebra entre los indios quichés en Guatemala (Tradiciones de Guatemala [Guatemala] 5, 1976, p. 301–311)

Distinguishes three types of dances common among Guatemalan Indians: 1) dramatic dances relating to historical or religious events; 2) dramatic dances relating to natural events; and 3) comic dances. Gives an account of a performance of a comic dance, the *baile de la culebra*, which involves the use of a live snake.

1191 Torres de Araúz, Reina. La danza de los Cuenecué: folklore afro-americano (*in* Actas del I Congreso Internacional de Folklorología en Panamá [see item **963a**] p. 33–43, bibl., plate)

Describes a dance that is seldom danced but still remembered by aged informants from the Azuero region of Panama. It contains elements of drama.

1192 Valenzuela O., Wilfredo. El corrido nacional (Tradiciones de Guatemala [Guatemala] 5, 1976, p. 131–154)

Briefly traces the development of the Guatemalan *corrido*, or ballad, from the Spanish tradition of the *romance*, and gives sample texts of some of the most popular types of ballads in Guatemala.

1193 Zárate, Dora P. Algunas consideraciones sobre las fiestas de San Juan Bautista en Panamá (IPGH/FA, 24, dic. 1977, p. 29–32)

A description of rites and customs associated with the fiesta of San Juan Bautista in Panama and an inquiry into their origins.

CHILE

1194 Araya, Guillermo. Algunos aspectos del ALESUCH (CEEP/RD, 32:1/4, 1976, p. 43–50)

Offers preliminary comments about the ALESUCH (acronym for *Atlas lingüístico-etnográfico del Sur de Chile*, begun in 1968 and published in 1973, see *HLAS 41:1336*). Gives examples of some of the phenomena that are beginning to be apparent in this important study of popular and regional speech.

1195 Camaño de Arias, María Esther. Pinceladas folklóricas chilenas (UCR/R, 41, julio 1975, p. 111–130, bibl.)

A miscellany of information about Chilean folklore. Among the subjects treated: the dance known as the *cueca*, the *guaso* and his life, crafts, religious fiestas and beliefs, superstitions, words without music of many songs, etc.

1196 Cárdenas Tabies, Antonio. Cuentos folklóricos de Chiloé. Prólogo de Yolando Pino Saavedra. Santiago: Editorial Nascimento, 1976. 190 p.

Texts of 38 tales narrated by the author's mother, who was born on the Island of Quehue. It is the first serious collection of tales from Chiloé. Yolando Pino Saavedra provides Aarne-Thompson and Hansen tale-type numbers and Thompson motif numbers.

1197 ———. Ngenechen, Dios de Arauco. Rancagua, Chile: Talleres Fournier, 1975. 99 p.

Consists of 20 valuable and interesting texts of tales and legends collected orally from Araucanian Indian informants. Unfortunately, no informant data or other scholarly information are provided.

1198 ———. Usos y costumbres de Chiloé. Santiago: Editorial Nascimento, 1978. 222 p., bibl.

Surveys the history and geography of the island-archipelago of Chiloé, then offers brief sections describing customs observed there. Treats such matters as birth, childhood and adolescence, everyday home life, religious practices, social life, sicknesses, death, etc.

1199 **Carvalho-Neto, Paulo de.** Rodolfo Lenz, 1863–1938: un precursor del folklore en América Latina (IPGH/FA, 21, junio 1976, p. 33–62, bibl.)

Offers a biography of the eminent pioneer folklorist of Chile and evaluates his scholarly contributions. Ends with a brief general summary of the history of folklore studies in Chile.

1200 **Castro Gatica, Omar.** Escultura mapuche. Ilustraciones de Guillermo Meriño Pedreros. Temuco, Chile: Imprenta Alvarez, 1976. 28 p., illus.

A brief ethnographic discussion of certain beliefs and practices of the Mapuche Indians of Chile. Drawings by Meriño Pedreros supplement the description of mostly material objects used in rituals. Students of material culture may find some of this of value.

1201 **Clouzet, Jean.** La nouvelle chanson chilienne. Paris: Editions Seghers, 1975. 259 p.

A long introductory essay tells the story of the "new Chilean song," a kind of protest and revolutionary music of the 1960s and 1970s with alleged roots in Chilean folklore and cultivated first by Violeta Parra and later by various Communist singers. A large collection of songs (words without music) follows with texts in Spanish and French translations. Contains discographies.

1202 **Dannemann R., Manuel.** El *Atlas del folklore de Chile* (UC/AT, 436, 1977, p. 137–151)

Explains the work of those scholars who are preparing the *Folklore atlas of Chile*, with particular attention to the theory and procedures upon which their work is based. An important theoretical statement because Dannemann and his associates are developing new anthropological concepts for studying folklore (e.g., folkloric communities, retraditionalization, etc.).

1203 ———. Bibliografía del folklore (Revista Chilena de Antropología [Santiago] 2, 1979, p. 3–78)

The entire issue of the *Revista* is given over to an excellent supplement to the author's earlier "Bibliografía del Folklore Chileno, 1952–1965" published in 1970. The new installment covers 1966–76 and contains 624 additional annotated items about Chilean folklore grouped according to a functional classification devised by the author. Includes indexes.

1204 ———. La disciplina del folklore en Chile (Archivos del Folklore Chileno [Santiago] 10, 1976, p. 23–74, bibl., plates)

A fine article that in Chap. 1 synthesizes theoretical and practical features of the scientific study of folklore. Chap. 2 is a history of the discipline in Chile followed by a basic bibliography of 152 items. Undoubtedly the most up-to-date treatment of these subjects available.

1205 ———. Folklore (*in* Cultura Chilena. Santiago: Universidad de Chile, 1977, p. 173–201, bibl.)

Establishes nine basic folklore areas of Chile and briefly characterizes each of them. Contains glossary.

1206 ———. Nuevas reflexiones en torno al concepto de folklore (IPGH/FA, 22, dic. 1976, p. 121–129, bibl.)

Adduces some theoretical concepts designed to redefine what folklore is and the ways in which it should be studied.

1207 ———. Plan Multinacional de Relevamiento Etnomusicológico y Folklórico: Organización de Estados Americanos, Instituto Interamericano de Etnomusicología y Folklore, Facultad de Ciencias y Artes Musicales y de la Representación, Universidad de Chile: Misión Chile—1977 (UCIEM/R, 32:141, enero/marzo 1978, p. 17–41)

A general report on research done by

the Misión Chile, with Dannemann as Head, in studying the ethnography of three areas. Emphasis was on ethnomusicology and folklore. The places chosen, all characterized by the existence of aboriginal groups, were Calama, province of El Loa; Santa Barbara, province of Bío-Bío; and Queilen, province of Chiloé.

1208 ———. Supersticiones, mitos y leyendas en la cultura tradicional chilena (Logos [Revista de la Facultad de Filosofía y Letras, Universidad de Buenos Aires] 13/14, 1977/1978, p. 183–200)

Inventories some representative Chilean superstitions, various mythical animals, objects, or beings, and a few legends.

1209 ——— and **Jorge Sapiaín.** Consecuencias del alcoholismo en la práctica del canto tradicional (Revista Chilena de Antropología [Santiago] 1, 1978, p. 111–123, bibl., music)

An anthropological study of the effects of chronic alcoholism upon two singers of traditional *cantos a lo pueta* and *cuecas.* The focus is on the pathology of the singers, but the songs treated are folkloric in character and the nature of the alterations caused in words and music by the singers' alcoholism might interest some folklorists.

1210 **Dedicatoria: curriculum vitae** [de Yolando Pino Saavedra] (Archivos del Folklore Chileno [Santiago] 10, 1976, p. 7–21, bibl.)

Introduces a special number of the *Archivos del Folklore Chileno* to the memory of the recently deceased Chilean folklorist. Offers a short biography of Pino Saavedra and a bibliography of his published works.

1211 **Dölz Blackburn, Inés.** Antología crítica de la poesía tradicional chilena. México: Instituto Panamericano de Geografía e Historia, 1979. 239 p., bibl. (Serie de folklore del IPGH. Colección Documentos; 8)

A scholarly and important critical edition of traditional Chilean poetry. Four chapters deal with various types of *romances,* mostly from general Hispanic tradition. Three chapters then treat other kinds of songs and poems and focus particularly on Chilean creations. Includes words without music of 156 texts of poems and songs.

1212 **Dölz Henry, Inés.** La muerte en la poesía tradicional chilena (IPGH/FA, 22, dic. 1976, p. 157–165)

Studies funeral poetry in Chile and the social customs and beliefs associated with funerals and death. Gives texts of some poems and prayers and words without music of some songs.

1213 ———. Los romances tradicionales chilenos: temática y técnica. Santiago: Editorial Nascimento, 1976. 270 p., bibl.

Studies themes and sometimes techniques of various types of Chilean *romances*: i.e., old *romances,* supernatural *romances,* erotic *romances,* and novelesque *romances.* Quotes parts of many ballad texts.

1214 ———. Temática y técnicas romancescas en la poesía infantil chilena (IPGH/FA, 23, junio 1977, p. 69–87)

Studies children's traditional poetry associated with songs and games in Chile. Discusses its basic themes and fundamental motifs.

1215 **Grebe, María Ester.** Aportes de Jorge Urrutia Blondel a la literatura musical chilena (UCIEM/R, 31:138, abril/junio 1977, p. 39–54, bibl.)

Surveys and evaluates the work of Urrutia Blondel, an important Chilean composer and musicologist. Deals mostly with art music, but there is a section about his study of traditional Chilean music and titles of his works in the field are listed in a bibliography. For musicologist's comment, see *HLAS 40:9084.*

1216 **Henry, Inés D.** Romances y canciones populares en la primera década del siglo XVII en Chile (UC/BF, 25/26, 1974/1975, p. 309–326)

Publishes texts of some *romances* and other songs as found in an early 17th-century Chilean manuscript in the Archivo O'Higgins of the Archivo Nacional de Santiago de Chile. An important collection.

1217 **Jorda, Miguel.** El catecismo criollo. Santiago: Editorial Salesiana, 1976. 344 p.

Offers a collection of poems in *décima* form that reflect Catholic ideas and precepts.

Kessel, Juan Van. Los conjuntos de bailes religiosos del Norte Grande: análisis del censo practicado en 1973. See *HLAS 41:1253.*

1218 **Pérez Ortega, Juan.** Música folklórica infantil chilena. Valparaíso, Chile: Ediciones Universitarias de Valparaíso, 1976, 294 p., bibl., music.

Offers orally collected songs, games, etc., divided in three parts: *Romances* (p. 15–66); *Canciones* (p. 67–117); and *Rondas y juegos* (p. 119–282). Transcribes the music using the system devised by Jorge Urrutia Blondel.

1219 **Plath, Oreste.** Geografía del mito y la leyenda chilenos. Santiago: Editorial Nascimento, 1973. 454 p.

An anthology of Chilean myths and legends gathered from oral, printed, and literary sources. Texts are arranged according to the province of origin.

1220 **———.** Lenguaje de los pájaros chilenos: avifauna folklórica. Santiago: Editorial Nascimento, 1976. 223 p., bibl.

A curious miscellany of popular lore about birds assembled by a capable folklorist. Attention to the types and names of birds, beliefs about each kind of bird, poetry and songs, some legends and tales about birds, etc. Includes index.

1221 **———.** Regionalización de las artes populares chilenas (UC/AT, 436, 1977, p. 169–237, plates)

Defines 10 different types of popular arts (e.g., *arte tradicional, arte popular, trabajo carcelario, artesanía,* etc.) and then divides Chile into 11 regions in order to describe the salient features of each in the production of popular arts. Includes many photographs.

1222 **Prado Ocaranza, Juan G.** En torno a algunas normas legislativas referidas al folklore en Chile (IPGH/FA, 26, dic. 1978, p. 83–91, bibl.)

Surveys chronologically from colonial times to the present various decrees, laws, regulations, etc., that had to do with such traditional activities and customs as bull fights, horse races, fiestas, cock fights, games, gambling in various forms, etc. Recent laws deal with the study or preservation of folklore, protection of churches as monuments, etc.

1223 **Uribe Echevarría, Juan.** Fiesta de la Virgen de la Candelaria de Copiapó. Valparaíso, Chile: Ediciones Universitarias del Valparaíso, 1978. 112 p., illus., music, plates.

Describes and studies the cult of the Virgen de la Candelaria: i.e., its history and the fiesta that honors her (including the procession, the *cofradías* that organize the fiesta, etc.). Includes words of some songs, a few with music, and many photographs.

1224 **Valderrama, Sara.** Pilgrimage to La Tirana (OAS/AM, 29:8, Aug. 1977, p. 17–20, plates)

Photographs and text describe a religious fiesta in the town of La Tirana in northern Chile.

1225 **Valenzuela Rojas, Bernardo.** Estudio etnográfico del carboneo artesanal y del horno, en Chile (Archivos del Folklore Chileno [Santiago] 10, 1976, p. 75–94, illus., maps)

A descriptive ethnographic study of the making of charcoal in Chile. Deals with woods used, characteristics of ovens, techniques of manufacture, some riddles associated with the activity, etc.

1226 **Van Kessel, Juan.** El desierto canta a María: bailes chinos de los santuarios marianos del Norte Grande. t. 1. Santiago: Ediciones Mundo, 1977? 304 p. (La Fe de un pueblo; 4)

Texts of a large collection of religious songs (no music) that are sung as part of dances performed by various "sociedades" in the areas of Arica, Iquique, and Victoria Alianza, Chile. Collected from both written and oral sources.

COLOMBIA

1227 **Abadía Morales, Guillermo.** Compendio general de folklore colombiano. 3. ed. corregida y aumentada. Bogotá: Instituto Colombiano de Cultura, 1977. 557 p., bibl., illus., tables, music.

Expanded ed. of *the* standard general work on Colombian folklore first published in 1970. Defines the field and offers individual chapters on practically every aspect of literary, musical, material, and other types of folklore. Good bibliography.

1228 **Beutler, Gisela.** Estudios sobre el romancero español en Colombia en su tradición escrita y oral desde la época de la conquista hasta la actualidad. Bogotá: Instituto Caro y Cuervo, 1977. 613 p.

A translation from the German of *Studien zum spanishchen Romancero in Kolumbien* (Heidelberg, FRG, 1969), the best study done thus far on the *romance* in Colombia.

1229 **Colombia. Ministerio de Gobierno. División Operativa de Asuntos Indígenas** [and] **Instituto Lingüístico de Verano.** Folclor indígena de Colombia. t. 1. Prólogo de Jaime Valencia y Valencia. Translators: Jorge Arbeláez G. and others. Bogotá: 1974. 383 p., bibl., illus., maps, plates, tables.

A compilation of tales and legends collected from nine indigenous groups in Colombia. For each tale there is an introduction, texts in the original Indian language, a literal and a free translation into Spanish, a vocabulary and an explanation of orthography, and a bibliography.

1230 **Dougherty, Frank T.** Romances tradicionales de Santander (ICC/T, 32:2, mayo/agosto, 1977, p. 242–272)

A useful collection of *romance* texts with annotations. Selects 17 of 75 that he collected in Santander, Colombia, in 1975.

Estrada U., Guillermo and others. Folclor indígena de Colombia. See *HLAS 39:1641*.

1231 **Gradante, William J.** A structural study of the *copla*, as text and as performance (Folklore Annual [Austin, Texas] 7/8, 1977, p. 78–94)

A structural analysis of the *copla* in both its textual and performance aspects. Focuses on the *coplas* sung in Huila, Colombia, during the fiestas of San Juan and San Pedro.

1232 **Granda, Germán de.** Fórmulas mágicas de conjuro en el departamento del Chocó, Colombia (ICC/T, 32:1, enero/abril 1977, p. 166–177)

Offers some oral conjurations that were collected through fieldwork among blacks in Chocó, Colombia. Shows their traditional character by comparing them to similar magic formulas found in papers of the Inquisition from the 17th century.

1233 **———.** Romances de tradición oral conservados entre los negros del occidente de Colombia (ICC/T, 31:2, mayo/agosto 1976, p. 209–229)

Gives literary texts without music of some ballads orally collected among blacks of the Pacific coast of Colombia. Includes comparative notes, commentary, etc.

1234 **———.** Técnicas y léxico de la minería tradicional del oro en las áreas de los ríos Telembí e Iscuandé: Nariño, Colombia (CEEP/RD, 1/4, 1976, p. 207–216)

Tells the history of gold mining in Colombia, then focuses attention on two widely separated areas of the province of Barbacoas where old methods of mining are still used. Compares the popular speech used in the two regions to refer to similar things having to do with the mining of gold.

1235 **Jaramillo Londoño, Agustín.** El folklore secreto del Pícaro Paisa. Medellín, Colombia: Editorial Bedout, 1977. 162 p.

Contains orally collected obscene folklore from the Antioquia region of Colombia: e.g., sexually oriented tales and anecdotes, songs, sayings, riddles, jokes, insults, graffiti, etc. Informant data are lacking.

1236 **Montes Giraldo, José Joaquín.** Voces a los animales usadas en Colombia (CEEP/RD, 32:1/4, 1976, p. 359–372)

Presents results of fieldwork on the words or sounds used in Colombia to deal with farm or domesticated animals (i.e., to call them, to shoo them away or scare them, etc.). Also lists many regional items of vocabulary used in referring to or dealing with animals.

1237 **Reichel-Dolmatoff, Gerardo.** Desana curing spells: an analysis of some shamanistic metaphors (UCLA/JLAL, 2:2, 1976, p. 157–219, bibl.)

Describes and analyzes ritual spells as one of the main procedures for the curing of illness among the Desana Indians of the Colombian Northwest Amazon. Contains verbatim texts of many curing sessions in the Indian language and in English translation.

1238 **———.** The loom of life: a Kogi principle of integration (UCLA/JLAL, 4:1, Summer 1978, p. 5–27, bibl., illus., plates)

An anthropologist studies the loom and the art of weaving among the Kogi Indians of northern Colombia, seeing the loom as a symbol of the cosmos, many aspects of human life, etc. Touches on many subjects of interest to folklorists: e.g., myths and tales, a weaving song, and certain beliefs and practices.

1239 **Soejarto, Djaja D.** Folclor y la búsqueda de sustancias vegetales para regularizar la fertilidad (UA/U, 51:196, enero/marzo 1976, p. 17–23)

Discusses the use of certain plants to regulate fertility and serve as alternatives to contraceptive methods now in use. Of interest to students of folk medicine.

ECUADOR

1240 **Carvalho-Neto, Paulo de.** Cuentos folklóricos de la costa del Ecuador. México: Instituto Panamericano de Geografía e Historia, 1976. 237 p., plates (Serie de Folklore del IPGH. Colección Documentos; 1)

The second installment of a collection of tales first published in Quito (Editorial Universitaria, 1966). This volume contains 27 tale texts collected on the coast of Ecuador in 1966. Also includes Stanley L. Robe's "Clasificación de Tipos y Motivos."

1241 **———.** Cuentos folklóricos del Ecuador. v. 3, Costa: provincia de Guayas. Clasificación de tipos y motivos por Stanley L. Robe. Quito: Editorial Casa de la Cultura Ecuatoriana, 1976. 259 p.

Consists of 17 orally collected tale texts carefully transcribed for use by scholars and accompanied by Aarne-Thompson numbers and notes prepared by Stanley L. Robe. Informant data also are provided. These texts bring to 95 the number published thus far in the series of three volumes.

1242 **———.** Decamerón ecuatoriano. México: Editorial V Siglos, 1975. 223 p.

A collection of 21 literary tales based directly upon folk themes that are identified and explained at the beginning of each story by the author, who is one of the most able Latin American folklorists working today. A most interesting projection of folklore into art literature.

1243 **———.** Historias de tramposos (IPGH/FA, 26, dic. 1978, p. 105–148)

The author, who earlier collected from oral tradition and published carefully transcribed texts of 139 Ecuadorian tales for use by scholars, here presents literary versions of 11 of the same tales. His purpose is to return to the Ecuadorian people polished and easily read retellings of their folktales.

1244 **Coba Andrade, Carlos A.** Estudio sobre el tumank o tsayantur: arco musical del Ecuador (IPGH/FA, 25, junio 1978, p. 79–100)

Discusses the musical bow, its history and origins, and its specific characteristics as found in several provinces of Ecuador.

1245 **Gallardo Moscoso, Hernán.** 400 [i.e. Cuatrocientos] años de cultura lojana. Loja, Ecuador: Editorial Universitaria, 1977. 334 p.

A jumbled miscellany of information about the province of Loja containing some folklore: e.g., texts of *coplas, villancicos* and other songs, proverbs, popular sayings, description of dances, etc. However, much that is presented as folklore is not.

1246 **Guevara, Darío.** Exégesis de toponímicos indígenas ecuatorianos. Quito, Editorial Ecuatoriana, 1975. 49 p.

A listing of Ecuadorian indigenous place names with historical and folkloric analysis of each.

1247 **Muriel, Inés.** Contribución a la cultura musical de los jívaros del Ecuador (IPGH/FA, 21, junio 1976, p. 141–157, bibl., music)

An essay on the music of the Jívaros of Ecuador, based on a field collection made by a missionary in 1942. Includes comments on the socioeconomic life of these Indians, their festivals, and their musical instruments. For musicologist's comment, see item **7124**.

1248 **Punín de Jiménez, Dolores.** La cerámica de Cera, Ecuador: un estudio socioeconómico y cultural (IPGH/FA, 25, junio 1978, p. 125–161, bibl.)

A very complete and detailed study of the potters and traditional pottery of Cera, Ecuador. Includes useful photographs.

Scheller, Ulf and others. Artesanía folclórica en el Ecuador. See *HLAS 41:1275*.

1249 **Townsend, Elizabeth Jane.** Festivals of Ecuador (OAS/AM, 30:4, April 1978, p. 9–16, plates)

Some interesting photographs of Ecuadorian fiestas accompanied by perfunctory explanatory notes.

1250 Ubídia, Abdón. Sobre el problema del estudio del cuento popular en el Ecuador (IPGH/FA, 26, dic. 1978, p. 149–176)

Explains succinctly and well differing methods of studying folktales (i.e., the historic-geographic or Finnish method, Propp's structural analysis and Lévi-Strauss' and Bremond's modifications of it, etc.) and then studies three specific Ecuadorian tales using structural methods.

GREATER ANTILLES

1251 Abrahams, Roger D. The Riddle of the Poisoned Animals (CFS/WF, 26:2, April 1977, p. 163–168)

About riddle-stories collected on several islands of the West Indies. Includes texts and commentary.

1252 ———. The training of the man of words in talking sweet (*in* Verbal art as performance. Edited by Richard Bauman. Rowley, Mass.: Newbury House Publishers, 1977, p. 117–132 [Series in sociolinguistics]).

Discusses different types of traditional language behavior and speechmaking performance in St. Vincent.

1253 Alexis, Gerson. Voudou et quimbois: essai sur les avatars du voudou à la Martinique. Port-au-Prince: Les Editions Fardin, 1976. 71 p., tables.

Considers some of the peculiarly localized forms of popular religions in Martinique with emphasis on voodoo and practitioners of magic.

1254 Alvarez, Roberto and **Tania García.** Anancy, el hombre araña del folklore jamaicano (UH/U, 203/204, 1976, p. 111–122)

About the man-spider hero of Jamaican folklore. Discusses his characteristics and notes how these have changed along with the history of blacks in Jamaica.

1255 Aretz, Isabel and **Luis Felipe Ramón y Rivera.** Un cursillo de folklore (UASD/U, 4, julio/dic. 1973, p. 11–98)

A compilation of data collected in a course about folklore of the Dominican Republic taught by the authors, both distinguished folklorists from Venezuela. Includes information about customs, material lore, recipes, dress, ceremonies, fiestas, dances, songs, poems, music, musical instruments, etc. Includes texts of some songs and poems. For musicologist's comment, see item **7073**.

1256 Baron, Robert. Syncretism and ideology: Latin New York *salsa* musicians (CFS/WF, 36:3, July 1977, p. 209–225)

Discourses on various aspects of the *salsa* music of Afro-Cuban origin which now is cultivated by Latin New Yorkers. Considers particularly the influence operating on *salsa* musicians to commercialize their music in order to appeal to a larger English-speaking audience.

1257 Barrett, Leonard E. The sun and the drum: African roots in Jamaican folk tradition. Kingston: Sangster's Book Stores *in association with* Heinemann, 1976. 128 p., bibl., illus.

Intended as an introduction to Jamaican folk tradition. Contains chapters on the African roots of the Jamaican heritage; proverbs, sayings, signs, and omens; healing; witchcraft and psychic phenomena; and some theoretical conclusions. Includes index.

1258 Bettelheim, Judith. Jamaican Jonkonnu and related Caribbean festivals (*in* Africa and the Caribbean: the legacies of a link [see item **2499**] p. 80–100)

Treats historically and descriptively a traditional Christmas parade found in Jamaica and other neighboring regions as well that dates back at least to the 18th century and was revived in 1951–52. Contains both African and English elements.

1259 Borrello, Mary Ann and **Elizabeth Mathias.** Botanicas: Puerto Rican folk pharmacies (AMNH/NH, 86:7, Aug./Sept. 1977, p. 64–73, plates)

Treats in text and photographs various aspects of Puerto Rican folk religions in New York City, particularly the *botánicas* that sell items and materials used in connection with spiritism and *santería*. Describes in detail one session with a medium.

1260 Brereton, Bridget. The Trinidad Carnival: 1870–1900 (Savacou [Caribbean Artists Movement, Kingston] 11/12, Sept. 1975, p. 46–57)

Traces the vicissitudes of Carnival celebrations in Trinidad as the obscenities, disturbances, and other excesses of the 1870s and 1880s were gradually suppressed when respectable classes of society gained control of the fiesta.

1261 Bushnell, Amy. "That demonic game:" the campaign to stop Indian *pelota* playing in Spanish Florida, 1675–1684 (AAFH/TAM, 35:1, July 1978, p. 1–19)

Describes an early Spanish crusade against Indian ball games in Florida. Within a historical framework examines the game and its associated myths and magic.

1262 Coll y Toste, Cayetano. Puerto Rican tales: legends of Spanish colonial times. Translated and adapted by José Ramírez Rivera. Mayagüez, P.R.: Ediciones Librero, 1977. 89 p., illus., maps.

Translations into English of 12 texts taken from Coll y Toste's *Leyendas puertorriqueñas* (1924–25). The originals were literary versions of historical, religious and supernatural tales and legends. Intended for the general reader.

1263 Deive, Carlos Esteban. El prejuicio racial en el folklore dominicano (MHD/B, 4:8, enero/marzo 1976, p. 75–96)

Cites turns of speech and texts of folksongs from the Dominican Republic that attest to the existence of racial stereotypes of the Negro and of popular beliefs in his inferiority.

1264 Droog, Jan. Biba Nanzi!: serie volksverhalen uit de Nederlandse Antillen. Vanuit het Papiaments naverteld door . . . Aruba, Netherlands Antilles: De Wit, 1977. 47 p.

Series of folktales about Compe Nanzi, a spider, translated from Papiamento by Jan Droog, Inspector of Schools in the Netherlands Antilles. [J. Darilek]

1265 Escabí, Pedro C. and **Elsa M. Escabí.** La décima: vista parcial del folklore. Hato Rey, P.R.: Editorial Universitaria, Universidad de Puerto Rico, 1976. 520 p., bibl., illus., tables.

Studies statistically by using charts and tables such things as literary form, rhyme, rhythm, metric structure, themes, etc., of about 3700 Puerto Rican *décima* texts. A massive compilation of quantitative data. Includes appendixes.

1266 García Arévalo, Manuel Antonio. Los gallitos de madera: historia de un artesano (MHD/B, 4:8, enero/marzo 1976, p. 47–61)

About Erasmo Puello, a woodcarver in the town of Cambita, San Cristóbal, in the Dominican Republic. He specializes in carving colorful roosters and other birds as well as more utilitarian objects such as wooden spoons.

1267 García Cisneros, Florencio. Santos of Puerto Rico and the Américas/Santos de Puerto Rico y las Américas. Translated from the Spanish by Roberta West. Detroit, Mich.: Blaine Ethridge, 1979. 122 p., bibl., illus.

An art critic offers a brief introductory appreciation of the carved figures of saints found in Puerto Rican tradition and places them in the general history of such art in America. His study, given in both English and Spanish, is followed by an excellent collection of 76 photographs and a good bibliography.

1268 García González, José. Algunas consideraciones lingüísticas a propósito de un nuevo cuento afrocubano (UCLV/I, 61, sept./dic. 1978, p. 129–139, music)

Offers an orally collected folktale, "La Muchacha y el Majá," in phonetic transcription and also a literary version. Comments on linguistic transculturation to be observed as a result of contact between African languages and the Spanish spoken in Cuba. Includes also a song that accompanies the tale.

1269 Gaviria, Moisés and **Ronald M. Wintrob.** Supernatural influences in psychopathology: Puerto Rican folk beliefs about mental illness (Canadian Psychiatric Association Journal [Ottawa] 21:6, Oct. 1976, p. 361–369, tables)

Explores attitudes toward mental disorder among Puerto Ricans in two Connecticut cities and defines popular concepts of such things as spiritism, witchcraft, *daño*, *susto*, etc. Discusses the effectiveness of folk healers in the Puerto Rican community. For sociologist's comment, see *HLAS 41:9157*.

1270 George, Philip Brandt. Reaffirmation of identity: a Latino case in East Chicago (Indiana Folklore [Bloomington] 10:2, 1977, p. 139–148)

Relates the author's personal experiences researching urban folklore in the

Region (i.e., East Chicago, Indiana) and characterizes the Latin-American community that he studies. Focuses particularly on one family of Puerto Rican origin which provided several informants.

1271 ———. Tales of a Puerto Rican storyteller (Indiana Folklore [Bloomington] 10:2, 1977, p. 149–158)

Translates into English five tape-recorded narratives collected from informants of Puerto Rican background in East Chicago, Indiana. Two texts are folktales, one is a legend, and two are personal accounts.

1272 Gilfond, Henry. Voodoo: its origins and practices. New York: Franklin Watts, 1976. 114 p., bibl., illus., map, plates.

A detailed general discussion of voodoo as practiced mainly in Haiti and Santo Domingo. Treats its origins, gods, initiation and other ceremonies and rites, dance, magic, voodoo and the Catholic Church, etc. Includes index.

1273 González, Mercedes R. Pinceladas folklóricas dominicanas. New York: Abra Ediciones, 1975? 82 p., illus., music.

Gives words of various songs, verses, riddles, games, etc. Music is provided for some songs.

González Canalda, María Filomena. Notas y entrevistas sobre etnobotánica en Santo Domingo. See *HLAS 39:1212.*

1274 Hedrick, Basil C. and **Jeanette E. Stephens.** In the days of yesterday and in the days of today: an overview of Bahamian folkmusic. Carbondale: University Museum, Southern Illinois University, 1976. 63 p., bibl. (University Museum studies; 8)

Discusses the qualities and the performance of religious and secular music in the Bahamas. Based on fieldwork conducted by the authors between 1974–76. Includes discography and appendix.

1275 Jardel, J.P. Notes sur les contes créoles des Petites Antilles (ASHSH/B, 5, 1977, p. 52–65)

Classifies folktales in the Lesser Antilles according to their themes, notes the occasions when they are told and comments on some of their stylistic features, and compares them to similar tales in Europe and Africa.

1276 Jha, J.C. The Hindu festival of Divali in the Caribbean (UWI/CQ, 22:1, March 1976, p. 53–61)

Describes the Divali festival of lights as it exists in India and as it is practiced in Trinidad.

1277 ———. The Hindu sacraments—Rites de Passage—in Trinidad and Tobago (UWI/CQ, 22:1, March 1976, p. 41–52)

A general description of various Hindu rites of passage. Actually specific attention to Trinidad and Tobago is quite limited.

1278 Juste-Constant, Voegeli. Approche ethnomusicologique du vovou [sic] haitien (IPGH/FA, 21, junio 1976, p. 95–140, bibl., illus., music, plates)

Discusses Haitian voodoo in general terms and then analyzes its songs and music through commentary and musical examples. For musicologist's comment, see item **7079**.

1279 Koss, Joan D. Religion and science divinely related: a case history of spiritism in Puerto Rico (UPR/CS, 16:1, April 1976, p. 22–43)

Traces by periods the history of spiritism in Europe and Puerto Rico from the 18th century to the present. Dwells on its relationship to folk religion and folk healings. For ethnologist's comment, see *HLAS 41:1047*.

1280 Lama, Sonia de. El habla cubana en las estampas de Eladio Secades; caudal de cubanismos, dichos y frases populares (AATSP/H, 60:3, Sept. 1977, p. 519–523)

Lists about 175 items from Cuban popular speech taken from *artículos de costumbres* (i.e., literary sketches about customs) written by Eladio Secades.

1281 Laurent, Joëlle and **Ina Césaire** *eds.* and *trans.* Contes de mort e de vie aux Antilles. Paris: Nubia, 1976. 248 p.

Offers 22 orally collected folktales gathered in Martinique and Guadeloupe. Texts are in Creole with French translations and are grouped according to themes. An introduction describes the tale-telling tradition and touches on various aspects of the materials collected.

1282 León, Julio Antonio. Afro-Cuban poetry: an unpublished treasure (OAS/AM, 29:9, Sept. 1977, p. 28–32, illus.)

Some brief comments on songs and

poetry found in Afro-Cuban tradition. Gives texts of a few examples.

1283 **Lizardo, Fradique.** Danzas y bailes folklóricos dominicanos. Santo Domingo: Editora Taller, 1975. 329 p., bibl., illus., maps, music.

Relates the history of music and dance in the Dominican Republic and then offers an exhaustive descriptive survey of the different dances known today. Gives music and words of many songs that accompany dancing. Illustrations and excellent bibliography enhance the work. Martha Ellen Davis provides an informative introduction. For musicologist's comment, see item **7080**.

1284 ———. Instrumentos musicales indígenas dominicanos. Santo Domingo: Alfa y Omega, 1975. 109 p., bibl., illus.

A classification and description of the indigenous folk instruments of the Dominican Republic. Offers little folkloristic interpretation or analysis (the author promises this in a future publication), but the work is useful as a source of data. For musicologist's comment, see *HLAS 40:9067*.

1285 **London, Clement B.G.** Carnival à la Trinidad and Tobago (OAS/AM, 29:2, Feb. 1977, p. 19–24, plates)

Describes and interprets Carnival celebrations in Trinidad and Tobago. Includes some good photographs.

1286 **Martínez Furé, Rogelio.** Diálogo imaginario sobre folklore: nuevos aportes al conocimiento de las tradiciones populares cubanas (IPGH/FA, 22, dic. 1976, p. 143–151)

Poses a series of questions about the nature of folklore in Cuba, its place in society, the proper approaches for studying it, etc. Fairly long answers set forth Marxist theories about these subjects.

1287 **Mejías de Díaz, María E.** Descripción de algunas manifestaciones folklóricas de Curazao (IPGH/FA, 20, julio/dic. 1975, p. 107–137, illus., music, plates)

Calls attention to some examples of Curazao's folklore in sections on three different fiestas, a funeral ceremony, a musical bow, and various kinds of musical instruments used on the island.

1288 **Midgett, Douglas K.** Performance roles and musical change in a Caribbean society (Ethnomusicology [Ann Arbor, Michigan] 21:1, Jan. 1977, p. 55–73, illus.)

Analyzes a particular West Indian musical event, La Rose singing in St. Lucia, focusing on the performances of the central characters and showing how the tradition is subject to both continuity and change.

1289 **Moldes, Rhyna.** Música folklórica cubana: con la historia, ritmos e instrumentos de origen hispano-africano. Hialeah, Fla.: Editors & Printers, 1975. 62 p., illus., music, plates.

Discusses briefly the nature of Cuban musical folklore, its Hispanic and African antecedents, the instruments associated with it, etc. Gives words of some songs and offers short chapters on various genres of dance. Includes some musical examples.

1290 **Morales P., Félix.** Un cuento folklórico anotado: "Velasquillo" (UCV/S, 8[11]: 1/2, 1975, p. 81–107)

Gives text in Spanish with phonetic transcription on facing page of a folktale called "Velasquillo." Detailed annotation covers such things as phonetic phenomena, grammar, parts of speech and their use, lexicon, and tale-type and motif numbers.

1291 **Murad, Timothy.** René Marqués' "Juan Bobo y la Dama de Occidente:" folklore as pantomime and the art of cultural affirmation (Revista Chicano-Riqueña [Gary, Indiana] 7:4, otoño 1979, p. 35–47)

Discusses Marqués' adaptation of the traditional trickster figure Juan Bobo and other folkloric elements such as music for use in a satirical play about Puerto Rican affirmation of its authentic cultural identity.

1292 **Newall, Venetia.** Selected Jamaican foodways in the homeland and in England (*in* Folklore today, a festschrift for Richard M. Dorson. Edited by Linda Dégh, Henry Glassie, and Felix Oinas. Bloomington: Research Center for Language and Semiotic Studies, Indiana University, 1976, p. 369–377)

Surveys the foods contained in the traditional Jamaican diet; also treats some customs and beliefs associated with them.

Rosa-Nieves, Cesáreo. Los bailes de Puerto Rico. See item **7084**.

1293 **Valdés Bernal, Sergio.** Sobre locuciones y refranes afrocubanos (BRP, 15:2, 1976, p. 321–328, bibl.)

Traces the history of the Negro in Cuba and then examines turns of speech and proverbial expressions of African origin that are found in Cuba today.

1294 Valdés-Cruz, Rosa. Lo ancestral africano en la narrativa de Lydia Cabrera. Barcelona, Spain: Editorial Vosgos, 1974. 113 p., bibl.

A critical study of the literary production of Lydia Cabrera, a cuban author who in her works, particularly three collections of stories published in the 1940s, draws heavily upon Negro culture, especially folklore (e.g., proverbs, stories, myths, speech, etc.). Includes excellent bibliography.

Wong, Wesley. Some folk medicinal plants from Trinidad. See *HLAS 39:1276*.

GUYANA

1295 An annotated glossary of folk medicines used by some Amerindians in Guyana. Editor, Walter F. Edwards. Researcher, Kean Gibson. Georgetown: Amerindian Languages Project, University of Guyana, 1978. 96 p., bibl., index.

Lists almost 200 words for plants, animals, and various materials from the Arekuna, Patamuna, Akawaio, and Makushi languages having to do with folk medicines. Translates and explains each item and describes its use.

1296 Carew, Jan. The fusion of African and Amerindian folk myths (UWI/CQ, 23:1, March 1977, p. 7–21)

Draws upon various Amerindian and African myths and legends in order to speculate upon the ways in which these were presumably fused in America, and more specifically in Guyana.

1297 Dictionary of Guyanese folklore. Georgetown: National History and Arts Council, 1975. 74 p.

A tentative but useful alphabetical listing of words that are in some way related to Guyanese folklore.

1298 Drummond, Lee. Structure and process in the interpretation of South American myth: the Arawak dog spirit people (AAA/AA, 89:4, Dec. 1977, p. 842–868)

Studies a clan origin myth collected from an Arawak Amerindian of the upper Pameroon River, Guyana. Attempts to show how differing approaches to the study of oral narratives and symbolic systems (i.e., the study of structure and process) contradict and complement each other. For ethnologist's comment, see *HLAS 41:1020*.

1299 Persaud, Satnarine. Names of folk spirits in Guyana (NHAC/K, 14, July 1976, p. 56–60)

Reports results of interviews in which 18 informants were asked to give the precise meanings of various spirit-names: *fair-maid*; *jumbie*; *dutchman*; *churile*; *ole-hique*; *bakoo*; *sukhanti*; *moon-gazer*; *Bush dai-dai*; and *massocouraman*.

MEXICO

1300 Arora, Shirley L. Proverbial comparisons and related expressions in Spanish, recorded in Los Angeles, California. Berkeley: University of California Press, 1977. 521 p., bibl.

A huge compilation with detailed annotation of "proverbial comparisons" (i.e., true proverbs, proverbial phrases and formulaic elements) collected from 517 Spanish-speaking informants of Greater Los Angeles, California. Entries are arranged by key words. Includes an introduction, data about informants, and an excellent bibliography. Contains appendix.

1301 Baudot, Georges. "La Belle et La Bête" dans le folklore náhuatl du Mexique central (UTIEH/C, 27, 1976, p. 53–61)

Translates into French a Náhuatl tale text collected by Pablo González Casanova in northern Morelos. Identifies two Aarne-Thompson tale types found in the tale and demonstrates that it is a version of "The Beauty and the Beast."

1302 Boggs, Ralph S. La vida de San Pedro (CEEP/RD, 32:1/4, 1976, p. 53–55)

Offers the text of a folktale about Saint Peter that was orally collected in San Pedro de Cholula, Mexico, in 1945.

1303 Boyd, Lola Elizabeth. Emiliano Zapata en las letras y el folklore mexicano. Madrid: Ediciones José Porrúa Turanzas, 1979. 171 p., bibl.

Studies the different views of the Mexican revolutionary leader, General Emiliano Zapata, expressed by historians, associates or enemies of Zapata who wrote about him, novelists, and poets. Also draws material from *corridos* (i.e., ballads) and includes 14 texts of *corridos* (no music) in an appendix.

1304 Brandes, Stanley H. Dance as metaphor: a case from Tzintzuntzan, Mexico (UCLA/JLAL, 5:1, Summer 1979, p. 25–43, bibl.)

Detailed ethnographic description of an elaborate dance associated with the major annual festival in the ritual cycle of Tzintzuntzan in central Mexico. Places the dance in cultural context and relates it to moral and religious codes, then shows how its performance may be viewed as a social metaphor.

1305 Bravo Ramírez, Francisco J. El artesano en México. México: Editorial Porrúa, 1976. 103 p.

About artisans throughout history and specifically in Mexico, with attention principally to the life of artisans in rural areas. Discusses their problems, official organizations that deal with them or foment the production of traditional arts and crafts, etc.

1306 Breve selección de fiestas tradicionales. México: Dirección General de Arte Popular, Secretaría de Educación Pública, 1975. 109 p. (mimeo)

A calendar that lists in approximate chronological order and describes in simple language a large number of fiestas celebrated in the Republic of Mexico. Intended for the general public, it is a useful listing for specialists as well.

1307 Bricker, Victoria Reifler. Historical dramas in Chiapas, Mexico (UCLA/JLAL, 3:2, Winter 1977, p. 227–248, bibl.)

Documents and analyzes the dance-dramas known as the Conquest and its variant, the Dance of the Moors and Christians, as they exist today in highland Chiapas, Mexico. Shows how, particularly in the dramas that depend on oral transmission, many diverse historical elements are jumbled together. Interprets the dramas as expressions of ethnic conflict.

1308 Brown, Betty Ann. Fiestas de Oaxaca. Oaxaca: Centro Regional de Oaxaca, Instituto Nacional de Antropología e Historia, 1977. 20 p. (Estudios de antropología e historia; 2) (mimeo)

Lists annual regional fiestas of the state of Oaxaca in chronological order. Indicates the names of towns and their districts and then describes briefly the nature of the fiesta.

1309 Brown, Lorin W.; Charles L. Briggs; and **Marta Weigle.** Hispano folklife of New Mexico: the Lorin W. Brown Federal Writers' Manuscripts. Albuquerque: University of New Mexico Press, 1978. 279 p., bibl., map, plates.

Briggs and Weigle edit some of the manuscripts about Hispano life and customs in New Mexico as described by Brown while working in the Federal Writers Project in the 1930s. Also included are bibliographies of Brown's writings and of selected works by other writers on New Mexican folklife of the same period. Contains appendix and index.

1310 Campa, Arthur Leon. Hispanic folklore studies. Introduction by Carlos E. Cortés. New York: Arno Press, 1976. 1 v. (Unpaged)

An anthology of previously published articles by Campa. Includes the following titles: "A Bibliography of Spanish Folklore in New Mexico;" "Spanish Folk-Poetry in New Mexico;" "The Spanish Folksong in the Southwest;" "Spanish Religious Folk-Theatre in Spanish Southwest;" and "Sayings and Riddles of New Mexico."

1311 Cancionero folklórico de México. t. 2, Coplas del amor desdichado y otras coplas de amor. Edited by Margit Frenk Alatorre and others. México, El Colegio de México, 1977. 510 p., bibl., table.

The second of a projected five-volume *cancionero*, this collection contains *copla* texts Nos. 2273a–5716. Frenk Alatorre provides an introduction. Includes comparative notes, an index of song titles, and another of first lines. For vol. 1 of this work, see *HLAS 38:1517*.

1312 Cardozo-Freeman, Inez. The *corridos* of Arnulfo Castillo (Revista Chicano-Riqueña [Gary, Indiana] 4:4, otoño 1976, p. 129–138)

Attempts to show how a *corrido*-singer's compositions reflect not only the world-view of his people, but his own personality.

1313 ———. Games Mexican girls play (AFS/JAF, 88:347, Jan./March 1975, p. 12–24)

Holds that the games played by Mexican girls are a rehearsal for female adult roles in a male-dominated folk culture.

1314 **Castillo Robles, Soledad** and **Blanca Irma Alonso Tejeda.** La Semana Santa en San Lucas Tecopilco, Tlax. (Boletín del Departamento de Investigación de las Tradiciones Populares [México] 3, 1976, p. 45–89)

Studies Holy Week in a rural community in the state of Tlaxcala. Gives ethnographic data about the town and then describes and analyzes customs, processions, ceremonies, and other activities related to Holy Week. Includes words without music of several songs.

1315 **Crumrine, N. Ross** and **M. Louise Crumrine.** Ritual symbolism in folk and ritual drama: the Mayo Indian San Cayetano Velación, Sonora, Mexico (AFS/JAF, 90:355, Jan./March 1977, p. 8–28, plates)

By way of analyzing ritual symbols and their relation to sociocultural conditions among the Mayo Indians of northwest Mexico, describes a dramatic ritual event or drama that focuses upon a trickster type of Saint, San Cayetano. For ethnologist's comment, see *HLAS 41:900*.

1316 **Díaz Mendoza, María del Carmen.** La teoría de la comunicación aplicada a la danza-drama de los arrieros (Boletín del Departamento de Investigación de las Tradiciones Populares [México] 3, 1976, p. 29–44, bibl., plates)

Seeks to demonstrate how to apply the theory of folk performance as communication to a dance-drama that takes place in San Martín Ocoyoacac, state of Mexico.

1317 **El Guindi, Fadwa.** Lore and structure: *Todos Santos* in the Zapotec system (UCLA/JLAL, 3:1, Summer 1977, p. 3–18)

Describes and analyzes beliefs about death and the dead as observed in a farming community in Oaxaca, Mexico. Focuses on the practices associated with All Saints' Day, Nov. 1. Includes texts of some oral narratives about the dead. For ethnologist's comment, see *HLAS 41:920*.

1318 **Espejel, Carlos.** Cerámica popular mexicana. México: Editorial Blume [and] Museo Nacional de Artes e Industrias Populares, 1975. 224 p., bibl., illus., maps, plates.

A general book with many black-and-white and color illustrations of pottery-making in various parts of Mexico. Written by the Director of the Museo Nacional de Artes e Industrias Populares, it inventories traditional ceramics, discusses techniques of manufacture, decorations, etc., and provides information about the artisans who make pottery. Includes glossary and index.

1319 **Espinosa, J. Manuel.** Spanish folklore in the Southwest: the pioneer studies of Aurelio M. Espinosa (AAFH/TAM, 35:2, Oct. 1978, p. 219–237, bibl.)

The author summarizes and evaluates the work of his father, Aurelio M. Espinosa, who pioneered research on Hispanic folklore of the Southwest of the US. Treats his studies of language, songs and ballads, folktales, proverbs, riddles, folk drama, etc. Includes Espinosa's personal bibliography of over 100 books and articles.

1320 **Furst, Jill Leslie.** The tree birth tradition in the Mixteca, Mexico (UCLA/JLAL, 3:2, Winter 1977, p. 183–226, bibl., illus.)

Notes a recently collected Mixteca origin myth from Oaxaca, Mexico, relating how in ancient times a tree gave birth to a sacred individual; then studies two versions of the myth in 16th and 17th-century books written by Spanish friars and also finds pictorial representations of it in prehispanic codices and bone carvings.

1321 **Galván, Roberto A.** and **Richard V. Teschner.** El diccionario del español de Tejas / The dictionary of the Spanish of Texas. Silver Spring, Md.: Institute of Modern Languages, 1975. 102 p., bibl.

A dictionary of non-standard Spanish vocabulary and phrases found among Chicanos in Texas. English translations are provided. Also has an appendix containing proverbs and sayings.

1322 **García, Ricardo.** Multi-ethnic literature in America: overview of Chicano folklore (English Journal [East Lansing, Mich.] 55:2, Feb. 1976, p. 83–87)

Suggests that folklore is the main basis of Chicano literature and gives brief descriptions of some important categories of Mexican-American lore: e.g., folksongs, legendary characters, folk drama, parables, proverbs, and riddles.

1323 Geijerstam, Claes af. Popular music in Mexico. Albuquerque: University of New Mexico Press, 1976. 187 p., bibl., music, plates.

A Swedish scholar surveys the whole field of Mexican "popular" music in its diverse manifestations. Folk music, folksongs, traditional dances, etc. are included in his purview. Includes copious notes. For musicologist's comment, see *HLAS 40:9109*.

1324 Giffords, Gloria Kay. Mexican folk retablos, masterpieces on tin. Tucson: University of Arizona Press, 1974. 160 p., bibl., plates.

A handsome art book that deals with Mexican folk paintings of saints, painted exvotos, etc. Contains good discussion of the artistic aspects of such paintings and 81 plates, most of them in full color. Also includes good indexes and useful bibliography.

1325 Gossen, Gary H. Translating Cuscat's War: understanding Maya oral history (UCLA/JLAL, 3:2, Winter 1977, p. 249–278, bibl.)

A fascinating study and commentary about how Cuscat's War, a rebellion of the Chamula people of Chiapas, Mexico (1867–70) is recalled and understood in contemporary Chamula oral tradition. Explains the Chamulas' cosmovision and their view of history as background for interpreting an orally collected narrative that is one informant's version of Cuscat's War.

1326 Granger, Byrd Howell. A motif index for lost mines and treasures applied to redaction of Arizona legends, and to lost mine and treasure legends exterior to Arizona. Tucson: University of Arizona Press, 1977. 277 p., bibl.

Contains texts of many Arizona lost mine and treasure legends, many of them from Spanish-speaking informants or from printed sources in Spanish. The motif index section, of course, treats motifs from both Hispanic and general American culture.

1327 Grimes, Ronald L. Symbol and conquest: public ritual and drama in Santa Fe, New Mexico. Ithaca, New York: Cornell University Press, 1976. 281 p., bibl., illus.

Studies public symbols in the processions and novenas of a Marian image in the city of Santa Fe. Provides a description of the Santa Fe fiesta showing how religion and drama are linked to ethnic and civil symbols in this modern urban context. Includes index.

1328 Gutiérrez, Electra and **Tonatiún Gutiérrez.** Oaxaca y su arte popular (ARMEX, 21:176, 1974, p. 72–81, illus.)

Traces the history of the Oaxacan fiesta of the *Guelaguetza* and then describes it. Dwells upon such things as regional dress, artifacts, dances, etc. Good photographs. The Spanish version of the article is on p. 72–78; on p. 79–81, there is a translation into English.

1329 Heisley, Michael. An annotated bibliography of Chicano folklore from the southwestern United States. Los Angeles: University of California, 1977. 188 p.

Consists of 1028 entries distributed by categories such as narratives, songs, dance, speech, games, etc. Also includes a useful section on Mexican folklore in general and indexes.

1330 Herrera-Sobek, María. The theme of drug smuggling in the Mexican *corrido* (Revista Chicano-Riqueña [Gary, Ind.] 7:4, otoño 1979, p. 49–61)

Examines a number of ballad (i.e., *corrido*) texts, both old and new, in order to ascertain Mexican attitudes toward the smuggling of drugs, and many other things as well, along the border between the US and Mexico.

Higgins, Cheleen Mahar. Integrative aspects of folk and western medicine among the urban poor of Oaxaca. See *HLAS 39:1082*.

1331 Hinds, Harold E., Jr. Tradiciones y leyendas de la colonia: Mexican folklore and colonial history for popular consumption (IPGH/FA, 25, junio 1978, p. 101–109)

Examines the authenticity of a popular Mexican comic strip series, *Tradiciones y leyendas de la colonia*, published since 1963 in Mexico City. Analyzes its main themes, the values it portrays, and its influence on the Mexican reader.

1332 Hispanic folktales from New Mexico. Edited by Stanley Robe. Berkeley: University of California Press, 1977. 223 p., bibl. (Folklore Studies; 30)

205 folktales translated into English from the R.D. Jameson Collection. Includes

Aarne-Thompson tale-type numbers provided by Robe; also information about informants, place and date of collecting, and the name of the field collector.

1333 Hispano culture of New Mexico. Introduction by Carlos E. Cortés. New York: Arno Press, 1976. 1 v. (Unpaged) illus., music.

An anthology of reprints of the following articles: Aurora Lucero White's, Eunice Hauskins' and Helene Mareau's "Los Hispanos," "The Folklore of New Mexico," and "Folk Dances of the Spanish Colonials of New Mexico;" Mela Sedillo's "Mexican and New Mexican Folk Dances;" and F.M. Kercheville's and George E. McSpadden's "A Preliminary Glossary of New Mexico Spanish."

1334 Holden, William Curry. Teresita. Illustrated by José Cisneros. Owings Mills, Md.: Stemmer House, 1978. 235 p., bibl., illus.

A semi-historical, partly fictionalized account of the life of Teresita Urrea, a healer who had a large following in the state of Chihuahua, Mexico, in the late 19th century. Known as La Santa de Cabora, she was revered by some revolutionaries who rebelled against the government of President Porfirio Díaz. Of interest to students of folk religion.

1335 Holscher, Louis M. Tiene arte valor afuera del barrio: the murals of East Los Angeles and Boyle Heights (Journal of Ethnic Studies [Bellingham, Wash.] 4:3, Fall 1976, p. 42–52, illus.)

Discusses the themes and significance of popular Mexican-American urban murals.

1336 Hunn, Eugene S. Tzeltal folk zoology: the classification of discontinuities in nature. New York: Academic Press, 1977. 368 p., bibl., illus., maps, tables.

An anthropologist compiles an extremely detailed encyclopedic dictionary of the zoological lexicon used by Indians in the central highlands of Chiapas. Based on fieldwork, it deals with more than 500 animals. Incorporates a great deal of folklore, particularly in treating the "medicinal" significance of animals, popular names for animals, etc. Includes appendix and indexes. For ethnologist's comment, see *HLAS 41:928*.

1337 Hunt, Eva. The transformation of the hummingbird: cultural roots of a Zinacantecan mythical poem. Ithaca, New York: Cornell University Press, 1977. 312 p., bibl., illus., maps, tables.

A fascinating attempt to use a historical approach combined with structural analysis to interpret the mythical symbolism found in "The Hummingbird," a poem from Zinacantan, Chiapas, that is related to prehispanic antecedents in Mesoamerican mythology. Includes appendixes.

1338 Irigoyen, Renan. Esencia del folklore de Yucatán. 2. ed. Mérida: Ediciones del Gobierno del Estado, 1976. 63 p., illus., music.

A cursory survey of various types of folklore (i.e., songs and dances, superstitions, customs, ceremonies, crafts, etc.) with stress on indigenous elements. Of interest only to non-specialists. Includes appendix.

1339 Jaquith, James R. *Cawboy [sic] de Medianoche*: Mexican highway folklore (UCSD/NS, 5:1, 1975, p. 39–72)

Reports on 900 bumper slogans seen on Mexican trucks. Divides them into categories and provides English translations or explanations of all of the slogans listed.

1340 Kanellos, Nicolás. Folklore in Chicano theater and Chicano theater as folklore (IU/JFI, 15:1, Jan./April 1978, p. 57–82, plates)

Tells something of the history of Chicano theater in the Southwest and Midwest, surveys Latino folk theaters and theatrical groups, offers a brief section on the *corrido* and its relationship to Chicano theater, etc. The author writes from eight years of personal experience with Chicano and Puerto Rican popular theater.

1341 Kearney, Michael. Oral performance by Mexican spiritualists in possession trance (UCLA/JLAL, 3:2, Winter 1977, p. 309–328, bibl.)

Discusses spiritualism in Mexico and specifically around the city of Ensenada, Baja California; then analyzes *doctrinas*, speech events engaged in by spiritualist mediums during possession trances.Gives textual examples of some *doctrinas*. Includes appendix.

1342 Lagarriga Attias, Isabel. Medicina tradicional y espiritismo: los espiritualistas trinitarios marianos de Jalapa, Veracruz. México: Secretaría de Educación

Pública, Dirección General de Divulgación, 1975. 158 p., bibl., illus., maps (Sep-Setentas; 191)

Reports the results of anthropological fieldwork that studied a group of spiritualists in the city of Jalapa, Veracruz. Describes their diagnosis of illnesses, healing practices and cures, ceremonies, etc. Contains appendixes.

1343 Lange, Yvonne. Santo Niño de Atocha: a Mexican cult is transplanted to Spain (SAR/P, 84:4, Winter 1978, p. 2–7)

Traces to the 19th century the rise of the cult of the Santo Niño de Atocha at Fresnillo, Zacatecas, Mexico. Then finds that in the 1920s the veneration of the Mexican saint appeared in Spain. Describes several statues and paintings of the Santo Niño.

1344 Lomelí, Francisco A. and **Donaldo W. Urioste.** Chicano perspectives in literature: a critical and annotated bibliography. Albuquerque, New Mexico: Pajarito Publications, 1976. 120 p.

A detailed, annotated bibliography of Chicano literature with a few entries on oral tradition.

1345 Martínez Peñaloza, Porfirio. Arte popular y artesanías artísticas en México: un acercamiento. México: Ediciones del *Boletín Bibliográfico* de la Secretaría de Hacienda y Crédito Público, 1972. 124 p., bibl., illus., tables.

Contains three useful articles: "Arte Popular en México: Cincuentenario de una Exposición y un Libro;" "Las Artes Populares en México, 1922;" "Desarrollo Artesanal en México: un Enfoque Orientado a la Exportación." The first and third had earlier been published elsewhere.

1346 Medina, Andrés and **Noemí Quezada.** Panorama de las artesanías otomíes del Valle del Mezquital: ensayo metodológico. México: Universidad Nacional Autónoma de México, Instituto de Investigaciones Antropológicas, 1975. 122 p.

Studies artisans in the Valle del Mezquital from a socioeconomic point of view. Describes the region in ethnographic terms and then considers the relationship between artisans and a capitalistic economy, their role in a rural agricultural society, the ideological and economic bases of programs to foment the production of traditional arts and crafts, etc.

1347 Mexican folk tales. Edited and translated by Anthony John Campos. Tucson: The University of Arizona Press, 1977. 136 p.

A collection of about 25 Chicano tales and legends of the southwestern US told to the editor in Spanish by his godmother, Lily Cornejo.

1348 Mexico. Dirección General de Arte Popular. Departamento de Extensión Educativa. Calendario de fiestas tradicionales. México: Coordinación de las Culturas Populares, Subsecretaría de Cultura y Difusión Popular, Secretaría de Educación Pública, 1977. 620 l., bibl., maps, plates (mimeo)

A huge and important listing of fiestas in all parts of Mexico. Groups and indexes them according to states of the Mexican Republic, months of the year, towns (by states and also in alphabetical order), etc. Includes indexes.

1349 Moedano N., Gabriel. Estado actual de la investigación folklórica en México (*in* Actas del I Congreso Internacional de Folklorología en Panamá [see item **963a**] p. 225–242, bibl.)

Surveys the activities of various groups or organizations that are doing folklore research in Mexico, principally the Departamento de Investigación de las Tradiciones Populares of the Secretaría de Educación Pública, but including also several other institutions working in the field.

1350 ———. Rubén M. Campos: un pionero de la investigación folklórica en México (Boletín del Departamento de Investigación de las Tradiciones Populares [México] 3, 1976, p. 5–27, bibl., plates)

Offers a brief biography of Campos, one of Mexico's earliest folklorists, and then surveys his work and comments upon it. Includes bibliography about Campos as well as a listing of Campos' own works.

1351 ———. La vida y la obra de Vicente T. Mendoza: 1894–1964. México: Departamento de Investigación de las Tradiciones Populares, Dirección General de Arte Popular, Secretaría de Educación Pública, 1976. 91 p., bibl., plates (Estudios de folklore y de arte popular; 1)

A biography of Mendoza, Mexico's most outstanding folklorist, and at the same time a history of the study of folklore in Mexico. Evaluates Mendoza's work and the methodology he employed. Includes a bibliography of works cited by Moedano, another of the works of Mendoza, and a third of works about the latter.

1352 **Morales Viramontes, María Cristina.** Los funerales en San Miguel Tenancingo, Tlax. (Boletín del Departamento de Investigación de las Tradiciones Populares [México] 3, 1976, p. 105–122, bibl., music)

Describes various funeral customs and rites as observed in a small town in the state of Tlaxcala. Includes words and music of some songs.

1353 **Nelson, Cynthia.** Supports for ethnic identity in a changing Mexican village (Ethnicity [New York] 5:1, March 1978, p. 33–41)

Discusses ethnicity in a Tarascan village of the state of Michoacán. Contains some information of interest to folklorists about such topics as historical narratives, religious rituals, nationalistic symbols, etc.

1354 **Núñez y Domínguez, José de Jesús.** El rebozo. Toluca: Gobierno del Estado de México, 1976. 67 p., illus.

A new ed. of a work first published in 1917. A kind of extended poetic essay that traces the history of the *rebozo,* the traditional shawl of Mexico, and ferrets out from many sources interesting facts about its use and significance.

1355 **Nutini, Hugo G.** Syncretism and acculturation: the historical development of the cult of the patron saint in Tlaxcala, Mexico: 1519–1670 (UP/E, 15:3, July 1976, p. 301–321)

Formulates a concept of syncretism for the folk religious system of Tlaxcala. Based on the historical development of the cult of the Virgin of Ocotlán.

1356 **Otomí parables, folktales and jokes.** Edited by H. Russell Bernard and Jesús Salinas Pedraza. Chicago: University of Chicago Press, 1976. 120 p. (*International Journal of American Linguistics.* Native American Texts Series; 1:2)

Transcriptions of texts collected in the Otomí language, along with literal and free English translations.

1357 **Paredes, Américo.** On ethnographic work among minority groups: a folklorist's perspective (UCSD/NS, 6, 1977, p. 1–32)

A Chicano folklorist of distinction analyzes and comments upon the pitfalls that many ethnographers fall into as they study Chicano culture. Suggests ways of avoiding errors of interpretation due to prejudices or stereotypes found in both the ethnographer and his informants.

1358 ———. A Texas-Mexican *cancionero:* folksongs of the Lower Border. Urbana: University of Illinois Press, 1976. 194 p., illus., map, music.

Words and music of 66 songs that are representative of the corpus of folksongs sung along the Texas-Mexican border from 1750–1960. English translations of the Spanish texts are provided, as are excellent extended commentaries on each type of song (they are grouped by types) and a fine general introduction. Includes glossary and index.

1359 ———. Yamashita, Zapata, and the Arthurian legend (CFS/WF, 36:2, April 1977, p. 160–163)

Comments upon various legends about deceased heroes who are supposedly not really dead but only waiting for the right moment to return and lead their people again. Gen. Tomobumi Yamashita of Japan and Emiliano Zapata of Mexico are two examples.

1360 **Pettit, Florence Harvey** and **Robert M. Pettit.** Mexican folk toys: festival decorations and ritual objects. New York: Hastings House Publishers, 1978. 192 p., bibl., illus.

Presents the traditional handmade toys and decorations of Mexico with the aid of text and hundreds of beautiful pictures. Includes glossaries and index.

1361 **Pineda del Valle, César.** Cuentos y leyendas de la costa de Chiapas. México: B. Costa-Amic, 1976. 103 p.

Short pieces that relate some episodes and tales from folkloric tradition. Of limited value to folklorists because they are rewritten in a highly literary style and no sources are given.

1362 **Posada's Mexico.** Edited by Ron Tyler. Washington: Library of Congress *in cooperation with the* Amon Carter Museum of Western Art, Fort Worth, Texas, 1979. 315 p., bibl., illus.

Contains a catalog of an important exhibition at the Library of Congress of the works of José Guadalupe Posada, the famous Mexican engraver of illustrations for newspapers, *corridos*, and various other kinds of popular literature. Besides hundreds of reproductions of Posada's work, there are five important studies about his art and times: Ron Tyler's "Posada's Mexico;" Jean Charlot's "Posada and His Successors;" Jas Reuter's "The Popular Traditions;" Joyce Waddell Bailey's "The Penny Press;" and Jacques Lafaye's "From Daily Life to Eternity." Includes appendixes and index.

1363 Reyna, José. Raza humor in Texas (Revista Chicano-Riqueña [Gary, Ind.] 4:1, invierno 1976, 27–33)

Studies Chicano jests, jokes, anecdotes, ethnic slurs, idiomatic phrases, etc., and shows how they reflect a specific sociocultural reality.

1364 Robe, Stanley L. Problems of a Mexican legend index (IU/JFI, 14:3, 1977, p. 159–167)

Robe, who is engaged in preparing an index of Mexican legend materials, explains some of the problems he faces in such areas as defining and identifying legends in the Mexican context, the difficulty of adapting procedures of European legend indexes to the task at hand, etc.

1365 Romero-Flores, Jesús. Corridos de la Revolución Mexicana. México: B. Costa-Amic, 1977. 340 p., illus.

Consists of 107 *corrido* (i.e., ballad) texts without music dated between 1879–1938, not counting two that are about Romero-Flores personally. Though not so stated, this work is a reissue in more handsome format of a book published in 1941.

1366 Romero Giordano, Carlos. Somera semblanza de las artesanías mexicanas (BBAA, 37:46, 1974/1975, p. 221–223)

Discusses the importance of artisans to the Mexican economy. Stresses workers in pottery, textiles, and wood.

1367 Sandoval, Rubén. Games, games, games/juegos, juegos, juegos: Chicano children at play—games and rhymes. Garden City, New York: Doubleday, 1977. 78 p., illus.

A collection of games, rhymes, and tongue-twisters with numerous photographs to illustrate them.

1368 Scheffler, Lilian. La celebración del Día de Muertos en San Juan Totolac, Tlaxcala (Boletín del Departamento de Investigación de las Tradiciones Populares [México] 3, 1976, p. 91–103, bibl., plates)

Describes Day of the Dead customs and practices in a small town in the state of Tlaxcala.

1369 ———. Juegos tradicionales del estado de Tlaxcala. México: Departamento de Investigación de las Tradiciones Populares, Dirección General de Arte Popular, Secretaría de Educación Pública, 1976. 108 p., bibl., illus., maps, plates (Estudios de folklore y de arte popular; 3)

Studies traditional games of both children and adults in four indigenous communities in the state of Tlaxcala. Provides detailed historical and ethnographic data as background for describing and analyzing games through commentary, drawings, photographs, etc. Includes words (no music) of many songs and data on informants.

1370 Simson, Eve. Chicano street murals (Journal of Popular Culture [Bowling Green, Ohio] 10:3, Winter 1976, p. 642–652)

Analyzes Mexican-American murals in east Los Angeles, calling attention to their depiction of traditional themes and values, Aztec designs and motifs, and legendary figures. Sees the murals as a source of religious and ethnic identity.

1371 Serna-Maytorena, M.M. Del corrido mexicano: su dimensión y proyección actual (UY/R, 20:117/118, mayo/agosto 1978, p. 19–30)

Notes the important role of the *corrido* in Juan Rulfo's *El llano en llamas* and then offers a personal appreciation of the *corrido* and its place in Mexican tradition. Cites texts of some *corridos* to illustrate certain points.

1372 Shutler, Mary Elizabeth. Disease and curing in a Yaqui community (*in* Ethnic medicine in the Southwest. Edited by Edward H. Spicer. Tucson: University of Arizona Press, 1977, p. 169–237)

A study of Yaqui beliefs and practices about health and sickness with consideration of Yaqui-Hispanic medical customs and how they flourish today.

1373 Stroessner, Robert J. Folk art of Spanish New Mexico (*in* How to know

American folk art: eleven experts discuss many aspects of the field. Edited by Ruth Andrews. New York: E.P. Dutton, 1977, p. 59–82, illus.)

Studies the Spanish legacy in New Mexico's early colonial architecture, furniture, decorative techniques, carved and painted religious images (i.e., *santos*), and textiles.

1374 Taggert, James M. Metaphors and symbols of deviance in Nahuat narratives (UCLA/JLAL, 3:2, Winter 1977, p. 279–307, bibl., table)

Gives texts in English translation of three orally collected Nahuat narratives from the state of Puebla, Mexico. Seeks to interpret their meaning in terms of deviance in patrilocal extended family relations. They deal with an unfaithful wife, a disobedient son who kills his father, and three quarrelsome brothers.

1375 Talavera S., Francisco. Cuaderno de la danza de la conquista (INAH/A, 7. época, 6:54, 1976, p. 149–178, bibl., plates)

Gives the complete literary text of a dance-drama about the conquest of Mexico by Cortés that is performed on Dec. 12, the day of the Virgin of Guadalupe, in Mezcala, Jalisco, Mexico. Said to be based on old oral traditions, it was written about 50 years ago by a man who still organizes and directs the dance.

1376 Tatum, Charles M. A selected and annotated bibliography of Chicano studies. Manhattan, Kansas: Society of Spanish and Spanish American Studies, 1976. 107 p. (SSSAS Bibliographies; 101)

Includes 307 entries arranged in sections on folklore, art, music, and literature. Valuable to any student interested in Chicano studies. Contains index.

1377 Tully, Marjorie F. and **Juan B. Rael.** An annotated bibliography of Spanish folklore in New Mexico and southern Colorado. New York: Arno Press, 1977. 124 p.

Reprint of a work published in 1950. Contains 702 items on such subjects as folktales, cookery, music, ceremonies, place names, folk medicine, games, drama, etc., and an index.

1378 Turok, Marta. Diseño y símbolo en el huipil ceremonial de Magdalenas, Chiapas (Boletín del Departamento de Investigación de las Tradiciones Populares [México] 3, 1976, p. 123–136, bibl., illus., tables)

Studies the *huipil* (i.e., woman's blouse) worn in a town in the state of Chiapas. Holds that contrary to past beliefs the meaning of designs and symbols used in Mesoamerican textiles has not been lost.

1379 Valle-Arizpe, Artemio de. Historia, tradiciones y leyendas de calles de México. México: Editorial Diana, 1978. 829 p.

Literary versions of historico-legendary material about Mexico City, about 100 short pieces in all. Interesting, but its value to folklorists is limited because of the author's overriding concern for literary excellence rather than legendary authenticity.

1380 Warren, Nancy. *La Función*: village fiestas in northern New Mexico (SAR/P, 84:2, Summer 1978, p. 23–29, plates)

A photographic essay that deals with fiestas in five villages. Photographs are accompanied by a brief introduction and short descriptive captions.

1381 Weigle, Marta. Brothers of light, brothers of blood: the Penitentes of the Southwest: Albuquerque: University of New Mexico Press, 1976. 300 p., bibl., illus., maps.

A comprehensive overview of *Los Hermanos Penitentes*, a lay religious society comprised of Hispanic men and having its headquarters in Santa Fe, New Mexico. Traces the history of the Brotherhood, describes its organization and rituals, and briefly discusses some legends and beliefs about ghostly Penitentes. Includes appendixes and index.

1382 ———. Ghostly flagellants and Doña Sebastiana: two legends of the Penitente Brotherhood (CFS/WF, 36:2, April 1977, p. 135–147, plate)

From 19th and 20th-century sources the author draws information about the Brothers of Our Father Jesus, commonly known as the Penitentes of northern New Mexico and southern Colorado. Discusses primarily beliefs concerning revenants who take part in the penitential processions and carved figures that represent death. These are known as Doña Sebastiana.

1383 ———. *comp.* A Penitente bibliography. Albuquerque: University of New Mexico Press, 1976. 162 p.

An annotated bibliography that supplements the author's book on a Hispanic folk religious group, the Penitentes. See item **1381**.

1384 **Winn, Robert K.** V.J.M. y J.: Viva Jesús, María y José: a celebration of the birth of Jesus: Mexican folk art and toys from the Collection of Robert K. Winn. Foreword by Everett H. Jones. Photos by Michael J. Smith. San Antonio: Trinity University Press, 1977. 103 p., bibl., illus.

Presents Robert K. Winn's collection of Mexican religious folk art through a beautiful display of photographs and commentaries.

1385 **Zaldívar Guerra, María Luisa.** Santa Apolonia Teacalco: un pueblo canastero. México: Departamento de Investigación de las Tradiciones Populares, Dirección General de Arte Popular, Secretaría de Educación Pública, 1976. 80 p., bibl., illus., plates, tables (Estudios de folklore y de arte popular; 2)

Studies basket-weaving in a town in the state of Tlaxcala, Mexico. Gives an ethnography of the community and then analyzes materials and techniques, types of baskets, etc.

PARAGUAY

1386 **Martínez-Crovetto, Raúl.** Folklore toba oriental: pt. 1, Los tabúes menstruales (UCNSA/SA, 9:1/2, dic. 1976, p. 139–149)

Discusses various taboos about menstruation found among the Tobas who live in the Chaco area. Explains the beliefs or seeks information about such matters as their origin, tales related to them, etc.

1387 **Ruiz Rivas de Domínguez, Celia.** Danzas tradicionales paraguayas: métodos de enseñanza. Asunción: Imprenta *Makografic,* 1974. 318 p., bibl., illus.

Discusses folklore and its relationship to dance and then surveys the history of dancing in Paraguay. With Chap. 4 begins a detailed descriptive survey of different traditional dances complete with diagrams and drawings to show choreography. Also includes brief sections on dress and fiestas and a comprehensive bibliography.

PERU

1388 **Alarco, Rosa.** Danza de "Los Negritos de Huánuco" (San Marcos [Lima] 13, oct./dic. 1975, p. 55–96, bibl., music, plates)

An ethnographic and historical study of a dance performed in Huánuco that represents the life of black slaves during the colonial period of Peru.

1389 **Alma serrana: más de 200 huaynos peruanos.** Lima: Producciones Ermes, Distribuidora Rivera, 197? 224 p., illus. (Los Exitos del folklore serrano)

A *cancionero* with words only of some Peruvian *huaynos.* Some are probably traditional songs.

1390 **Arguedas, José María.** Señores e indios: acerca de la cultura quechua. Introducción de Angel Rama. Montevideo: Arca Editorial, 1976? 259 p.

Consists of 38 articles by Arguedas published between 1940–69 and dealing with his vision of the Indian and his culture. Most treat various aspects of folklore: e.g., fiestas, rites, dances, myths, songs, etc. Angel Rama provides an excellent introduction about Arguedas as a literary artist. For anthropologist's comment, see *HLAS 41:1277.*

1391 **Arteaga León, Arcadio.** Mitos y leyendas andinos. Lima: n.p., 1976. 30 p.

Literary versions of a collection of 28 tales and legends collected in the province of Canta by a primary schoolteacher.

1392 **Bernal, Dionicio Rodolfo.** La muliza: teorías e investigaciones, origen y realidad folklórica, su técnica literaria y musical: folklore del Perú. 2. ed. corregida y aumentada. Lima: G. Herrera Editores, 1978. 269 p., bibl., illus., music.

First published in 1947. An introductory study traces the history of the *muliza* of Cerro de Pasco, a type of traditional song, and seeks to establish its relationship to Hispanic tradition. A collection of texts (some with music) and a chapter about the *mulizas* of Tarma, also with some representative texts, complete the work.

1393 Black rainbow: legends of the Incas and myths of ancient Peru. Edited and translated by John Bierhorst. New York: Farrar, Straus and Giroux, 1976. 131 p., illus.

A very superficial introduction deals with the Incas and their legends and leads into an anthology of legends, myths, fables, and animal tales, mostly old ones taken from various Spanish sources. All are translated into literary English. Of very limited value.

1394 Bolton, Charlene and **Ralph Bolton.** Rites of retribution and restoration in Canchis (UCLA/JLAL, 2:1, 1976, p. 97–114, bibl., tables)

Describes and analyzes comparatively the Earth Payment Ritual and the Enclosure Ritual as performed by a shamaness in the Cuzco region of southern Peru. They were performed in order to protect the authors themselves against robbery or other harm.

1395 Brown, Michael F. Notas sobre la chonguinada de Junín (III/AI, 36:2, abril/junio 1976, p. 375–384, bibl.)

Studies a dance from the provinces of Junín and Tarma that fuses colonial and prehispanic traditions. Describes it and discusses such matters as its organization, its function as a mechanism for social integration, etc.

1396 Calderón, Eduardo and **Douglas Sharon.** Terapia de la curandería. Trujillo, Perú: Edigraf, 1976. 135 p.

Sharon publishes here tapes of conversations he held with Calderón, a *curandero* from northern Peru. In the first person the latter discusses illnesses, folk cures, rituals, etc. He is, however, an educated *curandero* who talks about modern medicine, psychosomatic illnesses, and the like. For another work about Calderón, see item **1404**.

Carlin Arce, Jorge. Antología documental del Departamento de Tumbes. See *HLAS 41:1288*.

1397 Caycho Jiménez, Abraham. Folklore médico y fitoalucinismo en el Perú (IPGH/FA, 23, junio 1977, p. 89–100)

Discusses traditional medicine and the use of hallucinogenic drugs among certain Peruvian groups. Provides a descriptive list of drugs so used with emphasis on their biomedical aspects. Ends with a glossary of terms.

1398 Chang-Rodríguez, Raquel. Tapadas limeñas en un cancionerillo peruano del siglo XVII (RIB, 28:1, enero/marzo 1978, p. 57–62)

Notes efforts of Spanish authorities to suppress the practice of colonial *limeñas* of covering themselves so completely with clothes and shawls that only one eye was visible. Then gives texts of three poems from a song-book that satirize the custom. One is a semi-popular *romance*.

Congreso Nacional de Folklorólogos, *I, Huancayo, Perú, 1972*. Actas. See *HLAS 39:1446*.

1399 Crumrine, N. Ross. The Peruvian pilgrimage: a ritual drama (OAS/AM, 30:8, Aug. 1978, p. 28–34, map, plates)

Gives basic information about three important centers of religious pilgrimage in Peru, all south of Lima: Yauca, San Pedro de Grocio Prado, and Humay.

1400 Cuentos folklóricos de los achual. Compiled by Gerhard Fast Mowitz. Yarinacocha, Perú: Instituto Lingüístico de Verano *bajo convenio con el* Ministerio de Educación, 1976. 242 p., illus. (Comunidades y culturas peruanas; 3)

Consists of 29 field-collected texts from the Achual people who live in the province of Alto Amazonas, Department of Loreto. Texts are in the Indian language with Spanish translations. Most are not really tales. Probably more valuable for folklorists interested in beliefs and customs than for folktale scholars.

1401 D'Ans, André-Marcel. La verdadera biblia de los cashinahua: mitos, leyendas y tradiciones de la selva peruana. Traducción del francés de Hermis Campodónico Carrión. Lima: Mosca Azul Editores, 1975. 351 p.

A collection of myths, tales, and legends of the Cashinahua people of Peru. Though collected from oral tradition, the narratives are rewritten here in literary form. Includes glossary.

1402 Flores Ochoa, Jorge A. *Enqa, Enqaychu, Illa* y *Khuya Rumi*: aspectos mágico-religiosos entre pastores (UCLA/JLAL, 2:1, 1976, p. 115–134, bibl., table)

Surveys and explains various propitiatory beliefs and ceremonies that are found among shepherds in the Puna Alta region of Peru. Includes good bibliography.

1403 Gómez G., Rodolfo A. Padre e hijo: narraciones arequipeñas. Arequipa, Perú: Imp. Editorial El Sol, 1977. 425 p., illus., music.

Newspaper articles about Arequipa's past written by Rodolfo Gómez G. and his father Domingo Gómez. Neither was a folklorist, but they touch on certain customs and practices dealt with in few other places: e.g., Carnival customs and songs, nicknames, regional food and drink, etc.

1404 Gushiken, José. Tuno: el curandero. Lima: Universidad Nacional Mayor de San Marcos, Seminario de Historia Rural Andina, 1977. 165 p. (mimeo)

An anthropological study of such matters as methods used by *curanderos* in Peru, witchcraft, and various psychic phenomena. Based in large part on fieldwork with a *curandero* named Eduardo Calderón. For a later work about Calderón, see also item **1396**.

1405 Ibáñez, Nito. Salas, Incahuasi, Penachí en la novelesca vida de los brujos. Lima: Offet-Tipografía, 1977. 138 p., plates.

A literary evocation of certain aspects of life in Salas, Department of Lambayeque, Peru, particularly beliefs about witchcraft and practices related to it. Not scholarly and the information is diffuse, but some of it is of interest to folklorists.

1406 Isbell, Billie Jean and **Fredy Amílcar Roncalla Fernández.** The ontogenesis of metaphor: riddle games among Quechua speakers seen as cognitive discovery procedures (UCLA/JLAL, 3:1, Summer, 1977, p. 19–49, bibl.)

An absorbing analysis of Quechua riddles collected in several communities in the Department of Ayacucho, Peru. Studies topics like their social context, social dynamics, structure, metaphors, etc.

1407 Matto de Turner, Clorinda. Tradiciones cuzqueñas completas. Lima: Ediciones Peisa, 1976. 204 p.

Consists of 57 literary pieces written around 1870–80 by the well known novelist-newspaperwoman Clorinda Matto de Turner. Some contain folklore since they are based on historico-legendary material.

1408 Merino de Zela, E. Mildred. Folklore coreográfico e historia (IPGH/FA, 24, dic. 1977, p. 67–94)

Hypothesizes that it is possible to establish a chronological sequence in the content of Peruvian dances that deal with historical themes. Seeks to show the value of choreographic studies as an aid to the understanding of history.

1409 Millikan, Louise C. A joyful art: the crafts of Peru (OAS/AM, 30:11/12, Nov./Dec. 1978, p. 49–54, plates)

Text and photographs offer some basic information about traditional arts and crafts in Peru: e.g., articles made of wool, ceramics, etc.

1410 Mitchell, Fergus, Jr. The foxes in José María Arguedas' last novel (AATSP/H, 61:1, March 1978, p. 46–56)

Analyzes the Peruvian novel, *El Zorro de arriba y el zorro de abajo* (*The fox from above and the fox from below*), the last work of Arguedas, famed as a novelist and folklorist. The two foxes are magic characters from an ancient Quechua myth whom Arguedas incorporates into his novel placed in contemporary Peru.

1411 Powlison, Paul. Bosquejo de la cultura yagua (IPGH/FA, 24, dic. 1977, p. 33–65)

A detailed study of the Yagua Indians who live on the Colombian border with Peru. Describes their subsistence activities, political organization, economy, medicine, fiestas, aesthetic and recreational activities, religion, and cosmology.

1412 Primer Congreso Interprovincial de Folklore y Concurso de Danzas (IPGH/FA, 20, junio/dic. 1975, p. 176–178)

Reports on a congress sponsored by the Univ. Nacional Federico Villarreal that took place in the city of Quichés, Ancash, Peru, 1–15 Sept. 1975.

1413 Químisha Yohuan Xení: cuentos folklóricos de los capanahua. Edited and translated by Thelma Schoolland. Yarinacocha, Perú: Instituto Lingüístico de Verano *elaborado bajo convenio con el* Ministerio de Educación, 976. 34 p. (Comunidades y culturas peruanas; 6)

Contains orally collected texts of three Capanahua folktales from the Amazonian region of Peru. Translations into Spanish are also provided. See also *HLAS 41: 1415.*

1414 **Shaver, Harold.** Los campa-nomatsiguenga de la Amazonia peruana y su cosmología (IPGH/FA, 20, julio/dic. 1975, p. 49–53)

A brief summary of some of the cosmological beliefs of a group that lives in the southern part of the central Andean region of Peru.

1415 **Smith, Robert Jerome.** A legend-set of Greece and Peru (*in* Folklore today, a festschrift for Richard M. Dorson. Edited by Linda Dégh, Henry Glassie, and Felix J. Oinas. Bloomington: Research Center for Language and Semiotic Studies, Indiana University, 1976, p. 463–472)

Points out similarities in saints' legends collected from Greek and Peruvian traditions, showing that two texts are related by patterns of association (or legend-sets) which reveal the world view of the informants.

1416 **Torre López, Fernando.** Notas etnográficas sobre el grupo anti o campa de la Amazona Peruana (IPGH/FA, 25, junio 1978, p. 43–71)

An ethnographic survey of the folklife and material culture of the Anti or Campa Indians of the Amazon region of Peru.

1417 **Weiss, Gerald.** Rhetoric in Campa narrative (IPGH/FA, 3:2, Winter 1977, p. 169–182, bibl., table)

Calls attention to various rhetorical devices used in narrating myths and other tales by the Campa people of the Montaña region of Perú. Analyzes their use descriptively and also quantitatively and compares them to similar rhetorical devices found in Western culture.

Zelenka, Georg. Das Fest der Virgen del Carmen in Paucartambo. See *HLAS 39:1583.*

URUGUAY

1418 **Assunçao, Fernando O.** Pilchas criollas. Ilustraciones de Federico Reilly. Montevideo: Edición de la Comisión Nacional de Homenaje del Sesquicentenario de los Hechos Históricos de 1825, 1976. 429 p., bibl., illus.

A large and handsome volume dedicated to a study of specifically Uruguayan gaucho traditions as distinguished from Argentine or Brazilian practices. The paintings by Reilly, some in full color, are superb. Assunçao's commentary describes gaucho life from mainly a historical perspective. Includes a great deal of folklore (e.g., customs, linguistic and material lore, particularly gaucho clothing and trappings, etc.). Includes index.

VENEZUELA

1419 **Acosta Saignes, Miguel.** El llanero en su copla. Caracas: Coorpoimpro, 1979. 9 p.

A brief sketch about the Venezuelan *llanero*'s life. Includes some texts of traditional songs.

1420 **Almoina de Carrera, Pilar.** Diez romances hispanos en la tradición oral venezolana. Caracas: Universidad Central de Venezuela, Facultad de Humanidades y Educación, Instituto de Investigaciones Literarias, 1975. 137 p.

An ed. with commentary of 41 *romance* texts representing 15 different panhispanic ballad text-types that are still found in Venezuelan oral tradition. Includes also an introduction that surveys Venezuelan ballad fieldwork and scholarship.

1421 **Aretz, Isabel.** El traje del venezolano. Caracas, Monte Avila Editores, 1977. 287 p., bibl., plates.

Combines text and innumerable photographs to produce a scholarly descriptive and historical survey of Venezuelan dress. Includes sections on Indian and European dress with numerous subdivisions. A basic book on the subject.

1422 **Domínguez, Luis Arturo.** Documentos para el estudio del folklore literario de Venezuela. San José: Talleres Gráficos de Trejos Hnos., 1976. 237 p., bibl. (Serie de folklore del IPGH. Colección Documentos; 2)

A large collection of orally collected texts of folktales, legends, humorous tales, songs, lullabies, riddles, dramas, proverbs, sayings, popular speech, etc. Includes complete informant data, tale-type numbers, a glossary, and bibliography. Lacks, however, any kind of introduction or explanation of procedures.

1423 ———. Encuentro con nuestro folklore. Caracas: Editorial Kapeluz Venezolana, 1975. 167 p., maps, plates.

A comprehensive book on Venezuelan folklore intended primarily for classroom use. In sections on material folklore, social folklore (e.g., fiestas, games, etc.), and spiritual-mental folklore (e.g., songs, tales, proverbs, riddles, superstitions, etc.), the author touches on practically all types of Venezuelan folklore. Includes appendixes.

1424 ———. Rafael Olivares Figueroa, 1893–1972: precursor de los estudios de folklore en Venezuela (IPGH/FA, 21, junio 1976, p. 63–94, bibl., plate)

A literary appreciation of the work of Olivares Figueroa as a poet, essayist, pedagogue, etc. Includes a short section on his contributions to the study of Venezuelan folklore.

1425 **García Tamayo, Malula.** En pos del folklore II. Barquisimeto, Venezuela: Departamento de Extensión, Instituto Universitario Pedagógico Experimental, 1978. 101 p.

A miscellany of brief notes on many aspects of Venezuelan folklore: e.g., regional dishes, fiestas, legends, dances, proverbs, songs, traditional furniture, games, witchcraft, etc. Unscholarly but provides information not easily found elsewhere.

1426 **Gonzáles, Norma** and **Luis Zelkowics.** Breves notas en torno a la funcionalidad de la décima en la poesía venezolana (IPGH/FA, 25, junio 1978, p. 119–123)

Brief comments on the Venezuelan *décima* and its aesthetic functions. Includes a few texts.

1427 **Juárez Toledo, J. Manuel.** Música tradicional de los yucpa-irapa del Estado Zulia, Venezuela (IPGH/FA, 26, dic. 1978. p. 59–81, bibl., music, plates)

An ethnomusicological and sociological study of field-collected songs of the Yucpa-Irapa subgroup of the Yucpa culture. The description and analysis are organized around the life cycle. Includes some texts and also musical examples.

1428 **Key-Ayala, Santiago.** Los nombres de las esquinas de Caracas: tradiciones y tradicionistas; contribucion al folklore venezolano. Caracas: Ediciones de la Presidencia de la República, 1976. 34 p., illus.

New ed. of a work first published in 1926. Reviews the names of a large number of streets in Caracas and explains the origins of many. Some are related to folklore or old local traditions.

1429 **Machado, José E.** Centón lírico. 2. ed. Caracas: Ediciones de la Presidencia de la República, 1976. 260 p.

New ed. of a work originally written in 1918–19. Although not done with modern methods of scholarship, it is important as a collection of many popular songs (words without music) from the early 19th century. Most are historical in nature. Includes index.

1430 **Perrin, Michel.** Le chemin des indiens morts: mythes et symboles goajiro. Paris: Payot, 1976. 268 p., bibl., map, plates, tables.

Gives French versions of tape-recorded myths and other narratives about death and the afterlife gathered among the Guajiro Indians of Venezuela. The second part of the work contains an analysis of Guajiro beliefs about these subjects and some thoughts on the present status of this isolated tribe that is increasingly under pressure to become acculturated to modern civilization. Includes index.

Pollak-Eltz, Angelina. Bibliografía afrovenezolana. See *HLAS 40:26*.

1431 ———. Indianische Relikte im Volksglauben der Venezolaner (IAI/I, 34, 1975, p. 133–145, bibl.)

Comments upon syncretism of Indian and Hispanic elements in the culture of mestizos in rural Venezuela. Examines religious beliefs and practices, tales and myths, popular medicine, magic rites, shamanism, the cult of María Lionza, etc.

1432 **Ramón y Rivera, Luis Felipe.** La música popular de Venezuela. Caracas: Ernesto Armitano Editor, 1976. 207 p., bibl., illus., music, plates.

A handsome book about "popular" music in Venezuela by the country's most distinguished folklorist. Deals with songs or dances such as waltzes, *pasillos, bambucos, contradanzas*, etc., genres that are "popular" rather than folkloric, though the lines of distinction are often blurred. Includes excellent photographs and many musical transcriptions. For musicologist's comment, see item **7162**.

1433 Unceín Tamayo, Luis Alberto. Folklore histórico de Venezuela: pts. 1/2 (CIF/FA, 20, junio/dic. 1975, p. 7–34; 21, junio 1976, p. 7–32)

Though rambling and diffuse, this two-part article contains interesting information. Pt. 1 discusses folklore during the colonial period (e.g., *coplas*, the *Baile de los Enanitos*, ecclesiastical attitudes toward dances and fiestas, etc.). Pt. 2 treats such topics as the celebration of Corpus Christi in Trujillo, the devils of Yare, Indian hair styles, regional recipes, and dances like the *burriquita*.

1434 Wilbert, Johannes. Geography and telluric lore of the Orinoco delta (UCLA/JLAL, 5:1, Summer 1979, p. 129–150, bibl., maps, plate)

Among other things, analyzes and interprets an origin myth of the Warao Indians of Venezuela.

JOURNAL ABBREVIATIONS FOLKLORE

AAA/AA American Anthropologist. American Anthropological Association. Washington.

AAA/AE American Ethnologist. American Anthropological Association. Washington.

AAFH/TAM The Americas. A quarterly publication of inter-American cultural history. Academy of American Franciscan History. Washington.

AATSP/H Hispania. American Association of Teachers of Spanish and Portuguese. Univ. of Cincinnati, Ohio.

AFS/JAF Journal of American Folklore. American Folklore Society. Austin, Tex.

AM/R Revista do Arquivo Municipal. Prefeitura do Município de São Paulo, Depto. Municipal de Cultura. São Paulo.

AMNH/NH Natural History. American Museum of Natural History. New York.

ANH/B Boletín de la Academia Nacional de Historia. Buenos Aires.

ARMEX Artes de México. Revista bimestral. México.

ASB/PP Philologica Pragensia. Academia Scientiarum Bohemoslovenica. Praha.

ASHSH/B Bulletin de l'Académie des Sciences Humaines et Sociales d'Haiti. Port-au-Prince.

BBAA B.B.A.A. Boletín Bibliográfico de Antropología Americana. Instituto Panamericano de Geografía e Historia, Comisión de Historia. México.

BRP Beiträge zur Romanischen Philologie. Rütten & Loening. Berlin.

CDFB/RBF Revista Brasileira de Folclore. Ministério da Educação e Cultura, Campanha de Defesa do Folclore Brasileiro. Rio.

CEEP/RD Revista de Dialectología y Tradiciones Populares. Centro de Estudios de Etnología Peninsular, Depto. de Dialectología y Tradiciones Populares del Consejo Superior de Investigaciones Científicas. Madrid.

CER/C Cuadrante. Centro de Estudios Regionales. Tucumán, Arg.

CFS/WF Western Folklore. Univ. of California Press *for the* California Folklore Society. Berkeley.

CIF/FA *See* IPGH/FA.

CSIC/A Asclepio. Consejo Superior de Investigaciones Científicas, Instituto Arnau de Vilanova de Historia de la Medicina, Archivo Iberoamericano de Historia de la Medicina y Antropología Médica. Madrid.

IAI/I Indiana. Beiträge zur Volker-und Sprachenkunde, Archäologie und Anthropologie des Indianischen Amerika. Ibero-Amerikanisches Institut. Berlin, FRG.

ICC/T Thesaurus. Boletín del Instituto Caro y Cuervo. Bogotá.

III/AI América Indígena. Instituto Indigenista Interamericano. México.

IILI/RI Revista Iberoamericana. Instituto Internacional de Literatura Iberoamericana *patrocinada por la* Univ. de Pittsburgh, Pa.

INAH/A Anales del Instituto Nacional de Antropología e Historia. Secretaría de Educación Pública. México.

INC/PH Patrimonio Histórico. Instituto Nacional de Cultura, Dirección del Patrimonio Histórico. Panamá.

IPGH/FA Folklore Americano. Instituto Panamericano de Geografía e Historia, Comisión de Historia, Comité de Folklore. México. (formerly CIF/FA)

IU/JFI Journal of the Folklore Institute. Indiana University. Bloomington.

MEC/C Cultura. Ministério da Educação e Cultura, Diretoria de Documentação e Divulgação. Brasília.

MHD/B Boletín del Museo del Hombre Dominicano. Santo Domingo.

MNDJG/A Anales del Museo Nacional David J. Guzmán. San Salvador.

NHAC/K Kaie. National History and Arts Council of Guyana. Georgetown.

OAS/AM Américas. Organization of American States. Washington.

PCCLAS/P Proceedings of the Pacific Coast Council on Latin American Studies. Univ. of California. Los Angeles.

RIB Revista Interamericana de Bibliografía [Inter-American Review of Bibliography]. Organization of American States. Washington.

SAA/R Relaciones de la Sociedad Argentina de Antropología. Buenos Aires.

SAR/P El Palacio. School of American Research, Museum of New Mexico [and] Archaeological Society of New Mexico. Santa Fe.

UA/U Universidad. Univ. de Antioquia. Medellín, Colombia.

UASD/U Universo. Univ. Autónoma de Santo Domingo, Facultad de Humanidades. Santo Domingo.

UC/AT Atenea. Revista de ciencias, letras y artes. Univ. de Concepción, Chile.

UC/BF Boletiń de Filología. Univ. de Chile, Instituto de Filología. Santiago.

UC/CA Current Anthropology. Univ. of Chicago, Ill.

UCIEM/R Revista Musical Chilena. Univ. de Chile, Instituto de Extensión Musical. Santiago.

UCL/LR Les Lettres Romanes. Univ. Catholique de Louvain, Fondation Universitaire de Belgique. Louvain, Belgium.

UCLA/JLAL Journal of Latin American Lore. Univ. of California, Latin American Center. Los Angeles.

UCLV/I Islas. Univ. Central de las Villas. Santa Clara, Cuba.

UCNSA/SA Suplemento Antropológico. Univ. Católica de Nuestra Señora de la Asunción, Centro de Estudios Antropológicos. Asunción.

UCR/R Revista de la Universidad de Costa Rica. San José.

UCSD/NS The New Scholar. Univ. of California, Center for Iberian and Latin American Studies [and] Institute of Chicano Urban Affairs. San Diego.

UCV/S Signos. Estudios de lengua y literatura. Univ. Católica de Valparaíso, Instituto de Literatura y Ciencia del Lenguaje. Valparaíso, Chile.

UFP/EB Estudos Brasileiros. Univ. Federal do Paraná, Setor de Ciências Humanas, Centro de Estudos Brasileiros. Curitiba.

UFP/RL Revista Letras. Univ. Federal do Paraná, Setor de Ciências Humanas, Letras e Artes. Curitiba.

UH/U Universidad de La Habana. La Habana.

UIA/C Comunidad. Revista de la U.I.A. Cuadernos de difusión cultural. Univ. Iberoamericana. México.

UNC/AAE Anales de Arqueología y Etnología. Univ. Nacional de Cuyo, Facultad de Filosofía y Letras. Mendoza, Arg.

UNTIA/R Revista del Instituto de Antropología. Univ. Nacional de Tucumán. San Miguel de Tucumán, Arg.

UP/E Ethnology. Univ. of Pittsburgh, Pa.

UPR/CS Caribbean Studies. Univ. of Puerto Rico, Institute of Caribbean Studies. Río Piedras.

USCG/TP La Tradición Popular. Univ. de San Carlos de Guatemala, Centro de Estudios Folklóricos. Guatemala.

UWI/CQ Caribbean Quarterly. Univ. of the West Indies. Mona, Jam.

UY/R Revista de la Universidad de Yucatán. Mérida, Mex.

HISTORY

ETHNOHISTORY: Mesoamerica

EDWARD E. CALNEK, *Associate Professor of Anthropology, The University of Rochester*

STUDIES OF SOCIOPOLITICAL ORGANIZATION and religion among the Nahua-speaking peoples of late prehispanic and early colonial-period, central Mexico were particularly abundant during the past two years. Prem's meticulously, detailed analysis of changing land tenure institutions in the Alto Atoyac region of Puebla, Mexico (item **1562**), together with Hicks' reassessment of the administrative system developed by the Texcocan emperor, Nezahualcóyotl (item **1540**), illustrate the main concerns of specialists who have chosen to concentrate on political and economic documentation. The several papers in *Economía política e ideología en el México prehispánico*, edited by Carrasco and Broda (item **1528**), argue for a greater complexity of preconquest societies than was assumed by most archaeologists and ethnohistorians until very recent years. Incidentally, the contributions by Broda and Erdheim demonstrate that religious ideologies actively shaped social realities, and were by no means merely "determined" by the supposedly *hard facts* of ecology and economic life (items **1513** and **1530**).

There is, on the other hand, a notable decline in contributions by archaeologists and other Mesoamericanists who, until recently, were actively involved in research which combined the data and theoretical interests of various related disciplines with ethnohistorical documentation. There is no clear reason why this growing tendency towards sub-specialization should have developed in the last five to 10 years, especially in a notably broad and open field such as Mesoamerican studies. Whether this trend will continue or whether it *should* continue, are questions which cannot, of course, be determined until the research interests of the many new scholars entering the field are better known.

1501 Acuña, René. Calendarios antiguos del altiplano de México y su correlación con los calendarios mayas (UNAM/ECN, 12, 1976, p. 279–314), bibl., table)

Attempts to coordinate lists of month names available both for central Mexico and the Maya region.

1502 Arizpe Scholesser, Lourdes. Un cuento y una canción náhuat de la sierra de Puebla (UNAM/ECN, 13, 1978, p. 289–299)

Text and translation of Nahuatl myth collected in the Sierra de Puebla in 1970, dealing with the origin of differences between Indians and mestizos.

1503 Ballesteros Gaibrois, Manuel. El lienzo de Tlaxcalla de la Casa de Colón de Valladolid. Valladolid. Spain: Casa-Museo de Colón, 1977. 15 p.; bibl.; 4 leaves of plates: ill.

Short preliminary description of early version of Tlaxcalla *lienzo* possibly prepared at instigation of Ramírez de Funleal or Viceroy Mendoza in 1530s.

1504 Bastarrachea Manzano, Juan Ramón. El sistema de parentesco entre los mayas peninsulares del siglo XVI (UY/R, 20:119, sept./oct. 1978, p. 11–22)

Brief review of kinship terms and documentary evidence relating to marriage, descent, and residence patterns in 16th-century Yucatan.

1505 Baudot, Georges. Fray Andrés de Olmos y su *Tratado de los pecados mortales* en lengua náhuatl (UNAM/ECN, 12, 1976, p. 33–59)

First publication of Nahuatl text and Spanish translation of missionary text composed by Olmos in 1551–1552, with brief outline of significance and content.

1506 ———. Un *Huehuetlatolli* desconocido de la Biblioteca Nacional de México (UNAM/ECN, 13, 1978, p. 69–87)

First publication of Nahuatl text and Spanish translation of address delivered by an older lord to a newly elected ruler, together with brief but useful introductory analysis by the author.

———. Utopie et historie au Mexique: les premiers chroniqueurs de la civilisation mexicaine, 1520–1589. See item **2012**.

1507 Berdan, Frances F. Distributive mechanisms in the aztec economy (*in* Peasant livelihood: studies in economic anthropology and cultural ecology. Edited by Rhoda Halperin and James Dow. New York: St. Martin's Press, 1977, p. 91–101)

Synoptic study of role of tribute, claimed to be a form of redistribution; foreign trade, said to be a form of reciprocity; and marketplace exchange in overall economic structure of Aztec empire.

1508 ———. Enculturation in an imperial society: the Aztec of Mexico (*in* Enculturation in Latin America: an anthology [see *HLAS 41:260*, p. 237–264, bibl., ill., tables)

Describes educational methods employed by Aztecs of Tenochtitlan and allied cities to teach skills and enculcate values deemed useful by the state at each of several levels of social differentiation.

1509 ———. La organización del tributo en el imperio azteca (UNAM/ECN, 12, 1976, p. 185–195, bibl.)

Outlines main characteristics of tribute system developed by Triple Alliance of Tenochtitlan, Texcoco, and Tlacopan, emphasizing close connections with complexly structured economic system of the "Aztec empire" as a whole.

1510 ———. Replicación de principios de intercambio en la sociedad mexica: de la economía a la religión (*in* Economía política e ideología en el México prehispánico [see item **1528**] p. 175–193, bibl.).

Brief review of ways in which modern social systems theory is useful for analysis of relations between economy, sociopolitical organization, and religious organization among the Mexica.

1511 ———. Tres formas de intercambio en la economía azteca (*in* Economía política e ideología en el México prehispánico [see item **1528**] p. 77–95, bibl.)

Describes trade, tribute, and market exchange in Aztec society from general standpoint of Karl Polanyi's theoretical interpretation.

1512 Broda, Johanna. Algunas notas sobre crítica de fuentes del México antiguo (IGFO/RI, 35:139/142, enero/dic. 1975, p. 123–165, tables)

Clearly written study of relations between primary and secondary sources dealing with late prehispanic Mesoamerica. Emphasizes need for higher standards of critical scholarship.

1513 ———. Consideraciones sobre historiografía e ideología mexicas: las crónicas indígenas y el estudio de los ritos y sacrificios (UNAM/ECN, 13, 1978, p. 97–111, bibl.)

Emphasizes ideological and religious functions and significance of certain mythlike interpolations in earlier Mexica historical texts.

———. Cosmovisión y estructura de poder en el México prehispánico. See *HLAS 41:274*.

1514 ———. Relaciones políticas ritualizadas: el ritual como expresión de una ideología (*in* Economía política e ideología en el México prehispánico [see item **1528**] p. 211–255)

Describes ceremonial activities by Aztec ruler, nobility, and other functionaries which express relations of domination and subordination characteristic of this strongly centralized political system.

1515 ———. El tributo en trajes guerreros y la estructura del sistema tributario mexica (*in* Economía política e ideología en el México prehispánico [see item **1528**] p. 115–174, bibl., ill., maps, tables)

Outstanding study of tributes consisting of warrior dress, shields, and ornamentation illustrated in *Matrícula de Tributos* and *Códice Mendocino.* Notes effects of tribute system on productive organization in subject provinces, and connections with elite social organization and ideology in the imperial center.

1516 Calnek, Edward E. The analysis of prehispanic central Mexican historical texts (UNAM/ECN, 13, 1978, p. 239–265, bibl., ill., tables)

Outlines potentially useful but not yet adequately tested for relating historical records committed to writing in colonial times to preconquest pictorial-glyphic manuscripts and oral texts.

1517 ———. El sistema de mercado en Tenochtitlan (*in* Economía política e ideología en el México prehispánico [see item **1528**] p. 97–114, bibl.)

Argues that economic development of Aztec capital, Tenochtitlan, powerfully influenced by strongly entrenched patterns of market-oriented commodity production, which still outweighed state-dominated sectors based on reallocation of tributary goods among social elites at time of Spanish conquest.

1518 Carrasco, Pedro. Las bases sociales del politeismo mexicano: los dioses tutelares (*in* International Congress of Americanists, XLII, Paris, 1976. Actes [see *HLAS 41:255*] v. 6, p. 11–17, bibl.)

Notes apparent concordance between certain aspects of preconquest social organization and religious pantheon.

1519 ———. La economía del México prehispánico (*in* Economía política e ideología en el México prehispánico [see item **1528**] p. 13–76, bibl.)

Emphasizes great complexity of late prehispanic economic system. Provides detailed summary of documentary evidence relating to Aztec-period economies to support view that state-centered redistributive apparatus predominated over *private enterprise* in determining main patterns of economic growth.

1520 ———. La jerarquía cívico-religiosa de las comunidades mesoamericanas: antecedentes prehispánicos y desarrollo colonial (UNAM/ECN, 12, 1976, p. 165–183, bibl.)

First publication in Spanish of Carrasco's important study of the civil-religious hierarchy in Mesoamerica which previously appeared in the *American Anthropologist* (v. 63, 1961).

1521 Castillo F., Víctor M. Aspectos económicos en las fuentes de tradición indígena: uso y aprovechamiento historiográfico (UNAM/ECN, 12, 1976, p. 155–163, bibl.)

Describes types of economic data available in various types of indigenous source materials, and degree to which these have been utilized by modern investigators.

1522 Davies, Nigel. Mixcoatl: man and god (*in* International Congress of Americanists, XLII, Paris, 1976. Actes [see *HLAS 41:255*] v. 6, p. 19–26, bibl.)

Outlines main aspects of god Mixcoatl noting relationship to both hunting and agriculture. Suggests that the warrior-hero of same name lived long after main characteristics of deity defined in religious sense.

1523 Dávila Bolaños, Alejandro. Calendarios indígenas de Nicaragua y sus relaciones con el santoral católico (BNBD, 22, marzo/abril 1978, p. 1–25)

Attempts to show that preconquest calendar transposed to forms which still regulate Catholic religious festivals for "the immense majority of the Nicaraguan people." Useful compilation of calendar-related data available for Nicaragua for all times up to the present.

1524 Dehouve, Danièle. Dos relatos sobre migraciones nahuas en el estado de Guerrero (UNAM/ECN, 12, 1976, p. 137–154, table)

Reproduces Spanish and Nahuatl texts from Ocotequila and Xalatzala which describe late prehispanic and early colonial migrations by Nahua-speaking peoples into Tlapanec region.

1525 Durand-Forest, Jacqueline de. Sistema de fechamiento en Chimalpahin (UNAM/ECN, 12, 1976, p. 265–277)

Shows that despite minor difficulties, the Chimalpahin texts dealing specifically with Tenochcan chronology are internally consistent and compatible with current understandings of central Mexican calendrical systems.

1526 ———. Tlaloc: dieu au double visage (*in* International Congress of Americanists, XLII, Paris, 1976. Actes [see *HLAS 41:255*] v. 6, p. 119–126, bibl.)

Reviews ceremonies, origin myth, and related calendrical data associated with Tlaloc.

1527 Duverger, Christian. La fleur létale: économie du sacrifice aztèque. Paris: Editions du Seuil, 1979. 249 p.; bibl.; ill. (Recherches anthropologiques)

Highly original and carefully documented study of human sacrifice conceived as the principal motor force involved in development of Aztec civilization.

1528 Economía política e ideología en el México prehispánico. Editores: Pedro Carrasco y Johanna Broda. México: Editorial Nueva Imagen [and] Instituto Nacional de Antropología e Historia, Centro de Investigaciones Superiores, 1978. 270 p.; bibl.; ill.; maps, tables.

Seven important papers dealing primarily with economic organization and politico-religious ideology in the late prehispanic central Mexico. For individual reviews of these articles see items **1510–1511, 1514–1515, 1517, 1519** and **1530**.

1529 Elzey, Wayne. Some remarks on the space and time of the "center" in Aztec religion (UNAM/ECN, 12, 1976, p. 315–334)

Insightful study of "the ways in which time and space were homologized at levels above that of the calendars," not only in myths and religious symbols, but in religiously motivated attitudes toward "*all* human actions from birth to death" among the Nahua speaking peoples of late prehispanic central Mexico.

1530 Erdheim, Mario. Transformaciones de la ideología mexica en realidad social (*in* Economía política e ideología en el México prehispánico [see item **1528**] p. 195–220, bibl.)

Skillfully conducted investigation of ideological concommitants of political power in Mexica society as exemplified in poetry and myth, as well as more straightforward historical narratives.

1531 Esqueva, Antonio. Nuevo estudio sobre la religión de los nicaraos (BNBD, 25, sept./oct. 1978, p. 1–9)

Brief review and analysis of data relating to Nicarao in 16th-century writings of Oviedo.

1532 Feldman, Lawrence H. and **Teresita Majewski.** A catalogue of animals: the zoo in Molina's vocabulario (UNAM/ECN, 12, 1976, p. 335–343, bibl., ill., tables)

Outlines method for utilizing early colonial period *vocabularios* to obtain ethnohistorical data not available in other sources. Includes comparison between Molina's entries and those provided by Sahagun in Book 11 of the *Florentine Codex*.

1533 Galarza, Joaquin. Lire l'image aztèque (EHESS/C, 29, 1978, p. 15–42)

Rigorous and insightful investigation of pictorial-glyphic representations of Aztec rulers based primarily on examples from the Codex Tovar. Important contribution to study of late prehispanic Mesoamerican "writing systems" in general.

1534 García Quintana, Josefina. Exhortación del padre que así amonesta a su hijo casado, *tlazopilli* (UNAM/ECN, 13, 1978, p. 49–67)

Introductory analysis with text and modern translation by author of *huehuetlatolli* probably collected by Olmos but first published by Juan Bautista Viseo in 1600.

1535 ———. El *huehuetlatolli*, antigua palabra: como fuente para la historia sociocultural de los nahuas (UNAM/ECN, 12, 1976, p. 61–71, bibl.)

Analytic discussion and classification of *huehuetlatolli* collected by Olmos, Sahagun, Bautista, and others.

1536 Garza Tarazona de González, Silvia. Códices genealógicos: representaciones arquitectónicas. México: Instituto Nacional de Antropología e Historia (INAH), Centro Regional del Sureste, 1978. 65 p.; bibl.; ill. (Colección Científica INAH; 62. Arqueología)

Utilizes architectural representations found in historico-genealogical codices from Mixtec region to complement data from archaeological research.

1537 Gurría Lacroix, Jorge. Andrés de Tapia y la Coatlicue (UNAM/ECN, 13, 1978, p. 23–33, bibl., ill., plates)

Compares Tapia's description of Tenochtitlan's ceremonial precinct with that given by other primary and secondary sources.

Harner, Michael. The ecological basis for Aztec sacrifice. See *HLAS 41:1451*.

———. The enigma of Aztec sacrifice. See *HLAS 41:1452*.

1538 Henderson, John S. The Valley of Naco: ethnohistory and archaeology in northwestern Honduras (ASE/E, 24:4, Fall 1977, p. 363–377, bibl., ill.)

Historical and archaeological evidence used to document important role of Naco within extensive trade networks that included both Maya groups to the west and non-Maya groups further east.

1539 Heyden, Doris. Flores, creencias y el control social (*in* International Congress of Americanists, XLII, Paris, 1976. Actes [see *HLAS 41:255*] v. 6, p. 85–97, bibl., figs.)

Examines pictorial representations of flowers used to indicate hierarchical status of men and gods.

1540 Hicks, Frederic. Los *calpixque* de Nezahualcóyotl (UNAM/ECN, 13, 1978, p. 129–151, bibl.)

Important study of social background, status, and functions of *calpixque* (stewards) within the imperial administration devised by the Texcocan ruler, Nezahualcoyotl, beginning in the 1430s. Includes significant new data from lawsuit over landholdings in Atenco conducted before the Royal Audience in 1573–75.

1541 ———. "Flowery War" in the Aztec history (AAA/AE, 6:1, Feb. 1979, p. 87–92, bibl.)

Suggests that famous "flowery wars" (*xochiyaotl*) fought in late preconquest central Mexico were concerned less with obtaining sacrificial victims than providing military training and practice needed for more serious campaigns for imperialistic expansion.

1542 Horcasitas, Fernando. La narrativa oral Náhuatl: 1920–1975 (UNAM/ECN, 13, 1978, p. 177–209, bibl.)

Interesting discussion and comparison of several types of oral narratives collected since 1920 with prehispanic literature of similar kinds.

1543 Hunt, Eva. The provenience and contents of the Porfirio Díaz and Fernández Leal Codices: some new data and analysis (SAA/AA, 43:4, Oct. 1978, p. 673–690)

Meticulous study of historical sections of two Cuicatec codices dealing "with the topic of community war about water rights." One of the most impressive examples of a genuinely rigorous historiographic investigation available in recent literature.

1544 Jäcklein, Klaus. Los popolocas de Tepexi, Puebla: un estudio etnohistórico. Wiesbaden: Steiner, 1978. 316 p.; bibl.; ill. (Das Mexiko-Projekt der Deutschen Forschungsgemeinschaft; 15)

Reports detailed archival investigations aimed at clarifying preconquest and early colonial period social, political and economic organization of this important but little studied group.

1545 Jimenez Moreno, Wigberto. De Tezcatlipoca a Huitzilopochtli (*in* International Congress of Americanists, XLII, Paris, 1976. Actes [see *HLAS 41:255*] v. 6, p. 27–34)

Argues that Huitzilopochtli, like the god Mixcoatl, was a hero figure deified in the image of Tezcatlipoca in last centuries before Spanish conquest.

1546 Kaspar, Oldrich. La imagen de la civilización azteca en la literatura de los siglos XVI y XVII conservada en bibliotecas checoslovacas (UCP/IAP, 10, 1976, p. 179–185)

Describes impact of Cortes' letters and other early accounts of the Spanish conquest of Mexico on Czech writers of 16th and 17th centuries.

Kinzhalov, R.V. Indian sources for the history and ethnography of highland Guatemala: the tenth to the sixteenth centuries. See item **2405**.

1547 Klor de Alva, Jorge. Notes on the teaching of prehispanic Mesoamerican intellectual history (*in* Pacific Coast Council on Latin American Studies, XXI, San Diego, Calif., 1976. Proceedings. San Diego, Calif.: The Campanile Press, 1977, v. 5, p. 101–104)

Thoughtful and useful review of

source materials—most available in English translations—for use by instructors proposing to deal with this theme.

1548 **León-Portilla, Miguel.** El libro inédito de los testamentos de Culhuacán, su significación como testimonio histórico (UNAM/ECN, 12, 1976, p. 11–31)

Describes main characteristics of Nahuatl wills and testaments, most dating to late 16th century, found in a single manuscript volume from Culhuacan, with transcription and translation of two sample testaments.

1549 ———. Un texto en Hahua Pipil de Guatemala, siglo XVII (UNAM/ECN, 13, 1978, p. 35–53, facsim.)

Reviews historical literature dealing with Pipil of Guatemala and discusses internal content and significance of brief text in local Nahua dialect published with Spanish translation by the author.

1550 **López Austin, Alfredo.** El fundamento mágico-religioso del poder (UNAM/ECN, 12, 1976, p. 197–240, bibl.)

Wide-ranging investigation of close interconnections between political and religious ideologies among Quiche and Uacúsechas (Tarascans), designed to exemplify method for historiographical investigation applicable to other groups.

1551 **MacLachlan, Colin M.** The eagle and the serpent: male over female in Tenochtitlán (*in* Pacific Coast Council on Latin American Studies, XXI, San Diego, Calif., 1976. Proceedings. San Diego, Calif.: The Campanile Press, 1977, v. 5, p. 45–56)

Provocative, witty and well argued study of preconquest attitudes towards sexuality.

1552 **Marcus, Joyce.** Zapotec writing (SA, 242:2, Feb. 1980, p. 50–64, maps, ill.)

Traces evolution of Zapotec writing system from origins possibly as early as 600 BC as part of more general investigation of this people's long, political history.

——— and **Ronald Spores.** The *Handbook of Middle American Indians*: a retrospective look. See *HLAS 41:941.*

1553 **Martínez, Marin.** Historiografía de la migración mexica (UNAM/ECN, 12, 1976, p. 121–135, bibl.)

Reviews and compares pictorial and annalistic texts dealing with early Aztec migrations.

1554 **Melgarejo Vivanco, José Luis.** Antigua historia de México. México: Secretaría de Educación Pública, 1976. 3 v.; bibl., ill. (Sep/Documentos)

Major attempt at synthesis of archaeological and documentary evidence dealing with all areas of Mesoamerican culture history. Most detailed treatment reserved for central Mexico.

1555 **Monjaras-Ruiz, Jesús.** Panorama general de la guerra entre los aztecas (UNAM/ECN, 12, 1976, p. 241–264, bibl.)

Well documented review of information dealing with military training, command hierarchies, warrior orders, arms, war-related gods and religious ceremonies, and pertinent topics dealing primarily with the Aztecs of Tenochtitlan.

1556 **Morera de Guijarro, Juan Ignacio.** Sobre la existencia de una filosofía azteca (IGFO/RI, 37:147/148, enero/junio 1977, p. 287–307)

Critical review of earlier work by Caso, Soustelle, León-Portilla, Garibay and others dealing with the quality and intent as well as simple content of Aztec religious thought and philosophy.

1557 **Nash, June.** The Aztecs and the ideology of male dominance (UC/S, 4:2, Winter 1978, p. 349–362, ill., plate)

Speculative interpretation of changing female roles as Aztec society was "transformed from the egalitarian traditions of a wandering tribe to those of a predatory empire."

1558 **Nicholson, Henry B.** Ehecatl Quetzalcoatl vs. Topiltzin Quetzalcoatl of Tollan: a problem of Mesoamerican religion and history (*in* International Congress of Americanists, XLII, Paris, 1976. Actes [see *HLAS 41:255*] v. 6, p. 35–47, bibl.)

Concise review of basic ethnohistorical and archaeological evidence aimed at clarifying major issues rather than providing definitive solutions.

1559 **Noguez, Xavier.** Tira de Tepechpan: códice colonial procedente del Valle de México. v. 1, Estudio del códice; v. 2, Reproducción del códice y apéndices. Edición y comentarios por Xavier Noguez; presentación de Fernando Horcasitas. México: Biblioteca Enciclopédica del Estado de México, 1978. 2 v.; bibl.; ill.; index (Biblioteca enciclopédica del Estado de México; 64/65)

Color reproduction of little studied, pictorial manuscript with materials derived from Mexica historical traditions as well as those from Tepechpan itself. Noguez provides commendably thorough review of content together with well organized discussion of similar documentation found in other historical sources.

1560 Oltra, Enrique. Paideia precolombina: ideales pedagógicas de aztecas, mayas e incas. Buenos Aires: Ediciones Castañeda, 1977. 211 p.; bibl.; ill. (Colección Estudios antropológicos y religiosos; 2)

Useful summary of documentary evidence relating to prehispanic child-rearing and educational practices among Aztecs and Maya, with very brief review of similar materials dealing with the Inca.

1561 Prem, Hanns J. Comentario a las partes calendáricas del *Codex Mexicanus*, 23–24 (UNAM/ECN, 13, 1978, p. 267–288, bibl.; ill.; tables)

Meticulous summary and analysis of calendrical data contained especially on p. 1–15 and 90–102. Concludes that the *Mexicanus* was probably elaborated in about 1579, with some items added until 1583. Compares dates given in both indigenous and European calendrical systems, concluding that the author of this codex prepared a largely fictitious system of correlation between the calendars used. An extremely important study.

1562 ———. Milpa y hacienda: tenencia de la tierra indígena y española en la cuenca del Alto Atoyac, Puebla, México: 1520–1650. Con contribuciones de Ursula Dyckerhoff y Günter Miehlich. Wiesbaden: Steiner, 1978. 325 p.; bibl.; index (Das Mexiko-Projekt der Deutschen Forschungsgemeinschaft. El Proyecto México de la Fundación Alemana para la Investigación Científica; 13)

Major study of changing land-tenure relations based on extensive study of colonial-period archives. Introduction includes best available synthesis of preconquest history for this region; reviews political and physical geography; and describes late prehispanic land-tenure systems. Main text deals extensively with both Spanish and Indian land-tenure systems from time of conquest until mid-17th century.

Riley, Carroll L. and **Basil C. Hedrick** *eds.* Across the Chichimec sea: papers in honor of J. Charles Kelley. See *HLAS 41:342*.

1563 Romero Galván, José Rubén. Dos atestaciones en la obra de Chimalpahin (UNAM/ECN, 13, 1978, p. 113–127)

Includes transcription and translation of Nahuatl text dealing with possession of certain lands near Amecameca, Chalco, appended to the *Primera Relación* by Chimalpahin, with very useful analytic commentary by Romero Galván.

1564 ———. Posible esquema de las diferentes historias originales de Chimalpahin (UNAM/ECN, 12, 1976, p. 73–78, bibl.)

Considers possible manner in which Chimalpahin may have viewed broader relationships connecting his several otherwise distinct historical works.

1565 Rounds, J. Lineage, class and power in the Aztec state (AAA/AE, 6:1, feb. 1979, p. 73–86, bibl.)

Argues that class stratification at Tenochtitlan developed mainly "as a strategy for coopting the traditional leaders of the lineage segments of the prestate polity . . . into a centralized state power system." New but controversial approach to long-standing theoretical problem.

1566 ———. The role of the tecuhtli in ancient Aztec society (ASE/E, 24:4, Fall 1977, p. 343–361, bibl.)

Argues that *tetecuhtin* (singular: *tecuhtli*) were originally leaders of clan-like groups called *capullis*. As a centralized, state-level administration developed in the late 14th and 15th centuries, the *tetecuhtin* became a ruling class.

1567 Smith, Mary Elizabeth. *Codex Becker II:* a manuscript from the Mixteca Baja? (MVW/AV, 33, 1979, p. 29–43, bibl.; ill., map, tables)

Information from pictorial text and written inscription viewed under ultra-violet light show that codex derives from Mixteca Baja region of northern Oaxaca and southern Puebla.

1568 Stenzel, Werner. Der angebliche vorkortesische Eingottglaube der texcocanischen Fürsten (MVW/AV, 33, 1979, p. 15–27, bibl.)

Provocative study of possible Old Testament influences on the historical writing of the Texcocan chronicler Don Fernando and Alva Ixtlilxochitl.

1569 Thompson, J. Eric S. Los Señores de la Noche en la documentación náhuatl y maya (UNAM/ECN, 13, 1979, p. 15–22, plate)

Translation by León-Portilla of study prepared by the distinguished Mayanist and Mesoamericanist shortly before his death.

1570 Torquemada, Juan de. Monarquía indiana: de los veinte y un libros rituales y monarquía indiana, con el origin y guerra de los indios occidentales, de sus poblazones, descubrimiento, conquista, conversión y otras cosas maravillosas de la mesma tierra. v. 1, Libros 1/3; v. 2, Libros 4/5; v. 3, Libros 6/10; v. 4, Libros 11/14;. v. 5, Libros 15/18. 3. ed. Preparada por el Seminario para el Estudio de Fuentes de Tradición Indígena, bajo la coordinación de Miguel León-Portilla. México: Universidad Nacional Autónoma de México, Instituto de Investigaciones Históricas, 1975/1977. 5 v.; ill. (Serie de historiadores y cronistas de Indias; 5)

This seven-volume edition (of which only five were available at press-time) is the first complete version of Torquemada's classic (of which the manuscript is lost). This major work is the result of a two-year effort by the INAH team headed by León-Portilla. Although the spelling and punctuation have been modernized for clarity's sake, archaisms were not changed. In v. 1, the Editor's introduction describes how the text of the original books has been redistributed among the volumes of this edition. In v. 7 (not received at the Library of Congress at press-time), the Editor explains other aspects of the edition (e.g., changes introduced, glossary, notes, archaisms, etc.).

1571 Troike, Nancy P. Fundamental changes in the interpretations of the Mixtec codices (SAA/AA, 43:4, Oct. 1978, p. 553–568)

Surveys major advances in interpretation of Mixtec codices accomplished by impressively large roster of scholars since mid-1974. Shows convincingly that "the field of Mixtec codex interpretation," is indeed "now a separate and firmly established area of specialization within Mesoamerican scholarship."

1572 Uchmany, Eva Alexandra. Las características de un dios tutelar Mesoamericano: Huitzilopochtli (*in* International Congress of Americanists, XLII, Paris, 1976. Actes [see *HLAS 41:255*] v. 6, p. 49–62, bibl.)

Outlines main stages in development of Huitzilopochtli related to historical progress toward imperialist ideal of late preconquest era.

1573 ———. Huitzilopochtli: dios de la historia de los azteca-mexitin (UNAM/ECN, 13, 1978, p. 211–237, bibl., ill.)

Comprehensive review and analysis of sources dealing with historical development of the *concept* of Mexica god, Huitzilopochtli.

1574 Viesca Treviño, Carlos and **Ignacio de la Peña Páez.** Las enfermedades mentales en el *Códice Badiano* (UNAM/ECN, 12, 1976, p. 79–84)

Describes attempts to reconcile Nahua and European concepts of mental illness and methods of treatment by Juan Badiano in codex bearing his name.

1575 Vollemaere, Antoon Léon. Codex Mendoza: topogliefen. 2800 Mechelen, Nieuw Beggaardenstraat 15: Vlaams Instituut voor Amerikanistiek, 1977. 184 p.; bibl.; ill. (Amerika antiqua)

Catalogue of name-glyphs for places described as "conquered regions" and "areas of taxation" in *Mendoza Codex*. Each name-glyph is annotated with an explanatory comment. The author plans follow-up study of name-glyphs for people.

1576 Von Hagen, Victor Wolfgang. The Aztec and Maya papermakers. Introduction by Dard Hunter. New York: Hacker Art Books, 1977. 120 p.; bibl.; 23 leaves of plates: ill.; index.

New edition of useful study of papermaking techniques, but with now outdated, historical and archaeological background material.

1577 Zantwijk, Rudolf van. Iquehuacatzin, un drama real azteca (UNAM/ECN, 13, 1978, p. 89–95)

Despite the title narrowing consideration to a single Aztec nobleman, this is an important and insightful study of several anomalies—including several involving females of royal rank—in the succession to kingship at Tenochtitlan.

1578 ———. El parentesco y la afiliación étnica de Huitzilopochtli (*in* International Congress of Americanists, XLII, Paris, 1976. Actes [see *HLAS 41:255*] v. 6, p. 62–68, bibl.)

Interesting but speculative attempt to place the god Huitzilopochtli in genealogical framework which includes both other deities and mortals prominent in early formation of Aztec state.

1579 **Zavala, José F.** Die psychische Entwicklung in altmexikanischer Symbolik: dargest. an e. altemexikan. Gesang im Lichte der Psychologie C.G. Jungs: mit ausführlichem Register im Anhang. Stuttgart: Bonz, 1977. 156 p.; bibl.; ill. (Psychologisch gesehen: Wissenschaft)

Intriguing study of religious poem from *Codice Matritense* viewed in light of Jung's system of analytic psychology.

1580 **Zemsz, Abraham.** Le tlacuilo et les deux conventions (EHESS/C, 29, 1978, p. 71–91)

Applies analytic method developed by J. Galarza (see item **1533**) to further clarify techniques evolved by colonial period manuscript painters to synthesize preconquest and European representational methods in *Codex Tovar.*

ETHNOHISTORY: South America

JOHN V. MURRA, *Professor of Anthropology, Cornell University*

A MAJOR PROBLEM IN ANDEAN ETHNOHISTORY is the scarcity of new primary sources dealing with the dynastic oral tradition, the so-called chronicles. Very few of these sources have been located in this century; the last major find was made in 1908; lesser but still significant sources were located and published by Hermann Trimborn in the 1930s. Recent developments such as the publication of better editions of eyewitness accounts of the invasion or the new interest in administrative records (e.g., litigations, inspections, census data) are useful but do not compensate for the lack of dynastic materials. This gap will be filled only by the collaboration of anthropologists and historians. But then, one wonders, how can this be achieved?

In other areas, however, there has been some progress. In 1956, Madrid's Biblioteca de Autores Españoles began republishing some of its early volumes, especially new and accessible editions of the classics. Pedro Cieza de León was among the major authors selected and Carmelo Sáenz de Santa María was assigned to edit his works in a uniform, multi-volume set. Unfortunately, the edition was delayed for years because certain chapters from part three were missing. It was known, however, that there existed copies of these chapters. One was owned by the late Rafael Loredo who preferred to release only a few chapters at a time through the *Mercurio Peruano* (see item **1726**). Another copy was in the library of a baronet who resided in Dublin. Father Sáenz's efforts to examine these texts were unsuccessful because their owners refused him access. Fortunately, a third copy was finally located and one looks forward to the first complete edition of Cieza's works. Moreover, Sáenz has solved the "mystery" of the missing decade in Cieza's life (before he went south in 1547 to answer La Gasca's call) by revealing that in Colombia he was well known as Pedro de León (see item **1725**).

In 1965, the above mentioned Biblioteca issued the memoirs of Pedro Pizarro as vol. 5 of a monographic series on civil wars. The Pizarro reminiscences concern the time when the Pizarro crowd attempted to separate Peru from the Spanish Crown. The inclusion of these memoirs in a series on civil wars was not entirely justified but one welcomed their publication in any form. In 1978, the reminiscences finally appeared in a definitive edition prepared by Guillermo Lohmann Villena (see item **1705**) who used the original manuscript located in California. His edition is well annotated and includes supplementary papers on the personality of the writer who, although barely an adolescent at the time of the invasion, managed to observe everything with a keen eye.

In addition to the Pizarro memoirs, another improved edition is underway. The original of Bernabé Cobo's first *History of the Andes* (1653) has been located in Sevilla by Roland Hamilton (item **1606**). And John H. Rowe has already compared the chapters on Cuzco's *ceque* lines as they appear in the original and published versions (see item **1721**).

When Pierre Duviols' analysis of the *extirpaciones de idolatrías* appeared in 1971 (see *HLAS 34:1155*), it encouraged a new approach to the study of Andean religion; a translation into Spanish was issued by the Universidad Nacional Autónoma de México. Recently, the Instituto de Estudios Peruanos announced plans to publish all 6,000 pages of the *extirpación* papers from the Archive of the Arzobispado of Lima. The editor is María Rostworowski and vol. 1, containing the interpretative essays, will appear after the publication of the texts.

Jorge Urioste has completed his translation into English of the oral traditions of Huarochiri and is preparing a new Spanish version. In addition, Gerald Taylor (see *HLAS 40:2118*) has issued a French version in Parish (see item **1589**). There are now several studies of this unique Quechua literary source whose access was a leading priority for a long time.

Two years ago I noted the collaborative use of ethnographic fieldwork, astronomic observations and early written sources for the Cuzco area promoted by R.T. Zuidema. Recently, additional results of such concerted efforts have been published by his students Jeanette Sherbondy and Gary Urton (see item **1735**). Settled in Ayacucho, John Earls offered further elaborations of his notions on Andean productivity in Inka times (item **1624**). Zuidema's original analysis (see *HLAS 29:2207*) of the *ceque* lines and their structural importance is receiving renewed attention. For example, when reflecting about Inka urbanism at Huánuco Pampa, a large administrative center in the central Andes, the archaeologist Craig Morris found that Zuidema's analysis was suggestive (see *HLAS 41:817*).

As usual in this section, we list journals that welcome ethnohistorical contributions. *Avances* of La Paz and *Chungara* of Arica have been delayed. Both Lima's *Historia y Cultura* and its Bolivian namesake have published new issues despite difficult circumstances. The *Revista del Museo Nacional* fell behind through no fault of the editors; the cost of volume 43 (dated 1977) was finally paid in 1979. Two issues of *Estudios Atacameños* appeared almost simultaneously. *Histórica* of Lima, under the editorship of Franklin Pease García Yrigoyen, consistently includes ethnohistorical materials. Pease's essays, collected and published by the Instituto de Estudios Peruanos, received the Ethnohistory Prize awarded by the Conference on Latin American History of the American Historical Association. María Rostworowski, a member of the Instituto's staff, continued to study coastal matters and promises a volume on fishermen and the sea (see item **1718**).

By selecting the "Historical Anthropology of the Andes" as the subject of a double issue of the Paris journal *Annales: Economies, Sociétés, Civilisations*, its editors gave a notable boost to the concerted effort involved in correlating insights drawn from written sources with data gathered in archaeological and contemporary fieldwork. Edited by Nathan Wachtel and J.V. Murra, this issue consists of 17 articles and 10 reviews by Argentine, British, Chilean, French, Peruvian and US students (items **1592–1593**, **1665**, **1706**, **1727**, **1732**, **1751** and **1758**). An English and a Spanish translation of this compilation will be published, respectively, by Cambridge University Press and Crítica of Barcelona.

1581 Adorno, Rolena. Felipe Guaman Poma de Ayala: an Andean view of the Peruvian viceroyalty, 1565–1615 (SA/J, 65, 1978, p. 121–143, ill.)

An excellent review of the current status of Waman Puma studies, with new suggestions for the European sources he used and quoted. He was familiar with Las Casas' work, with Fray Luis de Granada, with local church workers. This is a preview of a new edition of Waman Puma's *Letter to the King* which Adorno is co-editing.

1582 ———. The *Nueva Coronica y Buen Gobierno*: a new look at the Royal Library's Peruvian treasure (Fund og Forskning i det kongelige samlinger [Copenhagen] 24, 1979/1980, p. 7–28, ill.)

Locates Waman Puma's text in the corpus of primary sources. Investigates what can be learned from the original about the composition of the manuscript: locates addenda to the first writing, notes changes in self-references, the date of the conclusion of the text, the possible route by which the text reached Copenhagen.

1583 ———. Paradigms lost: a Peruvian Indian surveys Spanish colonial society (Studies in the Anthropology of Visual Communication [Society for the Anthropology of Visual Communication, Washington] 5:2, April 1979, p. 78–96, bibl., ill.)

Centers on pictorial text (some 400 full-page drawings) which contains two levels of meaning: not just what is represented but also arrangement of images in space. The latter "expresses his [the Peruvian Indian's] virulent criticism of the Spanish colonialists in a secret text-within-a-text." Three models of Andean spatial design are analyzed, the changes these have undergone noted. "The perfect model (i.e. the original paradigm) consists of four sectors . . . which was a system both autonomous and complete . . . The great majority of the drawings are but broken bits of the prototypical scheme."

1584 Agurto Calvo, Santiago. Medidas de longitud en el Incario (Cuadernos del Consejo Nacional de la Universidad Peruana [Lima] 24/25, 1977, p. 7–24, bibl., tables)

Since no original sources have come to light beyond those surveyed in 1962 by María Rostworowski, Agurto decided to supplement such eyewitness accounts with his own measurements of Inca buildings. A set of units emerges with regularity, apparently based on the human body and its subdivisions, most of them 80 centimeters. While the decimal system was used for counting, buildings were measured anthropomorphically. Distances were assessed with paces, *tupu* or *wamanin*. Mendizábal's work is ignored.

1585 Alcina Franch, José and **Remedios de la Peña.** Patrones de asentamiento en Esmeraldas durante los siglos XVI y XVII (*in* International Congress of Americanists, XLII, Paris, 1976. Actes [see *HLAS 41:255*] v. 9-A, p. 283–301, bibl., ill., maps)

Reports on research carried out in Esmeraldas by a Spanish team, directed by Alcina, are becoming available. This one, for example, compares archaeological evidence on house form and settlement patterns with colonial written reports. The comparison produces a chart of several activities which are compared with those of present-day settlements and other forest regions.

1586 Andía Chávez, Juan. El cronista Felipe Huamán Poma de Ayala. Lima: n.p., 1976. 23 p.; ill.

1587 Antúnez de Mayolo R., Santiago E. La alimentación en el Tawantinsuyu (Etnohistoria y Antropología Andina [Museo Nacional de Historia, Lima] 1, 1978, p. 277–298, tables)

It is frequently heard in the Andean republics that traditional Andean nutrition provided both quantity and quality. This report includes the most thorough documentation on behalf of this argument.

1588 **Argentina. Comando General del Ejército. Dirección de Estudios Históricos.** Política seguida con el aborigen: 1750–1819. v. 1. Buenos Aires: Círculo Militar, 1973. 546 p.; ill., maps.

Vol. 2 will cover *Las luchas contra el indígena: 1850–1852*. Based on published sources, vol. 1 is organized as a sort of handbook. However, one chapter, by José A. Buruena about late 18th-century Patagonia, refers to sources in the Archivo General de la Nación: "Una explícita referencia al deslinde de jurisdicciones entre el estado y el aborigen y, si bien en la práctica no fue respetado, demostró una vez más el próposito de las autoridades por afianzar y proteger las zonas fronterizas."

1589 **Avila, Francisco de.** Rites et traditions Huarochiri: manuscrit quechua du début de 17e. siècle. Texte établi, traduit et comenté par Gerald Taylor. Paris: L'Hartmattan, 1980. 243 p. (Série Ethnolinguistique amérindienne; ISSN 0245-4343)

A new version of this unique example of the Andean oral tradition. See also *HLAS 29:2137b* and *HLAS 32:1120* as well as the Introduction by editor Gerald Taylor, annotated below, item **1743**.

1590 **Ayala Queirolo, Víctor.** Los chiriguanos y la preparación y entrenamiento para la guerra del Avá (APH/HP, 16, 1978, p. 21–42)

Survey based on secondary sources.

1591 **Ballesteros Gaibrois, Manuel** and **María del Carmen Martín Rubio.** Supervivencias del "ayllu" andino y sus características (RUC, 28:117, 1979, p. 431–460, bibl., ill., maps)

After a short review of primary sources and later commentaries, authors describe contemporary functions of the *ayllu* in towns near Cuzco. Kinship has been replaced by propinquity in creating and maintaining bonds.

1592 **Bérthelot, Jean.** L'exploitation des métaux précieux au temps des Incas (AESC, 33:5/6, sept./déc. 1978, p. 948–966, bibl., maps, tables)

The most detailed examination of mining in Inka society, the resumé of a doctoral thesis on the subject. The location of the mining studied was the area of Lake Titicaca and covers both silver and gold. Both state and ethnic mines are discussed; the latter were more dispersed and multi-ethnic as suggested by patterns of complementarity. The technology of mining and the rituals accompanying the extraction are also examined.

1593 **Bittman, Binte.** Cobija y alrededores en la época colonial: 1600–1750 (*in* Congreso de Arqueología Chilena, VII, Altos de Vilche, 1977. Actas. Santiago: Sociedad Chilena y Arqueología del Maule, 1978? v. 1, p. 327–356, bibl., tables)

On the basis of parish records, author tries to identify ethnicity of coastal populations in a province which once was Bolivia's. Classified as Uru or Camanchaca, these people were fishermen and hunters of sea lions who maintained barter relations with inland Atacama dwellers. In the early 18th century, French visitors reported on them. All of this information provides a less desolate view of these populations.

1594 **Boschin, María Teresa** and **Lidia Rosa Nacuzzi.** Ensayo metodológico para la reconstrucción etnohistórica: su aplicación a la comprensión del modelo tehuelche meridional (*in* Congreso de Arqueología Chilena, VII, Altos de Vilche, 1977. Actas. Santiago: Sociedad Chilena de Arqueología, Sociedad Arqueológica de Maule, 1978? v. 1, p. 327–356, bibl., tables)

Provides demographic evidence and information on distribution of the Tehuelche both before and after their adaptation to nomadism on horseback. Hunters of ostriches and guanacos, they moved easily, roaming over extensive territory. The title of this article does not reflect its content.

1595 **Bouysse-Cassagne, Thérèse.** L'espace aymara: *urco* et *uma* (AESC, 33:5/6, sept./déc. 1978, p. 1057–1080, bibl., ill., maps)

Dual organization in the Andes is assuming greater importance. Bouysse contrasts Aymara and Inka dual division: the first centered on Lake Titicaca, the second on Cuzco. The ritual use of space differs according to the political center.

1596 **Bravo, G.** Revitalización del mito de origen en la etapa final de la historia incaica (*in* International Congress of Americanists, XLII, Paris, 1976. Actes [see *HLAS 41:255*] v. 4, p. 327–333, bibl.)

Analyzes political use of the *amaru* serpent myth by king Atawallpa, as prisoner of the Europeans.

1597 Bravo Guerreira, María Concepción. La economía andina del siglo XVI: continuidad y cambio en los mecanismos de producción y distribución (RUC, 28:117, 1979, p. 289–396, bibl., tables)

If ethnic groups in Tawantinsuyu were responsible for duties only within their own territory, who undertook long-distance transport duties? A variety of *mitmaqkuna*, answers Bravo; their antecedents remain unclear. Transport became particularly important in colonial times with the increasing trade in coca leaf, cloth and other commodities.

1598 ———. ¿Fue Francisco de Xerex el autor de la *Relación de Samano*? (EEHA/AEA, 33, 1975 [i.e. 1978] p. 33–55)

Suggests author was the pilot Bartolomé Ruíz, who in the 1520s reached as far south as Chincha and informed Pizarro about what he had seen before the Marquis went to Spain to ask the Crown for Peru. Secretary Xerex (presumed by Porras to have been the author of the account) is shown to have left the territory earlier.

1599 Busto Duthurburu, José Antonio del. Peru incaico. Lima: Editorial Studium, 1977. 380 p.; ill.

Organized as a college level textbook, this work reproduces copious quotes from traditional sources about legendary and historical kings. Includes excellent illustrations by Abraham Guillén. Separate chapters are devoted to the following organizational aspects: political, social, administrative, military, economic and religious.

1600 Caillavet, Chantal. Le sel d'Otavalo, Equateur: continuités indigènes et ruptures coloniales (Mélanges de la Casa de Velázquez [Paris] 15, 1979, p. 329–363, bibl., ill., map)

Once the saltlick, known by the Europeans as Salinas, was a prosperous place where the Otavalo "hazen gran rescate" with cotton and coca leaf from other ecologic zones. Some of the *myndalaes*, traders, came from as far away as Pasto. Caillavet tries to distinguish how much of today's exchange activity is commercial, how much barter, how much ancient or influenced by the Inka.

1601 Camino, Alejandro. Trueque, correrías e intercambios entre los quechuas andinos y los piro y machiguengas de la montaña peruana (Etnohistoria y Antropología Andina [Museo Nacional de Historia, Lima] 1, 1978, p. 79–100, bibl.)

Highland-Amazonian relations included efforts by the Inca to implant garrisons and other outliers in the lowlands. In addition, there were trading and other exchanges. Since different lowland ethnic groups had distinct settlement patterns, it is possible to trace predatory dependence of some upon others. The Piro of the lower Urubamba used to row upriver, prey upon the Machiguenga and maintain exchange links with the highlanders, using the booty they acquired. In the process, they covered distances of up to 300 kms.

1602 Cardich, Augusto. Puscanturpa: un posible recuerdo mítico sobre las fluctuaciones de los límites superiores del cultivo (SAA/R, 9, 1977, p. 179–183, bibl.)

In 1955, Cardich heard oral traditions in the region of Lauricocha where he was doing his archaeological fieldwork. They confirmed his observations that the maximum altitude of field cultivation varied significantly from century to century.

1603 Castelli, Amalia. Tunupa: divinidad del altiplano (Etnohistoria y Antropología Andina [Museo Nacional de Historia, Lima] 1, 1978, p. 201–204)

Although most studies of Tunupa are archaeological (see *HLAS 34:1208*), there is historical material identifying this deity. Further north, Tunupa is the equivalent of Wiraqucha as creator deity. This article examines attempts to adapt Tunupa to European religious requirements.

1604 Choque Canqui, Roberto. Coca in the historical development of Bolivia (*in* Traditional use of coca leaf in Bolivia: multidisciplinary study, final report. La Paz, Museo de Etnografía y Folklore, 1978, p. 151–157)

A thin, superficial account. Given the seriousness of the contemporary study, the lack of attention given to history is startling.

1604a ———. Empleo de caciques aymaras en la socioeconomía colonial (Etnohistoria y Antropología Andina [Museo Nacional de Historia, Lima] 1, 1978, p. 73–77)

Study of primary sources on Aymara lords in colonial times indicates that they took advantage of early dispositions in order to acquire new powers and privileges. Their aim was private ownership of land which was not an option in earlier times.

1605 Civrieux, Marc de. Los caribes y la conquista de la Guayana española: etnohistoria kari'ña. Caracas: Universidad Andrés Bello, Instituto de Investigaciones Históricas, 1966. 155 p.; maps.

Many ethnic groups of Venezuela were called Caribs by foreign observers. Author argues that the "real" ones were *kari'ña*. They lived on both sides of the Orinoco; an eastern branch reached the Esequibo River in Guayana. The material is listed chronologically from the 1520s to 1820. Includes indexes of proper names, particularly those of Carib leaders and place names in their territories. (Although published in 1966, this work was not annotated in *HLAS*.)

1606 Cobo, Bernabé. History of the Inca Empire. Translated and edited by Roland Hamilton. Foreword by John H. Rowe. Austin: University of Texas Press, 1979. 279 p.

The editor has located the original of this 1653 history of "the Indians' customs and their origin . . ." in an ecclesiastic archive in Sevilla. He translated here Books XI and XII, those dealing most directly with the aboriginal population, the dynastic traditions, and the administration of the Inka state. Rowe has expanded his introductory remarks in other publications, see item **1723**.

1607 Cock Carrasco, Guillermo. Ayllu, territorio y frontera en los Callaguas (Etnohistoria y Antropología Andina [Museo Nacional de Historia, Lima] 1, 1978, p. 29–32, bibl.)

Territoriality and land tenure must be added to considerations of how Andean peoples achieved "vertical complementarity." While patterns of settlement were dispersed, there existed enclaves within the nuclear area. Author finds that the "multi-ethnic" label Murra applies to peripheral outliers is misleading.

1608 Cook, N. David. Estimación sobre la población del Perú en el momento de la conquista (PUCP/H, 1:1, 1977, p. 37–60, bibl., maps, tables)

Author returns to his earlier estimates with new data, from several regions in earliest years of European settlement. Several models exist to help historians: seven are outlined and data tested against each. Rate of population decrease was particularly violent before 1572. Cook's calculation provides a population of some six million in 1532 with an absolute minimum of three million and a maximum of eight. Territory considered is approximately that of Peru today. Article includes demographic charts.

1609 Crespo, Juan Carlos. Chincha y el mundo andino en la *Relación de 1558* (PUCP/H, 2:2, 1978, p. 185–212, bibl.)

After publishing a new, more accurate version of one of the few coastal descriptions (see *HLAS 40:2040*), Crespo analyzes now its contents and relations to other sources. He reviews the importance of Chincha as a terminal for long-distance travel as one of the earliest grants to the Spanish Crown as well as Chincha's relations to other coastal polities and to the highlands. An important evaluation of a first-class source.

1610 Culagovski, Mauricio J. La visitación de los chupachu y la unidad doméstica andina (PUCP/H, 2:2, 1978, p. 213–223, bibl., tables)

Re-analysis of Gordon Hadden's population figures derived from a house-to-house survey (see *HLAS 29:2156a*). Concludes that household sizes proposed by Hadden are too large and 4.79 persons per "fire" is more likely.

1611 Curatola, Marco. El culto de crisis del "Moro Oncoy" (Etnohistoria y Antropología Andina [Museo Nacional de Historia, Lima] 1, 1978, p. 179–192)

Ambitious attempt to link the catastrophic population decrease in the 16th-century Andes with messianic cults of the period. These involved not only the *taki unquy* of the 1560s (see *HLAS 34:1192*) but, according to new data, later movements as well which would make the loss of so many comprehensible if not manageable.

1612 ———. Mito y milenarismo en los Andes: del Taki Onqoy a Inkarri (IPA/AP, 10, 1977, p. 65–92, bibl.)

Examines millenarian movements from colonial period to their present-day manifestations. Stresses their rebelliousness but also their adaptive features in extremely difficult colonial and hacienda times. It was assumed that in the long run, the native divinity would defeat foreign rule. Stages in the resistance and the perception of future victory can be traced in the versions of the myth.

1613 Deustua, José. Acceso a recursos en Yanque-Collaguas 1591: una experiencia estadística (Etnohistoria y Antropología Andina [Museo Nacional de Historia, Lima] 1, 1978, p. 41–51, tables)

In 1591, the lords of Collaguas had greater access to maize and quinua lands than the bulk of the population. The figures of the visita allow comparisons of population, lineage by lineage, including weavers.

1614 ———. Derroteros de la etnohistoria en el Perú (IPA/AP, 15, 1980, p. 173–178, bibl.)

A survey of recent publications with a stress on the work of María Rostworowski.

1615 Duque Gómez, Luis. Introducción al apasado aborigen. Bogotá: Editorial Retina, 1976. 157 p.; bibl.; ill. (Breviarios colombinos; 5)

1616 Durand, José. Perú y Ophir en Garcilaso Inca, el Jesuita Pineda y Gregorio García (PUCP/H, 3:2, 1979, p. 35–55, bibl.)

After a long delay (see *HLAS 29: 2149a–2149b*), Durand returns to the study of Garcilaso's sources and acquaintances among the clergy of Andalusia. The lack of connections between the name of Peru and Ophir is well understood by Garcilaso and other writers and first-hand Andean experience such as Acosta.

1617 Duviols, Pierre. La Capacocha (IPA/AP, 6, 1976, p. 11–57, bibl.)

Human sacrifice in the Andes has received occasional attention but this is a major essay concerned not with apologetics but with understanding the rite. Duviols examines three dimensions of the latter: spatial, economic, and semantic. He perceives human sacrifices as part of tribute offered by a conquered ethnic group to the Crown, mediated by the chief beneficiary: a state cult. Duviols came across some of these primary sources while studying the campaign "to extirpate idolatries" (see *HLAS 36:1390–1392*). Other sources are being prepared for publication by the Instituto de Estudios Peruanos.

1618 ———. La dinastía de los incas: ¿monarquía o diarquía? (SA/J, 66, 1979, p. 67–83)

Elaborates Zuidema's well-known thesis (see *HLAS 29:2207*) that the "long count" of Cuzco kings does not take into account the possibility of two of them reigning simultaneously. Where earlier writers preferred the longer list, Duviols demonstrates that there are additional reasons for accepting the short count.

1619 ———. La guerra entre el Cuzco y los chanca: ¿historia o mita? (RUC, 28:117, 1979, p. 363–371, bibl.)

Duviols compares two versions of the war against the Chanca, one of the earliest steps in the extension and actual creation of the Inka state. While superficially very different, Duviols finds that, at the symbolic level, there are similarities between these two versions and promises further elaborations on them.

1620 ———. Lo indígena en la *Relación* de Pedro Pizarro (*in* Pizarro, Pedro. Relación del descubrimiento y la conquista de los Reinos del Perú [see item **1705**] p. lxxxviii–xciii)

Stresses that Pizarro's work contains a rich and varied image of pre-European institutions. Because 40 years elapsed between Pizarro's arrival in the first wave and the writing of his *Relación,* he was able to reflect on what he had seen and not always understood in the 1530s. Duviols' point is confirmed by the textual comparisons which reveal how much Cobo copied from Pizarro.

1621 ———. Los nombres quechua de Viracocha, supuesto Dios Creador de los evangelizadores (IPA/AP, 10, 1977, p. 53–63)

The missionaries assigned creator deity functions to Viracocha—why and how did they do so? Western ideological considerations led friars sympathetic to the Andean population to insist they had knowledge of such a divinity. Duviols tries to weed out the later accretions and comes to the following translation: "Viracocha, Father of the People, teacher who has known and knows how to put order in the world."

1622 ———. Un symbolisme andin du double: la lithomorphose de l'ancêtre (*in*

International Congress of Americanists, XLII, Paris, 1976. Actes [see *HLAS 41:255*] v. 4, p. 359–364, bibl., table)

Contrasts the *huaqui*—a statuette which accompanied both Cuzco kings and ethnic lords into their graves—with the *huanca*, a stone erected to stand in for the ancestor, colonizer or whoever defined the group's territory. The *huanca* was "the protector of the means of production and also its catalyst through the huanca's symbolic fecundating action."

1623 ———. Un symbolisme de l'occupation, de l'aménagement et de l'exploitation de l'espace: le monolithe *huance* et sa fonction dans les Andes préhispaniques (EPHE/H, 19:2, avril/juin 1979, p. 7–31)

In each human settlement, and occasionally in a subdivision, there would be a stone shrine. Its functions were both military and religious and it was also closely related to the original establishment of the settlement. In this inquiry into the process of "lithification" of the ancestor, Duviols suggests that it coincides with the arrival in pre-Inka times of *llacuash* or herding migrants. Incaic Cuzco exemplifies such an establishment in pre-imperial days.

1624 Earls, John. Astronomía y ecología: la sincronización alimenticia del maíz (IPA/AP, 14, 1979, p. 117–135, bibl., tables)

Agrees with estimates that there was a large population in the Central Andes before 1532. The feeding of such numbers required efficient coordination among various crops and the zones in which they were grown. Part of this effort consisted in the careful selection of varieties of crops. Since the state's chief interest was maize, the selection effort is most apparent in this crop. Because maize grows at many altitudes, well-adapted varieties were selected and their total numbers decreased.

1625 ——— and **Irene Silverblatt.** Ayllus y etnias de la región Pampas-Qaracha: el impacto del Imperio Inca (*in* Congreso Peruano: el Hombre y la Cultura Andina, III, Lima, 1977. El hombre y la cultura andina [see *HLAS 41:782*] v. 1, p. 157–177, bibl., maps)

A good introduction to regional organization in the Huamanga area based on new primary material. Wari political hegemony succeeded by accelerating the fragmentation of ethnic groups. An effort is made to trace the location and spatial arrangements of particular polities.

1626 ——— and ———. Investigaciones interdisciplinarias en Moray, Cuzco (Etnohistoria y Antropología Andina [Museo Nacional de Historia, Lima] 1, 1978, p. 115–122)

How does one coordinate temperature charts, the several varieties of land and the kinds of labor mobilized in Inca times? One mechanism can be examined at Moray, on whose terraces were conducted both astronomical observations and experimental projects. Evidence from both written sources and contemporary practice suggest that a variety of micro-climates were reproduced at the Moray amphitheatre. Terraces were designed to recreate the microclimates found in nature. There is a possibility that the custodians were women.

1627 ——— and ———. La realidad física y social en la cosmología andina (*in* International Congress of Americanists, XLII, Paris, 1976. Actes [see *HLAS 41:255*] v. 4, p. 299–325, bibl., ill.)

Certain principles of order, comparable to Western scientific laws, appear to govern Andean social relations. Dualism is one of them; but here Earls and Silverblatt present a "geometry" which involves many other relations. Principles of reciprocity, modified by state exactions, are correlated with indigenous concepts of space such as *tinku* and *amaru*. Special stress is placed on chart of the world provided by Salcamayhua in 1613 which is redrawn to encompass both the agricultural calendar and kinship data.

1628 Espinoza Soriano, Waldemar. La base territorial del ayllu andino: siglos XV y XVI (Inca [Centro de Estudiantes de Arqueología, Lima] 3:6, 1979, p. 70–89, bibl., maps)

Territoriality was not an indispensable trait of the ayllu but access to it by land was always important. In coastal areas there were also artisan ayllus. In the North, where the decimal system was older and part of the social fabric, the ayllu overrode kinship and ayllu ties. Sometimes the 100 household units—the *pachaca*—coincided with the ayllu.

1629 ———. El habitat de la etnia Pinagua: siglos XV y XVI (PEMN/R, 40, 1974, p. 157–220, bibl., map)

Pinahua is mentioned in several dynastic traditions as a pre-Inka lord of the Cuzco area but it is also the name of a place whose inhabitants were deported by early Inka kings. After 1532, some of them returned and sued to recover their lands. Present article is based on the litigation records.

1630 ———. Los mitmas cañar en el Reino de Yaro, Pasco: siglos XV y XVI (IRA/B, 10, 1976, p. 63–82, bibl., map)

The resettlement of Cañari rebels throughout the Inka domain has been studied by Oberem (see *HLAS 40:2089*). Most studies have emphasized those Cañari who made up a standing army attached to the person of the king in the Cusco region. Espinoza, who has located Cañaris in many other parts of the Andes, documents here their distribution in the basin of the upper Huallaga River. In early colonial times, there was friction between the Cañaris and the aboriginal population.

1631 ———. Los orejones del Cuzco o la clase ociosa en el imperio inca: siglos XV y XVI (Proceso [Huancayo, Peru] 1977, p. 65–108, bibl., facsim.)

Argues that in pre-1532 Cuzco, the Inca were both a class and a nation, dominating the local inhabitants as well as the rest of the empire. The entire society was "una sociedad perteneciente al denominado científicamente como modo de producción asiática . . ." Reproduces a 1580 claim presented to European authorities by some surviving Inca descendants of mighty rulers, who had never performed servile work, became poorer than some of their former subjects who could work for a living.

1632 ———. Los orejones o los productores indirectos del Imperio Inca: siglos XV y XVI (*in* Congreso Peruano: el Hombre y la Cultura Andina, III, Lima, 1977. El hombre y la cultura andina [see *HLAS 41:782*] v. 1, p. 202–206)

What we have ruling in Cuzco is "un estado imperial que es despótico, teocrático, guerrero y clasista." The North Coast was the most "progressive" region in the Andes, "porque sus fuerzas productivas logran desarrollar y descomponer las estructuras asiáticas a su debido tiempo."

1633 ———. La poliginia señorial en el Reino de Caxamarca: siglos XV y XVI (PEMN/R, 43, 1979, p. 399–466, bibl.)

Dynastic polygyny among the major ethnic lords is well documented. There is usually less information about multiple marriages at more humble levels. The data emerge from litigation about the lineage of one of the pretenders to overall Caxamarca lordship in 1573. New information about the vocabulary of pairing, plus data on succession and inheritance. Only 14 of the pages are devoted to reproducing the original text of the litigation.

1634 ———. La vida pública de un príncipe inca residente en Quito: siglos XV y XVI (IFEA/B, 7:3/4, 1978, p. 1–31)

Reproduces petition by an Inca descendant of close relatives of the royal house of Cuzco, who soon after 1532 threw in his lot with the Europeans. The witnesses included old men who could remember kings who died before the coming of Pizarro; they testified that kinsmen of the king were entitled to receiving a village or two of their very own and also to drawing from produce stored in state warehouses. Their descendant produces evidence that he has faithfully served the European Crown in repressive campaigns against highlanders urging rebellion.

1635 Fernández, Jorge. Los chichas, los lipes y un posible enclave de la cultura de San Pedro de Atacama en la zona limítrofe argentino-boliviana (Estudios Atacameños [San Pedro de Atacama, Chile] 6, 1978, p. 19–35, bibl., ill., maps)

Laments scarcity of archaeological information about all groups whose existence has been documented in the region shared by Bolivia, Chile and Argentina. Reexamines information provided by one P. Sande to Lozano Machuca and published in the *Relaciones geográficas de Indias* which states that some groups from what today is Jujuy were not included in the mita to Potosí but occasionally reached that city. Fernández examines the Uru label applied to some of these peoples, both highlanders and city dwellers.

1636 Flores Galindo, Alberto. Marxismo y sociedad: derrotero de un malentendido (IPA/AP, 14, 1979, p. 139–143)

José Carlos Mariátegui's characterization of the Inka state as "comunismo agrario," brought him much criticism. Flores tries to explain the context of debates among Marxists at the time Mariátegui chose this designation. The experience of agrarian communities able to produce surpluses seemed to offer an alternative route to socialism which bypassed the classic evolutionary stages.

1637 **Frankowska, Maria.** Sistemas de propiedad en la sociedad incaica (Etnologia Polona [Warsaw] 4, 1979, p. 125–139, bibl.)

Author reviews published sources on land tenure and suggests that three-fold division of lands reported by early European observers is inadequate. Some data suggest presence of private land holdings. Draws comparisons with Mesoamerican data.

1638 **Gade, Daniel B.** Inca and colonial settlement, coca cultivation and endemic disease in the tropical forest (Journal of Historical Geography [Academic Press, London] 5:3, 1979, p. 263–279, bibl., ill., maps, tables)

Although the cultivation of coca leaf was an important activity, both economic and ceremonial, access to the Eastern slopes where the crop grew was dangerous because of *leishmaniasis*, a serious and disfiguring illness, endemic below 2,300 m. Gade suggests Inca expansion downriver was halted because of this danger. However, permanent settlement by kamayuq may have avoided the worst of the threat.

1639 **Gasparini, Graziano** and **Luise Margolies.** Arquitectura Inka. Caracas: Universidad Central de Venezuela, Facultad de Arquitectura y Urbanismo, Centro de Investigaciones Históricas y Estética, 1977. 357 p., bibl., ill., maps, plates, tables.

A significant compilation, most of it based on the authors' fieldwork. Ethnohistoric sources have been verified and systematically used. Both domestic and state architecture were studied. The photographs are superb. An English translation by Patricia J. Lyon has been published by Indiana University Press in 1980.

1640 **Gentille Lafaye, Margarita E.** Distintos aspectos del tributo entre los yauyos de Chaclla: siglo XV–XVIII (IFEA/B, 5:3/4, 1976, p. 77–89, bibl.)

Since the publication of the oral tradition of Huarochiri, the Yawyu have become one of the best documented ethnic groups. Favored by the Inka, this preference brought them enemies who harassed them in European times. Author has used primary sources to expand the colonial data.

1641 **———.** Mitimaes de Nasca en Arequipa, siglo XVI (Etnohistoria y Antropología Andina [Museo Nacional de Historia, Lima] 1, 1978, p. 135–140, bibl.)

The attempt to map the many kinds of *mitmaq* continues. Late 16th-century administrative sources locate Nasca colonies in several provinces further south. It is still not clear why such a large proportion of displaced ethnic groups was made up by the Nasca.

1642 **Golte, Juergen.** Redistribución y complementaridad regional en la economía andina del siglo XVIII (*in* International Congress of Americanists, XLII, Paris, 1976. Actes [see *HLAS 41:255*] v. 4, p. 64–87, bibl., maps, tables)

Inquires into the likelihood of drawing an analogy between the Corregidor's forcible distribution of goods among the Andean population in the 18th century and earlier Inka redistribution. In both cases the self-sufficiency of the ethnic community was threatened, but the colonial case is "mucho más burdo e impositivo." Also there is a fundamental difference between the two: "la separación de un sector estatal y un sector privado en la sociedad colonial."

1643 **González Luna, María D.** Características de las Gobernaciones de Santa Marta y Cartagena en relación al tema de los resguardos indígenas (UB/BA, 29, 1979, p. 65–82, bibl., maps)

Stresses the pre-European distribution of population and ethnic groups as a determinant in the kinds of *resguardos* that were set up in colonial times. The coastal population was more dispersed and of less interest to the invaders. Author has used primary sources in both Colombia and the Iberian peninsula.

1644 **Guillén Guillén, Edmundo.** Restauración geográfica del itinerario bélico seguido por los españoles, desde el puente de Chuquichaca a la ciudad de Vilcabamba (Etnohistoria y Antropología Andina [Museo Nacional de Historia, Lima] 1, 1978, p. 145–150, map)

Efforts initiated by Hiram Bingham to locate Vilcabamba—the "lost" capital of the refugee Inca regime after 1532—continue. Guillén combines fieldwork in the area with the use of primary sources and believes he has located the site.

1645 ———. Visión peruana de la conquista: la resistencia incaica a la invasión española. Lima: Editorial Milla Batres, 1979. 142 p.; bibl., 4 leaves of plates: ill.

Some years ago Guillén published the testimony of 14 survivors of the European invasion. Although witnesses were obviously reluctant to testify, Guillén demonstrates the existence of indigenous sources. Now a commercial publisher has added illustrations, maps, and "suggestions for further readings," and, in passing, reverted to an older orthography. This edition is meant to help "teachers" revise their sources. Essential point of both books was made in 1946 by Kubler when he argued that a neo-Inka state had survived until 1572 in the Eastern lowlands. Unfortunately, what was fresh and valuable in Guillén's original pamphlet is drowned in this commercialized edition.

1646 Habich, Eduardo de. Los libros de la Biblia peruana. Lima: Ediciones Eduardo de Habich, 1974. 90 p.; ill.

Reproduces selected pages from Montesinos and Waman Puma which author feels have been neglected about the origin of Andean states. The combination of these pages is alleged to be the Bible of Andean origins.

1647 Hardman, Martha J. Quechua y Aymara: lenguas en contacto (Antropología [La Paz] 1, 1979, p. 69–84, bibl.)

The political supremacy of the Quechua language at the time of the invasion, explains why it still enjoys a certain prestige in the Andes. This article examines attempts to relate Quechua to Aymara and other languages and finds these efforts wanting. Hardman has long insisted that Aymara influenced Quechua for millenia and that traces of Jaqi speech in the mountains above Lima indicate a past, much wider distribution.

1648 Hemming, John. Red gold: the conquest of the Brazilian Indians. Cambridge, Mass.: Harvard University Press, 1978. 677 p.; bibl.; index; 8 leaves of plates: ill.

A readable, exhaustive survey of the centuries of contact with the Europeans. Documents the gradual destruction of the Amazonian population through the 18th century and promises a follow-up volume which will bring the story up to date. The attempts to enslave the Amazonians is particularly well documented.

1649 Heredia, Edmundo A. Los tributos indígenas en el siglo XIX (JPHC/R, 5, 1977, p. 59–66, bibl.)

Reproduces an 1815 *Cedula* of Fernando VII, reestablishing tribute which had been abolished at the time of the Cortes of Cádiz.

1650 Hidalgo, Jorge. Incidencias de los patrones de poblamiento en el cálculo de la población del Partido de Atacama desde 1752 a 1804: las revisitas inéditas de 1787–92 y 1804 (Estudios Atacameños [San Pedro de Atacama, Chile] 6, 1978, p. 53–111, maps, tables)

Author used inspection reports from archives in Sucre and Santiago and detects major fluctuations when comparing earlier and later records. It appears that during the period noted above authorities changed their criteria for enumeration. Whereas Atacameños who were early residents of Salta were enumerated according to "vertical complementarity" with their original ethnic group, later residents were enumerated according to a "modern" criterion of residence.

1651 ———. Revisita de los Altos de Arica en 1750. Arica, Chile: Universidad del Norte, 1978. 209 p.; bibl.; index; tables.

Among the papers taken from the occupied northern region to Santiago, Hidalgo found the protocol of a detailed, house-to-house inspection of the *cacicazgo* of Codpa. It had been surveyed as early as 1575 when attempts were made to "reduce" the dispersed hamlets. Hidalgo considers this *cacicazgo* as part of a larger polity, that of the Ara, resident in Tacna. And 1750 records show that the local lord was still able to pool resources, up and down the valley.

1652 Huertas Vallejos, Lorenzo. Dioses mayores de Cajatambo. Ayacucho: Universidad Nacional de San Cristóbal de Huamanga, Dirección Universitaria de Investigaciones, 1978. 46 p.; bibl.

Reproduces historical material taken from interviews conducted in the 17th century as part of the "destruction of idolatries" in the highlands northeast of Lima. Distinguishes local deities from those imposed by the Inka.

1653 ———. Ideología campesina: Cajatambo, siglo XVII (Wari [Ayacucho, Peru] 1, 1977, p. 43–48)

The study of papers dealing with the extirpation of idolatries has been growing since Duviols' pioneer work (see *HLAS 34:1155*). In this article, Huertas uses data regarding confession and the cult of the dead as foci of Andean resistance in a region near Lima. He draws a contrast between the treatment of local worship by the Inka and Europeans.

1654 ———. Testimonios referentes al movimiento de Tupac Amaru II: 1784–1812 (IPA/AP, 11/12, 1978, p. 7–16)

Tupac Amaru's revolutionary message spread widely north of Cusco. Even after the defeat of his rebellion in the south, his followers in Huamanaga and elsewhere continued to express hopes of eventual victory. As late as 1784, alleged "brothers" of the rebel leader were apprehended.

1655 **Jave Calderón, Noé.** Vilcas Huaman: las tierras y collcas del Sol y del Inca (Inca [Centro de Estudiantes de Arqueología, Lima] 3:6, 1979, p. 92–120, bibl., maps)

In 1586, a European settler claimed as his own some unused land and corrals. Witnesses testified that the buildings standing there had been warehouses for wool, coca leaf and charqui belonging to the Sun. Another witness added that hot peppers and maize were also stored. The latter felt that an abandoned administrative center could hold "10,000 Indians" without infringing upon the disputed lands.

1656 **Julien, Catherine.** Investigaciones recientes en la capital de los qolla (*in* Arqueología peruana. Editor: Ramiro Matos Mendieta. Lima: Seminario Investigaciones Arqueológicas en el Perú, 1979, p. 199–213, bibl.; maps)

Recent archaeological work helped locate the storage area for this region mentioned by Cieza. Author discusses the problem of resettlement by the Inca of Aymara-speaking groups in lake area.

1657 **Klumpp, Kathleen M.** El retorno del Inga: una expresión ecuatoriana de la ideología mesiánica andina (CCE/CHA, 44, 1976, p. 99–135, bibl.)

Andean messianic ideology includes the notion of the Inka's return, since his defeat was explained as a *pachakuti*, a cyclic upheaval provided for in Andean history. In 1666, Don Alonso de Arenas y Florencia Inga, a mestizo of known Inka ancestry, was appointed Corregidor. Only six months later he was in jail; eventually he was deported to Lima. In rallying support for his cause, he used the painting of a genealogical tree which revealed how local lords were related to the royal house. Author shows how Don Alonso's claims fitted pre-existing notions of the Inka's return.

1658 **Larraín B., Horacio.** Análisis de las causas de despoblamiento entre las comunidades indígenas del Norte de Chile, con especial referencia a las hoyas hidrográficas de las quebradas Aroma y Tarapacá (UCC/NG, 1:2, dic. 1974, p. 125–154, bibl., tables)

Surveys demographic data available for northern Chile and causes leading to its depopulation. In addition to the more usual factors such as mines, Larraín points to the gradual dessication of the area, some of it cyclical in nature.

1659 **Llagostera Martínez, Agustín.** El Tawantinsuyo y el control de las relaciones complementarias (*in* International Congress of Americanists, XLII, Paris, 1976. Actes [see *HLAS 41:255*] v. 4, p. 39–50, bibl., tables)

Given complementary organization of production in widely separated areas, Llagostera stresses the role of the Inka state in expanding redistributive circulation.

1660 **Lobsiger, Georges.** La fin de l'Indianité péruvienne vue à travers *El primer nuevo coronica ibuen gobierno conpuesto por Don phelipe Poma guaman de Aialaprincipe*, 1613–1615 (SSA/B, 42, 1978, p. 23–45)

Stresses the "good government" part of Waman Puma's *Letter to the King*. Explains the author's concern about a growing mestizo population, why his attitude about collaborationist Andean lords was so ambivalent and his feelings about Christianity. Author suggests Waman Puma may have written in Quechua first and later translated the work into Spanish.

1661 Lohmann Villena, Guillermo. Una depredación inaudita: ¿Dónde están los documentos sobre Pedro Pizarro desaparecidos en Arequipa? (PUCP/H, 2:1, 1978, p. 89–91)

While preparing a new edition of Pedro Pizarro's eyewitness account (see *HLAS 38:3109*), Lohmann found that important memoranda and notarial records concerning this kinsman of the marquis and listed in a published bibliography, have disappeared. Lohmann is too polite to indicate who were the buyers of this loot. A well-known Middle Western collection of Andean sources could earn merit by returning these materials.

1662 López-Baralt, Mercedes. La Contrarreforma y el arte de Guaman Poma: notas sobre un política de comunicación visual (PUCP/H, 3:1, 1978, p. 81–96, bibl.)

Continuing her studies of Waman Puma's illustrations, the author examines his European antecedents, particularly the effect of the Counter-Reformation on Peruvian ecclesiastical circles. The Second and Third Councils of Lima took up the resolutions of the Council of Trent and emphasized the correct representation of the true faith in images, icons and illustrations. The Jesuits were particularly active in this matter. Waman Puma had close contacts with them and knew of Phillip II's affection for illustrations. The author draws together all references to images and ornamentation in the 1615 text.

1663 ———. Millenarism as liminality: an interpretation of the Andean myth of Inkarrí (Point of Contact [New York] 2:2, Spring 1979, p. 65–80, bibl.)

Several contemporary versions of the myth promising the return of the Inka were collected and are reproduced here. They should not be equated "with a desire for the restoration of the historical Incaic empire" but rather with "the order" which prevailed in the past and which now fuels contemporary expression. There is no cult of Inkarrí: "it embodies the millenarian hopes which once triggered messianic movements in the Andes . . ."

1664 Lorandi, Ana María. Arqueología y etnohistoria: hacia una visión totalizadora del mundo andino (*in* Obra del centenario del Museo de La Plata. La Plata, Argentina: Universidad Nacional de La Plata, Facultad de Ciencias Naturales y Museo, 1977, v. 2, p. 27–50, bibl.)

An effort to reinterpret the "horizons" of Andean archaeology through the application of ethnohistoric models. Lorandi stresses the importance of llama caravans in the functioning of "vertical" ecologic complementarity. In addition to these, she suggests that Cardich's changes in the upper limits of cultivation also correlated with presence or absence of "horizons."

1665 Lounsbury, Floyd G. Aspects du système de parenté inca (AESC, 33:5/6, 1978, p. 991–1005, bibl.)

Consists of an early (1964) attempt to understand the Inka kinship system utilizing data from early dictionaries and grammars. Suggests it was a parallel system, in which women descended from women and men from men.

1666 Lumbreras, Luis G. Acerca de la aparición del estado inca (*in* Congreso Peruano del Hombre y la Cultura Andina, III, Lima, 1977. El hombre y la cultura andina [see *HLAS 41:782*] v. 1, p. 101–109)

Any state arises out of the class struggle. There are two levels at which emergence of the Inca state can be understood: 1) before the reign of Pachacuti, and 2) afterward. Author discusses the roles of the Chanka as age-old enemies of the Inca and of the Colla as traditional allies. In circumstances such as the ones described the class struggle does not depend on control of means of production but on the appropriation of the labor-power which generates the wealth. The archaeology of Wari and of urbanism is treated in the above framework.

1667 ———. Los incas y los modos de producción (ANA, 4, 1978, p. 95–98)

The debate about which "mode of production" best fits the Andean data continues (see item **1678**). In cases where "slavery" or the "Asiatic mode" prevailed, Lumbreras believes the "primitive community" was more likely to reach "el nivel más alto del desarrollo de fuerzas productivas."

1668 Macierewicz, Antoni. La ciudad incaica como el centro del poder: las funciones y el papel de las ciudades en la estructura económica del Tawantinsuyu (Etnologia Polona [Warsaw] 2, 1976, p. 45–61, bibl.)

Starting from the premise that a significant percentage of the population was "enslaved and dependent," Macierewicz argues that they were concentrated in the "cities." The dramatic increase in their numbers coincided with "a sharp crisis" posing the "Qusqu aristocracy" against the state's central authority.

1669 Marsicotti de Görlitz, Ana María. Los curi y el rayo (*in* International Congress of Americanists, XLII, Paris, 1976. Actes [see *HLAS 41:255*] v. 4, p. 365–376, bibl.)

A long-lasting, Andean belief is that twins are dangerous to society. One consequence of their birth was frost and one way of eliminating them was infanticide. Lightning, the "Lord of Meterological Phenomena," was another manifestation of their appearance. Commanding thunder, rain, hail, and snow, this powerful deity threatens to this day.

1670 Martínez, Eduardo N. Etnohistoria de los pastos. Quito: Editorial Universitaria, 1977. 176 p.; bibl.; ill.; maps.

Despite the title, most of the work summarizes archaeological findings, some of them still unpublished such as Alice Francisco's thesis. Toponyms and other ethnographic data are reproduced from published sources.

1671 Maxwell, Thomas J. Inca Huacas: idols or fetishes? (El Dorado [University of Northern Colorado, Museum of Anthropology, Greeley] 2:2, July 1977, p. 87–92, bibl., ill.)

1672 Micheli, Catalina Teresa. Condiciones ecológicas de la región cuyana a la llegada de los españoles (Publicaciones [Universidad de San Juan, Instituto de Investigaciones Arqueológicas, San Juan, Argentina] 6, 1979, p. 11–36, bibl.)

Consists of a compilation of published sources concerned with the ecology of the Cuyo region. Author notes continuities with present-day climatic conditions.

1673 ———. Los puelches (Publicaciones [Universidad de San Juan, Instituto de Investigaciones Arqueológicas, San Juan, Argentina] 4, 1978, p. 1–39, bibl.)

A useful compilation from secondary sources of materials about an important ethnic group inhabiting Neuquen and Mendoza. A comparison with the entry on "Puelche" in the *Handbook of South American Indians* shows that progress has been made on this topic in the last 30 years.

1674 Millones, Luis. Los ganados del Señor: mecanismos del poder en las comunidades andinas (PMNH/HC, 11, 1978, p. 7–43, maps)

The access of ethnic lords to ecclesiastical authorities continued well into colonial times. An indispensable feature of this access was the lords' collaboration with "sacerdotes indígenas." Despite the almost immediate destruction of state religion after 1532, ensuing prohibitions and extensive baptisms, many ethnic cults were revitalized. Millones provides good detail from the late colonial era and emphasizes how individuals in charge of Andean worship drew clandestine revenues from their herds.

1675 ———. Religión y poder en los Andes: los curacas idólatras de la Sierra Central (Etnohistoria y Antropología Andina [Museo Nacional de Historia, Lima] 1, 1978, p. 253–273)

Where as many earlier studies of Andean lords dealt with the decades which followed the invasion, Millones examines their activities 100 years later. The cases of several lords of the Ancash region are surveyed: they were denounced, sometimes by their own subjects, sometimes by rivals. Much of their power was still operative but their societies included people who were ready to challenge them. The most difficult charges to resist were those concerning idolatry because its definition was so vague.

1676 ———. Las religiones nativas del Perú: recuento y evaluación de su estudio (IFEA/B, 8:1/2, 1978, p. 35–48, bibl.)

Annotated bibliography, reaching from the chronicles to contemporary studies.

1677 Miño Grijalva, Manuel. Los cañaris en la conquista española del Perú (Etnohistoria y Antropología Andina [Museo Nacional de Historia, Lima] 1, 1978, p. 151–157)

Although mostly based on secondary sources, this article manages to avoid studies by Oberem. Suggests formal but no functional distinctions between those transplanted as *yana* vis-à-vis those sent as *mitmaq*.

1678 Los modos de producción en el imperio de los Incas. Compilación de Waldemar Espinoza Soriano. Lima: Editorial Mantaro, 1978. 390 p.; bibl.; ill.

A reader reproduces three articles by the editor and one each by: Edmundo Guillén Guillén, Juergen Golte, Maurice Godelier, and Emilio Choy.

1679 Monteiro, Mário Ypiranga. História da cultura amazonense. v. 1, A colônia. Manaus, Brazil: Edição do Governo do Estado do Amazonas, Administração Ministro Henoch da Silva Reis, 1977. 399 p.; bibl.; ill. (some col.).

While most of the text deals with the European penetration of the Amazon, both Spanish and Portuguese, there are frequent references to the region's native population. Also considers the rise of the *mameluco*, a mestizo social type.

1680 Moreno Yáñez, Segundo. Elementos para un análisis de la sociedad indígena en la Audiencia de Quito (Sarance [Instituto Otavaleño de Antropología, Otavalo, Ecuador] 6, 1978, p. 79–89, bibl.)

Traditional historiography has neglected events, personalities and institutions of the vanquished population. Moreno surveys authors who did offer some pertinent information in the past and outlines recent work at the Universities of Bonn and Illinois.

Morris, Craig. The archaeological study of Andean exchange systems. See *HLAS 41:817*.

1681 Murra, John V. Derechos a las tierras en el Tawantinsuyu (RUC, 28:117, 1979, p. 273–287, bibl., tables)

The vogue to determine "modes of production" runs into an almost total lack of information concerning land rights in the Andes. Here, Murra picks up a chart which he discussed in 1959 in Mexico and wonders why so little progress has been made to fathom how land was held, claimed and defended.

1682 ———. La guerre et les rébellions dans l'expansion de l'état Inka (AESC, 33:5/6, sept./déc. 1978, p. 927–935, bibl.)

The political organization of the Inka state used local ethnic lords in the administration. Since this encouraged both expansion and rebellion, the Inka responded by reorganizing its forces and shifting from rotating troops to a standing army.

1683 ———. Los olleros del Inka: hacia una historia y arqueología del Qollasuyo (*in* Historia, problema y promesa. Edición a cargo de Francisco Miró Quesada C., Franklin Pease G.Y. and David Sobrevilla A. Lima: Pontificia Universidad Católica del Perú, 1978, p. 415–423, bibl.)

Suggestions for an archaeology which would take its inspiration from written sources. Litigation records from the Bolivian National Archives suggest a way to approach Andean textile and ceramic technology.

1684 ———. La organización económica del estado inca. Traducción de Daniel R. Wagner. México: Siglo Veintiuno, 1978. 270 p.; bibl. (Colección América nuestra; 11. América antigua)

Spanish version of 1955 thesis.

1685 Naranjo, Marcelo F. Zonas de refugio y adaptación étnica en el Oriente: siglos XVI–XVII (*in* Temas sobre la continuidad y adaptación cultural ecuatoriana [see *HLAS 41:1274*] p. 105–169, bibl.)

Scrutiny of many groups which reportedly inhabited the Alto Amazonas (i.e., the valleys of the Bobonaza and Napo Rivers) reveals that they were mostly the same people called by different names. They were swidden agriculturists who moved frequently and were reluctant to establish the *pueblos* urged on them by missionaries. Thus, Jívaros, Oas, Coronados, Zapas, Canelos, and Gayes all know each other. Both ethnogenesis and ethnocide were familiar processes in the forest.

1686 Nectario María, Brother. Los indios teques y el Cacique Guacaipuro. 2. ed. Madrid: Villena, 1975. 106 p.; bibl.; 3 leaves of plates: ill.; map.

The original population of the region which later became Caracas was given in encomienda in 1568. Details emerge from testimony collected a few years later as part of litigation. Selected passages of the latter are reproduced in this edition.

1687 Núñez Atencio, Lautaro and **T.D. Dillehay.** Movilidad giratoria, armonía social y desarrollo en los Andes meridionales: patrones de tráfico e inter-acción económica. Antofagasta, Chile: Universidad del Norte, 1979. 170 p.; bibl.; maps; tables.

This study constitutes a major effort to expand our understanding of complementary relations between highland societies and their settlements on the western highlands. Stresses the importance of camelid herders and their caravans who are not integrated into any agricultural society. Much of their "gyratory" movement implies "social harmony" or truces between potentially competitive ethnic groups, and in Tiwanaku times, even states.

1688 Oberem, Udo. El acceso de recursos naturales de diferentes ecologías en la sierra ecuatoriana: siglo XVI (*in* International Congress of Americanists, XLII, Paris, 1976. Actes [see *HLAS 41:255*] v. 4, p. 51–64)

Differences between the *páramo* of the northern Andes and the *puna* regions to the south affect the pattern of economic complementarity between ecological zones in each region. Oberem suggests the concept of "micro-verticality" to describe the distinctive situation found in the Ecuadorian sierra. Resources were rarely located very far from the main settlement, particularly since ethnic groups were small. In addition, one can distinguish settlements that were multiethnic and charged with certain state duties such as the supervision of the transplanted *camayo* group, who grew coca and occasionally cotton. It is unclear if all such colonization was pre-European, since pressure to expand coca growing was an integral part of colonial economics. It should also be noted that in the North, there were groups of traders (see *HLAS 32:1055*), called *mindala,* who specialized in long-distance exchanges.

1689 ———. Ein Beispiel für soziale Selbsteinschäntzung des Indianischen Hochadels im kolonialzeitlichen (IAA, 5:3, 1979, p. 215–224, bibl.)

Further studies of Atawallpa's descendants (see *HLAS 38:2141*) reveal that early in the 17th century they continued to petition for pensions owed them by the Crown. Doña Bárbara, whose claims are reproduced here, was a great-granddaughter of Atawallpa. She stressed that Don Melchior Inca, a well-provided for resident of Spain, was no closer to the royal line than she was and compared her status to that of dukes and marquises in the peninsula. Oberem notes differences in the adaptation of royal relatives in Quito and Cuzco. The former maintained kinship ties with both Europeans and local ethnic lords.

1690 ——— and **Roswith Hartmann.** Indios cañaris de la sierra sur del Ecuador en el Cuzco del siglo XVI (RUC, 128:117, 1979, p. 373–390, bibl.)

The long resistance of ethnic groups in the northern part of the realm to Cuzco's armies led to innovations. Among them was the massive resettlement of groups like the Cañari who were transferred from their home base to the Yucay valley, near the capital (see *HLAS 40:2089*). Their military skill is frequently mentioned in the sources; shortly before the European invasion they had replaced Aymara troops as potential elements of a standing army. After 1532, they sided with the Europeans against the Inka whenever there were attempts at resistance or accommodation.

1691 O'Phelan Godoy, Scarlett. Cuzco 1977: el movimiento de Maras, Urubamba (PUCP/H, 1:1, 1977, p. 113–128, bibl.)

Tupac Amaru's rebellion was not an isolated incident; in the years prior to 1780 various movements arose against the corregidores and forced purchases. Such sales affected both criollo and Andean populations.

1692 ———. La rebelión de Tupac Amaru: su organización interna, dirigencia y alianzas (PUCP/H, 3:2, 1979, p. 89–122, bibl., tables)

Examines records in Sevilla which permit better appreciation of role of Tupac Amaru's kin in the rebellion. The percentage of mestizos and muleteers was high.

1693 ———. El sur andino a fines del siglo XVIII: ¿cacique o corregidor? (IPA/AP, 11/12, 1978, p. 17–32, bibl.)

After the defeat of Tupac Amaru and the abolition of the corregidores, what happened to local Andean leadership? Colonial administrators pressured local ethnic lords to assume some of the corregidor's functions. These new responsibilities weakened the authority of local leaders and led to many community complaints. Their written records are analyzed here.

1694 Ossio, Juan M. Las cinco edades del mundo según Felipe Guaman Poma de Ayala (Etnohistoria y Antropología Andina [Museo Nacional de Historia, Lima] 1, 1978, p. 241–252)

While the "five ages" so frequently studied by archaeologists may have an idiosyncratic dimension, they mostly correspond to one Andean tradition. Time, space and social relations were perceived as dual. Thus, the world was divided between Andeans and non-Andeans. The five ages also provided the genealogical explanation for the final stage of the Inca as unifying what had previously been split into two. Christianity continued the process by reinforcing this perception. Parallels with China are offered.

1695 ———. Los mitos de origen de la comunidad de Andamarca (IPA/AP, 10, 1977, p. 105–113)

Whereas some local myths refer to families and their land rights, others deal with a settlement's origin. The legend of the four Mayo Brothers whose adventures are related to the town's creation is reproduced here.

1696 Paradowska, Maria. The role of external factors in the formation of the leadership institution among Araucanians (Ethnologia Polona [Warsaw] 3, 1977, p. 161–174, bibl.)

Resistance to European rule encouraged the emergence of war leaders whose tendency was to perpetuate their authority. Based on secondary sources. Apparently, the more recent studies of the Mapuche, particularly by Chilean scholars, are unavailable in Warsaw.

1697 Parejas Moreno, Alcides J. Los pueblos indígenas del Oriente boliviano en la época de su contacto con los españoles. Santa Cruz de la Sierra, Bolivia: Universidad Boliviana Gabriel René Moreno, Departamento de Publicaciones, 1976. 24 p.; bibl.

See *HLAS 38:2142.*

1698 Pease G.Y., Franklin. La formación del Tawantinsuyu: mecanismos de colonización y relación con unidades étnicas (PUCP/H, 3:1, 1979, p. 97–120, bibl.)

Well-documented summary of current status of debate. The very notion of what constituted an ethnic group is in doubt, partly because so many regions had multiethnic resettlement policies and the state encouraged them. Author also examines the degree of consent implied in the rapid spread of Tawantinsuyu and the nature of royal redistribution effected to gain loyalties. The kind of consent would also affect state-ethnic group institutions.

1699 ———. Inkarri en Collaguas (Etnohistoria y Antropología Andina [Museo Nacional de Historia, Lima] 1, 1978, p. 237–240)

The texts of these myths have been included in a previous article by Pease (see *HLAS 40:2094*). The versions are distinct from others dealing with this deity. One concerned agricultural assignments, the other settlement patterns.

1700 ———. Los últimos incas del Cuzco. 2. ed. Lima: P. L. Villanueva, 1977. 143 p.; bibl.

Second edition of *HLAS 38:2144.*

1701 Pérez, Aquiles R. La minúscula nación de Nasacota Puento resiste la invasión de la gigantesca de Hauina Capac. Quito: Editorial Casa de la Cultura Ecuatoriana, 1978. 20 p.

In the continued debate about the veracity of Velasco's claim that there was a large polity in pre-Inka times on what today is Ecuadorian territory, Pérez quotes very early testimony by priests who talk about the resistance to the Inka penetration in the Cayambi area. Such resistance depended on extensive political organization, confirmed by the prevalence of anti-Inka fortresses.

1702 Pérez T., Aquiles R. Los cañaris. Quito: Casa de la Cultura Ecuatoriana, 1978. 501 p.

Further installment in a long-range effort to define the territory, linguistic affiliation and whatever fragments of social organization can be discerned of Andean populations inhabiting Ecuador. Moving from north to south, Pérez has used Jijón's identifications through toponimies; he has also consulted notarial and church archives. The definition of Cañari territory is essentially post-European and the dispersion of this ethnic group towards the Cuzco region and even further south is ignored.

1703 *Pesquisas: História.* Universidade do Vale do Rio dos Sinos, Instituto Anchietano de Pesquisas. No. 18, 1975– . São Leopoldo, Brazil.

Consists of two articles (total 49 p.): José de Moura e Silva's "Fundação da Missão de Diamantina," and Alonso Silveira de Mello's "A Missão do Mangabal do Juruena in Prelazia de Diamantina." Both report brief observations culled from Jesuit archives and secondary sources about the aboriginal populations at various times since 1840. Most of the material dates from this century.

1704 Pinckert Justiniano, Guillermo. La guerra chiriguana. Santa Cruz de la Sierra, Bolivia: Talleres Gráficos Los Huerfanos, 1978. 143 p.; bibl.; index.

A survey of Chiriguano resistance from Inka times, through the colony and their eventual acceptance of a defeated status.

1705 Pizarro, Pedro. Relación del descubrimiento y conquista de los Reinos del Perú. Edición de Guillermo Lohmann Villena. Lima: Pontificia Universidad Católica del Perú, 1978. 277 p.; indexes.

Guillermo Lohmann has prepared a new edition of this 1571 account by a Pizarro kinsman, eyewitness of the invasion. Based on the original, in the Huntington Library, it provides many relatively minor improvements over earlier versions. Lohmann has provided supplementary materials on Pizarro's life in Arequipa and his comments on the work and the author are first class.

1706 Platt, Tristan. Symétries en miroir: le concept de *yanantin* chez les Macha de Bolivie (AESC, 33:5/6, 1978, p. 1081–1107, bibl., maps)

A revised and translated version of author's suggestions about the relevance of mirrow images in Andean thinking (see *HLAS 38:2146*).

1707 Poma de Ayala, Felipe Huamán. *Letter to a King*: a Peruvian chief's account of life under the Incas and under Spanish rule. Arranged and edited with an introduction by Christopher Dilke. New York: Dutton, 1978. 248 p.; ill.; index.

This first English version of the *Letter* translated many of its pages and was prepared for the Human Relations Area Files where it was made available to researchers. This edition, designed for a more popular audience, consists of portions of the original and additional translations edited and rearranged for readability.

1708 ———. Nueva corónica y buen gobierno. Edición crítica preparada por John V. Murra y Rolena Adorno. Traducción de los textos quechuas de Jorge Urioste. México: Siglo XXI, 1980. 1700 p.; ill.; indexes.

Editions of this classic *Letter to the King* of 1615 have been multiplying. This one transcribes written text from a fresh examination of the Copenhague manuscript by Adorno, who adds a detailed commentary of the sources used by Waman Puma and of his colonial relevance. Urioste has translated anew the songs, prayers, sermons and occasional remarks and includes a commentary on the Quechua used and how it influenced the author's Spanish.

1709 Radicati di Primeglio, Carlos. El sistema contable de los incas: yupana y quipu. Lima, Perú: Librería Studium, between 1976 and 1980. 116 p.; bibl.; ill.

Useful summary of past efforts to interpret knot records and bookkeeping. Offers new solution for the use of the counting board illustrated by Waman Puma (facsimile on p. 360). The *yupana* is said to permit all four arithmetic operations. Eventually, results were recorded on *khipu*.

1710 Ramírez-Horton, Susan E. Chérrepe en 1572: un análisis de la Vista General del Virrey Francisco de Toledo (PMNH/HC, 11, 1978, p. 79–121, bibl., tables)

Whereas several financial resumés of the 1572 inspection have been published (see *HLAS 38:2103*), there are very few available protocols of the visita itself. Chérrepe was a small ethnic group on the North Coast, consisting of both fishermen and cultivators, which suffered a drastic population decline by 1572. Ramírez is able to trace the group's demographic fate through 1610 with occasional glimpses beyond. After the inspection, the inhabitants were subjected to a *reducción* with consequent impoverishment, particularly through loss of irrigation rights. Reproduces full text of the *visita*.

1711 Remy, Pilar. El sacerdocio cusqueño: problemática (Etnohistoria y Antropología Andina [Museo Nacional de Historia, Lima] 1, 1978, p. 221–224)

Our knowledge of Andean religion is weakest where it concerns specialists of several cults who were annihilated or driven underground by the invasion. This article surveys some research questions raised by this dearth in our information without offering any new sources.

1712 Reynal, Vicente. El indio motilón: nuevas aportaciones históricas y algunos datos antropológicos (UPR/RO, 2:2, junio 1978, p. 93–113)

Several lowland ethnic groups along the Colombia-Venezuela border have been known in colonial and even modern times as *motilones*. Author, who knew one such group as a missionary, has also consulted records in Sevilla and Colombia. Under the pen-name of A. de Alcocer he already published a book about them: *El indio motilón y su historia* (1962).

1713 Rivière, Gilles. Intercambio y reciprocidad en Carangas (Antropología [La Paz] 1, 1979, p. 85–113, bibl.)

Most of the article concerns contemporary phenomena in a region which has received minimal attention. Rivière, however, has considerable archival experience and is particularly intrigued by the "historical memory" of the inhabitants concerning distant holdings they lost. They "remembered" lands they had controlled and which lay towards Cochabamba, a 25-day walk, but not their holdings towards the Pacific, a five-day walk. Present-day contacts occur through annual caravans, facilitating barter.

1714 Robles, Román. Destrucción y supervivencia dc las prácticas religiosas prehispánica en Mangas: Cajatambo-Bolognesi (Etnohistoria y Antropología Andina [Museo Nacional de Historia, Lima] 1, 1978, p. 225–235)

Among the many "idolatry" records available in the Archbishop's Archive in Lima, one from 1663 concerns a region near the vice-regal capital. Well over a century after the European invasion, local cults flourished. Many of these are familiar because of earlier sources, but details of their practices are frequently new. Mangas' reputation in the region was that of a "pueblo de brujos." An attempt to chart hierarchical relations between cults is included.

1715 Roel Pineda, Virgilio. Sobre el modo de producción inca (*in* Congreso Peruano del Hombre y la Cultura Andina, III, Lima, 1977. El hombre y la cultura andina [see *HLAS 41:782*] v. 1, p. 110–111)

The reciprocity principle in Inca productive process constituted a great advance in Inca technology. Personal services were the only loans. No known mode of production describes what author proposes we call the Inca one.

1716 Romoli, Kathleen. El Alto Chocó en el siglo XVI: pt. 2., Las gentes (ICA/RCA, 20, 1976, p. 25–77, bibl., maps, plates, tables)

Some 19 ethnic groups, independent of one another, can be located in early maps and eyewitness reports. Some used rivers for traffic but others knew the forest and could cross the cordilleras. Some managed to reject European rule for decades. Romoli made a serious effort to disentangle contradictory demographic data in earliest accounts.

1717 ———. Las tribus de la antigua jurisdicción de Pasto en el siglo XVI (ICA/RCA, 21, 1977/1978, p. 11–55, bibl., maps, tables)

Careful attempt, published posthumously, to clarify location of and relations among ethnic groups on the Ecuador-Colombia border. Quechua place-names cluster only near European settlements and are supposed to be a late, post-1532 influence. Other ethnic groups and their languages can be identified and located through the *Visita* of 1558 which includes a list of encomiendas and numbers of *tributarios*. Provides brief accounts of Pasto, Abad and Quillacinga and outlines their demographic fate towards the end of the century.

1718 Rostworowski, María. La costa peruana prehistórica (RUC, 28:117, 1979, p. 461–473)

Because of their concentration on the highlands, most investigators have neglected the coast. Only archaeologists have given it the attention it deserves. Stresses the need to study specialized coastal populations such as fishermen, high-sea navigators or those who used nearby inland territories.

1719 ———. Una hipótesis sobre el surgimiento del estado inca (*in* Congreso Peruano del Hombre y la Cultura Andina, III, Lima, 1977. El hombre y la cultura andina [see *HLAS 41:782*] v. 1, p. 89–100)

Stresses the importance of many ethnic groups of various sizes. As the Lord of the Cuzco achieved hegemony over others, he used well known redistributive tactics to secure and attract loyalties. Rostworowski stresses importance of coastal data for testing and adding to our knowledge of Inca expansion.

1720 ———. Señoríos indígenas de Lima y Canta. Lima: Instituto de Estudios Peruanos, 1978. 280 p.; bibl.; maps; tables.

This close follow-up to the author's volume of essays on coastal ethnic groups (see *HLAS 40:2110*) concentrates on the inhabitants of valleys above the new capital. The book is a revelation for those who think they know about the history of the City of the Three Kings. The publishers have padded the volume with the text of the 1549 Inspection of Canta.

1721 Rowe, John Howland. An account of the shrines of ancient Cuzco (IAS/ÑP, 17, 1979, p. 1–80)

Roland Hamilton's recent discovery of the original of Barnabé Cobo's *Historia* (see item **1606**) allows Rowe to restudy the chapters dealing with *ceque* lines radiating from the Inka capital. Rowe provides corrections to Jiménez's edition and comments on the identification and location of shrines. He also corrects prevailing opinion that Cobo copied his list from Polo de Ondegardo.

1722 ———. La fecha de la muerte de Wayna Qhapaq (PUCP/H, 2:1, 1979, p. 83–88, bibl.)

Examines several versions of what was the date of death of the last Inka king. The date is important since it determines the duration of the war of succession waged by his sons. Rowe finds evidence favoring a late date, a very few years before the invasion. This clarifies the contradictory claims of Inka historiography.

1723 ———. Religión e historia en la obra de Bernabé Cobo (Antropología Andina [Cuzco, Peru] 3, 1979, p. 31–39, bibl.)

Defense of the historical skill of Father Cobo whose 1653 compilation is widely admired (see item **1606**) partly because of his use of sources now unavailable. Of the latter, Rowe thinks Cobo had the greatest trust in Cristóbal de Molina's *History of the Inka*. The article also includes an attempt to explain how Cobo tried to combine Garcilaso's "long count" of Inka kings with the much shorter list transmitted by dynastic oral tradition.

1724 Rozo G., José. Cultura material de los muiscas. Bogotá: Ediciones Ideas, 1977. 99 p.; bibl.

Study based on secondary sources. Its supplement reproduces a survey of placer mines in 1580–90 from Tunja's Notarial Archive.

1725 Sáenz de Santa María, Carmelo. Hacia un pleno conocimiento de la personalidad de Pedro Cieza de León (EEHA/AEA, 32, 1975 [i.e. 1978] p. 329–373)

In his search for the "lost" third part of Cieza's early account of Andean history, Sáenz has checked his hero's career in New Granada, before joining LaGasca in Perú in 1547. After establishing that the writer used "Pedro de León" and not Cieza during that period, Sáenz could trace his activities. A partisan of Jorge Robledo, he was awarded several small encomiendas and was on the whole glad LaGasca's call to arms offered him the opportunity to leave. Sáenz traces Cieza's kin ties with several traders and notaries active in the Andes and suggests Cieza himself was an occasional trader.

1726 ———. Los manuscritos de Pedro Cieza de León (IGFO/RI, 36:145/146, 1977, p. 185–215)

The request to prepare a complete edition of Cieza's works meant finding the "missing" text of the third part of his chronicle. Parts of it had been published in the *Mercurio Peruano* by Rafael Laredo, who died without revealing the location of the original. Another copy was hoarded by an Irish collector. Certain parts had been pirated by Herrera. Sáenz outlines here the required detective work.

1727 Saignes, Thiérry. De la filiation à la résidence: les ethnies dans les vallées de Larecaja (AESC, 33:5/6, 1978, p. 1160–1181, bibl., maps, tables)

We learned from Garci Diez (the year 1567, see *HLAS 29:2151*) that Aymara polities maintained permanent establishments in the warm valleys east of the lake. Following the hint, Saignes located these peripheral settlements and made a major contribution to our understanding of ecologic complementarity in both colonial and pre-European times.

1728 ———. Indios de abajo, ideología e historia: los chiriguanos en los ojos del otro (Antropología [La Paz] 2, 1979, p. 78–120, bibl.)

After studying the history of the Chiriguanos, Saignes began working on ethnic groups in the lowlands east of La Paz. This is the first installment of his final report. In colonial times, the Chiriguanos were perceived as prototypical barbarians who resisted all demands to join or be eliminated. Saignes studied them as they saw themselves by using religious reports from several centuries culminating in a 1912 monograph by Father Bernardino de Nino. In the late 18th century, colonists began intruding into Chiriguano territory with predictable consequences. Even recent land reforms have failed to return their lost lands.

1729 ———. Niveles de segmentación y de interdigitación en el poblamiento de los valles de Larecaja (Etnohistoria y Antropología Andina [Museo Nacional de Historia, Lima] 1, 1978, p. 141–144)

The Aymara lords' control of Lake Titicaca's numerous warm-weather "islands" continued in colonial times. Propitious for commercial agriculture, this region underwent early alienation when European planters began supplying the miners of Potosí. In the process, highland lords lost some of their privileges but compensated for the loss by purchasing lands. Both maize and coca leaf were "democratized" when they became available through commercial channels that disregarded traditional Andean patterns of access.

1730 ———. Valles y punas en el debate colonial: la pugna sobre los pobladores de Larecaja (PUCP/H, 3:2, 1979, p. 141–164, bibl., tables)

Further study of the fate of the colonists sent out from their nuclei at Lake Titicaca by the Aymara kingdoms. Both planters and corregidores in lowerlands to the east tried to detach the colonists from their ethnic allegiances in the altiplano. Use of new and unpublished sources allows Saignes to follow the quantitative presence of the highlanders through the 17th century.

1731 Salazar Zapatero, Héctor. Reflexiones sobre la metalurgia de la sociedad inca (*in* Congreso Peruano del Hombre y la Cultura Andina, III, Lima, 1977. El hombre y la cultura andina: actas y trabajos. Editor: Ramiro Matos Mendieta. Lima: Editorial Lasontay, 1978, v. 1, p. 178–201)

Surveys previous classifications of Inca state which characterized its modes of production as feudal, slave or Asiatic. Considers that servile populations were numerous and significant.

1732 Salomon, Frank. Systèmes politiques verticaux aux marches de l'Empire Inca (AESC, 33:5/6, 1978, p. 967–989, bibl., maps)

The slow-down of Tawantinsuyu's northward expansion was largely due to the resistance of local ethnic groups and new ecologies facing the conquerors. Salomon suggests that stages in the Inka's advance can be reconstructed from both ethnohistorical evidence and a typology of state settlements.

1733 Schaedel, Richard P. Formation of the Inca state (*in* Congreso Peruano del Hombre y la Cultura Andina, III, Lima, 1977. El hombre y la cultura andina [see *HLAS 41:782*] v. 1, p. 112–156, bibl., maps, tables)

Wars against ethnic groups both towards the North and to the South of Cuzco took place at "the crucial period of transformation from Chiefdom to state." At this early period in their expansion, the Inca presented "all the characteristics of an Oppenheimer conquest state." After a predatory period, author discerns a change in the technological relations of production, with massive reallocation of manpower going to projects in the circum-Cuzco area. These go beyond "verticality" and redistribution, since the stress is on *yana* and *mitmaq*. Considerable space is devoted to bureaucracy and religion.

1734 Sharon, Douglas G. The Inca Warachikuy initiations (*in* Enculturation in Latin America [see *HLAS 41:260*] p. 213–236, bibl.)

Summarizes and translates available pages by Cristóbal de Molina (the one from Cuzco) dealing with the initiation of young royals. Cites comparative materials from other sources.

——— and **Christopher B. Donnan.** The magic cactus: ethnoarchaeological continuity in Peru. See *HLAS 41:1460*.

1735 Sherbondy, Jeanette. Les réseaux d'irrigation dans la géographie politique de Cuzco (SA/J, 66, 1979, p. 45–66, bibl., maps, tables)

Author coordinates contemporary field-work on irrigation with ethnohistoric data. Certain canals were controlled by a given *panaca* of royals; some by a reigning king, others by priests. Documents the association with shrines and the *ceque* lines connecting them. This is a significant contribution to both land tenure and irrigation studies.

1735a Silva Celis, Eliécer. Relaciones comerciales precolombinas de los muiscas con los nativos de la provincia de Santa Marta (*in* Congreso Nacional de Historiadores y Antropólogos, I, Santa Marta, Colombia, 1975. Memorias. Medellín, Colombia: Editorial Argemiro Salazar, 1976, p. 178–188, bibl.)

Glosses over secondary sources and emphasizes the presence of earliest markets. Suggests their precolumbian character.

1736 Silva Galdames, Osvaldo. Consideraciones acerca del período inca en la cuenca de Santiago, Chile Central (Boletín [Museo Arqueológico de la Serena, Chile] 16, 1977/1978, p. 211–243, bibl.)

Careful review of published sources dealing with the southernmost extensions of Inka rule. Although there were colonies of *mitmaqkuna* on the banks of the Maipo Maipo, Silva suggests that this region was part of the royal patrimony, as distinguished from state holdings. Military incursions may have reached further south.

1737 Silva Holguín, Raúl. Naciones y tribus que habitaban la provincia de Santa Marta antes de la fundación de la ciudad (*in* Congreso Nacional de Historiadores y Antropólogos, I, Santa Marta, Colombia, 1975. Memorias. Medellín, Colombia: Editorial Argemiro Salazar, 1976, p. 197–208, bibl., map)

Summarizes secondary sources on ethnic distribution in earliest days of European occupation.

1738 Silva Santisteban, Fernando. El tiempo de cinco días en los mitos de Huarochiri (Etnohistoria y Antropología Andina [Museo Nacional de Historia, Lima] 1, 1978, p. 210–220, bibl.)

Relates myths recorded by Francisco de Avila with data on Waman Puma. In both authors, creation, regeneration and fertility were connected to a five-day cycle. Suggests parallels with Mesoamerica.

1739 Silverblatt, Irene and **John Earls.** Mito y renovación: el caso de Moros y los aymaraes (IPA/AP, 10, 1977, p. 93–104, bibl.)

There are papers which confirm the colonial origin of the village of Sarhua as a *reducción*. One of the components was a recognized ceremonial center, known today as Moros (Muru). Several villages claim to descend from Moros, an Aymara center. Abandonment is correlated with fertility and sterility. Authors use mythic materials which they refer to pre-Inca and the transition from colonial to modern times. Nothing in Andean history is perceived as catastrophically as the European invasion: it is still used as a "modelo simbólico para la codificación de otros procesos históricos de transición."

1740 Soldi, Ana María. Nuevos datos sobre la antigua provincia de Chucuito (Etnohistoria y Antropología Andina [Museo Nacional de Historia, Lima] 1, 1978, p. 123–133)

There were changes in the numbers and composition of lineages among the Lapaqa between 1573–1685 with some lineages disappearing during this period. A list of later date provides more functional detail such as how several ethnic lords or "provinces" as well as some lineages lived intermixed on the same lands, how camelid herds held by lineages shrunk and how weights and measures became Europeanized.

1741 Stern, Steve J. Algunas consideraciones sobre la personalidad histórica de Don Felipe Guaman Poma de Ayala (PUCP/H, 2:2, 1978, p. 225–228)

Recent publication of details of Waman Puma's participation in colonial administrative affairs as interpreter and scribe suggest to Stern that he was caught between two worlds. He is also "miembro de la raza o cultura dominada, incapaz por su origen y vida social de adoptar perfectamente las modalidades hispánicas . . ."

1742 Susnik, Branislava. Los aborígenes del Paraguay. v. 1, Etnología del Chaco Boreal y su periferia: siglos XVI y XVII; v. 2, Epoca colonial. Asunción: Museo Etnográfico Andrés Barbero, 1978. 2 v. (156, 332 p.); bibl.; maps.

These extremely useful volumes were conceived as the first two of eight devoted to the native peoples of Paraguay. They bring together data from primary sources about the Alto Paraguay, the Guaraní and the inhabitants of the Chaco. Vol. 2 deals with the colonial Guaraní, and vol. 3 will follow them through the period after 1811.

1743 Taylor, Gerald. Avant-propos: texte établi, traduit et commenté (*in* Avila,

Francisco de. Rites et traditions Huarochiri [see item **1589**] p. 5–23)

Suggests that the text of the 33 oral traditions collected at Huarochiri, which form our only serious Quechua literary text-source, may have been collected before Avila began his treatise in 1608. Most likely though, Avila did encourage a local literate man to assemble the material. Draws a comparison with Waman Puma as an example of a bilingual—if not trilingual—man capable of writing the traditions of his people. Useful philological notes.

1744 Torres, Luiz B. A terra de Tilixi e Txiliá: Palmeira dos Indios dos séculos XVIII e XIX. Maceió, Brazil: Serviços Gráficos de Alagoas, 1975. 358 p.: ill.

Reproduces numerous unpublished documents from the history of Palmeira and of the Xurucú and Keriri, local aboriginal groups. As early as 1665 they were objects of missionary efforts and by the 18th century they were under the complete control of the *Diretorio Indígena.*

1745 Trimborn, Hermann. El Reino de Lamabayeque en el antiguo Perú. St. Augustin, FRG: Haus Völker und Kulturen Anthropos Institut, 1979. 88 p.; bibl.; ill.; maps (Collectanea Institut Anthropos; 19)

While most of the text and illustrations are concerned with the study of ceremonial centers, the first half of the book examines both primary and secondary sources on the North Coast. Author compares the historicity of materials first recorded by Cabello Valboa (1586) dealing with rulers reaching Lambayeque on rafts with later accounts and the archaeological evidence.

1746 Urbano, Henrique-Osvaldo. La symbolique de l'espace andin (*in* International Congress of Americanists, XLII, Paris, 1976. Actes [see *HLAS 41:255*] v. 4, p. 335–345, bibl., tables)

The concept *pacha* covers both space and time and, in certain contexts, it can also mean earth. It is present in *pachacuti*, the upheaval, the reversal of an existing order. These are all related to Inka myths of the peopling of Cuzco and reformulated for our time, in which a new cycle is imminent.

1747 Varallanos, José. Guamán Poma de Ayala: cronista precursor y libertario. Lima: G. Herrera Editores, 1979. 242 p.; bibl.; 5 leaves of plates: ill.; index. (Colección Biblioteca de cultura andina)

As soon as Rivet brought out in 1936 his facsimilar edition, Varallanos began studying the unusual manuscript, following the fate of this text and the commentaries it has generated. Here, he argues for the anthropological veracity of Waman Puma and offers ample confirmation of his complaints against European rule contained in the second part.

1748 Velasco, Juan de. Historia del Reino de Quito en la América Meridional. v. 1, Historia natural; v. 2, Historia antigua; v. 3, Historia moderna. Quito: Editorial Casa de la Cultura Ecuatoriana, 1977/1979. 3 v. (504, 445, 531 p.) bibl.; tables.

The long debate about the value of Juan de Velasco's 18th-century history continues. The newest contribution does not reproduce the copy in the Quito Archives but an earlier "original" in Madrid. Alfredo Costales has sponsored this edition and Juan Freile Granizo provides an introduction defending the value of the Jesuit's information.

1749 Velasco de Tord, Emma. La *k'apakocha*: sacrificios humanos en el incario (Etnohistoria y Antropología Andina [Museo Nacional de Historia, Lima] 1, 1978, p. 193–199)

Although most data in support of the existence of human sacrifice among the Inca are well known, the author uses primary sources which further corroborate the fact of this practice. Some sacrifices were designed by the Inca to serve as punishment. There are allegations that the practice persists to this day.

1750 Villanueva, Horacio and **Jeanette Sherbondy.** Cuzco: aguas y poder. Cuzco, Peru: Centro de Estudios Rurales Andinos Bartolomé de las Casas, 1979. 153 p.; bibl. (Archivos de historia rural andina; 1)

This first-rate contribution is based on field work as well as archival materials. It concerns the distribution of waters in the Cusco area, the prevalence of irrigation, the differential relation of the latter several crops, and the references to water in so many of the shrines surrounding the Inka capital. The sources range from the 17th to the 19th centuries and are also useful for the study of how the European takeover of Andean irrigation spread throughout the region.

1751 Wachtel, Nathan. Hommes d'eau: le problème Uru, XVI–XVIIIème siècles (AESC, 33:5/6, 1978, p. 1127–1159, bibl., maps, tables)

This is a major reevaluation of the role and fate of the Uru, the "fishermen" of classical European sources. It includes serious reexamination of their location among Aymara and Puquina speakers. Wachtel was able to locate villages where they constituted the majority and occasionally the entire population. It was noted early in the colony that their numbers were decreasing faster than altiplano dwellers. One of the explanations offered by Wachtel suggests that the Uru took advantage of European policies in order to become "Aymarized." Many ethnic identifications prevailing before 1532 were ignored thereafter.

1752 Yáñez Quirola, Francisco G. Historia cuatrisecular del pueblo de San Andrés Xunxi, Chimborazo. n.p.: The Author, n.d. 105 p.; bibl.; plates.

Although most of the data in this book are culled from printed sources, the author also uses some parish records to describe what was essentially an Andean population.

1753 Zapater, Horacio. Aborígenes chilenos a través de cronistas y viajeros. 2. ed. Santiago: Editorial Andrés Bello, 1978. 184 p.; bibl.; 2 fold. leaves of plates: ill.

Consists of reading notes, classified in a systematic way, of the earlier observers of the indigenous population of what today is Chile. For the earlier edition published in 1973, see *HLAS 38:2159.*

1754 ———. La autoridad del Inca y la dominación española en el Norte de Chile: 1534–49 (*in* Congreso de Arqueología Chilena, VII, Altos de Vilche, 1977. Actas. Santiago: Sociedad Chilena de Arqueología, Sociedad Arqueológica del Maule, 1978?, v. 1, p. 393–408)

Reading notes on secondary sources.

1755 Zavala, Silvio. La monarquía del mundo en Guamán Poma de Ayala (IAI/I, 4, 1977, p. 179–186)

Zavala has been reading Waman Puma's *Letter to the King* as part of his study of Indian labor in the mines of Potosí. In this article, he stresses Waman Puma's conception of the world after the European conquest of the Indies. The Castilian king is portrayed as sitting at the center of a world which is divided into four parts one of which is governed by a descendant of the Incas and another by a black ruler from Guinea.

1756 Zevallos, Pilar O. de and **Lía del Río de Calmell.** Las lagunas como fuentes de recursos naturales en el siglo XVI (Etnohistoria y Antropología Andina [Museo Nacional de Historia, Lima] 1, 1978, p. 59–62, bibl.)

The sweet-water lagoons along the Pacific coast were more numerous in the 16th century when they provided fish and other resources for the population. Fish production began early in the region and the most widely cultivated fish was the *liza.*

1757 Zorrilla A., Juan C. La posesión de Chiara por los yndios chachapoyas (Wari [Ayacucho, Peru] 1, 1977, p. 49–64)

The search for evidence of Waman Puma's activities in his native Ayacucho region has intensified. Although some of the evidence reproduced here was already known (see *HLAS 32:1053*), Zorrilla adds proof of litigation in 1594. It claims that Waman Puma's European name was not Felipe but Lázaro and thoroughly confirms his claim in *Letter to the King* that he had been active in protecting local land rights.

Zuidema, R. Tom. The Inca kinship system: a new theoretical view. See *HLAS 41:1329.*

1758 ———. Lieux sacrés et irrigation: tradition historique, mythes et rituels au Cuzco (AESC, 33:5/6, 1978, p. 1037–1058, bibl., maps, tables)

Author returns to his earlier work concerning the *ceque* lines that radiated from the Inka capital. This time Zuidema follows them on the ground and locates many shrines listed by Cobo in 1653. He documents a close correlation among sources of water, irrigation canals and shrines. The city itself was divided by rivers and a ritual dual division of kings and kingdom is also documented.

1759 ———. Mito e historia en el antiguo Perú (IAP/AP, 10, 1977, p. 15–52, bibl., tables)

Zuidema offers a new analysis of Huarochiri's legendary materials (see *HLAS 29:2207*) in the light of his study of Cuzco's *ceque* organization. He draws a comparison between the above mythological materials and those compiled by Lévi-Strauss while studying the Borro. This parallel enables Zuidema to reiterate his belief that existing continuities between the forest and the Andes permit a reconsideration of the dynastic tradition.

1760 ———. Mito, rito, calendario y geografía en el antiguo Perú (*in* International Congress of Americanists, XLII, Paris, 1976. Actes [see *HLAS 41:255*] v. 4, p. 347–357, bibl., maps, tables)

Correlates earlier studies of ancient Cuzco's *ceque* lines with calendrical and astronomical observations. The four-fold division of the Inka state corresponded to observations set along lines determined by the solstice and equinox. Shrines as far away as Lake Titicaca were located along these lines. Zuidema suggests that current ethnographic data can shed light on these questions.

1761 ———. El ushnu (RUC, 28:117, 1979, p. 317–362, bibl., ill., tables)

It was common in Inka cities and administrative centers for elaborate buildings of fine masonry to be located at the center (referred to in Quechua as *ushnu*). In the course of his astronomical studies, Zuidema located an *ushnu* in Cuzco. Important for solar observations, the *ushnu* also had religious significance and represented an opening in the earth which "sucked" the sky's waters.

1762 ——— and **Gary Urton.** La constelación de la llama en los Andes peruanos (IPA/A, 9, 1976, p. 59–120, bibl., ill.)

A major effort to relate rituals organized in Cuzco in Inka times, bit of mythology from the same area but also from the provinces with astronomical observations. The few calendars available but particularly those of Waman Puma are related to rituals concerned with camelids, both the herded and those visible in the constellations of the southern sky.

HISTORY: GENERAL

DONALD E. CHIPMAN, *Professor of History, North Texas State University*
JAMES D. RILEY, *Professor of History, The Catholic University of America*

IN *HLAS 40*, THIS SECTION CONTAINED many more items, especially in the first subsection entitled "General" and in the last one corresponding to "20th Century." The decline in the number of book-length monographs and interpretative essays annotated in this volume is a result of economic constraints which have reduced the quantity as well as affected the quality of books published in this biennium. In contrast to *HLAS 40*, most interpretative syntheses published in the last two years were found in articles. Nevertheless, the best general interpretative essay appeared in a book on US-Latin American relations by the Venezuelan Carlos Rangel Guevara, *Del buen salvaje al buen revolucionario* (see *HLAS 41:7065*) now available in English as *The Latin Americans: their love-hate relationship with the United States* (item **1809**). Two noted works of reference in the general category were Hardoy's excellent bibliography on urbanization (item **1782**) and Lavrin's compilation of essays on women (item **1791**). Likewise, two noted works of interpretation also in the general category and impressive because of their insights and provocative approaches, were Bauer's article on peonage (item **1766**) and Hennessy's book on frontiers (item **1786**).

Despite economic constraints, some outstanding works were published on the colonial period concerning discovery, exploration and colonization. They combined careful scholarship with a visually attractive format and the most important among them was Davies' study of voyagers to the New World (item **1838**). Also worthy of special mention in the colonial category were: Gibson's presidential address to the American Historical Association in 1977 (item **1848**); studies of Columbus by Rumeu (item **1873**) and Hulme (item **1851**); Ramos' work on restrictions affecting foreign immigration to the Spanish colonies (item **1868**); and Zavala's work on the evolution of rules governing early discoveries and conquests (item **1892**). Morison's landmark volumes on the Northern and Southern Voyages (see *HLAS 38:3009*) were reissued in a handsome abridgement which retains the flavor and essence of the original (item **1861**). Burrus' massive project on the writings of Alonso de la Vera Cruz concluded with the publications of vols. 4 and 5 (item **1889**). Andrews prepared a fine synthesis of Spanish trade and plunder in the Caribbean (item **1826**) and Gibson compiled an excellent survey of the literature published in the last 25 years on Spanish colonial institutions (item **1849**). Works of particular merit on the late colonial period were Pike's on penal servitude (item **1866**), Sánchez-Barba's on Atlantic security (item **1877**) and Campbell's on Bourbon enlightened despotism (item **1900**). Among the best monographs devoted to specific topics were two on black slavery, one by Russell-Wood (item **1874**) and another by Sweet (item **1883**), as well as one on matrimonial practices by Rípodas Ardanaz (item **1870**). Two useful reprints on colonial subjects were Mercado's study of Sevillan business practices (item **1859**) and Madariaga's work on the rise and fall of the Spanish empire (item **1857**).

Important studies of the Independence and 19th-century periods were Anna's examination of what motivated Ferdinand VII to launch the Buenos Aires expedition (item **1894**) and Bartley's analysis of Russian Czar Alexander I and his interest in the New World (item **1896**). Burns provided a useful study of ideology in 19th-century Latin American historiography (item **1899**) and Bosch García presented a broad survey of Anglo-Spanish independence movements and the ensuing period of transition (item **1898**).

In contrast to *HLAS 40*, the majority of 20th-century works annotated below dwelt on development themes and international relations but the general lack of innovative historical approaches to the study of these topics resulted in a preponderance of undistinguished works. One leading exception was Peter Winn's essay on the uses of factory studies in labor history (item **1954**). Two additional analyses of 20th-century topics were also worthwhile: Parkinson's volume on Cold War politics (item **1936**) and Child's article on the strategic thinking of government planners, illustrated by an interesting use of military contingency plans (item **1924**).

This section reflects a collaborative effort. The two middle subsections, entitled "Colonial" and "Independence and 19th Century," were prepared by Chipman and the remaining first and last, corresponding to "General" and "20th Century," by Riley. Chipman wishes to acknowledge continuing support from the faculty research committee of North Texas State University and the assistance of Mrs. Olga Paradis.

GENERAL

1763 **Al'perovich, M.S.** Principal trends in Soviet research on the history of Latin America (*in* Soviet historians on Latin America [see item **1817**] p. 30–57)

A description of the interests and work of Russian scholars since 1950. Most interest has focused on Indian cultures, 20th-century changes and diplomatic relations.

1764 **Arbitration treaties** among the American nations, to the close of the year 1910. Edited by William Ray Manning. Reprint of the edition published by Oxford University Press. Millwood, N.Y.: Kraus, 1978. 472 p.

Reprint of 1924 publication. Contains English translations of 228 arbitration treaties negotiated between various nations of the Western Hemisphere.

1765 Baretta, Silvio R. Duncan and **John Markoff.** Civilization and barbarism: cattle frontiers in Latin America (CSSH, 20:4, 1978, p. 587–620)

An interesting but oversimplified interpretative essay on the causes and nature of the "culture of violence" found on the cattle frontiers in Latin America. Explains the violent lifestyle as an outgrowth of the economic and social structure of the activity.

1766 Bauer, Arnold J. Rural workers in Spanish America: problems of peonage and oppression (HAHR, 59:1, Feb. 1979, p. 34–63, tables)

An excellent and provocative essay which attempts to create a general picture of the evolution of the system of labor recruitment and retention between the early colonial period and 1930. It is based on careful reading of the enormous amount of recent research on rural history. The author argues that we must abandon the old stereotypes of debt-peonage and rural oppression as descriptive of labor relations. The system must be seen, rather, as one of "give and take, choice and accommodation."

1767 La burguesía mercantil gaditana: 1650–1868. Cádiz, Spain: Instituto de Estudios Gaditanos, 1976. 319 p.

Estudios presentados en el XXXI Congreso Luso-Español para el Progreso de las Ciencias, celebrado de Cádiz. La mayor parte trata de las relaciones de dicha ciudad con América, especialmente en el aspecto comercial. Tales los siguientes: Antonio Domínguez Ortiz "La Burguesía y el Comercio de Indias desde Mediados del Siglo XVII hasta el Traslado de la Casa de la Contratación;" Luis Navarro García "La Casa de la Contratación en Cádiz;" María Cristina García Bernal "Los Españoles Hijos de Extranjeros en el Comercio Indiano;" Antonio Heredia "Asiento con el Consulado de Cádiz para el Despacho de Avisos;" Julián Ruiz Rivera "La Casa Ustáriz, San Ginés y Compañía;" y Ramón Serrera "La Técnica de la Fabricación de la Jarcia en los Arsenales Reales del Departamento Marítimo de Cádiz en el Siglo XVIII." Otros varios trabajos versan directamente sobre la historia del comercio hispano-americano, y los restantes interesan en su mayoría a la historia de América—al menos de forma indirecta—en cuanto ayudan a entender el carácter de una ciudad que fue el más importante punto de arranque del tráfico con las Indias españolas. [L.G. Canedo]

1768 Comparative perspectives on slavery in New World plantation societies. Edited by Vera Rubin and Arthur Tuden. New York: New York Academy of Sciences, 1977. 618 p.; bibl.; maps; tables (Annals of the New York Academy of Sciences; 292)

Consists of 41 papers plus commentaries from conference of same name. Most of them concern the non-Hispanic Caribbean with the bulk of the remainder on Brazil. The time period ranges from 1500 to 1900 and topics include overviews of slave societies, economics of slavery, slave codes, social institutions, slave revolts and resistance, research problems and research tools. (For annotations of individual papers in this *HLAS*, look up author's name in Author Index.)

1769 Cortada, James W. Two nations over time: Spain and the United States, 1776–1977. Westport, Connecticut: Greenwood Press, 1978. 305 p.; bibl. (Contributions in American history; 74)

Examines US-Spanish diplomatic relations with emphasis on economic and cultural factors. Both nations sought to establish political and economic hegemony over the New World, but their rivalry was also exacerbated by lack of understanding and respect for each other's society and culture.

1769a Cortés Alonso, Vicenta. Archivos de España y América: materiales para un manual. Madrid: Editorial de la Universidad Complutense, 1979. 382 p.; bibl.; tables.

Anthology of articles on archival principles and practices in Spain and Spanish America by a leading authority, Vicenta Cortés Alonso, Inspector General of Spain's Corps of Archivists and Librarians. Given their depth and breadth, these "materials" constitute a manual in effect on what archival principles and practices should be, their evolution and present state in the Hispanic world. Historians will appreciate Cortés' detailed introductions to "Archival Resources in Mediterranean Europe, The Vatican and Latin America," the Archivo General de Indias, the Archivo de San Agustín de Santa Fe de Bogotá, the Map Collection of the Archivo Nacional de Colombia, and the Colonial Section of the latter, and bibliography on Spanish archives. [M.T. Hamerly]

Cuevas Cancino, F. Del Congreso de Panamá a la Conferencia de Caracas. See *HLAS 41:8786.*

1770 Davis, Harold Eugene; John J. Finan; and F. Taylor Peck. Latin American diplomatic history: an introduction. Baton Rouge: Louisiana State University Press, 1977. 301 p.; bibl.

A textbook with a new approach to Latin American international history emphasizing viewpoints within the nations rather than from the outside. Authors divided responsibilities for the chapters which treat topics from the origins of foreign policies to the present. For political scientist's comment, see *HLAS 41:8524.*

1771 Dealy, Glen C. The public man: an interpretation of Latin American and other Catholic countries. Introduction by Richard M. Morse. Amherst: University of Massachusetts Press, 1977. 128 p.

Examines behavioral patterns in Latin American and other monolithically Catholic countries. Rejects traditional explanations that Latin American behavior is the result of Latin culture, maintaining rather that its roots can be traced to certain characteristics of Catholicism. To an extent, perceives Latin American cultures as akin to those of Ireland, Poland and Austria in addition to Italy and Spain.

1772 Dependency unbends: case studies in inter-American relations. Edited by Robert H. Claxton. Carrollton: West Georgia College, 1978. 112 p. (Studies in the social sciences; 17)

Nine articles on varied aspects of political and economic relations of United States with various countries. Topics include activities of specific individuals in Brazil, Chile, Honduras and Mexico, the W.R. Grace company in Peru, involvement in Panamanian politics under Taft and Cuban politics under Wilson, and Mexican oil diplomacy. For political scientists's comment, see *HLAS 41:8515.*

1773 De Platt, Lyman. Genealogical historical guide to Latin America. Detroit: Gale Research Company, 1978. 272 p.; tables (Gale genealogy and local history series; 4)

A research tool intended for laymen attempting to research genealogies in Spanish and Portuguese American archives. The guide identifies the major sections of national and local archives in 20 Ibero-American countries. Also describes type of information found in various types of documents and offers a number of research aids to assist with paleography.

1773a Domínguez, Jorge I. Insurrection or loyalty: the breakdown of the Spanish American Empire. Cambridge, Mass.: Harvard University Press, 1980. 307 p.; bibl.

Political scientist's fascinating, rigorously comparative, and (to historian) redundantly theoretical treatment of Mexico, Cuba, Venezuela, Chile as case studies of rebellion vs. loyalty. Author's conclusion that "nature of elite participation and government response" mainly determined whether and how a colony would rebel is less interesting than his comprehensive review of ethnic, economic, ecological and other factors that influenced elite and government and produced significant differentiation even before 1808. [D. Bushnell]

1774 Duncan, W. Raymond. Latin American politics: a developmental approach. New York: Praeger, 1976. 277 p.; maps; tables.

Brief survey of a variety of topics such as political parties, social structure, geography, and pressure groups. Author sees developmental approach as illustrative of how some elements of Latin America's population bring demands on governments toward goal of more equitable distribution of national resources. For political scientists's comment, see *HLAS 39:7025.*

1775 Elites, masses and modernization in Latin America, 1850–1930. Edited by Virginia Bernhard. Austin: University of Texas Press, 1979. 156 p. (Texas Pan American series)

Contains two articles derived from lectures given at the University of St. Thomas in 1978: E. Bradford Burns' "Cultures in Conflict: the Implications of Modernization in 19th-Century Latin America" and Thomas Skidmore's "Workers and Soldiers: Urban Labor Movements and Elite Responses in 20th-Century Latin America."

1776 Fell, Barry. America B.C.: ancient settlers in the New World. New York: Pocket Books, 1978. 312 p.; bibl.; maps; plates; tables.

Advances questionable evidence of voyages and settlements in America by Celts as early as 3,000 years ago. Asserts that Celts were followed by Basques, Libyans, and Egyptians whose precolumbian presence is documented by inscriptions on buried temples, tablets, gravestones, and cliffs.

Ferrer Benimeli, José Antonio. Bibliografía de la masonería: introducción histórico-crítica. See *HLAS 41:26.*

1777 Frei, Eduardo. Latin America: the hopeful option. Translation by John Drury. Maryknoll, New York: Orbis Books, 1978. 271 p.

An idealistic and personal analysis of latent and overt crises that face western democracy with special emphasis on Latin America. Frei examines historical and sociological roots of democracy's problems and outlines the essentials for maintaining "modern, effective, living democracy grounded on humanism." For comment on Spanish original, see *HLAS 41:7402.*

1778 García Oro, J. La América franciscana: a propósito de una obra reciente y su autor (PF/AIA, 39:153/154, enero/junio 1979, p. 207–215)

Brief homenaje honoring prolific Franciscan scholar Lino Gómez Canedo on occasion of his 70th birthday. Author summarizes Father Lino's career spanning 50 years and the significance of his many publications, including most recent book, *Evangelización y conquista* (1977).

1779 González Casanova, Pablo. Imperialismo y liberación en América Latina: una introducción a la historia contemporánea. México: Siglo Veintiuno Editores, 1978. 297 p.; bibl. (Historia)

Author defines contemporary Latin American history as encompassing years 1880 to present. The central and unifying theme for nations throughout the era, which is divided into five stages of development, is the continuing and multifaceted struggle against imperialism. Imperialism as it affected both dominant and working classes is examined by Mexican political scientist noted for neo-Marxian writing.

1780 Grieshaber, Erwin P. Hacienda-Indian community relations and Indian acculturation: an historiographical essay (LARR, 14:3, 1979, p. 107–128)

Revises the popularly held belief that the entry of the hacienda into Indian areas led to forced Hispanization. Analyzes the recent literature on hacienda-peasant relations from conquest to early 20th century to show that other variables such as the density of the Indian population, the strength of the community organization, the proximity to cities and type of production dictated the degree of acculturation which would take place.

1781 Haciendas and plantations in Latin American history. Edited by Robert G. Keith. New York: Holmes & Meier, 1977. 200 p.; bibl.

Collection of 19 essays, all previously published, which examines haciendas and plantations in Brazil, Costa Rica, Mexico, Peru, Ecuador, Chile, and Argentina. Selections are equally divided into colonial period, 19th and 20th centuries.

1782 Hardoy, Jorge Enrique. Urbanización en América Latina: una bibliografía sobre su historia. v. 1/3. Buenos Aires: Centro de Estudios Urbanos y Regionales, Instituto Torcuato di Tella, 1977. 3 v. (Serie celeste, planeamiento regional y urbano)

Vol. 1 contains 1,400 titles, some 80 of which have accompanying annotations. Entries include articles, books, and documents and are grouped into three broad sections: 1) Precolumbia, 2) Colonial, and 3) Independence—although latter contains items encompassing years 1870–1930. Likewise in vol. 2 only a small number of total items are annotated. It, however, is devoted entirely to the Spanish colonial period. Five subsections incorporate general works and works devoted to viceroyalties of New Spain, Peru, New Granada, and Rio de La Plata. Vol. 3 contains bibliographic citations to Portuguese empire and other European outposts in Latin America.

1783 Hellwege, Johann D. Frontier und Conquista: Zur amerikanischen Entwicklungsdivergenz am Beispiel eines fragwürdigen historischen Vergleichs (IAA, 2:1, 1976, p. 1–37, bibl.)

Sees divergence in development patterns of Anglo and Ibero America as the result of manner of initial colonization and colonial institutions.

1784 **Hemispheric perspectives** on the United States: papers from the New World Conference. Edited by Joseph S. Tulchin. Westport, Connecticut: Greenwood Press, 1978. 445 p.; plates; tables (Contributions in American studies; 36)

Consists of 28 papers of very uneven quality on a wide variety of topics but generally dealing with the American impact on the rest of the hemisphere. Subsections deal with perspectives on the American Revolution and its impact on the hemisphere, art and culture in the Americas, US political and economic relations with the hemisphere, views of ethnicity and American studies outside the US.

1785 **Henderson, James D.** and **Linda Roddy Henderson.** Ten notable women of Latin America. Chicago: Nelson-Hall, 1978. 257 p.; bibl.; maps; plates.

Contains 10 biographical sketches of Latin American women who rose above limitations of female's usual role in Spanish culture to carve historical nitches for themselves in a man's world. Subjects range from Malinche to Eva Perón and Che's guerrilla companion Tania in the 20th century.

1786 **Hennessy, Alistair.** The frontier in Latin American history. Foreword by Ray Allen Billington. Albuquerque: University of New Mexico Press, 1978. 202 p.; bibl.; maps (Histories of the American frontier)

Compares frontier history of Latin America with that of US, Canada, South Africa, and Australia. Stresses inapplicability of Turner thesis to the frontier in Latin America and offers insightful comparisons of varied frontier experiences. An important work.

1787 **Hispanic-American essays** in honor of Max Leon Moorhead. Edited by William S. Coker. Maps by Jerome F. Coling. Index by Polly Coker. Pensacola: Perdido Bay Press, 1979. 193 p.; bibl.; 5 leaves of plates: ill.; index.

Consists of eight articles, four of which are annotated separately and entered under author's name in the appropriate *HLAS* section (see item number after title).

Edgar Wickberg "Spanish Frontiers in the Western Pacific, 1662–1700" p. 12–36 (see item **2166**)

Oakah L. Jones, Jr. "Spanish Civil Communities and Settlers in Frontier New Mexico, 1790–1810" p. 37–60 (see item **2137**)

William S. Coker "John Forbes and Company and the War of 1812 in the Spanish Borderlands" p. 61–98 (see item **2546**)

Karla Robinson "The Merchants of Post-Independence Buenos Aires" p. 111–132 (see item **3414**). [Ed.]

1788 **Homage to Irving A. Leonard:** essays on Hispanic art, history and literature. Edited by Raquel Chang Rodríguez and Donald A. Yates. East Lansing: Michigan State University, Latin American Studies Center, 1977. 230 p.; bibl.; plates.

Brief essays by 21 contributors offer an appropriate tribute to an outstanding scholar of colonial history, culture, and literature—Irving A. Leonard.

1789 **Jackson, Richard L.** Black writers in Latin America. Albuquerque: University of New Mexico Press, 1979. 224 p.; bibl.

Analyzes historically the place of black writers in Latin American literature. Emphasis is on the themes specific writers dealt with in three periods, 1821–1921, 1922–49, and 1950–present.

1790 **König, Hans Joachim.** Liberación nacional y cambio social (FJB/BH, 45, sept. 1977, p. 285–314)

A standard treatment of the causes and goals of revolutions in Latin American history. Compares independence movements with modern social upheavals in Bolivia, Cuba and Mexico. Emphasizes demand for agrarian reform as key component in the latter three.

Kutscher, Gerdt. Berlín como Centro de Estudios Americanistas: ensayo biobibliográfico. See *HLAS 41:121*.

Lara F., Celso A. Algunas consideraciones metodológicas sobre la aplicación del folklore a los estudios históricos. See item **982**.

———. Implicaciones del folklore como fuente histórica. See item **985**.

1791 **Latin American women:** historical perspectives. Edited by Asunción Lavrin. Westport, Conn.: Greenwood Press, 1978. 343 p.; bibl.; 5 leaves of plates: ill.;

index (Contributions in women's studies; 3)

Series of essays which seek to revise the traditional image of women in Latin American society and attempts to show that women of all classes—not just exceptional individuals—had an important influence. Topics range from colonial era to the twentieth century.

1792 Lavrin, Asunción. Some final considerations on trends and issues in Latin American women's history (*in* Latin American women: historical perspectives [see item **1791**] p. 302–332)

Author assesses trends in research and calls for new avenues of study on Latin American women. Among suggestions are broadening the sample of women, thereby selecting personalities who are truly representative of their times and classes, and an endorsement of the genre of collective biography pioneered by Irving A. Leonard.

1793 Llinas Alvarez, Edgar. La educación y el proceso integrador de América Latina (CAM, 223:2, marzo/abril 1979, p. 40–48, bibl.)

Sees Latin American education as afflicted by continued imitation of imposed foreign models. Only by breaking out of this pattern will Latin Americans escape a continuing cultural imperialism.

1794 Maier, Joseph and **Richard W. Weatherhead.** The Latin American university. Albuquerque: University of New Mexico Press, 1979. 237 p.; bibl.

Essays by 10 scholars analyzing different aspects of the organization and functioning of Latin American universities. Topics include the origin and philosophy of Spanish American and Brazilian universities, European and US influences on 19th and 20th century developments, university reform in the 1920s, and the characteristics of students, faculties and rectors.

1795 Martinière, Guy. Les Amériques Latines: une histoire économique. Grenoble: Presses Universitaires de Grenoble, 1978. 362 p.; bibl.; map (Actualités-recherche: Série Dossiers du développement)

Survey of economic institutions and thought from precolumbian period to 1940. A standard treatment emphasizing land tenure patterns and the export economy.

1796 Mauro, Frédéric. Les investissements Français en Amérique Latine des origines a 1973 (Revue d'Histoire Economique et Sociale [Editions Marcel Rivière *avec le concours du* Centre National de la Recherche Scientifique, Paris] 55:1/2, 1977, p. 234–262)

Statistical analysis of type of French investments by country and period. Depends mainly on other secondary sources and emphasizes the period since 1960.

1797 Mesa-Lago, Carmelo. Latin American studies in Europe. Pittsburgh: University of Pittsburgh Press, 1979. 190 p.; bibl.; maps; tables (Latin American monograph and document series; 1)

Reference work identifying size, orientation, personnel, sources of funding, publications and library resources for Latin American studies programs in 17 European nations. Ends with an analytical essay.

1798 Mörner, Magnus. Historia social latinoamericana: nuevos enfoques. Caracas: Universidad Católica Andrés Bello, 1979. 376 p.; bibl.; ill.; maps; tables (Colección Manoa)

Presents eight essays on three themes: 1) immigration; 2) rural, social, and economic conditions; and 3) the treatment of black slaves and freedmen. The purpose is to illustrate the findings, methods, and sources of the social history currently being written by scholars of Latin America. The essays follow the author's own research interests over the past 15 years and provide an excellent résumé of the state of social history in Latin America today.

———. Los movimientos campesinos de Latinoamérica y del Caribe en la investigación histórica. See *HLAS 41:9173*.

1799 ———. Recent research on Negro slavery and abolition in Latin America (LARR, 13:2, 1978, p. 265–290, bibl.)

A bibliographical essay considering work on these issues appearing between 1969 and 1977. Lauds recent researchers for their increasing sophistication in handling the relationship between slavery and racism, and regional variations in behavior. Also notes increasing use of quantification. Bibliography contains 175 items.

1800 Morse, Richard M. Latin American intellectuals and the city, 1860–1940 (JLAS, 10:2, Nov. 1978, p. 219–238)

Explores attitudes of three 19th and three 20th-century intellectuals towards city life and the city's role in nation building. The writers include Miguel Samper of Colombia, Joaquín Capelo and Jorge Basadre of Peru, Gilberto Freyre of Brazil, and Juan Agustín García and Ezequiel Martínez Estrada of Argentina.

1801 *Nova Americana.* Giulio Einaudi Editore. Vols. 1/2, 1978/1979– . Torino, Italy.

Vols. 1 and 2 of a new annual, multilingual and multidisciplinary journal devoted to Latin American studies and published in Torino, Italy. Editors are Ruggiero Romano and Marcello Carmagnani. Vol. 1 (380 p.) focuses on market themes and consists of the following articles:

Juan Carlos Garavaglia "Un Capítulo del Mercado Interno Colonial: el Paraguay y su Región, 1537–1682"

Carlos Sempat Assadourian "El Sector Exportador de una Economía Regional del Interior Argentino: Córdoba, 1800–1860"

Roberto Cortés Conde "El Mercado de Tierras en Argentina 1880–1913"

Marcello Carmagnani and Chiara Vangelista "Mercati Monetari e Ferrovie Inglesi in Argentina: 1880–1914"

Joanne Fox Przeworski "Mines and Smelters: the Role of the Coal Oligopoly in the Decline of the Chilean Copper Industry"

Chiara Vangelista "Per una Ricera sul Mercato del Lavoro: la Mobilità della Monodopera in una Filatura Paulista"

John V. Murra "Personal Documents of Aymara Lords in the Study of Andean Society"

Elizabeth Dore "Social Relations and the Barriers to Economic Growth: the Case of the Peruvian Mining Industry"

R.J. Bromley "Precolonial Trade and the Transition to a Colonial Market System in the Audiencia of Quito"

Scott Cook "Petty Commodity Production and Capitalist Development in the 'Central Valleys' Region of Oaxaca, Mexico"

Sidney W. Mintz "Caribbean Marketplaces and the Caribbean History"

Marcos Winocur "Cuba: Ventura y Desventura de una Burguesía Azucarera"

Vol. 2 (398 p.) is devoted to:

Enrique Montalvo Ortega "Caudillismo y Estado en la Revolución Mexicana: el Gobierno de Alvarado en Yucatán"

Miguel Izard "Tanto Pelear para Terminar Conversando: el Caudillismo en Venezuela"

Benjamin S. Orlove "The Breaking of Patron-Client Ties: the Case of Surinam in Southern Peru"

Daniela Violini-Elisabetta Bertola "L'Oligarchia Cilena nel 1920: i Meccanismi di Riproduzione, di Coesione e di Organizzazione"

Rubén H. Zorrilla "Estructura Social y Caudillismo en la Argentina: 1810–1870"

José Pedro Barrán-Benjamín Nahum "Proletariado Ganadero, Caudillismo y Guerras Civiles en el Uruguay del Novecientos"

Brooke Larson "Caciques, Class Structure and the Colonial State in Bolivia"

José Carlos Chiaramonte "Coacción Extraeconómica y Relaciones de Producción en el Río de la Plata durante la Primera Mitad del Siglo XIX"

Malcolm Deas "Poverty, Civil War and Politics: Ricardo Gaitán Obeso and his Magdalena River Campaign in Colombia, 1885"

Antonio Annino "La Fine del Populismo in Cuba"

Elizabeth de G.R. Hansen "Middle Class Formation and Political Stages in 20th Century Brazil."

1802 O'Gorman, Edmundo. Apocalypse and gospel: thoughts on the historian's responsibility (*in* Pacific Coast Council on Latin American Studies, XXI, San Diego, Calif., 1976. Proceedings. San Diego, Calif.: The Campanile Press, 1977, v. 5, p. 1–10)

Eloquent assessment of "the state of the discipline of history." Author decries the trend toward a consuming passion for facts and a disposition to regard history as a science or social science. He also reminds us that history is an art that "should glow with the light of man's individual natural rich variety." In this manner the discipline can serve as a bastion and expression of individual liberty.

1803 Pan American Institute of Geography and History. Commission on History. El proyecto de historia general de América: antecedentes y perspectivas. Caracas: La Comisión, 1976. 235 p.; map.

Explores the genesis of a project sponsored by the PAIGH concerning the writing of a general history of the Americas as well as problems of coordinating such an effort.

Reports by several scholars address questions of focus, periodization, and textual balance.

1804 Pescatello, Ann M. The Afro-American in historical perspective (*in* Old roots in new lands [see *HLAS 40:2214*] p. 3–35, map, tables)

A brief overview of the context within which slavery developed in the New World. Considers the nature of slavery in Africa and the New World, the transference of African cultural traits and the impact of abolition on cultural patterns.

1805 Pinto, Aníbal and **Armando Di Filippo.** Desarrollo y pobreza en la América Latina: un enfoque histórico-estructural (FCE/TE, 46[3]:183, julio/sept. 1979, p. 569–590)

A brief synthesis of the author's ideas on the origin of poverty in LA and a possible strategy for producing a more equitable distribution of income.

1806 The politics of antipolitics: the military in Latin America. Edited by Brian Loveman and Thomas M. Davies, Jr. Lincoln: University of Nebraska Press, 1978. 309 p.; tables.

Editors have included six topics of "antipolitics" in five Latin American countries covering century and one-half of independence. Similarities of outlook, ideology, and practice of military governments are studied while using historical, thematic, and case-study approaches. Also includes selection of military speeches.

1807 Portes, Alejandro and **John Walton.** Urban Latin America: the political condition from above and below. Austin: University of Texas Press, 1976. 217 p.; bibl.; tables (Texas Pan American series)

Categorizing Latin American urbanization as a political problem, authors have constructed a new approach to integrating research on social organization. The structure of urban politics is studied by examining power elites and marginal classes as well as city planning, demography and economics.

1808 Rama, Carlos M. Historia de América Latina. Barcelona: Bruguera, 1978. 280 p.; bibl.; map (Libro blanco)

A brief popular history of Latin America from Independence to the end of World War II.

1808a Randall, Laura Regina Rosenbaum. A comparative economic history of Latin America: 1500–1914. v. 1, Mexico; v. 2, Argentina; v. 3, Brazil; v. 4, Peru. Ann Arbor, Mich.: University Microfilms International, 1977. 4 v. (292, 268, 269, 231 p.); bibl.; index (Monograph publishing on demand; sponsor series)

Comprehensive and highly readable economic history. Consists of four volumes, one per country: Mexico, Argentina, Brazil and Peru, from precolonial times through the eve of World War I. Their differential economic developments, however, are compared where appropriate and in the introductory and concluding chapters in vols. 1 and 4. Written between 1967–69—publication was delayed through no fault of the author—Randall's accounts of the economies of colonial Mexico and of 19th-century Mexico, Argentina, Brazil and Peru are still valid in the main as are also most of her interpretations. Her accounts of the economies of colonial Argentina, Brazil and Peru are incomplete and less valid in light of the considerable work done subsequently. Nonetheless, a superior piece of scholarship which goes far towards filling the gap in the literature on the economic history of post-independence Latin America. [M.T. Hamerly]

1809 Rangel Guevara, Carlos. The Latin Americans: their love-hate relationship with the United States. Translated from the French by Ivan Kats. New York: Harcourt Brace Jovanovich, 1977. 302 p.; bibl. (A Helen and Kurt Wolff book)

A provocative and well-written essay by a Venezuelan journalist and diplomat on the character of Latin American political and cultural life. The major thesis is that, historically, many Latin American problems are caused by a weak sense of national identity stemming, in turn, from a deep sense of inferiority vis-à-vis the US and its culture. For comment on Spanish version, see *HLAS 41:7065* and for political scientist's comment, see *HLAS 41:8582*.

1810 Reflexiones sobre la historia. Montevideo, Uruguay: Centro Latinoamericano de Economía Humana, 1977. 39 p.; bibl. (Serie Estudios. Centro Latinoamericano de Economía Humana; 5)

Contains reprints of two brief interviews with Fernand Braudel (1971 and 1977) and of two articles by Ernesto Laclau (1963) and Torcuato S. Di Tella (1977).

1811 Reid, John T. The rise and decline of the Ariel-Caliban antithesis in Spanish America (AAFH/TAM, 34:3, Jan. 1978, p. 345–355)

Examines the origin and decline of the Ariel-Caliban antithesis popularized by Rodó. Noting that it was not original with Rodó, author suggests that the most immediate influence was propaganda associated with French Pan-Latin propaganda. Points out that as early as 1910, key intellectuals were rejecting the identification of the US with Caliban.

1812 ———. Spanish American images of the United States. Gainesville: The University Presses of Florida, 1977. 298 p.

Changing images of the US as held by the educated classes of Spanish America are examined for the years 1790–1960. Offers guarded conclusion that images of the US have altered very little over the years surveyed. For political scientist's comment, see *HLAS 41:8585*.

1812a Rodríguez de Alonso, Josefina. El siglo de las luces visto por Francisco de Miranda. Liminar de J.L. Salcedo-Bastardo. Prefacio de Edmond Giscard d'Estaing. Caracas: Presidencia de la República, 1978. 517 p.; bibl.; facsims.; maps; plates.

Mainly an extended summary of Miranda's North American and European travels and impressions, 1783–89. No new data or insights, but convenient. [D. Bushnell]

Sable, Martin Howard. Latin American Jewry: a research guide. See *HLAS 41:45*.

1813 Shur, Leonid A. Russian travelers of the 18th and 19th centuries: source materials on the geography, history and ethnology of Latin America (IAA, 3:4, 1977, p. 395–402, bibl.)

Brief description of types of travelers' accounts existing in Russian archives. While it does not include a list of these documents with archival citations, it does include a list of works which cite them (see also *HLAS 34:1294–1295*).

1814 Simposio Latinoamericano de Historia, *Tunja, Colombia, 1975.* Historiografía contemporánea de América Latina: problemas generales y especiales de la investigación histórica contemporánea de Latinoamérica. Tunja: Ediciones La Rana y el Aguila, 1975. 91 p.; bibl.

Stanley Ross, Eduardo Arcila Farías, Moisés González Navarro, and Elías Pino Iturrieta discuss problems encountered by scholars who research contemporary topics and methodological approaches.

Simpson, George Eaton. Black religions in the New World. See *HLAS 41:1091*.

1815 Smith, Robert Freeman. The American Revolution and Latin America: an essay in imagery, perceptions and ideological influence (UM/JIAS, 20:4, Nov. 1978, p. 421–441)

Reviews external-internal debate on US influence in Latin American independence movements. Author concludes that the American Revolution's influence on Latin American revolutions from 1800s to present was mostly symbolic and calls for reevaluation of influence thesis in an atmosphere less charged emotionally and ideologically.

1816 Sofer, Eugene F. and **Mark D. Szuchman.** City and society: their connection in Latin American historical research (LARR, 14:2, 1979, p. 113–129)

Examines general trends in current treatment of social history and presents the specific documentation and problems encountered in the authors' own research on Buenos Aires and Córdoba, Argentina.

Solari, Aldo E. *comp.* Poder y desarrollo: América Latina. See *HLAS 41:9046*.

1817 Soviet historians on Latin America: recent scholarly contributions. Edited and translated by R.H. Bartley. Madison: University of Wisconsin Press, 1978. 345 p.; bibl. (Conference on Latin American History; 5)

Consists of 16 articles by Russian scholars. Topics include: trends in Russian research; 19th-century descriptions of Latin America by Russians; plantation slavery; precolumbian society in Guatemala; the discovery of America; Romanticism and positivism; labor unions; the Cuban and Mexican Revolutions; and diplomatic history.

1817a Stoetzer, O. Carlos. The scholastic roots of the Spanish American revolution. New York: Fordham University Press, 1979. 300 p.; bibl.; index.

Work of impressive erudition and bound to be highly useful as reference, especially on colonial thinkers and on political formulas of early phase of independence period itself, one which Stoetzer catalogues and classifies at some length. His thesis that the Spanish American revolution was scholastic-inspired traditionalist reaction will satisfy mainly those already convinced, as causal relationships between particular sets of ideas and subsequent actions are often assumed rather than proven and considerable contrary evidence is ignored. Be that as it may, this is an important publication, which naturally builds upon author's earlier *El pensamiento político en la América española durante el período de la emancipación* (see *HLAS 30:1815a*). [D. Bushnell]

1818 Storia dell'America Latina. Edited and compiled by Marcello Carmagnani. Firenze, Italia: La Nuova Italia, 1979. 456 p.; bibl.; tables.

Organizado alrededor de los grandes problemas de la historia contemporánea latinoamericana, el volumen trata de ilustrar las carácteristicas básicas del fenómeno histórico, las diferentes interpretaciones de los estudiosos y los problemas aun no suficientemente estudiados. Los temas del libro son: burguesía nacional; caudillismo; Iglesia; desarrollo industrial; frontera y ocupación del territorio; guerrilla; inmigración; imperialismos; problema étnico; independencia; haciendas; marginalidad social y subproletariado; movimiento obrero; nacionalismo; panamericanismo; populismo; regímenes militares; reforma agraria; revoluciones (mexicana, boliviana y cubana) y esclavitud. Contiene colaboraciones de numerosos historiadores latinoamericanos (José Luis Romero, Roberto Cortés Conde, Cristóbal Kay, etc.), americanos (Karen Spalding, Herbert S. Klein, etc.) y europeos (Werner H. Tobler, Antonio Annino, etc.). [M. Carmagnani]

1819 Subero, Efraín. Pregón de la Hispanidad: España en América bajo el signo caudal del descubrimiento (FJB/BH, 46, enero 1978, p. 58–72)

Appeal by Venezuelan man of letters for thorough interchange of books, people, ideas, methodology, etc., among Hispanic communities of Spain and America. Sees benefits redounding from destruction of provincialism's "corrosiva soledad."

1820 Sunkel, Osvaldo; Pedro Paz; and **Yves Lacoste.** El proceso de subdessarrollo: una perspectiva histórica. Tegucigalpa: Programa de Capacitación Campesina para la Reforma Agraria, 1975. 88 p.; bibl. (Serie Didáctica; 5)

Brief, generalized account divided into two parts. Sunkel and Paz trace the progress of development over past two centuries followed by Lacoste's analysis of the causes of underdevelopment.

1820a Tanzi, Héctor José. El tema ideológico de la revolución norteamericana y su influencia en Hispanoamérica (PAIGH/R, 86, julio/dic. 1978, p. 169–191)

Overview with numerous specific citations. Downplays influence of ideology generally and *political* importance of Enlightenment thought for Latin America, but accepts importance of Anglo-American model in formation of Latin American institutions once revolution got underway. [D. Bushnell]

1821 Torres Gaytán, Ricardo. La tecnología como factor dependencia de los países de Indoamérica (CAM, 216:1, enero/feb. 1978, p. 45–62)

Examines social and economic consequences of technological progress. Author acknowledges benefits for humanity derived from scientific advances in chemistry and biochemistry, but maintains that insufficient attention has been directed toward lack of improvement in conditions for working classes in dependent countries.

1822 Tulane University of Louisiana. Middle American Research Institute. Philological and documentary studies. v. 2. New Orleans: 1977. 286 p., facsims. (Publication; 12)

Six items included in this publication all of which have been issued previously are of value to researchers. Each has an unusually descriptive title that serves as a brief annotation: 1) S.K. Lowe's "Paleographic Guide for Spanish Manuscripts, Fifteenth-Seventeenth Centuries: Roman Numerals" (1943); 2) Silvia Rendón's "Ordenanza del Señor Cuahtémoc: Paleografía, Traducción, y Noticia Introductoria" (1952); 3) William Griffith's "The Hasinai Indians of East Texas as Seen by Europeans, 1687–1772" (1954); 4) Marshall Durbin's "An Interpretation of Bishop Diego de Landa's Maya Alphabet" (1969); 5) Ross Parmenter's "The Identification of Lienzo A: a Tracing in the Latin American Library of Tulane University" (1970); 6) William Griffith's "The Personal Archive of Francisco Morazán" (1977).

1823 Urbanski, Edmund Stephen. Hispanic America and its civilizations: Spanish Americans and Anglo-Americans. Translated from the Spanish by Frances Kellam Hendricks and Beatrice Berler. Forewords by Carl Benton Compton and Manuel M. Valle. Norman: University of Oklahoma Press, 1978. 332 p.; bibl.; maps; plates.

Study of transplantation of Western culture to New World with cultural, anthropological, historical, and sociological perspectives that affected Hispanic-American civilizations. Resulting complexities shaped contemporary multi-ethnic, Hispanic society. Author utilizes cultural-anthropological approach to present comparative studies of civilization of both Americas to promote intercontinental understanding.

1824 Wiarda, Howard J. Corporatist theory and ideology: a Latin American development paradigm (BU/JCS, 20:1, Winter 1978, p. 29–56, bibl.)

Brief analysis of corporatism as an organizing element in Hispanic society and the application of the concept in the organization of states in contemporary Latin America.

COLONIAL

1825 Abellán, José Luis. Los orígenes españoles del mito del "buen salvaje:" Fray Bartolomé de Las Casas y su antropología utópica (IGFO/RI, 145/146, julio/dic. 1976, p. 157–179)

Traces Spanish origins of the myth that man is the "good savage" and the influence of this theme on the literature of the Enlightenment. Abellán examines the works of Peter Martir, Luis Vives, and Las Casas, focusing on the latter's exaggerated descriptions of the American Indian's humanity and utopian life styles.

1826 Andrews, Kenneth R. The Spanish Caribbean trade and plunder, 1530–1630. New Haven, Conn.: Yale University Press, 1978. 267 p.; fold. maps; plates; tables.

Despite absence of bibliography, footnotes reflect extensive archival research by author as well as familiarity with printed materials. Andrews traces 100 years of maritime history-including intermittent warfare and its destructive impact, influence of foreign traders and pirates, lack of adequate Spanish responses to problems of region, and foreign settlement. Highly recommended and significant synthesis.

1827 Aramayo Alzérreca, Carlos. Forjadores de América. Buenos Aires: Editorial Francisco de Aguirre, 1975. 175 p.; bibl.; 7 leaves of plates: ill.; index. (Biblioteca Antartica; 29)

Dramatic accomplishments of explorers and conquistadors (Columbus, Balboa, Magellan, Orellana, and Valdivia) and liberators (O'Higgins and Bolívar) as well as those of lesser fame such as painter Melchor Pérez de Holguín are recounted.

Aretz de Ramón y Rivera, Isabel. Música y danza: América Latina continental, excepto Brasil. See item **7002**.

1828 Ariza S., Alberto E. Notas y textos: acotaciones sobre Fray Bartolomé de las Casas (ISTM/MH, 34:100/102, 1977, p. 333–334)

Important events in Las Casas' life such as birthdate, ecclesiastical studies, and transatlantic voyages, corrected by recent scholarship are noted.

1828a Armas Medina, Fernando de. Estudios sobre historia de América. Las Palmas de Gran Canaria, Spain: Cabildo Insular de Gran Canaria, 1973. 350 p.; bibl. (Ediciones del Cabildo Insular de Gran Canaria; 3. Geografía e historia; 8)

Collection of nine articles on colonial history by the author. Topics include the church in 17th-century Peru, governmental institutions in Cuba, organization of the audiencias in Puerto Príncipe, Puerto Rico and the Canaries, and general articles on colonial treasury officials, organization of doctrinas and the legal justifications for the conquests.

1829 Arnall Juan, María Josefa. El *Itinerario de Indias: 1673–1679*, del Padre Fray Isidoro de la Asunción, C.D.: Manuscrito 514 de la Biblioteca Provincial y Universitaria de Barcelona (UB/BA, 20:28, 1978, p. 197–252)

Transcription of a portion of Father Isidoro de la Asunción's *Itinerario de Indias.* Among his first but detailed descriptions are Puebla (Mexico), the royal place in Mexico City, how Indians lived, race mixture, royal mines, and city of Havana during years 1673–1679.

1830 Arranz Márquez, Luis. La herencia colombina en los primeros proyectos de descubierta y colonización (IGFO/RI, 37:149/150, julio/dic. 1977, p. 425–469)

Lengthy article which details actions of Ferdinand of Aragon that effectively halted further projects of exploration and discovery by Columbus' family. While Ferdinand tacitly acknowledged rights of the Second Admiral to sponsor expeditions into areas peripheral to Española, he nevertheless granted capitulations to others, such as Juan Ponce de León and Diego Velázquez.

1832 Caballero, Enrique. La Casa de Contratación de Sevilla responsable del subdesarrollo de la América española (BCV/REL, 11:43, 1975, p. 105–115, bibl.)

Places responsibility for economic underdevelopment in America as well as in Spain on restrictive commercial policies of Casa de Contratación and on special interest groups whose selfish interests dictated policies.

1833 Campillo y Cosío, Joseph del. Nuevo sistema de gobierno económico para la América. Introducción de Eduardo Arcila Farías. Mérida, Venezuela: Universidad de los Andes, Facultad de Humanidades y Educación, 1971. 219 p.

Second edition of work originally published in Madrid in 1789. Of particular interest is the introduction by Eduardo Arcila Farías which establishes Campillo y Cosío (d. 1743) as an *arbitrista,* compares his recommendations for reform with those subsequently adopted by Charles III, and establishes by textual comparisons that Bernardo Ward's *Proyecto económico* (Madrid: 1779) constituted unconscionable plagiarism of Campillo y Cosío's then unpublished manuscript.

1833a Canedo, Lino Gómez. Evangelización y conquista: experiencia franciscana en Hispanoamérica. México: Editorial Porrúa, 1977. 393 p.; bibl.; index (Biblioteca Porrúa; 65)

Superior analysis of the Franciscan missionary experience in Spanish America, based on a lifetime of research in Old and New World archives. Canedo examines three major themes: the organization of the Franciscan Order in the Indies, their policies towards the Indians, and the methods employed to christianize them. Includes extensive documentary appendix and a chronology and biobibliographical sketches of all known *comisarios generales.* [M.T. Hamerly]

1834 Casas, Bartolomé de las. Brevísima relación de la destrucción de Indias. Introducción y notas de Manuel Ballesteros Gaibrois. Madrid: Fundación Universitaria Española, 1977. 135 p.; bibl. (Publicaciones de la Fundación Universitaria Española. Facsímiles; 2)

Facsimile reproduction of 1552 edition of the *Brevísima.* Introduction by Ballesteros Gaibrois summarizes the varied facets of Las Casas' personality as well as "repercussions" of his famous work. Also included are a brief bibliography. a list of other editions of the *Brevísima,* and notes on the text.

1835 Cebrián, Alfredo Moreno. El ocio del indio como razón teórica del repartimiento (IGFO/RI, 35:139/142, enero/dic. 1975, p. 167–185)

Examines references to Indians as lazy, indolent creatures in "official" publications such as *Recopilación de las leyes de Indias* and *Política indiana.* These beliefs provided the theoretical bases for the exploitative actions of corregidores as documented in the late colonial era.

1836 Cipriano de Utrera, *Father.* Los restos de Colón en Santo Domingo. Santo Domingo: Editora Taller, 1977. 390 p.; index (Publicaciones de la Academia Dominicana de la Historia; 44)

Compiled after author's death. Utrera left a manuscript with incomplete and unconnected paragraphs, with pages obviously missing and the remainder not paginated, and with no designated chapters, this detailed study adds additional evidence that Columbus' remains repose in Santo Domingo, not in Seville.

1837 Contreras, Remedios. Encomiendas, repartimientos, obrajes y mita en la Colección Mata Linares, Real Academia de la Historia (IGFO/RI, 36:143/144, enero/junio 1976, p. 353–384)

Valuable reference work for research on encomiendas, repartimientos, obrajes, and mita. A total of 303 documents in the Colección Mata Linares relate to these topics. Distribution is as follows: encomiendas (1), repartimientos (25), obrajes (13), and mita (174). Includes especially useful geographic and onomastic indices.

1838 Davies, Nigel. Voyagers to the New World. New York: William Morrow, 1979. 287 p., bibl., maps, plates.

Author of excellent works on Aztecs and Toltecs provides a highly readable and well reasoned summation of continuing controversy over Old World influences on American cultures. While intended for the general reader, theories are examined in light of most recent archaeological and anthropological research and current knowledge of navigation.

1839 Delgado Ribas, José María. América y el comercio de Indias en la historiografía catalana: 1892–1978 (UB/BA, 20:28, 1978, p. 179–187)

Provides survey of historiographical writing (1892–1978) on subject of Catalonia's commercial ties with the Indies and suggests need for additional research on topic to resolve conflicting interpretations.

1840 Desroche, Henri. L'utopism Euroaméricain et ses pratiques migratoires: XVIIe–XIXe siècles (UP/TM, 19:75, juillet/sept. 1978, p. 495–511)

Brief article which points out the attractiveness of North and South American ambiance vis-à-vis European for Utopian ventures. Lists communities that were religiously, economically, and politically motivated ranging from Vasco de Quiroga's in Mexico to Robert Owen's in Indiana.

1841 Días Avelino, Yvone. Institução do comércio livre na mudança estrutural do sistema colonial espanhol (PAIGH/H, 85, enero/junio 1978, p. 59–84)

The institutionalization of "free trade" within the Spanish empire under Charles III is perceived by the author as an outgrowth of more than half a century of structural change initiated under the first two Bourbon monarchs. The institutionalization reflected a maturing accommodation to foreign ideas, and a growing liberalism among the Spanish intelligentsia. [L. Huddleston]

1842 Domínguez Compañy, Francisco. Ordenanzas municipales hispanoamericanas (PAIGH/H, 86, julio/dic. 1978, p. 9–60)

Analyzes nature and content of selected municipal ordinances issued in colonial era. The earliest considered emanated from Cortés in 1525 and the latest, from the municipality of Cúcuta in 1793. Author concludes that more ordinances were intended to modify existing conditions, thereby suggesting flexibility in policies implemented by local officials.

1843 Efimov, A.V. On the discovery of America (*in* Soviet historians on Latin America: recent scholarly contributions. [see item **1817**] p. 67–76)

Russian author addresses question of discovery of America which he sees as a multi-staged continuum of geographical processes rather than a singular, spectacular incident.

1844 Ezquerra Abadía, Ramón. Los primeros contactos entre Colón y Vespucio (IGFO/RI, 36:143/144, enero/junio 1976, p. 19–48)

Examines identity and testimony of witnesses, the most important of whom was Amerigo Vespucci, in an *información* dated 1510. Vespucci acknowledged personal contact with Columbus. By correlation of known whereabouts of two explorers, author speculates on date of their initial meeting.

1845 Fikes, Robert, Jr. José de Acosta's window on the New World (OAS/AM, 30:6/7, June/July 1978, p. 29–31)

Examines the views of José de Acosta who lived for 16 years in Peru and Mexico as explorer, theologian, and author of books, including his famous work, *Historia natural y moral de las Indias*. His writings were designed to promote a better understanding of the New World by Europeans of his day.

1846 Gabaldón Márquez, Edgar. El coloniaje: la formación societaria peculiar de nuestro continente. Caracas: Academia Nacional de la Historia, 1976. 526 p.; bibl.; index (Serie Estudios, monografías y ensayos; 3. Biblioteca de la Academia Nacional de la Historia; 1)

Presented as a history of ideas, this volume contains a hodgepodge of comments made by writers ranging from Plato to present-day authors. Includes "Layers of Opinion" on topics such as theory and practice of imperialism (from the Sumerians to Lenin); panorama of imperialism (spanning 4,733 years); and theory and practice of colonialism (from Phoenician to contemporary times).

1846a García-Baquero González, Antonio. Cádiz y el Atlántico, 1717–1778: el comercio colonial español bajo el monopolio gaditano. Sevilla: Escuela de Estudios Hispano-Americanos, 1976. 2 v. (570, 296 p.); bibl.; plates; tables (Publicación; 237)

This quantitative study of trade and navigation between Spain and her American colonies via Cádiz, from the transference of the Board of Trade from Sevilla in 1717 through the promulgation of the Free Trade Act of 1778, is based on considerable research in archives of Cádiz, Sevilla and Simancas. Vol. 1 examines sources and methodology; polity and theory of imperial trade; organization of the *carrera de Indias*; customs and consular duties and other taxes; frauds; the ships themselves; their construction and type; routes; exports and imports; vicissitudes suffered by ships and the trade; merchant societies and merchants of Cádiz foreign as well as national; questions of capital; and economic cycles. Vol. 2 contains 45 time series; 17 charts on the ships' names, owners, types, country of fabrication and tonnage; sailings and destinations; specific exports by year and quantity; and imports by quantity, estimated values and assess prices. See also García-Baquero's *Comercio colonial y guerras revolucionarias* (Sevilla: Escuela de Estudios Hispano-Americanos, 1972; Publicación; 206, not annotated in *HLAS*) which examines the final years of trade (i.e., 1797–1824) with the mainland colonies as well as with the Leeward Islands with equal care and attention to detail. Both monographs compare favorably with Chaunus' *Seville et l'Atlantique, 1504–1650*. Their focal point, however, is Cádiz and Spain, not the colonies. [M.T. Hamerly]

1847 Garzón Pareja, Manuel. El riesgo en el comercio de Indias (IGFO/RI, 35:139/142, enero/dic. 1975, p. 187–227, tables)

Examines the manifold dangers and incumbrances that affected commerce between Spain and the Indies. Author assesses problems of piracy, Atlantic security, restrictive commercial ordinances, and financial guarantees assumed by ship masters for their cargoes. Statistical data include the *Registro de Pólizas* for Cádiz during years 1760–81.

1848 Gibson, Charles. Conquest, capitulation, and Indian treaties (AHA/R, 83:1, Feb. 1978, p. 1–15)

Presidential address delivered at annual meeting of American Historical Association (1977). Gibson draws parallels or lack thereof between Reconquest and Conquest, defines precisely capitulation, and speculates on absence of Spanish treaties and *pactos* with Indians. Problems raised are then examined in broader context.

1849 ———. Spanish institutions and the colonial history of Latin America (UCSD/NS, 7:1/2, 1978 [i.e. 1979] p. 1–27)

Superb survey of literature published since 1955 on the Iberian background of Spanish America. Gibson notes that general background bibliography over past two decades reflects a trend away from political-legal-institutional history toward socioeconomic history. He also points out lacunae in historical knowledge regarding adaptations and modifications of Spanish institutions transplanted to Spanish colonies. In doing so, he charts potential research topics for Hispanic and Latin American scholars. (Gibson's essay is intended as a companion piece to an article by Charles Julian Bishko published in the *Hispanic American Historical Review*, 36, 1956, p. 50–80.)

1850 González González, Alfonso Federico. El Consejo de Indias en la crisis de los Consejos y en el nacimiento de la estructura administrativa contemporánea (UB/BA, 20:28, 1978, p. 165–177)

Sketches fundamental changes in structure and administrative responsibilities of Council of Indies from its creation in 1524 to its demise in 1834. Author enumerates weaknesses of Council in 17th century and documents its further decline during years 1700–1834.

Heyerdahl, Thor. Early man and the ocean. See *HLAS 41:1453*.

1851 Hulme, Peter. Columbus and the cannibals: a study of the reports of anthropophagy in the *Journal* of Christopher Columbus (IAA, 4:2, 1978, p. 115–139, bibl.)

Intriguing analysis of Columbus' *Jour-*

nal which employs liberal use of psychology. Author develops two motivations of the Admiral—a conscious search for the Grand Khan and an unconscious but dominant search for native gold. A concomitant rationalization of the dominant motive was European projection of bestial and cannibalistic traits on natives.

1852 Humble, Richard. The explorers. Alexandria, Va.: Time-Life Books, 1978. 176 p.; bibl.; ill.; index. (The Seafarers)

Attractive, well-written book in *Time-Life* series. Text is enhanced with superb illustrations from world-wide libraries and museums and the expertise of consultants, John Horace Parry and William Avery Baker.

1853 Jara, Alvaro. Estructuras coloniales y subdesarrollo en Hispanoamérica (SA/J, 65, 1978, p. 145–171, tables)

Provides, as point of departure for historical consideration, an explanation of underdevelopment in Latin America resulting from Interaction of Hispanic-Indian society and Spanish imperial interests. Statistical data are reproduced from printed sources.

1854 Juan Ginés de Sepúlveda y su *Crónica Indiana:* [De rebus hispanorum gestis ad Novum Orbem Mexicumque]: en el IV centenario de su muerte 1573–1973. Valladolid: Seminario Americanista de la Universidad de Valladolid, 1976. 498 p.; bibl.; 7 leaves of plates: ill. (Bernal, Serie Americanista; 8)

In commemoration of 400th anniversary of Juan Ginés de Sepúlveda's death, the ayuntamiento of his birth place, Pozoblanco, commissioned a team of scholars headed by Demetrio Ramos to write a series of brief studies of the great humanist's life and to produce an excellent, new translation with accompanying notes of his *Crónica Indiana.*

1855 Lewis, James A. New Spain and the American Revolution: a view from the Valley of Mexico, 1779–1783 (RIB, 28:1, enero/marzo 1978, p. 37–45)

Author theorizes on reasons why inhabitants of New Spain were largely indifferent to revolution in England's North American colonies. Explanations include high rate of illiteracy and lack of political consciousness, lack of empathy for causes of war, and Spanish perceptions of English race.

1856 López de Lara, Guillermo. Ideas tempranas de la política social en Indias: apología de los indios, bula de la libertad. México: Editorial Jus, 1977. 355 p.; bibl.; 3 leaves of plates: ill.

Title and subtitles are headings for this curious, fragmented, three-part study of events and ideas which shaped Spanish Indian policy from 1492 through reign of Charles V. Author's previous works consisted of poetry and literary criticism.

1857 Madariaga, Salvador de. El auge y el ocaso del imperio español en América. Madrid: Espasa-Calpe, 1977. 735 p.; bibl.; index; 2 leaves of plates: map.

Attractive new edition of Madariaga's work first published in 1945. Chapter notes have been relocated as footnotes in this printing (for comments on earlier editions, see *HLAS 11:1971* and *HLAS 20:2455*).

1858 Mendelson, Johanna S.R. The feminine press: the view of women in the colonial journals of Spanish America, 1790–1810 (*in* Latin American women: historical perspectives [see item **1791**] p. 198–218, tables)

Excellent contribution which analyzes the role served by journal articles in articulating the position of 18th-century, Spanish women. Journalists (all male) readily acknowledged that women had an inferior status while advocating education to improve it, especially through women's influence on children as extensions of themselves. Articles pay only token attention to the movement and do not suggest alternate roles.

1859 Mercado, Tomás de. Suma de trates y contratos. v. 1/2. Madrid: Instituto de Estudios Fiscales del Ministerio de Hacienda, 1977. 795 p.; plates.

Attractive reprint of 16th-century Dominican's magnum opus on ethics of business practices employed by merchants and businessmen of Seville. Addresses controversial topics such as just price, usury, and rational for monopolies. Ranks a classic among Spanish economic studies of Golden Century.

1860 Mohler, Stephen C. Publishing in colonial Spanish America: an overview (RIB, 28:3, julio/sept. 1978, p. 259–273)

Brief description of limitations placed on development of colonial Spanish American publishing and printing. Topics include suppression of native works, problems of illiteracy, censorship by civil and ecclesiastical authorities, press and marketing regulations, scarcity of supplies and presses, and attitudes and taste for subjects. For literary critic's comment, see item **5134**.

1861 Morison, Samuel Eliot. The great explorers: the European discovery of America. New York: Oxford University Press, 1978. 752 p.; plates.

Handsome abridgement of parent volumes devoted to *The northern voyages, A.D. 500–1600* (1971), and *The southern voyages, 1492–1616* (1974). For comments on both, see *HLAS 38:3009*.

1862 New York (City). **Public Library.** Colonial Latin American manuscripts and transcripts in the Obadiah Rich collection: an inventory and index. By Edwin Blake Brownrigg. New York: New York Public Library [and] Astor, Lenox and Tilden Foundations, 1978. 159 p.; bibl.

First comprehensive guide to the Obadiah Rich Collection in New York Public Library. Excellent introduction provides provenance of documents and relates them to the Muñoz Collection in Madrid. This valuable and much-needed guide for researchers also includes name and title indexes as well as inventory and chronological arrangements of documents. For another comment, see *HLAS 41:68*.

1863 El Ocaso del orden colonial en Hispanoamérica. Compilador: Tulio Halperín Donghi. Buenos Aires: Editorial Sudamericana, 1978. 247 p.; bibl. (Colección Historia y sociedad)

Collection of five essays, four of which have been published elsewhere, on socioeconomic crises that beset the colonial order prior to independence. Contributors are: Herbert Klein on Peru (1975, see *HLAS 38:3160*); Oscar Cornbilt on Peru and Bolivia (1970, see *HLAS 36:2572*); Tulio Halperín Donghi on Buenos Aires (1968, see *HLAS 32:2462*); and Torcuato S. Di Tella on Mexico (1973, see *HLAS 36:2017*). Nicolás Sánchez Albornoz's contribution treats the abolition of Indian tribute to independence and its subsequent reinstitution in the Bolivarian Republics.

1863a Parry, John Horace. The discovery of South America. New York: Taplinger Pub. Co., 1979. 320 p.; bibl.; ill.; index.

A retelling of the discovery and early exploration of the Caribbean, Mexico and Central America as well as South America, largely in the words of the discoverers, conquistadores and early explorers themselves and mostly of their initial impressions of the people and places, flora and fauna of the New World. Includes many reproductions of coeval maps and woodcuts. Parry's text, however, includes some errors and he is more familiar with traditional accounts than with recent studies and reinterpretations. [M.T. Hamerly]

1864 Pérez, Joseph. Los movimientos precursores de la emancipación en Hispanoamérica. Madrid: Alhambra, 1977. 156 p.; bibl. (Estudios)

Brief study which analyzes social, economic, and political factors underpinning independence in Paraguay, Venezuela, Ecuador, Peru, and Bolivia. Author concludes that deep seated problems worsened throughout 18th century fostering solidarity among previously disparate elements of colonial society who were increasingly allied against Spain.

1865 Pérez de Barradas, José. Los mestizos de América. Madrid: Espasa-Calpe, 1976. 249 p.; bibl. (Colección austral; 1610)

Reprint minus illustrations of volume first published in 1948 (*HLAS 14:576*).

1866 Pike, Ruth. Penal servitude in the Spanish empire: presidio labor in the eighteenth century (HAHR, 58:1, Feb. 1978, p. 21–40, tables)

Compares use of prisoners in providing cheap labor both in Spain and Spanish America by state and private sectors. Author notes that the two sectors were less sharply defined in the Americas, and she concentrates on the application of penal labor to strengthen the military fortifications of Havana and San Juan after the Seven Years War.

1867 Pugliesi, Haidée Marquiafave. O regime do Porto Unico no mercantilismo espanhol: Razão de Estado (PAIGH/H, 85, enero/junio 1978, p. 85–101)

After reviewing the beginnings of the Sevillan monopoly of American trade, the author argues that the system derived from Western monarchical traditions of personalism and Machiavellian "reasons of state." The monopoly was impelled by Spain's capitalistic immaturity and the need to protect the power of absolute monarchy. [L. Huddleston]

Ramos Pérez, Demetrio. El mito del Dorado: su génesis y proceso. See item **996**.

1868 ———. La prevención de Fernando el Católico contra el presumible dominio flamenco de América: la primera disposición contra el paso de extranjeros al nuevo continente (JGSWGL, 14, 1977, p. 1–46)

Addresses question of whether restrictions on emigration of non-Castilians to Indies were relaxed by Ferdinand of Aragon after the death of Isabella in 1504. In well-researched article, author examines conflicting views of chroniclers on subject, concludes with few exceptions that Ferdinand's policies were a continuation of Isabella's and credits Ferdinand with statesmanship that transcended provincial considerations.

1869 Rementería, Carlos J. Díaz. El regimen jurídico del Ramo de Tributos en Nueva España y las reformas peruanas de Carlos III (CM/HM, 28:3, enero/marzo 1979, p. 401–437)

Careful study of influence of José de Gálvez's visitation to New Spain (1765–71) and his recommendations for improvement in collection and administration of royal revenue. Author concludes that newly imposed system in Mexico was essentially duplicated in Peru, and documents his case by citing increases in revenue from South American viceroyalty of more than 500,000 pesos between years 1773–80.

1870 Rípodas Ardanaz, Daisy. El matrimonio en Indias: realidad social y regulación jurídica. Buenos Aires: Fundación para la Educación, la Ciencia y la Cultura, 1977. 454 p.; bibl.; 8 leaves of plates: ill.

Significant work in social history that examines marriage in colonial period among peninsulares, Creoles, Indians, blacks, and castes. Author's research in Spanish, Argentine, and Chilean archives, her extensive bibliography of printed sources, and her careful analysis of the institution of marriage within juridical framework of state and Church make this a landmark study.

1871 Rodríguez Vicente, María Encarnación. Apelaciones de la Casa de Contratación y Consulado de Cádiz ante el Consejo de Indias: inventario de la documentación existente en el Archivo Histórico Nacional de Madrid (RUC, 26:107, enero/marzo 1977, p. 143–244, tables)

This inventory of documentation contained in Archivo Histórico Nacional de Madrid relates to cases carried on appeal to Consejo de Indias from Casa de Contratación and Consulado de Cádiz. Significantly, documentation originating in late colonial period was not sent to Archivo General de Indias to accompany lawsuits of earlier provenance located in sections Justicia and Escribanía de Cámara de Justicia of AGI, rather it was dispatched to section Consejos of AHN. Bulk of AHN cases covers years 1760–1830. Valuable index at end of inventory.

1872 ———. La contabilidad privada como fuente histórica (IGFO/RI, 37:147/148, enero/junio 1977, p. 159–176)

Examination of private papers in AHN (Madrid) relating to the estate of a Spaniard, who emigrated to Mexico where he died in 1771 after acquiring a sizable hacienda in Sonora. Reveals social as well as economic insights into colonial life. Author advocates study of private accounts as untapped avenue of research.

1873 Rumeu de Armas, Antonio. El *Diario de a bordo* de Cristobal Colón: el problema de la paternidad del extracto (IGFO/RI, 143/144, enero/junio 1976, p. 7–17)

Renowned Columbus scholar examines the holographic compendium of the lost *Diario de a bordo*, kept by Columbus on his first voyage. He concludes, contrary to popular belief, that Las Casas did not author the extract.

1874 Russell-Wood, A.J.R. Iberian expansion and the issue of black slavery: changing Portuguese attitudes, 1440–1770 (AHA/R, 83:1, Feb. 1978, p. 16–42)

Excellent article which synthesizes an impressive range of literature dealing with moral, philosophical, and economic consequences of black slavery in Portugal and Brazil. Of particular interest are Russell-Wood's observations on the Portuguese "struggle for justice." Intensity of debate in Portugal over black slavery did not equal that in Spain over Indian slavery, but the tempering of theological and moral doctrines by political and commercial considerations is a familiar theme in both countries.

1875 **Saint-Lu, André.** Fondements et implications de l'indigénisme militant de Bartolomé de las Casas (JGSWGL, 14, 1977, p. 47–56)

Brief assessment of implications of Las Casas' militant defense of Indians. Author concludes that despite significant influence of Las Casas on royal legislation, the inevitable resistance of colonial interest to change did not materially alter New World conditions. Nevertheless, the Dominican's example serves to inspire continuing regard for justice and brotherhood.

1876 **Sánchez, Víctor** and **Cayetano S. Fuertes.** España en Extremo Oriente: Filipinas, China, Japón, presencia franciscana. Madrid: Editorial Cisneros, 1979. 671 p.

Número extraordinario de la revista *Archivo Ibero-Americano* (Madrid) dedicado a conmemorar el cuarto centenario de la llegada de los franciscanos a Filipinas. Contiene trabajos de varios especialistas distinguidos (tres en inglés, uno en italiano y otros en portugués; los nueve restantes están en español, y 17 ilustraciones). La obra tiene importancia especial para los americanistas, no sólo por el hecho de que algunos misioneros ejercieron antes su apostolado en América y casi todos pasaron al Oriente a través de México—y aquí tuvieron su principal punto de apoyo—sino por las referencias que se hacen en ella a métodos misionales ensayados antes en el Nuevo Mundo. [L.G. Canedo]

1877 **Sánchez-Barba, Mario Hernández.** El bicentenario de 1776: América y la estrategia de seguridad atlántica en el reformismo español (RUC, 26:107, enero/marzo 1977, p. 9–47)

Broad analysis by expert on subject of policy affecting Spanish empire in America in reign of Charles III. Author assesses Spanish posture in context of Anglo-French colonial rivalry, reviews administrative organization of three viceroyalties in 1776, and comments on problems of Atlantic security in context of European Enlightenment and Bourbon reform in Spain.

1878 **Sanz, Carlos.** La primitiva historia de América: pts. 1/2 (RSG/B, 108:1/12, enero/dic. 1972, p. 185–194, 110:1/12, enero/dic. 1974, p. 221–226)

Pt. 1 reviews publication of books and maps in Europe which stirred Old World interest and expansion into the New World. Pt. 2 idealistically calls for sensitive scholarship to promote harmonious integration of humanity in the two worlds.

1879 **Sanz, Eufemio Lorenzo.** Esplendor y quiebra de la sociedad mercantil más poderosa del comercio indiano de mediados del siglo XVI (IGFO/RI, 37:147/148, enero/junio 1977, p. 23–50)

Impressive research in Spanish archives documents rise and financial ruin of a Sevillan consortium engaged in commercial ventures in the Indies and in Europe. The firm had incurred debts of 183,700,000 maravedís by 1567. Its bankruptcy was hardly unique, for at least 51 powerful Sevillan merchants suffered a similar fate that year.

1880 ———. La producción y el comercio de las plantas medicinales, alimenticias, maderas preciosas, cueros vacunos y productos diversos recibidos de Indias en el Reinado de Felipe II (UB/BA, 20:28, 1978, p. 137–164, tables)

Title of this impressively documented article is descriptive of its contents. Statistical data have been painstakingly assembled from several sections of AGI and other Spanish archives on products arriving in Seville, primarily from New Spain, Honduras, Puerto Rico, Cuba, and Española during years 1550–1600.

1881 **Sepúlveda, Juan Ginés de.** Hechos de los españoles en el Nuevo Mundo y México. Edición y estudios de Demetrio Ramos y Lucio Mijares, con la colaboración de Jonas Castro Toledo. Valladolid, Spain: Seminario Americanista de la Universidad de Valladolid, 1976. 400 p.; bibl.; ill.

New edition of Sepúlveda's work, with an introduction and editorial annotations.

1882 **Solano, Francisco de.** Política de concentración de la población indígena: objectivos, proceso, problemas, resultados (IGFO/RI, 36:145/146, julio/dic. 1976, p. 7–29)

Examines what author calls multidimensional explanations for urbanization policies applied both deliberately and accidentally to Indian populations in colonial era.

Steele, Colin. English interpreters of the Iberian New World from Purchas to Stevens:

a bibliographical study, 1603–1726. See *HLAS 41:5282.*

1883 Sweet, David G. Black robes and "black destiny:" Jesuit views of African slavery in 17th century Latin America (PAIGH/H, 86, julio/dic. 1978, p. 87–133)

Excellent article which challenges the Tannenbaum thesis regarding role of Catholic clergy in the enslavement of blacks. Author argues that priests often provided essential justification of slavery, aided in disciplining recalcitrant slaves, and helped diminish threat of slave insurrections. Sees spiritual welfare of slaves as distinctly secondary to economic exploitation of both African and Indian slaves.

1884 Traboulay, David M. The Church and the university in colonial Latin America (ZMR, 63:4, Okt. 1979, p. 283–294)

Interesting article which explores origins of colonial Latin American universities and their close association with major religious orders. Included are comments on academic organization, degrees, curricula, and codes of conduct for professors and students.

1885 Turner, E. Raymond. Los libros del Alcaide: la biblioteca de Gonzalo Fernández de Oviedo y Valdés (IGFO/RI, 31:125/126, julio/dic. 1971, p. 139–198, bibl.)

As in previous publications (see *HLAS 30:1097* and *HLAS 32:979*), Turner continues his work on the first chronicler of the Indies, Gonzalo Fernández de Oviedo y Valdés. This is a speculative reconstruction of Oviedo's library. Included are author, title, publication language and data, etc., of books and documents probably used by Oviedo in composing his *Historia general y natural de las Indias.*

1886 Tyacke, Sarah. The long way home for Sir Francis Drake (GM, 50:2, Nov. 1977, p. 105–111, col. plates, col. maps, facsim., map, plates)

Author contends that Drake's unintentional circumnavigation of globe (1577–1580) challenged Spanish and Portuguese hegemony in New World. While the plunder of Spanish possessions was Drake's own plan, his voyage brought spices, charts of unknown South Sea areas, and 10 tons of silver bullion for England.

1887 Valera Marcos, Jesús. El Seminario de Marinos: un intento de formación de los marineros para las armadas y flotas de Indias (PAIGH/H, 87, enero/junio 1979, p. 9–36)

Notes need for reform in Spanish maritime service at beginning of 17th century, and traces successful efforts of Admiral Diego Brochero, a catalyst of reform, to create in 1606 a school for mariners in province of Guipúzcoa. Failure of the *seminario* to produce desired results is assessed.

1888 Velasco, B. La vida en alta mar en un relato del P. Antonio Vázquez de Espinosa, 1602 (IGFO/RI, 36:143/144, enero/junio 1976, p. 287–352)

Edited version of Antonio Vázquez de Espinosa's account of 100 days at sea in 1602. His detailed and graphic descriptions of bad weather, plagues of rats, and general discomfort aboard ship are interesting and are reflective of rigors endured by Spaniards on trans-Atlantic voyages.

1889 Vera Cruz, Alonso de la. The writings of Alonso de la Vera Cruz. v. 4, Defense of the Indians: their privileges; v. 5, pt. 2, Spanish writings. Translated and with an introduction by Ernest J. Burrus. St. Louis, Missouri: Jesuit Historical Institute, 1976. 2 v. (889, 382 p.) bibl.; plates (Sources on studies for the history of the Americas, 11/12)

Vol. 4 and 5 complete Father S.J. Burrus' monumental project to publish and translate 31 significant writings of the University of Salamanca's and University of Mexico's distinguished professor and Augustinian friar. Vol. 4 (actually published after vol. 5) deals with the controversy of Indian tithing, and papal privileges in the Mexican Apostolate; vol. 5 presents all letters and reports written or signed by Vera Cruz.

Vigneras, Louis-André. La búsqueda del paraíso y las legendarias Islas del Atlántico. See item **1007**.

1889a Vila, Enriqueta. The large-scale introduction of Africans into Veracruz and Cartagena (*in* Comparative perspectives on slavery in New World societies [see item **1768**] p. 267–280, tables)

Revisionist study of the number of slaves introduced into Viceroyalties of New

Spain and Peru between 1595–1640 which is largely based on sources in the Archivo General de Indias. Taking issues with Gonzalo Aguirre y Beltrán, Philip D. Curtin and Rolando Mellafe, Vila contends that the actual number of slaves introduced into Spanish South America by the Portuguese during the 45 years in question was about 150,000 or somewhat more than twice as many as were introduced into New Spain (70,800). Preview of a larger, quantitative work (in preparation) on the Portuguese asiento. [M.T. Hamerly]

1890 Villapalos, Gustavo. Los recursos en materia administrativa en Indias en los siglos XVI y XVII (INEJ/AHD, 46, 1976, p. 7–75)

Trabajo bien documentado. Estudia la competencia de los distintos órganos administrativos y las posibilidades de recurrir por vía administrativa contra sus excesos. [L.G. Canedo]

1890a Walker, Geoffrey J. Spanish politics and imperial trade, 1700–1789. Bloomington: Indiana University Press, 1979. 397 p.; bibl.; 4 leaves of plates: ill.; index.

Detailed political, economic study examines the trade between Spain and her American colonies in the 18th century, particularly with New Spain via the *flotas* until finally suppressed in 1789—the last of which sailed in 1776—and with Peru via the *galeones*, abolished a half century earlier. Also describes the fairs at Jalapa and Portobello, French and English legal participation in trade and interloping, and the role of Mexican and Peruvian merchants in the trade and their attitudes towards the fleet and its replacement by "free trade." Includes some quantitative data, but its primary contribution is the elucidation of the "struggle for supremacy between the merchants of the metropolis and the merchants of the colonies." Based primarily on research in Sevilla and Lima. [M.T. Hamerly]

1891 Wallis, Helen. Silver medal for the Golden Hind (GM, 50:2, Nov. 1977, p. 112–117, maps, plates)

Interesting article which establishes Drake's knowledge upon completion of 1577–80 circumnavigation that a strait separated Tierra del Fuego from South American continent. For reasons of security, his discovery of strait and return voyage were kept secret, but have been reestablished by new documentary evidence.

1892 Zavala, Silvio. Reglas sobre descubrimiento y entradas (USP/RH, 50:100, 1974, p. 117–131)

Traces evolution of rules governing discoveries and conquests from early 16th century to issuance of *Recopilación* in 1680. Impact of major legislation, such as New Laws and 1573 Ordinances, as it influenced restrictive clauses in royal capitulations is noted.

INDEPENDENCE AND 19TH CENTURY

1893 Acevedo, Edberto Oscar. La formación de las nacionalidades americanas (UNC/RHAA, 7:13/14, 1968/1969, p. 97–110)

Printed version of a lecture given in 1969 concerning the reasons for the great difficulties Latin Americans had in the 19th century with establishing stable nations. The author argues that these difficulties are attributable to characteristics of the independence movements.

Alberich, José. Bibliografía anglo-hispánica 1801–1850: ensayo bibliográfico de libros y folletos relativos a España a Hispanoamérica impresos en Inglaterra en la primera mitad del siglo diecinueve. See *HLAS 41:15*.

1894 Anna, Timothy E. The Buenos Aires expedition and Spain's secret plan to conquer Portugal, 1814–1820 (AAFH/TAM, 34:3, Jan. 1978, p. 356–380)

Excellent article which examines the misguided and unrestrained power of Ferdinand VII, the bankruptcy of his policies toward America, and the significance of the Riego Revolt. Instead of concentrating on reform within Spanish kingdoms, the King engaged in the highrisk Buenos Aires expedition which was secretly designed to provoke war with Portugal and legitimize Spain's annexation of the metropolitan nation.

Arosemena, Justo. Estudio sobre la idea de una Liga Americana. See *HLAS 41:8504*.

1896 Bartley, Russell H. Imperial Russia and the struggle for Latin American independence, 1808–1828. Austin: University of Texas, Institute of Latin American Studies, 1978. 236 p.; bibl.; plates; tables (Latin American monographs; 43)

Extensive research by author and study of works by Russian scholars provide basis for much-needed examination of New World interest of Tsar Alexander I. Bartley sees Alexander's responses to break up of Iberian colonial empires as part of ongoing Russian imperial expansion and international circumstances. An important contribution to works on Latin American policies of major European powers at time of independence.

1897 Bolkhovitinov, N.N. On the threat of intervention in Latin America by the Holy Alliance: from the background of the Monroe Doctrine (*in* Soviet historians on Latin America [see item **1817**] p. 132–157)

Concludes that threat of armed intervention in Latin America by Holy Alliance was a "myth" created by US and England in order to strengthen their economic and political positions in the hemisphere. Author contends that no member nation of the Holy Alliance approved of plan to threaten Latin American independence, and that the chief danger to the latter came from US.

1897a Bollo Cabrios, Palmira S. Instrucciones del gobierno español a sus representantes en Francia y Gran Bretaña, años 1808–1844: pts. 1/2 (ANH/IE, 23, julio/dic. 1977, p. 409–445; 24, enero/junio 1978, p. 481–515)

Pt. 1 is a "preliminary study" that reviews Spanish diplomatic initiatives relating to retention, reconquest, and ultimate recognition of independence of American colonies; pt. 2 consists of a series of "instructions," mostly through 1824, from Argentina's Archivo del Ministerio de Relaciones Exteriores. [D. Bushnell]

1898 Bosch García, Carlos. Latinoamérica, una interpretación global de la dispersión en el siglo XIX. México: Universidad Nacional Autónoma de México, Instituto de Investigaciones Históricas, 1978. 437 p.; bibl. (Serie de historia general; 10)

In keeping with objectives defined by meetings of "Programa de Historia de América," this important synthesis adopts approach of general history of America from independence to 20th century. Approximately one-half of text treats independence of Anglo and Spanish America. The second part analyzes period of transition after independence, followed by development of "three Americas;" one molded by political and economic leaders, a second composed of workers, and a third influenced by intellectuals and ideologies.

1899 Burns, E. Bradford. Ideology in nineteenth-century Latin American historiography (HAHR, 58:3, Aug. 1978, p. 409–431)

Impressive profile of 63 Latin American historians of the 19th century whose rather myopic and exclusive historiography is attributed to the following factors: similar class background and life-styles, predilection for Europeanizing their countries and residing in their major cities. For another comment, see item **7626**.

1900 Campbell, Leon G. Recent research on Bourbon enlightened despotism, 1750–1824 (UCSD/NS, 7:1/2, 1978 [i.e. 1979] p. 29–50)

Well-written essay emphasizing different approaches of social historians to the internal rebellions of the 1780s against Bourbon authoritarianism. Today's revisionists view Bourbon century as one characterized by fiscal and administrative innovations distrusted by Latin Americans who regarded them not as reforms but as disruptive and unwarranted examples of Bourbon absolutism.

1901 Cardoso, Ciro F.S. Características básicas de la economía latinoamericana del siglo XIX: algunos problemas de la transición neocolonial (UNCR/R, 2:4, enero/junio 1977, p. 47–76, bibl.)

Broadly interpretative article which examines: a) circumstances promoting emancipation of blacks in America as well as economic realities confronting freedmen, and b) the economic impact of 19th-century liberal reform programs. Author sees significant transition from colonial to more capitalistic economies, while admitting that capitalism perpetuated antiquated methods of production.

1902 Carreras, Charles. An early venture in trade promotion: the NAM's Caracas center, 1895–1901 (IAMEA, 31:1, Summer 1977, p. 51–64)

Examines aftermath of panic and depression of 1893 which led to creation of the National Association of Manufacturers in the late 1890s.

1902a Cuesta Domingo, Mariano. El Consejo de Estado ante la independencia hispanoamericana, 1821 (RUC, 26:107, enero/marzo 1977, p. 245–264)

Most of the vacillation and incoherence of Spanish policy toward rebellious colonies, featuring new research on proceedings of Consejo de Estado. [D. Bushnell]

1903 Cummins, Light T. John Quincy Adams and Latin American nationalism (PAIGH/H, 86, julio/dic. 1978, p. 221–231)

Broad view of President Adam's foreign policy toward Latin America. Author sees President's goals of hemispheric solidarity in context of nationalistic commonalities as failing in his lifetime, only to emerge 60 years later as pan-Americanism supported by commercial, not nationalistic, underpinnings.

1904 Davis, Harold Eugene. Jaime Balmes, Spanish traditionalist: his influence in Spanish America (AAFH/TAM, 35:3, Jan. 1979, p. 341–351)

Author singles out Balmes as an exception to the assumption that traditionalists were universally conservative in the 1840s, a decade of revolution and intellectual ferment. Evidence is presented of Balmes' liberal inclinations on Church-state relations and personal religious freedom.

1905 Duarte French, Jaime. América de Norte a Sur: ¿Corsarios o libertadores? Bogotá: Biblioteca Banco Popular, 1975. 581 p.; bibl.; ill. (some col.); index.

Examines the activities of mercenaries and filibusters in the Caribbean area and Northern South America during the wars of Independence. Heavily quotes from letters to, from, and about the individuals. The main figures studied are Louis Aury, Louis Peru de Lacroix and Gregor McGregor.

Elkin, Judith Laikin. Jews of the Latin American republics. See item **1927a**.

1905a Ferro, Carlos A. Vida de Luis Aury: corsario de Buenos Aires en las luchas por la independencia de Venezuela, Colombia y Centroamérica. Buenos Aires: Editorial Cuarto Poder, 1976. 269 p.; bibl. (Colección Historia de Latinoamérica)

Workmanlike, unpretentious history by an Argentine diplomat concerning a significant figure, of French origin, in Caribbean privateering warfare. About one-third documentary appendix. [D. Bushnell]

1905b Gandía, Enrique de. La política secreta de la Gran Logia de Londres (ANH/B, 49, 1979, p. 207–242)

After reviewing at some length and dismissing as imaginary the Masonic activities widely attributed to Francisco de Miranda in London, Gandía here seeks to determine just what can be documented concerning Cádiz and London lodges—*not* founded by Miranda—that spurred Carlos de Alvear and San Martín on to Argentina in 1812. [D. Bushnell]

1905c Graham, Robert Bontine Cunninghame. The South American sketches of R.B. Cunninghame Graham. Selected and edited, with an introduction, notes, glossary and bibliography, by John Walker. Norman: University of Oklahoma Press, 1978. 292 p.; bibl.

An anthology of colorful portraits of people and places in late 19th-century Argentina, Uruguay, Paraguay and Brazil, and early 20th-century Colombia and Venezuela. Graham (1852–1936), who is virtually forgotten today, spent much of his youth and early manhood in southern South America, and remained enamoured of the pampas and the gauchos all his life, on both of which he wrote prolifically. [M.T. Hamerly]

1906 Kinsbruner, Jay. The *pulperos* of Caracas and San Juan during the first half of the nineteenth century (LARR, 13:1, 1978, p. 65–85, tables)

Preliminary report of economic activities of *pulperos*, officially designated and supervised storekeepers who operated small, independent shops. Majority of pulperos appear to have been unmarried Catalonians or Canarians. Their profits on non-perishable inventories, especially alcoholic beverages, often reached an annual rate of 100 percent or more.

1908 Kossok, Manfred. Das Dalz der Revolution: Jakobinismus in Lateinamerika; Versuch einer Positionsbestimmung (*in* Universalhistorische Aspekte und Dimensionen des Jakobinismus. Berlin, GDR: Akademie der Wissenschaften, Klässe für Gesselschaftswissenschaften, 1976, p. 124–159)

East German historian sketches differences between French Jacobinism and its counterpart in Latin America (especially Argentina, Haiti, Mexico, Paraguay, Uruguay, and Venezuela). Special reference is made to the effect of Jacobinism on agrarian reform movements. [M. Kossok]

1909 Lucena Salmoral, Manuel. El donativo patriótico hecho por Venezuela a España para ayudar a sufragar los gastos de la Guerra de Independencia Peninsular (VANH/B, 61:241, enero/marzo 1978, p. 109–127, facsim., tables)

Addresses problem of amount of patriotic donations made by Venezuela to Spain during first two years of Peninsular War. The author's minimum rather than precise figures are due to incomplete statistical data resulting from vague accounting records, missing documentation, and lack of information for all Venezuelan ports.

1909a ———. La orden apócrifa de 1810 sobre la "Libertad de Comercio" en América (UB/BA, 20:28, 1978, p. 5–21)

Nice piece of historical detective work showing that the May 1810 royal order—destroyed even before it could be put into effect—did not really offer "free trade" as some historians have alleged but incorporated various lesser provisions that taken singly would have been quite unremarkable. Episode nevertheless does illuminate ongoing debate on trade policy. [D. Bushnell]

1910 Mörner, Magnus. La imagen de América Latina en Suecia en los siglos XIX y XX (PAN/ES, 6, 1980, p. 237–285, bibl., tables)

Examination of the factors and interests which shaped the image of Latin America among Swedish elites since 1810. Notes how information from Latin America has expanded enormously in the second half of the 20th century.

1911 Morgan, Iwan. French policy in Spanish Amerca: 1830–48 (JLAS, 10:2, Nov. 1978, p. 309–328)

Concludes that Orléanist policy in Latin America had little success and little to recommend it. Errors in policy making were in part due to self-seeking goals of French agents in Spanish America who entangled their government in ill-advised ventures and misconceptions that prevented realistic assessment of conditions in the Republics.

1911a Pensamiento político de la emancipación. Prólogo de José Luis Romero. Selección, notas y cronología de José Luis Romero y Luis Alberto Romero. Caracas: Biblioteca Ayacucho, 1977. 2 v. (324, 359 p.)

Best anthology yet of political thought of Latin American independence. Broad coverage (even Haiti represented) and excellent prologue by José Luis Romero, which specifically takes note of limitations of ideology. Unfortunately, the introductory notes to specific selections are a bit too brief. [D. Bushnell]

1912 Peskin, Allan. Blaine, Garfield and Latin America: a new look (AAFH/TAM, 36:1, July 1979, p. 79–89)

Although credit for dynamic foreign policy in Garfield's administration is traditionally given to Secretary of State, James G. Blaine, Peskin argues that the President himself was actually responsible. Garfield's interest in international relations and Latin America in particular began during his congressional days when basic principles for his future administration's policies were established.

1913 Poyo, Gerald E. Cuban revolutionaries and Monroe County reconstruction politics, 1868–1876 (FHS/FHQ, 55:4, April 1977, p. 407–422, plates)

Explores process of how Cuban citizens, concerned with their country's independence, became involved in Florida and national politics in 1868 through Republican Party.

1913a Seckinger, Ron L. South American power politics during the 1820s (HAHR, 56:2, May 1976, p. 241–267)

Excellent piece of original research and analysis. Examination of "intra South American relations during the 1820s" leads to a definition of issues and interests at stake and to conclusion that conditions for a true "continental system" were notably lacking. [D. Bushnell]

1914 Slëzkin, L. Yu. The Congress of Aix-la-Chapelle and the pacification of Spain's colonies in America: the position of tsarist Russia (*in* Soviet historians on Latin America [see item **1817**] p. 120–131)

Brief account of Spain's failure to gain admission to Congress of Aix-la-Chapelle and subsequent rejection of recommendations of that Congress relating to her rebel colonies. This left Spain solely responsible for pacification and precluded acceptance of mediation offer by Duke of Wellington.

1915 Smith, Joseph. Illusions of conflict: Anglo-American diplomacy toward Latin America, 1865–1896. Pittsburgh: University of Pittsburgh Press, 1979. 276 p.; bibl.; index (Pitt Latin American series)

Examines diplomatic rivalry between the US and the British government after the US Civil War and before the Venezuelan Boundary Crisis. Suggests that there were no real conflicts because the British Foreign Office took no interest in Latin America and recognized US interests in the area. Thus, the British pursued a conciliatory policy toward the US.

1916 ———. New World diplomacy: a reappraisal of British policy toward Latin America, 1823–1850 (IAMEA, 32:3, Autumn 1978, p. 3–24)

Traces three stages of British policy toward Latin America: initial diplomatic recognition of the newly independent Latin American nations, followed by a period of active involvement in their internal affairs, and concluding with a posture of diplomatic and military non-intervention assumed by mid-century. By 1850s, British goals were exclusively commercial.

Wilgus, Alva Curtis. Latin America in the nineteenth century: a selected bibliography of books of travel and description published in English. See *HLAS 41:5286*.

1917 Zéndegui, Guillermo de. Romantic chronicles of America (OAS/AM, 30:4, April 1978, p. 25–28, facsims., plates)

Consists of François-René de Chateaubriand's travels in the US in 1791 and the account of his experiences written in *Travels in America* and published around 1830.

20TH CENTURY

1918 Boils Morales, Guillermo. Progresismo militar en América Latina durante el período entre guerras (UNAM/RMS, 40:3, julio/sept. 1978, p. 851–866)

Weak study of role of military reformers in Brazil, Bolivia, Cuba, Chile, and Mexico during 1920s and 1930s.

1919 Borón, Atilio A. El fascismo como categoría histórica: en torno al problema de las dictaduras en América Latina (UNAM/RMS, 39:2, abril/junio 1977, p. 481–528)

Examines the historical concept of fascism to see if it is being correctly applied to the ideology and intent of Latin American military regimes of the 1970s. The author argues that it can not be so applied.

1920 The breakdown of democratic regimes: Latin America. Edited by Juan J. Linz and Alfred Stepan. Baltimore: The Johns Hopkins University Press, 1978. 216 p.; tables (Breakdown of democratic regimes; 3)

Focuses on breakdown of six democratic regimes in Argentina, Colombia, Venezuela, Brazil, and Peru. Dynamics of political process, structural strain, actions or inactions of leaders, recurring patterns, and crisis are studied.

1921 Cabal, Hugo Latorre. The revolution of the Latin American Church. Translated by Frances K. Hendricks and Beatrice Berler. Norman: University of Oklahoma Press, 1978. 192 p.; tables.

Translation of a volume originally written in 1969. Latorre superficially examines the changing values of the Roman Catholic Church in Latin America in light of Pope John XXIII's influence. Sheds little light on fundamental ecumenical issues.

1921a Calafut, George. An analysis of Italian emigration statistics, 1876–1914 (JGSWGL, 14, 1977, p. 310–331, tables)

Relatively accurate analysis, by period and country, of emigration figures compiled by Direzione Generale di Statistica for 1876–1920 and Commissariato Generale dell'Emigrazione for 1902 (emphasizes Argentina, Brazil and US). Also comments on and corrects "errors" in Marcello Carmagnani and Giovanna Mantelli's recent study on Italian emigration to Latin America (see *HLAS 40:3069*). [M.T. Hamerly]

1922 Cancian, Francesca M.; Louis Wolf Goodman; and **Peter H. Smith.** Capitalism, industrialization, and kinship in Latin America: major issues (NCFR/JFH, 3:4, Winter 1978, p. 319–336, bibl.)

Looks at the evolution of the family since the conquest emphasizing the modern period in order to show how kinship structures have adapted to meet economic changes. Suggests that industrialization has had a different impact on the family in Latin America than it had in other regions because of cultural differences.

1923 Cardoso, F.H. Current theses on Latin American development and dependency: a critique (CEDLA/B, 22, junio 1977, p. 53–64)

Cardoso presents five theses of dependency theory and imperialism in Latin America and points out how these theses have been incorrectly used in prior studies.

1924 Child, John. From "color" to "rainbow:" U.S. strategic planning for Latin America, 1919–1945 (UM/JIAS, 21:2, May 1979, p. 233–259)

Examines shift in US defense thinking from emphasis on planning for unilateral interventions in Latin American countries to the bi-lateral approaches using as evidence military contingency plans. Declares that the US military considered hemispheric defense approaches impractical and drew up no multilateral defense plans during World War II.

1925 Conflict, order and peace in the Americas. v. 1, Dialogue on the central issues; v. 2, Analyses of the issues. Edited by Norman V. Walbek and Michael E. Conroy. Austin: University of Texas, The Lyndon B. Johnson School of Public Affairs, 1978. 2 v. (125, 167 p.) tables.

Vol. 1 consists of transcripts of panel discussions held at the conference of the same name in 1976. Jacques Chonchol and William Colby examine intervention and violence in the Americas; Arnold Harberger and Enrique Iglesias, the roots of maldevelopment; and Kenneth Boulding and Johan Galtung, dependence and interdependency as determinants of hemispheric peace. In vol. 2 Marina Bandeira discusses conflict and culture in the Latin American experience; Richard Sinkin, violence in contemporary Latin America; Irving Horowitz, from dependency to determinism; the emergence of militarism in the region; James Petras and Dale Tomich, images and realities of violence: the US and Latin America; and Hugh Holley, the roots of "disdevelopment" in the Southern Cone.

1926 Costello, Gerald M. Mission to Latin America: the successes and failures of a twentieth century crusade. Maryknoll, N.Y.: Orbis Books, 1979. 306 p.; bibl.

A study by a Catholic journalist of the response of the US Catholic Church to Pope John XXIII's call in 1961 for priests and religious to serve in Latin America. Analyzes the reasons why those who went accomplished little.

1927 Dix, Robert H. Non-urban oppositions in Latin America (IAMEA, 31:3, Winter 1977, p. 75–91)

Believes that political scientists focus too narrowly on opposition to ruling parties formed in core/urban areas. To counter this, he examines historically the types of opposition groups which have developed outside of the urban core area.

1927a Elkin, Judith Laikin. Jews of the Latin American republics. Chapel Hill: University of North Carolina Press, 1980. 298 p., bibl.; ill., index.

Thorough, highly literate study with the purpose of showing how Jewish immigrants in 19th and 20th centuries adapted to "Catholic societies that reject cultural pluralism as a valid ideal." Examines immigration patterns, demography, Jewish involvement in the economy, community life, and relations with the wider culture. Based on printed sources.

1928 Gaspar, Edmund. United States-Latin America: a special relationship? Washington: American Enterprise Institute for Public Policy Research, 1978. 90 p.; tables (Hoover Institution series; 63)

A superficial essay on the causes of tension and conflict between the US and Latin America. The main theme is the danger of bipolarization in the hemisphere if Latin American nations choose to perceive themselves as a part of the Third World rather than of the West. For political scientist's comment, see *HLAS 41:5837*.

1929 Gonzalo, Marisol de. Relaciones entre Estados Unidos y América Latina a comienzos de la primera guerra mundial: formulación de una política comercial (FJB/BH, 47, mayo 1978, p. 181–241, bibl.)

A study of the role of the I Panamerican Financial Congress held in 1915 in regularizing the financing of US trade with Latin America.

1930 Hanke, Lewis. Proposición para un proyecto de historia oral—para historiadores (CAM, 36[215]:6, nov./dic. 1977, p. 17–30)

Surveys the progress of oral history projects in Latin America and calls for a special project devoted specifically to interviews with historians regarding their professional careers.

1931 Johnson, Kenneth and **Miles W. Williams.** Democracy, power and intervention in Latin American political life: a study of scholarly images. Tempe: Arizona State University, Center for Latin American Studies, 1978. 68 p.; tables (Center for Latin American Studies special studies; 17)

Brief suggestive essay on how literary and scholarly perceptions can be used to validate social science models concerning democracy, or lack of it, and how personality and psychic needs affect, or are affected by, political systems. The analysis involved interpretation of the answers of Latin American intellectuals to items on a modified Fitzgibbon index of democratic images, the relevance of Gabriel García Márquez's novel, *One hundred years of solitude*, to understanding current political behavior, and the relationship between US aid and political democracy.

1932 La Roche, Humberto J. América Latina y la revolución de las esperanzas en aumento (UZ/R, 57, enero/dic. 1977, p. 4–30, tables)

A rambling essay on the problems of development. Discusses nationalism as a directive ideology, the relationship between Latin America's situation and that of Asia and Africa, and the general problems hindering the development process.

Lipp, Solomon. The university reform in Latin America: background and perspective. See *HLAS 41:4326*.

1933 Money and politics in Latin America. Edited by James Wilkie. Los Angeles: UCLA Latin American Center Publications, 1977. 91 p.; tables (Statistical abstract of Latin American supplement; 7)

Three articles which examine political implications of budgeting and financial policy. Enrique Baloyra compares budgets of Prío Socarrás and Batista in Cuba; James Hansen examines Mexican budgets of the 1940s and 1950s to see if they offer evidence of a shift from personalist to more institution politics; and David Eiteman describes the financial strategy of Argentine industrial development between 1955–66.

1933a Nitoburg, E.L. From the "big stick" to the Good Neighbor Policy (*in* Soviet historians on Latin America: recent scholarly contributions [see item **1817**] p. 273–298, table)

Emphasizes economic factors as cause of policy shifts; specifically the needs of US investors moving into South America where they confronted competition with English investors and emerging popular natonalism.

1933b Nunn, Frederick M. European military influence in South America: the origins and nature of professional militarism in Argentina, Brazil, Chile and Peru, 1890–1940 (JGSWGL, 12, 1975, p. 230–252)

Examines the importance of French and German military influence on and training of the officer corps of the four countries specified during the half century. Stresses that the most significant result "was stimulation rather than lessening of political interests, and motivation of elitist, professional army officers." Like their French and German counterparts, the South American military were highly politicized by the turn of the century. [M.T. Hamerly]

1934 ———. Latin American military-lore: an introduction and a case study (AAFH/TAM, 35:4, April 1979, p. 429–474)

Discusses the need to examine attitudes of military officers toward both professional questions and national issues. Suggests a methodology for using military professional literature to accomplish this and offers a case study of Chile to show its application.

1935 **Ogelsby, J.C.M.** A Trudeau decade: Canadian-Latin American relations, 1968–1978 (UM/JIAS, 21:2, May 1979, p. 187–208, tables)

Description of Canadian government's initiatives in the area of increasing relations with Latin America.

1936 **Parkinson, F.** Latin America, the Cold War, and the world powers, 1945–73. Beverly Hills, Calif.: Sage Publications, 1974. 288 p.; bibl. (Sage library of social research; 9)

An interesting examination of the Latin American reaction to Cold War politics in the hemisphere. Argues that Latin American nations expected the 1947 Rio Treaty to result in growing cooperation between the US and the rest of the hemisphere. While initially accepting the fact that the US merely utilized the treaty to enforce diplomatic conformity, since the late 1950s the Latin American nations have grown increasingly skeptical of, and resistant to, US leadership.

1937 **Pérez Brignoli, Héctor.** El ciclo en las economías agrícolas de exportación de América Latina, 1880–1930: hipótesis para su estudio (UNCR/R, 3:5, julio/dic. 1977, p. 9–46, tables)

Wants more emphasis on analysis of internal factors such as technology, characteristics of capital and cycles of agricultural crisis to offset current emphasis among economists on external demand and stimuli as explanation for behavior of Latin America's economies. Illustrates with brief case studies of Argentine cereal grains and Costa Rican coffee.

1938 **Picón-Salas, Mariano.** Americas desavenidas (CAM, 22:5, sept./oct. 1979, p. 57–66)

Philosophical examination of Rodó's "Ariel" from perspective of contemporary times. Picón-Salas sees much *inquietud* and tension in the Americas, observing that the anguish and tension of the present hardly isolates the continents from experiences common to universal history.

1939 **Powelson, John P.** The strange persistence of the "terms of trade" (IAMEA, 30:4, Spring 1977, p. 17–28, bibl., tables)

Examines statistically the relation between commodity and industrial prices since 1948 and concludes that, contrary to what Latin American politicians and economists believe, the "terms of trade" are not worsening, but rather have shown basically no movement. For economist's comment, see *HLAS 41:2877*.

1940 **Quantitative Latin American studies:** methods and findings. Edited by James W. Wilkie and Kenneth Ruddle. Los Angeles: UCLA, Latin American Center, 1977. 91 p.; tables (Statistical abstracts of Latin America supplement; 6)

Consists of five articles: 1) Donald Keesing on employment in Mexico, 1900–70; 2) Roderic AiCamp on Mexican precanditates in gubernatorial elections, 1970–75; 3) Jorge Pérez-López on Cuban industrial output, 1930–58; 4) James Wilkie and Maj-Britt Nilsson on projecting the health-education-communication index for Latin America back to 1940; and 5) Kenneth Johnson on research perspectives on the revised Fitzgibbon-Johnson index, 1945–75.

1941 **Rachum, Ilan.** The Latin American revolutions of 1930: a non-economic interpretation (CLAPCS/AL, 17, 1976, p. 3–17)

Rejects the idea that the Depression caused the wave of coups in Latin America in 1930 and 1931. Sees them rather as the culmination of a continental, political crisis caused by generational conflicts developing during the 1920s.

1942 **Randall, Stephen J.** The diplomacy of modernization: Colombian-American relations, 1920–1940. Toronto: University of Toronto Press, 1977. 239 p.; maps; plates; tables.

Examines relationship between public and private sectors in US and Colombia which shaped diplomacy of both countries in 1920s and 1930s. Also offers evidence of how economic and strategic interests of US were reconciled in context of Good Neighbor Policy.

1943 Sánchez-Albornoz, Nicolás. The land population balance in Latin America (CUH, 68:406, June 1975, p. 254–257, tables)

Brief overview of reasons for demographic explosion in Latin America and the problem of whether it will be able to meet its food needs in the year 2000 without having to import. Believes that because agricultural land is under-utilized in most countries, expansion of production is possible.

1944 Schröder, Hans-Jürgen. Hauptprobleme der deutschen Lateinamerikapolitik, 1933–1941 (JGSWGL, 12, 1975, p. 408–433)

Reviews East and West German, as well as US historiography about the Third Reich's Latin American policy. Research bears out that after the National Socialist Party ascended to power, economic concerns dominated Germany's Latin American policy especially during 1933–37. After that year, cultural exchange and ideological concerns became an integral part of Germany's policy towards the hemisphere. For political scientist's comment, see *HLAS 41:8592*. [G.M. Dorn]

1945 Síntesis informativa iberoamericana: 1972. Madrid: Centro de Documentación Iberoamericana, Instituto de Cultura Hispánica, 1974. 375 p.; ill.

Contains mostly summaries of major and minor news events of 1972 for Latin America and Central America in general, Puerto Rico, and 19 Latin American countries (excluding Haiti).

1946 Sori, Ercole. L'emigrazione italiana dall'Unità alla seconda guerra mondiale. Bologna, Italia: Il Mulino, 1979. 512 p.; bibl.; tables.

Excelente síntesis de la vasta temática económica, social y política relativa a la emigración italiana entre 1861 y 1940. De particular interés para los latinoamericanistas son los capítulos octavo y noveno dedicados a la emigración hacia las Américas entre 1861 y 1914. [M. Carmagnani]

1947 Tambs, Lewis A. The changing geopolitical balance of South America (The Journal of Social and Political Studies [Council on American Affairs, Washington] 4:1, Spring 1979, p. 17–35)

Sees as the key geopolitical theme of the 1970s, a drawing away of Brazil and Venezuela from alliances with the US, and a rivalry among Argentina, Venezuela, and Brazil over leadership of the continent. Believes that Brazil emerged dominant.

1948 The underside of Latin American history. Edited by John F. Bratzel and Daniel M. Masterson. East Lansing: Latin American Studies Center, Michigan State University, 1977. 106 p.; bibl. (Monograph series. Latin American Studies Center, Michigan State University; 16)

Contains five essays on recent and contemporary topics: George Heaps-Nelson's "Emilio Civit and the Politics of Mendoza;" Daniel Masterson's "Soldiers, Sailors, and *Apristas*: Conspiracy and Power Politics in Peru, 1932–1948;" Richard Super's "The Seguro Obrero Massacre;" Michael Grow's "The Good Neighbor Policy and Paraguay;" and John Bratzel's "The Chaco Dispute and the Search for Prestige."

1949 United Nations. Economic Commission for Latin America. Series históricas del crecimiento de América Latina. Santiago de Chile: Naciones Unidas, CEPAL, 1978. 206 p.; bibl.; tables (Cuadernos estadísticos de la CEPAL; 3)

Statistics for gross domestic product (1900–76) for the region and each country broken down into economic sectors. Also tables for percentage rates of growth and product per capita. All data is given in constant prices 1970.

1950 Vanden, Harry E. The peasants as a revolutionary class: an early Latin American view (UM/JIAS, 20:2, May 1978, p. 191–206)

Analyzes views of Mariátegui on the potential of Peruvian peasants as revolutionaries. The author believes that he was the first Latin American Marxist thinker to assert that peasants would support a revolution, and could perhaps even initiate one. For political scientist's comment, see *HLAS 41:7081*.

1951 Vargas Hidalgo, Rafael. Africa en las miras de América Latina (CAM, 22:6, nov./dic. 1978, p. 21–26)

Decries general ignorance of Latin American people and their official agencies of conditions in Africa and calls for increased awareness through better newspaper coverage and improvement of other sources of information.

1952 Wiarda, Howard J. Critical elections and critical coups: state, society and the military in the processes of Latin American development. Athens: Ohio University Center for International Studies, 1978. 75 p.; tables (Papers in international studies. Latin American series; 5)

Argues that military coups must be seen as a regular part of the political process, not as an aberration, in Latin America. He then examines "critical coups" since Independence, meaning those which resulted from a realignment of political forces.

1953 Wilkie, James W. and **Edna Monzón de Wilkie.** Dimensions of elitelore: an oral history questionnaire (UCLA/JLAL, 4:2, 1978, p. 183–223, table)

Stresses importance of oral history projects which gather data on how elites perceive, organize and justify their own actions. Presents a methodology and hypothetical questions for gathering material in interview situations.

1954 Winn, Peter. Oral history and factory study: new approaches to labor history (LARR, 14:2, 1979, p. 130–140)

To avoid danger of becoming confined to "institutional chronologies and ideological controversies," author believes labor historians must expand studies to look more fully at lives of individual workers and conditions of the workplace. Believes studies of individual factories are a means to this end and presents the results of his own study of the Yarur textile mill in Chile.

MEXICO: General and Colonial Period

ASUNCION LAVRIN, *Associate Professor of History, Howard University*
EDITH B. COUTURIER, *Chevy Chase, Maryland*

AS OF THIS VOLUME, *HLAS 42*, all works on colonial Spanish Florida will be annotated in the section devoted to the Caribbean and the Guianas (see p. 000–000). The change is justified by Florida's history which is more interconnected with the Caribbean's than with northern New Spain's. Florida was colonized and governed from Cuba and maintained close administrative and commercial ties with the Caribbean. Only works on Florida that are directly relevant to New Spain will be included in this section. In other respects, the organization of the latter continues as noted in *HLAS 40* (see p. 128).

In said volume, we also noted that social history continues to lead in the study of New Spain. The selection of labor as the theme of the Fifth Meeting of historians of Mexico and the US held in Pátzcuaro in 1977 strengthened this trend. Over 40 papers presented at the meeting provided much new knowledge on labor history (item **1979**). Colonial historians discussed slave, Indian, hacienda, mine and *obraje* labor in studies such as Tutino's (item **2100**), Riley's (item **2084**), Carroll's (item **2022**) and Kagan's (item **2055**).

Additional new topics and the application of innovative methodology to the study of social history are enriching our understanding of colonial society. See for example, William B. Taylor's suggestive work on social, familial, criminal and political problems (item **2097**) and Julia Hirschberg's analysis of the settlement and early society of Puebla (item **2049**). The history of women, marriage and the family received considerable attention in a work edited by Lavrin (item **1791**) which includes three monographs on women in colonial New Spain (items **1968**, **2029** and

2034). Other significant contributions by Carreño Alvarado (item **2019**), Duke (item **2030**), and Lavrin and Couturier (item **2057**) indicate a growing sensitivity to this aspect of social history. Specific studies of marriage patterns such as those by Arrom (item **2009**) and Swann (item **2159**) apply quantification techniques to this area of research.

The study of blacks and slavery commanded limited but discerning attention as exemplified in works by Alberro (item **2005**), Carroll (item **2022**) and Naveda (item **2070**). As usual, studies devoted to Indians are not only more numerous but more eclectic. In addition to Taylor's work mentioned above, important contributions are those by Cintrión Tiryakian (item **1987**), Rojas Rabiela (item **2087**) and Borah and Cook (item **2014**). Indeed, several topical or regional studies mentioned throughout this introduction deal, in varying degrees, with indigenous groups or related topics. Earlier estimates of New Spain's Indian population and its Spanish Indian policy by Cook and Borah were critically reevaluated in articles by B.H. Slicher van Bath (item **1981**) and Francis O. Guest (item **2128**). While there is no final verdict on these issues, doubts have been cast on some of the conclusions reached by Cook and Borah in their pathbreaking studies.

A favorite topic in economic history was mining. Worthy of note are the careful studies by Heredia Herrera on the mercury monopoly (item **1991**), Garner's work on Zacatecas (item **2037**), the contributions of Roberto Moreno on the historic circumstances surrounding the promulgation of 18th-century mining ordinances (items **1996**, **2063** and **2065**), and Bakewell's note on the industry (item **2010**). Although work on hacienda history has levelled off in the last several years, the momentum gained during the last decade continues in important studies such as those by Brading on the Bajío region (item **2016**), and Nickel's work on the Puebla-Tlaxcala region and the hacienda system (items **1976** and **2071**). Worthwhile inroads into new fields of economic history such as market and credit studies offer promise for a timely broadening of research in this field. See, especially, the works by van Young (item **2101**), and Greenow (item **2042**).

The increase in studies of Yucatan and southern Mexico during this biennium indicates a greater scholarly concern for an area which is usually neglected. Several stimulating works in demography, historical geography and economic history merit special recognition, and the reader's attention is directed to the following authors: García Bernal (item **2036**), Farriss (item **2031**), Gerhard (item **2038**), and Path (item **2075**). With the exception of Yucatán, regional history has not achieved the professionalism, nor maintained the high standards set by historians such as Luis González y González.

For the North and Borderlands, recent publications reflect the growing sophistication and wide-ranging interests of historians of these areas. David Weber's collection of essays (item **2148**) illustrates aspects of the new research undertaken during the last decade. Philip W. Powell's work on Miguel Caldera (item **2149**) is an innovative effort to tie biography and political history through the use of official records. Janet Fireman's work on the Spanish Royal Corps of Engineers (item **2123**) is a good example of collective biography. A number of titles in this biennium continued to deal with bicentennial themes. Especially worthy of note are the works of Gilbert C. Din (item **2119**), Jack Holmes (item **2132**), and Weddle and Thonoff (item **2165**).

One of the most commendable publication achievements of the last biennium is the series of indexes, guides and catalogues to the *Ramos* or sections of Mexico's National Archives of the Nation (AGN). Since 1977, 46 guides have been prepared or published with additional numbers planned. They include 20th-century materials, which are receiving increased attention by this institution. Undoubtedly, this outstanding effort, supported by a reorganization of the archives and its public service, makes the resources of this repository truly accessible both to historians and the general public (see item **1965**).

In terms of chronology, studies of the 18th century continue to prevail over those of earlier periods. This is partly due to the wealth of archival material for that period, as well as to the interest of most historians in the processes of socioeconomic change taking place during the last decades of the century. The conquest and the 16th century continues to attract research attention, but to a lesser degree than the 18th century. The interest in the 17th century noted in *HLAS 38* seems to have ebbed, as less than half a dozen works were published on this period. In sum, political, biographical and administrative history continue to lag behind socioeconomic topics, and should command more attention from historians. Other areas which would benefit from further research are family history, ethnohistory, historical demography, urban and intellectual history and regional microhistory.

Historians should always check the section devoted to Bibliography and General Works which appears yearly in both the social sciences and humanities volumes of *HLAS* (for this volume, see items **1–236** and *HLAS 41:1–171*) as well as the section on Geography: Mexico (see *HLAS 41:5332–5377*). Both these sections usually contain additional listings and annotations of interest on colonial Mexico.

GENERAL

1955 Alessio Robles, Vito. Acapulco, Saltillo y Monterrey en la historia y en la leyenda. Presentación de Vito Alessio Robles Cuevas. México: Editorial Porrúa, 1978. 670 p.; bibl.; 4 leaves of plates: ill. (Biblioteca Porrúa; 66)

Consists of historical vignettes of these three areas from the colonial period through the 20th century narrated in the author's masterful, anecdotic style. A treasure chest of entertaining reading. Professional historians, however, will never forgive the scarcity of footnotes and bibliographical references. [AL]

1956 Archivos (*in* Reunión de Historiadores Mexicanos y Norteamericanos, 5th, Pátzcuaro, México, 1977. El trabajo y los trabajadores en la historia de México [see item **1979**] p. 823–863)

A series of six papers ranging from contributions to the microfilming of documents in various repositories, to aspects of the history of Mexican archives, a description of the Mormon microfilm collection to the unexpected bonus of a list of documents in the AHN in Madrid, on the Jesuits, residencias, and the Mexican law suits in the Escribanía de Cámara. [EBC]

1957 Arreola Cortés, Raúl. Morelia. Morelia, Mex.: Gobierno del Estado de Michoacán, 1978. 393 p.; ill. (Monografías municipales del Estado de Michoacán)

Part of a series on the history of Michoacán's municipalities. Traces the history of the city of Morelia from precolumbian times to the present in about 300 p. Descriptive work with emphasis on political history. [AL]

Beltrán, Enrique. Desarrollo histórico de la enseñanza de la biología en México. See *HLAS 41:4501*.

1958 *Bibliografía Histórica Mexicana: 1976–1978.* El Colegio de México, Centro de Estudios Históricos. Vol. 10, 1979– . México.

Biennial bibliography includes brief annotations and is divided into topics and periods of Mexican history, as well as states of the Republic. For bibliographer's comment, see *HLAS 41:18*. [EBC]

1959 *Boletín del Archivo Histórico de Jalisco.* Vol. 2, No. 1, enero/abril 1978– . Guadalajara, México.

First volume was published under the title *Boletín Bibliográfico del Archivo Histórico de Jalisco.* Historians of 19th and 20th-century Jalisco should welcome this new publication. Consists of articles on local history, reproduces documents and will publish, in each edition, catalogued entries for the Archive's rich documentation. The latter should be very useful to potential researchers. Although the colonial period is not well represented in this archive, the publication occasionally provides material on this period. [AL]

1960 **Borah, Woodrow.** Discontinuity and continuity in Mexican history (UC/PHR, 48:1, Feb. 1979, p. 1–25)

In his presidential address to the Pacific Historical Association, Borah suggests new hypotheses for the periodization of Mexican history. Postulates one division based on cycles in the exploitation of the land. Also proposes that decisive political and economic breaks occurred in 1760 and 1890, rather than at the Wars of Independence and the Revolution. A stimulating review of the literature in the field. [EBC]

1961 **Cabrera Ypiña, Octaviano** and **Matilde Cabrera Ypiña.** San Francisco Javier de La Parada. San Luis Potosí, México: Editorial Universitaria Potosina, 1978. 127 p.; 2 leaves of plates: ill.

History of this hacienda since the late 16th century through 1910. Although author has obviously used archival sources, there are no notes or bibliography, making his general account suitable only for general readers. [AL]

1962 **Ciudad de México:** ensayo de construcción de una historia. Edited by Alejandra Moreno Toscano. México: Secretaría de Educación Pública, Instituto Nacional de Antropología e Historia, Departamento de Investigaciones Históricas, 1978. 235 p.; ill.; maps; tables (Colección Científica; 61. Historia)

A collection of papers concentrating largely on the history of Mexico City in the 19th and early 20th centuries, although there are several short papers on colonial themes. Includes valuable collection of maps illustrating aspects of the city's growth. Some of the papers are in a preliminary state, but all are based on research in primary sources. A promising collection of materials. [EBC]

1963 **Esparza Sánchez, Cuauhtémoc.** Historia de la ganadería en Zacatecas: 1531–1911 (Zacatecas [Anuario de historia. Universidad Autónoma de Zacatecas, Departamento de Investigaciones Históricas] 1, 1978, p. 13–160, facsims., plates, tables)

Work of synthesis based on printed sources and several smaller archival repositories. Includes valuable information on the cattle industry of Zacatecas and on cattle destined for bullfights and beef-markets during the Profirian period. Useful contribution. [AL]

1964 *FEM.* Publicación femenina. Nueva Cultura Feminista. Vol. 3, No. 11, nov./dic. 1979– . México.

Edited by Lourdes Arizpe, the issue is dedicated to "La Mujer en la Historia de México." Among other items, this issue contains a general article by Josefina Vázquez; an oral history of a revolutionary soldadera; Carmen Ramos' review of new works on the history of Mexican women; Anne Staples on feminine amusements in 1842; Elena Urrutia on Leona Vicario; Ana Macías on the feminist magazine of the 1920s called *Mujer*, as well as excerpts from new and old works containing sections about women. [EBC]

Gerhard, Peter. Continuity and change in Morelos, Mexico. See *HLAS 41:5347*.

1965 *Guías y Catálogos.* Archivo General de la Nación. No. 1, 1977– . México.

Excellent monographic series published by Mexico's National Archive consisting of guides and catalogues to their manuscript collections which are divided into *Ramos* (Sections). For an introductory guide to all the Ramos, see item **1972**. Annotated below are several monographs published between 1977–79, running from Nos. 1 through 46. Others in the same series are *not* listed here (e.g., *Ramo Correspondencia de Diversas Autoridades*; *Bienes Nacionalizados*; *Archivo Francisco Bulnes*; *Mexican Codices in the Bibliothèque Nacionale de Paris*; and material from the Archivo de Francisco Bulnes, and from the presidential administrations of Obregón, Calles and Abelardo Rodríguez; as well as catalogues of illustrations):

No. 1, *Vocabulario de términos en documentos históricos* (1977, 55 p., bibl.): a useful guide for the researcher on historical terminology.

No. 2, *Caminos y calzadas* (1977, 126 p., index): this branch of the AGN consists of

24 vols. of 450 separate *expedientes* dealing with transportation, freight and roads.

No. 3, *Indice del Ramo de Californias* (1977, 2 v. of 237 p.): a guide to the 82 bound vols. of California materials.

No. 4, *Catálogo del Ramo Cofradías y Archicofradías* (1977, 41 leaves, index): this guide includes a long introduction and a listing of the materials in the 19 vols. of the *Ramo.*

No. 5, *Indice del Ramo Filipinas* (1977, 71 leaves): a catalogue of the 63 vols. of 936 *expedientes* issued between 1718 and 1817 dealing largely with administrative matters and voyages.

No. 6, *Guía del Archivo de Leyva* (1977, 27 p., 7 leaves, index): material from the 1860s on the French Intervention.

No. 7, *Indice del Ramo de la Junta Protectora de las Clases Menesterosas* (1977, 67 p., 2 leaves, indexes): materials from 1865–67 dealing with the local history of Maximilian's empire.

No. 8, *Ramos Hospitales y Protomedicato* (1977, 116 p., 6 leaves): *Ramo Hospitales* consists of 78 bound vols. of 1031 *expedientes*, largely from the 18th century and beginning the 19th, although the range is 1582–1828. The *Ramo Protomedicato* has 5 vols.

No. 9, *Guía del Ramo, Títulos y Despachos de Guerra: copias* (1977, 63 leaves): this Ramo consists of one vol. of 509 p. and consists of 1810 and 1811 materials.

No. 10, *Ramo Colegios* (1977, 41 p.): a collection of 42 vols. of 394 *expedientes*, is largely 18th century, and deals with the Jesuit and Mercederian colleges and the College of Mines. The materials on economic and administrative matters concern elections. Includes the accounts of the Hacienda of San José Acolman.

No. 11, *Guía del Ramo de Desagüe* (1977, 129 leaves): a reprinting of the catalogue made by Manuel Carrera Stampa in 1944.

No. 12, *Ramo Acordada* (1978, 166 p.): 768 *expedientes* bound in 31 vols. that include material from the second half of the 18th century to 1816, on this branch of Justice and the police.

No. 13, *Comisión Nacional Agraria* (1977, 167 p.): organized by towns and villages, this catalogue covers material for 1916–27, and includes the texts of presidential resolutions.

No. 14, *Ramos Pensiones y Montepíos* (1977, 76 leaves): consists of 624 *expedientes* of materials collected between 1723 and 1825 providing much information on soldiers killed during the wars of independence, as well as on marriages and the Monte de Piedad.

No. 15, *Catálogo del Ramo Tributos* (2 v. of 351 p., indexes): the history and geography of Indian pueblos in 62 vols. with a total of 1092 *expedientes.*

No. 16, *Ramo Misiones* (1978, 166 p., index): this Ramo has material largely from the North and Borderlands.

No. 17, *Ramo Provincias Internas* (1978, 4 v. unpaged): first 2 vols. not available for comment, but vols. 3 and 4 are an analytic index in 311 p. (see *HLAS 32:1560* and *HLAS 36:1948*).

No. 18, *Ramo Real Fisco de la Inquisición* (1977, 231 p.): materials from 1570 to 1823, which include inventories, costs of maintaining prisoners, and information on Church and nobility's properties. There are 247 vols. in the Ramo.

No. 19, *Catálogo del Ramo de Indios* (1979, 1 v. unpaged): not available for annotation in this *HLAS.*

No. 20, *Ramo Instrucción Pública y Bellas Artes: catálogo de partituras, siglos XIX y XX* (152 leaves): of interest to the historian of music.

No. 21, *Ramo de Edictos de la Santa y General Inquisición* (1978, 62 p.): this guide is based on 2 vols. of printed works consisting of materials from 1613–1819. It contains lists of prohibited books, and "edicts on behavior in confessions with special reference to women."

No. 22, *Ramo Clero Regular y Secular* (1978, 244 p.): mostly 18th-century materials on baptisms, marriages, divorces, pensions and censuses. It also has lists of convents, accounts for church buildings, missions, jobs, inventories of the principal colleges.

No. 23, *Ramo de Diezmos* (1978, 40 p.): 18th-century materials bound in 23 vols. which include information on tithes, tributes and salaries.

No. 24, *Manual de Paleografía* (1978, 172 p., bibl., ill., tables, transcriptions): a useful guide which also includes an introduction to the history of writing, charts of different kinds of alphabets, and descriptions of different kinds of documents and forms.

No. 25, *Ramo Consolidación* (1978, 35 p.): incomplete listing, not all documents have yet been incorporated into the Ramo. There is material as early as the 17th century on chaplaincies and the documents continue until 1808. Lists 29 vols. with 273 *expedientes*.

No. 26, *Ramo Expulsión de Españoles* (1978, 139 p., index): materials from 1828–29 describing the contents of 36 vols. in the AGN.

No. 27, *Ramo Universidad* (1979, 314 p.): covers such diverse topics as the administration of the university, professors, and catalogues of graduates and complements an earlier index of the faculty of medicine by Guillermo Fernández de Recas.

No. 37, *Ramo Cárceles y Presidios y Presidios y Cárceles* (1979, 60 p.): reprint of a catalogue published in the *Boletín* of AGN in 1971. A total of 51 vols. of 674 *expedientes* consisting of materials on the construction and administration of jails, casas reales, and presidios. There is also information on fugitives, women placed in *recogimientos*, and exiling of prisoners to presidios. Includes other information on law suits, assassinations, adultery, desertion and treason. Useful for Borderlands. The bulk of the documents fall between 1760 and 1820.

No. 41, *Ramo Bulas y Santa Cruzada* (1979, 55 p., 6 p.): materials from 1634 to 1815 on the money borrowed from the Santa Cruzada. There are 475 *expedientes* in 28 vols.

No. 42, *Ramo Inquisición I* (1979, 167 p.): consists of charts and tables of organization. Revised and corrected catalogue of materials from 1522–80.

No. 46, *Bienes de Comunidad* (1979, 176 p.): collections dealing with special tributes, real estate, censos, petitions to the treasury, testimonies on the poverty of certain communities, and loans. Seven vols. of documents from the last third of the 18th century to the beginning of the 19th century. [EBC]

1966 Historia de Yucatán: antología de textos. Recopilación, Carlos Castillo Peraza. México: Fondo Editorial de Yucatán, 1979. 365 p.: ill.

An anthology of reprints of articles by several well-known authors such as J. Eric Thompson, R.S. Chamberlain and Eligio Ancona. Covers the history of Yucatan from prehispanic times to mid-19th century. [AL]

1967 Historiografía de Michoacán (*in* Reunión de Historiadores Mexicanos y Norteamericanos, 5th, Pátzcuaro, México, 1977. El trabajo y los trabajadores en la historia de México [see item **1979**] p. 801–822)

Five brief contributions on the modern and colonial history of Michoacán underline the most important recent work, pinpoint research in progress, and suggest directions of future investigations. [EBC]

1968 Lavrin, Asunción. In search of the colonial woman in Mexico: the seventeenth and eighteenth centuries (*in* Latin American women: historical perspectives [see item **1791**] p. 23–59, tables)

The didactic literature on women prescribed her ideal behavior and characterized an unchanging personality over two centuries. This view is contrasted with women's historical experience as reflected in law and revealed in an examination of a variety of primary sources. The dimensions of historical change and the class differences in the life of colonial women are described through an analysis of marriage customs, measures for the protection of women, and their economic and religious roles. [EBC]

Lindvall, Karen. Research in Mexico City: a guide to selected libraries and research centers. See *HLAS 41:124*.

López Rosado, Diego G. Los servicios públicos de la Ciudad de México. See *HLAS 41:5355*.

1969 Meade, Joaquín. La huasteca tamaulipeca. Introducción de Mercedes Meade de Angulo. Ciudad Victoria, México: Universidad Autónoma de Tamaulipas, Instituto de Investigaciones Históricas, 1977. 3 v. (322, 376, 147 p.) bibl.; ill.; indexes; plates (Monografías huastecas; 2)

A general history of the region of Tamaulipas in three volumes. Like similar general works the coverage of the historical development is uneven with many gaps in the information. Vol. 3 furnishes a potpourri of information on 20th-century Tamaulipas. [AL]

1970 Mendirichaga Cueva, Tomás. El municipio de San Nicolás de los Garzas: antecedentes históricos (UNL/H, 19, 1978, p. 295–316, bibl.)

Historical survey of the municipality of San Nicolás de los Garzas, Monterrey. Author has used archival sources but treatment of the topic is uneven, highlighting some years of the 16th century, skimming over the 18th and focusing on the mid years of the 19th. Half of the article deals with property records of some of the settlers in the colonial period, while second half treats the municipality in mid-19th century. [AL]

1971 **Mesa Redonda de Historiografía de Durango,** *1978.* Memoria. Durango, México: Universidad Juárez del Estado de Durango, Escuela de Derecho, 1979. 165 p.; bibl.

Documents and bibliography on the history of Durango presented at a round table in Aug. 1978. [EBC]

1972 **Mexico. Archivo General de la Nación. Departamento de Publicaciones.** Guía descriptiva de los Ramos que constituyen el Archivo General de la Nación. Elaborado por Miguel Civeira Taboada y María Elena Bribiesca Sumano. México: 1977. 124 leaves.

Consists of a brief description of each of the 159 Ramos of the AGN, a note on its relation to other branches of the archive, a bibliography, and the inclusive dates of the bulk of the documents. A brief description of the official source of the documents; the office which generated them, or the law which required centralization of information on a certain topic, concludes the work. [EBC]

1973 **Meyer, Michael C.** and **William L. Sherman.** The course of Mexican history. New York: Oxford University Press, 1979. 696 p.; bibl.; ill.; index.

Balanced survey of Mexican history since precolumbian times. The indigenous past and the colonial period up to independence receive fair space and treatment. Although the discussion since 1825 is largely political, authors have made special effort to consider economic, social and cultural issues. Attractively illustrated and up to date in scholarly literature, this survey is highly recommended. [AL]

1974 **Mounce, Virginia N.** An archivist's guide to the Catholic Church in Mexico. Palo Alto, Calif.: R&E Research Associates, 1979. 90 p.; bibl.

Aims at acquainting uninitiated archivists with the structure and history of the Catholic Church in Mexico. Contains useful list of translation of terms usually found in ecclesiastical manuscripts. This is not a guide to ecclesiastical archival sources, only a reference tool for archivists. Researchers must go elsewhere for direction. [AL]

Muría, José María. Historia de las divisiones territoriales de Jalisco. See *HLAS 41:5358.*

1975 ———. La jurisdicción de Zapotlan el grande del siglo XVI al XIX (INAH/A, 6:54, 1976, 7. epoca, p. 23–42, maps, tables)

Survey of the civil and religious division of the jurisdiction of Zapotlan (Ciudad Guzmán). Potentially useful for regional microhistory. [AL]

1976 **Nickel, Herbert J.** Soziale Morphologie der mexikanischen Hacienda = Morfología social de la hacienda mexicana. Wiesbaden: Steiner, 1978. 432 p.; bibl.; indexes (Das Mexiko-Projekt der Deutschen Forschungsgemeinschaft; 14)

Thorough study of the morphology of the Mexican hacienda system begins with a general history of haciendas, and includes a second section on haciendas in the Puebla-Tlaxcala regions, and ends with a history of San José Ozumba. The emphasis in the last section is largely on the 19th and 20th centuries, through the first years of the agrarian reform. Also includes an interesting collection of photographs. This volume is the 14th work produced by the German inter-disciplinary project on the Puebla Tlaxcala region. [EBC]

Nuevo León (state), *Mexico.* **Oficialía Mayor. Dirección del Registro Civil. Archivo General del Estado.** Asuntos Eclesiásticos. Indice y catálogos de la Sección Asuntos Eclesiásticos existentes en el Archivo General del Estado: 1568–1874. See *HLAS 41:85.*

1977 **Ochoa, Alvaro.** Jiquilpan. Morelia, Mexico: Gobierno del Estado de Michoacán, 1978. 231 p.; bibl.; map; plates (Monografías municipales del Estado de Michoacán)

Surveys history of this municipality in Michoacán through four centuries. Although the author has consulted archival sources, their uneven use has resulted in a somewhat shallow work. [AL]

1978 **O'Gorman, Edmundo.** México, el trauma de su historia. México: Universidad Nacional Autónoma de México, Coordinación de Humanidades, 1977. 119 p.

Essay on the philosophy of Mexican history which contains an analysis of paradoxes in the ideological conflicts of 19th century politics between Liberals and Conservatives. Suggests new ideas for periodization. [EBC]

Péano, Pierre. L'activité littéraire des Franciscains du Méxique, XVIe–XIXe siècles. See item **5137**.

1979 Reunión de Historiadores Mexicanos y Norteamericanos, *5th, Pátzcuaro, México, 1977.* El trabajo y los trabajadores en la historia de México = Labor and laborers through Mexican history: ponencias y comentarios presentados en la V Reunión de Historiadores Mexicanos y Norteamericanos, Pátzcuaro, 12 al 15 de octubre de 1977. Compiladores: Elsa Cecilia Frost, Michael C. Meyer, Josefina Zoraida Vázquez y con la colaboración de Lilia Díaz. México: Colegio de México; Tucson: University of Arizona Press, 1979. 954 p. (3 fold.); bibl.; ill.; index.

Conference devoted to Mexican labor history from colonial times to present. List of contributors and papers follows:

Pt. 1:

El Trabajo durante la Epoca Cortesiana y la Conquista:

Josefina Cintrón Tiryakian "The Indian Labor Policy of Charles V"

Teresa Rojas Rabiela "La Organización del Trabajo para las Obras Públicas: el Coatequitl y las Cuadrillas de Trabajadores" *Trabajo Indígena y Procesos de Aculturación*:

Murdo J. MacLeod "Forms and Types of Work, and the Acculturation of the Colonial Indian of Mesoamerica: Some Preliminary Observations"

Ignacio del Río "Sobre la Aparición y Desarrollo del Trabajo Libre Asalariado en el Norte de Nueva España: siglos XVI–XVII"

El Trabajo de los Negros:

Patrick J. Carroll "Black Laborers and their Experience in Colonial Jalapa"

Solange B. de Alberro "Negros y Mulatos en los Documentos Inquisitoriales: Rechazo e Integración"

Adriana Naveda Chávez "Trabajadores Esclavos en las Haciendas Azucareras de Córdoba, Veracruz, 1714–1763"

Trabajo Forzado:

William L. Sherman "Some Aspects of Forced Labor in Chiapas: Sixteenth Century"

Samuel Kagan "The Labor of Prisoners in the Obrajes of Coyoacán: 1660–1693"

Trabajo en Haciendas y Minas:

James D. Riley "Landlords, Laborers and Royal Government: the Administration of Labor in Tlaxcala, 1680–1750"

Roberto Moreno "Régimen de Trabajo en la Minería del Siglo XVIII"

Vestigios Coloniales: Burocracia y Gremios:

Linda Arnold "Social, Economic, and Political Status in the Mexico City Central Bureaucracy: 1808–1822"

Dorothy Tanck de Estrada "La Abolición de los Gremios"

Trabajadores en Haciendas Agrícolas:

John Tutino "Life and Labor on North Mexican Haciendas: the Querétaro-San Luis Potosí Region, 1775–1810"

Jan Bazant "El Trabajo y los Trabajadores en la Hacienda de Atlacomulco"

Trabajadores no Asalariados:

Frederick J. Shaw "The Artisan in Mexico City"

Beatriz Ruiz Gaytán F. "Un Grupo Trabajador Importante no Incluido en la Historia Laboral Mexicana: Trabajadoras Domésticas"

Los Trabajadores Mexicanos en los Estados Unidos:

Juan Gómez Quiñones "The Origins and Development of the Mexican Working Class in the United States: Laborers and Artisans North of the Rio Bravo, 1600–1900"

Pedro Castillo "The Making of the Mexican Working Class in the United States: Los Angeles, California, 1800–1920"

Jorge A. Bustamante "La Migración hacia la Frontera Norte y los Estados Unidos"

Condiciones de Trabajo Agrícola, Siglo XX:

Raymond Th. J. Buve "Movilización Campesina y Reforma Agraria en los Valles de Nativitas, Tlaxcala, 1917–1923: Estudio de un Caso de Lucha por Recuperar Tierras habidas durante la Revolución Armada"

Roberto Gallaga "La Historia del Trabajo de los Campesinos Cañeros en el Siglo XX"

Movimiento Obrero:

Barry Carr "The Casa del Obrero Mundial, Constitutionalism and the Pact of February 1915"

S. Lief Adleson "Coyuntura y Conciencia: Factores Convergentes en la Fundación de los Sindicatos Petroleros de Tampico durante la Década de 1920"

Organizaciones Sindicales:

Fernando Talavera and Juan Felípe Leal

"Organizaciones Sindicales Obreras de México: 1948–1970, Enfoque Estadístico"
Aurelio de los Reyes "El Sindicato de Empleados de Cinematógrafo"
Síntesis:
John Womack, Jr. "The Historiography of Mexican Labor"
Enrique Florescano "Evaluación y Síntesis de las Ponencias sobre el Trabajo Colonial"
Pt. 2:
Historiografía de Michoacán:
Lyle C. Brown "Political and Military History of the State of Michoacán, 1910–1940"
David L. Raby "Importancia y Problemas de la Historiografía de Michoacán en el Siglo XX"
Lydia Espinosa Morales "La Historiografía Económica del Obispado de Michoacán en la Epoca Colonial"
Jorge Gurría Lacroix "Historiografía sobre la Conquista de Occidente"
Francisco Miranda "Perspectivas y Problemas de la Historiografía Michoacana"
Archivos:
Marvin D. Bernstein "The Organization and Functioning of the Mexican-American Consultative Committee on the Microfilming of Historical Documents (Comisión Consultiva Mixta para la Microfilmación de Documentos Históricas de México)"
Lewis Hanke "Problemas del Pasado, Proyectos de Hoy, Posibilidades para el Futuro"
Ernesto de la Torre Villar "Custodia y Utilización de las Fuentes Históricas en México: Panorama Global"
Francisco de Solano "Fuentes para la Historia del Trabajo en México en los Archivos de Madrid"
Xavier Tavera Alfaro "Los Archivos en Michoacán"
Dale M. Valentine "Preservación de Registros de la Sociedad Genealógica de Utah en México"
Temas en Busca de Historiador:
Stanley R. Ross "Daniel Cosío Villegas y las Reuniones de Historiadores Mexicanos y Norteamericanos"
David C. Bailey "El Pasado Reciente"
John H. Coatsworth "Questions in Search of Historians"
Asunción Lavrin "La Iglesia en la Economía Novohispana"
Clara E. Lida "México y el Internacionalismo Clandestino del Ochocientos"
Andrés Lira "Las Actividades Desplazadas"
Jorge Alberto Manrique "La Historia del Arte por el otro Cabo"
Jean Meyer "Los Intelectuales y el Estado en México en el Siglo XX"
Metodología:
CEUSMO "La Experiencia Institucional en el Estudio de la Historia Obrera"
Rita Eder "Algunos Aspectos Metodológicos de las Ciencias Sociales y su Aplicación a la Historia del Arte." [AL]

Rodríguez de Lebrija, Esperanza. Indice analítico de la *Guía del Archivo Histórico de Hacienda*. See *HLAS 41:94*.

1980 Simposio de Historia de Sonora, *2nd, Hermosillo, Mexico, 1976*. Memoria. Hermosillo, México: Universidad de Sonora, Instituto de Investigaciones Históricas, 1976. 443 p.

Consists of 17 essays on the history of Sonora originally presented at the Second Symposium of the History of Sonora in 1976, including several on archaeology, ethnology, folklore, etc. Some of the articles by historians are: Germán Zúñiga's on landed property; Cynthia R. de Murrieta's on land and community in Primería Alta Missions of 1824–42; J.A. Ruibal Corella's on Gastón Raousset de Boulbon, the failed conqueror of Sonora; Héctor Pesqueira's on García Morales; Margarita Urías' on historiography and economic studies of 1821–67; etc. [AL]

1981 Slicher van Bath, B.H. The calculation of the population of New Spain, especially for the period before 1570 (CEDLA/B, 24, June 1978, p. 66–95, tables)

Important critical demographic study written by a historian of European agriculture, is part of a larger research project. Suggests revision of Cook and Borah's population figures for the 16th and early 17th centuries, by using different conversion factors to turn the original tribute lists into modern population counts. While this critique is based on a portion of Cook and Borah's work, the author concludes that their calculations should be altered by 15 percent, that their figures from 1570 to 1605 are too low, and that Indian demographic recovery only began in 1650. [EBC]

Trabulse, Elías. El erasmismo de un científico: supervivencias del humanismo cristiano en la Nueva España de la Contrarreforma. See item **7656**.

1982 van Oss, Adrian C. Mendicant expansion in New Spain and the extent of the colony: sixteenth century (CEDLA/B, 21, Dec. 1976, p. 32–56, maps, tables)

Through an extensive series of maps and documentary tables, the geographic extension and withdrawal of the mendicant clergy is traced. Conflicts between the regular orders and the secular clergy at the end of the century stemmed from a declining Indian population rather than a loss of missionary fervor, as the early Franciscans had believed. [EBC]

1983 Velázquez, María del Carmen. Bibliographical essay: the Colección SepSetentas (OAS/A, 35:3, Jan. 1979, p. 373–389)

An alphabetical listing of the 315 titles which were published by the Secretariat for Public Education between 1970–76, is preceded by an essay which outlines the purposes of the series, categorizes the kinds of books, and points out special works of interest to historians of Mexico. [EBC]

COLONIAL PERIOD: GENERAL

1984 Alanís Boyso, José Luis. Elecciones de República para los pueblos del corregimiento de Toluca, 1729–1811. México: Biblioteca Enciclopédica del Estado de México, 1978. 319 p.; bibl.; ill.; index (Biblioteca enciclopédica del Estado de México; 62)

Useful guide to documents in Section Hospital de Jesús, National Archives, on the neglected topic of election of Indian town officials. [AL]

Arnall Juan, María Josefa. El *Itinerario de Indias: 1673–1679*, del Padre Fray Isidoro de la Asunción, C.D.: Manuscrito 514 de la Biblioteca Provincial y Universitaria de Barcelona. See item **1829**.

1985 Bialostosky, Sara. Situación social y jurídica de los judíos y sus descendientes en la Nueva España (UNAM/RFD, 26:101/102, enero/junio 1976, p. 115–128)

Surveys legal and social status of Jews in New Spain. A synthesis based on secondary sources, it provides few new insights. [AL]

1986 Carreño Alvarado, Gloria Celia. Guía de los materiales de los archivos de las notarías parroquiales de la ciudad de Morelia, Michoacán (Anuario [Universidad Michoacán de San Nicolás de Hidalgo, Escuela de Historia, Morelia, México] 2, 1977, p. 97–120)

Brief guide to material in the parochial archives of Morelia. Lists available volumes in chronological order on baptisms, confirmation, marriage information and deaths. Archives are richer on material from mid-17th century onwards. [AL]

1987 Cintrón Tiryakian, Josefina. The Indian labor policy of Charles V (*in* Reunión de Historiadores Mexicanos y Norteamericanos, 5th, Pátzcuaro, México, 1977. El trabajo y los trabajadores en la historia de México [see item **1979**] p. 9–41)

Study of the evolution of Caroline policy toward Indians, which mostly followed Castilian patterns. Although the encomienda system represented a regression to feudal patterns, Charles V's aim was to rectify this feudal character of Spanish legislation, as part of his overall policy of political centralization. Interesting synthesis. [AL]

1988 Documentos para la historia de Tabasco. t. 1/2, siglos XVI y XVII. Recopilados y ordenados por Manuel González Calzada. México: Comisión del Grijalva, 1976. 2 v. in 1 (258 p.)

Miscellaneous documents originally catalogued by Luis Chávez Orozco. Legal suits and inventories form the bulk of a collection of 14 documents, mostly of the 16th and 17th centuries. [AL]

1989 Florescano, Enrique. Evaluación y síntesis de las ponencias sobre el trabajo colonial (*in* Reunión de Historiadores Mexicanos y Norteamericanos, 5th, Pátzcuaro, México, 1977. El trabajo y los trabajadores en la historia de México [see item **1979**] p. 756–797)

An original analysis of the historical literature on colonial labor from the chroniclers to the present is followed by a re-examination of 10 papers presented at the Pátzcuaro conference. Florescano reorders this new data under the rubrics of the principal topics in labor history, and connects the new contributions to previous research. [EBC]

1990 Gruzinski, Serge. Algunas fuentes para el estudio de las mentalidades en el

México colonial (MAGN/B, 2[4]:6, oct./dic. 1978, p. 40–41)

Brief survey of some archival sources which may help develop *mentalité* studies for the colonial period. Author suggests potential wealth of religious sources, especially, the Inquisitorial records. [AL]

1991 Heredia Herrera, Antonia. La renta del azogue en Nueva España: 1709–1751. Sevilla: Escuela de Estudios Hispanoamericanos, Consejo Superior de Investigaciones Científicas, 1978. 277 p.; bibl.; 12 leaves of plates: ill. (Publicaciones de la Escuela de Estudios Hispano-Americanos de Sevilla; 250)

A study of the 44 years when the mercury monopoly in New Spain was administered independently of the Viceroy. Based on AGI materials, and a wide variety of published works, this study deals with costs, transportation, packaging, distribution, prices, and royal revenues. A contribution to both mining and administrative history. [EBC]

1992 Lavrin, Asunción. Women in convents: their economic and social role in colonial Mexico (*in* Liberating women's history: theoretical and critical essays. Edited by Berenice A. Carroll. Urbana: University of Illinois Press, 1976, p. 250–271)

A descriptive and analytic overview of the principal issues determining the role of feminine religious orders. The article covers the reasons for choosing the profession of nun, the intellectual and educational role of convents, and the financing of these institutions through patrons, dowries, and investment in rural and urban real estate. [EBC]

1993 MacLeod, Murdo J. Forms and types of work, and the acculturation of the colonial Indian of Mesoamerica: some preliminary observations (*in* Reunión de Historiadores Mexicanos y Norteamericanos, 5th, Pátzcuaro, México, 1977. El trabajo y los trabajadores en la historia de México [see item **1979**] p. 75–92)

Analytic study suggesting three variables for measuring acculturation: taxation, economic geography and comparative demography of Indians and others. All of these variables depend upon labor. Suggests that the poor documentation on the sociology of work might be remedied by describing the methods of producing various commodities as these techniques might explain which ethnic group would retain control. Uses indigo, cochineal and sugar as examples of how labor illuminates other social processes. [EBC]

1994 Martínez Montiel, Luz María. Integration patterns and the assimilation process of Negro slaves in Mexico (*in* Comparative perspectives on slavery in New World societies [see item **1768**] p. 446–454)

Impressionistic, inaccurate and naive brief survey. [AL]

1995 Morales, Francisco and **Dorothy Tanck de Estrada.** Inventario del Fondo Francisco del Museo de Antropología e Historia de México. Washington: Academy of American Franciscan History, 1978. 395 p. (Bibliographical series; 4)

Inventory of 100 volumes out of a total of 193 of the manuscripts of the Convent of Saint Francis, Mexico City, which are housed at the National Museum of Anthropology and History. Introduction provides useful information on the Franciscan Archives and a clear guide to the contents of this volume. [AL]

1996 Moreno, Roberto. Régimen de trabajo en la minería del siglo XVIII (*in* Reunión de Historiadores Mexicanos y Norteamericanos, 5th, Pátzcuaro, México, 1977. El trabajo y los trabajadores en la historia de México [see item **1979**] p. 242–267 and 272–279, tables)

The special character of each mining camp is underlined in this review of labor ordinances from 1584 to 1783. Using the 1766 and 1771 ordinances from the Real del Monte disputes, the author describes the political background of the last colonial ordinances of 1783. This original contribution to legal history, based on archival research, is classified in three tables by Elías Trabulse. [EBC]

1997 Muro Orejón, Antonio. Régimen legal de los indios de la Nueva España según el Cedulario del doctor Vasco de Puga: 1563 (UNAM/RFD, 26:101/102, enero/junio 1976, p. 485–520)

Summarizes all the legislation dealing with Indians in the earliest compilation of law known in New Spain, the Cedulario compiled by *oidor* Vasco de Puga. A short biography of Puga opens the work. Contains legislation starting in 1493 and ending in 1563, on such topics as tributes, labor, encomienda, enslavement, etc. [AL]

1998 O'Gorman, Edmundo. Al rescate de Motolinía: comentarios al libro *Utopie et histoire au Mexique*, de Georges Baudot (IGFO/RI, 37:149/150, julio/dic. 1977, p. 375–424)

Author engages in a polemic with Georges Baudot. This is a work for specialists who know the works of Motolinía very well. [AL]

1999 Palerm, Angel. Sobre la formacion del sistema colonial: apuntes para una discusión (*in* Ensayos sobre el desarrollo económico de México y América Latina: 1500–1975. Compiled by Enrique Florescano. México: Fondo de Cultura Económica, 1979, p. 93–127)

Presents a hypothesis that Mexico's colonial economic development was increasingly affected by the demands of the world market. Also examines such issues as the transition between feudalism and capitalism, and the exploitation of the northern mining centers. Makes interesting use of secondary sources. [EBC]

Rementería, Carlos J. Díaz. El regimen jurídico del Ramo de Tributos en Nueva España y las reformas peruanas de Carlos III. See item **1869**.

2000 Ronan, Charles E. Francisco Javier Clavigero, S.J., 1731–1787: figure of the Mexican Enlightenment, his life and works. Roma: Institutum Historicum S.I.; Chicago, Illinois: Loyola University Press, 1977. 396 p.; bibl.; index (Bibliotheca Instituti Historici S.I.; 40)

Definitive, new biography of Clavigero describes his life and discusses his works exhaustively. Ronan argues for the originality of Clavigero's history of California, while the *Storia antica* owes a far greater debt to Torquemada than the author acknowledged. Clavigero's contribution to the history of the Aztecs lay in his readable style, his philosophical views, and in his making vast quantities of earlier works available to the 18th-century public. [EBC]

2001 Los salarios y el trabajo en México durante el siglo XVIII. Selección de documentos por Luis Chávez Orozco. 2. ed. México: Centro de Estudios Históricos del Movimiento Obrero Mexicano, 1978. 103 p. (Cuadernos obreros; 23)

Republication of the 1934 document collection of laws governing mining, agricultural and obraje labor. The mining collection includes Gamboa's 1766 ordinances and other materials on Real del Monte and the Count of Regla. [EBC]

2002 Serrera Contreras, Ramón María. El indio y su acceso a la propiedad individual de la tierra (*in* Jornadas Americanistas, III, Valladolid, Spain, 1974 [see *HLAS 40: 2298*] t. 3, p. 261–274, ill.)

Surveys the problem of Indian access to private ownership of land through regulation and reports on the thinking of leading statesmen on this issue. Author concludes that the prevailing negative legislation and the stress on latifundia ownership conspired against the Indians. [AL]

2003 Tanck de Estrada, Dorothy. Las Cortes de Cádiz y el desarrollo de la educación en México (CM/HM, 29:1, julio/sept. 1979, p. 3–34)

Analyzes the influence on the evolution of Mexican independence during its first decades of both 18th-century Spanish educational concepts and ideas emanating from the Cortes of Cádiz in 1812 and 1820. Stresses the growing influence of the state in determining educational policies. [AL]

2004 Torre Villar, Ernesto de la. La ilustración en La Nueva España: notas para su estudio (PAIGH/H, 87, enero/junio 1979, p. 37–63)

Survey of the Enlightenment in New Spain with stress on its intellectual aspects. Based on well known sources. [AL]

CENTRAL AND SOUTH

2005 Alberro, Solange B. de. Noirs et mulatres dans la société coloniale mexicaine, d'après les Archives de l'Inquisition: XVIe–XVIIe siècles (CDAL, 17, 1978, p. 57–87)

Careful study of blacks and mulattoes in colonial Mexico based on Inquisitorial records. Stresses problems such as uprootedness, rebelliousness, magic practices and social integration. Detailed qualitative analysis stressing personal and social nuances. Fascinating reading. [AL]

2006 ———. Proceso y causa criminal contra Diego de la Cruz (MAGN/B, 2[4]:6, oct./dic. 1978, p. 8–17, ill.)

Transcription of an inquisitorial inquiry against a black slave, for unorthodoxy (1612, Vol. 504, Archives of the Inquisition). [AL]

2007 Alvarado Morales, Manuel. El Cabildo y regimiento de la Ciudad de México en el siglo XVII: un ejemplo de oligarquía criolla (CM/HM, 28:4, abril/junio 1979, p. 489–514, bibl.)

Study of the City Council of Mexico City in the first third of the 17th century. Suggests that *regidores* had firmly established themselves in the social elite of colonial Mexico by that time. Case studies of several personalities provide useful information. [AL]

2008 Arnold, Linda. Social, economic, and political status in the Mexico City central bureaucracy: 1808–1822 (*in* Reunión de Historiadores Mexicanos y Norteamericanos, 5th, Pátzcuaro, México, 1977. El trabajo y los trabajadores en la historia de México [see item **1979**] p. 281–310, map, tables)

This paper is part of a much larger study of the Mexican bureaucracy between 1763–1835. Author describes here the sources she used to identify and provide biographical data, then the criteria used for evaluating the relative position or status of subjects. The tables outline characteristics of jobs, rates of entry and exit from public service, salaries of selected bureaucrats, and the information used to construct a status index. Our understanding of both the locus of political power, and its relationship to the elite will be enormously increased by this work. [EBC]

2009 Arrom, Silvia M. Marriage patterns in Mexico City: 1811 (NCFR/JFH, 3:4, Winter 1978, p. 376–391, bibl., tables)

Analyzes the 1811 census of Mexico City in order to establish whether Spanish marriage patterns prevailed in 19th-century Mexico and what marital customs reveal about women's role in society. Different marriage patterns prevailed among different sectors of the population. The Spanish, white population had the largest proportion of single persons. Author discusses several hypotheses to explain marriage patterns and poses interesting questions. A significant contribution. [AL]

2010 Bakewell, P.J. Notes on the Mexican silver mining industry in the 1590's (UNL/H, 19, 1978, p. 383–409, tables)

Describes the state of the mining industry in the districts of New Spain, Zacatecas, Guadiana and Guadalajara in 1597. Based on a manuscript at the British Museum, this work offers important data on the labor force, the provision of mercury to the industry and the silver production of each of the regions. [AL]

2011 Barrett, Ward. *Jugerum* and *caballería* in New Spain (AHS/AH, 53:2, April 1978, p. 423–437, map, tables)

Part of a larger work in progress on weights, measures, and money. Thesis is that the measurements for *caballerías* and estancias were related to each other and were based on the Roman standard of the *jugerum*. An original work of historical reconstruction. [EBC]

2012 Baudot, Georges. Utopie et historie au Mexique: les premiers chroniqueurs de la civilisation mexicaine, 1520–1569. Toulouse: Privat, 1977. 554 p.; bibl.; 5 leaves of plates (1 fold.): ill.; index; maps.

An important work both in historiography and ethnohistory, this detailed archival examination of early texts describing Mexican Indians, is followed by extensive analyses of the lives and works of Friars Olmos, Motolinía, de las Navas, and materials on the *Relación de Michoacán*. An interesting explanation for the suppression of these works in 1577 concludes the study. An important book on the intellectual and political history of New Spain. [EBC]

2013 Benavides H., Artemio. De la historia social a la historia de la sociedad: el Sermón en la Colegiata de Guadalupe de Fray Servando Teresa de Mier en 1794 (UNL/H, 19, 1978, p. 317–330)

Proposes a reinterpretation of the sermon on the Virgin of Guadalupe delivered in 1794 by Fray Servando Teresa de Mier. Author's thesis is that Mier was expressing a growing national consciousness by asserting that Virgin of Guadalupe had arrived in Mexico prior to Spanish conquest and extolling privileged character of Mexican nation vis-à-vis Spain. [AL]

2014 Borah, Woodrow and **Sherburne F. Cook.** A case history of the transition from precolonial to the colonial period in Mexico: Santiago Tejupan (*in* Social fabric and spatial structure in colonial Latin America. Edited by David J. Robinson. Syracuse, N.Y.: Syracuse University, Department of Geography [and] University Microfilms International, 1979, p. 409–432, ill., tables)

History of a small town in the Mixteca region from the prehispanic period through the 18th century, with emphasis on the 16th century. Author stresses physical and demographic changes. Attention is paid to social hierarchy and town government. Concise and well written. [AL]

2015 Borchart de Moreno, Christiana. Los miembros del Consulado de la Ciudad de México en la época de Carlos III (JGSWGL, 14, 1977, p. 134–160)

This fact-studded work analyzes the merchants of the Consulado of Mexico City in the period 1759–78. The topics probed are regional origin of the merchants, areas of trade, control of merchandise, financing, use of *mayorazgo*, land purchases, etc. This very useful essay is a summary of a longer work by the author which makes extensive use of archival sources. [AL]

2016 Brading, D.A. Haciendas and ranchos in the Mexican Bajío, León, 1700–1860. Cambridge; New York: Cambridge University Press, 1978. 258 p.; bibl.; index (Cambridge Latin American studies; 32)

A significant series of essays on the agrarian history of the Bajío, centered on León and emphasizing the 18th century. Beginning with an analysis of the region, and continuing with materials on León's demography, structure, rents and profits of haciendas, the expansion of agriculture at the expense of stock-breeding, and including biographical sketches of hacendados and rancheros, the book concludes with an epilogue of the history of the agrarian reform. Although some of this material has appeared in a different form in previous publications (see *HLAS 40:2419–2421*), the author has examined and analyzed a huge body of primary material, contributed substantively to the subject of latifundia history, and detailed the rise of the rural middle class in the Bajío region. [EBC]

2017 Broda, Johanna. Las comunidades indígenas y las formas de extracción del excedente: época prehispánica y colonial (*in* Ensayos sobre el desarrollo económico de México y América Latina: 1500–1975. Compiled by Enrique Florescano. México: Fondo de Cultura Económica, 1979, p. 54–92)

On the basis of secondary sources, the author concludes that "the equalitarian nature of the peasant community was a result of colonial policies, and not of the continuity of pre-hispanic forms" (p. 77). She finds this to be a common reaction to conquest. Tribute, however, remained a common factor in the exploitation of the village. [EBC]

2018 Calvento, María del Carmen. Intereses particulares y política de abastecimiento en México (IGFO/RI, 36:143/144, enero/junio 1976, p. 159–211)

Discusses the legislation controlling the preparation and sale of bread in Mexico City, with emphasis on the period 1770 onwards. The study reveals the internal problems confronted by the bakers and distributors of bread, and the government in the task of regularizing the quality and supply of bread in Mexico City. Includes two useful Appendixes: Reglamento del Gremio de Panaderos (1770) and a list of bakeries and their owners in 1770. [AL]

2019 Carreño Alvarado, Gloria. El Colegio de Santa Rosa María de Valladolid: 1743–1810. Morelia, México: Universidad Michoacana de San Nicolás de Hidalgo, 1979. 209 p.; maps; tables.

Well-documented history of a colonial school for women in Valladolid. Based on local and school archives, work focuses on foundation, financial affairs and academic goals of the institution. Informative and useful contribution. [AL]

2020 ———. Mortalidad en el Obispado de Michoacán a consecuencias de la crisis económica de 1785–1786 (Anuario [Universidad Michoacana, Escuela de Historia, Morelia, México] 3, 1978, p. 187–198)

Reports the number of dead (89,445) which resulted from the well-known famine of that period in the Bishopric of Michoacán and breaks down figures by parishes. [AL]

2021 Carrillo y Ancona, Crescencio. El Obispado de Yucatán: historia de su fundación y de sus obispos desde el siglo XVI hasta el XIX, seguida de las constituciones sinodales de la diócesis y otros documentos relativos. t. 2, 1677–1887. Mérida, México:

Fondo Editorial de Yucatán, 1979. 1 v. (1102 p.) bibl.

Reissue of the 1895 first edition of this book. An Appendix contains a polemic between the Yucatecan historian Juan Francisco Molina Solís and the author, and brief biographies of the Bishops of Yucatán from 1898 to the present (1970s). [AL]

2022 Carroll, Patrick J. Black laborers and their experience in colonial Jalapa (*in* Reunión de Historiadores Mexicanos y Norteamericanos, 5th, Pátzcuaro, México, 1977. El trabajo y los trabajadores en la historia de México [see item **1979**] p. 119–132, tables)

Asserting that the experience of blacks in Jalapa was representative of other places in Mexico, Carroll summarizes the results of a longer study tracing the demographic history and work experiences of urban and rural slaves as they earned manumission and mixed with other groups. Particularly valuable for its study of race mixture. [EBC]

2023 Cepeda, Fernando de; F.A. Carrillo; and J. Alvarez Serrano. Relación universal: 1637. Advertencia preliminar de Luis E. Bracamontes. Nota bibliográfica de Francisco González de Cosío. 3. ed. México: Secretaría de Obras Públicas, 1976. 452 p.; bibl.; 12 leaves of plates: facsims.; indexes (Obras públicas en México; 1)

Reprinting of a rare 1637 book on the history of the Desagüe, which contains much general information on the history of Mexico City. Indexed, but not annotated. [EBC]

2024 Chipman, Donald. The will of Nuño de Guzmán: President, Governor and Captain General of New Spain and the province of Pánuco, 1558 (AAFH/TAM, 35:2, Oct. 1978, p. 238–248)

Transcription of the will of this famous conquistador with some preliminary comments. [AL]

2025 Ciudad Real, Antonio de. Tratado curioso y docto de las grandezas de la Nueva España: relación breve y verdadera de algunas cosas de las muchas que sucedieron al padre fray Alonso Ponce en las provincias de la Nueva España, siendo comisario general de aquellas partes. Edición, estudio preliminar, apéndices, glosarios, mapas de índices por Josefina García Quintana y Víctor M. Castillo Farreras. Prólogo de Jorge Gurría Lacroix. 2. ed. México: Universidad Nacional Autónoma de México, Instituto de Investigaciones Históricas, 1976– . 2 v. (272, 482 p.) bibl.; ill.; maps.

An account of the travels, observations, and political difficulties of the Comisario General of the Franciscan Order. The events described occurred between 1584–89, and his investigations covered the area between Nayarit and Nicaragua. Extensive biographical, bibliographical materials, as well as maps and catalogues of Franciscan constructions are provided in a lengthy introduction. [EBC]

2026 Colección de documentos sobre Coyoacán. t. 1, Visita del Oidor Gómez de Santillán al pueblo de Coyoacán y su sujeto Tacubaya en el año de 1553. Compiled by Pedro Carrasco P. and Jesús Monjarás-Ruiz. México: Secretaría Educación Pública, Instituto Nacional de Antropología e Historia, Centro de Investigaciones Superiores, 1976. 1 v. (unpaged) bibl.; index (Colección científica; 39. Fuentes historia social; 39)

Contains documents of the visita of Oidor Gómez de Santillán in 1553, originally housed at the Archives of the Indies in Seville. [AL]

2027 Connell, Tim. New Spain and the tribute system in the 16th century, Diego Ramírez and Jerónimo de Valderrama: "Justo Juez" and "Azote de Indios" (IAA, 4:2, 1978, p. 161–170, bibl.)

Brief but helpful analysis of the *visitas* of Diego Ramírez (1555–63) and Jerónimo de Valderrama (1563–66), royal emissaries in charge of regularizing the Indian tribute system. While the former stressed relieving the Indians from unjust taxation, the latter was more interested in raising the level of the Crown's income. [AL]

2028 *Correo Americano del Sur.* México: Partido Revolucionario Institucional, 1976. 318 p.; ill.

Facsimile edition of José María Morelo's newspaper. Also reprints a weekly irregular publication issued in Oaxaca: *Sud* (Nos. 51/53 for Jan. 25, 1813). Printed in sepia with illustrations. [AL]

2029 Couturier, Edith. Women in a noble family: the Mexican Counts of Regla, 1750–1830 (*in* Latin American women: historical perspectives [see item **1791**] p. 129–149, tables)

Explores the role of women in the colonial family, using the example of four generations of women in the powerful Regla class. Spectrum of women ranges from the strong-willed to the passive wife, revealing their potentially diverse roles. Study is based on private and public archival sources and underscores the importance of women as central characters in the basic social unity of colonial society. [AL]

2030 Duke, Cathy. The family in eighteenth-century plantation society in Mexico (*in* Comparative perspectives on slavery in New World societies [see item **1768**] p. 226–241)

Analysis of the institution of marriage in four social groups of late colonial Córdoba. Author argues that "the family served as the vehicle through which individuals in Cordobés society understood their economic and social goals" (p. 240). Study focuses on haciendas, ranchers, workers and slave families, providing comparisons across class and race lines. Broadens the narrow scope of available studies of colonial family. [AL]

Ewald, Ursula. The von Thünen principle and agricultural zonation in colonial Mexico. See *HLAS 41:5344.*

2031 Farriss, Nancy M. Nucleation versus dispersal: the dynamics of population movement in colonial Yucatan (HAHR, 58:2, May 1978, p. 187–216)

Thoughtful study of patterns of settlement among Yucatecan Mayas from 1550 through 1810. Explains opposite forces in process of settlement: integration into towns and dispersal over land. Argues that religious congregations imposed by Spaniards were artifically imposed and failed. Maya society harbored dispersal forces which were "integral part of Maya cultural dynamics by the time the Spanish landed in Yucatán." This explains why Mayas were as dispersed at the end of the colonial period as at the beginning. [AL]

2032 Fluctuaciones económicas en Oaxaca durante el siglo XVIII. Coordinación: Elías Trabulse. México: Colegio de México, 1979. 112 p.; bibl.; ill. (Nueva serie—Centro de Estudios Históricos; 29)

This exercise in quantitative history, based on the Oaxaca tithe figures between 1700–1800, was conceived partly as a teaching tool. A series of short essays explain the meaning of 44 p. of tables and graphs, and relate this new information to economic cycles in other parts of New Spain. Contains valuable clues to the economic history of the 18th century. [EBC]

2033 Galaviz de Capdevielle, María Elena. Crónica del Padre Fray Luis de Guzmán de la rebelión de los jonaces en 1703 (UCEIA/H, 18, 1977, p. 387–401)

An account of the rebellion of the Jonaces Indians, of Sierra Gorda. Based on two archival manuscripts which provide information on the events and the actions undertaken by settlers and civil and ecclesiastical authorities. [AL]

2034 Gallagher, Ann Miriam. The Indian nuns of Mexico City's Monasterio of Corpus Christi: 1724–1821 (*in* Latin American women: historical perspectives [see item **1791**] p. 150–172, tables)

Detailed study of the nuns of the first convent for Indian women in Mexico City based on the documents required for their profession. Provides significant information on social status of families of nuns, and on attitudes of Indian population towards the Church and the religious profession. Study broadens our limited knowledge of Indian women during the colonial period. [AL]

2035 García Bernal, Manuela Cristina. Indios y encomenderos en el Yucatán español: evolución demográfica y relaciones interraciales (UY/R, 20:116, marzo/abril 1978, p. 16–38)

Abstract of a longer work by the author on the encomienda in Yucatan during the Habsburg period. Author explains her methodological approach and advances some conclusions. Encomiendas lasted longer in Yucatan than elsewhere in Spanish America, although their value was small. Points out correlation between control of encomienda and membership in the small ruling class. [AL]

2036 ———. Yucatán: población y encomienda bajo los Austrias. Prólogo de Luis Navarro García. Sevilla: Escuela Hispano-Americanos, 1978. 595 p.; fold. maps; tables (Publicación; 252)

Major study of population and encomienda in Yucatán from 1550 through 1700. The population section of this lengthy study is based on examination of new documentary sources which support a revision of estimates suggested by other authors. The study of encomiendas is also based on meticulous research and subject to exhaustive treatment concerning their allocation, succession, fiscal policies, economic productivity, geographical distribution and socioeconomic implications. The wealth of information and solid foundation single out this work as an important contribution to the study of colonial Yucatán. [AL]

2037 Garner, Richard L. Reformas Borbónicas y operaciones hacendarias: la Real Caja de Zacatecas, 1750–1821 (CM/HM, 27:4, abril/junio 1978, p. 542–587, bibl., tables)

In-depth study of the reforms and subsequent performance of the Real Caja of Zacatecas. Author studies the administration of the silver tithes, the mercury, tobacco and salt monopolies, and the *alcabala*, *pulque* and other sources of revenue under the purview of the Caja. He concludes that the carefully administered and thoroughly enforced reforms of the Bourbon period were ultimately exploitative insofar as Spain reaped the largest share of the greatly expanded revenues. [AL]

2038 Gerhard, Peter. The southeast frontier of New Spain. Princeton, N.J.: Princeton University Press, 1979. 213 p.; bibl.; index; maps.

Carefully documented and illustrated, this study of the Southeast of New Spain is a timely sequel to the author's previous work on the viceroyalty's central area. For each region Gerhard furnishes information on encomiendas, political government, Church affairs, population and a list of sources. Most useful work for both scholars and students. [AL]

2039 González Cicero, Stella María. Perspectiva religiosa en Yucatán, 1517–1571: Yucatán, los franciscanos y el primer Obispo Fray Francisco de Toral. México: Colegio de México, 1978. 254 p.; bibl.; 4 leaves of plates: ill. (Nueva serie. Centro de Estudios Históricos; 28)

A factual re-statement of aspects of Yucatan's 16th-century history based on published secondary sources, and a selection of AGI materials. The description of the conflict between Bishop Toral and the Franciscans is an interesting example of the reasons for intra-Church conflicts, but is not analytically tied to the previous events, nor related to the subsequent history of Yucatan. [EBC]

2040 González Domínguez, María del Refugio. Notas para el estudio de las Ordenanzas de Minería en México durante el siglo XVIII (UNAM/RFD, 26:101/102, enero/junio 1976, p. 157–167)

Description of the legal literature regulating the mining industry of New Spain in the 18th century. This brief article mentions the works of Francisco J. Gamboa, José A. Areche, José de Gálvez and Joaquín Velázquez de León. [AL]

2041 González Salar, Carlos. Dos cronistas franciscanos del nuevo Santander: Simón del Hierro y Vicente de Santa María (UCEIA/H, 18, 1977, p. 427–437)

Brief review of the lives and written work of these distinguished missionaries. This is a narrative rather than an interpretive account. [AL]

2042 Greenow, Linda L. Spatial dimensions of the credit market in eighteenth century Nueva Galicia (*in* Social fabric and spatial structure in colonial Latin America. Edited by David Robinson. Syracuse, N.Y.: Syracuse University, Department of Geography [and] University Microfilms International, 1979, p. 227–279, maps, tables)

Examines registered loans from three sample decades in late colonial New Galicia to show the extent to which credit was the key element of the colonial economy. Analyzes dependence on markets, groups controlling credit, social and institutional ties, and underlines roles of the Church in the credit market. Study indicates that Spanish and Creole property-owners had a tight grip on the economy by monopolizing capital and credit. Excellent analysis which should serve as a model for the study of other geographic area. [AL]

2043 Gruzinski, Serge. Indios reales y fantásticos en documentos de la Inquisición (MAGN/B, 2[4]:6, oct./dic. 1978, p. 18–39, ill.)

Reprint of two documents usually issued prior to the Inquisitorial investigation. It sheds light on "deviant," religious practices of rural indigenous groups and the practice of magic and witchcraft rites among Spanish women. [AL]

2044 Gurría Lacroix, Jorge. Narciso Mendoza y Juan N. Almonte en el sitio de Cuauhtla (UNAM/E, 7, 1979, p. 43–65, bibl., facsim., plates)

Furnishes new data on the children's battalion which participated in the Morelos campaign, especially in the siege of Cuautla. [AL]

2045 ———. La población de Tabasco durante el virreinato (UNAM/EHN, 6, 1978, p. 65–88, tables)

Attempt to estimate the population of this area based on contemporary chronicles, tribute assessments, *relaciones* and censuses. The varied character of the sources makes appraisal difficult, especially for the early colonial period. Except for the 1794 census, all figures remain conjectural. [AL]

2046 Hamill, Hugh M. Un discurso formado con angustia: Francisco Primo Verdad, el 9 de agosto de 1808 (CM/HM, 28:3, enero/marzo 1979, p. 439–474, ill.)

Unveils newly-discovered manuscripts of the several drafts of Primo Verdad's speech of 9 Aug. 1808 in which he allegedly called for the sovereignty of people to rule in the absence of the monarch. The succession of drafts suggest an increasingly guarded posture to protect Verdad from Audiencia's ire. Interesting example of historical detection. [AL]

2047 Hamnett, Brian R. The abortive reestablishment of the Jesuits in Mexico: 1815–1820 (IAA, 4:4, 1978, p. 265–288, bibl., tables)

The Society of Jesus was restored in 1815 as part of Ferdinand VII's policy of bolstering royal authority, to revive clerical influence on education, and to root out political dissent. This brief study stresses the efforts of Mexican conservatives on behalf of the Society and the financial sources used to support it during its short revival. [AL]

2048 ———. Anastasio Bustamante y la guerra de independencia: 1810–1821 (CM/HM, 28:4, abril/junio 1979, p. 515–545, bibl.)

Traces Anastasio Bustamante's activities during the period 1810–21 as a useful exercise in understanding the attitudes of royalist Creoles who eventually became the republic's conservatives. Author argues that Bustamante and others like him aimed at stopping social revolution and securing political power for the Creole elite. These attitudes matured slowly prior to 1821 as bourgeoisie decided that Spaniards had lost claim to legitimacy. [AL]

2049 Hirschberg, Julia. An alternative to *Encomienda*: Puebla's *Indios de Servicio,* 1531–45 (JLAS, 2:2, Nov. 1979, p. 241–264, tables)

Study of labor allocation in early Puebla. The *indios de servicio* system provided limited, officially supervised and more equitable distribution of labor, and was an alternative to encomienda. Draft system became a model for repartimiento. Well-documented study with careful analysis of the Spanish population receiving the labor allocations. [AL]

2050 ———. La fundación de Puebla de los Angeles: Mito y realidad (CM/HM, 28:2, oct./dic. 1978, p. 185–223, bibl.)

Discussion of the foundation of the city of Puebla in terms of ideal goals and contradictory realities encountered in the process. Slightly different from the following work in English (see item **2051**). This article deals in greater length with the historiographical issues posed by the sources and their interpretations rather than with the prosopographical analysis of the population. [AL]

2051 ———. Social experiment in New Spain: a prosopographical study of the early settlement at Puebla de los Angeles, 1531–1534 (HAHR, 59:1, Feb. 1979, p. 1–33)

This revisionist work tests previously held assumptions on the meaning and goals of the foundation of Puebla. Close examination of cabildo and notarial records are the base for a prosopographical study of the early settler population which examines various parameters such as age, gender, occupation, wealth, geographical mobility, etc. The conclusion is that Puebla did not fulfill most of the proposed but incompatible goals of bureaucrats and theologians. A very good study with new insights and challenging new data and interpretation. [AL]

2052 Horcasitas, Fernando. Los descendientes de Nezahualpilli: documentos del cacicazgo de Tetzcoco, 1545–1855 (UNAM/EHN, 6, 1978, p. 145–185)

Consists of 10 documents relative to the cacicazgo of Texcoco ranging from 1545 through 1855. Useful documentary sources. [AL]

2053 Hurtado, Flor. Dolores Hidalgo en el siglo XVIII: una aproximación cuantitativa (CM/HM, 27:4, abril/junio 1978, p. 507–541, bibl., tables)

Partial revision of author's previous study of Dolores Hidalgo. She offers suggestions to overcome problems inherent to colonial data and revised versions of earlier results on the production of corn, wheat, beans and wool. [AL]

Jara Hantke, Alvaro. Plata y pulque en el siglo XVIII mexicano. See *HLAS 40:283*.

2054 José Ignacio Bartolache: *Mercurio Volante,* 1772–1773. Edición de Roberto Moreno. México: UNAM, 1979. 202 p.

Prosiguiendo sus valiosos estudios sobre la cultura "ilustrada" en México, Roberto Moreno reedita en este pulcro volumen de la "Biblioteca del Estudiante Universitario" el *Mercurio Volante,* una interesante empresa del médico José Ignacio Bertolache en pro de la difusión de los conocimientos. La introducción sobre él y su obra por Moreno es excelente. [L.G. Canedo]

2055 Kagan, Samuel. The labor of prisoners in the obrajes of Coyoacán: 1660–1693 (*in* Reunión de Historiadores Mexicanos y Norteamericanos, 5th, Pátzcuaro, México, 1977. El trabajo y los trabajadores en la historia de México [see item **1979**] p. 201–214, tables)

Richly descriptive study of working conditions in the textile industry based upon *visitas,* Inquisition and criminal cases, all of which underline the persistence of forced labor. [EBC]

2056 Ladd, Doris M. Mexican women in Anahuac and New Spain: Aztec roles, Spanish notary revelations, Creole genius. Austin: University of Texas, Institute of Latin American Studies, 1979. 87 p.

One of a series of teaching aids developed by the University of Texas, this valuable collection of documents would be useful for units in social and colonial history as well as women's studies. It includes excerpts from the Florentine Codex, and translations of the Millares y Mantecón summaries of Mexico City notaries, including land sales, wills, dowries, commercial transactions, slave sales and manumissions. There is a final section on Sor Juana Inés de la Cruz with biographical data, and selections from her works. Also includes study guides, and other pedagogical materials. [EBC]

2057 Lavrin, Asunción and **Edith Couturier.** Dowries and wills: a view of women's socioeconomic role in colonial Guadalajara and Puebla, 1640–1790 (HAHR, 59:2, May 1979, p. 280–304, tables)

Discusses the use and value of dowries and wills as sources for the history of colonial women. Provides new data on how wills, dowries, property and marriage affected women's role in society. Authors suggest that women are more powerful than previously assumed because of the legal system's special structure, and they propose a reinterpretation of the status of women in New Spain. [AL]

2058 Lewis, James A. New Spain and the American Revolution: a view from the Valley of Mexico, 1779–1783 (RIB, 28:1, enero/marzo 1978, p. 39–45)

Concise survey of the impact of the rebellion of the 13 British colonies on colonial New Spain. Author concludes that neither the lower classes nor the elites were highly aware of the events. Residents of New Spain had no common interests with English colonials and "felt no common bond as victims of European exploitation" (p. 44). [AL]

2059 ———. Nueva España y los esfuerzos para abastecer La Habana, 1779–1783 (EEHA/AEA, 33, 1976, p. 501–526)

During Spain's war with England (1779–83), the supply of flour to Spanish troops stationed in Cuba was assigned to New Spain. Nevertheless, numerous transportation problems—both by land and by sea—prevented reliable deliveries, forcing Cuba to turn to the US market and resulting in a large amount of Spanish bullion being channelled to the US. Article highlights the significance of internal problems of transportation on the course of trade and history. [AL]

2060 López Lara, Ramón. Zinapécuaro: monografía del municipio. 2. ed. Morelia, México: Talleres Fimax Publicistas, 1979. 253 p.; bibl.; maps; plates.

This attempt at writing the local history of a Michoacán municipality is very uneven in quality. Of limited interest or use for the historian. [AL]

2061 Marcus, Raymond. La conquête de Cholula: conflit d'interprétations (IAA, 3:2, 1977, p. 193–213, bibl., table)

Mentalité study of the conquest of Cholula based on accounts by Hernán Cortés, Bernal Díaz del Castillo, Diego Muñoz Camargo, and Fathers Motolinía and Las Casas. Cortés compared Indians to the Muslim mental archetype and wanted rapid assimilation. Bernal thought more like a soldier and emphasized the Indians' barbarity and the greatness of the conquest. The two missionaries stressed, in different ways, the role of the conquerors but both manifested their European mentality by wishing to convert the Indians. Although the conclusions reached by the author in his analysis are not surprising, he succeeds in presenting a new perspective to the narrative of the conquest. [AL]

2062 Mier Noriega y Guerra, José Servando Teresa de. Fray Servando: biografía, discursos, cartas. Monterrey, México: Gobierno del Estado de Nuevo León, Universidad Autónoma de Nuevo León, Dirección General de Investigaciones Humanísticas, 1977. 347 p.

Reprint of a series of Fray Servando's letters and several of his speeches. Six brief studies of Fray Servando's personality and work introduce the material. [AL]

2063 La Minería en México: estudios sobre su desarrollo histórico. Coordinador: Miguel León-Portilla. México: Universidad Nacional Autónoma de México, 1978. 183 p.; bibl.; 14 leaves of plates: ill.

An innovative study of the causes and effects of the Bourbon Reforms in mining. Moreno's work "Las Instituciones de la Industria Minera Novohispana" is the central piece in this compilation of essays by León-Portilla, Gurría Lacroix and Madero Bracho. By concentrating on the period 1761–75, Moreno identifies a crisis in mining beginning around 1761. He delineates the events and describes the personalities such as Gamboa, the Count of Regla, Gálvez, Bucareli, Velázquez de León that led to formulating the 1784 Ordinances and establishing the Mining Tribunal and the School of Mines. Moreno finds that the source of both successes and failures of these institutions was rooted in the political conflicts of the 1760s and 1770s. [EBC]

2064 Moreno, Roberto. Joaquín Velázquez de León y sus trabajos científicos sobre el Valle de México, 1773–1775. México: Universidad Nacional Autónoma de México, Instituto de Investigaciones Históricas, 1977. 407 p.; bibl.; 6 fold. leaves of plates: ill.; index (Série de historia novohispana; 25)

Complete edition of the works of Joaquín Velázquez de León dealing with the Mexican basin. The scientist was a member of the enlightened, Mexican Creole elite who were most active during the period 1768–88. Moreno stresses the role of Velázquez de León as a precursor of modernity. Introduction provides biographical data and evaluation of the scientist's contribution to scientific and philosophical renewal in late colonial New Spain. [AL]

2065 ———. Salario, tequío y partido en las Ordenanzas para la Minería Mexicana del siglo XVIII (UNAM/RFD, 26:101/102, enero/junio 1976, p. 465–483)

Author surveys solutions offered by four legal experts to problems of labor unrest and limited capital in the mines of New Spain. The experts are: Francisco Xavier de Gamboa, José Antonio de Areche, José de Gálvez and Joaquín Velázquez de León. These men offered different solutions to problems of wages, forced labor, and the laborers' share of the mineral findings of the mines (*partido*). Long excerpts from their proposals encourage comparison of values and attitudes among them. [AL]

2066 Morin, Claude. Sentido y alcance del siglo XVIII en América Latina: el caso del centro-oeste mexicano (*in* Ensayos sobre el desarrollo económico de México y América Latina: 1500–1975. Compiled by Enrique Florescano. México: Fondo de Cultura Económica, 1979, p. 154–170, tables)

Revisionist view of 18th-century economic development, based on research in the Bishopric of Michoacán, suggests that the recovery from the 17th century depression began in 1680 or 1690 and continued only until 1760. The "Reforms" of Gálvez and Charles III created new ties of dependency without any important new wealth except in the southern part of the bishopric. [EBC]

2067 Motín de los indios de Ajacuba, 1774 (MAGN/B, 3[1]:7, enero/marzo 1979, p. 24–37)

Selection of documents of Vol. 53 of Criminal Section, National Archives of the Nation, dealing with litigation over land by Otomí Indians of Ajacuba, State of Hidalgo. [AL]

2068 Muría, José María. La dependencia y la autonomía de Nueva Galacia: México (FJB/BH, 45, sept. 1977, p. 327–335)

Popularized account of the colonial history of present Jalisco and its interdependence with New Spain. [AL]

2069 Muriel, Josefina. En torno a una vieja polémica: erección de los primeros conventos de San Francisco en la ciudad de México, siglo XVI (UNAM/EHN, 6, 1978, p. 7–38, bibl., ill., plate)

Discusses the site and construction of the two first Franciscan convents of Mexico City and ably uses the scant data available. [AL]

2070 Naveda Chávez-Hita, Adriana. Trabajadores esclavos en las haciendas azucareras de Córdoba, Veracruz: 1714–1763 (*in* Reunión de Historiadores Mexicanos y Norteamericanos, 5th, Pátzcuaro, México, 1977. El trabajo y los trabajadores en la historia de México [see item **1979**] p. 162–182, tables)

This thorough analysis of the slave population in 15 out of 33 sugar haciendas reveals demographic patterns, slave prices, values, and the structure of production. [EBC]

2071 Nickel, Herbert J. Reclutamiento y peonaje de los gañanes indígenas de la época colonial en el altiplano de Puebla-Tlaxcala (IAA, 5:1, 1979, p. 71–104, bibl., facsims., tables)

Explores complexities of the recruitment process of peons and seasonal workers in the Puebla-Tlaxcala area. Concludes that debt peonage was not a simple procedure to obtain labor, and explains nuances in the method of tying labor to land. Focuses mostly on the late 18th century and uses hacienda records. Useful contribution. [AL]

2072 Nunn, Charles F. Foreign immigrants in early Bourbon Mexico, 1700–1760. Cambridge; New York: Cambridge University Press, 1979. xi, 243 p.; bibl.; index (Cambridge Latin American studies; 31)

Studies policies and actions of Spanish Crown towards foreigners. Unlike preceding centuries, the years under study were characterized by toleration of useful foreigners willing to adapt to Spanish basic demands. Religion, security and trade were main concerns of Spanish policies. Coverage of subject is thorough in this well-researched work which may be considered the definitive study of the topic. [AL]

2073 Ortiz de la Tabla Ducasse, Javier. Comercio exterior de Veracruz, 1778–1821: crisis de dependencia. Sevilla: Escuela de Estudios Hispano-Americanos, 1978. 456 p.; bibl.; 12 leaves of plates: ill.; index (Publicaciones de la Escuela de Estudios Hispano-Americanos de Sevilla; 243)

The economic reforms promulgated by Spain at the end of the 18th century sharply affected the exterior commerce of Veracruz. Until the 1790s, this change was essentially one of quantity. After this decade, however, the traditional trade of Veracruz with Spain and neighboring colonies in the New World was replaced by new commercial patterns. At no time did the events of these years resolve the struggle within New Spain between those advocating free trade and those supporting protectionism. Useful work. [James A. Lewis]

2074 Parodi, Claudia. Algunos aspectos léxicos relativos al repartimiento forzoso o cuatequitl del centro de México, 1575–1599 (UNAM/EHN, 6, 1978, p. 47–64)

Linguistic study of the terms used in the 16th century to refer to forced labor. Although not strictly a historical subject, this study should be useful to historians trying to determine meaning of words in manuscripts. [AL]

2075 Patch, Robert. El mercado urbano y la economía campesina en Yucatán durante el siglo XVIII (UY/R, 20:116/118, mayo/agosto 1978, p. 83–96)

This is a study of Yucatan's internal colonial market in the second half of the 18th century. According to Patch the internal market was far more important than the export market. The chief article of exchange was corn, and most of the producers were small Indian peasants. Yet, the Spanish cabildo subordinated their interests to those of the city. The author concludes that this unequal relationship was one of the bases of internal colonialism. [AL]

2076 Pérez-Mallaína Bueno, Pablo Emilio. Comercio y autonomía en la intendencia de Yucatán, 1797–1814. Sevilla: Escuela de Estudios Hispano-Americanos de Sevilla, Consejo Superior de Investigaciones Científicas, 1978. 268 p.; bibl.; 6 leaves of plates (2 fold.): ill.; index (Publicaciones de la Escuela de Estudios Hispano-Americanos de Sevilla; 248)

Detailed study of trade and population tied to trade interests in Yucatán during the period between royal approval of free trade to friendly nations and the year Yucatán unilaterally opened its ports to free trade. Good survey but somewhat mechanical in the presentation of information. [AL]

2077 Pérez-Rocha, Emma. Mayordomías y cofradías del pueblo de Tacuba en el siglo XVIII (UNAM/EHN, 6, 1978, p. 119–131, tables)

Describes the structural organization, economic assets, administration and similar activities of the Indian confraternities of Tacuba, mostly in the 18th century. Given the scarcity of information on this aspect of ecclesiastical history, this brief contribution is welcome. [AL]

2078 Piratas en la costa de Nueva Galicia en el siglo XVII. Estudio, transcripción y notas por W. Michael Mathes. Guadalajara: Librería Font, 1976. 81 p.; index (Documentación histórica mexicana; 6)

Collection of manuscripts on the piratical spree of J. Van Spilbergen (1615) and the expected but never received Dutch attack of 1673. Consists of 13 manuscripts including letters, legal reports and royal cédulas on these two events. [AL]

2079 Poma y Poma, Antonio. Historia y sociología de una gran ciudad (UNL/H, 19, 1978, p. 481–496)

Synthesis of the early history of the city of Guanajuato prior to 1556. Author describes precolumbian settlement, first land grants and cattle raising stages. Although based on primary sources, the absence of footnotes is regrettable. [AL]

2080 Porras Muñoz, Guillermo. Un golpe de estado contra Hernán Cortés (UNL/H, 19, 1978, p. 361–382)

Retells the story of the 1525 rebellion against Hernán Cortés and the leading role played by Gonzalo de Salazar. [AL]

2081 Porro, Antonio. Un nuevo caso de mileranismo maya en Chiapas y Tabasco, Mexico, 1727 (UNAM/EHN, 6, 1978, p. 109–117, map)

Studies an unsuccessful revolt among Indians of Chiapas and Tabasco in 1712, which the author claims is the logical precursor of the 1727 revolt, and part of a long line of messianic uprisings in the peninsula. Brief but useful. [AL]

Rees, Peter W. Origins of colonial transportation in Mexico. See *HLAS 41:5365*.

2082 Reid, Paul Joseph. The Constitution of Cádiz and the independence of Yucatán (AAFH/TAM, 36:1, July 1979, p. 22–38)

Studies the activities of the Patriotic Confederation and the Yucatecan Provincial Deputation throughout the second decade of the 19th century. Evaluates their contribution to the independence movement and the attitude of the latter toward the Spanish Cortes and Iturbide's regime. [AL]

2083 Relaciones del Desagüe del Valle de México: años de 1555–1823. 2. ed. Advertencia preliminar de Luis E. Bracamontes. México: Secretaría de Obras Públicas, 1976. 564 p.; facsim.; fold. map; index; tables (Obras públicas en México. Documentos para su historia; 3)

A collection on the history of Mexico City's Desagüe (drainage system), including a brief introduction and seven articles by: Enrico Martínez; Fray Luis Flores; Fray Manuel de Cabrera; Francisco de Cuevas Aguirre y Espinosa; and a memorial to José María Mora. Valuable information on the history of Mexico City. [EBC]

2084 Riley, James D. Landlords, laborers and royal government: the administration of labor in Tlaxcala, 1680–1750 (*in* Reunión de Historiadores Mexicanos y Norteamericanos, 5th, Pátzcuaro, México, 1977. El trabajo y los trabajadores en la historia de México [see item **1979**] p. 221–241)

Sheds new light on the old issue of debt peonage through an examination of legal cases brought against Tlaxcalan hacendados by their resident work force. Measures these cases against legislation on the status of Indian workers. Concludes that an Indian born on an estate usually remained attached to it, whether he owned money or not. [EBC]

2085 Rodríguez Losa, Salvador. La encomienda, el indio y la tierra en el Yucatán colonial (UY/R, 20:115, enero/feb. 1978, p. 50–79)

A synthesis of views, facts and opinions on the encomienda, land ownership and the status of Indians in colonial Yucatan. Based mostly on secondary sources copiously quoted, this is a typical example of "scissors and paste" history. [AL]

2086 Rojas, Alfonso Villa. El cambio social y cultural del maya desde el siglo XVI (UY/R, 20:117/118, mayo/agosto 1978, p. 75–96)

Brief analysis of the persistence of certain forms of Maya culture such as the *calpulli* social unit, *nagualismo* (magic beliefs) and religious ceremonies. [AL]

2087 Rojas Rabiela, Teresa. La organización del trabajo para las obras públicas: el coatequitl y las cuadrillas de trabajadores (*in* Reunión de Historiadores Mexicanos y Norteamericanos, 5th, Pátzcuaro, México, 1977. El trabajo y los trabajadores en la historia de México [see item **1979**] p. 41–66)

Explores the relation between precolonial and colonial forms of recruiting and utilizing labor for public works. Also discusses the methods of task assignment and the length of service. Based on secondary works and published primary sources. [EBC]

2088 Rubial García, Antonio. La insulana: un ideal franciscano medieval en Nueva España (UNAM/EHN, 6, 1978, p. 38–64)

Briefly describes the unsuccessful attempts at founding a hermitic branch of the Franciscan Order in New Spain shortly after the conquest. [AL]

2089 El Santo desierto de los Carmelitas de la Provincia de San Alberto de México: Santa Fe 1605, Tenancingo 1801: historia documental e iconográfica. Revisión paleográfica, introducciones y notas por Dionisio Victoria Moreno y Manuel Arredondo Herrera. México: Patrimonio Cultural y Artístico del Estado de México, 1978. 699 p.: ill. (Biblioteca Enciclopédica del Estado de México; 66)

This annotated collection of materials about two Carmelite institutions in the state of Mexico, consists of chroniclers accounts, biographies of important members of the order, information on the life of their principal patron, daily life at the convents, and architectural data. An excellent example of a well-produced documentary publication. [EBC]

2090 Sarabia Viejo, María Justina. Don Luis de Velasco, Virrey de Nueva España, 1550–1564. Sevilla: Escuela de Estudios Hispanoamericanos, 1978. 341 p.

Obra basada principalmente en referencias documentales sacadas en su mayoría del Archivo General de Indians (Sevilla) pero también del Archivo General de la Nación (México) *Ramo de Mercedes* y del *Familiar del Duque del Infantado.* Es asimismo copiosa la información bibliográfica. Buena base para un ulterior estudio analítico de este gran virrey. [L.G. Canedo]

2091 Sepúlveda, Juan Ginés de. Hechos de los españoles en el Nuevo Mundo y México = De rubus Hispanorum gestis de novum orbem Mexicumque. Edición y estudios de Demetrio Ramos y Lucio Mijares, con la colaboración de Jonas Castro Toledo. Valladolid, Spain: Seminario Americanista de la Universidad de Valladolid, 1976. 400 p.; bibl.; ill.

New edition of Sepúlveda's work, with an introduction and editorial annotations. [AL]

2092 Sherman, William L. Some aspects of forced labor in Chiapas, sixteenth century (*in* Reunión de Historiadores Mexicanos y Norteamericanos, 5th, Pátzcuaro, México, 1977. El trabajo y los trabajadores en la historia de México [see item **1979**] p. 191–201)

Brief review of some cases of slavery or forced labor among Chiapas Indians, based upon AGI materials, and adding economic and political information. [EBC]

2093 Soberanes Fernández, José Luis. La Audiencia de México en la primera mitad del XVIII (UNAM/RFD, 28:109, enero/abril 1978, p. 187–197)

Brief consideration of the institutional reforms that were proposed for the Audiencia to encourage more efficiency in the administration of justice. Focuses on *Cédulas* of 1736 and 1746. [AL]

2094 Solano, Francisco de. La modelación social como política indigenista de los franciscanos en la Nueva España, 1524–1574

(CM/HM, 28:2, oct./dic. 1978, p. 297–322, bibl.)

Interpretive study of goals of early Franciscan missionaries in New Spain. They had the double task of Christianizing the indigenous population and providing it with technical knowledge necessary to adapt to a new social and economic order. Emphasis is laid on the conceptual aspects of the evangelizing task. [AL]

2095 Strecker, Matthias and **Jorge Artieda.** *La Relación de algunas costumbres,* 1582, de Gaspar Antonio Chi (UNAM/EHN, 6, 1978, p. 89–108)

Complete transcription of the existing parts of document written in 1582 by distinguished indigenous chronicler. Authors state that previously published English translations either missed several sections or were abridged. [AL]

2096 Tanck de Estrada, Dorothy. La abolición de los gremios (*in* Reunión de Historiadores Mexicanos y Norteamericanos, 5th, Pátzcuaro, México, 1977. El trabajo y los trabajadores en la historia de México [see item **1979**] p. 311–329)

Examines the political and economic rationale for the abolition of the gremios in Cádiz and Mexico City. Describes the sources and some of the kinds of data which would elucidate the history and operations of the *gremios* and their *cofradías.* Based on the Archivo de Ayuntamiento in Mexico City. [EBC]

2097 Taylor, William B. Drinking, homicide and rebellion in colonial Mexican villages. Stanford, Calif.: Stanford University Press, 1979. 242 p.; appendices; maps; tables.

Selecting three indexes of village life, and comparing their characteristics and frequency in Oaxaca and in Central Mexico, Taylor demonstrates the continued vitality of the rural Indian community from the late 17th to the early 19th century. He concludes that drinking continued to be a village ritual rather than a symptom of individual despair; that incidence of murder was more frequent because of personal disputes in Oaxaca, and because of intra-village disputes in Mexico; and that rebellions were caused by extraordinary economic demands. [EBC]

Tibón, Gutierre. Historia del nombre y de la fundación de México. See *HLAS 41:1431.*

2098 Torre Villar, Ernesto de la. El Decreto Constitucional de Apatzingán y sus fuentes legales (Boletín Mexicano de Derecho Comparado [UNAM, Instituto de Investigaciones Jurídicas, México] 10:28/29, enero/agosto 1977, p. 76–85)

Consiste de más dos largos apéndices sin paginar: el primero contiene un cuadro comparativo de la Constitución de Apatzingán de 1814 con la Constitución de los Estados Unidos, y en el segundo se hace lo mismo respecto de las constituciones francesas de 1793 y 1795, y de la española de 1812. Trabajo valioso para la historia de las ideas políticas. [L.G. Canedo]

2099 Trabulse, Elías. El erasmismo de un científico: supervivencias del humanismo cristiano en la Nueva España de la Contrarreforma (CM/HM, 28:2, oct./dic. 1978, p. 224–296, bibl., ill.)

In-depth study of the *Doctrina Christiana,* a catechism written by a layman, Francisco Hernández, *protomédico* of New Spain in the late 16th century. A broad study of Erasmian ideas and of the Erasmian group of Spanish scholars from which Hernández emerged precedes the examination of this unique document. The author shows his thorough knowledge of the development of philosophical and theological ideas in New Spain. [AL]

———. El problema de las longitudes geográficas en el México colonial. See *HLAS 41:5370.*

Trautmann, Wolfgang. Ergebnisse der Wüstungsforschung in Tlaxcala, Mexiko. See *HLAS 41:5371.*

2100 Tutino, John. Life and labor on north Mexican haciendas: 1775–1810 (*in* Reunión de Historiadores Mexicanos y Norteamericanos, 5th, Pátzcuaro, México, 1977. El trabajo y los trabajadores en la historia de México [see item **1979**] p. 339–378, tables)

Heavily tabulated, as well as lucidly written analysis of seven haciendas with a work force of 650 people based on University of Texas materials and censuses from the AGN (Mexico). Identifies an intermediate stage between the sparsely populated estates of the north, and the densely nucleated villages of the south. Also examines family structure, population trends, debt peonage and the *avio* system, working conditions and the internal structure of haciendas and their relationships with the ecology of the regions. Author documents a deterioration of living standards in the decades before independence. A major contribution to hacienda studies. [EBC]

2101 van Young, Eric. Urban market and hinterland: Guadalajara and its region in the eighteenth century (HAHR, 59:4, Nov. 1979, p. 593–635, map, tables)

Study of demand and supply relations in colonial Guadalajara for three major products: beef, wheat and corn. Rapid growth of the population spurred a significant increase in consumption. While cereal production rose to meet the challenge, beef supply was more unelastic due to insufficiency of livestock. Detailed study of market structure and the institutions regulating it. Excellent contribution to local economic history. [AL]

2102 Warren, J. Benedict. Vasco de Quiroga y sus hospitales, pueblo de Santa Fé. Morelia, México: Difusión Cultural, Editorial Universitaria, 1977. 206 p.; bibl.; plates (Ediciones de la Universidad Michoacán)

Translation of the original book published in the US in 1963 (never annotated in *HLAS*). The author has made some revisions in the text and added new material in the Appendix. The work consists of a detailed study of the life of Bishop Vasco de Quiroga who served as *oidor* (member) of the Audiencia of Mexico. He also founded the pueblo-hospitals, socioeconomic units where the Indian population lived according to the rules of a model society devised by Quiroga, and closely inspired by Thomas Moore's *Utopia.* Based on extensive manuscript material, this work unearths considerable information on this aspect of Quiroga's life. [AL]

2103 Wills, John E. Dutch ships on Mexico's Pacific coast: 1747 (HSSC/SCQ, 61:4, Winter 1979, p. 337–350)

In 1747, the Dutch East Indian Company tried to establish a trading port near Tepic in order to take advantage of the colony's hunger for foreign merchandise during the Anglo-Spanish war. The purpose of the article is to use this incident to illustrate the importance of the Dutch East Indian Company Archives as source for the commercial affairs of New Spain. [EBC]

2104 Winfield Capitaine, Fernando. Trapiches e ingenios azucareros en la jurisdicción de Xalapa, durante el siglo XVIII (UV/PH, 11, julio/sept. 1974, p. 19–26, ill.)

Comparative study of the sugar mills of the region of Japala, especially in the late 18th century. Author comments on the organization of their operations, area of cultivation, slave population, demographic changes in the area, etc. Based on archival sources, the work could have profited from a more in-depth treatment. [AL]

2105 *Yucatán: Historia y Economía.* Revista de análisis socioeconómico regional. Universidad de Yucatán, Centro de Investigaciones Regionales, Departamento de Estudios Económicos y Sociales. Año 1, No. 6, marzo/abril 1978 [and] Año 2, No. 7, mayo/junio 1978– . Mérida, México.

Bimonthly journal devoted to regional economic history. It published original contributions and an occasional older work of historiographical interest. Interpretations of many of the articles stress class struggle. [AL]

NORTH AND BORDERLANDS*

*Materials on Florida have been placed in the Caribbean section, see p. 265

2106 Alessio Robles, Vito. Coahuila y Texas en la época colonial. 2. ed. México: Editorial Porrúa, 1978. 751 p.; bibl.; 18 leaves of plates (7 fold.): ill.; index (Biblioteca Porrúa; 70)

Reprint of the 1938 edition of a classic (see *HLAS 4:2614*) designed to reach a new generation of scholars and aficionados of borderland history. [AL]

2107 Archer, Christon I. The Spanish reaction to Cook's third voyage (*in* Captain James Cook and his times. Edited by Robin Fisher and Hugh Johnston. Seattle: University of Washington Press, 1979, p. 99–119, map, plates)

Focuses on Spanish expeditions predating and following Cook's expedition to the Northwest. Spain had sent expeditions to the area since 1773 but under a policy of secrecy. After Cook's voyage this policy changed in an effort to assert Spanish claims to the area. Late 18th-century expeditions such as Alcalá

Galiano's, Malaspina's, Martínez' and Valdés' produced excellent profits, but it was too late by then to detract from Cook's fame. Well-documented and useful study for early history of the Northwest. [AL]

2108 Archibald, Robert. Acculturation and assimilation in colonial New Mexico (UNM/NMHR, 53:3, July 1978, p. 205–217)

The continuation of Indian slavery on the New Mexican frontier produced a group of people called *genizaros*. Ethnically Plains Indians, but culturally Hispanic, when manumitted from slavery, they were often settled in frontier towns. Article provides another angle on Spanish Indian policy. [EBC]

2109 Bannon, John Francis. The mission as a frontier institution: sixty years of interest and research (WHQ, 10:3, July 1979, p. 303–322)

A review of scholarly work on the mission on the 60th anniversary of Bolton's paper on the subject. Bannon finds the mission "one of the more humane approaches of a conquering people." [EBC]

2110 Beers, Henry Putney. Spanish & Mexican records of the American Southwest: a bibliographical guide to archive & manuscript sources. Tucson: University of Arizona Press, 1979. 493 p.; bibl.; ill.; index.

Written by a noted archivist, this collection of government, local, ecclesiastical, land and some private records scattered throughout many places treats Texas, New Mexico, Arizona and California in separate sections. [EBC]

2111 Benedict, H. Bradley. Hacienda management in late colonial Northern Mexico: a case study of Juan Bustamante and the Hacienda of Dolores (APS/P, 123:6, 28 Dec. 1979, p. 391–409, tables)

Thorough and well-documented study of an ex-Jesuit hacienda in Chihuahua. Information on labor, administration, salaries, production, profits, etc. [AL]

2112 Berman, Eric. The death of an old conquistador: new light on Juan de Oñate (UNM/NMHR, 54:3, Oct. 1979, p. 305–319)

Describes the last years of Juan de Oñate as he tried to clear charges against him for his work in New Mexico, entered the order of Santiago, and became an inspector of mines in southern Andalusia. [EBC]

2113 Bringas de Manzaneda y Encinas, Diego Miguel. Friar Bringas reports to the King: methods of indoctrination on the frontier of New Spain, 1796–97. Translated and edited by Daniel S. Matson and Bernard L. Fontana. Tucson: University of Arizona Press, 1977. 177 p.; bibl.; ill.; index (The Documentary relations of the Southwest. The Franciscan relations)

Handsomely produced work, this translation of a manuscript account written by the *visitador* from the Colegio de Santa Cruz to the Pimería deals with the history of the Franciscan missions during 1768–96. It also touches on problems of frontier organizations and conversion. A useful edition. [EBC]

2114 Cavazos Garza, Israel. Controversias sobre jurisdicción espiritual entre Saltillo y Monterrey: 1580–1652. Saltillo, Mexico: Colegio Coahuilense de Investigaciones Históricas, 1978. 21 p.

Deals with Franciscan and secular Church antagonism over tithes and clerical income after Monterrey developed a cattle bonanza in the 1740s. Little known but interesting chapter on the history of the Church in the borderlands. [AL]

2115 Chandler, R.E. Eyewitness history: O'Reilley's arrival in Louisiana (Louisiana History [University of Southwestern Louisiana, Louisiana Historical Association, Lafayette] 20:3, Summer 1979, p. 317–324)

Translation of a diary and letters recording the voyage of O'Reilley from Havana to Louisiana in 1769. Supplements earlier published documents. [EBC]

2116 ———. Ulloa and the Acadians (Louisiana History [University of Southwestern Louisiana, Louisiana Historical Association, Lafayette] 21:1, Winter 1980, p. 87–91)

Translation of a letter from Ulloa to Grimaldi in 1766, which describes the problems of an immigrant group and juxtaposes them to the issues of imperial defense and economic development. An interesting addenda to the problems faced by Ulloa as Governor of Louisiana. [EBC]

2117 Coutts, Brian E. An inventory of sources in the Department of Archives and Manuscripts, Louisiana State University, for the History of Spanish Louisiana and

Spanish West Florida (Louisiana History [University of Southwestern Louisiana, Louisiana Historical Association, Lafayette] 19:2, Spring 1979, p. 213–250)

An inventory of 172 collections, mostly originals, which are described with dates and number of items. Some transcriptions are included. [EBC]

Crosby, Harry. El Camino Real in Baja California: Loreto to San Diego. See *HLAS 41:5340*.

2118 Cutter, Donald C. Plans for the occupation of Upper California: a new look at the "Dark Age" from 1602 to 1769 (SDHS/J, 24:1, Winter 1978, p. 78–90, bibl., facsims.)

Popularly written account of the various plans made in the 17th and 18th centuries for the occupation of California including details on the final expedition of 1769. [EBC]

2119 Din, Gilbert C. Protecting the "barrera:" Spain's defenses in Louisiana, 1763–1779 (Louisiana History [University of Southwestern Louisiana, Louisiana Historical Association, Lafayette] 19:2, Spring 1978, p. 183–211)

Argues that between 1766 when Antonio de Ulloa arrived in Louisiana, and 1779, Spain built up her military capacity in the southeastern borderlands, thus facilitating the successful attack on Pensacola. Article based on a wide variety of primary and secondary sources, and is well reasoned. [EBC]

2120 The documentary relations of the Southwest: project manual. Compiled by Charles William Polzer, Thomas C. Barnes, Thomas H. Naylor. Tucson: University of Arizona, Arizona State Museum, 1977. 160 p.; bibl.

A guide to a series of projected publications entitled *Documentary Relations of the Southwest (DRSW)* which will serve as a counterpart to the *Jesuit Relations of North America*. This manual includes sections on the computer access bibliography, description of the kinds of documents, money and currency, ethnic tribal names, and a list of colonial borderlands officials. [EBC]

2121 Engstrand, Iris Wilson. The occupation of the Port of San Diego de Alcalá, 1769 (SDHS/J, 24:1, Winter 1978, p. 91–96, map)

Popular account of the founding of San Diego. [EBC]

2122 Etnología y misión en la Pimería Alta, 1715–1740: informes y relaciones misioneras de Luis Xavier Velarde, Giuseppe Maria Genovese, Daniel Januske, José Agustín de Campos y Cristóbal de Cañas. Edited by Luis González R. México: Universidad Nacional Autónoma de México, 1977. 359 p.; bibl.; 1 leaf of plates; index; map (Serie de historia novohispana; 27)

Consists of a quarter century of ethnographic and historical descriptions of Sonora and Arizona, following the death of Kino. Also draws on several previously unpublished descriptions from Mexico's Archivo Histórico de Hacienda at the AGN, as well as a richly annotated edition of Luis Velarde's works. [EBC]

2123 Fireman, Janet R. The Spanish Royal Corps of Engineers in the western borderlands: instrument of Bourbon reform, 1764 to 1815. Glendale, Calif.: A.H. Clark Co., 1977. 250 p.; bibl.; index; maps (Spain in the West; 12)

An important contribution to borderlands history based on extensive archival research into the lives of the commanders of the Corps of Engineers. Beginning as soldiers, most of these men became military fortifications specialists, as well as map makers. Includes valuable material on Teodoro de Croix's use of the Engineer's Corps in the Provincias Internas, and on civil military relations in central New Spain. [EBC]

2124 Garner, Van Hastings. The dynamics of change: New Mexico 1680 to 1690 (JW, 18:1, Jan. 1979, p. 4–13)

By examination of presidio records, and other primary materials, author reassesses events in the decade after the Pueblo revolt. Settlers adjusted to the loss of the encomienda and independent political power, and gained economically through entry as soldiers into the presidio. [EBC]

2125 Garr, Daniel. Villa de Branciforte: innovation and adaptation on the frontier (AAFH/TAM, 35:1, July 1978, p. 95–109)

An examination of the history of town planning on the frontier, followed by a description of the misfortunes besetting the last colonial town to be founded in America. [EBC]

2126 Griffen, William B. Indian assimilation in the Franciscan area of Nueva Vizcaya. Tucson: University of Arizona Press, 1979. 122 p.; bibl.; ill. (Anthropological papers of the University of Arizona; 33)

Surveys history of Concho Indians from early 17th century through 1816. Well-documented and clearly written, this is a useful work for the historian and the ethnohistorian. [AL]

2127 Guest, Francis. An examination of the thesis of S.F. Cook on the forced conversion of Indians in the California missions (HSSC/SCQ, 61:1, Spring 1979, p. 1–77, appendices)

An extensive and intensive review of the sources used by Cook in his 1943 book alleging the forcible conversion in missions (see *HLAS 9:2771*). Also adds additional primary and secondary materials, and concludes that the Cook thesis will not stand the test of thorough scrutiny. An interesting work of historical criticism. [EBC]

2128 ———. Mission colonization and political control in Spanish California (SDHS/J, 24:1, Winter 1978, p. 97–116, facsim.)

An earlier model for the colonization of California might be found in the policies of Escandón in the Sierra Gorda and Nuevo Santander whereby Indians were integrated with Spanish settlers. The author also reviews the policy proposals of other military men and missionaries. A fresh look at an old issue. [EBC]

2129 Guillén, Clemente. Clemente Guillén, explorer of the South: diaries of the overland expeditions to Bahía Magdalena and La Paz, 1719, 1720–1721. Translated and edited by W. Michael Mathes. Los Angeles: Dawson's Book Shop, 1979. 99 p.; bibl.; 1 fold. leaf of plates: map (Baja California travels series; 42)

English translation and annotation of the diary of a Mexican Jesuit explorer. The work emphasizes ethnography and geography. [EBC]

2130 Habig, Marion A. and **Benedict Leutenegger.** Puelles' report of 1827 on the Texas-Louisiana boundary (Louisiana History [University of Southwestern Louisiana, Louisiana Historical Association, Lafayette] 19:2, Spring 1978, p. 133–181, map)

Biography of a Franciscan missionary who lived in Texas between 1797 and 1807. In the last five years of his residence, he studied the boundary between Louisiana and Texas. In 1828, the Mexican government asked Father Puelles to summarize the case. This summary history of the borderlands, long out of print, is translated by Leutenegger and introduced and annotated by Habig in this serial. [EBC]

2131 Hale, Duane. California's first mining frontier and its influence on the settlement of that area (JW, 18:1, Jan. 1979, p. 15–21)

Brief review of silver mining in upper California from mid-17th century until 1848. Based on secondary materials including professional mining journals. Concludes that despite the discovery of silver and sporadic mining, the poverty of the area and waterlogged mines prevented their full exploitation before 1848. [EBC]

2132 Holmes, Jack. The historiography of the American Revolution in Louisiana (Louisiana History [University of Southwestern Louisiana, Louisiana Historical Association, Lafayette] 19:3, Summer 1978, p. 309–326)

Urging greater attention to the borderlands historiography of the American Revolution, Jack Holmes outlines work that has been done in the past, points out new sources, and exhorts US colonial historians to consider these issues. Galvez' victories during the Revolution were based on years of preparation. Despite enormous difficulties, Spain defended Louisiana during the war, and conquered West Florida. [EBC]

2133 ———. A new look at Spanish Louisiana census accounts: the recent historiography of Antonio Acosta (Louisiana History [University of Southwestern Louisiana, Louisiana Historical Association, Lafayette] 21:1, Winter 1980, p. 77–85)

A "preview" of a soon to be published dissertation written by a Spanish historian concerning the population of Louisiana between 1763–1803. Also contains a list of the 74 local censuses used by Antonio Acosta in his computer aided demographic study. [EBC]

2134 Hoyo, Eugenio del. La diputación de mineros en las minas ricas de los zacatecas: democracia corporativa (UCEIA/H, 18, 1977, p. 299–319, bibl.)

Established the existence of a peculiar form of local government, the *diputación*, in the mines of Zacatecas and several others in the 16th century, prior to the establishment of regular municipalities. A newly discovered archival source sustains the hipothesis that the early government of several mines was based on provisions enacted for pearl fishery settlements. *Diputados* chosen from among wealthy *vecinos* were elected to assist in the government of the mines. [AL]

2135 ———. Notas y comentarios de la *Relación* de las personas nombradas por Luis de Carvajal y de la Cueva para llevar al descubrimiento, pacificación y población del Nuevo Reino de León, 1580 (UNL/H, 19, 1978, p. 251–281)

Article is based on a recently discovered list of immigrants brought from Spain to New León by Luis de Carvajal in 1580. By comparing this document with other sources, the author uncovers several inaccuracies and discusses the limitations of the list. [AL]

2136 Jones, Oakah L., Jr. Los paisanos: Spanish settlers on the northern frontier of New Spain. Norman: University of Oklahoma Press, 1979. 351 p.; maps.

Civilian settlers, not soldiers or missionaries are the stars of this new borderlands history. The author divides the region north from Mexico into four geographic regions, and considers demography, education, economic life, land tenure, epidemics, and popular culture for each of the regions. [EBC]

2137 ———. Spanish civil communities in frontier New Mexico, 1790–1810 (*in* Hispanic-American essays in honor of Max Leon Moorhead [see item **1787**] p. 37–60)

Author stresses need to study broad social structures of Spanish colonial frontier. Using the 1790 census as a basis, he focuses on ethnic mixtures, class and family structure, forms of labor and internal migration. Results point to considerable intermixture, extended families, widespread manual labor and significant migration from central and northern New Spain. This is a commendable effort towards understanding society as a whole. Census analysis could have been more sophisticated. [AL]

2138 Kelsey, Harry. The California Armada of Juan Rodríguez Cabrillo (HSSC/SCQ, 61:4, Winter 1979, p. 313–336)

Thorough examination of both primary and secondary sources on the first expedition to upper California. Valuable for its information about sailing ships, as well as the process of assembling exploring expeditions in the 16th century. Includes lively and interesting details. [EBC]

2139 Kinnaird, Lawrence. Spanish treaties with Indian tribes (WHQ, 10:1, Jan. 1979, p. 39–48)

A unique chapter in Spanish-Indian relations in the Borderlands was written in 1771, 1784 and 1793 when diplomacy was substituted for conquest in Louisiana and West Florida. [EBC]

2140 ———. The western fringe of revolution (WHQ, 7:3, July 1976, p. 253–270, ill.; map)

Description and analysis of the importance of events in the Mississippi Valley during the revolutionary war. Underlines the role of a merchant, Olivier Pollack, in relations between Spain and the North Americans. An interesting summary based on complete familiarity with published primary and secondary sources. [EBC]

2141 ——— and **Lucia Kinnaird.** Secularization of four New Mexican missions (UNM/NMHR, 54:1, Jan. 1979, p. 35–41)

Introduction to and translation of the 1767 letters ordering the transferral of four of the 28 New Mexico missions from the Franciscans to the secular clergy. [EBC]

2142 Langum, David J. *Californios* and the image of indolence (WHQ, 9:2, April 1978, p. 181–196)

This review of European and US travel literature about the *californios* between 1800–45, reports that all observers agreed that local male residents were indolent. According to the author, visitors from industrialized countries such as these travelers tend to perceive people from less developed societies as indolent. A facile explanation for the complex origins of European and US racism (for another view, see item **2164**). [EBC]

2143 León, Gerardo de. Conflicto socio-histórico en el Cerralvo colonial (UNL/H, 19, 1978, p. 427–440)

Contains paraphrases of a late 18th-century matrimonial litigation in Cerralvo, New León. Brief local history vignette which suggests the potential usefulness of local archives for social history. [AL]

2144 Leutenegger, Benedict; Marion A. Habig; and **Barnabas Diekemper.** Notes and documents: memorial of Father Benito Fernández concerning the Canary Islanders, 1741 (TSHA/SHQ, 82:3, Jan. 1979, p. 265–296)

This annotated translation with explanatory material of the report of a Franciscan missionary clarifies a previously misunderstood incident in the history of the settlement of Texas. The memorials, presented by the settlers and the missionary response, admirably summarize the frequent conflicts between these two adversaries on the frontier. The materials also recount efforts of the government in Mexico City to resolve the issues. [EBC]

2145 McCarty, Kieran. Desert documentary: the Spanish years, 1767–1821. Tucson: Arizona Historical Society, 1976. 150 p.; ill.; index (Historical monograph; 4)

Translation of documents, with a brief introduction and notes. Suitable for text. [EBC]

2146 Mason, Bill. The garrisons of San Diego Presidio: 1770–1794 (SDHS/J, 24:4, Fall 1978, p. 399–424, plates)

Listings of the members of the San Diego garrison at several points in the first 24 years after its foundation is accompanied by some descriptive and anecdotal materials. Lacks references to modern secondary works. [EBC]

2147 Mirafuentes Galván, José Luis. La insurrección de los Seris, 1775 (MAGN/B, 3[1]:7, enero/marzo 1979, p. 3–23, ill.)

Reprint of documents from *Jails and Presidios Section* of Mexico's National Archives detailing rebellion of Seri Indians (Sonora) against Spanish settlers. [AL]

2148 New Spain's far northern frontier: essays on Spain in the American West, 1540–1821. Edited by David J. Weber. Albuquerque: University of New Mexico, 1979. 321 p.; bibl.; ill.

A much expanded version of the work in Spanish was reviewed in *HLAS 40:2583*. This English edition also includes articles by Worcester on the importance of the Borderlands to the US; Myres on ranching; Tjarks on Texas depopulation; Navarro García on the northern areas as a political problem; Schroeder, Park and Phillips on Indian policy; and Wroth on Santeros; among other contributors. Excellent selection of articles with informative introductions. [EBC]

2149 Powell, Philip Wayne. Mexico's Miguel Caldera: the taming of America's first frontier, 1548–1597. Tucson: The University of Arizona Press, 1977. 322 p.; appendices; bibl.; index; map; plates.

Life-and-times biography of a mestizo frontiersman, a discoverer of San Luis Potosí, who participated in the Chichimeca Wars. Caldera pioneered in the formation of such frontier institutions as the *presidio* and mission, he promoted Tlaxcalan migration and was an economic enterpreneur. The author uses Caldera's achievements as a method of telling the story of the 16th-century northern exploration and conquest. [EBC]

2150 Rarámuri, a Tarahumara colonial chroniclc, 1607–1791. Edited by Thomas E. Sheridan and Thomas H. Naylor. Foreword by Charles W. Polzer. Flagstaff, Ariz.: Northland Press, 1979. 144 p.; bibl.; 2 leaves of plates: ill.; index.

First publication of the *Documentary Relations of the Southwest Project of the Arizona State Museum*. A collection of representative manuscripts illustrates the Franciscan missionary efforts among the Tarahumara in 17th and 18th-century Chihuahua. Useful teaching aid. [AL]

2151 Rey, Agapito. La labor civilizadora de los misioneros en Nuevo México (ANLE/B, 2/3, 1977/1978, p. 23–33)

Extolls activities of conversion and acculturation of Franciscan friars in New Mexico. Based on well-known sources. [AL]

2152 Río, Ignacio del. Sobre la aparición y desarrollo del trabajo libre asalariado en el norte de Nueva España, siglos XVI y XVII (*in* Reunión de Historiadores Mexicanos y Norteamericanos, 5th Pátzcuaro, México, 1977. El trabajo y los trabajadores en la historia de México [see item **1979**] p. 92–111)

After a thorough and careful examination of printed primary and secondary sources, the author concludes that Indian mine workers rapidly became acculturated to a regime of free labor. Discusses issues of migration, debts and labor shortages. [EBC]

2153 Rodack, Madeline. The "lost" manuscript of Adolph Bandelier (UNM/NMHR, 54:3, July 1979, p. 182–207)

The odyssey of Bandelier's manuscript history of the Borderlands until 1700 is narrated. Manuscript has ethnographic and historical importance. [EBC]

2154 Roedl, Bohumir. La historia de José Neumann sobre la sublevación de los Tarahumaras como fuente historiográfica (UCP/IAP, 10, 1976, p. 197–209, map)

Historiographical analysis of Joseph Neumann's work on the many rebellions of the Tarahumara Indians throughout the mid-years of the colonial period. Author stresses the value of this work as a source for the study of missionaries' role, indigenous cultures and colonial socioeconomic history. [AL]

2155 Sepúlveda, César. Tres ensayos sobre la frontera septentrional de la Nueva España. México: Editorial Porrúa, 1977. 101 p.; bibl.; index; maps.

Three addresses by the noted Mexican diplomat-historian on the borderlands which deal with the disintegration of the frontier, the wars of independence, and with Luis de Onís. A popular explication which uses some of the more recent secondary sources. [EBC]

2156 Serrera Contreras, Ramón María. Pedro de Fages (*in* Congreso Commemorativo del II Centenario de la Independencia de los Estados Unidos, Madrid, 1978. n.p.: n.p., n.d., p. 243–253)

Brief but useful biography and assessment of the historical role of Pedro de Fages, twice Governor of California, career military and author of a little known but excellent *Description* of that province. [AL]

2157 Stagg, Albert. The Almadas and Alamos, 1783–1867. Tucson: University of Arizona Press, 1978. 173 p.; genealogical chart; ill.

Local history of the town of Alamos, Sonora, as it relates to the Almada family, descendants of a nephew of the first Bishop of Sonora. Largely based on secondary sources. [EBC]

2158 Strout, Clevy Lloyd. The resettlement of Santa Fe, 1695: the newly found muster roll (UNM/NMHR, 53:3, July 1978, p. 260–274, map)

Publication of a document from the Gilcrease Institute Collection which lists the settlers collected for the Juan Páez Hurtado expedition of 1695. The muster roll contains ages, family ties, provenance, and the amounts portioned out for expenses. [EBC]

2159 Swann, Michael M. The spatial dimensions of a social process: marriage and mobility in late colonial Northern Mexico (*in* Social fabric and spatial structure in colonial Latin America. Edited by David J. Robinson. Syracuse, N.Y.: Syracuse University, Department of Geography [and] University Microfilms International, 1979, p. 117–180, maps, tables)

This analysis of marriage patterns designed to determine social and spatial mobility of the population is based on the records of various parishes of Durango between the periods 1769–79 and 1792–1809. Study takes into consideration geographical origin of partners, seasonal marriage patterns of migration and racial and jurisdictional endogamy. Concludes that racial exogamy increased during periods of crisis when frequency of marriages decreased. Most cases of racial endogamy were among the white population, but between 1769 and 1809 there was a relative increase of racially exogamous marriages. A solid demographic study. [AL]

2160 Tjarks, Alicia V. Demographic, ethnic and occupational structure of New Mexico, 1790 (AAFH/TAM, 35:1, July 1978, p. 45–88, tables)

This thorough examination of 18th-century population counts from New Mexico, with special emphasis on the 1790 census, modifies earlier estimates. Includes a complete review of the literature, and an analysis of the population from the viewpoint of occupation, ethnic composition and family characteristics. [EBC]

2161 Velázquez Chávez, María del Carmen. Tres estudios sobre las provincias internas de Nueva España. México: Centro de Estudios Históricos, El Colegio de México, 1979. 170 p.; 1 leaf of plates: map (Jornadas—El Colegio de México; 87)

Contains three essays: "Los Reglamentos," "Los Indios Gentiles Apóstatas y Enemigos," and "Bernardo Bonavía y Félix María Calleja, Rivales." Author offers informative material on *presidio* regulations through the 18th and 19th centuries, indigenous groups and personal relationships among military commanders. [AL]

2162 Vizcaya Canales, Isidro. En los albores de la independencia: las Provincias Internas de Oriente durante la insurrección de don Miguel Hidalgo y Costilla, 1810–1811. Monterrey: Instituto Tecnológico y de Estudios Superiores de Monterrey, 1976. 340 p.; bibl.; index (Publicaciones del Instituto Tecnológico y de Estudios Superiores de Monterrey. Serie Historia; 14)

Surveys the history of northwest Mexico during the first six months of the war of independence. Follows the activities of the protagonists of the insurrection in the area. Well-documented study with useful comments on the sources. [AL]

2163 Walker, Billy D. Copper genesis: the early years of Santa Rita del Cobre (UNM/NMHR, 54:1, Jan. 1979, p. 5–20, plate)

Review of mining history and techniques from before the conquest to the Mexican period based on secondary sources and published primary documents. [EBC]

2164 Weber, David J. Here rests Juan Espinosa: toward a look at the image of the "indolent californios" (WHQ, 10:1, Jan. 1979, p. 61–69)

In reply to another article on the Californios and the Image of Indolence (see item **2142**) surveys the Black Legend as applied to Borderland peoples, reviewing the primary sources and examining the conditions which vitiated individual enterprise, such as lack of markets and conflicts with the missions. [EBC]

2165 Weddle, Robert S. and **Robert H. Thonhoff.** Drama & conflict: the Texas saga of 1776. Illustrated by Marvin L. Jeffreys. Austin, Tex.: Madrona Press, 1976. 210 p.; bibl.; ill.; index.

Popularly written account of Texas in 1776 focuses on the biographies and politics of four men: Hugo O'conor, Athanse de Mézières, Antonio Bucareli, and Juan María Vicencio de Ripperdá. The book also includes information on Indians, population, living conditions, trade, military and naval engagements with well-chosen selections from primary sources. An interesting work. [EBC]

2166 Wickberg, Edgar. Spanish frontiers in the Western Pacific, 1662–1700 (*in* Hispanic-American essays in honor of Max Leon Moorhead [see item **1787**] p. 12–36, maps, tables)

Drawing upon a wide collection of recent research in the history of the European powers in the Far East in the 17th century, the author concludes that the Philipines and the Marianas were a "western frontier" of New Spain rather like her Caribbean frontier. He uses abundant commercial data and describes the military and missionary aspects of the Spanish presence in the Far East. [EBC]

2167 Worcester, Donald E. The significance of the Spanish borderlands to the United States (WHQ, 7:1, Jan. 1976, p. 6–18)

New appraisal of the borderlands as an expansion of a northern frontier, fully as important as the western frontier. Appeals for serious historical consideration of the importance of growing urban Spanish-speaking or Spanish-surnamed population for the development of the US. [EBC]

MEXICO: 19th Century, Revolution and Post-Revolution

RICHARD E. GREENLEAF, *Director, Center for Latin American Studies, Tulane University*
DON M. COERVER, *Assistant Professor of History, Texas Christian University*

SEVERAL EXCELLENT HISTORIOGRAPHICAL STUDIES appeared during the last biennium. Among the best were: David Bailey on the Mexican Revolution (item **2265**); Niblo and Perry on the 19th century (item **2227**); and John Womack on the economy during the Revolution (item **2370**). Other good studies were prepared by: Benjamin (item **2173**); Mabry (item **2329**); and Velázquez (item **2255**). Border studies past and present continued to attract scholars with most of them falling into one of two categories: Contemporary-Economic (items **2294**, **2339** and **2367**) or Revolutionary-Diplomatic (items **2309–2310**, **2338** and **2365**). The excellent study of Ciudad Juárez by Oscar Martínez was an outstanding contribution (item **2332**).

Massively researched, solid studies on the 19th century continued to appear indicating a particularly productive biennium: Costeloe on the Church (item **2184**); Barker on the French in Mexico (items **2170** and **2171**); Arrom on Mexican divorce and the status of women (item **2169**); Coerver on Manuel González (item **2180**); Knowlton on the Church in Jalisco (item **2209**); and Perry on Juárez and Díaz (item **2229**). The publication of the extensive 15-volume Benito Juárez Archivo Series (1972–75) is a landmark in 19th-century Mexican documentary historiography (item **2208**).

The Revolution and Post-Revolution era also produced some interesting and well researched contributions. Among the outstanding ones were Hart on anarchism (item **2312**); Salamini on agrarian radicalism in Veracruz (item **2353**); Falcón's study of agrarianism under Cárdenas (item **2293**); González Navarro's article on forced labor (item **2199**); Katz's offering on Villa (item **2321**); and the revisionist, groundbreaking study of Harris and Sadler on the Plan of San Diego (item **2310**).

The financial fallout from the Echeverría administration and recent economic history were also the subject of much attention. The energy crisis produced a predictable output of studies of which George Grayson's two articles provided the most incisive observations (items **2304** and **2305**). Other useful works on the topic were those by Mancke (item **2330**) and Williams (item **2368**). The debate over the economic policies of the Echeverría administration continues with Fitzgerald absolving Echeverría of blame for Mexico's economic woes in the 1970s (item **2296**), with Clement and Green attributing part of the trouble to Echeverría's mismanagement (item **2281**), and with Mixon and others concluding that devaluation made Mexico even more economically dependent upon the US (item **2287**). Topical subjects such as oil and finance did not completely overshadow more traditional, economic interest in agrarian history, a field in which solid studies continue to command the interest of scholars (e.g., items **2185**, **2269**, **2280**, **2283**, **2293** and **2355**). The works by Bazant (item **2269**), Cross (item **2185**), and Schryer (item **2355**) continue the revisionist trend of recent years concerning rural working conditions. The survey of the economic scene concludes with two excellent accounts of railroad construction in the late 19th century by Hardy (item **2204**) and Juan Felipe Leal and Antonio Gálvez Gussy (item **2211**).

19TH CENTURY

2168 Arenas, Francisco Javier. Francisco Ignacio Madero, el creador de la Revolución Mexicana. México: Federación Editorial Mexicana, 1977. 249 p.; bibl.; port. (Colección Pensamiento actual)

A biographical work with appeal to younger readers; contains shrewd comment and anecdotes; portrays Madero very patriotically. The work has solidly moral air for the youth of Mexico, promoting national pride and combating discreditors of national valour.

2169 Arrom, Silvia M. La mujer mexicana ante el divorcio eclesíastico: 1800–1857. México: Secretaría de Educación Pública, Dirección General de Divulgación, 1976. 222 p. (SepSetentas; 251)

A study of divorce judgements found in the AGN, followed by a selection of nine especially interesting cases; excellent sources of information for the study of women and family and daily life; covers the arch-bishopric of Mexico, 1800–57; includes cases from all social classes, colonial as well as republican; part of the author's doctoral dissertation (Stanford University, 1976).

2170 Barker, Nancy Nichols. The factor of "race" in the French experience in Mexico, 1821–1861 (HAHR, 59:1, Feb. 1979, p. 64–80)

After carefully delineating the factor of race which was "highly elastic and subject to imaginative improvisation," the author shows the influence of French racial attitudes on policy toward Mexico as exemplified by the Pastry War of 1838–39 and the intervention of the 1860s.

2171 ———. The French experience in Mexico, 1821–1861: a history of constant misunderstanding. Chapel Hill: University of North Carolina Press, 1979. 264 p.; bibl.; ill.; index.

Solid and well-documented narrative study of the French in Mexico from Independence to Maximilian. Impressive command of French sources.

2172 Bazant, Jan. Joseph Yves Limantour: 1812–1885 y su aventura californiana (CM/HM, 28:1, julio/sept. 1978, p. 1–23)

An account of the misadventures of Limantour resulting from his acquisition of a large land grant in the San Francisco Bay area in 1843. The author details Limantour's legal problems in defending his title in the 1850s, a defense which produced large profits but which also led to Limantour being briefly jailed on charges of fraud and perjury.

2173 Benjamin, Thomas. Recent historiography of the origins of the Mexican War (UNM/NMHR, 54:3, July 1979, p. 169–181)

Acknowledging that the Mexican War has provoked more historical interest for its results than its origins, the author provides a useful survey of the literature dealing with the War's origins. He finds that the slave-power conspiracy thesis has been largely abandoned but that the Whig thesis (Polk plotted the War and the US is to blame) and the Polk-Democratic thesis (the primary responsibility for the War lies with Mexico) have gained new adherents.

2174 Blázquez, Carmen. Miguel Lerdo de Tejada, un liberal veracruzano en la política nacional. México: El Colegio de México, 1978. 201 p.; bibl.; 4 leaves of plates: ill.; index (Nueva serie—Centro de Estudios Históricos; 27)

Insightful overview of "the other" Lerdo de Tejada. Well researched.

2175 Bojorquez Urzaiz, Carlos. Estructura agraria y maíz a partir de la "Guerra de Castas" (UY/R, 20:120, nov./dic. 1978, p. 15–35)

Good description of the interplay of political, military, and agrarian policies before and during the Caste War of Yucatán. The author stresses regional differences, labor problems, and the traffic in maize in understanding the political and economic developments of the period.

2176 Bretos, Miguel A. Indices de inventarios parroquiales conservados en el Archivo de la Arquidiócesis de Mérida (UY/R, 19:115, nov./dic. 1977, p. 65–71)

Lists the legajos containing inventories of the material possessions of the churches of the Archdiocese of Yucatan. There are over 100 of such inventories, mostly belonging to the 19th century.

2177 Canto López, Antonio. La guerra de castas en Yucatán. Mérida: Universidad de Yucatán, 1976. 204 p.; bibl.

Analysis of the Caste War based on thesis that the struggle was originally a "class conflict" that degenerated into a race war because of the action of the whites.

2178 Chávez, Thomas E. Don Manuel Alvarez (de las Abelgas): multi-talented merchant of New Mexico (JW, 18:1, Jan. 1979, p. 22–31)

Description of the career of Manuel Alvarez, leading businessman and US Consul in Santa Fe in the years before the Mexican War.

2179 ———. The trouble with Texans: Manuel Alvarez and the 1841 "invasion" (UNM/NMHR, 53:2, April 1978, p. 133–144)

Background to and description of the "Santa Fe Expedition" launched by the Republic of Texas in 1841 and the problems this caused for the US Consul in Santa Fe, Manuel Alvarez.

2180 Coerver, Don M. The Porfirian interregnum: the presidency of Manuel González of Mexico, 1880–1884. Fort Worth: Texas Christian University Press, 1979. 322 p.; bibl.; index (Texas Christian University monographs in history and culture; 14)

In this historical evaluation of the González regime the author argues that González, though loyal to Díaz while in office, was really his own man while president. Author perceives economic development of Mexico under González as his greatest achievement but also the cause of his downfall.

2181 Cole, Harold L. The birth of modern Mexico, 1867–1911: American travelers' perceptions (North Dakota Quarterly [University of North Dakota, Grand Forks] 45:2, Spring 1977, p. 54–72)

The author draws on the writings of a wide variety of American travelers in Mexico to describe not only the modernization process taking place but also the American attitude toward progress in less-developed areas.

2182 Colín, Mario. Guía de documentos impresos del Estado de México, 1824–1835. México: Biblioteca Enciclopédica del Estado de México, 1976– . 1 v. (440 p.) facsims.; index (Biblioteca enciclopédica del Estado de México; 56)

A guide to published documents in state of Mexico, 1824–35; particular importance to documents concerning Lorenzo de Zavala, Coronel Melchor Múzquiz: includes some reproductions of work represented in the guide.

2183 Cortada, James W. España y Estado Unidos ante la cuestión mexicana: 1855–1868 (CM/HM, 27:3, enero/marzo 1978, p. 387–426, bibl.)

Analysis of US-Spanish rivalry over Mexico during the turbulent 1850s and 1860s. Author emphasizes the connection between Spain's Mexican policy and Spanish domestic politics and Spain's concern for her Caribbean possessions in face of US expansionism. He concludes that Mexico never figured as prominently in the diplomacy of Spain as it did in that of US and France. For political scientist's comment, see *HLAS 41:8615*.

2184 Costeloe, Michael P. Church and State in independent Mexico: a study of the patronage debate, 1821–1857. London: Royal Historical Society, 1978. 207 p.; bibl.; index.

Examination of the controversy over government control of ecclesiastical patronage from independence to the establishment of an official policy of separatism in the Constitution of 1857. The discussion often expands to include other Church-State related topics such as the economic role of the Church.

2185 Cross, Harry E. Living standards in rural nineteenth century Mexico: Zacatecas, 1820–80 (JLAS, 10:1, May 1978, p. 1–19, tables)

Another in the recent series of revisionist studies on rural living and working conditions. Analyzing the Hacienda del Maguey near the city of Zacatecas, the author concludes that the rural workers had an adequate diet, did not suffer from a declining standard of living, enjoyed discretionary income, were rarely debt peons, and were able to purchase goods at the tienda de raya at or below the prevailing market prices. For geographer's comment, see *HLAS 41:5341*.

2186 Cutter, Donald C. The legacy of the Treaty of Guadalupe Hidalgo (UNM/NMHR, 53:4, Oct. 1978, p. 305–315)

Examination of the formulation of the Treaty of Guadalupe Hidalgo and the various problems it spawned concerning Indians, boundaries, water, land, mineral rights, women's rights, and citizenship.

2187 Davids, Jules. American political and economic penetration of Mexico, 1877–1920. New York: Arno Press, 1976. 436 p.; bibl. (American business abroad)

An examination of the origins, development and fulfillment of American foreign policy in Mexico from 1821 to climax in the Mexican Revolution arranged as follows: Pt. 1, "The Seeds: Historical Introduction, 1821–1868;" Pt. 2, "The Fulfillment: the Reign of Porfirio Díaz;" Pt. 3, "The Crisis: the Madero Revolution;" and Pt. 4, "The Consummation: Triumph of Carranza," Ph.D. dissertation (Georgetown University, 1947).

2188 DeVolder, Arthur L. Guadalupe Victoria: his role in Mexican independence. Albuquerque: Artcraft Studios, 1978. 143 p.; bibl.; ill.; index.

A generally complimentary plaudit to the first president of Mexico and his struggle to override the personal ambitions and conflicting powers among the Church, the Spanish and the *criollos* as well as the rising strength of the mestizos and peons.

2189 Díaz y de Ovando, Clementina. La vida mexicana al filo de la sátira: la Intervención Francesa y el Segundo Imperio (IIE/A, 46, 1976, p. 81–108, plates)

Survey of the satire directed against the French Intervention and the Second Empire; includes satire in press, plays, art, poetry; contains several plates of contemporary political satire.

2190 Documentos: introducción a los documentos sobre la huelga en el siglo XIX (CEHSMO, 4:13, julio 1978, p. 2–27, plates)

Selection of documents illustrative of the incipient worker's movement in the second half of the 19th century in Mexico; selected from period 1870–80; questions the legality of the strikes and their results; opinions of artisans and industrialists, particularly the textile workers' strike of Hercules de Zuerétaro (1877) and the miners' strike of Real del Monte in Pachuca (1872).

2191 Ebright, Malcolm. Manuel Martínez's ditch dispute: a study in Mexican period custom and justice (UNM/NMHR, 54:1, Jan. 1979, p. 21–34)

Case study of water dispute in New Mexico in 1830s gives good insight into workings of Mexican legal system as well as into relations between the government and the ayuntamientos which were increasingly independent in their actions.

2192 El Federalismo en Jalisco: 1823. Selección de documentos e introducción de José María Muría. México: Instituto Nacional de Antropología e Historia, SEP, Centro Regional de Occidente, 1973. 79 p.; bibl.; ill.; index (Colección científica. Instituto Nacional de Antropología e Historia; 4: Historia)

A modest collection of documents concerning federalism and political life in Guadalajara in 1823; gathered from archives in Jalisco and Guadalajara municipal archives.

2193 Ferrocarriles en México: reseña histórica-reglamentos: siglo XIX. Advertencia preliminar de Luis E. Bracamontes. México: Secretaría de Obras Públicas, 1976. 456 p. in various pagings; 9 leaves of plates: ill. (Obras públicas en México; 2)

A review of the principal railroads constructed in Mexico in 1892; contains regulations governing railways in Mexico published in 1892, 1894 and 1895; photoprints of the original documents, maps, a glossary explaining railroad terminology by Luis E. Bracamontes, Secretario de Obras Públicas.

2194 Figueroa, José. Manifesto to the Mexican Republic, which Brigadier General José Figueroa, Commandant and Political Chief of Upper California, presents on his conduct and on that of José María de Híjar and José María Padrés as directors of colonization in 1834 and 1835. Translated, with an introduction and notes by C. Alan Hutchinson. Berkeley: University of California Press, 1978. 156 p.; bibl.; index.

Contains both a new translation and a facsimile of Figueroa's *Manifesto* plus a 16-p. introduction by C. Alan Hutchinson. Explanatory notes for the text clarify and offer biographical and historical information essential to understanding of the work. Hutchinson challenges Figueroa's views in light of contemporary events in Mexico and California, exonerates Híjar and Padrés of treason; a prime source of material on the Mexican period in California history.

2195 Fitchen, Edward D. Self-determination or self-preservation: the relations of independent Yucatán with the Republic of Texas and the United States, 1847–1849 (JW, 18:1, Jan. 1979, p. 32–40)

Analysis of Yucatan's separatist movements in the 1840s and the efforts of the Yucatecans to obtain aid from Texas and later the United States. Outbreak of the Caste War in 1847 changed the motivation of the separatists from self-determination to self-preservation and ultimately forced Yucatan's reincorporation into Mexico.

2196 Gibbs, William E. Díaz's executive agents and United States foreign policy: pts. 1/2 (UM/JIAS, 45:2, Spring 1977, p. 36–53; 20:2, May 1978, p. 165–190, bibl.)

Mildly revisionist interpretation of struggle in 1877–78 over US recognition of Díaz administration. Author maintains that greater emphasis should be placed on the role played by Díaz's executive agents in propagandizing the Congress and the American public into pressing the US government to extend recognition. For political scientist's comment, see *HLAS 41:8623*.

2197 Giron, Nicole. Heraclio Bernal: ¿bandolero, cacique o precursor de la Revolución? México: Secretaría de Educación Pública, Instituto Nactional de Antropología e Historia, 1976. 156 p.; bibl.; ill.; maps; tables.

Drawing on everything from archival sources to *corridos*, the author traces the career of one of Mexico's most famous bandits, Heraclio Bernal of Sinaloa. The author generally assumes a favorable attitude toward Bernal who is seen as part bandit, part cacique, and part precursor of the Revolution.

2198 González Navarro, Moisés. Anatomía del poder en México: 1848–1853. México: El Colegio de México, 1977. 498 p.; bibl.; ill.; index (Nueva serie. Centro de Estudios Históricos; 23)

Massively researched study of a crucial and relatively neglected period when Mexico was consolidating its political power after the defeat as the decision to end the era of Santa Anna was being made.

2199 ———. El trabajo forozoso en México: 1821–1917 (CM/HM, 27:4, abril/junio 1978, p. 588–615, bibl.)

In a well-written and well-organized narrative, the author tackles a major subject in both its evolution and in its regional variations. Legal approaches to forced labor to a great extent represented elaborations of colonial laws on vagrancy. The Constitution of 1857 unsuccessfully addressed the question, and various restraints on labor continued into the 20th century. The economic crisis of 1907 weakened the system which was definitively abolished by the Constitution of 1917.

2200 Graebner, Norman A. Lessons of the Mexican War (UC/PHR, 47:3, Aug. 1978, p. 325–342)

The author expertly delineates the problem President Polk encountered in trying to convert a successful war into a successful peace. The "lessons" of the war were that military invasions of backward countries more easily lead to military successes than diplomatic victories and that peace could be secured because US demands were kept "limited, tangible, and precise" (p. 342).

2201 Green, Robert Michael. *Activo Batallón de Tres Villas*: February–April 1836 (Military History of Texas and the Southwest [Military History Press, Austin] 14:1, 1976, p. 53–59)

History and organization of Mexican military unit which participated in the massacre at Goliad during the Texas Revolution.

2202 Hale, Duane. California's first mining frontier and its influence on the settlement of that area (JW, 18:1, Jan. 1979, p. 15–21)

Brief description of the influence of mining discoveries on settlement of Alta California prior to 1848.

2203 Halleck, Henry Wager. The Mexican War in Baja California: the memorandum of Captain Henry W. Halleck concerning his expeditions in Lower California, 1846–1848. Introduced and edited by Doyce B. Nunis, Jr. Los Angeles: Dawson's Book Shop, 1977. 208 p.; bibl.; 5 leaves of plates (1 fold. in pocket): ill. (Baja California travels series; 39)

"Memorandum" of one of the participants of the fighting in Lower California, Captain Henry W. Halleck, with a lengthy and excellent introduction by the author who has also added other official reports to the volume.

2204 Hardy, B. Carmon. The Sonora, Sinaloa and Chihuahua Railroad (JGSWGL, 12, 1975, p. 253–283)

An interesting and exhaustively researched account of the free-wheeling environment which surrounded railroad construction during the Porfiriato as exemplified by the building of what is now called the Chihuahua al Pacífico railway. The author assembles a fascinating cast of characters, all of whom tried unsuccessfully to build the line which was not completed until 1961.

2205 Hemerografía sobre las huelgas en el siglo XIX (CEHSMO, 4:13, julio 1978, p. 28–48)

Annotated bibliography which contains articles, organized in chronological order, from two periodicals: *El Socialista* and *El Hijo de Trabajo.*

2206 Huelga de Cananea, 1906. Edición preparada por Felipe Molina Roqueñi. México: PRI, Comisión Nacional Editorial, 1976. 35 p.: ill.

Provides brief account of the Cananea copper-mine strike of 1906 against the Green Consolidated Mining Company. Includes testimonial of miner Plácido Ríos.

2207 Hutchinson, C. Alan. General José Antonio Mexía and his Texas interests (TSHA/SHQ, 82:2, Oct. 1978, p. 117–142)

Account of the checkered career of man who played a major role in both land speculation in Texas and politics in Mexico as a supporter of federalism.

2208 Juárez, Benito Pablo. Documentos, discursos y correspondencia. Prólogo a la 2. ed. por Luis Echeverría Alvarez. Selección y notas de Jorge L. Tamayo. 2. ed. México:

Editorial Libros de México, 1972–1975. 15 v. (964, 976, 897, 871, 866, 938, 950, 925, 928, 1038, 1123, 1167, 1257, 1162, 1322 p.); ill.; indexes.

Important compilation of Juárez writings organized as follows: Vol. 1: Introduction by Jorge L. Tamayo; "Apuntes para mis Hijos" (p. 31–279); an autobiography up to 1857; his diary from Oct. 1857–July 1872; a collection of documents of Juárez's personal life; documents, speeches, press releases during Juárez's period in Oaxaca, 1833–53; the period in New Orleans and his Plan of Ayutla, 1854–55. Vol. 2: Contains documents and correspondence from 1855 up to end of the three years' war in 1860; Juárez in the Ministry of Justice; new Governor of Oaxaca, 1856; the transformation of Oaxaca, 1857; Government in crisis, 1857; Raising the banner of legality; Legal government installed in Veracruz; Constitutionalist mission at Veracruz; Issuance of Reform laws, 1859; The War of the Reform up to 1860. Vol. 3: Deals with the period of war up to 1860, particularly the Ocampo-McLane Treaty negotiations of 1859 (i.e., the Gadsden Purchase, rights of passage in Tehuantepec and Forsyth's role in the negotiations). Vol. 4: Contains diplomatic correspondence up to the end of 1860 between Mexico and President Buchanan, also diplomacy with President Lincoln; the polemical debate between Ocampo and Lerdo de Tejada. Vol. 5: Covers from the renunciation of Juárez in Sept. 1861 to the beginning of the French Intervention; contains much of the negotiations for the Tripartite Intervention. Vol. 6: March 1862–Sept. 1862; Negotiations with the allies; Napoleon's decision to put Maximilian on the Mexican throne Oct. 1861 to March 1862; the British attitudes to Juárez Feb.–April 1862; the Invasion and commencement of hostilities; the Battle of May 5 and aftermath; events of the summer of 1862. Vol. 7: Sept. 1862, González Ortega takes command; activities of Doblado and Vidaurri; Juárez in Puebla; problems with Comonfort; regional warfare; the siege of Puebla; French government in Mexico. Vol. 8: Aug. 1863 crises in Michoacán, Colima, Sonora and Sinaloa. Warfare in the provinces; the United States reaction to intervention; relations between Maximilian and Napoleon; Maximilian accepts the crown; Juárez in exile. Vol. 9: May 1864 to May 1865. Relations with US; Juárez in Monterrey; Profirio Díaz in Oaxaca; the diplomatic scene in London and Washington; Warfare in the north. Vol. 10: April 1865 to May 1866, Assassination of Lincoln; Imperial government; Juárez and his government in the north. Vol. 11: Covers from 1866 to May 1867; Porfirio Díaz's triumph in Oaxaca; crisis in Maximilian's empire; Juárez's victories in Chihuahua, Matamoros, Tamaulipas; Carlota's departure for Europe and the fall of Maximilian. Vol. 12: Covers the trial and execution of Maximilian; the late intervention of Garibaldi, Victor Hugo and Francisco José of Austria; the beginning of the new republic under Juárez; the Caste War in Yucatán; floods in Matamoros; up to Jan. 1868. Vol. 13: Contains documents, correspondence from Jan. 1868 to Oct. 1869; Sinaloa rebellion, 1868; problems with Porfirio Díaz in Oaxaca; Santa Anna and the filibusters; Juárez's reconciliation with the Díaz brothers; crisis in Querétaro. Vol. 14: Covers from Aug. 1869 to Sept. 1871; William H. Seward's visit to Mexico; Juárez's interest in women's education; death of Francisco Zarco; Zacatecas rebellion, Jan. 1870; insurrections in Jalisco, Michoacán; Mexico's policy on Cuban independence; ministerial crisis, Jan.–Feb. 1871; political intrigue, June–Sept. 1871. Vol. 15: From July 1871 to the death of Juárez, July 1872; the Díaz role in Oaxacan revolt, Aug.–Sept. 1871; administration of the Sixth Congress of the Union; rebellion in Nuevo León; revolt of La Naria; Juárez's political strategy, reelection, Dec. 1871; assassination of Félix Díaz; last acts and letters of Juárez.

2209 Knowlton, Robert J. La individualización de la propiedad corporativa civil en el siglo XIX: notas sobre Jalisco (CM/HM, 28:1, julio/sept. 1978, p. 24–61)

An excellent sub-national examination of the disamortization of corporate civil property during the 19th century. After a review of anti-corporate land legislation prior to 1856, the author deals with the impact of liberal reform legislation on both municipal and indigenous properties, focusing particularly on the financial and legal results. Suggestive of new avenues of research.

2210 Ladd, Doris M. The Mexican nobility at Independence, 1780–1826. Austin: Institute of Latin American Studies, University of Texas, 1976. 316 p.; bibl.; ill.; index (Latin American monographs; 40)

Focusing on the titled nobility, the author demonstrates that this group was Mexico's principal entrepreneurial class and was more concerned with its wealth than its noble attributes. Revisionist view of the conservative interpretation of the Revolution of Iguala.

Langum, David J. *Californios* and the image of indolence. See item **2142**.

2211 Leal, Juan Felipe and **Antonio Gálvez Gussy.** Grupos empresariales en los ferrocarriles mexicanos: el Consorcio Southern Pacific-Union Pacific, 1880–1914 (UNAM/RMCPS, 21:82, oct./dic. 1975, p. 71–119)

One in a series of studies on the 10 consortiums that dominated Mexican railroads in the late 19th and early 20th centuries. In a systematic, balanced account the authors describe the activities of one of the consortiums that they consider most important, the Central Pacific-Union Pacific group.

2212 Lecomte, Janet. La Tules and the Americans (UA/AW, 20:3, Autumn 1978, p. 215–230)

Entertaining account of the life of Gertrudis Barceló ("La Tules") social leader and gambling-hall proprietor in Santa Fe, N. Mex., in the 1830s and 1840s.

2213 Lee, James H. Church and State in Mexican higher education, 1821–1861 (BU/JCS, 20:1, Winter 1978, p. 57–72)

Examination of the relationship between Church and State in higher education within the context of an increasingly bitter conflict between the two. Author concludes that growing state intervention did not lead to a major confrontation and that educational matters played only a minor role in the increasingly violent struggle between Liberals and Conservatives.

2214 López y Rivas, Gilberto. La guerra del 47 y la resistencia popular a la ocupación. México: Editorial Nuestro Tiempo, 1976. 207 p.; bibl. (Colección Teoría e historia)

Despite the title, the author directs considerable attention to the background of the war. He concludes that the Mexican ruling class deliberately restrained the growth of popular resistance to the American occupation in order to protect their own privileged position.

2215 McCutchan, Joseph D. Mier Expedition diary: a Texas prisoner's account. Edited by Joseph Milton Nance. Foreword by Jane A. Kenamore. Austin: University of Texas Press, 1978. 246 p.; bibl.; 4 leaves of plates: ill.; index (The Elma Dill Russell Spencer Foundation series; 8)

McCutchan's diary of his experiences on the Tampico to Mexico City episode of the Mier Expedition and of his imprisonment at Perote from Dec. 1842 to Sept. 1844. Contains annotated footnotes with much detail.

2216 McGowan, Gerald L. Prensa y poder, 1854–1857: la revolución de Ayutla, el Congreso Constituyente. Prólogo de María del Carmen Ruiz Castañeda. México: El Colegio de México, 1978. 376 p.; bibl.; ill.; tables.

The author identifies three stages in government-press relations between 1854–57 which coincide with the administrations of Santa Anna (strict control of press); Juan Alvarez (complete freedom); and Ignacio Comonfort (relative freedom). Author also concludes that there was complete freedom of press during a change of administration and that there was a tendency for the press to come under tighter control as each administration evolved.

2217 Maciel, David R. Ideología y praxis. Ignacio Ramírez y el Congreso Constituyente, 1856–1857 (CAM, 221:6, nov./dec. 1978, p. 119–129)

Description of role played by Ignacio Ramírez, radical liberal, at the Constitutional Convention with particular emphasis on his views on federalism, anticlericalism, and civil rights.

2218 Maldonado L., Celia. Estadísticas vitales de la Ciudad de México: siglo XIX. México: Instituto Nacional de Antropología e Historia, SEP, Departamento de Investigaciones Históricas, Seminario de Historia Urbana, 1976. 179 p.; bibl.; map; tables (Colección científica. Instituto Nacional de Antropología e Historia; 31: Fuentes)

Contains births, deaths and marriages in Mexico City by parish for the 19th century; charts arranged by month and year; excellent sources for demographic history.

2219 Márquez, Viviane Brachet de and **Margarita Nettel.** La población de los estados mexicanos en el siglo XIX: 1824–1895. México: Instituto Nacional de Antropología e Historia, SEP, Departamento de Investigaciones Históricas, 1976. 141 p.; bibl.; ill. (Colección científica. Instituto Nacional de Antropología e Historia; 35)

First stage of a regional investigation of Mexican history in 19th century (i.e., the demography of the 19th-century in Mexico). Discusses sources, methodology, conclusions.

2220 Mexico. Archivo General de la Nación. Indice del ramo de la Junta Protectora de las Clases Menesterosas. Elaborado por Alfonso Angel Alfiero Gallegos y Miguel González Zamora. México: Archivo General de la Nación, 1977. 67 p.; 2 leaves; indexes (Serie Guías y catálogos; 7)

An index of materials in the *Archivo General de la Nación* concerning relief measures to aid the poor in Mexico from 1865–67 during Maximilian's regime; also pertains to labour administration in this period (for an excellent guide to AGN archival holdings, see item **1965**.

2221 ———. Secretaría de Fomento, Colonización, Industria y Comercio. Caminos de la República a la época de la Reforma, años de 1856–1857. Advertencia preliminar de Luis E. Bracamontes. México: Secretaría de Obras Públicas, 1976. 129, 71 p.; 8 leaves of plates (7 fold.): ill. (Obras públicas en México; 4)

Reprint of the 1857 issue of the Memoria de la Secretaría de Estado y del Despacho de Fomento, Colonización, Industria y Comercio; contains maps of roads, bridge plans, statistical information.

2222 ———. Secretaría de Relaciones Exteriores. Representantes diplomáticos de México en Washington, 1822–1973. Tlatelolco, México: Secretaría de Relaciones Exteriores, 1974. 118 p.: ill.; index (Colección del archivo histórico diplomático mexicano; 3. época. Serie documenta; 8)

A short chronology given with each representative; useful for researchers in Mexican foreign relations.

2223 México y la Gran Bretaña durante la Intervención y el Segundo Imperio mexicano, 1862–1867. Introducción, selección y traducción de Gloria Grajales. Tlatelolco, México: Secretaría de Relaciones Exteriores, 1974. 237 p.; bibl.; facsims.; index (Colección del archivo histórico diplomático mexicano; 3. época. Serie documental; 10)

Contains varied opinions concerning the trial of Maximiliano. The appendix (p. 107–220) summarizes the contents of all the documents of the Foreign Office in London on matters concerning this period in Mexican history.

2224 Milligan, James C. José Bernardo Gutiérrez de Lara; Governor of Tamaulipas (Red River Valley Historical Journal [Red River Valley Historical Association, Durant, Okla.] 2:4, Winter 1977, p. 379–394)

Description of the organizational problems faced by the first governor of Tamaulipas following the overthrow of Iturbide's Empire. Gutiérrez is best known for his military activities and his connection with the execution of Iturbide.

2225 Moyano Pahissa, Angela. El comercio de Santa Fe y la Guerra del 47. México: Secretaría de Educación Pública, 1976. 175 p. (SepSetentas; 283)

Investigates the commercial relations established after Mexican independence between Santa Fe and St. Louis, Missouri; often viewed as a profound economic and cultural invasion of Mexican territory by American scholars, the author claims that the influence of the Anglo-American merchants on the Mexican population was transitory and superficial. Using Mexican archival sources, the author challenges the "myths" created by North American scholars concerning the invasion of 1847 and the effects of North American commerce in Santa Fe.

2226 Naylor, Thomas H. The Mormons colonize Sonora (UA/AW, 20:4, Winter 1978, p. 325–342)

Description of the establishment of the Mormon colony known as Colonia Oaxaca in the Rio Bavispe in northeastern Sonora in the 1890s. The author focuses on the early years of settlement, particularly the financial problems of the colony. The colony, one of the last "wilderness experiments" of the Mormons, finally fell victim to natural disasters and the Revolution of 1910.

2227 Niblo, Stephen R. and **Laurens B. Perry.** Recent additions to nineteenth-century Mexican historiography (LARR, 8:3, 1978, p. 3–45)

Excellent review of materials published since 1969. The approach is chronological; the periodization is political; but the greatest emphasis is on the economic, particularly dependency analysis.

Nuevo León (state), *México.* **Oficialía Mayor. Dirección del Registro Civil. Archivo General del Estado. Asuntos Eclesiásticos.** Indice y catálogos de la Sección Asuntos Eclesiásticos existentes en el Archivo General del Estado: 1568–1874. See *HLAS 41:85*.

2228 Pasquel, Leonardo. Manuel Gutiérrez Zamora. México: Editorial Citlaltépetl, 1977. 120 p.; bibl.; 13 leaves of plates: ill. (Serie Gobernantes del estado. Colección Suma veracruzana)

First of series of brief biographies of governors of Mexican states. This one concerns Veracruz and Manuel Gutiérrez Zamora, governor from April 1856–57 under Presidents Comonfort and Juárez.

Penot, Jacques. Primeros contactos diplomáticos entre México y Francia: 1808–1838. See *HLAS 41:8643*.

2229 Perry, Laurens Ballard. Juárez and Díaz: machine politics in Mexico. DeKalb: Northern Illinois University Press, 1978. 467 p.; bibl.; ill.; index (The origins of modern Mexico)

Massively researched study of the transition from Reform to Dictatorship. The political underpinnings of the Porfiriato are here found in the Restored Republic. A significant contribution.

2230 Reid, Paul Joseph. The constitution of Cádiz and the independence of Yucatán (AAFH/TAM, 36:1, July 1979, p. 22–38)

An examination of the mixed groups and mixed motives that led Yucatán to declare for independence. A desire to maintain the liberalizing measures of the Constitution of Cádiz against both Spanish and Mexican authorities is a central theme.

2231 Reilly, Tom. Newspaper suppression during the Mexican War: 1846–48 (AEJ/JQ, 54:2, Summer 1977, p. 262–270, 349)

Description of censorship activities of US Army during Mexican War. Censorship was aimed not so much at preventing publication of sensitive military information as it was concerned with silencing criticism of American occupation. American-operated newspapers were censored as frequently as Mexican-operated publications.

2232 Reyna, María del Carmen. La prensa censurada, durante el siglo XIX. México: Secretaría de Educación Pública, Dirección General de Divulgación, 1976. 189 p.; bibl. (SepSetentas; 255)

An analysis of Mexican history and government custom and style of press censorship during the 19th century; contains 21 denounced articles and an appendix of authors and publications censored, along with comment on the outcome of each case.

2233 Rodríguez Losa, Salvador. Población y "Guerra de Castas" (UY/R, 20:120, nov./dic. 1978, p. 123–135)

After reviewing census data for 1846–81, author concludes that the decline in population caused by the Caste War has been exaggerated and that the population was not reduced by approximately one-half (500,000 to 250,000) as widely believed. The author attributes this error primarily to the failure to include those Indians in revolt in later census counts but does not give a specific figure himself for the decline.

2234 Romero Quiroz, Javier. Santiago Tianguistenco: Villa Tianguistenco de Galeana, primera centenario 1878–1978. México: Gobierno del Estado de México, Oficialía Mayor, 1978. 208 p.; bibl.; ill. (Colección Historia)

Brief notes for the history of this village near Chalma. Includes excerpts from some documents and nuggets of information on its toponymy, rivers, geography, dependent villages, haciendas and important citizens. [E.B. Couturier]

2235 Rosales, Amanda; Sergio Chávez; and **Mario Gijón.** La huelga en México: 1857–1880 (CEHSMO, 3:12, abril 1978, p. 2–13, plates)

Investigates the strike phenomena in Mexico following the Constitution of 1857; relations of the press to strikes; the collaboration of the Gran Círculo de Obreras with the interests of capital and labour; opens new possibilities of labor investigations.

2236 Salomon, Noël. Juárez en la conciencia francesa, 1861–1867. Tlatelolco, México: Secretaría de Relaciones Exteriores, 1975. 161 p.; bibl.; index (Colección del archivo histórico diplomático méxicano; 3. época. Obras monográficas; 7)

This work on Franco-Mexican relations received the first prize among French scholars for a study on the subject, on the 100th anniversary of Juárez's death. Author portrays the French as interventionists and opposes those who justified the French as liberal defenders of Mexican sovereignty such as Picard, Favre, Henon, Darimon and Ollivier.

2237 Sánchez D., Gerardo. El suroeste de Michoacán: estructura económico-social, 1821–1851. Morelia, México: Universidad Michoacana de San Nicolás de Hidalgo, Departamento de Investigaciones Históricas, 1979. 143 p.; bibl.; maps; tables (Colección Historia nuestra; 2)

Impressive research and use of tithe documentation to uncover economic and social patterns.

2238 Sánchez Gómez, María del Pilar. Catálogo de fuentes de la historia de Tamaulipas. v. 1, Archivo General de la Nación; v. 2, Biblioteca Nacional de México, Departamento de Manuscritos. México: Editorial Jus, 1974. 2 v.

A catalogue of materials in the AGN covering the state of Tamaulipas; 18th and 19th-centuries; materials organized under 26 headings.

2239 Schoonover, Thomas David. Dollars over dominion: the triumph of liberalism in Mexican-United States relations, 1861–1867. Baton Rouge: Louisiana State University Press, 1978. 316 p.; bibl.; index.

Viewing US-Mexican relations within the framework of a worldwide struggle between liberalism and conservatism, author contends that the US was shifting from a policy of territorial expansion to one of economic penetration (see *HLAS 40:2659*).

2240 Schwatka, Frederick. In the land of cave and cliff dwellers. Glorieta, N.M.: Rio Grande Press, 1977. 391 p.; bibl.; ill.; index (A Rio Grande classic)

Reprint of 1893 account of travels and description of Sonora and Chihuahua by Arctic explorer and former US Army officer.

2241 La servidumbre agraria en México en la época porfiriana. Introducción y selección de Friedrich Katz. Traducción de Antonieta Sánchez Mejorada. México: Secretaría de Educación Pública, Dirección General de Divulgación, 1976. 183 p.; bibl. (SepSetentas; 303)

A collection of essays dealing with working conditions in haciendas during the Porfiriato. Describes effects of capitalism on living conditions, work of peasants and tenant farmers. Consists of seven parts: Editor Katz's essay on working conditions in haciendas and six contemporary accounts of social conditions in Mexican haciendas towards end of 19th century and beginning of the 20th (three concern Yucatán, one Tabasco-Chiapas, one Central Highlands, and two the North).

2242 Sierra, Justo. Ensayos y textos elementales de historia. Edición ordenada y anotada por Agustín Yáñez. México: Universidad Nacional Autónoma de México, 1977. 517 p.; bibl.; 1 leaf of plates: port. (His Obras completas; 9. Nueva biblioteca mexicana; 57)

Pt. 1 contains essays, memoirs of the illustrious dead, contemporary celebrities, comments on books and historical events. Pt. 2 consists of three elementary texts composed by Sierra for primary school instruction on the history of Mexico: *Elementos de historia general* (1888); *Elementos de patria* (v. 1, 1894; v. 2, 1912) written for third and fourth year of primary instruction; and *El catecismo de historia patria* (1894). These three texts were complemented by 24 *Cuadros de historia patria*, descriptions of 24 murals of scenes, personages, depictions of Mexican historical events. The works are all arranged in chronological order.

Stagg, Albert. The Almadas and Alamos, 1783–1867. See item **2157**.

2244 Staples, Anne. El abuso de las campanas en el siglo pasado (CM/HM, 27:2, oct./dic. 1977, p. 177–194, bibl.)

Analysis of the role played by church bells in 19th-century life and the noise problem associated with them which produced ecclesiastical and civil efforts to curb abuse.

2245 ———. La Iglesia en la Primera República Federal Mexicana, 1824–1835. Traducción de Andrés Lira. México: Secretaría de Educación Pública, Dirección General de Divulgación, 1976. 167 p.; bibl. (SepSetentas; 237)

Sees the patronage issue and the question of diplomatic recognition as the principal issues of Church-State relations. Individual states dealt with the problem of Church relations on their own with state actions setting the stage and perhaps forcing actions at the national level under Gómez Farías in 1833. Reforms of 1833 seen as culmination of process in late colonial period rather than as forerunners of more extensive actions of Reform period.

2246 **Stapp, William Preston.** The prisoners of Perote: containing a journal kept by the author, who was captured by the Mexicans, at Mier, December 25, 1842, and released from Perote, May 16, 1844. Foreword by Joe B. Frantz. Illustrations by Charles Shaw. Austin: University of Texas Press, 1977. 226 p.; ill. (Barker Texas History Center series; 1)

Vol. 1 in the Barker Texas History Center Series; a republication of Stapp's diary of the fateful prisoners of the Mier Expedition of Dec. 1842. Frantz's foreword provides a perspective of Texan-Mexican relations in both 1842 and now. Includes vivid illustrations by Charles Shaw but unfortunately lacks maps.

2247 **Suárez Molina, Víctor M.** Espíritu y características de las regiones yucatecas en la primera mitad del siglo XIX (UY/R, 20:116, marzo/abril 1978, p. 69–83)

Author is concerned with regionalism not in the political sense of periphery vs. center but rather regional differences as they exist among various sections of the Yucatán Peninsula. Identifying four basic regions, the author outlines the social, cultural, and economic causes of these differences, many of which were eliminated by the Caste War which started in 1847.

2248 **Sweet, David.** An experiment with nineteenth-century Mexican travel accounts (PCCLAS/P, 5, 1976, p. 115–120)

Report on class project aimed at greater utilization of travel accounts in classroom situations. Includes model index for such accounts.

2249 **Tenenbaum, Barbara A.** Merchants, money, and mischief: the British in Mexico, 1821–1862 (AAFH/TAM, 35:3, Jan. 1979, p. 317–340)

Description of the confusion that existed on the part of the Mexican government over the connection—if any—between British public interests and private interests. Focusing on the career of Ewen MacKintosh, British Consul in Mexico City and leading agiotista, the author demonstrates that British merchants were able to exploit this confusion to their personal financial advantage and to Mexico's financial disadvantage.

2250 **Time-Life Books.** The Mexican War. Text by David Nevin. Alexandria, Va.: Time-Life Books, 1978. 240 p.; bibl.; ill.; index (The Old West)

Mexican-American War; contains maps of maneuvers in both sea and land operations, interesting early photographs, cartoons, flags, uniforms, arms and weapons used.

Topete, María de la Luz. Labor diplomática de Matías Romero en Washington: 1861–1867. See *HLAS 41:8652*.

2251 **Torre Villar, Ernesto de la.** Los Estados Unidos de Norteamérica y su influencia ideológica en México (UCEIA/H, 18, 1977, p. 439–474)

A longtime student of Mexican political thought skillfully blends a discussion of the positive and negative influences exercised by the US with a description of the ambivalent feelings of fear and admiration that the US has generated among Mexican thinkers. Primary emphasis is on Lorenzo de Zavala and Justo Sierra. For political scientist's comment, see *HLAS 41:8653*.

2252 **Towner, Margaret.** Monopoly capitalism and women's work during the Porfiriato (LAP, 4[12/13]:1/2, p. 90–105, bibl., tables)

Analysis of the incorporation of women into the work force, the resulting politicization of women, and their role in political movements. Presentation is hampered by the imposition of a framework of "monopoly capitalism" which is never adequately explained nor demonstrated. Based solely on secondary sources.

2253 **Tutorow, Norman E.** Texas annexation and the Mexican War: a political study of the Old Northwest. Palo Alto, Calif.: Chadwick House, 1978. 320 p.; bibl.; ill.; index.

Of interest primarily for US historians,

this work examines the political divisions that developed in Illinois, Indiana, Michigan, and Ohio over the issue of annexation of Texas and war with Mexico. The author concludes that the growing importance of the slavery issue led to greater emphasis on sectional interests and less on party advantage.

2254 Valdés, José C. Alamán, estadista e historiador. México: Universidad Nacional Autónoma de México, 1977. 576 p.; bibl.; 8 leaves of plates: ill.; index.

Biography of Lucas Alamán, reprint of 1938 ed.

2255 Velázquez, Gustavo G. La diputación del Estado de México en el supremo Congreso Constituyente de 1824: notas bibliográficas. Presentación de Mario Colín. Toluca: Dirección del Patrimonio Cultural y Artístico del Estado de México, 1977. 75 p.; bibl. (Serie Chimalphin; 2)

A study in prosopography drawn from archival sources and printed documents.

Velázquez, María del Carmen. Bibliographical essay: the Coleccion SepSetentas. See item **1983**.

Vizcaya Canales, Isidro. En los albores de la independencia: las Provincias Internas de Oriente durante la insurrección de don Miguel Hidalgo y Costilla, 1810–1811. See item **2162**.

2257 La voz de los trabajadores: periódicos obreros del siglo XIX. v. 1, *El Pueblo, La Justicia, La Voz del Obrero, El Ancora*; v. 2, *El Obrero Internacional, La Unión de los Obreros*; v. 3, *La Internacional, El Obrero Mexicano*. México: Centro de Estudios Históricos del Movimiento Obrero Mexicano, 1975. 3 v. (92, 94, 102 p.); ill.

A collection of workers' periodicals selected at random from the 19th century; most were of short duration with anthologies of longer running works. V. 1 contains: *El Pueblo* (1873–74), *La Justicia* (1875), *La Voz del Obrero* (1877) and *El Ancora* (1878); v. 2, *El Obrero Internacional* and *La Union de los Obreros* (1877); v. 3, *La Internacional* (1878) and *El Obrero Mexicano* (1894).

2258 Wasserman, Mark. Foreign investment in Mexico, 1876–1910: a case study of the role of regional elites (AAFH/TAM, 36:1, July 1979, p. 3–21)

Using Chihuahua as a case study, author provides a fascinating insight into the complex relations that evolved among national elites, regional elites, and foreign investors. The author is especially good at showing the mechanics through which these different groups interacted and their mutual economic impact. Useful example for similar regional studies.

2259 Weber, David J. Mexico's far northern frontier, 1821–1845: a criticial bibliography (UA/AW, 19:3, Autumn 1977, p. 225–266)

Valuable annotated bibliography on the Mexican period, which contains some material on the early part of the 19th century. [E.B. Couturier]

2260 Weeks, Charles A. El mito de Juárez en México. Translated by Eugenio Sancho Riba. México: Editorial Jus, 1977. 231 p.; bibl.; ill.; index.

An examination of the uses to which the myth of Juárez has been put by various individuals, groups, and governments in the century following his death in 1872. Ironically it was Porfirio Díaz, Juárez's bitter enemy, who helped make the myth an integral part of Mexican political life.

2261 Zavala, Silvio. Somero análisis de las relaciones culturales entre Francia y México (UY/R, 20:120, nov./dic. 1978, p. 47–57)

The author in his role as former Mexican Ambassador to France discusses the official and unofficial cultural relations that have existed between France and Mexico with special emphasis on the Yucatán.

2262 Zerecero, Anastasio. Memorias para la historia de las revoluciones en México. Estudio historiográfico de Jorge Gurría Lacroix. 2. ed. México: Universidad Nacional Autónoma de México, Dirección General de Publicaciones, 1975. 346 p.; bibl.; 1 leaf of plates: ill.; index (Nueva biblioteca mexicana; 38)

First published in 1869, the author wrote a liberal interpretation of Mexican independence utilizing the ideas common with other 19th-century historians (e.g., Zavala, Mora Alamán, Lerdo de Tejada). Also contains an historiographical study of the author by Jorge Gurría Lacroix (p. vii–lxx).

REVOLUTION AND POST-REVOLUTION

2263 Aguilar Camín, Héctor. La frontera nómada: Sonora y la Revolución Mexicana. México: Siglo Veintiuno Editores, 1977. 450 p.; bibl. (Historia)

Investigates the reasons for Sonora's isolation prior to the Revolution and the conditions which permitted its breakdown; describes the indigenous world of Sonora, the Yaqui war; socioeconomic conditions of prerevolutionary Sonora. The author describes post-Revolution Sonora as a triumph under the banner of *carrancistas*; part of the author's doctoral dissertation in history at El Colegio de México, 1974.

Alcocer Andalón, Alberto Historia de la Escuela de Medicina de la Universidad Autónoma de San Luis Potosí, S.L.P. (México), 1877–1977. See *HLAS 41:4500*.

2264 Authoritarianism in Mexico. Editors: José Luis Reyna and Richard S. Weinert. Philadelphia: Institute for the Study of Human Issues, 1977. 241 p.; bibl.; graphs (Inter-American politics series; 2)

Collection of nine studies from a 1975 conference dealing with authoritarianism in Mexico under the PRI. The concepts of "authoritarianism" and "cooperatism" prove troublesome as does the effort to relate authoritarianism to foreign economic dependency. Peter Smith's contribution on "elites" highlights the work. For political scientist's comment, see *HLAS 41:7137*.

2265 Bailey, David C. Revisionism and the recent historiography of the Mexican Revolution (HAHR, 58:1, Feb. 1978, p. 62–79)

Insightful survey of revolutionary scholarship since the mid-1960s. Author concludes that the traditional consensus interpretation of the Revolution has broken down but that no new "revisionist" consensus has arisen to take its place. Historians have generally directed their attention to revising limited aspects of the traditional interpretation without formulating a new, all-embracing interpretation. Important historiographical contribution.

2266 Barnhill, John H. The punitive expedition against Pancho Villa: the forced motorization of the American army (Military History of Texas and the Southwest [Military History Press, Austin] 14:3, 1976, p. 135–145)

Author demonstrates how the demands of the Pershing Expedition brought the US Army out of the 19th century and forced it to mechanize, a valuable preparation for World War I.

Barreda, Gabino. La educación positivista en México. See item **7538**.

2267 Basurto, Jorge. El proletariado industrial en México, 1850–1930. México: Universidad Nacional Autónoma de México, Instituto de Investigaciones Sociales, 1975. 298 p.; bibl.

Utilizing a larger time span than most recent labor studies, the author examines Mexico's working class movement with particular attention to the complicated period of the 1920s.

2268 Bazant, Jan. A concise history of Mexico from Hidalgo to Cárdenas, 1805–1940. Cambridge; New York: Cambridge University Press, 1977. 222 p.; bibl.; index.

Essentially a political history of Mexico during the national period, the author focuses on the struggle for land as the central theme in modern Mexican history. Such a focus brings with it built-in limitations, not the least of which is the cut-off date of 1940. Withal, a good survey of the time period involved.

2269 ———. La hacienda azucarera de Atlacomulco, México, entre 1817 y 1913 (JGSWGL, 14, 1977, p. 245–268, tables)

Analysis of a relatively small sugar hacienda near Cuernavaca by one of the leading figures in hacienda studies. Study is of interest due to the long run of accounts upon which it is based, the connection between the hacienda and the Lucas Alamán family, and the hacienda's obviously commercial orientation in the face of absentee ownership. Numerous financial tables.

Bibliografía histórica mexicana: 1976–1978. See *HLAS 41:18*.

2270 Bose, Johanne Caroline Wehmeyer. Farewell to Durango: a German lady's diary in Mexico, 1910–1911. Translated by John Carlos Bose. Edited by Robert W. Blew. Lake Oswego, Or.: Smith, Smith, and Smith Pub. Co., 1978. 93 p.; bibl.; ill.; index (A Western Americana book)

Acute observations of the beginnings of the Mexican Revolution; no profound reflections but much of the daily anxieties of civil war; also contains problems encountered by immigrants in the New World, class prejudices, pro-Díaz view of the business sector, and the strength and determination of the middle-class Victorian women.

2271 Braddy, Haldeen. The paradox of Pancho Villa. Illustrations by Manuel Acosta. El Paso: Texas Western Press, 1978. 95 p.; bibl.; 2 leaves of plates: ill.; index.

The author explores the impact of Villa on the US, the contradictions in his bizarre personality, and relates examples of his reputation as a madman. The book seeks to find the major facts and legends with which to reconcile the puzzling aspects of Villa's paradoxical character. Braddy is recognized as the dean of Villa writers.

2272 Britton, John A. Carlton Beals on the ambiguities of revolutionary change in Mexico and Peru (Studies in the Social Sciences [West Georgia College, Carrollton] 17, June 1978, p. 89–97)

Examination of Beals' attitude toward elite-led revolutionary change among the rural masses. Beals, often accused of being blindly pro-revolutionary, was often critical of the agrarian policies of the leftist Mexican government and the Apristas of Peru.

2273 ———. Teacher unionization and the corporate state in Mexico, 1931–1945 (HAHR, 59:4, Nov. 1979, p. 674–690)

Analysis of the evolution of Mexican teachers' unions with particular emphasis on efforts by the state to dominate these unions. Government efforts to extend its influence over the teachers led to considerable friction in the 1930s, but the 1940s saw greater cooperation between the two with the corporate state finally coopting the teachers.

2274 Broussard, Ray F. The Puebla revolt: first challenge to the Reform (JW, 18:1, Jan. 1979, p. 52–57)

Description of the abortive Conservative revolt at Puebla in 1856 against the Comonfort regime. Provides a good picture in miniature of the problems that would later lead to the War of the Reform.

2275 Cabrera, Luis. Obras completas. v. 1, Obra jurídica; v. 2, Obra literaria; v. 3/4, Obra política. México: Ediciones Oasis, 1975. 4 v. (1097, 580, 1007, 1074 p.); appendix; glossary; tables.

The collected works of the lawyer-journalist turned rebel who was best known as an advisor to Carranza. Collection demonstrates that Cabrera may have been a rebel but he was never a social revolutionary.

2276 Camp, Roderic Ai. La campaña presidencial de 1929 y el liderazgo político en México (CM/HM, 27:2, 1977, p. 231–259, bibl., tables)

The author argues convincingly that the unsuccessful Vasconcelos presidential campaign of 1929 had a long-range impact on the political leadership. He analyzes the sources of Vasconcelos' support particularly among the university students and the reasons for their support. Defeat in 1929 encouraged rather than discouraged greater political participation by the Vasconcelistas most of whom subsequently dropped their opposition stance and went over to the official party. For political scientist's comment, see *HLAS 41:7097*.

2277 ———. Mexican political biographies, 1935–1975. Foreword by Peter H. Smith. Tucson: University of Arizona Press, 1976. 468 p.; appendices; bibl.

Author provides biographical information on 902 persons using 12 different categories. Valuable reference tool for students of 20th-century Mexican history. For political scientist's comment, see *HLAS 41:7099*.

2278 Cárdenas, Lazaro. La única acción anti-imperialista latinoamericana (CAM, 218:3, mayo/junio 1978, p. 163–171)

Copy of President Cárdenas' Decree of 18 March 1938 nationalizing the foreign-owned oil companies.

2279 Chassen de López, Francie R. Lombardo Toledano y el movimiento obrero mexicano, 1917–1940. México: Editorial Extemporáneos, 1977. 285 p.; bibl.; tables.

The author does a good job of blending a description of the career of Lombardo Toledano with a discussion of the urban labor movement in the 1920s and 1930s while placing both in the broader context of Mexican political development.

2280 Chevalier, François. Un factor decisivo de la Revolución agraria en México: el levantamiento de Zapata, 1911–1919

(CNC/RMA, 8:2, abril/junio 1975, p. 61–84)

One of the leading authorities on Mexican land tenure analyzes the role played by the Zapatista movement in the agrarian revolution. The author does an excellent job of placing the movement in its historical context, provides a good portrait of Zapata, furnishes a survey of the various agrarian reform measures adopted, and explains why Zapata and Morelos played such central roles in agrarian unrest.

2281 Clement, Norris and **Luis Green.** The political economy of devaluations in Mexico (IAMEA, 32:3, Winter 1978, p. 47–75, bibl., tables)

Analysis of the causes, timing and initial results of Mexico's devaluation of the peso in 1976. The authors attribute Mexico's deteriorating financial-economic position in 1976 to long-term development policies, international economic conditions, and Echeverría's mismanagement. While the devaluation has apparently achieved its intended goals, more fundamental changes are needed to solve Mexico's economic problems. For economist's comment, see *HLAS 41:2951.*

2282 Clements, Kendrick A. Emissary from a revolution: Luis Cabrera and Woodrow Wilson (AAFH/TAM, 35:3, Jan. 1979, p. 353–372)

Description of Cabrera's diplomatic role in three major issues between the US and Mexico: the lifting of the arms embargo, the Niagara Falls Conference, and the Joint Commission negotiations of 1916–17. The author concludes that, while Cabrera was not always successful in his negotiations, he played a major role in influencing Woodrow Wilson's attitude toward the Revolution and in restraining Wilson's interventionist tendencies.

2283 Climo, Jacob. Collective farming in northern and southern Yucatán, Mexico: ecological and administrative determinants of success and failure (AAA/AE, 5:2, May 1978, p. 191–205, bibl.)

Author contends that it is misleading to compare the ejido with the private sector in view of the different constraints and incentives under which the two function. Local variables involving both administrative and ecological considerations play a critical role in the success or failure of the ejido. For anthropologist's comment, see *HLAS 41:897.*

2284 Coatsworth, John H. Obstacles to economic growth in nineteenth-century Mexico (AHA/R, 83:1, Feb. 1978, p. 80–100, tables)

The author rejects the traditional interpretation that the principal obstacles to economic growth were Spanish colonial rule, the land-tenure system, and the economic activities of the Catholic Church. He postulates that the two main obstacles to economic growth in the 19th century were: an inadequate transportation system and an inefficient economic organization, largely the product of the political-legal environment. Very well organized with the emphasis on the pre-1877 period.

2285 Cosío Villegas, Daniel. Memorias. México: J. Mortiz, 1977. 320 p.; indexes; 4 leaves of plates (Confrontaciones: Los Testigos)

Contains author's memoirs from early childhood up to Luis Echeverría; describes the details of the founding of El Colegio de México; the compilation of his *Historia moderna de México;* contains abundant reference to political events, foreign travels, his studies at home and abroad, completed before his death in 1976.

Cottler, Susan M.; Roger M. Haigh; and **Shirley A. Weathers.** Preliminary survey of the Mexican Collection. See *HLAS 41:72.*

2286 Craig, Richard B. La campaña permanente: Mexico's antidrug campaign (UM/JIAS, 20:2, May 1978, p. 107–131, bibl.)

Analysis of Mexico's drug problem, the federal government's campaign in regard to it, and its effect on US-Mexican "narcotics diplomacy." For biological anthropologist's comment, see *HLAS 41:1647.*

2287 Las crisis en el sistema política mexicano, 1928–1977. México: El Colegio de México, Centro de Estudios Internacionales, 1977. 217 p.; bibl.; ill. (Colección Centro de Estudios Internacionales; 19)

Collection of essays dealing with both historical and contemporary political and economic crises. Topics range from divisions within the PAN to the impact of the 1976 devaluation on the political system.

2288 Documents on the Mexican Revolution. v. 3, The election of Madero, the rise of Emiliano Zapata and the Reyes plot in

Texas. Edited by Gene Z. Hanrahan. Salisbury, N.C.: Documentary Publications, 1978. 446 p.; facsims., indexes.

Continuation of earlier documentary publications (see *HLAS 40:2725*).

Dorantes, Alma; José María Muría; and **Jaime Olveda.** Inventario e índice de las misceláneas de la Biblioteca Pública del Estado de Jalisco. See *HLAS 41:73*.

2289 Enríquez Coyro, Ernesto. El Tratado entre México y los Estados Unidos de América sobre Ríos Internacionales: una lucha nacional de noventa años. México: Universidad Nacional Autónoma de México, 1975. 2 v. (671, 1338 p.) appendices; bibl.; chronology; index; maps (Serie Estudios; 47)

An important study of a major topic in US-Mexican relations by a man who was actively involved in negotiations over international waters. (He produced the legal study which was the basis for the Mexican diplomatic position in 1944.) The author traces the problem from the Treaty of La Mesilla in 1853 to the Treaty on International Waters in 1944. Based on exhaustive research in Mexican archives and the records of the International Boundary and Water Commission. For political scientist's comment, see *HLAS 41:8618*.

2290 Essays on the Mexican Revolution: revisionist views of the leaders. By William H. Beezley and others. Introduction by Michael C. Meyer. Edited by George Wolfskill and Douglas W. Richmond. Austin: University of Texas Press, 1979. 136 p.; bibl.; 8 leaves of plates: ill. (The Walter Prescott Webb memorial lectures; 13)

Diverse and balanced anthology with a fine introduction by Michael C. Meyer.

2291 La expropiación petrolera. Introducción y selección de Juan Barona Lobato. Tlatelolco, México: Secretaría de Relaciones Exteriores, 1974. 303 p. (Colección del archivo histórico diplomático mexicano; 3. época. Serie documental; 11)

Includes the most important judicial documents related to the oil expropriation and the diplomatic despatches related to the question. Introduction discusses its relevance to Mexico today with regard to the energy crisis of the 1970s.

2292 Fabela, Isidro. Mis memorias de la Revolución. Editadas por la Comisión de Investigaciones Históricas de la Revolución Mexicana. México: Editorial Jus, 1977. 316 p. (Documentos históricos de la Revolución Mexicana)

With a predictably pro-Carranza bias, the First Chief's former Minister of Foreign Relations offers his insights and observations on the late Porfiriato and early years of the Revolution.

2293 Falcón, Romana. El surgimiento del agrarismo cardenista: una revisión de las tesis populistas (CM/HM, 27:3, enero/marzo 1978, p. 335–386, bibl.)

A lengthy examination of the continuities and differences between the Cardenist regime and its predecessors. With extensive research and excellent organization, the author revises the "populist" interpretation of Cárdenas as put forward by authors such as Arnaldo Córdova. The author challenges the idea that Calles regime was "overthrown" by popular pressure and depicts Cárdenas as pro-agrarian but moderate. He maintains that agrarian unrest and influence have been exaggerated and that Cárdenas owed his position as much to military support as mass support.

2294 Fernández, Raúl A. The United States-Mexico border: a politico-economic profile. South Bend, Ind.: University of Notre Dame Press, 1977. 174 p.; index; maps; tables.

Defining the border region in economic terms, the author identifies the uneven economic development of the region as its principal source of difficulties, a situation which he attributes most recently to the activities of multinational corporations in the region. He views the Border Industrialization Program as repressive and exploitative and generally sees a gloomy future for the border zone.

2295 Ferrua, Piero. Gli anarchici nella Rivoluzione Messicana: Praxedis G. Guerrero. Ragusa, Italy: La Fiaccola, 1976. 163 p.; bibl.

First in a proposed series of monographs dealing with the role played by anarchists in the Mexican Revolution. The author maintains that Guerrero's influence on the Revolution should be upgraded but his efforts to connect Guerrero with contemporary guerrilla movements in Latin America seems strained.

2296 FitzGerald, E.V.K. The state and capital accumulation in Mexico (JLAS, 10:2, Nov. 1978, p. 263–282)

Survey of Mexican economic development since 1940, focusing on the changing role of the state in capital accumulation and culminating in the "fiscal crisis" of the 1970s. Author concludes that public sector activities have not crowded out private sector activities and that the crisis of the 1970s was not the result of economic mismanagement by Echeverría but rather due to structural problems in the Mexican development model.

2297 Furman, Necah S. *Vida Nueva*: a reflection of Villista diplomacy, 1914–1915 (UNM/NMHR, 53:3, April 1978, p. 171–192)

Using Villa's official newspaper, *Vida Nueva*, the author traces the domestic rise and fall of Pancho Villa as well as his changing attitude toward the US during the crucial years of 1914–15.

2298 The future of Mexico. Edited by Lawrence E. Koslow. Tempe: Center for Latin American Studies, Arizona State University, 1977. 241 p.; bibl.

Collection of papers presented at conference at Arizona State University divided into four main categories: economic, political, demographic, and international.

2299 Gilderhus, Mark T. Diplomacy and revolution. Tucson: University of Arizona Press, 1977. 159 p.; bibl.; index; map.

Mildly revisionist examination of Wilsonian relations with revolutionary Mexico. The author maintains that Wilson sought to maintain the Revolution within the bands of "liberal capitalism" which came into conflict with Carranza's effort to follow another widely-espoused Wilsonian principle, national self-determination. Well researched from US and Mexican archives. For political scientist's comment, see *HLAS 41:8624*.

2300 Gómez, Marte R. Historia de la Comisión Nacional Agraria. México: Centro de Investigaciones Agrarias, Secretaría de Agricultura y Ganadería, 1975. 359 p.; bibl.; port.

Compiled from documents left by Marte R. Gómez, Secretario de Agricultura from 1929–30 and from 1941–46; covers the history of the organization from 1916–24.

2301 Gómez Jara, Francisco. Anarquismo y populismo en Costa Grande bajo el obregonismo (CNC/RMA, 8:1, enero/marzo 1975, p. 95–112)

The author uses three biographical case studies to demonstrate the formation of "Mexican bonapartism" in the state of Guerrero during the 1920s. Weakly documented and often polemical, the author's own phrase describes the basic problem of the work: "there exists great ideological confusion" (p. 112).

2302 González, Heliodoro. The ultimate cosmetic touch for U.S.-Mexican relations (IAMEA, 33:3, Winter 1979, p. 85–96)

Title refers to appointment of Robert Krueger as Ambassador-at-Large to Mexico. Author depicts President Carter's Mexican policy as a bungled affair, beginning with the appointment of Ambassador Lucey, a "politician who would have had difficulty distinguishing between *braceros* and bananas" (p. 87).

2303 González Loscertales, Vicente. La colonia española de México durante la Revolución Maderista, 1911–1913 (RUC, 26:107, enero/marzo 1977, p. 341–365)

Concentrating primarily on the period before Madero's rise to power, the author demonstrates that Spainards in Mexico underestimated the Madero revolt while overestimating the strength of Díaz. Spanish nationals generally did not take sides in fighting prior to the overthrow of Díaz, but there was some support afterwards for anti-Madero forces, especially for Félix Díaz. Based on Archives of the Spanish Ministry of Foreign Relations.

González-Polo, Ignacio *comp.* Bibliografía general de las agrupaciones y partidos políticos mexicanos: 1910–1970. See *HLAS 41:30*.

2304 Grayson, George W. Mexico and the United States: the national gas controversy (IAMEA, 32:3, Winter 1978, p. 3–27)

While partially outdated by rapidly changing events in the international energy picture, this is an excellent survey of the natural-gas dispute which complicated US-Mexican relations between 1977 and 1979. The author concludes with some thoughtful policy recommendations that are still relevant to the US-Mexican energy relationship. For political scientist's comment, see *HLAS 41:8627*.

2305 ———. Oil and US-Mexican relations (UM/JIAS, 21:4, Nov. 1979, p. 427–456, bibl.)

Veteran observer of Mexico's oil development discusses energy and its effects on US-Mexican relations, particularly in terms of its "linkage" to other issues such as illegal aliens. Research partially based on 30 interviews with high-level officials of both governments. Article of interest to historians, economists, and political scientists.

2306 Guerrero, Práxedis G. Artículos literarios y de combate, pensamientos, crónicas revolucionarias, etc. México: Centro de Estudios Históricos del Movimiento Obrero Mexicano, 1977. 109 p. (Cuadernos obreros; 14)

A collection of writings and chronicles of the pre-revolutionary anarchist who died at age 28 after a confrontation with federal troops in Chihuahua on 30 Dec. 1930; also contains a prologue by Ricardo Flores Magón. For a recent historical study of Guerrero, see item **2295**.

2307 Hansis, Randall. The political strategy of military reform: Alvaro Obregón and revolutionary Mexico, 1920–1924 (AAFH/TAM, 36:2, Oct. 1979, p. 197–233)

Analysis of Obregón's efforts to modernize, depoliticize, and "moralize" the Mexican Army. Extensive discussion of the Murguía revolt of 1922 and the De la Huerta revolt of 1923 as examples of success of Obregón's reforms. Based on US and Mexican archival resources.

2308 Harper, James W. The El Paso-Juárez Conference of 1916 (UA/AW, 20:3, Autumn 1978, p. 231–244)

Well-researched analysis of Scott-Obregón conference called to deal with status of Pershing Expedition in Mexico. While conference produced no official accord, author concludes that it reduced tensions on border and helped buy time for Wilson administration to deal with German problems.

2309 ———. Hugh Lenox Scott y la diplomacia de los Estados Unidos hacia la Revolución Mexicana (CM/HM, 27:3, enero/marzo 1978, p. 427–445, bibl.)

Examination of the role played by the "old soldier of the frontier," Gen. Hugh Scott in Wilson's Mexican policy from his first contacts with Villa in 1914, through the Naco crisis of 1914–15, down to the de facto recognition of Carranza which Scott opposed. The author does not deal with the Scott-Obregón conference of 1916 which is covered in another article. For political scientist's comment, see *HLAS 41:8630*.

2310 Harris, Charles H., III and **Louis R. Sadler.** The Plan of San Diego and the Mexican-United States war crisis of 1916: a re-examination (HAHR, 58:3, Aug. 1978, p. 381–408)

Utilizing a broad array of sources, the authors demonstrate that the Plan of San Diego was not a Huertista operation but rather a Carrancista action that helped bring not only diplomatic recognition to Carranza but also came close to precipitating a war between the US and Mexico. It is well written and includes a cast of colorful characters (some Japanese were included, but probably not the Germans). This is one of the best articles of the biennium.

2311 Harrison, Benjamin T. Chandler Anderson and business interests in Mexico, 1913–1920: when economic interests failed to alter U.S. foreign policy (IAMEA, 33:3, Winter 1979, p. 3–23, bibl.)

Focusing on the activities of Chandler Anderson, former State Department official and lobbyist for several major firms doing business in Mexico (Phelps-Dodge, Doheny, International Harvester), the author demonstrates that business interests were consistently unsuccessful in influencing Wilson's Mexican policy.

2312 Hart, John Mason. Anarchism & the Mexican working class, 1860–1931. Austin: University of Texas Press, 1978. 249 p.; bibl.; ill.; index.

The author traces the evolution of Mexican anarchism from its mostly Spanish origins to its virtual suppression under Porfirio Díaz to its rebirth in the early 20th century under the Flores Magón brothers and its influence on the Revolution through the Casa del Obrero Mundial. Author concludes that the anarchist movement did not achieve its goals but did seem to promote a more militant agrarianism and working class activism.

2313 ———. The urban working class and the Mexican Revolution: the case of the Casa del Obrero Mundial (HAHR, 58:1, Feb. 1978, p. 1–20)

Reexamination of the role of the Casa in the Revolution from its organizational stage beginning in 1909 down to its climatic and unsuccessful showdown with the Constitutionalist government during the general strike of July–Aug. 1916.

2314 Hellman, Judith Adler. Mexico in crisis. New York: Homes & Meier Publishers, 1978. 229 p.; bibl.; 6 leaves of plates: ill.; index.

One of the better offerings in the recent works analyzing the "crisis" in the Mexican political system. The familiar items of unfulfilled promises, favoritism of the rich, exploitation of the poor, and unresponsiveness of the PRI are all examined with an especially good discussion of the cooptation process in the political system.

2315 Henderson, Peter V.N. Mexican exiles in the borderlands, 1910–13. El Paso: Texas Western Press, 1979. 55 p.; bibl.; 4 leaves of plates: ill. (Southwestern studies; 58)

Vigorously written story of Madero and anti-Madero exiles in the American southwest as the Revolution accentuated 1910–13.

2316 Hernández, Salvador. El magonismo 1911: la otra revolución (CP, 4, abril/junio 1975, p. 26–41)

Analysis of the Magonista revolution in Baja California in 1911. The author does a good job of tying in the Magonista revolt with the Madero revolution and political movements in the US but his conclusion about the reasons for the failure of the revolt (the machinations of North American annexationists and capitalists) is strained.

2317 Herrera, Ana María A. Vida y obra del periodista Luis B. Herrera Juárez (UCEIA/H, 18, 1977, p. 321–361, bibl.)

Biography of the journalist-historian Luis B. Herrera Juárez with special emphasis on his political writings on the government of Nuevo León. Exhaustive bibliography of subject's works.

2318 Horn, James J. Mexican oil diplomacy and the legacy of Teapot Dome (Studies in the Social Sciences [West Georgia College, Carrollton] 17, June 1978, p. 99–112)

Author demonstrates how the Teapot Dome scandal and its aftermath helped to create a domestic situation which moderated the American response to Calles' policies toward American oil companies.

2319 Interpretaciones de la Revolución Mexicana. Adolfo Gilly and others. Prólogo de Héctor Aguilar Camín. México: Universidad Nacional Autónoma de México, 1979. 150 p.

Five interpretative essays on the Mexican Revolution, presented at a seminar of UNAM's Economics Faculty, June 1977. Adolfo Gilley explores the rural revolutionary struggle and its impact on the historical conscience of Mexico's masses; Arnaldo Córdova follows the transition from a national oligarchic state to the modern state, capable of institutionalizing the politics of the masses; Armando Bartra writes of the Revolution from the perspective of "magonismo;" Manuel Aguilar Mora refers to the Revolution as "Bonapartist;" Enrique Semo describes the revolution as a capitalist development.

2320 Iwańska, Alicja. The truths of others: an essay on nativistic intellectuals in Mexico. Cambridge, Mass.: Schenkman Pub. Co., 1977. 124 p.; bibl.

Study of two popular issues in Mexican history—incorporation of the Indian into modern society and the question of identity—through the case studies of two Indianist organizations, one "realist" (the Association of Mexican Indian Professionals & Intellectuals) and the other "utopian" (the Movement of Reappearance of Anauk).

2321 Katz, Friedrich. Pancho Villa and the attack on Columbus, New Mexico (AHA/R, 83:1, Feb. 1978, p. 101–130, plates)

Revisionist interpretation of the motivation behind Villa's attack on Columbus. Author maintains that traditional motives offered (anger at Wilson's recognition of Carranza; desire for revenge against cheating arms dealers and/or bankers; need for supplies and arms; effort to attract German aid) are at best secondary in importance. Primary motive was Villa's belief that Carranza had sold out to US.

Keesing, Donald B. Employment and lack of employment in Mexico: 1900–70. See *HLAS 41:2963*.

2322 Kirchner, Louisa D. México, en busca de su identidad: la faz cultural de su Revolución. Prólogo de Joaquín Ruiz-Giménez. Traducción del inglés. Madrid:

Ediciones Iberoamericanas, 1973. 229 p.; bibl.

Concise and eloquent description of the Ateneo de la Juventud and the extraordinary cast of personalities (e.g., Alfonso Reyes, José Vasconcelos, Pedro Henríquez Ureña, A. Caso, etc.) whose writings reflected the most significant cultural and intellectual changes caused by the Mexican Revolution. [Pedro F. Hernández]

2323 **Krauze, Enrique; Jean Meyer;** and **Cayetano Reyes.** La reconstrucción económica. México: El Colegio de México, 1977. 323 p.; bibl.; ill.; index (Historia de la Revolución Mexicana; 10. Período 1924–1928)

Covers public finance, the public debt, transportation, the economy and agriculture, social classes and laws.

2324 **La France, David G.; Fred Lobdell;** and **Maurice Leslie Sabbah.** Fuentes históricas para el estudio de Puebla en el siglo XX (CM/HM, 27:2, oct./dic. 1977, p. 260–272)

Detailed description of bibliographical tools and archives (including addresses) of use to students of history of Puebla in 20th century.

2325 **Lavrov, N.M.** The Supreme Revolutionary Convention: from the history of the Mexican Revolution, 1910–1917 (*in* Soviet historians on Latin America [see item **1817**] p. 256–272)

Another treatment of the Convention at Aguascalientes in 1914–15. Despite the author's Marxist framework, his presentation differs from earlier accounts primarily in terminology rather than interpretation. Carranza is dismissed as a bourgeois landowner whereas Villa and Zapata are presented as sincere—if disorganized—leaders of the radical masses. Undoubtedly, Obregón would have been surprised to find himself regarded as part of the "anarchosyndicalist" government leadership.

2326 **Lecturas** de política mexicana. México: El Colegio de México, Centro de Estudios Internacionales, 1977. 376 p.; bibl.

Collection of 11 articles previously published in *Historia Mexicana* or *Foro Internacional* dealing with a wide variety of topics ranging from the army to the PAN.

2327 **León, Samuel.** Alianza de clase y cardenismo: junio de 1935–febrero de 1936 (UNAM/RMCPS, 23:89, julio/sept. 1977, p. 25–76)

An investigation of the alliance of the working class with the Cárdenas faction, el Comité Nacional de Defensa Proletaria.

Lindvall, Karen. Research in Mexico City: a guide to selected libraries and research centers. See *HLAS 41:124.*

2328 **Lyon, Jessie Sanders.** Huerta and Adachi: an interpretation of Japanese-Mexican relations, 1913–1914 (AAFH/TAM, 34:4, April 1978, p. 476–489)

An interesting account of the triangular relationship involving US, Mexican, and Japanese diplomacy during the Huerta administration. While each party attempted to exploit differences between the other two parties, the author concludes that all three wound up as losers: Adachi's activities aroused fears about Japanese expansionism; Huerta was overthrown, and Woodrow Wilson was forced to intervene militarily. Based primarily on Department of State records. For political scientist's comment, see *HLAS 41:8631.*

2329 **Mabry, Donald J.** Mexican anticlerics, bishops, cristeros, and the devout during the 1920's: a scholarly debate (BU/JCS, 20:1, Winter 1978, p. 81–92)

An historiographical essay on the five major works on Church-State relations in Mexico in the 1920s written by historians from four different countries (Robert Quirk, David Bailey, Nicolas Larin, Alicia Olivera Sedaño, and Jean Meyer). The author concludes that Meyer's work is the best of the lot, a fact partly attributable to his nationality (French).

2330 **Mancke, Richard B.** Mexico's petroleum resources (CUH, 76:444, Feb. 1979, p. 74–77, 90)

Brief review of Mexico's rising position in oil production in the 1970s with particular attention to potential US markets and indirect economic benefits to the US. Author's viewpoint is essentially American and economic which may account for the optimistic view of López Portillo's willingness and ability to help meet US energy needs.

2331 **Markets in** Oaxaca. Edited by Scott Cook and Martin Diskin. Foreword by Sidney W. Mintz. Austin: University of Texas Press, 1976. 329 p.; bibl.; ill.

Consists of 12 essays by 10 authors describing one of the largest and oldest native market systems in Mexico. For ethnologist's comment, see *HLAS 39:1040.*

2332 Martínez, Oscar Jáquez. Border boom town: Ciudad Juárez since 1848. Austin: University of Texas Press, 1978. 231 p.; bibl.; 8 leaves of plates: ill.; index.

An excellent, well-researched history of "The Queen of the Bordertowns;" particularly focuses on the dynamics of trade which have shaped the growth and development of Juárez. Concludes that Juárez has developed an economy with a strong external orientation. Also treats aspects of local social history, i.e., migration, political and military events; provides valuable insights into understandings of international boundaries and the economy of the whole Mexican northern border.

2333 México en el siglo XX [i.e. veinte]: textos y documentos. t. 1, 1900–1913; t. 2, 1913–1920. Compiladores: Mario Contreras y Jesús Tamayo. México: Universidad Nacional Autónoma de México, Facultad de Filosofía y Letras, Centro de Estudios Latinoamericanos, 1975. 2 v. (528, 408 p.) bibl. (Lecturas universitarias; 22)

An undergraduate's anthology of history, economics, literature, politics. Sections are devoted to land tenure, social oppression, foreign capital, the political and labor struggle according to three periods: 1) the Porfiriato; 2) the pre-revolutionary stage; 3) the Maderista stage. Very useful as a college text.

2334 Meyer, Lorenzo. El conflicto social y los gobiernos del Maximato. México: El Colegio de México, 1978. 335 p.; bibl.; ill.; index (Historia de la Revolución Mexicana; 13. Período 1928–1934)

Covers the economy, the workers' movement, agrarian reforms, state relations in Veracruz, Chihuahua, and San Luis Potosí.

2335 ———. Los grupos de presión extranjeros en el México revolucionario, 1910–1940. Tlatelolco, México: Secretaría de Relaciones Exteriores, 1973. 102 p.; bibl. (Colección del archivo histórico diplomático mexicano; 1)

A study of foreign pressure groups affecting Mexican economic and political stability during the Revolution from 1910 to 1930; uses documents from Mexican Foreign Affairs Secretary, US Department of State and personal archives of US Ambassador Josephus Daniels and President Woodrow Wilson, with particular emphasis on mining and petroleum interest groups.

2336 ———; Rafael Segovia; and **Alejandra Lajous.** Los inicios de la institucionalización: la política del Maximato. México: El Colegio de México, 1978. 314 p.; bibl.; ill.; index (Historia de la Revolución Mexicana; 12. Período 1928–1934)

Covers the consolidation of power from the death of Obregón to the rise of Lázaro Cárdenas to the presidency.

2337 Millett, Richard. John Wesley Butler and the Mexican Revolution, 1910–1911 (Studies in the Social Sciences [West Georgia College, Carrollton] 17, June 1978, p. 73–87)

Impressions of the Madero revolution by one of the leading Protestant ministers and prominent member of the American community in Mexico City.

Montoya Briones, José de Jesús. Estructura de poder y desarrollo social en la sierra de Hidalgo. See *HLAS 41:946.*

2338 Mumme, Stephen P. The Battle of Naco: factionalism and conflict in Sonora, 1914–15 (UA/AW, 21:2, Summer 1979, p. 157–186)

Analysis of the Maytorenista-Carrancista confrontation at Naco, Sonora, with its international and internal implications. The author provides an excellent description of the series of broken agreements that marked the affair and the US role in the ultimate settlement. For another study of the subject, see *HLAS 40:2724.*

2339 ———. Mexican politics and the prospects for emigration policy: a policy perspective (IAMEA, 32:1, Summer 1978, p. 67–94)

Examination of the illegal immigration problem as an issue in Mexican politics with emphasis on the institutional constraints confronting the Mexican government in dealing with it. Author concludes that, because of political and economic restraints, there is little likelihood that the Mexican government will formulate a comprehensive emigration policy. For political scientist's comment, see *HLAS 41:7128.*

2340 Ochoa Campos, Moisés. Calles, el estadista. México: Editorial Trillas, 1976. 175 p.; bibl.; ill. (Colección Occidente; 5)

The author covers a broad range of topics from Calles' views on women to his attitudes towards banks. The author's approach is to let the Calles' record speak for itself with the result that the work is considerably less than the political biography implied by the title.

O'Gorman, Edmundo. México, el trauma de su historia. See item **1978**.

2341 Ojeda, Mario. Alcances y límites de la política exterior de México. México: El Colegio de México, 1976. 220 p.; bibl. (Colección Centro de Estudios Internacionales; 17)

Analysis of Mexico's foreign policy since World War II. Author maintains that, despite Mexico's geographic position and economic dependence upon the US, Mexico was able to pursue a relatively more independent foreign policy than any other Latin American nation. For political scientist's comment, see *HLAS 41:8638*.

2342 La otra cara de México, el pueblo chicano. Prólogo: Carlos Monsiváis. Compilador: David R. Maciel. México: Ediciones El Caballito, 1977. 369 p. (Colección Fragua mexicana; 29)

Collection of 13 essays with vaguely Marxist focus aimed at countering the negative attitude in Mexico toward Chicanos and at analyzing the formation and significance of the Chicano population in the US.

2343 Pancho Villa: intimate recollections by people who knew him. Edited by Jessie Peterson and Thelma Cox Knoles. New York: Hastings House, 1977. 279 p.; bibl.; 8 leaves of plates: ill.; index; map (on lining papers).

Interviews reflecting both the *norteño* and American attitudes toward Villa. Much of the information is secondhand and of questionable historical value.

2344 Paoli, Francisco J. and **Enrique Montalvo.** El socialismo olvidado de Yucatán; elementos para una reinterpretación de la revolución mexicana. México: Siglo Veintiuno Editores, 1977. 232 p.; appendices; bibl.; 2 leaves of plates: ill. (Historia)

Effort to fit the early revolutionary history of Yucatán into a broader framework of political evolution from traditional oligarchy to middle-class populism to a populist government based on socialism and class struggle. According to the authors, the Porfiriato represents the first stage, the regime of Salvador Alvardo the second, and the administration of Felipe Carrillo Puerto the third.

2345 Pellicer de Brody, Olga and **Esteban L. Mancilla.** El entendimiento con los Estados Unidos y la gestación del desarrollo estabilizador. México: El Colegio de México, 1978. 299 p.; bibl.; ill.; index (Historia de la Revolución Mexicana; 23. Período 1952–1960)

Final installment in the multi-volume work on the Mexican Revolution and the second of two volumes directed to the 1950s. As with the previous volume a topical approach is employed in discussing political and economic developments during the period. See also item **2346**.

2346 ——— and José Luis Reyna. El afianzamiento de la estabilidad política. México: El Colegio de México, 1978. x, 222 p.; bibl.; ill.; index (Historia de la Revolución Mexicana; 22: Período 1952–1960)

Next-to-last volume in monumental study of Mexican Revolution started under the direction of Daniel Cosío Villegas. Collection of topical essays on political and economic activities of the 1950s. See also item **2345**.

Popp, Kilian and **Konrad Tyrakowski.** Der caserío Metepec, Atlixco: zur Entwicklung einer frühen Industreisiedlung in Mexiko. See *HLAS 41:5362*.

2347 Raby, David L. Ideology and state-building: the political function of rural education in Mexico, 1921–1935 (IAA, 4:1, 1978, p. 21–37, bibl.)

Classifying the Obregón-Calles era as a "Bonapartist" interlude between the factionalism of the early Revolution and the mass movements of the 1930s, the author analyzes the Sonoran dynasty's emphasis on education, especially in rural areas. Education involved an "official" history, a national mythology, and a strident anticlericalism which actually became an obstacle to the development of a national revolutionary bloc. For comment by education specialist, see *HLAS 41:4520*.

Ramírez Casteñeda, Rafael. La escuela rural mexicana. See *HLAS 41:4521.*

2348 Reisler, Mark. By the sweat of their brow: Mexican immigrant labor in the United States, 1900–1940. Westport, Conn.: Greenwood Press, 1976. 298 p.; bibl.; index.

Mildly polemical but still useful study of the immigration work, and settlement patterns of Mexican workers. Extensive use of US archival sources.

Reunión de Historiadores Mexicanos y Norteamericanos, *5th, Pátzcuaro, México, 1977.* El trabajo y los trabajadores en la historia de México—Labor and laborers through Mexican history: ponencias y comentarios presentados en la V Reunión de Historiadores Mexicanos y Norteamericanos, Pátzcuaro, 12 al 15 de octubre de 1977. See item **1979**.

2349 *Revista Coahuilense de Historia.* Colegio Coahuilense de Investigaciones Históricas. Vol. 1, No. 1, mayo/junio 1978– . Saltillo, México.

New journal devoted to the history of Coahuila consists of articles on the origins of the city of Saltillo, Coahuila during the Reforma, the foundation of Parras (ca. 100 p.). The rest of the journal provides documents and bibliography (ca. 30 p.). For bibliographer's comment, see *HLAS 41:168.* [Ed.]

2350 Ricardo Flores Magón: su vida, su obra, en un estudio de B. Cano Ruiz y 42 cartas (en faccimil [sic] escritas en inglés durante los dos últimos años de su prisión y de su vida. Traducidas al castellano por Proudhon Carbó. México: Editores Mexicanos Unidos, 1976. 221 p.: ill.

Contains a brief biography of Flores Magón plus a Spanish translation of his 42 letters to Ellen White written in English during the last two years he served at Fort Leavenworth prison.

2351 Robles, Martha. Educación mexicana: una incógnita y tres programas (CAM, 217:2, marzo–abril 1978, p. 51–67)

Survey of Mexican education through three "programs" or stages: 1) educational developments under Vasconcelos during the 1920s; 2) a period of efforts to adjust education to an environment of increasing industrialization lasting through the mid-1960s; and 3) a period of educational crisis and attempted reform stretching through the 1970s. The "unknown" factor is the new National Plan for Education introduced in 1977. For the author's book on education and society in Mexican history, see *HLAS 41:4524.*

Rodríguez de Lebrija, Esperanza. Indice analítico de la *Guía del Archivo Histórico de Hacienda.* See *HLAS 41:94.*

2352 Roman, Richard. Church-State relations and the Mexican Constitutional Congress, 1916–1917 (BU/JCS, 20:1, Winter 1978, p. 73–80)

Analyzing the debate at the Constitutional Convention, the author concludes that the Church question was a political issue not a religious issue and that the restrictions placed upon the Church were nationalistic in motivation and aimed at promoting the ideological domination of the emerging nation-state.

2353 Salamini, Heather Fowler. Agrarian Radicalism in Veracruz, 1920–38. Lincoln: University of Nebraska Press, 1978. 239 p.; bibl.; index; maps.

Traces the course of the Veracruz peasant movement from its origins in Porfirian Mexico; focuses on the dynamics of peasant organization and examines the changing nature of peasant leadership over a 50-year period; compares types of organizational techniques used by state and national peasant caudillos; views Tejada and Cárdenas in a new historical light; employs archival materials and interviews with a large number of peasant leaders and public officials involved in the events of the Veracruz peasant movement.

2354 Schmidt, Henry C. The roots of *lo mexicano*: self and society in Mexican thought, 1900–1934. College Station: Texas A&M University Press, 1978. 195 p.; bibl.; index.

Examines the origins and development of *lo mexicano* in the works of Ramos' intellectual antecedents, i.e., Justo Sierra, Antonio Cuso, José Vasconcelos, Alfonso Reyes, and Cosío Villegas; explains how Mexicans went about defining national character in this period; shows the growth of Mexican self awareness as the intellectual foundation of nationalism. For philosopher's comment, see item **7654**.

2355 Schryer, Frans J. A ranchero economy in northwestern Hidalgo, 1880–1920 (HAHR, 59:3, Aug. 1979, p. 418–443)

Focusing on the Sierra Alta region of Hidalgo, the author challenges the traditional interpretation of rural life in which a small number of hacendados are arrayed against a mass of landless peasants and instead finds a significant role played by the ranchero class.

2356 Shapira, Yoram. Mexico's foreign policy under Echeverría: retrospect (IAMEA, 31:4, Spring 1978, p. 29–61)

While some may disagree with the author's conclusions concerning the significance and persistence of foreign policy changes under the Echeverría administration, he clearly demonstrates the linkage between Echeverría's domestic and foreign policies and extensively discusses various areas where Echeverría departed from traditional Mexican policy. For political scientist's comment, see *HLAS 41:8649*.

2357 Siller Rodríguez, Rodolfo. La crisis del Partido Revolucionario Institucional. México: B. Costa-Amic, 1976. 219 p. (Colección Ciencias sociales; 15)

The author identifies not a single crisis but several crises including the declining power of the party, the concentration of power in the executive, the possibility of a split between the government and the party, and the threat of a split within the ranks of the PRI. For political scientist's comment, see *HLAS 41:7141*.

2358 Sloan, John W. United States policy responses to the Mexican Revolution: a partial application of the bureaucratic politics model (JLAS, 10:2, Nov. 1978, p. 203–308)

Good survey of US-Mexican relations between 1911–41 in which the author tests two popular interpretations: the bureaucratic-politics model and dependency theory. The author concludes that relations during this period tend to support the bureaucratic-politics model and that dependency theory proves overly simplistic.

2359 Smith, Peter H. The Mexican Revolution and the transformation of political elites (CEDLA/B, 25, dic. 1978, p. 3–20, tables)

Concludes that the Mexican Revolution was led by the middle class; Smith also discovers the increased participation of the middle class, a decrease in the presence of the upper class and a gradual rise in the lower class participation among the political elites; the Revolution redistributed political power among relatively dispossessed segments of the middle class, compares Mexico's political elites with other nation's elites.

Stavenhagen, Roldofo and others. Neolatifundismo y explotación: de Emiliano Zapata a Anderson, Clayton & Co. See *HLAS 41:2972*.

2360 Taracena, Alfonso. La vida en México bajo Avila Camacho. México: Editorial Jus, 1976. 2 v.

A highly critical account of the Avila Camacho years by the well-known political commentator of *Novedades*. The author accuses Avila Camacho of selling out to the US during World War II and places considerable emphasis on political corruption during the period.

2361 Townsend, William Cameron. Lázaro Cárdenas, Mexican democrat. With a foreword by Frank Tannenbaum. 2. ed. Waxhaw, N.C.: International Friendship, 1979. 408 p.: ill.

This second edition includes six additional chapters on Cárdenas from 1951 to his death in 1970.

2362 Ulloa Ortiz, Berta. La encrucijada de 1915. México: El Colegio de México, 1979. 267 p.; bibl.; ill.; index (Historia de la Revolución Mexicana; 5. Périodo 1914–1917)

Vigorously written and well researched with fresh material on Carrancismo 1914–17.

2363 Vaughan, Mary K. Women, class, and education in Mexico, 1880–1928 (LAP, 4[12/13]:1/2, 1977, p. 135–152, bibl.)

Description of the impact that the extension of education and other public services had on the socioeconomic role of women. Effectiveness of presentation is reduced by effort to force it into questionable ideological framework.

2364 Views across the border: the United States and Mexico. Edited with an introduction by Stanley R. Ross. Albuquerque: University of New Mexico Press, 1978. 456 p.; bibl.; index.

Collection of articles growing out of 1975 conference on border. A wide variety of topics are discussed (ecology to economics) by an equally diverse group of academicians and politicians. For political scientist's comment, see *HLAS 41:8647*.

2365 Vigil, Ralph H. Revolution and confusion: the peculiar case of José Inés Salazar (UNM/NMHR, 53:2, April 1978, p. 145–170)

Fascinating account of one of the most colorful military figures to arise during the early years of the Revolution along the border. Salazar was successively: a Magonista, a Maderista, a Vasquista, an Orozquista, a Huertista, a would-be Carrancista, and finally a Villista.

2366 Vollard, Klaus. Das Dritte Reich und Mexiko. Bern, Switzerland: Verlag Peter Long, 1976. 364 p.; bibl.; index.

Analysis of the shifting fortunes of German-Mexican relations during the volatile period from 1933 to 1942. Relations were uneventful between 1933 and 1936 but soured between 1936 and 1938 over Hitler's more aggressive foreign policy especially toward Spain. Mexico's expropriation of the foreign oil companies and its political fallout led to closer relations between the two countries, a relation which ended when German submarines sank Mexican tankers and Mexico declared war.

2367 Walker, William O., III. Control across the border: the United States, Mexico, and narcotics policy, 1936–1940 (UC/PHR, 47:1, Feb. 1978, p. 91–106)

Examination of the relation between US narcotics diplomacy and Mexican narcotics policy. Author clearly documents the success of American efforts in the late 1930s to have Mexico adopt a more punitive and legalistic approach to narcotics problem.

2368 Williams, Edward J. Oil in Mexican-US relations: analysis and bargaining scenario (FPRI/O, 22:1, Spring 1978, p. 210–216)

Analysis of the energy issue within the framework of US-Mexican relations in general with particular emphasis on the factors conditioning Mexico's position. The author connects the energy issue with trade/debt relations, illegal immigration, the drug traffic, technological aid, and nationalism. General outlook for settlement of problems is optimistic. For political scientist's comment, see *HLAS 41:8655*.

2369 Williman, John B. La Iglesia y el Estado en Veracruz, 1840–1940. México: Secretaría de Educación Pública, 1976. 189 p.; appendix; bibl. (SepSetentas; 289)

Survey of Church-State relations at state level highlighted by lengthy period of peaceful coexistence from 1863 to 1929. The calm ended in 1929 when radical governor Adalberto Tejeda instituted strict enforcement of anticlerical legislation. Anticlerical campaign came to an end under Cárdenas administration as a result of pressure from federal government.

2370 Womack, John. The Mexican economy during the Revolution, 1910–1920: historiography and analysis (RU/MP, 1:4, Winter 1978, p. 80–104)

Excellent review of the literature—or lack of it—dealing with the economic results of the Revolution. The author challenges the traditional idea that the 1910–20 period can be dismissed simply as a destructive period economically, maintains that too much emphasis has been placed on institutional change, particularly in terms of liberating the economy, and concludes that the judgements of social and political histories must be grounded in the history of production and distribution.

CENTRAL AMERICA

MURDO J. MACLEOD, *Professor of History, University of Arizona*

POLITICAL TURBULENCE AND CHANGE have spread throughout Central America in the last two years, a development which has greatly affected publishing in most of the countries.

In Panama where the question of the canal appears to be settled, writings of varying quality have been issued. Many Panamanian writers were at pains to point out that nationalism and rejection of Colombian sovereignty antedated US intervention. As in previous years, the question of the canal became a bonanza enterprise for those interested in other aspects of Panamanian history. Many primary documents were printed in the last two years, usually as appendices to books or articles.

The revolution which overthrew the Somoza dynasty in Nicaragua dominated events throughout the country, overshadowing everything else. Several biographies of the Revolution's hero and martyr, Augusto César Sandino, were published including some of high quality such as those by Fonseca (item **2449**), Ramírez (item **2475**) and Selser (item **2486**). In the meantime, the Banco de América in Managua continued its program devoted to reprinting Nicaraguan classics and unknown writers, many of them carefully edited by Franco Cerutti who also contributed further additions to his study of the Jesuit Order in Nicaragua (items **2438** and **2439**).

In El Salvador as in Guatemala, continuing guerrilla warfare inhibited publication. Certainly works issued in the last two years are generally disappointing.

Honduras continues to be somewhat of a backwater as far as the writing of history is concerned, with most of its publications consisting of traditional biographies of notable men, and nostalgic evocations and mood pieces about days gone by. There are, however, some notable exceptions, including a fine pioneering essay by Mario Posas on the origins of the Honduran working class movement (item **2473**).

Costa Rican historians continue to lead as the most sophisticated in Central America. Several combine careful archival research with imaginative, statistical manipulations of large quantities of data. Gudmundson's works exemplify this social science approach (items **2452** and **2453**). Belizean history has also made noticeable advances, as exemplified by Bolland's recent works (items **2373–2374** and **2394**).

Certain types of history are more dominant in Central America than elsewhere. The political biography, a vanishing genre in some Latin American countries, is still very common, and in the last two years, in addition to the above mentioned books on Sandino, there have been biographies published on José Figueres, Ramón Villeda Morales, and Manuel Barahona Jiménez.

Although colonial history attracted only a handful of new authors, some of the established ones produced outstanding books. Rubio Sánchez's series on colonial ports told us much about Realejo and Trujillo, and about the colonial economy in general (item **2416**). And finally, the most important book of the last two years on Central American colonial history is William Sherman's (item **2422**). Indeed, works on the colonial era continue to excel those on the national period, at least in quality if not in quantity.

GENERAL

2371 Ashdown, Peter D. The perversion of history: a critique of Stephen L. Caiger's *British Honduras: past and present* (JBA, 6, Jan. 1978, p. 37–50)

A ferocious but often well-argued attack on Caiger's work. Caiger is accused of white ethnocentrism, elitism, and romanticism.

2372 Becerra, Longino. Síntesis de la historia de Honduras. 4. ed. Tegucigalpa: Editorial R. Amaya Amador, 1976. 25 p. (Colección Cultura)

A sketchy history of Honduras told as a struggle between exploiters and exploited. The argumentation is strident and thin.

2373 Bolland, O. Nigel. Slavery in Belize (JBA, 6, Jan. 1978, p. 3–36, tables)

Belizean slavery was not associated with plantations but with lumbering. The nature, economics, and geography of Belize and of logging, especially after the shift to mahogany, enabled the slaves to obtain somewhat better treatment and to escape to Maroon communities more frequently. An interesting attempt to combine the Tannenbaum national-legal view of slavery, and the economic determinism of the opposing view.

2374 ——— and **Assad Shoman.** Land in Belize, 1765–1871. Mona: Jamaica: Institute of Social and Economic Research, University of the West Indies, 1977. 142 p.; bibl.; 1 fold. leaf of plates; index; map (Law and society in the Caribbean; 6)

A history of land tenure patterns from the early days of settlement, through the period of elite settler domination, to the Crown colony era (1838–71). The book concludes with a chapter which discusses the impact of these historical patterns on present-day land ownership, land use, and agricultural development. Several interesting primary documents can be found in the appendices. For anthropologist's comment, see *HLAS 41:1008.*

2375 Calderón Ramírez, Salvador. Aquino, Morgan y Paterson. 2. ed. San Salvador: Ministerio de Educación, Dirección de Publicaciones, 1974. 141 p. (Biblioteca popular; 9)

A series of impressionistic essays about Anastasio Aquino, the leader of an Indian revolt in El Salvador in 1833; Henry Morgan, the pirate, his life and his raids in Panama; and William Paterson, leader of the ill-fated Scots colony in Darién.

2376 Castellanos García, J. Efraín. El diario de una patria, 1976: almanaque nacional, agenda histórica y turística de Honduras. 2. ed. n.p.: Imprenta Calderón, 1976. 431 p.; bibl.; ill.

An almanac, organized in a confusing way, of the most notable events of Honduran history. The reader must know the exact date of an event before looking it up.

2377 Flores Andino, Francisco A. El Reino de la Mosquitía (YAXKIN, 1:2, enero 1976, p. 43–50, bibl., plate)

Anecdotes and snippets of archival information about the kings, royal families and Kingdom of Mosquitía.

2378 Flores Macal, Mario. Orígenes de las formas de dominación en El Salvador. San José: Universidad de Costa Rica, Facultad de Ciencias Sociales, 1977. 185 p.; bibl.; maps; tables (Avances de investigación; 4:29)

A thorough study from printed sources of labor exploitation and monopolization of land and production in their various forms, going back to the early colonial period.

2379 Goytía, Víctor Florencio. Estampas del acontecer. San José, Costa Rica: Lehmann, 1974. 350 p. (His Crónicas breves; 2. Publicaciones del Instituto Panameño de Cultura Hispánica)

In vol. 2 of his *Crónicas breves,* Goytía offers a large collection of short essays, many of a page or two, taken from Panamanian newspapers, in which he comments on news of the day, Panamanian history, and world affairs. The tone is light and amusing, and occasionally shrewd.

2380 Guatemala. Secretaría de Relaciones Exteriores. Breve resumen de la disputa guatemalteca con la Gran Bretaña sobre el territorio de Belice: 1783–1977. Guatemala: Ministerio de Relaciones Exteriores, 1977. 36 p.; maps.

A brief statement of the official Guatemalan government view on this old and difficult dispute.

2381 Gudmundson, Lowell. Aspectos socioeconómicos del delito en Costa Rica: 1725–1850 (UNCR/R, 3:5, julio/dic. 1977, p. 101–148, tables)

Gudmundson now turns to late colonial and early national crime to give us insights to the laws and morality of the period in Costa Rica. As usual in the work of this author the research is thorough and the analysis fresh and stimulating.

2382 Jáen Suárez, Omar. Los llanos de Chirú: evolución del primer latifundio de Coclé desde 1690 hasta 1977 (USMLA/LA, 6:9, nov. 1977, p. 233–258, maps, tables)

Describes the formation of a great rural estate on the Pacific coast, southwest of the city of Panama. Ownership, land use, and labor force are all studied. Well documented.

Láscaris, Constantino. Algunos pensadores centroamericanos. See item **7581**.

2383 Lemaitre Román, Eduardo. Panamá y su separación de Colombia. Prólogo de Abelardo Forero Benavides. 2. ed., corr. y aumentada. Bogotá: Banco Popular, 1972. 724 p.; bibl.; ill.; index (Biblioteca Banco Popular)

A long detailed history of Panamanian difficulties with Colombia. Panama's early attempts to break away, foreign interest in the isthmus, the attempted French canal, the role of Theodore Roosevelt, and the final break with Colombia, are all explained lucidly. A major contribution from the Panamanian point of view.

2384 Menon, P.K. The Anglo-Guatemalan territorial dispute over the colony of Belize (British Honduras) (JLAS, 2:2, Nov. 1979, p. 343–371)

A history of the background to the dispute and an analysis of the treaties and agreements involved. Menon favors an independent Belize, free from ties to Great Britain or Guatemala, and attacks modern Guatemalan insistence on its claims to the area.

2385 Miranda Flamenco, Jaime. El añil en El Salvador (MNDJG/A, 50, 1977, p. 43–63)

A short history of the indigo dye industry in El Salvador drawn mostly from secondary sources.

2386 Noriega Hurtado, Luis C. La lucha heróica de un pueblo por su independencia y liberación (LNB/L, 263, enero 1978, p. 17–34)

A chronological and rudimentary listing of Panama's struggles for independence and for ownership of the canal.

2387 Pector, Desire. Exposición sumaria de viajes y trabajos geográficos sobre Nicaragua durante el siglo XIX (BNBD, 18, julio/agosto 1977, p. 66–69)

A very brief, schematic review of some 19th-century writers who discussed Nicaragua.

2388 Pérez Estrada, Francisco. Ensayos nicaragüenses. Managua: Fondo de Promoción Cultural, Banco de América, 1976. 191 p.; bibl.; index (Serie Ciencias humanas; 1. Colección Cultural Banco de América)

An anthropologist looks at the Nahuas of Nicaragua; magical thought and rituals from an historical point of view; the Nicaraguan folk hero, the Güegüense; and a socioeconomic history of land tenure in Nicaragua.

2389 *Revista Lotería.* Lotería Nacional de Beneficencia. No. 228, feb. 1975– Panamá.

Lotería continues to be one of the best historical journals of the isthmus. This issue contains excellent articles on early slavery in Panama, on the Latin American wars of independence, and on the influence of the Enlightenment in America in general.

Veblen, Thomas T. Native population decline in Totonicapán, Guatemala. See *HLAS 41:5326*.

2390 Zepeda-Henríquez, Eduardo. Folklore nicaragüense y mestizaje (BNBD, 18, julio/agosto 1977, p. 173–184)

A light discussion of the picaresque Nicaraguan folkloric figure, the mestizo Güegüense. His history is traced from its remotest origins.

COLONIAL

2391 Arellano, Jorge Eduardo. Oviedo y la provincia de Nicaragua (BNBD, 24, julio/agosto 1978, p. 1–5)

A quick biography of Oviedo and a discussion of his journeys in Nicaragua and description of the area.

2392 ———. El prócer centroamericano Tomás Ruiz (BNBD, 17, mayo/junio 1977, p. 1–22, bibl.)

This whole issue is devoted to the Nicaraguan priest and scholar Tomás Ruiz, a forerunner of Central American independence. In addition to Arellano's article on Ruiz's life and activities, the volume (total 91 p.) includes essays by Gene A. Muller on Ruiz's formation as a revolutionary, and by Conde de Pecchio on his impact on others. Ruiz's own writings are represented by two sermons and a petition to the Crown for clemency. The volume concludes with a bibliography of works on Ruiz and a list of his writings and sermons. An essential compilation for students working on Ruiz, and useful for an understanding of the early 19th century and of independence in Nicaragua.

2393 Barrantes Ferrero, Mario. Un caso de la esclavitud en Costa Rica. 2. ed. corr.

San José: Instituto Geográfico Nacional, 1973. 5 p.

By following the life of a slave, mainly through notarial records, the author is able to make some suggestions about master-slave relations and the lives of slaves in late colonial Costa Rica.

2394 **Bolland, O. Nigel.** The social structure and social relations of the settlement of the Bay of Honduras, Belize, in the 18th century (UWI/JCH, 6/7, May/Nov. 1973, p. 1–42, tables)

An interesting and chatty attempt to move away from the traditional diplomatic and political histories of British Honduras towards a social history of the first settlers and of relations among them and with their slaves.

2395 **Buhler, Richard.** How the British won the Battle of St. George's Caye (BISRA/BS, 7:5, Sept. 1979, p. 11–17)

The British won by preventing the Spanish forces from bringing to bear their superior numbers. The Spanish lost because of poor planning and unfamiliarity with these coastal waters. The victory gave Belize permanency and the Spanish never returned. For another article on this subject, see item **2403**.

2396 **Cabezas, Horacio de Jesús.** Los primeros veinticinco años del régimen de tierras en el Reino de Guatemala 1527–1563 (IGFO/RI, 36:145/146, julio/dic. 1976, p. 31–50, plates, tables)

A study of the first official distributions of urban lots and farm lands to the conquerors and first settlers around the capital city.

2397 **———.** Las reducciones indígenas en Guatemala durante el siglo XVI. Guatemala: Facultad de Humanidades, Universidad de San Carlos de Guatemala, 1974. 105 p.; appendix; bibl.

A solid little monograph based on published and archival sources. Author deals with the juridical and governmental background of the *reducciones,* how Indians were gathered together in these new concentrated villages, Bishop Marroquín's role, the monastic orders, Indian leaders in the operation, and changes which occurred in some Indian villages because of the *reducciones.* Guatemala (1547) was the first area where *reducciones* were carried out systematically. There is an appendix of useful documents.

2398 **Carlés, Rubén Darío.** Historia (USMLA/LA, 6:9, nov. 1977, p. 25–40)

An anecdotal, narrative study of early Spanish penetration of Panama and of Santa María la Antigua del Darién.

2399 **Estrada Monroy, Agustín.** Andrés de las Navas y Quevedo: Obispo de Nicaragua (BNBD, 25, sept./oct. 1978, p. 20–42, plate)

A brief biography of the 17th-century Bishop, born in Andalucia and Bishop of Nicaragua (1677), enemy of the civil governors, and, in this article at least, defender of the Indians and other oppressed groups. The essay consists mostly of long letters from the Bishop to the authorities in Spain. In 1683, Navas y Quevedo was promoted to the bishopric of Guatemala and Verapaz.

2400 **Fernández, León.** Colección de documentos para la historia de Costa Rica. v. 1, Conquista y poblamiento en el siglo XVI: relaciones histórico-geográficas; v. 2, Encomiendas y reducciones: indios no sometidos, Matina. San José: Editorial Costa Rica, 1976. 2 v. (452, 446 p.); bibl. (Biblioteca Patria; 2, 4)

Selections in two volumes from a very important, 10-volume, documentary collection on the Costa Rican colonial period. The conquest, demographics, *reducciones* of Indians, and the cacao plantations of the Matina valley are all emphasized.

2401 **Gudmundson, Lowell.** Los juegos prohibidos y el régimen colonial en Costa Rica (UNCR/R, 3:5, julio/dic. 1977, p. 171–186, bibl.)

By studying forbidden games and sports and some of the laws and cases involved, the author offers some insights into the nature of social control in colonial society. Most cases are drawn from the early 18th century.

2402 **Hernández Aparicio, Pilar.** Problemas socioeconómicos en el Valle de Guatemala: 1670–1680 (IGFO/RI, 37:149/150, julio/dic. 1977, p. 585–637, maps, tables)

Deals with abuses of the labor repartimiento and with the *visitas* of Juan de Solís (1670) and of Jerónimo Chacón Abarca (1679) to the area to correct the situation. Wheat farmers reacted strongly to the possible labor restrictions, but new regulations were promulgated in 1680. The essay and appendices contain a wealth of information on the Valle.

2403 Humphreys, H.F. The Battle of St. George's Caye; a new analysis: pt. 2 (BISRA/BS, 7:5, Sept. 1979, p. 1–10)

A detailed analysis of the battle and its aftermath, which tries to stick to facts and to deglamorize the events. The essay concludes by discussing the various competing claims to sovereignty over Belize.

2404 Hurtado y Plaza, Blas. Memorial de mi vida. Presentado, trascrito y anotado por Carlos Molina Argüello. Nicaragua: Banco de América, 1977. 332 p.; bibl.; index (Serie Ciencias humans; 7. Colección Cultural)

A manuscript by an 18th-century Nicaraguan Franciscan found in the AGI by Carlos Molina Argüello. Largely autobiographical, it also tells us much about the ambiance in Nicaragua and Costa Rica at that time. In a long, informative prologue, the editor puts Hurtado y Plaza in the setting of his times and compares him to other writers of the period.

2405 Kinzhalov, R.V. Indian sources for the history and ethnography of highland Guatemala: the tenth to the sixteenth centuries (*in* Soviet historians on Latin America [see item **1817**] p. 77–88)

A brief but thorough review of ethnohistorical sources. Especially valuable for review and reference purposes.

2406 Luján Muñoz, Jorge. Fundación de villas de ladinos en Guatemala en el último tercio del siglo XVIII (IGFO/RI, 36:145/146, julio/dic. 1976, p. 51–81, tables)

Settlement patterns of the Indian and ladino population of Guatemala were highly dispersed in the 18th century. Bishop Cortés y Larraz and the civil authorities of the time deplored this fact and tried to change these patterns by concentrating the population in accordance with the Laws of the Indies.

2407 Markman, Sidney David. Colonial Central America: a bibliography including materials on art and architecture, cultural, economic, and social history, ethnohistory, geography, government, indigenous writings, maps and plans, urbanization, bibliographic and archival documentary sources. Tempe: Center for Latin American Studies, Arizona State University, 1977. 345 p.; indexes.

A bibliography of considerable importance and generally astute commentary. Sections on writings from the colonial period and modern writing on the colonial period are followed by two sections devoted to the compiler's speciality, art and architecture. Section V is a bibliography of bibliographies on colonial Central America, a short but very valuable chapter. Section VI is a bibliography of catalogs of documentary collections. Sections VII and VIII are a surprise and do not quite "belong," but are of great usefulness. They consist of a guide to maps and plans of the area governed by the Audiencia de Guatemala, and a catalog to some of the documents in the Archivo General de Gobierno in Guatemala City. A long index of authors, people, places and subjects completes this very satisfactory research aide. For bibliographer's comment, see *HLAS 41:36.*

2408 Mejía, Medardo. José Cecilio del Valle, gran precursor del movimiento de liberación nacional de la América Latina: conferencia en ocasión del segundo centenario de su nacimiento en el auditorium municipal, patrocinada por la Alcaldía Municipal de San Pedro Sula y el Centro Universitario Regional del Norte. 2. ed. San Pedro Sula, Honduras: n.p., 1977. 47 p.

A brief, minor biography of the Central American precursor of independence. A transcribed lecture.

2409 Meléndez, Carlos. Costa Rica: tierra y poblamiento en la colonia. San José: Editorial Costa Rica, 1977. 211 p.; bibl.; ill.; charts; maps.

Consists of previously published essays in a new collection. Subjects include Indian reducciones in the central valley, land tenure patterns in the colonial period, studies of the foundation of the cities of Cartago and Liberia, and a nostalgic look at wheat farming and the fiestas and customs surrounding it.

2410 Miró, Rodrigo. Aspectos de la cultura colonial en Panamá. Panamá: Instituto de Investigaciones Históricos Ricardo J. Alfaro, Academia Panameña de la Historia, 1976. 93 p.; bibl.; ill.

Four brief essays on the cultural life of

colonial Panama. A general survey of intellectual life is followed by an essay on education in the 17th and 18th centuries. The last two essays deal with the influence of Friar Hernando de la Cruz on the Quiteño school of painting, and with a play by Víctor de la Guardia y Ayala.

2411 Molina de Lines, María; Josefina Piana de Cuestas; and **Ana I. Fuentes de May.** El escenario geográfico de Costa Rica en el siglo XVI según los informes de Gonzalo Fernández de Oviedo en la *Historia general y natural de las Indias.* Ciudad Universitaria Rodrigo Facio: Universidad de Costa Rica, Facultad de Ciencias Sociales, Escuela de Historia y Geografía, 1979. 231 p.; bibl.; fold. map (Avances de investigación; 2)

An attempted reconstruction of the 16th-century flora and fauna of Costa Rica, mostly the Pacific slope, using Fernández de Oviedo as the source.

2412 Nicaragua en los cronistas de Indias. v. 2/3. Managua: Fondo de Promoción Cultural, Banco de América, 1975. 2 v. (579, 300 p.) bibl.; ill.; indexes (Serie Cronistas; 1. Colección cultural Banco de América)

Another two volumes in the Banco de América's series on the *cronistas.* The introductions are knowledgeable and helpful, but the reader may feel ambivalent about the idea of extracting from the famous chroniclers (e.g., Herrera, Fernández de Oviedo, Remesal, etc.) only the Nicaraguan material. But then, these published extracts may be useful to researchers working on colonial Nicaragua.

2413 Pinto Soria, Julio César. Centroamérica en la época de la Independencia (BNBD, 25, sept./oct. 1978, p. 43–56, plates)

Competent, general survey of the situation in the area at the time of independence. Favors the thesis that independence served the interests of the economic elite who led the movement, especially in El Salvador.

2414 Polo Sifontes, Francis. Los cakchiqueles en la conquista de Guatemala. Guatemala: Universidad de San Carlos de Guatemala, Facultad de Humanidades, Departamento de Historia, 1974. 88 p.; bibl.: ill.

A history of the cakchiquels in the period of the conquest, this is a general survey of the first encounters with the Spaniards, and of the later rebellions. It is derived from published sources and adds little new.

2415 Polson, Jno. Interrogatorio del 27 de abril de 1780 (BNBD, 16, marzo/abril 1977, p. 7–9)

A translation of an interrogation of two Indians and a Spanish soldier captured by the English on Lake Nicaragua in 1780. It contains some snippets of interest on population, tribute, cattle, and numbers of troops.

2416 Rubio Sánchez, Manuel. Historial de El Realejo. Notas de Eduardo Pérez-Valle. 2. ed. Managua: Fondo de Promoción Cultural, Banco de América, 1977. 843 p.; bibl.; 12 leaves of plates: ill.; indexes (Serie Fuentes históricas; 4. Colección Cultural Banco de América)

Another exhaustive study of a colonial port by Rubio Sánchez. This one consists of a very detailed history of Realejo, the Nicaraguan Pacific port which served the Audiencia de Guatemala during the colonial period. Notwithstanding the lengthy section devoted to institutional history which precedes the main topic, the history of the town and its people is written with the author's usual care and with an abundance of archival documentation. As in Rubio's other works, the section on the late colonial period is especially strong.

2417 ———. Historia del puerto de Trujillo. Tegucigalpa: Banco Central de Honduras, 1975. 3 v. (689 p.) (continuous pagination) bibl.; facsims.

Study of the colonial port of Trujillo in Honduras which for many years served as colonial Central America's main link with the mother country and other colonies in the Caribbean. Author traces the port's founding, growth, repeated destruction by pirates, decadence, and revival in the 19th century. As the author admits, this is a chronological narrative rather than an analytical history.

2418 Sáenz de Santa María, Carmelo. Historia de la educación jesuítica en Guatemala. v. 1, Período español: siglos XVII y XVIII. Madrid: Instituto Gonzalo Fernández de Oviedo, 1978. 314 p.; ill.

Obra de fundamental importancia no sólo para conocer la labor educativa que en Guatemala realizaron los jesuitas sino otros aspectos de la historia cultural de dicho país.

Basada casi enteramente en fuentes de archivo: Archivo General de Indias, Archivo de la Compañía de Jesús en Roma y Archivo General de Centro América en Guatemala, principalmente. Bien organizada y escrita, y bien impresa. [L.G. Canedo]

2419 ———. La vida económica del Colegio de los Jesuitas en Santiago de Guatemala (IGFO/RI, 37:149/150, julio/dic. 1977, p. 543–584)

A detailed survey of Jesuit landholdings and economic activities, told with the author's usual care and solid documentation. An interesting side product is the attempt to establish an average cost-of-living for Santiago de Guatemala.

2420 Sanchíz Ochoa, Pilar. Los hidalgos de Guatemala: realidad y apariencia en un sistema de valores. Sevilla: Universidad de Sevilla, 1976. 193 p.; bibl.; ill.; charts; tables (Publicaciones del Seminario de Antropología Americana; 13)

Based on research in the AGI and on analysis of the conquistador class and the first two generations of its heirs. The hopes, fears, ambitions and behaviors of the *hidalgo* class are thoroughly discussed, but there is a certain lack of Guatemalan context and economic background.

2421 Selva, Salomón de la. Ideas de la emancipación norteamericana y de la independencia de Hispanoamérica (BNBD, 18, julio/agosto 1977, p. 45–65, ill.)

A survey of North American, European and Spanish thought as each played a role in the Latin American movements for independence.

2422 Sherman, William L. Forced native labor in sixteenth-century Central America. Lincoln: University of Nebraska Press, 1979. 496 p.; bibl.; index.

This book constitutes the publishing event of the past two years as far as the Central American colonial period is concerned. Long, carefully researched and well written, the work covers much more than the title suggests and includes additional information on the Cerrato reforms, the fate of the native aristocracy under Spanish rule, and lengthy statistical appendices on the early colonial population, etc. Although somewhat old fashioned in its narrative approach, the book challenges many theoretical assumptions and recent arguments. The bibliography is long, useful, and exhaustive. Of first importance for colonial specialists.

2423 Solano y Pérez-Lila, Francisco de. Tierra, comercio y sociedad: un análisis de la estructura social agraria centroamericana durante el siglo XVIII (IGFO/RI, 31:125/126, julio/dic. 1971, p. 311–365, bibl., tables)

A pioneering, well-documented study of land use and tenure in 18th-century Central America. Prices, crops, *composiciones*, and social classes are all treated at some length.

Torres de Araúz, Reina. Las culturas indígenas panameñas en el momento de la conquista. See *HLAS 41:979*.

2424 Valverde, José G. Apariencia y realidad en el movimiento emancipador de Centroamérica. Nanterre: Université Paris X-Nanterre, Centre de Recherches de Linguistique et de Sciences Humaines, 1975. 56 p.; bibl. (Publications du Centre de Recherches de Linguistique et de Sciences Humaines; 9)

Well-researched dissertation which takes a close revisionist look at the people and events of the period of independence. The attack on the "historiografía de exaltación localista" is especially effective. Nevertheless, the author does find the beginnings of an ideology in the independence movement, one with many local characteristics. His main point is that since the whole phenomenon of Central American independence is more complex than assumed so far a new and more thorough history of the subject is required.

NATIONAL

2425 Aldana, Carlos. Biografía de Ramón Amaya Amador: apóstol de la liberación (CHE/PE, 1:3, julio/sept. 1975, p. 24–28)

A brief, adulatory biography of the Honduran Marxist politician, journalist and novelist who died in 1966.

2426 Ameringer, Charles D. Don Pepe: a political biography of José Figueres of Costa Rica. Albuquerque: University of New Mexico Press, 1978. 324 p.; bibl.; map.

A detailed, sympathetic, but not uncritical biography of the Costa Rican political leader, based on interviews, documentary research, and a scrutiny of Figueres' personal papers. It is clear that Ameringer wishes that Figueres had left Costa Rican politics before the last few embarrassing years.

2427 Amnesty International, *New York.* Reporte sobre la República de Nicaragua incluyendo los resultados de una misión, 10–15 de mayo de 1976 (RCPC, 32:157, oct./dic. 1977, p. 112–152, map)

A report condemning torture and judicial and extra judicial government repression in Nicaragua between 1974 and 1976. Several cases are described in detail.

2428 Arellano, Jorge Eduardo. Los "incunables" de Nicaragua: 1829–1859 (BNBD, 24, julio/agosto 1978, p. 92–103, bibl.)

A list of the 88 products of the first years of the printing press in Nicaragua, an interesting view of cultural life in the decades following independence.

2429 Ashdown, Peter D. Antonio Soberanis and the disturbances in Belize: 1934–1937 (UWI/CQ, 24:1/2, March/June 1978, p. 61–74)

Rioting in Belize City because of unemployment fails to bring improvement because of poor organization and leadership in the protest movement.

2430 Aybar de Soto, José M. Dependency and intervention: the case of Guatemala in 1954. Foreword by Fred Warner Neal. Boulder, Colo.: Westview Press, 1978. 374 p.; bibl.; index (A Westview replica edition)

The overthrow of Guatemalan president, Jacobo Arbenz in 1954 by US supported rebels is treated as a case study in the intervention of a metropole or developed nation in the affairs of a peripheral or dependent one. The role of US corporations and of the US government is explained in detail. A useful book for an understanding of present-day Guatemala in spite of the sometimes dense cloud of theory.

2431 Baciu, Stefan. Ramón Villeda Morales, ciudadano de América. San José, Costa Rica: A. Lehmann, 1970. 214 p.; bibl.

A favorable biography of the Honduran ex-president and Liberal Party leader. A list of writings about Villeda, and a collection of some of his speeches follow.

2432 Barahona Jiménez, Luis. Manuel de Jesús Jiménez. San José, Costa Rica: Ministerio de Cultura, Juventud y Deportes, Departamento de Publicaciones, 1976. 245 p.; bibl. (Serie ¿Quién fue y qué hizo?; 25)

A favorable biography of the Costa Rican politician, journalist and historian (1854–1916), best known for his nostalgic, romantic *Cuadros de costumbres,* herein reprinted in the text.

2433 Bolaños, Pío. Obras de Don Pío Bolaños. Introducción y notas de Franco Cerutti. Managua: Fondo de Promoción Cultural, Banco de América, 1976/1977. 2 v. (714, 345 p.); bibl.; indexes (Serie Ciencias humanas; 2/6. Colección Cultural Banco de América)

Over the past few years, Cerutti's efforts to edit the works of distinguished but little known Nicaraguans have been carefully carried out and are of great value. These works by Pío Bolaños include his long history of Granada, *Granada, la ciudad trágica,* his personal reminiscences, his examination of Nicaragua's economic backwardness, and much else.

2434 Bonilla, Harold H. Figueres and Costa Rica: an unauthorized political biography. San José: Editorial Texto, 1975. 214 p.; bibl.; 5 leaves of plates: ill.; index.

An awkwardly written biography, which sees Figueres as a great man tainted by the sin of hubris.

Bray, Wayne D. The Common Law Zone in Panama: a case study in reception with some observations on the relevancy thereof to the Panama Canal Treaty controversy. See *HLAS 41:8660.*

———. The controversy over a new Canal Treaty between the United States and Panama: a selective annotated bibliography of United States, Panamanian, Colombian, French, and international organization sources. See *HLAS 41:8661.*

2435 Burguess, Paul. Justo Rufino Barrios: una biografía. Guatemala: Editorial del Ejército, 1971. 285 p.; plate (Sociedad de Geografía e Historia de Guatemala; 17)

A Spanish translation of the 1926 English edition by a Protestant missionary who lived for many years in Quetzaltenango.

2436 Calderón Ramírez, Salvador. The last days of Sandino: a moral document revealing the pathos of the Nicaraguan tragedy (FIU/CR, 7:4, oct./dec. 1978, p. 4–11, plates)

A passionate account of the last days of Sandino and of the emergence of Somoza. A reprint of the 1934 edition, containing many primary documents.

2437 Castañeda Fuertes, Digna. El nacionalismo y la lucha contra la dependencia en Guatemala: 1944–1954 (Santiago [Universidad de Oriente, Santiago de Cuba] 30, junio 1978, p. 9–45)

A short essay on recent Guatemalan history from a Marxist point of view, followed by an extended discussion which includes assessments of the Arévalo and Arbenz regimes.

2438 Cerutti, Franco. Historia de la Compañía de Jesús en Nicaragua: 1876–1880 (RCPC, 32:157, oct./dic. 1977, p. 101–110)

Cerutti's history of the Nicaraguan Jesuits, published as various essays, will be compiled into a book on the subject.

2439 ———. Jesuitas en la Nicaragua de 1853 (IGFO/RI, 36:145/146, julio/dic. 1976, p. 257–270)

Another of Cerutti's articles on the Jesuits. Although the order was not readmitted officially to Nicaragua until 1871, some Jesuits visited the country briefly in 1853 on their way to Guatemala.

2440 Comando Juan José Quezada. Frente Sandinista, diciembre victorioso. México: Editorial Diógenes, 1976. 112 p.; bibl.; 8 leaves of plates: ill.

The author describes both the Sandinista seizure of hostages on 20 Dec. 1976, and the history of Sandino, Somoza, and the US in Nicaragua. Interspersed are attacks on Howard Hughes, US Ambassador Turner Shelton, and the US. The book includes a brief bibliography, two Sandinista documents, and a *pronunciamiento* to the Nicaraguan people.

2441 Cuadra Pasos, Carlos. Obras. v. 1, El libro de familia. Casos sueltos de mi memoria. Historia de medio siglo; v. 2, Estudios históricos. Escritos políticos. Escritos culturales. Discursos y conferencias. Managua: Fondo de Promoción Cultural, Banco de América, 1976/1977. 2 v. (701, 769 p.); indexes (Serie Ciencias humanas; 4/6. Colección Cultural Banco de América)

A large collection of the works of the well-known Nicaraguan intellectual and journalist. Most of the selections are short and cover Nicaraguan history, politics and elite culture. The book also contains illuminating, personal reminiscences. Many of the essays are taken from *El Diario Nicaragüense* (1912–28), and *La Semana*, which Cuadra directed 1925–26.

2442 Diez hojas sueltas del siglo pasado (BNBD, 24, julio/agosto 1978, p. 45–54)

Ten political pamphlets from Nicaragua issued in the 1870s and 1880s.

2443 Dodd, Thomas. The papers of Tomás Herrán during the Panama crisis: 1901–1904 (RIB, 28:4, 1978, p. 359–372)

A discussion of the life and papers of Tomás Herrán, Colombian negotiator of the Hay-Herrán convention, later rejected by the Colombian senate. Herrán had warned the Senate that Panamanian nationalists and the US would exploit such a rejection.

2444 Dumaytray, Alonso and **Pedro Rouhaud.** Opúsculo sobre la República de Centroamérica (BNBD, 25, sept./oct. 1978, p. 57–63, facsims.)

A reprint of the general survey first published in 1833.

Fallas Monte, Carlos Luis. Alfredo González Flores. See *HLAS 41:8669*.

2445 Fielding, John. La diplomacia norteamericana y la reincorporación de la Mosquitía (BNBD, 26, nov./dic. 1978, p. 15–24, map)

A translation of an article which discusses the US role in Nicaragua's acquisition of the Mosquito Shore from Great Britain.

2446 Figueroa Navarro, Alfredo. Aproximación a la sociología histórica del grupo dominante coclesano: 1821–1850 (USMLA/LA, 6:9, nov. 1977, p. 207–221)

A study of Panama's neglected rural elite, distant from the dynamic transit and export economy, and somewhat turned in upon itself. Unlike the urban elite which fears the black masses, the rural dominant groups fear and distrust the Indians. It was not until the second half of the 18th century that a strong rural elite developed.

2447 ———. Tensiones sociales en el arrabal según la correspondencia consular francesa: 1850–1880. Panamá: Ediciones de la *Revista Tareas*, 1977. 13 p. (Separata; 39)

A 13-page pamphlet drawn from the French consular records, in which the author continues his studies of the development of early Panamanian elites. In this essay we catch a glimpse of the role played by the discontent and revolutionary potential of the urban poor.

2448 Finney, Kenneth V. Rosario and the election of 1887: the political economy of mining in Honduras (HAHR, 59:1, Feb. 1979, p. 81–107)

Because of the persistence of archaic features, or because of the process of capitalistic center-periphery underdevelopment, the mining boom of the late 1870s and 1880s failed to bring more than transitory economic development to Honduras.

2449 Fonseca, Carlos. Ideario político de Augusto C. Sandino (BNBD, 30, julio/agosto 1979, p. 65–82, plates)

Sandino's ideas on liberty and independence, exploitation, revolutionary politics,
democratic elections, Latin American solidarity, Central American unity, and much else, all backed up by quotations from his speeches and writings.

Gerome, Frank. Secretary of State Philander C. Knox and his good will tour of Central America: 1912. See *HLAS 41:8672*.

2450 González Saravia, Miguel. Documentos del último gobernador español de Nicaragua (BNBD, 18, julio/agosto 1977, p. 31–44)

Brigadier Miguel González Saravia, last Spanish colonial governor of Nicaragua, writes to the Iturbidean empire on a variety of matters. In these 23 documents, previously published by Rafael Heliodoro Valle in his *La anexión de Centroamérica a México*, González Saravia shows himself to be a faithful servant of the new regime.

2451 González Víquez, Cleto. Obras históricas. 2. ed. Ciudad Universitaria Rodrigo Facio: Universidad de Costa Rica, 1973. 510 p. (Serie Historia y geografía; 17. Publicaciones de la Universidad de Costa Rica)

A collection of some of the essays of this little known political historian of the 19th century in Costa Rica. The period covered in the essays is approximately 1824–70. A long appendix of useful documents completes the book. The table of contents is inaccurate and does not include all that is in the book.

Grieb, Kenneth J. Guatemala and the Second World War. See *HLAS 41:8674*.

2452 Gudmundson, Lowell. Documentos para la historia del distrito minero del Guanacatse: ¿enclave minero? (UNCR/R, 3:6, enero/junio 1978, p. 129–162, bibl., maps, tables)

Documents on mining in the Guanacaste province of Costa Rica.

2453 ———. Nueva luz sobre la estratificación socio-económica costarricense al iniciarse la expansión cafetalera (UNCR/R, 2:4, enero/junio 1977, p. 149–189, bibl., tables)

A revisionist, debunking article which attacks the Costa Rican myth of rural egalitarianism. The article is well argued and shows signs of considerable scholarship.

2454 Guzmán Selva, Enrique. Editoriales de *La Prensa*, 1878. Introducción y notas de Franco Cerutti. Managua: Fondo de Promoción Cultural, Banco de América, 1977. 459 p.; bibl.; index (Serie literaria; 8. Colección Cultural Banco de América)

An example of Nicaragua's Banco de América's laudable effort to publish all works by notable Nicaraguans. This is one of several devoted to Guzmán Selva, Nicaragua's noted 19th-century Liberal and man of letters. In 1878, he founded *La Prensa* in Managua and wrote the editorials for several years. Compiled and introduced by Franco Cerutti, the latter cover a variety of social, and especially political, topics. Written from the point of view of a 19th-century Liberal, the editorials reveal much about political life in Nicaragua at the time. For more on Guzmán Selva, see items **2455–2457**.

2455 ———. Escritos biográficos de Enrique Guzmán. Introducción y notas de Franco Cerutti. Managua: Fondo de Promoción Cultural, Banco de América, 1976. 232 p.; bibl.; index (Serie literaria; 7. Colección Cultural Banco de América)

Consists of the biographical writings of Guzmán, also compiled and introduced by Cerutti.

2456 ———. Las gacetillas, 1878–1894. Introducción y notas de Franco Cerutti. Managua: Fondo de Promoción Cultural, Banco de América, 1975. 206 p.; bibl.; index (Serie literaria; 4. Colección Cultural Banco de América)

Contains Guzmán's shorter newspaper contributions, and shows him as politician, journalist, and man of letters.

2457 ———. Las pequeñeces cuiscomeñas de Antón Colorado. Managua: Fondo de Promoción Cultural, Banco de América, 1974. 170 p.; bibl.; index (Serie literaria; 1. Colección Cultural Banco de América)

Another compilation of writings by Guzmán, this time a series of ironic essays written in 1896. They satirize the fads and politics of the period in Nicaragua, under the guise of "Letters to the Editors" of various newspapers.

Helms, Mary W. Negro or Indian?: the changing identity of a frontier population. See *HLAS 41:1038.*

2458 **Hoffman, Carl.** Viajes por Costa Rica. Presentado por Carlos Meleñdez Ch. San José, C.R.: Ministerio de Cultura, Juventud y Deportes, Departamento de Publicaciones, 1976. 217 p.; bibl.; ill. (Serie Nos ven; 6)

A Spanish translation of the observations made by Karl Hoffman, the German scientist and naturalist, as he travelled through Costa Rica in the mid 19th century. The introductory essay by Carlos Meléndez Ch. is informative and detailed.

2459 **Honduras. Oficina Central de Información.** El conflicto de un siglo. Tegucigalpa: Comisión Publicitaria de la Oficina Central de Información de la Secretaría de Cultura, Turismo e Información, 1976. 29 p.; bibl.; 1 fold. leaf of plates: map.

A polemical statement of the Honduran case in its boundary disputes and other quarrels with El Salvador.

2460 **Irías de Rivera, María Amalia** and **Irma Violeta Alfaro de Carpio.** Guatemalan working women in the labor movement (LAP, 4[12/13]:1/2, 1977, p. 194–202)

A description and analysis of the role played by three women in a workers' action in Guatemala City, Feb. 1975.

Koch, Charles W. Jamaican blacks and their descendants in Costa Rica. See *HLAS 41:1045.*

2461 **Linares, Julio E.** Juicio crítico sobre la independencia de Panamá (UNL/H, 19, 1978, p. 537–554)

Yet another critical examination of what really happened when Panama became independent. He believes that while the US and Roosevelt played a large role, the Panamanian struggle was also important.

López, Lorenzo. Estadística general de la República de El Salvador. See *HLAS 41:3006.*

2462 **McCain, William David.** Los Estados Unidos y la República de Panamá. Estudio preliminar y notas de Celestino Andrés Araúz. Traducción de Nina Shirer. Panamá: Editorial Universitaria, 1976. 281 p.; bibl.; index (Serie Monografía. Sección Historia)

A Spanish translation of McCain's work, first published in 1937 (see *HLAS 3:3012*) on US-Panamanian contractual relations and other difficulties. The book was written almost entirely on the basis of US sources and from a US point of view. In a long prologue Celestino Andrés Araúz points out that Panamanians should try to study and understand materials of this kind.

2463 **Marcoleta, José de.** Documentos diplomáticos de Don José de Marcoleta, Ministro de Nicaragua en los Estados Unidos, 1854. 2. ed. Managua: Banco de América, Fondo de Promoción Cultural, 1976. 84 p. (Colección Cultura. Serie Fuentes históricas; 3)

Another valuable reprint by the Banco de América in Managua, this time of Marcoleta's 1869 volume of documents on diplomatic history. Most of the contents are related to the great fire in San Juan del Norte in 1855, and to the Kenney filibustering project against Nicaragua of that same year.

2464 **Marroquín, Alejandro D.** Estudio sobre la crisis de los años treinta en El Salvador (*in* América Latina en los años treinta. México: UNAM, Instituto de Investigaciones Sociales, 1977, p. 113–190)

El Salvador was peculiarly susceptible to the 1930 world Depression because of the simple monocultural nature of its coffee export economy. Several years of poor harvests, a distorted land tenure structure, and inflexibility in production exacerbated the crisis. Like other essays in this volume, this one contains a mass of information and well-thought out analysis.

2465 Marure, Alejandro. Memoria histórica sobre el canal de Nicaragua (BNBD, 24, julio/agosto 1978, p. 15–32)

A reprint of Marure's Guatemalan essay of 1845 on the pros and cons of a Nicaraguan canal. Useful for its review on colonial attempts to organize a transisthmian route through Nicaragua.

2466 Miranda, Hernany. A redeeming light looking for social justice: educational pamphlet about Alberto Masferrer, a great Latin American visionary. San Salvador, El Salvador: Miranda, 1976. 38 p.

An adulatory biography of Alberto Masferrer (1868–1932), the Salvadorian civil rights advocate, and author of the document, *The vital minimum.*

2467 Miró, Rodrigo. La imprenta y el periodismo en Panamá durante la primera mitad del siglo XIX. Panamá?: Instituto de Investigaciones Históricas Ricardo J. Alfaro, Academia Panameña de la Historia, 1976. 152 p.; bibl.; ill.

A misleading title. An essay on printing and journalism before 1850 is followed by one on 19th-century poetry; a biography of the journalist Mariano Arosemena; and an essay on literary journalism. The appendix reprints, not altogether appropriately, some important political documents from 1824 to 1831, most of them related to early Panamanian nationalism and separatism.

2468 Molina Chocano, Guillermo. Estado liberal y desarrollo capitalista en Honduras. Tegucigalpa, Honduras: Banco Central de Honduras, 1976. 122 p.; bibl.; ill.

The author argues that the period 1862–76 saw the decline of local caudillismo and the emergence of a national state in Honduras. The growth of numbers of the national liberals was, he argues, linked to foreign investment and the resultant revival of mining in the highlands. Thus a dependent mini-state was created.

2469 Monge Alfaro, Carlos. Nuestra historia y los seguros. San José: Editorial Costa Rica, 1974. 542 p.; bibl.

A book written to celebrate the 50th anniversary of the Costa Rican National Institute of Social Security. This is a history of those 50 years, beginning with its origins in fire insurance and work accident compensation, and ending with its modern diversification and growth. A large bibliography adds to the value of a solid work.

2470 Muñoz Pinzón, Armando. La huelga inquilinaria de 1932. Panamá: Editorial Universitaria, 1974. 73 p.; bibl. (Editorial universitaria. Sección Historia. Serie Monografías)

A study of the neglected but important rent strike by the urban working class in Panama in 1932. (A larger one in 1925 had been crushed by US troops, invited in by the Panamanian government.) The Great Depression and the accompanying unemployment and falling wages caused a resurgence of grievances. For the first time, thanks to the doggedness of the strikers, the national government was forced to intervene and impose rent ceilings, and the strike broke "laisser faire" government in such matters.

2471 Obregón Loría, Rafael. De nuestra historia patria. Costa Rica en la independencia y la Federación. San José: Editorial Costa Rica, 1977. 254 p.; bibl. (Biblioteca Patria; 8)

This volume brings together two of the author's works: *Los primeros días de la independencia* (first published in 1971) and *Costa Rica en la federación* (1974). The period covered is 1800–25, and the history is told in great detail. There is a documentary appendix and a brief bibliography.

Olien, Michael D. The adaptation of West Indian blacks to North American and Hispanic culture in Costa Rica. See *HLAS 41:955.*

2472 Pérez-Venero, Alex. Before the five frontiers: Panama, from 1821–1903. New York: AMS Press, 1978. 199 p.; bibl.; index.

A thoroughly researched account of 19th-century Panama with emphasis on what were the advantages and disadvantages for the Panamanian people of the country's isthmian position and the transitory nature of the population. The author points out that the Panamanian separatist movement was well on its way to success before US intervention, and that the canal created a new form of dependency and self depreciation. A reasonable and well-reasoned book.

2473 Posas, Mario. Notas sobre las sociedades artesanales y los orígenes del movimiento obrero hondureño: a propósito de la obra de Graciela A. García, *Páginas de lucha revolucionaria en Centroamérica*, Ediciones Linterna, México, 1971. Tegucigalpa?: ESP Editorial, 1978? ii p.; bibl.

The author has several purposes in this pamphlet. He wishes to write a critical but favorable review of Graciela A. García's *Páginas de lucha revolucionaria en Centroamérica* (Mexico: Ediciones Linterna, 1971). He also examines the artisan origins of the labor movement in Honduras, and attempts to put it in a larger Marxist perspective. Organizations of skilled trades began in 1908 but grew slowly until the 1920s. Then the long dictatorship of Tiburcio Carías Andino further inhibited development. Growth resumed in the early 1950s and has continued since. The appendices consist of valuable early documents and a brief biography of the Honduran labor martyr Juan Pablo Wainright, executed in Guatemala at Gen. Ubico's orders. A valuable introduction to a little known and important topic.

2474 Quesada Camacho, Juan Rafael. Algunos aspectos de la historia económica del cacao en Costa Rica: pts. 1/2 (UNCR/R, 3:5, julio/dic. 1977, p. 65–100, map, tables; 3:6, enero/junio 1978, p. 69–110, bibl.)

A long, two-part article on the cacao plantations and industry in Costa Rica. Theoretical underpinnings include discussions on enclave economies and dependency. Only the national period is covered.

2475 Ramírez, Sergio. El muchacho de Niquinohomo (BNBD, 30, julio/agosto 1979, p. 1–56, plates)

Long, rambling account, with valuable documents interspersed, of the life, aspirations, and activities of Augusto Sandino.

2476 Rodríguez, René and **Antonio Acevedo.** Augusto C. Sandino: bibliografía (BNBD, 30, julio/agosto 1979, p. 124–128)

A brief, incomplete bibliography of the Nicaraguan nationalist hero.

2477 Rosa, Marco Antonio. La Tegucigalpa de mis recuerdos. Tegucigalpa: Centro Técnico Tipo-Litográfico Nacional, 1978. 205 p.; ill.

Costumbrista essays on the Honduran capital, its history and people. Contains a list of the presidents of Honduras.

2478 Rosenberg, Mark B. La política social, el estado y la cuestión social en Costa Rica: 1845–1939 (UNCR/R, 2:4, enero/junio 1977, p. 113–148, bibl.)

A study of the delayed state role in organizing a social security system in Costa Rica, and of the increasing tempo since the presidency of Rafael Calderón Guardia. The essay concentrates on the first 40 years of this century. A solid study.

2479 ———. Reforma social y conflicto político: la huelga médica como preludio a la guerra civil costarricense de 1948 (UNCR/R, 3:5, julio/dic. 1977, p. 149–170, tables)

Costa Rican physicians struck against President Calderón Guardia's attempt to broaden the Costa Rican social security system, thus helping to provoke the civil war and revolution of 1948.

2480 Salabarría Patiño, Max. Por la reivindicación de Pedro Prestán (LNB/L, 264/265, feb./marzo 1978, p. 118–134, bibl.)

An attempted rehabilitation of the Panamanian Liberal caudillo who was blamed, tried, and executed as the perpetrator of the great Colón fire of 1885. The author claims that Prestán was falsely accused by the Colombian Conservatives and the US, both of whom he opposed at various stages.

2481 Salas Víquez, José Antonio. El liberalismo positivista en Costa Rica: la lucha entre ladinos e indígenas en Orosí, 1881–1884 (UNCR/R, 3:5, julio/dic. 1977, p. 187–217, bibl.)

Documents concerning a dispute over land between Indians and intruders is presented as a case study of how liberal positivism treated marginal peoples.

2482 Salisbury, Richard V. Costa Rica and the 1920–1921 Union Movement: a reassessment (UM/JIAS, 19:3, Aug. 1977, p. 393–418, bibl.)

While 1920–21 seemed a propitious moment for union, Salisbury finds that the usual obstacles were present. Nicaraguan obstruction hindered negotiations. Costa Rican President Julio Acosta seemed pro-unionist, but his stand was related to winning a share of a Nicaraguan transisthmian canal. When union failed as a means to this end Acosta and the Costa Rican Congress reverted to isolationism and "purely national objectives."

2483 Sanabria Martínez, Víctor. Anselmo Llorente y Lafuente, primer Obispo de Costa Rica: apuntamientos históricos. 2. ed. San José: Editorial Costa Rica, 1972. 397 p.; bibl.

Biography of Costa Rica's first bishop (1850–71), after the diocese became a separate one from Nicaragua. Apart from being a detailed biography of the bishop, this book is useful because of its large statistical appendices. They include counts of the numbers of churches and hermitages in 1851, numbers of priests ordained (1850–71), and births, marriages and deaths by parish (1851–75).

2484 Sandino, Augusto César. Augusto César Sandino. Prólogo, selección y notas de Sergio Ramírez. Managua: Ministerio de Cultura, Juventud, y Deportes, 1978. 408 p.; 11 leaves of plates: ill. (Pensamiento de América; 11)

An invaluable collection of Sandino's widely scattered manifestos, interviews, letters and documents. Well presented by the editor, Sergio Ramírez, whose introduction, list of documents, and brief biography are all most useful, this volume gives a clearer picture of the rebel leader and his political beliefs.

2485 Scott, Joseph Newton. El testimonio de Scott: declaración del Capitán Joseph N. Scott, como testigo de la defensa en juicio entablado por el depositario de la Compañía Accessoria del Tránsito contra Cornelius Vanderbilt en 1861, en Nueva York. Traducción del original en inglés y anotaciones por Alejandro Bolaños Geyer. Managua: Fondo de Promoción Cultural, Banco de América, 1975. 363 p.; bibl.; 12 leaves of plates: ill.; index (Serie Fuentes históricas; 5. Colección Cultural Banco de América)

A Spanish translation of the testimony of Captain James Scott who served for six years as agent for the Accessory Transit Company in Nicaragua. He saw the bombardment of Greytown, the Walker intervention and the war against him, and the diplomatic negotiations between England, the US, Costa Rica and Nicaragua. He wrote up none of these experiences but, fortunately, was called upon to testify in a suit vs. Cornelius Vanderbilt in New York in 1861. While in court he recounted a mass of detail about events and personalities—all of great value to interested historians.

Seligson, Mitchell A. Agrarian policies in dependent societies: Costa Rica. See *HLAS 41:7160.*

2486 Selser, Gregorio. Sandino: general de hombres libres. México: Editorial Diógenes, 1978. 334 p.

One of the better histories of the origins of the Sandino movement, and of the activities of the movement and its leader. The book is an apologia for Sandino and condemns the roles of the US and Somoza.

2487 Serrano Gómez, Gustavo. Panamá, la República que nosotros perdimos. Bucaramanga: Consejo del Gobierno Departamental de Santander, 1975. 177 p.; bibl.; ill.

An argument that it was the Colombian leadership which "lost" Panama and the canal rather than the US which seized it. The Colombian author claims that there is still a basic unity between Panama and Colombia which should be fostered.

Sibaja Chacón, Luis Fernando. Nuestro límite con Nicaragua: estudio histórico. See *HLAS 41:8694.*

2488 Somoza, Anastasio. El verdadero Sandino: o, El calvario de las Segovias. 2. ed. Managua: Editorial y Litografía San José, 1976. 566 p.; bibl.; 1 leaf of plates: ill.

A republication of Anastasio Somoza's 1936 attack on Sandino and defense of his own actions. Documents of the period, some of them of dubious validity, are scattered among the pages.

Thiel, Bernardo A. and others. Población de Costa Rica y orígenes de los costarricenses. See *HLAS 41:9128.*

2489 Tjarks, Germán O.E.; Julio César Espinoza Guadamuz; and **Carlos Paniagua Vargas.** Un procedimiento estadístico para resolver muescas de población: el caso de Heredia (UNCR/R, 3:6, enero/junio 1978, p. 111–127, tables)

An exercise in statistical manipulation with some interesting results. For example, the article shows a clearer picture of the demographic devastation caused by the cholera epidemic of 1856.

2490 Tobis, David. ¿Qué es la United Fruit Co.? (CHE/PE, 1:3, julio/sept. 1975, p. 29–47, tables)

A Marxist description of the history of the United Fruit. Explores its links with the new bourgeoisie of the "Banana Republics."

2491 Torres, Edelberto. Influencia de la crisis del 29 en Nicaragua (*in* América Latina en los años treinta. México: UNAM, Instituto de Investigaciones Sociales, 1977, p. 89–112)

The fall of prices during the world crisis affected Nicaragua's export economy but her subsistence peasantry was largely immune to its effects. Of more national consequence was the US intervention and the civil war. Central Nicaragua was devastated. A solid essay offering a mass of economic detail and information on class structure.

2492 Urbanski, Edmund Stephen. Dr. José Leonard y sus actividades en América Central: afinidades ideológicas entre Leonard y Darío (UNL/H, 19, 1978, p. 217–235)

Describes travels, residence, and intellectual activities of the Polish savant in Central America, and discusses his dealings with the poet Rubén Darío who was Leonard's student and friend. The same essay was published in *Revista Interamericana de Bibliografía* (Washington, 29:1, 1979, p. 15–31).

2493 Uribe, Juan de Dios. José Santos Zelaya (BNBD, 24, agosto/junio 1978, p. 70–91, table)

A 19th-century Ecuadorian Liberal exile, who arrived in Nicaragua with Gen. Eloy Alfaro, gives a first hand impression of José Santos Zelaya and his policies. A reprint of the 1897 Quito edition.

2494 Valladares, Paulino. Hondureños ilustres en la pluma de Paulino Valladares. Tegucigalpa: Oficina de Relaciones Públicas, Presidencia de Honduras, 1972. 240 p.

Sketches of national leaders and notables, some deservedly rather obscure, plus a few essays on events and historical questions, culled from the writings of Valladares.

Velásquez Díaz, Max. Las cuestiones pendientes entre Honduras y El Salvador. See *HLAS 41:8704*.

2495 Woodward, Ralph Lee. Dr. Pedro Joaquín Chamorro, 1924–1978: the Conservative Party, and the struggle for democratic government in Nicaragua (SECOLAS/A, 10, March 1979, p. 38–46)

Consists of praise for Chamorro's struggle vs. the Somoza regime, and a brief description of his activities.

2496 ———. Las impresiones de un general de las Fuerzas Confederadas sobre Centroamérica en los años finales del siglo XIX (UCR/AEC, 4, 1979, p. 39–66)

US Confederate Gen. Edward Porter Alexander offers his impressions of travels and experiences in Nicaragua and Costa Rica towards the end of the 19th century.

2497 ———. Liberalism, Conservatism, and the response of the peasants of La Montaña to the Government of Guatemala: 1821–1850 (Plantation Society [University of New Orleans, La.] 1:1, Feb. 1979, p. 109–129)

Carrera's peasant support allowed him to play off Conservatives and Liberals against one another, and also led, perhaps, to "a better life for the masses than had the progressivism of the Gálvez Liberals," at least in the early years of his career. Peasants and lumpen had successfully and conservatively driven out cosmopolitan, 19th-century Liberalism.

2498 Zorina, A.M. The Clayton-Bulwer Treaty of 1850 and Russian diplomacy (*in* Soviet historians on Latin America [see item **1817**] p. 209–220)

A Marxist interpretation of the US role in Central America, and a précis of Russian diplomatic analyses of what was going on at the time. The tsarist government decided to refrain from endorsing the Clayton-Bulwer Treaty.

THE CARIBBEAN AND THE GUIANAS

FRANKLIN W. KNIGHT, *Professor of History, The Johns Hopkins University*

AS OF THIS VOLUME, *HLAS 42,* all of the literature on the Spanish borderlands of Florida and Louisiana (1510s–1820s) will be annotated in this section instead of in the one devoted to "Mexico: Colonial Period," subsection "North and Borderlands." The reasons for the change are set forth in the introduction to said section (see p. 000). Much of the literature dealing with the Spanish borderlands in Florida and Louisiana concern military, commercial and Indian relations, but the multi-disciplinary work edited by Samuel Proctor, *Eighteenth-century Florida and the Caribbean* (item **2542**) places the area in a wider framework. There are some useful contributions to the Caribbean's early colonial period such as: Mendel Peterson's article in the *National Geographic* (item **2522**); Frank Moya Pons' *Historia colonial de Santo Domingo* (item **2533**); Cristina Campo Lacasa's *Historia de la Iglesia en Puerto Rico* (item **2530**), a study conducted with keen sensitivity to social and architectural developments; and, finally, David Henige's article on the contact population of Hispaniola (item **2532**), the most reasoned rebuttal to the escalating estimates of early populations proposed by Sherburne Cook and Woodrow Borah. Howard Fergus' article "The Early Laws of Monserrat: 1668–1680, the Legal Schema of a Slave Society" (item **2537**) is the most sophisticated analysis of Caribbean slave laws since Elsa Goveia's brilliant contribution in 1965 on the same subject (see *HLAS 30:1774*).

The quality and breadth of studies of the modern period are impressive and encouraging. Cuba continues to attract most of the attention and the best single volume to date on the island for the period 1940s–1970s is Jorge Domínguez's *Cuba: order and revolution* (item **2598**). Two works on pre-revolutionary Cuba worthy of notice are: *United Fruit Company: un caso del dominio imperialista en Cuba* (item **2625**) which, despite an undeniable political slant, succeeds in portraying the social and political consequences for the island of the company's economic expansion; and Oscar Pino Santos' *El asalto a Cuba por la oligarquía financiera yanqui* (item **2618**) which provides varied data on American economic penetration of the country during the first part of the 20th century. Finally, Mario Llerena's memoir *The unsuspected revolution: the birth and rise of Castroism* (item **2610**) sheds much light on the origins of the Cuban Revolution.

With respect to the rest of the Caribbean, one should note Kenneth Post's *Arise ye starvelings* (item **2619**) an outstanding study of the development of Jamaica's labor movement which will not be superseded in the near future. Bridget Brereton's *Race relations in colonial Trinidad: 1870–1900* (item **2555**), although awkwardly written and poorly edited, consists of a brilliant analysis of the genesis of social fragmentation in a complex society. Finally, Gordon Lewis' article on the mass suicides at Jonestown, Guyana, offers a perceptive discussion of the significance as well as of the regional implications of this event (item **2609**).

GENERAL

2499 Africa and the Caribbean: the legacies of a link. Edited by Margaret E. Crahan and Franklin W. Knight. Baltimore: Johns Hopkins University Press, 1979. 159 p.; bibl. (Johns Hopkins studies in Atlantic history and culture)

Seven multidisciplinary essays look at the impact of the African connection on art, culture, language, literature, family patterns, and religious traditions. For individual annotations of the articles, see items **1258, 2572** and **6567** in this volume and the forthcoming one on the social sciences, *HLAS 43*.

2500 Arana Soto, Salvador. Puerto Rico peculiar. San Juan de Puerto Rico: Biblioteca de Autores Puertorriqueños, 1978. 104 p. (Biblioteca de autores puertorriqueños)

Collection of articles, published previously in other sources of the impact which the insularity, size, and physical features of Puerto Rico had on the population.

2501 Austin, Diane J. History and symbols in ideology: a Jamaican example (RAI/M, 14:3, Sept. 1979, p. 497–514, tables)

Austin asserts that ritual communication is an all-pervasive social manifestation in Jamaica, and challenges Maurice Bloch's distinction between ritual and normal communication, or Marx's distinction between ideology and knowledge.

Bailey, Wilma. Social control in the pre-emancipation society of Kingston, Jamaica. See *HLAS 41:999*.

Bayrón Toro, Fernando. Elecciones y partidos políticos de Puerto Rico: 1809–1976. See *HLAS 41:7244*.

2502 Bibliografía de la Guerra de Independencia: 1895–1898. Compilador: Araceli García Carranza. La Habana: Biblioteca Nacional José Martí, Instituto Cubano del Libro, Departamento Colección Cubana, Editorial Orge, 1976. 746 p.

Surprisingly thorough, and usefully divided into works done by Cubans and those done abroad, with mention of the literature, and based on the holdings of the Biblioteca Nacional de Cuba.

2503 Brathwaite, Edward. Nanny, Sam Sharpe, and the struggle for people's liberation. Kingston, Jamaica: Published by API *for the* National Heritage Week Committee, 1977. 64 p.; bibl.; ill.

Has a very good bibliography, and although geared for a popular audience, is solid.

Clarke, Colin G. The quest for independence in the Caribbean: review article. See *HLAS 41:8719*.

2504 Cripps, Louise L. The Spanish Caribbean, from Columbus to Castro. Boston: G.K. Hall, 1979. 251 p.; bibl.; index.

Essentially a political history designed for a general audience.

2505 Cuba in the world. Edited by Cole Blasier and Carmelo Mesa-Lago. Pittsburgh: University of Pittsburgh Press, 1979. 343 p.; bibl.; index (Pitt Latin American series)

Based on a conference at Pittsburgh in 1976, this is an outstanding collection of articles on a wide variety of topics, including Angola, Puerto Rico, the English-speaking Caribbean, the Arab-Israeli conflict, as well as international economic affairs. For political scientist's comment, see *HLAS 41:8713*.

2506 Farley, Ena L. African survivals and the Jamaican heritage (UCSD/NS, 7:1/2, 1978 [i.e. 1979] p. 305–310)

A review of the literature with special reference to the works of Leonard Barret, Orlando Patterson, and Edward Brathwaite.

2507 Franco, José Luciano. La Diáspora africana en el Nuevo Mundo. La Habana: Editorial de Ciencias Sociales, 1975. 425 p.; plates.

This collection of essays, covering various aspects of the African experience in the Americas and published in various places during the period 1960–78, demonstrates the author's amazing scope.

2508 ———. Las minas de Santiago del Prado y la rebelión de los cobreros, 1530–1800. La Habana: Editorial de Ciencias Sociales, 1975. 153 p.; bibl. (Nuestra historia)

A case study of a successful slave rebellion in Cuba, which began in 1677 and finally won the approval of the Crown in 1800.

———. La política de expansión imperialista norteamericana en el Caribe. See *HLAS 41:8730*.

2509 Gastmann, Albert L. Historical dictionary of the French and Netherlands Antilles. Foreword by Curtis Wilgus. Metuchen, N.J.: Scarecrow Press, 1978. 162 p.; bibl. (Latin American historical dictionaries; 18)

Useful, but not very sophisticated in content or arrangement.

2510 Honychurch, Lennox. The Dominica story: a history of the island. Maps and drawings, Lennox Honychurch. Photos, Curtis Henry and Peter Green. Roseau?, Dominica: Honychurch, 1975. 112 p.; bibl.; ill.

Readable account, but recent period rather brief. Has a helpful bibliography.

2511 Hostos y Bonilla, Eugenio María de. Obras. Compilación y prólogo de Camila Henríquez Ureña. La Habana: Casa de las Américas, 1976. 723 p. (Colección Pensamiento de Nuestra América)

This collection illustrates the breadth and fine literary style of Hostos.

2512 Jacobs, H.P. The French influence on Jamaica (JHS/R, 21, 1978, p. 5–48, plates)

Reviews the irregular nature of French contact with Jamaica, and states that only in the 19th century did the impact become important.

Jimenes Grullón, Juan Isidro. Sociología política dominicana: 1844–1966. See *HLAS 41:9165*.

Joseph, Cedric L. The strategic importance of the British West Indies: 1882–1932. See *HLAS 41:8739*.

2513 Lauring, Palle. Dansk Vestindien: historien og øerne. Med fotografier af Kirsten Kyhl. København: Forum, 1978. 305 p.; bibl.; 32 leaves of plates: ill.

From 1666 until 1917, the Virgin Islands were known as the Danish West Indies. This book is a history of the Danish period which began with the islands as plantation colonies for sugar, tobacco and guajak trees. Slaves were brought to the islands yearly and the first uprising took place in 1733. Slaves were finally set free in 1848 and the sugar trade simultaneously deteriorated because of new sources for raw sugar. It no longer was profitable for Denmark to rule the islands; thus in 1917, they were sold to the US. Includes bibliography and black-and-white photographs. [R.V. Shaw]

2514 Lawaetz, Eva. Free coloured in St. Croix, 1744–1816: the history, statistics, and selected information concerning the free coloured in the Danish West Indies, with special reference to St. Croix, from 1744–1816. Christiansted, V.I.: Lawaetz, 1979. v, 51 p.; bibl.; ill.

Reprint of archival material with little analytical elaboration.

2515 Maldonado-Denis, Manuel. Betances, revolucionario antillano y otros ensayos. Río Piedras, P.R.: Editorial Antillana, 1978. 175 p.; bibl.

Four essays on the Puerto Ricans, Betances and Albizu Campos, as well as Martí, Guevara and Camilo Torres, trace the concept of "Revolution" in the Caribbean.

2516 Mathurin, Lucille. The arrivals of black women (Jamaica Journal [Institute of Jamaica, Kingston] 9:2/3, 1975, p. 2–9, bibl.)

Argues that women were important in African societies, and this preserved her from the "total defeminisation" in the slave and post-slave societies of the New World.

2517 Mavrogordato, Olga J. Voices in the street. Port of Spain, Trinidad: Inprint Caribbean, 1977. 183 p.; bibl.; ill.; index.

Interesting as much for its information as well as its illustrations, this convenient volume is a nice tourist guide to Trinidad and Tobago for someone wanting something more than hotel prices.

2518 Musson, Nellie Eileen. Mind the onion seed: Black "roots" Bermuda: presented during Bermuda's First Heritage Week, May, 1979. Hamilton, Bermuda: Musson's, 1979. 329 p.; bibl.; ill.

A tribute to the women of Bermuda and their contribution to the history of their country.

2519 Newson, Linda. Inmigrantes extranjeros en América Española: el experimento colonizador de la isla de Trinidad (PAIGH/H, 87, enero/junio 1979, p. 79–103, tables)

Examines the reasons for the modest success of the Spanish colony.

2520 Ortiz Fernández, Fernando. Historia de una pelea cubana contra los demonios. Prólogo a la segunda edición de Mariano Rodríguez Solveira. La Habana: Editorial de Ciencias Sociales, 1975. 625 p.; bibl.; 8

leaves of plates: ill.; index (Pensamiento cubano)

This second edition of the famous study by Ortiz is greatly enhanced by the biographical prologue of Rodríguez Solveira which includes incidents concerning Ortiz's early life not usually found elsewhere.

2521 Peñate, Florencia. José Martí y la primera Conferencia Panamericana. La Habana: Editorial Arte y Literatura, 1977. 141 p.; bibl.; tables.

Less about Martí than the general picture of the Americas in the 19th century, and the process of developing an American perspective by the Latin Americas.

2522 Peterson, Mendel. Reach for the New World (NGS/NGM, 152:6, Dec. 1977, p. 724–767, plates)

Interesting article for the collection of beads and *manillas* used in the slave trade and recovered from a wreck discovered in 1966 off the Bermuda coast. The *National Geographic Magazine* deserves credit for its efforts in producing this article, one of the best available graphic presentations of the complex nature of trade in the 18th century. David L. Arnold took the photographs and Richard Schlecht prepared the paintings.

Pierce, B. Edward. The historical context of Nengre kinship and residence: ethnohistory of the family organization of lower status Creoles in Paramaribo. See *HLAS 41:1076*.

2523 Pope, Dudley. The buccaneer king: the biography of Sir Henry Morgan, 1635–1688. New York: Dodd, Mead, 1978, 1977. 379 p.; bibl.; 8 leaves of plates: ill.; index.

Perhaps the best biography of Morgan to date, with an account of the times which produced the man.

2524 *Revista de la Biblioteca Nacional José Martí.* Biblioteca Nacional José Martí. Año 67, Vol. 18, No. 2, 3. época, mayo/agosto 1976– . La Habana.

José Luciano Franco examines trade relations between Cuba and West Africa; Jordi Maluquer de Motes analyzes economic relations between Catalonia and Cuba and provides extensive figures; Pedro Méndez Díaz has an interesting article on David Turnbull; and Araceli García-Carranza provides an index to the *Revista de la Biblioteca Nacional José Martí* for the years 1970–75.

2525 Santos, Danilo de los and **Valentina Peguero.** Visión general de la historia dominicana. Santiago, República Dominicana: Universidad Católica Madre y Maestra, 1978. 516 p.; bibl.; ill. (Colección Textos; 40)

Detailed account of the Dominican Republic from pre-hispanic times to the age of Trujillo, with documentary evidence and an extensive bibliography.

Sanz Tapía, Angel. Los militares emigrados y los prisioneros franceses en Venezuela durante la guerra contra la revolución: un aspecto fundamental de la época de la preemancipación. See item **2757**.

Sherwin, Martin J. and **Peter Winn.** The U.S. and Cuba. See *HLAS 41:8753*.

2526 Tous Rodríguez, José M. Desarrollo histórico-político y jurídico del Estado Libre Asociado de Puerto Rico. Prólogo de Luis Sánchez Agesta. San Juan, P.R.: Master Typesetting, 1977. 259 p.; bibl.; plates.

Long on documentation, short on analysis.

Wilkinson, Audine. The Caribbean sugar industry: a select bibliography. See *HLAS 41:54*.

2527 Woll, Allen L. Puerto Rican historiography. New York: Gordon Press, 1978. 134 p.; bibl. (Studies in Puerto Rican culture, history, and literature)

Indispensable start for any investigation into the history of Puerto Rico, the references are extensive, and the notes careful.

EARLY COLONIAL

2528 Alegría, Ricardo E. El Rey Miguel: héroe puertorriqueño en la lucha por la libertad de los esclavos (PAIGH/H, 85, enero/junio 1978, p. 9–26, bibl.)

An attempt to recognize the Puerto Rican-born slave who tried to undermine the system of slavery in New Granada in the 1550s and 1560s.

Andrews, Kenneth R. The Spanish Caribbean trade and plunder, 1530–1630. See item **1826**.

Arnall Juan, María Josefa. El *Itinerario de Indias: 1673–1679,* del Padre Fray Isidoro de la Asunción, C.D.: Manuscrito 514 de la Biblioteca Provincial y Universitaria de Barcelona. See item **1829**.

2529 **Balzerova, Eva.** Portocolos del Cabildo de La Habana, 1616–1624 (UCP/IAP, 10, 1976, p. 187–196)

Review of the publications.

2530 **Campo Lacasa, Cristina.** Historia de la Iglesia en Puerto Rico, 1511–1802. Prólogo de Francisco Morales Padrón. San Juan de Puerto Rico: Instituto de Cultura Puertorriqueña, 1977. 326 p.; bibl.; 7 leaves of plates: ill.

Despite some deficiencies, this makes a modest contribution to the early history of Puerto Rico, with extensive research, and a valiant attempt to incorporate other aspects of society into its history.

2531 **Cantos, Angel López.** El comercio canario-puertorriqueño: cien años de su historia (JGSWGL, 14, 1977, p. 78–91)

Useful description of the trade between Puerto Rico and the Canary Islands during the years 1650–1783 with cargo content, and infrequency of sailing. Illustrates the marginal relationship of the commerce within the context of Spanish empire.

Cipriano de Utrera, *father.* Los restos de Colón en Santo Domingo. See item **1836**.

García del Pino, César and **Alicia Melis Cappa.** Catálogo parcial de los fondos de la Sección XI, Cuba, del Archivo General de Indias. See *HLAS 41:78*.

2532 **Henige, David.** On the contact population of Hispaniola: history as higher mathematics (HAHR, 58:2, May 1978, p. 217–237, tables)

This is the most skeptical analysis and the best criticism of the highly implausible estimates of Hispaniola's early population formulated by Sherburne Cook and Woodrow Borah. Henige concludes that, contrary to their assertions, it is not possible to measure the rate of the decline of the original population since it is impossible to ascertain the size of that population.

Manón Arredondo, Manuel J. Importancia arqueológica de los ingenios indohispánicos de las Antillas. See *HLAS 41:500*.

2533 **Moya Pons, Frank.** Historia colonial de Santa Domingo. 2. ed. Santiago, República Dominicana: Universidad Católica Madre y Maestra (UCMM), 1976. 488 p.; bibl.; indexes (Colección Estudios; 17)

In what may be the best history of early colonial Santo Domingo, author shows a keen sensitivity to wider Caribbean and European affairs. An important contribution to the literature. Impressive bibliography.

2534 **Vigneras, Louis André.** Diego Méndez, secretary of Christopher Columbus and Alguacil Mayor of Santo Domingo: a biographical sketch (HAHR, 58:4, Nov. 1978, p. 676–696, table)

Méndez' biography reflects the turbulence and insecurity of the age.

2535 **Zerquera, Carlos J.** and **Fernández de Lara.** La villa india de Trinidad en el siglo XVI (BNJM/R, 19:2, mayo/agosto 1977, p. 71–94)

Traces the decline of the predominantly Indian village of Trinidad and its replacement by a Spanish town.

LATE COLONIAL

Caron, Aimery. Inventory of French documents pertaining to the US Virgin Islands: 1642 to 1737. See *HLAS 41:69*.

2536 **David, B.** La Paroisse de Case-Pilote, 1760–1848: notes d'histoire social. Fort-de-France: Société d'Histoire de la Martinique, 1975. 113 p.; tables (Mémoires; 4)

Detailed description of the population of a parish of Martinique which exemplified the island's demographic configuration during the indicated period.

Dreyfus, Simone. Territoire et résidence chez les Caribes insulaires au XVIIème siécle. See *HLAS 41:1138*.

2537 **Fergus, Howard A.** The early laws of Monserrat, 1668–1680: the legal schema of a slave society (UWI/CQ, 24:1/2, March/June 1978, p. 34–43)

A valuable article showing that the laws reflected an "obsessively materialistic and exploitative" society, and that since penalties for infringement of the laws were expressed in tobacco, indigo and cotton, the society of Monserrat did not become monocultural during the 17th century.

Handler, Jerome S.; Frederick W. Lange; and **Robert V. Riordan.** Plantation slavery in Barbados: an archaeological and historical investigation. See *HLAS 41:1034*.

2538 *Historical Reflections/Reflexions Historiques.* University of Waterloo, Department of History. Vol. 6, No. 1, Summer 1979– . Waterloo, Canada.

Contains proceedings of a conference held at the University of Waterloo in March 1979. A fair number of the articles deal with the Caribbean, directly or indirectly, but in general, the material is derivative of works submitted at the 1976 New York conference edited by Vera Rubin and Arthur Tuden (see item **1768**).

Kopytoff, Barbara Klamon. The early political development of Jamaican Maroon societies. See *HLAS 41:1046*.

2539 Kuethe, Allan J. La introducción del sistema de milicias disciplinadas en América (SHM/RHM, 23:47, 1979, p. 95–112, plates, tables)

Kuethe argues that the English capture of Havana in 1762 led the Spanish to reorganize the colonial militias, beginning in Cuba, and this partly resulted in the improved defenses which lasted until the end of the Spanish colonial period.

Lent, John A. Third World mass media and their search for modernity: the case of Commonwealth Caribbean, 1717–1796. See *HLAS 41:7182*.

2540 López Cantos, Angel. El comercio de Puerto Rico con las posesiones españolas de América: 1700–1783 (IAA, 4:1, 1978, p. 57–79, bibl., tables)

Discusses the importance of trade as an index of exchanges between metropolis and colonies. The case of Puerto Rico exemplifies the wider pattern of trade.

Pike, Ruth. Penal servitude in the Spanish empire: presidio labor in the eighteenth century. See item **1866**.

Poyo, Gerald E. Cuban revolutionaries and Monroe County reconstruction politics, 1868–1876. See item **1913**.

2541 Solano, Francisco de. Geopolítica española y conflictividad en el Mar de las Antillas durante la guerra de independencia norteamericana: 1776–1783 (RUC, 26:107, enero/marzo 1977, p. 49–69)

Demonstrates that the wars of American independence did not seriously disrupt Caribbean trade, although exports of some products declined. The war was an important watershed in international relations.

Thoden van Velzen, H.U.E. The origins of the Gaan Gadu movement of the Bush Negroes of Surinam. See *HLAS 41:1097*.

SPANISH BORDERLANDS OF FLORIDA AND LOUISIANA

2542 Bicentennial Symposium, *2d, Florida International University, 1973.* Eighteenth-century Florida and the Caribbean. Edited by Samuel Proctor. Gainesville: University Presses of Florida, 1976. 103 p.; bibl. (A University of Florida book)

An excellent collection of papers and comments on a variety of themes linking Florida and the Caribbean: Richard Sheridan "British Sugar Planters and the Atlantic World, 1763–1775;" William Coker "Entrepreneurs in the British and Spanish Floridas, 1775–1821;" Orlando Patterson "The Development of Kinship and Social Organization among the Slaves of Jamaica, 1655–1830;" Barry Higman "The Slave Populations of the British Caribbean;" Duncan Mathewson "Archaeological Analysis of Material Culture . . . in Eighteenth Century Jamaica;" and Charles Fairbanks "The Changing Nature of Eighteenth Century St. Augustine." Comments are by Jack Greene, Thomas Mathews and John Griffin.

Bushnell, Amy. "That demonic game:" the campaign to stop Indian *pelota* playing in Spanish Florida, 1675–1684. See item **1261**.

2543 ———. The Menéndez Marqués cattle barony at La Chua and the determinants of economic expansion in seventeenth-century Florida (FHS/FHQ, 56:4, April 1978, p. 407–431)

A substantive contribution to the revisionist view of 17th-century Florida as a productive contributor to the colonial economy. After examining a wide variety of materials on a large cattle estate, the family history of its owners, and the political ambiance of the peninsula, the author has enlarged our knowledge of the "forgotten century," and informed us about the rise and fall of rural enterprises. [E.B. Couturier]

2544 Coker, William S. The financial history of Pensacola's Spanish Presidios, 1698–1763. Pensacola, Fla.: Pensacola Historical Society, 1979. 20 p.; bibl.; ill. (Pensacola Historical Society quarterly; 9:4)

Describes the middle period of Spanish occupation of the Pensacola region, with expenses for construction and defense as well as pictures of some of the coins used during the period. The number and denomination of French coins indicate a high volume of illegal trade.

2545 ———. Historical sketches of Panton, Leslie and Company. Pensacola: The University of West Florida, 1976. 44 p.; bibl.; ill.

This important article on trading in late 18th-century Florida also includes rich bibliographic information on the important firms of Panton, Leslie and Company and Forbes and Company. Coker is among the most prolific writers on the Southeastern borderlands.

2546 ———. John Forbes and Company and the War of 1812 in the Spanish Borderlands (*in* Hispanic American essays in honor of Max Leon Moorhead [see item **1787**] p. 61–97)

Well-researched account of the company fortunes during war and peace, and the complex and delicate nature of trade during periods of international strife. In 1818, Forbes went into the sugar business in Matanzas, Cuba.

2547 Forbes, John. John Forbes' *Description of the Spanish Floridas*, 1804. Edited and introduced by William S. Coker. Translated by Vickie D. Butt and others. Maps by Jerome F. Coling. Index by Polly Coker. Pensacola: Perdido Bay Press, 1979. 45 p.; bibl.; ill.; index.

Includes a good introduction to this very interesting description of an active frontier inhabited by Indians, Americans, Spanish and English.

2548 Lyon, Eugene. The enterprise of Florida: Pedro Menéndez de Avilés and the Spanish Conquest of 1565–1568. Gainesville: University of Florida Press, 1976. 253 p.; ill.

Detailed account of the first Spanish settlement of Florida based on extensive use of primary materials underlines the importance of the *adelantamiento* as a technique for the discovery, conquest and peopling of new lands. Author emphasizes the "private" character of the enterprise by recounting the business deals of the main protagonists. Footnotes specify location of variant copies of documents. Exceptionally wide use of Spanish archives. [E.B. Couturier]

2549 Miller, Janice Borton. Rebellion in East Florida in 1795 (FHS/FHQ, 57:2, Oct. 1978, p. 173–186)

Political history, almost entirely based on primary sources, reviews the struggle for control of East Florida from both rebel and Spanish points of view. [E.B. Couturier]

2550 Rivera y Villalón, Pedro de. Pedro de Rivera's *Report on the presidio of Punta de Sigüenza, alias Panzacola*, 1744. Edited and introduced by William S. Coker. Cover illustrations by Dianne Dusevitch. Pensacola, Fla.: Pensacola Historical Society, 1975. 22 p.; bibl.; ill. (Pensacola Historical Society quarterly; 8:4)

Transcription of Pedro de Rivera's description of Panzacola (sic) in 1744. Rivera was a long-time servant of the Spanish Crown, an experienced traveler and a member of the high bureaucracy. Viceroy Fuenclara asked him to prepare a report of the Presidio of Santa Rosa Island (later Penzacola). Coker provides an informative introduction to the document. [AL]

19TH CENTURY

2551 Badura, Bohumil. Sobre la inmigración alemana en Cuba durante la primera mitad del siglo XIX (UCP/IAP, 10, 1976, p. 111–136)

Provides breakdown of occupations and activities of German immigrants to Cuba during the early 19th century.

2552 Bergad, Laird W. Agrarian history of Puerto Rico: 1870–1930 (LARR, 8:3, 1978, p. 47–94, bibl.)

Contrasts the socioeconomic and political impact of sugar and coffee on the development of a national bourgeoisie in Puerto Rico.

2553 Berleant-Schiller, Riva. The failure of agricultural development in post-emancipation Barbuda: a study of social and economic continuity in a West Indian community (CEDLA/B, 25, dic. 1978, p. 21–36)

An interesting case study of how small-scale peasant production based on semi-communal land tenure expanded despite attempts to promote a plantation-export economy.

2554 **Bibliografía** de la Guerra Chiquita: 1879–1880. Compiladora: Miriam Hernández Soler. La Habana: Biblioteca Nacional José Martí, Instituto Cubano del Libro, 1975. 265 p.

Annotated bibliography consists of 714 articles.

Bolland, O. Nigel and **Assad Shoman.** Land in Belize, 1765–1871. See item **2374**.

2555 **Brereton, Bridget.** Race relations in colonial Trinidad, 1870–1900. New York: Cambridge University Press, 1979. 251 p.; index; map.

Brilliant examination of the development of Trinidadian society and its segmentation by race, class and color. Nicely complements works by Donald Wood (see *HLAS 30:1783*), Edward Brathwaite (see *HLAS 35:1132*) and Michael Smith (see *HLAS 25:505*). Essential reading.

2556 **Carreras, Julio Angel.** Los bandoleros de la tregua en Santa Clara (UCLV/I, 60, mayo/agosto 1978, p. 127–146)

Analyzes the rise of banditry and the official attempts to suppress it after the Ten Years War.

2557 **Chez Checo, José** and **Rafael Peralta Brito.** Azúcar, encomiendas y otros ensayos históricos. Portada de Leonardo Alvarado. Santo Domingo: Editores Fundación García-Arévalo, 1979. 218 p.; bibl.; ill. (Serie Investigaciones; 10)

Based on a fairly good and up-to-date bibliography, these interesting essays clarify the process of development in the 19th century more thoroughly than other sources.

2558 **Cifre de Loubriel, Estela.** La formación del pueblo puertorriqueño: la contribución de los catalanes, baleáricos y valencianos. San Juan, Puerto Rico: Instituto de Cultura Puertorriqueña, 1975. 485 p.: ill.

A valuable tool for the prosopographical study of Puerto Rico during the 19th century.

2559 **Clément, Job B.** History of education in Haiti, pt. 1, 1804–1915 (PAIGH/H, 86, enero/junio 1979, p. 141–181, maps, tables)

Discusses some factors which have retarded the development of Haitian education. Notes that expansion of facilities was impressive during the period in question and attributes most deficiencies to poor administration.

2560 **Colthurst, John Bowen.** *The Colthurst journal*: journal of a special magistrate in the islands of Barbados and St. Vincent, July 1835–September 1838. Edited by Woodville K. Marshall. Millwood, N.Y.: KTO Press, 1977. 255 p.; bibl.; ill. (The Caribbean: historical and cultural perspectives)

The most detailed account written by the peculiar overseer of an ambiguous apprenticeship system introduced in the Caribbean by the English to serve as transition from slavery to full freedom. This journal provides as valuable an insight into the new Caribbean as does Lady Nugent's more famous account.

2561 **Las Conspiraciones de 1810** [i.e. mil ochocientos diez] y 1812 [i.e. mil ochocientos doce]. Compilación e introducción de José Luciano Franco. La Habana: Editorial de Ciencias Sociales, 1977. 220 p. (Nuestra historia)

Documents taken from Seville—but mostly from Cuba—support the extent of the conspiracies, and demonstrates, according to Franco, that the island was not exempt from the political and economic influences of the time.

2562 **Cortada, James W.** A case of international rivalry in Latin America: Spain's occupation of Santo Domingo, 1853–1865 (PAIGH/H, 82, julio/dic. 1976, p. 53–82)

Examines the causes for Spanish reoccupation of Santo Domingo, and shows that both the US and Spain were there for military and economic purposes.

2563 ———. Economic issues in Caribbean politics: rivalry between Spain and the United States in Cuba, 1848–1898 (PAIGH/H, 86, julio/dic. 1978, p. 233–267, tables)

Author asserts that during 1800–98 there was little change in the economic relations among Spain, Cuba, Puerto Rico, and the US and that there was intertwining of economic, cultural and politcal issues.

2564 Deschamps Chapeaux, Pedro. Rafael Serra y Montalvo, obrero incansable de nuestra independencia. La Habana: Unión de Escritores y Artistas de Cuba, 1975. 189 p.; bibl.

Traces the career of Serra through exile and the struggle for independence.

2565 Domínguez, Jaime de Jesús. Economía y política en la República Dominicana, años 1844–1861. Santo Domingo: Editora de la Universidad Autónoma de Santo Domingo, 1977. 204 p.; bibl. (Colección Historia y sociedad; 29. Publicaciones de la Universidad Autónoma de Santo Domingo; 236)

Although somewhat schematic, this study includes some important data, and complements the edition by Mejía Ricart (see item **2590**).

2566 Estrade, Paul. Las huelgas de 1890 en Cuba (BNJM/R, 70[21]: 1, enero/abril 1979, p. 27–52, tables)

Strikes constituted only one form of worker protest, and were vital in the development of working-class solidarity.

2567 Foner, Philip Sheldon. Antonio Maceo: the "Bronze Titan" of Cuba's struggle for independence. New York: Monthly Review Press, 1977. 340 p.; bibl.; index.

A sympathetic account which fills a void in the English language of one of the most outstanding Cubans of the 19th century, and a hero of the Cuban nation. Very few non-military aspects are discussed here, but the account is most readable.

2568 García-Baquero González, Antonio. Estados Unidos, Cuba y el comercio de neutrales (RUC, 26: 107, enero/marzo 1977, p. 117–142, tables)

Author uses good bibliography and import-export figures for the period 1794–1860 in order to demonstrate the increasing dependency of the Cuban economy on that of the US.

2569 García Martínez, Orlando. Estudio de la economía cienfueguera desde la fundación de la colonia Fernandina de Jagua hasta mediados del siglo XIX (UCLV/I, 55/56, sept. 1976/abril 1977, p. 117–169, maps, tables)

Describes the growth of the city of Cienfuegos in relation to the expanding sugar industry.

2570 González Vales, Luis E. Alejandro Ramírez y su tiempo: ensayos de historia económica e institucional. Río Piedras: Editorial Universitaria, Universidad de Puerto Rico, 1978. 283 p.; bibl.; ill.

The four essays cover an important period in Puerto Rican history, and the essay on Ramírez connects him with service in Cuba. Most of the volume consists of documentation.

2571 Guyanese sugar plantations in the late nineteenth century: a contemporary description from the *Argosy*. Edited and introduced by Walter Rodney. Georgetown: Guyana: Release Publishers, 1979. 97 p.; bibl.; ill.

The introduction is excellent, and the descriptions of all major Guyanese plantations in the late 1880s done by local authors and giving size, location, crops, labor force and much other relevant data, comprise a most valuable record.

Helly, Denise. Idéologie et ethnicité: les Chinois Macao à Cuba: 1847–1886. See *HLAS 41: 1036*.

2572 Higman, Barry W. African and Creole slave family patterns in Trinidad (NCFR/JFH, 3: 4, Winter 1978, p. 163–180, bibl., maps, tables)

Important contribution to the demographic history of the Caribbean, especially concerning the origins of sugar-plantation society. Also appeared in item **2499**.

2573 Joachim, Benoît. Aux sources d'un blocage du dévéloppement: la dépendance néocoloniale d'Haïti vue à travers les problèmes de la terra du capital: XIXe.—début XXe. siécles (CDAL, 17, 1978, p. 3–21, bibl.)

Examines the process of economic transition in Haiti and attributes the country's underdevelopment to its relations with highly-developed capitalist states.

2574 Lacerte, Robert K. The evolution of land and labor in the Haitian Revolution, 1791–1820 (AAFH/TAM, 34: 4, April 1978, p. 449–459)

Describes the progressive reduction of size of landholdings in Haiti, and reason that the emphasis on coffee virtually condemned the state to poverty.

2575 Lepkowski, Tadeusz. ¿Fué la abolición de la esclavitud el fin del feudalismo en las Antillas? (PAN/ES, 3, 1976, p. 207–216)

This attempt to understand the Caribbean through a Caribbean lens is intelligently aware of the contradictions of 19th-century slave society. Modern slavery, the author suggests, was a variant on the theme of transition from feudalism to capitalism.

Lesassier, Miguel. Mapa histórico de Cuba. See *HLAS 41:5821*.

Menezes, Mary Noel. British policy towards the Amerindians in British Guiana: 1803–1873. See *HLAS 41:1064*.

Moore, Brian L. The retention of caste notions among the Indian immigrants in British Guiana during the nineteenth century. See *HLAS 41:1069*.

2576 Morales Carrión, Arturo. Auge y decadencia de la trata negrera en Puerto Rico: 1820–1860. San Juan: Centro de Estudios Avanzados de Puerto Rico y el Caribe, Instituto de Cultura Puertorriqueña, 1978. 259 p.; bibl.; 12 leaves of plates: ill.; index.

Meticulously researched and ably presented, this study makes an important contribution to the study of the general disintegration of Caribbean slave systems. The work also deals with a much neglected aspect of the transatlantic slave trade.

2577 Moreno Fraginals, Manuel. El ingenio: complejo económico social cubano del azúcar. Editado de Luis M. Traviesas. La Habana: Editorial de Ciencias Sociales, 1978. 3 v. (350, 245, 270 p.); bibl.; ill. (Nuestra historia)

This new edition of the classic includes a vol. 3 consisting of substantiating data on which the earlier two-volume edition was based (see *HLAS 27:2026*). For sociologist's comment which includes a complete description of contents, see *HLAS 41:9175*.

2578 Opatrny, Josef. Los checos y eslovacos en los EE.UU. y la guerra contra el colonialismo español en Cuba, 1895–1898 (UCP/IAS, 10, 1976, p. 211–218)

Suggests that the reaction of the two immigrant groups did not differ from the rest of the American public, and that the Czech and Slovak presses tended towards more conservative views than the workers.

2579 Padrón Valdés, Abelardo. El general Flor: apuntes históricos de una vida. La Habana: Editorial Arte y Literatura, 1976. 574 p.; bibl.; ill.

Unorthodox as history, the work provides the example of a French immigrant family (originally from Grenada) and shows the development of their career in the expanding Cuba of the 19th century.

2580 Pérez, Louis A., Jr. Cubans in Tampa: from exiles to immigrants, 1892–1901 (FHS/FHQ, 57:2, Oct. 1978, p. 129–140)

Like Poyo's article (see item **2585**), this one traces the complex interrelations between Cuba and the US and the conditions which led to Cuban emigration with profound consequences for both countries.

2581 Pérez de la Riva, Juan. El barracón: esclavitud y capitalismo en Cuba. Prólogo de Jordi Maluquer de Motes. Barcelona: Crítica, 1978. 185 p.; bibl. (Crítica/historia; 6)

Some of these articles have appeared already, but this collection demonstrates the methodological competence as well as the commanding span of one of Cuba's most distinguished historians. Essays cover the following topics: barracoons; moneys used in commerce along the African coast; the Chinese indentured laborers of the 19th century; and the history of the latifundio Puercos Gordos.

2582 Pérez Guzmán, Francisco. La Batalla de las Guásimas. La Habana: Editorial de Ciencias Sociales, 1975. 231 p.; bibl.; fold. map; fold. plates.

The Battle of Guásimas was important for the reputation of Máximo Gómez, and was widely hailed among the Cuban insurgents in the Ten Years War.

2583 Perotin, Anne. Los planes económicos de los grandes hacendados habaneros (BNJM/R, 19:2, mayo/agosto 1977, p. 5–50, tables)

Offers a content analysis of the political ideas of the Cuban bourgeoisie at the beginning of the great economic transformation of the island. Perotin's argument is an interesting intellectual tour-de-force.

2584 Porter, David Dixon. Diario de una misión secreta a Santo Domingo, 1846. Traducción: Gustavo Amigó Jensen. Santo Domingo: Editora de Santo Domingo, 1978. 268 p. (Colección de cultural dominicana; 28)

Porter was President Polk's emissary to the Dominican Republic, and his report offers a fascinating look at the country in the middle of the 19th century.

2585 Poyo, Gerald E. Key West and the Cuban Ten Years War (FHS/FHQ, 57:3, Jan. 1979, p. 289–307)

Traces the development of the Key West exile community of Cubans and its interrelationship with the political events in Cuba. The permanent community became a cradle for Cuban independence after the temporary reversal of the Ten Years War.

2586 Sánchez Bermúdez, Juan A. La posición del autonomismo entre 1878 y 1895 (UCLV/I, 59, enero/abril 1978, p. 115–162, bibl.)

Examines the basis of political affiliation during the 19th century, with documents and a good bibliography.

2587 Senior, Olive. The Colón people (IJ/JJ, 11:3/4, 1978, p. 62–71, plates)

Discusses the various factors which accounted for the large number of Jamaicans who went to Panama to build the Canal and remained to form the nucleus of the English-speaking community in the later Republic of Panama.

2588 Serrano León, Isabel. El libro *Los ingenios*: reflejo de la producción material del siglo XIX en Cuba (BNJM/R, 70[21]:1, enero/abril 1979, p. 85–110, bibl.)

After reviewing the luxury edition of *Los ingenios*, which portrays the great Cuban sugar estates of the 19th century, the author shows how this work reveals the deep contradictions created by the sugar revolutions and slavery.

2589 Shur, L.A. Russian volunteers in the Cuban War of National Liberation: 1895–98 (*in* Soviet historians on Latin America [see item **1817**] p. 221–233)

Account of three Russians who volunteered to fight with Antonio Maceo and his insurgents in the Cuban war of independence.

2590 La sociedad dominicana durante la Primera República, 1844–1861: curso monográfico, Santo Domingo, 1977. Editor: Tirso Mejía Ricart. Santo Domingo: Editora de la Universidad Autónoma de Santo Domingo, 1977. 449 p.; bibl. (Historia y sociedad; 31. Publicaciones de la Universidad Autónoma de Santo Domingo; 258)

The essays are heavily political and narrative, with little attempt to examine the social and cultural bases of the transformation being described. For another work on the subject, see item **2565**.

2591 Zaragoza Ruvira, Gonzalo. Tres interpretaciones de la Guerra de Independencia cubana (IGFO/RI, 37:147/148, enero/junio 1977, p. 249–264)

Consists of views of Cuban, American and Spanish historians concerning the Cuban war of independence.

20TH CENTURY

2592 Baecker, Thomas. Deutschland im karibischen Raum im Spiegel amerikanischer Akten: 1898–1914 (JGSWGL, 11, 1974, p. 167–237)

Major contribution which presents a well-documented overview of German policy toward the Caribbean from the Spanish-American War to the outbreak of World War I. The author used mainly US documents in the National Archives of Washington. He also analyzes US policy towards the Caribbean and Germany as well. [G.M. Dorn]

2593 Baptiste, Fitzroy A. The anti-Vichyite movement in French Guiana, June to December 1940 (UWI/SES, 26:3, Sept. 1977, p. 294–307)

The repercussion of World War II in a distant corner of the world—microhistory with macrohistorical ramifications.

Barrett, Leonard E. The Rastafarians: sounds of cultural dissonance. See *HLAS 41:1001*.

2594 Cabrera, Olga. Guiteras: la época, el hombre. La Habana: Editorial de Arte y Literatura, Instituto Cubano del Libro, 1974. 539 p.; bibl.; 35 leaves of plates: ill.

Not merely a good biography of Antonio Guiteras, this study also provides an excellent analysis of the general background of Cuba in the 20th century.

2595 Calder, Bruce J. *Caudillos* and *gavilleros* versus the United States Marines: guerrilla insurgency during the Dominican intervention, 1916–1924 (HAHR, 58:4, Nov. 1978, p. 649–675, maps)

Examines the socioeconomic backgrounds of the guerrillas who resisted the US occupation and refutes the assertion that they were bandits.

2596 Chester, Edward. The United States and six Atlantic outposts: the military and economic considerations. Port Washington, N.Y.: Kennikat Press, 1980. 259 p.; bibl.

Study of US interest in obtaining bases on islands in the North Atlantic. Involvement in the Bahamas, Bermuda, Jamaica, Iceland, Greenland and the Azores examined. [J.D. Riley]

Comitas, Lambros. The complete Caribbeana 1900–1975: a bibliographic guide to the scholarly literature. See *HLAS 41:1014*.

2597 Díaz Ruiz Soto, Antonio; Mercedes Humpierre Alvarez; and **René Márquez Castro.** Las corrientes ideológicas en la Cuba neocolonial a partir de 1930 (UCLV/I, 61, sept./dic. 1978, p. 23–63, bibl.)

Posits the origins of the Cuban Revolution in the context of three major ideological currents: reactionary, nationalist and proletarian. Nothing surprisingly new here.

2598 Domínguez, Jorge I. Cuba: order and revolution. Cambridge, Mass.: Belknap Press of Harvard University Press, 1978. 683 p.; bibl.; index.

This book ranks among the best ever written on Cuba. Starting with 1902, Domínguez covers the entire period trading an evolving pattern which culminates in the Revolution. Pt. 3 analyzes the Revolution itself and focuses on some shortcomings but overall the work constitutes a fair attempt at objectivity. The best chapters deal with mass political organizations and the Communist Party. For political scientist's comment, see *HLAS 41:3058*.

2599 D'ou, Lino. Papeles del Tte. Coronel Lino D'ou. La Habana: Unión de Escritores y Artistas de Cuba, 1977. 151 p.: ill. (Cuadernos de la *Revista Unión*)

The importance of D'ou's papers lies in his being a mulatto "who made good."

2600 Doubout, Jean Jacques. Haïti, féodalisme ou capitalisme?: Essai sur l'évolution de la formation sociale d'Haïti depuis l'indépendance. Port-au-Prince: Imprimerie Abécé, 1973. 32 leaves; bibl.

Author believes that capitalism ruptured the harmony of the Haitian masses and thus accounts for the latent instability of the society.

2601 Dynamics of the Cuban Revolution: the Trotskyist view. Compiled by Joseph Hansen. New York: Pathfinder Press, 1978. 393 p.; index.

The introductory essay explains why these articles, written in the first years or so of the Cuban Revolution, still constitute a valid attempt at understanding the Cuban revolutionary process as well as Cuba's appeal to the rest of the world. For political scientist's comment, see *HLAS 41:7200*.

Fernández Valledor, Roberto. El mito de Cofresí en la narrativa antillana. See item **5299**.

2602 García Godoy, Federico. El derrumbe. Prólogo de Juan Bosch. Santo Domingo: Editora de la Universidad Autónoma de Santo Domingo, 1975. 177 p. (Publicaciones de la Universidad Autónoma de Santo Domingo; 170. Colección Historia y sociedad; 16)

Offers a valuable insider's view of the situation which brought about the US intervention in the Dominican Republic, but does not provide a broad analysis of the relations between both countries.

2603 Gilbert, Gregorio Urbano. Mi lucha contra el invasor yanqui de 1916. Santo Domingo: Editora de la Universidad Autónoma de Santo Domingo, 1975. 289 p. (Colección Historia y sociedad; 19. Publicaciones de la Universidad Autónoma de Santo Domingo; 187)

Memoirs of a guerrilla fighter who began resisting the US occupation of the Dominican Republic at age 17, and ended up as an opponent of the Trujillo regime.

2604 Guerra, Sergio and **Rosa Pulpeiro.** Política demográfica de la United Fruit (UH/U, 200, 1973, p. 60–92, tables)

Demonstrates that the United Fruit Company's policy which favored population increase was closely related to its need of additional manpower for its sugar enterprises.

2605 Guerra Díaz, Carmen; Liana Bosch Rodríguez; and Juan Sánchez Bermúdez. Mella en la historia (UCLV/I, 58, 1978, p. 23–72)

Reaffirms the importance of Mella in the development of the Cuban Communist Party.

2606 Guevara, Ernesto. El socialismo y el hombre nuevo. Edición preparada por José Aricó. México: Siglo XXI Editores, 1977. 429 p.; plates (Colección América nuestra: los hombres y las ideas; 9)

Two sections consist of selections of Guevara's writings, while the third contains essays on Cuban economic problems during the early 1960s. Unfortunately, both the selections by Che as well as the comments sound rather dated today. For political scientist's comment, see *HLAS 41:7199*.

2607 Henríquez Ureña, Max. Los yanquis en Santo Domingo: la verdad de los hechos comprobada por datos y documentos oficiales. pt. 1, La verdad de los hechos comprobada por datos y documentos oficiales; pt. 2, En pos de la justicia. Santo Domingo: Editora de Santo Domingo, 1977. 322 p.; bibl.

More narrative than analysis, this book exemplifies the newly emerging Dominican historiography. Unfortunately, the author offers few new insights.

Hidalgo, Ariel. Orígenes del movimiento obrero y del pensamiento socialista en Cuba. See *HLAS 41:9160*.

Instituto de Historia del Movimiento Comunista y la Revolución Socialista en Cuba, *La Habana.* El movimiento obrero cubano: documentos y artículos. See *HLAS 41:9161*.

2608 Johnson, Howard. The West Indies and the conversion of the British official classes to the development idea (ICS/JCCP, 15:1, March 1977, p. 55–83)

Argues that West Indian labor disturbances of the 1930s stimulated British awareness of the problem which led to new concepts of economic development and social welfare for the Caribbean. For political scientist's comment, see *HLAS 41:7180*.

Levesque, Jacques. L'URSS et la Révolution Cubaine. See *HLAS 41:8740*.

2609 Lewis, Gordon K. "Gather with the saints at the river:" the Jonestown Guyana holocaust of 1978: a description and interpretative essay on its ultimate meaning from a Caribbean viewpoint. Río Piedras, P.R.: Institute of Caribbean Studies, University of Puerto Rico, 1979. 50 p.; bibl.

The most intelligent analysis of the People's Temple Cult and its unfortunate demise in Guyana. Lewis explains why an independent nationalist state such as Guyana was hospitable to the cult's location, and suggests that the episode reveals as much about modern American society as it does about Jones and Guyana.

2610 Llerena, Mario. The unsuspected revolution: the birth and rise of Castroism. Ithaca, N.Y.: Cornell University Press, 1978. 324 p.; bibl.; ill.; index.

This book constitutes vital reading for anyone interested in the genesis of the Cuban Revolution. The US representative for the 26th of July Movement and an insider for part of the time, Llerena presents a fairly open report on his relations with the 26th of July Movement, despite occasional use of adverse terms. For political scientist's comment, see *HLAS 41:7207*.

Maldonado Denis, Manuel. Las perspectivas del nacionalismo latinoamericano: el caso de Puerto Rico. See *HLAS 41:8741*.

2611 Mil fotos Cuba: territorio libre de América. Colaboraron el Museo de la Revolución y la Academia de Ciencias de Cuba. s.l.: s.n., between 1965 and 1979. 435 p.; 1 fold. leaf of plates: ill.

Reminiscent of Anita Brenner's *The wind that swept Mexico*, this book of photographs concentrates on the Cuban Revolutionary period. A more explanatory text would have enhanced the volume.

2612 Millet, Kethly. Les paysans haïtiens et l'occupation américaine d'Haïti, 1915–1930. La Salle, Québec: Collectif Paroles, 1978. 197 p.; maps.

Author insists that the American occupation intensified the pressures of the Haitian peasantry, and by forcing them into a state of revolt heightened nationalist sentiment.

Payne, Anthony. From Michael with love: the nature of socialism in Jamaica. See *HLAS 41:7235*.

2613 Peña Rivera, Víctor A. Trujillo: la herencia del Caudillo. Río Piedras,

P.R.: Publicaciones y Distribuciones San Juan, 1978. 318 p.: ill.

In an interesting, readable style, author describes the worse aspects of the Trujillo dictatorship and the significance of this legacy for the Dominican Republic.

2614 Pérez, Louis A., Jr. "La Chambelona:" political protest, sugar, and social banditry in Cuba, 1914–1917 (IAMEA, 31:4, Spring 1978, p. 3–27)

Describes the rise of social banditry in the central and eastern provinces during the period, and suggests that although government action drove the activity underground, it reappeared to support Fidel Castro's 26th of July Movement in the late 1950s.

2615 ———. In the service of the Revolution: two decades of Cuban historiography, 1959–1979 (HAHR, 60:1, Feb. 1980, p. 79–89)

Pérez shows how Cuban historians were in the forefront of Cuban nationalism and, as a result, generated a "revisionist historiography before [Cuba] possessed a body of policy history." Their revisions, therefore, coincided with ideological perceptions of the Revolution after 1959. As Pérez sees it, the problem lies in the tendency of Cuban historians to justify the overthrow of the ancient regime without offering any insight into current and/or future problems.

2616 ———. Intervention, revolution, and politics in Cuba, 1913–1921. Pittsburgh: University of Pittsburgh Press, 1978. 198 p.; bibl.; index (Pitt Latin American series)

Consists of a valuable analysis of the collapse of party politics in Cuba, and the emergence of US hegemony after 1912. Although much of the source material derives from US sources, the interpretation does justice to the Cuban point of view.

2617 Pierre-Charles, Gérard. Génesis de la Revolución Cubana. México: Siglo Veintiuno Editores, 1976. 194 p.; bibl. (Sociología y política)

Based on extensive bibliography, traces the development of Cuba's economic dependency, and the subsequent political discontent which created the conditions for the Revolution. A good summary of the transformation brought about by the Revolution after 1959.

2618 Pino Santos, Oscar. La oligarquía yanqui en Cuba. Epílogo por Fidel Castro. México: Editorial Nuestro Tiempo, 1975? 207 p.; bibl. (Colección Teoría e historia)

Essential reading for anyone who seeks to understand the development of US economic hegemony in Cuba, as well as to the strong anti-American sentiment which resulted from the political changes of the Cuban Revolution. For economist's comment, see *HLAS 41:3073*.

2619 Post, Kenneth William John. Arise ye starvelings: the Jamaican labour rebellion of 1938 and its aftermath. The Hague; Boston: Nijhoff, 1978. 502 p.; bibl.; index (Series on the development of societies; 3)

Best Marxist analysis of the development of the labor movement and the political party in Jamaica—vital for understanding the period after World War II.

2620 Quintero Rivera, Angel G. La dominación imperialista del Estado en Puerto Rico y la política obrera: 1900–1934 (UNAM/RMS, 40[40]:3, julio/sept. 1978, p. 1119–1141, maps, tables)

On the basis of theories by Georg Lukacs and Antonio Gramsci, author analyzes the development of political consciousness among the Puerto Rican labor force. Explains why capitalist hegemony was incomplete in Puerto Rico.

2621 Ricardi, Antonio and others. La revolución dominicana de abril vista por Cuba. Presentación de Emilio Cordero Michel. Santo Domingo: Editora de la Universidad Autónoma de Santo Domingo, 1974. 251 p. (Publicaciones; 164. Colección Historia y sociedad, 10)

All papers oppose the US intervention of the Dominican Republic in 1965 and Antonio Ricardi chronicles the history of US intervention in Latin America. For political scientist's comment, see *HLAS 39:7248*.

2622 Rigual, Néstor. Incidencias parlamentarias en Puerto Rico. v. 2, La década del '30. San Juan, P.R.: Instituto de Cultura Puertorriqueña, 1977. 477 p.; ill.; index.

Summary of parliamentary debates and matters attended by the legislature during the 1930s. For vol. 1, see *HLAS 38:2938*.

2623 Rodríguez-Loeches, Enrique. Bajando del Escambray. La Habana: Unión de

Escritores y Artistas de Cuba, 1976. 212 p.; plates.

This study is important not only as a contribution to the history of the Cuban Revolution, but also because the author was one of the founders of the Directorio Revolucionario which fought against Batista and Trujillo in the 1940s and 1950s. The description of the action, however, is little novelesque.

2624 Soto, Lionel. La Revolución del 33. La Habana: Editorial de Ciencias Sociales, 1977/1978. 3 v. (534, 435, 446 p.) bibl. (Nuestra historia)

A basic reference for those interested in the 1933 revolution, this work includes much valuable data on population, land holdings, foreign sugar interests, prices, wages, and other commercial statistics of the period. A bit tedious at times, the book includes a lengthy introduction on the 19th century.

Toro González, Carlos del. Algunos aspectos económicos sociales y políticos del movimiento obrero cubano: 1933–1958. See *HLAS 41:9191.*

2625 United Fruit Company, un caso del dominio imperialista en Cuba. La Habana: Editorial de Ciencias Sociales, 1976. 450 p.; bibl.; 26 leaves of plates: ill. (Nuestra historia)

A valuable study based on actual records of the company, depicting the development of the holdings in eastern Cuba, and analyzing the effect which this fact had on Cuban life and conditions, both locally and nationally. A solid contribution to the historiography of the subject.

Useem, Bert. Peasant involvement in the Cuban Revolution. See *HLAS 41:7220.*

Wessman, James W. The sugar cane hacienda in the agrarian structure of southwestern Puerto Rico in 1902. See *HLAS 41:1103.*

2626 Yglesia Martínez, Teresita. Cuba, Primera República, segunda ocupación. La Habana: Editorial de Ciencias Sociales, 1976. 432 p.; 19 leaves of plates: ill. (Nuestra historia)

The bibliography is extensive with a broad socioeconomic orientation and strong political overtones. The integration of documentation and commentary, however, is often disconcerting.

SPANISH SOUTH AMERICA: General

MICHAEL T. HAMERLY, *Visiting Senior Lecturer, The Hebrew University, Jerusalem*
JOHN HOYT WILLIAMS, *Professor of History, Indiana State University, Terre Haute*

2627 Academia Nacional de la Historia, *Caracas.* Catálogo, 1958–1978. Recopilación y catalogación por Santiago-Gerardo Suárez. Caracas: Academia Nacional de la Historia, 1978. 185 p.: ill. (Serie Fuentes para la historia colonial de Venezuela)

A catalogue of the "Biblioteca de la Academia Nacional de la Historia" from its inception in 1958 through 1978. More specifically of the "Serie Sesquicentenario de la Independencia" (53 vols.), the "Fuentes para la Historia Colonial de Venezuela" (89 vols. as of 1978), the "Serie para la Historia Republicana de Venezuela" (25 vols. as of 1978), and lesser series. Describes the "Fuentes para la Historia Colonial . . ." in detail. [MTH]

2628 Alvarez, Antonio. Crónica de la Patagonia y tierras australes desde el descubrimiento hasta la colonización. Buenos Aires: Talleres Gráficos Editorial Lito, 1978. 189 p.

An interesting episodic account of expeditions of exploration and colonization in the Argentine South, from Magellan in the 16th century through Amundson and Scott in the 20th. While there are no notes or maps, the bibliography is adequate. Contains considerable information on the Malvinas, Chubut, Neuquén, Deseado, Santa Cruz, Río Negro and Tierra del Fuego. A useful publication for the specialist as well as the general reader. [JHW]

2629 Arcila Farías, Eduardo. Historia de un monopolio: el estanco del tabaco en Venezuela, 1779–1833. Caracas: Facultad de Humanidades y Educación, Instituto de Estudios Hispanoamericanos, Universidad Central de Venezuela, 1977. 364 p.; bibl.; 1 leaf of plates (fold.): ill.

Exhaustively researched for all practical purposes, quantitative study of the heretofore poorly known Tobacco Monopoly in Venezuela from its establishment as a royal monopoly in 1779 through its suppression by independent Venezuela in 1833. Includes chapters on opposition to the monopoly, its administration, illicit cultivation and contraband trade as well as on production and intracolonial, intraimperial and international trade in the leaf, cigar and cigarettes, snuff and plug. A major and original contribution not only to the economic history of Venezuela but also to the history of royal and state monopolies in Spanish America. [MTH]

2630 Bischoff, Efraín U. Las viejas imprentas de la Universidad (UNC/R, 1:1/5, marzo/dic. 1977, p. 1–72, facsims., plates)

Well documented and written, this article traces the origins of the Córdoba University Press from its inception in 1766 to the end of the Rosas period in 1852. Stresses the technical and financial aspects but not slighting the cultural impact of the *imprenta* in Córdoba and beyond. [JHW]

2631 Bromley, Rosemary D.F. The functions and development of "colonial" towns: urban change in the Central Highlands of Ecuador, 1698–1940 (Transactions of the Institute of British Geographers [London] 4:1, 1979, p. 30–43, maps, tables)

A succinct overview of the differential growth and development of Ambato, Latacunga and Riobamba in highland Ecuador from the earthquake of 1698 through the early 20th century. Includes demographic data and an analysis of the 1832 cadastral surveys. See also items **2632** and **2786**. [MTH]

2632 ———. Urban-rural demographic contrasts in highland Ecuador: town recession in a period of catastrophe, 1778–1841 (Journal of Historical Geography [Academic Press, London] 5:3, July 1979, p. 281–295, maps, tables)

Demonstrates the extent to which the towns of Latacunga, Ambato and Riobamba lost population absolutely and relatively in terms of their previous numbers and those of their districts during the neocolonial period. At play were the continuing economic depression, several epidemics, a major earthquake which hit the towns particularly hard, civil disorders, especially the wars of independence, and out migration. Also delineates the differences in the characteristics of the urban and rural populations. Based primarily on analysis of the *padrones* of 1778–81 and 1814 and the censuses of 1836–41. See also item **2786**. [MTH]

2633 Bushnell, David. El proceso inicial del liberalismo en Colombia y en la Argentina: un esquema comparativo (UNCR/R, 2:4, enero/junio 1977, p. 77–91, bibl.)

Perspicacious, comparative study of liberalism in Argentina and Colombia during the independence and early national periods. [MTH]

2634 Cenni storici suls emigrazione italiana nelle Americhe e in Australia. A cura di Renzo De Felice. Scritti di Claudia Belleri Damiani. Milano: F. Angeli, 1979. 184 p.; bibl.

El volumen presenta una serie de estudios sobre la emigración italiana. De especial interés para el área latinoamericana son el excelente estudio de Eugenia Scarzanella sobre el rol de la inmigración italiana en la colonización agrícola argentina (p. 15–36), el de Giorgio Erler sobre la emigración italiana al estado de Rio Grande do Sul (p. 37–74), y el de José de Souza Martins sobre el rol de la emigración italiana en la formación del mercado de trabajo brasileño (p. 165–184). [M. Carmagnani]

Cobo, Bernabé. History of the Inca Empire. See item **1606**.

2635 Crespo R., Alberto. Esclavos negros en Bolivia. La Paz: Academia Nacional de Ciencias de Bolivia, 1977. 220 p.; bibl.; ill.

Consists of a somewhat sketchy account of black slavery in Bolivia from the Spanish conquest through emancipation in the mid 19th century. Nonetheless, it is worth consulting as a first attempt to pull together what is known about the history of slaves in the former Audiencia of Charcas and because it contains some new data from the archives of La Paz. [MTH]

2636 Duviols, Jean-Paul. Voyageurs français en Amérique: colonies espagnoles et portugaises. Paris: Burdas, 1978. 272 p.; ill.

Annotated bibliography of 16th through early 19th-century French travel accounts of the Spanish American colonies and Brazil. Organized thematically and chronologically, this well done and useful guide covers accounts of: voyages of discovery and colonization; missionary activities; spies, smugglers, pirates and slavers; scientific, military and commercial voyages. Includes a summary table, excerpts and illustrations from sample accounts. [MTH]

2637 Estrada Ycaza, Julio. Regionalismo y migración. Guayaquil: Archivo Histórico del Guayas, 1977. 296 p.; bibl.; index; maps (Colección Monográfica—Archivo Histórico del Guayas; 10)

Semi-impressionistic, semi-quantitative study concerns the history of migration in Ecuador, especially on the coast and from the highlands to the coast. The study includes significant demographic and social data (partly supplied by M.T. Hamerly). [MTH]

2638 Estudios bolivianos en homenaje a Gunnar Mendoza L. Edited by Martha Urioste de Aguirre et al. La Paz: s.n., 1978. 328 p.: ill.; bibl.; index; maps; tables.

Publishes 13 essays in honor of Gunnar Mendoza, Director of the National Archive and Library in Sucre, six on the colonial period (see items **2799**, **2805**, **2808** and **2814**) and seven on the national period. The contributors are young Bolivian historians of promise, commited to original research and interested in demographic, economic, ethno- and social history. A valuable set, available only in a limited printing. Includes a bibliography of Mendoza's works (item **33**). [MTH]

Fell, Eve-Marie. Sources françaises du courant racist en Amérique du Sud. See item **7634**.

2639 Fleming, William J. Regional research in Argentina: a critical evaluation of the archives and libraries of Mendoza province (AAFH/TAM, 35:1, July 1978, p. 110–120)

Succinctly describes holdings and facilities of major and minor archives and libraries in the city of Mendoza. Exemplifies their research potential insofar as the colonial as well as the national period are concerned, and comments on the historiography of Mendoza and its province. [MTH]

2640 Hamerly, Michael T. Registros parroquiales e inventarios de iglesias del litoral (AHG/R, 6:12, dic. 1977, p. 25–69, tables)

Lists all known parish registers through 1901 and inventories of churches in what are now the Archdiocesis of Guayaquil and the Prelacies of Los Ríos and El Oro. Preceded by an analysis of the registers and the uses they may serve. Includes notes on the origins of the colonial parishes in said dioceses. [MTH]

2641 Hernández Rodríguez, Guillermo. De los chibchas a la Colonia y a la República: del clan a la encomienda y al latifundio en Colombia. Bogotá: Instituto Colombiano de Cultura, Subdirección de Comunicaciones Culturales, 1975. 361 p.; bibl.; index (Biblioteca básica colombiana; 9)

New edition with updated notes of work first published in 1949, but not annotated in *HLAS*. A traditionalistic account of the Chibchas prior to and after the conquest. Still useful for data, but dated in interpretations. [MTH]

2642 Herrera de Weishaar, María Luisa; María Leonor Ferreira Ferreira; and **Carlos Nestor Alvarez Cabrera.** Parroquia La Vega: estudio micro-histórico. Caracas: Consejo Municipal del Distrito Federal, 1977. 176 p.; bibl.; 3 leaves of plates: ill.; maps.

Historical and sociological study of La Vega, formerly a rural parish and now an urbanized part of the Distrito Federal of El Libertador or Greater Caracas. The historical portion delineates the population growth and economic development of La Vega from colonial times through the present. Includes a documentary appendix (e.g., 1769 *matrícula* of La Vega). [MTH]

2643 Klein, Herbert S. The impact of the crisis in nineteenth-century mining on regional economies: the example of the Bolivian Yungas, 1786–1838 (*in* Social fabric and spatial structure in colonial Latin America. Edited by David J. Robinson. Ann Arbor, Mich.: University Microfilms International, 1979, p. 315–338, tables)

Utilizes the results of the censuses of 1786, 1803, 1829 and 1838, to establish the impact of mining cycles at Potosí on the population and economy of the coca producing haciendas and Aymara ayllus of the Yungas during the late colonial, independence and early national periods. A methodologically sophisticated and revisionist study with far reaching conclusions, among others, that the peasantry was neither stable nor unresponsive to the market, and that *yanaconas* may not have been all that dependent upon *hacendados*. [MTH]

Levene, Ricardo. Lecturas históricas argentinas. See items **2850** and **3375**.

2644 **Lombardi, John V.** The rise of Caracas as a primate city (*in* Social fabric and spatial structure in colonial Latin America. Edited by David J. Robinson. Ann Arbor, Mich.: University Microfilms International, 1979, p. 433–472, maps)

Masterful survey of the emergence of Caracas as a primary city. Lombardi focuses on four periods: 1) the creation of the city, 1560–1600; 2) the mature colonial city, 1750–1850, to which he devotes the most space as it was during the neocolonial years that Caracas consolidated its position as the central city of Venezuela; 3) "the commercial bureaucratic empire," 1860–1930; and 4) the petroleum metropolis, 1935–1978. At the same time Lombardi attempts to establish a paradigm of primacy applicable with modifications to other major cities of Latin America such as Lima, Mexico City or Rio de Janeiro. [MTH]

Loveman, Brian. Chile: the legacy of Hispanic capitalism. See item **3233**.

McCaa, Robert. Chilean social and demographic history. See item **3235**.

2645 **Macera dall'Orso, Pablo.** Trabajos de historia. Lima: Instituto Nacional de Cultura, 1977. 4 v. (312, 460, 352, 499 p.) bibl.

A welcome anthology of many of the writings of one of Peru's most prolific, professional and productive historians, Pablo Macera (b. 1929). The volumes consist of the following: 1) his theoretical studies and those on sources; 2) his research on language, ideas and art mostly but not exclusively of the 18th century; 3) his work on the economy of the 18th century; and 4) his essays on sugar estates in the 19th century and on guano. In brief, historians of the national as well as of the colonial period will find much of interest and importance in this major set. [MTH]

2646 **Martínez, Carlos.** Bogotá: sinopsis sobre su evolución urbana. v. 1, 1536–1900; v. 2, Bogotá reseñada por cronistas y viajeros ilustres, 1572–1948. Bogotá: Escala Fondo Editorial, 1976–1978. 2 v. (162, 168 p.) bibl.; fold. plates; ill.; maps; plates; tables (Colección Historia; 2)

Anthology of 45 descriptions of 16th-, 17th-, 18th-, 19th- and 20th-century Bogota, excerpted from the writings of chroniclers and travellers (for vol. 1, see *HLAS 41:5509*). [MTH]

2647 **Los Mercedarios en Bolivia:** documentos para su historia, 1535–1975. Recopilación: Eudoxio de Jesús Palacio y José Brunet. La Paz: Universidad Mayor de San Andrés, 1977. 385 p.; bibl.; 9 leaves of plates: ill.

Chronologically organized anthology of archival sources and notes on the Mercedarians in Bolivia. Covers the 16th through the 20th century. Compiled primarily by Palacio and upon his death, completed by Brunet who also added the notes. Sources selected included data on Indians and blacks, *censos* and haciendas as well as on convents and friars. [MTH]

2648 **Middleton, DeWight R.** The growth of a city: urban, regional, and national interaction in Ecuador (UA, 5:2, Summer 1976, p. 125–141, bibl.)

Methodologically sophisticated essay on the role of Manta in the prehistory, history and present of Ecuador in its regional or coastal as well as national context. Based on some but not all of the appropriate literature. Manta was a major port in the coastal trade between Central America, northern and central South America prior to the arrival of the Spaniards, all but depopulated in the 16th century, abandoned in the 18th except as a roadstead, reoccupied in the late 19th century, and is again today a relatively important maritime community. [MTH]

2649 **Miranda, Francisco de.** Colombeia. t. 1, 1750–1780. Prefacio de J.L. Salcedo-Bastardo. Introducción, bibliografía, prólogo y notas de Josefina Rodríguez de Alonso. Caracas: Ediciones de la Presidencia de la República, 1978. 1 v. (631 p.) bibl.; ill.

Inaugural volume of a new, chronologically reorganized and textually modernized edition of the *Archivo del General Francisco de Miranda* (24 vols.; Caracas: 1929–50). Covers the first 30 years of his life. Includes documents on Miranda's family, his education, sojourn in Spain between 1771 and 1780, and return to the colonies in 1780, as well as Miranda's correspondence of those years. [MTH]

2650 Norris, Robert E. Guía bibliográfica para el estudio de la historia ecuatoriana. Austin: Institute of Latin American Studies, University of Texas at Austin, 1978. 295 p.; indexes (Guides and bibliographies series; 11)

Lists with occasional commentary 4,000 plus items relating to the history of Ecuador. Somewhat more comprehensive on the independence and national than the colonial period. Primarily useful as guide to articles and published sources in Ecuadorian periodicals. [MTH]

2651 Paraguay. Archivo Nacional. Archivo Nacional de Asunción: primer ensayo de índice, el documento más antiguo, documentos inéditos. Recopilador, Viriato Díaz-Pérez. Prólogo, Marco Antonio Laconich. Palma de Mallorca: Luis Ripoll, 1978. 2 v. (Archivo Familia Díaz-Pérez; 14/15)

Viriato Díaz-Pérez, a Spanish *pensador*, and well-known and prolific literary figure, arrived at Asunción in 1906. The following year he became Director of the chaotic National Archive, which post he held until 1923. During his tenure, he really *created* the archive, organized its documents into sections, bound the papers, and, also wrote scores of articles for the *Revista del Instituto Paraguayo* and other periodicals. Díaz Pérez published hundreds of what he considered to be the most important of the archive's papers. This small, two-volume work reproduces about 40 of those documents (mostly from late 18th and 19th centuries) and includes a bio-bibliography of Díaz Pérez by Marco Antonio Laconich. [JHW]

2652 Philip H. & A.S.W. Rosenbach Foundation. A calendar of the Peruvian and other South American manuscripts in the Philip H. & A.S.W. Rosenbach Foundation, 1536–1914. Compiled and edited by David M. Szewczyk. Philadelphia: The Foundation, 1977. 190 p.; bibl.; facsims.; index.

A calendar of documents in the Rosenbach Foundation collection on Peru, Ecuador, Bolivia and Chile. Most of the manuscripts are on Peru, the earliest of which dates from 1536 and the latest, 1915. The entry format, descriptions and indexing leave something to be desired. Of interest to specialists only. For bibliographer's comment, see *HLAS 40:80*. [MTH]

2653 Pinto, Sonia; Luz María Méndez; and **Sergio Vergara.** Antecedentes históricos de la Contraloría General de la República. Santiago de Chile: La Contraloría General, 1977. 456 p.; bibl.; ill.

A detailed, documented account of the colonial and 19th-century antecedents of the Comptroller Generalcy in Chile, which was established in 1927. Includes a documentary appendix. Of considerable interest to economic historians. [MTH]

2654 Portugal Ortiz, Max. La esclavitud negra en las épocas colonial y nacional de Bolivia. La Paz: Instituto Boliviano de Cultura, 1978. 111 p.; bibl.

Not a monograph, but a collection of notes and sources, mostly archival, on black slavery in Bolivia, especially during the 18th and 19th centuries. Of research value only. [MTH]

2655 Rodríguez, Simón. Obras completas. Caracas: Universidad Simón Rodríguez, 1975. 2 v. (Colección Dinámica y siembra)

Likely to be definitive edition of writings of significant thinker of independence and early national periods who is too often remembered only as Bolívar's tutor. Contains useful extra features including Manuel Pérez Vila's "Estudio Bibliográfico," and Alfonso Rumazo González's "El Pensamiento Educador de Simón Rodríguez." [D. Bushnell]

2656 Romero Carranza, Ambrosio; Alberto Rodríguez Varela; and **Eduardo Ventura.** Manual de historia política y constitucional, Argentina, 1776–1976. Buenos Aires: AZ Editora, 1977. 432 p.

Although devoid of bibliography and notes, this is an impressive review of the development of the Argentine constitution and its frequent abrogation. Ranges from discussions of 16th-century, Spanish juridical thought and other foreign influences in the 18th century (chap. 1) to "Subversión y Corrupción," which deals with Cámpora, Lastiri and both Peróns (chap. 20). [JHW]

Sater, William. A survey of recent Chilean historiography, 1965–1976. See item **3264**.

2657 Spalding, Karen. Estructura de clases en la sierra peruana: 1750–1920 (ANA, 1, enero/marzo 1977, p. 25–35)

Presents working hypothesis or model as to structural changes in the rural society of highland Peru from the mid-18th century through the early 20th century. Argues that conventional interpretations notwithstanding, local census data indicates that the hacienda did not become the dominant agrarian institution, at least in the southern highlands, until the beginning of the 20th century, and that all-pervasive power of the hacendados resulted from an alliance between the political elite of the sierra and the nouveau richeau of the coast. [MTH]

2658 Williams, John Hoyt. The Archivo General de la Nación of Uruguay (AAFH/TAM, 36:2, Oct. 1979, p. 257–268)

Detailed description of the *fondos* of the National Archives of Uruguay. The majority of the holdings of this repository date from the 19th and 20th centuries, but it also has some materials from and on the 17th and 18th centuries. The archive itself is divided into four sections, an inventory of each of which has been published. [MTH]

SPANISH SOUTH AMERICA: Colonial Period

MICHAEL T. HAMERLY, *Visiting Senior Lecturer, The Hebrew University, Jerusalem*
JOHN HOYT WILLIAMS, *Professor of History, Indiana State University, Terre Haute*

BY AND LARGE CONTINUITY characterizes recent writings on the colonial period of the nine Spanish South American countries. For the most part the same themes are being addressed by the same individuals. And although more is published on colonial Venezuela and Peru than on any other former colony, much of the work on all former colonies is impressive. The volume of production continues to increase as scholars trained in the 1960s and early 1970s, especially in the US, begin to publish. In contrast to North American and European scholars whose preferences are eclectic in terms of periods and themes, most South American researchers continue to concentrate on either the early or late colonial periods. Therefore, the majority of studies on the 17th century are by foreign scholars.

Among changes worthy of note, regional history, never entirely neglected, has come into its own. Many of the studies annotated below can be regarded as works of regional history that are not only detailed and well documented but methodologically sophisticated and thematically varied. In contrast to the US, where only a few new researchers have emerged in recent years, there has been a marked increase in the ranks of colonialists in Spain and South America. Indeed, foreign as well as national scholars have been publishing more and better studies on colonial Ecuador, Bolivia, and Paraguay.

Finally and in order to improve access to users of this section—in which the bibliography is already geographically subdivided—we have organized the more specific comments in this introduction topically and chronologically, that is to say, according to eight major subjects and periods of interest to colonialists: 1) General Works; 2) Bibliography and Historiography; 3) Discovery and Conquest; 4) The Sixteenth Century; 5) The Seventeenth Century; 6) The Eighteenth Century; 7) Historical Demography; and 8) Sources.

1) GENERAL WORKS: There is a need for syntheses on the state of knowledge in the colonial period of the Spanish South American countries as well as for balanced overviews of their entire histories. The lack of such syntheses and overviews is

largely due to the belief shared by most productive scholars that more specific studies are needed prior to the writing of satisfactory and equitable general histories. Examples of general histories which lack balance by neglecting the colonial period are: Henry E. Dobyns and Paul L. Doughty, *Peru: a cultural history* (see *HLAS 40:3510*) and Brian Loveman, *Chile: the legacy of Hispanic capitalism* (item **3233**). Dobyns and Doughty slight the 17th century and the first half of the 18th; and Loveman devotes only 21 percent of his text to the colonial period. Also skimpy is David P. Werlich's section on the colonial period in *Peru: a short history* (item **3130**). Nevertheless what little Loveman and Werlich convey on the period is cogently said. One general work that is balanced as well as up-to-date in scholarship is Sergio Villalobos', Fernando Silva's, Osvaldo Silva's and Patricio Estellé's recent *Historia de Chile* (see *HLAS 40:3089*).

2) BIBLIOGRAPHY AND HISTORIOGRAPHY: Many major and minor bibliographies, historiographical studies and research guides appeared during the past five years. The most monumental are the six-volume *Author Catalog of the Peruvian Collection of the National Library of Peru* (Boston: G.K. Hall, 1979); and the six-volume *Argentine Bibliography: a Union Bibliography of Argentinian Holdings in the Libraries of the University of Buenos Aires* (Boston: G.K. Hall, 1980). According to the publisher, "The books and other materials listed in the latter are available on interlibrary loan, directly from the University of Buenos Aires." The only other noteworthy national bibliography is Robert E. Norris' *Guía bibliográfica para el estudio de la historia ecuatoriana* (item **2650**).

Angelina Lemmo reviews many but not all writings on colonial Venezuela in *Historiografía colonial de Venezuela* (item **2742**). William F. Sater notes a few items not caught by *HLAS* contributing editors in "Survey of Recent Chilean Historiography" (item **3264**). And José Vásquez Machicado's long awaited *Catálogo descriptivo del material del Archivo General de Indias referente a la historia de Bolivia* (see *HLAS 40:3244*), and Eduardo Arze Quiroga's *Papeles de Cochabamba* (item *2794*) facilitate research on colonial Bolivia.

The following specialized reviews and guides also deserve special attention: Leon G. Campbell's very good review article on Tupac Amarú and related studies (item **2686**); Michael T. Hamerly's solid guide to parish registers and Church inventories of the Ecuadorian coast (item **2640**); Robert McCaa's excellent piece on sources for the reconstruction of the demographic and social history of Chile (item **3235**); Julio Retamal Avila's extensive bibliography of articles on ecclesiastical history in Chilean journals (see *HLAS 40:3048*); and John Hoyt Williams' four-part discourse on Paraguayan repositories, sources and historiography (see *HLAS 40:3091*, and *The Americas*, Washington, 34:2, Oct. 1977, p. 274–284, 34:3, Jan. 1978, p. 407–418, and 34:4, April 1978, p. 537–552).

3) DISCOVERY AND CONQUEST: The discovery, exploration and conquest of Spanish South America continue to elicit attention, but most of the ensuing studies are prosaic. The following, however, are important because they pull together what is now known or contribute new data and interpretations: John Hemming's popular but more or less accurate and handsomely illustrated retelling of the discovery, exploration and conquest of what are now Venezuela and Colombia, *The Search for El Dorado* (item **2666**); Juan Friede's thoroughly researched biography of Jiménez de Quesada (item **2764**); José Antonio del Busto Duthurburu's new general history of 16th-century Peru (item **2684**), which is rich in information on the conquistadores on whom Busto Duthurburu is an authority; and Raúl Porras Ba-

rrenechea's posthumous *Pizarro* (item **2713**). The latter republishes Porras Barrenechea's several specialized studies on Pizarro and his heretofore unpublished and incomplete but nonetheless basic biography of the conqueror of Peru. And, Nathan Wachtel's classic analysis of the other side of the conquest of the Tahuantinsuyu is now available in English as *Vision of the vanquished* (item **2721**).

4) THE SIXTEENTH CENTURY: Perhaps the most exciting of recent monographs are: María Angeles Eugenio Martínez's dissertation on encomiendas, Indian population; tribute and labor in the Provinces of Santa Fé and Tunja (item **2763**); and Silvia Padilla Altamirano's thesis on Indian population, tribute, and encomiendas in the Governorship of Popayán (item **2777**). Eugenio Martínez complements Julián Bautista Ruíz Rivera's dissertation on those same themes and provinces for the 17th century (see *HLAS 40:3156*). And, Padilla Altamirano's thesis is part of a conjointly published and researched set on *La encomienda en Popayán: tres estudios*. The other two parts are: María Luisa López Arellano's "Las Encomiendas de Popayán en los Siglos XVII y XVIII", and Adolfo Luís González Rodríguez's "La Sociedad Encomendera en la Gobernación de Popayán durante el Siglo XVII." These five monographs were all produced by graduates of the Universidad de Sevilla, and add appreciably to knowledge of encomiendas and encomenderos, Indian labor systems in general, tribute and population movements, especially the decline in tributaries, in colonial Colombia.

Apparently no important studies appeared on 16th century Venezuela during the last biennium. Turning to Ecuador, the only noteworthy items appearing in this volume of the *Handbook* are: the articles by José Alcina Franch and his Universidad de Madrid group on *entradas* in Esmeraldas, which covers the entire colonial period (item **2785**), and John C. Super's article on early merchants of Quito (item **2791**). As for 16th-century Peru, with the exception of Guillermo Lohmann Villena's monograph on ideological aspects of the rebellion of the encomenderos (item **2704**) and Keith A. Davies' piece on land ownership and rural society in Arequipa (item **2695**), almost all of the work which has come to our attention is ethnohistorical. In addition to the studies annotated by John V. Murra in the ETHNOHISTORY: SOUTH AMERICA section of this volume (see p. 135–159), see also items **2696** and **2717**.

Peter J. Bakewell has published two more articles on Potosí, one on the introduction of the patio process and the subsequent boom of the 1570s (item **2797**), and the other on registered output between 1550 and 1735 (item **2796**). Bakewell and Daniel J. Santamaría (see *HLAS 40:3242*) have been joined by the Brazilian Jaciro Campante Patrício, who also stresses the importance of the patio process in bolstering output in item **2804**. And finally, the *cacicazgos* of Upper Peru are being studied at last (see item **2814**).

Insofar as early colonial Chile is concerned, the most important studies are Marcello Carmagnani's seminal paper on the market sector of the economy (item **2818**), and Rolando Mellafe's call for research on "neglected" aspects of the economy (see *HLAS 40:3253*). As for 16th-century Río de la Plata, the only noteworthy work is Héctor Adolfo Cordero's encyclopaedic account of daily life in early Buenos Aires (item **2837**).

5) THE SEVENTEENTH CENTURY: Clearly this is no longer a "forgotten" century. Stephanie Blank pulls together many of her findings on patron client relationships in late 16th century and early 17th-Caracas (item **2725**). In addition to López Arellano's and González Rodríguez's monographs on encomiendas and encomen-

deros of Popayán and Pasto, Peter Marzahl has published a book on 17th-century Popayán (item **2775**), which confirms many of their findings. Lawrence A. Clayton treats ship-building and ship-builders in depth in *Los astilleros de Guayaquil colonial* (item **2788**). Robson B. Tyrer delineates "The Demographic and Economic History of the Audiencia of Quito, 1600–1800" (Ph.D. dissertation, Berkeley, University of California, 1976). Although unpublished dissertations are not annotated in *HLAS*, important ones such as Tyrer's should be mentioned and commended. Another sophisticated study is the one by Spanish historian Javier Ortiz de la Tabla, "El Obraje Colonial Ecuatoriano" (item **2789**), which treats much the same themes as Tyrer's dissertation. But whereas the latter drew on Colombian and Ecuadorian repositories, Ortiz de la Tabla's study is based on sources in the Archivo General de Indias.

Peter T. Bradley, a British historian, has reexamined the defenses of the Viceroyalty of Peru during the 17th century especially those of Lima and Callao (see *HLAS 40:3192–3193*, and in this volume, items **2659** and **2678**); Fred Bronner of the Hebrew University of Jerusalem has enlightened us on encomenderos circa 1630 (see *HLAS 40:3195*), "Elite Formation in Seventeenth-Century Peru," *Boletín de Estudios Latinoamericanos y del Caribe* (24, 1978, p. 3–26), Viceroy Chinchón (item **2680**), and the population of Lima in the late 16th and early 17th centuries (item **2681**). And, there are several other important studies on 17th-century Peru as for example, Katharine Coleman's pioneering study of Trujillo (item **2689**).

Perhaps the most innovative study is Armando de Ramón's extraordinarily detailed reconstruction of real estate and proprietorship in Santiago de Chile during the second half of the 17th century (see *HLAS 40:3254* and in this volume, item **2821**). Also fascinating is his study of Santiago artisans during the same period (item **2820**).

6) THE EIGHTEENTH CENTURY: There are so many good works on the 18th century—notwithstanding continued neglect of the first half—that is difficult to select the best. Proceeding north to south, there is Eduardo Arcila Farías' definitive history of the tobacco monopoly in Venezuela (item **2629**), the only comprehensive account of that monopoly for any of the Spanish South American countries. Two works which complement one another and clarify many aspects of the Bourbon reforms and their consequences in what is now Colombia are: Allan J. Kuethe's *Military reform and society in New Granada, 1773–1808* (item **2772**) and John Leddy Phelan's *The people and the King: the Comunero Revolution in Colombia, 1781* (item **2779**). Kuethe's work is also noteworthy because it encompasses the viceregal dependencies of Panama and Quito. And, Ann Twinam joins the ranks of colonialists with her revisionist "Enterprise and Elites in Eighteenth-Century Medellín" (item **2782**).

As has become usual, there are several major new works on late colonial Peru: Leon G. Campbell, *The military and society in colonial Peru, 1750–1810* (item **2685**); John R. Fisher, *Silver mines and silver miners in colonial Peru: 1776–1824* (see *HLAS 40:3205*), also available in Spanish (item **2697**); the anthology of traditional and new-approach studies on the Tupac Amarú rebellion; Guillermo Lohmann Villena's monograph on the ministers of the Audiencia of Lima (see *HLAS 40:3215*); the compendium of many of Pablo Macera's studies on economic and other aspects of the 18th and 19th centuries (item **3094**); Magnus Mörner's quantitative study of rural Cuzco (item **2706**); and Alfredo Moreno Cebrian's monumental monograph on *El corregidor de indios* (item **2707**).

Several significant studies on late colonial Ecuador and Bolivia are discussed under the next subheading: *Historical Demography*. Insofar as Chile is concerned, only two items are important: Jacques A. Barbier's revisionist "Tradition and Reform in Bourbon Chile: Ambrosio O'Higgins and Public Finances" (item **2817**)—see also his just published *Reform and Politics in Bourbon Chile, 1755–1796* (Ottawa: University of Ottawa Press, 1980)—and Eulogio Zudaire Huarte's thoroughly researched study of Captain General Jáuregui y Aldecoa (item **2823**).

The bicentennial of the establishment of the Viceroyalty of the Río de la Plata in 1776 did not stimulate much in the way of significant publications, but see items **2832** and **2869**. Much more important and significant, certainly the most sophisticated work on 18th-century Spanish South America published during the last biennium, is Susan Migden Socolow's *The merchants of Buenos Aires, 1778–1810* (item **2865**). Turning to Paraguay, see Jerry W. Cooney's article on the cable industry (item **2836**), and Father José Luis Mora Mérida's social history of the late colonial Church (item **2858**). As for Uruguay or the Banda Oriental, nothing at all worthy of mention came to our attention with the exception of the article on the National Archives of Montevideo (item **2658**).

7) HISTORICAL DEMOGRAPHY: Judging from the great number of important contributions, historical demography may be evolving into a separate discipline. The overwhelming interest in the early and late colonial periods evident in the works noted below reflects the availability and accessibility of sources rather than indifference towards long-term trends. Demographic research in the intermediate colonial period, especially for those interested in non-Indian groups or vital events, requires much digging in local archives, an exceptionally time-consuming process. That the result is worth the effort, is exemplified by Noble David Cook's article on the demography of 17th-century Vegueta, an Indian parish in the central highlands of Peru (see *HLAS 40:3201*). For works based on the historical demographic sources of local archives in Ecuador, Peru, and Chile, see items **2640**, **2685** and **2822**.

Because these studies concern pre-industrial societies in which the economy and the population were closely intertwined, they shed much light on economic developments. This is why the twin questions of tributaries and Indian population movements are addressed by Eugenio Martinez, Padilla Altamirano and López Arellano in their monographs on the encomienda in 16th-century Santa Fé and Tunja and 16th- and 17th-century Popayán and Pasto (items **2763** and **2777**).

The only contribution in historical demography that can be regarded as general, in a chronological if not thematic sense, is Nicolás Sánchez-Albornoz's *Indios y tributos en el Alto Perú* (item **2811**). It deals with the demography and ethnohistory of highland Indians of Bolivia, from conquest through early 20th century, and should be mandatory reading for all colonialists. Valuable are Sánchez-Albornoz's comparative approach and his illumination of the issue of *forasteros*, who they were and how their presence or absence in the sources affects estimates of number of tributaries or Indians at large. It could be that the presence of many *forasteros* in the highlands of Ecuador—apparently an area of refuge during the intermediate colonial period—led some scholars to assume that the Indian population of Ecuador did not suffer as severe a decline as those of Mexico and Peru. On this and other points see Ortiz de la Tabla's above-mentioned study on the *obrajes* of Quito, and Rolando Mellafe's seminal paper on internal migration in the Viceroyalty of Peru (item **2670**).

The majority of historical demographic studies noticed in this *Handbook* concern the late colonial period, and occasionally the independence and early national periods as well. Rosemary D.F. Bromley, a British historical geographer, has begun to delineate the demographic and economic history of the central highlands of Ecuador and their capitals; Latacunga, Ambato and Riobamba (items **2631–2632** and **2786**). David G. Browning and David J. Robinson reexamine the reliability of late colonial "censuses" of Peru, the later ones consisting of more or less verbatim restatements of earlier ones (item **2682**). Herbert S. Klein delineates and elucidates the impact of mining cycles on the population and economy of the Bolivian *yungas* (item **2643**), and Daniel J. Santamaría, describes patterns of Indian land holdings throughout the *altiplano* (item **2813**), and the extent to which agriculture was commercialized in the Partido of Larecaja (item **2812**). See also Alcides Parejas Moreno's demographic and ethnohistorical study of 18th-century Moxos (item **2802**).

The following studies are also worth noting: Lyman L. Johnson's excellent studies of the size of Buenos Aires' population during the late colonial period (item **2844**), his work on the manumission of slaves (item **2845**), and together with Susan Migden Socolow, their fascinating reexamination of the characteristics of and changes in the population of Buenos Aires between 1774 and 1810 (item **2847**); and David J. Robinson's microanalysis of the demography of Córdoba 1779 (item **2861**) illustrates the utility of *padrones* as samples, their proclivity to understate the sizes of populations.

8) SOURCES: An outstanding number of quality items have appeared or come to our attention in the last few years: a) a compendium of all records of marriages between *peninsulares* and/or *criollos* in the Cathedral registers of Caracas for 1578 through 1831 (item **2729**) is a monumental source which students of social as well as demographic history will be mining for decades to come; b) as of 1978, at least 89 volumes had appeared in the "Fuentes para la Historia Colonial de Venezuela" series, for a list of which see item **2627**; c) the original version of Pedro Pizarro's *Relación del descubrimiento y conquista . . .* has appeared at long last (item **1705**); d) Jorge Juan and Antonio de Ulloa's *Relación histórica del viaje a la América meridional* (which covers much of Spanish South America, not just Ecuador and Peru) has been reissued in its entirety in a photo offset reprint (item **2674**), their *Noticias secretas* is available in an abridged but critical translation: *Discourse and political reflections on the Kingdoms of Peru* (item **2667**), it cannot be over-emphasized that the *Noticias secretas* reflect Juan and Ulloa's experiences in what is now Ecuador as much as, if not more so than in Peru proper; and e) the English abridgement of *Letter to a King* (item **1707**) from Poma de Ayala's *Nueva crónica y buen gobierno* which is not satisfactory.

The most voluminous and in many ways the most critical group of sources to be reissued or published for the first time is the compendium of viceregal *relaciones de mando* and *juicios de residencias* being brought out by Lewis Hanke and Celso Rodríguez (item **2675**). Although limited to the 16th and 17th centuries, their *Los virreyes españoles en América durante el gobierno de la Casa de Asturias: Perú*, of which the final two volumes just came off the press, includes supplementary materials and research notes on the interregnum *Audiencias* as well as on the viceroys themselves. One should also note Hanke and Rodríguez's introduction to and sampling of the *visita general* of 1590–93 (see *HLAS 40:3208*), and Pedro Rodríguez Crespo's "Fichero de Cédulas Reales: 1607–1615" (item **2672**).

GENERAL

2659 Bradley, Peter T. Maritime defense of the Viceroyalty of Peru, 1600–1700 (AAFH/TAM, 36:2, Oct. 1979, p. 155–175, tables)

Review of the changing composition and role played by the Armada del Mar del Sur—especially of the ships, the majority of which were built at Guayaquil—in the defense of the southern viceroyalty during the 17th century. [MTH]

2660 Burkett, Elinor C. In dubious sisterhood: class and sex in Spanish colonial South America (LAP, 4[12:13]:1/2, Winter/Spring 1977, p. 18–26, bibl.)

Self-critique of author's dissertation, abstracted below, on the urban and female experience in early colonial Peru. Burkett now argues that racial and class attitudes were more improtant than sexism in shaping roles played by and determining options open to black and Indian women. [MTH]

2661 ———. Indian women and white society: the case of sixteenth-century Peru (*in* Latin American women: historical perspectives [see item **1791**] p. 101–128)

Examines the differential impact of Spanish conquest on Indian men and women. Examples are drawn from Quito and Potosí as well as Arequipa and Lima. Argues that the initial need of conquistadores for women facilitated their incorporation into Spanish society, and afforded them some opportunities for socioeconomic mobility. Concludes that "While the economic activity of indigenous women strengthened their position within Hispanic society, it nonetheless broke down the relationships between these families and indigenous males, tying the women into a sex-based, rather than a race-based, social network." [MTH]

2662 ———. La mujer durante la conquista y la primera época colonial (UP/EA, 5[12]:1, 1976, p. 1–35, bibl.)

Preliminary version of item **2661**. [MTH]

Campbell, Leon G. Recent research on Andean peasant revolts, 1750–1820. See *HLAS 41:21.*

2663 Crahan, Margaret E. Civil-ecclesiastical relations in Hapsburg Peru (BU/JCH, 20:1, Winter 1978, p. 93–111)

Schematic overview of tensions between the State and the Church throughout the Viceroyalty of Peru during the 16th and 17th centuries. Considers the extension of the *patronato* to the Indies, the right of presentation, appointments to benefices, control over the clergy and Church finances, and the Indian question. Crahan finds that "conflicts increased and became less reconcilable" between the civil and ecclesiastical bureaucracies, especially in the 17th century under the weakened monarchy, which was no longer able to mediate effectively. [MTH]

2664 Cross, Harry E. Commerce and orthodoxy: a Spanish response to Portuguese commercial penetration in the Viceroyalty of Peru, 1580–1640 (AAFH/TAM, 35:2, Oct. 1978, p. 151–167, tables)

Reexamination of imperial and local, especially limeño, response to commercial competition with the Portuguese during the union of the two Crowns, in the Viceroyalty of Peru, which then embraced all of Spanish South America except for what is now Venezuela. Cross demonstrates that the Consulado de Comercio de Lima was able to cope with the competition threat on its own—in fact had to do so as Madrid was unwilling to act in the matter—by having the Inquisition eliminate the interlopers. [MTH]

2665 Díaz Rementería, Carlos J. En torno a un aspecto de la política reformista de Carlos III: las matrículas de tributarios en los Virreinatos de Perú y Río de la Plata (IGFO/RI, 37:147/148, enero/junio 1977, p. 51–139, tables)

Comparative study of the instructions issued to Visitadores Generales José Antonio de Areche and Jorge de Escobedo in 1778 and 1784 on the taking of the new censuses of the Indian population, especially tributaries, both of which documents are given in appendix. It is important to note that although many of the resultant, extraordinarily detailed *revisitas* have been recovered, many more remain to be found, and that even those which are known have yet to be exploited in their entirety. [MTH]

2666 Hemming, John. The search for El Dorado. New York: Dutton, 1979. 223 p.; bibl.; 16 leaves of plates: ill.; index (A Sunrise book)

Fast moving, handsomely illustrated account of the search for the fabled *El Do-*

rado (the King or Kingdom of Gold) throughout northern South America in the 16th and early 17th centuries by visionary Germans, Spaniards and Englishmen. Although intended for the general public, the work is of interest to specialists because of its use of appropriate secondary studies and published sources, and first hand reexploration of the area. The illustrations, many in color, include photographs of artifacts from the Museo de Oro in Bogotá. [MTH]

2667 Juan y Santacilia, Jorge and **Antonio de Ulloa.** Discourse and political reflections on the Kingdoms of Peru, their government, special regimen of their inhabitants, and abuses which have been introduced into one and another, with special information on why they grew up and some means to avoid them. Edited and with an introduction by John J. Tepaske. Translated by John J. TePaske and Besse A. Clement. Norman: University of Oklahoma Press, 1978. 326 p.; bibl.; index; map.

The first acceptable English translation and the most scholarly version to date of the well known *Noticias secretas de América*, authored primarily by Ulloa. Prepared from a coeval copy in the New York Public Library and the original in the Royal Palace of Madrid. Competently edited by TePaske. The Spanish and English titles notwithstanding, this classic account of political corruption and socioeconomic abuses in the Viceroyalty of Peru during the 1730s and 1740s, largely reflects the experience of Juan and Ulloa in the Audiencia of Quito. Regrettably, three chapters of the original were omitted. [MTH]

2668 Levillier, Roberto. El Paititi, El Dorado y las Amazonas. Buenos Aires: Emecé Editores, 1976. 304 p.; bibl.; ill.

Levillier, long a leading figure in Argentine historiography, has given us a pleasant recounting, in episodic form, of 16th-century expeditions, most of them failures, to penetrate the South American rain forests and savannas. While the search for El Dorado and the exploration of the Amazon are treated, the principal part of the book deals with explorations and expeditions North and West from Paraguay into the Chaco and today's Mato Grosso, the prominent figures being Cabeza de Vaca, Domingo Martínez de Irala and Ñuflo de Chaves. The individuals, their times and the environment are lavishly described. Complemented by an excellent bibliography. [JHW]

2669 Medina, José Toribio. El piloto Juan Fernández, descubridor de las islas que llevan su nombre y Juan Jufré, armador de la expedición que hizo en busca de otras en el mar del sur: estudio histórico. 2. ed. Santiago de Chile: Gabriela Mistral, 1975. 257 p.; bibl.; facsim. (Historia y documentos)

Reprint of a classic study by a noted Chilean scholar on two 16th-century Spanish pilots and explorers of the South Pacific. Includes an extensive documentary appendix. Originally published in 1918. [MTH]

2670 Mellafe, Rolando. Esquema del fenómeno migratorio en el Virreinato Peruano (IGFO/RI, 36:143/144, enero/junio 1976, p. 147–158)

Calls attention to an extremely important but little studied variable in the colonial history of Spanish South America, internal migration which was more extensive and intensive than many realize. Mellafe proposes a tentative general chronology and a typology of areas of in and out migration. [MTH]

Moreno Cebrián, Alfredo. Venta y beneficios de los corregimientos peruanos. See item **2709**.

2671 Ortiz, Sergio Elías. Informe del intendente Don Bartolomé Tienda de Cuervo, sobre la situación económica del Nuevo Reino de Granada, año 1734 (ACH/BHA, 61:705, julio/agosto 1974, p. 365–392)

Republishes little known, succinct but unusually well informed 1734 account by the Intendant of the Treasury in Bogotá on economic conditions, resources and problems throughout the then suppressed Viceroyalty of New Granada, including the eventual Captaincy General of Venezuela. A valuable coeval source, replete with useful facts and figures. [MTH]

2672 Rodríguez Crespo, Pedro. Fichero de cédulas reales, 1607–1615 (PUCP/CSH, 8/10, enero 1970/dic. 1972, p. 71–117)

Regrettably not noticed in an earlier *HLAS*, this is a very useful chronological guide to and summary of the contents of *cédulas* from the Council of Indies to the Viceroys of Peru for the years 1607–15, as found in the Archivo General de Indias, Audiencia de Lima, *Legajos No. 570–571*. The *cédulas* themselves touch upon virtually every aspect of administration in the colonies. [MTH]

Sáenz de Santamaría, Carmelo. Los manuscritos de Pedro Cieza de León. See item **1726**.

2673 Salmoral, Manuel Lucena. Los movimientos antirreformistas en Suramérica, 1777–1781: de Tupac Amarú a los comuneros (RUC, 26:107, enero/marzo 1977, p. 79–113)

Makes a strong case that the uprisings of the late 1770s and early 1780s in what are now Colombia, Ecuador, Peru and Bolivia, were movements of protest against the fiscal reforms of the Bourbons, then being introduced by the Visitadores José de Areche in the Viceroyalty of Peru, Joseph García de León y Pizarro in the Audiencia of Quito, and Francisco Gutiérrez de Piñeras in Nueva Granada, rather than movements for independence, precursor or otherwise. [MTH]

2674 Ulloa, Antonio de and **Jorge Juan y Santacilia.** Relación histórica del viaje a la América meridional. Introducción y edición de José P. Merino Navarro y Miguel M. Rodríguez San Vicente. Madrid: Fundación Universitaria Española, 1978. 2 v. (682, 603 p.) bibl.; ill.; fold. maps; fold. plans; fold. plates (Publicaciones de la Fundación Universitaria Española. Facsímiles; 4)

Welcome photo offset reprint of original 1748 account by Spanish naval Lieutenant Juan Y Santacilia and Ulloa. It describes first their joint French-Spanish expedition which was sent to the equator in 1735 to measure the earth, and then their subsequent 11-year sojourn in the Viceroyalty of Peru, first as members of the expedition and then as military advisors to the viceroy. Important not only for the data on the expedition but as a major source, replete with illustrations and maps, on peoples and places, flora and fauna of what are now Panama, Colombia, and especially Ecuador and Peru. Apparently Ulloa was the principal author of this classic as well as *Kingdoms of Peru* (see item **2667**). The introduction by Merino Navarro and Rodríguez San Vicente includes a history of the original printing. [MTH]

2675 Los Virreyes españoles en América durante el gobierno de la Casa de Austria: Perú. Edición de Lewis Hanke, con la colaboración de Celso Rodríguez. Madrid: Atlas, 1978. 5 v. (296, 284, 286, 306, 296 p.) bibl. (Biblioteca de autores españoles; 280–284)

Major set of sources and research notes on the 16th- and 17th-century Viceroys of Peru, interregnum Audiencias, and the viceroyalty as a whole, then inclusive of all Spanish South America except for what is now Venezuela. These five volumes (1/5) cover Viceroys Blasco Núñez Vela (1544–46) through Melchor de Linán y Cisneros (1678–81), and the interregnum Audiencias of 1606–07, 1666–67, and 1672–74. The final two volumes (6/7, in press) will cover the viceregencies of the final quarter of the 17th century. The first five volumes include instructions issued to each viceroy, the account he or the Audiencia left of his/its reign (*relaciones de mando*)—most of which are newly transcribed and several of which appear here for the first time—and summaries of the review of term (*juicios de residencia*). Vols. 1/5 also include bibliographical notes on each viceroy or interregnum Audiencia and a list of the dispatches remitted to the Crown by him/it as published by others, especially Roberto Levillier, or to be seen in the Archivo General de Indias, Audiencia de Lima *legajos*. The shorthand references to studies and published sources in the notes are keyed to Hanke and Rodríguez's *Guía de las fuentes en el Archivo General de Indias para el estudio de la administración virreinal española en México y en el Perú: 1535–1700* (see *HLAS 40:2293* and see also their set on the Mexican viceroys, *HLAS 40:2461*). [MTH]

PERU

Adorno, Rolena. Felipe Guamán Poma de Ayala: an Andean view of the Peruvian viceroyalty, 1565–1615. See item **1581**.

2676 Arcila Farías, Eduardo. El pensamiento económico hispanoamericano en Baquíjano y Carrillo. Caracas: Consejo Nacional de la Cultura, Centro de Estudios Latinoamericanos "Rómulo Gallegos," 1976. 150 p. (Colección Repertorio americano)

Analyzes the political economic thought of Baquijano, a late 18th-century

Peruvian reformer and thinker, and reprints Baquijano's 1791 *Disertación histórica y política sobre el comercio del Perú*, which originally appeared in *Mercurio Peruano*. [MTH]

Basto Girón, Luis J. Salud y enfermedad en el campesino peruano del siglo XVII. See *HLAS 41:1441*.

2677 Birckel, Maurice. Sobre los extranjeros en Lima: el proceso inquisitorial contra un catedrático francés en la Universidad de San Marcos, siglo XVI (PUCP/H, 1:2, dic. 1977, p. 161–182, bibl.)

Case study of political uses to which the Inquisition was sometimes put, in this instance to investigate Diego Corne, a French professor of Latin in Lima and who was suspect because of his nationality. Prelude to a larger study on limeño attitudes toward the treatment of foreigners. [MTH]

2678 Bradley, Peter T. The lessons of the Dutch blockade of Callao, 1624 (PAIGH/H, 83, enero/junio 1977, p. 53–68)

Reexamination of the frustrated 1624 Dutch blockage of Callao. Sheds new light on what happened, why and the consequences. Among these were the strengthening of the fortifications of Callao and Lima and a project—never realized—to redouble the Armada del Mar del Sur with a peninsular contingent. [MTH]

———. Maritime defense of the Viceroyalty of Peru, 1600–1700. See item **2659**.

2679 Bravo Guerreira, María Concepción. La muerte de Huayna Capac, 1530: precisiones cronológicas (IGFO/RI, 37:147/148, enero/junio 1977, p. 7–22)

Argues that native chronicles of the conquest demonstrate that Huayna Capac, the penultimate Inca, died in late 1529 or early 1530, rather than in the mid 1520s. If true, the chronology of the twilight of the Tahuantinsuyu, especially of the power struggle between Huascar, Atahualpa and others, will have to be revised. [MTH]

2680 Bronner, Fred. Perfiles humanos y políticos del conde Chinchón, virrey del Perú: 1629–1639 (IGFO/RI, 37:149–150, julio/dic. 1977, p. 639–677)

Exceptionally well researched monograph on a major early 17th-century viceroy of Peru. Primarily a study of Chinchon's efforts to reconcile crown demands, mostly for money, with those of the dominant interest groups in the colony. Examines the viceroy's personality, Chinchon as a politician, as an administrator, his relations with *corregidores* and with the Audiencia of Lima and its members. The section of the *Acuerdo* or joint sessions of the Viceroy and Audiencia, is especially enlightening. [MTH]

2681 ———. The population of Lima, 1593–1637: in quest of a statistical bench mark (IAA, neuer Folge, 5:2, 1979, p. 107–119, bibl., tables)

Careful assessment of the several late 16th- and early 17th-century censuses and estimates of the population size and composition of Lima. Bronner concludes that whereas the 1614 census may be relatively accurate, that of 1619 is not. Furthermore he argues the demography of colonial Lima can only be reconstructed more or less accurately from the city's parish registers, in which task he is now engaged. [MTH]

2682 Browning, David G. and **David J. Robinson.** The origin and comparability of Peruvian population data: 1776–1815 (JGSWGL, 14, 1977, p. 199–223, maps, tables)

Critical reexamination of late colonial population sources on Peru proper. Browning and Robinson demonstrate that the so called censuses of 1795 and 1812 were no more than almost verbatim restatements of the census of 1791/92, and that even the latter, upon which many scholars have relied in their studies of the period, was not entirely original. In other words, the census of 1791/92 was based in part, at least upon the *padrones* of the late 1770s and early 1780s. Depending upon the use to which such data are put, considerable caution may have to be exercized. For ethnohistorian's comment, see *HLAS 40:2029*. [MTH]

Burkett, Elinor C. In dubious sisterhood: class and sex in Spanish colonial South America. See item **2660**.

———. Indian women and white society: the case of sixteenth-century Peru. See item **2661**.

2683 Busto Duthurburu, José Antonio del. Francisco Pizarro, el marqués gobernador. 2. ed. corr. y aumentada. Lima: Librería Studium, 1978. 291 p.; bibl.

Revised edition of a popular biography of the conqueror of Peru. Based on archival research as well as standard sources. Pro-Pizarro but not apologetic. [MTH]

2684 ———. Historia general del Perú: descubrimiento y conquista. Lima: Librería Studium, 1978. 563 p.; fold. tables; ill.; maps; plates.

Detailed, more or less integral account of the discovery and conquest of Peru. Especially rich in data on minor as well as major conquistadores, on which Busto Duthurburu is an authority. Apparently intended as a text. [MTH]

2685 Campbell, Leon G. The military and society in colonial Peru, 1750–1810. Philadelphia: American Philosophical Society, 1978. 254 p.; bibl.; ill.; index (Memoirs of the American Philosophical Society; 123)

Diachronic study of military developments and their impact on society in late colonial Peru. Campbell demonstrates that Viceroy Amat did not militarize the colony in the 1760s and 1770s as has often been alleged, the recruitment of thousands of militiamen notwithstanding, as their failure to put down the rebellions of 1780 on their own subsequently demonstrated, and that Visitador Areche abandoned reliance on the ineffectual militia in favor of "veteran Spanish and fixed infantry regiments." Campbell also finds that the privileges accorded the military were insufficient to challenge the civil bureaucracy, the Church or the merchant corporation when these groups came into conflict, and that there did not emerge a military class prior to independence. This revisionist study is sound in so far as military developments per se are concerned. It is less satisfactory as to economic and especially social developments, however, partly because the chronological approach does not lend itself well to this kind of study, partly because Campbell did not consult all the appropriate related literature. [MTH]

2686 ———. Rebel or royalist?: Bishop Juan Manuel de Moscoso y Peralta and the Tupac Amaru revolt in Peru, 1780–1784 (PAIGH/R, 86, julio/dic. 1978, p. 135–168)

Examines the role of the Bishop of Cuzco in the Indian rebellions of the 1780s. Campbell argues that Moscoso, a criollo, was an opportunist who initially sought to manipulate Tupac Amarú and other native leaders, only to revert to loyalism to the Crown, when it became obvious that the movement possessed its own dynamic. Such Machiavelian behavior, however, does not necessarily make Moscoso "a unique and atypical individual" as Campbell concludes given the fact that many of the bishop's compatriots were also men on the make. [MTH]

2687 ———. Recent research on Andean peasant revolts, 1750–1820 (LARR, 14:1, 1979, p. 3–49, bibl.)

An incisive review of 20th-century work by Peruvian and foreign scholars on Indian rebellions in late colonial Peru. Focuses primarily on the Tupac Amaru uprising of 1780, on which Campbell is preparing a book. The full bibliography includes published sources as well as monographic studies. [MTH]

2688 Castro, Ignacio de. Relación del Cuzco. Prólogo de Carlos Daniel Valcárcel. 2. ed. Lima: Universidad Nacional de San Marcos, Dirección Universitaria de Biblioteca y Publicaciones, 1978. 190 p.; ill.

First complete edition of coeval work heretofore available only in manuscript or the incomplete Madrid edition of 1795, on the establishment of the Audiencia of Cuzco in 1788, and the celebration of that event. Castro (1732–92), the rector of the local seminary, includes a valuable description of Cuzco and its inhabitants. [MTH]

2689 Coleman, Katharine. Provincial urban problems: Trujillo, Peru, 1600–1784 (*in* Social fabric and spatial structure in colonial Latin America. Edited by David J. Robinson. Ann Arbor, Mich.: University Microfilms International, 1979, p. 369–408, maps, tables)

Able summary of ongoing, original research into the demographic, economic and social history of the city of Trujillo and northern Peru during the colonial period. This study is largely limited to Trujillo itself and examines the city's war during the 17th century and subsequent wane. A significant contribution to the regional as well as urban history of Peru. [MTH]

Crahan, Margaret E. Civil-ecclesiastical relations in Hapsburg Peru. See item **2663**.

Cross, Harry E. Commerce and orthodoxy: a Spanish response to Portuguese commercial penetration in the Viceroyalty of Peru, 1580–1640. See item **2664**.

2690 Cúneo-Vidal, Rómulo. Diccionario histórico-biográfico del sur del Perú. Lima: s.n., 1978. 577 p.; 1 leaf of plates: port. (His Obras completas; 6/11)

Useful biographical dictionary of Spanish *vecinos* and Indian caciques of colonial Arequipa, Arica, Tacna and other cities and towns in southern Peru. Includes a documentary appendix. Based on considerable research in local as well as national and Spanish archives. Cúneo-Vidal (1865–1931) was a journalist, diplomat, poet and novelist as well as an amateur historian and philogist. Fortunately his diligence compensates for his lack of method. Except where otherwise noted, this and the following items are posthumous publications, not reeditions. [MTH]

2691 ———. Guerras de los últimos incas peruanos. 2. ed. Lima: s.n., 1978. 172 p.; 1 leaf of plates: ill. (His Obras completas; 3/4)

Prosaic but well documented narrative of post-conquest resistance of the Incas to Spanish conquest, from Manco Yupanqui's rebellion in 1534 through Vilcabamba's fall in 1572. Originally published in 1925. Cúneo-Vidal was among the first to recognize that the conquest of Peru was neither as complete nor as heroic as traditionally believed, that is to say that some Incas held out for some time and that the Spaniards would not have succeeded in conquering as much territory as rapidly as they did had it not been for Indian allies. [MTH]

2692 ———. Historia de la civilización peruana. Historia de los antiguos cacicazgos hereditarios del sur del Perú. Editor: Ignacio Prado Pastor. Lima: s.n., 1977. 489 p.; ill. (His Obras completas; 1:1/2)

Two volumes in one. The first is only of historiographic interest. The second (p. 295–489), on the cacicazgos of the Peruvian South, is still quite useful. Contains much archival local data on 16th-, 17th- and 18th-century caciques or *kurakas* of Tacna, Codpa. Tarata, Ilabaya, Arica, Pica, and Tarapacá. [MTH]

2693 ———. Historia de la fundación de San Marcos de Arica. Leyendas de Arica, Tarapacá y Atacama. Editor: Ignacio Prado Pastor. Lima: s.n., 1977. 451 p.; ill. (His Obras completas; 5:9/10)

This is not an account of the foundation of Arica in 1574, but a series of notes on the history of Arica from the conquest through the 19th century. Useful volume, given the lack of more scholarly works. The *Leyendas* are of the *palmista* genre. [MTH]

2694 ———. Vida del conquistador del Perú: Don Francisco Pizarro. Editor: Ignacio Prado Pastor. 2. ed. Lima: s.n., 1978. 403 p.; 1 leaf of plates: ill. (His Obras completas; 2/3)

Reprint of a 1925 narrative account of the lives of Francisco Pizarro and his brothers, and of the conquest of Peru. Relatively dispassionate and modern in interpretation. Reflects some archival research. [MTH]

2695 Davies, Keith A. La tenencia de la tierra y la sociedad rural arquipeña en los siglos XVI y XVII (PUCP/H, 1:2, dic. 1977, p. 183–197, bibl.)

A sequel to *HLAS 40:3203*, this article is a précis of the structure of and changes in the economy of the district of Arequipa during the 16th and 17th centuries. Rich in data, but lacking in cohesiveness. [MTH]

2696 Espinoza Soriano, Waldemar. Huaraz: poder, sociedad y economía en los siglos XV y XVI, reflexiones en torno a las visitas de 1558, 1594 y 1712. Lima: Universidad Nacional Mayor en San Marcos, Seminario de Historia Rural Andina, 1978. 165 p.; 1 leaf of plates: bibl.; maps, tables.

Analyzes demographic and economic data in the 1558 *visita* of Ichoc- and Allauca-Huaraz, the 1594 land *composición* of Huambo, and the 1712 *composición* of various *parcialidades*, the texts of which are appended. An important contribution to the ethno- and early colonial history of the north central coast. [MTH]

Estudios bolivianos en homenaje a Gunnar Mendoza L. See item **2638**.

2697 Fisher, John Robert. Minas y mineros en el Perú colonial, 1776–1824. Presentación de Heraclio Bonilla. Lima: Instituto de Estudios Peruanos, 1977. 253 p.; bibl.; tables (Serie Estudios históricos; 4)

Spanish translation of *HLAS 40:3205*. Includes an introduction by Heraclio Bonilla. [MTH]

2698 ———. Royalism, regionalism, and rebellion in colonial Peru, 1808–1815 (HAHR, 59:2, May 1979, p. 232–257)

A fresh and original reexamination of unrest in the final years of the colony. Fisher first reviews the literature on "precursor movements," stressing in passing that the rebellion of Tupac Amarú was primarily "a violent social protest"—an interpretation with which most North American and European scholars would agree—and then focuses on Cuzco, the primary scene of renewed unrest. He demonstrates that the rebellion of 1814–15 was motivated by economic dissatisfaction, and that it "was a revolution for independence which enjoyed widespread support from both whites and Indians in southern Peru." [MTH]

2699 Fuentes documentales para la historia de Arequipa. v. 1, El Obispo Pedro José Cháves de la Rosa. Arequipa, Perú: Universidad Nacional de San Agustín, Seminario de Palografía Hispanoaméricana, 1975. 84 p.; bibl.

The first volume in a new set on the history of Arequipa. Publishes a 1788 inventory of the library holdings of Bishop Chaves de la Rosa, his last will and testament, and deeds to houses he purchased. [MTH]

Guillén Guillén, Edmundo. Visión peruana de la conquista: la resistencia incaica a la invasión española. See item **1645**.

2700 Harth-Terré, Emilio. Lima: ensayos. Lima: Editorial J. Mejía Baca, 1977. 155 p.; 2 leaves of plates: ill.

Collection of some of Harth-Terré's essays on prehispanic and colonial Lima. Particularly interesting are "El Cabildo de los Reyes" (1945) and "El Mestizaje en los Primeros Años de la Fundación de Lima, 1538–1539" (1965). Harth-Terré (b. 1899), an architect and engineer, has long been interested in the history of the lower strata and produced a number of important studies over the years (see also *HLAS 36:2577a* and *HLAS 40:3209*). [MTH]

2701 Heras D., P. Julián. Los franciscanos en el Pongoa, Tambo y Alto Ucayali a fines del siglo XVII (CAAAP/AP, 2:3, oct. 1978, p. 199–221)

Historical geographic introduction to the accounts of Father Manuel Biedma and his Franciscan brethren of their mission to the Cunibos of the Upper Ucayali and neighboring tribes in the 1670s and 1680s. The *informes* themselves will be published proximately in *Amazonia Peruana*. [MTH]

2702 Hernández Aparicio, P. El Obispo D. Francisco Verdugo: apuntes para una historia de Huamanga, 1623–1636 (ISTM/MH, 34:100/102, 1977, p. 5–20)

Primarily a summary of the detailed inspection realized by the second bishop of Guamanga of his diocesis in 1624–25. Hopefully Verdugo's *visita* and related documentation will be published as it is apparently an exceptionally rich source on the demography, economy and society as well as the state of the Church in this southern highland area. [MTH]

Juan y Santacilia, Jorge and **Antonio de Ulloa.** Discourse and political reflections on the Kingdoms of Peru, their government, special regimen of their inhabitants, and abuses which have been introduced into one and another, with special information on why they grew up and some means to avoid them. See item **2667**.

Lavallé, Bernard. Les Péruviens à la recherche de leur XVIIIe siècle. See item **5132**.

2703 León Borja de Szásdi, Dora. Los traslados de ciudades en la nueva Castilla (UNAM/RFD, 26:101/102, enero/junio 1976, p. 227–241)

Examines the problematics of shifting sites of cities as legal entities during the early years of the colony, especially during the conquest period. León Borja suggests that San Miguel (Piura) might have been founded initially at Puerto Viejo on the central coast of Ecuador, and argues that Xauxa (Juaja) became Los Reyes or Lima, and Santiago de Quito, Santiago de Guayaquil. Such conjectures rest on the juridical approach to the past, prevalent in Hispanic historiography. [MTH]

2704 Lohmann Villena, Guillermo. Las ideas jurídico-políticas en la rebelión en Gonzalo Pizarro: la tramoya doctrinal de levantamiento contra las Leyes Nuevas en el Perú. Valladolid: Casa-Museo de Colón y Seminario Americanista, Secretariado de Publicaciones, de la Universidad de Valladolid, 1977. 112 p.; bibl.; 3 leaves of plates: ill. (Serie americanista Bernal; 11)

Well researched, written and organized study of the ideological aspects of the rebellion of the *encomenderos*. Includes a chapter on men of the cloth and of the law involved in the uprising. [MTH]

Macera dall'Orso, Pablo. La imagen francesa del Peru: siglos XVI–XIX. See item **3094**.

———. Trabajos de historia. See item **2645**.

Mendoza, Diego de. Chronica de la Provincia de S. Antonio de los Charcas del Orden de Nro. Seraphico P.S. Francisco en las Indias Occidentales, Reyno del Peru. See item **2801**.

2705 Mörner, Magnus. Continuidad y cambio en una provincia del Cuzco: Calca y Lares desde los años 1680 hasta los 1790 (PMNH/HC, 9, 1975, p. 79–117, bibl., tables)

Consists of a preliminary version of the section on and at the same time a more extended treatment of the demography and economy of the Province of Calca and Lares during the late colonial period than is to be found in Mörner's recent book on Cuzco (item **2706**). [MTH]

2706 ———. Perfil de la sociedad rural del Cuzco a fines de la colonia. Lima: Universidad del Pacífico, Departamento Académico de Ciencias Sociales y Políticas, 1978. 186 p.; bibl.; fold. maps; maps; tables.

This major contribution to the little-known post-conquest history of the Peruvian *altiplano* is a quantitative study of the demographic and economic infrastructures of the Intendancy of Cuzco and its component provinces during the late 17th and throughout the 18th centuries. Based primarily on two sets of extraordinarily detailed *informes*, those of 1689–90, which were compiled by parish priests at the order of the Bishop of Cuzco and are here analyzed for the first time in the literature, and the well known *relaciones* of 1786. Includes a chapter on the causes and effects of the rebellion of 1780. Unfortunately, the printer left out the table of contents. [MTH]

———. La sociedad rural cusqueña en la perspectiva histórica. See item **3099**.

2707 Moreno Cebrián, Alfredo. El corregidor de indios y la economía peruana del siglo XVIII: los repartos forzosos de mercancías. Madrid: Consejo Superior de Investigaciones Científicas, Instituto Gonzalo Fernández de Oviedo, 1977. 801 p.; bibl.; index; plates; tables.

Monumental work on the *corregidores de indios* and their impact on the rural economy of 18th-century Peru. Primarily an extraordinarily detailed, quantitative analysis of the *repartimiento* system or forced distribution of merchandise among Indians. Examines the institution of the *corregimiento* and the *corregidores* themselves, abuses they committed, especially through the *repartimiento*, attempts to regulate the system, the *residencia*, the massive information gathered by the Crown in the 1770s from bishops throughout the colonies regarding *repartimiento* abuses, subsequent attempts to suppress the repartimiento, and its rebirth under the intendants and subintendants. In brief, this is an exceptionally important contribution to the institutional and socioeconomic history of the late colonial period. [MTH]

2708 ———. *La Descripción del Perú*, de Joaquín Bonet, y *La Ordenanza de Intendentes de 1803* (IGFO/RI, 37:149/150, julio/dic. 1977, p. 723–788, tables)

Publishes with a brief introduction a 1795 description of Peru by a knowledgeable viceregal bureaucrat. Bonet y Abascal's *Descripción de las provincias o partidos de este Virreynato del Perú . . .* (p. 736–788) is a detailed *partido*-by-*partido* account of boundaries, population as of 1792, agricultural and/or mineral output, value of the *repartimiento*, collection of tributes and salaries paid subintendants and corregidores. [MTH]

2709 ———. Venta y beneficios de los corregimientos peruanos (IGFO/RI, 36:143/144, enero/junio 1976, p. 213–246, tables)

Includes significant data found by author in the Archivo General de Indias on specific sales of corregimientos in 17th and 18th-century Peru. The extensive tables give names of purchasers, dates of appointment, and amounts paid. Also includes some information on the worth of corregimientos elsewhere in the Viceroyalty (e.g., Chile and Upper Peru). [MTH]

2710 O'Phelan Godoy, Scarlett. El norte y los movimientos antisfiscales del siglo XVIII (PUCP/H, 1:2, dic. 1977, p. 199–222, bibl.)

Conceptually sophisticated and systematic examination of known and fresh data from the archives of Trujillo and Lima on 18th-century tax riots in the Provinces of Cajamarca, Huamachucho and Saña or Lambayeque. [MTH]

Philip H. & A.S.W. Rosenbach Foundation. A calendar of the Peruvian and other South American manuscripts in the Philip H. & A.S.W. Rosenbach Foundation, 1536–1914. See item **2652**.

Pizarro, Pedro. Relación del descubrimiento y conquista de los Reinos del Perú. See item **1705**.

2711 Polo y La Borda, Jorge. La Hacienda Pachachaca: segunda ruta, del siglo XVIII (PUCP/H, 1:2, dic. 1977, p. 223–247, bibl.)

Argues that haciendas were feudal rather than capitalistic institutions, i.e., that their owners attempts to maximize returns from the sale of one or two basic products to more or less closed markets by promoting self sufficiency of the estates. Believes that the Jesuit developed sugar estate of Pachachaca in the Province of Abancay within the Intendancy of Cuzco constitutes an example albeit imperfectly realized of such "feudalistic" principles. [MTH]

Poma de Ayala, Felipe Huamán. *Letter to a King:* a Peruvian chief's account of life under the Incas and under Spanish rule. See item **1707**.

2712 Ponce, Fernando and **Eusebio Quiroz Paz-Soldán.** Observaciones críticas a la información demográfico-histórica de Arequipa, 1549–1820 (LARR, 13:2, 1978, p. 170–181, tables)

Considers the several groups of extant sources, including parish registers, available for the reconstruction of the demography of colonial Arequipa. These record groups have been brought together in the recently formed Archivo Departamental de Arequipa. See also the authors' *Informe de datos bibliográficos-documentales de orden demográfico de la ciudad de Arequipa, Perú* (México: CELADE, 1975). [MTH]

2713 Porras Barrenechea, Raúl. Pizarro. Prólogo de Luis Alberto Sánchez. Portada e ilustraciones de Félix Nakamura. Lima: Editorial Pizarro, 1978. 686 p.; bibl.; 20 leaves of plates: ill.

Reprints Porras' preliminary studies on Pizarro and publishes for the first time Porras' never completed yet exceptionally important magnum opus on the conqueror and conquest of Peru. Not definitive, but by far and above the most thorough and well researched study in conjunct of Pizarro ever produced. [MTH]

Pouncey, Lorene. The Library Convent of Ocopa. See *HLAS 41:93*.

Ramírez-Horton, Susan. Chérrepe en 1572: un análisis de la Visita General del Virrey Francisco de Toledo. See item **1710**.

2714 Roche, Paul. Les corrections *almagristes* dans l'éditions princeps de l'*Histoire du Pérou* d'Agustín de Zárate (UTIEH/C, 31, 1978, p. 5–16)

That there are marked differences between the 1577 and the 1555 or first edition of Zárate's *Historia del descubrimiento y conquista del Perú* has long been known—the "second" edition is anti-Pizarro, pro-Almagro and somewhat pro-Indian. According to Roche, there was another, intermediate version, discovered by him in the Bibliothèque Mazarine and printed in 1563(?). Roche, however, leaves us in doubt as he does not give the bibliographic particulars of this unknown version. [MTH]

Rodríguez-Buckingham, Antonio. The establishment, production, and equipment of the first printing press in South America. See *HLAS 41:156*.

Rodríguez Crespo, Pedro. Fichero de cédulas reales, 1607–1615. See item **2672**.

2715 Rodríguez Tena, Fernando. Sigue la misión de Panatahaus. Transcripción de María del Carmen Urbano (Amazonia Peruana [Centro Amazónico de Antropología y Aplicación Práctica, Lima] 1:2, julio 1977, p. 157–168)

Continues the transcription of a 1774 manuscript by a Franciscan chronicler on the activities of his order in Peru. This part corresponds to Chap. 2 of Book 3, and covers the mission of Pantahaus in the Oriente for the years 1652–1711. Chap. 1 appeared in the inaugural issue of *Amazonia Peruana.* [MTH]

2716 Rosas Cuadros, Emilio Eduvino. La Provincia de Chancay en la colonia y emancipación, Chancay-Huaral. Lima: s.n., 1976. 274 p.; bibl.; 21 leaves of plates: ill.

A miscellany of data culled from archives and published studies and sources on what are now the Provinces of Chancay and Huaral during the colonial and independence periods. [MTH]

2717 Rostworowski, María. Algunos comentarios hechos a las Ordenanzas del Doctor Cuenca (PMNH/HC, 9, 1975, p. 119–154, bibl.)

Publishes ordinances issued by Dr. Gregorio Gonzales de Cuenca in 1566 to cacique of Jayanca (p. 126–154). Contains ethnohistorical data not only on Indian customs and traditions for the northern highlands, but more importantly also the coast, particularly the area around Trujillo, in the *visita* of which Cuenca was engaged. [MTH]

Spalding, Karen. Estructura de clases en la sierra peruana: 1750–1920. See item **2657**.

2718 Tord Nicolini, Javier. Sociedad colonial y fiscalidad (UP/A, 4:7, 1977, p. 3–28, tables)

The use of treasury accounts as sources for the compilation of time series on different aspects of the economy (e.g., mining output, trade patterns and cycles and land exchanges) is a recent development. In this précis of his forthcoming *Las Cajas Reales y la sociedad colonial peruana, 1700–1820*, which will include time series for Upper as well as Lower Peru, Tord Nicolini reviews the literature on treasury accounts and their use as sources. He also discusses sources for the Bourbon years, the problems they pose, and exemplifies the extent to which the data in the *cartas cuentas* are indicative of economic trends. [MTH]

2719 Túpac Amaru II [i.e. Segundo]-1780 [i.e. mil setecientos ochenta]: sociedad colonial y sublevaciones populares. Compilación de Alberto Flores Galindo. Lima: Retablo de Papel Ediciones, 1976. 323 p.; bibl.; ill.

A useful compendium of traditional and revisionist studies by foreign and national scholars on the Tupac Amarú rebellion of 1780. Those by Scarlett O'Phelan, Lorenzo Huertas and Alberto Flores Galindo appear here for the first time. [MTH]

2720 Valcárcel Esparza, Carlos Daniel. Túpac Amaru, precursor de la independencia. Lima: Universidad Nacional Mayor de San Marcos, Dirección Universitaria de Biblioteca y Publicaciones, 1977. 201 p.; bibl.; ill.; index.

Restatement by Valcárcel of his views on Tupac Amarú and the rebellion of 1780. See *HLAS 34:1228* and *2289*. [MTH]

Los Virreyes españoles en América durante el gobierno de la Casa de Austria: Perú. See item **2675**.

2721 Wachtel, Nathan. The vision of the vanquished: the Spanish conquest of Peru through Indians eyes, 1530–1570. Translated by Ben and Siân Reynolds. Hassocks, Eng.: Harvester Press, 1977. 328 p.; bibl.; 12 leaves of plates: ill.; index.

English translation of the basic work on the subject which, regrettably, was not revised. For comment on the 1971 French original, see *HLAS 34:1235*. [MTH]

Werlich, David P. Peru: a short history. See item **3130**.

CARACAS

Academia Nacional de la Historia, *Caracas*. Catálogo, 1958–1978. See item **2627**.

2722 Acosta Saignes, Miguel. Historia de los portugueses en Venezuela. Caracas: Librería Suma, 1977. 116 p.; bibl.; ill.

Consists of chronologically ordered but uninterpreted notes on Portuguese active in colonial Venezuela. Based on archival research and published studies and sources. Interestingly illustrated. [MTH]

2723 Andrews, G. Reid. The Archivo Arquidiocesano of Caracas (AAFH/TAM, 35:4, April 1979, p. 479–485)

A succinct description of the very important Archbishop's Archive of Caracas, its *fondos*, and their utility for research, especially on the colonial period. [MTH]

Arcila Farías, Eduardo. Historia de un monopolio: el estanco del tabaco en Venezuela, 1779–1833. See item **2629**.

2724 Beaujón, Oscar. Las primicas de Coro (VANH/B, 60:239, julio/sept. 1977, p. 435–454)

Miscellany of well documented notes on the history of Coro on the northwest coast of Venezuela during the colonial and independence periods. Important for the leads it provides as to sources for systematic research on this city and its district. [MTH]

2725 **Blank, Stephanie.** Patrons, brokers and clients in the families of the elite in colonial Caracas, 1595–1627 (AAFH/TAM, 36:1, July 1979, p. 90–115, tables)

Carefully analyzed and thoroughly researched case study of patron-client relationships in early colonial Caracas. Includes charts of the patron families (i.e., those holding "proprietary municipal offices"). A major contribution to the social history of the colony. For related studies by Blank, see *HLAS 36:2492* and *HLAS 38:3015*. [MTH]

2726 **Brito Figueroa, Federico.** La estructura económica de Venezuela colonial. 2. ed. Caracas: Universidad Central de Venezuela, Ediciones de la Biblioteca, 1978. 455 p.; bibl.; 3 leaves of plates: ill.; maps; tables (Colección Ciencias económicas y sociales; 22)

Reprints Brito Figueroa's doctoral dissertation in anthropology (originally published in 1963, see *HLAS 28:866a*). [MTH]

La Capitanía General de Venezuela: 1777–1778. See *HLAS 41:5909*.

2727 **Capriles Ayala, Carlos.** Evolución demográfica de la Provincia de Cumaná, según las observaciones de Fray Iñigo Abad, 1773, y. J.J. Dauxion Lavaysse, 1807 (FJB/BH, 46, enero 1978, p. 35–57)

Impressionistic study of the growth of the population of the Province of Cumaná in northeastern Venezuela during the late colonial period. [MTH]

2728 **Caracas. Cabildo.** Actas. t. 12, 1664–1668. Transcripción de Leopoldo Méndez M. Prólogo de Manuel Alfredo Rodríguez. Caracas: Consejo Municipal del Distrito Federal, 1975. 403 p.

Literal transcription of the remainder of Book 12, continued from Tomo 11, and Book 13 of the minutes of the Cabildo of Caracas. Covers the years 1664–68. Well indexed. Rodríguez's prologue is a précis of sorts. For earlier volumes in this continuing series, see *HLAS 32:2106*. [MTH]

2729 ———. **Catedral.** Matrimonios y velaciones de españoles y criollos blancos celebrados en la Catedral de Caracas desde 1615 hasta 1831: extracto de los primeros once libros parroquiales. Compilador: Carlos Iturriza Guillén. Prólogo de Luis Báez Díaz. Caracas: Instituto Venezolano de Genealogía, 1974. 1006 p.; indexes.

Abstracts all extant records of marriages of "whites" (i.e., peninsulares and criollos) in the registers of the Cathedral of Caracas, the only parish in the city until 1751, from the years 1578 through 1831. Each register is separately indexed. An invaluable demographic as well as genealogical source for family reconstruction. [MTH]

2730 **Castillo Lara, Lucas G.** Materiales para la historia provincial de Aragua. Caracas: Academia Nacional de la Historia, 1977. 417 p.; bibl.; index. (Fuentes para la historia colonial de Venezuela. Biblioteca de la Academia Nacional de la Historia; 128)

A chatty account of sundry aspects of the colonial history of Aragua, useful only for occasional tidbits of hard core data and as a guide to sources. [MTH]

2731 ———. Nuestra Señora de la Victoria de los Valles de Aragua (VANH/B, 61:241, enero/marzo 1978, p. 69–102)

Detailed account of the foundation of Aragua in the late 1610s and its early history. Contains some new data on local missions, Indian resettlements and *encomiendas*, mostly culled from the Archivo Arquidiocesano de Caracas. [MTH]

2732 **Drenikoff, Ivan.** Impresos relativos a Venezuela desde el descubrimiento hasta 1821. Caracas: Fundación para el Rescate del Acervo Documental Venezolano, 1978. 233 p.; ill. (Colección Manuel Segundo Sánchez)

Alphabetical list of works published in Europe and the Americas prior to 1821, on or relating to Venezuela. Provides locations in Venezuelan repositories. Notes are weak. [MTH]

2733 **Farré, Joseph.** Relations commerciales entre la Catalogue et le Venezuela à la fin du XVIIIe. siècle (UTIEH/C, 32, 1979, p. 19–38, tables)

A quantitative study of trade between Barcelona and Venezuelan ports during the late colonial period, especially after 1778, when direct sailings were legalized. Largely based on secondary studies and published sources, but includes some new data from Barcelona archives. [MTH]

2734 Felice Cardot, Carlos. Tomás Valero, humanista venezolano del siglo XVIII (ANH/B, 60:240, oct./dic. 1977, p. 635–644)

Brief account of the life and doctoral dissertation of the little known but apparently important *tocuyense* and Franciscan priest Tomas Valero (1711–88), a humanist theologian and educator. [MTH]

2735 González González, Alfonso F. El oriente venezolano a mediados del siglo XVIII: a través de la visita del Gobernador Diguja. Caracas: Academia Nacional de la Historia, 1977. 244 p.; bibl.; 1 leaf of plates; indexes; map; tables (Fuentes para la historia colonial de Venezuela. Biblioteca de la Academia Nacional de la Historia; 129)

Detailed portrait of the Governorship of Nueva Andalucía as of the mid 18th century, drawn from the 1761 *visita* of Governor José Diguja Villagómez. Nueva Andalucía then included the districts of Cumaná, Barcelona and Guayana. An integral as well as quantitative study, rich in demographic, economic and social data. [MTH]

2736 Grases, Pedro. Andrés Bello, humanista caraqueño. Caracas: LAGOVEN, Departamento de Relaciones Públicas, 1977. 35 p.; ill. (Cuadernos LAGOVEN. Documentos)

Authoritative, elegantly illustrated piece of historical popularization, on the intellectual formation and early career of Andrés Bello in late colonial Venezuela. [D. Bushnell]

2737 Gutiérrez de Arce, Manuel. El Sínodo Diocesano de Santiago de León de Caracas de 1687: valoración canónica del Regio Placet a las constituciones sinodales indianas. Caracas: Academia Nacional de la Historia, 1975. 2 v. (432, 336 p.) bibl.; indexes (Fuentes para la historia colonial de Venezuela. Biblioteca de la Academia Nacional de la Historia; 124/125)

Vol. 1 consists of a detailed, well documented study of the 3rd Ecclesiastical Council of Venezuela or the Synod of 1687; of the decrees it issued; preparations for the Synod; the sessions themselves; the quarrel between the Governor of Caracas and the Audiencia of Santo Domingo with Bishop Diego de Baños y Sotomayor, a staunch defender of Church supremacy, over the tenor and certain provisions of the decrees; the appeal to the Council of Indies, and the latter's modification of synodal decisions. Also examines the issue of canonical vis-à-vis royal right. Vol. 2 publishes the *constituciones* of the Synod and the *autos acordados* of the Council of Indies modifying them. [MTH]

Herrera de Weishaar, María Luisa; María Leonor Ferreira Ferreira; and **Carlos Nestor Alvarez Cabrera.** Parroquia La Vega: estudio micro-histórico. See item **2642**.

2738 Humbert, Jules. Los orígenes venezolanos: ensayo sobre la colonización española en Venezuela. Traducción: Feliciana de Casas. Corrección y revisión: Claudine de Francia. Caracas: Academia Nacional de la Historia, 1976. 306 p.; bibl.; indexes (Fuentes para la historia colonial de Venezuela. Biblioteca de la Academia Nacional de la Historia; 127)

Spanish version of work originally published in French in 1905. Primarily useful nowadays for the material it contains on the Compañía Guipuzcoana de Caracas. [MTH]

2739 Humboldt, Alexander, Freiherr von. El Humboldt venezolano: homenaje en el bicentenario de su nacimiento. Compilación y notas de Miguel S. Wionczek. Prólogo de Jaime Labastida. Presentación de Luis Pastori. Caracas: Banco Central de Venezuela, 1977. 306 p.; bibl.; 10 leaves of plates: ill.

Useful compilation of writings by the great German naturalist and savant and accompanying illustrations, some of which are reproduced in color, on people and places, flora and fauna of Venezuela. Includes 28 letters of Humboldt, written between 1799 and 1841, relating to Venezuela. Competently edited and translated by Wionczek. [MTH]

2740 Izard, Miguel Ll. Contrabandistas, comerciantes e ilustrados (UB/BA, 20:28, 1978, p. 23–86, tables)

Reexamines primary questions such as whether the intendancy system was the driving force of the expanding economy of the late colonial period and to what extent the intendants were able to reestablish imperial control over the economy. Maintains that for the most part the growth and diversification of the economy of Venezuela began prior to 1777, and that at best the intendants were successful in collecting more taxes, but not in minimizing contraband. Based on reexamination of the papers of the first Intendant of Caracas José Abalos (1777–88), i.e., the first 50 volumes of the *fondo* of Intendencia del Ejército y Real Hacienda in the Archivo General de la Nación. [MTH]

2741 Juicios de residencia en la provincia de Venezuela. v. 1, Los Welser. Estudio preliminar de Marianela Ponce de Behrens, Diana Rengifo y Letizia Vaccari de Venturini. Caracas: Academia Nacional de la Historia, 1977. 73 p.; bibl.; indexes (Fuentes para la historia colonial de Venezuela. Biblioteca de la Academia Nacional de la Historia; 130)

Publishes the judicial reviews held in 1538 and 1546 of the governorships of the Welser, members and agents of the Augsburg merchant-banker family remunerated by Charles I with what would become Venezuela, and of their rival Juan de Carvajal. Competently transcribed, edited and introduced by an able team of researchers of the Departamento de Investigaciones of the Academia Nacional de la Historia. An exceptionally important and rich group of sources on the conquest and colonization. This is the initial volume in a subseries devoted to *juicios de residencia*. [MTH]

2742 Lemmo B., Angelina. Historiografía colonial de Venezuela. Caracas: Facultad de Humanidades y Educación, Universidad Central de Venezuela, 1977. 421 p.; bibl.; 3 p. (Serie Varia. Universidad Central de Venezuela, Escuela de Historia; 16)

This is a series of essays on the colonial historiography of Venezuela and historiography on colonial Venezuela rather than a survey of the latter. In pt. 1, Lemmo offers critical evaluation of general reviews on the historiography of the colonial period (e.g., Arístides Rojas, Mario Briceño Irragorry, Ramón Díaz Sánchez, Miguel Acosta Saignes and Germán Carrera Damas) and reviews of 12 major colonial authors, most of whom were priests or friars, beginning with 16th-century Pedro Aguado and ending with 18th-century Ramón Bueno. She also examines many but hardly all 19th- and 20th-century writings on the colonial period in general and the component regions of Venezuela in particular. In pt. 2, she takes up works of and on the naturalists and travelers of the 18th and early 19th centuries, especially Humboldt, Depons and Dauxion Lavaisse. In sum, a competent review of much of the literature of and on the colonial period, from which specialists as well as beginners will profit. [MTH]

Lombardi, John V. The rise of Caracas as a primate city. See item **2644**.

Martínez, Carlos. Bogotá: sinopsis sobre su evolución urbana. See item **2646**.

Miranda, Francisco de. Colombeia. See item **2649**.

2743 Morazzani de Pérez Enciso, Gisela. Materiales para el estudio de una Ordenanza del siglo XIX (UNAM/RFD, 26: 101/102, enero/junio 1976, p. 447–464, bibl.)

Preliminary analysis of sources in the Archivo General de Indias and the Archivo General de la Nación (Caracas) on the Audiencia of Caracas as an institution. Particularly concerned with its ordinances of 1805. [MTH]

2744 Morón, Guillermo. Historia de la Provincia de Venezuela. Caracas: Consejo Municipal del Distrito Federal, 1977. 390 p.; bibl.; ill.

Detailed, well researched but prosaic history of the colonial Province of Venezuela or the Governorship of Caracas. Rich in information on the creation and limits of the Province, its governors and the Cabildo of Caracas, settlement, cities and towns. [MTH]

2745 ———. El proceso de integración de Venezuela, 1776–1793. Caracas: Academia Nacional de la Historia, 1977. 177 p.; bibl. (El Libro menor; 3)

Reexamines the institutional origins of modern Venezuela. Deemphasizes the importance of the Captaincy Generalship, created in 1777, as a unifying force and emphasizes the importance of the Intendancy established the preceding year, and of the Audiencia, created a decade later. [MTH]

2746 Nectario María, *hermano.* Datos históricos sobre la fundación y primeros años de la ciudad de San Carlos de Cojedes, Venezuela (VANH/B, 62:246, abril/junio 1979, p. 327–346)

Chronologically organized archival sources and notes on the foundation of San Carlos de Austria in 1678 and the first 42 years of the city. [MTH]

Ortiz, Sergio Elías. Informe del intendente Don Bartolomé Tienda de Cuervo, sobre la situación económica del Nuevo Reino de Granada, anõ 1734. See item **2671**.

2747 Pollak-Eltz, Angelina. Slave revolts in Venezuela (*in* Comparative perspectives on slavery in New World societies [see item **1768**] p. 439–445)

An overview of black resistance to slavery in Venezuela during the colonial and early national periods (i.e., through the abolition of slavery in 1854). Apparently there were relatively few rebellions per se. Rather most unwilling slaves found it comparatively easy to escape to the bush or to join Maroon communities. [MTH]

2748 Ramírez F., Joaquín A. La lucha de los alcaldes por el gobierno de la Provincia· el formidable pleito entre el licenciado don Juan de Padilla Guardiola y el Cabildo Caraqueño de 1675. Caracas: Banco Central de Venezuela, 1975. 358 p.; bibl.; port.; tables.

Well documented study of dispute between the governor and Cabildo of Caracas, which prompted issuance of a *cédula* authorizing *alcaldes* to act as governors of entire province during interregnums or absences of the governor, which privilege remained in effect until 1736. Includes considerable genealogical data on 17th century *cabildantes* and other local office holders. [MTH]

2749 Ramos Guédez, José Marcial. El Valle del Tuy en 1768: una visión geohistórica (VANH/B, 61:242, abril/junio 1978, p. 385–387, tables)

Brief analysis of the 1768 *relación geográfica* of the Valley of Tuy, published in *Boletín de la Academia Nacional de la Historia* (Caracas, 56:223, julio/sept. 1973, p. 523–529). Tuy was a major cacao producing area in the central coastal highlands. [MTH]

2750 Ramos Pérez, Demetrio. Estudios de historia venezolana. Caracas: Academia Nacional de la Historia, 1976. 821 p.; bibl.; indexes (Serie Fuentes para la historia colonial de Venezuela. Biblioteca de la Academia Nacional de la Historia; 126)

This welcome anthology is based on 30 years of research by distinguished Spanish historian. Consists of 24 studies which Ramos Pérez has updated and revised where necessary, incorporating his own and others' findings. His contributions are organized chronologically and also indexed. Of the 24 studies, 13 have to do with the 16th century, and the other 11 with the 18th. Thematically they range from where Columbus took possession of South American for Spain through the attempts by Captains General to subvert the authority of Intendants. [MTH]

2751 *Real Cédula de Intendencia de Ejército y Real Hacienda:* diciembre 8 de 1776. Estudio preliminar de Gisela Morazzani de Pérez-Enciso. Caracas: Presidencia de la República, 1976. 128 p.; bibl.; ill.

Publishes in facsimile and transcription the *cédula* establishing the Intendancy of Caracas in 1776. Preceded by a competent introduction to and brief analysis of this basic source. [MTH]

2752 Rey Fajardo, José del. Los jesuitas en la historia de la educación en Coro (VANH/B, 61:242, abril/junio 1978, p. 325–354)

Research notes on abortive attempt of 1750s and 1760s to found a Jesuit school in Coro. Although the Jesuits were forced to abandon the venture in 1764, they were able to offer some classes during the preceding eight years. Supplemented by an extensive documentary appendix. [MTH]

2753 ———. Misiones jesuíticas en la Orinoquía. v. 1, Aspectos fundacionales. Caracas: Universidad Católica Andrés Bello, 1977. 231 p.; bibl.; indexes (Colección Manoa; 4)

This initial volume, in a projected multi-volume history of Jesuit missions in eastern Venezuela, reviews pertinent historiography and archival sources, 17th-century failures and 18th-century successes, and what Rey Fajardo calls "pedagogía misionera." The culmination of many years of research in Old and New World repositories. [MTH]

2754 ———. El proceso fundacional del Colegio Jesuítico de Caracas: 1731–1752 (VANH/B, 61:244, oct./dic. 1978, p. 729–770)

Publishes and comments on documentation relating to renewed, this time successful efforts of 1731–52, to obtain royal permission to found a Jesuit colegio in Caracas. See also item **2755**. [MTH]

2755 ———. Proyectos educacionales jesuíticos en la Venezuela del siglo XVI (FJB/BH, 43, enero 1977, p. 40–43)

Short note on unsuccessful attempt of Jesuits and local supporters in Venezuela to obtain permission in 1570s to send 12 Jesuits to educate the sons of Spanish conquerors and mission Indians. [MTH]

2756 Robinson, David J. and **Michael M. Swann.** Geographical interpretations of the Hispanic-American colonial city: a case study of Caracas in the late eighteenth century (*in* Conference of Latin Americanist Geographers, 5th, Boca Raton, Fla., 1974. Latin America: search for geographic explanations; proceedings. Chapel Hill, N.C.: CLAG Publications, 1976, p. 1–15, maps, tables)

A case study of residential density by blocks, patterns of ownership, household size, and turn-over in property in Caracas *intramuros* between 1766–70. Exemplifies ways in which enumerator books or raw returns of late colonial censuses, civil and ecclesiastical, may be used to reconstruct and to monitor changes in the demography and morphology of urban Latin America. [MTH]

Rodríguez, Simón. Obras completas. See item **2655**.

2757 Sanz Tapía, Angel. Los militares emigrados y los prisioneros franceses en Venezuela durante la guerra contra la revolución: un aspecto fundamental de la época de la preemancipación. Caracas: Instituto Panamericano de Geografía e Historia, Comisión de Historia, Comité Orígenes de la Emancipación, 1977. 273 p.; bibl. (Publicación; 21)

Though burdened with excessive administrative detail, this is an important addition to literature on late colonial Venezuela and the Caribbean repercussions of the French Revolution. Strictly on a basis of original research, it reviews the problems posed by French royalist refugees and revolutionary prisoners (including slaves), all of which led not to revolutionary contagion but to conservative backlash. [D. Bushnell]

2758 Suárez, Santiago Gerardo. Fortificación y defensa. Caracas: Academia Nacional de la Historia, 1978. 510 p.; bibl.; index; tables (Fuentes para la historia colonial de Venezuela. Biblioteca de la Academia Nacional de la Historia; 131)

Well chosen anthology of 163 previously unpublished documents from Spanish, Venezuelan and Colombian repositories, ranging in time from 1657 through 1806, relating to the fortification and defense of cities and towns, ports and harbours and other military matters such as salaries and the *situado*. Preceded by a useful introduction. [MTH]

2759 Tandrón, Humberto. El Real Consulado de Caracas y el comercio exterior de Venezuela. Prólogo de Eduardo Arcilla Farías. Caracas: Instituto de Estudios Hispanoamericanos, Facultad de Humanidades y Educación, Universidad Central de Venezuela, 1976. 314 p.; bibl.

A new study on the Consulado de Comercio of Caracas, which focuses on the patterns of trade of the Intendancy of Venezuela with foreign countries, especially Holland, England and the US. Includes new data but suffers from lack of quantification. [MTH]

2760 Troconis de Veracoechea, Ermila. Historia de El Tocuyo colonial: período histórico, 1545–1810. Caracas: Facultad de Humanidades y Educación, Universidad Central de Venezuela, 1977. 479 p.; bibl.; 1 fold. leaf of plates: indexes; plates; tables.

Fascinating, well written, thoroughly researched history of Tocuyo, which is in the western highlands. This work covers virtually every aspect of the colonial past of the city and its district in considerable detail. Divided into nine parts on the foundation of the city and settlement of the district, the Indian population, land tenure and use, the Church, society, economy, culture, conclusions, and documentary appendixes. Especially fascinating is the account of urban and rural *cofradías*, which were mutual aid societies as well as religious brotherhoods. This is the most outstanding contribution to the local history of Venezuela to date. [MTH]

NUEVA GRANADA

2761 Ariza S., Alberto E. Fray Tomas Ortíz y Berlanga: apuntes para su reivindicación (ACH/BHA, 63:713, abril/junio 1976, p. 181–194)

Consists of chronologically ordered notes with incorporated citations on the first Protector of Indians in what was then the recently founded Diocesis of Santa Marta. Friar Tomás, a Dominican, was appointed in

1528, took up his post almost immediately and his duties seriously. Consequently he was opposed and vilified by the governor, encomenderos and other resident Spaniards. [MTH]

2762 Briceño, Manuel. Los comuneros. Prólogo de Carlos Vidales. Bogotá: C. Valencia Editores, 1977. 162 p.; index.

Reprint of a late 19th-century account (1880) on the rebellion of the comuneros, by General Manuel Briceño (1849–85), one of Colombia's first serious historians. Nowadays primarily useful for the appended documents (p. 59–158), most of which were culled from the Archivo Nacional. [MTH]

2763 Eugenio Martínez, María Angeles. Tributo y trabajo del indio en Nueva Granada: de Jiménez de Quesada a Sande. Prólogo de Luis Navarro García. Sevilla: Escuel de Estudios Hispano-Americanos, Consejo Superior de Investigaciones Científicas, 1977. 654 p.; bibl.; 1 leaf of plates; index; map; tables (Publicaciones de la Escuela de Estudios Hispano-Americanos de Sevilla; 240)

Major, new work on Indian tribute and labor in the Provinces of Santa Fe and Tunja during the early colonial period. Pt. 1 delineates the establishment and organization of the encomienda system among the Chibchas; pt. 2, the interplay between population decline and tribute pressure; and pt. 3, Indian labor legislation and practices. Includes *repartimiento* specific time series on tribute schedules, tributaries, total population, encomiendas and encomenderos. Does for the 16th century what Ruiz Rivera's comparable study did for the 17th (see *HLAS 40:3156*). [MTH]

2764 Friede, Juan. El adelantado don Gonzalo Jiménez de Quesada. Bogotá: C. Valencia Editores, 1979. 2 v. (287, 472 p.); bibl.

The most detailed and well researched biography of Jiménez de Quesada to date by a leading authority on 16th-century Colombia. Adds appreciably to our knowledge of the *adelantado* himself, the conquest of the Chibchas and initial colonization of the highlands. Vol. 2 consists of 87 archival sources, many of which are published for the first time. [MTH]

2765 Fuentes documentales para la historia del Nuevo Reino de Granada desde la instalación de la Real Audiencia en Santafé. t. 1, 1550–1552; t. 2, 1553–1555; t. 3, 1556–1559; t. 4, 1560–1562; t. 5, 1563–1567; t. 6, 1568–1575; t. 7, 1576–1580; t. 8, 1581–1590. Compilador: Juan Friede. Bogotá: Banco Popular, 1975/1976. 8 v. (308, 371, 398, 346, 427, 474, 375, 442 p.) (Biblioteca Banco Popular; 89/96)

Publishes 1,237 documents from the Archivo General de Indias on the emerging "political, social and economic formation of colonial society." This major collection, which also includes demographic sources, covers the years 1550 through 1590 (as of this writing) and continues Friede's earlier *Fuentes documentales para la historia de Colombia* (10 vols., Bogotá: 1955–1965). Hopefully the final volume will include comprehensive indexes which the individual volumes lack. [MTH]

2766 Gálvez Piñal, Esperanza. La visita de Monzón y Prieto de Orellana al Nuevo Reino de Granada. Prólogo de Luis Navarro García. Sevilla: Escuela de Estudios Hispano-Americanos, 1974. 153 p.; bibl.; 3 fold. leaves of plates; 3 maps; index (Publicaciones de la Escuela de Estudios Hispano-Americanos de Sevilla; 225)

Useful summary of the major *visita* of 1579–1584, begun by Juan Bautista Monzón, Oidor of the Audiencia of Lima, and concluded by Licenciado Juan Prieto de Orellana when Monzón and the Audiencia of Santa Fe reached an impasse. Relations between them deteriorated to the point where the latter imprisoned the former. Both *visitadores* found the Audiencia to be corrupt, co-opted by the local elite, and active in the despoliation of the Indians. This visita was unusual because it was instigated by Diego Torres, the mestizo cacique of Turmeque, who was deeply concerned over the Indians and whose brother was the local encomendero. [MTH]

2767 Gómez, Tomás. Indiens et terre en Nouvelle-Grenade 1539–1843, les *resguardos*: structures de protection ou spoliation désguisée? (UTIEH/C, 28, 1977, p. 11–31, tables)

Documented survey of the *resguardos* in what is now Colombia from their inception through their suppression. Gómez concludes that the relegation of Indians to reduced reserved lands amounted to more or less systematic expropriation of their original, extensive holdings—which was the case (see item **2874**)—and was also one of the means employed to coopt their services as laborers. [MTH]

2768 González, Margarita. Ensayos de historia colombiana. Bogotá: Editorial La Carreta, 1976. 333 p.; bibl.; map, tables.

Reprints three articles—not previously annotated in *HLAS*—which appeared in *Cuadernos Colombianos* between 1974 and 1975: 1) a useful synthesis of what was then known about Indian labor during the colonial period; 2) an original study of the Royal Tobacco Monopoly; and 3) a cogent reexamination of the suppression of slavery during the independence and early national periods. [MTH]

2769 González Luna, María Dolores. La política de población y pacificaciones indígenas en las poblaciones de Santa Marta y Cartagena: Nuevo Reino de Granada, 1750–1800 (UB/BA, 20:28, 1978, p. 87–118, maps)

Diachronic study of largely futile Spanish efforts of the second half of the 18th century to reduce and collect tribute from the previously pacified Indians of the Province of Cartagena and to pacify the hostile Chimila in the Province of Santa Marta. Illuminates Viceroy Esclava's attempt of the 1740s and *fiscal* Moreno y Escandon's efforts of the late 1770s to deal with Indian problems by reorganizing their populations through the corregimiento system. Also adds appreciably to the inadequately known history of the interior of the Caribbean coast. [MTH]

2770 Huarte, Eulogio Zudaire. Juan Martín de Sarratea y Goyeneche, Superintendente de la Ceca de Santa Fe: Albacea de Virreyes y Contador Mayor (ACH/BHA, 62:709, abril/junio 1975, p. 281–348, tables)

Detailed and original study of a major peninsular bureaucrat whose career in New Granada spanned the second half of the 18th century. Sarratea y Goyeneche was Accountant General of the Cajas Reales in Bogota from 1750 through 1774, and Superintendent of the Royal Mint there from 1775 until his death in 1797. An important contribution to the little-known history of the vicerequal exchequer and the men who ran it. Huarte also includes data on the operation and output of the mint. [MTH]

2771 Isacsson, Sven-Erik. Fray Matías Abad y su diario de viaje por el Río Atrato en 1649 (ACH/BHA, 61:706, sept./dic. 1974, p. 457–475)

Documentary notes on mid 17th-century missionary and other *entradas* into the River Atrato area, especially that of the Franciscan friar Matías Abad who gave his life in one such attempt in 1649. [MTH]

2772 Kuethe, Allan J. Military reform and society in New Granada, 1773–1808. Gainesville: University Presses of Florida, 1978. 234 p.; bibl.; map (Latin American monographs; 2d ser., 22)

Excellent monograph on the Bourbon military reforms per se, their impact on administration as well as society, and the role played by the regular army and the militia (e.g., the Comunero rebellion of 1781) throughout the Viceroyalty of Nueva Granada. Kuethe delineates and compares military and related developments in Cartagena, Panama, Guayaquil, Popayán and elsewhere, and examine their long-term consequences. A significant study which illuminates many heretofore clouded aspects of the late colonial history of northern South America. [MTH]

2773 Laviña, Javier. La sublevación de Túquerres de 1800: una revuelta antifiscal (UB/BA, 20:28, 1978, p. 189–196)

Routine essay on Indian riot of May 1800 in Tuquerres in southern Colombia. The riot was provoked by local corregidor's attempt to collect the tithe on domestic animals and produce, previously exempted. [MTH]

2774 Martínez Reyes, Gabriel. Funcionamiento socio-económico de la parroquia virreinal en Málaga, Servitá y pueblos anexos, especialmente en los años de 1801 a 1810. Bogotá: Pontificia Universidad Javeriana, Facultad de Filosofía y Letras, 1975. 2 v.; bibl.; facsims.; ill.; map; tables.

Well researched, quantitative case study of social and economic aspects of the Catholic Church at the parish level, especially of the Parish of Málaga and the Doctrina of Servitá, both in the Province of Santander del Sur, between 1801–10. Also contains data on the 17th and 18th centuries and neighboring parishes. Particularly strong on sources of parish income. Vol. 2, which I have not seen, is a documentary appendix. Poorly written, but nonetheless a unique as well as valuable contribution to the local and ecclesiastical history of Colombia. [MTH]

2775 Marzahl, Peter. Town in the empire: government, politics and society in seventeenth-century Popayán. Austin: Institute of Latin American Studies, University of Texas at Austin, 1978. 218 p.; bibl.; index; maps (Latin American monographs; 45)

A more or less integral history of Popayán and its region in the 17th century, largely based on cabildo and notarial records. Marzahl focuses on three basic themes: 1) the role of the environment in shaping Spanish settlement in southern New Granada, particularly Popayán; 2) the structure of that society; and 3) relations between imperial authorities, colonial governments in Bogotá and Quito, and Spanish settlers. Also includes chapters on the economy, Indians and blacks, and the Church. One of the few major studies on the urban history of Colombia as well as on that of the seventeenth century. [MTH]

2776 Molino García, María Teresa. La encomienda en el Nuevo Reino de Granada durante el siglo XVIII. Sevilla: Escuela de Estudios Hispano-Americanos, 1976. 206 p.; bibl.; 5 leaves of plates (4 fold.): ill.; index (Publicaciones de la Escuela de Estudios Hispanoamericanos de Sevilla; 236)

Solid, quantitative study of the much diminished yet still somewhat important encomiendas of the eighteenth century and their at long last elimination through attrition. Includes a chapter on the encomenderos. [MTH]

2777 Padilla Altamirano, Silvia; María Luisa López Arellano; and **Adolfo Luis González Rodríguez.** La encomienda en Popayán: tres estudios. Sevilla: Escuela de Estudios Hispano-Americanos, 1977. 393 p.; bibl.; index; maps; tables (Publicaciones de la Escuela de Estudios Hispano-Americanos de Sevilla; 238)

Consists of three separate but conjointly researched and related monographs on tributary Indians, encomiendas and encomenderos in the Governorship of Popayán, which encompassed much of western as well as southern Colombia, during the 16th and 17th centuries. Silvia Padilla Altamirano studies the initial distribution of encomiendas, the decline of the native population, and tribute as regulated by *visitadores* in the 16th century. Padilla finds that the number of tributaries declined by 52.7 percent between 1559–82, that more than half of the tributary population of the Governorship was in the district of Pasto, which also had the largest encomiendas, twice as large on the average than those elsewhere in the Governorship. María Luisa López Arellano studies the continuing decline of the Indian population, changes in tribute schedules, encomienda distribution and rentability, and labor services and abuses in the 17th century. López Arellano finds that by 1668, the number of tributaries was only 16.5 percent of what it was 86 years earlier, and that encomiendas continued to be held. She also examines the demography of the increasing black, white and mixed components of the population. Adolfo Luis González Rodríguez studies encomenderos as a social group in the 17th century, employing prosopographic analysis. He examines their entrepreneurial and mercantile activities, social role, and political power base, the Cabildo, and relations with the governor. González Rodríguez finds that of 50 families holding encomiendas in the 17th century, those who prevailed in numbers of encomiendas held power, prestige and wealth and as members of the local elite were these six family names: Caicedo, Mosquera y Figueroa, Velasco, Campo Salazar, Hurtado del Aguila, and Godoy y Prado, the history of which he sketches. Altogether an important set which illuminates and details many aspects of the demographic, economic, ethno- and social history of Popayán, Pasto, other towns and their districts in western and southern Colombia during the first two centuries of the colonial period. [MTH]

2778 Phelan, John Leddy. El auge y la caída de los criollos en la Audiencia de Nueva Granada, 1700–1781 (ACH/BHA, 59:697/698, nov./dic. 1972, p. 597–618)

A more detailed statement of the re-peninsularization of the Audiencia of Bogotá or "revolution in government" than is to be found in chap. 1 of Phelan's *The people and the King* (see item **2779**). Regrettably, this important companion piece to the revisionist literature on the administrative reforms of the Bourbons did not reach the Library of Congress in time for inclusion in an earlier volume of the *Handbook*. [MTH]

2779 ———. The people and the King: the Comunero Revolution in Colombia, 1781. Madison: University of Wisconsin Press, 1978. 309 p.; bibl.; ill.; index.

On the one hand, this is an essentially correct account, replete with new details, of the Comunero movement of 1781, the events leading up to it, especially of the Bourbon reforms as they related to what is now Colombia, and of the successful efforts of Viceroy Caballero y Góngora to defuse the rebellion and continue the implementation of reforms while tempering imperial demands with regional needs. And on the other hand, it is a thought-provoking reexamination of the significance of the rebellion and its aftermath. Phelan argues that the Comunero movement was neither a precursor of political independence nor a frustrated social revolution but rather a demand for return to what he calls the "unwritten constitution" theretofore prevalent in the colony, that is to say, pragmatic, semi-autonomous government. [MTH]

2780 ———. La trayectoria enigmática de Manuel García Olano durante la revolución comunera (ACH/BHA, 61:704, abril/junio 1974, p. 157–185)

Examines the alliance between the supporters of the comuneros in Bogotá and its leaders in Socorro through a case study of a member of the former group, Manuel García Olano, a minor peninsular-born bureaucrat. Although much of this article is incorporated in Phelan's book (item **2779**), it is still interesting for the light shed on the problems and attitudes of the lesser bureaucracy, about which much remains to be learned. [MTH]

2781 **Tovar Pinzón, Hermes.** Estado actual de los estudios de demografía histórica en Colombia (UNC/ACHSC, 5, 1970, p. 65–142, tables)

Regrettably not noticed in an earlier *HLAS*, this review of the state of study on the size of precontact populations and their postconquest decline is still useful if somewhat dated. Tovar Pinzón evaluates and adds appreciably to the findings of Friede, Jaramillo Uribe, Colmenares and Fajardo on the Chibcha populations of the highland Provinces of Cartago, Tunja, Pamplona and Vélez, drawing upon his own considerable research, especially in the "Visitas" *fondo* of the Archivo Nacional in Bogotá. Tovar also examines the problem of sources. [MTH]

2782 **Twinam, Ann.** Enterprise and elites in eighteenth-century Medellín (HAHR, 59:3, Aug. 1979, p. 444–475, tables)

A first rate prosopographic study of the identity and activities, origins and attitudes of the late colonial elite of Medellín. Twinam is concerned not merely with the time and place, but the larger question of why antioqueños have played such an important role in the economic history of Colombia. She argues that the distinguishing feature of *medellinenses* is their dedication to mining and commerce, generation after generation, rather than abandonment of either for land and the seigneurial life style. She attributes this dedication to an environment which left them no viable alternative and to the development of an ingrained entrepreneurship. [MTH]

2783 **Uribe, Carlos Alberto.** La rebelión Chimila en la Provincia de Santa Marta, Nuevo Reino dc Granada, durante al siglo XVIII (UP/EA, 7:13, 1977, p. 113–165, bibl., maps, tables)

Ethnohistorical study of Chimila resistance to Spanish attempts to pacify and reduce them during the 18th and early 19th centuries. The Chimila were a coastal group, who raided shipments along the Magdalena. More detailed than item **2769**. [MTH]

2784 **Villamarín, Juan A.** and **Judith E. Villamarín.** Chibcha settlement under Spanish rule, 1537–1810 (*in* Social fabric and spatial structure in colonial Latin America. Edited by David J. Robinson. Ann Arbor, Mich.: University Microfilms International, 1979, p. 25–84, maps, tables)

An excellent case study of the *resguardos* in the Sabana de Bogotá, rich in ecological and socioeconomic data. The Villamaríns delineate not only Spanish attempts to reduce the Chibcha to nucleated, concentrated settlements but also the latter's resistance, and changes in the underlying patterns and motivations of the movement (i.e., Spanish and mestizo takeover of Indian pueblos and *resguardos*). A very important contribution to the ethnohistory and historical geography of highland Colombia. [MTH]

Zambrano Pantoja, Fabio. La economía colombiana en la primera mitad del siglo 19, 1820–1850. See item **2999**.

QUITO

2785 **Alcina Franch, José; Encarnación Moreno;** and **Remedios de la Peña.** Penetración española en Esmeraldas, Ecuador: tipología del descubrimiento (IGFO/RI, 36:143/144, enero/junio 1976, p. 65–121, bibl., maps, tables)

Systematic reexamination and summary of military expeditions to, missionary endeavours in, and attempts to open a road through Esmeraldas to the sea during the colonial period. Authors stress wealth of ethnographic data to be found in accounts of the 65 Spanish *entradas* of one sort or another between 1526 and 1804. One in a series of reports on the ongoing project "Arqueología de Esmeraldas, Ecuador" directed by senior author Alcina Franch (see also *HLAS 37:964, HLAS 39:876–877*, and *HLAS 40:3163*).

Bradley, Peter T. Maritime defense of the Viceroyalty of Peru, 1600–1700. See item **2659**.

2786 **Bromley, Rosemary D.F.** Disasters and population change in central highland Ecuador, 1778–1825 (*in* Social fabric and spatial structure in colonial Latin America. Edited by David J. Robinson. Ann Arbor, Mich.: University Microfilms International, 1979, p. 85–115, maps, tables)

Quantifies the differential impact of natural disasters, especially the earthquake of 1797, and the loss of the textile market of Peru to European competition, on the population and economy of Latacunga, Ambato, Riobamba and their districts during the late colonial and independence periods. In addition to the earthquake of 1797, Bromley finds that the wars of independence were also largely responsible for the loss of population, at least in the towns, which argument she refines in item **2632**. She also analyzes the ethnic composition and distribution of the population. [MTH]

———. The functions and development of "colonial" towns: urban change in the Central Highlands of Ecuador, 1698–1940. See item **2631**.

2787 **Castillo, Abel Romeo.** Los gobernadores de Guayaquil del siglo XVIII: notas para la historia de la ciudad durante los años de 1763 a 1803. Prólogo de Rafael Altamira. 2. ed. aumentada. Guayaquil: Archivo Histórico del Guayas, 1978. 398 p.; bibl.; 8 leaves of plates: ill.; indexes (Colección monográfica; 12)

Castillo's doctoral dissertation still is the standard account on the late 18th-century governors of Guayaquil. Includes additional biobibliographical notes on the author but is a reprint and not a true second edition of work of same title published in Madrid in 1931. [MTH]

2788 **Clayton, Lawrence A.** Los astilleros de Guayaquil colonial. Prólogo de Julio Estrada Ycaza. Edición de Julio Estrada Ycaza y Michael T. Hamerly. Versión castellana de Carmen Victoria Flores de Hamerly y Michael T. Hamerly. Guayaquil: Archivo Histórico de Guayas, 1978. 230 p.; bibl.; ill.; maps; plates (Colección Monográfica; 11)

Revised and translated version of Clayton's dissertation on the 16th- and 17th-century shipyards of Guayaquil and Puná, the most important on the Pacific coast of Spanish America throughout the entire colonial period. Includes considerable material on related aspects of the early history of the port city as for example, the guilds, and the Castro family, who for many years dominated the industry and the Cabildo as well. Based primarily on research in Sevilla and Lima. [MTH]

Hamerly, Michael T. Registros parroquiales e inventarios de iglesias del litoral. See item **2640**.

Juan y Santacilia, Jorge and **Antonio de Ulloa.** Discourse and political reflections on the Kingdoms of Peru, their government, special regimen of their inhabitants, and abuses which have been introduced into one and another, with special information on why they grew up and some means to avoid them. See item **2667**.

Kuethe, Allan J. Military reform and society in New Granada, 1773–1808. See item **2772**.

Leon Borja de Szásdi, Dora. Los traslados de ciudades en la nueva Castilla. See item **2703**.

Middleton, DeWight R. The growth of a city: urban, regional, and national interaction in Ecuador. See item **2648**.

Norris, Robert E. Guía bibliográfica para el estudio de la historia ecuatoriana. See item **2650**.

2789 Ortiz de la Tabla Ducasse, Javier. El obraje colonial ecuatoriano: aproximación a su estudio (IGFO/RI, 37:149/150, julio/dic. 1977, p. 471–541, tables)

Fascinating, pioneering study on a basic but virtually unstudied aspect of Ecuadorian history, the colonial *obraje* or textile industry. Drawing on several *fondos* of the Archivo General de Indias, Ortiz de la Tabla examines the demographic aspects of the industry, the actual labor force, salaries, costs and profits, the *obraje*'s relationship with the tributary and encomienda system, and includes a chronology and genealogical charts of those Spaniards who established the *obrajes* and their descendants. Moreover, Ortiz de la Tabla is properly cautious in interpretation, being fully aware of the need for more research on *obrajes*, especially in Ecuadorian archives which he was unable to consult. [MTH]

2790 ———. Panorama económico y social del corregimiento de Quito 1768–1775 (IGFO/RI, 36:145/146, julio/dic. 1976, p. 83–98, tables)

Quantitative study of the rural economy of the Corregimiento of Quito (i.e., more or less the modern Province of Pichincha) c. 1770. Based on a detailed *encabezamiento de alcabalas* found in the Archivo General de Indias. [MTH]

2791 Super, John C. Partnership and profit in the early Andean trade: the experiences of Quito merchants, 1580–1610 (JLAS, 11:2, Nov. 1979, p. 265–281, tables)

Well documented case study of merchants in late 16th-century Quito, the problems they faced, the companies they formed, profits earned and disposal thereof. Enriched by comparisons to emerging portrait of merchants elsewhere in the colonies. [MTH]

ALTO PERU

2792 Archivo Histórico Nacional (PAIGH/RHA, 77/78, enero/dic. 1974, p. 151–203)

Publishes without introduction or notes a major ethnohistorical source, a lengthy late 18th-century *expediente* which enables one to trace the succession to the *cacicazgo* of Asangaro, initially only to the *hanan* moiety and subsequently to the whole pueblo and governorship, by members of the Chunquihuanca family from at least 1587 through the 1790s. [MTH]

2793 Arzáns de Orsúa y Vela, Bartolomé. Tales of Potosí. Edited, with an introduction by R.C. Padden. Translated from the Spanish by Frances M. López-Morillas. Providence: Brown University Press, 1975. 209 p.; bibl.

Popular distillation in English of the more colorful parts of Arzáns, *Historia de la Villa Imperial de Potosí*, an indispensable source on that mining town from its foundation through 1736. Scholars will prefer Hanke and Mendoza's edition original (see Bartolomé Arzáns de Orsúa y Vela's *Historia de la Villa Imperial de Potosí*. Edición de Lewis Hanke y Gunnar Mendoza. Providence, R.I.: Brown University Press, 1965. 3 vols.). For literary critic's comment on the above translation, see *HLAS 38:6444*. [MTH]

2794 Arze Quiroga, Eduardo. Papeles de Cochabamba en el Archivo General de la Nación Argentina. La Paz: Banco Hipotecario Nacional, 1975. 81 p.

A calendar of papers from 1762–86 and 1810–15 in the National Archives of Buenos Aires relating to the Corregimiento/Intendencia of Cochabamba. [MTH]

2795 Avila, Federico. Don Luis de Fuentes y Vargas y la fundación de Tarija. Potosí: Departamento de Extensión Universitaria de la Universidad Boliviana Tomás Frías, 1975. 265 p.

Posthumous publication of an incomplete work on the foundation of Tarija in 1574. Anachronistic in approach, it is of value because of the sources published contextually. [MTH]

2796 Bakewell, Peter J. Registered silver production in the Potosí District,

1550–1735 (JGSWGL, 12, 1975, p. 67–103, map, tables)

From treasury accounts in the Archivo General de Indias and the Casa de la Moneda (Potosí), Bakewell has compiled a time series of the Crown's share of silver mined in Potosí and its district, and from them computed minimum production figures. He is aware of the shortcomings of this approach as much silver was never reported, but argues cogently that the derived figures are indicative of medium and long-range trends. Curiously, Bakewell makes no reference to late colonial Royal Treasurer Lamberto de Sierra's *Manifiesto de la plata extraída de Potosí, 1556–1800* (see *HLAS 36:2598*) with whose figures Bakewell's ought to be compared as Sierra not only utilized the same method but had access to more complete data. [MTH]

2797 ———. Technological change in Potosí: the silver boom of the 1570s (JGSWGL, 14, 1977, p. 57–77, tables)

Detailed examination of introduction of *patio* process or refining by amalgamation and its impact on production of silver in Potosí, where output had stagnated once richer ores depleted. Bakewell demonstrates patio process was more important than *mita*—to be treated separately by him—in bolstering producting, and that among other things, it underlays the ousting of Indians as refiners. This article and item **2796** are preludes to Bakewell's forthcoming book on silver mining in Potosí (see also *HLAS 38: 3155*). [MTH]

2798 Ballivián y Rojas, Vicente de. Archivo boliviano: colección de documentos relativos a la historia de Bolivia durante la época colonial, con un catálogo de obras impresas y de manuscritos, que tratan de esa parte de América Meridional. 2. ed. La Paz: Casa Municipal de la Cultura Franz Tamayo, 1977. 352 p. (Biblioteca paceña)

Reprints work heretofore available only in first Paris edition of 1872: Intendant Sebastián Segurola's *Diary* of the 1781–82 siege of La Paz by forces of Tupac Amarú and supplementary documents; Bartolomé Martínez Vela's 1705 *Anales de la Villa Imperial de Potosí* which chronicles the history of the city through 1702; and Ballivián's own *Biblioteca Boliviana*. The latter lists colonial manuscripts found by Ballivián in the Archivo General de Indias, the Academia de la Historia of Madrid, and the British Museum, and 321 imprints from the 16th, 17th and 18th centuries relating to Bolivia. [MTH]

2799 Cajías de la Vega, Fernando. La población indígena de Paria en 1785 (*in* Estudios bolivianos en homenaje a Gunnar Mendoza L. [see item **2638**] p. 41–100, map, tables)

Analyzes and tabulates population data, repartimiento by repartimiento, *ayllu* by *allyu*, contained in the 1785 revista of the Partido of Paria in the Lake Poopo area. [MTH]

2800 El Conato de José Pablo Conti en La Paz. Compilador: Carlos Urquizo Sossa. Documentación: Carlos Ponce Sangines. Transcripción: René Arze. La Paz: Casa Municipal de la Cultura Franz Tamayo, 1977. 187 p.; bibl. (Jornadas Peruano Bolivianas de Estudios Científico del Altiplano Boliviano y del Sur del Perú; 5. Biblioteca paceña)

Publishes a 1795 *expediente* concerning disturbances in La Plata (Sucre), provoked in part at least by quarrel between José Pablo Conti, Oidor of the Audiencia of Charcas (1794–1802) and Commandant Joaquín Antonio Mosquera. Urquizo Sossa's introduction fails to clarify the incidents and their significance remains to be determined. [MTH]

Coplas a la muerte de Don Diego de Almagro, primer gobernador de la Nueva Toledo. See item **5115**.

Crespo R., Alberto. Esclavos negros en Bolivia. See item **2635**.

Estudios bolivianos en homenaje a Gunnar Mendoza L. See item **2638**.

Klein, Herbert S. The impact of the crisis in nineteenth-century mining on regional economies: the example of the Bolivian Yungas, 1786–1838. See item **2643**.

2801 Mendoza, Diego de. Chronica de la Provincia de S. Antonio de los Charcas del Orden de Nro. Seraphico P.S. Francisco en las Indias Occidentales, Reyno del Perú. Dedicada al Illmo. y Rmo. S.D.F. Gabriel de Guillestegui del Consejo de su Magd. y Obispo del Paraguay. 2. ed. La Paz: Editorial Casa Municipal de la Cultural Franz Tamayo, 1976. 601 p.

Welcome photo offset reproduction of rare 1665 chronicle of Franciscans and Poor Clares in Upper Peru from the creation of their Province of San Antonio de los Charcas, which included Cuzco, in 1553 through 1663. Hagiography notwithstanding, this is an important source on the early history of women as well as religious in the Bolivian/Peruvian altiplano. [MTH]

Los Mercedarios en Bolivia: documentos para su historia, 1535–1975. See item **2647**.

2802 Parejas Moreno, Alcides. Historia de Moxos y Chiquitos a fines del siglo XVIII. La Paz: Instituto Boliviano de Cultura, 1976. 157 p.; bibl.

A detailed, well researched and balanced monograph on 18th century Moxos in eastern Bolivia. Rich in demographic and ethnohistorical data which are professionally handled. The inclusion of Chiquitos in the title is a typographical error. [MTH]

2803 Patrício, Jaciro Campante. As instituições monetário e bancária de Potosí no decurso do século XVIII (USP/RH, 56:111, julho/set. 1977, p. 51–72, tables)

Quantitative study of monetary and banking institutions in Potosí between 1750 and 1825. Includes time series on minting and the circulation of Potosí coinage and on the activities and movements of the Banco de Azogueros and the Banco de San Carlos. [MTH]

2804 ———. Significativas conotações entre as técnicas de mineração e a produção argentífera potosina: 1550–1650 (FFCLM/EH, 16, 1977, p. 17–50, tables)

Excellent summary of what is known about the interrelationships between the supply of mercury and silver output at Potosí, once the *patio* method was introduced there, during the first century of production, and about that technological innovation itself. Includes some new archival data. [MTH]

2805 Platt, Tristan. Mapas coloniales de la Provincia de Chayanta: dos visiones conflictivas de un solo paisaje (*in* Estudios bolivianos en homenaje a Gunnar Mendoza L. [see item **2638**] p. 101–118, bibl., maps)

Publishes—regrettably in poor reproduction—and analyzes two 1651 maps of Pocoata in the Province of Chayanta (nowadays the northern part of the Department of Potosí), the one drawn by the local priest according to information provided by the Indians of Pocoata and the other as prepared by Jacinto de Carvajal, a Spanish miner, with whom the Indians were in dispute. The discrepancies between the two maps are resultant neither from geographic errors nor cartographic imperfections, but from fundamental differences in cosmographic conceptions, the one Andean, the other European. [MTH]

Portugal Ortiz, Max. La esclavitud negra en las épocas colonial y nacional de Bolivia. See item **2654**.

2806 Ramos Gavilán, Alonso. Historia de Nuestra Señora de Copacabana. 2. ed. completa, según la impresión principe de 1621. La Paz: Academia Boliviana de la Historia, 1976. 257 p. (Publicaciones culturales)

A modernized but complete and accurate edition of the scarce 1621 *Historia del celebre Santuario de Nuestra Señora de Copacabana, y sus milagros, e invención de la Cruz de Carabuco*, a basic ethnohistorical as well as ecclesiastical source. [MTH]

Rementería, Carlos J. Díaz. El regimen jurídico del Ramo de Tributos en Nuevo España y las reformas peruanas de Carlos III. See item **1869**.

2807 Romero, Gonzalo. Conquista de Nueva Toledo: el alzado de Charcas. La Paz: s.n., 1976. 549 p.; bibl.; index.

A traditionalistic account of the conquest and early colonization of what is now Bolivia. Based on some of, but not all the appropriate literature. [MTH]

2808 Saignes, Thierry. Historia de Cumbay: derrotero de un lider chiriguano (*in* Estudios bolivianos en homenaje a Gunnar Mendoza L. [see item **2638**] p. 125–129)

Research notes on a major Indian leader, Cumbay of the Ava or Chiriguanos, who resisted white and mestizo encroachments in the Valley of Ingre in the early 19th century, and later sided with guerrilla patriots against royalist forces. One of the problems in researching the career of such native personages is that they changed names several times in their lives. [MTH]

2809 Sanabria Fernández, Hernando. Crónica sumaria de los gobernantes de Santa Cruz, 1560–1810. La Paz: Librería Editorial Juventud, 1975. 166 p. (Publicaciones de la Universidad Boliviana Gabriel Cruz de la Sierra)

Consists of brief but nonetheless detailed sketches of the lives and career of the governors of Santa Cruz de la Sierra. Based on considerable original research. These kind of data are hard to come by elsewhere. [MTH]

2810 Sánchez-Albornoz, Nicolás. Una dicotomía indigena: originarios y forasteros en el Alto Perú (UCP/IAP, 10, 1976, p. 87–110, tables)

Original version of chap. 2 of item **2811**. [MTH]

2811 ———. Indios y tributos en el Alto Perú. Lima: Instituto de Estudios Peruanos, 1978. 224 p.; bibl.; maps; tables (Historia andina; 6)

Important collection of five excellent studies on demographic and social aspects of postconquest history of highland Indians of Bolivia. Sánchez-Albornoz probes extent to which increasing numbers of *forasteros,* who were not taxed and usually not registered in the 16th and 17th centuries, render fiscal data unreliable indicator of native decline; examines origins, importance and status of *forasteros,* and coeval terminology; reproduces with corrections and an additional appendix *El indio en el Alto Perú a fines del siglo XVII* (on which see *HLAS 36:1439* and *HLAS 38:3164*); offers a case study of demographic and socioeconomic vicissitudes suffered by Indians in the Partido of Tapacarí in the Corregimiento of Cochabamba; and sketches the abolition and subsequent restoration of tribute during the independence and national periods, the tax on Indians having been retained through 1882 at the national level and well into the 20th century at the departmental. Both contextually and in notes, Sánchez-Albornoz compares and contrasts changes and continuities in Bolivia with those elsewhere in Spanish America. Required reading for colonialists as well as Andeanists. [MTH]

2812 Santamaría, Daniel J. La estructura agraria del Alto Perú a fines del siglo XVIII: un análisis de tres regiones maiceras del Partido de Larecaja en 1795 (IDES/DE, 18:72, enero/marzo 1979, p. 579–595, map, tables)

Quantitative analysis of three maize-producing districts of Ayata, Aucapata and Chuma as of 1795 in the Partido of Larecaja in the Intendancy of La Paz. Examines number, type and size of estates, their estimated or declared value, output in maize, wheat, potatoes, kind of ownership, capital input, and the makeup of the labor force. [MTH]

2813 ———. La propiedad de la tierra y la condición social del indio en el Alto Perú, 1780–1810 (IDES/DE, 17:66, julio/set. 1977, p. 253–271, tables)

Utilizes late colonial tributary sources, especially *matrículas, padrones* and *revisitas* as found in the Archivo General de la Nación in Buenos Aires, to delineate patterns of Indian land holdings in Upper Peru by coeval classification group, administrative units and ecological zones during the years in question. A fascinating article, which among other important findings, demonstrates that the *archipielago*-model of multiple ecological control propounded by Murra and others, was still prevalent albeit to a lesser extent as of the late 18th and early 19th centuries. [MTH]

2814 Urioste de Aguirre, Marta. Los caciques Guarache (*in* Estudios bolivianos en homenaje a Gunnar Mendoza L. [see item **2638**] p. 131–140, tables)

Traces the succession to the cacicazgo of Jesús de Machaca, held uninterruptedly by members of the Guarache family from prior to the Inca conquest through the entire colonial period. Includes data on their *servicios y méritos* as found in a *memorial* of 1805 and other coeval sources. [MTH]

CHILE

2815 Anadón, José. Pineda y Bascuñán, defensor del araucano: vida y escritos de un criollo chileno del siglo XVII. Santiago de Chile: Editorial Universitaria, 1977. 287 p.; bibl.; 9 leaves of plates: ill.; index.

Well documented and written biography of the author of *Cautiverio feliz.* Includes considerable new archival data. [MTH]

2816 Aquila, August J. Alonso de Ercilla y Zúñiga: a basic bibliography. London: Grant & Cutler Ltd., 1975. 96 p. (Research bibliographies and checklists; 11)

Useful checklist of editions and translations of *La araucana,* other works by Ercilla, critical studies of and related materials based on *La araucana.* See also item **5077.** [MTH]

2817 Barbier, Jacques A. Tradition and reform in Bourbon Chile: Ambrosio O'Higgins and public finances (AAFH/TAM, 34:4, Jan. 1978, p. 381–399)

On the one hand, a carefully done case study of a so-called Bourbon reformer, Ambrosio O'Higgins as Captain General of Chile (1788–96), and on the other, a highly revealing reexamination of the "revolution in government" carried out by José de Galvez and his subordinates in the colonies. Barbier focuses on O'Higgins' relations with the Cabildo of Santiago, the Audiencia of Chile, other local bureaucracies, the Spanish Ministries, and the Viceroy of Peru. He demonstrates that O'Higgins was primarily a pragmatist, and that it was not the local elite as a group who lost power "but rather some members of it." [MTH]

2818 Carmagnani, Marcello. Formación de un mercado compulsivo y el papel de los mercaderes: la región de Santiago de Chile, 1559–1601 (JGSWGL, 12, 1975, p. 104–133, tables)

Seminal study of the market sector of the economy of early colonial Chile. Carmagnani attempts to establish both its characteristics and chronology. "Compulsivo" may be translated as forced and/or superimposed, which the author argues was the prevalent characteristic of the market through the end of the 17th century. Carmagnani also examines early colonial merchants as a group and the goods in which they traded. And he supports his interpretations with carefully analyzed statistics culled from the coeval notarial *protocolos* of Santiago de Chile, the only ones extant for that period. [MTH]

2819 Muñoz Olave, Reinaldo. Historia de la Diócesis de Concepción. Santiago: Fundación Alemana para el Desarrollo [and] Universidad Católica de Chile, Instituto de Historia, 1973. 342 p.; bibl.; port.

Written in 1926 but not published until now, this is a detailed study of the first half century of the Diócesis of Concepción, created in 1563. Includes data on the clergy as well as the prelates. Although somewhat dated, it is still useful for the wealth of archival data it contains. [MTH]

Pinto, Sonia; Luz María Méndez; and **Sergio Vergara.** Antecedentes históricos de la Contraloría General de la República. See item **2653.**

2820 Ramón, Armando de. Producción artesanal y servicios en Santiago de Chile, 1650–1700 (JGSWGL, 12, 1975, p. 134–166, map, tables)

Pioneering study of commercial and industrial establishments in Santiago of Chile during the second half of the 17th century. Particularly concerned with crafts, trades and the service sector, the individuals who made their living at them, and their role in the growth as well as the economy of the city. An outgrowth of the work cited below. [MTH]

2821 ———. Santiago de Chile, 1650–1700: pt. 2 (UCCIH/H, 13, 1976, p. 97–270, fold. map, tables)

Completes a socioeconomic analysis of real estate in Santiago de Chile during the second half of the 17th century. For pt. 1, see *HLAS 40:3254*. Pt. 2 covers the remainder of Santa Ana parish and that of San Isidro. Includes a map of the properties in question and indexes of lots, *vecinos*, buildings and places. Altogether a fundamental piece of ground-breaking research. [MTH]

2822 Salinas Meza, René. Fuentes para el estudio de la demografía histórica en el Norte Chico chileno, 1600–1854 (LARR, 13:2, 1978, p. 98–103)

Describes and evaluates extant sources from the colonial and early national period on the demography of the Norte Chico. [MTH]

2823 Zudaire Huarte, Eulogio. Don Agustín de Jáuregui y Aldecoa. v. 1, Presidente, Gobernador y Capitán General del Reino de Chile. Pamplona: Diputación Foral de Navarra, Institución Príncipe de Viana, Consejo Superior de Investigaciones Científicas, 1978. 253 p.; bibl.; ill.; indexes; plates; tables.

Thoroughly researched study of a major late colonial administrator Jaúregui y Aldecoa (1708–84), President, Governor and Captain General of Chile (1773–80) and Viceroy of Peru (1780–84). Vol. 1 sketches his military career in Spain and details his years in Chile. Includes chapters on Indian policies, the frontier, military reforms, economic policies, the epidemic of 1779, and cultural developments, and a documentary appendix. In brief, a major monograph on late 18th-century Chile and its rule. Vol. 2, not yet received at the Library of Congress, covers Jaúregui's viceregency. [MTH]

RIO DE LA PLATA

Academia Nacional de la Historia, *Buenos Aires.* Catálogo de la Colección Enrique Fitte. See item **3282**.

2824 Alvarenga Caballero, Pedro Antonio. La Villa Real de la Concepción y la defensa de la "marca hispánica" del norte (UCNSA/EP, 4:2, dic. 1976, p. 115–128)

Scantily-documented article details how Concepción in the Paraguayan North was originally settled by Governor Pinedo in 1773–74 in order to slow down penetration of the area by both Portuguese and hostile Indians. New documents show exactly who the colonists were, where they settled and stress correctly that until 1812, the area was virtually besieged by Indians. [JHW]

Alvarez, Antonio. Crónica de la Patagonia y tierras australes desde el descubrimiento hasta la colonización. See item **2628**.

Argentina. Comando General del Ejército. Dirección de Estudios Históricos. Política seguida con el aborigen: 1750–1819. See item **1588**.

2825 Arias Divito, Juan Carlos. Breve noticia de la factoría del Paraguay (CEHA/NH, 11:21, 1978, p. 180–182)

Describes the 1779 establishment of the Real Renta de Tabacos in Paraguay designed to monopolize and increase production of local, black tobacco. By 1802, the Renta was shipping south an impressive 49,165 *arrobas* and was running its own experimental finca at San Lorenzo, outside the capital. [JHW]

2826 Asdrúbal Silva, Hernán. La grasa y el sebo: dos elementos vitales para la colonia; Buenos Aires en la primera mitad del siglo XVIII (UNC/RHAA, 8:15/16, 1970/1971, p. 39–53, bibl.)

A well-documented study of the supply of basic cattle staples to Buenos Aires. Regulations setting prices and governing slaughter were adopted by the *porteño* cabildo because of: the city's growing demands, the resulting *faenas* which soon stripped surrounding territory, increasing shortages caused by recurrent Indian wars, and the drainage effect of Portuguese Colonia do Sacramento across the estuary. Impressive bibliography and notes are appended. [JHW]

2827 Avellá Cháfer, Francisco. Don Francisco Zaldívar, 1568–1638: Primer Deán del Cabildo Eclesiástico de Buenos Aires; crónica biográfica (ANH/IE, 21, julio/dic. 1976, p. 307–334, bibl.)

Biography of Zaldívar, an Asunción criollo educated for the priesthood at San Marcos, in Lima, and who filled a number of important positions in the ecclesiastical hierarchy of the Río de la Plata. More important for what it has to say about the functioning and internal squabbling of the Platense Church than for what it reports on the priest himself. Documentation is drawn from four important archives and sound secondary sources, and the work helps fill a gap in the history of Church in Río de la Plata. [JHW]

2828 Bacigalupo, Mario Ford. Bernardo Ibáñez de Echavarri and the image of the Jesuit missions of Paraguay (AAFH/TAM, 35:4, April 1979, p. 475–494)

An excellent piece on the impact of a man twice expelled from the Jesuit Order who went on to become a major figure and synthesizer of anti-Jesuit polemics, helping prepare the climate of opinion which led to the expulsion of the Order in 1767. His greatest work of propaganda was the famous *Reyno jesuítico del Paraguay,* which appeared in the 1760s and was soon translated into numerous languages. [JHW]

2829 Barrios Pintos, Aníbal. Una conferencia inédita de Guillermo Furlong S.J. (UBN/R, 17, 1977, p. 35–53)

Consists of brief bio-bibliography of the great Argentine Jesuit scholar (who wrote 53 books and 616 articles), followed by the text of a talk he delivered in Montevideo in 1972 concerning the role of the Church in Uruguay in the last decades of the colonial era. Describes founding of churches, chapels and schools in the hinterland. A thoughtful piece. [JHW]

———. Paysandú en escorzo histórico. See item **3482**.

2830 Bejarano, Ramón César. Caciques guaraníes de la época colonial. Asunción: Editorial Toledo, 1979. 16 p.; ill.; map; plate.

Alphabetical list of 125 Guaraní caciques' names includes a short description of each drawn from Nicolás del Techo's *Historia de la Provincia del Paraguay*. Of possible interest to ethnographers. [JHW]

2831 Beverina, Juan. La expedición de D. Pedro de Cevallos en 1776–77. Introducción, notes y selección documental y cartografía por Alfredo G. Villegas. Buenos Aires: Editorial Rioplatense, 1978. 212 p.; bibl.; ill.

Competent treatment of the successful expulsion of Luso-Brazilians from extreme southern Brazil and the Banda Oriental (Uruguay) by Viceroy and General Cevallos. Beverina examines the long standing strife in and contention over the region and describes the military operations—in which Cevallos appears as military genius. Complemented by good maps, and a long documentary appendix. [JHW]

2832 Bicentenario del Virreinato del Río de la Plata. Buenos Aires: Academia Nacional de la Historia, 1977. 2 v. (392, 403 p.) bibl.; ill.

A major collection of 30 scholarly articles on various aspects and regions of the Viceroyalty (e.g., black slaves in Bolivia by Alberto Crespo or the growth of cattle ranching in Corrientes by Ernesto J.A. Maeder). Most of the pieces are well-documented and appear here for the first time. In brief, a compendium of some excellent, albeit specialized articles by several of Argentina's leading historians. [JHW]

Biraghi, Roberto I. Reseña histórica de la zona de San Lorenzo, el país de las batatas. See item **3304**.

Bischoff, Efraín U. Córdoba: los ratones y las llaves. See item **3305**.

2833 ———. ¿Quién fué Bamba? (PJHC/R, 6, 1977, p. 11–42, plate)

The article traces the evolution of the lengendary "Bamba" from viceregal times to the present. Essentially, Bischoff proves that "Bamba" existed and was most probably one Juan Esteban Bemba, a black slave, who, in order to escape punishment from some wrong-doing, fled into the deserted hinterland of Córdoba where he remained, tilling the soil and establishing a settlement. [JHW]

———. Las viejas imprentas de la Universidad. See item **2630**.

2834 Blujaki, Agustín. Los primeros sacerdotes y el primer Obispo electo de la Asunción del Paraguay (APH/HP, 16, 1978, p. 43–101, bibl.)

This lengthy, well thought out article deals with the first priests in Paraguay, from the Mercedarian Juan de Salazar, present at the foundation of Asunción in 1537 through the arrival of first Bishop of the Diocesis, Juan de los Barrios in 1553. Stress is on the contributions of the Church to early 16th-century Paraguay. [JHW]

Boletín. Provincia de Santa Fe. Año 6, No. 6, 1974– . See item **3306**.

Brown, Jonathan C. A socioeconomic history of Argentina, 1776–1860. See item **2947**.

Casais de Corne, Alicia Elena; Fiz Antonio Fernández; and **Julio Lardies González.** Panorama histórico de la medicina argentina. See item **3315**.

2835 Cestau, Saúl D. Historia del notariado uruguayo desde la época colonial hasta la sanción de la Ley No. 1421. Montevideo: Asociación de Escribanos del Uruguay, 1976. 270 p.; bibl.; index.

A turgid volume dealing with the 18th- and 19th-century functioning of notaries and *escribanías* in Uruguay. Well researched and carefully documented, but poorly organized and tediously written. [JHW]

2836 Cooney, Jerry W. A colonial naval industry: *The Fábrica de Cables* of Paraguay (PAIGH/H, 87, enero/junio 1979, p. 105–126)

This fine study provides "an example of the mobilization of men, material and capital" to fill an emergency need for ship-ropes, hawsers and cables during the war-torn 1790–1810 period. Cooney rightly notes that without cordage the fleet was immobilized and describes Governor Ribera's rapid response of 1797 to urgent Crown demands for these items. They were met with the use of cordage made from indigenous *güembé* and *caraguatá* fibers (there being no hemp grown in Paraguay). A revealing study of a forgotten, but vital product. [JHW]

2837 Cordero, Héctor Adolfo. El primitivo Buenos Aires: comercio, político, religión, instrucción pública, artesanos, gobernantes, médicos, fiestas populares. Buenos Aires: Plus Ultra, 1978. 317 p.; bibl.

A good, worthwhile social history of Buenos Aires and its *cercanías*, during the late 16th and early 17th centuries. Rich in information on everything from the types of trees growing in the city to the type of medicine and medical help available to the porteño. In fact it is in the treatment of the "lesser" activities that this work makes its contribution (e.g., descriptions of the arrival of a new barber, of bull fights and card games, of the new jail). [JHW]

2838 De Rosas, Marta Duda and **Marta Herrera.** La acción estatal de la organización de la campaña cuyana a mediados del siglo XVIII: aportaciones demográficas (UNC/RHAA, 7:13/14, 1968/1969, p. 29–96, tables)

Vast, well-documented work on the Junta General de Poblaciones of Santiago de Chile, which in 1735 began to implement an organic plan to found a series of pueblos and expand those few existing in the Cuyo area. Detailed census data shows the growth of population in the area (especially after 1750) in poblaciones centered around individual churches. Despite Indian raids from Chile and the Chaco, and the resistance of estancieros who claimed enormous expanses of the area, the plan essentially succeeded and the gap between Chile and the more settled areas of the Río de la Plata was gradually filled. [JHW]

2839 Destéfani, Laurio H. Informe sobre Nombre de Jesús, una población fundada en 1584 por Sarmiento de Gamboa (ANH/B, 49, 1979, p. 201–205, ill.)

Well-documented article deals with settlements (chiefly Nombre de Jesús) founded to safeguard the Straits of Magellan by Pedro Sarmiento de Gamboa in 1584. Shortly thereafter, the 338 inhabitants became ill from the damp cold and hunger. Their sufferings ended in 1587 when the English pirate Cavendish destroyed the settlements in a devastating raid. Excavations to locate Nombre de Jesús began as late as 1954 ending with its discovery in 1975. The dig is still underway and the government has designated the site as a historic landmark ("lugar histórico"). [JHW]

Fleming, William J. Regional research in Argentina: a critical evaluation of the archives and libraries of Mendoza province. See item **2639**.

2839a Flores, Moacyr. Aspectos culturais das missões jesuíticas (PUC/V, 33:90, junho 1978, p. 142–162, illus., maps, tables)

A survey, based on secondary sources, of the structure and conditions of the Jesuit missions in Paraguay. Tries to set them in the context of the other New World missions of the Jesuits. [Colin MacLachlan]

2840 Fonrouge de Baliña, Julia Elena. Los fuertes de Corpus Christi y la colonización del Río Paraná (ANH/IE, 20, enero/junio 1976, p. 341–359)

A short study of the short-lived forts of Corpus Mendoza (80 and 84 leagues respectively, north of Buenos Aires) in mid-1536 to serve as bases for his expedition further up the Paraná in search of the fabled Sierra de Plata. Both were constantly under Indian attack, the former was slaughtered twice before evacuation in 1539, two years prior to the abandonment of Buenos Aires itself. These Indian troubles discouraged Spanish interest in the Río de la Plata for a century. [JHW]

2841 Garavaglia, Juan Carlos. El ritmo de la extracción de metálico desde el Río de la Plata a la Península, 1779–1783 (IGFO/RI, 36:143/144, enero/junio 1976, p. 247–268, tables)

In this short period, Buenos Aires became the chief exporter of silver from Alto Perú and gold from Chile, partly because of Spain's war with Britain. Author concludes that most of the gold went to Cádiz for immediate use in Spain's foreign trade and debt service, while much of the silver was funneled through Montevideo (legal) to Brazil (illegal). Much of the precious metal which reached Spain did so "informally," aboard neutral ships consigned to private individuals to avoid British capture. A thorough piece of research. [JHW]

2842 García Belsunce, César A. La aduana de Buenos Aires en las postrimerías del régimen virreinal (ANH/IE, 19, julio/dic. 1975, p. 463–486, tables)

The author deals with the years 1805–10, mining the wealth of information in the nearly complete *registros* of the Aduana. Most of the article is a description of the different *ramas de ingreso*, rates of taxation, and regulations of the institution, followed by charts and tables showing the collections, expenses and credits. One consequence of these chaotic years was the inability of merchants to meet their installment payments for taxes levied in previous years. [JHW]

Gianello, Leoncio. Historia de Santa Fe. See item **3354**.

2843 Haubert, Maxime. Bons sauvages et bonne nouvelle au Paraguay (UP/TM, 19:75, juillet/sept. 1978, p. 469–494)

Haubert presents a rather glowing (if not naive) account of the Paraguayan system of reducciones, after admitting that "le totalitarisme qui régit la Compagnie de Jesus imprime aussi sa marque a la vie quotidienne." Notes in concluding that prior messianic movements among the precolombian Guaraní greatly aided their adaptation to Jesuit control. [JHW]

2844 Johnson, Lyman L. Estimaciones de la población de Buenos Aires en 1774 y 1810 (IDES/DE, 19:73, abril/junio 1979, p. 107–119, tables)

Utilizes vital statistic data, derived from parish registers of Buenos Aires, to test relative accuracy of the *padrones* of 1774, 1778 and 1810. The total population resultant from the enumeration of 1774 is more or less acceptable; that resultant from the enumeration of 1778 is between 53.5 and 22.8 percent below the mark, assuming the mean crude birth rate to have been between 40 and 50 per 1,000; and that resultant from the enumeration of 1810 is off by between one half and two thirds. A methodologically sophisticated and stimulating essay. [MTH]

2845 ———. La manumisión de esclavos en Buenos Aires durante el virreinato (IDES/DE, 16:63, oct./dic. 1976, p. 333–348, tables)

Quantitative study of manumission in late colonial Buenos Aires. Johnson finds that most ex-slaves had to purchase their freedom and were not freed by magnanimous *padrinos* or would-be lovers, the importance of both of whom has been exaggerated in the literature. [MTH]

2846 ———. La manumisión en el Buenos Aires colonial: un análisis ampliado (IDES/DE, 17:68, enero/marzo 1978, p. 637–646, tables)

This article deals with the last three decades of the colonial era and compares, decade by decade the characteristics of manumission. Among the conclusions: the disproportionate number of women manumitted, the increasing rate of manumission, and the increase of self-purchase as a primary vehicle of manumission. Johnson includes comparative data from Brazil for the same epoch, and the work is very well-documented. [JHW]

2847 ——— and **Susan Migden Socolow.** Population and space in eighteenth century Buenos Aires (*in* Social fabric and spatial structure in colonial Latin America. Edited by David J. Robinson. Ann Arbor, Mich.: University Microfilms International, 1979, p. 339–368, ill., tables)

Stimulating spin-off from ongoing research into the growth and composition of late colonial Buenos Aires. Based on the fairly complete censuses of 1744, 1778 and 1810, presents a variety of tentative social and demographic conclusions. Among these: the non-white population increased faster than the white; there was great demographic fluidity; the free black segment of society increased more slowly than did the slave community; there was a large and fluctuating Luso-Brazilian immigration; the physical limits of the city expanded little while density in city center notably increased; immigrants got the most prestigious and remunerative urban jobs, thus limiting social mobility for the creoles; and the wealthy remained in the city's center while the poor dwelt in the outskirts. A very valuable article which, we hope, will be followed by many others. [JHW]

2848 Labougle, Raúl de. Historia de San Juan de Vera de las Siete Corrientes, 1588–1814. Buenos Aires: Distribuidor, Librería Platero, 1978. 341 p.

Good, standard history of colonial Corrientes, Argentina, and by extension, of the Argentine Northeast. Flawed by a lack of maps, the volume, however, is well-documented, with precise notes. Especially interesting is the author's discussions of the absolutely Byzantine boundary and jurisdictional squabbles between Paraguay and Corrientes, both in the Misiones area and from Pilar (Paraguay), south to the Paraná. While not replacing Mansilla's classic, two-volume history of Corrientes, this tome admirably updates it. [JHW]

2849 Levaggi, Abelardo. Las instituciones de clemencia en el derecho penal rioplatense (UNAM/RFD, 26:101/102, enero/junio 1976, p. 243–297)

Levaggi wrote this article to correct the common view of the Spanish and Spanish American penal codes as basically cruel and harsh. Quite to the contrary, he persuasively argues—there were in the Río de la Plata (and elsewhere) many institutions and legal devices which operated "siempre en beneficio de la parte delincuente," such as pardons of various types, indultos (both collective and individual), rights of asylum, etc. According to the author, these were applied frequently. [JHW]

2850 Levene, Ricardo. Lecturas históricas argentinas. v. 1, Decubrimiento, conquista y colonización. Los cabildos. El Virreinato. Buenos Aires: Editorial Belgrano, 1978. 249 p. (Colección La Argentina histórica)

Reprint of Levene's still useful 1913 compendium of sources on the history of Argentina. Vol. 1 on the colonial period, is organized into three sections: 1) discovery, conquest, and colonization; 2) the cabildos; and 3) the viceroyalty. Includes documents ranging in time from 1514 through 1806, in place from Madrid to Corrientes, and in theme from *aranceles de gremios* (guild tariffs) through *sublevaciones de indios*. For comment on vol. 2 (independence and national period), see item **3375**. [MTH]

2851 Maeder, Ernesto J.A. La expansión de la frontera interior de Corrientes entre 1750 y 1814: de la ciudad a la provincia (ANH/IE, 19, julio/dic. 1975, p. 423–462, map, tables)

Maeder has given us another very professional piece of work, based for the most part on documentation from five major archives. He neatly shows the expansion of the Province of Corrientes from a small triangle wedged between the Paraná and Alto Paraná outwards into five geographical districts to the East and South. This dramatic expansion, predicated largely on stock-raising and orchestrated by the Corrientes Cabildo, brought this body into conflict and litigation with Paraguay, Entre Ríos and the Jesuit Order. Through patient negotiating and "irregular" migration into the interior, Corrientes gained the major portions of the lands it coveted. [JHW]

2852 Mariluz Urquijo, José María. Orígenes de la burocracia rioplatense: la Secretaría del Virreinato. Buenos Aires: Ediciones Cabargón, 1974. 132 p.; bibl.; ill.

A thoroughly researched work on the composition and duties of the Viceregal Secretariat in general, and its establishment and functioning within the Río de la Plata. The scribes, lawyers and advisors which composed the Secretaría were a true bureaucracy, with a force and a drive of their own, often eclipsing the Viceroy. Excellent study which should be consulted. [JHW]

2853 ———. La situación del mitayo en las glosas de Benito de la Mata Linares al código carolino (JGSWGL, 14, 1977, p. 161–198)

This piece, one half of which is composed of a detailed appendix, deals with the comments and criticisms of Mata Linares (probably written in 1807) on the late 18th century mining code for the New World. In short, he did not like it, finding from his own extensive experience in Peru that its provisions were both harsh and unrealistic. For the specialist. [JHW]

2854 Martiré, Eduardo. El estatuto legal del oficial de la administración pública al crearse el Virreinato del Río de la Plata (UNAM/RFD, 26:101/102, enero/junio 1976, p. 417–436)

With extensive documentation, Martiré deals with a late 18th-century concern. Because of the rapid growth of the Río de la Plata's bureaucracy, legislation was promulgated to tighten regional administration and define the duties and obligations of civil servants. While this article notably avoids drawing conclusions, it does offer a wealth of detail concerning innovations introduced by the legislation such as: placing new stress on merit; recognizing the need to treat the public "con mucha cortesía;" implementing the seven-hour day; requiring new educational qualifications; *ad infinitum.* A good article. [JHW]

2855 Mayo, Carlos A. Los *pobleros* del Tucumán colonial: contribución al estudio de los mayordomos y administradores de encomienda en América (PAIGH/H, 85, enero/junio 1978, p. 27–57)

A very worthwhile study of agents who were appointed by absentee encomenderos of Tucumán and known as *pobleros.* Since they had day-to-day dealings with the encomienda and the Indians, Mayo finds that they were key elements in that institution and prime movers of cultural adjustment and mestizaje. They were in charge of supervising most work, listing births and deaths, collecting tribute, and even performing some religious duties. A very well-documented article which opens a new door and should be read by all colonialists. [JHW]

2856 Melía, Bartomeu. Las reducciones jesuíticas del Paraguay: un espacio para una utopía colonial (USNSA/EP, 6:1, sept. 1978, p. 157–167)

A thoughtful attempt to show how the Jesuits, in their Paraguayan Mission system, preserved much of Guaraní culture by confining their "spatial organization" to a new urban setting which limited their "historical mobility." The missions might have presented "un espacio de libertad . . . reducida," but it was also "un área compacta libre de otras intromisiones coloniales," a utopia of sorts, protecting the Indians and much of their culture from the depredations of secular colonial society. [JHW]

2857 Montes, Alberto. Santiago Montenegro, fundador de la Ciudad de Rosario. Rosario: Ediciones IEN, 1977. 164 p.; bibl.; ill.

A brief history of Santiago Montenegro and the province of Rosario. Well-researched and contains a good bibliography and notes, a long documental appendix and quite a few "documentos inéditos" within the text. It deals primarily with the city's foundation in the early 18th century, and its later growth. A useful but not major work. [JHW]

Montevideo. Biblioteca del Poder Legislativo. Departamento de Relaciones Públicas y Publicaciones. Cronología de Montevideo en los 250 años de su proceso fundacional. See item **3496**.

2858 Mora Mérida, José Luis. Iglesia y sociedad en Paraguay en el siglo XVIII. Sevilla: Escuela de Estudios Hispanoamericanos de Sevilla, 1976. 162 p.; bibl.; index (Publicaciones de la Escuela de Estudios Hispanoamericanos de Sevilla; 235)

This is a superbly documented social history of the Paraguayan Church in the first two-thirds of the 18th century by a leading authority on colonial Paraguay. The focus is less on the Revolt of the Comuneros and the Expulsion of the Jesuits than upon the day-to-day impact and nature of the Church in this imperial backwater. Of great interest are Mora Mérida's profiles of Bishop Manuel Antonio de la Torre and of regular and secular clergymen. A highly recommended work. [JHW]

2859 *Noticias del Correo Mercantil de España y sus Indias:* sobre la vida económica del Virreinato del Río de la Plata. Advertencia de Enrique M. Barba. Estudio preliminar de José M. Mariluz Urquijo. Buenos Aires: Academia Nacional de la Historia, 1977. 156 p.; bibl. (Colección de historia económica y social; 1)

This volume consists of a brilliant, 12-page historical introduction by José María Mariluz Urquijo, and 131 p. of extracts from the Spanish journal dealing specifically with the Río de la Plata. Much of the information concerning the Viceroyalty came from Manuel Belgrano, the Buenos Aires Consulado, of which he was a member, and the nascent porteño press. The excerpts date from 1792 (when the *Noticias* was founded in Madrid) through 1803, and deal with virtually every part of the Viceroyalty. [JHW]

Ortega, Exequiel César. Historia de la provincia de Buenos Aires: su panorama de 460 años, 1516–1978. See item **3396**.

2860 Oyarzun Iñarra, Javier. Expediciones españoles al Estrecho de Magallanes y Tierra del Fuego. Madrid: Ediciones de Cultura Hispánica, 1976. 294 p.; bibl.; 12 leaves of plates: 12 ill.

An excellent, narrative account of 11 major Spanish expeditions to the Straits and Tierra del Fuego, from Magellan's, which discovered both in 1520, to that of Malaspina in the late 18th century. Includes a discussion of the known sources on each expedition. A fine addition to the growing literature on the history of the Argentine South. [JHW]

Paraguay. Archivo Nacional. Archivo Nacional de Asunción: primer ensayo de índice, el documento más antiguo, documentos inéditos. See item **2651**.

Prost, Gérard. Ganados sin hombres ou: la latifundium em Uruguay résiste au temps. See item **3499**.

2861 Robinson, David J. Córdoba en 1779: la ciudad y la campaña (Gaea [Sociedad Argentina de Estudios Geográficos, Rosario, Argentina] 17, 1979, p. 279–312, maps, tables)

Goes beyond the usual macroanalysis of *padrones* and parish registers to reconstruct and analyze in extraordinary detail the demographic, economic and social structure of Córdoba del Tucumán and its immediate hinterland c. 1779. An impressive and highly original piece of scholarship, which demonstrates rather than merely suggests the many uses to which such sources may be put. [MTH]

Romero Carranza, Ambrosio; Alberto Rodríguez Varela; and **Eduardo Ventura.** Manual de historia política y constitución, Argentina, 1776–1976. See item **2656**.

2862 Sanabria Fernández, Hernando. Cristóbal de Mendoza, el apóstol de los guaraníes. La Paz: Biblioteca del Sesquicentenario de la República, 1976. 132 p.; bibl. (Biblioteca del Sesquicentenario de la República, 18)

A popular biography of the Jesuit missionary (b. Santa Cruz de la Sierra, 1589) who, in the missions of Guairá fought against the *bandeirantes* to defend his charges, accompanied Father Montoya on the epic migration of 12,000 surviving Guaraní neophytes to new missions near the alto Paraná and Uruguay Rivers, and who was then sent to today's Rio Grande do Sul in Brazil. There, in 1632, he founded the mission of San Miguel, in 1634, inaugurated cattle ranching in the region, and the following year was killed by hostile Indians. Cristóbal de Mendoza was a fascinating character, but the author shows him in one dimension only, and with a bare minimum of notes and bibliography. [JHW]

Sánchez Quell, Hipólito. Los 50,000 documentos paraguayos llevados al Brasil. See *HLAS 41:95*.

2863 Sanz, Francisco de Paula. Viaje por la Virreinato del Río de la Plata: el camino del tabaco. Estudio preliminar por Daisy Rípodas Ardanaz. Buenos Aires: Librería Editorial Platero, 1977. 95 p.; bibl. (Documentos. Universidad de Buenos Aires, Centro de Estudios Interdisciplinario de Hispanoamérica Colonial; 1)

Sanz, a peninsular bureaucrat, was sent to establish and serve as director of the *Renta del Tabaco* in the Río de la Plata in 1778. This volume contains his 1778–81 reports, province by province, section by section, concerning actual and and potential tobacco culture throughout the Viceroyalty. The originals are in the Archivo General de la Nación, in Buenos Aires and the Archivo General de Indias in Seville. A valuable source for the agricultural history of the late colonial period. [JHW]

2864 Segreti, Carlos A. Contribución al estudio de la condición del aborigen en Córdoba de la Nueva Andalucía hasta las Ordenanzas del Visitador Francisco de Alfaro (ANH/IE, 19, julio/dic. 1975, p. 181–258, bibl., tables)

This lengthy article is a valuable examination of the poor conditions of Indians in the Argentine Northwest in the late quarter of the 16th century. Their lamentable state was due to the following: overly rapacious *encomenderos*; their even more greedy *pobleros* or contract overseers; an almost startling absence of clergy; the area's relative isolation; a series of devastating epidemics in the 1590s; an unusual drop in the Indian birth-rate; and Indian revolts. A well-researched and written study. [JHW]

Seminario de Historia de la Medicina Argentina, *Córdoba, Argentina, 1976.* Historia general de la medicina argentina. See item **3422**.

2865 Socolow, Susan Migden. The merchants of Buenos Aires, 1778–1810: family and commerce. Cambridge, Eng.: Cambridge University Press, 1978. 253 p.; bibl.; ill.; index (Cambridge Latin American studies; 30)

A carefully researched, skillfully analyzed and well-written prosopographic study of porteño merchants during the viceregal period. Primarily a social rather than an economic history of this group. Includes a case study of Gaspar de Santa Coloma, a "typical" merchant. In the conclusion, Socolow compares her findings to those of Brading, Lockhart and Ruth Poke on merchants in 18th-century Mexico and 16th-century Lima and Seville. [MTH]

2866 Storni, Hugo. Jesuitas italianos en el Río de la Plata: antigua provincia del Paraguay, 1585–1768 (AHSI, 48:95, gen./luglio 1979, p. 3–64, bibl., tables)

A useful, biobibliographical listing of 114 Jesuits of Italian origin from Acquarone to Zipoli who served in Paraguay from 1587 (e.g., De Arminio) through the expulsion (e.g., Stella). There is a short paragraph, written in abbreviated form on each, and a section with less information on 44 more Italian Jesuits "relacionados" with the Jesuit Province of Paraguay. Includes an excellent bibliography, detailed footnotes and four indexes: a general index provides different spellings of the Jesuits names; another lists dates of their arrival in Paraguay; and two final ones concern their geographic origin. A trove of information. [JHW]

Tejerina Carreras, Ignacio G. El Archivo del Arzobispado de Córdoba: breve guía para el conocimiento de la documentación existente. See *HLAS 41:96*.

2867 Urbano Salerno, Marcelo. Aplicación en el Virreinato de Río de la Plata del Auto Acordado del 31 de junio de 1792 sobre arrendamiento de casas de Madrid (UNAM/RFD, 26:101/102, enero/junio 1976, p. 773–784)

This law, caused by a Madrid housing shortage, limited the liberty of contract of homeowners—except those who lived on their properties—by essentially forcing them to rent them. It was adopted in housing-short Buenos Aires in 1804 by the Audiencia after a decade of argument between the municipal government and those who owned homes. The article is thoroughly researched, but very cautious in its conclusions. [JHW]

Urquiza Almandoz, Oscar F. Las primeras industrias entrerrianas: 1600–1850. See item **3432**.

2868 Velázquez, Rafael Eladio. Iglesia y educación en el Paraguay colonial (APH/HP, 25, 1978, p. 97–154)

Buttressed by heavy, almost lavish documentation, this major article deals with virtually all aspects of the Church's educational work in colonial Paraguay, from decisions of its ecclesiastical cabildo, to activities of militia chaplains and the *cofradías*, through the late 18th century founding of the Real Seminario to train local clerics. A very useful piece. [JHW]

2869 El Virreinato del Río de la Plata, 1776–1810. Buenos Aires: Sociedad Rural Argentina, 1976. 137 p.; bibl.; ill.

This slim volume contains nine brief articles dealing with the 18th-century Río de la Plata, some of which are excellent (e.g., Adolfo Luis Ribera "Los Pintores del Buenos Aires Virreinal" and José María Peña "Vivienda y Mobilario en Tiempos del Virreinato"). The basic thrust is social history, but there are no pieces on sheep and cattle ranching and the global significance of the creation of the viceroyalty. Generally, a good and well-documented collection. [JHW]

Williams, John Hoyt. The Archivo General de la Nación of Uruguay. See item **2658**.

2870 Zapata Gollán, Agustín. La primera urbanización hispanoamericana en el Río de la Plata: Santa Fe (UNL/U, 88, sept./dic. 1977, p. 171–188)

Zapata believes Santa Fe was the first town in the Río de la Plata built according to a strict grid urban pattern. He attributes the origin of this Iberian characteristic to the wars of the Reconquista in Spain and stresses its military *raison d'être*. Juan de Garay, probing south from Asunción, founded Santa Fe in 1573 as a fortified settlement: "That military character of the foundation demanded a city laid out regularly . . . which would facilitate the rapid deployment of the scant military force" available. A century later, due to the flooding Paraná, the city was moved to a new site, but the original has been unearthed and studied through a program begun in 1949. This is a well-researched and valuable article. [JHW]

Independence Period

DAVID BUSHNELL, *Professor of History, University of Florida*

FOR LATIN AMERICAN HISTORIANS generally, the most important new book on the independence of Spanish South America is without much doubt Miguel Izard's provocatively titled *El miedo a la Revolución* (item **2907**). It represents a survey of the struggle in Venezuela, both interpretative and detailed, by a modern Spanish historian. Among the other volumes listed in this section, those by Brown on the scope and social impact of economic changes in Argentina (item **2947**) and Hamnett on counter-revolution in Mexico and Peru (item **2928**) are also notable but either chronologically or geographically extend beyond the topic of Spanish South American independence per se. The *Handbook* section devoted to works classified as General History (see p. 000–000) includes two more items with which anyone working on the independence period should become familiar even though neither is limited to the Bolivarian and San Martinian theaters, the settings that provide most of the content of this section: Russell Bartley's excellent study of Russia and Latin American independence (item **1896**) and O. Carlos Stoetzer's examination of the ideological roots of the movement in Spanish America as a whole (item **1817a**). Many will disagree with Stoetzer's thesis, but he does at last provide a full statement in English of a viewpoint that has long been influential in the Hispanic world.

None of the works just mentioned was written in Spanish South America itself. This seems to be one more indication that, among historians from the Andean and Platine nations, independence topics continue to hold special attraction for amateurs and traditionalists, while the more innovative and, by and large, the more professionally trained historians seek topics elsewhere. However, some of the better amateurs or traditionally oriented professionals continue producing history on the independence period that is both workmanlike and a net addition to knowledge, even if trail-blazing in neither method nor interpretation and generally of more specialized interest than the titles cited previously. A fine example is Pilar Moreno de Angel's new life of José María Córdova (item **2899**); another is the study of Cochrane by Alamiro de Avila Martel (item **2871**); and still another is the study of the Uruguayan revolt of 1822–23 by Martha Campos Thévenin de Garabelli (item **2968**). The fact that two of these three examples are books written by women is at least noteworthy.

If the monographic literature is on the whole disappointing, historians can take heart from the appearance of a very good crop of scholarly articles. To be sure, once again there is a disproportionate number by foreign scholars. The Spanish historian Manuel Lucena Salmoral has contributed two somewhat revisionist articles on aspects of Venezuelan and imperial economic history during the early phases of the independence period (items **1909a** and **2909**). Also on economic themes, but dealing specifically with Chile, there are two good articles by John Rector (item **2941**) and Claudio Véliz (item **2944**). For its combination of originality and broad interest of the topic treated, one more contribution on Chile—the analysis of naval recruitment by David J. Cubitt (item **2940**)—is difficult to surpass. Yet John Fisher's interpretation of Peruvian alignments (item **2927**) is no less important, and there are several good articles by Peruvian scholars in the collaborative volume *Primer Simposio Nacional de Historia de la Independencia* (item **2930**). Nor should the independence specialist overlook two articles listed elsewhere under a General rubric: Héctor José Tanzi's discussion of ideology (item **1820a**), which represents the same philosophical school as Stoetzer's volume but is more *matizado* in interpretation, and Ron Seckinger's stimulating analysis of intra-South American international relations of the immediate post-independence years (item **1913a**).

For the rest, students of Spanish South American independence are referred to the entries that follow. Each item has lasting value of some sort, but few will rate as landmarks in the development of the field, and those interested in specific areas can locate the pertinent titles without further guidance from the contributing editor.

GENERAL

2871 Avila Martel, Alamiro de. Cochrane y la independencia del Pacífico. Santiago: Editorial Universitaria, 1976. 306 p.; facsims.; ill.; plates.

Excellent account of naval warfare in Pacific theater and role of Cochrane in particular. Defends Cochrane against San Martín and other critics, but on basis of solid scholarly research. Well illustrated, clearly written.

Bartley, Russell H. Imperial Russia and the struggle for Latin American independence, 1808–1828. See item **1896**.

2872 Bolívar, Simón. Escritos del Libertador. t. 11, Documentos Nos. 1971–2290, 15 septiembre–31 octubre 1817; t. 12, Documentos Nos. 2291–2582, 1 noviembre–30 diciembre 1817. Caracas: Sociedad Bolivariana de Venezuela, 1974/1976. 2 v.; facsims.

Further installments of *HLAS 36: 2651*.

Bromley, Rosemary D.F. The functions and development of "colonial" towns: urban change in the Central Highlands of Ecuador, 1698–1940. See item **2631**.

Campbell, Leon G. Recent research on Andean peasant revolts, 1750–1820. See *HLAS 41:21*.

Duarte French, Jaime. América de Norte a Sur: ¿Corsarios o libertadores? See item **1905**.

2873 García Godoy, Christián. San Martín: bibliografía principal en inglés (selected bibliography in English). Washington: Sociedad Sanmartiniana (The San Martín Society), 1978. 63 leaves.

Not exhaustive, but helpful for those who do not read Spanish. Also valuable as demonstration of how little has been done in English on San Martín.

2874 Grases, Pedro. Cartas inéditas de José Joaquín de Olmedo al General José de San Martín: 1821–1822 (BANH/V, 62:246, abril/junio 1979, p. 449–474, facsim.)

Consists of 27 letters (from Indiana's Lilly Library) sent by Olmedo, as President of Junta de Guayaquil, with news of military events and requests for help.

2875 Grigulevich, Iosif R. Fransisko de Miranda i bor'ba za nezavisimost' Latinskoi Ameriki (Francisco de Miranda and the struggle for the independence of Spanish America). Moscow: Izdatel'stvo 'Nauka,' 1976. 273 p.; bibl.; plates.

A biography of Miranda—rather unexpectedly sponsored by the Institute of Ethnography of the Academy of Sciences—with but a few notes (all, evidently, to previously published material) and an index. The sponsorship may account for its peculiar documentation. [R.V. Allen]

2876 Heredia, Edmundo A. Réplicas españolas a los planes continentales de Bolívar y San Martín (JPHC/R, 8, 1978, p. 5–20)

Treats Spanish perceptions of both liberators as well as counter-measures considered or adopted. See also item **2953**.

2877 König, Hans-Joachim. Bolívar visto por Carlos Marx (SBV/R, 32:106, julio 1975, p. 79–87)

West German historian's very good short critique of Marx's infamous (and embarrassing to Marxists) biographical article.

Kossok, Manfred. Probleme einer vergleichenden Analyse der lateinamerikanischen Unabhängigkeitsrevolution. See *HLAS 41:7036.*

2878 Lima, Nestor dos Santos. La imagen del Brasil en las cartas de Bolívar. Caracas: Gráficos Bloch, 1978. 67 p.; plates.

Handsomely illustrated edition of article earlier published in *Revista de la Sociedad Bolivariana de Venezuela* (34:114, 24 julio 1977, p. 60–86) which reviews familiar sources to extract coherent picture of Bolívar's attitude toward his largest immediate neighbor. Sees evolution from indifference and omission to active hostility to final comprehension. Also contains short general item by author, a Brazilian diplomat, on Brazil-Venezuelan relations.

2879 Martí Gilabert, Francisco. La primera misión de la Santa Sede a América. Pamplona, Spain: Ediciones Universidad de Navarra, 1967. 359 p.; bibl. (Colección Canónica)

Missed by *HLAS* when first published and still worth listing: solidly researched study of Muzi mission to Chile via Buenos Aires, including both antecedents and issues dealt with, which concerned impact on Church of coming of independence. Competently professional, also bears imprimatur.

2880 Rayfield, Jo Ann. Daniel F. O'Leary as a historian (*in* Rocky Mountain Council on Latin American Studies, 25th, Tucson, Arizona, 1977. Proceedings. Lincoln: University of Nebraska, 1977, p. 31–38)

Useful, brief analysis focusing chiefly on classic *Narración* of Bolívar's aide, still a key source on independence period in Bolivarian theater.

2881 Rodríguez S., Luis A. Ayacucho: la batalla de la libertad americana, 1824–1974. Quito: Editorial Casa de la Cultura Ecuatoriana, 1975. 504 p.; bibl.

Combines general narrative of final liberation of Ecuador and that of Peru with detailed presentation (transcribing numerous documents) of Ecuadorian financial, material and other contributions to the latter.

2882 Ross, Stanley R. San Martín as seen in United States textbooks (RIB, 29:1, 1979, p. 41–52)

Brief survey of references contained in 11 Latin American history texts for US students.

2883 Santa-Cruz Schuhkrafft, Andrés de. Archivo histórico del Mariscal Andrés de Santa-Cruz. t. 1, 1820–1828. La Paz, Bolivia: Universidad Mayor de San Andrés, Instituto de Investigaciones Históricas, 1976. 411 p.; port.

Wholly devoted to letters written by Santa Cruz during war of independence and its immediate aftermath but prior to his first presidency of Bolivia. Some published in other compilations, but also much new material, particularly from the Santa Cruz Family Archive. Valuable for history of both Peru and Bolivia; unfortunately has only name index, not even full list of contents.

2884 Scovozza, Antonio. Bolivar e la rivoluzione panamericana. Bari, Italy: Dedalo Libri, 1978. 284 p.; bibl.

El libro se presenta dividido en dos partes: en la primera analiza la epopeya bolivariana y en la segunda presenta una selección de los escritos más importantes de Bolívar. La síntesis de la actuación de Bolivar, si bien no aporta originalidad al tema se basa en la extensa bibliografía existente. [M. Carmagnani]

Slëzkin, L.Yu. The Congress of Aix-la-Chapelle and the pacification of Spain's colonies in America: the position of tsarist Russia. See item **1914**.

2885 Sucre, Antonio José de. Archivo de Sucre. t. 4, 1823–1824. Caracas: Fundación Vicente Lecuna, 1976. 615 p.

Continuation of *HLAS 40:3333.*

2886 Townsend Ezcurra, Andrés. Las ideas de Bolívar en la integración de los pueblos latinoamericanos. Lima: Comisión Nacional del Sesquicentenario de la Independencia del Perú, 1975. 120 p.; bibl.

Title should be "*sobre* la integración;" yet a concise and coherent, if unoriginal, exposition.

2887 *Universidad.* Universidad Nacional del Litoral. No. 90, mayo/agosto 1978– . Santa Fe, Argentina.

Special issue devoted to the bicentennial of San Martín's birth consisting of many articles of merit. However, only those by Roverano and Livi contribute any new data. Both deal with San Martín's relations with the Argentine interior provinces (especially Santa Fe) during the preparation and execution of his Peruvian campaign:

Andrés A. Roverano "San Martín y Estanislao López" p. 23–92; bibl.; documentary appendix

José Rafael López Rosas "San Martín y Sus Ideas Políticas" p. 93–143

Victorio M. Bonamín "La Religiosidad de San Martín" p. 145–191

Federico Guillermo Cevera "Las Enfermedades en la Trayectoria del Libertador San Martín" p. 193–220; bibl.

Hebe Livi "San Martín: Misión Gutiérrez de la Fuente" p. 221–266; bibl.; documentary appendix

Julio A. Caminos "Notas sobre el General Don José de San Martín" p. 267–276

Francisco Cignoli "San Martín en Lima: Proclamación y Jura de la Independencia Peruana: Crónicas y Testimonios Directos" p. 277–291; bibl.

Estela Mónica Cirulli de César "Acerca de la Concreción y Desarrollo del Plan Sanmartiniano en el Perú" p. 293–313; bibl.

Juan María Rafael Funes "San Martín y la Estrategia de la Aproximación Indirecta" p. 315–347.

GRAN COLOMBIA

2888 Castellanos, Rafael Ramón. Pedro Gual: ideólogo de la libertad (VANH/B, 60:240, oct./dic. 1977, p. 707–738)

With slightly different title, this is the same as *HLAS 40:3340.*

2889 Cherpak, Evelyn. The participation of women in the independence movement in Gran Colombia: 1780–1830 (*in* Latin American women: historical perspectives [see item **1791**] p. 219–234)

Useful if unremarkable overview based (not always critically) on wide range of sources.

2890 Congreso Grancolombiano de Historia, *2nd, Ocaña, Colombia, 1978.* Sesquicentenario de la Convención de Ocaña: 1828. Publicación dirigida por José M. de Mier. Bogotá: Academia Colombiana de Historia, 1978. 419 p.; facsims.; plates (Biblioteca de Historia Nacional; 138)

Collected papers presented at session honoring Great Convention that failed to preserve Great Colombia. Many quite marginal; will be most useful for amount of information provided on men who were delegates to Convención de Ocaña.

2891 Cubitt, David J. La anexión de la provincia de Guayaquil, 1822: estudio del estilo político bolivariano (PAIGH/R, 86, julio/dic. 1978, p. 193–219)

Reconstructs final steps leading to incorporation of Guayaquil into Colombia, revising previous accounts on some details and emphasizing both Bolívar's political astuteness and San Martín's passivity.

2892 García Chuecos, Héctor. Pedro León Torres. Caracas: Archivo General de la Nación, 1977. 130 p.; bibl.; 1 leaf of plates: port. (Biblioteca venezolana de historia; 24)

Military biography of Venezuelan officer promoted to general on battlefield of Bomboná (1821), where he had been mortally wounded. In traditional vein but well researched.

2893 Guerra, José Joaquín. La Convención de Ocaña. Nota preliminar e índice por Luis C. Adames Santos. Cali, Colombia: Banco Popular, 1978. 2 v. (530 p.); indexes (Biblioteca Banco Popular; 101/102)

Reissue of solid and useful piece of traditional historiography, on 1828 constituent convention whose failure led to formal establishment of Bolívar's last dictatorship.

2894 Indice de la Sección Venezolana del Archivo de la Gran Colombia (FJB/BH, 43, enero 1977, p. 102–156)

Concluding installment of important reference aid which has been appearing intermittently in the *Boletín Histórico* of the Fundación John Boulton. Of value whether one proposes to use original documents in Colombia's Archivo Histórico Nacional or microfilm copies at Fundación John Boulton in Caracas; and for much more than studying Venezuela *in* Gran Colombia, as selection criteria are generous.

2895 Lecompte Luna, Alvaro. Castillo y Rada: el grancolombiano. Prólogo de Lucio Pabón Núñez. Bogotá: Instituto Caro y Cuervo, 1977. 170 p.; bibl.; facsim.; plates (Serie La granada entreabierta; 19)

Attractively produced, somewhat anecdotal amateur biography of man who was significant figure in all phases of revolution, best known as Finance Minister of Gran Colombia and collaborator in Bolívar's last dictatorship. Although Castillo y Rada deserves better than this work, it is annotated here because there is so little on him.

2896 **Lozano Cleves, Alberto.** Campaña de 1819. Bogotá: Editorial Kelly [and] Academia Colombiana de Historia, 1977. 90 p.; maps; plates (Bolsilibros; 29)

With abundant *gráficos* of battles and campaigns, provides clear and rapid overview of decisive Boyacá campaign. Naturally, some points of interpretation will be disputed by rival bands of exegetes.

2897 **Martínez Zulaica, Antonio.** Cólicos republicanos; patobiografía del General Santander. Tunja: Universidad Pedadógica y Tecnológica de Colombia, Secretaría de Investigaciones y Extensión Universitaria, 1978. 241 p.; bibl. (Ediciones La Rana y el águila)

Better book than title may suggest. A medicopsychological analysis is the primary thread running through this anecdotal and somewhat discursive study of Santander, but it offers a good bit more and is in fact more useful than most existing Santander biographies.

2898 **Miró, Rodrigo.** El Istmo de Panamá y la empresa libertadora de Bolívar (LNB/L, 268, junio 1978, p. 1–18)

Broader than title suggests: a good synthesis of Panama in the strategy of Bolívar and subsequent history of Gran Colombia.

2899 **Moreno de Angel, Pilar.** José María Córdova. Bogotá: Editorial Kelly, 1977. 669 p.; bibl.; plates (Academia Colombiana de Historia. Biblioteca de Historia Nacional; 137)

Massive study that rests on impressive amount of research, including use of European as well as Colombian repositories and Córdova's correspondence previously edited by author (see *HLAS 40:3227*). In style it is a somewhat conventional biography, sympathetic toward its subject. Its greatest strength lies not in coverage of Córdova as foremost *granadino* military hero of independence, but in treatment of his post-Ayacucho career (to his death fighting Bolívar's dictatorship), which occupies half the volume.

2900 **Ocampo López, Javier.** La independencia de los Estados Unidos de América y su proyección en Hispanoamérica: el modelo norteamericano y su repercusión en la independencia de Colombia; un estudio a través de la folletería de la independencia de Colombia. Caracas: Instituto Panamericano de Geografía e Historia, Comisión de Historia, Comité Orígenes de la Emancipación, 1979. 162 p.; appendixes (Publicaciones; 22)

This work, adequately described by title, is a further elaboration of same scholar's earlier study (see *HLAS 40:3364*). It is followed by two appendices: Miguel de Pombo's essay on the US Constitution, published in Bogotá in 1811, which though little known today is one of the key documents for studying the impact of US independence in Latin America; and David Bushnell's "El 'Modelo' Angloamericano en la Prensa de la Emancipación: una Aproximación Cuantitativa de su Impacto."

2901 **Vargas Tejada, Luis.** Recuerdo histórico. Bogotá: Academia Colombiana de Historia, 1978. 171 p.; plate (Bolsilibros; 34)

Transcription of 1894 Bogotá ed. of important source on conflict between followers of Santander and Bolívar, by one of latter's would-be assassins.

VENEZUELA

Arcila Farías, Eduardo. Historia de un monopolio: el estanco del tabaco en Venezuela, 1779–1833. See item **2629**.

Beaujon, Oscar. Las primicias de Coro. See item **2724**.

2902 **Bencomo Barrios, Héctor.** El ilustre prócer de la independencia: Coronel Luis María Rivas Dávila (VANH/B, 62:247, julio/sept. 1979, p. 641–652)

Brief but documented tribute to a secondary patriot hero from Mérida, who died in the collapse of the Second Republic.

2903 **Cuando los militares votaban:** 1819 (FJB/BH, 46, enero 1978, p. 106–159)

Brief note by Manuel Pérez Vila introduces *actas* of voting for Deputies to Congress of Angostura in Cumanacoa and of *escrutinio* for entire Province of Cumaná. Though suffrage was broader than usual, procedures illustrated by these documents are fairly representative of those used at other times and places in early post-independence Spanish America.

2904 Estudios y discursos sobre el general Carlos Soublette. Caracas: Academia Nacional de la Historia, 1977. 240 p.; bibl.; port (Fuentes para la historia republicana de Venezuela. Biblioteca de la Academia Nacional de la Historia; nueva serie; 22)

Good collection of previously published materials—by both 19th century and more recent authors—concerning *mantuano* staff officer who became Secretary of War in Gran Colombia and later President of Venezuela, as Páez ally, during Conservative Oligarchy.

2905 Fernández Avelló, Manuel. Bobes: mariscal asturiano para la historia. Oviedo: Asturex, 1974. 129 p.; ill.

Deluxe Spanish tribute to scourge of Venezuelan patriots, José Tomás Boves. Rather thin treatment except of his Spanish origins, but useful also for illustrations and for references to literature on Boves.

2906 Instrucción para la Dirección, Buen Orden, Régimen y Gobierno de los Jueces y Pueblos del Distrito de estas Provincias (VANH/B, 61:242, abril/junio 1978, p. 391–409)

Rules laid down in 1817 by Captain General Juan Bautista Pardo for regularization of civil and judicial administration in royalist areas.

2907 Izard, Miguel. El miedo a la Revolución: la lucha por la libertad en Venezuela, 1777–1830. Prólogo de Sergio Bagú. Madrid: Editorial Tecnos, 1979. 205 p.; bibl.; maps; tables (Serie de historia)

Though creation of Captaincy-General is given as starting date, this study focuses mainly on Venezuela from outbreak of independence struggle to dissolution of Gran Colombia. It is easily the best general account of that period, giving special attention to evolution of economic and social structures. Title is indicative of central theme that *mantuano* dominant class was guided at every turn by its desire to prevent real revolution. Interpretative yet highly factual, with much of the detail crammed into textual footnotes.

2908 Juicios sobre la personalidad del General José Antonio Páez. Caracas: Academia Nacional de la Historia, 1974. 384 p.; bibl.; ill. (Fuentes para la historia republicana de Venezuela. Biblioteca de la Academia Nacional de la Historia; nueva serie, 17)

Anthology of mostly brief, mostly favorable, and mostly Venezuelan views of Páez, both as fighter for independence and as later ruler of Venezuela. Good historiographical reference material.

2909 Lucena Salmoral, Manuel. El "donativo patriótico" hecho por Venezuela a España para ayudar a sufragar los gastos de la guerra de independencia peninsular (VANH/B, 61:241, enero/marzo 1978, p. 109–127, tables)

Careful examination of intriguing and neglected topic: Venezuela's contributions in specie and in kind to beleaguered Spain. They were intended at least in part to elicit commercial concessions. Inadequacy of Spain's appreciation, it is suggested, helped trigger the revolt of 1810.

2910 Maracaibo y la independencia de Venezuela, 1810–1812: documentos. Transcritos y prologados por Agustín Millares Carlo. Caracas: Archivo General de la Nación, 1977. 193 p.; bibl.; index (Biblioteca venezolana de historia; 23)

With very helpful prologue by Millares Carlo, presents documentation from both Venezuelan and Spanish archives on activities of revolutionary sympathizers in royalist-controlled Maracaibo, 1810–12.

2911 Morales Padrón, Francisco. Francisco Tomás Morales, último Capitán General de Venezuela (EEHA/AEA, 33, 1976, p. 641–712, appendix)

Without trying to decide whether Morales was really "worse than Boves," as patriots charged, author gives a good account of Canarian-born soldier of relatively humble origin who fought effectively for Spain throughout independence period. Documentary appendix.

2912 Perazzo, Nicolás. Crónica de San Felipe: cuando la ciudad perteneció a Carabobo (FJB/BH, 44, mayo 1977, p. 203–221, bibl.)

Some interesting social and political local history, mainly of Gran Colombian period. Appears mostly based on archival sources.

2913 Pérez Vila, Manuel. La accidentada misión diplomática de Juan Vicente Bolívar Palacios (FJB/BH, 47, mayo 1978, p. 267–282, facsim.)

Good review of mission to US by Simón's brother, for initial Caracas junta; on it he also dealt with Spanish minister. Introduces three pertinent items from Spanish diplomatic correspondence.

Rodríguez, Simón. Obras completas. See item **2655**.

2914 Romero, Mario Germán. Un documento interesante sobre la independencia de la ciudad de Barcelona (VANH/B, 62:247, julio/sept. 1979, p. 607–619, facsim.)

Brief introduction precedes some anonymous royalist listing of "traitors" and narration of events. Original document is in Instituto Caro y Cuervo, Bogotá.

2915 Tres testigos europeos de la Primera República, 1808–1814: apéndice documental de la prensa contemporánea. Edición e introducción de Ramón Escovar Salcedo. Caracas: Presidencia de la República, 1974. 245 p.; 9 leaves of plates: ill. (Colección viajeros y legionarios; 1)

Three important sources on revolution in Venezuela: Robert Semple's "Sketch of the Present State of Caracas;" Luis Delpech's "Relación Sucinta de los Ultimos Acontecimientos de Caracas;" and H. Proudenx's "Memoir pour Servir à l'Histoire de la Révolution de la Capitainerie Générale de Caracas." The sources are translated into Spanish and include a selection of Venezuelan press articles and broadsides of the same period, which cover the Second as well as the First Republic.

NUEVA GRANADA

2916 Archivo Central del Cauca, *Popayán, Colombia.* Catálogo general detallado del Archivo General del Cauca formado por José María Arboleda Llorente. t. 1 [and] t. 6/7, Archivo Histórico de Popayán: época de la Independencia. Popayán, Colombia: Universidad del Cauca, Instituto de Investigaciones Históricas José María Arboleda, 1944 [i.e. 1969]/1977. 3 v. (355, 350, 360 p.)

The first volume (t. 1) of this important tool was published in 1969 (despite erroneous imprint date 1944) and was never annotated in *HLAS*. The other two volumes (t. 6 and t. 7) were published in 1977. For more information on this valuable series, see *HLAS 34:2410* and *HLAS 38:3246*.

2917 Arias de Greiff, Jorge. Una Sociedad Democrática en 1816 (ACH/BHA, 65:722, julio/sept. 1978, p. 319–330)

Research note on society formed at Popayán as Patria Boba neared its end, whose members vowed last-ditch resistance to Spanish Reconquest.

2918 Miramón, Alberto. Política secreta de Napoleón en Nueva Granada. Bogotá: Editorial Kelly [and] Academia Colombiana de Historia, 1978. 159 p.; bibl.; facsims.; plates (Bolsilibros; 30)

Treats French and Bonapartist activities that came to nothing and accordingly have not received much attention. Contents somewhat miscellaneous and not all equally pertinent; but based on archival research as well as published sources.

2919 Restrepo, José Félix de. Obras completas. Medellín: Secretaría de Educación y Cultura Departamental, 1978. 449 p. (Pensamiento vivo antioqueño; 1)

Misleadingly titled but nevertheless useful anthology, which contains not just writings of but documents relating to and assorted tributes and anecdotes about *antioqueño* educator, magistrate, and civil patriot José Félix Restrepo (1760–1832).

QUITO

Bromley, Rosemary D.F. Disasters and population change in central highland Ecuador, 1778–1825. See item **2786**.

2920 Correspondencia del Libertador con el general Juan José Flores: 1825–1830. Quito: Banco Central del Ecuador, 1977. 581 p.; facsims; plates (Publicaciones del Archivo Juan José Flores de la Pontificia Universidad Católica del Ecuador)

Important collection of source materials on Ecuador as part of Gran Colombia, with further value for study of Gran Colombia itself. Bolívar's letters contained in it are printed from originals in Archivo Flores even if published before; most of Flores' letters are published for the first time. They are preceded by Jorge Salvador Lara's "La República del Ecuador y el General Juan José Flores," which covers latter's entire career, and also specific introductions to both sets of correspondence. They are followed by notes to specific letters and index of proper names.

Estrada Ycaza, Julio. Regionalismo y migración. See item **2637**.

2921 Loor, Wilfrido. Guayaquil y Manabí en 1820. Guayaquil, Ecuador: Editorial Gregorio Portoviejo, 1976. 162 p.

Collection of short pieces by a leading local historian, mostly concerning Guayaquil revolution of 1820. Miscellaneous but useful, based on wide familiarity with published sources plus original research.

2922 Quito (Dept.), *Ecuador.* Colección de Oficios y Documentos dirigidos por las autoridades del Departamento de Quito al Cabildo de la Ciudad: 1823–1826. Transcripción de Gustavo Chiriboga C. Quito: Imprenta Municipal, 1972. 460 p.; ill.; indexes; plates (Publicaciones del Archivo Municipal de Quito; 35)

Valuable collection of documents from municipal archives, covering wide range of topics of local and national, political-military and socioeconomic interest.

2923 Ramos Pérez, Demetrio. Entre El Plata y Bogotá: cuatro claves de la emancipación ecuatoriana. Madrid: Ediciones Cultura Hispánica del Centro Iberoamericano de Cooperación, 1978. 408 p.; bibl.; 4 leaves of plates: ill.; index.

Disappointing study of movements for independence in and affecting San Francisco de Quito. Reflects biases and inadequacies of quiteño historiography, upon which Ramos Pérez, a Spanish historian, relies excessively. Slights role of Guayaquil and importance of 9 de Octubre. The four keys to which subtitle refers, are Colombian and Peruvian pretensions to Ecuador, Quito's alleged attempts to maintain territorial integrity, and rivalry between Quito and Guayaquil. [M.T. Hamerly]

PERU

2924 Beltrán Gallardo, Ezequiel. Las guerrillas de Yuayos en la emancipación del Perú, 1820–1824. Lima: Editores Técnicos Asociados, 1977. 168 p.; facsims.; fold. maps; tables.

Another account of resistance activities (including material contributions to patriot cause) of a specific highland region. Crammed with facts from original archival research.

2925 *Colección Documental de la Independencia del Perú.* Comisión Nacional del Sesquicentenario de la Independencia. Tomo 1 [through] tomo 27, 1971– . Lima.

Several additional installments have been published in this collection of 27 tomos (each tomo generally consisting of several volumes). Of those listed here, one should note: t. 11, v. 1, which contains the correspondence of Peruvian agents in other American republics, especially Chile; and t. 12, which consists of San Martín's correspondence, from Peru, to the Chilean government (1820–22) now in Chilean diplomatic archives (for previously published tomos and volumes, see *HLAS 38:3529*). The recent additions are: t. 1, *Los ideólogos* (consisting of v. 1, *Juan Pablo Viscardo y Guzmán*, and v. 10, *José Faustino Sánchez* Carrión); t. 2, *La rebelión de Tupac Amaru* (consisting of vols. 3/4 of the same title); t. 5, *La acción patriótica del pueblo en la emancipación* (consisting of vols. 5/6, *Guerrillas y montoneras*); t. 11, *Misiones peruanas; 1820–1826* (consisting of v. 1, *Las primeras misiones diplomáticas en América*); t. 12, *Misiones y documentación de cancillerías extranjeras*; and t. 13, *Obra gubernativa y epistolario de San Martín* (consisting of v. 2 of the same title).

2926 Cook, Noble David. Education and the leaders of Peruvian independence (*in* Historia, problema y promesa. Edición a cargo de Francisco Miró Quesada C.; Frank Pease G.Y.; y David Sobrevilla A. Lima: Pontificia Universidad Católica del Perú, Fondo Editorial, 1978, v. 1, p. 62–88, bibl.)

Of approximately 200 Peruvians, discusses relative numbers educated in different kinds of institutions who supported or opposed independence. Suggestions as to political influence of education are quite plausible even though mostly based on correlation rather than hard proof.

2927 Fisher, John. Royalism, regionalism, and rebellion in colonial Peru, 1808–1815 (HAHR, 59:2, May 1979, p. 232–257)

Excellent article that stresses both seriousness of revolutionary activities in Peruvian interior and role of regional and racial divisions within the colony in frustrating early moves toward independence.

2928 **Hamnett, Brian R.** Revolución y contrarrevolución en México y el Perú: liberalismo, realeza y separatismo, 1800–1824. México: Fondo de Cultura Económica, 1978. 454 p.; bibl. (Sección de obras de historia)

An important study that combines some redundancy of archival data with often suggestive interpretation to throw new light on the structure of forces and their internal divisions on royalist side. Emphasizes legacy of unresolved issues and tensions from revolutionary to early national periods.

Rosas Cuadros, Emilio Eduvino. La Provincia de Chancay en la colonia y emancipación, Chancay-Huaral. See item **2716**.

2929 **Salas Olivarri, Elsa.** Periódicos de la preemancipación, 1795–1819 (PEBN/B, 69/72, 1974, p. 5–25, bibl.)

Annotated listing of earliest Peruvian periodicals, with summary index of titles and of names of editors, printers, etc.

2930 **Simposium Nacional de Historia de la Independencia,** *1st, Ayacucho, Perú, 1974.* I [Primer] Simposium Nacional de Historia de la Independencia: 25–30 noviembre 1974. Ayacucho, Perú: Universidad Nacional de San Cristóbal de Huamanga, Departamento de Ciencias Histórico-Sociales, 1975. 162 p.; bibl.; tables.

Mimeographed work of presumably limited circulation, which is too bad as it contains some very good material (along with some that is marginal). Interdisciplinary group of collaborators includes Pablo Macera, Virgilio Roel, Luis Millones, other well known scholars. Both interpretative pieces and detailed research notes; on background, development, and consequences of independence. On the whole, a certain emphasis on socioeconomic aspects.

2931 *El Sol de Cuzco:* 1825–1826. Caracas: Comisión Nacional del Sesquicentenario de las Batallas de Junín y Ayacucho y de la Convocatoria del Congreso Anfictiónico de Panamá, 1974. 2 v. (245, 230 p.); facsims.

Facsimile reprint edition of newspaper founded after Cuzco came under patriot control. Includes all issues printed 1825–26, interspersed with *impresos varios,* consisting of broadsides and pamphlets published in Cuzco during the same period.

ALTO PERU

2932 **Condarco Morales, Ramiro.** Orígenes de la Nación Boliviana: interpretación histórico sociológica de la Fundación de la República. La Paz: Instituto Boliviana de Cultura, 1977. 171 p.; bibl.

Succinct exposition of inevitability of process whereby colonial Charcas became an independent nation.

Costa de la Torre, Arturo. Bibliografía de la Revolución del 16 de Julio de 1809: año del protomártir Pedro Domingo Murillo. See item **3147**.

2933 **———.** Estirpe y genealogía del protomártir Pedro Domingo Murillo. La Paz: Editorial Casa Municipal de la Cultura Franz Tamayo, 1977. 552 p.; bibl.; plate (Biblioteca paceña. Nueva serie)

Combination of documentary collection, anthology, and study by author himself, with primary emphasis on personal background and family (including descendants) of hero of La Paz 1809 revolution. Confusingly organized but does make some contribution.

2934 **———.** Mujeres en la independencia. La Paz: Ultima Hora, 1977. 326 p.; bibl. (Biblioteca popular boliviana. Colección Historia)

Properly called "notes" by author, a volume with much miscellaneous information on independence heroines, including bibliographical/historiographical data.

2935 **Gantier, Joaquín.** Historia del gran republicano Jayme de Zudáñez y de la emancipación americana. Cochabamba, Bolivia: Editorial Canelas, 1971. 297 p.; bibl.; plates.

Traditional but documented biography of a leading figure in Chuquisaca's May 1809 revolt who was later active in Chile, Argentina, and Uruguay (where he died in 1832).

Klein, Herbert S. The impact of the crisis in nineteenth-century mining on regional economies: the example of the Bolivian Yungas, 1786–1838. See item **2643**.

2936 **Ovando Sanz, Jorge Alejandro.** La invasión brasileña a Bolivia en 1825: una de las causas del Congreso de Panamá. La Paz: Ediciones Isla, 1977. 182 p.; bibl.

Looks at abortive annexation of Bolivian province of Chiquitos to Brazil, and includes numerous documents but without examining all pertinent secondary sources. Somewhat more serious than the highly exaggerated subtitle would suggest.

2937 Saavedra, Bautista. La aurora de la independencia hispanoamericana. La Paz: Fundación Manuel Vicente Ballivián, 1977. 154 p.; plate.

Excellent prologue by Alberto Crespo Rodas on "Bautista Saavedra y la Historia" introduces previously unpublished writings by Bolivian intellectual and president (1920–25) on his understanding of history and on the La Paz revolution of 1809.

2938 Valencia Vega, Alipio. Ildefonso de las Muñecas: el sacerdote que hizo culto de la libertad en la republiqueta de Larecaja. La Paz: Librería Editorial Juventud, 1978. 93 p. (Colección Tradición, historia)

Popular biography of patriot priest who took part in 1814 Cuzco uprising and subsequent guerrilla resistance in Alto Peru.

———. Manuel Victorio García Lanza: el guerrillero devorado por la propia revolución. See item **3183**.

2939 Villarroel Triveño, Augusto. La fundación de Bolivia: documentos para su historia. Cochabamba, Bolivia: Centro de Investigaciones Históricas de la Normal Superior Integrada Católica, 1975. 224 p.; bibl.; facsims.

Contains correspondence and other documents on conclusion of military struggle and convocation and proceedings of 1825 assembly that created an independent Bolivia (e.g. minutes of the assembly's sessions). Compiler's preliminary discussion is not especially noteworthy; but the documentary collection is good.

CHILE

Atenea. No. 437, 1978– . See item **3192**.

2940 Cubitt, David J. The manning of the Chilean Navy in the War of Independence: 1818–1823 (Mariner's Mirror [Society for Nautical Research, Greenwich, London] 63:2, May 1977, p. 115–127, bibl.)

Original and quite fascinating piece of social military history. Looks at numbers, national origin (predominantly Chilean), and varieties of recruitment of common seamen.

2941 Rector, John. Transformaciones comerciales producidas por la independencia de Chile: el mercader y su casa comercial (SCHG/R, 144, 1976, p. 62–80)

Brief but good case study of commercial operations, during independence and early post-independence periods, of firm founded in late colonial period by Spanish merchant.

2942 *Revista Chilena de Historia y Geografía.* Sociedad Chilena de Historia y Geografía. No. 146, 1978– . Santiago.

Issue devoted to the bicentennial of Bernardo O'Higgins consists mostly of articles on that central theme. The majority are personal and anecdotal in emphasis, including the Matte Varas piece which deals with O'Higgins' Peruvian haciendas during his exile. Other articles examine aspects of his political and military career. The longest contribution, by Donoso Vergara, is loosely organized but incorporates (among other things) some original research on family and associations. There is no one article of exceptional merit but the volume as a whole is competent and useful. Consists of the following:

Guillermo Donoso Vergara "Los Avatares de O'Higgins junto al Maule" p. 5–71

Julio Heise González "O'Higgins y la Organización de la República" p. 72–93 (including "Anexo Documental")

Julio Jiménez Berguecio "Don Bernardo O'Higgins: Primer Gobernante Americano en Relaciones con la Santa Sede" p. 93–116

José J. Matte Varas "Montalván y Cuiba" p. 117–130, ill.; map

Manuel Reyno Gutiérrez "Primeras Campañas del General O'Higgins" p. 131–149

Rafael González Novoa "Cronología de la Vida del General Bernardo O'Higgins" p. 151–171

Fernando Campos Harriet "O'Higgins y Concepción" p. 173–180

Sergio Flores Farías and Juan Saavedra Avila "El Valparaíso de O'Higgins en la Observación de los Viajeros, 1817–1825" p. 181–211; bibl.

L. Omar Retamal Parra "La Casa de O'Higgins en Talca" p. 227–237; bibl.

Manuel Escala Escobar "La Policía durante el Gobierno de O'Higgins" p. 251–267

Guillermo Krumm Saavedra "Actuaciones de Don Bernardo O'Higgins en la Isla de la Laja" p. 269–279, bibl.

Reyno Gutiérrez, Manuel. La Patria Vieja no se perdió en Rancagua. See item **3258**.

Stegmaier Rodríguez, Juan L. Lord Tomás Alejandro Cochrane. See item **3268**.

2943 **Vázquez de Acuña, Isidoro.** El General Quintanilla y su gobierno en Chiloé: 1817–1826 (ACH/B, 41:88, 1974, p. 287–310)

With brief but good introduction by Isidoro Vázquez de Acuña, presents previously inedited memorial by last-ditch royalist defender of Chiloé.

2944 **Véliz, Claudio.** The Irisarri loan (CEDLA/B, 23, dic. 1977, p. 3–20)

Solidly researched article on "unwanted and unnecessary loan" raised in 1822 in London by Antonio José Irisarri for Chilean government of O'Higgins, covering both details of negotiations and adverse political and economic repercussions. Excellent case study in international finance of independence period.

2945 **Walker Trujillo, Osvaldo.** La Orden de San Agustín y la independencia de Chile (SCHG/R, 146, 1978, p. 281–303)

Patriotic-pietistic review of Augustinians' participation in independence movement. Well documented, gives at least some data on great number of friars.

RIO DE LA PLATA

2946 **Acevedo, Edberto O.** Notas sobre organización jurídica y sociedad en Mendoza hacia 1820 (Revista de Historia del Derecho [Buenos Aires] 2, 1974 [i.e. 1975] p. 9–37)

Tidbits mainly from provincial archives, on crime, punishment, and establishment of a higher court.

Anna, Timothy E. The Buenos Aires expedition and Spain's secret plan to conquer Portugal, 1814–1820. See item **1894**.

Boletín. Provincia de Santa Fe. Año 6, No. 6, 1974– . See item **3306**.

2947 **Brown, Jonathan C.** A socioeconomic history of Argentina, 1776–1860. New York: Cambridge University Press, 1979. 302 p.; bibl.; ill.; index (Cambridge Latin American studies; 35)

This history is socioeconomic but not "of Argentina;" it really is a history of productive and trade relationships centered on Buenos Aires, with only cursory glance at the interior. Breezily written, includes much good information. Brown points out many positive aspects of export-led growth, while repeatedly claiming to refute "dependency theory," loosely defined.

Castedo Franco, Eliana. El proceso social de la revolución del 14 de mayo de 1811: un estudio socio-histórico. See item **3451**.

2948 **Cornejo, Atilio.** Semblanza del guerrero de la independencia Coronel Mayor Don Juan José Fernández Campero, Marqués del Valle de Tojo (ANH/IE, 23, julio/dic. 1977, p. 99–130)

Though his properties extended into present-day Bolivia, Fernández Campero was Argentina's one creole marquis and for that reason, if no other, a significant figure. Cornejo admits his early wavering, but insists he ultimately became a true patriot.

2949 **Demicheli, Alberto.** Artigas, el fundador: su proyección histórica. Buenos Aires: Ediciones Depalma, 1978. 280 p.; facsims.

This winning entry in an OAS prize contest on Artigas is not strictly biography. Rather, it treats Artigas as exponent of democratic, republican, federalist principles in Platine area and follows these to ultimate vindication of Artigas in Argentine constitutional organization. Mainly political; does not feature Artigas the agrarian reformer.

2950 **Documentos** sobre el General Güemes (Revista del Archivo General de la Nación [Buenos Aires] 4, 1974, p. 51–278)

Continuation of *HLAS 38:3291*.

2951 **Durnhofer, Eduardo.** Mayo y el antecedente norteamericano. Buenos Aires: Instituto Bonaerense de Numismática y Antigüedades, 1976. 89 p.; bibl.; facsims.

In homage to both US Bicentennial and the "liberalism" of Mariano Moreno, reproduces and comments on his somewhat modified Spanish version of the US Constitution, billing it as "El Primer Proyecto Constitucional Argentino."

2952 **Gárate Córdoba, José María.** Las raíces del alma militar de San Martín y el Cuerpo de Granaderos a Caballo: pts. 1/2 (SHM/RHM, 23:46, 1979, p. 7–46; 23:47, 1979, p. 41–94, bibl., facsims., plates, tables)

Good article on San Martín's intellectual formation, emphasizing moral precepts in military indoctrination and in books to which he was exposed, rather than technical aspects. Also provides information on Spanish antecedents of mounted grenadiers corps that San Martín organized on his return to Argentina.

2953 **Heredia, Edmundo A.** España y la independencia del Río de la Plata: capítulos de su historia. Córdoba, Argentina: 1977. 120 p.; bibl. (Junta Provincial de Historia de Córdoba; 2)

Group of well-researched, short, monographic chapters, all dealing with Spanish military and political responses to Spanish American independence movement and Platine counter-responses. Complements same author's previous work, especially *HLAS 38:2360*.

2954 **Lastarria, Miguel.** Portugueses y brasileños hacia el Río de la Plata: un informe geopolítico, 1816. Introducción de Aníbal Abadie-Aicardi and Oscar Abadie-Aicardi. Recife, Brazil: Pool Editorial, 1977. 216 p.

Another creole loyalist memorial, by one Miguel Lastarria, analyzing problems of patriot insurgency and Portuguese designs and recommending measures to deal with them. Includes appendix of documents compiled by Lastarria himself.

2955 **Livermore, H.V.** Captain Gillespie and the 58 Anglophiles of Buenos Aires in 1806 (HAHR, 60:1, Feb. 1980, p. 69–78)

Identifies, tentatively, just one of *porteños* who supposedly pledged voluntary allegiance to British Crown.

2956 **Lobos, Héctor Ramón.** La frontera norte de Córdoba, 1810–1820 (ANH/IE, 21, julio/dic. 1976, p. 367–412)

Detailed examination of military defense of Córdoba province against hostile Indians, with much information on status, organization, and functioning of local militia.

2957 **Peña, Roberto I.** Los jueces pedáneos en la provincia de Córdoba: 1810–1856, algunos aspectos de sus atribuciones (Revista de Historia del Derecho [Buenos Aires] 2, 1974 [i.e. 1975] p. 121–148)

Mainly concerns just second decade of 19th century, but title otherwise is correct. From provincial archives, a miscellany of information on functioning of rural justice in Córdoba.

2958 **Pérez Amuchástegui, A.J.** San Martín y el Alto Perú: 1814. San Miguel de Tucumán, Argentina: Fundación Banco Comercial del Norte, 1976. 414 p.; map; plates (Ediciones; 5)

This study of San Martín as commander of Argentina's northern front prior to his transfer to Mendoza and organization of expedition to Chile was author's doctoral thesis and apparently not revised for publication. Nevertheless, it is still worth having, particularly for discussion of numerous doubtful points, including genesis of plan to free Peru via Chile. Pérez Amuchástegui is systematic as usual in analysis even though his format is somewhat unconventional.

2959 **Piccinali, Héctor Juan.** Vida de San Martín en España. Buenos Aires: Ediciones Argentinas, 1977. 133 p.; bibl.; facsims.; ill.

Detailed survey of San Martín's military education and career in Spain until his departure in 1811. Well-researched though without source references; contains good selection of maps and tables in "Anexos."

2960 **Ramos, R. Antonio** and **Teresita Tessari de Bellasai.** El dictador José Gaspar Rodríguez de Francia y la ciudad de Concepción (APH/H, 25, 1978, p. 25–43)

This substantial article is both a contribution to Paraguayan local and regional history and a description of Francia's militarization of the vital northern frontier, 1814–40. Well-documented, this work credits Francia with checking the advance of Brazil southwards from the Mato Grosso. [J.H. Williams]

2961 **Segreti, Carlos S.A.** La aurora de la independencia: 1810–1815. t. 2. Buenos

Aires: Ediciones La Bastilla, 1976. 237 p.; bibl.; table (Memorial de la patria)

Readable and nonpolemical summary of period following May Revolution, to 1815. Deals mainly with rest of viceroyalty, not Buenos Aires; mainly political, but with quick review of socioeconomic and cultural highlights.

2962 Serrano, Mario Arturo. Cómo fue la revolución de los orilleros porteños. Buenos Aires: Editorial Plus Ultra, 1972. 304 p.; bibl.; ill.

Examination of a topic always mentioned in passing, seldom studied in its own right: the April 1811 "popular" uprising against the *morenistas,* here approvingly compared with 17 October 1945. Polemical but documented. Provides more information on background to events than on events themselves, but still worth noting.

2963 Shtrakhov, Aleksei Ivanovich. Voina za nezavisimost Argentini. Moscow: Izdatelstvo "Nauka," 1976. 425 p.; bibl.

Copious footnotes and a 38-p. bibliography attest to the breadth of research of this fact-crammed but somewhat conventional survey.

2964 Tanzi, Héctor José. El clero patriota y la Revolución de Mayo (IGFO/RI, 37:147/148, enero/junio 1977, p. 141–158)

Analyzes sermons of Argentine patriot priests to show that they expounded an ideology basically derived from Hispanic antecedents (same as that of revolutionists throughout Spanish America). A rather good summary of theses of author's *El poder político y la independencia argentina* (see *HLAS 40:2378*).

2965 Tonda, Américo A. Juan Bernardo Alzugaray y la revolución (ANH/IE, 23, julio/dic. 1977, p. 341–363)

Research note on vicissitudes of Creole priest whose promising career was ruined by suspicions of disloyalty to patriot cause.

URUGUAY

2966 *Archivo Artigas.* Comisión Nacional Archivo Artigas. t. 11, 1974 [through] t. 14, 1976– . Montevideo.

Contains documents of 1813–14, edited with the highest technical standards and grouped according to the titles of the four volumes listed below (for previous volumes in this series, see *HLAS 36:2803*). Tomos 11, 13 and 14 contain prefaces or "Advertencias" by Juan E. Pivel Devoto, all of which provide good introductions to the topics covered. The "Advertencia" in t. 11 also surveys both contemporary sources and later treatment of 1813 events in Platine historiography. The tomos are: t. 11, *Definición soberana del Pueblo Oriental. Proyección del artiguismo en el Litoral, 1813;* t. 12, *La Provincia Oriental en 1813. El gobierno económico;* t. 13, *Segundo sitio de Montevideo. Embargos dispuestos por el Gobierno de Montevideo, el de la Provincia Oriental y por el General José Rondeau sobre los bienes de los emigrados de ambos campos;* and t. 14, *La marcha secreta. Segundo sitio y capitulación de Montevideo.*

2967 Artigas, inauguración de su mausoleo y glosario de homenajes. Compilación de Fernando O. Assunção, Wilfredo Pérez. Montevideo: República Oriental del Uruguay, Palacio Legislativo, Biblioteca, 1978. 605 p.: ill.

On occasion of inauguration of Artigas mausoleum, an anthology of tributes past and present. Fine introduction to study of Artigas cult.

2968 Campos Thévenin de Garabelli, Martha. La Revolución Oriental de 1822–1823: su génesis. v. 1/2. Montevideo: Junta Departamental de Montevideo, 1972 [i.e. 1973]/1978. 2 v. (577, 450 p.); bibl. (Biblioteca Jose Artigas)

Lavishly documented (1424 footnotes), detailed, and wide-ranging study of movement that was unsuccessful forerunner of definitive 1825 rebellion against Brazilian rule. Examines political antecedents, state of economy, socioeconomic alignments, growth of nationalism, relationships with Argentine provinces. Impressive original contribution.

2969 Comisión Nacional de Homenaje del Sesquicentenario de los Hechos Históricos de 1825. El Ejército Oriental de 1825: apéndice documental. Montevideo: Comisión Nacional de Homenaje del Sesquicentenario de los Hechos Históricos de 1825, 1977. 5 vols. (Various pagings)

Each volume contains military rosters, detailing participants in Uruguayan uprising of 1825.

Demicheli, Alberto. Artigas, el fundador: su proyección histórica. See item **2949**.

2970 Roca, C. Alberto. La frustrada erección de una Real Audiencia en Montevideo, 1810–1814 (Revista de Historia del Derecho [Buenos Aires] 4, 1976, p. 209–230)

Carefully documented examination of one facet of political and bureaucratic activity in loyalist Montevideo: abortive move to reestablish there the Audiencia expelled from Buenos Aires.

19th and 20th Centuries Colombia, Venezuela and Ecuador

WINTHROP R. WRIGHT, *Associate Professor of History, University of Maryland, College Park*

DESPITE PETROLEUM REVENUES and urgent requests from the Academia Nacional de la Historia to place more emphasis upon contemporary history (1830–present), Venezuela has not produced an impressive array of new studies. With the exception of Marc Dufumier's article on the crisis of agriculture (item **3017**) and a study of racial attitudes and immigration laws during the 20th century (item **3046**) most of the Venezuelan works deal with well worn political themes. Two factors explain this unhappy situation. First, few young historians have been trained in modern methodology. Colonial and independence themes still attract the interest of the most competent historians. Furthermore, most writers remain reluctant to investigate modern topics because of the relative inaccessibility of archival material. Second, Venezuela has no major publishing houses. With the exception of government and university presses, most publishers do not show any judgement in selecting authors. With any luck, the hiring of Hugh Thomas to write the Carlos Andrés Pérez story and a quasi-official history of Acción Democrática years may alter this trend. But even this development centers attention on political topics, and excludes economic and social history.

As in the past, Venezuelans excel in the publication of documentary collections. A new series, sponsored by the Congreso de la República (*Boletín del Archivo Histórico*), presents documents from the archives of the National Congress (item **3011**). Unfortunately, the first volume lacks coherent organization. But the effort is well intentioned and should make a significant contribution in the future. Edgard Rodríguez Leal has compiled a useful inventory of documents found in the Archives of France's Ministry of Foreign Affairs for the period between 1832 and 1895 (item **3039**). His annotations will assist any researcher who wishes to study relations between France and Venezuela for those years. A brief collection from the vast archives of Gen. José M. Hernández, edited by José Antonio Armas Chitty, provides information on an important turn-of-the-century politician (item **3006**). Further light is shed on the early 20th-century political scene by the series of documents published in the *Boletín* of the Archivos de Miraflores (item **3012**). In a useful but limited collection of correspondence between leading positivists and Juan Vicente Gómez, Elías A. Pino Iturrieta gives a clear record of the involvement of intellectuals in the Gómez administration (item **3036**). The work comprises yet another part of the series organized by the Castro/Gómez project of the Universidad Central de Venezuela.

Only two monographs have dealt adequately with 19th-century topics. Both treat the mid-century political disturbances that Federico Brito Figueroa interpreted as manifestations of class conflict in his *Tiempo de Ezequiel Zamora* (see *HLAS 38:3373*). Robert Matthews' study of rural violence between 1840 and 1858, offers a well documented but fairly conventional study of the political turmoil on the Venezuela llanos (item **3030**). He sees the participants in the struggle more as competing bandit gangs than as ideologically inspired politicians. In a similar manner, Adolfo Rodríguez R. has made a thorough investigation of Zamora and his time in an effort to refute Brito Figueroa, and he views the Venezuelan leader as a member of the commercial class at the time of his death, rather than one of the masses (item **3040**).

The Gómez era continues to command attention as Venezuelans openly express their love-hate feelings towards their immediate past. The traditional anti-gomecista views appear in several edited memoirs. The accounts of the struggles against Gómez by José Garbi Sánchez (item **3021**), Rafael Arévalo González (item **3004**), and Rafael Vegas (item **3007**), all leave vivid impressions of the jails, years of exile, and oppression that the dictator's foes experienced. These books also offer some interesting descriptions of contemporary Venezuela, especially in the case of Garbi Sánchez's characterization of the llanos of the Venezuelan-Colombian frontier. Like most of the memoirs that have appeared in recent years, these works show the fierce opposition to Gómez, and the dedication of those who tried to overthrow him, but they also make it obvious that the anti-Gómez forces had no specific programs in mind. In other words, they stood united against Gómez, but had not worked out any long-term political or economic solutions to the nation's basic problems. Another colorful memoir appears in José Manuel Sánchez's recollection of his life as a Caracas merchant, in which he offers especially good information about changes that occurred between 1900 and 1936 (item **3042**). Two studies of Rubén González, one written by his son César González (item **3023**) and the other published by the Ministerio de Educación (item **3041**) offer contrasting perspectives of the Gómez years. In an attempt to show Venezuelans that not all of their ancestors were evil, venal, and anti-humanitarians, these two books pay homage to a progressive educator who served as Minister of Education between 1922 and 1929. González authored the Ley Orgánica de Educación of 1924, and refused to work as a servant of Gómez. These books will probably set the tone for future studies of the Gómez period, as Venezuelans will attempt to demonstrate that the era was not a completely sterile one, nor without men and women of strong convictions and character.

The post-Gómez period has received increasing attention from Venezuelan and foreign historians. Harrison Howard and Steven Ellner offer sympathetic accounts of the development of Acción Democrática, and the left in general, between 1936 through the World War II era (items **3018** and **3027**). In a related study, Charles Ameringer describes the clandestine resistance campaign that Leonardo Ruíz Pineda led for Acción Democrática against the dictator Pérez Jiménez between 1949 and 1952 (item **3003**). The publication of a facsimile of Ruíz Pineda's *Venezuela bajo el signo del terror: Libro Negro 1952* (item **3045**), complements the Ameringer article, and offers further testimony to the commitment of Venezuelans to overthrow the Pérez Jiménez regime. In a number of books, Rómulo Betancourt has become the focus of a debate as to whether or not he will emerge as a great leader or as the latest Venezuelan caudillo. Attacked by foes, such as Guillermo Morón (item **3033**) and revered by allies, such as Luis González Herrera and Manuel Caballero (items **3015** and **3024**) the number of books indicates that Rómulo Betancourt will hold the attention of scholars for the next decade.

In contrast to their Venezuelan counterparts, historians of modern Colombia have paid much more attention to economic and social topics. Though too few in number, the quality of most of these economic studies is far above that found in either Venezuela or Ecuador. The most outstanding of these works, Marco Palacios' *Coffee in Colombia 1850–1970* (item **2989**), sets high standards in inter-disciplinary study. Palacios has written an extraordinary account of the impact of coffee upon merchants, landowners, laborers, and politicians, as well as upon banking, politics, the state, and landowning. Palacios offers the most critical and conclusive response to William McGreevey. The appearance of Charles Bergquist's *Coffee and conflict in Colombia: 1886–1910* (item **2974**) also sets a high level for the study of political and economic development in Latin America. He argues quite effectively that the growth and decline of the coffee industry explained in large part the tensions and complexities of the internal splits that occurred during the Regeneration and ultimately led to the War of the Thousand Days. Another study of coffee, Mariano Arango's *Café e industria* (item **2971**) relates the profits from coffee production to the industrial development that took place in western Antioquia. Two other authors also challenge McGreevey's economic interpretations. In his study of mid-19th century capital accumulation, Mario Arango Jaramillo views the 1850s as a period of economic growth rather than decadence (item **2972**). A series of Frank Safford's essays, mostly translations of previously published articles, includes an extended review of McGreevey, whom Safford criticizes for methodological reasons as well as for historical inaccuracies (item **2992**). The rise of capitalism, class development, and syndicalism have received serious consideration by Antonio García, Luis Darío Bernal Pinilla, and Miguel Urrutia (items **2975**, **2980** and **2997**). Like Bergquist and Arango, García writes of the impact of modernization on politics and economic development. Both Bernal Pinilla and Urrutia treat the growth of Colombia's commercial class, as well as the growth of artisan organizations during the 1850s. By using family history, Keith H. Christie shows that the colonization of Caldas, Risaralda, and Quindío led to large profits for Antioqueño merchants (item **2977**). His work clearly challenges Parsons and others who have argued that Antioqueño expansion followed egalitarian patterns. The emphasis on economic history is capped, at least in a symbolic way, by the republication of the writings of Aníbal Galindo, the 19th-century economist, thus making available a source of information long out of print.

Jane Loy has investigated a previously overlooked aspect of Colombia's history, the little known llanos region of the eastern frontier (item **2985**). Though she uses a conventional narrative style, she writes well, and has broken important ground in explaining the isolation of the Colombian/Venezuelan borderlands.

Colombia lacks the wealth of its neighbor Venezuela. For that reason few government subsidized-documentary studies have been published during the past decade. Banks and commercial organizations have taken up some of the slack, such as the beautifully illustrated collection of travel accounts written by Colombians about their own country, published for the Fondo Cultural Cafetero (item **2998**).

The inclusion of Ecuador in this section has posed some short-term problems. To date very little of note has crossed this contributor's desk. This trend will probably change, but as my predecessor has noted for several volumes (see *HLAS 36*, p. 255–256; *HLAS 38*, p. 282; and *HLAS 40*, p. 250–251) the quantity and quality of Ecuadorian publications pale when contrasted to those of other Andean nations.

COLOMBIA

2971 Arango, Mariano. Café e industria, 1850–1930. Bogotá: C. Valencia Editores, 1977. 260 p.; bibl.; indexes.

Study of land use and policy, especially in areas occupied by Antioqueñan colonization. States that eastern *hacendados* were not capitalists. Wealth provided by campesino producers of coffee was concentrated in hands of the export merchants. Demonstrates importance of coffee production to industrial development that took place in the west, due to accumulation of capital in that region.

2972 Arango Jaramillo, Mario. El pensamiento económico político de la generación de 1850 en Colombia (UM/R, 21, enero/marzo 1976, p. 35–58)

Studies accumulation of capital at midcentury. Shows the impact of the reforms passed in early 1850s upon the struggle between free traders and the artisans. Differs with McGreevey, who sees same period as one of economic decadence, by stressing importance of capital accumulation that occurred.

Arrubla, Mario. Síntesis de historia política contemporánea. See *HLAS 41:7271.*

2973 Bejarano, Jesús Antonio. El fin de la economía exportadora (*in* La nueva historia de Colombia. Bogotá: Instituto Colombiano de Cultura, 1976, p. 659–739)

Quantitative analysis of employment between 1925 and 1939 compiled by young economist. Shows impact of 1929 crash on export sector and development of national industry.

2974 Bergquist, Charles W. Coffee and conflict in Colombia, 1886–1910. Durham, N.C.: Duke University Press, 1978. 277 p.; bibl.; ill.; index.

An important book, in which the author has dealt with a period of great political instability and economic difficulty. Argues that the growth and decline of the coffee industry explained in large part the tensions and complexities of the internal splits that occurred during the Regeneration and ultimately led to the War of the Thousand Days. As much a social history of the struggle between elites as a political and economic study. Includes a treatment of warfare between guerrilla troops and government conscripts. Also points out the internal difficulties that hampered Colombians as they negotiated the Panama Canal Treaty with the US. Concludes that (p. 262) "Such unique characteristics of twentieth-century Colombian politics as the continued vitality of the traditional parties, the limited success and moderate goals of social reformers, and the continuing strength of the Catholic Church are all related in part to the special structure of the Colombian coffee economy." The old order of the coffee economy depended upon the small-firm nature of coffee production.

2975 Bernal Pinilla, Luis Darío. Siglo XIX: los comerciantes vs. Colombia (*in* El nuevo pensamiento colombiano. Bogotá: FEDELCO, 1977, p. 187–248)

Traces rise of commercial class in Colombia from late colonial period through the mid-19th century, and sees them as pro-imperialists and supporters of free trade, with hurt Colombian enterprises. Then deals with artisan organizations at the mid-century, and the challenge that organized artisans posed to commercial interests.

2976 Bonilla Plata, Jaime. Jurista y general Luis Enrique Bonilla: episodios de la vida civil y militar de Colombia. Bogotá: Canal Ramírez-Antares, 1978. 495 p.; 12 leaves of plates: ill.

A rather disjointed biographical homage, written by the son of a leading Cauca politician and general.

Bushnell, David. El proceso inicial del liberalismo en Colombia y en la Argentina: un esquema comparativo. See item **2633**.

2977 Christie, Keith H. Antioqueño colonization in western Colombia: a reappraisal (HAHR, 58:2, May 1978, p. 260–283, maps, tables)

Challenges Parsons and others who argue that Antioqueño colonization followed egalitarian pattern. Colonization of Caldas, Risaralda, and Quindío was undertaken by wealthy merchants who made large profits from expansion. Based upon careful study of surnames of leading families. Identifies oligarchs who had disproportionate influence in Caldas and at national level. For geographer's comment, see *HLAS 41:5493.*

Colombia. Departamento Administrativo Nacional de Estadística (DANE). Medellín de cifras: ciudad tricentenaria, 1965–1975. See *HLAS 41:5494*.

2978 Echavarría M., Guillermo. Camilo C. Restrepo. Medellín, Colombia: Servigráficas, 1979. 97 p.; bibl.; 4 leaves of plates: ill.

A hodgepodge of photos, text and copies of documents make a biography of Restrepo (1864–1933) as railway advocate, governor of Antioquia, and national political figure. Interesting photos of the construction of the Ferrocarril de Amagá.

2979 Galindo, Aníbal. Estudios económicos y fiscales. Bogotá: ANIF, 1978. 289 p. (La Economía colombiana en el siglo XIX. Biblioteca popular de economía Anif-Colcultura; 1)

Reprint of writings of an important 19th-century economist. Makes available a book long out of print. Useful statistical data for 1830–80.

2980 García, Antonio. Colombia: medio siglo de historia contemporánea (*in* América Latina: historia de medio siglo. Edited by Pablo González Casanova. v. 1, América del Sur. México: Siglo XXI Editores, 1977, p. 173–225, bibl.)

Writes about the rise of capitalism, sindicalism, new politics, and dependency, which have defined Colombia's recent history. Part of an ongoing debate over landless peasants, egalitarian frontiers, and coffee as a national or regional product. In essence, an essay on the impact of capitalistic modernization on politics and economic development.

2981 Gilhodès, Pierre. La violence en Colombie, banditisme et guerre sociale (UTIEH/C, 1976, p. 69–81, tables)

An attempt to deal with the peculiar aspect of Colombia's violence between 1948–68, that owed to the rural base of the political struggle. Interesting interpretation, but no new information.

Gómez, Tomás. Indiens et terre en Nouvelle-Grenade 1539–1843, les *resguardos*: structures de protection ou spoliation désguisé? See item **2767**.

2982 Gómez Rodríguez, Ramiro. General Francisco Albornoz. Bogotá: Editorial Kelly, 1977. 194 p.; bibl.; ports.

Anecdotal political biography of a 19th-century Liberal general.

Gónzález, Margarita. Ensayos de historia colombiana. See item **2768**.

Hernández Rodríguez, Guillermo. De los chibchas a la Colonia y a la República: del clan a la encomienda y al latifundio en Colombia. See item **2641**.

2983 Jaramillo Uribe, Jaime. La personalidad histórica de Colombia y otros ensayos. Bogotá: Instituto Colombiano de Cultura, Subdirección de Comunicaciones Culturales, 1977. 270 p.; bibl. (Biblioteca básica colombiana; 28)

Collection of essays written between 1956–77. Ranges in topics from the influence of Rousseau in Colombia, personalism, and the influence of French Romanticism and the Revolution of 1848 upon 19th-century Colombia, through a review of Solaún and Kronis, *Discrimination without violence*, a study of race and class in modern Cartagena.

2984 Lorenzana, Fernando. Recuerdos de su vida: diario de su viaje a Bogotá en 1832, y su correspondencia con el primer representante de Colombia en Roma. Edición de Germán Arciniegas. Bogotá: Instituto Caro y Cuervo, 1978. 426 p.; 2 leaves of plates: ill. (Serie La Granada entreabierta; 22)

Includes letters and diary of a Papal representative who arrived at Bogotá in 1832. Shows early states of Colombia's relations with Rome. Introduction by Arciniegas consists of short biography of Fernando Lorenzana. Also contains account books and similar items.

2985 Loy, Jane M. Rebellion in the Colombian Llanos: the Arauca affair of 1917 (AAFH/TAM, 34:4, April 1978, p. 502–531, map)

Well written. The author uses an uprising in Arauca by Humberto Gómez as a means of undertaking a multifaceted discussion and description of llanero life in eastern Colombia during the early 20th century. Touches on the land and people, as well as the political and economic dimensions of the llanero/andino relationships. Illustrates the degree and type of cooperation practiced by Colombian and Venezuelan governments in maintaining order along their common llano frontier. On the isolation of the region, the author concludes that "as long as the development of the core areas is not dependent on progress in the Llanos, the region will remain a frontier in a permanent state of semi-abandonment" (p. 531).

Martínez, Carlos. Bogotá: sinopsis sobre su evolución urbana. See item **2646**.

2986 Orígenes de las guerras civiles en Colombia: un análisis marxista. Bogotá: Ediciones Historia y Sociedad, 1977? 70 p.

Marxist analysis of major civil wars during the 19th century by anonymous author who claims they have not received fair treatment by either Liberal or Conservative historians.

2987 Orlando Melo, Jorge. Colombia 1880–1930: La República Conservadora (*in* La nueva historia de Colombia. Bogotá: Instituto Colombiano de Cultura, 1976, p. 601–656)

Tries to argue that modernization and displacement of rural population brought downfall of Conservatives in 1930. Mostly taken from secondary sources.

2988 Ortiz Márquez, Julio. El hombre que fue un pueblo. Bogotá: Carlos Valencia Editores, 1978. 263 p.

Very detailed, journalistic, and partisan account of the period of Gaitán's most successful political career, 1942–48/49. Partly personal, mostly anecdotal. Based largely on newspaper accounts.

2989 Palacios, Marco. Coffee in Colombia, 1850–1970: an economic, social, and political history. Cambridge; New York: Cambridge University Press, 1980. 338 p.; bibl.; ill.; index (Cambridge Latin American studies; 36)

The most outstanding study of coffee written to date. Takes advantage of interdisciplinary methodology to present a complete study of the impact of coffee upon the state, land owning, labor, foreign and internal trade, the economy in general, and politics. Excellent sections on land tenure/labor relationships. A convincing attack of William McGreevey's analysis. One of the best studies of economic history to appear in recent years. Wise use of quantitative data and traditional empirical evidence.

2990 *Papel Periódico Ilustrado:* Año 1, Tomo 1, agosto 1881 a Año 5, Tomo 5, mayo 1888. Presentación de Eduardo Santa. Cali, Colombia: Carvajal & Campañía, 1975. 5 v. (400, 424, 402, 408, 324 p.); ill.; plates.

Five-volume offset reproduction of 1881–88 issues of a Colombian newspaper dedicated to arts, science, history, and customs. Stopped publication in Aug. 1888.

Poveda Ramos, Gabriel. Políticas económicas, desarrollo industrial y tecnología en Colombia: 1925–1975. See *HLAS 41:3109*.

2991 Rodríguez Garavito, Agustín. Jorge Eliécer Gaitán: biografía de una sombra: oligarquía, burguesía, democracia, oclocracia en Colombia. Bogotá: Ediciones Tercer Mundo, 1979. 160 p.

Written by a newspaper correspondent. No new evidence. Popularly written for mass distribution. Treats Gaitán (1902–48) as a combination of socialist, Liberal, and opportunist, who died when his time came. Conservatives, Liberals, communists, and just about everyone else is excused of responsibility for Gaitán's death.

2992 Safford, Frank. Aspectos del siglo XIX en Colombia. Medellín: Ediciones Hombre Nuevo, 1977. 284 p.; bibl. (Serie Historia; 2)

Collection of five essays, previously published separately between 1965–75, two of which were translated from English to Spanish. Four deal with economic and social topics found in Safford's previously published works. The late chapter consists of provocative criticism of William P. McGreevey's economic history of Colombia, whom Safford attacks as much for methodological reasons as for historical inaccuracies. The latter is well worth reading.

2993 Samper, Miguel. Selección de escritos. Selección y prólogo de Héctor Charry Samper y Santiago Samper Trainer. Bogotá: Instituto Colombiano de Cultura, Subdirección de Comunicaciones Culturales, 1977. 340 p. (Biblioteca básica colombiana; 22)

Collection of writings by 19th-century Liberal politician and thinker. Called a progressive bourgeois by Héctor Charry Samper, who wrote the introduction. Miguel Samper's career spanned 1867 to 1890s. Writings touched economic and social/class topics.

2994 Sanín Echeverri, Jaime. Ospina supo esperar. Bogotá: Editorial Andes, 1978. 267 p.; 2 leaves of plates: ports.

Glowing praise in form of a biography. Undocumented. Lists Ospina's accomplishments but gives little analysis of his career.

Seminario Nacional de Desarrollo Rural, *I, Bogotá, 1976.* El agro en el desarrollo histórico colombiano: ensayos de economía política. See *HLAS 41:3117.*

2995 Tirado Mejía, Alvaro. Las guerras civiles en Colombia (*in* El nuevo pensamiento colombiano. Bogotá: FEDELCO, 1977, p. 249–267)

Argues that Colombia has had a violent and bloody record of civil discord, despite its reputation as a center of intellectual brilliance. Regards regionalism as one cause of the strife. Article is part of a book entitled *Aspectos sociales de las guerras civiles en Colombia* (see *HLAS 40:3438*).

2996 ———. La tierra durante la República (*in* La nueva historia de Colombia. Bogotá: Instituto Colombiano de Cultura, 1976, p. 457–528)

Land use and labor relations from 1820s through the present. Based on "New History" economic perspectives, but drawn essentially from secondary sources. Stresses landless peonage and its political/economic repercussions during the 20th century. Too broad to be new.

2997 Urrutia, Miguel. El sindicalismo durante el siglo XIX (*in* La nueva historia de Colombia. Bogotá: Instituto Colombiano de Cultura, 1976, p. 531–597)

An economist views the period 1853–54 as an exceptional one during which class struggle did exist in Colombia, fomented in part by the government. La Sociedad de Artesanos began in 1847 as a guild and political group, opposed to the government's free trade policy. Support of López in 1848 marked the society's entry into political activity. Other artisan groups appeared in the 1850s, setting up class conflict between radical bourgeoisie and Liberal artisans. Shows influence of the French Revolution of 1848 upon both groups. Liberal reforms of the early 1850s affected artisans adversely, for the most part.

2998 Viajeros colombianos por Colombia. Prólogo de Gabriel Giraldo Jaramillo. Ilus. de la Comisión Corográfica y de Le Tour du Monde. Bogotá: Fondo Cultural Cafetero, 1977. 276 p.: ill. (8 col.)

Beautifully illustrated collection of travel accounts written by Colombians about their own country. An excellent source of cultural and social observations, as well as information on transportation and industry.

2999 Zambrano Pantoja, Fabio. La economía colombiana en la primera mitad del siglo 19, 1820–1850. Medellín, Colombia: Centro de Investigaciones Económicas, Facultad de Ciencias Económicas, Universidad de Antioquia, 1977. 65 p.; bibl.

First part of a projected economic study of agrarian property between 1819 and 1936 by a research group at the Universidad de Antioquia. Much of the data seems to have been collected from secondary sources, including Restrepo, Aníbal Galindo, Safford, Bushnell, as well as the *Gaceta de Colombia.* Despite title, most of the work treats late colonial and 1820s. A nominally useful but not essential study.

3000 Zeuske, Max. Volksbewegung und Bourgeoisie in Neugranada, Kolumbien: 1849–1854 (*in* Rolle und Formen der Volksbewegung im bürgerlichen Revolutionszyklus. Berlin, GDR: Akademie Verlag, 1976, p. 264–294)

East German analysis of the populist movements in Colombia in 1849–54. Examines conflict between Liberals and Conservatives, the Liberal reforms which paved the way for the development of capitalism in the "Prussian manner." [M. Kossok]

VENEZUELA

Academia Nacional de la Historia, *Caracas.* Catálogo, 1958–1978. See item **2627**.

3001 Aizenberg, Isidoro. Hoheb/Yepes: polémica sobre la libertad religiosa en 1840 (FJB/BH, 38, mayo 1975, p. 202–211)

David Hoheb, a Jewish immigrant to Coro from Curaçao, became a naturalized Venezuelan citizen in 1829, after five years residence. Article discusses Hoheb's attempts to deal with the anti-Semitism of a priest in Barquisimeto during 1839–40, who tried to exclude Hoheb from attending several church functions. Interesting observations on relative religious tolerance in Venezuela.

3002 ———. Los intentos de establecer un cementerio judío en la Caracas del siglo XIX (FJB/BH, 47, mayo 1978, p. 243–254)

A history of the efforts of the Jewish community in Caracas to establish a cemetery. Between 1843 and 1850s, Jews were buried in the British cemetery founded by Sir Robert Ker Porter. After 1890, Sephardic and Ashkenazi Jews used sections of the Cementerio General del Sur.

3003 **Ameringer, Charles D.** Leonardo Ruiz Pineda: leader of the Venezuelan resistance, 1949–1952 (SAGE/JIAS, 21:2, May 1979, p. 209–232, bibl.)

Short study of Acción Democrática's efforts to make Leonardo Ruiz Pineda a hero of the party's struggle against the dictatorship of Pérez Jiménez. Ruiz Pineda remained in Venezuela during a period in which most of the AD leadership was in exile. Killed by Pérez Jiménez's policemen in 1952, Ruiz Pineda carried on a successful campaign against the dictatorship, including the publication of a clandestine book chronicled AD's tragic fight: *Venezuela bajo el signo del terror: 1948–1952, libro negro de una dictadura* (published in 1952 and reissued in 1974, see item **3045**). AD used Ruix to establish its role in the struggle against Pérez Jiménez.

Arcila Farías, Eduardo. Historia de un monopolio: el estanco del tabaco en Venezuela, 1779–1833. See item **2629**.

3004 **Arévalo González, Rafael.** Memorias. Prólogo de Luis Villalba-Villalba. Caracas: s.n., 1977. 291 p.; 3 leaves of plates: ill.

Detailed biography of Rafael Arévalo González, a newspaper writer who was a victim of Gómez's tyranny and prisons. Born in 1866 in Miranda, he died in 1935. First quarter of the book consists of an introduction written by Luis Villalba-Villalba. Anecdotal and popular in style and lacking in documentation and bibliography, the work shows Arévalo González as director of *El Pregonero* and *Linterna Mágica*. Mostly deals with political history and intrigue. Last three quarters are memoirs of Arévalo, which Villalba-V. synthesized in his introduction.

3005 ——— and others. Pío Gil, beato de la libertad. Caracas: Senado de la República, 1975. 307 p.

A collection of short sketches of Pío Gil [Pedro María Morantes]. Published as a tribute. Articles by Andrés Eloy Blanco, Julio Febres Cordero, Ramón J. Velásquez and others. Pío Gil attacked both Castro and Gómez in his works. He died in Paris in 1918.

3006 **Armas Chitty, José Antonio de.** El Mocho Hernández: papeles de su archivo. Caracas: Facultad de Humanidades y Educación, Instituto de Antropología e Historia, Universidad Central de Venezuela, 1978. 316 p.; appendix; bibl.

First 80 p. constitute a political biography of general José Manuel Hernández (1858–1921), who opposed Castro's regime before going into exile. The rest of the book includes correspondence for the years 1892–1911, taken from the vast archives of the general found at the Archivo de la Academia Nacional de la Historia. Concludes with an exchange of long and heated letters with Gómez. Collection affords a minor glimpse of an impressive source of political data.

3007 **Bastidas, Arístides.** Rafael Vegas: reportaje biográfico. Barcelona: Ariel, 1978. 268 p.; index (Horas de Venezuela; 1)

Written by a newspaper reporter. Deals with an *antigomecista* who took part in the 1929 *Falke* incident at Cumaná. Vegas escaped from Venezuela and lived in France and Spain, until Franco came to power. In 1943 he became Minister of Education. He broke with his old teacher and friend Rómulo Gallegos when the latter joined the golpe against Medina Angarita. Book is written in popular, undocumented style. More a romantic and anecdotal novel than a biography.

3008 **Bello, Andrés.** Caracas en el epistolario de Bello. Caracas: Casa de Bello, 1979. 69 p.

Letters from Bello to friends written between 1815 and 1865, while Bello lived in London and Santiago, Chile. Letters mention Caracas, his family, and his old friends. Strictly for the Bello-buffs.

3009 **Betancourt, Rómulo.** Venezuela: oil and politics. Translated by Everett Bauman. Foreword by Arthur M. Schlesinger, Jr. Introduction by Franklin Tugwell. Boston: Houghton Mifflin, 1979. 418 p.; bibl.; index.

English edition of Betancourt's famous political statement (see *HLAS 21:1353*). Edited to make the Venezuelan case clearer to North American reader. Some important revisions appear in this edition.

3010 Blonval López, Adolfo. Páez, de guerrillero a magistrado y legislador. Carabobo: Universidad de Carabobo, Dirección de Cultura, Departamento de Publicaciones, 1976. 332 p.; bibl.

A collection of documents, mostly decrees, dictated by José Antonio Páez between 1830 and 1863. Nothing new is stated in the brief introductory essay.

3011 *Boletín del Archivo Histórico.* Congreso de la República. Año 1, Nos. 1/4, 1978– . Caracas.

New quarterly serial consisting of documents from the archives of Congress. These issues concern 1830 materials. Unfortunately little rhyme or reason has been applied to organizing them. Subjects include the Congreso de Valencia, fiscal affairs, economic information, and revolts. Valuable for research, if used with patience.

3012 *Boletín del Archivo Histórico de Miraflores.* Año 17, No. 91, mayo/junio 1977– . Caracas.

Collection includes material from the Castro era. The defeat of Pedro Julián Acosta; the Constitution of 1901; affairs in Zulia and Falcón in 1901; bubonic plague and other calamities in 1905; and the assassination of Carmelo Montenegro.

3013 ———. Año 19, Nos. 98/100, julio/dic. 1977– . Caracas.

Includes sections on Santos Matute Gómez and the petroleum workers in 1923; 1901 reclamations by H. Savignoc, a Frenchman who lived in Venezuela since 1860; the situation in the Andes as of 1901; Castro as provisional president of the Republic in 1901; and Rafael Bolívar Coronado (1913–16). Other sections touch upon a projected peace program in early 1901, a revolt in the Oriente in the same year, as well as the problem of Simón Bello in Zulia and Falcón.

Brito Figueroa, Federico. La formación de las clases sociales en Venezuela. See *HLAS 41:9196*.

3014 ———. Las repercusiones de la revolución socialista de octubre de 1917 en Venezuela: conferencia sustentada el 11 de noviembre de 1977, con ocasión del 60° aniversario de la revolución socialista de octubre, Caracas, Venezuela. Caracas: Ediciones Vanguardia, 1977. 37 p.; bibl.

Short pamphlet by Marxist historian. Reviews the treatment of the 1917 Russian Revolution in the Gómez press, which perceived Lenin and the Bolsheviks as Ivan the Terrible and enemies of family, state and religion. During the 1920s, Venezuelan Marxists published newspapers in the US, and slipped material in through clandestine routes. Russian books reached Venezucla through similar channels. Brito F. claims that Betancourt was not a founder of the Frente Popular Venezolano. Reconstitution of the Partido Comunista in 1937 was "possibly the most important of the repercussions of the Socialist Revolution of October in Venezuela" (p. 29).

3015 Caballero, Manuel. Rómulo Betancourt. Caracas: Ediciones Centauro, 1977. 302 p.; appendixes; bibl.; ill.

Written by a former adversary, who sees Betancourt as the most brilliant bourgeois politician in Venezuela's history. Essays in book were written between 1971 and 1976. Appendixes include copies of the Plan of Barranquilla, along with Betancourt speeches.

3016 Carreño, Eduardo. Vida anecdótica de venezolanos. Prólogo de Santiago Key Ayala. 5. ed. Caracas: Consejo Municipal del Distrito Federal, 1978. 229 [i.e. 231] p.; indexes; ports.

Fifth edition of a popular collection of anecdotes about famous Venezuelans. Handy for lectures and colorful tales.

Carreras, Charles. An early venture in trade promotion: the NAM's Caracas center, 1895–1901. See item **1902** and *HLAS 41:2776*.

3017 Dufumier, Marc. L'agriculture au Venezuela (FDD/NED [Problèmes d'Amérique Latine, 47] 4457, 24 fév. 1978, p. 113–128, tables)

Chronicles the crises of Venezuelan agriculture during the 20th century. Emphasis placed upon the entry of modern agriculture and capitalism, and the rise of agribusiness, its arrival in the market place, and recent measures to redress the balance. Sub-employment and exodus from rural areas have not been resolved. For economist's comment, see *HLAS 41:3141*.

3018 Ellner, Steven. The Venezuelan left in the era of the Popular Front: 1936–45 (JLAS, 2:1, May 1979, p. 169–184)

Traces national policies of Acción Democrática and the Venezuelan Communist Party from post-Gómez era through World War II. Based largely on interviews and newspaper files. Explains parties' relationship with Medina, and the differences between the two factions. Says that during this period AD was "the main alternative to orthodox Marxism" (p. 184).

3019 Etchepareborda, Roberto. Impresiones sobre Venezuela en la época de Guzmán Blanco: la misión de Miguel Cané en 1881 ante la Guerra del Pacífico; vivencias de los argentinos en Caracas (FJB/BH, 44, mayo 1977, p. 222–249)

Argentine historian discusses the impressions of two Argentines, Miguel Cané and Martín García Merou, who visited Caracas in 1881 as part of a diplomatic mission. Based on the published accounts of these two distinguished visitors. Deals with their observations of the country, the city of Caracas, the customs, culture and history of the nation.

3020 Felice Cardot, Carlos. Páginas biográficas y críticas. Caracas: Academia Nacional de la Historia, 1978. 245 p.; bibl.; facsims.; index (Biblioteca de la Academia Nacional de la Historia; 2. Serie Estudios, monografías y ensayos. Academia Nacional de la Historia)

Series of short, well-researched, and clearly written biographical essays on "meritorious" Venezuelans. Includes sketches on the lives of Gil Fortoul, Arcaya, Parra Pérez, and Verocoechea.

3021 Garbi Sánchez, José. Alzamientos, cárceles y experiencias: historia contemporánea. Prólogo de J.A. de Armas Chitty. Caracas: s.n., 1977. 175 p.; bibl.; ill.

Episodes in the life of an individual who fought with Arévalo Cedeño against Gómez. Spent time in jails. Useful information concerning the Venezuelan-Colombian border of the llanos.

3022 Gilhodès, Pierre. Venezuela: genèse de son système de partis (UTIEH/C, 32, 1979, p. 71–105)

A standard chronology of Venzuelan political organization, based on Venezuelan secondary sources, especially Brito Figueroa, Magallanes, Fuenmayor, Rangel, Pérez Vila, and Betancourt.

3023 González, César. Rubén González, una vida al servicio de Venezuela. Caracas: Ministerio de Educación, Dirección General de Administración y Servicios, Departamento de Imprenta, 1975. 170 p.; port (Colección Homenajes; 1)

Written by the son of Rubén González, Minister of Education and educational reformer during the Gómez administration. Author was his father's secretary (see also item **3041**).

3024 González Herrera, Luis. Rómulo en Berna: un documento para la historia de Acción Democrática. Caracas: Ediciones Centauro, 1978. 2 v.; bibl.; ill.

Vol. 1 comprises a personalized history of "the ultimate caudillo and first modern leader," written for the Acción Democrática Party and its grandchildren. Vol. 2 includes assorted documents that deal with the founding of the party, statutes of the party, other important party papers, as well as a section on opinions of Rómulo Betancourt by noted personages and the press.

3025 Grases, Pedro. Bibliografía de Don Arístides Rojas, 1826–1894. 2. ed. ampliada. Caracas: Fundación para el Rescate del Acervo Documental Venezolano, 1977. 169 p.; index (Colección "Manuel Segundo Sánchez")

Expanded second edition of a work first published in 1944. Guide to works of Andrés Bello and works about him.

Herrera de Weishaar, María Luisa; María Leonor Ferreira Ferreira; and **Carlos Nestor Alvarez Cabrera.** Parroquia La Vega: estudio micro-histórico. See item **2642**.

3026 Un hombre llamado Rómulo Betancourt: apreciaciones críticas sobre su vida y su obra. Caracas: Catalá/Centauro/Editores, 1975. 331 p.; ill.

A tribute to Rómulo Betancourt. Includes articles and speeches about Betancourt by those who have praised him between 1928 and the 1960s.

3027 Howard, Harrison Sabin. Rómulo Gallegos y la revolución burguesa de Venezuela. Traducción del ingles: Martín Sagrera. Caracas: Monte Avila Editores, 1976. 358 p.; bibl. (Colección Estudios)

A sympathetic but critical, political biography of Gallegos and the party he came to lead. Spanish translation of the author's Ph.D. dissertation. Well worth reading for any student of recent political history of Venezuela.

Izard, Miguel. Política y economía en Venezuela: 1810–1976. See *HLAS 41:3149.*

Lemmo, Angelina. La educación en Venezuela en 1870. See *HLAS 41:4576.*

3028 León, Ramón David. El brujo de la mulera. Prólogo de Raúl Torres Gámez. Caracas: Fondo Editorial Gomún, 1976. 167 p.; plates.

A rethinking of the experience of the dictatorship of Juan Vicente Gómez by a journalist who lived and practiced his profession during the period. [P.B. Taylor, Jr.]

3029 Liss, Sheldon B. Diplomacy & dependency: Venezuela, the United States, and the Americas. Salisbury, N.C.: Documentary Publications, 1978. 356 p.; bibl.; index; map.

A survey of the basic manifestations of Venezuelan foreign policies during its history as an independent state. Descriptive rather than analytical. Mentions highlights only, with little or no discussion of the formation of policy.

Lombardi, John V. The rise of Caracas as a primate city. See item **2644**.

Mártinez, Aníbal R. Gumersindo Torres. See *HLAS 41:3155.*

3030 Matthews, Robert Paul. Violencia rural en Venezuela, 1840–1858: antecedentes socio-económicos de la Guerra Federal. Traducción, Marie Françoise de Petzolde, revisida por el autor. Caracas: Monte Avila Editores, 1977. 210 p.; bibl. (Colección Temas venezolanos)

Spanish translation of the author's Ph.D. dissertation. A well documented study of violence on the central llanos during the 1840s and 1850s, which the author treats as the origins of the Federal War. War between competing bandit/Liberal factions and their economic and political consequences serves as the focus of this study. Based on extensive use of Venezuelan archives and newspapers. Records the destruction of the cattle industry on the llanos. Demonstrates how the Federalists evolved into a more mature political movement during the 1840s and 1850s as they gained the faith of the people.

3031 Maza Zavala, D.F. Historia de medio siglo en Venezuela, 1926–1975 (*in* América Latina: historia de medio siglo. Edición de Pablo González Casanova. v. 1, América del Sur. México: Siglo XXI Editores, 1977, p. 450–543, bibl.)

Studies dependency relationships within the world capitalist system. Breaks down into four convenient periods: 1926–35; 1936–45; 1946–57; and 1958–75. Tries to describe the formation of classes in Venezuela during the 20th century. Stresses political organizations, their leaders and their objectives.

Mendoza, Rafael Martínez. Breves consideraciones sobre el sistema tributario de Venezuela. See *HLAS 41:3160.*

3032 Mesa, Salom. Por un caballo y una mujer: relato autobiográfico. 2. ed. Valencia, Venezuela: Vadell Hermanos, 1978. 361 p.

Autobiographical statements written by Salom Mesa while in jail. Makes for interesting reading about the formation of a "radical" Venezuelan politician during the Betancourt era. Author attacks Rómulo Betancourt and Carlos Andrés Pérez. In so doing, he sheds some light on the split within Acción Democrática that led to Prieto Figueroa's break away faction. Mesa charges that police officials acted as killers for AD politicians. He also sees CIA activity everywhere, claiming that they helped Carlos Andrés Pérez win in 1973.

3033 Morón, Guillermo. Historia política contemporánea de Venezuela, 1936–1976 (JGSWGL, 14, 1977, p. 350–368)

Depicts recent history since 1936 as a recurring struggle between dictatorship and democracy. López Contreras seen as father of modern democracy. Rómulo Betancourt called one of Venezuela's four great caudillos, along with Páez, Guzmán Blanco, and Gómez. Betancourt organized Acción Democrática for personal purposes. Attacks inability of Venezuelans to study Betancourt.

3034 Mudarra, Miguel Angel. Andrés Eloy Blanco: perfiles biográficos. Caracas: Garza Impresores, 1978. 296 p.; ill. (Perfiles biográficos)

Adulatory and traditional biography of the Cumaná poet and AD politician. Treats literary themes as well as political topics.

3035 Ocando Yamarte, Gustavo. Historia político-eclesiástica de Venezuela, 1830–1847. Caracas: Academia Nacional de la Historia, 1975. 2 v.; bibl.; ill.; indexes (Fuentes para la historia republicana de Venezuela. Biblioteca de la Academia Nacional de la Historia; nueva serie, 18/19)

Traces, in chronological order, major issues concerning Church-state relations during the Páez era. Extensive use of archdiocesan archives, showing richness of this source for the study of modern Venezuela. Includes sections on question of Church privileges, fear of Protestants, tithes, and foreign (Royalist?) priests, as well as newspapers, published collections, and memoirs. Best coverage is for the period between 1830 and 1836. An excellent collection with good editorial interpretation.

3036 Pino Iturrieta, Elías A. Positivismo y gomecismo. Caracas: Facultad de Humanidades y Educación, Instituto de Estudios Hispanoamericanos, Universidad Central de Venezuela, 1978. 153 p.; bibl.; ports.

Lacking in new observations, this work offers a useful synopsis of relations during 1913–31 between leading positivists (e.g., Arcaya, Gil Fortoul, Vallenilla Lanz, and Zumeta) and Gómez. Includes copies of letters from these men to Gómez and several good photographs.

3037 Plaza, Helena. El 23 [i.e. veintitrés] de enero de 1958 y el proceso de consolidación de la democracia representativa en Venezuela: ensayo de interpretación sociopolítica. Caracas: Garbizu & Todtmann, 1978. 239 p.; bibl.; ill. (Monografías G&T)

A fairly traditional and conservative treatment of a "reform" movement. Based on secondary sources and interviews.

Pollak-Eltz, Angelina. Slave revolts in Venezuela. See item **2747**.

3038 Ricardo Montilla. Recopilado por Gosvinda Rugeles de Montilla. Caracas: Editorial Binev, 1977. 102 p.

Tribute to a leading Acción Democrática member and founder of the modern party. Poems, essays, and the like discuss the many contributions of Montilla to agriculture, education, and politics.

Rodríguez Campos, Manuel. Venezuela, 1902: la crisis fiscal y el bloqueo: perfil de una soberanía vulnerada. See *HLAS 41:3170*.

3039 Rodríguez Leal, Edgard. Relaciones entre Francia y Venezuela, 1832–1918. v. 1, Correspondencia política, 1837–1895. Caracas: Facultad de Humanidades y Educación, Instituto de Antropología e Historia, Universidad Central de Venezuela, 1977. 1 v.; indexes.

An inventory of documents found in the Archives of the Ministry of Foreign Affairs in France, 1832–95. Brief annotations help researcher. A very useful research tool.

3040 Rodríguez Rodríguez, Adolfo. Ezequiel Zamora. Caracas: Ministerio de Educación, 1977. 352 p.; bibl.

A carefully researched refutation of Brito Figueroa's last book on Ezequiel Zamora (see *HLAS 38:3373*). Factual and detailed, it treats Zamora as part of the commercial class by birth, not as one of the "masses." Based on documentation found at the National Archives, as well as local archives and from newspapers. The author tries to offset the Zamora myth by pointing out what he was like at the time of his death.

3041 Rubén González visto por varios autores. Caracas: Ministerio de Educación Dirección de Administración, Departamento de Imprenta, 1976. 141 p.; port. (Colección Homenajes; 2)

Rubén González served as Minister of Education between 1922 and 1929. This book marked the 100th anniversary of his birth. Various authors prepared mostly anecdotal tributes. González defended Cecilia Núñez Sucre in 1928 from government attacks on the university. The work shows a definite effort to revise the image of some of the men who served in official capacities during the Gómez era. Minister of Education Peñalver wanted to pay homage to a good guy. González authored the Ley Orgánica de Educación of 1924, setting limits to freedom in teaching and a balance between public and private education. The book tries to establish that González was an educational reformer; not a servant of Gómez. See also item **3023**.

3042 Sánchez, José Manuel. Mis primeros noventa años, 1887–1977. Caracas: s.n., 1977. 141 p.: ill.

A rambling autobiography of recollections of life and changes by an old Caracas merchant (Sánchez y Compañía). Includes good photographs of Caracas and Venezuela. Gives idea of cost of living and style of living in 20th-century Venezuela. Best on the 1900–36 period.

3043 Schael, Guillermo José. L.Q.Q.D. Caracas: s.n., 1977. 238 p.; bibl.; ill.

Popularistic account of the political history of modern Venezuela, roughly 1900–45. Contains many very good photographs.

3044 Sullivan, William M. The harassed exile: General Cipriano Castro, 1908–1924 (AAFH/TAM, 33:2, Oct. 1976, p. 282–297)

A detailed description of Castro's beleaguered travels after he left Venezuela in 1908 in order to seek medical treatment in Germany. Strictly a log of Castro's comings and goings between 1908 and 1924.

3045 Venezuela bajo el signo del terror: Libro Negro 1952. Caracas: J.A. Catalá, 1974. 354 p.: ill.

Reproduction of a clandestine book printed under the direction of Ruiz Pineda and members of Acción Democrática in 1952, documenting the bloody excesses of the regime of the dictator Marcos Pérez Jiménez. Presented AD's position against the dictatorship. Outlines the AD's program. Includes testimonies of many victims of Pérez Jiménez's police torture, along with lists of those arrested and expelled (see item **3003**).

3046 Wright, Winthrop R. Race, nationality, and immigration in Venezuelan thought, 1890 to 1937 (Canadian Review of Studies in Nationalism. Revue Canadienne des Etudes sur le Nationalisme [University of Prince Edward Island, Charlottetown] 6:1, Spring 1979, p. 1–12)

Reviews the evolution of racial thinking by leading positivists who contributed to the idea of "whitening" Venezuela by encouraging European immigration and excluding the entry of blacks, Asians, and other "undesirables."

3047 Zawisza, Leszek M. Colonización agrícola en Venezuela (FJB/BH, 37, enero 1975, p. 15–59)

Chronological presentation of attempts by various Venezuelan governments since the 1820s to establish agricultural colonies of European immigrants. Most early ones failed due to nature of tropical agriculture for which the Europeans were not prepared, or due to poorly worded and non-enforced legislation. Wars and diseases gave Venezuela a bad image in Europe. In sum, most colonization projects failed because of a lack of realistic and well-studied organization and economic bases. Today agricultural development is no longer associated with immigration. For economist's comment, see *HLAS 41:5587*.

ECUADOR

Bromley, Rosemary D.F. The functions and development of "colonial" towns: urban change in the Central Highlands of Ecuador, 1698–1940. See item **2631**.

———. Urban-rural demographic contrasts in highland Ecuador: town recession in a period of catastrophe, 1778–1841. See item **2632**.

Cerutti Guldberg, Horacio. Aproximación a la historiografía del pensamiento. See item **7557**.

Estrada Ycaza, Julio. Regionalismo y migración. See item **2637**.

Fitch, John Samuel. The military coup d'état as a political process: Ecuador, 1948–1966. See *HLAS 41:7319*.

Hamerly, Michael T. Registros parroquiales e inventarios de iglesias del litoral. See item **2640**.

3048 Jouanen, José. Los jesuítas y el Oriente ecuatoriano, 1868–1898: monografía histórica. Guayaquil, Ecuador: Editorial Arquidiocesana Justicia y Paz, 1977. 231 p.; bibl.; 4 leaves of plates: ill.

A highly documentary account of the 28 years that the Jesuits were allowed to work in eastern Ecuador, between their return under García Moreno and their expulsion under Eloy Alfaro. Author died in 1952. Drawn from Jesuit archives. Extensive use of quotations from Jesuit documents makes for a very descriptive but not interpretative narrative. Rich information on Indians of eastern Ecuador, the Jesuits who served them, and the relations between them. Much information on health conditions of the Indians and the missionaries.

3049 Loor, Wilfrido. Gobernadores de Manabí y mandatarios de Guayaquil, 1822–1945. Portoviejo: Editorial Gregorio, 1976 or 1977. 119 p.

Governor-by-governor account of administrations that served at Manabí post before 1845. Old fashioned political narrative.

Middleton, DeWight R. The growth of a city: urban, regional, and national interaction in Ecuador. See item **2648**.

3050 Miranda Ribadeneira, Francisco. García Moreno y la Compañía de Jesús: historial e interpretativa. Quito: Imprenta y Ediciones Lexigrama, 1976. 120 p.; bibl. (Colección Desarrollo y paz)

Written from material found in Jesuit archives. Argues that García Moreno wanted an educated and intelligent clergy to come to Ecuador since the Ecuadorian priests were ignorant. García Moreno thought that the Jesuits would promote national progress by means of introducing education and encouraging a mature religious conviction among the citizenry.

3051 Muñoz Vicuña, Elías. La guerra civil ecuatoriana de 1895: una epopeya de la revolución burguesa antifeudal: el triunfo del Partido Radical de Eloy Alfaro. Guayaquil: Departamento de Publicaciones de la Universidad de Guayaquil, 1976. 520 p.; bibl.; 9 leaves of plates: ill.

Short chapters, mostly documents and quotations from the late 19th century, showing the background and completion of what the author calls an anti-feudal bourgeois revolution, the triumph of Eloy Alfaro and the Radical Party in 1895.

Norris, Robert E. Guía bibliográfica para el estudio de la historia ecuatoriana. See item **2650**.

3052 Paul Rivet, 1876–1976: selección de estudios científicos y biográficos. Quito: Editorial Casa de la Cultura Ecuatoriana, 1977. 365 p.; bibl.; 4 leaves of plates (Colección de estudios científicos ecuatorianos; 1)

Homage to a French scientist who had a long career as ethnographer in Ecuador between 1903 and 1958. Short biography, followed by bibliography of works, and short excerpts from major works, articles, and speeches.

Sampedro V., Francisco. Atlas geográfico del Ecuador "SAM:" con las básicas nociones históricas de la nacionalidad. See *HLAS 41:5833*.

Peru

VINCENT C. PELOSO, *Associate Professor of History, Howard University*

POLITICAL AND HISTORICAL EVENTS of the past two years coincided in fortuitous ways to dramatize a rise in the quantity and quality of Peruvian historical studies. The centenary of the start of the War of the Pacific (1879–83), the end of the military government of 1969–80, and its replacement by a constitutional regime, coming in the aftermath of the death of Víctor Raúl Haya de la Torre, inaugurated a new, important political phase in the country's history.

Momentous political changes were accompanied by shifts in the state of historical production. The latter are exemplified by two developments: Magnus Mörner's announcement of the Cuzco Agrarian Project—a cooperative venture of the Institute of Latin American Studies, Stockholm, and the Institute of Peruvian Studies, Lima (see item **3099**)—and by the decision to devote an issue of *Allpanchis*, normally an anthropology journal, to the history of peasant movements in Peru. A regrettable prospect for social historians however, was the recent rumor that the

Archivo del Fuero Agrario (AFA), formerly the Centro de Documentación Agraria, a fledgling depository of invaluable plantation records, would close for lack of funds. If so, this development would signal a lamentable disregard for scholarship on the part of the new constitutional government. The closing of such an archive might forestall a recent and commendable effort to use manuscript sources in order to document agrarian history for the post-1880 period, a trend rare not only in Peru but in all of Latin America. Only in the last few years has the impact of this new archive on the modern history of Peru begun to register. Its closing would severely cripple the work undertaken by enthusiastic, highly competent and under-funded Peruvian scholars. One hopes that some means will be found to maintain such a seminal depository as the AFA.

True, not all the good work on Peruvian topics is generated by the sources of the AFA. Strictly political or diplomatic studies, traditional biographies and narratives of standard themes also draw the attention of scholars, though this work receives much less favor from publishers nowadays than was the case a decade or so ago. Most publishing historians have risen to the challenges posed by *Annales* and Marxist scholarship, and their responses help to clarify our understanding of Peru's past. Although social historians—and the formation of a social history of Peru—have benefitted from these challenges far more than is true of other branches of the discipline, the impact of these canons is especially notable when they are applied to a familiar topic or a traditional problem. A case in point is the splendid biographical study of José Carlos Mariátegui by Jesús Chavarría (item **3065**), the most inspiring work reviewed in this biennium. Skillfully and stylistically, the book interweaves dependency theory with interviews and traditional sources to clarify the formative process in the emergence of this widely influential 20th-century *pensador*, and to suggest the extent and depth of his contribution to ideology in Latin America.

On the other hand, studies based on AFA materials have encouraged historians to search out provincial archives, resulting in the reemergence of regional themes in the republican history of Peru. The most notable pattern that is distinguishable among the good regional studies appearing in this volume is that 20th-century regional affairs drew far more attention than did their 19th-century antecedents. Nevertheless, in both cases regional questions seem most interesting to researchers either for the impact they made upon national politics or for the way they represented the tensions that shape deeply rooted local traditions. Students were drawn to the local history of Arequipa, Cuzco and Huancayo, while few of them turned their attention to the provinces of Piura, Cajamarca and Loreto. In addition, their works discussed social and economic themes rather than formal politics; even political events were subject to sociological scrutiny. José Tamayo's work on Cuzco (item **3123**) is an example in which the author applies an *Annales* model to the social history of the area in order to seek out the *mentalité* that bred such distinctive institutions as the Universidad de San Antonio Abad. Farther north in the highlands, a team of sociologists gathered together by Norman Long and Bryan Roberts (item **3105**) examined historical stages in order to clarify the links that bind communities throughout the Huancayo region. Among students of Arequipa, José Luis Rénique (item **3115**) followed the path of Alberto Flores Galindo (see *HLAS 40:3515*) and studied the conflicts between local interests and Arequipeño desires for national leadership.

The other major focus of study is the nature of the republican state. At a theoretical level, Ronald Berg and Frederick S. Weaver (item **3058**) suggest that control of the state during the guano era was wrested from landowners by an urban elite, while Stephen Gorman (item **3082**) views the problem somewhat differently when he suggests that a plutocratic ruling class was able to govern by interposing the military between themselves and the masses. Heraclio Bonilla (item **3060**) and Nelson Manrique (item **3096**) examine another dimension of state control when they argue that during the War of the Pacific the rural masses often were aware of the weaknesses of their own ruling class. They suggest that peasant opposition to the Chilean invaders represented a commitment to the larger interests of the community rather than to the landlords.

Historical debate over the relationship between the state and the ruling class has entered a theoretical phase. Foremost among those who try to conceptualize the dynamics of state and society in the republican era is Julio Cotler whose succinct essay (item **3069**) is a chapter of a larger work, *Clases, estado y nación en el Perú* (Lima: Instituto de Estudios Peruanos, 1978), which had not yet been received at the Library of Congress by press time, and Aníbal Quijano's incisive overview of 20th-century imperialism, class and the state (item **3108**), which places a different emphasis on the problem. In a less theoretical and more methodological vein, Rosemary Thorp and Geoffrey Bertram (item **3125**) delineate the state's role in the export economy, and in the last section of a collection of essays by Jorge Basadre (item **3057**), he speculates on the meaning of the 20th-century praetorian state.

Discussion of the state invariably recalls APRA, the political party most frustrated in its efforts to gain control of it. These days the party's relationship to the Church is under scrutiny in the work of Jeffrey Klaiber (item **3090**), who explores the Church's legitimizing role in APRA's successes, and in the interpretive essay by Frederick Pike which probes the nexus of religious and collectivist ideas in the formation of mass behavior (item **3107**). No doubt the recent publication of the complete works of Victor Raúl Haya de la Torre will fuel this issue to the benefit of interested Peruvianists.

It is easy to predict that Peruvian historians and historical-minded social scientists will remain tireless in their quest for useful perspectives on the republic's problems, but one hesitates to foretell their future prospects. The continued low-budget priority given to national archives and libraries, the need to open provincial archives and the likely disappearance of the AFA are symptomatic of the critical problems faced by historians of the Andean world.

A further note. Professor Bryce Wood pointed out to me that two items in my last contribution (see *HLAS 40:3494* and *3538*) were in error. In the first one, a reference to a "border war" was an exaggeration because there was no fighting in 1910, and in the last item I erroneously ascribed the leadership of the Peruvian campaign against Ecuador in that year to Gen. Oscar Benavides when in fact it was led by Gen. Eloy Ureta. I wish to thank Professor Wood for pointing out these errors.

3053 Alisky, Marvin. Historical dictionary of Peru. Metuchen, N.J.: Scarecrow Press, 1979. 157 p.; bibl. (Latin American historical dictionaries; 20)

One of a decade-old series on Latin America and the Caribbean, this slim volume reflects the weaknesses and strengths of such undertakings. More heavily political than economic in orientation, it contains few of the names of politically powerful families in the 20th century, yet many items reflect broad knowledge of the military government of 1968–80. No cross references are made, hence inconsistencies such as the information given on Melgar Márques and Luis Sánchez Cerro tend to appear. On the whole, however, it contains useful introductory material.

3054 Aranda, Arturo and **María Escalante.** Lucha de clases en el movimiento sindical cusqueño, 1927–1965. Lima: G. Herrera, 1978. 143 p.; bibl.; 3 leaves of plates: ill.

A Marxist-Leninist analysis of how the class struggle is reflected directly within working class and peasant organizations, a phenomenon of ruling-class hegemony which in turn is seen as the key to the problem of organization. The authors warn that labor unions do not necessarily reflect either the interests or the ideology of the working class, and can even be converted into an instrument of bourgeois oppression. With this problem raised, labor history in Peru as it is reflected in this study of labor in Cuzco reached a more difficult and potentially more fruitful level. Written expressly as a guide to action, this tightly woven analysis devotes most attention to the problem of ideology. Sources include newspapers, trade union files and interview accounts of the Cuzco movement. Sets the development of labor unions in Cuzco within the general labor movement in Peru with attention given to labor and artisan unions as well as peasant organizations. Ends with judgements on the ideological and political influences on the movement by all segments of the left. Both authors have been active in the labor movement in Cuzco since the fateful mid-1960s.

3055 Baella Tuesta, Alfonso. El miserable. Lima: Baella Tuesta, 1978. 447 p.: ill.

Personal account of his exile on 5 Aug. 1975, by a former official of *El Comercio*, a journalist who until he was deported had worked cooperatively with the military government. Includes brief, impressionistic biographies of the generals involved in the coup of Aug. 1975. A goodly part of the volume details relations between Velasco and the leadership of the Peruvian press and scores government press controls. Ends with the death of Velasco on 24 Dec. 1977.

3056 Basadre, Jorge. Apertura: textos sobre temas de historia, educación, cultura y política escritos entre 1924 y 1977. Selección, edición y notas introductorias de Patricio Ricketts. Lima: Ediciones Taller, 1978. 592 p.; bibl.; index.

A selection of the famed historian's essays on history, culture and politics written over his prolific lifetime. They begin with essays published in Tacna in the 1920s, move to pieces on the writing and teaching of history, and a third section on "historical themes," including an eclectic collection of short works on such subjects as "feudalism in Peru," Flora Tristán, an interview on the Battle of Tarapacá (1879), and valuable thoughts on the recent historiographical trends in Peru. The final section contains thoughts on recent events in his country. A diverse and widely useful volume that once more demonstrates why the author is one of Latin America's most widely respected historians.

3057 ———. Leyes electorales peruanas, 1890–1917: teoría y realidad (PUCP/H, 1:1, julio 1977, p. 1–36)

Study of the changes in electoral laws and their social meaning over the period as reflected not merely in the formal documentation but also in the literature and literary organs of the epoch. Attempts to broaden democracy met with heated parliamentary opposition which sometimes produced extraordinary satirical comment from insightful provincial congressmen. An unusual juxtaposition of parliamentary debates and literary expression.

3058 Berg, Ronald H. and **Frederick Stirton Weaver.** Toward a reinterpretation of political change in Peru during the first century of independence (UM/JIAS, 20:1, Feb. 1978, p. 69–84, bibl.)

Argues that the magnitude of political change in Peru in the first century of independence was most clearly shown in the relations between the central government and the sources of socioeconomic power in society. Examines three periods, 1825–40, the 1840s through the 1850s, and the 1880s through the 1920s, and links the expansion of central government power to guano revenues, while the formation of regional elites is linked to other raw materials exports and the rise of a related working class, a relationship which is said to have fundamentally altered the character of Peruvian national politics. In contrast to some "dependency" formulations, this one stresses the articulation of international market forces with the mediating social structure of the country.

3059 Bocchio Rejas, Luis Orlando. Los tacneños y el corredor para Bolivia.

Pueblo Libre: Bocchio Rejas, 1978. 102 p.; bibl.; maps.

Sponsored by the Departmental Club of Tacna, this essay surveys the passage of national political events through the region, especially concentrating on the negotiations that led to the war of 1879–83, and especially the role of Tacna officials in the offer of a plan to give Bolivia a corridor to the sea just above Río Lluta, with tripartite sovereignty in the territory north of Arica. Rejected by Chile in 1976 negotiations between the Banzer regime of Bolivia and the Pinochet government in Chile.

3060 Bonilla, Heraclio. The War of the Pacific and the national and colonial problem in Peru (PP, 81, Nov. 1978, p. 92–118)

Through use of the archives of Anthony Gibbs and Sons, Ltd., organizers of the guano and nitrate trades, this study examines the deep cleavages within the oligarchy which weakened it in the face of the Chilean wartime advance, and it argues that the following civil war reflected these social divisions and made the ruling class desire peace with continued Chilean occupation. In addition to the conflicts between ruling and subordinate classes, and cleavages between ruling class sectors and their sponsors, this study finds deep-set, violent ethnic divisions that cut across class lines. Suggests that a social leveling process and a shift from ethnic to national consciousness accompanied postwar readjustment and points out areas for future research on this issue. A succinct, invaluable study. The colonial problem, however, is not always clearly linked to the national issue.

3061 ———; Lía del Río; and **Pilar Ortiz de Zevallos.** Comercio libre y crisis de la economía andina: el caso del Cuzco (PUCP/H, 21:1, julio 1978, p. 1–25, bibl., tables)

Part of a cooperative study of agrarian history of the Cuzco region conducted by Swedish and Peruvian scholars, this essay uses British PRO documentation, French, AGN Lima, and local Cuzco sources to evaluate the commercial policy of early Peruvian governments as they affected Cuzco. Discusses British textile imports and changes in Peruvian import regulations, pointing out state ambivalence on the issue. Consequences included the slow saturation of the internal Peruvian market. The purchase of local factories by Europeans, thoroughly destroying local procedures and paralyzing the local economy, offers strong evidence against the arguments of Mathew and Platt on the impact of British commerce on the national political structure.

Britton, John A. Carlton Beals on the ambiguities of revolutionary change in Mexico and Peru. See item **2272**.

Campbell, Leon G. Recent research on Andean peasant revolts, 1750–1820. See item **2687**.

3062 Caravedo, Baltazar. El problema del centralismo en el Perú republicano (IPA/A, 12/13, 1979, p. 19–50, bibl.)

Notes the differences between 19th-century and 20th-century variations on centralism in Peru and suggests the nature and degree of change in the two types, the one a process of state formation on the basis of an "archipelago" economy made over into regional, autonomous markets; the other impelled toward market centralization in Lima and the subordination of the national economy to international capital. The expansion of the state, 1968–75, despite its intentions, wiped out local autonomy, crowded Lima and aggravated the unequal development of the economy, and especially limited new industrialization. A synthesis and interpretation based largely upon illustrations from the 1950s and 1960s.

Carlin Arce, Jorge. Antología documental del Departamento de Tumbes. See *HLAS 41:1288*.

3063 Cerda Catalán, Alfonso. La guerra entre España y las repúblicas del Pacífico, 1864–1866: pt. 1, Antecedentes diplomáticos, militares y económicos (UMHN/RH, 49:145/147, nov. 1977, p. 1–210)

Based upon research in the Archivo del Ministerio de Asuntos Exteriores, Madrid, puts the war in the context of the "violent intervention" of European powers in Spanish America in the 1860s. Pt. II describes the diplomatic confrontations, legal arguments, negotiations, and military gestures, as they related to domestic politics in Spain and Peru, 1860–1864. Though it overemphasizes a continental nationalist perspective and gives economic factors minimal attention, this detailed, traditional narrative gives a lively account of the main political features of the war.

3064 Chavarría, Jesús. The colonial heritage of national Peru: an overview (CEDLA/B, 25, dic. 1978, p. 37–49)

Argues that despite a picture of general 18th-century decadence, some sectors were economically attractive in that era but that on the eve of independence formerly active sectors declined and capital flight was widespread. The early independence population rate declined, internal migration increased and precious metals fled, devastating the hinterland. Peru, heavily burdened by the colonial experience, now was exceptionally predisposed toward neo-colonialism. Guano transformed this economy: though its effect was largely domestic, the net result was the encouragement of imports. Capital accumulated with merchant houses and the economy faltered; modernization took place slowly and unevenly. Thoughtful interpretive review of previously published studies.

3065 ———. José Carlos Mariátegui and the rise of modern Peru, 1890–1930. Albuquerque: University of New Mexico Press, 1979. 247 p.; bibl.; 4 leaves of plates: ill.; index.

Creatively woven tapestry that sets the formation of Mariátegui's ideas in their proper perspective while surpassing all other biographies in demonstrating both European and Latin American—especially Peruvian nationalist—threads of the man's ideas. They are shown to reflect his experiences as well as his responses to the writings and teachings of the preceding "generation of 1900" in Peru. Mariátegui's "generation of 1919" overcame positivism and wrought Peruvian socialism to formulate ideas and to create a political counterweight to imperialism, racism and class oppression. The resulting socialism was open and receptive. This penetrating study is based on wide-ranging knowledge of European and Latin American political philosophy, extensive interviews with the family and friends of the subject, and unpublished materials. An excellent bibliographic essay accompanies a superlatively written text.

3066 Chirinos Soto, Enrique. Historia de la República, 1821–Peru–1978. Lima: Editorial Andina, 1977. 578 p.; bibl.; index.

Sets the history of republican Peru in the context of Latin American politics, never wanders outside of a political and diplomatic narrative, concentrates on personalities from Bolívar to Morales Bermúdez, and does it all in anecdotal fashion, with relish.

3067 Claverías, Ricardo. El mercado interno y la espontaneidad de los movimientos campesinos: Puno, 1950–1968 (IPA/A, 11/12, 1978, p. 151–173)

Important study of the rural labor movement on the large haciendas of the Puno altiplano where Social Christian and Community Party unions operated in spontaneous shepherd-wage worker uprisings which were a response to demands for increased production, in turn encouraged by industrial and mining development. Changes in tenant rent and changes in administration of the haciendas are examined for their social implications, as is the effectiveness of peasant unions. Relies largely upon plantation records.

La Confederación Perú-Boliviana: el Mariscal Santa Cruz y la Santa Sede: documentos inéditos. See item **3146**.

3068 Congrains Martín, Eduardo. Batalla de San Juan: pt. 2, Chorrillos. Lima: Editorial Ecoma, 1976. 204 p.; plate (Biblioteca histórica Ecoma. Serie Reivindicación; 9)

Account of the tactics, problems, movements of the Chilean army in the occupation of the south coast and the capture of Lima in 1880–1881. Hagiographic, undocumented digest of more serious studies. Part of an extended popular series.

3069 Cotler, Julio. Perú: estado oligárquico y reformismo militar (*in* América Latina: historia de medio siglo. v. 1, América del Sur. Edited by Pablo González Casanova. México: Siglo XXI Editores, 1977, v. 1, p. 373–423)

A sociohistorical interpretation of Peru since the 1920s, from the intellectual response to the linkage of international capital and landlord control through a weak state, through the shape of the crisis of the 1930s which defined the political struggle in Peru for decades as one of the popular masses against the army. Offers an explanation of why APRA rather than the Communist Party led the popular sector, and argues that the imperialist sector blocked creation of a nationalistic bourgeoisie in the era. Reflects further on the democratic experience of 1945–48, the new imperialist penetration in the Odría period, the oligarchic crisis of the Prado period, the unraveling of the 1960s, and finally the "revolution from above," whose peculiarity derived from its anti-oligarchic and nationalistic reforms without the participation of mass organizations. Notes that the military revolution has become more repressive and more favorable to bourgeois and pro-imperialist policies since 1976. A concise statement of a larger work examining classes, parties and the state.

3070 ———. A structural-historical approach to the breakdown of democratic institutions: Peru (*in* The breakdown of democratic regimes: crisis, breakdown and reequilibration. Edited by Juan J. Linz and Alfred J. Stepan. Baltimore, Md.: The Johns Hopkins University Press, 1978, p. 178–206)

Argues that analysis of a sudden crisis inadequately demonstrates the weaknesses of democracy and that more accuracy can be obtained from historical examination of the structure of democracy in society. Example of Peru before 1968 used to show that democracy can exist in form without its content; that the 1968 coup was only the collapse of an oligarchic rather than a democratic system. Dependency framework focuses on the subordination of the oligarchy to the needs of foreign capital and the related failures of popular mobilization before and after 1950, stressing the roles of a split within the oligarchy and the awakened nationalist and populist sentiments of army and Church. The ineffectiveness of the Belaúnde AP regime is laid to structural control of the oligarchy through parliament. Pre-1968 scandal, including the "page eleven" episode of Sept. 1968, involving the IPC, helped the military launch its planned coup. Concludes that a precarious bourgeois state with an enclaved economy in alliance with international capital which strove to avoid popular mobilization through APRA intensified class struggle. Sweeping survey with a clear point of view that presents a useful framework for analysis of particular elements of the argument.

Di Ció, Miguel Angel. Chile contra Bolivia y Perú, 1879–1883: la guerra de los diez centavos. See item **3213**.

3071 Documents del siglo XIX [i.e. diecinueve] para la historia de Tumbes. Compilado por Jorge Carlín Arce. Lima: Talleres de la Imprenta del Ministerio de Guerra, 1978. 294 p.: ill.; index.

Collection of 167 documents on an official level which have no single focus, suggesting nothing distinctive about the region.

3072 Durand A.N., Francisco. Movimientos sociales urbanos y problema regional: Arequipa, 1967–1973 (IPA/A, 12/13, 1979, p. 79–108)

Regional perspective dramatizes the intensity and importance of general strikes in Arequipa in the period which were based on labor and popular movements with regional and national claims. Explores the force of those movements, their place in Peruvian society, and their regional character. Finds that a local pole of industrial development was consolidated on the basis of continued labor union advances, which passed from a frontist to a popular character. The general strike was the principal weapon of these movements but the state responded with successful divide and conquer tactics. A useful illustration of the problem of contemporary centralism and export orientation in Peru.

3073 Erasmus, Charles J.; Solomon Miller; and **Louis C. Faron.** Contemporary change in traditional communities of Mexico and Peru. Foreword by Julian H. Steward. Urbana: University of Illinois Press, 1978. 302 p.; bibls.; maps; plates; tables (Illini books)

Paperback reprint of well-known seminal works on plantation society resulting from fieldwork conducted in the mid 1960s. Contains the studies on the Peruvian north coast by Solomon Miller and the study of the central coastal peasant society by Louis Faron, both still valuable as points of departure.

Escobari Cusicanqui, Jorge. Historia diplomática de Bolivia: política internacional. See item **3152**.

3074 Fernández Prado Effio, Alberto. La aviación en el Perú. t. 2/3. Lima: Editorial Universo, 1975. 2 v. (532, 520 p.); bibls.; facsims.; ill.; tables.

This work amounts to an amplified, detailed calendar of events in the history of flight in Peru, both civilian and state supported. Lists of names of those attending social affairs or graduated from academies pad the pages of these volumes. Moreover, there is no analysis of the political or social role of the air force or of commercial companies in events.

3075 Fitzgerald, Edmund Valpy Knox. The political economy of Peru, 1956–78: economic development and the restructuring of capital. Cambridge; New York: Cambridge University Press, 1979. 360 p.; bibl.; index.

Sets out a series of theoretical problems specific to the post-World War II sources of underdevelopment in Peru, including discussion of the problems of dependency and dualism, and the development strategies of state capitalism. With this overview in hand, the author reviews the class forces in the history of Peru since 1956, and within that context he analyzes the patterns of production, ownership of resources and income distribution, accumulation of capital and the role of the state in overall planning and in industrialization. Closely and carefully reasoned, this is a highly important study as much for the sources made available to the author as for the argument and conclusions it presents.

3076 Flores Galindo, Alberto. Apuntes sobre las ocupaciones de tierras y el sindicalismo agrario: 1945–1964 (IPA/A, 11/12, 1978, p. 175–185, plates, table)

Points out that in addition to all the known agrarian reforms conducted in Peru since 1964 yet another should be noted, the one conducted in 1963 and 1964 by the peasants themselves, in which 300,000 peasants participated all around the country. This program was characterized by "voluntary" landowner surrender of lands for fear of peasant rebellion. These were not land "invasions" but rather "recuperations," wherein the power of landlords was fundamentally attacked. Suggests the importance of flags as signs of a new peasant nationalism in these movements.

3077 Flores González, Demetrio. Medio siglo de vida sindical en Vitarte, 26 de mayo 1911–26 de mayo 1961. Camaná: EETSA, 197?. 131 p.; bibl.

To commemorate the 50th anniversary of the founding of the Vitarte Textile Workers' Union, this essay was written by one of its most active officers in the 1940s through the 1950s presumably to celebrate the occasion in 1961. Without saying so, this edition appears to be neither an original printing of the manuscript nor a copy of an original publication. It constitutes a chronology of the public social and economic activities of the Vitarte union down to 1961 and does not raise important political issues.

3078 Flores Marín, José and **Rolando Pachas Castilla.** Luchas campesinas en el Perú. t. 1, 1900–1920; t. 2, 1881–1900. Lima: Universidad Nacional Mayor de San Marcos, Seminario de Historia Rural Andina, 1973/1977. 2 v.; facsims.

A catalogue of news items in *El Comercio* in which peasant activities were recorded for posterity. Enough news items were found through careful review of the extant issues in the Biblioteca Nacional, Lima, to question long-held notions. Among them, that peasants did not react to repressive conditions in a massive way in the crucial period of agro-commercial expansion, 1880–1920, and that rural society constitutes an undifferentiated, unchanging mass of peasants. A valuable compilation organized under a half dozen topics, including peasant conflicts, rural worker movements, banditry, miner strikes, oil worker strikes, textile strikes and service worker strikes.

3079 Gavrikov, Iurii P. Peru: ot Inkov do nashikh dnei (Peru: from the Incas to our days). Moscow: Izdatel'stvo Nauka, 1977. 131 p.; plates.

A short Soviet survey of Peruvian history. One of a series of what are, in the USSR, "scholarly-popular" works on the peoples and countries of the world. Includes notes, short bibliography, and index. [R.V. Allen]

3080 Giesecke Sara-Lafosse, Margarita. Masas urbanas y rebelión en la historia: golpe de estado, Lima, 1872. Lima: Centro de Divulgación de Historia Popular (CEDHIP), 1978. 161 p.; ill.; plates; tables.

Aimed as study of the Lima crowd that hanged two military officers in protest against militarism and in favor of civilism as the episode is represented in standard works, which always emphasized the grisly details of mutilation and hanging from the cathedral façade. Seen in the context of the economic and social conditions of the era, the event reveals that a severe rupture within the ruling class led one group, the Baltistas, to plot the downfall of the other, the Gutierristas, by manipulation of out-of-favor sectors of the urban working class whose condition had worsened with the increased inflation that accompanied the guano crisis. Uses police records, death records, newspapers and contemporary sources to good advantage.

3081 González Prada, Manuel. Sobre el militarismo, antología: *Bajo el oprobio.* Selección y presentación de Bruno Podestá. Lima: Editorial Horizonte, 1978. 112 p.; bibl.

Presents the anti-military writings (1904–15) of the famous Peruvian rebel son of the aristocracy and anarchist, one of which, *Bajo el oprobio*, appeared first in Paris, long after he died. Most important, the reliability of these essays is demonstrated in the fastidious retention of marginal notations from the original. The value of the ideas presented here, and in the introduction, lie in their appeal for a new and more complete biography than *Don Manuel* (1930).

3082 Gorman, Stephen M. The state, elite, and export in nineteenth century Peru: toward an alternative reinterpretation of political change (SAGE/JIAS, 21:3, Aug. 1979, p. 395–417, bibl.)

Disagrees with the Berg-Weaver analysis (see *Journal of Inter-American Studies and World Affairs*, 20:1, Feb. 1978), of the relationship of the ruling class to the 19th-century state. Argues that the new urban elite abused state power and thus prefigured Peruvian society. Also says that the post-1895 state took the form of a republic under the control of a plutocracy which, after a brief hiatus, renewed its links with the military, after which a pre-1912 democratic facade disintegrated. The plutocracy of the late guano era is viewed as a proto-bourgeoisie whose power was based on an export enclave economy. The Lima elite, not the state, was the primary beneficiary of enclaved guano export, and if it was too weak to take firm control of the state it also was strong enough to prevent emerging classes from doing so. Theoretical and provocative, based on respected secondary sources including new dissertations.

Graig, Alan K. Placer gold in eastern Peru: the great strike of 1942. See *HLAS 41:5547*.

3083 La Guerra con Chile en sus documentos. Selección y notas de Fernando Lecaros. Lima: Ediciones Rikchay Perú, 1979. 156 p.; map (Rikchay Perú; 6)

Published on the centenary of the war's start, this small group of documents represent the major phases of the war. Each section is preceded by a brief explanatory introduction and a chronology of that phase of the conflict. An overall chronology of military events appears in the front, and appendixes make this a helpful publication. Although the editor claims that many of the documents are inaccessible, in fact most are from public (and here unacknowledged) repositories.

3084 Guerrero, Julio C. 1879–1883 [i.e. Mil ochocientos setenta y nueve a mil ochocientos ochenta y tres]: la guerra de las ocasiones perdidas; con el texto de los Tratados de Ancón y de Arica. Edición, documentación gráfica y epígrafes: Carlos Milla Batres. Lima: Editorial Milla Batres, 1975. 84 p.; 12 leaves of plates: ill.

Strictly surveys the military and diplomatic highlights of the war while the author defends the heroism of General Andrés Cáceres and blames the diplomatic losses of Peru on US stubbornness in following its narrow economic interests. The "lost occasions" refer to military tactics. Based on well-known histories. Excellent plates of major Peruvian and Chilean figures made prominent by the war, and appends war messages and the Treaty of Ancón that followed it. Of minor usefulness.

3085 Hünefeldt, Christine. Los negros en Lima: 1800–1830 (PUCP/H, 3:1, julio 1979, p. 17–51)

Though black slaves constituted only 1/35 of the population of early 19th-century Peru, study of their activities in Lima illuminates the formation of the Peruvian republic. Examines intra-ethnic tensions, role of institutions in the lives of slaves and free persons—divisive as well as cohesive aspects—and notes that free black artisans favored a Spanish victory in independence war because English goods were ruining their business. Concludes, however, that blacks participated in the social formation of Lima and made gains from the independence movement. Differential relations within black society led to advantages for those with skills who also turned out to be lighter skinned and less mixed with Indians. Institutional structures thus hampered unified action among blacks vs. dominant whites, supported the status quo and maintained black society against itself. A strong argument based on fragmentary evidence and subject to further research.

3086 Kaerger, Karl. Condiciones agrarias de la Sierra Sur Peruana: 1899. Prefacio y notas de Magnus Mörner. Lima: Instituto de Estudios Peruanos, 1979. 58 p.; tables (Serie Historia socioeconómica del Cuzco; 2)

One of the best trained observers of Peru at the turn-of-the-century—in the tradition of von Tschudi and Raimondi—was Kaerger, a professor of agronomy in Berlin who published studies of rural society in Europe, Africa and Brazil. This book consists of excerpts from a two-volume work on agriculture and colonization in South America, which covered Argentina, Bolivia, Peru, Ecuador and Mexico. The author spent a week in the Peruvian sierra as part of a longer journey and depended heavily for his information upon large landowners. Nevertheless, his insights make this report invaluable. This extract contains the sections in which he described working conditions in the sierra, and agricultural characteristics of the sierra and lower valleys. Includes a helpful introductory essay and amplificatory notes by Magnus Mörner. Gives agricultural wages, farming technology in the Juliaca-Sicuani and Arequipa regions, land and product measurements and prices, cattle raising and other activities. This translation is part of a larger history in progress of rural society in the Cuzco region.

3087 Kapsoli E., Wilfredo. Las luchas obreras en el Perú, 1900–1919: por las ocho horas de trabajo. Lima: Delva Editores, 1976. 176 p.; bibl.

Republication—with contemporary observations by L. Curletti and F. Mostajo on living-and-working conditions in the early 20th century appended—of a short work first published in 1968 and which formed the basis of later, much amplified studies by this author of working class history.

3088 ———. Los movimientos campesinos en el Perú, 1879–1965: ensayos. Lima: Delva Editores, 1977. 300 p.; plates.

Author-editor sees four major stages in the development of peasant movements in Peru: 1) 1879–1896, an "anti-fiscal" period; 2) millenarianism in 1919–1930; 3) reformist movements in 1945–1948; and 4) revolutionary movements in 1956–1965. Discussion of these stages is followed by: a textual analysis of a document from the Atusparia revolt of 1885 by Manuel Valladares and Jean Piel; an essay on Ezequiel Urviola, a Puno peasant leader of the early 20th century, by Antonio Rengifo; a brief study of Arequipa peasant uprisings related to wool exports by A. Flores Galindo; an essay on 20th-century peasant movements in the Jequetepeque Valley of the coast by M. Burga; a study of peasant actions in Hacienda Lauramarca near Cuzco in the 1920s; and a study of settlements and struggles for control of land in the Perené River region of the Peruvian jungle, between the Peruvian Corporation and local settlers, during the 1950s and 1960s. A dispersed though useful collection.

3089 ———. Movimientos sociales en Cayaltí: 1915–1919 (IPA/A, 11/12, 1978, p. 103–121, bibl., tables)

Comparison of an uprising in 1915 with another in 1919 on the same plantation, discusses social context, motives, issues and their resolution, narrowly confining comment to the immediate property. Documented with plantation records in the Archivo del Fuero Agrario, Lima.

3090 Klaiber, Jeffrey L. El APRA: religión y legitimidad popular (UP/A, 4:8, 1978, p. 49–58)

Argues that APRA's longevity is due not only to its ideology but also to its ability to absorb, select and channel popular myths and sentiments in the advancement of a party cause. Using religious symbols and images of the 1930s and 1940s, and their use by APRA, this study explores the ramifications of the important concept of political legitimacy and its popular support. An effective means for examining the contradictory phenomenon of a historically anti-clerical party winning the support of deeply religious masses in Peru in part through manipulation of religious symbols. Sources include interviews with major Aprista founders and leaders. For political scientist's comment, see *HLAS 41:7336*.

3091 ———. Los cholos y los rotos: actitudes raciales durante la Guerra del Pacífico (PUCP/H, 21:1, julio 1978, p. 27–37, bibl.)

Insightful study of the attitudes of leading intellectuals and politicians of both Chile and Peru, among others, revealing a racist bias in the way they blamed the loss of the War of the Pacific on the one hand, and laid a basis for a Chilean victory on the other, on the genetic or ethnic characteristics of the national populations involved in the struggle. This work suggests that the War of the Pacific released many of these irrational arguments on both sides. Based on newspaper and contemporary accounts.

3092 ———. Religión y revolución en los Andes en el siglo XIX (PUCP/H, 1:1, julio 1977, p. 93–111, bibl.)

Studies five Indian uprisings of the 19th century, especially the one in Huaraz in 1885, to sharpen our view of the role of the Church among Indians. Asserts that contrary to the ideas promoted by Manuel González Prada, the late 19th-century men of the cloth participated along with and in support of a pastoral ideology of social justice and that they saw in popular Catholicism an inspiration and legitimation of their cause. A thought-provoking, insightful study which makes limited use of primary documentation.

Kuczynski, Pedro-Pablo. Peruvian democracy under economic stress: an account of the Belaúnde Administration, 1963–1968. See *HLAS 41:3265*.

3093 Luna Vegas, Ricardo. Mariátegui, Haya de la Torre y la verdad histórica. Lima: Retama Editorial, 1978. 139 p.; bibl. (Historia política; 3)

Popular level, biographical account of the organizing and theorizing activities of both men which plays down the issues which separated the two major Peruvian ideologues of the 20th century. Of little scholarly value.

3094 Macera dall'Orso, Pablo. La imagen francesa del Perú: siglos XVI–XIX. Lima: Instituto Nacional de Cultura, 1976. 174 p.; bibl.

This work is based on research undertaken when the author began his studies in France. He traces the development of and changes in the image of Peru in the writings of French scholars and travelers since the 16th century, by evaluating the writers' veracity and perceptual abilities. In the final third of the essay, the author discusses the commentators themselves and places their views in the proper social context, an analysis not undertaken before. Valuable chronological bibliography of travelers appended.

3095 ———. Población rural en haciendas: 1876. Lima: Universidad Nacional Mayor de San Marcos, Seminario de Historia Rural Andina, Dirección Universitaria de Proyección Social, 1976. 82 p.; tables.

Extracts the tables of this particular sub-heading of the national census of 1876, and supplies the information given in table form. Limited comments by way of endnotes and no introductory essay. A hasty job.

———. Trabajos de historia. See item **2645**.

3096 Manrique, Nelson. Los movimientos campesinos en la Guerra del Pacífico (IPA/A, 11/12, 1978, p. 71–101)

Studies uprisings of peasant communities around Huancayo which occurred while Chilean armies were present in the region, and provides evidence that the peasant guerrilla armies that fought the Chileans were not under the command or control of the Peruvian government-in-exile, but that they fought on the basis of agreed upon class and community goals. A perceptive, detailed class analysis of high historical merit, this is part of a larger study of peasants and nationalism.

Martín, José Carlos. Manuel Pardo en Chile. See item **3237**.

3097 Masterson, Daniel M. Soldiers, sailors, and apristas: conspiracy and power politics in Peru, 1932–1948 (*in* The underside of Latin American history. Edited by John I. Bratzel and Daniel M. Masterson. East Lansing: Michigan State University, The Latin American Studies Center, 1977, p. 24–42, bibl. [Monograph series; 16])

Author draws insightful distinction, as of 1932, between military hatred for APRA and military need for civilian support in conspiracies to subvert legal processes. Stresses APRA instigation of these plots and willingness to participate in order to gain power, and infers that APRA-military tactics persist.

However, study devoid of suggestion that principles, ideology or any objective other than power underlay these conspiracies.

3098 Melgar, Jorge. A Belaúnde lo que es de Belaúnde. Lima: n.p., 1973. 278 p.; tables.

The work of an early Belaúnde organizer, journalist and Acción Popular congressional representative in 1963 whose effort to set out the impact of his candidate on the political process in Peru during the 1960s becomes a more important source with the passage of the 1980 election. Lists of Belaúnde cabinets by position (1963–68) appended.

3099 Mörner, Magnus. La sociedad rural cusqueña en la perspectiva histórica (IPA/A, 12/13, 1979, p. 219–229)

Announces and outlines a project to study the evolution of the agrarian structures of Cuzco from the end of the colonial period to 1969. Begun in 1977 and sponsored by the Instituto de Estudios Peruanos, Lima, and the Institute of Latin American Studies of the University of Stockholm, Sweden, the project's intention is the study of factors of change and structural resistance over a long period in a "traditional" rural society, from a quantitative point of view. Regional, provincial, district and production unit (plantation/community) studies are underway. Describes the division of labor among the collaborators in the project, the sources under examination, and some early publications that appeared in the early stages of the project.

3100 Moya Obeso, Alberto. Sindicalismo aprista y sindicalismo clasista en el Perú, 1920–1956. Lima: Pontificia Universidad Católica del Perú, Programa de Perfeccionamiento en Ciencias Sociales, 1977. 2 v.; bibl.

Highly disciplined, carefully organized study of the labor history of Peru in the 20th century which stresses a singularly important theme: the relation between the ideology of the labor movement and its organization. The study aims to illustrate to the working class movement the difference between anti-imperialism and "its true historic interests." Heavily influenced by the work of Sulmont and Quijano, it concentrates on the formation of the CGTP on the basis of enclaved industries to the north and center, places the formation of the CGTP in the context of international labor movements, "popular front" tactics, and the consequent failure of Community Party direction. The subsequent rise and fall of APRA, greater penetration of US investment and labor organization weaknesses are laid ultimately to the uneven processes of capitalist expansion. Vol. 2 contains copies of important labor documents of the period covered.

3101 Normano, João Frederico and **Antonello Gerbi.** The Japanese in South America: an introductory survey with special reference to Peru. New York: AMS Press, 1978. 135 p.; bibl.; index.

Reprint of a 1943 study, over half of which is devoted to Peru, and a chapter deals with Brazil. A brief historical background is followed by demographic-economic analysis, trade between Japan and Peru, and anti-Japanese legislation in Peru. Immigration and migration tables cover both Peru and Brazil. A wartime atmosphere prevails.

Nunn, Frederick M. European military influence in South America: the origins and nature of professional militarism in Argentina, Brazil, Chile and Peru, 1890–1940. See item **1933b**.

3102 Ortiz, Dionisio. El Perené: reseña histórica de una importante región de la selva peruana. Lima: Imprenta Editorial San Antonio, 1978. 465 p.; appendix; bibl.; ill.

Narrative survey by a Franciscan who wishes to draw attention to the missionary possibilities of his famous area of settlement plans and failures. Helpful chronology of events appended.

3103 Pachas Castilla, Rolando. Economía y sociedad en el Valle de Chincha: 1860–1919. Lima: Universidad Nacional Mayor de San Marcos, Seminario de Historia Rural Andina, 1976. 129 p.

Study of the rise of agrarian capitalist structure in a south coast valley, including the impact of export on the region. Relies upon prefectural exports of Ica department, sub-prefectural reports of Chincha, scarce and poorly preserved as they are, along with 20th-century government publications and newspapers. In a search for critical junctures around which social change occurred, discusses production of wine, cotton and sugar raising, the rise of a labor movement around

1917, and subdivisions within peasant society—tenants, sub-tenants and contracted day-labor.

Palma, Ricardo. Cartas a Piérola sobre la ocupación chilena de Lima. See item **3249**.

3104 Palomino, Abdón. Andahuaylas, 1974: un movimiento de reivindicación campesina dentro del proceso de reforma agraria (IPA/A, 11/12, 1978, p. 187–211, plate)

A discussion of the events that encouraged the peasant land occupations in Andahuaylas province in the mid-1970s from a class perspective. The agrarian reform of 1969 was not applied to all peasants here until 1974 because of the "segmentary" agrarian policy of the government. In the meantime, an agrarian union movement took shape and seized lands long under claim. Examines the actions of peasants, landlords (all local *mestizos*), and the repressive response of the military state, making this one of the earliest documented studies of the provincial impact of the agrarian reform of 1969.

3105 Peasant cooperation and capitalist expansion in central Peru. Edited by Norman Long and Bryan R. Roberts. Austin: University of Texas, Institute of Latin American Studies, 1978. 349 p.; bibl.; maps; tables (Latin American monographs; 46)

A regional study of the Mantaro region that provides a number of examples of rural social antagonism at the village level and whose overall purpose is to examine the validity of sociological research which influenced the 1969 military agrarian reform. Varied in scope, from re-study of Muquiyauyo cooperativism to industrial cooperativism in Huancayo, 1960s land occupations in Huasicancha, monopoly politics in Pucará and coalition politics in Matahuasi, the cases are always set in historical perspective, pointing out the abrupt changes in agricultural production and social organization of the late 19th century, and all of them are copiously documented from local archival sources and extensive interviews collected over two years of residence in the region. The conclusions of the editors offer significant challenges to the dependency perspective as well as to a more Parsonian framework for study of rural development—or underdevelopment. Essential reading for social historians of Peru.

3106 Pease García, Henry. Los caminos del poder: tres años de crisis en la escena política. Lima: Centro de Estudios y Promoción del Desarrollo, 1979. 363 p.

A class analysis of the "second phase" of the 12-year military regime in Peru which sets the fall of Velasco (1975) within the global meaning of the government that followed him. Pt. 2 periodizes the accomplishments of Velasco and the popular response to him, and reviews the search by his successors for a political escape from his policies. The isolation of the military government from non-military institutional or sectoral support is said to have occurred when a broad spectrum of intellectual leaders suddenly was exiled in Aug. 1975. Also notes the importance of various popular strikes and movements against the "second phase" government since 1976. Sources consist largely of data previously collected and subsequently published by the author along with colleagues. A useful analysis of recent events because it is set in historical perspective.

Philip H. & A.S.W. Rosenbach Foundation. A calendar of the Peruvian and other South American manuscripts in the Philip H. & A.S.W. Rosenbach Foundation, 1536–1914. See item **2652**.

3107 Pike, Fredrick B. Religion, collectivism, and intrahistory: the Peruvian ideal of dependence (JLAS, 10:2, Nov. 1978, p. 239–262)

An interpretation of a central process in Peruvian history: the nexus of collectivist and religious ideas and attitudes, and their impact upon Peruvian society and politics. "Intrahistory" refers to the nearly unrecorded behavior of the masses. An expression of considerable insight but with essentially pessimistic conclusions and assumptions.

3108 Quijano, Aníbal. Imperialismo, clases sociales y estado en el Perú: 1895–1930 (*in* Clases sociales y crisis política en América Latina: seminario de Oaxaca. Edited by Benítez Zenteno. México: Siglo XXI Editores, 1977, p. 113–205)

Originally a presentation made in Oaxaca in 1977, this thought piece is extremely valuable for its perspective on the relation between imperialist domination and the shape of both social classes and the state—and their consequences for revolutionary politics. Generated by ideas on the "structural dependency" of Latin American social formations, the essay examines the outlines of the historical formation of Peruvian classes. Especially focuses on the imperialist phase in the 19th century, arguing that capitalist trade did not require the establishment of capitalist relations of production but rather relations he calls capitalist-imperialist, marked specifically by the class rather than the national character of investments. These relations are viewed in several stages, from semicolonial through imperialist hegemonic, in which their impact on social classes and the state is considered. In the end the author speculates on the meaning of hegemonic imperialism for the weakened oligarchic state. Perceptive essay rooted in advanced Marxist theories worth testing, followed by the comments of Octavio Ianni, Orlando Fals Borda, José Luis Reyna and Manuel Villa (p. 151–205). For sociologist's comment, see *HLAS 41:9237*.

3109 ———. El Perú en la crisis de los años 30 (*in* Antezana, Luis and others. América Latina en los años treinta. México: Universidad Nacional Autónoma de México, Instituto de Investigaciones Sociales, 1977, p. 239–302)

Uses internal developments of the 1930s, whose revolutionary and counter-revolutionary character was so outstanding in Peru, as they were made more acute by the international crisis of capitalism, and which form the most immediate context for present-day tendencies in this author's view, to illuminate contemporary political problems. Examines three major periods, 1898–1919, 1919–30, and further subdivides 1930–33, examining financial and political events in turn which, when their consequences for the popular masses are suggested, demonstrate the seriousness of the crisis of that era for subsequent Peruvian politics. A thought-provoking essay, marred by the author's failure to cite recent studies.

3110 Ramos Alva, Alfonso. Siete tesis equivocadas del marxismo-leninismo sobre Indoamérica. 3. ed. Lima: IDEA, 1978. 63 p.; bibl. (Publicaciones del Instituto de Estudios Antimperialistas; 2)

Not much to be learned here about Aprista analysis of historical development, underdevelopment, social theory or theory of any sort; more a polemical effort than a serious essay setting out a position.

Randall, Laura Regina Rosenbaum. A comparative economic history of Latin America: 1500–1914. See item **1808a**.

3111 Real de Azúa, Mario Federico. La misión diplomática del peruano Manuel Corpancho: 1862–1863 (CM/HM, 28:1, jul./sept. 1978, p. 62–81)

An episode in the diplomatic relations of Peru and Mexico which shows that the tradition of political exile is more deeply rooted in Peru than has been thought to be the case. Focuses on the relations of Peru with the Benito Juárez government. Appendix and references.

3112 Reátegui Cháves, Wilson. Explotación agropecuaria y las movilizaciones campesinas en Lauramarca-Cusco. Lima: Universidad Nacional Mayor de San Marcos, 1977. 2 v. (230 p.) (Continuous pagination); tables.

Originally a thesis at San Marcos, this study focuses on the political economy of Hacienda Lauramarca in the Cuzco region in order to clarify its relations of authority and servility between owners and peasants, as well as their conflicts, through the mechanisms of exploitation in a pastoral system since the 1920s. Based on documents from the Ministerior de Trabajo y Asuntos Indígenas—until recently a branch of SINAMOS—census data, official and organization bulletins, newspapers, periodicals, pamphlets and field interviews. Details the process of marketing of pastoral production while the process of expropriation occurred after 1940, directed by the major landlords, the Lomellini family, who consigned most of their production to the international market. Community movements since 1923 against exploitation also are analyzed, and the role of the state is examined. Vol. 2 consists of bibliography and reprints of documents on community struggles, among others.

3113 Rénique, Gerardo. Comunidades campesinos y "recuperaciones" de tierras: Valle de Mantaro. Lima: Universidad Nacional Agraria La Molina, Taller de Estudios Andinos, n.d. 1 v. (Unpaged) (Serie: Andes Centrales; 4)

A compilation of documents illustrating the struggles of various peasant communities against Hacienda Laive near Huancayo on a number of issues (1930–47) coupled with two brief studies of the conflict between village shepherds and the centralizing process conducted by major landowners. Unfortunately the repository for the edited documents is not made clear, nor is there an introduction setting them in context.

3114 ———. Movimientos campesinos en la Sociedad Ganadera del Centro: 1910–1950 (IPA/A, 11/12, 1978, p. 129–150, table)

Analysis of peasant movements on a group of haciendas owned by the company in the context of modifications in the productive structure over the period. The extension of cattle-raising (1900–30) was followed by modernization of the means of production (1930–60). In the early period shepherds fled indebtedness but in the later era they fought cattlement to reclaim the land. Radicalization of shepherds after World War II was led by local APRA organizers while national APRA leadership merely sought to legislate agrarian reform. This disarticulation is documented with newspaper and materials from the Archivo del Fuero Agrario, Lima.

3115 **Rénique, José Luis.** Los descentralistas arequipeños en la crisis del 30 (IPA/A, 12/13, 1979, p. 51–78)

An exacerbation of regional differences in the 1930s provides the opportunity for this examination of commercial and professional Arequipa sectors which demanded economic and political autocracy in order to achieve local development. Interests formed by the rise of a local wool, flour and wheat economy developed within the context of the Sánchez Cerro movement. Together with a base of popular support for the colonel, the two sectors formed the Decentralist Party in 1931. The party won military support but failed to achieve its national goals when its agro-export leaders were unable to overcome their localist aspirations with a nationally appealing ideology. Based on AGN materials for the 1930s and personal archives of involved individuals plus newspapers. An impressive study.

Reyno Gutiérrez, Manuel. Algunos antecedentes históricos sobre la contraposición peruana para otorgar una salida al Pacífico a Bolivia. See item **3177**.

3116 **Rodríguez Pastor, Humberto.** Una rebelión de culíes chinos Pativilca, 1870 (IPA/A, 11/12, 1978, p. 59–69)

Analysis of uprisings by Chinese plantation workers in north coast Lima department that spread to the towns and were crushed in 14 hours by government troops. Concludes that the limited goals of these groups were shaped by their isolation on different plantations and the cause of their discontent was a combination of repressive conditions of work and low chances for escape. Comments that repressive sexual conditions encouraged celibacy among Chinese population contractees at best and homosexuality at worst. Based on wide reading in plantation records and considerable anthropological field work.

3117 ———. Los trabajadores chinos culíes en el Perú: artículos históricos. Lima: n.p., 1977. 53 p.; ill.; tables (mimeo)

A compilation of articles on draft Chinese plantation laborers, stressing their resistance to oppressive conditions. Much of the material was gathered in the Archivo del Fuero Agrario collection, of which the author was a founder and is currently a co-director. Most of the articles appeared in various periodicals, including *La Prensa, El Correo,* and *Marka,* between 1975–77. Marred by a poor job of reproduction. Includes helpful tales on the movement of Chinese through plantations.

3118 **Samaniego L., Carlos** and **Bryan Roberts.** El significado de la SAIS de la sierra central del Perú: el caso de las SAIS Cahuide. Lima: Universidad Nacional Agraria La Molina, Centro de Investigaciones Socio-Económicos, 1976? 1 v. (Unpaged) (mimeo)

Analyzes the application of the 1969 agrarian reform to the plantation region formerly known as Sociedad Ganadera del Centro and three other entities, altogether forming one-half million hectares, which became SAIS Cahuide, located in the Mantaro valley. Analysis is made in terms of the local social structure and political process that went into the formation of the SAIS, especially gives attention to the shepherd economy and political movements, and concludes that the problems faced by the SAIS since its inception in 1970 are due to the broader structure of agricultural capitalism within which community needs were made to fit.

3119 Scott, C.D. Peasants, proletarianisation and the articulation of modes of production: the case of sugar cane cutters in northern Peru, 1940–69 (JPS, 3:3, April 1976, p. 321–342, bibl., map)

Examines the theoretical problem of the articulation of capitalist with pre-capitalist modes of production, specifically examining problems of labor abundance and scarcity under conditions of seasonal migration, illustrating with the case of sugar cane cutters on the Peruvian north coast, sketchy from the 1890s to the 1940s, 1940 to 1960 in detail and less so in the period of military agrarian reform of the 1970s. Important and rigorous description and analysis of the *enganche* system (obligatory labor recruitment) followed by a discussion of changes in the labor market as a result of increased surplus of labor and mechanization of agriculture. Suggests political consequences of these changes. Based on important plantation records, official publications and over two years research and interviews in Peru. Valuable study for economists and historians. For economist's comment, see *HLAS 41:3289*.

3120 Skinner, Geraldine. José Carlos Mariátegui and the emergence of the Peruvian socialist movement (SS, 43:4, Winter 1979/1980, p. 447–471)

Aims to extract Mariátegui from the common misuse of his ideas by current political groups. To do so, this essay ignores his European travels and concentrates on the Peruvian influence on his socialism. Discusses his ideas on capitalist development and the formation of social classes in Peru in light of the general strike of 1919, the rise of conflict between Mariátegui and Haya, the creation of the PSP and the CGTP, and concludes that Mariátegui rejected Leninism in favor of Sorelian socialism. Based almost exclusively upon his writings.

3121 Slater, David. El capitalismo subdesarrollado y la organización del espacio, Perú, 1920–1940 (IPA/A, 12/13, 1979, p. 109–143, map)

Re-issue in translation of a study that appeared earlier in the *Revue Tiers Monde* (see *HLAS 38:3513*).

3122 Smith, Gavin A. Socio-economic differentiation and relations of production among rural-based petty producers in central Peru: 1800 to 1970 (JPS, 6:3, April 1979, p. 286–310, bibl.)

Argues that the process of sub-division within society wherein fundamental conflict arises between formerly harmonic groups only becomes visible by study of specific situations over long periods of time, and uses the case of events among Huasicancha shepherds to illustrate the point. Based on interviews and local archival materials in Huancayo.

Soto Quijano, Clemente; Arturo Urbano San Martín; and **Zenón E. Vargas Morales.** Empobrecimiento absoluto y relativo: Paramonga. See *HLAS 41:1320*.

Spalding, Karen. Estructura de clases en la sierra peruana: 1750–1920. See item **2657**.

3123 Tamayo, José Armando. Historia social del Cuzco republicano. Lima: s.n., 1978. 335 p.; bibl.; 12 leaves of plates: ill.; index.

Thoughtful prologue by Jorge Basadre notes influence of *Annales* studies for the opening of local archives and reflects on the meaning of Cuzco as a center of power throughout its history before 1814. Study suggests that Cuzco region is *sui generis*, linked permanently with Apurimac and Madre de Dios, in the Andean south of Peru. Thus, the model for its history comes from within its own mode of production and the peculiarities of its cultural form. Sees Cuzco as a space dominated by its landlord class until 1969, with its contradictions worked out in three stages: a 19th-century epoch of decadence and stagnation, and two 20th-century dynamic cycles called the first modernization (1895–1945) and the second modernization (1945–75). A historiographical study as well as a social history, this work also examines threads that link Cuzco with the intellectual history of Peru and finds that the binding is uneven. Wide exploration of the sources, written and oral, statistical and literary, published and unpublished, to determine the intellectual, economic, political, climatic and social bases of changes in the Cuzco region. Special emphasis is placed on the role of the University of San Antonio Abad in the process, and ends with a discussion of the impact of the agrarian reforms of 1961–75. A genuine *tour de force* in the local and regional history of Peru, this study will provoke many future research efforts.

Tantaleán Arbulú, Javier and **Augusto Pérez-Rosas Cáceres.** Referencias bibliográficas para el estudio de la economía peruana: 1830–1977. See *HLAS 41:49*.

Testimonios y recuerdos de la Guerra del Pacífico. See item **3272**.

3124 Thompson, Stephen I. Assimilation and nonassimilation of Asian-Americans and Asian-Peruvians (CSSH, 21:4, Oct. 1979, p. 572–588, bibl.)

Takes issue with findings of Bernard Wong (see item **3131**) that attitudes of the larger society determined successful assimilation of Chinese migrants to Lima and New York, by studying Japanese immigrants in both areas. Concludes that Wong's criteria were too narrow. More sociology than history but of potential use of the historian even if author has not used the work of C. Harvey Gardiner on Japanese in Peru (see *HLAS 38:3472*).

Thorndike, Guillermo. Vienen los chilenos. See item **3274**.

3125 Thorp, Rosemary and **Geoffrey Bertram.** Peru, 1890–1977: growth and policy in an open economy. New York: Columbia University Press, 1978. 475 p.; bibl.; index; tables.

Seeks to establish growth patterns quantitatively and by sector, to test growth and development theory, and to evaluate the Peruvian experience in its present historical stage. Sources drawn from government agencies, contemporary accounts, business periodicals and recent works. The authors examine the hypothesis that agents of change in the Peruvian economy which were imported from abroad were successful primarily because of the needs of the internal bourgeoisie and only secondarily because of the demands by outside capitalists. Early chapters study export crops (1890–1930) under the direction of progressive entrepreneurs which, with little state help, failed to stimulate a home market. When control of mining by foreign enterprises received state blessings, the combination of processes acted as a severe handicap to growth in the non-export sector over the early 20th century. The period 1930–48 is seen as an era of opportunity for renewed economic autonomy which was missed or forsaken, resulting in a post-1948 era of laissez-faire export-led growth whose difficulties brought on the military government of 1969 and after. This volume provides close scrutiny of dependency theory while it makes careful use of existing studies. It is replete with statistical data and offers a strong corrective of extreme dependency arguments. For economist's comment, see *HLAS 41:3292*.

3126 Tigner, James L. The Ryukyuans in Peru: 1906–1952 (AAFH/TAM, 35:1, July 1978, p. 20–44, tables)

Numbers of immigrants, stages of immigration, public policy and public opinion in Peru and among the Ryukyuan settlers, both first generation and later, all are examined in this survey of the economic and social history of Japanese immigrants to Peru. Effective use is made of Japanese as well as Peruvian sources. Important distinctions between generations and occupation groups are noted in the tables.

3127 Urquiaga, José. Indios: Puno, 1916. Lima: Universidad Nacional Mayor de San Marcos, Seminario de Historia Rural Andina, 1977. 60 p.

Written in 1916 as a response to the Puno uprising of 1915, this study also includes a description of Indian life in Puno, especially emphasizing social analysis of the region, and ends with a description of the Rumi Maqui movement. This mimeograph reprint puts the movement in context.

Vanden, Harry E. Mariátegui: marxismo, comunismo, and other bibliographic notes. See *HLAS 41:14*.

———. The peasants as a revolutionary class: an early Latin American view. See item **1950**.

3128 Vassallo, Manuel. Rumi Maqui y la nacionalidad quechua (IPA/A, 11/12, 1978, p. 123–127, facsim.)

A fragment of knowledge of a Quechua "nationalist" movement at the turn of the 20th century in Chucuito in the Puno region, led by a Jauja-born former prefect who shed his criollo identity, and which ended in a massacre by government troops. With evidence of signed documents and a suggestion of reluctance to publicize the repression on the part of locals for fear of their lives, this one is a real teaser.

3129 Vietmeyer, Noel D. Incredible odyssey of a visionary Victorian peddler

(Smithsonian [Smithsonian Institution, Washington] Aug. 1978, p. 91–102)

Incident of British entrepreneur's effort to smuggle alpacas out of Peru to Australia for breeding. The effort failed for lack of government support and competition from merino sheep. Also details Charles Ledger's other smuggling venture—to transplant cinchona trees. Through theft the effort finally resulted in the transplanting of high-quinine seedlings to Dutch-held plantations of southeast Asia in the 1870s, where by the 1930s Java produced 87 percent of the world's supply. Author does not give sources but inclusion of Ledger's personal correspondence makes this essay useful for the classroom. For geographer's comment, see *HLAS 41:5396*.

3130 Werlich, David P. Peru: a short history. Carbondale: Southern Illinois University Press, 1978. 434 p.; bibl.; index; maps.

An introductory survey welcome because it stresses 20th-century events, this volume reaches for a popular audience and on the whole succeeds. Contains a bibliographic essay which, though it is policy oriented, will be useful for those who wish to pursue the subject in a number of directions.

3131 Wong, Bernard. A comparative study of the assimilation of the Chinese in New York City and Lima, Peru (CSSH, 20:3, July 1978, p. 333–358, bibl.)

Concludes on the basis of interviews, recent census data and work in assimilation theory that the Lima Chinese community was better assimilated than that of New York. The approach used concentrates on the degree to which the study populations have met assimilation criteria lodged in the structure of the larger society. An ahistorical but nevertheless useful essay. For another opinion, see item **3124**.

3132 Yang, Alexander Chung Yuan. O comércio dos "coolie" (USP/RH, 56:112, out./nov. 1977, p. 419–428, tables)

A general survey of the social and political problems raised by the trade in Chinese laborers. Of interest to scholars of every area where such labor was used.

3133 Zitor (pseudonym). Historia de las principales huelgas y paros obreros habidos en el Perú, 1896–1946. Lima: Universidad Nacional Mayor de San Marcos, 1976. 74 p. (mimeo)

Reprint of an essay first done in typescript, this work surveys the 19th century and, after noting some outstanding labor conflicts in largely urban centers after 1883, describing essential events, examines the early 20th century and ends with the Trujillo uprising of 1931. This typescript was located in the Biblioteca Nacional and now joins other, better organized and presented works on the subject.

Bolivia and Chile

ANN HAGERMAN JOHNSON, *Lecturer, History Department, University of California, Davis*

THE HISTORIOGRAPHY OF 19th- AND 20th-CENTURY Bolivia and Chile continues to generate two types of works: 1) patriotically motivated political-military histories and documents (especially noticeable this biennium in which the centennial of the War of the Pacific led to an extraordinary outpouring of memoirs, analyses and diatribes); and 2) detailed social or economic investigations with little or no analysis and unclear usefulness. However, the record number of publications listed in this section (for example, this volume of *HLAS* lists 60 percent more work on Bolivian history than did volumes 38 or 40) includes many well-motivated and researched studies which may foreshadow the increasing relevance of historical inquiry.

For Bolivia, the tired topics of wars, revolutions and politics were subject to some fresh reinterpretations, such as the Bratzel article on the Chaco dispute (item **3141**), Mayorga's analysis of the 1952 revolution (item **3163**), and the three publications by Lora on political parties, organized labor and recent national problems (items **3160–3162**). Perhaps more significant, several Bolivian scholars consciously attempted, with varying success, to write histories of the long-ignored common people and their environment. The best of these, Fernando Cajías de la Vega's intensive study of Atacama, was originally his university thesis, and may indicate the new emphasis of younger Bolivian historians (item **3142**).

For Chile, there is finally a good brief general history in English (item **3233**) to replace, with updated themes and interpretations, the aged work by Luis Galdames. Mamalakis' ambitious work on Chilean economic history (item **3236**), when supplemented by Cariola and Sunkel's essay on the 1830–1930 period (item **3206**), provides a new general overview of that topic. Also, there are a few fine new monographs, such as Heise's work on the early independence period (item **3226**), Kirsch's study of early industrialization (item **3231**), and Drake's timely analysis of socialism (item **3215**).

In other areas of Chilean history, serious scholarship commands a few topics. The causes and impact of foreign control of mining and commerce continues to be a favorite theme, with about a dozen thoughtful analyses annotated in the following pages. The flood of critiques of the Allende years, 1973 coup, and its aftermath, continues, though at a somewhat diminished rate (see *HLAS 41*, p. 506–516, for a more extensive bibliography of recent publications on the subject). Chilean intellectual history benefitted recently from several thoughtful reinterpretations: 1) Rafael Caldera "Andrés Bello" (item **3204**); 2) Edgard Greene "La generación literaria chilena de 1938" (item **3225**); 3) Peter J. Sehlinger "Valentín Letelier" (item **3265**); and 4) Allen Woll "Positivism and History in Nineteenth Century Chile" (item **3279**). The articles by Salinas (item **2822**), McCaa (item **3235**), and Johnson (item **3230**), indicate the tantalizing potential of demographic history.

Of the new bibliographic resources, the annotations of Cariola and Sunkel (item **3206**) provide an outstanding guide to primary sources for the economic and social history of Chile (1830–1930). Mamalakis' overview of Chilean statistical sources is the leading edge of his monumental work on this topic entitled *Historical statistics of Chile* (see *HLAS 41:3229*). Finally Sater's informed bibliographic essay (item **3263**) provides a valuable guide to recent secondary works on political, economic and social Chilean history.

BOLIVIA

3134 Alvarez España, Waldo. Los gráficos en Bolivia de la organización y luchas de los trabajadores de este sector social. La Paz: s.n., 1977. 179 p.; bibl.

In a conscious attempt to write the history of the "submerged mass" rather than that of great men and war, the author does a valiant pioneering study of the printing industry since 1905, focusing on the post-1935 period. Includes extensive reproductions of documents from newspapers, legislation, union publications, and speeches.

3135 Antezana, Luis E. Bolivia en las crisis de los años treinta (*in* Antezana, Luis and others. América Latina en los años treinta. México: UNAM, Instituto de Investigaciones Sociales, 1977, p. 193–213)

After a brief statement of the general economic and political effects of the 1930 depression on Bolivia, analyzes the response of the labor movement to new conditions. Author's novel thesis contends that the governing class used the Chaco War in an unsuccessful attempt to sidetrack a social revolution.

3136 Ayala Z., Alfredo. Historia de Bolivia en cuadros sinópticos. La Paz: Editorial Don Bosco, 1976. 424 p.

Written as a chronological outline, this work by a well-qualified historian provides a handy guide to the key events and personalities of Bolivian history from preconquest to 1972.

3137 Ballivian y Rojas, Vicente de. Archivo Boliviano: colección de documentos relativos a la historia de Bolivia, durante la época colonial con un catálogo de obras impresas y de manuscritos, que tratan de ese parte de la América Meridional. t. 1. 2. ed. La Paz: Editorial Casa Municipal de la Cultura Franz Tamayo, 1977. 352 p. (Biblioteca Paceña. Nueva serie)

This valuable research aid is a reprinting of an 1872 publication by a foremost Bolivian historian. Contains: 1) the documents of Sebastián de Segurola on the seige of La Paz, 1781–82; 2) a 1771 summary of major annual events of Potosí, 1545–1702; and 3) a catalogue of manuscripts and published documents on Bolivian history located in Madrid, London, and private collections.

3138 Barnadas, Josep María. Apuntes para una historia aymara. 2. ed. La Paz: Centro de Investigación y Promoción del Campesinado, 1978. 113 p.; bibl.; index (Cuadernos de investigación CIPCA; 6)

A sympathetic and intelligent, although brief, history of the Aymara Indians from conquest to 1952, based on a variety of primary sources. An important first-step toward a more complete history of this indigenous people.

3139 Barrero, Francisco. Radepa y la Revolución Nacional. La Paz: Empresa Editora Urquizo, 1976. 398 p.

Although passionately written, this book better than most cuts through the inflamed literature to present an indepth discussion of the origins, course and suppression of the National Revolution. Focuses on the role of the dissident group of Chaco War soldiers called Radepa, short for "Razón de Patria."

Bermúdez Miral, Oscar. Repercusiones en Cobija de la guerra con España. See item **3198**.

Bolivia. Corte Supreme de Justicia. Sesquicentenario, 1827–16 de julio–1977. See *HLAS 41:7370*.

3140 Botelho Gosálvez, Raúl. Breve historia del litoral boliviano: la misión Jaimes Freyre en Santiago. La Paz: Ediciones Populares Ultima Hora, 1978. 151 p.; bibl.; maps (Colección Litoral boliviano. Biblioteca popular boliviana de Ultima Hora)

Reargues the legitimacy of original and current claims to the Charaña area, discusses the Bolivian mission to Chile in 1922 to negotiate a port, and reprints relevant documents. Written from a Bolivian viewpoint, this contains no really new information or insights.

3141 Bratzel, John F. The Chaco dispute and the search for prestige (*in* The underside of Latin American history [see item **1948**] p. 88–106, bibl.)

Theorizes that Paraguay's and Bolivia's need to regain prestige led to the Chaco War, and that competition between neighboring countries, the US, and the League of Nations for the role of key mediator complicated the war's resolution. An innovative perspective on inter-American relations.

3142 Cajías de la Vega, Fernando. La Provincia de Atacama, 1825–1842. La Paz: Instituto Boliviano de Cultura, 1975. 390 p.; bibl.; 6 leaves of plates: ill.

Written by a Bolivian to justify his nation's claim to the Atacama desert, this work's merit lies in its abundant and carefully documented facts on such topics as population, religion, education, governmental expenditures, agriculture, mining, and cost of living, drawn from Bolivian, Chilean and Spanish sources. An essential reference for future analyses.

3143 Capriles Villazón, Orlando. Historia de la minería boliviana. La Paz: Banco Minero de Bolivia, 1977. 268 p.; bibl. (Biblioteca Bamin)

Sponsored by the Banco Minero de Bolivia to form a base for more effective mineral resource management, this work is a compendium of information on production, legislation, policies, institutions, and working conditions for the mining industry from conquest to 1970.

3144 Carvalho Urey, Antonio. Del ignorado Mojos. Trinidad, Bolivia: s.n., 1978. 145 p.

A collection of the author's sympathetic though journalistic essays on the history and people of the Mojos province, Bolivia.

3145 Centellas C., Juan. En dos frentes de lucha. La Paz: s.n., 1977. 213 p.: ill.

Entertaining and insightful memoirs, focusing on the two major events of the author's life, the Chaco War and the National Revolution of 1952. Well illustrated with photos and sketches.

3146 La Confederación Perú-Boliviana: el Mariscal Santa Cruz y la Santa Sede: documentos inéditos. Colegidos y comentados por Manuel Frontaura Argandoña. La Paz: Banco Central de Bolivia, 1977. 143 p.; facsims. (Biblioteca cultural histórica; v. 3)

The transcripts and facsimiles of documents from the Vatican archive published here suggest that the Church backed the Peru-Bolivia Confederacy fomented by Bolivian President Andrés de Santa Cruz between 1836 and 1839. The introduction discusses the Church's role in the Confederacy and attempts to exonerate Santa Cruz with a brief biography. Documents useful to the studies of Church-state relations in the early 19th century, as well as to studies of the Confederacy.

3147 Costa de la Torre, Arturo. Bibliografía de la Revolución del 16 de Julio de 1809: año del protomártir Pedro Domingo Murillo. La Paz: Empresa Editora Universo, 1974. 127 p.; index.

An extensive bibliography, organized by date of publication, on Pedro Domingo Murillo and other participants of the 1809 La Paz uprising for independence from Spanish rule. The comments and references on women's roles in the Independence movement are especially valuable.

———. Estirpe y genealogía del protomártir Pedro Domingo Murillo. See item **2933**.

3149 Crespo R., Alberto. Alemanes en Bolivia. La Paz: Amigos del Libro, 1978. 246 p.; bibls.; ill.

Very general introduction to the social, economic and cultural contributions of Germans in Bolivia since the colonial period. Focuses on principal people. Interesting photo collection.

———. Esclavos negros en Bolivia. See item **2635**.

Di Ció, Miguel Angel. Chile contra Bolivia y Perú, 1879–1883: la guerra de los diez centavos. See item **3213**.

3150 Dómich Ruiz, Marcos. Ideología y mito: los orígenes del fascismo boliviano. La Paz: Editorial Los Amigos del Libro, 1978. 319 p.; bibl.; diagrs.

A lucid and well-documented, albeit polemical, essay tracing the evolution of "fascist" thought in Bolivian literature. Maintains that fascist inclinations, being an inevitable result of upper class economic and social domination, have long been evident in Bolivia, as elsewhere in Latin America.

3151 Echevarría, Evelio. Panorama y bibliografía de la novela social boliviana (RIB, 27:2, 1977, p. 143–152)

An intelligent commentary on the change in themes and emphasis in the social protest novel occasioned by the National Revolution of 1952. Divides the bibliography into two periods: 1904–52 and 1952–70. For literary critic's comment, see *HLAS 40: 6801*.

3152 Escobari Cusicanqui, Jorge. Historia diplomática de Bolivia: política internacional. La Paz, Bolivia: Casa Municipal de la Cultura Franz Tamayo, 1975. 519 p.; bibl.

A laudatory but thoughtful work by a noted Bolivian diplomat and historian. Comprehensive treatment of Bolivian relations with neighbors. A major work which supersedes other syntheses of Bolivian international relations. For political scientist's comment, see *HLAS 41:8796*.

Estudios bolivianos en homenaje a Gunnar Mendoza L. See item **2638**.

Fernández Solís, Jorge. Tema: el petróleo. See *HLAS 41:3308*.

3153 Fletcher, G. Richard. Santa Cruz: a study of economic growth in eastern Bolivia (IAMEA, 29:2, 1975, p. 23–41)

A cursory survey of economic change in the department of Santa Cruz since 1824, emphasizing the role of the central government in regional development. For economist's comment, see *HLAS 39:3363*.

Francovich, Guillermo. Alcides Arguedas y otros ensayos sobre la historia. See item **7850**.

3154 Gómez, Walter. Bolivia: problems of a pre- and post-revolutionary export economy (JDA, 10:4, 1976, p. 461–487)

This informative article discusses the effect of government policies on the mining sector (1900–58) and the consequent impact of mining on general economic development. For economist's comment, see *HLAS 41:3310*.

3155 Greño Velasco, José Enrique. Bolivia y su retorno al mar (IEP/RPI, 150, 1977, p. 199–230)

Another impassioned discussion of Bolivia's efforts to gain a corridor to the sea, emphasizing attempts made since the War of the Pacific.

3156 Historia gráfica de la Guerra del Pacífico. Bajo la dirección de Mariano Baptista Gumucio. La Paz: Ultima Hora, 1978. 119 p.; 44 leaves of plates: ill. (Colección Litoral boliviano. Biblioteca popular boliviana de Ultima Hora)

Interesting collection of photographs of Bolivian generals, towns, ships, soldiers, documents, battle scenes and maps of the War of the Pacific, followed by a brief chronological outline of the war and reprints of major documents.

3157 Ibáñez Franco, Alfredo. Dr. Melchor Pinto Parada: arquetipo y vigía de la Cruceñidad. Santa Cruz, Bolivia: s.n., 1978. 301 p.: ill.

A laudatory, journalistic account of how this medical doctor and political leader of the province of Santa Cruz brought about the enforcement of an ignored petroleum law in the late 1950s. Author sees Pinto Parada as the embodiment of the virtues of the citizens of Santa Cruz. Extensive quotes of newspaper articles.

Klein, Herbert S. The impact of the crisis in nineteenth-century mining on regional economies: the example of the Bolivian Yungas, 1786–1838. See item **2643**.

3158 Kohl, James V. Peasant and revolution in Bolivia: April 9, 1952–August 2, 1953 (HAHR, 58:2, May 1978, p. 239–259)

A competent article contending that the Bolivian peasantry was more militant before 1952 and more important in revolutionary ideology than formerly believed. Shows that peasant revolutionary activities and landowner reaction to it depended on local variables and that generalization is thus dangerous.

3159 López Videla, Winsor. Documentos para la historia: sinopsis del Chaco Boreal, acciones del III Cuerpo de Ejército, calendario de las acciones de guerra, 1932–1935. La Paz: s.n., 1977. 109 p.

This patriotically motivated work begins with a brief analysis of the origins and course of the Chaco War, followed by a reprinted article, "La Guerra en el Paraguay," and a lengthy listing of Bolivian statistics on manpower, equipment, leaders, etc., of the various battles of the Chaco War (1932–35).

3160 Lora, Guillermo. Contribución a la historia política de Bolivia. t. 2. La Paz: Ediciones Isla, 1978. 521 p. (Colección Historia y documentos)

Primarily a history (volume 2 covers the period from 1946 to 1977) of the political party of this prominent activist, based heavily on his former works, with valuable personal insights. Vol. 1 was never received at the Library of Congress.

3161 ———. Estudios histórico-políticos sobre Bolivia. La Paz: Ediciones El Amauta, 1978. 333 p.

A collection of four nationalistic historical essays by this prominent socialist, including two on Bolivia's territorial problems.

3162 ———. A history of the Bolivian labour movement, 1848–1971. Edited and abridged by Lawrence Whitehead. Translated by Christine Whitehead. New York: Cambridge University Press, 1977. 408 p. (Cambridge Latin American studies; 27)

An abridged English version of this valuable analysis of Bolivian labor history by a major labor activist. Although much of Lora's political argumentation has been cut, this is a major contribution for the English-language reader. For comment on the 1967 Spanish original, see *HLAS 32:2653*.

3163 Mayorga, René Antonio. National-popular state, state capitalism and military dictatorship in Bolivia: 1952–1975 (LAP, 17, Spring 1978, p. 89–119)

Argues, by using an analytical framework, that although the National Revolution of 1952 was the work of an armed proletariat, it resulted in a bourgeois economic and political order. Based on secondary sources.

Los Mercedarios en Bolivia: documentos para su historia; 1535–1975. See item **2647**.

3164 Mitre, Antonio F. Estructura económica social de la minería boliviana de la plata en el siglo XIX (UFMG/DCP, 5, março 1979, p. 45–71, bibl., tables)

An intelligent introduction to Bolivian silver mining based on company records. Demonstrates, once again, that mining, agricultural, and international interests overlapped.

3165 Monasterio da Silva, Aurelio. La caída de Salamanca. s.l.: s.n., between 1973 and 1978. 147 p.: ill.

A reprint of Gen. Angel Rodríguez's *Autopsia de una guerra*, plus an eulogistic introduction by a military colleague. This memoir of the Chaco War by a principal actor and later political dissident was, until recently, almost unavailable.

3166 Moscoso, Oscar. Recuerdos de la Guerra del Chaco. v. 1, Laguna Chuquisaca. Boquerón. La Cuarta División. Cochabamba, Bolivia: Editorial Canelas, 1976. 447 p.; ill.; maps; tables.

Written in 1939 by an appointee of President Salamanca to "set the record straight," this adds to the growing collection of memoirs of the Chaco War. Vol. 1 assesses the causes and selected events of the conflict. Contains maps and other documents.

3167 Moya Quiroga, Víctor. Internacionalización de Arica: documentos para la historiografía de una salida al mar. La Paz: s.n., 1977. 29 p.

A polemical defense of Bolivia's right to an outlet to the sea as a prelude to a call for the internationalization of the Chilean city of Arica.

3168 Nash, June. Mi vida en las minas: la autobiografía de una mujer boliviana (UP/EA, 5[5]:1, 1976, p. 139–150)

An entertaining, lively written account of an interview with a poor 58-year-old Bolivian woman, giving insights into her work, family experiences and perceptions.

3169 Ocampo Moscoso, Eduardo. Historia del periodismo boliviano. La Paz: Librería Editorial Juventud, 1978. 714 p.; bibl.; 10 leaves of plates: ill.

This serious work primarily describes major Bolivian publications from the colonial period to the present. Some insight into the relationship between the press and sociopolitical trends.

3170 O'Connor d'Arlach, Octavio. Calendario histórico de Tarija. La Paz: Talleres-Escuela de Artes Gráficas del Colegio Don Bosco, 1975. 281 p.; bibl.

A listing of the major historical events associated with each day of the year for the department of Tarija. Compiled as part of Bolivia's sesquicentennial celebration.

3171 Ortiz Sanz, Fernando. Jaime Mendoza and the new Bolivia (AAFH/TAM, 28:9, 1977, p. 21–26)

Brief descriptive survey of the contributions of Jaime Mendoza, noted doctor, intellectual and artist, 1874–1939.

3172 Otero, Gustavo Adolfo. Memorias de Gustavo Adolfo Otero: Nolo Beaz. La Paz: Litografías e Imprentas Unidas, 1977. 232 p.

This autobiography of the noted Bolivian historian, journalist, and politician (1896–1958) provides potentially valuable insights into political, social and intellectual conditions in Bolivia in the first half of the 20th century.

3173 Paredes, Alfonsina. El indio Laureano Machaka: esbozo biográfico de un líder. La Paz: Ediciones Isla, 1977. 58 p.

A sympathetic, though undocumented, narrative of an Aymara Indian leader's unsuccessful attempt in 1956 to foment a revolution for the independence of his people.

3174 Paredes Candia, Antonio. Anécdotas bolivianas. La Paz: Ediciones Isla, 1975. 117 p.; index.

A collection of anecdotes about and sayings by famous Bolivians. Possibly useful for social histories as they give insights into social customs and values.

3175 Pentland, Joseph Barclay. Informe sobre Bolivia. Traducción al español por Jack Aitken Soux. Potosí: Editorial Potosí,

1975. 200 p.; 2 fold. leaves of plates: ill. (Colección de la cultura boliviana; 13. Colección segunda. Autores del siglo XIX; 7)

A welcome Spanish translation of the fascinating and highly informative *Report on Bolivia* dealing with the political, economic, and social situation of Bolivia in 1827. Pentland was one of many British officials requested to make such reports as part of the British attempt to develop markets in Latin America.

Portugal Ortiz, Max. La esclavitud negra en las épocas colonial y nacional de Bolivia. See item **2654**.

3176 Qué se rinda su abuela, carajo: vida y epifanía de Eduardo Avaroa. Bajo la dirección de Mariano Baptista Gumucio. La Paz: Ultima Hora, 1978. 223 p.; 1 leaf of plates: ill. (Biblioteca popular boliviana de Ultima Hora. Colección Litoral boliviano)

A collection of documents and secondary commentaries to commemorate Eduardo Avaroa's leadership of the Bolivian defenders in the 1879 Battle of Calama. Some of the documents are quite interesting and will be useful to historians studying the War of the Pacific.

3177 Reyno Gutiérrez, Manuel. Algunos antecedentes históricos sobre la contraposición peruana para otorgar una salida al Pacífico a Bolivia (SCHR/R, 144, 1976, p. 7–20)

After discussing early 19th-century documents which define Bolivia's right to a seaport, the author argues that Bolivia should accept Chile's recent offer to port access and that Peru's counter proposition belies an attempt to interfere in Bolivia's internal affairs. For political scientist's comment, see *HLAS 41:8869*.

3178 Rivero Egüez, Victorino. Historia de Santa Cruz durante la 2a. [i.e. segunda] mitad del siglo XIX. Santa Cruz, Bolivia: Fundación Cultural Ramón Darío Gutiérrez, 1978. 189 p.

An insider's version of the history of the city of Santa Cruz (1850–1900) with comments on political and religious events, living conditions, and natural disasters. Informative but impressionistic.

3179 Rojas Camacho, Alfredo. El pensamiento andino: la expresión de un autor, Fernando Díez de Mendina. La Paz: Distribuidores exclusivos Los Amigos del Libro, 1978. 127 p.; bibl.

A synthesis and analysis of Díez de Medina's books *Thunupa* (1947) and *Nayjama* (1950). Whether writing essays, histories, or fiction, this sensitive and refreshing author looks for a Bolivian identity in the precolumbian and Indian heritage and natural setting rather than in generals, wars and political problems.

3180 Saavedra Pinochet, Rafael. Nacionalismo: ensayo. La Paz: Empresa Editora Urquizo, 1977. 141 p.; bibl.

Examines the nature of Bolivian nationalism in various political periods. Most interesting as an example of current intellectual concerns.

3181 St. John, Ronald Bruce. Hacia el mar: Bolivia's quest for Pacific port (IAMEA, 31:3, 1977, p. 27–73)

Reviews Bolivia's attempts since 1825 to gain a Pacific outlet. For political scientist's comment, see *HLAS 41:8875*.

3182 Salinas Mariaca, Ramón. Vida y muerte de José Manuel Pando. La Paz: Ultima Hora, 1978. 184 p.; 3 leaves of plates: ill. (Biblioteca popular boliviana de Ultima Hora)

Eulogistic biography of a Bolivian politician, diplomat, and general in the War of the Pacific written by a relative.

Sánchez-Albornoz, Nicolás. Indios y tributos en el Alto Perú. See item **2811**.

Testimonios y recuerdos de la Guerra del Pacífico. See item **3272**.

Thorndike, Guillermo. Vienen los chilenos. See item **3274**.

3183 Valencia Vega, Alipio. Manuel Victorio García Lanza: el guerrillero devorado por la propia revolución. La Paz: Librería Editorial Juventud, 1978. 88 p.; bibl. (Colección Tradición, historia)

This essay, largely undocumented and based on secondary materials, deals with the socio-intellectual context and political events of the Wars of Independence. The purpose is to show that Manuel Victoria García Lanza, an upper class leader of the common people in an unsuccessful challenge to a

Church-led counterrevolution, is a symbol of "the great ideas of liberty and independence."

3184 ———. Simona Josefa Manzaneda: por patrioto, pero "chola," un infamante suplicio acabó con su vida. La Paz: Librería Editorial Juventud, 1978. 87 p. (Colección Tradición, historia)

While commendably attempting to document the role of the lower class and women in Bolivian history, this commentary on a female participant in the War of Independence is polemical and shallowly researched.

3185 Vaughn, Courtney Ann. By hook or by crook: Alfalfa Bill Murray, colonizer in Bolivia (JW, 18:1, Jan. 1979, p. 67–72)

Describes an Oklahoman's unsuccessful attempt to establish a colony in Bolivia in the 1920s. While the incident had little significance for Bolivian history, it is another example of a North American trying to create in Latin America something unattainable in the US. Pertinent to the history of US-Latin American relations.

3186 Velarde Vizcarra, Nicanor. Remembranzas de la Guerra del Chaco: apreciaciones y realidades de lo acontecido en la pasada campaña internacional con el Paraguay, en el cautiverio, en mi evasión y en la post-guerra. La Paz: s.n., 1976. 323 p.: ill.

One of the more interesting and well-written memoirs of the Chaco War and aftermath by a Bolivian general.

3187 Yeager, Gertrude Matyoka. Gabriel René-Moreno and the intellectual context of late nineteenth-century South America (UT/SSQ, 59:1, June 1978, p. 77–92, bibl.)

A perceptive analysis of Bolivia's foremost 19th-century historian's stance on such 19th-century controversies as race mixture, the impact of Spanish heritage, and positivism as developed by Chilean and Argentine intellectuals. For philosopher's comment, see item **7660**.

3188 Zavaleta Mercado, René. Consideraciones generales sobre la historia de Bolivia, 1932–1971 (*in* América Latina: historia de medio siglo. Edited by Pablo González Casanova. v. 1, América del Sur. México: Siglo XXI Editores, 1977, p. 74–126)

Maintains that with the Chaco War, Bolivia discovered a need to fight for its national identity and that the struggle has continued, not against neighbors but against imperialism. Within this framework, author analyzes major political and social themes of the past 50 years.

CHILE

3189 Alexander, Robert Jackson. Arturo Alessandri: a biography. Ann Arbor: Published for Latin American Institute, Rutgers University by University Microfilms International, 1977. 2 v. (986 p.) (Continuous pagination); bibl. (Monograph publishing on demand: Sponsor series)

An authoritative and flattering biography of one of Chile's foremost presidents. Based on personal interviews as well as extensive library research.

3190 Alvear Godoy, Aníbal. Por los caminos de Chile: ayer y hoy, hechos históricos y anécdotas, 1810–1976. 2. ed., corr. y ampliada. Santiago de Chile: Gráficos Corporación, 1977. 257 p.: ill.

This autobiography, with reflections on Chile's political and cultural heritage, is particularly valuable as a commentary by a general of the *Carabineros* (National Police) on the personalities, events, and meaning of the Allende years.

3191 Araneda Bravo, Fidel. La iglesia catedral de Santiago: pt. 2 (SCHG/R, 142, 1974, p. 95–118)

A continuation of the detailed description of Chile's chief church containing a wealth of painstakingly gathered information of uncertain value. Details such topics as the locations and inscriptions of tombs, the history of the bells, and the process of constructing the building. For pt. 1 of this study, see *HLAS 38:9091*.

3192 *Atenea.* Revista de ciencia, arte y literatura. Universidad de Concepción. No. 437, 1978– . Concepción, Chile.

This issue in honor of Bernardo O'Higgins contains some fine, even elegant, essays on Chile's liberator and first president. Topics include the cultural environment of O'Higgins' era, his foreign politics, the England he knew, his legal legacy, and his handling of the political rivalry between Santiago and Concepción.

3193 Bahamonde Silva, Mario. El caudillo de Copiapó: Copiapó, 1859. Santiago, Chile: Editorial Nascimento, 1977. 70 p.

A popular, journalistic narrative of the role of Pedro León Gallo Goyenechea in the 1859 insurrection in Copiapó when miners, the unemployed and the local elite united against the clergy and central government to retain control of local affairs.

3194 Balmori, Diana and **Robert Oppenheimer.** Family clusters: generational nucleation in nineteenth-century Argentina and Chile (CSSH, 21:2, April 1979, p. 231–261)

Using research from judicial and notorial archives and biographical dictionaries, this study attempts to explain how and why a group of families, within three generations of intermarriage and cooperation, comes to control a region. Despite its cumbersome prose, this article adds to our understanding of kinship politics and is an innovative attempt at comparative history.

3195 Barros Charlín, Raymundo. Consideraciones sobre la integración latinoamericana en el siglo XIX, con particular referencia a la política de Chile. Santiago: Departamento de Estudios Internacionales, Universidad de Chile, 1975. 76 leaves; bibl. (Serie de Publicaciones especiales; 8)

A thoughtful analysis of the development of a "Latin American" awareness in 19th-century Chile using legislation, political philosophy, and executive actions as well as international treaties and organizations. Concludes that Latin Americans for generations have recognized the need for regional integration. For political scientist's comment, see *HLAS 41:7380.*

3196 Barros Lezaeta, Luis and **Ximena Vergara Johnson.** El modo de ser aristocrático: el caso de la oligarquía chilena hacia 1900. Prólogo de Tomás Moulian. Santiago: Ediciones Aconcagua, 1978. 190 p.; bibl. (Colección Lautaro)

A fascinating, though controversial, analysis of 19th-century aristocratic attitudes toward money, idleness, and lineage based on novels, newspaper articles, polemics, and other literary sources.

3197 Bermúdez Miral, Oscar. Estudios de Antonio O'Brien. Antofagasta, Chile: Ediciones Universitarias, 1975. 120 p.

A summary and publication of much of the writing of Anthony O'Brien, an Irish military engineer employed by the king of Spain to survey the Atacama desert. His maps, charts, and comments form one of the few sources of information on this region during the colonial period.

3198 ———. Repercusiones en Cobija de la guerra con España (SCHG/R, 143, 1975, p. 46–72)

Bermúdez first describes the port of Cobija (important nitrate center, now in the province of Antofagasta) as it was in 1866, then details the subject matter of the relevant documents found in the archive of the intendencia, and finally transcribes 30 documents dealing with the War with Spain, 1864–66. The information awaits analysis.

3199 Biblioteca Nazionale Centrale di Firenze, *Italy.* Un popolo unito, Cile: 1970–1974; dal governo di Unità Popolare alla giunta di Pinochet, bibliografia ragionata. Milano, Italy: La Pietra Editore, 1978. 253 p.

This excellent annotated bibliography reflects the great interest aroused in Italy by the Chilean experience of Unidad Popular. It consists of 1,095 items and several indexes (e.g., subject, author, personalities interviewed, etc.). [M. Carmagnani]

3200 Blakemore, Harold. Gobierno chileno y salitre inglés, 1886–1896: Balmaceda y North. Traducción de Sofía Varela. Santiago: Editorial Andrés Bello, 1977. 281 p.; bibl.; plate.

A much needed Spanish translation of this fundamental synthesis resulting from decades of careful research and critical interpretation. For comment on original English version, see *HLAS 36:2970.*

3201 ———. Limitation of dependency: an historian's view and case study (CEDLA/B, 18, junio 1975, p. 74–87)

Challenges the dependency theorists by documenting an instance where Chilean national economic interests thwarted foreign interests. Based on research of the Chilean government's handling of Peruvian bondholders following the War of the Pacific.

Botelho Gosálvez, Raúl. Breve historia del litoral boliviano: la misión Jaimes Freyre en Santiago. See item **3140**.

3202 Bravo Lira, Bernardino. Chile 1925–1932 [i.e. mil novecientos veinticinco-mil novicientos treinta y dos]: de la nueva Constitución al nuevo régimen de gobierno. Santiago: Contraloría General de la República, 1977. p. 20–53; bibl.

The first part of a law professor's larger synthesis of Chilean legal history. This part gives an overview of intent and historical background, and then discusses the Constitution of 1925 and its implementation to 1932. Shows obvious interest in recent legal history, especially that of the Allende years.

3203 Bunster, Enrique. Crónica portalianas. Santiago de Chile: Editorial del Pacífico, 1977. 221 p.; 9 leaves of plates: ill. (Alta mar)

Published posthumously to honor this prolific historian, this book is a collection of Enrique Bunster's short histories on Diego Portales and contemporaries. These essays add to the author's repertoire of well-written though laudatory political biographies. The thoughtful opening essay by Guillermo Izquierdo Araya discusses Bunster's works in general.

Cajías de la Vega, Fernando. La Provincia de Atacama, 1825–1842. See item **3142**.

3204 Caldera, Rafael. Andrés Bello: philosopher, poet, philologist, educator, legislator and statesman. Translated by John Street. London: George Allen & Unwin, 1977. 165 p.

A sympathetic and elegant biography and critique of the intellectual contributions of Andrés Bello. The author, future Venezuelan President, was only 19 when he wrote this in 1935.

3205 Campos Harriet, Fernando. Historia constitucional de Chile: las instituciones políticas y sociales. 5. ed. Santiago: Editorial Jurídica de Chile, 1977. 431 p.; bibl.

An updating and republication of this basic text of Chilean legal history. Deals with key institutions, personalities, and legislation from conquest to 1970. Its outline, organization, extensive citations, and careful documentations makes it a particularly valuable reference.

Canclini, Arnoldo. Cómo fue civilizado el sur patagónico. See item **3313**.

Cárdenas Tabies, Antonio. Usos y costumbres de Chiloé. See item **1198**.

3206 Cariola, Carmen and **Osvaldo Sunkel.** Chile (*in* Latin America: a guide to economic history, 1830–1930 [see *HLAS 40:2386*] p. 273–363, bibl.)

This monumental article (90 p.) comments on virtually every published primary source, major archival collection, and periodical relevant to Chilean economic history (1830–1930). It is extraordinarily valuable given the inadequate subject index of Chile's National Library. The introductory essay interprets Chile's economic history from 1830 to 1930 within a dependency framework.

3207 Casassas Canto, José María. Avance informativo sobre algunos precios y otros aspectos económicos en la región Atacameña durante el siglo XVIII (Revista de Historia [Universidad de Concepción, Instituto de Antropología, Historia y Geografía, Chile] 2:2, 1977, p. 71–92, bibl.)

As in other articles, the author publishes the unanalyzed data found in the parish archives of San Pedro de Atacama and Chiuchiu, this time on the prices of goods and services in the 18th century. Due to unusually detailed descriptions and citations, this can almost substitute for the original documents.

3208 Cavarozzi, Marcelo. El orden oligárquico en Chile, 1880–1940 (IDES/DE, 18:70, 1978, p. 231–262)

Based on secondary works, develops an analytical framework for understanding the changes in the composition and function of Chile's ruling class which accompanied the changes in Chile's position in the world market system (1880–1940).

3209 Chacón del Campo, Julio. La prensa de Linares, 1871–1972 (SCHG/R, 144, 1976, p. 124–145)

A descriptive synopsis of the literary and popular magazines and newspapers published in the city of Linares from 1871 to 1972. Contains the name, dates, editor, and theme of each publication, along with a brief comment on the circumstances of publication. The article does not justify the significance of this information, but such a catalogue may be useful to researchers using provincial publications.

3210 Chile: the land and the people (OAS/AM, 28:6/7, 1976, p. sl-sl6)

Brief, very general information on the geography, history (since 1750), and current conditions of Chile.

3211 Concha, Jaime. Martín Rivas o la formación del burgués (CDLA, 15:89, 1975, p. 4–17)

Brief biography of author Blest Gana (1837–91), and a critique of the historical and intellectual significance of his novel, *Martín Rivas* (1862).

Cubitt, David J. The manning of the Chilean Navy in the War of Independence: 1818–1823. See item **2940**.

Cuccorese, Horacio Juan. La cuestión limítrofe con Chile: tiempo de agudización del conflicto, 1900–1901. See item **3323**.

3213 Di Ció, Miguel Angel. Chile contra Bolivia y Perú, 1879–1883: la guerra de los diez centavos. Buenos Aires: Editorial Moharra, 1979. 108 p.; bibl.; maps.

Another work on the War of the Pacific to commemorate its 100th anniversary. The unusual thesis of this study explains the causes of the confrontation in terms of colonial rivalry and wars.

3214 Donoso Vergara, Guillermo. La revolución de 1851 en Talca: pts. 1/5 (SCHG/R, 141, 1973, p. 88–115; 142, 1974, p. 54–94; 143, 1975, p. 5–45; 144, 1976, p. 21–61; 145, 1977, p. 5–62)

This book-length monograph, published in five serial installments, is the most comprehensive study available on the slightly-known civil strife of 1851. Based on in-depth research, this work is a detailed, and unfortunately dull, analysis of the local grievances and actions which culminated in the uprising. Contains lengthy citations of archival documents and letters from private collections.

3215 Drake, Paul W. Socialism and populism in Chile, 1932–52. Urbana: University of Illinois Press, 1978. 418 p.; bibl.; index.

An authoritative history of Chilean socialism dealing chiefly with the socialist movement's socioeconomic base and the "decline" of the Socialist Party from 1942–52, with insightful comments on the implications of this history through the Allende years. This major work: 1) places the Chilean socialist experience in the context of populist movements in Latin America and Europe in general; 2) provides a crucial perspective for understanding the failure of Marxism in Chile; and 3) offers an intelligent social analysis of Chilean politics from 1932–52.

3216 Duncan, Roland E. Chilean coal and British steamers: the origin of a South American industry (Mariner's Mirror [Society for Nautical Research, Sussex, UK] 61:3, 1975, p. 271–281)

Another of the author's intelligent contributions to business history. Discusses the role of William Wheelwright and the British merchant service in the development of the coal industry south of Concepción, Chile (1834–50).

3217 Durand Florez, Guillermo. El padrón de contribuyentes de Tarapacá en 1845 (PEAGN/R, 4/5, 1977, p. 115–199)

Publishes the potentially useful taxation list for Tarapacá for 1845 from the collection of the Archivo Histórico de Hacienda, Peru.

3218 Elgueta, Belarmino and **Alejandro Chelén R.** Breve historia de medio siglo en Chile (*in* América Latina: historia de medio siglo. Edited by Pablo González Casanova. v. 1, América del Sur. México: Siglo XXI Editores, 1977, p. 226–285, bibl.)

Using leftist terminology and perspectives, evaluates Allende's rule and overthrow by analyzing the evolution of social and political structures from 1920 to 1970.

3219 Escala Escobar, Manuel. Una semblanza del Batallón Bulnes (SCHG/R, 144, 1976, p. 167–185)

Written by a ranking official of the Chilean National Police (*Carabineros*), this study documents the participation of Santiago's police force in the War of the Pacific. Although written chiefly to glorify the *Carabineros*, the study is carefully researched and presented.

Escobari Cusicanqui, Jorge. Historia diplomática de Bolivia: política internacional. See item **3152**.

3220 Estellé Méndez, Patricio. *Informe sobre la situación de Chile en 1829* del Cónsul Británico Henry William Rouse (SCHG/R, 142, 1974, p. 119–169)

Consists of a translation (by Estellé) of the 1829 report of the first British Consul to Concepción, describing the chaotic political situation of the period; related correspondences of Joaquín Prieto, Juan Manuel Basso, and José Antonio Rodríguez Aldea; and Estellé's concise and informed introduction on the life of Henry Rouse and the circumstances surrounding his report. A valuable source for early 19th-century political history.

Etchepareborda, Roberto. La intervención argentina en el conflicto chileno-norteamericano de 1892: el caso del "Baltimore." See item **3340**.

3221 Fuenzalida Contreras, Abraham. Memorias de un proscrito: pts. 1/3 (SCHG/R, 143, 1975, p. 127–152; 144, 1976, p. 81–99; 145, 1977, p. 235–268)

A publication of the memoirs of an ardent *balmacedista,* recording his experiences in and opinions of the 1891 Civil War. Although written years later and resorting to citations of other documents for collaboration, frequent candid observations provide the new insights of a participant.

3222 Gazmuri Riveros, Cristián; Mariana Aylwin; and **Juan Carlos González.** Perspectiva de Jaime Eyzaguirre. Prólogo de Ricardo Krebs. Santiago, Chile: Ediciones Aconcagua, 1977. 214 p.; bibl.; facsim. (Colección Lautaro)

A fine collection of critical essays on the life and work of one of Chile's foremost historians. Ezaguirre's "Hispanic" perspective, which considers Chile as part of the Christian world, has been severely criticized. However, as these essays show, it has also simulated much thoughtful reconsideration of Chilean history.

3223 Godoy Urzúa, Hernán. El carácter chileno: estudio preliminar y selección de ensayos. Santiago de Chile: Editorial Universitaria, 1976. 458 p.; bibl. (Ediciones universitarias)

Although not as provocative in theme or content as the earlier *Estructura social de Chile,* this is an interesting historical probe by a sociologist into the development of diverse image of the Chilean character. Reprints selections of key primary and secondary works to illustrate principal themes.

3224 González Salinas, Edmundo. La Guerra del Pacífico, la historia militar, y los historiadores (SCHG/R, 145, 1977, p. 173–183)

A well-written critique of the major Chilean historiography of the War of the Pacific. In particular, challenges Encina's interpretation which, the author claims, defames many of Chile's traditional heroes.

3225 Greene, Edgard. La generación literaria chilena de 1938: apuntes histórico-críticos (SCHG/R, 145, 1977, p. 199–234)

An able discussion of the intellectual climate in Chile in the 1930s and the national and international sources of literary inspiration, followed by critiques of the works of 10 of the era's foremost authors.

Greño Velasco, José Enrique. Bolivia y su retorno al mar. See item **3155**.

Hakim, Peter and **Giorgio Solimano.** Development, reform, and malnutrition in Chile. See *HLAS 41:1609*.

3226 Heise González, Julio. Años de formación y aprendizaje políticos, 1810–1833. Santiago de Chile: Editorial Universitaria, 1978. 286 p.; bibl.

A thoughtful, carefully written, refreshing analysis of the early republican period in Chile contending that the chaos symptomized a necessary learning period in self-government. Gives a favorable interpretation of the early authoritarian leaders and concludes with an evocative section on social, political, and cultural achievements.

3227 Hervey, Maurice H. Dark days in Chile: an account of the revolution of 1891. With a new introduction by Frank N. Manitzas. Philadelphia: Institute for the Study of Human Issues, 1979. 331 p. (ISHI reprints on Latin America and the Caribbean)

Reprint of the first-class eyewitness report of the 1891 Civil War by a correspondent of *The Times* of London. New introduction points out the similarities between the "dark days" of 1891 and those of 1973.

3228 Historia de Chile. Sergio Villalobos R. and others. Santiago de Chile: Editorial Universitaria, 1976. p. 580–977; ill. (Colección Imagen de Chile. Cormorán)

This fourth and final volume of the valuable survey of Chilean history covers the period from 1861–1970. An easy-to-use introduction to historical events and issues. For previous volumes, see *HLAS 40:3089*.

3229 History of the health care system in Chile (APHA/J, 67:1, Jan. 1977, p. 31–36)

A very general history of Chilean health care, with scant information on the pre-1952 period. Focus on Allende and post-Allende periods.

3230 Johnson, Ann Hagerman. The impact of market agriculture on family and household structure in nineteenth-century Chile (HAHR, 58:4, Nov. 1978, p. 625–648, map, tables)

A notable pioneering analysis of the economic determinants of lower-class family structure. Using census manuscripts for different years, the author is able to trace changes in the headship and composition of households on estates and small holdings in a region changing from self-sufficient to market agriculture. [Thomas C. Wright]

3231 Kirsch, William W. Industrial development in a traditional society: the conflict of entrepreneurship and modernization in Chile. Gainesville: University Presses of Florida, 1977. 210 p.; bibl.; tables (Latin American monographs; 21)

A fundamental contribution to Chilean entrepreneurial history. Convincingly argues that industry expanded between the War of the Pacific and the First World War, and that industrial entrepreneurs were not in conflict with the landed elite. Explains why industry did not form a "growth pole" for economic development. Interesting appendix on Chilean imports prior to World War I. For economist's comment, see *HLAS 41:3225*.

Leuchter, W. Zur Rolle der staatlichen Investitionspolitik im Rahmen der Strategie und Taktik der herrschenden Klassen Chiles in den fünfziger und sechziger Jahren. See *HLAS 41:7422*.

3232 Lira Montt, Luís. Estudiantes chilenos en la Real Universidad de Córdoba del Tucumán, 1670–1815 (SCHG/R, 142, 1974, p. 7–53)

Begins with a summary of the history of the University of Córdoba, and then lists Chilean students alphabetically, giving dates of attendance, course of study, and eminent relatives of each. Relevance of work remains to be shown; perhaps useful in kinship studies.

3233 Loveman, Brian. Chile: the legacy of Hispanic capitalism. New York: Oxford University Press, 1979. 429 p.; bibl.; index; maps (Latin American histories)

Part of the fine Oxford Latin American Histories series. With this, the English language audience finally has a concise general history of Chile, incorporating the latest historical findings and interpretations.

3234 Luigi, Juan de. Justo Abel Rosales Justiniano, su labor histórica y literaria: pts. 1/2 (SCHG/R, 144, 1976, p. 186–229; 145, 1977, p. 125–144)

Carefully documented and well-written, this essay describes the life and work of one of Chile's lesser known 19th-century intellectuals. Of value to scholars of Latin American intellectual history.

3235 McCaa, Robert. Chilean social and demographic history (LARR, 13:2, 1978, p. 104–126)

McCaa first cautions researchers about traditional methodologies and sources of social and demographic history and then presents titillating bits from his own fascinating, unpublished research. The issues, conclusions, and techniques suggested here foreshadow a major advance in Latin American social history.

3236 Mamalakis, Markos. The growth and structure of the Chilean economy: from independence to Allende. New Haven: Yale University Press, 1976. 390 p.; bibl.; ill.; index (A Publication of the Economic Growth Center, Yale University)

In this long-awaited work, the economist-author applied his analytical framework of sectoral conflict to his vast collection of historical statistics to explain the evolution of production, distribution, and capital formation in Chile from 1840–1973. Unfortunately, 19th-century economic history is touched too briefly, data and source selection are somewhat capricious, and most importantly, Chilean economic change is not viewed in the context of its place within the world market system. Nevertheless, this work provides the English language audience with a fact-filled reference on Chilean economic change, especially since 1930. For economist's comment, see *HLAS 39:3396*.

———. Historical statistics of Chile: national accounts. See *HLAS 41:3229*.

3237 Martín, José Carlos. Manuel Pardo en Chile. Lima: s.n., 1978. 111 p.; appendix; bibl.; 5 leaves of plates.

Although highly eulogistic, this account of the exiled Peruvian President's residency in Chile on the eve of the War of the Pacific is based on interesting personal correspondence, much of which is reproduced here. As such, this work contributes to the historiography of the War of the Pacific and Chilean social history of the 1870s.

Martinić Beros, Mateo. Actividad lobera y ballenera en litorales y aguas de Magallanes y Antártida, 1868–1916. See *HLAS 41:5472*.

3238 Mayo, John. Before the nitrate era: British Commission Houses and the Chilean economy, 1851–80 (JLAS, 2, [pt. 2] Nov. 1979, p. 283–302)

This serious work provides a wealth of information on the Chilean economy 1851–80. By scrutinizing the operation of commission houses, author explains how the British came to control Chilean commerce, and assesses the benefits and liabilities of foreign control.

3239 Méndez García de la Huerta, Alejandro. La escuadra ante la dictadura, 1891 (SCHG/R, 145, 1977, p. 63–112)

A chronological account of the Navy's role in the Civil War of 1891. Discusses the reasons the navy sided with the Congress-led revolutionary movement against President Balmaceda, and the effect of naval support on the war's outcome.

3240 ———. Juntas revolucionarias de los años 1890 y 1891 (SCHG/R, 143, 1975, p. 73–106)

Based on writing of revolutionary leaders, the author argues that the revolutionary committees formed in 1890 and 1891 in reaction to the usurpation of local prerogatives by President Balmaceda, and were pushed into a more militant stand by the President's actions. Provides a useful perspective on this controversial experience.

3241 Millas, Orlando. La presencia de Bernardo O'Higgins en las luchas sociales actuales (URSS/AL, 4, 1978, p. 5–12)

A journalistic and basically undocumented essay asserting that Bernardo O'Higgins was a champion of anti-imperialism and a role-model for the current working-class struggle against oppression.

3242 Monteón, Michael. The *enganche* in the Chilean nitrate sector, 1880–1930 (LAP, 6:3[22], Summer 1979, p. 66–79)

Rather than illuminating the method and social implications of "hooking" Chileans from the central zone for the nitrate mines in the north, this paper mostly discusses the recruitment and control of the foreign-miner minority. Information on foreign miners' relationship to labor unrest is particularly interesting.

Moya Quiroga, Victor. Internacionalización de Arica: documentos para la historiografía de una salida al mar. See item **3166**.

Muñoz Gomá, Oscar and **Ana María Arriagada.** Orígenes políticos y económicos del estado empresarial en Chile. See *HLAS 41:3233*.

3243 Neumann, Gerald Jacob. La gestación del poder naval en Chile y su evolución hasta la Guerra del Pacífico (Revista de Historia [Instituto de Antropología, Historia y Geografía, Universidad de Concepción, Chile] 2:2, 1977, p. 7–17)

Written to describe and extoll the foresight of the early proponents of the Chilean Navy, this narrative contains some potentially useful, though unfortunately undocumented, information.

Nunn, Frederick M. European military influence in South America: the origins and nature of professional militarism in Argentina, Brazil, Chile and Peru, 1890–1940. See item **1933b**.

3244 ———. Latin American militarylore: an introduction and a case study (AAFH/TAM, 35:4, April 1979, p. 429–474)

Tackles the awesome task of defining the historical development of the military's perception of itself and its social and political role by using interviews and analyzing military literature and actions. Nunn uses his analysis to explain the Chilean coup of 1973. Adds an important perspective to understanding the Latin American military.

3245 O'Brien, Thomas F., Jr. The Antofagasta Company: the case study of peripheral capitalism (HAHR, 60:1, Feb. 1980, p. 1–31, tables)

A micro-level critique of the dependency theory based on a careful analysis of the Antofagasta Company, a major Chilean-English owned nitrate enterprise. Shows that the foreign connections allowed such a modern enterprise to exist without disrupting traditional society and that this, rather than foreign domination of domestic politics or exploitation of surplus labor, doomed Chile to "underdevelopment" by impeding the formation of a non-traditional economic interest group.

3246 ———. Chilean elites and foreign investors: Chilean nitrate policy, 1880–1882 (JLAS, 2:1, May 1979, p. 101–121)

This authoritative reassessment of Chile's early nitrate policy shows that foreign control of the industry was the most pragmatic alternative and was well attuned to the interests of Chile's ruling class.

3247 **Ondarza O., Antonio.** Grandeza y ruina de Cobija (SCHG/R, 144, 1976, p. 119–123)

A brief and lively-written discussion of the earthquakes in 1867 and 1877 which changed Cobija from the most important port in the Atacama desert into a quasi-deserted shantytown.

3248 **Orrego Luco, Augusto.** Recuerdos de la Escuela. Prólogo de Leónidas Aguirre Mac-Kay. Semblanza del autor por Amelia Orrego Cifuentes. Buenos Aires: Editorial Francisco de Aguirre, 1976. 176 p.; 17 leaves of plates: ill.; index (Colección Historia de la medicina; 2. Biblioteca Francisco de Aguirre; 59)

The third printing of the memoirs of this eminent physician, educator, and writer who shaped as well as observed Chilean medical practice from 1874 to 1933. These memoirs form a key source of information on Chile's medical profession and society in general at that time.

3249 **Palma, Ricardo.** Cartas a Piérola sobre la ocupación chilena de Lima. Introducción y notas, Rubén Vargas Ugarte. 2. ed. Fotografías, Archivo Eugene Courret. Edición y epigrafías, Carlos Milla Batres. Lima: Editorial Milla Batres, 1979. 140 p.; 8 leaves of plates: ill.

Republication of the letters of Ricardo Palma, curator of the Peruvian National Library, to President Nicolás de Piérola. Most letters concern the Chilean occupation of Lima during the War of the Pacific.

3250 **Philippi, Federico.** Viaje de Don Federico Philippi por el desierto de Atacama en 1885 (SCHG/R, 143, 1975, p. 171–261)

The first publication of Federico Philippi's fascinating diary of his scientific expedition to Antofagasta and Tarapacá in 1885. More than the formerly published summary reports, this diary deals with the people and society, as well as the flora and fauna, of the Atacama desert. Preceded by Julio Philippi's introduction.

3251 **Pike, Frederick B.** Chilean local government and some reflections on dependence (IAMEA, 31:2, Autumn 1977, p. 63–70)

Drawing from the recent research of Valenzuela (see *HLAS 41:7454*) and Remmer (see *HLAS 39:7684*), the author argues that local government officials preferred to ask the "core" (i.e., the national government in Santiago)—for funds rather than to generate revenue locally. This cemented ties of "dependence." An interesting interpretation. For political scientist's comment, see *HLAS 41:7432*.

3252 **Pinochet de la Barra, Oscar.** La Antártica chilena. 4. ed. Santiago: Editorial Andrés Bello, 1976. 210 p.

This seminal study on Antarctica, first published in 1944, continues to play an important role in justifying Chile's claim to a sector of Antarctica.

Pinto, Sonia; Luz María Méndez; and **Sergio Vergara.** Antecedentes históricos de la Contraloría General de la República. See item **2653**.

3253 **Pinto-Cisternas, J.; B. Lazo; C. Campusano;** and **S. Ballesteros.** Some determinants of mating structure in a rural zone of Chile, 1810–1959 (Social Biology [Society for the Study of Social Biology, New York] 24:3, Fall 1977, p. 234–244)

Novel study by biologists which correlates the incidence of consanguineous marriages in Puchuncaví, Chile from 1810 to 1954 with marital status, legitimacy, incidence of extramarital relations with blood-kin, and frequency of legal kinship via marriage. Shows marked decreases in consanguineous marriages over time, but does not attempt economic or social explanation of changes. For biological anthropologist's comment, see *HLAS 41:1495*.

3254 **Presa Casanueva, Rafael de la.** Venida y aporte de los españoles a Chile independiente. Santiago de Chile: s.n., 1978. 686 p.: port.

A detailed listing of notable Spaniards in Chile and Spanish-Chilean relation from Independence to 1973. Extolls the contributions of Spaniards to Chilean political, economic, cultural and intellectual development, as well as their role in the Independence movement. Although inadequately footnoted, contains a wealth of information of possible value to studies on the social composition of political and economic groups.

3255 **Puente, Mario.** Chile, enseñanzas y balance de un proceso revolucionario. Lima: Taller de Estudios Políticos, Programa Académico de CCSS, Universidad Católica del Perú, 1975? 51 p. (Serie Procesos políticos latinoamericanos; 3)

A polemical assessment by an exiled Chilean of the Allende government, the causes of the coup, and the "temporary failure" of the revolutionary movement in Chile. Most valuable to those studying post-1973 political thought.

3256 **Quiroz, Abraham** and **Hipólito Gutiérrez.** Dos soldados en la Guerra del Pacífico. Prólogo de Guillermo Feliú Cruz. Introducción y notas de Yolando Pino Saavedra. Buenos Aires: Editorial Francisco de Aguirre, 1976. 241 p.: ill.; index (Colección Guerra del Pacífico; 9. Biblioteca Francisco de Aguirre; 60)

An inside and personal document of the feelings, perceptions, training, daily life, and even language of the common soldiers during the War of the Pacific. Such rare accounts are valuable for studies of social history, as well as the history of the war.

3257 **Rector, John.** Transformaciones comerciales producidas por la independencia de Chile: pts. 1/2 (SCHG/R, 143, 1975, p. 107–126; 144, 1976, p. 62–80)

A thoughtful and well-founded analysis of the changes in Chilean commerce from 1808 to 1828. Deals with such topics as the amount and type of commerce, the role of foreigners, operation of the merchant companies, and regulations. Particularly valuable for understanding the dominance of foreign merchants in Chile.

3258 **Reyno Gutiérrez, Manuel.** La Patria Vieja no se perdió en Rancagua (SCHG/R, 143, 1975, p. 153–170)

A lucid essay, rather than a research-based analysis, claiming that neither Bernardo O'Higgins nor José Miguel Carrera were culpable for the disaster of the Battle of Rancagua in 1811. Argues that both leaders, though inexperienced and perhaps self-centered, were dedicated to the independence of Chile.

3259 **———.** Quién fué el vencedor de Yungay? (SCHG/R, 145, 1977, p. 161–171)

Written to correct the statement in a recent newspaper article that Peruvian General Ramón Castilla, and not the Chilean hero, Manuel Bulnes, won the battle of Yungay during the war with the Peruvian-Bolivian Confederacy in 1839. Those unfamiliar with the controversy will find this argument hard to follow.

3260 **Richards, Alan R.** The political economy of commercial estate labor systems: a comparative analysis of Prussia, Egypt, and Chile (CSSH, 21:4, Oct. 1979, p. 483–518, table)

A provocative comparative analysis of the economic motivations of resident estate labor which criticizes existing analytical frameworks. Argues that the threat of expulsion precluded any need for oppressive control and gave landowners a cheap, docile labor force. Based on secondary sources.

3261 **Román, Charles G. Pregger.** Economic interest groups within the Chilean government, 1851 to 1891: continuity and discontinuity in economic and political evolution (SS, 43:2, Summer 1979, p. 202–233)

Interprets the uprisings of 1851, 1859 and 1891 as the results of the political exclusion of major economic interest groups. Fails to recognize and excuse kinship ties between economic interests. Oddly, the primary source here is consular dispatches. Thesis has been set out more convincingly in Crisóstomo Pizarro's *La revolución de 1891*

(Valparaíso, Chile: Universidad Católica de Valparaíso, 1975? 98 p.; bibl.).

3262 ———. Role of the banking and insurance sector in the failure of the industrial revolution in nineteenth-century Chile (RU/SCID, Oct. 1978, p. 76–96)

Presents some new and interesting data to demonstrate and explain anew why the foreign-dominated, export-oriented business sector did not direct capital toward the development of industry and other internal enterprises.

Salinas Meza, René. Fuentes para el estudio de la demografía histórica en el Norte Chico Chileno, 1600–1854. See item **2822**.

3263 **Sater, William F.** Chile and the world depression of the 1870s (JLAS, 2:1, May 1979, p. 67–99, tables)

Takes the unusual though debatable position that: 1) Chile's economic problems in the late 1870s were part of the worldwide depression, rather than the result of declining mineral and agricultural exports as usually assumed, and that 2) the Chilean government consciously sought economic self-suffiency. A serious study with authoritative descriptions of the impact of the depression on different economic sectors.

3264 ———. A survey of recent Chilean historiography: 1965–1976 (LARR, 14:2, 1979, p. 55–88)

A heroic and well-executed synthesis of the recent outpouring of historical writing on Chile, dividing the literature into political, economic and social categories. Besides providing a valuable reference to recent publications, the article synthesizes the major current theories and arguments.

3265 **Sehlinger, Peter J.** Valentín Letelier and positivist historiography in nineteenth-century Chile (*in* Rocky Mountain Council on Latin American Studies, XXV, Tucson, Ariz., 1977. Proceedings. Lincoln: University of Nebraska, 1977, p. 39–45)

A readable, thoughtful, and well-documented analysis of the intellectual underpinnings of late 19th-century Chilean historiography, emphasizing Valentín Letelier's optimistic "scientific" rationale for historical research. For Spanish translation, see *Revista Chilena de Historia y Geografía* (Santiago, 145, 1977, p. 113–124).

3266 **Shazo, Peter de.** The Valparaíso maritime strike of 1903 and the development of a revolutionary labor movement in Chile (JLAS, 2:1, May 1979, p. 145–168)

A fundamental analysis of Chile's organized labor movement (1898–1927) and particularly the 1903 strike. Maintains that the Chilean labor movement, unlike others in Latin America, assumed leftist leanings early-on because brutal repression fostered class unity while neither employers nor civil authorities attempted to redress grievances nor eradicate resistance.

3267 **Shurbutt, Ray T.** The personnel approach to United State's relations with Chile, 1823–1850 (*in* Dependency unbends: case studies in inter-American relations. Carrollton: West Georgia College, 1978, p. 37–48)

Documents the lack of concern within the US State Department toward Chile (1823–50) by looking at the contact of the State Department with its representative in Chile.

Stallings, Barbara. Class conflict and economic development in Chile, 1958–1973. See *HLAS 41:7446*.

3268 **Stegmaier Rodríguez, Juan L.** Lord Tomás Alejandro Cochrane (SCHG/R, 144, 1976, p. 146–166)

A descriptive chronological outline of the major events in the life of this charismatic English naval captain who figured prominently in the independence of South America. This easy-to-use presentation only gives the most basic information on Cochrane's life.

3269 **Stemplowski, Ryszard.** Chile y las compañías petroleras, 1931–1932: contribución al estudio del entrelazamiento dominación-dependencia (IAA, 4:1, 1978, p. 1–19, bibl.)

Based on consular reports, shows the ties between economic and political interests in North Atlantic countries by analyzing the reaction of the governments of the US and Great Britain to the threatened Soviet takeover of the Chilean oil market in 1928. A serious work. For economist's comment, see *HLAS 41:3239*.

3270 **Subercaseaux Browne, Julio.** Reminiscencias. Santiago, Chile: Editorial

Nascimento, 1976. 322 p. (Biblioteca popular Nascimento)

These memoirs offer colorful insight into the life and concerns of the Chilean upper class in the last third of the 19th century. The descriptions of piano lessons, horse racing, gala parties, and foreign travels are a non-fictional confirmation of the "good life" portrayed in the famous novel *Casa Grande.*

3271 Super, Richard R. The Seguro Obrero massacre (*in* The underside of Latin America [see item **1948**] p. 43–66)

Details the circumstances of this little known event in 1938 in which the national police massacred 61 Nazi youths, probably by the orders of President Alessandri. Contends the episode demonstrates that unsavory political incidents occurred in Chile as elsewhere in Latin America.

3272 Testimonios y recuerdos de la Guerra del Pacífico. Edited by Oscar Pinochet de la Barra. Santiago de Chile: Editorial del Pacífico, 1978 or 1979. 284 p.; bibl.; 1 leaf of plates: ill.

Reproductions of excerpts of letters, diaries, and memoirs of a cross-class and country selection of participants in the War of the Pacific. Organized by battles, giving various perspectives. At times colorful and fascinating, these accounts are valuable documents for social history as well as history of the war.

3273 Thomas, Jack Ray. The impact of the generation of 1842 on Chilean historiography (PAT/TH, 41:4, Aug. 1979, p. 705–720)

Looks at the writings of lesser as well as famous Chilean intellectuals of the early republican period. Studies their opinions on education and the purpose of history.

3274 Thorndike, Guillermo. Vienen los chilenos. Lima: Promoinvest Compañía de Inversiones, 1978. 420 p.; 3 leaves of plates: maps (HKIS Guerra del salitre; 3)

A lively written historical novel about the War of the Pacific, complete with maps and some documents.

3275 Valenzuela, Arturo. Political brokers in Chile: local government in centralized polity. Durham: University of North Carolina Press, 1977. 272 p.

Fundamental work on the role of local government in Chilean national politics in the early 1970s. Pt. 3 deals with the historical evolution of local governments' prerogatives. For political scientist's comment, see *HLAS 41:7454.*

3276 ———. Political participation, agriculture, and literacy: communal versus provincial voting patterns in Chile (LARR, 12:1, 1977, p. 105–114)

A replication of Sinding's (see *HLAS 35:7782*) pioneering analysis of the ecological correlations between voting patterns and socio-economic variables in Chile, 1912–1973, based, this time, on communal rather than provincial data. Shows that province is too large a unit for analysis, and suggests that, due to ecological diversity between regions of this exceptionally long country, correlations are not possible for Chile as a whole. Anyone attempting a statistical analysis for Chile will have to deal with the issues raised here. For political scientist's comment, see *HLAS 41:7455.*

3277 Veliz, Claudio. The Irisarri loan (CEDLA/B, 23, 1977, p. 3–20)

A carefully researched study of the terms of negotiation and impact of the 1822 British loan to Chile. Offers a new perspective on the downfall of O'Higgins and rise of Portales.

3278 Vergara Quiroz, Sergio. Economía y sociedad en Magallanes, 1843–1877. Santiago: Universidad de Chile, Facultad de Ciencias Sociales, Departamento de Historia, Cátedra de Historia de Chile, Editorial Universitaria, 1979; 84 p.; ill. (Cuadernos de historia; 3)

A comprehensive, extensively researched study of Magallanes' early history discussing such topics as the penal colony at Punta Arena, population increase, Swiss immigration, and commercial activity.

Winn, Peter. Oral history and the factory study: new approaches to labor history. See item **1954**.

3279 Woll, Allen L. Positivism and history in nineteenth century Chile: José Victoriano Lastarria and Valentín Letelier (JHI, 37:3, 1976, p. 493–506)

A thoughtful critique of Chilean positivism, asserting that due to religious restraints and a fractured intellectual school, Chilean positivists were unable to produce the scientific history advocated by Auguste Comte.

3280 Yeager, Gertrude Matyoka. Barros Arana, Vicuña Mackenna, Amunátegui: the historian as national educator (UM/JIAS, 19:2, May 1977, p. 173–200)

This interesting article, based on thorough reading of the sources, deals with the trio of 19th-century historians from the viewpoint of their impact on Chilean political and civic values. Through analysis of the major themes of their works, the author demonstrates the ways in which these professional historians were able to inculcate their brand of eclectic liberalism in generations of elite youth and thus influence the country's pattern of development. [Thomas C. Wright]

3281 ———. The Club de la Unión and kinship: social aspects of political obstructionism in the Chilean Senate, 1920–1924 (AAFH/TAM, 35:4, April 1979, p. 539–572)

Contends that the elitist *Unionista* party, after failing in the election of 1920, nevertheless blocked social legislation and political change during the Alessandri presidency. Although the article as a whole is disjointed, each of the three sections—on party competition in the 1920 election, kinship links and class composition of the Club de la Unión, and the voting behavior of Chilean Senators from 1920 to 1924—is sound and interesting.

Zapata, Francisco. Las relaciones entre el movimiento obrero y el gobierno de Salvador Allende. See *HLAS 41:9251.*

Argentina, Paraguay and Uruguay

HOBART A. SPALDING, JR., *Professor of History, Brooklyn College, CUNY*

ARGENTINA: In previous volumes, we noted how this section was shrinking, a trend which continues despite the fact that, in the last two years, a number of interesting new topics have been the subject of historical investigation. While some relatively unpublished authors produced important articles and books, many familiar names published on areas and themes about which they had previously written. Popular works still poured off the presses but the seemingly endless controversies on Rosas and Perón suffered a marked reduction.

In English, at least three monographs deserve more than passing attention. Reid Andrews' book (item **3291**) fulfilled much of the promise evident in his articles (items **3290** and **3292**). His work on Afro-Argentines in Buenos Aires from 1800–1900 will help dispel the mystery of their "disappearance" in the 19th century. Donna Guy continued her studies of Tucumán and sugar, showing how local and national politics intertwined to influence the development of agroindustry (item **3360**). Carl Solberg's general history of the petroleum industry in national politics to the 1930s provided a competent synthesis and raised questions for further investigation (item **3425**).

Foreign and local merchants in the early 19th century received varied treatment in works by Vera Blinn Reber, Jonathan Brown, and Karla Robinson (items **2947**, **3411** and **3414**). All three examined the impact of British merchants and the evolution of their role as local and international economic conditions changed. In conjunction with Henri Arnoux's article on French investment in later decades (item **3294**), they suggest the need for a fresh look at the relative importance of British, French, and local capital in the period.

Several books appeared in Spanish on conservative politics, perhaps reflecting the current situation. Natalio Botana wrote what may be the best single volume on the

Régimen (1880–1916) from a sympathetic yet critical point of view (item **3311**). Félix Luna's biography of President Ortiz revived interest in that key but relatively unknown figure (item **3382**). Mafalda Díaz Melian's detailed work on the crisis of 1890 broadens our knowledge about the event (item **3333**). The yellow fever epidemic of 1871 received lengthy treatment in Miguel Angel Scenna's study (item **3419**). César García Belsunce edited a second volume about Buenos Aires in the early decades of the 19th century (item **3312**) as rich in data as was the first (see *HLAS 40:3760*). Also worth mentioning is Enrique Barba's short monograph on the 1868–78 reform movement in Buenos Aires province which links it to contemporary and future national events (item **3300**). Yaácov Oved's careful monograph on anarchism at the turn of the century, not available at press time, will be annotated in *HLAS 44*.

A number of articles raised suggestive hypotheses and explored new themes for the period 1853–1930. Glyn Williams continued his work on Welsh settlements in this case suggestively arguing that the "Conquest of the Desert" could have occurred in a different fashion through peaceful settlement (item **3443**). Henri Arnoux did a fine summary of the impact of the French and particularly French capital in late 19th- and early 20th-century economic development, a theme which merits further attention (item **3294**). Ezequiel Gallo contributed yet another seminal article on provincial history providing additional building blocks for future synthesis on the integration of immigrants into political and economic structures at the local and national levels (item **3350**). A worthy study of a populist movement in the provinces is Rodríguez' book on Mendoza politics in the 1920s (item **3415**). Jorge Balán and Nancy López persuasively argue that provincial finances rested on a much more rational basis than is often assumed, at least in Tucumán and Mendoza between 1873 and 1914 (item **3299**), a theme supported by Guy (item **3360**) and by William Fleming (item **3346**). Two veteran historians of Argentina published interesting contributions: Samuel Baily struck another blow against the melting-pot thesis by examining immigrant marriage patterns in Buenos Aires (1882–1923), and finding a continuing homogamy among first and second generations (item **3298**). Richard Walter looked at electoral patterns (1916–22) and provided some empirical evidence for the accepted differentiated class backing for the Socialists, Radicals, and the PDP (item **3438**). A host of well-known Argentine historians continued to investigate varied aspects of their country's past, particularly the 19th century. For example, Néstor Auza looked at the frontier in mid-century (items **3295** and **3296**), Beatriz Bosch finished two works on Entre Ríos (items **3308** and **3309**), Horacio Juan Cuccorese wrote on the economic history of the late 19th century (item **3325**), Roberto Etchepareborda presented a detailed article on the 1892 *Baltimore* Affair (item **3340**), and Leoncio Gianello did more work on the provinces of the Litoral (item **3353**).

For the more recent period, Louise Doyon (item **3335**), Daniel James (item **3368**), and Spencer Wellhofer (item **3442**) all added fuel to the debate about the exact nature of support for peronism and the reasons why that tendency survived within the labor movement after 1955.

At a different level, popular historical publications continued to appear: *Todo es Historia* published more anthologies of articles from that magazine (items **3403** and **3424**), the "Memorial de la Patria" series (see *HLAS 40*, p. 280) neared completion, and a series of books based on conversations with leading figures of recent years also competed to capture the interest of non-professionals in contemporary and historical themes (items **3320**, **3334**, **3380** and **3399**).

PARAGUAY: These were vintage years for Paraguayan historiography marked by the appearance of three major monographs in English and a handful of useful articles. John Hoyt Williams, Richard White, and Harris Gaylord Warren all published notable items. Williams produced what surely will be the basic book on the period of 1800–70 (item **3477**). White launched a revisionist interpretation of the Franciata set within dependency theory which is sure to stir controversy (item **3475**). Warren's book initiated the process of unraveling the long transitional period after the Paraguayan War by studying the postwar decade and particularly the genesis of political groups that would eventually dominate the country (item **3472**). In addition, Thomas Whigham's article on the iron works of Ybycuí marks him as a rising scholar in the field (item **3473**). All the above authors share a marked sympathy for the area and a constant theme, explicit or tacit, that runs through their work is the degree to which outside forces have impinged upon Paraguayan history and almost always to the detriment of that nation's balanced development. Also of note is Corinne Choay's article on French immigration (item **3453**)—one of a number of articles on the three countries annotated in this section and written by French authors—and Omar Díaz de Arce's provocative, controversial, and lengthy essay on the course of Paraguayan development between 1925–75 (item **3454**). Otherwise, the usual number of publications on the Chaco War or related themes continued to appear.

URUGUAY: In contrast to Paraguay, historical work on Uruguay remained at a virtual standstill. A few items, nevertheless, deserve mention. Nelson Díaz' work on English railroads in the 19th century makes a good beginning for a study into an important topic (item **3486**). Martha Marenales Rossi and Guy Bourdé contributed to our knowledge on French influences in the country (item **3492**). Juan E. Pivel Devoto continued his detailed studies in the *Revista Histórica* where a lengthy article on banks makes available much useful data on that particular topic in the last century (item **3502**). And finally, Gerónimo de Sierra's interpretative essay provides a provocative departure point for potential reinterpretation of Uruguay's past 100 years (item **3504**). In addition, four more volumes of the popular series on Uruguayan political leaders were also published (items **3483**, **3490–3491** and **3495**).

ARGENTINA

3282 Academia Nacional de la Historia, *Buenos Aires.* Catálogo de la Colección Enrique Fitte. Presentación de Carlos S.A. Segreti. Introducción y catalogación por Alicia Mercedes Ubeira. Buenos Aires: La Academia, 1977. 170 p.; 4 leaves of plates: ill.; index (Biblioteca de publicaciones documentales; 13)

Chronologically arranged catalogue of 940 items dating from 16th through 20th centuries, but mostly from 19th century. Index by name and brief description of item.

3283 Acevedo, Edberto Oscar. Proceso a un hereje en Mendoza: aporte para la historia de las ideas en el interior (ANH/IE, 19, julio/dic. 1975, p. 275–304)

Concerns a heresy trial against a "freethinker" in Mendoza during 1824 showing collaboration between religious and civil authorities as guardians of the morals and cultural well-being of the community.

3284 ———. El regreso de los emigrados (ANH/B, 49, 1979, p. 263–270)

Brief commentary on petitions by exiles or their families asking the Mendoza government to return in 1832. While the reasons and motives, as well as responses, vary the government acceeded to most. A step towards further outlining the rules of the game for 19th-century provincial politics.

3285 **Alén Lascano, Luis C.** Yrigoyen y la guerra mundial. Buenos Aires: Editorial Korrigan: distribuidora Rubbo, 1974. 96 p.: ill. (Colección Testimonio; 2)

Short monograph defending Yrigoyen's policies during World War I which the author sees as nationalist, pacifist, and anti-imperialist.

3286 **Alexander, Robert Jackson.** Juan Domingo Perón: a history. Boulder, Colo.: Westview Press, 1979. 177 p.; bibl.; index.

A short interpretive study which presents a mostly unflattering picture of Perón. Concludes that character flaws (lack of political philosophy, cynicism, and authoritarian tendencies) prevented Perón's becoming a true leader but converted him into a tragic figure.

Allub, Leopoldo. Estado y sociedad civil: patrón de emergencia y desarrollo del Estado Argentino. See *HLAS 41:7461*.

3287 **Alvarado, Ricardo.** L'évolution historique du syndicalisme argentin entre 1955 et 1973 (FDD/NED [Problèmes d'Amérique Latine, 50] 4499/4500, 29 déc. 1978, p. 93–130, tables)

A broad summary article outlining the basic trends within the labor movement and primarily its majoritarian Peronist component. Contrasts the coalition basis of the first Peronist regime with that of 1973 to show the lessened possibilities for a united movement and the strengthened anti-Peronist forces grouped around foreign monopoly capital.

Alvarez, Antonio. Crónica de la Patagonia y tierras australes desde el descubrimiento hasta la colonización. See item **2628**.

3288 **Alzola Zárate, José Daniel.** La organización de archivos históricos. Buenos Aires: Ediciones C.I.C.H.A.L., 1977. 16 p.

Based on author's work and experiences in the Archive of La Rioja Province and the University of Buenos Aires Historical Archive.

3289 **Anadón, Carlos A.** and **María del Carmen Muratur de Badaracco.** La colectividad italiana en Victoria, E. Ríos. Victoria, Argentina: Los Gráficos, 1976. 76 p.; bibl.; plates; tables.

Brief historical sketch of Italian colony with material on leading citizens, associations, etc.

3290 **Andrews, George Reid.** The Afro-Argentine officers of Buenos Aires Province, 1800–1860 (ASNLH/J, 64:2, Spring 1979, p. 85–100, tables)

Excellent article showing that contrary to common assertions, Afro-Argentines did hold positions as officers in the Army of Buenos Aires Province between 1800 and 1860. Explores the limitations placed upon these officers in terms of advancement and within the society as a whole. Hypothesizes that this phenomena was not limited to Argentina but holds true for all Latin America.

3291 ———. The Afro-Argentines of Buenos Aires, 1800–1900. Madison: University of Wisconsin Press, 1980. 286 p.; bibl.; ill.; index.

An excellent, pathbreaking monograph on the Afro-Argentine community from the 18th century to 1900. Examines slave trade and slavery, transition to freedom, the early 19th century, Afro-Argentines in the military, community organization, the arts, and the post-1850s. Concludes that the oft cited "disappearance" of the Afro-Argentines, while partially true statistically, was also the product of changing racial attitudes which eliminated the group by ignoring it. The community suffered from discriminatory practices found elsewhere in the Americas (differences being mainly in degree). Modernization and growth only reinforced mechanisms which excluded Afro-Argentines from social and economic competition, despite laws (largely unenforced) to the contrary. Hypothesizes that Argentine patterns resemble those found elsewhere in Latin America.

3292 ———. Race versus class association: the Afro-Argentines of Buenos Aires, 1850–1900 (JLAS, 2:1, May 1979, p. 19–39)

An excellent article which convincingly argues that the Afro-Argentine community remained a caste apart, but divided into classes which paralleled those of the larger society. Based on primary sources, the work seriously challenges assimilationist theories for both Argentina, and by implication, the rest of Latin America.

3293 **Argentine Republic. Ministerio de Guerra y Marina.** Campaña de los

Andes al sur de la Patagonia, año 1883: partes detalladas y diario de la expedición, Ministerio de Guerra y Marina. 2. ed. Buenos Aires: Editorial Universitaria de Buenos Aires, 1978. 438 p.: map (1 fold. col. in pocket) (Lucha de fronteras con el indio)

Includes a variety of documents, reports, *memorias*, official orders, etc. about the expedition.

Armani, Roberto. Trenel, un pueblo de La Pampa: estudio histórico-geográfico. See *HLAS 41:5402*.

3294 Arnoux, Henri. Le role des Français dans la fondation de l'industrie argentine à la fin du XIXe et au début du XXe siècle (CDAL, 16, 1977, p. 79–104)

Interesting article on role of French people and capital during the 19th and early 20th centuries. French immigrants helped found some of the largest units in the wine, tannin, sugar, textiles, beer, and meat-packing industries. Distinguishes two periods: 1850–90 when Frenchmen came and founded industrial establishments, and 1890 to 1930 when French capital was invested in the railroad system and in banking.

3295 Auza, Néstor Tomás. Lucio V. Mansilla: la Confederación. Buenos Aires: Plus Ultra, 1978. 191 p.: ill. (Colección Los Argentinos; 8)

A detailed study of Mansilla's life from his exile of 1856 to entry in military in 1860. Good summary of the Confederation, local politics, and the man.

3296 ———. El periodismo de la Confederación, 1852–1861. Buenos Aires: Editorial Universitaria de Buenos Aires, 1978. 287 p.; bibl. (Colección Argentina)

An excellent monograph which includes a chapter on each of 12 newspapers studied and several chapters on *El Nacional*. Includes a general historical background summary and lists of all the newspapers believed published at the time. Shows a vibrant press flourished in these years.

3297 Avellaneda, Nicolás. El baúl de Avellaneda: correspondencia y documentos, 1861–1885. Compilados y comentados por Julio Avellaneda. Buenos Aires: Emecé Editores, 1977. 802 p.: ill.

Includes 172 letters each with brief commentary. Mostly personal material but names of correspondents indicates how small was the world of politics in that era. Includes little if any material for a substantial re-evaluation of the man.

Bagú, Sergio. José Luis Romero: evocación y evaluación. See item **7619**.

3298 Baily, Samuel L. Marriage patterns and immigrant assimilation in Buenos Aires, 1882–1923 (HAHR, 60:1, 1980, p. 32–48)

An excellent article based on primary materials which argues that "ethnicity continued to be important in the selection of a spouse and homogamy continued high among first and then second generation immigrants." Assimilation "did not take place very rapidly or completely" and "cultural pluralism is a more valid conceptualization of the assimilation process." Another strong attack on the once accepted melting pot thesis.

Balán, Jorge. Una cuestión regional en la Argentina: burguesías provinciales y el mercado nacional en el desarrollo agroexportador. See *HLAS 41:3375*.

3299 ——— and **Nancy G. López.** Burguesías y gobiernos provinciales en la Argentina: la política impositiva de Tucumán y Mendoza entre 1873 y 1914 (IDES/DE, 17:76, oct./dic. 1977, p. 391–435, bibl., tables)

An innovative and suggestive article based on a study of taxation from 1873 to 1914. Argues that traditional oligarchies pursued a far more enlightened fiscal policy than hitherto assumed and that new industries or political outs did not suffer necessarily extreme taxation. Indeed tax policies often followed pragmatic considerations.

Balmori, Diana and **Robert Oppenheimer.** Family clusters: generational nucleation in nineteenth-century Argentina and Chile. See item **3194**.

3300 Barba, Fernando Enrique. Los autonomistas del 70: auge y frustración de un movimiento provinciano con vocación nacional: Buenos Aires entre 1868 y 1878. Buenos Aires: Editorial Pleamar, 1976. 158 p.; bibl.; 3 leaves of plates: maps (Testimonios nacionales)

A solid study of a generation which sought to reform their province in matters of education, social legislation, and agriculture. Links this generation with that of 1880, a comparison few historians have attempted.

3301 Barnes, John. Evita, First Lady: a biography of Eva Perón. New York: Grove Press: distributed by Random House, 1978. 195 p.; 8 leaves of plates: ill.; index.

A journalistic account with more sensationalism than historical interpretation. Perpetuates most of the traditional myths.

Bartolomé, Leopoldo. Movimientos milenaristas de los aborígenes chaqueños entre 1905 y 1933. See *HLAS 41:1113*.

3302 Benencia, Julio Arturo. Partes de batalla de las guerras civiles. t. 3, 1840–1852. Buenos Aires: Academia Nacional de la Historia, 1977. 650 p. (Biblioteca de publicaciones documentales; 12)

Good primary source. A brief historical introduction by Benencia precedes the 238 documents he compiled. For previous volume (covering 1840–52), see *HLAS 40: 3699*.

Biagini, Hugo E. El progresismo argentino del ochenta. See item **7625**.

3303 Bidart Campos, Germán José. Historia política y constitucional argentina. Buenos Aires: EDIAR, 1976. 2 v.; bibl.

Vol. 1 covers 1810–53, mostly constitutional history; vol. 2, 1854–1976, is devoted to political history and less detailed than the first. Both summarize constitutional developments and main political trends. Written from an anti-Marxist, anti-revisionist viewpoint.

3304 Biraghi, Roberto I. Reseña histórica de la zona de San Lorenzo: el país de las batatas. Rosario, Argentina: Escuela de Artes Gráficas del Colegio Salesiano San José, 1973. 323 p.; bibl.; 8 leaves of plates: ill.

Local history from pre-colonial times to early 20th century.

3305 Bischoff, Efraín U. Córdoba: los ratones y las llaves (ANH/IE, 21, julio/dic. 1976, p. 175–221)

Leading provincial historian expounds on the Municipal Archive and its development from colonial period. Mostly anecdotal.

———. Las viejas imprentas de la Universidad. See item **2630**.

3306 *Boletín*. Provincia de Santa Fe. Ministerio de Gobierno. Archivo General de la Provincia. Año 6, No. 6, 1974– . Santa Fe, Argentina.

Contains numerous documents, biographical materials, short articles by local writers from the past, as well as longer historical studies covering colonial, independence, and national periods.

3307 Bonura, Elena. Notas sobre la Aduana de Buenos Aires: la "Unión Aduanera Argentina" (CEHA/NH, 9:18, dic. 1976, p. 340–348)

Short article on role of port of Buenos Aires during first decades of 19th century. Reassesses the position that Buenos Aires choked off commerce within the platine basin.

3308 Bosch Vinelli, Julia Beatriz. Historia de Entre Ríos, 1520–1969. Buenos Aires: Plus Ultra, 1978. 334 p.: ill.; index (Colección Historia de nuestras provincias; 3)

Basic historical overview by a leading provincial historian concentrating mostly upon 19th century and political events.

3309 ———. Notas sobre navegación fluvial: 1843–1853 (ANH/IE, 19, julio/dic. 1975, p. 325–345, facsims., tables)

Describes sail traffic on the Paraguay and Uruguay rivers in Entre Ríos, during 1843–53, providing assorted data on ports, number of ships, cargoes, ownership of bottoms, etc. By mid 1850s the predominance of sail finally ended.

3310 Bossio, Jorge Alberto. Argentina: la historiografía en crisis. Buenos Aires: Ediciones C.I.C.H.A.L., 1977. 135 p.; bibl.

An interpretive essay which argues that it is necessary to place historical phenomena inside their larger cultural settings in order to understand the country's evolution.

3311 Botana, Natalio. El Orden Conservador: la política argentina entre 1880 y 1916. Buenos Aires: Editorial Sudamericana, 1977. 345 p.; bibl.; ill. (Colección Historia y sociedad)

An astute examination of the oligarchy and its political rule. Examines the ideological origins of the hegemonic project from Alberdi to its political triumph with Roca.

Details relationships between national and provincial authorities. Contrasts intent behind Sáenz Peña Law and its destructive results for the regime. Based on many primary sources and author's keen insights into the conservative mind. Argues ultimately that a loss of political, and with it socioeconomic, vision cost the conservatives (although not entirely unwillingly) their dominance. An excellent contribution.

Bratzel, John F. The Chaco dispute and the search for prestige. See item **3141**.

Brown, Jonathan C. A socioeconomic history of Argentina, 1776–1860. See item **2947**.

3312 Buenos Aires, 1800–1830. t. 2, Salud y delito. Edited by César García Belsunce. Buenos Aires: Emece Distribuidora, 1977. 297 p.; plates; tables.

Contains wealth of data about health, medicine, and public safety. Argues that health facilities improved slowly and that a cosmopolitan medical community existed attuned to latest European advances. Also notes increasing harshness of the law after 1820 directly related to political instability. A valuable contribution. For vol. 1, on *Su gente,* see *HLAS 40:3760.*

Buljevic, Ossandon. La concepción de una filosofía americana en Alberdi. See item **7552**.

Bushnell, David. El proceso inicial del liberalismo en Colombia y en la Argentina: un esquema comparativo. See item **2633**.

Calafut, George. An analysis of Italian emigration statistics, 1876–1914. See item **1921a**.

3313 Canclini, Arnoldo. Cómo fue civilizado el sur patagónico. Prólogo de Armando Alonso Piñeiro. Buenos Aires: Editorial Plus Ultra, 1977. 319 p.; appendixes; bibl. (Colección Esquema históricos; 27)

Expanded version of 1951 publication centering around missionary efforts of Sociedad Misionera de la Patagonia from 1830s to end of century. Also material on society in northern Argentina and Chile. Documentary appendixes.

3314 Capdevila, Pedro V. La estancia argentina. Buenos Aires: Editorial Plus Ultra, 1978. 409 p.; bibl.; 19 leaves of plates: ill. (Grandes obras de la literatura gauchesca)

Divided into four parts: 1) history of the estancia; 2) evolution of the livestock industry; 3) daily life around the estancia; and 4) the estancia as a social, economic, political, and military nucleus. Contains historical and anecdotal materials, photos and statistics.

3315 Casais de Corne, Alicia Elena; Fiz Antonio Fernández; and **Julio Lardies González.** Panorama histórico de la medicina argentina. Buenos Aires: Todo es Historia, 1977. 147 p.; bibl.; plates.

Brief synthesis from pre-colonial period to 1950. Biographies and short histories of institutions such as the Argentine Red Cross, etc.

3316 Castro, Ana E. Mendoza ante los intentos constitucionales: 1827–1830 (UNC/RHAA, 8:15/16, 1970–1971, p. 83–98)

A summary article on the viscissitudes of the federalist-unitario struggles and Mendoza's role in the several attempts to find a way to constitute a national entity. Part of a larger study in progress on the 1824–52 period.

3317 Castro Nevares, Federico. El Archivo de la Confederación (Revista del Archivo General de la Nación [Buenos Aires] 5:5, 1976, p. 49–79, tables)

Argues that the Archive of the Confederation (1853–61) which many thought lost exists but dispersed among other collections in the capital. A nice detective job, if accurate.

Cenni storici sull'emigrazione italiana nelle Americhe e in Australia. See item **2634**.

3318 Chávez, Fermín. Historicismo e iluminismo en la cultura argentina: Juan Cuello, Rosas, Vico, Herder, Alberdi, Castañeda, Castellani, Nimio de Anquín. Buenos Aires: Editora del País, 1977. 135 p.; bibl.; index (Ideas del pensamiento nacional)

A series of short essays on intellectual history. Attacks *iluminismo* as predominant among Argentine ideologues and argues that its false values have no application for the true Argentine national being.

3319 100 [i.e. Cien] años, Iglesia Danesa Tandil: 28 de octubre, 1877–1977. Tandil, Argentina: Congregación Protestante del Tandil, 1977. 92 p.; ill.; plates.

Study of Lutheran church and community in Tandil. Text in Spanish and Danish.

3320 Corbière, Emilio J. Conversaciones con Oscar Alende. Buenos Aires: Colihué-Hachette, 1978. 215 p.: ill. (Colección Diálogos polémicos)

A veteran Radical politician discusses his 40 years in politics including his administration as Governor of Buenos Aires Province (1958–62). Like others in this series mostly of interest for anecdotes and political details of period and personage.

3321 Cortés-Conde, Roberto. Trends of real wages in Argentina, 1880–1910. Cambridge, UK: Cambridge University, Centre of Latin American Studies, 1976. 45 p.; tables (Working papers; 26)

Argues that real wages increased from 1883 to 1899 reaching a peak in that year not again matched even in 1912. A steady decline set in after 1900 with slight improvement from 1910–12. Based on official figures and series taken from records of Bagley Brothers, a previously untapped source. For Spanish version of this article, see *Económica* (Universidad Nacional de la Plata, 22:2/3, mayo/dic. 1976, p. 131–159).

3322 Cresto, Juan José. La correspondencia que engendró una guerra: nuevos estudios sobre los orígenes de la Guerra con el Paraguay. Prólogo de Enrique de Gandía. Buenos Aires: Ediciones Convergencia, 1974. 59 p.

Argues that Blanco foreign policy, in turn a product of the internal threat represented by the Colorados, ultimately lay behind the Paraguayan War.

3323 Cuccorese, Horacio Juan. La cuestión limítrofe con Chile: tiempo de agudización del conflicto, 1900–1901 (ANH/IE, 19, julio/dic. 1975, p. 305–323)

Lays out conflicting positions of Zeballos and Pellegrini concerning the border conflict with Chile based on a private letter between the two. Shows how each sought to fulfill nationalist goals, Zeballos by a strong stance, Pellegrini through a subtler approach.

3324 ———. Historia sobre el origen del Banco de la Nación Argentina: acción y reacción en Buenos Aires y Londres (ANH/IE, 21, julio/dic. 1976, p. 125–174, bibl.)

Continuation of an earlier article which examines the circumstances around the founding of the Bank and the arguments advanced for and against it.

3325 ———. La versión histórica argentina sobre la crisis de Baring Brothers & Co. en 1890 (ANH/IE, 20, enero/junio 1976, p. 265–322, bibl.)

Argues that Baring Brothers' poor administration led to its troubles in 1890 and that the Argentine government under Pellegrini provided support for the beleaguered financial house.

3326 D'Amico, David F. Religious liberty in Argentina during the first Perón regime, 1943–1955 (ASCH/CH, 46:4, Dec. 1977, p. 490–503)

Discusses why the Catholic Church supported Perón, the reasons behind the eventual break between the two, and Perón's curtailment and then relaxation of measures against Protestants and other non-Catholic groups. The analysis is primarily political and religious and weak on social aspects of Perón-Church relations.

3327 Daró, Delmo F.M. Apuntes históricos de la colonia y el pueblo Armstrong, Santa Fe: desde su orígenes hasta 1972. Santa Fe, Argentina: Librería y Editorial Colmegna, 1978. 400 p.; bibl.; ill.

A detailed local history covering 1870s to 1970s. Material on institutions, politics, and local notables.

3328 ———. Orígenes de la colonia y el pueblo de Armstrong, Santa Fe: precedidos por una reseña sobre las etapas en el dominio de la región, desde la época prehispánica hasta la colonización del F.C.C.A., y referencias sobre los primitivos núcleos de pobladores, dependencia político-administrativa y primeras autoridades del territorio. t. 1. Rosario, Argentina: Talleres Gráficos del Colegio Salesiano San José, 1977. 80 p.; ill.; maps; plates; tables.

First of four projected volumes covers the origins of the township of Armstrong through late 19th century.

3329 Davis, Thomas B. A young Argentine in the United States: 1824 (PAIGH/H, 82, julio/dic. 1976, p. 83–109)

Describes Tomás de Iriarte's stay in the US as Secretary of the Argentine legation when Carlos de Alvear first opened official relations.

3330 Díaz de Molina, Alfredo. José Figueroa Alcorta, de la oligarquía a la democracia: 1898–1928. Buenos Aires: Plus Ultra, 1979. 414 p.; bibl.; ill. (Colección Política e historia)

An essentially sympathetic biography concentrating upon the political aspects of Figueroa Alcorta's career and particularly his crucial presidency. Sees him as the key to the transition process between the old oligarchy and the "new democracy" in Argentina.

3331 ———. La oligarquía argentina: su filiación y régimen, 1840–1898. v. 1. Buenos Aires: Ediciones Pannedille, 1972. 345 p.; facsims.; plates.

Covers from independence through the Revolution of 1880 in detail. Mostly political history centering around historical mission of the oligarchy, and in particular the province of Córdoba.

3332 Díaz González, Argentino. Tiempo y región de los pringleses . . . : historia integral ilustrada: pasado, evolución, presente y porvenir al partido y ciudad. Con 53 fotograbados y 1400 nombres propios, araucanos, geográficos y agropecuarios. Coronel Pringles, Argentina: s.n., 1977. 165 p.; bibl.; 1 leaf of plates: ill.

Local history concentrating on individuals, institutions, and historical locations.

3333 Díaz Melián, Mafalda Victoria. La revolución argentina de 1890 [i.e. mil ochocientos noventa] en las fuentes españolas. Buenos Aires: Plus Ultra, 1978. 389 p.: ill. (Colección Política e historia)

A solid study which delivers more than the title promises. In reality, a work on the Revolution of 1890 as a whole based on primary sources. Includes documents and photos.

3334 Domínguez, Nelson. Conversaciones con Juan José Taccone sobre sindicalismo y política. Buenos Aires: Colihue/Hachette, 1977. 207 p.: ill. (Colección Diálogos polémicos)

A series of conversations about labor and politics with emphasis upon the post-1955 period by two persons who participated in many of the events of those years. Contains interesting material about specific labor leaders and politicians as well as about politics in general.

3335 Doyon, Louise M. Conflictos obreros durante el régimen peronista: 1946–1955 (IDES/DE, 1776, oct./dic. 1977, p. 437–473, tables)

A challenging and important article arguing that strikes during the early Perón period (1946–48) represented the attempt by workers to transfer their political victory of 1946 into the economic realm. Similarly, the wave of worker actions and increased level of participation at the grass roots level in 1953–54 can be viewed as signs of renewed combativity, one key to the survival of peronist labor organizations after 1955.

3336 Dyster, Barrie. Argentine and Australian development compared (PP, 84, Aug. 1979, p. 91–110)

Argues that Australian and Argentine development in the 19th century diverged mainly due to internal structural differences and their relative insertion into the international capitalist system. In Australia, internal forces interested in growth of internal markets and capitalization of land commanded a stronger position than in Argentina where export oriented groups held a dominant position.

3337 Elizalde, Luis de. Estudios de historia argentina. Salta: Editorial DEA, 1977. 191 p.; bibl.; 1 leaf of plates: port.

Newspaper and magazine articles published (1957–69) on diverse historical themes, most discuss the 19th century from the Liberal perspective.

3338 Endrek, Emiliano S. Defensa de la frontera cordobesa en la época de Bustos, 1820–1839 (JPHC/R, 5, 1977, p. 11–30, bibl., ill.)

Describes the defense of Córdoba's frontiers in detail.

3339 Entraigas, Raúl A. El mancebo de la tierra, Ceferino Namuncurá. Buenos Aires: s.n., 1974. 333 p.; bibl.; ill.

Sympathetic biography of Ceferino Namuncurá.

Etchepareborda, Roberto. Historia de las relaciones internacionales argentinas. See *HLAS 41:8800*.

3340 ———. La intervención argentina en el conflicto chileno-norteamericano de

1892: el caso del "Baltimore" (ANH/IE, 19, julio/dic. 1975, p. 161–179)

Argues that Argentina never offered the US logistical support should it invade Chile over the Baltimore affair of 1892, but that both President Pellegrini and Foreign Minister Zeballos knew and liked Balmaceda. Includes supporting documents.

3341 **Ezquerra, Ramón.** La vida y la obra de Roberto Levillier (IGRO/RI, 31:125/126, julio/dic. 1971, p. 387–395)

A tribute to the late (1886–1969) Argentine historian outlining his life and work.

Fabry, Julio R. San Francisco: la tierra prometida. See *HLAS 41:5417*.

3342 **Falcoff, Mark.** Was war per Peronismus von 1946 bis 1955? (BESPL, 1:4, März/April 1976, p. 3–17)

In this succinct examination of Perón's first presidency, the author discusses the significance of his ideology in Argentine political life. Author notes his agreements and divergences with revisionist historians of Peronism. [G.M. Dorn]

3343 **Ferrari, Gustavo.** Apogeo y crisis del liberalismo, 1886–1890. Buenos Aires: Ediciones La Bastilla: distribuidor exclusivo, Editorial Astrea de A. y R. Depalma, 1978. 262 p.; bibl. (Memoria de la Patria)

The rise and fall of Juárez Celman with a chapter devoted to the epoch as a whole.

Ferré, Dominique. La Perónisme: un passé en quête de futur. See *HLAS 41:7477*.

3344 **Ferreira Soaje, José V.** Alborotos revolucionarios en Córdoba en 1832 (JPHC/R, 5, 1977, p. 105–117)

Details the unsuccessful plots against the Reynafé administration during 1832, showing links to national politics as well as local impact.

3345 **Ferrer, Francisco M.** Evocación de Carlos Eduardo Carranza y su tiempo (UNL/U, 88, set./dic. 1977, p. 9–21)

Biographical article on santefecino journalist and writer (1881–1936).

3346 **Fleming, William J.** The cultural determinants of entrepreneurship and economic development: a case study of Mendoza Province, Argentina: 1861–1914 (EHA, 39:1, March 1979, p. 211–224)

Uses Mendoza as a case study to examine conditions under which economic development may proceed. In contrast to classical theories, argues that local cultural variables per se do not determine the outcome of development plans, but that any development attempts must conform to local cultural norms.

———. Regional research in Argentina: a critical evaluation of the archives and libraries of Mendoza province. See item **2639**.

3347 **Fontana, Andrés.** Alianzas y organización nacional en la Argentina, 1852–1862. Buenos Aires: Centro de Estudios de Estado y Sociedad, 1977. 34 p.; bibl. (Estudios sociales; 7)

Looks at shifting alliances within the Buenos Aires provincial elites to show how economic divisions crossed political boundaries leading to eventual consolidation of the nation.

3348 **Francavilla, Cayetano.** Historia de Villa Crespo. Buenos Aires: s.n., 1978. 180 p.; bibl.; 18 leaves of plates: ill.

Local history about culture, institutions, personages, etc.

3349 **Freijo, Adrián Enrique.** Lecciones de nuestra historia reciente: treinta años de vida argentina, 1945–1975. Buenos Aires: Editorial Sudamericana, 1977. 1 v.

An interpretive exposition about Argentina since the 1940s to 1976 from an essentially Liberal viewpoint. Argues at once "a plague on all our houses" and that "everyone has their strong points" and ends with a nationalistic plea for future unity and peace.

3350 **Gallo, Ezequiel.** Farmers in revolt: the revolutions of 1893 in the province of Santa Fe, Argentina. London: University of London, 1976. 97 p.; bibl.; index; map (University of London. Institute of Latin American Studies monographs; 7)

Another excellent article by this leading historian on provincial themes (see also *HLAS 38:3716–3717* and *HLAS 40:3756*). Examines three agricultural revolts in 1893 and concludes that there was the greatest participation in areas that were integrated and colonized by the Swiss. In contrast to standard interpretations, shows that the Radical Party responded with specific programmatic proposals to the colonists' demands.

Consequently, these areas remained Radical strongholds long after the revolts. For Spanish version, see *Colonos en armas: las revoluciones Radicales en la Provincia de Santa Fe: 1893* (Buenos Aires: Editorial del Instituto Torcuato Di Tella, 1977, 90 p.; bibl.).

García Costa, Víctor O. Un capítulo de una negra historia: la CIADE. See *HLAS 41:7483*.

3351 **Gasío, Guillermo** and **María C. San Román.** La conquista del progreso, 1874–1880. Buenos Aires: Ediciones La Bastilla: distribuidor, Editorial Astrea, 1977. 272 p.; bibl. (Memorial de la Patria)

Covers political history from the elections of 1874 to the federalization of Buenos Aires.

3352 **Gianello, Leoncio.** Estampas del Brigadier. Santa Fe, Argentina: Colmegna, 1977. 162 p.; port.

Re-publication of 1855 newspaper articles from *El Litoral.* Shows life and times of Estanislao López, patriarch of the Federation, from a favorable viewpoint.

3353 ———. La formación del Poder Legislativo en las provincias del litoral histórico (UNL/U, 86, enero/abril 1977, p. 9–78, facsims.)

Noted provincial historian examines the ideological and historical background, the immediate setting, and formal constitution of the legislative power in Santa Fe, Buenos Aires, Entre Ríos, and Corrientes between 1819–24.

3354 ———. Historia de Santa Fe. 3. ed., ampliada y actualizada. Buenos Aires: Plus Ultra, 1978. 475, 5 p.; bibl.; ill. (Colección Historia de nuestras provincias; 5)

Leading provincial historian ably narrates provincial history from founding through end of 19th century. Mostly political with less material on social or economic history. Briefly touches 20th century. For 1955 edition, see *HLAS 21:3055*.

3355 **Girbal de Blacha, Noemí M.** Comercio exterior y producción agrícola de la República Argentina: 1890–1900 (ANH/IE, 21, julio/dic. 1976, p. 343–366, tables)

Competent summary examines overseas trading partners, potential markets, and correlations between internal trade policies and larger world events.

3356 **Gravil, Roger** and **Timothy Rooth.** A time of acute dependence: Argentina in the 1930s (The Journal of European Economic History [Banco de Roma] 7:2/3, Fall/Winter 1978, p. 337–378, tables)

Argues specifically against André Gunder Frank's contention that periods of world depression lessen ties of dependency and allow for autonomous local development. Contends that during the 1930s "Argentine foreign trade was dragooned into the service of the British economy more thoroughly than ever before." The authors' use of the Argentine case to refute Frank is persuasive but further research is needed to apply their argument to peripheral areas in general.

3357 **Guaglianone, Adam.** Usted cometió un grave error: escudriñando un apasionante episodio de nuestra historia. Buenos Aires: Editorial Nordus, 1976. 101 p.; bibl. (Colección El Río de la historia)

Short, popularized biography of López Jordán.

3358 **Guaglianone de Delgado Fito, Manón Violeta.** El 13 [i.e. trece] de diciembre: los universitarios reformistas de 1871. Buenos Aires: s.n., 1976. 54 p.

Treats the abortive university reform attempt of 1871, a precursor of later student movements which culminated in 1918. Interesting to note that many of the demands are relevant for those made by Argentine students 100 years later.

3359 **Guerrero, César H.** Tres biógrafos de Sarmiento. San Juan, Argentina: Municipalidad de la Ciudad de San Juan, 1978. 107 p.; bibl.; ill.

Historical sketches of three earliest biographers of Sarmiento from San Juan.

3360 **Guy, Donna J.** Argentine sugar politics: Tucumán and the generation of eighty. Tempe, Arizona: Center for Latin American Studies, Arizona State University, 1980. 180 p.; bibl.; index; map; photos.

A fine monograph on the development of the sugar industry in Tucumán from late 19th through early 20th centuries. Focuses on provincial and national economics and politics, showing how they intertwined in encouraging expansion, to create local political upheavals (1887 and 1890), and to both aid and frustrate attempts to bolster the industry in lean years and/or protect it from external competition and those wishing to tax it. Adds greatly to understanding local-national economic and political relations.

3361 ———. Carlos Pellegrini and the politics of early Argentine industrialization: 1873–1906 (JLAS, 2:1, May 1979, p. 123–144)

Uses figure of Pellegrini as a vehicle to explore the attempts to develop a coherent policy to promote industrialization. Notes that in the long run protectionists lost out with the important exception of those in agro-industry, most notably sugar and wine. By 1906 the first important rounds in the battle for early industrialization had been fought and lost by industrialists. For Spanish version of this article, see *Desarrollo Económico* (73:19, abril/junio 1979, p. 1–23)

3362 Harbinson, W.A. Evita: a legend for the seventies. Designed by Mike Ricketts. London: W. H. Allen, 1977. 128 p. (A star book)

Most of the credit for this popularized (no footnotes, no bibliography) biography of Evita Perón belongs to Ann Horton who carried out the picture research. Obviously inspired by the musical, the book's chief value lies in the large and excellent collection of photographs documenting the life and career of Perón's first wife. [Ed.]

3363 Heaps-Nelson, George. Emilio Civit and the politics of Mendoza (*in* The underside of Latin American history [see item **1948**] p. 5–23, bibl.)

A study of provincial politics and corruption based on Civit's career in early 20th-century Mendoza. Discusses distribution of land and water rights as well as use of political repression.

3364 Homenaje a Gorostiaga, 1891–3 de octubre–1977. Santiago del Estero: Instituto Cultural Dr. José Benjamín Gorostiaga, 1977. 29 p.: ill.

Short essays in praise of life and work of 19th-century statesman and jurist.

3365 Ibarguren, Federico and others. La historia argentina. Buenos Aires: Editorial de Belgrano, 1977. 254 p.

Consists of conversations with specialists about a course in Argentine history given at the University of Belgrano. Topics include: the Revolution of May; Unitarios and Federales; Rosas; 1853; the Generation of 80; the Radical period; the 1930s; and the triumph of populism. Participants are: Fermín Chávez, Julio Irazusta, Néstor Aúza, Ezequiel Gallo, Natalio Botana, Carlos Fayt and Félix Luna. The compilation is most valuable as an introduction to these authors for those unfamiliar with their work.

3366 Irazusta, Julio. Gobernantes, caudillos y escritores. Buenos Aires: Ediciones Dictio, 1978. 435 p.; bibl. (Biblioteca Dictio; 31. Sección Historia)

Consists of 17 studies in all, two of which are lengthy pieces: one on Groussac and his literary career, the other on Urquiza and his revolt against Rosas. The remainder concern themes which the author has treated in depth elsewhere (e.g., books on San Martín, Rosas, etc.).

3367 ———. La política, cenicienta del espíritu. Buenos Aires: Ediciones Dictio, 1977. 330 p. (Biblioteca Dictio; 17: Sección Política)

A collection of short articles on Argentina and Europe. Most of the Argentine pieces date from 1927–1931 and as a whole present a coherent version of the author's conservative, nationalist position.

3368 James, Daniel. Power and politics in peronist trade unions (UM/JIAS, 20:1, Feb. 1978, p. 3–36)

Examines relationships between an undemocratic and hierarchical leadership and rank and file in terms of the role of the former within national politics and political bargaining between 1955 and 1973. Sees Frondizi's presidency as key in growth of bureaucratic unionists power as a result of demobilization and demoralization of Peronist labor after 1955. For political scientist's comment, see *HLAS 41:7488.*

3369 Kaplan, Marcos. 50 [i.e. Cincuenta] años de historia argentina, 1925–1975: el laberinto de la frustración (*in* América Latina: historia de medio siglo. v. 1, América del Sur. Edited by Pablo González Casanova. México: Siglo XXI Editores, 1977, v. 1, p. 1–73, bibl.)

An often insightful socioeconomic analysis asking the question: What went wrong? Demonstrates that no one social group succeeded in imposing its view, but fails to propose a convincing answer to current problems.

3370 *Karukinka.* Instituto de Investigaciones Históricas de Tierra del Fuego. No. 5, julio 1973 [through] No. 13, julio 1975– . Buenos Aires.

Each issue contains short historical articles about Tierra del Fuego, often including documents and photos. Also anthropological and geographical material. Under the general editorship of Juan E. Belza.

Labastié de Reinhardt, María Rosa. Una polémica poco conocida: Germán Ave-Lallemant—José Ingenieros, 1895–1896. See item **7639**.

3371 **Lacasa, Pedro** and **Mariano A. Pelliza.** Vida militar y política del general argentino Don Juan Lavalle. Buenos Aires: Editorial del Belgrano, 1977. 260 p. (Colección La Argentina histórica)

Re-edition of two 19th-century classics.

3372 **Landi, Oscar.** La tercera presidencia de Perón: gobierno de emergencia y crisis política. Buenos Aires: Centro de Estudios de Estado y Sociedad, 1978. 70 p.; bibl.; graphs (Documento CEDES/G.E. CLACSO; 10)

A sociological autopsy of Perón's third presidency. Examines competing socioeconomic forces and their ideological bases as manifested at the level of permanent political crisis to show that an inevitable deterioration of the regime led to the 1976 coup against a by then untenable government.

3373 **Lapido, Graciela** and **Beatriz Spota de Lapieza Elli.** De Rivadavia a Rosas: *The British Packet.* v. 1, 1826–1832. Buenos Aires: Solar/Hachette, 1976. 464 p. (Biblioteca dimensión argentina)

Selections from this important newspaper published in Buenos Aires covering a multitude of current economic and political topics. Selections are chronological but indexed by themes. Brief introduction by authors.

Lascano, Marcelo Ramón. El crecimiento económico: condición de la estabilidad monetaria en la Argentina: 1900–1968. See *HLAS 41:3401.*

3374 **Lemos, Manuel.** Relato de un relato: vida de un mendocino ilustre, Dr. Manuel Lemos. Edited by Néstor Lemos. Buenos Aires: Francisco A. Colombo, 1973. 184 p.

A short sketch based on the autobiography of Manuel Lemos about his youth and education in Mendoza at the end of the century and then educational career at the Colegio Nacional.

3375 **Levene, Ricardo.** Lecturas históricas. v. 2, La Revolución y la emancipación. El caudillismo y la época de Rosas. La organización nacional. Presidencias constitucionales. Buenos Aires: Editoral Belgrano, 1978. 407 p. (Colección La Argentina histórica)

Re-edition of 1913 work. Vol. 2 covers independence through 1880. In addition to historical summary includes documents from each period. More illustrative of Levene's ideas on Argentine history than of utility for the contemporary historian. For vol. 1 (colonial period), see item **2850**.

3376 **Levrey, Bernardo Félix.** Memorias de la Ciudad de Haedo. Mariano J. Haedo, Argentina: The Author, 1977. 150 p.; bibl.; map.

Local history, anecdotes, etc.

Lira Montt, Luís. Estudiantes chilenos en la Real Universidad de Córdoba del Tucumán, 1670–1815. See item **3232**.

3377 **Little, Cynthia Jeffress.** Education, philanthropy, and feminism: components of Argentine womanhood, 1860–1926 (*in* Latin American women: historical perspectives [see item **1791**] p. 235–253)

Explores the ways in which some Argentine women broke from traditional patterns and emerged as participants, albeit second-class, in the nation's gowth. Looks at females in teaching, education, bourgeois philanthropic efforts, and socialist women. Curiously ignores women in the labor movement where perhaps the truest equality existed in these years.

Llorente, Ignacio. Alianzas políticas en el surgimiento del peronismo: el caso de la provincia de Buenos Aires. See *HLAS 41:7493.*

3378 **López, Norberto Aurelio.** El pleito de la patria. Buenos Aires: Círculo Militar, 1975. 431 p.; bibl.; maps (20 in pocket) (Colección histórico-militar; 683/684)

A detailed study of Argentine frontiers in historical perspective from a nationalist position.

3379 **Loudet, Osvaldo.** Ensayos de crítica e historia. Buenos Aires: Academia Argentina de Letras, 1975. 274 p.; bibl. (Biblioteca de la Academia Argentina de Letras. Serie Estudios académicos; 21)

Consists of 16 essays chiefly on scientific or educational themes of the 19th and early 20th centuries (e.g., Guillermo Rawson, Víctor Mercante, El Instituto de Libre Enseñeanza, etc.).

Luca de Tena, Torcuato. Yo, Juan Domingo Perón: relato autobiográfico. See *HLAS 41:9268*.

3380 **Luna, Félix.** Conversaciones con José Luis Romero sobre una Argentina con historia: política y democracia. 2. ed. Buenos Aires: Editorial de Belgrano, 1978. 213 p. (Colección Figuras contemporáneas)

A series of five edited conversations between the author and one of Argentina's leading historians until his recent death. Topics covered include the Middle Ages, historiography, and Argentina in the colonial, modern, and contemporary periods. Reveals the impressive depth and scope of Romero's ideas and his factual knowledge. A monument to the man.

3381 **———.** De comicios y entreveros. Montevideo: Schapire Editor, 1976. 205 p.; bibl. (Colección Historia)

Two unpublished essays by one of Argentina's leading historians and journalists. The first written in 1949 describes La Rioja at the time of the Paraguayan War; the second, dating from 1975, concerns the election of Avellaneda in that same province. Both show military-civilian conflicts, the origins of public opinion at the provincial level, and the importance of this in the formation of Argentine civil society of the time.

3382 **———.** Ortiz, reportaje a la Argentina opulenta. Buenos Aires: Editorial Sudamericana, 1978. 347 p.; bibl.; 4 leaves of plates: ill.

A life-and-times biography and excellent political history based on both anecdotal material and personal interviews with numerous protagonists of the period. In addition to its fine narrative which evokes the epoch, the work raises some interesting points and hypotheses about Ortiz. Speculates that Ortiz would and could have succeeded in revitalizing a decaying system by ending the fraudulent decade and providing an opening to forces gathering in the wings. That Ortiz failed to realize this—and herein lies his tragedy—meant that the process would be delayed until after 1943, by which time the results would be vastly different.

3383 **Macchi, Manuel E.** and **Alberto J. Masramón.** Entre Ríos: síntesis histórica. 2. ed. Concepción del Uruguay, Argentina: Editorial Sacha, 1977. 183 p.; bibl.; maps; tables.

Expanded edition of 1962 publication aimed at primary school level.

3384 **McLynn, F.J.** The Argentine presidential election of 1868 (JLAS, 2:2, Nov. 1979, p. 303–323)

Detailed examination of the key 1868 election. Perceives Sarmiento's triumph as the result of the personalities of both Mitre and the mitristas as well as the decade's conjunctural factors, chiefly the Paraguayan War.

3385 **———.** The causes of the War of the Triple Alliance: an interpretation (IAMEA, 33:2, Autumn 1979, p. 21–43)

A British scholar argues that the "primary cause of the Paraguayan War was the policy of the Argentine government under President Bartolomé Mitre after 1863," who, in the author's view, sought to impose a uniform order on the Platine basic. Rejects suggestions that foreign capital (especially British) played a significant role.

Mafud, Julio. La vida obrera en la Argentina. See *HLAS 41:9270*.

3386 **Martinelli, Andrés Juan.** La Argentina en el Océano Pacífico. Buenos Aires: Ediciones Depalma, 1978. 125 p.; bibl.

Argues for the historic claim of Argentina to the Pacific and that its establishment is a necessity for the country and for continental unity.

3387 **Martínez, Pedro Santos.** Política y riqueza agropecuaria durante el peronismo, 1946–1955 (JGSWGL, 14, 1977, p. 332–349, tables)

A competent summary of the main features of peronist agricultural policies in their economic and social aspects.

3388 Martínez Ruiz, Bernabé. La colonización galesa en el Valle del Chubut. Buenos Aires: Editorial Galerna, 1977. 150 p.; bibl.; ill.

History of Welsh colony in Chubut.

3389 Matijevic, Nicolás. Imprenta bahiense. Bahía Blanca, Argentina: Departamento de Ciencias Sociales, Universidad Nacional del Sur, 1978. 92 p.

Local historian studies the evolution of publishing industry in Bahía Blanca. Lists 561 publications there. Index by name.

3390 Mechlowicz, Bronislaw and **Zdzislaw Kurnikowski.** Los ucranianos en la Argentina (PAN/ES, 3, 1976, p. 289–307)

Essentially two documents from the Polish legation in Buenos Aires dated 1935 and 1939 discussing the cultural and political activities of central Europeans in Argentina.

3391 Méndez Avellaneda, Juan M. Alejandro Heredia; Marco Avellaneda: Tucumán, 1838–1841. Buenos Aires: Imprenta del Congreso de la Nación, 1977. 316 p.; bibl.

Two, inter-locking and detailed monographic studies centering on Tucumán, 1838–41 and in particular on the assassinations of Alejandro Heredia and Marco Avellaneda. Shows influence of local and national politics. Lengthy documentary appendix.

Merkx, Gilbert W. Charisma in Latin American politics: some general comments and the case of Juan Domingo Perón. See *HLAS 41:7494*.

3392 Moncaut, Carlos Antonio. Estancias bonaerenses: con la menuda historia de algunos establecimientos, entre otros, de los partidos de Chascomús, Ranchos, Magdalena, General Lavalle y Luján: historia y tradición. City Bell: Editorial El Aljibe, 1977. 244 p.; bibl.; ill.

Brief histories and descriptions of estancias from the 18th and 19th centuries with some material from 1900s.

Müller, María S. La mortalidad en Buenos Aires entre 1855 y 1960. See *HLAS 41:1492*.

3393 Newton, Ronald C. Social change, cultural crisis and the origins of Nazism within the German-speaking community of Buenos Aires (NS, 1:1/2, 1976, p. 62–105)

Argues, as in *HLAS 40:3821*, that the appeal Nazism generated among the Argentine German community can only be understood in the local context and, particularly, in terms of the community's class structure and its fears of assimilation. The bourgeoisie's tendency to support Nazism was less a reflection of ideology than of its need to hold on to their leadership position. For political scientist's comment, see *HLAS 41:7497*.

3394 Nicolau, Juan Carlos. Dorrego gobernador: economía y finanzas: 1826–27. Buenos Aires: Editorial Sadret, 1977. 129 p.; bibl.

Argues forcefully that the deteriorating economic situation contributed to the total undermining of Dorrego's administration. Faulty economic policies, in turn, stemmed from self-serving rather than nationalistic attitudes of the commercial and land-owning community.

Nunn, Frederick M. European military influence in South America: the origins and nature of professional militarism in Argentina, Brazil, Chile and Peru, 1890–1940. See item **1933b**.

3395 Odena, Isidro J. Libertadores y desarrollistas, 1955–1962. Buenos Aires: Ediciones La Bastilla: distribuidor exclusivo, Editorial Astrea de A. y R. Depalma, 1977. 393 p.; bibl. (Memorial de la Patria)

Covers from the fall of Perón to fall of Frondizi and is generally favorable to the latter. Includes chapters on literature and art, labor movement, petroleum, international politics, and education in addition to material on the government and the military and Fondizi's relations to other opposition groups.

3396 Ortega, Exequiel César. Historia de la provincia de Buenos Aires: su panorama de 460 años, 1516–1978. Buenos Aires: Plus Ultra, 1978. 333 p.: maps (Colección Historia de nuestras provincias; 4)

Popular historical overview of Province of Buenos Aires from colonial period to 1930 with brief chapter on subsequent years.

3397 Ortiz, Tulio Eduardo. Los ciclos históricos argentinos. Buenos Aires: Plus Ultra, 1977. 237 p.; bibl. (Colección Política e historia)

An attempt to apply the theories of Toynbee to Argentina. Unconvincing, except for Toynbee fans.

3398 Páramo de Isleño, Martha Susana. Notas para un análisis de la Provincia de Mendoza en la Convención Nacional de Santa Fe (UNC/RHAA, 8:15/16, 1970/1971, p. 57–81, bibl.)

Study on the short lived and ill-fated Convención and the delegates from Mendoza.

3399 Pavón Pereyra, Enrique. Conversaciones con Juan Domingo Perón. Buenos Aires: Colihué: distribución exclusiva Librería Hachette, 1978. 222 p.; bibl.; ports (Colección Diálogos polémicos)

A series of short conversations between the author and Perón from the 1960s and 1970s. A lot of material about individuals and particular incidents and thus valuable for future biographers, but little to make a reevaluation of the central characters.

3400 Pelliza, Mariano A. La dictadura de Rosas. Buenos Aires: Editorial de Belgrano, 1977. 346 p. (Colección La Argentina histórica)

Re-edition of 19th-century classic.

3401 Pérez, Daniel E. Los italianos en Tandil: centenario de la Sociedad Italiana de Socorros Mutuos. Prólogo de Enrique de Gandía. Tandil, Argentina: Sociedad Italiana de Socorros Mutuos (S.I.S.M.), 1977. 176 p.; plates.

Brief outline of Italian immigration and some local history, but focuses on the Italian Mutual Aid Society. Documents.

3402 Perón, Eva Duarte. Evita by Evita: Eva Duarte Perón tells her own story. London: Proteus Publishing Co., 1978. 235 p.; facsims.; plates.

English translation of Evita's classic credo/confession of faith, *La razón de mi vida*. Includes two appendixes of old newspaper clippings about key events in the careers of both Peróns.

Le peronisme: bibliographie. Compiled by Dominique Ferré. See *HLAS 41:25*.

3403 El Petróleo nacional. Buenos Aires: Todos es Historia, 1976. 150 p.; bibl.; ill. (Todo es historia; 6)

Three articles published in *Todo Es Historia* (see *HLAS 40:3878–3879*) treating the life and work of Mosconi, the abortive attempts at nationalization around 1930, and the petroleum industry in the 1930s to 1950s. United by an at times strident nationalism, the articles nevertheless present an interesting and in places highly critical view of foreign petroleum companies and the government's attempts to control or limit their operations in Argentina.

3404 Pezzarini, Heriberto María. Batalla de Arroyo Grande. Santa Fe, Argentina: Librería y Editorial Colmegna, 1976 or 1977. 197 p.; appendix; bibl.; ill.

A succinct monograph on this important battle by local historian from a nationalist perspective. Includes lengthy documentary section.

3405 Poggi, Rinaldo Alberto. Derrotado pero no vencido: Calfucurá después de San Carlos (CEHA/NH, 11:21, 1978, p. 134–157)

Examines relations between the government and the cacique Calfucurá after the 1872 invasion and defeat. Says that failure to follow up aggressively only prolonged the struggle on the frontier.

3406 Ponce, Aníbal. Sarmiento, constructor de la nueva Argentina y La vejez de Sarmiento. Estudio preliminar de Luis F. Iglesias. Buenos Aires: Solar, 1976. 282 p. (Biblioteca Dimensión Argentina)

Re-edition of two classic essays on Sarmiento dating from 1932 and 1927 respectively.

Portes, Alejandro. Perón and the Argentine national elections. See *HLAS 41:9278*.

3407 Prieto, Ramón. Treinta años de vida argentina, 1945–1975. Buenos Aires: Editorial Sudamericana, 1977. 286 p.

An interpretive essay which argues for the necessity of basic changes evolving from the agreement reached by a solid majority. In 1976, peronism had such a mandate, but remained stuck within the limits of Perón's own politics, as of 1943 or 1946.

3408 Pyenson, Lewis. The incomplete transmission of a European image: physics at greater Buenos Aires and Montreal, 1890–1920 (APS/P, 122:2, April 1978, p. 92–114, plates)

A groundbreaking article which examines science in peripheral areas and asks why certain types of sciences, in this case physics, did not take root. Concludes that a lack of "commitment to place students in positions commensurate with their new training," isolation, and lack of advanced facilities all contributed to prevent scientific development.

3409 Ramallo, Jorge María. La acción de la Iglesia y la masonería durante la epidemia de fiebre amarilla en Buenos Aires (CEHA/NH, 9:18, dic. 1976. p. 363–372)

Looks at the activities of Masons and the Church during the 1871 yellow fever outbreak in Buenos Aires. Both actively participated in combatting the disease and even cooperated together.

3410 Randall, Laura Regina Rosenbaum. An economic history of Argentina in the twentieth century. New York: Columbia University Press, 1978. 322 p.; bibl.; indexes.

An economist views 20th-century Argentina. Topical chapters discuss various sectors of the economy and then Argentina's relations with other nations. Concludes that "for the last fifty years, Argentina has not been part of another nation's economic empire" but "economically independent in all essentials." Explicitly argues against both Marxist interpretations and dependency theory analysis. For economist's comment, see *HLAS 41:3412*.

3411 Reber, Vera Blinn. British mercantile houses in Buenos Aires, 1810–1880. Cambridge: Harvard University Press, 1979. 1 v.; bibl.; index (Harvard studies in business history; 29)

A compact monograph based on research in Buenos Aires and England which details the practices, fortunes, and social experiences of British merchants and merchant houses. Shows how they aided growth of nascent capitalistic economy first through trade and then by investments in land, rails, processing, and banking (but seldom industry). In the late 19th-century, technological innovation and growth of the market led to specialization and joint stock companies or subsidiaries of English houses replacing old merchant houses. Concludes that the British contributed to Argentine development and that they took little out of the country while re-investing profits which spurred economic activity. Also notes the considerable cultural impact of the British among Argentine entrepreneurial types.

3412 Rimondi Rómulo, Juan. Humanizando los próceros: San Martín, Belgrano, Beltrán, Brandsen, Esquiú, González, Paz, Rivadavia, Sarmiento. Buenos Aires: Plus Ultra, 1978. 99 p.; bibl. (Colección Política e historia)

Brief anecdotal sketches about San Martín, Belgrano, Beltrán, Brandsen, Esquiú, Sarmiento, González, Paz, and Rivadavia.

3413 ———. El viaje de Sarmiento por el viejo y nuevo mundo (JPHC/R, 6, 1977, p. 127–142, bibl.)

Recounts the travels, work, writings, and impressions of Sarmiento during his wanderings from Argentina to Chile in 1804 and thence to Europe and back, 1840–49.

3414 Robinson, Karla. The merchants of post-independence Buenos Aires (*in* Hispanic-American essays in honor of Max Leon Moorhead [see item **1787**] p. 111–132, tables)

An interesting article which argues that the role of British merchant capital in the 1820s has been exaggerated and that Creole and Spanish merchants played a larger role in trade than hereto supposed. Also suggests that urban capital turned to rural investment in this period. This may lead to reevaluation of Rosas period.

3415 Rodríguez, Celso. Lencinas y Cantoni: el populismo cuyano en tiempos de Yrigoyen. Buenos Aires: Belgrano, 1979. 377 p. (Conflictos y armonías en la historia argentina)

This is a well-documented and well-written account of the 1920s populist governments of José Néstor Lencinas and Carlos Washington Lencinas in Mendoza and Federico Cantoni and his group in San Juan. Although the emergence of these provincial movements coincided with the rise of the Radical Party in national politics, both manifested greater populist tendencies than Irigoyen's movement. The Cuyo politicians represented regional forces formed to improve social conditions and to promote the political participation of the masses; both groups met with the unrelenting opposition of local presses and oligarchic forces. This work is the first in a new series of publications edited by Félix Luna which has as its intention the dissemination of unpublished or long-out-of-print research on Argentine political development. [J.R. Hébert]

Romero Carranza, Ambrosio; Alberto Rodríguez Varela; and **Eduardo Ventura.** Manual de historia política y constitución: Argentina, 1776–1976. See item **2656**.

3416 Rosa Olmos, Ramón. José Angelini Carafa: un educador olvidado (UNC/RHAA, 7:13/14, 1968/1969, p. 151–179, appendix)

Biographical study of Italian educator who lived and worked in Catamarca (1855–66) and then in Rosario and Córdoba until his death in 1909. Documentary appendix reproduces legislation he wrote or drafted.

3417 Roverano, Andrés A. Estanislao López, gobernador interno: la revolución de julio de 1818 (UNL/U, 85, julio/dic. 1976, p. 9–82, bibl.)

A detailed, lengthy examination of the 1818 revolution in Santa Fe. Argues that López clearly guided the province into the federal camp as best means to insure political and economic stability.

Sable, Martin Howard. Latin American Jewry: a research guide. See *HLAS 41:45*.

3418 Saint Geours, Yves. La France et l'opinion argentine, 11 novembre 1918–14 juillet 1919 (CDAL, 16, 1977, p. 125–151)

Examines *La Prensa* and *La Nación* to argue that Argentine opinion sided with the Allies against the Central Powers between Nov. 1918 and July 1919. Says that cultural identification with the Allies led to this result.

3419 Scenna, Miguel Angel. Cuando murió Buenos Aires: 1871. Buenos Aires: Ediciones La Bastilla, 1974. 503 p.; tables (Serie A sangre y fuego)

An exhaustive monograph on the yellow fever epidemic of 1871 based on contemporary materials and subsequent studies. Shows state of health facilities at the time, how various citizens groups and government mobilized to combat the disease, and its toll on the city. Indicates that most Argentines blamed the outbreak on the immigrants.

3420 Scroggins, Daniel C. Leopoldo Lugones' defense of the Monroe Doctrine in the *Revue Sud-Américaine* (RIB, 28:2, abril/junio 1978, p. 170–175)

Examines Lugones' defense of the Doctrine as modified by Drago and his support of the Wilsonian principles. Also discusses the impact of these articles and counter-attacks against Lugones.

3421 Segreti, Carlos S.A. La aurora de la independencia: 1810–1815. Buenos Aires: Ediciones La Bastilla, 1976. 354 p. (Colección Memorial de la patria)

Covers the confusing political scene after 1810 from both the local, platine, and international perspectives.

3422 Seminario de Historia de la Medicina Argentina, *Córdoba, Argentina, 1976.* Historia general de la medicina argentina. Antonio Aguilar and others. Introducción de Enrique P. Aznárez. Córdoba, Argentina: Universidad Nacional de Córdoba, Instituto y Cátedra de Historia de la Medicina, Dirección General de Publicaciones, 1976. 366 p.; bibls. (Publicación; 1)

Covers from pre-colonial period up through 1920s and includes chapters on teaching, publications, famous doctors, hospitals. Consists of 37 articles by 33 different authors.

Skidmore, Thomas E. The economic dimensions of populism in Argentina and Brazil: a case study in comparative public policy. See item **3752**.

3423 Smith, Peter H. The breakdown of democracy in Argentina: 1916–30 (*in* The breakdown of democratic regimes: crisis, breakdown and reequilibration [see item **1920**] p. 3–27, tables)

Develops argument presented in *HLAS 38:3855* that 1930 coup resulted from breakdown of political legitimacy and was not caused by economic situation. Concentrates on the political level and sees that the type of economic and subsequent social development led to democracy. This, in turn, aroused expectations which the political system could not fulfill, making a coup inevitable.

3424 El Socialismo. Buenos Aires: *Todo Es Historia*, 1976. 1 v.; bibl.; ill. (Todo es historia; 7)

Contains two articles: Juan Carlos Torre on the first socialist electoral victory of 1904 and a longer piece by Ernesto Goldar on Alfredo Palacios. Torres' is more interesting than Goldar's summary biography. The former shows that Palacios' 1904 triumph was a product of socialist-mitrista collaboration. Both previously published in the journal *Todo es Historia*.

3425 **Solberg, Carl E.** Oil and nationalism in Argentina: a history. Stanford, Calif.: Stanford University Press, 1979. 245 p.; bibl.; map; plates; tables.

A competent and useful monograph on oil policy mainly on the period 1907–30s. Links politics and the rise of oil to nationalism, showing ebb and flow of state vs. private vs. foreign company solutions. Discusses Argentine and international contexts. Denies that oil companies played significant role in the 1930 coup.

3426 ———. The origins of Yacimientos Petrolíferos Fiscales: prototype of state monopoly petroleum companies (UCSD/ND, 7:1/2, Spring 1978 [i.e. 1979] p. 121–129)

Summary of material contained in item **3425**.

3427 **Sousa, José Antônio Soares de.** A Batalha de Monte Caseros ou de Morón (IHGB/R, 318, jan./março 1978, p. 17–35)

A short introduction about Caseros, primarily from a Brazilian point of view, precedes an eyewitness account of the battle by a Brazilian engineer.

3428 **Stemplowski, Ryszard.** Las potencias anglosajonas y el neutralismo argentino: 1939–1945 (PAN/ES, 3, 1976, p. 129–160)

Leading Polish Latin Americanist summarizes material contained in his recently published book. Examines US-British-Argentine triangle from 1939–45, focusing on tensions created by US "hard line" vs. British "soft line" toward Argentine neutrality. Concludes, among other things, that in the final analysis, imperialist rivalries, not the war, determined each major power's attitude.

3429 **Stoppini, Juan Luis.** Pasado y presente de Lomas de Zamora, provincia de Buenos Aires: Coordinator: Julio Centenari. Asesor: Adrián Acevedo. Lomas de Zamora, Argentina: Centro de Periodistas de Lomas de Zamora, 1975. 66 p.; ill.; plates (Colección Historia; 1)

Local history from mid 19th century to present.

3430 **Tamagno, Rubén A.** Amargo testimonio: crónica histórica, 17 de agosto de 1951–17 de agosto de 1976. s.l.: s.n., 1978. 171 p.

Essentially a chronological presentation with commentary.

Tedesco, Juan Carlos. Clases sociales y educación en la Argentina. See *HLAS 41:9284*.

Tejerina Carreras, Ignacio G. El Archivo del Arzobispado de Córdoba: breve guía para el conocimiento de la documentación existente. See *HLAS 41:96*.

3431 **Tonda, Américo A.** Rosas, Corrientes y la nunciatura del Brasil. Rosario: Universidad Católica Argentina, Facultad de Humanidades de Rosario, Centro de Investigaciones, Sección Historia, 1972. 32 p.; bibl. (Monografías y ensayos; 9)

Short articles on the conflict between the government of Rosas and religious authorities in Corrientes.

3432 **Urquiza Almandoz, Oscar F.** Las primeras industrias entrerrianas: 1600–1850 (ANH/IE, 21, julio/dic. 1976, p. 223–275, tables)

An excellent summary article on the industrial development of Entre Ríos from late 18th to early 19th century. Shows external and internal factors and changes in export patterns. Although it was for the most part the "age of hides" (*edad de cuero*), other industries flourished too.

3433 **Vico, Humberto P.** Historia de Gualeguay, 1910–1940. Santa Fe, Argentina: Librería y Editorial Colmegna, 1977. 271 p.; bibl.

Local history in somewhat broader perspective than most.

3434 **Villegas, Osiris Guillermo.** En conflicto con Chile en la región austral. Buenos Aires: Editorial Pleamar, 1978. 196 p.; maps.

History of boundary conflicts between Chile and Argentina from colonial period to the Acta de Puerto Montt of 1978. Shows how Argentina has steadily lost territory and warns that the country must be prepared to defend its claim if a just solution for all involved is to emerge. Maps and documents.

3435 **Vuotto, Pascual.** Vida de un proletario: el proceso de Bragado. Prólogo de Osvaldo Bayer. 5. ed. Buenos Aires: R. Alonso Editor, 1975. 182 p. (Colección Argumentos argentinos)

Autobiographical account by anarchist

jailed in 1931 with two others for unproven crimes. This incident, often called the Argentine Sacco and Vanzetti case, stirred public opinion until the release of the prisoners in 1942. A moving and human story with contemporary relevance.

3436 **Wainerman, Catalina** and **Marysa Navarro.** El trabajo de la mujer en la Argentina: un análisis preliminar de las ideas dominantes en las primeras décadas del siglo XX. Buenos Aires: Centro de Estudios de Población, 1979. 49 p.; bibl. (Cuadernos del CENEP; 7)

A preliminary study of women in the labor force during the early 20th century. Lays out methodological and theoretical bases, initial source materials, and essential problems and questions.

3437 **Waldmann, Peter.** Stagnation als Ergebnis einer "Stückwerkrevolution" Entwicklungshemmnisse und -Versäumnisse im perionistischen Argentinien (UB/GG, 2:2, 1976, p. 160–187, tables)

Author examines the economic and social stagnation which followed Perón's first government in Argentina. Depriving the Peronista segment of political power, in the decades that followed, created recurring unrest in Argentine society. [G.M. Dorn]

3438 **Walter, Richard J.** Elections in the city of Buenos Aires during the first Yrigoyen administration: social class and political preferences (HAHR, 58:4, Nov. 1978, p. 595–624, tables)

Another fine article by this historian on early 20th-century Argentina. Uses voting statistics and social composition of electoral districts in the capital to suggest class and party allegiances from 1916–22. Concludes that Socialists won most support from workers but failed to attract substantial backing from other groups; middle sectors supported the Radicals; upper groups tended to side with the PDP.

3439 **Wasilewitsch, G.** Die Grosse Sozialistische Oktoberrevolution und die gesellschaftliche Entwicklung in Argentinien, 1917–1921 (Asien, Afrika, Lateinamerika [Deutscher Verlag der Wissenschaften, Berlin, GDR] 5:6, p. 1015–1024)

Describes the influence of the Russian Revolution of 1917 in Argentina (1917–21). [M. Kossok]

3440 **Weinberg, Félix** and others. Manual de historia de Bahía Blanca. 2. ed., corr. Bahía Blanca, Argentina: Departamento de Ciencias Sociales, Universidad Nacional del Sur, 1978. 288 p.; bibl.; 8 leaves of plates: ill.

Consists of contributions by 12 authors arranged in eight chapters covering prehistory, geography, and events up to the 1970s. Largest section covers 1880–1930, a good basic introduction to the area.

3441 **Weisbrot, Robert.** The Jews of Argentina: from the Inquisition to Perón. With the research assistance of Robert Murciano. Philadelphia: Jewish Publication Society of America, 1979. 348 p.; bibl.; 12 leaves of plates: ill.; index.

A somewhat rambling, disjointed account of Jews in Argentina. Covers immigration history, culture, acculturation, historical anti-semitism, and its present virulent manifestations. Laments the loss of Jewishness among the community and is pessimistic about its future survival as a separate entity.

3442 **Wellhofer, E. Spencer.** Peronism in Argentina: the social base of the first regime; 1946–1955 (JDA, 11:3, Spring 1977, p. 335–356, tables)

A political scientist tests recent hypotheses about peronism's electoral support outside Buenos Aires by using 1946 and 1954 national voting statistics. Concludes among other things: Peronism drew on a broad coalition, that women did not especially favor peronism, and that no evidence suggests that peronism depended upon mobilization of less experienced voters or that it lost significant sectors due to specific policies.

3443 **Williams, Glyn.** Welsh settlers and native Americans in Patagonia (JLAS, 2:1, May 1979, p. 41–66)

Continuation of author's previous work on Welsh in Argentina (see *HLAS 40:3883*). Discusses relations between the Welsh and the Indian population noting reciprocal influences. Argues that Welsh colonization pushed frontier outward with cooperation between the settlers and Indians, while the "Conquest of the Desert" was a "tragedy which could have and should have been avoided" had the government used the Welsh model.

3444 **Wolff, Inge.** Peronismus und Gewerkschaften: Ein Dokument zur Oktoberkrise des Jahres 1945 (JGSWGL, 10, 1973, p. 375–385)

The Central Committee of the Confederación General del Trabajo met 16 Oct. 1945 in an unscheduled session to consider a proposal made the day before. It called for a general strike in order to have Juan D. Perón released from prison. This article consists of a thorough examination of the documents of that extraordinary session. [G.M. Dorn]

3445 **Wright, Ione Stuessy** and **Lisa M. Nekhom.** Historical dictionary of Argentina. Metuchen, N.J.: Scarecrow Press, 1978. 1113 p.; bibl.; maps (Latin American historical dictionaries; 17)

A useful compendium of places, dates, people, concepts, organization, etc., although one could quarrel with the selections. For example, Liniers is given two and a half pages, the FORA gets four lines; Pampin House also gets four lines, while anarchism and anarcho-syndicalism have no entry or cross-reference; these instances are a clear statement of priorities and viewpoint. For bibliographer's comment, see *HLAS 41:145.*

3446 **Zinn, Ricardo.** Argentina: a nation at the crossroads of myth and reality. Preface by Robert C. Hill. New York: Robert Speller & Sons, 1979. 211 p.; bibl.; tables.

A highly personalistic account of Argentina past and present which defends the present military regime as possible saviour of the country from "sixty years of decadence" and "uncontrolled and misrepresented populism" as well as the "international Marxist conspiracy" to which the US at present is blind. Preface is by the ex-US Ambassador to Argentina.

3447 **Zorraquín Becú, Ricardo.** Algunas cartas del General Roca (ANH/B, 49, 1979, p. 243–249)

An analysis of 24 letters from Roca to Miguel M. Nogués, mostly from 1870s, with commentary on local and national politics revealing Roca's constant political preoccupations and incessant maneuvering for advantage among local politicians. Also shows his consistent views on larger topics such as the international situation with Chile and hopes for solution.

PARAGUAY

3448 **Alperovich, M.S.** Revolution von oben in Paraguay?: Zur Frage der historischen Wertung der Diktatur Francias (*in* Role und Formen der Volksbewegung im bürgerlichen Revolutionszyklus. Berlin, GDR: Akademia Verlag, 1976, p. 101–121)

Describes the causes and historic determinants which led to Francia's dictatorship in Paraguay. Also notes the advantages of the latter for Paraguayan independence. [M. Kossok]

3449 **Barreto, Sindulfo.** Campaña del Chaco: imagen de una pequeña unidad. Asunción: Fuerzas Armadas de la Nación, Dirección de Publicaciones, Imprenta Militar, 1977. 289 p.; facsims.; fold. maps; maps; plates; tables.

Story of company of sappers during Chaco War.

Bratzel, John F. The Chaco dispute and the search for prestige. See item **3141**.

3450 **Cardozo, Efraim.** Hace cien años: crónicas de la Guerra de 1864–1870 publicades en *La Tribuna* de Asunción en el centenario de la epopeya nacional. t. 9, 1° de junio de 1868 a 30 de setiembre de 1868. Asunción: Ediciones Emasa, 1977. 395 p.; map.

Continuation of series. For previous volumes, see *HLAS 40:3895.*

3451 **Castedo Franco, Eliana.** El proceso social de la revolución del 14 de mayo de 1811: un estudio socio-histórico (UCNSA/EP, 6:2, dic. 1978, p. 141–195)

Roughly half this article consists of a theoretical-methodological introduction. It then looks at the revolutionary process in Paraguay, seeking to identify pro- and anti-revolutionary social sectors (seeing them essentially as landed Creoles vs. peninsular merchants). Appendixes offer name lists and genealogical tables. [D. Bushnell]

3452 **Chiavenatto, Julio José.** Genocídio americano: a Guerra do Paraguai. Capa por Silvio Dworecki. São Paulo: Editora Brasiliense, 1979. 188 p.; bibl.; ill.

A critical if at times sensationalist view of the war. Agrees with the position that British interests lay behind the conflict.

3453 Choay, Corinne. L'echec d'une colonisation française au Paraguay au milieu du XIXe siècle (CDAL, 16, 1977, p. 7–30)

Discusses French immigration between 1850 and 1880 showing how hostile local conditions and lack of government effort helped reduce it to a trickle. Based on some original materials and containing some interesting vignettes of individual experiences.

Cresto, Juan José. La correspondencia que engendró una guerra: nuevos estudios sobre los orígenes de la Guerra con el Paraguay. See item **3322**.

3454 Díaz de Arce, Omar. El Paraguay contemporáneo 1925–1975 (*in* América Latina: historia de medio siglo. Edited by Pablo González Casanova. v. 1, América del Sur. México: Siglo XXI Editores, 1977, p. 322–372)

A Marxist interpretation which raises interesting problems and questions about Paraguay's internal class structures and its dependent economic status. In places probably overly optimistic about the possibility for and forces favoring significant social change in the near future.

3455 Domínguez Dibb, Humberto. Presencia y vigencia árabes en el Paraguay. Prólogo de Adolfo Bittar Nazer. Asunción: Editorial Cromos, 1977. 127 p.; facsims.; plates.

Short historical presentation of Arab colony in Paraguay with material on present social, cultural, and economic activities. Also material on Arab associations in Southern South America.

3456 Duarte Prado, Bacon. 5 [i.e. Cinco] semblanzas republicanas. Prólogo de Jorge Báez. Asunción: Imprenta Alborada, 1976. 123 p.; plates.

Brief summaries of life and work of Gen. Bernadino Caballero, Blas Garay, Ignacio A. Pane, Pedro P. Peña, and Manuel Talavera.

3457 ———. Juan Manuel Frutos: estilo y autenticidad. Prólogo de Ezequiel González Alsina. Asunción: Editorial Universo, 1978. 186 p.

Laudatory biography of Colorado caudillo (1879–1960) who briefly occupied the presidency in 1948. Divided thematically.

Escobari Cusicanqui, Jorge. Historia diplomática de Bolivia: política internacional. See item **3152**.

3458 Flores de Zarza, Idalia. Seis grandes de la historiografía nacional (APH/HP, 16, 1978, p. 153–192, bibl.)

Conference delivered at author's incorporation into Paraguayan Academy of History includes brief sketches on the work and place in Paraguayan historiography of: Cecilio Báez, Blas Manuel Garay, Manuel Domínguez, Fulgencio B. Moreno, Manuel Gondra, and Juan E. O'Leary.

3459 González Alsina, Ezequiel. El Doctor Francia del pueblo y ensayos varios. Asunción: Instituto Colorado de Cultura, 1978. 365 p. (Biblioteca Colorados contemporáneos; v. 3)

Series of essays on 19th and 20th-century historical themes (Francia, López, Chaco War) as well as political parties in the 19th century and an essay on Gen. Stroessner. Favors the Colorado position.

3460 Grow, Michael. The Good Neighbor Policy and Paraguay (*in* The underside of Latin American history [see item **1948**] p. 67–87, bibl.)

Argues that inter-American relations have been shaped by a two-way flow of reciprocal exploitation motivated by competing national interests, partisan domestic party politics, and personal ambitions. Uses late 1930s and early 1940s as case study showing how Paraguayan politicians used pro-Axis threats to exact concessions from the US and how the US used financial measures to influence and support "friendly" governments, regardless of their internal politics. For political scientist's comment, see *HLAS 41:8816*.

3461 Kaputi Mennonita: arados y fusiles en la Guerra del Chaco. Compilación de Peter P. Klassen. Adaptación al castellano y notas de Kornelius Neufeld. Asunción: Imprenta Modelo, 1976. 218 p.; ill.; map; plates.

Short sketches on background and history of Mennonite colonies during Chaco War. Based on newspapers, books, and personal testimonies.

López Videla, Winsor. Documentos para la historia: sinopsis del Chaco Boreal, acciones del III Cuerpo de Ejército, calendario de las acciones de guerra, 1932–1935. See item **3159**.

McLynn, F.J. The causes of the War of the Triple Alliance: an interpretation. See item **3385**.

Paraguay. Archivo Nacional. Archivo Nacional de Asunción: primer ensayo de índice, el documento más antiguo, documentos inéditos. See item **2651**.

3462 Pastor Cantero, Darío. Batallón 40 de la Guerra del Chaco: relato histórico. Prólogo de Antonio E. González. Asunción: Fuerzas Armadas de la Nación, Imprenta Militar, 1977. 124 p.; plates.

War record of a Paraguayan batallion.

3463 Pastore, Carlos. Introducción a una historia económica del Paraguay en el siglo XIX (APH/HP, 16, 1978, p. 103–126, bibl.)

A brief overview of the economy in the 19th century.

3464 Pérez Pardella, Agustín. Cerro Corá. Buenos Aires: Plus Ultra, 1977. 155 p.

A narrative of the last days of the Paraguayan War.

3465 Pitaud, Henri. Madama Lynch. Con prólogo de Juan E. O'Leary. Traducida del francés por Ricardo Anaya. Henri Pitaud en las letras paraguayas por Raúl Amaral. 4. ed. Asunción: France-Paraguay, 1978. 398 p.; bibl.; 34 leaves of plates: ill.

Fourth edition of historical novel which presents a somewhat romanticized and decidedly nationalistic version of Elisa Lynch's remarkable life in Paraguay.

3466 Plá, Josefina. Ida y vuelta de Whytehead (UCNSA/EP, 6:1, sept. 1978, p. 135–156)

Translation of a chapter from book reviewed in *HLAS 40:3909*.

3467 Rodríguez Alcalá de González Oddone, Beatriz. Testimonios veteranos: evocando la Guerra del Chago. Asunción: Talleres Gráficos de Casa América, 1977. 608 p.; maps; plates.

Testimonials from 21 officers who fought in the Chaco War.

3468 Salum-Flecha, Antonio. Historia diplomática del Paraguay de 1869 a 1938. 2. ed. Asunción: EMASA, 1978. 243 p.; bibl.; 1 leaf of plates: ill. (Fruto y flor)

A pro-Paraguayan summary designed as a university text. Useful for beginners.

Sánchez Quell, Hipólito. Los 50,000 documentos paraguayos llevados al Brasil. See *HLAS 41:95*.

3469 Soler, Carlos A. Andrés Barbero: su vida y su obra. Asunción: Fundación "La Piedad," 1977. 141 p.; bibl.; port.

Biography of doctor who pioneered the concept of preventive medicine as well as the growth of educational facilities for health services and the Red Cross.

3470 Speratti, Juan. Historia de la educación pública en el Paraguay, 1812–1932: origen y evolución histórica de la Escuela España de San Lorenzo, 1869–1975. San Lorenzo, Paraguay: s.n., 1979. 210 p.; bibl.; ill.

A series of essays on education. Central essay is a general history of public education from independence to the 1930s.

3471 Tate, E. Nicholas. Britain and Latin America in the nineteenth century: the case of Paraguay, 1811–1870 (IAA, 5:1, 1979, p. 39–70)

Documented entirely from sources available in Britain, this is a useful survey of British/Paraguayan relations during the dictatorships of Francia and the two López. The emphasis, necessarily, is on the 1853–70 period, and the author at length refutes those who claim that British had tremendous influence over a "dependent" Paraguay and helped cause the War of the Triple Alliance to complete its dominance. A good piece of work. [J.H. Williams]

Velarde Vizcarra, Nicanor. Remembranzas de la Guerra del Chaco: apreciaciones y realidades de lo acontecido en la pasada campaña internacional con el Paraguay, en el cautiverio, en mi evasión y en la post-guerra. See item **3186**.

3472 Warren, Harris Gaylord and **Katherine F. Warren.** Paraguay and the Triple Alliance: the postwar decade, 1869–1878. 376 p.; bibl.; ill.; index (Latin American monographs; 44)

A careful and detailed study of the post-war decade focusing primarily on national and international politics. Shows how the Allies, more concerned with each other, systematically neglected Paraguay's problems. Sees the genesis of Liberal and Colorado parties in this period as well as the seeds of future socioeconomic change. A solid contribution.

3473 **Whigham, Thomas Lyle.** The iron works of Ybycuí: Paraguayan industrial development in the mid-nineteenth century (AAFH/TAM, 35:2, Oct. 1978, p. 201–218, tables)

A young historian examines the works within the context of Paraguay's independent development showing their significant economic contribution and noting the shortcomings. Argues that deliberate destruction in 1869 formed part of the Allied plan to subject the country's economy.

3474 **White, Richard Alan.** The denied revolution: Paraguay's economics of Independence (LAP, 6:2, Spring 1979, p. 4–24)

A resumé of the arguments found in author's book, *Paraguay's autonomous revolution* (see item **3475**).

3475 ———. Paraguay's autonomous revolution, 1810–1840. Albuquerque: University of New Mexico Press, 1978. 295 p.; bibl.; ill.; index.

An attempt to apply dependency theory to Paraguay during the Franciata. Argues that Paraguay underwent a unique autonomous revolution which established a "popular" government. Strongest on the economic side, but lacks convincing proof to establish the exact nature of popular participation and real social benefits for the masses. A more explicit continental comparative approach might have highlighted Paraguay's uniqueness more effectively. Nevertheless, an important revisionist work.

3476 ———. La política económica del Paraguay popular, 1810–1840: la primera revolución radical de América (UCNSA/EP, 4:1, dic. 1976, p. 5–128, charts, graphs, maps, tables)

Article consists of Spanish translation of several chapters of item **3475**.

3477 **Williams, John Hoyt.** The rise and fall of the Paraguayan Republic, 1800–1870. Austin: Institute of Latin American Studies, University of Texas at Austin: distributed by University of Texas Press, 1979. 286 p.; bibl.; ill.; index (Latin American monographs; 48)

A basic history of this relatively uncharted period. By far the best summary to date in English or Spanish. Based on prime sources as available. Sympathetic to Paraguay and strongest on regimes of Francia and López. Primarily political history, although contains some socioeconomic material.

URUGUAY

3478 **Acevedo Díaz, Eduardo.** Viaje de Montevideo a Londres (UBN/R, 18, mayo 1978, p. 177–252, plate)

Travel diary (1903) with comments on the US, Mexico, and Cuba. Includes an introduction by Alicia Casas de Barran and Sergio Pittaluga.

3479 **Baracchini, Hugo.** Historia de las comunicaciones en el Uruguay. Montevideo: Universidad de la República, División Publicaciones y Ediciones, 1977 or 1978. 236 p.; bibl.; ill.

Essentially a summary and chronology from 1825 to present, thinner for post-World War II period.

3480 **Barbagelata, Aníbal Luis.** El constitucionalismo uruguayo a mediados del siglo XIX: la Constitución de 1830 y el régimen de la defensa. Montevideo: Fundación de Cultura Universitaria, 1978. 82 p.; bibl. (Colección mayor. Fundación de Cultura Universitaria)

Re-edition of 1957 publication studies 1830 Constitution and its application to 1860. Confined to legalistic aspects.

3481 **Barrios Pintos, Aníbal.** Los libertadores de 1825. Montevideo: Ediciones de la Banda Oriental, 1976. 95 p.; bibl.; facsim.; plates.

Popular biographies.

3482 ———. Paysandú en escorzo histórico. Paysandú, Uruguay: Intendencia Municipal de Paysandú, Dirección de Cultura, 1979. 339 p.; bibl.; maps; plates; tables.

Descriptive history of area and city from colonial period to 1976.

3483 **Castellanos, Alfredo Raúl.** Timoteo Aparicio: el ocaso de las lanzas. Montevideo: Ediciones de la Banda Oriental, 1977. 110 p.; bibl.; 4 leaves of plates: ill. (Historia uruguaya. Segunda serie, Los Hombres; 8)

Competent summary of life and times of 19th-century caudillo. For other volumes in this popular series, see *HLAS 40:3928.*

3484 Chelle, Luis Edelmiro. Principales hechos históricos del año 1825. Asesoría histórica de Flavio A. García. Montevideo: Comisión Nacional de Homenaje del Sesquicentenario de los Hechos Históricos de 1825, 1975. 102 p.; bibl.; plates.

Chronology.

Cresto, Juan José. La correspondencia que engendró una guerra: nuevos estudios sobre los orígenes de la Guerra con el Paraguay. See item **3322.**

3485 Deus, Sergio. Eduardo Acevedo Díaz: el caudillo olvidado. Montevideo: Acali Editorial, 1978. 261 p.; bibl.

Biography concentrating on 1897–1903 period and political career of central figure. Based on primary sources.

3486 Díaz, Nelson González. Los ferrocarriles ingleses en Uruguay desde sus orígenes hasta la crisis del noventa (RUC, 26:107, enero/marzo 1977, p. 265–340, tables)

A solid exposition on British railroads up to 1890. Could use more synthesis, but clearly shows how British capital, despite promises, acted consistently in its own interests, a pattern found elsewhere in Latin America. Based mostly on Uruguayan sources.

3487 Echenique, Carlos A. Junta Económico Administrativa de Cerro Largo 1852–1867: aspectos de su gestión como muestra de un proceso histórico, ensayos. Montevideo: IMCO, 1977. 61 p.

Short monograph focusing on Junta's activities in education, agriculture, public works, and local economic problems in general. Shows problems of local economy in unstable context.

3488 Ellis, Roberto J.G. Crónicas y viejas quintas de Montevideo. Montevideo: Imprenta Mercur, 1978. 113 p.

Series of short anecdotal essays about contemporary Uruguay, elites, Catholic social programs, and English colony.

3489 González Albistur, J. Joaquín Suárez: El Gran Ciudadano. Montevideo: Universidad de la República, División Publicaciones y Ediciones, 1978. 449 p.; ill. (Aguasdulces; 1)

Biography in the humanistic tradition of leading 19th-century political figure. Reproduces some original documents.

3490 Hierro, Luis Antonio. Batlle: democracia y reforma del estado. Montevideo: Ediciones de la Banda Oriental, 1977. 102 p.; bibl.; facsim.; plates (Historia uruguaya. Segunda serie: los hombres; 13)

Popular series noted in *HLAS 40: 3928,* consists mostly of political analysis.

Jacob, Raúl. El Uruguay en las crisis de 1929: algunos indicadores económicos. See *HLAS 41:3348.*

3491 Lacalle, Luis Alberto. Herrera, un nacionalismo oriental. Montevideo: Ediciones de la Banda Oriental, 1978. 175 p.; bibl.; 4 leaves of plates: ill. (Historia uruguaya: Segunda série, Los Hombres; 14)

Favorable study of figure. For other volumes in this popular history series, see *HLAS 40:3928.*

Lerin, François and **Cristina Torres.** La politique économique du gouvernement uruguayen. See *HLAS 41:3349.*

McLynn, F.J. The causes of the War of the Triple Alliance: an interpretation. See item **3385.**

3492 Marenales Rossi, Martha and **Guy Bourdé.** L'immigration française et le peuplement de l'Uruguay, 1830–1860 (CDAL, 16, 1977, p. 7–30)

A detailed study of French immigration and activity in Uruguay between 1830 and 1860. Material on economic and cultural influences.

3493 Martínez Montero, Homero. Armada nacional: estudio histórico biográfico. Montevideo: Club Naval, 1977. 385 p.; plates.

Study of Uruguayan navy from colonial times to 1975. Narrative approach including short biographies on 26 navy people.

3494 Mederos, Araceli F. Luis Alberto de Herrera, Fiscal de la Nación: porque puse Facundo a mi hijo. Montevideo: s.n., 1977. 77 p.

Short sketches about Herrera combined with laudatory opinions of contemporaries about him.

3495 Mena Segarra, Enrique. Aparicio Saravia: las últimas patriadas. Montevideo: Ediciones de la Banda Oriental, 1977. 190 p.; bibl.; 10 leaves of plates: ill. (Historia uruguaya. Segunda serie, Los Hombres; 12)

Mostly military but some social history in this popular biography. For other volumes in this series, see *HLAS 40:3928*.

3496 Montevideo. Biblioteca del Poder Legislativo. Departamento de Relaciones Públicas y Publicaciones. Cronología de Montevideo en los 250 años de su proceso fundacional. Montevideo: Biblioteca del Palacio Legislativo, 1976. 2 v. (743, 326 p.); ill.

A day-by-day calendar of events from colonial times to 1970s. Emphasis on political events, personages, or happenings such as major fires, etc.

3497 ———. Intendencia Municipal. Gobernantes municipales de Montevideo: datos biográficos-fotografías. Montevideo: Intendencia Municipal de Montevideo, Dirección de Publicaciones y Prensa, 1972. 72 p.: ill.

Brief one or two paragraph sketches of office holders from 1909 to 1972.

3498 Petrillo de Lagomarsino, María Teresa. Ana Monterroso de Lavalleja. Montevideo: Universidad de la República, División Publicaciones y Ediciones, 1977. 35 p.

A short biographical essay on wife of caudillo, but essentially portrays her as his adjunct.

Pimienta, Juan *comp.* Centenario de la Ley de Educación Común. See *HLAS 41:4558*.

3499 Prost, Gérard. Ganados sin hombres ou: la latifundium em Uruguay résiste au temps (UTIEH/C, 28, 1977, p. 105–122)

A brief historical exposition on the persistence of the latifundia from 18th century to present. For economist's comment, see *HLAS 41:3353*.

3501 Ramírez, Carlos María. Páginas de historia. Prólogo de Raúl Montero Bustamante. Montevideo: Ministerio de Educación y Cultura, 1978. 291 p.; bibl. (Colección de clásicos uruguayos; 152. Biblioteca Artigas)

Vol. 1 of collected works contains newspaper articles from 19th century. Two long series, one in defense of Artigas' ideas against those of Mitre; another on the Misiones boundary disputes from nationalist perspective.

3502 *Revista Histórica.* Museo Histórico Nacional. Año 70, Vol. 48, Nos. 142/144, dic. 1976– . Montevideo.

Includes the first part of a major article by Juan E. Pivel Devoto on banks and banking from 1824 to 1868 (p. 1–428). Details the ill-fated attempts to found permanent banking institutions in the early 19th century, the influence of Mauá and foreign capital after mid-century, and final formal establishment of a banking network. Includes documents. No. 142 includes a continuation of article on diplomatic reports of Spanish envoys noted in *HLAS 40:3947*.

3503 Schinca, Milton A. Boulevard Sarandí: 250 años de Montevideo; anécdotas, gentes sucesos. t. 2. Montevideo: Ediciones de la Banda Oriental, 1977. 148 p.; bibl. (Publicaciones; 62)

More anecdotes and brief sketches of Montevideo life. For vol. 1 of this set, see *HLAS 40:3950*.

3504 Sierra, Gerónimo de. Consolidación y crisis del "capitalismo democrático" en Uruguay (*in* América Latina: historia de medio siglo. Edited by Pablo González Casanova. v. 1, América del Sur. México: Siglo XXI Editores, 1977, v. 1, p. 424–449)

An at times insightful sociological interpretation of Uruguay's evolution from 1870 to present. Concentrates upon hegemonic blocs within the polity and the course of dependent capitalist development. Concludes that system at present is totally bankrupt and incapable of generating an acceptable social project.

3505 El Uruguay y sus visitantes, 1926–1967. Compilador: José María Firpo. Montevideo: Fundación de Cultura Universitaria, 1978. 115 p.

A collection of impressionistic sketches by foreign visitors, many anecdotal or humorous.

3506 Visca, Arturo P. Artículos sobre la Guerra de 1904 publicados en *La Tribuna Popular* (UBN/R, 18, mayo 1978, p. 41–158, plates, tables)

Consists of two sets of articles by Visca edited and compiled by José Pedro Barrán. One is an eyewitness account of the end of the 1904 conflict and surrender of Blanco forces, from *Tribuna Popular*. The second one, taken from *La Razon* of 1908, describes Uruguayan-British frontier life at the time.

Williams, John Hoyt. The Archivo General de la Nación of Uruguay. See item **2658**.

3507 **Zubillaga, Carlos.** Ciencias sociales en el Uruguay: historia (CLAEH, 20, 1978, p. 77–89)

Brief résumé of development of social sciences, and history in particular, since World War II. Specific suggestions about topics and general areas which historians should investigate.

———. Herrera: la encrucijada nacionalista. See *HLAS 41:7612*.

3508 ———. Luis Alberto de Herrera: filias y fobias (CLAEH, 10, abril/junio 1979, p. 39–55, ill., plates)

Mostly anecdotal.

BRAZIL

RODERICK J. BARMAN, *Associate Professor of History, University of British Columbia, Vancouver, Canada*
JEAN A. BARMAN, *University of British Columbia, Vancouver, Canada*
MICHAEL L. CONNIFF, *Associate Professor of History, University of New Mexico, Albuquerque*

THE HISTORICAL LITERATURE reviewed in this issue is perhaps best described as more of the same: no major historiographical departures, no great seminal works. In part this continuity has been due to the absence of any suitable anniversary such as 150 years of Independence (see *HLAS 36*, p. 306) or the centenaries of Italian and German immigration (see *HLAS 40*, p. 309) to inspire and fund new departures.

The only area where attention has markedly increased is Church history; and here the impetus has clearly come, not from historians *per se*, but from within the Church itself. The most ambitious—and most telling—recent work has been a new history of the Church in colonial Brazil (item **3583**), part of a major project to interpret the Latin American Church from within and to inspire a popular readership to social action. Lyra has written a useful synthesis of one religious order, the Franciscans (item **3532**). Many of the studies are little more than transcriptions or accumulations of source materials but, as such, do provide a useful base for subsequent analyses (items **3518**, **3539**, **3551**, **3564**, **3584**, **3588**, **3678** and **3748**). The University of São Paulo master's thesis by Lustosa (item **3696**) on 19th-century Church reform represents one of the few attempts to re-examine the Church from outside. North Americans have so far not participated in this surge of interest in Church history, although mention should be made of Soeiro's related but much more broadly based study of the function of convents (item **3614**).

Of the historiographical trends which have maintained themselves over the past two years, the most promising is the continued publication of Brazilian graduate theses, some of high quality and originality. Three theses stand out as deserving to be read by all serious historians of Brazil: Mesgravis' Ph.D. dissertation at the University of São Paulo on the Santa Casa da Misericórdia of São Paulo (item **3537**), Faria's master's thesis at the University of Paraná on the National Guard in Minas Gerais (item **3651**), and Santos' master's thesis at the Federal University of Pernambuco on the role of ideology at the time of the Praieira (item **3746**). The University of São Paulo continues to generate a majority of the theses. An inevitable consequence of this fact is that most of them are devoted to the history of the state of

São Paulo, which is fine except in cases where the paulista experience is perceived as a general one that applies to all of Brazil.

Another welcome continuation—without marked expansion—is what may be broadly regarded as social history. In their scrutiny of the socioeconomic bases of protest, Amado's and Domingues' analyses of the Muckers (items **3618** and **3648**), Leitman's and Flores' studies of the Farroupilha (items **3654** and **3685**), and Moniz's examination of the Canudos uprising (item **3719**) are worthy successors to the late Duglas Teixeira Monteiro's interpretation of the Contestado (see *HLAS 40:4136*). The role of women has received some attention in Russell-Wood's and Soeiro's studies of the colonial period (items **3604** and **3614**) and in Hahner's works on the national period (items **3667–3670**). Several complementary studies of the demographic basis of society in the late colonial period deserve mention: the analyses by Graham (item **3576**) and Santos of the slaves of the Fazenda Santa Cruz (item **3608**) and those by Ramos (items **3548** and **3601**) and Costa of Vila Rica (item **3570**). Maria Luiza Marcílio, whose doctoral dissertation at the Sorbonne on São Paulo city (see *HLAS 36:3526*) pioneered the field, continues to develop her demographic research (items **3533** and **3709**). And, most importantly, Mesgravis' study, mentioned above, underlines the importance of social history for understanding the Brazilian experience.

In the last two years the chronological emphasis has shifted perceptibly away from the Empire and toward the colonial period, while interest in the 20th century has grown steadily. The drop in the number of works on the 19th century is partially explained by the decline of interest in slavery, a theme which dominated the scholarship of the last decade. The new studies are either theoretical, primarily Marxist expositions (items **3524** and **3580**), or extensions of previous approaches. Conrad's thoughtful and thorough research bibliography on slavery (item **3517**) may, however, provide the impetus for a Brazilian equivalent of a Gutman or a Genovese. The most significant works on the Empire are undoubtedly two new urban histories, Mattoso's analysis of Salvador (item **3713**) and Lobo's of Rio de Janeiro (item **3530**), the latter also covering the late colonial period and the 20th century to 1945.

In contrast, the colonial period is alive and well, commanding many dynamic and exciting studies, most of them by non-Brazilians. New works by Hemming (item **3581**), Schwartz (item **3610**), and Thomas (item **3616**) examine previously neglected areas in the fields of Indian population, Portuguese-Indian contacts, and Indian acculturation. Three articles in American journals exemplify the innovative nature of recent research: Flory and Smith's examination of the relationship between planters and merchants in Bahia (item **3575**), Morton's study of royal economic policy, also in Bahia (item **3598**), and MacLachlan's analysis of the ideology of slavery (item **3594**). Two new syntheses of the colonial period based on secondary materials, by Lang and Mauro (items **3586** and **3596**)—neither one primarily a historian of Brazil—point up not only the breadth of materials that have become available but the attraction the field exerts on other scholars.

The history of the 20th century is fast becoming a respectable field, as indicated by the large production of the last two years. A few general histories merit note: Old-Republic in the *História Geral* series (item **3674**), Merrick and Graham's important study on demographic and economic history (item **3716**), and Flynn's political analysis (item **3655**). The neglect of political history is disturbing (excepting items **3638** and **3751**), but the flood of quality biographies and memoirs offers hope for coming years. Representative of the latter are works by Carneiro, Debes, Dulles,

Geribello, Lacerda, and Martins (items **3631**, **3646**, **3649**, **3661**, **3681** and **3712**). Moreover, regional studies of the Old Republic have prospered as exemplified by the innovative contributions of Levine, Love, and Pang (items **3687**, **3695**, **3727** and see also *HLAS 40:4187*).

Socioeconomic history is another important area of recent research on the 20th century. Labor studies continue to dominate, as seen in the contributions of Brandão, Canedo, Fausto, Moisés, Rodrigues and Vianna (items **3628**, **3630**, **3652**, **3718**, **3744** and **3773**). Malloy's book on the related field of social security is also important (item **3705**). Economic history, while less popular, is well-represented (items **3529–3530**, **3713** and **3752**). Interest continues in rural social problems (items **3639** and **3688–3689**). Urban history has been enriched by several studies (items **3664–3665a**, **3679** and **3706**).

Scholarship on the military in the present century is quite deficient, given its central role in the polity. Coelho, Fernandes, Manor, Mercadante, and Vale are, however, useful (items **3536**, **3641**, **3653**, **3707** and **3767**). The *tenentes* continue to attract interest (items **3642**, **3643**, **3656–3657**, **3717** and **3754**). Studies of authoritarianism have dominated intellectual history (items **3640**, **3714** and **3725**). Finally, it appears that the US role in the 1964 crisis has now been revealed in several works (items **3626**, **3683** and **3730**).

GENERAL

3509 Azeredo, Paulo Roberto de. Classe social e saúde na cidade no Rio de Janeiro: primeira metade do século XIX (MP/R, 25, nova série, p. 129–165, bibl., facsims.)

Uses contemporary travel and medical accounts to paint a graphic portrait of sanitary conditions and disease, particularly among the poor of Rio de Janeiro (1800–40). Author's conclusion that only the rich benefitted from medical care is paradoxical in view of the horrendous remedies of orthodox medicine. The poor were well out of it! Recommended. The same article appears in *Ciência e Cultura* (30:12, dez. 1978, p. 1406–1421, facsim.).

Azevedo, Thales de. Igreja e estado em tensão e crise: a conquista espiritual e o padroado na Bahia. See *HLAS 41:7511*.

3510 Bastide, Roger. The African religions of Brazil: toward a sociology of the interpenetration of civilizations. Translated by Helen Sebba. Baltimore, Md.: Johns Hopkins University Press, 1978. 494 p.

Excellent and long-awaited translation of this classic work on Afro-American religion and cultural mixing, first published in 1960. Theory, method, documentation are brilliant.

Bento, Cláudio Moreira. O negro e descendentes na sociedad do Rio Grande do Sul: 1635–1975. See *HLAS 41:9302*.

3511 Brazil. Departamento Nacional de Saúde Pública. Os serviços de saúde pública no Brasil (1808–1907). pt. 1, Esboço histórico; pt. 2, Legislação. Colaboradores: Plácido Barbosa e Cássio Barbosa de Rezende. São Paulo: s.n., 1978. 2 v. (1023 p.) (Continuous pagination); ill. (Oswaldo Cruz monumenta histórica; 4. Brasiliensia documenta; 6)

Reproduction of two-volume documentary work, originally published 1909, on the history of public health efforts in Rio de Janeiro (1808–1907). Includes all legislation.

3512 Bresciani, Maria Stella Martins. História: conceito e obra (SBPC/CC, 30:7, julho 1978, p. 805–812)

This long, involved and passionate article expresses the author's realization that the concepts guiding history are not neutral and external but very much a product of existing preconceptions and current concerns. The author uses the abolition period as her case study but, evidence to her own point, restricts her data totally to the province of São Paulo!

3513 Brito, Rubens da Silveira and **Eleyson Cardoso.** A febre amarela no Pará. Belém, Brazil: Ministério do Interior, Superintendência do Desenvolvimento da Amazônia (SUDAM), 1973. 241 p.; bibl.; facsims.; fold. tables; plates; tables.

A compilation of documents, statistics and facts, mainly from late 19th century, of possible use to social or medical historian.

3514 Carneiro, Daví. A vida gloriosa de José Bonifácio de Andrada e Silva e sua atuação na Independência. Rio de Janeiro: Civilização Brasileira, 1977. 431 p.; bibls. (Coleção Retratos do Brasil; 98)

Written, in the author's words, to supply "the real hunger for systematic knowledge about the Man of Independence." The result is a graceful panegyric based on the standard sources.

3515 Catálogo do Arquivo Cochrane: Edição comemorativa do bicentenário de nascimento do primeiro-almirante Lord Thomas Cochrane, Marquês do Maranhão: 1775–1860. Rio de Janeiro: Serviço de Documentação Geral da Marinha, 1975. 330 p.

Chronological catalogue of the Cochrane Archive located in the Scottish Record Office, Edinburgh (with microfilm copies available in Brazil). Summaries of the documents are so complete as to make the catalogue itself a primary source for the history of independence.

Coleção Nosso Brazil: Estudos Sociais. See *HLAS 41:5614.*

3516 Colóquio de Estudos Teuto-Brasileiros, *2d, Recife, 1968.* II [i.e. Segundo] Colóquio de Estudos Teuto Brasileiros: trabalhos de intelectuais brasileiros e alemães, vários ligados a universidades e institutos científicos dos dois países, sobre aspectos diversos da matéria que motivou o Colóquio. Recife, Universidade Federal de Pernambuco, Editora Universitária, 1974. 624 p.; bibl.; 1 leaf of plates: map.

A clutch of not very inspired articles on German influence in and on Brazil. Most useful as a general guide to subject.

3517 Conrad, Robert. Brazilian slavery: an annotated research bibliography. Boston: G.K. Hall, 1977. 163 p.; index.

Well-annotated bibliography including not only studies of slavery itself but more general works containing relevant material. An invaluable new research tool. For bibliographer's comment, see *HLAS 41:24.*

3518 Endres, José Lohr. Catálogo dos bispos, gerais, provinciais, abades e mais cargos de Ordem de São Bento do Brasil, 1582–1975. Salvador: Mosteiro de São Bento, 1976. 510 p.; bibl.; 1 leaf of plates: ill.; index.

This large volume, a biographical dictionary of all significant members of the Order of São Bento, is one of the more useful of a large number of new specialist works on Brazilian Church history.

3519 Essays concerning the socioeconomic history of Brazil and Portuguese India. Edited by Dauril Alden and Warren Dean. Gainesville: The University Presses of Florida, 1977. 247 p.

Consists of essays unified by their common preparation for an abortive Luso-Brazilian colloquium. For individual annotations, see items **3531**, **3665**, **3670**, **3675**, **3699–3700** and **3708**.

3520 Fernandes, Florestan. Slaveholding society in Brazil (*in* Comparative perspectives on slavery in New World societies [see item **1768**] p. 311–342)

A highly theoretical explication by a leading Brazilian sociologist of the nature and development of society during the colonial and imperial epochs. While valuable to the specialist, the less experienced reader may have difficulty with the poor translation and dependence on Marxist terminology.

3521 Flory, Thomas. Fugitive slaves and free society: the case of Brazil (ASNLH/J, 64:2, Spring 1979, p. 116–130)

An interpretive article essentially based on printed materials. While asserting that the study of slavery has been overly simplistic and oftimes extreme in its categorizations, author seems to suggest that the continued existence of runaway-slave communities is best understood by a single dominant factor, white economic priorities.

Fontes, Lucy Gonçalves. Relação das coleções de documentos dos séculos XVIII e XIX existentes na cidade de Tiradentes. See *HLAS 41:76.*

3522 Franco, Sérgio da Costa. Soledade na história. Porto Alegre: s.n., 1975. 136 p.; 3 leaves of plates: ill.

Straightforward chronology of an agricultural settlement in northeastern Rio Grande do Sul. Most interesting for its description of how town officials coped with such external upheavals as the Farroupilha or the 1932 uprising.

3523 Galvão, Flávio. Um português, o primeiro réu de crime de imprensa no Brasil (IHGSP/R, 72, 1975, p. 59–70, bibl.)

A case study of the use of law, after 1821, to control the press and to suppress unwelcome opinion. The victim, João Soares Lisboa, typified the group of immigrants from Portugal who turned politically radical.

3524 Gorender, Jacob. O escravismo colonial. São Paulo: Editora Atica, 1978. 592 p.; bibl. (Ensaios; 29)

This sociological analysis, incorporating Marxist theory, perceives slavery as being, despite capitalist externals, essentially a pre-capitalist mode of production. A thorough knowledge of the secondary literature allows the author to consider slavery in the general context of the colonial economy, which he views as enduring up to 1888.

3525 Janotti, Maria de Lourdes Mónaco. João Francisco Lisboa: jornalista e historiador. São Paulo: Atica, 1977. 253 p.; bibl. (Ensaios; 31)

Excellent biography of this 19th-century liberal historian (1812–63) dealing with the evolution of his ideas and writings. Chronology and bibliography appended.

3526 Komissarov, Boris N. The Archive of the G.I. Langsdorf Expedition to Brazil: 1821–29 (*in* Soviet historians on Latin America [see item **1817**] p. 177–187)

Despite its title, this is a short account of the life of G.H. Langsdorf, of the Russian expedition to Brazil (1821–29), and of the fate of the expedition's reports and materials. A fair example of Russian scholarship. For the author's book on the subject in Russian, see item **3527**.

3528 Levine, Robert M. Historical dictionary of Brazil. Metuchen, N.J.: Scarecrow Press, 1979. 297 p.; bibl. (Latin American historical dictionaries; 19)

A sadly disappointing work lacking any sense of the dynamic, substance or integrity of Brazilian history. The alphabetical entries, unevenly selected and phrased, frequently play up the peripheral or exotic to the total neglect of the essential. Not recommended for students or researchers.

3529 Levy, Maria Bárbara. História da Bolsa de Valores do Rio de Janeiro. Rio de Janeiro: IBMEC, 1977. 659 p.; bibl.; 26 leaves of plates: ill.

Massive, lavishly documented and illustrated volume, treating the rise of a banking class in colonial times, the formation of a guild of brokers in the 19th century, and the emergence of a highly articulated and regulated stock market in recent times. Originally a doctoral dissertation at the University of Paris, this work will be required reading for economic historians. Extensive statistical documentation in 64 tables.

Lima, Nestor dos Santos. La imagen del Brasil en las cartas de Bolívar. See item **2878**.

3530 Lobo, Eulália Maria Lahmeyer. História do Rio de Janeiro: do capital comercial ao capital industrial e financeiro. Rio de Janeiro: IBMEC, 1978. 2 v. (994 p.) (Continuous pagination); bibl.; ill.

This two-volume omnibus study of the economic development of greater Rio de Janeiro city (1760–1945) is a landmark, both for the breadth of source materials gathered together and for the sophistication of its data analysis. While the plentitude of facts sometimes gets in the way of general synthesis, the result is always intelligently written and highly illuminating. The volumes' 250 tables not only detail the city's economic life but reveal much of its social structure. A basic work for the researcher.

Lorenzo-Fernández, O.S. A evolução da economia brasileira. See *HLAS 41:3485*.

3531 Lugar, Catherine. The Portuguese tobacco trade and tobacco growers of Bahia in the late colonial period (*in* Essays concerning the socioeconomic history of Brazil and Portuguese India [see item **3519**] p. 26–70)

A detailed history of Brazilian tobacco growing (1620–1835) coupled with a close examination of the demographic characteristics of tobacco growers of the Cachoeira area of Bahia (1775–1835). Argues that the growers were very much at the mercy of fluctuating world markets and of Portuguese middlemen.

3532 Lyra, Sophia A. São Francisco de Assis e o Brasil. Rio de Janeiro: Livraria José Olympio Editora, 1978. 296 p.; ill.

Well-written, sympathetic summary of the Franciscan Order in Brazil, from the 16th to the 20th centuries.

3533 Marcílio, Maria Luiza. Croissance de la population pauliste de 1798 à 1828 (Annales de Démographie Historique [Société Demographie Historique, Paris] 1977, p. 249–269)

A short, clear summary of the author's research on the population of São Paulo. Mainly concludes that the richness of agricultural and natural resources of the region precluded the "crises of subsistence" typical of Europe and allowed for a consistent long-term growth in the free population, especially since epidemics were not an important factor. Recommended.

Margolis, Maxine. Historical perspectives on frontier agriculture as an adaptive strategy. See *HLAS 41:5667.*

3534 Marques, Xavier. Ensaios históricos sobre a Independência. 2. ed. São Paulo: Instituição Brasileira de Difusão Cultural, 1977. 173 p. (Biblioteca História; 25)

This 1924 work is republished to defend the author's reputation as a historian against the accusation of stupidity levelled by José Honório Rodrigues in *HLAS 38:4118.* While the essay is very much the child of its times, it does not seem to warrant the intensity of the denunciation.

3535 Martins, Wilson. História da inteligência brasileira. v. 6, 1915–1933. São Paulo: Editora Cultrix, 1978. 596 p.; plates.

Vol. 6, 1915–1933, consists of a historico-literary review and continues this ambitious attempt to trace the development of Brazilian thought and letters from 1500 to the present (for previous volumes, see *HLAS 40:3996* and *7692* and item **6424** in this *HLAS*). Most of the attention is devoted to the Modernists; to intellectuals such as Oliveira Vianna and Gilberto Freyre; and to less prominent writers whose careers spilled over into politics. Hundreds of others, including many foreigners, are also mentioned briefly. The volume lacks logical organization, wandering from one event to the next, and the table of contents does not reveal chapter subjects. Encyclopedic without the advantage of careful compilation. The sources are contemporary magazines and newspapers, the literary bookshelf, and the author's immense knowledge.

3536 Mercadante, Paulo. Militares & [i.e. e] civis: a ética e o compromisso. Rio de Janeiro: Zahar Editores, 1978 [1977]. 218 p.; bibl. (Atualidade)

Intellectual history of civil-military relations from colonial times until the 1920s. Many good insights into the role of the soldier available in this highly synthetic philosophical essay.

3537 Mesgravis, Laima. A Santa Casa da Misericórdia de São Paulo: 1599?–1884: contribuição ao estudo da assistência social no Brasil. São Paulo: Conselho Estadual de Cultura, 1977. 253 p.; bibl.; ill. (Coleção Ciências humanas; 3)

Skillfully accounts for the Santa Casa's longevity not only in terms of its good works but as an opportune means for social groups seeking upward mobility to gain visible status-by-association. Originally a doctoral thesis at the University of São Paulo, this study represents social history at its finest. Highly recommended.

3538 Mesquita, Eni de. O papel do agregado na região de Itu: 1780 a 1830 (Série de História [Coleção Museu Paulista, Universidade de São Paulo, Brazil] 6, 1977, p. 7–121, bibl., tables)

Using census data and qualitative evidence, the author examines the socioeconomic role of free labor in a sugar economy dominated by master and slave. Argues that the *agregados'* position was unstable with a larger percentage employed in urban areas than previously supposed. A well-constructed and very readable University of São Paulo master's thesis.

Miranda Neto, Manoel José de. O dilema da Amazonia. See *HLAS 41:3492.*

3539 Mosteiro de São Bento, *São Paulo, Brazil.* Livro do tombo do Mosteiro de São Bento: edição diplomática-interpretativa de manuscritos setecentistas do Arquivo do Mosteiro de São Bento de São Paulo. Feita por Martinho Johnson. São Paulo: O Mosteiro, 1977. 268 p.; bibl.; 11 leaves of plates: ill.; indexes.

Well-edited and indexed transcription of the property register of the São Bento monastery in São Paulo, 1571–1877. Good introduction.

3540 Mott, Luiz R.B. A população sergipana do Rio São Francisco no primeiro quartel do século XIX (Mensário do Arquivo Nacional [Rio de Janeiro] 9:9, 1978, p. 3–15, tables)

A short analysis of the population of Sergipe in 1802-08-25-29. Useful as a counterpoint and comparison to the demographic studies of São Paulo in the same period.

3541 Mulher brasileira: bibliografia anotada. Coordinado por Elba Siqueira de Sá Barreto. São Paulo: Editora Brasiliense, 1979. 1 v.

Covers history, family, ethnic groups, feminism, with rather length annotations. Not all entries are relevant.

3542 A mulher no Brasil. Edited by June E. Hahner. Rio de Janeiro: Civilização Brasileira, 1978. 175 p. (Retratos do Brasil; 112)

Basically a series of readings taken from contemporary writings on the condition of women in Brazil from colonial times to the present. The readings are linked and explained by the author's commentary which is, in the words on the back cover, "destined more to raise queries than to answer them and to stimulate new research."

Peláez, Carlos Manuel and **Mircea Buescu.** A moderna história econômica. See *HLAS 41:3497.*

3543 Petrone, Maria Thereza Schorer. O Barão de Iguapé, um empresário da época da independência. São Paulo: Companhia Editora Nacional, 1976. 177 p.; bibl.; ill. (Brasiliana; 361)

Despite the title, a major pioneering study of the development of the important mule and cattle trade in southern Brazil in the early 19th century, based on the surviving papers of the baron. Essential reading.

Piauí, Francelino S. Cinco séculos de reportagem econômica: síntesis histórica da economia brasileira. See *HLAS 41:3502.*

3544 Piazza, Walter Fernando. A Igreja em Santa Catarina: notas para sua história. Florianópolis: Governo do Estado de Santa Catarina, 1977. 313 p.; bibl.; ill. (Coleção Cultura catarinense. Série História)

A chronology of significant events, primarily administrative. Includes biographies of all relevant clergy. Useful to the specialist.

3546 Pires, Mario. Valinhos; tempo e espaço. Campinas: Brasil: s.n., 1978. 131 p.; bibl.; ill. (Publicações da Academia Campinense de Letras; 37)

Local history of a Campinas suburb organized in a vague chronological order.

Porter, Dorothy B. Afro-Brazilian: a working bibliography. See *HLAS 41:41.*

3547 Querino, Manuel Raimundo. The African contribution to Brazilian civilization. Translation and introduction by E. Bradford Burns. Tempe: University of Arizona, Center for Latin American Studies, 1978. 20 p.; ill. (Special studies; 18)

Brief essay by an early black student of slavery, showing that Africans contributed heartily to Brazil's material and cultural progress. Burn's introduction provides a sketch of Querino's life (1851–1923) in Bahia.

3548 Ramos, Donald. City and country: the family in Minas Gerais, 1804–1838 (NCFR/JFH, 3:4, Winter 1978, p. 361–375, bibl., tables)

An innovative, if essentially descriptive, application of family-history techniques to five communities of Minas Gerais. The author both details household composition and hypothesizes why significant differences existed between the Brazilian household and its Western European counterpart.

3549 Randall, Laura Regina Rosenbaum. A comparative economic history of Latin America: 1500–1914. v. 3, Brazil. Ann Arbor, Mich.: University Microfilms International, 1977. 269 p.; bibl.; index; tables (Monograph publishing on demand. Sponsor series)

A welcome addition to the limited English-language texts on Brazilian economic history. Its succinct analysis of events and summary tables make the volume particularly useful for student reference. A dependence on secondary sources impedes any innovative penetration beneath the surface of events. For comments on other volumes of this work, see item **1808a**.

3550 Reis, Arthur Cézar Ferreira. Santarém, seu desenvolvimento histórico. 2. ed. Rio de Janeiro: Civilização Brasileira, 1979.

198 p., bibl. (Coleção Retratos do Brasil; 124)

A straightforward account of Santarem's development through the 19th century. Very much on par with the author's many other studies of the Amazon region.

3551 **Rubert, Arlindo.** Clero secular italiano no Rio Grande do Sul: 1815–1930. Santa Maria, Brasil: Livraria Editora Pallotti, 1977. 151 p.; bibl.; ill.

A series of biographies strung together chronologically by short introductory sections. Based on wide research in Italian and Brazilian Church archives. Good raw material for the historian.

3552 **Sampaio, Theodoro Fernandes.** São Paulo no século XIX [i.e. dezenove] e outros ciclos históricos. Introdução de Arthur Cézar Ferreira Reis. Petrópolis: Editora Vozes, 1978. 399 p.; bibl. (Dimensões do Brasil; 11)

Reprints a number of previously uncollected articles on Brazil and its history by a leading technical engineer, intellectual and writer of the Old Republic who was also born illegitimate, black, and in the shadow of the *senzala*. Historiographically, essays have value due to author's strong sense of the role of geography in history.

3553 **Santos, Itazil Benício dos.** Vida e obra de Pirajá da Silva. Rio de Janeiro: Livraria J. Olympio Editora, 1977. 116 p.; bibl.; ill.

Biography of discoverer of Brazilian type of schistosomiasis, useful for medical historians.

3554 **Schwartzman, Simon.** Formação da comunidade científica no Brasil. São Paulo: Financiadora de Estudos e Projetos, Companhia Editora Nacional, 1979. 481 p.; bibl. (Biblioteca Universitária série; 8. Estudos em ciência e tecnologia; 2)

An excellent overview of the development not just of science per se but of all institutions, events, and publications that fostered a "modern" notion of empirical investigation. Particularly strong on the 20th century due to the author's interviews of about 65 leading figures in the field. Also contains an invaluable annotated chronology, 1500–1945, and full bibliography.

3555 **Silva, Colemar Natal e.** A missão da história na conjuntura atual (IHGB/R, 317, out./dez. 1977, p. 31–37)

If you think that Auguste Comte does not still have adepts in Brazil, read this assertion that sociology is shaping history and that sociology is a science created by you know who.

Sylos, Honório de. São Paulo e seus caminhos. See *HLAS 41:5703*.

3556 **Tavares, Luís Henrique Dias.** A Independência do Brasil na Bahia. Rio de Janeiro: Civilização Brasileira, 1977. 190 p.; bibl. (Coleção Retratos do Brasil; 104)

Collection of five essays by leading Bahian historian on episodes in the independence period in Bahia. Includes some original documents. Of interest to specialists.

3557 **Teles, José Mendonça.** Vida e obra de Silva e Souza. Goiânia, Brasil: Oriente, 1978. 194 p.; 4 leaves of plates: ill.

Reproduces documents on the life of a priest who was a journalist and writer in Goiás in the early 19th century, together with his two major works of 1812 and 1832 on the history and geography of Goiás. Useful as source materials.

3558 **Willeke, Venâncio.** Franciscanos no Maranhão e Piauí, 1600/1878, 1952/1977. São Luís, Brasil: Distribuidora, Convento de Nossa Senhora da Glória, 1978. 146 p.; bibl.; 8 leaves of plates: ill.; index.

A very short account of the Franciscans in the far North up to 1878 coupled with a longer section on the German Franciscans working in the same area since 1950. Based on archival sources.

3559 ———. Missionen und glaubensboten der Brasilianischen antoniusprovinz (AFH, 71, ian./iun. 1978, p. 112–129)

Useful compilation of data on the missions to Indian tribes and on the missionaries of the Franciscan province of St. Antony which covered most of the Northeast, 1679–1863. Limited analysis.

COLONIAL

3560 **Almeida, Luiz Castanho de.** Agonia, morte e sepultura em São Paulo, de 1722 a 1822 (IHGSP/R, 73, 1977, p. 7–13)

A short but able analysis by one of São Paulo's senior historians (under his alias of Aluísio de Almeida) of the rites of passage surrounding death in colonial São Paulo.

3561 *Anais.* Arquivo Histórico do Rio Grande do Sul. Vol. 1, 1977– . Porto Alegre, Brazil.

Vol. 1 of this new annual (350 p.) reproduces in full the Register Book of Acts of the first military commanders of the Rio Grande de São Pedro Presidio (1737–53). Includes index.

3562 Barbacena, Felisberto Caldeira Brant Pontes, *marques de.* Economia açucareira do Brasil no século XIX: cartas. Transcrição de Carmen Vargas. Rio de Janeiro: M.I.C., Instituto do Açúcar e do Alcool, Departamento de Informática, Divisão de Informações, Documentação, 1976. 210 p. (Coleção Canavieira; 21)

This transcription of the out-letters (1819–21) of a leading Bahian planter, merchant and soldier is an invaluable source on the actual functioning of the Brazilian export economy as it existed at the time of independence and on the mentality of those who ran that economy. Book suffers from poor editing but highly recommended.

3563 Barreiros, Eduardo Canabrava. Roteiro das esmeraldas: a bandeira de Fernão Dias Pais. Rio de Janeiro: José Olympio [and] Instituto Nacional do Livro, Brasília, 1979. 133 p., ill.; maps (Coleção Documentos brasileiros; 188)

Scholarly and authoritative account of the famous bandeira which lasted from 1672 to 1681.

3564 Benci, Jorge. Economia cristão dos senhores no governo dos escravos: livro brasileiro de 1700. Estudo preliminar de Pedro de Alcântara Figueira e Claudinei M. M. Mendes. São Paulo: Editorial Grijalbo, 1977. 224 p.; bibl.; 2 facsims. (Brasil ontem e hoje; 3)

A most welcome re-edition of a book published in Rome in 1705 by an Italian Jesuit then serving in Bahia. The work conveys the writer's distaste for the whole system of slavery and is a useful source: his advice to owners on how slaves should be treated is, for instance, indicative of how they were not being treated.

Besouchet, Lídia. Renan e o Imperador do Brasil. See item **7623**.

3565 Brásio, Antônio. O problema missionário brasileiro de século XVIII nos manuscritos de Casa Cadaval (IHGB/R, 319, abril/junho 1978, p. 49–64)

A slight account of the main concerns of both missionaries and of administration as they were reflected in the papers of a late 17th-century governor of Bahia.

3566 Brazil. Ministério da Marinha. Serviço de Documentação Geral da Marinha. História naval brasileira. v. 1, t. 1/2. Rio de Janeiro: O Serviço 1975– . 1 v. (622 p.) (Continuous pagination); bibl.; facsims.; fold. maps; ill.; maps; plates.

A very complete narrative chronicling all aspects of the navy's role (vol. 2 only reaches 1633). Superb illustrations and maps; useful sections discussing bibliographic and cartographic resources.

3567 Bruxel, Arnaldo. Os trinta povos Guaranis: panorama histórico-institucional. Porto Alegre, Brazil: Universidade de Caxias do Sul [and] Livraria Sulina Editora, 1978. 162 p.; ill.

Useful synthesis of the Indian missions of the Uruguay-Paraguay river basin, nicely illustrated.

3568 Carvalho, José Geraldo Vidigal de. Ideologia e raízes sociais do clero da conjuração, século XVIII, Minas Gerais. Viçosa, Brasil: Imprensa Universitária, Universidade Federal de Viçosa, 1978. 86 p.; bibl.

Although slight in scope, this work contains interesting data for the study of the background and outlook of the clergy of Minas Gerais at the time of the Inconfidência of 1788.

3569 Cascudo, Luís da Câmara. O Príncipe Maximiliano de Wied-Neuwied no Brasil, 1815/1817: biografia & notas, com versões para o inglês e alemão. Ilustrado com reproduções de originais da expedição. Rio de Janeiro: Livraria Kosmos Editora, 1977. 179 p.; bibl.; 8 leaves of plates: ill.

A tri-lingual edition (Portuguese, English and German) of a short essay written by Câmara Cascudo in 1935 on the life and expedition of Prince Maximilian. While not great history, a pleasant literary interlude.

3570 Costa, Iraci del Nero da. A estrutura familial e domiciliária em Vila Rica no alvorecer do século XIX (USP/RIEB, 20, 1978, p. 17–34, tables)

A demographic analysis of what is

present-day Ouro Preto in 1804, comparable to, but less complex, than the one by Ramos (see item **3601**).

3571 Delson, Roberta Marx. Colonization and modernization in eighteenth century Brazil (*in* Social fabric and spatial structure in colonial Latin America. Edited by David J. Robinson. Ann Arbor, Mich.: University Microfilms International, 1979, p. 281–313, ill., map)

Basically repeats at greater length, but with no more data, author's analysis of royal policy of urban development found in item **3572**. Assumes Portuguese Crown motivated by 20th-century concerns.

3572 ———. New towns for colonial Brazil: spatial and social planning of the eighteenth century. Ann Arbor, Mich.: Published for Department of Geography, Syracuse University, by University Microfilms International, 1979. 212 p.; bibl.; ill.; index (Dellplain Latin American studies; 2. Monograph publishing. Sponsor series)

Close innovative study of a neglected area of colonial history. Examines Crown policy of planned urban development, which in its origins represented a commitment to Enlightenment ideas and in its implementation a means of closer royal control. Also useful for its many reproductions of town plans. Conclusions may be overstated, since by author's own count planned settlements represented at most a third of new towns created during 18th century.

3573 A Febre amarela no século XVII no Brasil. Rio de Janeiro: Fundação Serviços de Saúde Pública, 1971. 99 p.; facsims.

Facsimile reproduction of the *Trattado unico da constituiçam pestilencial de Pernambuco* by João Ferreira da Rosa, published in 1694, with transcription into modern Portuguese and English translation. Accompanied by short modern essay claiming that the disease was yellow fever.

Ferguson, Stephen. Recently identified Braziliana. See item **41**.

3574 Ferrez, Gilberto. O Rio de Janeiro e a defesa do seu porto, 1555–1800. Rio de Janeiro, Serviço de Documentação Geral da Marinha, 1972. 232 p. and atlas 8 p.; 80 plates.

Basically a collection of documents, given in full or in part with running commentary, on the plans for the defense of Rio de Janeiro, particularly in respect to its many forts. Possibly of use to the military historian.

Figueiredo, Ariosvaldo. O negro e a violência do branco: o negro em Sergipe. See *HLAS 41:9325*.

3575 Flory, Rae and **David Grant Smith.** Bahian merchants and planters in the seventeenth and early eighteenth centuries (HAHR, 58:4, Nov. 1978, p. 571–594, tables)

A well-written, finely argued analysis of Recôncavo society (1600–1740). Does not see planters and merchants as in opposition, although latter were usually immigrants, but as being strongly linked both socially and economically. Most successful of the merchants were absorbed by planters. Highly recommended.

3576 Graham, Richard. Slave families on a rural estate in colonial Brazil (UCP/JHS, 9:3, 1976, p. 383–402, tables)

A careful demographic analysis of the slave population on the Fazenda Santa Cruz in 1791, the Crown-owned property previously belonging to the Jesuits. Although the author cautions against generalizing his unexpected findings due to the dearth of comparable studies, both the student and the specialist will find the study well worth reading. (Also available as a monograph from University of Texas Press, Austin, ILAS offprint series No. 173.) For a broader survey of the same fazenda, see item **3608**.

3578 Guerra, Flávio. Uma aventura holandesa no Brasil. Recife: Companhia Editora de Pernambuco, 1977. 275 p.; bibl. (His Evolução histórica de Pernambuco; 2)

A well-written narrative, intended for popular audience, of the Dutch occupation of the Northeast, based on existing literature in Portuguese and some original research. Good of its kind and does present the "Pernambucan" view of the *tempo dos flamengos*.

3580 Hell, Jurgen. Der brasilianische Plantagenkomplex, 1532–1808: ein Beitrag zur Charakteristik der Sklaverei in Amerika (Asien, Afrika, Lateinamerika [Deutscher Verlag der Wissenschaften, Berlin, GDR] 6:1, 1978, p. 117–138)

Analysis by East German author of

Brazilian slavery and the fazenda (1532–1808) and the role they played in the evolution of the country. [M. Kossok]

3581 Hemming, John. Red gold: the conquest of the Brazilian Indians. Cambridge, Mass.: Harvard University Press, 1978. 677 p.; bibl.; 8 leaves of plates: ill.; index.

This work, representing an incredible amount of hard research into a wide range of sources, is really a series of very detailed essays on Portuguese contact with the Amerindians, on the original settlements and subsequent advance inland, and on the Jesuit missions. Analysis is rather traditional and tends to get lost in the descriptions, perhaps because the author lacks anthropological training. Despite this drawback, easily the most comprehensible book on the subject in English and probably the most accessible, due to its commercial success. For ethnohistorian's comment, see item **1648**.

3583 Hoornaert, Eduardo and others. História da Igreja no Brasil: ensaio de interpretação a partir do Povo, primeira época. Petrópolis: Editora Vozes, 1977. 442 p.; bibl.; 8 leaves of plates: ill.; index (História geral da Igreja na América Latina; 2)

This volume, which covers colonial Brazil, is part of a major project to reinterpret the history of the Catholic Church in Latin America critically and from a distinctly Latin American perspective, emphasizing the Church's role among the poor so as to inspire a popular readership to social action (for a critique of the project, see *HLAS 40:2146a*). While the writing style is direct and somewhat simplistic, the content is soundly based on printed contemporary documents nicely listed at the beginning of each section. The result is a useful reference tool for both the general reader and the specialist.

3584 Ilha, Manuel da. Narrativa da Custódia de Santo Antônio do Brasil, 1584–1621. Texto bilíngüe. Introdução, notas e tradução portuguesa por Ildefonso Silveira. Petrópolis, Brasil: Vozes, 1975. 148 p.; bibl. (História; 4. Publicações CID)

Annotated transcription of hitherto unpublished account, contemporaneous but second-hand, of early Franciscan missionary activity in Brazil. Gives original Latin text parallel with Portuguese translation.

3585 Kuznesof, Elizabeth Anne. Clans, the militia and territorial government: the articulation of kinship with polity in eighteenth-century São Paulo (*in* Social fabric and spatial structure in colonial Latin America. Edited by David J. Robinson. Ann Arbor, Mich.: University Microfilms International, 1979, p. 181–226, map, tables)

Basically a study of how the militia and *ordenança* posts of the 18th century provided an institutional structure around which solidified the previously fluid and personalistic clans in frontier São Paulo. While informative, suffers from too ambitious a scope and insufficient evidence.

3586 Lang, James. Portuguese Brazil: the King's plantation. New York: Academic Press, 1979. 266 p.; bibl. (Studies in social discontinuity)

Companion volume to *HLAS 38:2290*, this study is a welcome addition to the small number of full-length, analytical overviews of colonial Brazil in English. The work reflects the author's training as a sociologist, lately come to Brazilian history. Its strong analytical framework and its concentration on *conjunctures* are its main strengths as is its placing of Brazil in the international context. But the author's lack of close knowledge means that the diversity of colonial Brazil is often lost in "reductionist" analysis.

Lastarria, Miguel. Portugueses y brasileños hacia el Río de la Plata: un informe geopolítico, 1816. See item **2954**.

3587 Leonzo, Nanci. As companhias de Ordenanças na capitania de São Paulo: das origens ao governo do Morgado de Matheus (Série de História [Coleção Museu Paulista, Universidade de São Paulo, Brazil] 6, 1977, p. 123–239, bibl.)

A fairly narrow, legalistic study of the origins and function of the paramilitary body which involved almost all adult males in colonial Brazil. Some specific data on *ordenanças* in São Paulo. Originally an USP master's thesis.

3588 Lima, Maurílio César de. Lourenço Caleppi: primeiro Núncio no Brasil, 1808–1816, segundo documentos do Arquivo Secreto Apostólico do Vaticano. Rio de Janeiro: Instituto Histórico e Geográfico Brasileiro, 1977. 257 p.; bibl.; index; port.

A close study essential both for the Church historian and for the specialist in foreign affairs.

3589 Lopes Serra, João. A Governor and his image in baroque Brazil: the funeral eulogy of Afonso Furtado de Castro do Rio de Mendoça. Edited by Stuart B. Schwartz. Translated by Ruth E. Jones. Minneapolis: University of Minnesota Press, 1979. 216 p.; bibl.; ill.; index.

Reprint of a manuscript funeral eulogy to the Viscount of Barbacena, Governor-General of Brazil (1671–75), which provides a graphic portrait not only of the man but of Bahian society. Beautifully introduced and edited by a leading colonial historian. Well worth reading.

3594 MacLachlan, Colin M. Slavery, ideology, and institutional change: the impact of the Enlightenment on slavery in late eighteenth-century Maranhão (JLAS, 11:1, May 1979, p. 1–17)

By analyzing three law cases in which slaves sought to compel their masters to sell them their freedom, the author shows how the prevailing ideology in 18th-century Brazil favored withdrawing from total commitment to slavery. An important and innovative essay recommended to students of Brazil and slavery.

3596 Mauro, Frédéric. Le Brésil du XVe à la fin du XVIIIe siècle. Paris: Société d'Edition d'Enseignment Supérieur, 1977. 253 p.; bibl.; maps (Regards sur l'histoire; 28. Histoire générale; 2)

While intended only as a popular introduction to colonial Brazil and not, in the author's words, as "a history according to our heart," the result is a well-written, concise synthesis of the secondary literature. Highly recommended to any reader at ease with elementary French. Compare with item **3586**.

3597 Meira Filho, Augusto. Evolução histórica de Belém do Grão-Pará: fundação e história. v. 1, Século XVII; v. 2, O século XVIII. Belém: s.n., 1976. 2 v. (893 p.) (Continuous pagination); bibl.; facsims.; ill.; maps.

These two large volumes, full of facts, documents and illustrations, form the colonial section of what will be a complete history of Belem do Pará. The traditional approach and narrowness of the data limit the work's potential. Perhaps most useful in conjunction with Ernesto Cruz's earlier study (see *HLAS 36:3431*).

3598 Morton, F.W.O. The royal timber in late colonial Bahia (HAHR, 58:1, Feb. 1978, p. 41–61)

Well-written, carefully researched study of the royal policy for the conservation and use of a commodity indispensable for the Portuguese navy and merchant marine. Also an excellent case study of the influence of the Enlightenment on the formation of royal policy and of the local potentates' ability to sabotage royal plans intended to achieve greater control at the local level. For geographer's comment, see *HLAS 41:5676*.

3599 Mota, Carlos Guilherme. Idéia de revolução no Brasil, 1789–1801: estudo das formas de pensamento. Petrópolis, Brasil: Editora Vozes, 1979. 145 p.; bibl. (Coleção História brasileira; 3)

Publication of the author's master's thesis written in 1967 and so preliminary to his later, more developed works. Emphasizes the conservative bent of "revolutionary" thought.

3600 Mott, Luiz R.B. Descrição da Capitania de São José do Piauí (USP/RH, 56:112, out./nov. 1977, p. 543–574, tables)

Transcribes a manuscript description of Piauí in 1772 by the *ouvidor* of the captaincy. Introduction contains excellent short study of the historiography of colonial Piauí. Useful source.

Pereira Júnior, José Anthero. Pesquisas arqueológicas no "Patio do Colegio." See *HLAS 41:673*.

3601 Ramos, Donald. Vila Rica: profile of a colonial Brazilian urban center (AAFH/TAM, 35:4, April 1979, p. 495–526)

Using a 1804 census, the author describes and tabulates virtually every demographic characteristic of family and household in the town now known as Ouro Preto. Perhaps most valuable as source material for the social historian; for such use of author's earlier work, see item **3606**.

3602 Richshoffer, Ambrósio. Diário de um soldado da Companhia das Indias Ocidentais: 1629–1632. 2. ed. Traduzido do raríssimo original alemão por Alfredo de Carvalho. Introdução de Mauro Mota. São Paulo: Instituição Brasileira de Difusão Cultural,

1978. 139 p.; bibl. (Biblioteca História; 27)

A welcome re-edition of the Alfredo de Carvalho translation (originally published 1897) of the account by a German soldier in Dutch pay of his service in the conquest of Recife and the Northeast (1629–32).

3603 **Rodrigues, José Honório.** História da história do Brasil. pt. 1, Historiografia colonial. São Paulo: Companhia Editora Nacional, 1979. 534 p.; bibl.; index (Brasiliana grande formato; 21)

A revised and expanded version of a study originally published in Spanish some two decades ago analyzing colonial writers on colonial Brazil. Without doubt a definitive reference work essential to the colonial historian.

3604 **Russell-Wood, A.J.R.** Female and family in the economy and society of colonial Brazil (*in* Latin American women: historical perspectives [see item **1791**] p. 60–100, tables)

An extremely useful overview of what is known about the role of the urban white female in colonial Brazil, together with suggestions for further research. Well worth reading.

3605 ———. Iberian expansion and the issue of black slavery (AHA/R, 83:1, Feb. 1978, p. 16–42)

A thorough, detailed survey of the place of African slavery in Portuguese society, its role in Imperial expansion, and Portuguese attitudes towards slavery. Makes some comparison to the Spanish experience. Not innovative but excellent as an introduction to the subject.

3606 ———. Technology and society: the impact of gold mining on the institution of slavery in Portuguese America (EHA/J, 37:1, March 1977, p. 59–86, table)

A close analysis of the organization of gold mining, its dependence on slave labor, and effects on the lives of slaves. Useful reminder that colonial slavery was not synonymous with the large plantation. Recommended. Includes a commentary by Joseph Love (p. 84–86).

3607 **Salvador, José Gonçalves.** Os cristãos-novos: povoamento e conquista do solo brasileiro, 1530–1680. São Paulo: Livraria Pioneira Editora, 1976. 406 p.; bibl.; ill.; index (Biblioteca Pioneira de estudos brasileiros)

Demonstrates that a great many of the original settlers in the "Captaincies of the South" may well have had Jewish ancestors but does not show that this inheritance engendered any special identity or separate consciousness among these people. Solidly based in manuscript sources, especially Portuguese.

3608 **Santos, Corcino Medeiros dos.** O trabalho escravo numa grande propiedade rural: a fazenda en Santa Cruz (FFCLM/EH, 16, 1977, p. 51–70, bibl., tables)

Places the condition of slaves on the Fazenda Santa Cruz at the end of the 18th century into a broad historical context. Particularly useful if read in conjunction with Graham's intensive study (see item **3576**).

3609 **Scarano, Julita.** Black brotherhoods: integration or contradiction? (UW/LBR, 16:1, Summer 1979, p. 1–17)

Although based on archival research, this article does no more than meander informatively throughout the subject. Centered on the 18th century.

3610 **Schwartz, Stuart B.** Indian labor and New World plantations: European demands and Indian responses in Northeastern Brazil (AHA/R, 83:1, Feb. 1978, p. 43–79, ill.)

Mildly disguised as a long article, this is really one section of what should be a monographic history of Indian-white relations in early colonial Brazil. The author focuses on the use of Indian labor on the sugar plantations of the Northeast and on its impact, both on Indians and on the whites, who increasingly preferred slaves from Africa. Required reading for historians of colonial Brazil.

3611 **Silva, Maria Beatriz Nizza da.** Análise de estratificação social: o Rio de Janeiro de 1808 a 1821. São Paulo: Faculdade de Filosofia, Letras e Ciências Humanas, Universidade de São Paulo, 1975. 183 p.; bibl. (Boletim Departamento de História; 6. Boletim Faculdade de Filosofia, Letras e Ciências Humanas; 7)

This work as well as items **3612** and **3613** compose a study, useful but not as developed as it could be, of public culture, social classes, and life styles in Rio de Janeiro (1808–21).

3612 ———. Cultura e sociedade no Rio de Janeiro, 1808–1821. Prefacio de Sérgio Buarque de Holanda. São Paulo: Companhia Editora Nacional, 1977. 246 p.; bibl. (Brasiliana; 363)

As noted in item **3611**, this is a well-researched recreation of the material and literary culture of pre-independence Rio city which, however, dwells more on specifics than on the import of the whole.

3612a ———. A primeira gazeta da Bahia: *Idade d'Ouro do Brasil.* São Paulo: Editora Cultrix, 1978. 208 p.; bibl.; ill.

Study of the first Bahian newspaper, showing through text and commentary the positions taken on various contemporary issues.

3613 ———. Produção, distribuição e consumo de livros e folhetos no Brasil colonial (IHGB/R, 314, jan./março 1977, p. 78–94)

An article on the book trade in colonial Brazil, see items **3611** and **3612**.

3614 **Soeiro, Susan A.** The feminine orders in colonial Bahia, Brazil: economic, social, and demographic implications, 1677–1800 (*in* Latin American women: historical perspectives [see item **1791**] p. 173–197, plates, tables)

Explains why convents were founded later and in fewer numbers in colonial Salvador than in Spanish America, and demonstrates how they functioned to buttress the social position of a privileged minority. A soundly argued, solidly researched contribution to the social history of colonial Brazil.

3615 **Studart Filho, Carlos.** História do Ceará holandés: considerações em torno de dois pontos controversos (Revista do Instituto do Ceará [Fortaleza, Brazil] 91:91, 1977, p. 7–47)

A refutation, slight and traditional in approach, of the common assumptions that: 1) Ceará was peopled by refugees from the Dutch regime in the Northeast, and 2) the Dutch were responsible for the "nordic" traits to be found in the Northeast.

3616 **Thomas, George.** Espírito Santo/Abrantes: die Entwicklung einer Indianersiedlung des brasilianischen Nordostens im Zeitalter Pombals (JGSWGL, 14, 1977, p. 97–133, graphs, tables)

A well-researched, intelligent article studying the fate of one of the Jesuit missions which was created an Indian "town" after the 1759 expulsion. Suggests that the change in status simply intensified a demographic decline already evident. Recommended, especially in conjunction with item **3610**.

3617 **Vasconcelos, Sílvio de.** Vida e obra de Antônio Francisco Lisboa, o Aleijadinho. São Paulo: Editora Nacional, 1979. 156 p.; ill. (Brasiliana; 369)

Valuable study, which concludes that the famous 18th-century sculptor-architect produced much more in his youth than is commonly thought; that he crystalized prevalent styles; and that his malady was not as debilitating as is often portrayed. Useful appendix with list of verifiable works. For art critic's comment, see item **460**.

Xavier, Carlos. Plantas indiáticas no Brasil. See *HLAS 41:5719.*

NATIONAL

3618 **Amado, Janaína.** Conflito social no Brasil: a revolta dos "Mucker," Rio Grande do Sul, 1868–1898. São Paulo: Edições Símbolo, 1978. 303 p.; bibl. (Coleção Ensaio e memória; 5)

First-class study of the conditions out of which emerged the Mucker sect in the Germanic area of settlement in Rio Grande do Sul and of the tensions between the sect and the local authority that produced the conflicts of July 1874. Fine analysis of German settlement in general. Highly recommended.

3619 **Andrade, Paulo René de.** Três revoluções: a atuação da Polícia Militar de Minas Gerais, a antiga Força Pública, nos movimentos revolucionários de 1924, 1930 e 1932: esboço histórico. Belo Horizonte: Imprensa Oficial, 1976. 538 p.; bibl.; plates; tables.

Factual account of the role of the Minas Gerais state police in the 1924 and 1930 revolutions. Based on state military records and recent memoirs, this study will only interest specialists working on regional or military history. Vol. 2 on the 1932 revolt is promised.

3620 Andréa, José. O Marechal Andréa nos relevos da história do Brasil. Capa e ilustrações por Murillo Machado. Rio de Janeiro: Biblioteca do Exército, 1977. 247 p.; bibl.; ill. (Coleção Taunay. Publicação Biblioteca do Exército; 475)

Despite a poor organization and a Baroque prose style, this biography contains a great deal of important material on the life and career of a soldier-administrator who, born in Portugal, played an important role in the emergence of Brazil as a nation in the 1830s.

Arinos Filho, Afonso [*pseud. for* **Afonso Arinos de Melo Franco Filho**]. Primo canto: memórias da mocidade. See item **6520**.

3621 Baggio, Sheila Brandão. A Força Pública de Minas na Primeria República (UMG/RBEP, 49, julho 1979, p. 201–232)

Preliminary research on administrative history of the Minas police force, based on legislation and internal regulations.

3622 Balhana, Altiva Pilatti. Santa Felicidade, uma paróquia vêneta no Brasil. Fotos por Altiva P. Balhana et al. Curitiba: Fundação Cultural de Curitiba, Prefeitura Municipal de Curitiba, 1978. 155 p.; bibl.; 12 leaves of plates: ill.

A concise, well-constructed socioeconomic and demographic analysis of an Italian colony established near Curitiba in the 1870s. Nicely illustrated.

3623 Barman, Roderick and **Jean Barman.** The prosopography of the Brazilian Empire (LARR, 13:2, 1978, p. 78–97)

An important methodological notice regarding authors' construction of a pool of some 15,000 computer entries on important figures during the Empire. Invites use and collaboration by other scholars interested in social history. For political scientist's comment, see *HLAS 41:7512*. [M.L. Conniff]

3624 Barral, Luisa Margarida Portugal de Barros, *condessa de.* Cartas a Suas Majestades, 1859–1890. Rio de Janeiro: Ministério de Justiça, Arquivo Nacional, 1977. 504 p.; bibl.; 6 leaves of plates: ill.; index (Publicações históricas; 83)

These well-edited letters offer the historian of the Empire excellent evidence on the ambience and intellectual outlook of court circles as well as indicating, on the more personal level, that the Condessa de Barral was not, despite Pedro II's hopes, his mistress.

3625 Besouchet, Lídia. Mauá e seu tempo. Rio de Janeiro: Editora Nova Fronteira, 1978. 193 p.; bibl.; port. (Coleção Vidas extraordinárias)

This reworked biography of Brazil's first "modern" entrepreneur does not improve on the original: not only is there no fresh evidence but the strong conceptual framework of the first edition is replaced by a confused narrative approach. Not recommended.

3626 Black, Jan Knippers. United States penetration of Brazil. Philadelphia: University of Pennsylvania Press, 1977. 313 p.; tables.

Well-researched and written account of US complicity in the military coup of 1964, based on interviews and government documents in Washington. Shows extraordinary range of public and private influence exerted, both before and after the coup. See also item **3730**.

3627 Boccia, Ana Maria Mathias. O contrabando de escravos para São Paulo (USP/RH, 56:112, out./nov. 1977, p. 321–379, bibl.)

Claims, on the basis of thin evidence drawn solely from São Paulo archives, that considerable contraband trade continued after 1850. Not convincing, showing only some reports of limited landings up to 1854.

3628 Brandão, Octávio. Combates e batalhas: memórias. Prefácio de Paulo Sérgio Pinheiro. São Paulo: Editora Alfa-Omega, 1978. 1 v. (Biblioteca Alfa-Omega de ciências sociais. Política; 5)

Fascinating memoir by labor and Communist Party leader, covering period from birth in Alagoas (1896) to his deportation for subversive activities (1931). An insider's account, it portrays figures and episodes from the early leftist movement in Rio.

3629 Brazil. Ministério da Indústria e do Comércio. Instituto Brasileiro do Café. O café no Brasil. Rio de Janeiro: 1978. 180 p.; tables.

Four monographs on coffee, written for a contest on the 250th anniversary of introduction of coffee into Brazil. They deal with social impact of coffee, its penetration into northern Paraná, the demand for migrants, and coffee's impact on Espírito Santo. All are well-documented.

Buescu, Mircea. Guerra e desenvolvimento: a economia brasileira durante a Segunda Guerra Mundial. See *HLAS 41:3451*.

Bunse, Heinrich A.W. Dialetos italianos do Rio Grande do Sul. See item **4627**.

Burton, Richard Francis. Viagem do Rio de Janeiro a Morro Velho. See *HLAS 41:5608*.

Calafut, George. An analysis of Italian emigration statistics, 1876–1914. See item **1921a**.

3630 Canêdo, Letícia Bicalho. O sindicalismo bancário em São Paulo no período de 1923–1944: seu significado político. São Paulo: Edições Símbolo, 1978. 220 p.; bibl. (Coleção Ensaio e memória; 13)

One of the few labor histories to focus on a single sector (São Paulo bank employees) and to discuss national policies from the viewpoint of union leadership. Thoroughly documented from union archives.

3631 Carneiro, Glauco. Lusardo, o último caudilho. pt. 1, Revolução de 1923; pt. 2, Entre Vargas e Perón. Rio de Janeiro: Editora Nova Fronteira, 1977. 1 v.; bibl.; ports (Coleção Brasil século 20)

Vol. 1 (in two parts) of this popular biography made best-seller lists in Brazil. Frankly admiring of the old-guard gaúcho politician, the author narrates major episodes from the mid-1920s until the 1960s. Of special interest are Lusardo's role in the Libertador party; his term as Rio police chief; his ambassadorships in Uruguay and Argentina; and what might be considered the transition from caudilho to populist national politics in the 1950s. The author, a journalist, interviewed Lusardo at length and consulted his private papers.

3632 Carone, Edgard. O Centro Industrial do Rio de Janeiro e sua importante participação na economia nacional, 1827–1977. Rio de Janeiro: Centro Industrial do Rio de Janeiro, 1978. 196 p.; ill.

Useful official history commemorating 150 years of this prestigious organization. Based on files and records of this and various predecessor associations.

3633 Carpeaux, Otto Maria. Alceu Amoroso Lima. Rio de Janeiro: Edições Graal, 1978. 173 p.; appendixes.

Contains biography of this leading Catholic intellectual, a chronology of his life, and a transcribed interview. Short, sympathetic.

3634 Carvalho, Afrânio de. Raul Soares, um líder da República Velha. Rio de Janeiro: Companhia Forense de Artes Gráficas, 1978. 318 p.; bibl.; 2 leaves of plates; index.

An admiring but useful biography of a leading mineiro politician who was governor of his state at the time of his death (1924). Based on Soares' private papers.

3635 Carvalho, José Murilo de. A Escola de Minas de Ouro Preto: o peso da glória. Rio de Janeiro: FINEP-Financiadora de Estudos e Projetos, 1978. 177 p.; bibl.; tables.

Part of a larger study on the development of science and technology in Brazil, this book traces the history of a major center of higher learning in Minas. Notes inculcation of scientific values and empirical methods.

3637 Cavalcanti, Orlando. Os insurretos de 43 [i.e. quarenta e três]: o manifesto mineiro e suas conseqüências. 2. ed., rev. e ampliada. Coordenação de Vladimir Luz. Rio de Janeiro: Civilização Brasileira, 1978. 76 p.; 8 leaves of plates (Coleção Retratos do Brasil; 118)

Reedition of the 1945 pamphlet which helped to immortalize the *manifesto mineiro*, including the original text, government retributions, and commentary.

Cenni storici sull'emigrzione italiana nelle Americhe e in Australia. See item **2634**.

3638 Chacon, Vamireh. Estado e povo no Brasil: as experiências do Estado Novo e da democracia populista, 1937–1964. Rio de Janeiro: Livraria José Olympio Editora, 1977. 259 p.; tables (Documentos brasileiros; 181)

Political and sociological analysis which is both broad and ultimately inconclusive. Much chronological detail, lengthy quotes, long footnotes slow down what is essentially an interpretive essay. For political scientist's comment, see *HLAS 41:7525*.

3639 Chandler, Billy Jaynes. The bandit king: Lampião of Brazil. College Station: Texas A&M University Press, 1978. 262 p.; bibl.; 6 leaves of plates: ill.; index.

Exhaustively documented study of the most famous of Brazil's rural bandits, whose career spanned the period 1921–37. Disproves "Robin Hood" myth which has arisen, by chronicling Lampião's activities and atrocities. Also reveals life in the *sertão* and the way Lampião's legends became incorporated into folk literature.

3640 Chasin, J. O integralismo de Plínio Salgado: forma de regressividade no capitalismo hípertardio. Prefácio de Antônio Cândido. São Paulo: Livraria Editora Ciências Humanas, 1978. 663 p.; bibl. (Brasil ontem e hoje; 4)

Exegesis of Plínio Salgado's philosophical position, which argues that its inspiration lay not fascism but constituted a reaction against urban industrial capitalism. Dense textual analysis and utilization of Lukacs' critical method will put off all but the most determined readers.

3641 Coelho, Edmundo Campos. Em busca de identidade: o exército e a política na sociedade brasileira. Rio de Janeiro: Forense-Universitária, 1976. 207 p.; ill. (Brazil análise e crítica)

First-rate study of a neglected subject, with some new information and penetrating analysis of the military. Covers from independence to the present, discussing military doctrines, roles, splits, and political behavior. Indispensable introduction to the subject. For political scientist's comment, see *HLAS 41:7528*.

3642 Conniff, Michael L. The *tenentes* in power: a new perspective on the Brazilian revolution of 1930 (JLAS, 10:1, May 1978, p. 61–82)

Argues that the Club 3 of Outubro phase (1931–32) of the *tenente* movement provided Vargas with policies and personnel indispensable for turning the regionalist rebellion of 1930 into the reformist-nationalist regime of 1932. Recommended reading, especially for its analysis of the important civilian group, typified by Pedro Ernesto, which was attached to the Club. [Barman]

3643 Corrêa, Anna Maria Martinez. A rebelião de 1924 em São Paulo. São Paulo: HUCITEC, 1976. 201 p.; maps (Coleção Estudos brasileiros; 2)

Thoughtful, documented, thorough account of the three-week capture of São Paulo by the tenentes in 1924. Concludes that the tenentes were unprepared to run the city, much less carry out any reform. When faced with a choice between labor and business alliances, they took the latter. Their flight northward followed their failure to govern the industrial metropolis.

3644 Costa, Levy Simões da. Cataguases centenária: dados para sua história. Juiz de Fora, Brazil: Esdeva Empresa Gráfica, 1977. 610 p.; plates; tables.

A very thorough compilation of materials about an agricultural town in the *zona da mata* of Minas Gerais. Could be reformatted as a useful local history or as source material for examining 20th-century social development of Brazil.

3645 Costa, Pedro Veloso. Medicina, Pernambuco, e tempo. Recife, Brazil: Universidade Federal de Pernambuco, 1978. 504 p.; bibl.; ill.; maps.

Major themes are introduction of X-rays, creation of the Institute of Forensic Medicine, psychiatry, and the creation of a public health service.

Costa, Rovílio and others. Antropologia visual da imigração italiana. See *HLAS 41:9316*.

Cupertino, Fausto. Raízes do atraso: país subdesenvolvido ou potência emergente? See *HLAS 41:3463*.

3646 Debes, Célio. Campos Salles; perfil de um estadista. v. 1, Na propaganda; v. 2, Na República. Rio de Janeiro: Livraria F. Alves Editora, 1978. 2 v. (664 p.); 18 leaves of plates; bibl.; ill.

A traditional and favorable biography, based on exhaustive primary documentation, about the man who did much to shape the Old Republic political system. Much of the text is dedicated to correspondence and newspaper articles, and little analysis is provided.

3647 ———. Um panfleto na propaganda republicana de São Paulo (MP/AN, 27, 1976, p. 119–156)

This transcription of a rare pamphlet written by Campos Salles in June 1888 is important to the specialist as marking his move from parliamentary to direct action against the Empire.

Delhaes-Guenther, Dietrich von. La influencia de la inmigración en el desarrollo y composición étnica de la población de Rio Grande do Sul. See *HLAS 41:9319*.

3648 Domingues, Moacyr. A nova face dos Muckers. São Leopoldo, Brazil: Editora Rotermund, 1977. 432 p.; bibl.

Violent repression of Protestant cult among German immigrants and their children in an isolated region of Rio Grande do Sul, led by João Jorge Maurer. Considerable detail on cult members and casualties from the attacks, based on family records.

3649 Dulles, John W.F. Castello Branco: the making of a Brazilian president. Foreword by Roberto de Oliveira Campos. College Station: Texas A&M University Press, 1978. 487 p.; 17 leaves of plates: ill.; index.

Flattering biography of the officer who led the 1964 coup and became first military president afterward. Based on Castello's archive and interviews with associates, the book covers only up to the assumption of presidential duties on 15 April 1964. Emphasizes early career, role in World War II, and his professionalism and neutrality in political affairs. For political scientist's comment, see *HLAS 41:7530*.

3650 Dutra, Eliana Regina de Freitas. A Igreja e as classes populares em Minas na década de vinte (UMG/RBEP, 49, julho 1979, p. 71–98)

Nicely executed study of the Catholic Labor Confederation and its attempts, through its newspaper, to promote a nonradical labor movement along the lines of the encyclical Rerum Novarum. Concludes that efforts largely succeeded in stemming independent labor and strikes.

3651 Faria, Maria Auxiliadora. A Guarda Nacional em Minas Gerais: 1831–1873 (UMG/RBEP, 49, julho 1979, p. 145–199)

Shortened version of author's master's thesis at the University of Paraná on the socioeconomic structure of the National Guard in Minas Gerais (1831–73). Shows that the Guard after 1851 was synonymous with the "have" section of Brazil and an effective weapon of the central authorities. Recommended, especially as a complement to Berrance de Castro (see *HLAS 40:4081*).

3652 Fausto, Boris. Trabalho urbano e conflito social: 1890–1920. São Paulo: DIFEL, 1976. 1 v.; ill.; tables (Corpo e alma do Brasil; 46)

An outstanding synthesis in a field heavily researched already. Balanced approach covering social system, economics, and politics. Primary research from newspapers fills gaps, and appendix enumerates strikes in the 1917–20 period, the apex of the Old Republican labor activity.

Fernandes, Florestan. Beyond poverty: the Negro and the mulatto in Brazil. See *HLAS 41:9322*.

3653 Fernandes, Heloisa Rodrigues. Política e segurança: força pública do estado de São Paulo, fundamentos histórico-sociais. São Paulo: Alfa-Omega, 1974. 259 p.; tables (Biblioteca Alfa-Omega de ciências sociais; 2)

Timely and well-researched study of police forces and repression in São Paulo from colonial times through the Old Republic. Fits subject into elaborate conceptual framework.

3654 Flores, Moacyr. Modelo político dos Farrapos: as idéias políticas da revolução farroupilha. Porto Alegre, Brazil: Mercado Aberto, 1978. 208 p.; bibl.; ill.

Fine study of the political goals of this famous rebellion, based on archival research and textual analysis of decrees, draft constitutions, and other documents.

3655 Flynn, Peter. Brazil: a political analysis. Boulder, Colo.: Westview Press, 1978. 564 p.; maps; plates; tables (Nations of the modern world)

Perhaps the best account of the 1960s and 1970s in English, preceded by lengthy historical sections which seek the origins of the military takeover. Stresses class relations in politics and often provides good insights in an otherwise detailed narrative. For political scientist's comment, see *HLAS 41:7538*.

3656 Forjaz, Maria Cecília Spina. Tenentismo a Aliança Liberal: 1927–1930. Prefácio de Sérgio Miceli. São Paulo: Livraria Editora Polis, 1978. 111 p.; bibl. (Coleção Teoria e história; 2)

Superficial treatment which adds little

to what is already available in the secondary literature.

3657 ———. Tenentismo e política: tenentismo e camadas médias urbanas na crise da primeira república. Rio de Janeiro: Paz e Terra, 1977. 117 p.; maps.

Useful examination of the tenente movement from 1922–27, based on memoirs and newspapers. Argues that the tenentes pursued urban middle class goals which arose during the crisis of traditional oligarchical rule. Undigested material and gaps between hypothesis and evidence mar this work.

3658 **Franco, Afonso Arinos de Melo.** The Chamber of Deputies of Brazil: historical synthesis: commemorative work marking the 150th anniversary of the inauguration of the first Chamber of Deputies. Translated from the Portuguese by Gilberto Antunes Chauvet, John Stephen Morris. Brasília: Câmara dos Deputados, Centro de Documentação e Informação de Publicações, 1977. 182 p.; ill.

While of limited value as a historical study, excellent for student use as an English-language text giving—straightfaced—the official "nationalist-republican" interpretation of Brazilian history, albeit from a Minas rather than São Paulo perspective.

3659 **Freitas, Décio.** Os guerrilheiros do Imperador. Rio de Janeiro: Graal, 1978. 170 p.; bibl. (Biblioteca de história; 1)

Interpretation of the Cabanada in Alagoas (1832–36) as a social uprising by the masses for land. Acknowledges but does not analyze the traditionalist ideas inspiring the revolt.

3660 **Galey, John.** Industrialist in the wilderness: Henry Ford's Amazon venture (UM/JIAS, 21:2, May 1979, p. 261–289, bibl.)

Well-written, enjoyable account of the Ford investments from 1928 to 1945, which amounted to nine million, and of the many causes for their failure to make their enterprises profitable. Notes Brazil's abiding fear of foreign exploitation of the basin.

3661 **Geribello, Wanda Pompeu.** Anísio Teixeira: análise e sistematização de sua obra. São Paulo: Atlas, 1977. 210 p.

A fine study combining biography, intellectual development, and writings by and about this great figure in Brazilian education and letters. Compare with biography by Hermes Lima (item **3690**).

3662 **Gobineau, Joseph Arthur.** O Conde de Gobineau no Brasil: documentação inédita. Compilador: Georges Raeders. São Paulo: Secretaria da Cultura, Ciência e Tecnologia, Conselho Estadual de Cultura, 1976. 212 p.; bibl. (Coleção Ensaio; 85)

Using Gobineau's private correspondence and other writings, the compiler recreates the French envoy's 14 unhappy months in Rio (1869–70). This volume together with item **3663** presents a good portrait of Rio de Janeiro and of Brazilian culture as it appeared to the European aristocrat.

3663 ———. Lettres brésiliennes. Edition établie et annotée par Marie-Louise Concasty. Paris: Les Bibliophiles de l'Originale, 1969. 247 p.; ill.

Well-edited transcript of the private letters of the French minister to Brazil (1869–70) giving intelligent if eccentric comments on Pedro II and society of Rio de Janeiro. See also item **3662**.

Graham, Ann Hartness. Subject guide to statistics in the Presidential Reports of the Brazilian provinces: 1830–1889. See *HLAS 41:115*.

3664 **Greenfield, Gerald Michael.** Dependency and the urban experience: São Paulo's public service sector, 1885–1913 (JLAS, 10:1, May 1978, p. 37–59)

Examines gas lighting and water concessions to determine applicability of dependency theory. Concludes that the principal restraint on policy-makers was lack of money and technology. Foreign concessionaires could make lucrative bargains but did not control the São Paulo elite.

3665 ———. Lighting the city: a case study of public service problems in São Paulo, 1885–1913 (*in* Essays concerning the socioeconomic history of Brazil and Portuguese India [see item **3519**] p. 118–149)

A rather repetitive demonstration that, in a rapidly growing city like São Paulo, private utility companies, national or foreign, look to their own profit and monopoly position, being in a much stronger position than the general public as a political force.

3665a ———. Streetcar squabbles in Old Sao Paulo: urban transportation development, 1872–1892. (South Atlantic Urban Studies [Columbia, S.C.], 2, 1978, p. 180–202)

Argues that the grant of monopoly concessions by competing municipal and state authorities and the lack of effective control prevented the swift building of the needed streetcar lines in the rapidly expanding Sao Paulo of the late nineteenth century.

3666 Grupo de Trabalho em Ciências Sociais e Humanas de Minas Gerais, *Belo Horizonte, Brazil.* Bibliografia de D. Pedro II [i.e. Segundo] e sua época, 1840–1889: levantamento realizado em Minas Gerais por ocasião das comemorações do sesquicentenário de nascimento do Imperador. Belo Horizonte: O Grupo, 1977. 162 p.; ill.; index.

A bibliography of books and articles relating to the Second Empire. Limited to items available in Minas libraries but still useful as a supplementary checklist.

3667 Hahner, June E. The beginnings of the women's suffrage movement in Brazil (Signs [Journal of women in culture and society, Chicago, Ill.] 5, 1979, p. 200–204)

Translation, with a short explanatory introduction, of the letter sent by Bertha Lutz to the *Revista da Semana* in 1918, which began the campaign for female suffrage achieved in 1932. Good for classroom use.

3668 ———. Feminism, women's rights, and the suffrage movement in Brazil, 1850–1932 (LARR, 15:1, 1980, p. 65–111)

Excellent survey of the feminist press in Brazil, highlighting women's roles in public life and their suffrage movement, which succeeded in 1932. Radically alters traditional picture of cloistered women, showing them active in many walks of life. However, these were a small group drawn from the middle and upper strata. See also item **3542**.

3669 ———. The nineteenth-century feminist press and women's rights in Brazil (*in* Latin American women: historical perspectives [see item **1791**] p. 254–285)

A welcome pioneer study of a crucial subject. Since the periodical press played so central a role in the political and cultural process, the article in effect discusses the whole range of the feminist movement. Soundly based on hitherto unused primary materials. Most effectively read in conjunction with item **3670**.

3670 ———. Women and work in Brazil, 1850–1920: a preliminary investigation (*in* Essays concerning the socioeconomic history of Brazil and Portuguese India [see item **3519**] p. 87–117)

A thoughtful and thorough examination of the kinds of employment open to Brazilian women and of the conditions under which women did begin to work outside the home. Firmly based on demographic and qualitative evidence. Recommended.

Hasenbalg, Carlos A. Diagnóstico sobre as desigualdades raciais no Brasil: notas para uma história social do negro brasileiro. See *HLAS 1:9330.*

Hilton, Stanley E. Suástica sobre o Brasil: a história da espionagem alemã no Brasil, 1939–1944. See *HLAS 41:8823.*

3672 Hirst, Mónica. Uma guia para a pesquisa histórica no Rio de Janeiro: os documentos privados nos arquivos públicos (LARR, 14:2, 1979, p. 150–171)

Useful guide to private archives in public repositories in Rio, covering especially the Old Republic.

3674 Holanda, Sérgio Buarque de. História geral da civilização brasileira. t. 3, O Brasil republicano: v. 1, Estrutura de poder e economia: 1889–1930; v. 2, Sociedade e instituições: 1889–1930. São Paulo: Difusão Editorial do Livro (DIFEL), 1975/1977. 2 v. (420, 431 p.); plates; tables.

This third tome of a multi-volume history of Brazil covers the Republic, and like preceding *tomos* (see *HLAS 34:2914*), consists of more than one volume. Vol. 1 concentrates on state power, coronelismo, changes in agricultural production, and Brazil's place in the world economy; v. 2 on social movements, immigration, the army, and culture. The two volumes, composed of contributions by leading Brazilian and American scholars, provide first satisfactory-in-depth analysis of the structures of the Old Republic. Highly recommended.

3675 Holloway, Thomas H. Immigration and abolition: the transition from slave to free labor in the São Paulo coffee zone (*in* Essays concerning the socioeconomic history of Brazil and Portuguese India [see item **3519**] p. 150–177)

Carefully examines the condition of São Paulo coffee growers in the last two decades of the Empire and argues that their change in attitude to favor abolition is explained by (a) an increase in available immigrant labor and (b) a desire to remove social unrest caused by the tactics of the abolitionist movement. A persuasive, well-written analysis.

3676 Hunsche, Carlos Henrique Trein. O ano 1826 [i.e. mil oitocentos e vinte e seis] da imigração e colonização alemã no Rio Grande do Sul, Província de São Pedro. Porto Alegre: Editora Metrópole, 1977. 637 p.; bibl.; 24 leaves of plates: ill.; index.

Continuation of *HLAS 38:4087* which covered years 1824–25. Equally overflowing with invaluable primary data (e.g., ships, passenger lists, genealogies, decrees, documents of all sorts).

3677 Instituto de Direito Público e Ciência Política, *Rio de Janeiro.* **Centro de Pesquisa e Documentação e História Contemporânea do Brasil.** Tenentismo: bibliografia. Editor: Paulo César Farah. Fotografia: Julio S.B. Alcântara. Rio de Janeiro: CPDOC, 1978. 37 p.; ill.

Comprehensive bibliography of books and articles on the tenentes, plus photos from the Pedro Ernesto Archive and summary descriptions of other unpublished material in the CPDOC collection.

3678 Jaeger, Luiz Gonzaga. Padre Pedro Lenz, S.J.: primeiro Provincial da Companhia de Jesus restaurada no Brasil, tópicos da vida; documentos relativos à Fundação da Província Sul-Brasileira da Companhia de Jesus. Textos a cargo de Arthur Rabuske. São Leopoldo, Brazil: Instituto Anchietano de Pesquisas, 1977. 92 p. (Publicações avulsas; 4)

Unfinished and undocumented biography of a Jesuit priest (1885–1938) born in Rio Grande do Sul of a German family. Interesting for data on his social background and his intellectual relationship with Europe.

3679 Katzman, Martin T. Cities and frontiers in Brazil: regional dimensions of economic development. Cambridge, Mass.: Harvard University Press, 1977. 255 p.; bibl.; index.

Stimulating analysis of the impact of urbanization and regional disparities on the welfare of rural population. Reexamines a number of accepted truths, using neoclassical economics. Discusses migration, wages, land development, transfer mechanisms, and popular models of economic growth. Important for several disciplines. For economist's comment, see *HLAS 41:3477*.

3680 Klarner, Izabela. Emigracja z królestwa polskiego do Brazylii, 1890–1914. Warszawa, Poland: Ksiaźka i Wiedza, 1975. 167 p.; bibl.; tables.

A solid, factual study of Polish emigration to Brazil based solely on Polish manuscript and printed sources.

3681 Lacerda, Carlos. Depoimento. Prefácio de Ruy Mesquita. Organização do texto, notas e seleção de documentos de Cláudio Lacerda Paiva. Rio de Janeiro: Editora Nova Fronteira, 1977. 469 p.; 12 leaves of plates: ill.; index (Coleção Brasil século; 20)

Fascinating and indispensable account of his life and career, by the prominent anti-Getulista and one-time governor of Guanabara. Based on 34 hours of interviews taped in 1977, the book contains fine material on the 1930s and after, plus several useful appendices. More candid and lucid than Góes Monteiro's famous *depoimento.* Lacerda's passion and amazing memory make this a most valuable source for contemporary history.

3682 Lacombe, Américo Jacobina. A sombra de Rui Barbosa. São Paulo: Companhia Editora Nacional/MEC, 1978. 226 p.; bibl. (Brasiliana; 365)

Useful contribution by Lacombe, dean of the *ruistas* and director of the Casa de Rui Barbosa since 1939. A 67-p. biographical synthesis is followed by nine essays and talks by Lacombe.

3683 Leacock, Ruth. JFK, business, and Brazil (HAHR, 59, Nov. 1979, p. 636–673)

Impeccably documented account of Kennedy's drift from neutrality to open sponsorship in US business interests in Brazil from 1961 until his death. Will interest specialists in US, Brazilian, diplomatic, and business history.

3684 Leitman, Spencer L. A Brazilian urban system in the nineteenth century; Pelotas and Rio de Janeiro (*in* Urbanization in the Americas from its beginnings to the present. Edited by Robert Schaedel; Jorge E. Hardoy; and Nora Scott Kinzer. The Hague: Mouton, 1978, p. 491–503)

Despite title, this is in fact a résumé of author's dissertation on the Farroupilha, published in Portuguese as item **3685**.

3685 ———. Raízes sócio-econômicas da Guerra dos Farrapos: um capítulo da história do Brasil no século XIX. Traduzido por Sarita Linhares Barsted. Rio de Janeiro: Edições Graal, 1979. 195 p.; bibl. (Biblioteca de história; 4)

Argues that the economic causes of the Farroupilha rebellión can bè traced to the discontent of the *charqueadors* of the *campanha* area who could not compete with Platine producers and were in 1835 facing increased taxation. War was ended, in author's view, by exhaustion of the cattle supplies of the *campanha* and fiscal concessions by Imperial government. Recommended. See item **3684** for précis in English.

3686 ———. Slave cowboys in the cattle lands of southern Brasil, 1800–1850 (USP/RH, 101, 1975, p. 167–177)

The use of slaves as cowboys, the epitome of freedom and individualism, is as the author suggests inherently inconsistent. Tries to suggest why and how slaves were so used by paucity of data does not allow any firm conclusions.

3687 Levine, Robert M. Pernambuco in the Brazilian Federation, 1889–1937. Stanford, Calif.: Stanford University Press, 1978. 236 p.; bibl.; ill.; maps; tables.

Highly innovative study of society, economy, polities in this northeastern state and of its relation with the nation. Demonstrates that Pernambuco could not take advantage of the great provincial autonomy afforded by the Old Republic and continued its secular decline vis-à-vis the urban-industrial South. Written as part of a larger project. See also *HLAS 40:4187* and item **3695**.

3688 Lewin, Linda. The oligarchical limitations of social banditry in Brazil: the case of the "good" thief Antônio Silvino (PP, 82, Feb. 1979, p. 116–146, map, table)

An engaging portrait of an archetypical cangaceiro and the way he was romanticized in folk literature. Concludes that cangaço protest ends up preserving the oligarchical system of the backlands by diffusing mass dissent.

3689 ———. Some historical implications of kinship organization for family-based politics in the Brazilian Northeast (CSSH, 21:2, April 1979, p. 262–292, tables)

Sophisticated analysis of family linkages among 303 members of the political elite of Paraíba between 1889–1930, revealing great adaptability and endurance of family-based politics.

Lima, Heitor Ferreira. 3 [i.e. Três] industrialistas brasileiros: Maúa, Rui Barbosa, Roberto Simonsen. See *HLAS 41:3482*.

3690 Lima, Hermes. Anísio Teixeira: estadista da educação. Rio de Janeiro: Civilização Brasileira, 1978. 212 p.

A fine, sympathetic account by a personal friend and colleague of one of Brazil's great educators. The lack of citations and scholarly apparatus should not detract from the book's utility for modern historians. See also item **3661**.

3691 Lima, Margarida Rosa de. Voyage d un Poitevin à Rio de Janeiro en 1830–1831 (BEPB, 35/36, 1973/1975, p. 121–143, plates)

Series of conventional descriptions of the physical aspects of Rio de Janeiro by a Frenchman who established himself briefly in that city. Contains nothing new.

3692 Lima Júnior, Olavo Brasil de. Evolução e crise do sistema partidário brasileiro: as eleições legislativas estaduais de 1947 a 1962 (DADOS, 17, 1978, p. 29–51, tables)

Stimulating examination of the disintegration of the party system, showing that all major parties gradually lost strength to minority parties. Party fragmentation undermined the system at the state level, as it did at the national level.

3693 Linhares, Maria Yedda. As listas eleitorais do Rio de Janeiro no século XIX (UMG/RBEP, 48, jan. 1978, p. 121–153, tables)

While the author's lengthy discussion shows importance of electoral lists for socioeconomic history, the substance is slight and the proposed code of occupations is so normative as to create as many problems as it solves.

3694 Lins, Etelvino. Um depoimento político: episódios e observações. Rio de Janeiro: Livraria José Olympio, 1977. 164 p.; ill.

Welcome memoir by unsuccessful presidential candidate in 1955 and Governor of Pernambuco.

3695 Love, Joseph L. São Paulo in the Brazilian Federation, 1889–1937. Stanford, Calif.: Stanford University Press, 1980. 393 p.; ill.; plates.

Without question the major book of the year. Outstanding analysis of Brazil's leading state during the crucial period of its rise to prominence. Synthesizes masses of secondary literature and makes superb use of much new data, especially on elites and budgets. See also item **3687** and *HLAS 40:4187*.

3696 Lustosa, Oscar de Figueiredo. Reformistas na Igreja do Brasil-Império. São Paulo: Universidade de São Paulo, Faculdade de Filosofia, Letras e Ciências Humanas, 1977. 180 p.; bibl. (Boletim Departamento de História; 10. Boletim Faculdade de Filosofia, Letras e Ciências Humanas; 17)

A master's thesis (University of São Paulo) which has special significance for being one of the first efforts, in the present surge of interest in Church history, to move beyond the descriptive to the analytic. Attempts with mixed success to place the reform movement of 1822–42 into a larger sociopolitical and religious context.

3697 Lutterbeck, Jorge Alfredo. Jesuítas no sul do Brasil: capítulos de história da Missão e Província Sul-Brasileira da Companhia de Jesus: em lembrança da passagem do 1° cinqüentenário de fundação da Província Sul-Brasileira S.J. Revisão dos textos e apresentação de Arthur Rabuske. São Leopoldo: Instituto Anchietano de Pesquisas, 1977. 172 p.; map (Publicações avulsas; 3)

A fairly simplistic account, without any sources given, of the return of the Jesuit order to the south of Brazil in 1842 and their achievements thereafter. Written in the 1940s, this study very much reflects the piety of the time. See also item **3678**.

3697a Lyra, Heitor. A educação dos príncipes: capítulo inédito da nova edição da *História de Dom Pedro II*: 1977 (BMA/BB, 38, jan./junho 1977, p. 39–79)

A traditional, descriptive—but well written—account of the upbringing of Pedro I's children (1831–40). Does not go a great deal beyond Alberto Rangel's work on the same subject.

3698 McBeth, Michael C. The Brazilian Army and its role in the abdication of Pedro I (UW/LBR, 15, Summer 1978, p. 117–129)

A short survey, based on secondary sources, showing that defeat in the war with Argentina, tensions within the officer corps, and deplorable conditions for the rank and file destroyed the effectiveness of the Brazilian Army by 1830 and prevented it from upholding Pedro I's rule in the April 1831 crisis. Recommended for students.

3699 ———. The Brazilian recruit during the First Empire: slave or soldier? (*in* Essays concerning the socioeconomic history of Brazil and Portuguese India [see item **3519**] p. 71–86)

Argues that the use of forced recruitment and the vile conditions in the Brazilian regular army under Pedro I explain the indiscipline which caused the Liberals to reduce the army's size and create the National Guard in the early 1830s.

3700 McCann, Frank D. The nation in arms: obligatory military service during the Old Republic (*in* Essays concerning the socioeconomic history of Brazil and Portuguese India [see item **3519**] p. 211–243)

Although only preliminary to a more developed study, this article demonstrates that conditions in the army (1900–20), were as deplorable as they had been under Pedro I (see item **3699**). The program for military reform, a national draft, and a volunteer reserve were, the author argues, pushed by the middle class which saw a strong army as indispensable for a strong nation. Only World War I enabled a partial fulfillment of this program.

3701 Macedo, Ubiratã Borges de. A liberdade no Império. São Paulo: Editora Convívio, 1977. 214 p.

Standard survey of 19th-century writers and thinkers, focused on the concept of liberty in the political, religious, and moral realms. Concludes that little interest existed in praxis, none in the dilemma of slavery.

3702 Maeyama, Takashi. Ethnicity, secret societies, and associations: the Japanese in Brazil (CSSH, 21:4, Oct. 1979, p. 589–610, bibl.)

A survey of associations among Japanese in Brazil, which concludes that they are not legacies of either parent culture but rather arise out of the peculiar situation of the immigrant in modern Brazil.

3703 Magalhães, Beatriz Ricardina de. Investimentos ingleses no Brasil e o Banco Londrino e Brasileiro (UMG/RBEP, 49, julho 1979, p. 233–252)

Using selected passages from the surviving letter books of the London and Brazilian Bank, tries to show that the bank, as an agent of foreign capital, dominated the Brazilian economy (1870–90). Unfortunately, neither the evidence given nor the author's understanding of the financial structure are sufficient to justify this assertion.

Malan, Pedro S. and others. Política econômica externa e industrialização no Brasil: 1939–52. See *HLAS 41:3488*.

3704 Mallon, Florencia E. Peasants and rural laborers in Pernambuco: 1955–1964 (LAP, 5[4]:19, Fall 1978, p. 49–70)

An attempt to determine which elements in the rural scene were more radical and how they acted, especially in the period prior to the 1964 coup. Based on secondary sources.

3705 Malloy, James M. The politics of social security in Brazil. Pittsburgh, Pa.: University of Pittsburgh Press, 1979. 200 p.; tables (Pitt Latin American series)

Theoretically exciting examination of the origins and development of Brazil's social security system, from the 1920s on. Uses social policy to elucidate the role of the state. Conclusion compares Brazil's system to those of other Latin American countries.

3706 Manchester and São Paulo: problems of rapid urban growth. Edited by John D. Wirth and Robert L. Jones. Stanford, Calif.: Stanford University Press, 1978. 234 p.; bibl.; index.

Stimulating comparative studies of two cities which shared much in common. Breadth of subjects addressed over past two centuries will interest students of urban history: ideology, literature, religion, etc., by well-known scholars. For sociologist's comment, see *HLAS 41:9411*.

Manfroi, Olívio. Religion d'attestation et créativité communautaire: l'immigration italienne au Rio Grande do Sul, 1875–1914. See *HLAS 41:9343*.

3707 Manor, Paul. Un prolétariat en uniforme et une révolution "honnête:" quelques considérations sur la rébellion des équipages de la Flotte Brésilienne de Haute Mer, en novembre 1910 (UTIEH/C, 30, 1978, p. 63–108)

Detailed account of the naval rebellion of 1910, with analysis of discontent among sailors and Brazil's rivalry with Argentina for naval supremacy.

3708 Maram, Sheldon L. The immigrant and the Brazilian labor movement, 1890–1920 (*in* Essays concerning the socioeconomic history of Brazil and Portuguese India [see item **3519**] p. 178–210)

Argues that the leadership of the labor movement by immigrants was undesirable, since it: a) caused conflicts between foreign and native groups within movement, and b) enabled employers and state to destroy movement by deporting leadership. However, does not show that any alternative and viable native leadership group existed.

3709 Marcílio, Maria Luiza. The price of slaves in XIXth century Brazil: a quantitative analysis of the registration of slave sales in Bahia (*in* Studi in memoria di Fedrigo Melis. Roma: Giannini Editore, 1978, v. 5, p. 83–97, tables)

Statistical analysis of the slave-sale records from the parish of Pilar, Salvador (1838–82), showing that the highest prices were: a) for slaves aged 25–34 who were field-hands of either sex or were male domestics, and b) for African over Brazilian-born slaves. Offers a tentative explanation of these findings.

3710 Marotti, Giorgio. Canudos: storia di una guerra. Roma: Bulzoni Editore, 1978. 185 p.; bibl.

El author reconstruye el desarrollo de la rebelión de Canudos y el impacto de la misma en la prensa, en la literatura y en la sensibilidad colectiva brasileña. De especial interés es su análisis sobre la transformación del hecho histórico en hecho legendario. La conclusión analiza el uso de la leyenda por parte de la clase dominante. [M. Carmagnani]

Martins, Eduardo. Coriolano de Medeiros: notícia biobibliográfica. See item **6423**.

3711 ———. A tipografia do Beco da Misericórdia: apontamentos históricos. Com um estudo de José Octávio. João Pessoa: Govêrno do Estado da Paraíba, Secretaria da Educação e Cultura, 1978. 215 p.; ill.

A narrow but well-researched, well-organized history of a printing press, its owners and its publications in João Pessoa, Paraíba (1834–92). Provides excellent data for the study of "official" culture in the provinces during the Empire.

3712 **Martins, José de Souza.** Conde Matarazzo, o empresário e a empresa: estudo de sociologia do desenvolvimento. 2. ed. 2. reimpressão. São Paulo: HUCITEC, 1976. 121 p.; bibl.; plates; tables (Coleção Estudos brasileiros; 1)

Sociological interpretation of the famous Italo-Paulista entrepreneur, his industrial empire, and the rise of São Paulo as manufacturing capital of the country. While not based on primary research, the book offers new insights on industrialization.

3713 **Mattoso, Katia M. de Queiros.** Bahia: a cidade do Salvador e seu mercado no século XIX. São Paulo: HUCITEC, 1978. 387 p.; ill.; maps (Coleção Estudos brasileiros; 12)

Superb socioeconomic history of Salvador, divided into three parts: Salvador and the hinterland; Salvador as a society; and Salvador as an international port. Much primary data from archives, showing population trends, prices, trade, etc.

3714 **Medeiros, Jarbas** *ed.* Ideologia autoritária no Brasil, 1930–1945. Rio de Janeiro: Fundação Getúlio Vargas, 1978. 625 p.

Handy compilation of articles which appeared in 1974 and 1975 in the *Revista de Ciência Política.* Consists of excerpts from the writings of Francisco Campos, Azevedo Amaral, Oliveira Vianna, Alceu Amoroso Lima, Plínio Salgado during the first Vargas presidency. Organized more or less topically with little commentary. Helpful index provided.

3715 **Mello, Evaldo Cabral de.** El norte, el sur y la prohibición del tráfico interprovincial de esclavos (Revista de Cultura Brasileña [Embajada del Brasil en España, Madrid] 49, julio 1979, p. 27–52)

Although largely a résumé of English-language works, this article does use the parliamentary debates (1875–82) to show that the idea of banning the internal slave trade was first proposed by the landowner politicians of the South on the grounds that the sale would: a) ruin the Northern sugar economy, and b) increase the social problems of the South.

3716 **Merrick, Thomas W.** and **Douglas H. Graham.** Population and economic development in Brazil: 1800 to the present. Baltimore, Md.: Johns Hopkins University Press, 1979. 385 p.; ill.

Extremely valuable essays on a variety of themes of interest to historians and social scientists. Especially good are chapters on slavery, immigration, migration, urban-rural change, and population growth. Loaded with tables and figures, intelligently documented.

3717 **Os militares** e a revolução de 30. Edição: Eurico de Lima Figueiredo. Tradução: José Augusto Drummond. Rio de Janeiro: Paz e Terra, 1979. 190 p.; table (Coleção Estudos brasileiros; 41)

Collection of six articles originally published in English, which deal with the tenente movement during the 1920s and 1930s.

3718 **Moisés, José Alvaro.** Greve de massa e crise política: estudo da greve dos 300 mil em São Paulo, 1953/54. Prefácio de Florestan Fernandes. São Paulo: Livraria Editora Polis, 1978. 167 p.; bibl.; ill. (Coleção Teoria e história; 3)

A very important account of the apogee of labor independence in recent history. Set in an innovative class analysis which elucidates the roles of the working class, communists, and Varguistas. Essential for 20th-century specialists.

3719 **Moniz, Edmundo.** A guerra social de Canudos. Rio de Janeiro: Civilização Brasileira, 1978. 282 p.; bibl. (Coleção Retratos do Brasil; 117)

A thoughtful and balanced synthesis of this primal struggle of the 1890s. With sympathy for the *sertanejos*, the author suggests that Canudos was a social uprising against an unfair land-tenure system and a government dominated by the bourgeoisie.

3720 **Monteiro, Frederico Mindêllo Carneiro.** Depoimentos biográficos. Rio de Janeiro: Gráfica Olympica, 1977. 391 p.; bibl.; facsims.; ill.

Personal memoir covering from 1920s to 1970s, including considerable time in the Northeast and abroad, as attaché. Useful insights on current events and revealing of officer attitudes.

3721 **Monteiro, Rolando.** Ruy e o exílio: motivação, consequências, agruras, documentário. Rio de Janeiro: s.n., 1978. 325 p.; appendix; bibl.

Detailed account of Ruy's 22-month exile following the naval revolt of 1893, followed by 81 documents from archives and contemporary press. Useful *ruiana*.

3722 **Morão Filho, Olympio.** Memórias: a verdade de um revolucionário. Porto Alegre: L&PM Editores, 1978. 1 v.

Controversial memoir by one of the principals in the 1964 military coup. Part diary, part reconstruction, the account is flawed, and Hélio Silva had problems finding a publisher. Specialists of the early 1960s will find it valuable.

3723 **Moura, Carlos Eugênio Marcondes de.** O Visconde de Guaratinguetá, um titular do café no Vale do Paraíba. São Paulo: Secretaria da Cultura, Ciência e Tecnologia, 1976. 295 p.; bibl.; 25 leaves of plates: ill.

Although basically a traditional biography of an important ancestor including full genealogy of descendents, the book includes so much original documentation and so much analysis of social background and attitudes that the result is an excellent study of a typical wealthy coffee planter of the Paraíba valley.

3724 **Muricy, José Cândido da Silva.** Viagem ao país dos jesuítas. Curitiba: Imprensa Oficial do Estado do Paraná, 1975. 405 p.; bibl.; ill.; fold. map; (Inserted)

A personal recollection of an *entrada* ("opening-up") expedition into the backlands of Paraná in 1896. Interesting for the attitudes it expresses and view of the rural society the expedition encountered.

Neuhaus, Paulo. História monetária do Brasil: 1900–45. See *HLAS 41:3494*.

Normano, João Frederico and **Antonello Gerbi.** The Japanese in South America: an introductory survey with special reference to Peru. See item **3101**.

Nunn, Frederick M. European military influence in South America: the origins and nature of professional militarism in Argentina, Brazil, Chile and Peru, 1890–1940. See item **1933b**.

Octavio, Rodrigo [*pseud. for* **Rodrigo Octavio de Langgard Meneses**]. Minhas memórias dos outros. See item **6532**.

3725 **Oliveira, Eliézer Rizzo de.** As Forças Armadas: política e ideologia no Brasil, 1964–1969. Petrópolis, Brazil: Vozes, 1976. 136 p. (Sociologia brasileira; 6)

Partly revised MA thesis from Campinas, with much stress on the Escola Superior de Guerra and national security doctrine. Central hypothesis is that the Escola gave the army a mandate to act when the Goulart government found itself without support from the US. Based on secondary and some archival sources. For political scientist's comment, see *HLAS 41:7566*.

Ornellas, Manoelito de. Gaúchos e beduínos: a origem étnica e a formação social do Rio Grande do Sul. See *HLAS 41:9367*.

3726 **Otaviano de Almeida Rosa, Francisco.** Cartas de Francisco Otaviano. Coligidas, anotadas e prefaciadas por Wanderley Pinho. Estabelecimento de texto de Alphonsus de Guimaraens Filho. Rio de Janeiro: Civilização Brasileira, 1977. 298 p.; bibl. (Coleção Octalles Marcondes Ferreira; 11)

A witty and charming running commentary on the politics, press and social life of the Second Reign by one of the most accomplished journalists and politicians of the day. Very much a counterpoint to his fellow Liberal, Tavares Bastos (see item **3761**).

Ovando Sanz, Jorge Alejandro. La invasión brasileña a Bolivia en 1825: una de las causas del Congreso de Panamá. See item **2936**.

Pacheco, Eliezer. Colonização e racismo: relações raciais em uma zona de colonização européia. See *HLAS 41:9370*.

3727 **Pang, Eul-Soo.** Bahia in the First Brazilian Republic: coronelismo and oligarchies, 1889–1934. Gainesville: University Presses of Florida, 1979. 256 p.; bibl.; 10

leaves of plates: ill.; index (Latin American monographs; 23)

An important study of Bahian politics, featuring oligarchic clans, coroneis, regional struggles, and ties with the federal government. Fine portrait of coronelismo and how it interacted with politics at different levels, persisting even to the present in some guises. Rich in detail, exhaustively documented.

3728 ———. O engenho central do Bom Jardim na economia baiana: alguns aspectos de sua história, 1875–1891. Rio de Janeiro: Ministério da Justiça, Arquivo Nacional, Instituto Histórico e Geográfico Brasileiro, 1979. 318 p.; bibl.; ill.; tables.

A compilation of letters, documents, genealogical data, photos and the like on the influential Recôncavo family, the Costa Pintos. Author's introduction places family in larger socioeconomic order. Very full bibliography. A useful case study for the Empire historian.

3729 ———. Modernization and slavocracy in nineteenth-century Brazil (JIH, 9:4, Spring 1979, p. 667–688, tables)

An interesting revisionist article questioning the thesis that modernization cannot occur in a slave-based society. Draws attention to attempts to improve Bahian agriculture through importation of new technology, but leaves unproven that the slavocracy itself was behind these efforts.

3730 Parker, Phyllis R. Brazil and the quiet intervention, 1964. Austin: University of Texas Press, 1979. 147 p. (Texas Pan American series)

A brief narrative of Goulart's troubles with the US, impeccably documented from the very best sources available, made possible through the Freedom of Information Act. Erases any doubt about US complicity in the 1964 coup.

3731 Peixoto Filho, Carlos. Discursos parlamentares. Seleção, introdução e comentários de David V. Fleischer. Brasília: Câmara dos Deputados, 1978. 720 p.; bibl.; 9 leaves of plates: ill.; indexes (Perfis parlamentares; 2)

Well-researched selection of speeches by prominent mineiro politician from the Old Republic. Fleischer's introduction sets the stage nicely, and the speeches are fully-indexed by subject. Important source of regional history. For a complete description of this valuable monographic series, "Perfís Parlamentares," see item **3732**.

Pereira, Eloy Lacava. O Brasil do imigrante. See *HLAS 41:9372*.

Pereira, Jesus Soares. Petróleo, energia elétrica, siderúrgia: a luta pela emancipação; um depoimento de . . . sobre a política de Vargas. See *HLAS 41:3500*.

3732 *Perfís* Parlamentares. 1– . Brasília: Câmara dos Deputados, 1977–

Monographic series issued by the Brazilian House of Representatives. Each volume is devoted to a particular congressman or senator and provides a brief biographical statement on the figure's importance in Brazilian politics, a description of his contribution to the development of congressional effectiveness, and excerpts from his speeches. The following figures covered so far are preceded by the monographic series number: 1) José de Alencar; 2) Carlos Peixoto Filho (see item **3731**); 3) Nunes Machado; 4) José Antônio Saraiva; 5) Affonso Celso (V. de Ouro Preto); 6) Francisco Campos; 7) Epitácio Pessoa; 8) João Neves de Fontoura; 9) Zacarias de Góis; 10) Otávio Mangabeira; 11) Gilberto Amado; 12) Teófilo Ottoni; 13) José Bonifácio, moço; 14) Silveira Martins; and 15) Leopoldo de Bulhões. Forthcoming are volumes on: Carneiro Leão (Marquês do Paraná); Nabuco de Araújo (Conselheiro Nabuco); Martim Francisco; and Santiago Dantas.

Piazza, Walter Fernando. Colonização italiana em Santa Catarina. See *HLAS 41:9373*.

3733 Pinheiro, José Juarez Bastos. A Força Expediciónaria Brasileira na Segunda Guerra Mundial: resumo histórico. Rio de Janeiro: Impressora Polar, 1976. 119 p.; bibl.; 4 leaves of plates: ill.

Useful synthesis by participant and amateur historian.

3734 Pinheiro, Paulo Sérgio and **Michael M. Hall.** A classe operária no Brasil, 1889–1930: documentos. v. 1, O movimento operário. São Paulo: Alfa-Omega, 1979. 320 p.; ill.

A fine, well-organized documentary collection, drawn from many European, US and Brazilian archives and libraries. Valuable supplement to growing monographic literature on labor.

3735 Pôrto, José da Costa. Os tempos de Lima Cavalcanti. Recife: Governo do Estado de Pernambuco, Secretaria de Educação e Cultura, 1977. 94 p. (Coleção pernambucana; 6)

Rather weak chronicle of Pernambuco history from 1930 to 1937, largely gleaned from the pages of Hélio Silva's *Ciclo de Vargas* (see *HLAS 40:4172*). Should be supplemented with Levine's *Pernambuco in the Brazilian Federation* (see item **3687**).

3736 Queiroz, Maria Isaura Pereira de. Cultura, sociedade rural, sociedade urbana no Brasil: ensaios. Rio de Janeiro: Livros Técnicos e Científicos [and] Universidade de São Paulo, São Paulo, 1978. 314 p.

Collection of essays dealing with rural and urban society, originally published in the late 1960s and early 1970s.

3737 Queiroz, Suely Robles Reis de. Escravidão negra em São Paulo: um estudo das tensões provocadas pelo escravismo no século XIX. Rio de Janeiro: Livraria J. Olympio Editora, 1977. 243 p.; bibl.; port. (Coleção Documentos brasileiros; 176)

While based on extensive primary research, this study of the tensions and violence created by slavery is neither well integrated nor analytically strong. Most useful for its data and documentation.

3738 Ravagni, Leda Almada Cruz de. Les investissements français au Brésil, 1890–1930 (CDAL, 16, 1977, p. 107–124)

A modest survey of French investments and loans to Brazil, based on official records in Paris. Special attention to problems arising during World War I.

3739 Reis, Jaime. The impact of abolitionism in Northeast Brazil: a quantitative approach (*in* Comparative perspectives on slavery in New World societies [see item **1768**] p. 107–122, tables)

Demonstrates that in 1880s slave prices were declining in Pernambuco, a decrease author attributes to planter anticipation of abolition. Suggests that the abolitionist movement thus had an indirect impact by so destabilizing the market for slaves and changing expectations that the collapse of slavery became virtually inevitable.

3740 Renault, Delso. Rio de Janeiro: a vida da cidade refletida nos jornais, 1850–1870. Rio de Janeiro: Civilização Brasileira, 1978. 317 p.; bibl. (Coleção Retratos do Brasil; 107)

A sort of gossip column for each year, based on bits of information that caught the author's eye while scanning the *Correio Mercantil.* Possibly useful as a reference tool.

3741 Resende, Maria Efigênia Lage de. Manifestações oligárquicas na política mineira: 1892–1897 (UMG/RBEP, 49, julho 1979, p. 7–69)

Exceedingly detailed narrative of political groupings and alliance-formation, together with analysis of rule-making. Lack of general framework limits its usefulness for nonspecialist.

Resor, Randolph R. Rubber in Brazil: dominance and collapse, 1876–1945. See *HLAS 41:5692.*

3742 Ridings, Eugene W. The foreign connection: a look at the business elite of Rio de Janeiro in the nineteenth century (UCSD/NS, 7:1/2, Spring 1978 [i.e. 1979] p. 167–182)

The author generalizes for all of Rio's businessmen from the directors of its commercial association who were, as he himself states, carefully proportioned by nationality. Thus, his central finding that the most significant characteristic of the business community was its foreign complexion is virtually predetermined.

3743 Rizzardo, Redovino. A longa viagem: os carlistas e a imigração italiana no Rio Grande do Sul. Porto Alegre: Escola Superior de Teologia São Lourenço de Brindes: distribuidora, Livraria Sulina, 1975. 137 p.; bibl.; ill. (Coleção Centenário da imigração italiana; 11)

Laudatory study of the missionary work of the Catholic priest, Father Scalabrini, among the Italian immigrants in Rio Grande do Sul, centering on his 1904 visit. Most interesting for its extensive use of his and others' contemporary observations.

3744 Rodrigues, Edgar. Novos rumos: história do movimento operário e das lutas sociais no Brasil, 1922–1946. Rio de Janeiro: Mundo Livre, 1978. 478 p.; bibl.; 18 leaves of plates: ill.

A flawed but passionate collection of chapters and documents from the anarchist movement. Based upon the anarchist press and interviews with militants, this book provides valuable raw material for labor history.

3745 Rodrigues, Inês Caminha Lopes. A Revolta de Princesa: uma contribuição ao estudo do mandonismo local, Paraíba 1930. João Pessoa: Estado da Paraíba, Secretaria da Educação e Cultura, Departamento de Assuntos Culturais, 1978. 181 p.; bibl.; 4 leaves of plates: ill.

A well-researched and valuable account of this backland civil war, a minor episode in the 1930 revolution. Based on newspapers and oral history interviews, the study portrays José Pereira and João Pessoa as coronéis.

Saito, Hiroshi. The integration and participation of the Japanese and their descendants in Brazilian society. See *HLAS 41:9394*.

3746 Santos, Mário Márcio de Almeida. Nascimento Feitosa e a Revolução de 1848. Recife: Universidade Federal de Pernambuco, Editora Universitária, 1978. 158 p.; bibl.

A series of essays (originally a master's thesis at the Federal University of Pernambuco) on the ideological outlook not only of Nascimento Feitosa but also Antonio Figueiredo ("o Cousin fusco"), demonstrating how it influenced their perception of social problems and their course of action. Extremely interesting for its original approach. Recommended.

3747 Scantimburgo, João de. José Ermírio de Moraes: o homen-a obra. Prefácio de Dario de Almeida Magalhães. São Paulo: Companhia Editora Nacional, 1975. 388 p.; bibl.; 8 leaves of plates.

Despite limited documentation and simplistic writing, this study of a Northeasterner who, through marriage, became head of the great industrial complex of Vortorantim is commendable. The work attempts to relate his career to existing socioeconomic conditions and shows how an ardent admirer of America could end up as an economic nationalist and last president of the PTB.

3748 Schupp, Ambros. Die deutsche Jesuiten-Mission in Rio Grande do Sul, Brasilien. Wiederherstellung und Herausgabe der Texte von Arthur Rabuske. São Leopoldo: Unisinos, 1974. 276 p.; bibl.

A series of historical essays on the German Jesuit missions to Rio Grande do Sul and on its German settlements, written in 1911–12 by one of the Jesuits. Best as source material for historians of the Church and immigration.

3748a Seckinger, Ron. O estado brasileiro e a political externa no seculo XIX (DADOS, 19, 1978, p. 111–134)

By quantifying data on the diplomatic posts and personnel during the Empire and by comparing the results with similar data from Chile, author draws inferences about the impact of modernization and state-building on Brazil.

3749 Silva, Hélio. O ciclo de Vargas. v. 16, 1954: um tiro no coração. Com a colaboração de Maria Cecília Ribas Carneiro. Edição ilustrada. Rio de Janeiro: Civilização Brasileira, 1978. 393 p.; plates; tables (Coleção Documentos da história contemporânea; 72)

Vol. 16 is the last one of an 18-year project tracing the entire career of Vargas. Unlike others (see *HLAS 38:4125* and *HLAS 40:4172*), this one covers a long period (1946–54), with most attention devoted to the last year of Vargas' life. Book lacks rationale and scholarly apparatus but contains some original material from oral history interviews conducted by author and Maria Cecília Ribas Carneiro.

3751 Silveira, Rosa Maria Godoy. Republicanismo e federalismo: um estudo da implantação da República Brasileira, 1889–1902. Brasília: Senado Federal, Centro Gráfico, 1978. 203 p.; bibl. (Coleção Bernardo Pereira de Vasconcellos; 4)

Well-documented study of the disjuncture between sociopolitical realities and the highly federalist 1891 Constitution. Concludes that the "política dos governadores" instituted by Campos Sales was a workable compromise. Based on presidential papers, newspapers, and contemporary sources.

Simonsen, Roberto Cochrane and **Eugênio Gudin.** A controvérsia do planejamento na economia brasileira: coletânea da polémica Simonsen e Gudin, desencadeada com as primeiras propostas formais de planejamento da economia brasileira ao final do Estado Novo. See *HLAS 41:3524*.

3752 **Skidmore, Thomas E.** The economic dimensions of populism in Argentina and Brazil: a case study in comparative public policy (UCSD/NS, 7:1/2, Spring 1978 [i.e. 1979] p. 129–166, tables)

An excellent comparative study of Perón and Vargas (second term), especially their handling of economic policy within existing political constraints. Demonstrates that redistribution was a real possibility in times of prosperity but that politically difficult choices prevented consistency.

3753 **Soares, Sebastião Ferreira.** Notas estatísticas sobre a produção agrícola e carestia dos gêneros alimentícios no Imperio do Brasil. Rio de Janeiro: Instituto de Planejamento Econômico e Social, Instituto de Pesquisas, 1977. 366 p.; facsim. (Série Pensamento econômico brasileiro; 2)

Reprint of a primary source on the economy of Brazil in the first half of the 19th century. Originally published in 1860.

3754 **Sodré, Nelson Werneck.** A coluna Prestes: análise e depoimentos. Rio de Janeiro: Civilização Brasileira, 1978. 119 p.; bibl. (Coleção Retratos do Brasil; 125)

A superficial review of the famous march, followed by brief but interesting recent statements by Luís Carlos Prestes, Emídio da Costa Miranda, and Arístides Corrêia Leal.

Sousa, José Antônio Soares de. A Batalha de Monte Caseros ou de Morón. See item **3427**.

3755 **Souto Maior, Armando.** Quebra-Quilos: lutas sociais no outono do Império. São Paulo: Editôra Nacional *em convênio com o* Instituto Nacional do Livro, Ministério da Educação e Cultura *e participação do* Instituto Joaquim Nabuco de Pesquisas Sociais, 1978. 213 p.; bibl. (Brasiliana; 336. Série Estudos e pesquisas; 10)

Rather than a new interpretation, this work is a series of overlapping articles on various aspects of the agrarian revolt that broke out in the Northeast in Nov. 1874. Soundly based on primary sources.

3756 **Souza, Carlos Alves de.** Um embaixador em tempos de crise. Rio de Janeiro: Francisco Alves, 1979. 361 p.; ill.

Readable memoir of a first-line diplomat, covering 50 years of political and international activities in this century. Close ties with Minas political families adds interest.

3757 **Stiel, Waldemar Corrêa.** História dos transportes coletivos em São Paulo. São Paulo: Editora McGraw-Hill do Brasil, 1978. 329 p.; bibl.; ill.; index.

Well-illustrated volume on *bondes* and tramways in São Paulo, based on newspapers, company records, and municipal laws. More encyclopedic than analytical.

3758 **Strauss, Norman T.** Brazil after the Paraguayan War: six years of conflict, 1870–1876 (JLAS, 10:1, May 1978, p. 21–35)

A précis of Argentine-Brazilian relations (1870–76) as reported in the dispatches of US envoys in Rio de Janeiro. The reliance on a single source without any analysis results in superficiality.

3759 **Sumaré:** São Paulo, Brasil. Direção geral: Leovigildo Duarte Júnior. Pesquisa histórica: Ulisses Pedroni. Pesquisa e estatística: Benedito de Assis Araújo. Coordenação editorial: José Lins Phenis. São Paulo: Editorial Focus, 1976. 107 p.: ill.

Local history of a town outside Campinas in which the extensive use of photos helps to recreate the life of the early mid-20th century.

Tambs, Lewis A. Five times against the system: Brazilian foreign military expeditions and their effect on national politics. See *HLAS 41:8893*.

3760 **Tavares, Aurélio de Lyra.** O Brasil de minha geração. Rio de Janeiro: Biblioteca do Exército-Editora, 1976/1977. w. v.; bibl.; ports. (Biblioteca do Exército; publicação 462/471. Coleção General Benício; 141/151)

Discrete but nonetheless revealing memoirs of a key military figure who sustained in various roles (Minister of War, 1969 junta member) the regime of 1964. Excellent source for understanding the psychology and outlook of the existing regime.

3761 **Tavares Bastos, A.C.** Correspondência e catálogo de documentos da coleção da Biblioteca Nacional. Brasília: Senado Federal, 1977. 246 p.

Since Tavares Bastos was the ideologue in the revival of "classic" Liberalism in the 1860s, this transcription of his letters will be of interest to specialists. Also provides some good material on the functioning of politics.

3762 Teffé, Tetrá de. Barão de Teffé, militar e cientista: biografia do almirante Antônio Luiz von Hoonholtz. Rio de Janeiro: Serviço de Documentação Geral da Marinha, 1977. 480 p.; bibl.; ill.

A long biography of an Imperial naval officer and Republic diplomat written by his daughter-in-law largely from family correspondence and related documents. While neither critical nor well organized, a close portrait of an important type in the ruling elite: the son of German immigrants with technical training and scientific capacity.

3763 Telarolli, Rodolfo. Poder local na República Velha. São Paulo: Editora Nacional, 1977. 222 p. (Brasiliana; 364)

Originally a Master's thesis at the University of São Paulo, this study recounts in great detail a violent conflict in Araraquara between rival coronéis and their bands. Exemplifies rural power structures in Old Republic.

3764 Toledo, Caio Navarro de. ISEB: fábrica de ideologias. São Paulo: Atica, 1977. 194 p.; (Ensaios; 28)

Useful survey and analysis of the Instituto Superior de Estudos Brasileiros, a liberal think-tank supported by the government between 1955–64.

3765 Topik, Steven. The evolution of the economic role of the Brazilian state, 1889–1930 (JLAS, 11:2, Nov. 1979, p. 325–342, tables)

Important correction of the general belief that the Old Republic was thoroughly laissez-faire in its economic policies. Demonstrates that some interventionism carried over from the Empire and new controls were imposed. However, intervention was piecemeal and reluctant.

3766 ———. Middle-class Brazilian nationalism, 1889–1930: from radicalism to reaction (UT/SSQ, 59:1, June 1978, p. 93–104, bibl.)

Brief comparison of the Jacobins and the Ação Social Nacionalista movements, which concludes that nationalism was converted from a progressive force to a defensive one, due to changing socioeconomic conditions and alliances.

3767 Vale, Osvaldo Trigueiro do. O General Dutra e a redemocratização de 45. Rio de Janeiro: Civilização Brasileira, 1978. 210 p.; bibl.; ill. (Coleção Retratos do Brasil; 120)

An unpretentious treatment of the subject, based largely on Dutra's personal papers. Lacks normal scholarly apparatus, contains no surprises, but is superior to Hélio Silva's *1945* (see *HLAS 40:4172*).

3768 Valla, Victor V. A penetração norte-americana na economia brasileira, 1898–1928: sempre de acordo ou nobre emulação? Rio de Janeiro: Ao Livro Técnico, 1978. 196 p.; bibl.; ill.; tables (Brasil séculos XIX e XX: relações internacionais)

Based on archives of the US State Department and Brazil's Foreign Ministry, as well as on many official publications. Competent survey of political and economic relations, treating both sides fairly. Based on master's thesis, University of São Paulo.

3769 Vasconcellos, Zachárias de Góes e. Da natureza e limites do poder moderador. Introdução de Pedro Calmon. Brasília: Senado Federal [and] Universidade de Brasília, 1978. 1 v. (Coleção Bernardo Pereira de Vasconcellos; 3)

Reedition of famous treatise, first published anonymously in 1860, part of polemic over Pedro II's use or misuse of the moderating power.

3770 Veiga, Gláucio. Estudos. v. 2, O Gabinete Olinda e a política pernambucana. O desembarque de Sirinhaém. Recife: s.n., 1977. 150 p.

These two unremarkable studies of Pernambucan politics in the 1850s reproduce original documents which may be of interest to specialists, but, writing as one of them, not much.

Versiani, Flávio Rabelo and **José Roberto Mendonça de Barros** *eds.* Formação econômica do Brasil: a experiência da industrialização. See *HLAS 41:3528*.

3771 Viana, Manoel. Paranaguá na história e na tradição. Curitiba: Gráfica Vicentina, 1976. 374 p.; bibl.

This local history of a port city of Paraná is a dotty accumulation of anecdotes and information for the years from 1850. Does include some interesting social data such as biographies of all school teachers and histories of clubs and festivals.

3772 Vianna, Lourival. Imprensa gaúcha, 1827–1852. Porto Alegre: Museu de

Comunicação Social Hipólito José da Costa, DAC-SEC, 1977. 68 p.; bibl. (Série Hipólito da Costa; 1)

A succinct, factual introduction to subject, but the annotated check list would be more useful if organized by date rather than alphabetically.

3773 **Vianna, Luiz Werneck.** Liberalismo e sindicato no Brasil. Rio de Janeiro: Paz e Terra, 1976. 288 p.; tables (Estudos brasileiros; 12)

Basically an analysis of Brazil's labor system as it was constructed in the 1930s, with some coverage of the entire period from 1889–1970. Using a sensible theoretical framework, the author examines major legislation and speeches in order to understand the intentions and outcomes of labor policy. For political scientist's comment, see *HLAS 41:7588.*

3774 **Vidal, Adhemar.** João Pessoa e a Revolução de 30 [i.e. trinta]. Rio de Janeiro: Graal, 1978. 539 p. (Coleção Depoimentos; 1)

Long narrative account, first published in 1933, of the events leading up to the assassination of João Pessoa and the articulation of the revolution in Paraíba. Reportorial but solid, by a partisan of the movement.

Vieira, Evaldo Amaro. Oliveria Vianna e o estado corporativo: um estudo sobre corporativismo e autoritarismo. See *HLAS 41: 7589.*

3775 **Vieira, Evantina Pereira.** Dinâmica das transformações eleitorais em Minas Imperial (UMG/RBEP, 49, julho 1979, p. 99–143, tables)

This article is part of the author's ongoing research on the development of the *zona da mata* in southeast Minas Gerais during the Empire. Full of excellent data which is not yet integrated or analyzed to best advantage.

Villela, Annibal V. and **Wilson Suzigan.** Government policy and the economic growth of Brazil: 1889–1945. See *HLAS 41:3529.*

3776 **Weffort, Francisco Correia.** O populismo na política brasileira. Rio de Janeiro: Paz e Terra, 1978. 181 p.; tables (Estudos brasileiros; 25)

A valuable collection of essays from the 1960s, with additional material from 1969 doctoral thesis. Seminal writings on the subject of populism, with special emphasis on São Paulo in the 1950s and 1960s. For political scientist's comment, see *HLAS 41: 7592.*

JOURNAL ABBREVIATIONS HISTORY

AAA/AE American Ethnologist. American Anthropological Association. Washington.

AAFH/TAM The Americas. A quarterly publication of inter-American cultural history. Academy of American Franciscan History. Washington.

ACH/B Boletín de la Academia Chilena de la Historia. Santiago.

ACH/BHA Boletín de Historia y Antigüedades. Academia Colombiana de Historia. Bogotá.

AEJ/JQ Journalism Quarterly. Association for Education in Journalism *with the cooperation of the* American Association of Schools, Depts. of Journalism [and] Kappa Tau Alpha Society. Univ. of Minnesota. Minneapolis.

AESC Annales: Économies, Sociétés, Civilisations. Centre National de la Recherche Scientifique *avec le concours de la* VIe Section de l'École Pratique des Hautes Études. Paris.

AFH Archivum Franciscanum Historicum. Firenze, Italy.

AHA/R American Historical Review. American Historical Association. Washington.

AHG/R Revista del Archivo Histórico del Guayas. Guayaquil, Ecuador.

AHS/AH Agricultural History. Agricultural History Society. Univ. of California Press. Berkeley.

AHSI Archivum Historicum Societatis Iesu. Rome.

ANA Análisis. Cuadernos de investigación. Apartado 11093. Correo Santa Beatriz. Lima.

ANH/B Boletín de la Academia Nacional de Historia. Buenos Aires.

ANH/IE Investigaciones y Ensayos. Academia Nacional de la Historia. Buenos Aires.

ANLE/B Boletín de la Academia Norteamericana de la Lengua Española. New York.

APH/H *See* APH/HP.

APH/HP Historia Paraguaya. Anuario de la Academia Paraguaya de la Historia. Asunción.

APHA/J American Journal of Public Health and the Nation's Health. The American Public Health Association. Albany, N.Y.

APS/P Proceedings of the American Philosophical Society. Philadelphia, Pa.

ASCH/CH Church History. American Society of Church History, Univ. of Chicago. Chicago, Ill.

ASE/E Ethnohistory. Journal of the American Society for Ethnohistory. Buffalo, N.Y.

ASNLH/J The Journal of Negro History. Association for the Study of Negro Life and History. Washington.

BCV/REL Revista de Economía Latinoamericana. Banco Central de Venezuela. Caracas.

BEPB Bulletin des Études Portugaises et Bresiliennes. Institut Français de Lisbonne *avec la collaboration de* Establissements Français d'Enseignement Supérieur, Instituto de Alta Cultura, et du Departamento Cultural do Itamarati. Lisbon.

BESPL Berichte zur Entwicklung in Spanien, Portugal, Lateinamerika. München, FRG.

BISRA/BS Belizean Studies. Belizean Institute of Social Research and Action [and] St. John's College. Belize City.

BMA/BB Boletim Bibliográfico. Biblioteca Mário de Andrade. São Paulo.

BNBD Boletín Nicaragüense de Bibliografía y Documentación. Banco Central de Nicaragua, Biblioteca. Managua.

BNJM/R Revista de la Biblioteca Nacional José Martí. La Habana.

BU/JCH *See* BU/JCS.

BU/JCS A Journal of Church and State. Baylor Univ., J.M. Dawson Studies in Church and State. Waco, Tex.

CAAAP/AP Amazonía Peruana. Centro Amazónico de Antropología y Aplicación Práctica, Depto. de Documentación y Publicaciones. Lima.

CAM Cuadernos Americanos. México.

CCE/CHA Cuadernos de Historia y Arqueología. Casa de la Cultura Ecuatoriana, Núcleo del Guayas. Guayaquil.

CDAL Cahiers des Amériques Latines. Paris.

CDLA Casa de las Américas. Instituto Cubano del Libro. La Habana.

CEDLA/B Boletín de Estudios Latinoamericanos. Centro de Estudios y Documentación Latinoamericanos. Amsterdam.

CEHA/NH Nuestra Historia. Centro de Estudios de Historia Argentina. Buenos Aires.

CEHSMO Historia Obrera. Centro de Estudios Históricos del Movimiento Obrero Mexicano. México.

CHE/PE Pensamiento Económico. Organo oficial de divulgación. Colegio Hondureño de Economistas. Tegucigalpa.

CLAEH Centro Latinoamericano de Economía Humana. Montevideo.

CLAPSC/AL América Latina. Centro Latino-Americano de Pesquisas em Ciências Sociais. Rio.

CM/HM Historia Mexicana. El Colegio de México. México.

CNC/RMA Revista del México Agrario. Confederación Nacional Campesina. México.

CP Cuadernos Políticos. Revista trimestral. Ediciones Era. México.

CSSH Comparative Studies in Society and History. An international quarterly. Society for the Comparative Study of Society and History. The Hague.

CUH Current History. A monthly magazine of world affairs. Philadephia, Pa.

DADOS Dados. Instituto Universitário de Pesquisas. Rio de Janeiro.

EEHA/AEA Anuario de Estudios Americanos. Consejo Superior de Investigaciones Científicas [and] Univ. de Sevilla, Escuela de Estudios Hispano-Americanos. Sevilla.

EHA *See* EHA/J.

EHA/J Journal of Economic History. New York Univ., Graduate School of Business Administration *for the* Economic History Association. Rensselaer.

EHESS/C Communications. École des Hautes Études en Sciences Sociales, Centre d'Études Transdisciplinaires. Paris.

EPHE/H L'Homme. Revue française d'anthropologie. La Sorbonne, l'École Pratique des Hautes Études. Paris.

FCE/TE El Trimestre Económico. Fondo de Cultura Económica. México.

FDD/NED Notes et Études Documentaires. France—Direction de la Documentation. Paris.

FFCLM/EH Estudios Históricos. Faculdade de Filosofia, Ciências e Letras, Depto. de História. Marília, Brazil.

FHS/FHQ The Florida Historical Quarterly. The Florida Historical Society. Jacksonville.

FIU/CR Caribbean Review. Florida International Univ., Office of Academic Affairs. Miami.

FJB/BH Boletín Histórico. Fundación John Boulton. Caracas.

FPRI/O Orbis. A journal of world affairs. Foreign Policy Research Institute, Philadelphia, Pa. *in association with the* Fletcher School of Law and Diplomacy, Tufts Univ., Medford, Mass.

GM The Geographical Magazine. London.

HAHR Hispanic American Historical Review. Duke Univ. Press *for the* Conference on Latin American History of the American Historical Association. Durham, N.C.

HSSC/SCQ Southern California Quarterly. Historical Society of Southern California. Los Angeles.

IAA Ibero-Amerikanisches Archiv. Ibero-Amerikanisches Institut. Berlin, FRG.

IAI/I Indiana. Beiträge zur Volker-und Sprachenkunde, Archäologie und Anthropologie des Indianischen Amerika. Ibero-Amerikanisches Institut. Berlin, FRG.

IAMEA Inter-American Economic Affairs. Washington.

IAS/ÑP Ñawpa Pacha. Institute of Andean Studies. Berkeley, Calif.

ICA/RCA Revista Colombiana de Antropología. Ministerio de Educación Nacional, Instituto Colombiano de Antropología. Bogotá.

ICS/JCCP Journal of Commonwealth & Comparative Politics. Univ. of London, Institute of Commonwealth Studies. London.

IDES/DE The Developing Economies. Institute of Developing Economies. Tokyo.

IEP/RPI Revista de Política Internacional. Instituto de Estudios Políticos. Madrid.

IFEA/B Bulletin de l'Institut Français d'Études Andines. Lima.

IGFO/RI Revista de Indias. Instituto Gonzalo Fernández de Oviedo [and] Consejo Superior de Investigaciones Científicas. Madrid.

IHGB/R Revista do Instituto Histórico e Geográfico Brasileiro. Rio.

IHGGB/R Revista do Instituto Histórico e Geográfico Guarujá/Bertioga. São Paulo.

IHGSP/R Revista do Instituto Histórico e Geográfico de São Paulo. São Paulo.

IIE/A Anales del Instituto de Investigaciones Estéticas. Univ. Nacional Autónoma de México. México.

IJ/JJ Jamaica Journal. Institute of Jamaica. Kingston.

INAH/A Anales del Instituto Nacional de Antropología e Historia. Secretaría de Educación Pública. México.

INEJ/AHD Anuario de Historia del Derecho Español. Instituto Nacional de Estudios Jurídicos. Madrid.

IPA/A Allpanchis. Instituto de Pastoral Andina. Cuzco, Peru.

IPA/AP *See* IPA/A.

IRA/B Boletín del Instituto Riva-Agüero. Pontificia Univ. Católica del Perú. Lima.

ISTM/MH Missionalia Hispanica. Instituto Santo Toribio de Mogrovejo [and] Consejo Superior de Investigaciones Científicas. Madrid.

JBA Journal of Belizean Affairs. Belize City.

JDA The Journal of Developing Areas. Western Illinois Univ. Press. Macomb.

JGSWGL Jahrbuch für Geschichte von Staat, Wirtschaft und Gesellschaft Lateinamerikas. Köln, FRG.

JHI Journal of the History of Ideas. City College. New York.

JHS/R The Jamaican Historical Review. The Jamaican Historical Society. Kingston.

JIH The Journal of Interdisciplinary History. The MIT Press. Cambridge, Mass.

JLAS Journal of Latin American Studies. Centers or institutes of Latin American studies at the universities of Cambridge, Glasgow, Liverpool, London and Oxford. Cambridge Univ. Press. London.

JPHC/R Revista de la Junta Provincial de Historia de Córdoba. Archivo Histórico Monseñor P. Cabrera. Córdoba, Argentina.

JPS The Journal of Peasant Studies. Frank Cass & Co. London.

JW Journal of the West. Los Angeles, Calif.

LAP Latin American Perspectives. Univ. of California. Riverside.

LARR Latin American Research Review. Univ. of North Carolina Press *for the* Latin American Studies Association. Chapel Hill.

LNB/L Lotería. Lotería Nacional de Beneficencia. Panamá.

MAGN/B Boletín del Archivo General de la Nación. Secretaría de Gobernación. México.

MNDJG/A Anales del Museo Nacional David J. Guzmán. San Salvador.

MP/AN Anais do Museu Paulista. São Paulo.

MP/R Revista do Museu Paulista. São Paulo.

MVW/AV Archiv für Völkerkunde. Museum für Völkerkunde in Wien und von Verein Freunde der Völkerkunde. Wien.

NCFR/JFH Journal of Family History. Studies in family, kinship and demography. National Council on Family Relations. Minneapolis, Minn.

NGS/NGM National Geographic Magazine. National Geographic Society. Washington.

NS NS NorthSouth NordSud NorteSur NorteSul. Canadian journal of Latin American studies. Canadian Association of Latin American Studies. Univ. of Ottawa. Ottawa.

OAS/A Annals. Organization of American States. Washington.

OAS/AM Américas. Organization of American States. Washington.

PAIGH/H Revista de Historia de América. Instituto Panamericano de Geografía e Historia, Comisión de Historia. México.

PAIGH/R *See* PAIGH/H.

PAIGH/RHA *See* PAIGH/H.

PAN/ES Estudios Latinoamericanos. Polska Akademia Nauk [Academia de Ciencias de Polonia], Instytut Historii [Instituto de Historia]. Warszawa.

PAT/TH The Historian. A journal of history. Phi Alpha Theta, National Honor Society in History. Univ. of Pennsylvania. University Park.

PCCLAS/P Proceedings of the Pacific Coast Council on Latin American Studies. Univ. of California. Los Angeles.

PEAGN/R Revista del Archivo General de la Nación. Instituto Nacional de Cultura. Lima.

PEBN/B Boletín de la Biblioteca Nacional. Lima.

PEMN/R Revista del Museo Nacional. Casa de la Cultura del Perú, Museo Nacional de la Cultura Peruana. Lima.

PF/AIA Archivo Ibero-Americano. Los Padres Franciscanos. Madrid.

PJHC/R *See* JPHC/R.

PMNH/C *See* PMNH/HC.

PMNH/HC Historia y Cultura. Museo Nacional de Historia. Lima.

PP Past and Present. London.

PUCP/CSH Cuadernos del Seminario de Historia. Pontificia Univ. Católica del Perú. Instituto Riva-Agüero. Lima.

PUCP/H Histórica. Pontificia Univ. Católica del Perú, Depto. de Humanidades. Lima.

RAI/M Man. A monthly record of anthropological science. The Royal Anthropological Institute. London.

RCPC Revista del Pensamiento Centroamericano. Centro de Investigaciones y Actividades Culturales. Managua.

RIB Revista Interamericana de Bibliografía [Inter-American Review of Bibliography]. Organization of American States. Washington.

RSG/B Boletín de la Real Sociedad Geográfica. Madrid.

RU/MP Marxist Perspectives. Transaction Periodicals Consortium. Rutgers Univ. New Brunswick, N.J.

RU/SCID Studies in Comparative International Development. Rutgers Univ. New Brunswick, N.J.

RUC Revista de la Universidad Complutense. Madrid.

SA Scientific American. Scientific American, Inc. New York.

SA/J Journal de la Société des Américanistes. Paris.

SAA/AA American Antiquity. The Society for American Archaeology. Menasha, Wis.

SAA/R Relaciones de la Sociedad Argentina de Antropología. Buenos Aires.

SAGE/JIAS Journal of Inter-American Studies and World Affairs. Sage Publication *for the* Center for Advanced International Studies, Univ. of Miami. Coral Gables, Fla.

SBPC/CC Ciência e Cultura. Sociedade Brasileira para o Progresso da Ciência. São Paulo.

SBV/R Revista de la Sociedad Bolivariana de Venezuela. Caracas.

SCHG/R Revista Chilena de Historia y Geografía. Sociedad Chilena de Historia y Geografía. Santiago.

SDHS/J The Journal of San Diego History. The San Diego Historical Society. San Diego, Calif.

SECOLAS/A Annals of the Southeastern Conference on Latin American Studies. West Georgia College. Carrollton.

SHM/RHM Revista de Historia Militar. Servicio Histórico Militar. Madrid.

SS Science and Society. New York.

SSA/B Bulletin. Société Suisse des Américanistes. Geneva.

TSHA/SHQ Southwestern Historical Quarterly. Texas State Historical Association. Austin.

UA Urban Anthropology. State Univ. of New York, Dept. of Anthropology. Brockport.

UA/AW Arizona and the West. Univ. of Arizona. Tucson.

UB/BA Boletín Americanista. Univ. de Barcelona, Facultad de Geografía e Historia, Depto. de Historia de América. Barcelona.

UB/GG Geschichte und Gesellschaft. Zeitschrift für Historische Sozialwissenschaft. Univ. Bielefeld, Fakultät für Geschichtswissenschaft. Bielefeld, FRG.

UBN/R Revista de la Biblioteca Nacional. Ministerio de Educación y Cultura. Montevideo.

UC/PHR The Pacific Historical Review. Univ. of California Press. Los Angeles.

UC/S Signs. Journal of women in culture and society. The Univ. of Chicago Press. Chicago.

UCC/NG Norte Grande. Revista de estudios integrados referentes a comunidades humanas del Norte Grande de Chile, en una perspectiva geográfica e histórico-cultural. Univ. Católica de Chile, Instituto de Geografía, Depto. de Geografía de Chile, Taller Norte Grande. Santiago.

UCCIH/H Historia. Univ. Católica de Chile, Instituto de Historia. Santiago.

UCEIA/H Humanitas. Boletín ecuatoriano de antropología. Univ. Central del Ecuador, Instituto de Antropología. Quito.

UCLA/JLAL Journal of Latin American Lore. Univ. of California, Latin American Center. Los Angeles.

UCLV/I Islas. Univ. Central de las Villas. Santa Clara, Cuba.

UCNSA/EP Estudios Paraguayos. Univ. Católica Nuestra Señora de la Asunción. Asunción.

UCP/IAP Ibero-Americana Pragensia. Univ. Carolina de Praga, Centro de Estudios Ibero-Americanos. Prague.

UCP/JSH Journal of Social History. Univ. of California Press. Berkeley.

UCR/AEC Anuario de Estudios Centroamericanos. Univ. de Costa Rica. Ciudad Universitaria "Rodrigo Facio." San Jose.

UCSD/ND *See* UCSD/NS.

UCSD/NS The New Scholar. Univ. of California, Center for Iberian and Latin American Studies [and] Institute of Chicano Urban Affairs. San Diego.

UFMG/DCP Cadernos DCP. Univ. Federal de Minas Gerais, Faculdade de Filosofia e Ciências Humanas, Depto. de Ciência Política. Belo Horizonte, Brazil.

UH/U Universidad de La Habana. La Habana.

UM/JIAS *See* SAGE/JIAS.

UM/R Revista Universidad de Medellín. Centro de Estudios de Posgrado. Medellín, Colombia.

UMG/RBEP Revista Brasileira de Estudos Políticos. Univ. de Minas Gerais. Belo Horizonte, Brazil.

UMHN/RH Revista Histórica. Museo Histórico Nacional. Montevideo.

UNAM/E Estudios de Historia Moderna y Contemporánea de México. Univ. Nacional Autónoma de México. México.

UNAM/ECN Estudios de Cultura Náhuatl. Univ. Nacional Autónoma de México, Instituto de Historia, Seminario de Cultura Náhuatl. México.

UNAM/EHN Estudios de Historia Novohispana. Univ. Nacional Autónoma de México, Instituto de Investigaciones Históricas. México.

UNAM/NMHR *See* UNM/NMHR.

UNAM/RFD Revista de la Facultad de Derecho. Univ. Nacional Autónoma de México. México.

UNAM/RMCPS Revista Mexicana de Ciencias Políticas y Sociales. Univ. Nacional Autónoma de México, Facultad de Ciencias Políticas y Sociales. México.

UNAM/RMS Revista Mexicana de Sociología. Univ. Nacional Autónoma de México, Instituto de Investigaciones Sociales. México.

UNC/ACHSC Anuario Colombiano de Historia Social y de la Cultura. Univ. Nacional de Colombia, Facultad de Ciencias Humanas, Depto. de Historia. Bogotá.

UNC/R Revista de la Universidad Nacional de Córdoba. Córdoba, Argentina.

UNC/RHAA Revista de Historia Americana y Argentina. Univ. Nacional de Cuyo, Facultad de Filosofía y Letras, Instituto de Historia. Mendoza, Argentina.

UNCR/R Revista de Historia. Univ. Nacional de Costa Rica, Escuela de Historia. Heredia.

UNL/H Humanitas. Univ. de Nuevo León, Centro de Estudios Humanísticos. Monterrey, Mex.

UNL/U Universidad. Univ. Nacional del Litoral. Santa Fe, Arg.

UNM/NMHR New Mexico Historical Review. Univ. of New Mexico [and] Historical Society of New Mexico. Albuquerque.

UP/A Apuntes. Univ. del Pacífico, Centro de Investigación. Lima.

UP/EA Estudios Andinos. Univ. of Pittsburgh, Latin American Studies Center. Pittsburgh, Pa.

UP/TM Tiers Monde. Problèmes des pays sous-développés. Univ. de Paris, Institut d'Étude du Développement Économique et Social. Paris.

UPR/RO Revista de Oriente. Univ. de Puerto Rico, Colegio Universitario de Humacao. Humacao.

URSS/AL América Latina. Academia de Ciencias de la URSS [Unión de Repúblicas Soviéticas Socialistas]. Moscú.

USMLA/LA La Antigua. Univ. de Santa María La Antigua, Oficina de Humanidades. Panamá.

USNSA/EP *See* UCNSA/EP.

USP/RH Revista de História. Univ. de São Paulo, Faculdade de Filosofia, Ciências e Letras, Depto. de História [and] Sociedade de Estudos Históricos. São Paulo.

USP/RIEB Revista do Instituto de Estudos Brasileiros. Univ. de São Paulo, Instituto de Estudos Brasileiros. São Paulo.

UT/SSQ Social Science Quarterly. Univ. of Texas, Dept. of Government. Austin.

UTIEH/C Caravelle. Cahiers du monde hispanique et luso-brésilien. Univ. de Toulouse, Institut d'Études Hispaniques, Hispano-Americaines et Luso-Brésiliennes. Toulouse, France.

UV/PH La Palabra y el Hombre. Univ. Veracruzana. Xalapa, Mexico.

UW/LBR Luso-Brazilian Review. Univ. of Wisconsin Press. Madison.

UWI/CQ Caribbean Quarterly. Univ. of the West Indies. Mona, Jamaica.

UWI/JCH The Journal of Caribbean History. Univ. of the West Indies, Dept. of History [and] Caribbean Universities Press. St. Lawrence, Barbados.

UWI/SES Social and Economic Studies. Univ. of the West Indies, Institute of Social and Economic Research. Mona, Jamaica.

UY/R Revista de la Universidad de Yucatán. Mérida, Mexico.

UZ/R Revista de la Universidad del Zulia. Maracaibo, Venezuela.

VANH/B Boletín de la Academia Nacional de la Historia. Caracas.

WHQ The Western Historical Quarterly. Western History Association, Utah State Univ. Logan.

YAXKIN YaxKin. Instituto Hondureño de Antropología e Historia. Tegucigalpa.

ZMR Zeitschrift für Missionswissenschaft und Religionswissenschaft. Lucerne, Switzerland.

LANGUAGE

D. LINCOLN CANFIELD, *Professor Emeritus of Spanish, Southern Illinois University*

THE SHIFT TOWARD sociolinguistics and bilingual studies in dialectology noted in *HLAS 40* continues in this volume. The accompanying phenomenon indicated is a shift from the general to the specific, and fully 25 percent of all books and articles examined deal with specific geographical or social lanaguage situations.

The publication of the papers of two important conferences is responsible for several studies such as the one edited by Mexico's very active linguist, Juan Lope Blanch, *Estudios sobre el español hablado en las principales ciudades de América* (item **4537**) and another edited by Humberto López Morales, *Corrientes actuales en la dialectología del Caribe hispánico: actas de un simposio* (item **4528**).

In line with the trends away from the general studies, it may be significant that there are some eight works on aspects of Mexico City Spanish. Although there are still many lacunae in the Spanish American language picture, it is evident that dialectologists are recognizing the need for detailed specifics of areas and of social and attitudinal factors. Rather important information has been added to existing data on the Spanish of Mexico, Costa Rica, Panama, Colombia, Venezuela, Peru, Chile, Argentina (several women linguists are active there), Uruguay, Cuba, Puerto Rico, the Dominican Republic, as well as New Mexico. Equally important dialect studies are now emanating from Brazil, and the book by Maria do Socorro Silva de Aragão on the Portuguese of Paraiba (item **4626**) could well serve as a model for regional investigation of Brazilian Portuguese. Noteworthy, too, is the article of João Alves Pereira Penha on the Portuguese of a rural community of Minas Gerais (item **4630**).

In the field of bilingualism, two significant articles appeared in 1978 based on experiences in New Mexico: Hannum's "Attitudes of Bilingual Students Toward Spanish" (item **4546**) and Valdes' "A Comprehensive Approach to the Teaching of Spanish to Bilingual Spanish-Speaking Students" (item **4583**). The second edition of *Bilingual schooling in the United States* by Theodore Andersson and Mildred Boyer (item **4516**, first ed. 1970), is still the best picture of definitions, rationale, planning, programs, in this area.

In spite of the continued publication of dictionaries with dates of late revision that are nevertheless not up to date, several special vocabularies have come out: *Terminología de urbanismo* (item **4596**); *Diccionario terminológico* (item **4587**); *Diccionario laboral* (item **4607**); *Dicionário profissional de relações públicas e comunicação* (item **4632**); *Dicionário de psicologia . . .* (item **4640**); *Dicionário técnico industrial* (item **4634**).

There continues to be considerable interest in Creole studies, notably in Haitian Creole.

RECENT DOCTORAL DISSERTATIONS
Spanish and Portuguese Languages and Linguistics
(1977–79)

Almeida, Francisco X. Structures in aeronautical phraseology: from English to Spanish. Univ. of Wisconsin (N.P. Sacks).

Anderson, Alice Long. Theories of evolution of the Spanish unstressed personal pronouns. Univ. of Illinois (M. Saltarelli).

Barasch, Ronald M. The application of set theory to the referents of Spanish event nouns. Univ. of California, Los Angeles (S. Robe).

Berk-Seligson, Susan. Phonological variants in a synchronic/diachronic sociolinguistic context: the case of Costa Rican Spanish. Univ. of Arizona (A. Lehrer).

Cordova, Robert H. Syntax and bilingual Chicano poetry. Univ. of Colorado (Anthony G. Lozano).

De Los Ríos, Rosa M.S. Aspectos sociolingüísticos del español de San Juan, Argentina. Univ. of New Mexico (D.B. Bills).

Escamilla, Pedro. A study of the aspects and mood characteristics of the Spanish of the Southwest United States. Univ. of Texas (C. Solé).

Holt, Candice. La desintegración sociolingüística en la narrativa contemporánea latinoamericana. Univ. of Iowa (J. Durán-Cerda).

Huerta, Ana G. Code-switching among Spanish-English bilinguals: a sociolinguistic perspective. Univ. of Texas (Ben Blount).

Koike, Dale April. A sociolinguistic analysis of the infinitive in colloquial Brazilian Portuguese. Univ. of New Mexico (J.J. Bergen).

Marrim, Stephanie. Logos and the word: the role of language in *Grande sertão: veredas* and *Tres tristes tigres*. Yale Univ. (E. Rodríguez-Monegal).

Mejías, Hugo. Préstamos de lenguas indígenas en el español hispanoamericano del siglo XVII. SUNY, Buffalo (P. Boyd-Bowman).

Merz, Geri W. A phonological study of the Spanish spoken in La Reforma neighborhood in Tucson, Arizona. Univ. of Arizona (Dolores Brown).

Montero, Joseph. Quantitive linguistic analysis of *Lazarillo de Tormes*, Segunda parte by Juan de Luna: a computer-aided study. Catholic Univ. (J.M. Solá-Solé).

Mugler, France. The pronoun system in Romance-based Creoles. Univ. of Michigan (E. Pulgram).

Silva-Corvalán, Carmen. Syntactic variation in monolingual and bilingual spoken Spanish. Univ. of California, Los Angeles (S. Thompson, B. Wald).

Smith, Karen Lynn. Common errors in the composition of students of Spanish as a second language. Univ. of Texas (Y.R. Solé).

Tuttle, Harry G. Effects of cultural presentations of similarities and dissimilarities of Puerto Rican daily life on the attitudes of field dependent and field independent second language learners. SUNY, Buffalo (Anthony Papalia).

Underwood, John Harvey. Spanish word order and a theory of stylistic rules. Univ. of California, Los Angeles (C.P. Otero).

SPANISH
GENERAL AND BIBLIOGRAPHY

4501 Alvar, Manuel. La gramática mosca de fray Bernardo de Lugo (ICC/T, 32:3, sept./dic. 1977, p. 461–500)

The principal interest of the Hispanist in a grammar of the Indian language of north central Colombia, which is usually referred to as Chibcha, is in the transcriptions made by a Spaniard of a language whose sound system was strange to him. Lugo wrote in the early 17th century, and Alvar rightly assumes, after careful analysis of his spellings of the Chibcha terms and sounds, that Spanish had already undergone some of the consonantal shifts.

4502 Guntermann, Gail. A study of the frequency and communicative effects of errors in Spanish (MLTA/MLJ, 62:5/6, Sept./Oct. 1978, p. 249–253)

The corpus for this study was taken from the taped oral interview tests of 30 Peace Corps volunteers who had completed 8-10 weeks of training in El Salvador. The tapes were listened to by native speakers, who in spite of the frequent errors in agreement, *ser-estar*, articles, prepositions, were able to get the message in most cases.

4503 Isaza Calderón, Baltasar. El español en América: enfoques y perspectivas de estudio. Panamá: Editorial Universitaria, 1976. 103 p., bibl. (Monografías)

A once-over of the evolution of Spanish in America that is largely a recapitulation of the work of Amado Alonso (1896–1952). Although the date of publication is 1976, countless books and articles written on the subject since the death of Alonso are not even considered. The perspective depicted is that of the first half of this century!

4504 Kirch, Max S. Non-verbal communication across cultures (MLTA/MLJ, 63:8, Dec. 1978, p. 416–423)

A very good discussion of gestures and postures and attitudes, in which there may be a certain universality and at least an apparent similarity between the Hispanic and the Arabic.

4505 Martínez, Fernando Antonio. A propósito de una gramática chibcha (ICC/T, 32:1, enero/abril 1977, p. 1–25)

Unfinished material written in 1968 and based on a manuscript in the library of the Palacio Real of Madrid. As in the case of the Lugo grammar (see item **4501**), one of the importances of this sort of record is the description of an "unknown" language in terms of Spanish for a picture of Spanish at the time.

4506 Neagu, Valeria. Los trabajos sobre lingüística hispánica en Rumania: 1960–1976 (UNAM/AL, 14, 1976, p. 303–346)

At the request of the Editorial Board of *Anuario de Letras*, this bibliography was written to complement Paul Alexandru Georgescu's work *Los estudios hispánicos en Rumania* (1964), which had considered material written before 1960. Much information is given concerning the Romanian School of Linguistics and the extensive investigations in phonology, morphology, lexicon and semantics, including material on American Spanish, Judeo-Spanish and Papiamento.

4507 Restrepo, Félix. Obras. t. 3, La cultura popular griega: a través de la lengua castellana y otros estudios semánticos; t. 4, La ortografía en América y otros estudios gramaticales. Selección de Horacio Bejarano Díaz. Bogotá: Instituto Caro y Cuervo, 1979. 2 v. (268, 271 p.) bibl. (Biblioteca colombiana; 16/17)

Vol. 3 contains four essays by Father Restrepo: 1) "La Cultura Popular a través de la Lengua Castellana" was his acceptance speech on becoming a member of the Academia Colombiana in 1933; 2) "Raíces Griegas" shows him as a good Hellenist and was written in 1956; 3) "Evolución Semántica en el Castellano de Gonzalo Jiménez de Quesada" written in 1959, is a useful contribution to the history of the Spanish language and although it deals chiefly with ships, armies and things military, it shows how much semantic change has occurred since the 16th century; and 4) "El Fonema Erre" is simply an effort to dispel misconceptions regarding the similarity of /r/ and /r̃/. Vol. 4, *La ortografía en América y otros estudios gramaticales*, was written for Spanish Americans who have doubts about spelling, syllabication, prefixes, etc., and was done sometime ago.

4508 Rodríguez Estrada, Mauro. Presencia del latín en el español. México: Editorial Edicol, 1976. 182 p.; ill.

A text that is designed to examine Spanish by going back to the roots of its forms and concepts, to develop a semantic perspective through etymology, and to learn common Latin words and phrases. The approach is morphological and quite thorough. Designed for Mexican students.

4509 Rosenblat, Angel. El criterio de corrección lingüística: unidad o pluralidad de normas en el español de España y América (UNPHU/A, 25, abril/junio 1978, p. 9–41)

Author cites the paradox that the linguistic theme that most concerns the speaker is that of the correction or incorrection, while this is what concerns the linguist least. In the Spanish of America, with its dialectal variations, there has to be a plurality of norms in the basic sense, but he insists that this does not excuse plain carelessness in communication. He believes that the "capas superiores" have an obligation in setting standards that are actually social rather than linguistic.

4510 Velleman, Barry L. Structuralist theory in Bello's *Gramática* (HR, Winter 1978, p. 55–64)

Writer believes that the 1847 *Gramática de la lengua castellana* by the Venezuelan humanist was a forerunner by several decades of the American structuralist technique of classification, and guesses that his long residence in London may have fostered this interest and the tendency to philosophize.

SPANISH PHONOLOGY AND GRAMMAR

4511 Cassano, Paul V. Vowel indistinction and splitting in American Spanish: internally derived or externally motivated? (CIDG/O, 25:2, 1976, p. 280–297)

Cassano is concerned over the very common indistinction or neutralization of /i/ and /e/ and /o/ and /u/ in the pretonic syllable in both Spain and Spanish America, and with the associated closure of final unstressed /e/ and /o/ to [i] and [u] respectively. He raises the question of whether the motivation is internal to Spanish or due to a language in contact, such as Quechua. Seems to doubt foreign influence in such cases as [disír], [confisjón], [hobentú], [póku], [nóči].

4512 Harris, James W. "Voiced" versus "voice" in Spanish obstruents (AATSP/H, 62:3, May/Sept. 1979, p. 342–344)

Criticizes Máximo Torreblanca's "El Fonema /s/ en la Lengua Española" en *Hispania* (61, 1978, p. 498–503) for misinterpreting some of his *Spanish phonology*. Expresses need for more attention to ranges of timing in onset of glottal vibrations and on states and activities of the vocal apparatus that underly timing phenomena dialect by dialect.

SPANISH DIALECTOLOGY AND SOCIOLINGUISTICS

4513 Academia Chilena, *Santiago.* Diccionario del habla chilena. Santiago: Editorial Universitaria, 1978. 260 p.; bibl.

Another valuable contribution to the growing store of regional lexicon. Contrary to what has not been done in so many regional vocabularies of the past, the Academy writers have researched the occurrence of the entries in other parts of America, and *chilenismos* often turn out to be *argentinismos* or even *guatemaltequismos.* The prólogo deals with the pronunciation of Spanish in Chile—but omits typical /x/ articulation as well as that of /č/. Discussion of the *voseo* of that country is appropriate: *cantai* in place of *cantás* and subjunctive *cantís* or *cantíh* instead of *cantés.*

4514 Alba, Orlando. Indigenismos en el español hablado en Santiago (UNAM/AL, 14, 1976, p. 71–100, tables)

Using 45 informants of both sexes and all ages, as well as of three levels of society, the testers found that nobody knew even 50 percent of the indigenous terms that had been considered a part of the Spanish of their native Dominican Republic. The vitality of the terms seems to be the big variable.

4515 Alvarez Nazario, Manuel. El influjo indígena en el español de Puerto Rico. Río Piedra: Universidad de Puerto Rico, Editorial Universitaria, 1977. 191 p.; bibl.; indexes (Colección Mente y palabra)

This very active scholar in the field of Puerto Rican Spanish gives us an excellent account of the insular world of the Arawaks at the time of the discovery of America, of the dialectal diversity of these people, of the period of bilingualism, of the extensive vocabulary of indigenous origin in Puerto Rico and in the Antilles generally. He describes typical phonology of the *tainismos*, the morphological adaptation to Spanish of the latter, as well as phrases and sayings of indigenous inspiration. He lists terms from other Indian languages, such as Nahuatl, that are common in Puerto Rico, and includes helpful indexes of words, phrases, *topónimos*, and *antropónimos* cited.

4516 Andersson, Theodore and **Mildred Boyer.** Bilingual schooling in the United States. 2. ed. Austin, Texas: National Educational Laboratory Publishers, 1978. 474 p.; bibl.; index.

A very thorough account of the nature and definition of bilingualism, the extent of bilingual schooling in the US, the rationale for its existence, the proper planning of such a program and the short and long-term implications. The bibliography is extensive, and the case studies of the appendices are very helpful to an understanding of benefits and obstacles.

4517 Arellano, Jorge Eduardo. Bibliografía fundamental del español en Nicaragua (BNBD, 19, sept./oct. 1977, p. 92–124, bibl.)

An extensive, critical review of 60 works on the Spanish of Nicaragua, most of which have to do with vocabulary and idioms. The details of the comments reveal many similarities with the Spanish of El Salvador, and the work of Heberto Lacayo (see *HLAS 26:1348*) seems to be the most scientific.

4518 Arnold, Marjorie R.; John W. Rosado, Jr.; and **Douglas A. Penfield.** Language choice by bilingual Puerto Rican children on a picture labeling task (MLTA/MLJ, 63:7, Nov. 1979, p. 349–354)

A diglossia study that examines the variables affecting language choice by bilingual Puerto Rican elementary school children: 20 from the second grade and 20 from the fourth. Although they had been initially monolingual in Spanish, the children show a marked preference for English this early, and although the home domain stimuli are great in certain areas, they seem to be sensitive to demand characteristics of the social setting.

4519 Bendezú Neyra, Guillermo E. Argot limeño: o, jerga criolla del Perú: teoría del argot, argot, jerga y replana, vocabulario y fraseología. Lima: Librería, Importadora, Editora y Distribuidora Lima, 1977. 339 p.; bibl.

The *jerga criminal* of Peru, often called *replana* seems to be closer to the mother tongue than the *lunfardo* of Buenos Aires, and it is replete with figures of speech. The expressions draw on Quechua (*La pachacama estuvo muy sabrosa*), and even more on English: *Tú luqueas Okey; Invito lonche a los que deseen; Es faite* (pendenciero).

4520 Bentivoglio, Paola. Formación de clíticos: análisis sobre el habla de Caracas (*in* Corrientes actuales en la dialectología del Caribe hispánico [see item **4528**] p. 13–33)

In the Spanish of Caracas it is necessary to postulate the existence of two rules to understand satisfactorily these forms, one obligatory in all dialects, the other, in some dialects, applicable to both direct and indirect objects.

4521 Berk-Seligson, Susan and **Mitchell A. Seligson.** The phonological correlates of social stratification in the Spanish of Costa Rica (LINGUA, 46:1, Sept. 1978, p. 1–28, bibl., tables)

Study examines Costa Rican Spanish phonology, relating linguistic variation to differences in socioeconomic status, as well as to differences in speech formality levels. Some of the variables considered were accent shift, vowel change, nasal combinations, stops and fricatives. As the level of formality increases, the use of prestige phonological forms increases. A fine contribution!

4522 Boretti de Macchia, Susana H. El español hablado en el litoral argentino: el pronombre. Rosario, Argentina: Consejo de Investigaciones, Universidad Nacional de Rosario, 1977. 47 p.; bibl. (Ciencias sociales)

A companion volume to that of Nélida Donni de Mirande (see item **4533**), this little book describes the pronominal use of the region whose center is Rosario, Argentina: personal, possessive, demonstrative, relative, interrogative, indefinite, numerals, and the subject pronouns, including *vos* and *che*. Notable, as in most of America, is the disuse of *aquel*.

4523 Canfield, D. Lincoln. La identificación de dialectos del español americano a base de rasgos distintivos (*in* Homenaje a Fernando Antonio Martínez: estudios de lingüística, filología, literatura e historia cultural. Bogotá: Instituto Caro y Cuervo, 1978, p. 168–174)

A reference to the work of Melvyn C. Resnick, *Phonological variants and dialect identification in Latin American Spanish* (see *HLAS 38:6104*) and a suggestion that a correlation of Resnick's data with those of Peter Boyd-Bowman on the Peninsular origins of the Spanish settlers of America (see *HLAS 28:1522*, *HLAS 30:2536a* and *HLAS 32:3035*) might be revealing as part of a diachronic study of American Spanish.

4524 Cantero, Gustavo. Pecularidades en el empleo del pronombre personal *yo* en el habla culta de la Ciudad de México (UNAM/AL, 14, 1976, p. 233–237, chart, graphs)

In this Mexico City study it was found that in 25 hours of conversation, *yo* was used three times as much as any other pronoun. Aside from the emphatic situation or the distinctive, the speaker of México, D.F., tends to use the pronoun with verbs of thinking or knowing more than is usually the case.

4525 Carrión Ordóñez, E. El léxico español en la región andina (PUC/L, 1:2, dic. 1977, p. 137–150, bibl.)

This is the first of a series of studies on aspects of the Spanish vocabulary of the Andes, although the author admits that the linguistic unity of the region is hypothetical. Using a diachronic approach, he examines the history of the term *soroche*, and finds that it was originally a word associated with a silver-bearing mineral. Records indicate that a mineral was blamed for the sickness that is most likely induced by lack of oxygen.

4526 Cassano, Paul V. La influencia maya en la fonología del español de Yucatán (UNAM/AL, 15, 1977, p. 95–113, tables)

With his usual role of iconoclast in the matter of influences in language-in-contact situations, Cassano examines the work of Manuel Alvar (see *HLAS 34:3070*) on the possible influences of Maya phonology on the Spanish of Yucatán. His knowledge of dialectal phenomena of other parts of Hispanic America lead him to the inevitable conclusion that such things as occlusive [b, d, g], [m] final and a tense -/s/ can very well be internal to Spanish.

4527 Cedergren, Henrietta J. En torno a la variación de la s final de sílaba en Panamá: análisis cuantitativo (*in* Corrientes actuales en la dialectología del Caribe hispánico [see item **4528**] p. 35–49)

Author believes variation is not a question of homogeneous groups in the population, but rather a matter of position, phonetic context, morphological condition, and at the same time, class, age, sex, and factors of style.

4528 Corrientes actuales en la dialectología del Caribe hispánico: actas de un simposio. Editadas por Humberto López Morales. Río Piedras: Universidad de Puerto Rico, Editorial Universitaria, 1978. 247 p.; bibl.

A collection of the papers presented at the symposium held at the University of Puerto Rico, 1–3 April 1976, and attended by linguists from the Dominican Republic, Venezuela, the US, Canada and Puerto Rico. In the introduction, editor Humberto López Morales writes on linguistic notation, describing the limitations of both generative and structural trends. Individual articles are annotated separately in this section, see items **4520**, **4527**, **4532**, **4544–4545**, **4550–4551**, **4553**, **4567**, **4578** and **4584**.

Corvalán, Grazziella. Estudios sociolingüísticos en el Paraguay. See *HLAS 41:1352*.

4529 ———. Paraguay: nación bilingüe. Presentación de Domingo M. Rivarola. Asunción: Centro Paraguayo de Estudios Sociológicos, 1977. 97 p.; bibl.

Interesting exploratory data on monolinguals and bilinguals by age groups, 15–44; study draws a great deal from the work of Joan Rubin (see *HLAS 32:3145–3147*), and considers the role of Guaraní in the acculturation of Paraguay in colonial times, and bilingualism in the educative process. The situation is more complicated than most realize, and any thorough analysis will have to consider factors of age, the urban-rural dichotomy, formal education, among others. While most Paraguayans are bilingual, there are fairly large groups who speak only Guaraní, and some city enclaves use only Spanish.

4530 Costa Sánchez, Manuel. Análisis acústico-articulatorio de las cinco vocales del español hablado en Cuba (UCLV/I, 57, 1977, p. 11–127, ills., tables)

Supported by drawings of articulatory positions and spectrograms of acoustic analysis, the study conducted in the Soviet Union, using three informants from Villa Clara, reveals the *frecuencia media* of the vowels of Cuba, but also a tendency to overlap slightly in certain situations.

4531 ———. Descripción de particularidades acústico-articulatorias de algunos sonidos consonánticos del español hablado en Cuba (UCLV/I, 55/56, sept. 1976/abril 1977, p. 3–42, plates, table)

Begun in Leningrad, USSR, and finished at the Universidad Central of Las Villas, Cuba, this paper examines especially the sonorization of intervocalic occlusives, the realization of /s/ preconsonantal, the sonorization of /x/ intervocalic and the simplification of /č/ to [š]. It also finds that Cuban Spanish /s/ before a voiced consonant generally does not voice and that /č/ is rapidly being pronounced as [š]. Many spectrograms support study.

4532 D'Introno, Francisco. Alternancia lo/le en el español de Venezuela. Análisis transformacional (*in* Corrientes actuales en la dialectología del Caribe hispánico [see item **4528**] p. 51–76)

The accusative *lo*(s) and *la*(s) alternates with *le*(s) on the basis of morphological readjustment in the context of *se* impersonal.

4533 Donni de Mirande, Nélida Esther. El español hablado en el litoral argentino: formas personales del verbo. Rosario, Argentina: Consejo de Investigaciones, Universidad Nacional de Rosario, 1977. 59 p.; bibl. (Ciencias sociales)

With characteristic precision, Donni describes verb forms of a region centered in Rosario, Argentina. Vital to such an examination is the typical *voseo*, which she does very thoroughly. She goes into the use of tenses with unusual time circumstances as well as verbs with non-Spanish stems (Italian, French, English). Pt. 2 deals with mood and aspect.

4534 Escobar, Alberto. Existe el castellano limeño? (PUC/L, 1:1, julio 1977, p. 39–49, bibl., tables)

The article is in a sense a "pilot" for a more extensive work on Peruvian Spanish that will consider not only local variations but also socio-linguistic phenomena. Stating that there is no identifiable *limeño* Spanish, the writer insists that there are socioeconomic factors that must be taken into account, as well as the fact that many of the present population are migrants from other sections of Peru. One is reminded of the good efforts of Fontanella in Argentina (see *HLAS 38:6077–6078*).

4535 ———. Lenguaje. 2. ed. Lima: Ministerio de Educación, Instituto Nacional de Investigación y Desarrollo de la Educación Augusto Salazar Bondy, 1976. 128 p.; bibl.; ill.

A recommendable text by the well-known Peruvian dialectologist. It is refreshing to see a book on *language* that has a linguistic approach and perspective, and that illustrates language phenomena through an account of the past and present of Peruvian linguistic reality. His chapter on "La Distribución Dialectal del Castellano del Perú" is one of the best pictures that we have today of the phonology of Spanish in that country.

4536 Espinosa, Aurelio M. Observaciones sobre el léxico nuevomejicano (ANLE/B, 2/3, 1977/1978, p. 9–19)

A very good selective study of the sources of New Mexico Spanish vocabulary. Copious examples are given of Spanish words that are either archaisms or neologisms, with their special meanings in that area. A section is devoted to terms of Indian origin, another to foreign words. The abundant use of prefixes and suffixes is noted, and in this and in other ways there would seem to be many similarities with Central America.

4537 Estudios sobre el español hablado en las principales ciudades de América. Editados por Juan M. Lope Blanch. México: Universidad Nacional Autónoma de México [and] Programa Interamericano de Lingüística y Enseñanza de Idiomas; Comisión de Lingüística Hispanoamericana, 1977. 569 p.; bibl. (Publicaciones del Centro de Lingüística Hispánica; 4)

In 1964, Juan Lope Blanch presented to the II Symposium of the Programa Interamericano de Lingüística y Enseñanza de Idiomas his *Proyecto de estudio coordinado de la norma lingüística culta de las principales ciudades de Iberoamérica y de la*

Península Ibérica. It was approved for action in 1966. A questionnaire was organized in 1968 (see *HLAS 34:3099*), and a director was appointed for each of the cities involved: Bogotá, Buenos Aires, Caracas, La Habana, Lima, Madrid, Mexico, San Juan, Santiago. Informants were to be 50 percent men and 50 percent women, of three generations (25–35; 36–50; 50 and over), people who had spent at least three-fourths of their life in the place and of Spanish-speaking parents. Several types of recordings were made: secret, dialogues between two informants, dialogues with investigator. The present volume contains many of the studies that have emanated from this project: three from La Habana, 16 from Mexico, one each from Caracas and San Juan, 11 from Buenos Aires, and three from Santiago de Chile. Some of these articles have been read as papers and several published. Many are important contributions to American Spanish dialectology: E.F. Haden and J.H. Matluck "El Habla Culta de la Habana" (see *HLAS 38:6087*); T.D. Terrell's "La Aspiración y Elisión en el Español Cubano" stresses the importance of position and grammatical considerations and yet-to-be-determined sociolinguistic implications. H. López Morales' "Tres Calas Léxicas en el Español de La Habana" studies indigenisms, Anglicisms, and *afronegrismos* in the vocabulary of La Habana in 21 areas of daily life; Anglicisms are numerous! I.I. Huyke Freiría's "Anglicismos en el Vocabulario Culto de San Juan" examines the occurrence of Anglicisms in the realms of transportation, communication and professions, and finds the list overwhelming (see *HLAS 38:6088*). A. Millán Orozco's "Anomalías en la Concordancia del Nombre en el Español de la Ciudad de México" encounters many cases of lack of agreement. E. Luna Traill's "Sobre la Sintaxis de los Pronombres Atonos en Construcciones de Infinitivo" (see *HLAS 34:3136*). J.G. Moreno de Alba's "Frecuencias de Formas Verbales en el Español Hablado en México" shows that the *arcaico* character of Mexican Spanish has left a wealth of verbal forms and many deviations. J.G. Moreno de Alba's "Transposiciones Temporales y Modales en las Formas de Indicativo" indicates a vast difference between the tenses in the matter of being subject to transformation. J.M. Lope Blanch's "Indigenismos en la Norma Culta Lingüística de México" finds that *nahuatlismos* are not as common in spoken Spanish of the capital as had been thought. J.M. Lope Blanch's "Anglicismos en la Norma Lingüística Culta de México" shows the greatest concentration to be in technology and the sports. P. Bentivoglio's "Observaciones sobre el Léxico del Cuerpo Humano en el Habla Culta de Caracas" indicates a vocabulary that is conservatively Spanish in this area. C. Wolf y E. Jiménez's "El Yeísmo Porteño" demonstrates an increased trend toward the articulation [š], notably in women and in the young. A.M. Rabanales' "*Queísmo y Dequeísmo* en el Español de Chile" shows a definite alteration, even in the same individual: *antes que* or *antes de que.*

Fernández Arévalos, Evelio. Presupuestos para uma "política lingüística" en el Paraguay. See *HLAS 41:1357.*

4538 Flórez, Luis. Sobre algunas formas de pronunciar muchos colombianos el Español: datos y problemas (ICC/T, 33:2, mayo/agosto 1978, p. 197–246, bibl., maps)

Written for teachers and students of Colombia, this is another spin-off of the extensive investigations and field work for the *Atlas lingüístico y etnográfico de Colombia* (see *HLAS 38:6063*) directed by Flórez. He describes peculiarities and differences in vowel and consonant articulation as well as sporadic phenomena. One misses one of the typical features, the occlusive [d, b, g] before another consonant.

4539 Fontanella de Weinberg, María Beatriz. La lengua española fuera de España: América, Canarias, Filipinas, judeoespañol. Buenos Aires: Editorial Paidós, 1976. 188 p.; bibl. (Biblioteca del hombre contemporáneo; 332)

A characteristically neat once-over of the work that has been done on American Spanish: historical studies, descriptive accounts (phonology, morphosyntactic phenomena, languages in contact); the Spanish of the Canary Islands, Judeo-Spanish in the New World and in the Old, the Spanish of the Philippines, which now is spoken by only two percent of the population. Fontanella's knowledge of dialectal variants is so thorough that her critiques and assessments are valuable additions to existing data.

4540 **García Piedrahita, Eduardo.** Disparates en el habla. Bogotá: Ediciones Cultural, 1978. 181 p.; indexes.

A series of articles from *El Espectador* (Bogotá, Colombia) that appeared between 27 March 1973 and 20 July 1975, under the motto: "Corrijamos el Lenguaje." They dealt with spelling mistakes; hesitation in the use of *de* and *por*; over-use of such words as *aparatoso* and *espectacular*; euphemisms like *antisocial*; the *gamín* of Bogotá; *el azúcar* vs. *la azúcar*; "algunos anglicismos; las voces de los animales."

4541 **González Tirado, Rafael.** Confrontación del inglés y el español en Puerto Rico. Santo Domingo: Editora Cultural Dominicana, 1973? 138 p.; bibl.; ills.

Results of work done in a course conducted by Alberto Escobar (Universidad de San Marcos) in Puerto Rico in 1971. Using 714 examples of signs seen throughout the island, the writer concludes that English is the element of between 50 and 60 percent of these, and that although Rubén del Rosario tends to minimize English influence, the language is used and understood much more in Puerto Rico than in any other part of the Spanish-speaking world. The text is cleverly illustrated with reproductions and photographs.

4542 **Granda, Germán de.** Dos campos léxicos arcaicos y sus implicaciones sociohistóricas en el área lingüístico de la costa pacífica de Colombia (IGFO/RI, 36:145/146, julio/dic. 1976, p. 243–255)

A spin-off from the field work toward the *Atlas lingüístico de Colombia.* The theme is that due to climate, poor conditions and lack of penetration, the Spanish of Colombia's Pacific coast retains the forms and structure of the colonial period: weights in *granos, onzas, libras* and the monetary terms *real, peseta, doblón.* In phonology, however, the conversion of /d/ to /r/ is described as restructuring.

4543 ———. Materiales para el estudio sociohistórico de la problemática lingüística del Paraguay (ICC/T, 33:2, mayo/agosto 1978, p. 254–279)

Granda believes that the Paraguayan sociolinguistic situation is going to be a popular and interesting object of study for several decades. With this in mind, he describes all sorts of sources of information (historical, sociological, linguistic, cultural and bibliographical). A very useful article for further investigation of this unique pattern of bilingualism.

4544 **Guitart, Jorge M.** A propósito del español de Cuba y Puerto Rico: hacia un modelo no sociolingüístico de lo sociodialectal (*in* Corrientes actuales en la dialectología del Caribe hispánico [see item **4528**] p. 77–92)

A study in *competencia y actuación.* Writer contends that speakers realize subconsciously that a sound can be pronounced in different ways, but he assigns a single meaning to the varieties.

4545 **Hammond, Robert M.** An experimental verification of the phonemic status of open and closed vowels in Caribbean Spanish (*in* Corrientes actuales de la dialectología del Caribe hispánico [see item **4528**] p. 93–143)

Testing the hypothesis that in regions where /s/ final is dropped at times a compensatory vowel quality develops to distinguish *casa* from *casas* or *tiene* from *tienes.* Using 20 listeners from Cuba, who heard four informants say 96 sentences, Hammond found that the eight-vowel hypothesis is not supported.

4546 **Hannum, Thomasina.** Attitudes of bilingual students toward Spanish (AATSP/H, 61:1, March 1978, p. 90–94)

An examination of attitudes based on a questionnaire filled by 64 undergraduate students of the University of New Mexico who were in the first semester of a Spanish course for Spanish-speaking people (90 percent of whom were born in the state). The students first listened to a tape of speakers from Spain, Argentina, Mexico, Puerto Rico, Costa Rica and two speakers from New Mexico, one with much greater fluency than the other. The taped speakers were graded on impressions of friendliness, education, humility, class, ambition, etc., and on language quality: relaxed-tense, smooth-harsh, careful-careless, clear-confusing. They rated the Spanish of New Mexico as high or higher than that of Spain, Costa Rica and Mexico, and higher than that of Argentina and Puerto Rico. Another test showed that these same students valued a knowledge of Spanish in their environment and especially a knowledge of both English and Spanish.

4547 Henríquez Ureña, Pedro. Observaciones sobre el español en América y otros estudios filológicos. Compilación y prólogo de Juan Carlos Ghiano. Buenos Aires: Academia Argentina de Letras, 1977. 260 p.; bibl. (Serie Estudios lingüísticos y filológicos; 1. Biblioteca de la Academia Argentina de Letras)

The famous *Observaciones* of the Dominican dialectologist, published first in 1921 in Madrid, and generally known through the BDH edition of 1938, along with previous writings of Espinosa, Marden, Hills, Semeleder and others, comes to us with a prologue by Juan Carlos Ghiano, and includes observations on the Spanish of Mexico, on the history of certain *americanismos*: *batata, papa, aje, boniato, Caribe*, and comments on the letters and chronicles of Las Casas, Oviedo, Pedro Mártir, Columbus.

4548 Hernández Aquino, Luis. Diccionario de voces indígenas de Puerto Rico. 2. ed., ampliamente aumentada y corregida. Río Piedras: Editorial Cultural, 1977. 456 p.; bibl.

Preceded by a congratulatory letter from Tomás Navarro, author of *El español en Puerto Rico* (Río Piedras: 1948), this second edition is a valuable contribution to Spanish American dialectology in that each entry has been thoroughly researched for significance historically and in relation to other similar terms. In a region where no Indian language is now spoken it is astounding how many geographical designations go back to the conquest and how much of the flora and fauna still bear native names.

Hilton, Ronald. El Padre Las Casas, el castellano y las lenguas indígenas. See item **5085**.

4549 Horton, James F. Two words of Chinese origin in present-day Peruvian Spanish (AATSP/H, 60:4, Dec. 1977, p. 956–957)

An interesting account of one result of the heavy Chinese immigration in Peru between 1850–74. The term *chifa* used so much in Peru for a Chinese restaurant is a corruption of two words of Cantonese origin that mean simply "eat rice."

4550 Huyke, Isabel. Indices de densidad léxica: anglicismos en la zona metropolitana de San Juan (*in* Corrientes actuales en la dialectología del Caribe hispánico [see item **4528**] p. 145–163)

Using informants native to the area and of Spanish speaking parents, and the PILEI questionnaire, the writer says that most Anglicisms are heard in the realism of transportation, communication, radio, cinema; the fewest in the professions and trades.

4551 Jiménez Sabater, Maximiliano A. Estructuras morfosintácticas en el español dominicano: algunas implicaciones sociolingüísticas (Ciencia y Sociedad [Instituto Tecnológica de Santo Domingo] 2:2, enero/junio 1977, p. 5–19, bibl.)

Since the work of Pedro Henríquez Ureña (*El español en Santo Domingo*, 1940) there have been gaps in the investigation of the Spanish of the Dominican Republic. Tomás Navarro's *Apuntes* of 1956 were actually based on field work of 1928. But in 1974 and 1975 there appeared two important descriptions: that of Elercia Jorge Morel (see *HLAS 38:6090*) and that of Jiménez Sabater (*HLAS 38:89*), the former dealt with the capital, the latter with the whole country. Writer points out that between 1950–70, the population has doubled to a total of 4,000,000, with extensive urbanization, and an increase of eight to 16 percent of the people in the capital, Santo Domingo. This has brought about changes in the Spanish of the cities, and morphological developments are often the result of phonetic changes, especially the loss of /s/ syllable final and /r/ as in *fuera* [fwa]; comieron [komjén]. The more primitive syntax of the countryside may now prevail in the city: *Es lluvia que hace falta*. This article was also published in *Corrientes actuales en la dialectología del Caribe hispánico* (see item **4528**, p. 165–180).

4552 Jorge Morel, Elercia. Estudio lingüístico de Santo Domingo: aportación a la geografía lingüística del Caribe e Hispano América. Palabras prologales de Manuel Alvarez Nazario. Santo Domingo: Editora Taller, 1974. 217 p.; bibl.; ill.

The first edition of this description of the Spanish of the capital city of the Dominican Republic appeared in 1974 (see *HLAS 38:6090*). It makes a good companion volume to the work of Jiménez Sabater (*HLAS 38:89* and item **4551** in this section), whose analysis is country-wide. Jorge Morel used 70 informants for her information, 20 "cultos," 23 "medios" and 27 "populares." She devotes special attention to the articulation of /x/

(her phonemic symbol is mistakenly /j/), to /s/ syllable final, to the leveling of /l/ and /r/, and to the pronunciation of /r̄/, which she finds is often not a multiple vibrant, and to /č/ as [š]. The indications of variations in articulation from class to class are valuable and the sections on syntax and lexicon are well written.

4553 Kvavik, Karen H. Directions in recent Spanish intonation analysis (*in* Corrientes actuales en la dialectología del Caribe hispánico [see item **4528**] p. 181–197)

The use of musical intervals as intonative units seems to be a promising direction for analyzing dialect intonations. The melodic shapes and intervals used by a Puerto Rican, for instance, are similar to those of the Mexican, but the Puerto Rican uses some shapes and semi-rises that are not used by the Mexican. The matter is complex!

4554 Lacayo, Herberto. Pronunciación y entonación del español en Nicaragua (BNBD, 19, sept./oct. 1977, p. 1–12, ills., tables)

Except for an explanation of symbols, this is the same article as "Como Pronuncian el Español en Nicaragua" (see *HLAS 26: 1348*). Still, it is the only accurate description of the phonology of Nicaraguan Spanish.

4555 Lagmanovich, David. La pronunciación del español en Tucumán, Argentina, a través de algunos textos dialectales (CIDG/O, 25:2, 1976, p. 298–315)

After tracing the history of the settlement of this smallest of Argentine provinces, the author describes pronunciation traits that are revealed in "Cartas de mi ñaña" from the traditional daily *La Gaceta: mos tao* (hemos estado); *salur, ciudar, novedar* (final /d/ as [r]); *dotor, vítimas, protesión.* And Tucumán is *yeísta.*

4556 Lama, Sonia de. El habla cubana en las estampas de Eladio Secades (AATSP/H, 60:3, Sept. 1977, p. 519–523)

Aptly called a *caudal de cubanismos, dichos y frases populares,* the writer defines such popular terms as *chévere* (nice person), *fulastre* (bad, deceitful), and *ñame con corbata* (dumb!). It is interesting to note that many of the words are also used in Colombia (coast) and Venezuela but with slight variations in meaning. For folklorist's comment, see item **1280**.

4557 López Morales, Humberto. En torno al léxico textil de Puerto Rico (UNAM/AL, 14, 1976, p. 23–49, tables)

The University of Puerto Rico's Instituto de Lingüística undertook this study because of the problems encountered in teaching textile skills in the industry. The extensive vocabulary deals with raw materials, cloth, thread, machines, products, operators, etc., and one finds that from 25 to 46 percent of the terms are Anglicisms.

4558 Mantica, Carlos. Dos textos sobre la lengua nicaraguënse (BNBD, 19, sept./oct. 1977, p. 60–76)

Essays on typically Nicaraguan expressions in the form of letters to Fernando Silva. Such terms as *chachalaca* (a woman who talks a lot) and Chorotega words like *lapa* (cotorra), *ñoca* (tortuga de mar), *nambira* (calabaza).

4559 Megenney, William W. El elemento subsahárico en el léxico venezolano (Revista Española de Lingüística [Madrid] 9:1, enero/junio 1979, p. 89–132)

Writes about the problem of identifying the 200 or more languages that came from Africa with the slaves, since there is little information on the slaves and their origins. Lists some 91 terms from Kikongo, Bozo, Dialonke, Kagoro, Kasonke, and many other languages.

4560 ———. El problema de "r" velar en Puerto Rico (ICC/T, 33:1, enero/abril 1978, p. 72–86)

Writer discounts the theory of the Negro origin of the velar /rr/. Indicates that there is an "island" of [r̄] among Negro populations of the Northeast of Puerto Rico, and invites an investigation of the possible indigenous influences in the early formation of the *Jíbaro* settlements of the interior and the west.

4561 Mendoza Cuba, Aída. Sustantivos en el habla coloquial de los niños de Cabana. Lima: Instituto Nacional de Investigación y Desarrollo de la Educación Augusto Salazar Bondy (INIDE), Subdirección de Investigaciones Educacionales, 1975. 138 p.

The study is one part of a project started in 1973 in 54 cities of Peru. Recordings have been made of the free conversations of children between the ages of five and 10. The survey of the nouns used by the children of Cabana (Ancash) was based on eight hours of recordings, 19 interviews, and tested 43 children. Variations that might be found in many other Spanish-speaking communities are common: *tamièn, sekia* (acequia), *djay* (common in Costa Rica). In addition there are several *quechuismos*, as might be expected. Incidentally certain phonological tendencies are apparent: the heightening of vowels, the distinction of *ll* and *y*.

4562 Mexico (City). **Universidad Nacional. Centro de Lingüística Hispánica.** El habla popular de la Ciudad de México: materiales para su estudio. México: Universidad Nacional Autónoma de México, 1976. 463 p. (Publicaciones del Centro de Lingüística Hispánica; 4)

In 1971, the Centro de Lingüística Hispánica published samples of the *habla culta* of Mexico City (see *HLAS 36:3847*) as a part of the project of determining the language norms of the major capitals of the Spanish-speaking world (see *HLAS 34:3099*); see also item **4537** in this volume. The present study was made for the sake of comparisons and includes 34 *muestras* of the "popular" speech of Mexico City. Pt. 1 is made up of interviews with a single informant; pt. 2 has dialogues with two informants; and pt. 3 has secret recordings. Although no detailed analysis is made of the material, it does show, among other things, many contractions, the diphthongization of hiatuses, acoustic equivalences, much closing of the vowels /o/ and /e/, especially final, much metathesis, many hesitations, gropings and repetitions, punctuated by *este, entons, ora, ps, ahá, essir* (es decir). This material would make a good corpus for several types of study.

4563 Moles, Jerry A. The influences of differential power and solidarity upon the predictability of behavior: a Peruvian example (IU/AL, 20:1, Jan. 1978, p. 38–51, bibl., tables)

Data for the study were collected during the 20-month period, 1968–70, in a barriada of 543 people on the outskirts of Arequipa, where most were migrants from the highlands. While the major thrust is sociological and shows the advantages of becoming non-Indian, it is revealed that in the population over 12 years of age, 63 percent speak both Quechua and Spanish, 30 percent speak only Spanish, and 11 percent only Quechua.

4564 Montes Giraldo, José Joaquín. Breve esbozo del ALEC: desarrollo, enseñanzas, resultados probables (UPRM/RL, 18, 1976, p. 185–194)

A handy history of the organization and formulation of the *Atlas lingüístico y etnográfico de Colombia* (see *HLAS 38:6063*), fruit of the enthusiasm of Luis Flórez, the initial inspiration of Tomás Navarro, the guidance of Tomás Buesa Oliver, and the efforts of many *encuestadores* over 15 years. After field work in some 262 communities, resulting materials are now being organized and many articles and books have already come out to increase knowledge of Spanish American Dialectology.

4565 ———. Fitónimos de sustrato y dialectos muiscas (ICC/T, 33:1, enero/abril 1978, p. 41–54)

Dialectal zones of the ancient Chibcha are established by the study of plant terminology and the alteration of /rr/ and /č/. One wonders if the assibilated /rr/ of Spanish is a factor!

4566 ———. Un tipo de composición nominal y el "español atlántico" (ICC/T, 32:3, sept./dic. 1977, p. 653–659)

The endocentric noun-adjective compounds, usually of the type *aliabiertos, bigotipintao, boquiabierto*, were found to be of the type *ciruelomacho, gallofino, yerbadulce* in northern Colombia in work done toward the *Linguistic atlas*. Illustrated by fairly detailed maps.

4567 Morales de Walters, Amparo. Léxico-estadística y dialectología: el léxico periodístico de Puerto Rico (*in* Corrientes actuales en la dialectología del Caribe hispánico [see item **4528**] p. 199–216)

Suggests a way of comparing standard language and dialect by word frequency count.

4568 Moreno de Alba, José G. Valores de las formas verbales en el español de México. t. 5, pt. 2, Estudio coordinado de la norma lingüística culta de la Ciudad de México. México: Universidad Nacional Autónoma de México, 1978. 254 p.; bibl. (Publicaciones del Centro de Lingüística Hispánica; 7)

Refers to decision to make a coordinated study of the "culta" linguistic norm of the principal cities of Ibero-America and the Iberian Peninsula, and to the questionnaire of 1972 (see *HLAS 34:3099*). Using recorded materials of some 400 hours of three generations, 25–35; 36–55; 55– , people who had spent at least 3/4 of the life in the city and who were up to "culta" standards, the study analyzes verbal usage in this segment of the population of Mexico City: indicative, imperative, subjunctive, and "verboides."

Morínigo, Marcos A. Impacto del español sobre el guaraní. See *HLAS 41:1399*.

4569 Ortiz Fernández, Fernando. Nuevo catauro de cubanismos. La Habana: Editorial de Ciencias Sociales, 1974. 526 p.; bibl. (Pensamiento cubano)

The *Catauro* (a Taíno word meaning a basket or catch-all) is the title of this work, a posthumous edition of the original one of 1923. Like many of the early part of the century, it is very good as far as local regional terms are concerned, but it does not readily take into consideration the occurrence of these terms in other parts of the Spanish-speaking world. The approach is argumentative. As an example, the compiler writes 15 pages on the word *conuco* to explain why the Royal Academy Dictionary does not have a complete list of *acepciones*. As far as Cuban Spanish is concerned, the *Catauro* is still a good "catch-all."

4570 Pardo Valle, Nazario. Mejoremos nuestro lenguaje. La Paz: n.p., 1975. 137 p.

Another in a long line of "repertorios de vicios," the book examines *vocablos mal empleados*, such as *evento* with the English sense, and *chocolatal* in Eastern Bolivia instead of the original Nahuatl *cacoatal*. A section is devoted to irregular verbs that are sometimes used regularly, and to spelling difficulties.

4571 Paredes Candia, Antonio. El apodo en Bolivia. La Paz: Ediciones ISLA, 1977. 203 p.

It would seem that Hispanic people everywhere are very fond of the *apodo* and have been clever over the years in formulating concepts based on physical characteristics, moral defects or on what they perceive as peculiarities of appearance. Bolivians naturally have these same tendencies, but due to the bilingual situation, many of the *motes* turn out to be a mixture of Spanish and Quechua. A person who has protruding chest may be called *waka pichón*. Although the first word is thought of as Quechua, it is actually the Spanish *vaca*. A *burro irpa* is one who does something stupid. The three-times President Victor Paz Estenssoro was often referred to as el *Mono Paz*. Many Bolivian politicians are called *pasa-pasa* because of the nature of the political scene. As in other Spanish-speaking regions, the apodo is apt to refer to an opposite quality: a short man is *rascacielos*.

4572 Perissinotto, Giorgio Sabino Antonio. Fonología del español hablado en la Ciudad de México: ensayo de un método sociolingüístico. Traducción de Raúl Avila. México: Colegio de México, 1975. 134 p.; bibl.; ill. (Serie Estudios de lingüística y literatura)

Preceded by a prologue by Juan Lope Blanch, Perissinotto has presented in relatively few pages an informative analysis of the phonology of Mexico City Spanish, especially with respect to sociolinguistic differences, following the lead of William Labov's *The social stratification of English in New York City* (1966). The corpus for the work is from the *cintoteca* of El Colegio de México (taped between 1963–68) and represents 110 informants of all sorts of educational background, three age categories, and both sexes. The sociolinguistic data gleaned were on several matters: synerisis vs. haitus; the neutralization of /p/, /b/, /t/, /d/, /k/, /g/ syllable final; the voicing of /s/ before a voiced consonant; [f] vs [Ø]; the assibilation of /r/; assibilation of /r̄/. The author concludes, among other things, that assibilation is a recent phenomenon and results seem to show that in the evolution of the language, women, old people, and the upper class tend to be conservative, although the picture is much more complicated than this.

4573 Perl, Matthias. Einige Gedanken zur Herausbildung der kubanischen Variante der spanischen Sprache (BRP, 15:1, 1976, p. 161–167, bibl., tables)

The morphosyntactic effects of the loss of /s/ syllable final, especially in verb forms, are noted in Cuban Spanish, as well as the possible hypercorrection (*vinistes; ves a la pizarra*). Many of the "Cuban" words and constructions cited by the writer are found in several other countries of Spanish America: *media loca, las otras noches te vi pasar, a ustedes es que hablo, habemos, tú lo que eres es un necio*.

Pottier, Bernard. La situation linguistique du Paraguay. See *HLAS 41:1409.*

4574 Rosa, Ramón. Diccionario de centroamericanismos (HUN/RU, 6:13, oct. 1977, p. 67–78)

Limited here to words and phrases from *a-* to *ach-*, the vocabulary would seem to have promise. It stresses difference between Central American Spanish and the "standard" in such expressions as *a la buena,a la fija, a mecate jalando, a la perra, abordar.*

4575 Rosell, A. Sobre dialectología uruguaya (UBN/R, 18, mayo 1978, p. 263–295, bibl.)

After a long discussion of what is implied by "dialecto," the writer describes attempts by Uruguayan linguists to divide the country into zones: Juan Carlos Sàbat Pebet and Horacio de Marsilio, José Pedro Rona, in fairly recent times. Generally, four zones are indicated: *la fronteriza, la litoral, la esteña,* Montevideo and its region of influence. In Rosell's critique of what has been done, he may stress too much the regional (Spain) origins of the settlers of the 17th and 18th centuries. The "dialect" was undoubtedly formed in the River Plate region long before.

Sánchez-Marco, Francisco. Acercamiento histórico a la sociolingüística. See *HLAS 41:1418.*

4576 Silva, Fernando. El habla nicaragüense (BNBD, 19, sept./oct. 1977, p. 52–59, ill.)

An informal account of the popular speech of Nicaragua, with a good expression of the feeling of *vos* compared to *tú*, and an extensive treatment of slang.

4577 Tamayo, Francisco. Léxico popular venezolano. Prólogo de Alexis Márques Rodríguez. Caracas: Dirección de Cultura, Universidad Central de Venezuela, 1977. 329 p.; bibl. (Colección Humanismo y ciencia; 13)

Written more like an encyclopedia than a dictionary, Tamayo's vocabulary has rather extensive comments and asides on most items. He classifies the terms included into six types: 1) Castilian words used with special meaning; 2) Castilian words with phonological changes; 3) New words created on the basis of older Spanish words; 4) New words created by onomatopoeia; 5) Words from foreign sources; 6) Indigenous terms. Typical of Venezuela is the verb *aguaitar* and related *aguaitadita* (*eche una agaitadita*) with the meaning of look, see.

4578 Terrell, Tracy D. Aportación de los estudios dialectales antillanos a la teoría fonológica (*in* Corrientes actuales en la dialectología del Caribe hispánico [see item **4528**] p. 217–237)

Considers the structural model vs. the generative model; the abstract generative model vs. the natural; universal aspects of the operation of variables. Goals are to determine the organization of a given phonology, determine the conditions of change, determine the conditions that govern variation.

4579 ———. Sobre la aspiración y elisión de /s/ implosiva y final en el español de Puerto Rico (CM/NRFH, 37:1, 1978, p. 24–38, tables)

After listening to some 20,000 cases of /s/ syllable final, Terrell has come to the conclusion that we must recognize the difference between the preconsonantal position and the final absolute. He finds in his corpus that the preconsonantal is aspirated about 92 percent of the time, while the final only 56 percent. Further, he suggests that phonetic context is a factor, as well as morphological and syntactic considerations. All this beyond the sociolinguistic parameters.

Teruggi, Mario E. Panorama del lunfardo: génesis y esencia del las hablas coloquiales urbanas. See item **1032**.

4580 Urtecho Sáenz, Rafael. Raíces nahuatl en el idioma nicaragüense (BNBD, 19, sept./oct. 1977, p. 13–27)

An extensive list of roots of the Pipil type of Nahuatl that apparently got to Central America in the fifth century. One notes several inaccuracies in the section called "El Alfabeto Nahuatl," especially in the sibilants.

4581 Urzaiz Jiménez, Carlos. El porvenir de la lengua nacional (UY/R, 21[21]:121, enero/feb. 1979, p. 27–39)

Writer is discouraged by the unnecessary influx of foreign words (chiefly English), the neologisms without sense, cliches, *esdrujulismo* and *cantinflismo* that have become so common in the Spanish of Mexico, and he shouts against *sopas secas, huevos tibios* and *cerveza de barril embotellada* with "¡No te entiendo, Sancho!"

4582 Valdés Bernal, Sergio. Sobre locuciones y refranes afrocubanos (BRP, 15:2, 1976, p. 321–328, bibl.)

After reviewing the history of the importations of African slaves, the writer classifies the idioms and proverbs under seven headings: 1) those limited to cult usage; 2) combinations of Spanish and African; 3) idioms translated into Spanish; 4) proverbs translated; 5) of limited coloquial use; 6) some retained as they were; and 7) sense translations from African languages.

4583 Valdés Fallis, Guadalupe. A comprehensive approach to the teaching of Spanish to bilingual Spanish-speaking students (MLTA/MLJ, 62:3, March 1978, p. 102–110)

A very good outline of the factors involved in the teaching of the "standard" dialect of Spanish to bilingual (English-Speaking) students of the Southwest. There has been, apparently, an unawareness among these students of differences, of grammar, of options in style, and often there is virtual illiteracy in Spanish. Valdés feels that the Profession should be deeply concerned about how it can serve the many students who have recently discovered the importance of their mother tongue.

4584 Vaquero de Ramírez, María. Hacia una espectrografía dialectal: el fonema /č/ en Puerto Rico (*in* Corrientes actuales en la dialectología del Caribe hispánico [see item **4528**] p. 239–247)

The well-known articulation of /č/ as [tj], first described by Navarro (*El español en Puerto Rico*, 1948), is only one way in which the sound is weakening toward a pure fricative, [š], according to the writer.

SPANISH LEXICON AND SEMANTICS

4585 Ayala, Francisco. Diccionario Atlantic. Bajo la dirección de Francisco Ayala. Con las pronunciaciones del inglés británico y inglés americano indicadas mediante el alfabeto de la Asociación Fonética Internacional por Ivar Dahl. Buenos Aires: Editorial Sudamericana, 1977. 2 v. in 1 (1068 p.)

This dictionary has much in its favor: it is quite up to date in scientific terminology, it has phonetic transcriptions of the English entries, using the International Phonetic Alphabet, and the important factor of syllable length is indicated for the English. Ivar Dahl gives a good description of Spanish phonology for speakers of English, although he may be overly influenced by River Plate models (he considers [ʒ] a common American trait and says it is absent in Spain). This articulation is common in Toledo and in parts of Estremadura and Andalucía, and in most of America the palatalization does not reach the extent of that of Eastern Argentina.

Borisov, Eugenio Felippovich and others. Diccionario de economía política. See *HLAS 41:2769*.

4586 Cassano, Paul V. Problems in language borrowing and lending exemplified by American Spanish phonology (CIDG/O, 26:1, 1977, p. 149–163)

In the belief that terminology has frozen our views, Cassano says that language borrowers are not indebted to language lenders. They do not request loans and the lenders do not agree to the granting of loans, and there is no impoverishment of the loaning language. Languages do not give or receive. A language will not normally select elements that it does not have or had.

4587 Compañía Telefónica Nacional de España. Centro de Investigación y Estudios. Diccionario terminológico de telecomunicaciones: inglés-español, español-inglés. Madrid: La Compañía, 1976. 327 p.

The result of four years of research and consultation, this manual should be highly recommended to communications personnel who for one reason or another work in a Hispanic setting. The terminology of radio, television, telephone, teleprinter, computer, is pretty well covered, although one notes that certain common terms, such as *tube* are taken for granted apparently. The first part is English to Spanish; the second, Spanish to English; the third some 50 pages of *siglas* (e.g. CAW—Channel address word: Palabra de dirección de canal). The role of correlative analogy in the vocabulary is tremendous.

4588 Córdova, Carlos J. Ecuatorianismos y colombianismos (Sarance [Instituto Otavaleño de Antropología, Otavalo, Ecuador] 1:1, oct. 1975, p. 19–27)

An interesting semantic study that demonstrates how much meaning difference can exist between contiguous countries. An example is *baboso* which in most places is a fool, turns out to be a *charlatán* in Colombia.

4589 Cuervo, Rufino José. Envidiar-escandalizar (*in* Diccionario de construcción y régimen de la lengua castellana. Bogotá: Instituto Caro y Cuervo, 1979, t. 3, fascículo 11, p. 721–784)

The Instituto Caro y Cuervo undertook the task of continuing the work started in 1872 and left unfinished at his death in 1911. Fernando Antonio Martínez was in charge of this until his death in 1972. The first volume was done in 1953, the second in 1954. The present Fascículo 11 of vol. 3 goes from *envidiar* to *escandalizar,* with Torres now in charge.

4590 Diccionario básico de la lengua española. Bilbao: Maves, 1976. 606 p.; ill.

A 30,000-word vocabulary, with maps of the continents, abbreviations, areas and volumes, but not up-to-date scientifically.

4591 Diccionario Karten ilustrado. Buenos Aires: Karten Editora, 1974. 1629 p., 16 leaves of plates: ill., maps (1 fold).

A combination dictionary and encyclopedia with entries similar to those of the *Pequeño Larousse.* Although it claims to be "rigurosamente al día," it is not so in all respects. In the astronautical sciences it does very well, but it is not up to date in computer terminology or statistics or missile launching. It has an extensive section on Spanish Grammar, a list of "Locuciones Latinas y Extranjeras" and colored maps.

4592 Diccionario manual ruso-español: 12000 palabras. Edición de J. Nogueira y G. Turover. Con nociones breves de la morfología y tablas morfológicas del ruso por A. Zalizniak. 3. ed., corregida y aumentada. Moscú: Idioma Ruso, 1976. 471 p.; bibl.

A revised and enlarged edition of a handy basic manual. Each entry is transcribed phonetically, and the vocabulary is followed by more than 100 p. of paradigms, declinations, conjugations, and morphological tables.

4593 Enciclopédico Universo: diccionario en lengua española. México: Fernández Editores, 1976. 1200 p., 24 leaves of plates: ill.

An up-to-date dictionary in matters of rocketry, astronautical science, computer terminology, etc. Definitions are rather curt.

4594 Enmiendas y adiciones a los diccionarios aprobados por la Real Academia Española durante los meses de enero, febrero y marzo de 1978 (ACO/B, 28:122, 1978, p. 284–302)

A useful list of revisions, eliminations, and additions, based on current usage in Spanish America. Example: "*Cachaco* . . . 2 bis. m. *Perú.* despect. *Policía;* militar en general."

4595 Haensch, Günther and **Reinhold Werner.** Un nuevo diccionario de americanismos: proyecto de la Universidad de Augsburgo (ICC/T, 33:1, enero/abril 1978, p. 1–40)

Authors state that the main reason for the projected dictionary is that those of Santamaría, Malaret, and Morínigo omit rather common Americanisms: *baúl* (of an auto); *palanca* (influence); *brasier* (brassiere); *cabinera* (airline hostess); *enganche* (down payment), and hundreds of others. They believe that the criteria of discrimination and contrastivity, along with actuality have been missing. They would use modern atlases and cut down the number of flora and *gentilicios.*

4596 Landa, Horacio. Terminología de urbanismo. México: Centro de Investigación, Documentación e Información sobre la Vivienda, Instituto Nacional para el Desarrollo de la Comunidad Rural y de la Vivienda Popular, 1976. 82 p.; bibl. (Publicaciones del CIDIV)

A very useful, little book for urban planners and others concerned with the status and growth of cities. Landa has taken special pains to examine variants in the largely sociological vocabulary that might help in overcoming semantic and conceptual problems occurring from country to country. Each entry has its English and French translations, and in the formulation of what is for many a new discipline, the book may aid in forming a fairly uniform body of terms. A case in point is the occurrence of both *planeamiento* and *planificación.* The bibliography is drawn mainly from Mexican, Puerto Rican and American sources.

4597 Lope Blanch, Juan M. Los indoamericanismos en el *Tesoro* de Covarrubias (CM/NRFH, 26:2, p. 296–315)

Although the *Tesoro de la lengua castellana* (1611) was written almost a century after the first settlement in America, it contains relatively few *americanismos*. Covarrubias probably did not know the work of the Indianists Molina, Córdoba, Gilberti, Santo Tomás, or that of the historians of the early 16th century. Lope points out that although it is in a sense the first etymological dictionary of the Spanish language, indigenous words known for many years are omitted. He does find *cacique, caimán, coca, Cuzco, hamaca, huracán, maíz, pita, tiburón, tuna,* and a few others.

4598 Montes Giraldo, José Joaquín. Otros calcos del inglés: *evidencia*(s) y algunos más (ICC/T, 31:3, sept./dic. 1976, p. 431–441, bibl.)

A useful discussion of English sense loans in Spanish: plurals where the normal is singular (*políticas*), and words used with English meanings: *evidencia(s).*

4599 Mora Monroy, Siervo Custodio. Breve estudio sobre apellidos y nombres propios de persona en Colombia (ICC/T, 31:3, sept./dic. 1976, p. 536–559, bibl.)

An interesting analysis of proper names by semantic groupings: animal kingdom, vegetable kingdom, minerals, colors, anatomical, etc.

4600 Morel, Héctor V. Diccionario mitológico americano. Buenos Aires: Distar Libros, 1978. 158 p.; bibl.; 8 leaves of plates: ill.

A once-over type of vocabulary that deals with the precolumbian civilizations of Mexico (Aztec and Maya only), the Inca of Peru, the Chibcha of Colombia, and certain groups of modern Argentina. Chief entries are names of gods, places, buildings, types of worship, symbols.

4601 Pichardo y Tapia, Esteban. Diccionario provincial casi-razonado de voces y frases cubanas. La Habana: Editorial de Ciencias Sociales, 1976. 639 p. (Lingüística)

Since Pichardo was born in 1799, this dictionary's main interest would be diachronic and in the realm of semantics. Editions appeared in 1836, 1849, 1862, so most definitions represent *acepciones* of the early 19th century. *Bozal* is described as "negro nacido en Africa" but also as "colono asiático." *Ladino* is "el negro o negra africanos que ya está bastante instruído . . . entendiendo suficientemente el castellano."

4602 Raluy Poudevida, Antonio. Diccionario Porrúa de la lengua española. Preparado por Francisco Monterde. 10 ed. México: Editorial Porrúa, 1976. 848 p., 1 leaf of plates; map.

It is a shame that a dictionary with such an attractive outer appearance should not have been updated much since its first edition (1969). Aside from a very brief definition of *astronauta*, science vocabulary in general is antiquated, including computer science, rocketry, linguistics (the definition for *fonema* is wrong).

4603 Sala, Marius; Dan Munteanu; Valeria Neagu; and **Tudora Sandru-Olteanu.** El léxico indígena del español americano; apreciaciones sobre su vitalidad. México: Academia Mexicana [and] Academiei Romane, Bucharest, 1977. 197 p.

Claiming that most vocabularies of this type try to list as many terms as possible, the authors have limited the list on three bases: geographical diffusion, productivity in terms of derivatives, and semantic richness (new meanings). Using distinctive feature techniques, they analyze the inventory on the first two bases and find that indigenous words in extensive use are not as many as has been believed.

4604 Schwauss, Maria. Wörterbuch der regionalen Umgangssprache in Lateinamerika: amerikaspan., dt.: mit e. Liste d. Indiostämme. Leipzig: Verlag Enzyklopädie, 1977. 692 p. (Lateinamerikanisches Sprachgut; 1)

Well done and quite extensive. Especially accurate in origins of Indian terms, and the list of Indian tribes and their groups and families is valuable. In any treatment of such a vast phenomenon there are bound to be gaps, and one finds certain fairly common terms of El Salvador missing, for example: *pacha* (bottle); *peche* (slim); *güisquil* (chayote); *taburete* (chair); *paila* (saucer); *seno* (sobaco; arm pit).

4605 Selva Andrade, Carlos. Vocabulario de ecología. Buenos Aires: Editorial Albatros, 1977. 109 p.

An interesting basic vocabulary of nature and such dangers as *contaminación*. It draws on related sciences such as biology, geology, chemistry, and even legal terminology.

4606 Sobre el vocablo *carajo*: lo referente o perteneciente al registro: del registro; escritura correcta: *El Dorado*; uso del relativo "que;" política; petofobia y no topofobia (ACO/B, 28:122, 1978, p. 270–283)

A series of letters to officers of the Academia Colombiana: the origins of *carajo* are still uncertain; *del registro* is to be preferred over *registral* or *registrorial*; *El Dorado* rather than *Eldorado*; *el que* is better than *el cual*; there is a distinction between *política* and *objetivos*.

4607 Velázquez, Francisco. Diccionario laboral. Hato Rey, P.R.: Master Typesetting of Puerto Rico, 1978. 269 p.; bibl.

The author (b. 1923, Ponce, Puerto Rico) has spent a great part of his life in workers' movements, having organized a syndicate in 1951, a cooperative in 1956, and finally in 1962 the Federación Puertorriqueña de Sindicatos Democráticos. It is interesting to note that the extensive vocabulary has many Anglicisms, and even titles of organizations show English influence; witness the *Federación* instead of the usual Spanish *Confederación*. Such terms as *forman, absentismo, abrazar una causa* are fairly common.

4608 Zamora, Antonio. Diccionario de sinónimos españoles. 7. ed. ampliada. Buenos Aires: Editorial Claridad, 1974. 326 p. (Colección Diccionarios; 2)

The first edition of this vocabulary appeared in 1954. It was revised in 1961, with the addition of 20,000 terms, but indications are that it has not been revised since. Scientific terminology is antiquated.

SPANISH SYNTAX

4609 Fontanella de Weinberg, María Beatriz. La constitución del paradigma pronominal de voseo (ICC/T, 32:2, mayo/agosto 1977, p. 227–241, bibl., tables)

In this follow-up of her excellent depiction of current verbal usage in the *voseo* regions of America (see *HLAS 40:6041*), Fontanella demonstrates that *os* arrived in America along with the other pronouns, but was finally lost in favor of *te*; further, that in the highlands of Ecuador and in Santiago del Estero, Argentina, the tendency is to use *vos* as subject with a second person singular verb form: *vos cantas*, rather than *vos cantás*.

4610 Lope Blanch, Juan M. Los pronombres átonos en las cartas de Diego de Ordaz (UPRM/RL, 18, 1976, p. 123–142)

Consists of a study of letters written by Ordaz to his nephew between 2 April 1529 and 15 Aug. 1530, when Castilian was changing with respect to pronoun position. After examining nine cases of atonic pronoun position, Lope finds that in this transitional period of the evolution of Spanish, the proclitic was the norm, except when the phrase began with a verb. Then, in about half of the cases, the pronoun followed: *vase a Béjar*. Such forms as *para vos dar parte* and *para los poder tomar* are common.

4611 Porto Dapena, José-Alvaro. Notas de sixtaxis: "enviar" y "mandar" infinitivo con "a" (ICC/T, 32:1, enero/abril 1977, p. 26–39)

Author classifies verbs that take preposition before infinitive as *verbos de lengua*: *decir, preguntar, pedir, llamar*.

4612 Prado, Marcial. El uso de los pronombres clíticos en español (AATSP/H, 60:4, Dec. 1977, p. 957–961)

Using three principal levels of speech, *Castellano coloquial, Español de Hispanoamérica* and *Español peninsular formal*, the writer shows how case differences are tending to disappear in the colloquial speech of Spain, but dative accusative distinction prevails in America.

4613 Radelli, Bruna. Los posesivos en español (CM/NRFH, 27:2, 1978, p. 235–257)

Questioning the traditional grammar definition of possessive, Radelli shows that it is more often indicative of a relation: *me das tu hora; el habla de la ciudad de México; tu error no fue grave*. In terms of *endofórico* and *exofórico*, there are more than twice as many of the latter as of the former.

PORTUGUESE GENERAL AND GRAMMATICAL

4614 Azevedo, Milton M. Identifying Spanish interference in learners of Portuguese (MLTA/MLJ, 62:1/2, Jan./Feb. 1978, p. 18–23)

The main difficulties seem to be failure to make phonemic vowel contrasts in the /o/ and /e/ areas, failure to nasalize, and a tendency to fricativize the voiced stops.

4615 Bisol, Leda. Predicados complexos do português: uma análise transformacional. Porto Alegre?: Editora Formação, 1975. 70 p.; bibl.

The transformational analysis of five structures leads to the conclusion that structures that are superficially similar are, in essence, different, because each of them possessed its own process of internal formulation, which brings about a specific sense.

4616 Câmara Júnior, Joaquim Mattoso. Para o estudo da fonêmica portuguesa. 2. ed. Preparada pelo professor Raimundo Barbadinho Neto, conforme indicações deixadas pelo author. Rio de Janeiro: Padrão, 1977. 140 p.; bibl.

Constructed on the model of Alarcos Llorach's *Fonología española* (1950), the book defines at length *fonético* and *fonémico* and gives a good thorough description of the phonemes and allophones of Portuguese. A third chapter discusses *Rima da poesia brasileira* as a literary application of phonology.

4617 ———. Princípios de lingüística geral: como introdução aos estudos superiores da língua portuguesa. 5. ed., com atualização ortográfica. Rio de Janeiro: Padrão, Livraria Editora, 1977. 333 p.; bibl.; ill.; index.

This text is still one of a very small number of introductory books available in Latin America that take a modern structural approach, but in some respects it has not been revised since the third edition of 1958. There is no reference to transformational generative grammar and to all the work that has been done in this realm since the middle 1950s. This was noted at the publication of the fourth edition in 1967 (see *HLAS 30: 2677c*).

4618 Castro, Antonio Veríssimo de. Harmonia mecânica de estilo. Teresina: COMEPI, 1976. 147 p.

An essay on poetic devices, figures of speech, *vícios de linguagem*, *ornatos de dição*, and onomatopoeic harmony.

4619 Damasceno, José Ribeiro. Introdução estruturalismo en lingüística. Petrópolis: Editora Vozes, 1977. 123 p.; bibl.; index. (Textos introdutórios; 4)

This little book would seem to be more of an essay on structuralism as an attitude, a point of view, than as an introduction to a type of linguistic notation. The treatment is historical-philosophical.

4620 Elia, Sílvio Edmundo. A unidade lingüística do Brasil: condicionamentos geoeconômicos. Rio de Janeiro: Padrão, 1979. 260 p.; bibl.; index.

An essay that tries to bring out the factors that through time favor the linguistic unity of Brazil. He considers ethnic, economic and geographical conditions that may have developed *perspectivas socioculturais* through the occupation of the *litoral*, through urbanization, capitalism, and "runs" to the interior of the country. He concludes that the language is still essentially that of Portugal and in its dialectal variations it represents stages in its evolution.

4621 Lima, Alexandre José Barbosa. A língua portuguesa e a unidade do Brasil. 2. ed. rev. Rio de Janeiro: Livraria J. Olympio Editora *em convênio com o* Instituto Nacional do Livro, 1977. 156 p.; bibl. (Coleção Documentos brasileiros; 99)

The first edition of this series of essays on the importance of a national language was published in 1958. The writer shows a good knowledge of dialectal variants in the Portuguese of Brazil, but since most of his previous work had been in literature, he tends to think in terms of anthologies of regional literature, and in terms of unity and "defense" of the language.

4622 Mattos, Geraldo. Curso de lingüística matemática. São Paulo: Difusão Editorial, 1977. 271 p. (Monografias de semiótica e lingüística; 2)

A long and complicated search for a *metalinguagem*, which would seem to be at the end of the rainbow!

4623 Naro, Anthony J. and **Mariam Lemle.** Syntactic diffusion (SBPC/CC, 29:3, março 1977, p. 259–268, bibl., tables)

The paper examines the nature of the implementation of syntactic change, especially across the relevant formal categories of the language in the possibility of a general principle that governs this change. They study in some detail several cases in which the syntax of agreement rules has changed, or is presently changing in Portuguese. Syntactic change tends to sneak through a language, and there is evidence that there are sociolinguistic factors.

4624 Sampaio, Maria Lúcia Pinheiro. Estudo diacrônico dos verbos ter e haver, duas formas em concorrência. Assis, Brazil: Tipografia Niro, 1978. 110 p.; bibl.

A good picture of the evolution of the two verbs from Latin through Old Portuguese in both the written and the spoken language. *Haver* was preferred to indicate possession and as an auxiliary for the compound tenses in early stages of the language. Changes began to develop in the 13th and 14th centuries and from the 16th century on *ter* invades the sphere of *haver* to the extent that now *haver* is found only in the written language.

4625 Vilanova, José Brasileiro Tenorio. Aspectos estilísticos da língua portuguesa. Recife: Casa da Medalha, 1977. 132 p.; bibl.

Writer considers stylistics a branch of linguistics: *estilística fonética, estilística léxica, estilística morfológica, estilística sintática, linguagem figurada.* Within these categories he proposes devices and selections that may improve expression, such as phrasal intonation, vocabulary selection, popular words, diminutives, superlatives, contrived phrase structure, metaphors, etc.

PORTUGUESE DIALECTOLOGY

4626 Aragão, Maria do Socorro Silva de. Análise fonético-fonológica do falar paraibano. João Pessoa: Editora Universitária da Universidade Federal de Paraiba, 1977. 207 p.; bibl.; ill. (Série Língua e literatura; 1. Coleção Estudos universitários)

This little book could well be a model for the regional investigation of Brazilian Portuguese. Done as part of the requirements for a doctoral thesis (São Paulo), the field work was accomplished by the author, who had divided the state into six sub-regions, and who had determined several sociolinguistic categories: age limits (15–45 in six sections); 10 gradations of educational experience (*analfabeto—pós-graduado*); four classes according to income; 21 professional categories. Valuable phonetic transcriptions of investigator-informant dialogues follow the main text.

4627 Bunse, Heinrich A.W. Dialetos italianos no Rio Grande do Sul. Porto Alegre: Universidade Federal do Rio Grande do Sul, Instituto de Letras, 1975. 68 p.; 2 leaves of plates; bibl.; maps (Monografias. UFRGS, Instituto de Letras; 1)

Convincing evidence of the Northern-Italian origins of the Italian immigrants of the Brazilian state of Rio Grande do Sul. Includes excellent maps of distribution of colonists' original homes.

4628 Cunha, Antônio Geraldo da. Dicionário histórico das palavras portuguesas de origem Tupí. Prefácio-estudo de Antônio Houaiss. São Paulo: Edições Melhoramentos *com a colaboração da* Editora da Universidade de São Paulo, 1978. 357 p.; indexes.

A very thoroughly wrought etymological dictionary of the Tupí element in Brazilian Portuguese, done in the manner of the famous Corominas Dictionary of Spanish. Two indexes follow the text: one of Tupí terms in phonetic notation followed by the ultimate Portuguese rendition, and another of Portuguese words of Tupí origin.

4629 Pereira da Costa, Francisco Augusto. Vocabulário pernambucano. Prefácio de Mário Souto Maior. 2. ed. Recife: Governo do Estado de Pernambuco, Secretaria de Educação e Cultura, 1976. 814 p.; bibl. (Coleção Pernambucana; 2)

The first edition of this good collection of popular regional words and phrases came out in 1937. Although some of the terms are now outdated, the vocabulary should be available as part of the history of Brazilian Portuguese lexicon.

4630 Pereira Penha, João Alves. Aspectos da linguagem de São Domingos tentativa de descrição da linguagem rural brasileira (FFCLM/A, 20/21, 1974/1975, p. 81–118, bibl., maps)

Using a community of Southern Minas Gerais with a population of about 1,000, the writer wishes to establish a model for the description of rural Portuguese in Brazil. The majority of informants were illiterate and racially they represented whites, blacks, and mulattos. Most of the article is dedicated to phonology and the notation is excellent: vowels, consonants, combinations, and sporadic phenomena such as assimilation, nasalization, epenthesis, palatalization, etc.

4631 **Santiago, Paulino.** Dinâmica de uma linguagem: o falar de Alagoas. Maceió: Universidade Federal de Alagoas, 1976. 228 p.; bibl.

A rather good study of the Portuguese dialect of Alagaos (capital Maceió) in Northeastern Brazil. After reviewing the origins of the popular speech, including the occurrence of African and Indian lexical elements, the author describes the phonology and morphology of the dialect, as well as syntactic features. The 2nd part of the book is a vocabulary of about 160 pages which is enhanced by the use of the terms in context. A contribution to the growing library of Brazilian dialectology.

Santos, Emmanoel. Mobilidade social e atitudes lingüísticas. See *HLAS 41:1419*.

PORTUGUESE LEXICON AND SEMANTICS

4632 **Andrade, Cândido Teobaldo de Souza.** Dicionário profissional de relações públicas e comunicação e glossário de termos anglo-americanos. São Paulo: Edição Saraiva, 1978. 134 p.; bibl.

The vocabulary is the result of an assigned task of the "Comisión Interamericana Para la Enseñanza de Relaciones Públicas" (Caracas, 1971). The list of terms and definitions shows strong American influence, as well as a great many Anglicisms. Although it is quite up-to-date, the word *printout* is missing. A glossary of some 1,000 Anglo-American terms follows the text, as well as a short bibliography.

4633 **Barbosa, Maria Aparecida.** Língua e discurso: contribuição aos estudos semântico-sintáxicos. São Paulo: Global Editora e Distribuidora, 1978. 413 p.; bibl. (Global universitária; 5. Série Linguagem, comunicação e sociedade)

Attempts to discover the semiotic systems responsible for perception that man has for the universe. Using the term *filhinha* as an example, the writer shows the strict dependence that exists between syntax and semantics and the impossibility of separating them in a study that pretends to be scientific.

4634 **Bini, Edson** and **Carlos Antonio Lauand.** Dicionário técnico industrial: tratando das principais áreas da engenharia e das ciências exatas: inglês/português/inglês. Supervisão, Maxim Behar. São Paulo: Hemus, 1978. 942 p.

Despite claims to the contrary, many of the dictionaries and special vocabularies emanating from Brazil are not up-to-date. This one is! In the realms of rocketry, space travel, computer science, missile launching, electronics, etc., it has extensive entries, subentries, and definitions. It is quite well illustrated, and has a Portuguese-English listing, limited and to the point, following the long English-Portuguese main part.

4635 **Blikstein, Izidoro.** As etimologías de Ménage (USP/LL, 6, 1977, p. 99–126)

In a rather wry assessment of 17th-century lexicography, the writer demonstrates that only about 75 percent of the definitions of G. Ménage's dictionary could be considered correct. Further, he believes that this is good for the period.

4636 **Buecken, Francisco J.** Vocabulario técnico, português, inglês, francês, alemão. 5. ed. São Paulo: Edições Melhoramentos, 1977. 600 p.

This fifth edition of what should be a very useful tool is not up-to-date in such things as space exploration, rocketry, meteorology, but it does have a good appendix on automotive terminology.

Cacciatore, Olga Gudolle. Dicionário de cultos afro-brasileiros com origem das palavras. See item **1064**.

4637 **Cardoso, Zelia de Almeida.** Zoonímia e metassemia (USP/LL, 6, 1977, p. 287–291)

Examines the extension of meanings especially among animals, and from animals to human qualities.

Carvalho-Neto, Paulo de. Diccionario de teoría folklórica. See item **960**.

4638 **Dicionário conciso** da língua portuguesa. Organizado por Antônio N. Machado. Rio de Janeiro: DIFEL, 1977. 768 p.

A dictionary of short definitions, but

barely touching on recent developments in science.

4639 Dicionário Melhoramentos da língua portuguesa. São Paulo: Melhoramentos, 1977. 1035 p.

Generally not up-to-date in recent scientific terminology. A good list of collective terms, another of the noises made by animals and things, and a vocabulary of Latin and foreign words and phrases.

4640 Dorin, E. Dicionário de psicologia abrangendo terminologia de ciências correlatas. Colaboradores, Maria Celisa Costa Couto de Moraes and others. São Paulo: Edições Melhoramentos, 1978. 300 p., 8 leaves of plates: ill.

The work of seven collaborators: two psychologists, two physiologists, one professor of Education and Statistics, one sociologist, and one biologist. The approach and the perspective of the authors would appear to have produced an instrument that fills a gap for scholars in the social sciences.

4641 Ferreira, Luíz Pinto. Dicionário de sociologia. São Paulo: J. Bushatsky, 1977. 361 p.; index.

A good vocabulary of terms, people, journals, preceded by an alphabetical index of entries. References draw heavily on American and German sources and include work done until about 1970.

4642 Gonçalves, Angela Jungmann. Lexicologia e ensino do léxico. Brasília: Thesaurus Editora, 1977. 135 p.; bibl.; ill.

The object of the book is to demonstrate how lexicology can contribute to the teaching of the mother tongue, especially vocabulary. Theories are examined and exercises are proposed for the improvement of the lexicon of one's own native language.

4643 Lopes, Edward. Discurso, texto e significação: uma teoria de interpretante. São Paulo: Editora Cultrix *em co-edição com a* Secretaria da Cultura, Ciência e Tecnologia do Estado de São Paulo, 1978. 111 p.: diagrams.

Supporting a semantic theory that he calls "interpretante ideológico," Lopes thinks that in discourse there tends to be a *manipulação dos sentidos,* and often the interpretation that the reader or listener presupposes is not actually that of the text. The real one is the one that the author (speaker) wanted to give, which in turn must be interpreted in order that the text make sense.

4644 Oliveira, Edison de. Todo o mundo tem dúvida, inclusive voce: português. Porto Alegre: Gráfica e Editora do Professor Gaúcho, 1974. 186 p.: ill.

Illustrated with humorous drawings, this little book attempts to right the wrongs of Brazilian Portuguese as it is commonly used: all sorts of errors, doubts and ambiguities. Such things as *fazem anos* instead of *faz anos* or *falou que chegaria atrasado* in place of *disse* . . . are discussed, as well as *vultosa* compared to *vultuosa* and mistakes in accentuation. A handy manual for learners as well as natives.

4645 Pais, Cidmar Teodoro. Ensaios semiótico-lingüísticos. Petrópolis: Editora Vozes, 1977. 103 p.; bibl.; ill.

A series of essays pointing toward a cybernetic model of meaning systems in the neverlagging search for "universals." Author maintains that the treatment of linguistic information at the speaker-hearer level in natural language is realized through a very complex process: elaboration, transmission, appreciation and re-elaboration, all of which presupposes the existence of different semiotic universals, related among themselves. Expresses need for semantic codification in linguistic communication.

4646 Paula, João Teixeira de. Dicionário enciclopédico ilustrado: espiritismo, metapsíquica, parapsicologia. 3. ed., corr. e atualizada. Porto Alegre: Bels, 1976. 293 p.; bibl.; ill.

An illustrated vocabulary of the occult and mysterious, including photos of "stigmatized" persons and a long International Directory of Parapsychological Associations. Much of the material is drawn from English, French, German, Italian and American sources.

4647 Pequeno dicionário filosófico. Compilado pelo Departamento de Redação. Colaboração de Márcio Pugliesi e Edson Bini. Revisão e adaptação, Eduardo Nunes Fonseca e Lauro S. Blandy. São Paulo: Hemus, 1977. 412 p.

A veritable encyclopedia of the terminology of the discipline of Philosophy, whose strength would seem to be in the shades of meaning discussed and the relation of each to currents of philosophical thinking.

4648 Vallandro, Leonel. Dicionário escolar inglês-português, português-inglês. 6. ed., de acordo com a ortografia oficial brasileira. Porto Alegre: Editora Globo, 1976. 981 p.

Although the introduction on English pronunciation and syllabication as well as the phonetic transcription of all English entries is in good order, the Dictionary has not been revised to any extent apparently since the first edition of 1965. The entries that might represent late developments in science are missing. There is not even an astronaut!

4649 Vogt, Carlos. O intervalo semântico: contribuição para uma teoria semântica argumentativa. São Paulo: Editora Atica, 1977. 282 p.; bibl.; ill. (Ensaios; 26)

Writer believes that semantics is to assume a pilot role in relation to other so-called human sciences. He tends to believe that the essence of semantic relevance is comparison—hence a *semântica argumentativa.*

CREOLE

4650 Allsopp, Richard. La influencia africana sobre el idioma en el Caribe (*in* Africa en América Latina [see *HLAS 41:9035*] p. 129–151, tables)

Suggests that influence from Ghana, Nigeria, Zaire and other sections of Africa on the English of the Caribbean is not only lexical but morphosyntactic, notably the use of particles and in word order. As an example, tears is expressed as *pi-wang* (eye water). Many Creole authorities, including Robert Hall, Jr., have insisted that the English pidgins have an English identity and a basically Indo-European structure.

4651 Castillo, Mathiew N. Léxico caribe en el Caribe insular (ICC/T, 32:2, mayo/agosto 1977, p. 316–373, bibl.)

This is a continuation of the study on Caribe lexicon in British Honduras (see *HLAS 40:6126*). At that time the writer had estimated the vocabulary to be about 200, but after consulting the Breton *Dictionnaire François-Caraïbe* and Taylor's *The black Carib,* he brings the number up to 568. One of the mysteries that he finds is the origin of *canoa.* The listing is of Indian terms learned originally by African slaves who had married into Indian tribes of the Caribbean coast of Central America.

4652 Craig, Dennis R. Conceptual repertoires and their communication through language (*in* Caribbean-American perspectives: proceedings and papers from the Caribbean-American exchange program. Washington: Phelps-Stokes Fund, 1978, p. 55–65)

In most contemporary societies, persons are prepared for society-wide oral communication through a lengthy process of formal schooling. If oral communication is to be used more extensively for imparting information to persons who have not been significantly conditioned within this process, there may be a possibility of problems in relation to the linguistic form of communication on the one hand and the conceptual content that is to be communicated on the other.

4653 Creole drum: an anthology of Creole literature in Surinam. Edited by Jan Voorhoeve and Ursy M. Lichtveld. With English translations by Vernie A. February. New Haven: Yale University Press, 1975. 308 p.; bibl.; ill.; index (Caribbean series; 15)

Surinam Creole apparently evolved after 1651 as a "lingua franca" between masters and slaves of several African origins, and remained the language of the mass of the people after emancipation in 1863. The *Drum* is a song of past events, and the volume has many of these as well as several folktales, notes on orthography and a good bibliography. It can be of scholarly importance to anthropologists and linguists because the corpus illustrates the participation of English, Dutch, and Portuguese in the formulation of a medium of communication for people who were African.

4654 Férère, Gérard A. Diglossia in Haiti: a comparison with Paraguayan bilingualism (UWI/CS, 23:1, March 1977, p. 50–60, bibl., tables)

To illustrate the vast difference between the Paraguayan and Haitian cases, a questionnaire was submitted to 50 bilingual (French and Creole) speakers of Haiti on their choice in 58 situations of home and society. Of the 2900 answers, 1730 chose French, 755, Creole, and 415 free choice. It was evident that French was given a higher social classification. One must consider, however, that in daily life situations, only a few speak French; also, that Creole is French based whereas Guaraní and Spanish are very distinct languages.

4655 Granda, Germán de. Algunos rasgos morfosintácticos de posible origen criollo en el habla de áreas hispanoamericanas de población negra (UNAM/AL, 14, 1976, p. 5–22)

Another spin-off from Granda's extensive investigations for the Colombian *Linguistic atlas,* especially along the Pacific coast. He believes that in the case of Spanish, much more than in French, Portuguese and English, the drift since slave days has been toward Spanish rather than toward a stable Creole.

4656 Haynes, Lilith M. The sociology of local names of plants in Guyana, South America (LING, 193, June 1977, p. 87–101, charts, tables)

In a population of whites, mixed African, Indian, Amerindian, Portuguese and Chinese, knowledge of the names of plants of the region was tested. It was found that this knowledge was concentrated in the three lowest classes of society, so that acquaintance with the flora may be said to diminish with upward social mobility, except among specialists. Racially, the African, the Indian and the Amerindian were the most knowledgeable.

4657 Hellinger, Marlis. A note on "Wowla" in Belizean Creole (Belizean Studies [Belize Institute of Social Research and Action (BISRA), Belize City] 5:5, Sept. 1977, p. 31–55, bibl., plates)

Using this one term as a key to the story of a complicated settlement pattern, writer tells of slaves who were shipwrecked near Gracias a Dios, married Indians, and eventually ended up in Belize. The Miskito Indian word for a type of snake also became the term for a long instrument used in making cassava bread.

4658 Mirville, Ernst. Précis de grammaire créole comparée. Port-au-Prince: Institut de Linguistique Appliquée de Port-au-Prince, 1977. 197 p. (Collection Coucouille. Bulletin de l'Institut de Linguistique Appliquée de Port-au-Prince, 1977; 3)

A synthesis of verbs, pronouns, adverbs, nouns, determinants, conjunctions, etc., as well as the peculiar order in the Creole phrase.

4659 Murray, Fernando Wright. Un análisis sintáctico del habla criolla de Limón (UCR/RF, 1:2, sept. 1975, p. 149–168, ill.)

The Creole described is English that has been brought from Jamaica into Costa Rica since 1872. The investigation examined the speech of three informants, ages 23, 29, and 49. The dialect was found to have a pattern of 19 consonants, eight vowels, three tones, and the syntax was described through transformational rules. One may doubt the writer's claim that this is a language unto itself.

4660 Naro, Anthony. Pidginization, Creolization, and natural change (SBPL/RBL, 5:1, 1978, p. 123–138, bibl.)

A need to establish effective linguistic communication arises when groups that have no language in common come into close contact. A compromise emerges. In a study of the evolution of the morphological and semantic structure of the Pidgin-Creole verb, Naro shows that substratum influences are rarer than a rapid comparison of pidgin and substratum might lead one to believe. The relative social status of the base and non-base speakers is a factor.

4661 Peleman, L. Dictionnaire créole-français. Port-au-Prince: Bon Nouvel, 1978. 209 p.

The fruit of 15 years of research in the Creole spoken in the northeastern part of Haiti, Peleman's vocabulary gives not only definitions, but in many cases, the cultural "fonction dynamique." The spelling system, always a problem among Creole languages, is carefully worked out by the author, and ample examples are given for symbols used.

4662 Pompilus, Pradel. Le colloque international des Créolistes et la question de l'écriture du Créole (ASHSH/B, 5, 1977, p. 14–28)

A review of the problems of adopting a common system for writing Creoles. Besides the many base language orthographies (French, English, Dutch, Portuguese, Spanish) involved already, there is the matter of homonyms, which would not be helped by a phonetic spelling.

Taylor, Douglas. Languages of the West Indies. See *HLAS 41:1096.*

4663 Ti diksyonnè kreyòl-franse = Dictionnaire élémentaire créole haïtien-français. Equipe de recherche: Pierre Nougayrol and others. Sous le direction de Alain Bentolila. Port-au-Prince: Editions Caraïbes, 1976. 511 p.

A good dictionary of Haitian Creole with French definitions. The corpus was made up of utterances of people who speak only Creole, in the center of the Republic, in the Saint Marc area (Senmak). The work was not done by questionnaire because of the unequal social status of investigators and informants and its effects on answers. A great deal of context is given with definitions to avoid confusion and ambiguities, since there has been extensive phonological levelling in the Creole.

4664 Washabaugh, William. Complexities in Creole continua (LINGUA, 46:2/3, Oct./Nov. 1978, p. 245–261)

Linguistic variation in English Creole of the Caribbean is not simply a product of decreolization. There are two processes which create complexities in post-Creole continua: 1) social pressure to avoid Creole; 2) different paths taken in original creolization.

JOURNAL ABBREVIATIONS LANGUAGE

AATSP/H Hispania. American Association of Teachers of Spanish and Portuguese. Univ. of Cincinnati, Ohio.

ACO/B Boletín de la Academia Colombiana. Bogotá.

ANLE/B Boletín de la Academia Norteamericana de la Lengua Española. New York.

ASHSH/B Bulletin de l'Académie des Sciences Humaines et Sociales d'Haiti. Port-au-Prince.

BNBD Boletín Nicaragüense de Bibliografía y Documentación. Banco Central de Nicaragua, Biblioteca. Managua.

BRP Beiträge zur Romanischen Philologie. Rütten & Loening. Berlin.

CIDG/O Orbis. Bulletin international de documentation linguistique. Central International de Dialectologie Générale. Louvain, Belgium.

CM/NRFH Nueva Revista de Filología Hispánica. El Colegio de México [and] the University of Texas. México.

FFCLM/A Alfa. Univ. de São Paulo, Faculdade de Filosofia, Ciências e Letras. Marília, Brazil.

HR Hispanic Review. A quarterly devoted to research in the Hispanic languages and literatures. Univ. of Pennsylvania, Dept. of Romance Languages. Philadelphia.

HUN/RU Revista de la Universidad. Univ. Nacional Autónoma de Honduras. Tegucigalpa.

ICC/T Thesaurus. Boletín del Instituto Caro y Cuervo. Bogotá.

IGFO/RI Revista de Indias. Instituto Gonzalo Fernández de Oviedo [and] Consejo Superior de Investigaciones Científicas. Madrid.

IU/AL Anthropological Linguistics. A publication of the Archives of the Languages of the World. Indiana Univ., Anthropology Dept. Bloomington, Ind.

LINGUA Lingua. North-Holland Publishing Co. Amsterdam.

MLTA/MLJ Modern Language Journal. The National Federation of Modern Language Teachers Associations [and] Univ. of Pittsburgh. Pittsburgh, Pa.

PUC/L Lexis. Revista de lingüística y literatura. Pontificia Univ. Católica del Perú. Lima.

SBPC/CC Ciência e Cultura. Sociedade Brasileira para o Progresso da Ciência. São Paulo.

SBPL/RBL Revista Brasileira de Lingüística. Sociedade Brasileira para Professores de Lingüística. São Paulo.

UBN/R Revista de la Biblioteca Nacional. Ministerio de Educación y Cultura. Montevideo.

UCLV/I Islas. Univ. Central de las Villas. Santa Clara, Cuba.

UCR/RF Revista de Filosofía de la Universidad de Costa Rica. San José.

UNAM/AL Anuario de Letras. Univ. Nacional Autónoma de México, Facultad de Filosofía y Letras. México.

UNPHU/A Aula. Univ. Nacional Pedro Henríquez Ureña. Santo Domingo.

UPRM/RL Revista de Letras. Univ. de Puerto Rico en Mayagüez, Facultad de Artes y Ciencias. Mayagüez.

USP/LL Língua e Literatura. Univ. de São Paulo, Depto. de Letras, Faculdade de Filosofia, Letras e Ciências Humanas. São Paulo.

UWI/CS Caribbean Studies. Univ. of the West Indies. Mona, Jamaica.

UY/R Revista de la Universidad de Yucatán. Mérida, Mexico.

LITERATURE

SPANISH AMERICA: GENERAL

ROBERTO GONZALEZ ECHEVARRIA, *Professor of Spanish, Yale University*

LIKE MODERN ART IN GENERAL and literature in particular, literary criticism thrives on crises and upheavals that not only bring about change but make of change the very condition for existence. Through the ritual discarding of old values and practices on behalf of the new, criticism justifies its changing mores and practices. In the past 15 or 20 years, Latin American literature has undergone a crisis so profound that the quality and nature of criticism has been radically altered leading, in effect, to new and surprising interactions between criticism and literature itself. The reasons for this transformation are varied. Perhaps the most important is that as Latin American literature extended its influence beyond the Spanish-speaking orbit, Latin American criticism was forced to follow suit and compete with older, more established critical traditions. Moreover, as the new Latin American literature revealed a new perspective on the writings of the colonial period, the 19th and the first half of our century, all criticism written before the 1960s and formulated according to values prevalent at that time, now appears tentative and obsolete. Because literature prior to the 1960s regarded itself as marginal and dependent, criticism was overtly defensive and needed to assert the historical depth and cultural uniqueness of an autochtonous literature generated from the very beginning by the New World. In contrast, Latin American literature and criticism are secure today in their knowledge of being and having always been, an integral part of modern literature. There is no longer a need to construct genealogies that legitimize current writing.

It is in the redefinition of literature and of its relation to culture that the most fundamental and ideological break with the past has occurred. The Romantic conception of culture linked language, community, and artistic expression in a metaphoric system of interconnections not unlike that of 19th-century natural science. The ideological nature of this 19th-century concept of literary expression has been exposed by Marxist-grounded criticism (including structuralism and post-structuralism). Nowadays, the most sophisticated criticism recognizes the importance of ideology in the formulation of literature and refutes the old notion of autonomy. This break distinguishes contemporary from older criticism of Latin American literature. Indeed, the pioneers of the field, figures such as Pedro Henríquez Ureña and Alfonso Reyes, are themselves increasingly subjects of criticism, a fact which underlines the decline of their influence.

The changes noted above are evident in a new group of journals, whose publication is scattered throughout Latin America. Nevertheless, the endemic evils of Latin American criticism continue in most cases (e.g., journalism and a tendency to politicize which often substitutes partisan fervor for critical thought and documentation). The (relatively) new magazines are: *Revista de Crítica Literaria Latinoamericana* (Peru); *Fragmentos* (Centro de Estudios Literarios Rómulo Gallegos);

Escritura (Caracas); and *Arte/Sociedad/Ideología* (Mexico). *Eco* (Colombia) continues to serve as an important bridge between European and Latin American criticism. Academic journals devoted to Hispanic studies such as *Publications of the Modern Language Association of America* (US) and *Hispanic Review* (US), *Bulletin of Hispanic Studies* (England) and *Bulletin Hispanique* (France) are devoting more space to Latin American literature, a welcome sign that Hispanists are becoming less defensive and chauvinistic. *Diacritics* (Cornell University) continues to publish on Latin American subjects at a high level of competence.

5001 Agustín, José. Literature and censorship in Latin America today: dream within a dream. Edited by John Kirk and Don Schmidt. Denver: Department of Foreign Languages and Literatures, University of Denver, 1978. 47 p., bibl., index (University of Denver occasional papers; 1)

Chatty, very personal lectures on three topics: 1) contemporary Latin American fiction; 2) Mexican fiction, and 3) censorship. The second is by far the best, for it provides an insider's view of the skirmishes among the various factions of Mexican writers.

5002 Antología de la literatura hispanoamericana. Compiled by Roberto Yahni. Madrid: Ediciones J. Porrua Turanzas, 1977. 204 p., bibl. (Ensayos)

This anthology is a minimal pedagogical contribution to the field because of the scarcity of notes and the absence of a general introduction.

5003 Arrom, José Juan. Esquema generacional de las letras hispanoamericanas: ensayo de un método. 2. ed. Bogotá: Instituto Caro y Cuervo, 1977. 261 p. (Publicaciones del Instituto Caro y Cuervo; 39)

This second edition of Arrom's well-known history of Latin American literature contains some substantial changes, particularly in the chapters dealing with the transition from the 16th to the 17th century, plus an expansion of the last chapter.

5004 Bellini, Giuseppe. Il mondo allucinante: da Asturias a García Márquez: studi sul romanzo ispano-americano della dittatura. Milano, Italy: Cisalpino-Goliardica, 1976. 196 p.

Good general overview of the emergence of the dictator-novel, and a thematic reading of the major ones by Carpentier, García Márquez and Roa Bastos. But Bellini's vaguely condescending view of Latin American social reality as a hallucinatory world mars the overall formulations.

5005 Benedetti, Mario. El escritor y la crítica en el contexto del subdesarrollo (CDLA, 18:107, marzo/abril 1978, p. 3–21)

The noted Uruguayan novelist surveys with alarm and scanty information the panorama of current critical theory. Benedetti makes the startling assertion that structuralism did away with French literature and makes a call for the kind of narrative, with characters, that he himself writes. An interesting piece for experts on Benedetti's fiction.

5006 Berger, Víctor. Luis Alberto Sánchez y la novela hispanoamericana: entrevista (INSULA, 34:394, sept. 1979, p. 3, plate)

An interesting interview with the author of *América, novela sin novelistas,* with observations about Gallegos, Rivera, Güiraldes and the new novel.

5007 Blacks in Hispanic literature: critical essays. Edited by Miriam DeCosta. Port Washington, N.Y.: Kennikat Press, 1977. 157 p., bibl. (National university publications. Literary criticism series)

These articles include a wealth of information on a subject that all Hispanists should become familiar with. The theme of this book is not ancillary to Hispanic studies but essential considering that, for five centuries, blacks have been an important part of Hispanic culture.

5008 Blasi, Alberto. Ricardo Güiraldes y la revista *Proa* (ANLE/B, 2/3, 1977/1978, p. 115–127)

Enlightening commentary on various unpublished letters of Güiraldes that help our understanding of the role played by the magazine *Proa* in River Plate and Latin American avant-garde movements. An important contribution for specialists.

5009 The Borzoi anthology of Latin American literature. v. 1, From the time of

Columbus to the twentieth century; v. 2, Twentieth century, from Borges and Paz to Guimarães Rosa and Donoso. Edited by Emir Rodríguez Monegal, with the assistance of Thomas Colchie. New York: Knopf, 1977. 2 v. (982, 493 p.)

Very useful anthology for English-language readers of Latin American literature compiled by the noted Uruguayan critic. Strong on the more recent periods in which the editor has been a shaping force, thus attesting to his tastes and biases. Particularly important for its inclusion of Brazilian authors and movements in the overall presentation of Latin American literary history. For a more comprehensive evaluation, see the review-article by this reviewer in *Modern Language Notes* (94, 1979, p. 394–404).

5010 Brotherston, Gordon. The emergence of the Latin American novel. Cambridge; New York; Cambridge University Press, 1977. 164 p., bibl., index.

Consists of a general introduction, eight chapters on individual authors and conclusion. The novelists studied are: Asturias, Carpentier, Onetti, Rulfo, Cortázar, Arguedas, Vargas Llosa and García Márquez. As a general introduction for English-speaking students the book should be a useful tool. The introduction, in which Brazilian authors are considered too, outlines current trends in the modern Latin American novel as clash between rural and cosmopolitan perspectives. The chapters on individual authors include remarks on nearly all the important works of the novelist, though they focus on the one given as the most representative. The specialist or advanced student will find the book less stimulating, though there are valuable observations throughout. The best chapter is on Vargas Llosa, the weakest on Carpentier. There is little on younger novelists.

5011 Bryant, Shasta M. A selective bibliography of bibliographies of Hispanic American literature. 2. ed. greatly expanded and revised. Austin: Institute of Latin American Studies (ILAS), The University of Texas at Austin, 1976. 100 p. (Guides and bibliographies series; 8)

This is an extremely useful tool for all Latin-Americanists. For bibliographer's comment, see *HLAS 41:20*.

Camacho Guizado, Eduardo. Sobre literatura colombiana e hispanoamericana. See item **5385**.

5012 Carilla, Emilio. Estudios de literatura hispanoamericana. Bogotá: Instituto Caro y Cuervo, 1977. 377 p., bibl., index (Publicaciones del Instituto Caro y Cuervo; 42)

Carilla is one of the few Latin-Americanists who can truly cover the range of Latin American literature from the colonial period to the present. This collection of papers is evidence of such a range. Carilla's return to Góngora and the American Baroque is particularly suggestive, for he was one of the first to study the topic in his book on Gongorism in America. A good collection.

5013 ———. Pedro Henríquez Ureña: biografía comentada (RIB, 27:3, julio/sept. 1977, p. 227–239)

Carilla divides Henríquez Ureña's life into seven periods and provides detailed comments for each one. He includes numerous quotations about the Dominican critic's work by others and himself. The very useful and well-organized introduction is, however, not as thorough as the one by Emma Susanna Speratti Piñero in her 1960 *Obra crítica* (see *HLAS 26:1483*).

Coluccio, Félix. Aproximación a la raíz folklórica en la novelística latinoamericana. See item **962**.

5014 Cometta Manzoni, Aída. El dictador en la narrativa latinoamericana (CONAC/RNC, 234, enero/feb. 1978, p. 89–111)

Good on background of dictator novels, though author claims that Spaniards brought the type to America when in fact it developed here. Rightfully stresses the importance of Echevarría's "El matadero" and Mármol's *Amalia* as the true precursors of the dictator-novel tradition.

5015 Congreso Internacional de Literatura Iberoamericana, *16th, Michigan State University, 1973.* Otros mundos, otros fuegos: fantasía y realismo mágico en Iberoaméricana: memoria del XVI Congreso Internacional de Literatura Iberoamericana. Edición al cuidado de Donald A. Yates. East Lansing: Michigan State University, Latin American Studies Center, 1975. 427 p., bibl.

Contains important pieces reassessing the whole question of *realismo mágico/real maravilloso*. Small print and many errata make this a difficult book to read.

5016 Cornejo Polar, Antonio. El indigenismo y las literaturas heterogéneas: su doble estatuto socio-cultural (RCLL, 4:7/8, 1./2. semestres 1978, p. 7–21)

Cornejo Polar concludes that the heterogeneity of *indigenismo* as a form of literary production reflects the heterogeneity of the cultural context from which the tradition derives. Conclusions of this article are not unduly original but their presentation is clothed in the language of various neo-Marxist approaches to literature. References to Ernst Robert Curtius' theory of *topoi* is in error and section on the colonial chronicles reveals a very superficial knowledge of those texts. A light, general piece that might serve as a good introduction for the non-specialist.

5017 La crítica literaria y estética en el siglo XIX cubano. Prólogo y selección de Cintio Vitier. La Habana: Biblioteca Nacional José Martí, 1974. 3 v., bibl.

Vitier's achievement in the edition of these three volumes is a remarkable achievement of continental significance. We now have access to a well chosen and edited corpus of critical material from the XIX century that broadens our knowledge of Hispanic thought on that period.

5018 Dellepiane, Angela B. Tres novelas de la dictadura: *El recurso del método*; *El otoño del patriarca*; *Yo, el Supremo* (UTIEH/C, 29, 1977, p. 65–87)

One of the more reliable pieces on the theme of the dictator novel, Dellepiane offers a good deal of pertinent information about the presence of the figure in Latin American literature and provides a creditable reading of the three main works. Underlines mythic quality of the dictator figure.

5019 Dessau, Adalbert. Realismo mágico y nueva novela latinoamericana: consideraciones metodológicas e históricas (*in* Simposio Internacional de Estudios Hispánicos, Budapest, 1976. Actas [see item **5067**] p. 351–358)

After going over a good deal of the material already explored by other critics (some of whom he mentions) author concludes that "la trayectoria 'interna' del realismo mágico va de la descripción de la conciencia prerracional y el comportamiento humano motivado por ella hasta su análisis y la demostración de su relatividad histórica en acciones que confrontan a sus protagonistas con procesos esenciales del mundo moderno . . ."

5020 ———. *Zivilisation und Barbarei* im lateinamerikanischen Roman (BRP, 14:2, 1975, p. 229–241)

Analyzes the trajectory of the theme "civilization vs. barbarism" in Latin American writing, starting with Sarmiento who introduced the concept in the 19th century and continuing with contemporary authors (e.g., García Márquez, Ariel Dorfman, etc.). [G.M. Dorn]

5021 *Diacritics*. A review of contemporary criticism. Johns Hopkins University Press. Vol. 8, No. 4, Winter 1978– . Baltimore, Md.

Entire issue devoted to Latin American literature, with pieces on Carpentier, Vallejo, Borges, Paz and Fernández Retamar.

5022 Dill, Hans Otto. El ideario literario y estético de José Martí. La Habana: Casa de las Américas, 1975. 204 p.

Naive, unimaginative account which uses Marxist jargon rather than Marxist analysis and points to the need for another study of this important subject.

5023 Donoso, José. The boom in Spanish American literature: a personal history. Translated by Gregory Kolovakos. New York: Columbia University Press in association with the Center for Inter-American Relations, 1977. 122 p., index.

English-speaking readers of the new Latin American novel will enjoy Donoso's inside view of an exciting period in Latin American literary history. Although not a particularly insightful critic, Donoso is a good storyteller. For Spanish original, see *HLAS 36:4429*.

5024 Durán Luzio, Juan. Creación y utopía: letras de Hispanoamérica. San José: Editorial de la Universidad Nacional, 1979.

The most complete history of the topic of utopia in Latin American literature, this book ranges from colonial literature to *Cien años de soledad*. It is particularly strong on the colonial period.

5025 Earle, Peter G. On the contemporary displacement of the Hispanic-American essay (HR, 46:3, Summer 1978, p. 329–341)

Earle maintains that the "dilution of the person as a literary subject" and the scientific tendency of current criticism have contributed to the demise of the essay in Latin America. Yet the French critics over whose work Earle voices his alarm—Derrida in particular—do practice the essay, as do many of their followers in Latin America. An interesting reaction by a recognized authority on the history of the Latin American essay.

5026 Fernández Retamar, Roberto. Calibán y otros ensayos. La Habana: Editorial Arte y Literatura, 1979. 294 p.

This re-edition of Retamar's well-known essay contains a number of new pieces. In them the author revises his position concerning the relationship between European and Latin American culture by using a progressively more Marxist approach. In his essay "*Calibán*," Retamar's strident *americanismo* and *tercermundismo* were based on a *Kulturgeschichte*'s view of Latin American culture originally formulated by Sarmiento and Rodó, a tradition he attempted to subvert. In essays such as "Nuestra América y Occidente," Retamar tries to analyze (though in very broad and vague terms) the economic and social transactions that determined relations between the Old and the New worlds since the 16th century.

5027 ———. Para una teoría de la literatura hispanoamericana y otros aproximaciones. La Habana: Casa de las Américas, 1975. 141 p., bibl. (Cuadernos Casa; 16)

Retamar is still grappling with the problem of the specificity of Latin American literature. This new edition contains two new essays, one of which ("La Contribución de las Literaturas de la América Latina en el Siglo XX") attempts unconvincingly to map out a historical scheme. Moreover, a progressive assimilation of Marxist ideology threatens the cogency of this book somewhat disrupted by visible stages in that process. It is, nevertheless, a book worth incorporating into any discussion of a theory of Latin American literature.

5028 Franco, Jean. From modernization to resistance: Latin American literature, 1959–1976 (LAP, 5:1, Winter 1978, p. 77–97, bibl.)

Overview of current Latin American literature by US-based British Latin Americanist. Franco's main argument about avant-garde writing is: "the greatest inconsistency in Paz's work—and one which characterizes much contempory writing—is that while attempting to reconcile the involvement of the reader in the text and the renunciation of the privileged status of the author as the sole creator of the work, it continues to idealize 'literature' and to address a highly specialized and competent reader." Roa Bastos' *Yo, el Supremo* is held up as an example of less complex narrative which also breaks with certain forms of populism. For Spanish version of this article, see *Escritura* (Univ. Central de Venezuela, 7, 2:3, enero/junio 1977, p. 3–19).

5029 Goić, Cedomil. Historia de la novela hispanoamericana. Santiago, Chile: Ediciones Universitarias de Valparaíso, Universidad Católica de Valparaíso-Chile, 1972. 304 p., bibl., index (Colección Aula abierta)

Sedulous effort to apply generational method to the history of the Latin American novel, beginning towards the end of the 18th century. The value of this manual lies in the careful reading of important novels whose level of acuity declines noticeably as we approach contemporary works. Main drawback is lack of reference to the impact of European and American novelistic tradition (one mention of Faulkner, one of Flaubert, none of Proust, Kafka, Joyce or even Sartre), and failure to notice the importance of Borges (whose name is a mere reference) in the development of the Latin American novel. Reasonably good bibliographies of main authors.

Gotthelf, René. Calibán como símbolo de la cultura latinoamericana. See item **7511**.

5030 Grossman, Rudolf. Der Indio in Dichtung und Erzählungskunst der Lateinamerikaner: Fiktion und Wirklichkeit (UH/RJ, 26, 1975, p. 326–342)

Traces the evolution of the image of the Indian in Latin American poetry and prose, in the context of the race mixture of Latin America. [G.M. Dorn]

5031 Henríquez Ureña, Pedro. Desde Washington. Selección e introducción de Minerva Salado. La Habana: Casa de las Américas, 1975. 128 p. (Cuadernos Casa; 14)

Sent as a correspondent to Washington by *El Heraldo de Cuba*, Henríquez Ureña published a series of articles in that newspaper between 1914–15 under the rubric "Desde Washington." The articles deal with American politics (Wilson, the beginnings of

World War I), cultural life in the city, and constitute an interesting side to his works.

5032 ———. Ensayos: selección. Prólogo de José Alcántara Almánzar. 2. ed. Santo Domingo: Ediciones de Taller, 1976. 386 p., table (Biblioteca Taller; 67)

This sound collection of essays by the Dominican scholar and essayist is basically a reprint of the 1965 Cuban edition. Fortunately, it includes José Rodríguez Feo's prologue to the early edition, which provides interesting glimpses into the life of Henríquez Ureña while at Harvard. There is a further treat: Rodríguez Feo quotes extensively from his correspondence with Henríquez Ureña, particularly one letter in which the author of *Seis ensayos* offers some very penetrating comments on Jorge Luis Borges.

5033 ———. Obras completas. t. 1, 1899–1909; t. 2, 1909–1914; t. 3, 1914–1920. Selección y prólogo de Juan Jacobo de Lara. Santo Domingo: Universidad Nacional Pedro Henríquez Ureña, 1976/1977. 3 v. (400, 384, 400 p.) bibl.

It is obvious that the complete works of Pedro Henríquez Ureña are necessary for any serious study of Latin American intellectual history. Nevertheless, this reviewer feels that his *Obra crítica* (see *HLAS 26:1483*) and *Las corrientes* (see *HLAS 15:2161a*) provide more than enough material to convey the breadth and depth of his works. This edition, in fact, does not appear as reliable as *Obra crítica* and the prologue does not dispel this impression.

5034 Jackson, Richard L. The black image in Latin American literature. Albuquerque: University of New Mexico Press, 1976. 174 p., bibl.

Though Jackson's point of view—that of an American black in the aftermath of the 1960s—somewhat distorts the image he perceives, his book is well-informed, clearly written and worthy of attention.

5035 Jozef, Bella. O espaço reconquistado: linguagem a criação no romance hispano-americano contemporâneo. Petrópolis, Brazil: Editora Vozes, 1974. 151 p., bibl. (Coleção Vozes do mundo moderno; 13)

Brief, introductory essays on Bioy, Carpentier, Vargas Llosa, Sarduy and others by the well-known Brazilian critic.

5036 Kulin, Katalin. Mítosz és valóság: Gabriel García Márquez. Budapest: Akadémiai Kiadó, 1977. 228 p.

Hungarian scholar provides a comprehensive analysis of myth and reality in the work of García Márquez. She begins with the forerunners, the chroniclers of the Conquest and follows the tradition all the way to Asturias, Carpentier, Cortázar and other contemporary writers of Latin American prose fiction. She concentrates her analysis on *Cien años de soledad.* Important contribution.

Latin-American literature today. See item **6620**.

5037 Leal, Luis. Pedro Henríquez Ureña: crítica de la literatura hispanoamericana (RIB, 27:3, July/Sept. 1977, p. 241–253)

Lucid overview of Henríquez Ureña's criticism with a very good sketch of the history of the study of Latin American history in general. An excellent article.

5038 Libertella, Héctor. Nueva escritura en Latinoamérica. Caracas: Monte Avila Editores, 1977. 110 p., bibl. (Colección Estudios)

Journalistic, uninformed on bibliography, rhapsodic rather than incisive.

5039 Lida de Malkiel, María Rosa. El cuento popular y otros ensayos. Buenos Aires: Editorial Losada, 1976. 172 p. (Estudios literarios)

Welcome re-edition of Argentine scholar's work first published in 1941 (see *HLAS 7:1949*).

5040 Lindstrom, Naomi. Feminist criticism of Latin American literature: bibliographic notes (LARR, 15:1, 1980, p. 151–159)

Good general introduction for the nonspecialist. Concentrates entirely on recent feminist criticism, excluding works by earlier writers such as Camila Henríquez Ureña and Victoria Ocampo.

5041 Losada, Alejandro. Estructura social y producción cultural en América Latina: las literaturas dependientes, 1780–1920 (*in* Simposio Internacional de Estudios Hispánicos, Budapest, 1976. Actas [see item **5067**] p. 93–110)

Losada's analysis of Peruvian Romanticism as a means to systematize our understanding of cultural productivity in Latin America is a serious enterprise. His sociological, Marxist approach allows him to articulate neatly a good deal of common but vague knowledge about the subject. The analysis of cultural productivity—particularly of the functioning of cultural elites and their relation to centers of power—is illuminating as is his innovative study of the ideology of Latin American Romanticism. His approach, however, seems better suited to the sociology of the literary tribe than to the reading of literature, even if his description of general tendencies and minor authors are plausible enough.

5042 ———. Rasgos específicos del realismo social en la América Hispánica (IILI/R, 45:108/109, julio/dic. 1979, p. 413–442)

By means of a minute analysis of *Facundo*, the various rhetorical strategies of the narrator's voice, Losada attempts to hit upon that which is specific to Latin American literature. Though at times Losada's rhetorical analysis is a bit crude, his perception of how Latin American literature constitutes itself is persuasive: "El paso del relator individual [in *Facundo*] al 'nosotros' colectivo y abstracto implica entonces la afirmación de este proceso de rechazo de la realidad dada que los condicionaba y la identificación con otra realidad que adoptan como propia sin pertenecer objetivamente a ella. [. . .] la situación del intelectual productor de cultura en América Latina se caracteriza por una pérdida de identidad de su modo objetivo de pertenencia a la sociedad americana y por la reestructuración de su personalidad social a través del mundo de la cultura. Con sus necesarias variantes, este paradigma se reformulará a lo largo de los próximos ciento cincuenta años, constituyendo el punto de partida diferencial de la producción cultural autónoma de los intelectuales marginales urbanos en América Latina hasta el presente." While it is not clear why this should be called *realismo social*, Losada is persuaded by the illusory cogency of the world created in literature. A more deconstructive reading of literature would have exposed the contradictions with that supposedly utopian world and the relations of the latter to society itself would prove more enlightening. An important piece that raises the level of discourse on the specificity of Latin American literature from the vagaries of journalism.

5043 Mallett, Brian J. Dictadura e identidad en la novela latinoamericana (ARBOR, 101:393/394, sept./oct. 1978, p. 59–73)

Mallett's is one of the more interesting pieces on the dictator novel. Author does not yield to the temptation to treat figure of the dictator merely as myth but perceives it, instead, as an important factor in the development of both *writing* and the Latin American identity.

5044 Martí, José. Páginas escogidas. t. 1/2. Selección y prólogo de Roberto Fernández Retamar. 3. ed. La Habana: Editorial de Ciencias Sociales, 1974. 2 v. (392, 363 p.) plates (Ediciones políticas)

A remarkably good paperback edition which places Martí within reach of the general public. The selection of texts and the introduction are by one of the more respected Martí scholars.

5045 Martínez, Z. Nelly. El carnaval, el diálogo y la novela polifónica (HISPA, 6:17, 1977, p. 3–21)

Well-informed synthesis of Bachtin's theories about the novel and its relation to Carnival. It is not clear whether or not the author is aware of the incompatibility between the dialogic metaphor of Bachtin, based on a phonocentric concept of the text, and the more modern intertextual model used by Kristeva. The phonic model functions well within the sacred ritual of the Carnival as conceived by Bachtin but may be incompatible with the lay nature of modern fiction. Application of Bachtin's model to Donoso and Cabrera Infante is cursory but suggestive. A very good article.

5046 Milliani, Domingo. El dictador, objeto narrativo en dos novelas hispanoamericanas: *Yo, el Supremo* y *El recurso del método* (*in* Simposio Internacional de Estudios Hispánicos, Budapest, 1976. Actas [see item **5067**] p. 463–490, tables)

This thorough analysis of the two novels concludes: "La historicidad reelaborada en el caso de *Yo, el Supremo* y la deshistorización globalizadora—abstractiva—de *El recurso del método* son dos modalidades de expresión artística cimentadas sobre una misma realidad concreta." This exemplifies Milliani's use of needlessly technical language for what seems a rather conventional study.

5047 Moreno, C.M. Don Quijano de la Marcha (INDEX, 8:2, March/April 1979, p. 38–42)

A personal testimony concerning the repression of the journal *Marcha* by Uruguay's military dictatorship who jailed the editorial staff. The article also includes a good historical overview of this very important Latin American literary magazine and of Carlos Quijano, its founder.

5048 Osorio T., Nelson. La nueva narrativa y los problemas de la crítica en Hispanoamérica actual (RCLL, 3:5, 1. semestre 1977, p. 7–26)

Broad, unconvincing generalizations about link between socio-historical changes in the Latin America of the 1960s and the emergence of the new novel.

5049 Paley Francescato, Martha. La novela de la dictadura: nuevas estructuras narrativas (RCLL, 5:9, 1. semestre 1979, p. 99–104)

Author calls attention to a dictator-novel by Argentine René Avilé. Fabila (*El gran solitario de palacio*).

5050 Panorama crítico de la literatura hispanoamericana. Selección y notas de Rigoberto Paredes. Tegucigalpa: Editorial Nuevo Continente, 1974. 300 p. (Manuales de literatura; 1)

Anthology of critical essays by various well-known critics, covering the range of Latin American literature. The essays have been drawn from published sources. Not of interest for the specialist, but useful to students (provided poor quality of paper does not "self destruct" the book).

5051 Perus, Françoise. Literatura y sociedad en América Latina. México: Siglo Veintiuno Editores, 1976. 139 p., bibl. (Sociología y política)

Although the socioeconomic background of this Marxist study is sketchy and its relation to literary production not very convincing, Perus makes a bold attempt to reassess *modernismo* and more current literary modes. Perus' problem—common to much of Latin American Marxism—is that she interprets the lack of certain evolutionary steps in Latin American socioeconomic history in terms of Marx's blueprint which is based on European history. But stages such as the missing "capitalistic democratic revolution" were never even remotely possible in the development of Latin American society for which a different model is necessary. Moreover, Perus wastes space by refuting a piece of Angel Rama's which should not have been considered in the first place. She does, however, offer a number of suggestive comments and her contribution should be acknowledged in future studies of *modernismo* and the origins of modern Latin American literature.

5052 Portuondo, José Antonio. La emancipación literaria de Hispanoamérica. La Habana: Casa de las Américas, 1975. 167 p. (Cuadernos Casa; 15)

A series of minor pieces published previously in journals or *actas*. Portuondo is at his best in descriptive, evocative pieces, and at his worst when attempting to theorize or make broad generalizations.

5053 Portuondo Zúñiga, Santiago. Cinco novelas y un tirano (Santiago [Universidad de Oriente, La Habana] 30, junio 1978, p. 47–76)

Strong on the historical background of dictatorship, weak on the analysis of dictator-novels.

5054 Rama, Angel. Los dictadores latinoamericanos. México: Fondo de Cultura Económico, 1976. 63 p., ill. (Colección Testimonios del Fondo; 42)

Of all the studies of the dictator-novel, this brief book is the most disappointing. It glosses over the works of García Márquez, Carpentier and Roa Bastos and includes several erroneous allusions to current critical theory. But chiefly, it is difficult to ascertain what the central argument is.

5055 Reid, John T. The rise and decline of the Ariel-Caliban antithesis in Spanish America (AAFH/TAM, 34:3, Jan. 1978, p. 345–355)

Good, analytic overview of the topic, with interesting study of Rodó's sources. Article is particularly good on the 19th century, particularly French background of ideas on what constitutes the "Latin race." It is weak on more recent manifestations of the topic. There is a conspicuous lack of mention of Fernández Retamar's contribution to this subject.

5056 Reyes, Alfonso. Epistolario Alfonso Reyes, José María Chacón. Edited by Zenaida Gutiérrez-Vega. Madrid: Fundación Universitaria Española, 1976. 285 p., bibl., 8 leaves of plates: ill., indexes (Biblioteca histórica hispanoamericana; 1)

Sedulously compiled, this correspondence sheds a good deal of light on the careers of both Reyes and Chacón y Calvó, and also provides a detailed picture of their life styles. The pleasant style of both writers makes the reading of this book a real treat, not to mention the tidbits about rivalries between various figures and the real opinion that Reyes and Chacón y Calvó had of various people. One of Reyes' most poignant scenes is the ridiculous display of oratory by Cuban Minister Mario García Kohly, whom Reyes describes as "un pobre borrachín juergista" (p. 97). Useful index of names and careful annotations (sometimes excessively so as when Cervantes' dates are indicated) make this volume a welcome addition to our knowledge of intellectual life in Spain and Latin America.

5057 Reyes, Alicia. Genio y figura de Alfonso Reyes. Buenos Aires: Editorial Universitaria de Buenos Aires (EUDEBA), 1976. 332 p., ill. (Genio y figura; 30)

Reyes' granddaughter, working out of the *capilla alfonsina,* gives us a doting portrait of her admired grandfather. This memoir does not pretend to offer a critical reassessment of Reyes' work but provides many useful facts about the man.

5058 Rivera Martínez, J. Edgardo. La literatura geográfica del siglo XVI en Francia como antecedente de lo Real Maravilloso (RCLL, 5:9, 1. semestre 1979, p. 7–19)

Explores the dissemination of various New World themes in the writings of French scholars, humanists, and poets of the 16th century: fabulous wealth, the noble savage, monsters. Author draws tenuous link with modern narrative but provides good background material.

5059 Robinson, Barbara J. Doctoral dissertations in Hispanic American literature: a bibliography of dissertations completed in the United States, 1964–1976. Austin, Tex.: SALALM Secretariat, 1979. 45 p., index (Bibliography — Seminar on the Acquisition of Latin American Library Materials; 5)

This is a useful research tool and an interesting gauge of trends in Latin American literary studies. An index of Latin American writers treated in the dissertations would have enhanced the volume.

5060 Rodríguez Monegal, Emir. Carnaval/Antropofagia/Parodia (IILI/R, 45:108/109, julio/dic. 1979, p. 401–412)

This survey of the application of Bachtin's theories to Latin American fiction, with emphasis on the work of Sarduy and Haroldo de Campos, is followed by suggestions for further uses of the theory of carnivalization. Author is aware of the incompatibility between Bachtin's medieval and Renaissance concept of Carnival and the latter's modern and lay manifestation. He attempts a recovery of the sacred by appealing to the concept of Latin American culture as an amalgam of carnivalesque cultures. Possibilities of the method are convincing in the cases of writers such as Sarduy or Carpentier, but less so in the case of Borges and Lezama.

5061 Saavedra, Desiderio. Nueva crítica para una nueva narrativa: problemas y perspectivas (*in* Simposio Internacional de Estudios Hispánicos, Budapest, 1976. Actas [see item **5067**] p. 85–91)

Survey of the crisis in Latin American criticism of the New Novel, with emphasis on the shortcomings of Structuralism and the promise of a Marxist approach. More symptomatic than enlightening.

Sábato, Ernesto. Significado de Pedro Henríquez Ureña. See item **7524**.

5062 Sainz de Medrano, Luis. Historia de la literatura hispanoamericana. v. 1, Hasta siglo XIX incl. Madrid: Guadiana de Publicaciones, 1976. 438 p., bibls. (Biblioteca universitaria guadiana)

This general overview for Spanish students is an important document attesting to Spain's growing interest in Latin American literature of the past few years. The study, however, offers nothing new in terms of bibliography, critical insights, or methodological *prise de position* on periodization.

5063 Salgués Cargill, Maruxa. La imagen de la mujer en las letras hispanoamericanas: enfoque feminista de la literatura hispanoamericana. Jaén, Spain: Gráfica Nova, 1975. 104 p., bibl.

General overview of the topic within the context of very vague and uncritical historical categories.

5064 Sánchez, Luis Alberto. Historia comparada de las literaturas americanas. v. 1, Desde los orígenes hasta el Barroco; v. 2, Del naturalismo neoclásico al naturalismo romántico; v. 3, Del naturalismo al posmodernismo; v. 4, Del vanguardismo a nuestros días. Buenos Aires: Editorial Losada, 1973/1976. 4 v. (401, 464, 371, 446 p.) bibl., facsims., ill., map, plates.

Unusual history which considers both Latin and North American literatures. The Latin American part—the most ample and reliable—is much like Sánchez's earlier historical work. A good reference.

5065 Sefchovich, Sara. El método estructuralista genético para el análisis de la literatura (UNAM/RMS, 39:2, abril/junio 1977, p. 733–741)

A summary of Lucien Goldman's theories that is largely though not always reliable.

5066 Seminario Latinoamericano: El Escritor y el Cambio Social, Santa Barbara, Costa Rica, 1972. El escritor y el cambio social. San José, Costa Rica: CEDAL, 1973. 77 p. (Colección Seminarios y documentos; 15)

Very brief, uninteresting pieces which offer far less than the Seminar's title promises.

5067 Simposio Internacional de Estudios Hispánicos, Budapest, 1976. Actas. Edición a cargo de Mátyás Horányi. Budapest: Akadémiai Kaidó, 1978. 520 p.

Consists of 52 articles, 45 of which are annotated separately and entered under author's name in the appropriate literature section of this volume. [Ed.]

5068 Suberscaseux, Bernardo. *Tirano Banderas* en la narrativa hispanoamericana: la novela del dictador, 1926–1976 (UC/A, 33, abril 1978, p. 57–82)

Traces the influence of *Tirano Banderas* on Latin American literature. A very well-documented article with insightful commentaries on the dictator-novel. The best study of this topic.

5069 Terra America: saggi sulla narrativa latinoamericana. Edited by Angelo Morino. Torino, Italy: Edizioni La Rosa, 197? 328 p., bibl.

Interesting compilation of articles by Italian scholars in Latin American literature who analyze the works of the following writers: Borges, Carpentier, Guimarães Rosa, Onetti, Arguedas, Bioy Casares, Rulfo, Roa Bastos, García Márquez, Fuentes, Vargas Llosa and Puig. [M. Carmagnani]

5070 Uslar-Pietri, Arturo. Breve historia de la novela hispanoamericana. 2. ed. Madrid: Editorial Mediterráneo, 1974. 183 p. (Colección de bolsillo EDIME; 79)

Written in 1954 (see *HLAS 21:3845*), this brief history of the Latin American novel is more interesting for what it reveals about the author of *Las lanzas coloradas* than for its insights into individual works or literary history. The volume should be used as a guide to Uslar's own Latin American library.

5071 Yurkievich, Saúl. La confabulación con la palabra. Madrid: Taurus, 1978. 169 p. (Persiles; 106)

Brief, somewhat frantic short essays on contemporary authors such as Cortázar, Lezama and Dalton.

COLONIAL PERIOD

DANIEL R. REEDY, *Professor of Spanish, University of Kentucky*

AT LONG LAST IT APPEARS that there is a kind of rebirth of interest in the literature of colonial Spanish America. In terms of the number of entries and in the quality of the research, the items which we have included in this listing show a noteworthy contrast with past years. We may speculate that in part the boom of critical interest in the modern Spanish American narrative during recent decades has shifted to the colonial narrative, in particular to the chroniclers: the Inca

Garcilaso, Alvar Núñez, Rodríguez Freile, Poma de Ayala, and others. This is not surprising when we consider the close affinities between the works of some contemporary prose writers and the imaginative narrative of the chroniclers of the 16th and 17th centuries. Also, developments in various disciplines, particularly linguistics and anthropology, offer valuable tools for innovative approaches to the study of colonial literature. Mercedes López-Baralt (item **5090**), Rolena Adorno (items **5072–5075**), and Nathan Wachtel (item **5139**) offer several different interpretations of Guamán Poma de Ayala and his *Nueva corónica y buen gobierno*, for example.

Interest in Sor Juana Inés de la Cruz never declines even if research on her works has been more peripheral than basic. Particularly noteworthy in this listing is Emil Volek's exegesis of Sor Juana's sonnet, "Detente, Sombra de mi Bien Esquivo" (item **5110**), a splendid example of the quality of scholarship deserved by the Monja's poetry. We are also pleased to note the edition of Esteban Terralla Landa's satirical poem, *Lima por dentro y fuera* (item **5121**), by Professor Alan Soons; first published in 1797, it has not been reprinted since 1925.

Undoubtedly, the significant increase in the number of articles on colonial Spanish American literature is largely due to the publication of the papers presented at the XVII Congreso del Instituto Internacional de Literatura Iberoamericana (item **5082**) which met in 1975 at the Universidad Complutense in Madrid. These three volumes contain more than 20 papers on the Baroque in Spanish America, the chief topic of the meeting. We also draw attention to several articles in the *Revista Iberoamericana* (item **5104**), published in an "Homenaje a Irving A. Leonard," distinguished professor, scholar and for 28 years, first contributing editor to this section of *HLAS* (i.e., from vol. 1, 1936, through vol. 26, 1964). Deserving of special attention, as well, is the collection of articles by several distinguished Latin Americanists, *Prosa hispanoamericana virreinal* (item **5099**), edited by Raquel Chang-Rodríguez.

Perhaps the past four to six years have set a trend. We hope that the enhanced quality of research and the increase in productivity during this period point to a resurgence of interest in the field of colonial Spanish American literature which will continue in the future.

INDIVIDUAL FIGURES

5072 Adorno, Rolena. Icon and idea: a symbolic reading of pictures in Peruvian Indian chronicles (The Indian Historian [American Indian Historical Society, San Francisco, Calif.] 12:3, 1979, p. 27–50, ill.)

Detailed description of 23 visual representations from Poma de Ayala's *Nueva corónica*. Author demonstrates that chronicle's iconography communicates a system of symbolic values rather than facts.

5073 ———. Of *caciques*, *coyas*, and kings: the intricacies of point of view (Dispositio [University of Michigan, Department of Romance Languages, Ann Arbor] 4:10, 1979, p. 27–47)

Deals with techniques of point of view through a comparison of selected textual examples from Poma de Ayala's *Nueva corónica*, utilizing both visual and verbal texts. Valuable approach to the topic.

5074 ———. Las otras fuentes de Guamán Poma: sus lecturas castellanas (UAEM/H, 2:2, dic. 1978, p. 137–158)

A general review of the identifiable Spanish sources in Guamán Poma's *Nueva corónica*. Sources, among others, include Las Casas, José de Acosta, and Fray Luis de Granada through Luis Gerónimo de Oré. English version of this article contains six illustrations taken from Adorno's original manuscript: "Felipe Guamán Poma de Ayala: an Andean View of the Peruvian Viceroyalty, 1565–1615" in *Journal de la Société des Americanistes* (Paris, 64, 1978, p. 121–143, ill.).

5075 ———. Paradigms lost: a Peruvian Indian surveys Spanish colonial society (Studies in the Anthropology of Visual Communication [Society for the Anthropology of Visual Communication, Washington] 5:2, Spring 1979, p. 78–96, ill.)

Author contends that Poma de Ayala's *Nueva corónica* provides criticism of Spanish colonialism through the use of the Quechua language and visual texts. Splendid article with numerous illustrations from the chronicle.

5076 **Aguirre, Mirta.** Del encausto a la sangre: Sor Juana Inés de la Cruz. La Habana: Casa de las Américas, 1975. 92 p., bibl. (Cuadernos Casa; 17)

Essentially biographical account of the life of Sor Juana based on her works and other documents, centering on important moments of her life. Contains no new information on the Monja.

5077 **Aquila, August J.** Alonso de Ercilla y Zúñiga: a basic bibliography. London, Grant and Cutler, 1975. 96 p.

A listing of some 480 items in four main sections: 1) editions; 2) translations; 3) other works by Ercilla; and 4) related materials. A useful, basic bibliography which is most welcome. See also item **2816**.

5078 **Carilla, Emilio.** Carrió de la Vandera y Quevedo (QIA, 47/48, 1976/1977, p. 329–335)

Author demonstrates Carrió de la Vandera's indebtedness to Quevedo throughout the *Lazarillo de ciegos caminantes*. Evidence of direct, indirect, and possible influences abound. Quevedo's *romance*, "Boda de Negros," may have been the source of Carrió's pseudonym, Concolorcorvo. Valuable contribution.

5079 **Caudet, Francisco.** Sor Juana Inés de la Cruz: la crisis de 1690 (CAM, 222:1, enero/feb. 1979, p. 135–140)

Suppositions based on the *Respuesta a Sor Filotea* suggest reasons for Sor Juana's silence after 1690 when rebuked by the Bishop of Puebla. Author downplays anti-feminism and anti-intellectualism as reasons for this convent isolation until her death.

5080 **Chang-Rodríguez, Raquel.** Elaboración de fuentes de "Carta Canta" y "Papelito Jabla Lengua" (UK/KRQ, 24:4, 1977, p. 433–439)

A tale from the Inca Garcilaso's *Comentarios reales* is the basis for one of Ricardo Palma's *Tradiciones peruanas* and for a *tradición* by Cuba's Alvaro de la Iglesia. The three works are compared to show the strong ties between different periods of Spanish American literature.

5081 **Chapman, Arnold.** Ercilla y el "Furor de Marte" (CAM, 221:6, nov./dic. 1978, p. 87–97)

Traces the theme of primitive justice through the three Araucanian wars described by Ercilla in the poem. Ercilla sees war as just and unjust, but always fatal for the Araucanians. An excellent article showing an important aspect of the *Araucana*.

5082 **Congreso Internacional de Literatura Iberoamericana,** *17th, Madrid, 1978.* XVII [i.e. Décimo Séptimo] Congreso del Instituto Internacional de Literatura Iberoamericana. v. 1, El barroco en América; v. 2, Literatura hispanoamericana; v. 3, Crítica histórico-literaria hispanoamericana. Madrid: Centro Iberoamericano de Cooperación, Ediciones Cultura Hispánica, 1978. 3 v. (1608 p.) (Continuous pagination) tables.

At its 17th Congress, meeting in Madrid at the Universidad Complutense, March 20–26, 1975, the Instituto Internacional de Literatura Iberoamericana chose as its main topic the Baroque in America. Papers of interest are included in all three volumes:

v. 1: A. Roggiano's "Acerca de Dos Barrocos: el de España y el de América" (p. 39–47) provides a comparison of characteristics of the Baroque in Europe and the New World; J. Durán Luzio's "Reflexión en Torno al Llamado Barroco Americano" (p. 49–56) sees certain characteristics of the Baroque of Spanish America as being distinctive from those of Spain; M. Camurati's "Academias y Fábulas Barrocas" (p. 57–62) describes the literary activities of the Marqués Castell-dos-Rius in the viceregal court of Lima (1709–10); G. Palau de Nemes' "Cuatro Obras Churriguerescas de la Literatura Colonial" (p. 62–70) finds aspects of Churrigueresque style in such writers as Las Casas, Rodríguez Freyle, Domínguez Camargo, Sor Juana; J. Simón Díaz's "Algunas Peculiaridades del Libro Barroco Mejicano" (p. 71–87) examines common characteristics of numerous books appearing in Mexico between 1642–84; A. Gallo's "Elementos Literarios en el Arte Barroco de la Antigua Guatemala" (p. 89–98) compares characteristics of the literary Baroque with the art of La Antigua Guatemala; S. Cro's "La Leyenda de los Césares y la Cultura Barroca" (p. 116–134) traces the topic of the Ciudad de los Césares through numerous chronicles; M. Peña Muñoz "Tres Poetas Criollos en el *Cancionero de Flores de Baria Poesía*" (p. 135–148) describes poems by Francisco de Terrazas, Carlos de Sámano and Martín Cortés contained in a 1577 manuscript from New Spain; A. Labandeira Fernández's "En Torno a la Historicidad de *El Vasauro*" (p. 149–171) investigates the historical authenticity of Pedro de Oña's *El Vasauro*; M.E. Bermúdez's "Juana de Asbaje, Poetisa Barroca Mejicana" (p. 173–186) combines summaries of critical views of others on Sor Juana with biographical details; N.J. Davison's "Primicias de un Análisis de Algunas Obras de Sor Juana a Base de Técnicas de Computadora" (p. 187–206) demonstrates the use of computer analysis in selected works by Sor Juana; R. Valdés-Cruz's "La Visión del Negro en Sor Juana" (p. 207–216) finds the roots of modern Afro-Caribbean poetry in the works of the Tenth Muse; V.G. Williamsen's "La Simetría Bilateral de las Comedias de Sor Juana Inés" (p. 217–228) examines structural symmetry in *Los empeños de una casa* and *Amor es más laberinto*; L. Fox-Lockert's "Comparación de Juan del Valle Caviedes con Sor Juana Inés de la Cruz" (p. 229–238) sketches a comparison between the two 17th-century poets; M. del Rosario Fernández Alonso's "Sor Juana Inés de la Cruz y Esther de Cáceres . . ." (p. 239–256) compares aspects of the personality and works of Sor Juana to those of Uruguayan poet Esther de Cáceres; C. de Zapata's "Dos Poetas de América: Juana de Asbaje y Sara de Ibáñez" (p. 257–267) compares similar attitudes in Sor Juana and Uruguayan poet Sara de Ibáñez; J. Martínez Gómez's "Visión Barroca de la Mujer en Caviedes" (p. 269–280) describes the attitude of the Peruvian poet toward women in several of his poetic works; L.A. Sánchez's "Barroco, Renacentismo, Gongorismo, Culteranismo y su Versión Hispanoamericana: Notas sobre *El Lunarejo*" (p. 281–288) comments on Juan de Espinoza Medrano and some distinguishing characteristics of the Baroque in America; J. Loveluck's "Lectura de un Texto Barroco: Un Romance de Domínguez Camargo" (p. 289–295) analyzes the *romance* "A un salto, por donde se despeña el arroyo de Chillo" by Domínguez Camargo; F. Sánchez-Castaner's "Don Juan de Palafox: Escritor Barroco Hispanoamericano" (p. 298–309) provides remarks on the life and works of Juan de Palafox y Mendoza, Bishop of Puebla; A. Porqueras-Mayo's "La Colección Palafox: Fondos Raros en la Universidad de Illinois" (p. 311–326) presents a detailed description of works in the Library of the Univ. of Illinois on Juan Palafox y Mendoza; S. Gostautas' "Un Escritor Picaresco del Perú Virreinal: Juan Mongrovejo de la Cerda" (p. 327–341) analyzes picaresque aspects of *La endiablada* by J. Mongrovejo y de la Cerda; C. Sáenz de Santa María's "Don Francisco Antonio de Fuentes y Guzmán: Representante del Barroco Literario Guatemalteco y sus Conexiones con el Culteranismo Peninsular" (p. 343–358) describes facets of *La recordación florida* (1690) by Fuentes y Guzmán, Guatemalan author.

v. 2: O. Arróniz's "Consideraciones y Alguna Novedad sobre el Teatro de Evangelización en Nueva España" (p. 1211–1217) provides an historical sketch of religious dramas presented in New Spain from 1533 through the early 18th century.

v. 3: E. Coll's "Lo Real Maravilloso Americano en los Cronistas de Indias" (p. 1327–1335) finds the seeds of Alejo Carpentier's *realismo mágico* in the writings of Columbus, Las Casas, Díaz del Castillo, Cortés, Inca Garcilaso, and others; P. Martínez's "En Busca del Tiempo de los Cronistas de Indias en México" (p. 1337–1343) deals with myths among the Cora and Huichol Indians and comments from the chronicles of Sahagún and Diego Durán; L. Tormo's and S. Woyski's "Los Memoriales a la Justicia Divina, de Alonso de Medina" (p. 1345–1359) gives an historical account and synthesis of several letters from Medina to Pedro de la Gasca on the subject of Divine Justice, written about mid-16th century; R. Chang-Rodríguez's "El *Cautiverio feliz* y la Narrativa Histórico-Literaria en Indias" (p. 1361–1370) analyzes various historical and literary characteristics of Núñez de Pineda y Bascuñán's *Cautiverio feliz*.

5083 Cueva, Agustín. El espejismo heroico de la conquista: ensayo de interpretación de *La araucana* (CDLA, 19:110, sept./oct. 1978, p. 29–40)

Author perceives the *Araucana* as the only example of an authentic heroic conscious growing out of the Conquest. Also includes remarks on Bernal Díaz, Inca Garcilaso, Oña, and Las Casas.

5083a Dauster, Frank. De los recursos cómicos en el teatro de Sor Juana (Caribe [University of Hawaii, Dept. of European Languages and Literatures, Honolulu] 2:2, otoño 1977, p. 43–54)

An excellent study finds in four plays by Sor Juana comic techniques typical of the 17th century, as well as others that seem to anticipate both Pirandello and Brecht. [G. Woodyard]

5084 Fitz, Earl E. Two Baroque poets in colonial Portuguese and Spanish America (INTI, 5/6, 1977, p. 134–150)

Compares major aspects of the poetry of Brazil's Gregório de Matos and Peru's Juan del Valle Caviedes. Special attention is given to Baroque aspects of the satirical, lyrical and sacred verse of these two 17th-century poets.

5085 Hilton, Ronald. El padre Las Casas, el castellano y las lenguas indígenas (CH, 331, enero 1978, p. 123–128)

Las Casas notes lack of interest in indigenous language and attributes it to unconcern about their importance and unawareness of their complexity. The linguistic unity of Spanish today still reflects this lack of concern for Andean Indians who speak little or no Spanish. Of possible interest to the linguist.

5086 Hopkins Rodríguez, Eduardo. Un problema de atribución en literatura colonial peruana: *Demofonte y Filis* o *Telémaco en la isla de Calipso* (UNMSM/L, 48:84/85, 2. semestre, 1976, p. 121–134, tables)

A comparison of two little-known poems, *Demofonte y Filis* by Lorenzo de las Llamosas and Pedro Joseph Bermúdez de la Torre y Solier's *Telémaco en la isla de Calipso*, provides convincing evidence that the former is based on a capricious re-elaboration of the second. Well-documented essay on two late 17th-century texts.

5087 Jara, René. El criollismo de Fray Servando Teresa de Mier (CAM, 221:1, enero/feb. 1979, p. 141–162)

Writings of Fray Servando Teresa de Mier reveal his ideas as a Creole writer of New Spain and pre-independence period. Comments on Las Casas, Sigüenza y Góngora and others as percursors. Of interest to study of subsequent development of *criollismo* in Mexico.

5088 Johnson, Julie Greer. Feminine satire in Concolorcorvo's *El Lazarillo de ciegos caminantes* (South Atlantic Bulletin [South Atlantic Modern Language Association, Chapel Hill, North Carolina] 45:1, Jan. 1980, p. 11–20)

Carrió de la Vandera's 18th-century description of his journey from Buenos Aires to Lima contains repeated instances of satire and criticism of women, including his own mother—in a uniformly uncomplimentary view. A well-documented study.

5089 Lagmanovich, David. Los *Naufragios* de Alvar Núñez como construcción narrativa (UK/KRQ, 25:1, 1978, p. 27–37)

In the episodic nature of the *Naufragios* by Alvar Núñez Cabeza de Vaca, the author finds a number of *relatos* which show close affinities with contemporary works. A noteworthy tension between the historical and literary aspects of the narrative is seen.

5090 López-Baralt, Mercedes. Guamán Poma de Ayala y el arte de la memoria en una crónica ilustrada del siglo XVII (CAM, 224:3, mayo/junio 1979, p. 119–151)

A splendid article which examines the relationship between the verbal and the visual texts in Guamán Poma's *Primer nueva corónica y buen gobierno*. The value of this piece is enhanced by several sketches from the chronicle and some 50 bibliographical entries.

5091 Magallanes, Manuel Vicente. La provincia de Coro en las elegías de Juan de Castellanos (CONAC/RNC, 39:233, sept./dic. 1977, p. 29–64)

An examination of various parts of Castellanos' *Elegías de varones ilustres de Indias* (1589) which deal with the coastal Venezuelan province of Coro. Of limited interest.

5092 Millán, María del Carmen. Sor Juana Inés de la Cruz. Toluca: Gobierno del Estado de México, Dirección del Patrimonio Cultural, 1976. 18 p., 2 leaves of plates: ill. (Testimonios del Estado de México)

Printed text of an oral presentation read at Nepantla to commemorate the 324th anniversary of the birth of the Tenth Muse. Of scant value.

5093 Montes Huidobro, Matías. La reacción antijerárquica en el teatro cubano colonial (CH, 334, 1978, p. 5–19)

Examines two representative plays of the colonial period, *El becerro de oro* and *Mefistófeles*, and finds a reactionary force against the musical, dramatic, and operatic world in which Cuban theatrical life was developing.

5094 Noreña, Carlos. Francisco de Vitoria, America, and the empire (UA/REH, 12:1, enero 1978, p. 71–89)

Author finds the writings of Francisco de Vitoria (1492–1545), Salamanca professor of moral theology, to be incomplete, historically naive and biased, but most influential in determining the foundations of modern colonialism as set up by Spain. Of value for study of ideas in early New World culture.

5095 Núñez C., Javier. Un impreso desconocido de Espinosa Medrano (FENIX, 24/25, 1977, p. 5–11)

Description of the content and significance of a "Censura" by Espinosa Medrano of a sermon by his teacher in Cuzco, D. Alonso Bravo de Paredes (20 April 1669). The original document, a copy of which is reproduced, is in the Biblioteca Nacional de Madrid. Of interest to the specialist.

Ortega, Julio. La cultura peruana: experiencia y conciencia. See item **5436**.

5096 Ortiz, Fernando. La "Leyenda Negra" contra Fray Bartolomé (CAM, 217:2, marzo/abril 1978, p. 84–116)

The Black Legend against Las Casas is the accusation that he supported slavery, introduced it in America, and was a racist. Author argues that Las Casas was the "apóstol" not only of the Indian but also of the black in the New World.

5097 Pardo, Isaac J. La ventana de Don Silverio. Caracas: Monte Avila Editores, 1978. 172 p. (Colección Temas venezolanos)

Volume contains previously published essays from journals and newspapers on works of Juan de Castellanos and on the influence of Old Spanish ballads on popular Venezuelan lyrics. Of varied interest.

5098 Pascual Buxó, José. Muerte y desengaño en la poesía novohispana: siglos XVI y XVII. México: Universidad Nacional Autónoma de México, Instituto de Investigaciones Filológicas, Centro de Estudios Literarios, 1975. 164 p., bibl., ill. (Textos y estudios; 2. Letras del XVI al XVIII)

Introductory essay examines the themes of *muerte* and *desengaño* in selected poets of the 16th and 17th centuries with special attention to several pieces by Luis de Sandoval Zapata. Documents section contains a long *romance*, 30 sonnets and two *décimas* by this 16th-century poet of New Spain.

5099 Prosa hispanoamericana virreinal. Edición, presentación y bibliografía de Raquel Chang-Rodríguez. Barcelona, Borrás Ediciones, 1978. 175 p.

Editor's introductory essay discusses major prose writers of viceregal Spanish America, pointing out significant critical attention in the past. Volume contains essays by: E. Pupo-Walker on the *Comentarios reales*; R. Chang-Rodríguez on *La endiablada*, a 17th-century Peruvian tale; J.J. Arrom on a *relato* contained in the chronicle (1657) authored by Fray Agustín de la Calancha and Fray Bernardo de Torres in Lima; A. Roggiano on Juan de Espinosa Medrano; L. Leal on the *Cautiverio feliz*; and a listing of Spanish-American colonial manuscripts in the Hispanic Society of America by T.J. Beardsley, Jr. Completing the tome is a bibliography of some 250 entries on Spanish-American colonial prose by the editor. A valuable contribution to the field.

5100 Puccini, Darío. Elementos de narración novelesca en *La florida* del Inca Garcilaso (CONAC/RNC, 40:240, enero/feb. 1979, p. 26–47, illus.)

An excellent article which defines novelesque narrative features of the Inca Garcilaso's *La florida*. Author sees *La florida* as perhaps the first appearance of a mannerist and pre-Baroque style in a work whose purpose and achievement is essentially historical. Clearly developed and convincing.

5101 Pupo-Walker, Enrique. La reconstrucción imaginativa del pasado en *El carnero* de Rodríguez Freyle (CM/NRFH, 27:2, 1978, p. 346–358)

Treats multiple aspects of *El carnero* with a lengthy discussion of the intercalated *relato*, "Un Negocio con Juana García," which shows close relationships with works of several literary predecessors (i.e., *Conde Lucanor, Libro de los engaños, La Celestina,* and Cervantes). Excellent, well-written study.

5102 ———. Sobre la configuración narrativa de los *Comentarios reales* (HIUS/R, 39:3, 1976/1977, p. 123–135)

An examination of the imaginative content and autobiographical nature of the *Comentarios,* owing to the episodic narrative organized around the Inca's personal experiences. Excellent article with ample documentation to support the author's assertions.

5103 Reedy, Daniel R. The writer as seer: Baroque views of natural phenomena in the New World (South Atlantic Bulletin [South Atlantic Modern Language Association, Chapel Hill, North Carolina] 43:4, Nov. 1978, p. 85–93)

Article focuses on Carlos de Sigüenza y Góngora's *Libra astronómica y filosófica* (1690) and his learned debate with Fray Eusebio Kino about the significance of natural phenomena. The debate marks a period of transition between the conflict of ideas from the Middle Ages and modern, scientific thought. Peripheral remarks on Sor Juana and Juan del Valle Caviedes.

5104 *Revista Iberoamericana.* University of Pittsburgh *for the* Instituto Internacional de Literatura Iberoamericana. Vol. 44, Nos. 104/105, julio/dic. 1978– . Pittsburgh, Pa.

Issue in honor of Irving A. Leonard who served as Contributing Editor for this section of *HLAS* from 1936 to 1964. The articles which contain information of interest on colonial Spanish-American writers and works are: Juan Adolfo Vásquez's "El Campo de las Literaturas Indígenas Latinoamericanas" (p. 313–349) lists numerous documents and sources on language, literature, religion, art of indigenous Latin America from pre-hispanic times to the present; Juan Durán Luzio's "Lo Profético como Estilo en la *Brevísima relación de la destrucción de Indias* de Bartolomé de las Casas" (p. 351–367) finds parallels between the prophetic voice and style of the Biblical Jeremiah as a model for Las Casas; José Juan Arrom's "Precursores Coloniales de la Narrativa Hispanoamericana: José de Acosta o la Ficción como Biografía" (p. 369–383) discusses José de Acosta's *Peregrinación de Bartolomé Lorenzo* as a narrative model for fictionalized biography of subsequent centuries; Enrique Pupo-Walker's "*Los comentarios reales* y la Historicidad de lo Imaginario" (p. 385–407) examines the motivating factors which produced the imaginative dimension of the Inca Garcilaso's *Comentarios,* and hence their literary qualities; Raquel Chang-Rodríguez's "Relectura de *Los empeños de una casa*" (p. 409–419) analyzes the relationship of Sor Juana's dramatic piece to its social and biographical context; Rafael Catala's "La Trascendencia en *Primero Sueño*: el Incesto y el Aguila" (p. 421–434) presents a Jungian analysis of the myth of incest and symbol of the eagle in the *Sueño* as signs of transcendence; Emilio Carilla's "Solórzano Pereira: Defensor de los Pobres" (p. 435–449) deals with the *Política Indiana* (1647) and Solórzano Pereira's defense of *criollos* in the New World; Luis Monguió's "Palabras e Ideas: 'Patria' y 'Nación' en el Virreinato del Perú" (p. 451–470) treats the concepts of *patria* and *nación* in the Inca Garcilaso, Peralta Barnuevo, *Mercurio peruano,* Túpac Amaru, and other sources; Julio Ortega's "El Inca Garcilaso y el Discurso de la Cultura" (p. 507–514) deals with the relationship of discourse to culture in the *Comentarios reales*; Julio Durán-Cerda's "Arauco domado: Poema Manierista" (p. 515–525) examines Oña's epic poem as a pre-Baroque work according to the percepts established by Helmut Hatzfeld; Raimundo Lida's and Emma Speratti's "Lacunza en México" (p. 527–533) deals with the *Venida del Mesías en gloria y majestad* (1790) by the Jesuit Manuel Lacunza (1731–1801) who wrote under the pseudonym of Juan Josafat Ben-Ezra; and William C. Bryant's "*La Relación de un ciego*: Pieza Dramática de la Epoca Colonial" (p. 569–575) presents the text of a short dramatic piece, by an unknown author, discovered in the Biblioteca Nacional de México.

5105 Robledo, Tey Diana. La poesía náhuatl de Machilxóchitl (RIB, 28:3, 1978, p. 283–289)

Analysis of fragments of náhuatl poetry by the only known female poet of Mexico-Tenochtitlan. Poem describes a single event in a particular military campaign around 1475.

5106 Rodríguez, Alfonso. El engaño: motivo estructurador en el *Popol Vuh* (CAM, 226:5, sept./oct. 1979, p. 192–209)

Studies the structure of the *Popol Vuh* following the structuralist theories of Roland Barthes. The *engaño* is seen as the essential paradigmatic unity of indigenous myths in general and of the *Popol Vuh* in particular. An innovative approach to an important text.

5107 Romero, Mario Germán. Aspectos literarios de la obra de don Juan de Castellanos. Palabras preliminares de Isaac J. Pardo. Bogotá: Editorial Kelly, 1978. 399 p., 3 leaves of plates: ill.

Single volume edition of studies published earlier as separate chapters in Bogota's *Boletín Cultural y Bibliográfico* (1965–68). Essays devoted to diverse aspects of Castellano's *Elegías*, in particular the stylistic and lexical peculiarities of the poems.

5108 Sáenz de Santa María, Carmelo. Aspectos literarios de la "Recordación Florida" del capitán guatemalteco Don Francisco Antonio de Fuentes y Guzmán (IGFO/RI, 37:147/148, enero/junio 1977, p. 309–328)

Contains comments on the life and works of Francisco Antonio de Fuentes y Guzmán (1642–99) and his principal chronicle, *Recordación florida*, an historical piece on the socio-cultural reality of 17th-century Guatemala. Valuable documentation in addition to the remarks.

Simmons, Merle E. Literary folklore in the *Historia verdadera* of Bernal Díaz del Castillo. See item **1003**.

5109 Torre Vilar, Ernesto de la. Autógrafos desconocidos de Sor Juana Inés de la Cruz en un libro de su biblioteca (*in* Les cultures ibériques en devenir: essais publiés en hommage à la memoire de Marcel Bataillon, 1895–1977. Paris: Fondation Singer-Polignac, 1979, p. 503–512)

Registra tres autógrafos de Sor Juana en los vols. 2/3 de las Obras del carmelita español Fray Juan de Jesús María (Colonia, 1622). Con éste son ya 133 los libros identificados de la biblioteca de la monja poetisa, 100 de ellos en latin. [L.G. Canedo]

5110 Volek, Emil. Un soneto de Sor Juana Inés de la Cruz "Detente, Sombra de mi Bien Esquivo" (CAM, 228:2, marzo/abril 1979, p. 196–211)

An exegesis of one of Sor Juana's most famous sonnets. Author demonstrates mystic overtones of poem through the textual labyrinth based on the anagram "Amor Iesu Nobiscum A(men)." Splendid example of type of scholarship the works of the Tenth Muse deserve.

5111 Williamsen, Vern G. Forma simétrica en las comedias barrocas de Sor Juana Inés (CAM, 224:3, mayo/junio 1979, p. 183–193)

Through an analysis of Sor Juana's *Los empeños de una casa* and *Amor es más laberinto*, the author finds that the dramatist uses specific actions and poetry to emphasize the aesthetic center of her works. Actions leading up to and following these scenes are symmetrically parallel, the one to the other, thus reinforcing the artistic concept inherent in the Baroque aesthetic.

5112 Wilson, S.R. The form of discovery: the Columbus letters announcing the finding of America (Revista Canadiense de Estudios Hispánicos [University of Toronto] 2:2, invierno 1978, p. 154–168)

Columbus' first letter (March 1493), as a literary piece, captures the essence of America by providing touches of fantasy to the reality which he had seen—a kind of narrative chronicle which interprets the aura of the New World.

5113 Zavala, Silvio. La monarquía del mundo según Guamán Poma de Ayala (CAM, 218:3, mayo/junio 1978, p. 119–125)

In his *Nueva corónica y buen gobierno*, Poma de Ayala treats the idea of sovereignty which passed from the Incas to the conquering Spaniards. His work reflects the colonial Indian society in which he wrote.

TEXTS

5114 Baudot, Georges. Un *huehuetlatolli* desconocido en la Biblioteca Nacional de México (UTIEH/C, 33, 1979, p. 5–18)

Presents the text of a precolumbian *huehuetlatolli* in the original Nahuatl and Spanish version. The text was probably recorded in the 16th century by a Franciscan, Fray Juan de Gaona. Text is modeled on a kind of dialogue or chat between an older leader and a young chief. Text seems to be one of the few authentic examples of its genre.

5114a Cabrera y Quintero, Cayetano Javier de. Obra dramática. Teatro novohispano del siglo XVIII. Edición crítica, introducción y notas de Claudia Parodi. México: UNAM, Instituto de Investigaciones Filológicas, Centro de Lingüística Hispánica, 1976. 257 p. (Nueva Biblioteca Mexicana, 42)

Edition of *El iris de Salamanca* plus a dozen lesser playlets by an 18th-century Mexican humanist and playwright. In a technique derivative of Calderón, the verse play exalts San Juan Sahagún through the theme of vengeance. A handsome edition with extensive introduction and supporting documentation. [G. Woodyard]

5115 Coplas a la muerte de don Diego de Almagro, primer gobernador de la Nueva Toledo. Introducción, transcripción paleográfica y notas de Juan Siles Guevara. La Paz: Instituto Boliviano de Cultura, 1975 [i.e. 1976]. 37 p., bibl., facsims. (Clásicos bolivianos; 3)

First known poem of Bolivian literature in praise of Diego de Almagro, written around 1539–40 by someone close to Almagro, with a prose introduction composed sometime after mid-century. Poem consists of 312 lines of *verso de arte mayor*, divided in octaves. Perhaps more valuable for historical content than for artistic qualities.

5116 Cortés, Hernando. Fernando [sic] Cortés: his five Letters of Relations to the Emperor Charles V. Translated and edited, with a biographical introduction and notes compiled from original sources by Francis Augustus MacNutt. Glorieta, New Mexico: Río Grande Press, 1977. 2 v. (354, 374 p.) appendixes, index.

Reprint of the first edition published in 1908. Vol. 1 contains John Greenway's "Introduction to an Age of Conquest" (p. 11–104) and includes an updated bibliography. The text by MacNutt consists of preface, biographical note (p. 1–119), and the translated texts of Cortés' five letters. Profuse notes, illustrations and appendixes enhance the value of the translation.

5116a Los dos primeros poetas coloniales ecuatorianos, Antonio Bastidas y Jacinto de Evia. Quito: Casa de la Cultura Ecuatoriana, 1975. 267 p.: facsim. (Colección básica de escritores ecuatorianos; 1)

Poesía a menudo imitativa y de méritos dispares, pero que ilustra bien un capítulo de la literatura colonial: la extendida influencia de Góngora en América. La edición es algo imprecisa en el registro de los datos de procedencia de los textos. Las informaciones y notas son mínimas, y aunque el carácter de la serie en que aparece explica estas ligerezas, ellas reducen también el interés de la publicación. [Pedro Lastra]

5117 Ercilla y Zúniga, Alonso de. La araucana. Estudio preliminar de Eduardo Solar Correa. Edición completa preparada por Olivo Lazzarin Dante. Buenos Aires, Editorial Francisco de Aguirre, 1977. 618 p. (Colección Reino de Chile, 6)

A new edition of *La araucana* based on Toribio Medina's text prepared early in this century. The preliminary study contains comments on the poem and Ercilla. Various illustrations and an index enhance the text. A reliable, accessible edition.

5118 Rodríguez Fresle [i.e. **Freyle**], **Juan.** El carnero. Con notas explicativas de Miguel Aguilera. Medellín: Editorial Bedout, 1976. 376 p., bibl. (Bolsilibros Bedout; 23)

General introduction with biographical information on Rodríguez Fresle [Freyle] and critical commentaries on the text precede the modernized text of *El carnero*. A reliable popular edition of this important work.

5119 Sahagún, Bernardino de. The war of conquest: how it was waged in Mexico. Translation by Arthur J.O. Anderson and Charles E. Dibble. Salt Lake City: University of Utah Press, 1978. 94 p., ill.

The first complete English translation of the Florentine Codex of Sahagún's *Historia de las cosas de Nueva España* (1569), a treasure of information on the history, religion, customs, literature and folklore of the time. Profusely illustrated with a very readable translation and explanatory notes.

5120 Solís y Valenzuela, Pedro de. El desierto prodigioso y prodigio del desierto. Edición de Rubén Páez Patiño. Introducción, estudios y notas de Jorge Páramo Pomareda, Manuel Briceño Jáuregui, and Rubén Páez Patiño. Bogotá: Instituto Caro y Cuervo, 1977. v. 1, bibl., ill. (Publicaciones del Instituto Caro y Cuervo; 45)

Edition of an unpublished 17th-century prose text, written by Pedro de Solís y Valenzuela (1624–1711). Contains several interrelated tales concerning the activities and adventures of three young men. Some *relatos* are historically based; others are novelesque. Bits of poetry and ascetic meditations are also inserted. The work was composed about 1647. Vol. 1 contains a lengthy bibliographical introduction and parts 1–11 of the text.

5120a Teatro en Honduras. Edición de Alma Caballero and Francisco Salvador. Tegucigalpa: Secretaría de Cultura, Turismo e Información, Depto. de Producción Intelectual, 1977. 103 p., plates.

Anthology of three anonymous Honduran plays (or fragments) of the colonial period: *Baile de las tiras o de las cintas: Tragedia del suplicio de San Sebastián; Coloquio de Doña Garbosa y Monzón.* Preceded by a concise overview of Honduran theatre history, with the accurate disclaimer that these are not the best plays but are collected here to stimulate further study and research on Honduran theatre.

5121 Terralla Landa, Esteban. Lima por dentro y fuera. Edited by Alan Soons. Exeter, U.K.: University of Exeter, 1978. 103 p. (Exeter Hispanic texts)

An important edition of a neglected work of colonial Peru. Andalusian-born Terralla Landa's *Lima por dentro y fuera* first appeared in 1797 and was last reprinted in 1925. The text reproduces the 1798 Madrid ed. It is preceded by a brief introduction and contains notes on variants, vocabulary, etc. The satirical nature of the poem provides interest for the literary scholar and historian as well.

5122 Tres piezas teatrales del Virreinato. Edición y prólogos de José Rojas Garcidueñas y José Juan Arrom. México: Instituto de Investigaciones Estéticas, Universidad Nacional Autónoma de México, 1976. 379 p., bibl. (Estudios de literatura; 3)

Three viceregal plays of New Spain published in a modern edition: *Tragedia del triunfo de los santos* (published 1578 and 1941); *Coloquio de los cuatro últimos reyes de Tlaxcala* (1935); *Comedia de San Francisco de Borja* (1641). Each piece is preceded by a valuable study of some length. A valuable contribution.

MISCELLANEOUS

Abellán, José Luis. Los orígenes españoles del mito del "buen salvaje:" Fray Bartolomé de Las Casas y su antropología utópica. See item **1825**.

5123 Antelo, Antonio. Literatura y sociedad en la América española del siglo XVI: notas para su estudio. Bogotá: Instituto Caro y Cuervo, 1973. 52 p., bibl.

Very general notes on the social context of the literary production in the New World during the 16th century. Of limited interest.

5123a Arrom, José Juan. Cambiantes imágenes de la mujer en el teatro de la América virreinal (UK/LATR, 12:1, Fall 1978, p. 5–15)

In studying various colonial plays, Arrom finds a slow but steady progress in the movement toward greater acceptance of women's rights and equality. [G. Woodyard]

———. Esquema generacional de las letras hispanoamericanas: ensayo de un método. See item **5003**.

5123b Arróniz, Othón. Teatro de evangelización en Nueva España. México: UNAM, 1979. 255 p.

To the already considerable literature on 16th-century Mexican theatre, this new book adds a play by Juan de Cigorondo and glosses the information earlier available on the catequizing theatre of the Franciscans, Dominicans, and Jesuits. [G. Woodyard]

5124 Banks, Russell. The New World (Ploughshares [A journal of the arts. Massachusetts Council on the Arts, Cambridge, Mass.] 3:2, 1976, p. 8–25)

Interweavings of fact with fiction to make an entertaining piece about Bernardo de Balbuena and life in Jamaica in the 17th century. Good reading but of no scholarly importance.

5125 Beutler, Gisela. Estudios sobre el Romancero Español en Colombia: en su tradición escrita y oral desde la época de la conquista hasta la actualidad. Bogotá: Instituto Caro y Cuervo, 1977. 613 p., bibl., music, plates (Publicación; 44)

Spanish translation of an earlier edition in German. An exhaustive study of the Spanish Romancero in Colombia in both written and oral tradition. Chaps. 1/3 deal with periods from the Conquest through the 18th century. Bibliography includes general as well as manuscript sources. An excellent resource book. For folklorist's comment, see item **1228**.

5126 Beyond the codices: the Nahua view of colonial Mexico. Translated and edited by Arthur J.O. Anderson, Frances Berdan, and James Lockhart. Linguistic essay by Ronald W. Langacker. Berkeley: University of California Press, 1976. 235 p., bibl., 16 leaves of plates: facsims. (UCLA Latin American studies series; 27)

Primarily of historical, anthropological and linguistic significance, these texts (wills and other documents) offer information on the cultural context of use to the literary historian of colonial Mexico. Nahuatl and Spanish texts are reproduced.

5127 Brundage, Burr Cartwright. The fifth sun: Aztec gods, Aztec world. Illustrated by Roy E. Anderson. Austin: University of Texas Press, 1979. 269 p., bibl., index (The Texas Pan American series)

Treats a variety of important subjects related to Aztec religion and religious organization. Major chapters deal with important gods—Tezcatlipoca, Quetzalcoatl, Huitzilopochtli—and goddesses. Volume serves as a kind of reference work with information for the research and interests of a wide variety of scholars. An excellent source book for critics of colonial and modern Mexican letters.

5128 Chang-Rodríguez, Raquel. Tapadas limeñas en un cancionerillo peruano del siglo XVII (IILI/RI, 28:1, enero/marzo 1978, p. 57–62)

Reproduces three poems (two sonnets and a *romance*) from the library of Juan de Solórzano Pereira (1575–1655) dealing with the "tapada" in Lima. Preliminary pages treat the background of the custom (i.e., of women covering their faces so that only one eye showed). Valuable note of cultural significance.

5129 Cúneo, Dardo. Esquema sobre el barroco (Zona Franca [Editorial Trazón, Caracas] 3, sept./oct. 1977, p. 41–43)

Author sees three primary sources of the Baroque aesthetic in Spanish America growing out of the indigenous/mestizo world, the popularized Baroque, and the Creole rebellion characterized by Sor Juana. Schematic article is primarily theoretical.

Durán Luzio, Juan. Creación y utopía: letras de Hispanoamérica. See item **5024**.

5130 González del Bosque, Hernán. Teatro inca: la escena enraizada (CH, 328, 1977, p. 116–130)

A succinct overview of the characteristics of the theater in Peru's Inca period, with attention to points of reference in rituals, dances, etc. Sources include the Inca Garcilaso, Guamán Poma de Ayala and others.

5131 ———. Teatro ritual americano: *El cautivo cristiano* (CH, 347, mayo 1979, p. 442–451)

Analysis of a ritualistic, one-act play, written in allegorical language on the baptismal sacrament. The play, presented usually in Northern Chile, deals with the confrontation between a Moorish king and Christian prince. Text involves several ritualistic scenes and dances.

Henry, Inés D. Romances y canciones populares en la primera década del siglo XVII en Chile. See item **1216**.

5132 Lavallé, Bernard. Les Péruviens à la recherche de leur XVIIIe siècle (UB/BH, 81:1/2, janvier/juin 1979, p. 173–179)

Reviews the extensive attention of recent books to aspects of Peruvian culture in the 18th-century. Of general interest, but with valuable sources for an understanding of the period historically and culturally.

5133 León, Julio A. Los cabildos afrocubanos y su poesía (Explicación de Textos Literarios [California State University, Department of Spanish and Portuguese, Sacramento] 7:2, 1978/1979, p. 171–176)

Figures of the Black Poetry Movement in Cuba (Ballagas, Guillén and others) were not inventing an essentially African point of view; rather, the African social and cultural tradition had been passed down from the Afro-Cuban *cabildos* by oral tradition. Contains excerpts of several poems and a brief glossary of Afro-Cuban works.

5134 Mohler, Stephen C. Publishing in colonial Spanish America: an overview (RIB, 28:3, 1978, p. 259–273)

Discussion of factors limiting the development of colonial Spanish American letters with particular attention to laws on printing and publishing. Contains a chronology and summary of laws from 1480–1814. An excellent article.

5135 Montejano y Aguiñaga, Rafael. Síntesis históricas de las letras potosinas

(*in* Bibliografía de los escritores de San Luis Potosí. México: UNAM, Instituto de Investigaciones Bibliográficas, 1978, p. 21–76)

Bibliographical data on major writers from San Luis Potosí during the period 1550–1821 (p. 30–50). Of interest to the bibliophile.

5136 Osuna, Rafael. Cuestiones de onomatología americana en los cronistas de Indias. Bogotá: Instituto Caro y Cuervo, 1973. 113 p. (Publicación series menor; 17)

A worthwhile piece of collateral material dealing with toponymics in the New World. Sources for information are more than 20 early chronicles and natural histories.

5137 Péano, Pierre. L'activité littéraire des Franciscains du Mexique, XVIe-XIXe siècles (AFH, 71, ian./iun. 1978, p. 168–184)

An extensive list of manuscripts and published works by Franciscans in Mexico from the 16th to 19th centuries. Most are on theological topics. Primarily of historical interest.

5138 Serralta, Frédéric. La biblioteca de Antonio de Solís (UTIEH/C, 33, 1979, p. 103–132)

An inventory of the library of Antonio de Solís y Ribadeneyra, chronicler and author of the *Historia de la conquista de Méjico* at the time of his death in 1686. Of special interest to bibliographers and persons in Golden Age culture.

5139 Wachtel, Nathan. The vision of the vanquished: the Spanish conquest of Peru through Indian eyes, 1530–1570. Translated by Ben and Siân Reynolds. New York: Barnes and Noble, 1977. 328 p., bibl., index, 12 leaves of plates: ill.

A translation of Wachtel's *La vision des vaincus* (1971, see *HLAS 34:1235*). Examines evidence of the annihilation of belief among the Indians after the Conquest. Of particular literary interest is pt. 2 of the book which examines the Indian dance-drama tradition in which Indian attitudes toward the conquerors are revealed. Important views of value for study of the early chronicles and drama.

PROSE FICTION and Other Prose Writings: 19th Century

NICOLAS SHUMWAY, *Assistant Professor of Spanish, Yale University*

WITH THIS SECTION, THE *HLAS* inaugurates a new division to accommodate growing interest in the literature of the past century and the influence of the Modernist movement on the prose fiction of the period. The creation of a new section suggests that works in these areas have been overlooked in the past. As a result, the editors will greatly appreciate information on significant studies of 19th-century prose fiction and other prose writings from recent years which have not been cited in the *Handbook*. All 19th-century poetry and drama will continue to be annotated in the respective POETRY (p. 563) and DRAMA (p. 606) sections of this volume.

During this biennium, Cuba has unquestionably led the way in republishing important, frequently scarce 19th-century works and in interpreting its heritage from the past century. Notable from Cuba are several anthologies of 19th-century poetry and drama, but particularly interesting are several studies on the abolitionist novel *Cecilia Valdés* (see items **5158** and **5163**) and an excellent book by Enrique Sosa, *La economía en la novela cubana del siglo XIX* (item **5165**) which should prove as useful to literary scholars as to historians. Also from Cuba comes a superb anthology of critical essays entitled *Recopilación de textos sobre la novela romántica latinoamericana* (item **5162**) by some of the foremost critics of the genre.

In other parts of Spanish America, several novels which have long been out of print were republished, namely, Julián Martel's *La Bolsa* (item **5143**), Vicente Grez's *Marianita* (item **5141**) and José Manuel Marroquín's *Entre primos* (item **5142**).

As for critical works aside from the *Recopilación de textos* (item **5162**) mentioned earlier, Noé Jitrik in his *Contradicciones del modernismo* (item **5862**) has written a challenging reexamination of Modernism and its principal spokesman, Rubén Darío, using as a theoretical framework many of the most recent ideas from European criticism. Also interesting are several articles and prologues which reexamine the difficult division between the early *cuentos* and the *cuadros de costumbres*, especially Enrique Pupo Walker's "El Cuadro de Costumbres, el Cuento y las Posibilidades de un Deslinde" (item **5161**).

The biennium also saw several successful attempts to reinterpret popular culture. Two anthologies are useful in this regard, namely *Narradores colombianos del siglo XIX* (item **5144**) which includes sketches and articles gleaned from the pages of popular newspapers and magazines from the last century, and another entitled *Fray Mocho desconocido* (item **5156**) which includes a large number of uncollected pieces plus an exceptionally fine introductory essay. Another excellent look at popular literature of the period is found in Angela B. Dellapiane's article "Los Folletines Gauchescos de Eduardo Gutiérrez" (item **5155**).

PROSE FICTION

5140 Armas y Céspedes, José de. Frasquito. Prólogo de Isaac Barreal. La Habana: Editorial de Arte y Literatura, 1976. 291 p.; bibl. (Ediciones Huracán)

Although published in 1894, this novel was written 30 years earlier, and was based on still earlier (1826) historical events; that is, the Venezuelan and Mexican inspired conspiracies against Spanish rule in Cuba, leading to the execution of Sánchez and Agüero in Puerto Príncipe. The novel is a name repository of the upper classes, including a brief appearance of Gertrudis Gómez de Avellaneda as a child, and is full of "cuadros de costumbres." [Carlos J. Cano]

Blasi, Alberto. Ricardo Güiraldes y la revista *Proa*. See item **5008**.

5141 Grez, Vicente. Marianita. Prólogo de José Promis Ojeda. Santiago: Editorial Nascimento, 1976. 200 p. (Biblioteca popular nascimento)

A recent edition of the last of Grez's novels. The prologue argues that this 1885 novel represents a transition point between Romanticism and Naturalism—a thesis supported by pointing to the novel's lack of moral purpose, Grez's tendency to associate the term "romantic" with old-fashioned, and his apparent interest in psychological and environmental determinism as opposed to fate.

Lecturas dominicanas. See item **5305**.

5142 Marroquín, José Manuel. Entre primos. Edición, glosario, y estudio por Cecilia Hernández de Mendoza. Bogotá: Instituto Caro y Cuervo, 1978. 500 p., 3 leaves of plates (1 fold) (Biblioteca colombiana; 14)

This quite sumptuous volume contains not only the complete text of Marroquín's sentimental novel but also one of the oddest attempts at literary criticism we are likely to see in a single lifetime. As well as providing us with several minutely boring reconstructions of Marroquín's quite simple plot, Ms. Hernández de Mendoza also computes the number of paragraphs dedicated to "*narración pura*," "*estilo directo*," and "*estilo indirecto*," descriptions of animals, of people, of *costumbres* and any one of a number of things. She then adds them up and proudly offers us the grand total. That she had the time to churn out 209 p. of this stuff is certainly less remarkable than the fact that the Instituto Caro y Cuervo had the money to publish it.

5143 Miró, José María [*pseud. for* **Julián Martel**]. *La bolsa* y "La Diputación de Alberto." Resúmenes históricos, biográficos y literarios, notas explicativas, bibliografía, juicios sobre el autor y sus obras y temas de estudio por Luis R. Lescano. Buenos Aires: Editorial Plus Ultra, 1975. 302 p. (Colección Clásicos hispanoamericanos; 20)

Another in the "Clásicos hispanoamericanos" series which has already reissued several important 19th-century works. The first work in the volume, Julián Martel's historically significant if artistically flawed novel *La bolsa* portrays the dog-eat-dog world of the Buenos Aires stockmarket in an interesting combination of Zola thematics and modernist sensibilities. The short story "La Diputación de Alberto" tells the tale of an honorable youth who is corrupted through ambition and the favors of a frustrated woman who hates her aging millionaire husband and eventually lands a lucrative government post for her young lover. The latter definitively proves that interesting ideas are not sufficient to make good stories, particularly when they do not seem to have anything to do with each other. Good introductory essay by Luis R. Lescano.

5144 **Narradores colombianos** del siglo XIX. Selección de Henry Luque Muñoz. Bogotá: Instituto Colombiano de Cultura, 1976. 643 p., bibl. (Biblioteca básica colombiana)

A large anthology of representative Colombian prose writers from the last century, most of whom are little known but worth knowing. An intelligent, short prologue provides essential background information, complete with descriptions of magazines and literary salons. The selections range from romantic sketches to humorous anecdotes to pious reflections on the Eternal Verities. A good sampling of 19th-century literary tastes, racial attitudes and social preoccupations. Short bibliography.

5145 **Noveletas cubanas.** Prólogo de Imeldo Alvarez García. La Habana: Editorial de Arte y Literatura, 1977. 524 p. (Ediciones Huracán)

Welcome collection of seven 19th-century Cuban novelettes, many of them out of print and difficult to obtain. They are useful in that they complete the historical and literary picture of the late Cuban colonial period. Works included are: Pedro José Morillas' *El rancheador*; Ramón de Palma's *El cólera en La Habana*; Cirilo Villaverde's *El guajiro*; José A. Echeverría's *Antonelli*; Francisco Calcagno's *Romualdo: uno de tantos*; Esteban Borrero Echeverría's *Aventura de las hormigas*; and Ramón Meza's *El duelo de mi vecino*. [Carlos J. Cano]

ESSAYS, ARTICLES, DIARIES, AND OTHER PROSE WRITINGS

Bello, Andrés. Caracas en el epistolario de Bello. See item **3008**.

5146 **Blanco Fombona, Rufino.** Rufino Blanco Fombona íntimo. Selección y prólogo de Angel Rama. Caracas: Monte Avila Editores, 1975. 327 p. (Colección Temas venezolanos)

A generous sampling from Blanco Fombona's three autobiographical books. The prologue provides a cursory look at the diaries' origins, the diary as a literary genre and several of Blanco Fombona's most important themes. The selections offer a useful glimpse of Blanco Fombona's life, attitudes and times, and are particularly interesting for their portrayal of the tawdry underside of Modernism. Mr. Rama justifies the book's lack of documentation and critical commentary by claiming that it is for "divulgación al gran público."

5147 **Costumbristas de América Latina.** Antología. Introducción, selección y notas preliminares de Susana Zanetti. Buenos Aires: Centro Editor de América Latina, 1973. 162 p. (Biblioteca fundamental del hombre moderno; 103)

A delightful collection of articles by 19th-century *costumbristas*, many of whom are little known. The introduction ambitiously presents a continental panorama of the *costumbristas* while resurrecting the debatable theory that the Spanish American short story derives from the *artículos de costumbre*.

5148 **Garrido, Miguel Angel.** Páginas de Miguel Angel Garrido. Edición de Julio Jaime Julia. Santo Domingo: Editora Taller, 1977. 200 p.

Polemical articles dating from the last decade of the 19th century to the first decade of the 20th. Garrido, a journalist, lived and wrote during a most interesting period of Caribbean history. His newspaper articles include political, sociological and religious editorials, as well as some interesting obituaries on such important figures as José Martí and Eugeno María de Hostos. Garrido's articles are of value primarily as historical documents for the late 19th century. [Carlos J. Hortas]

Martí, José. Our America: writings on Latin America and the struggle for Cuban independence. See item **6661**.

5149 **Sierra, Justo.** Obras completas. v. 3, Crítica y artículos literarios. Edición y notas de José Luis Martínez. México: Universidad Nacional Autónoma de México, 1977. 499 p., 1 leaf of plates: ill.; bibl., index (Nueva biblioteca mexicana; 51)

Between 1869 and 1911, Sierra wrote some 76 essays of literary criticism, mostly short, journalist commentaries. The most interesting are the prologues to books by Darío, Gutiérrez Nájera, and Luis G. Urbina, and a long essay on the image of Blue Beard. In these essays Sierra takes the time to develop his ideas in depth and provides a very useful source for the study of the literary environment of the Porfiriato. Good introduction and index of names. [J. Bruce-Novoa]

5150 **Zorrilla de San Martín, Juan.** Juan Zorrilla de San Martín en la prensa: escritos y discursos. Recopilación, ordenación, estudio preliminar y notas por Antonio Seluja Cecín. Montevideo: Publicaciones de la Comisión Nacional de Homenaje del Sesquicentenario de los Hechos Históricos de 1825, 1975. 300 p. (Ediciones del sesquicentenario)

A fine collection of Zorrilla de San Martín's newspaper pieces and speeches, some of which are republished here for the first time. Particularly useful for those who know Zorrilla primarily as a poet and find the 1930 edition of the *Obras completas* unavailable or intimidating. Organized according to theme: personal portraits, art criticism, literary criticism, political and historical essays and religious pieces. Useful prologue.

LITERARY CRITICISM AND HISTORY

5151 **Alonso, Carlos J.** *Facundo* y la sabiduría del poder (CAM, 38:5, sept./oct. 1979, p. 116–130)

This insightful article does indeed address the subject of the title, but in the process, it also demonstrates that *Facundo*, inspite of the accusations of its critics, possesses not only a thematic unity, but a unity demonstrable in the textual discourse itself.

5152 **Babín, María Teresa.** Genio y figura de Nemesio R. Canales. San Juan, Puerto Rico: Editorial Andina, 1978. 78 p. (Biblioteca de autores puertorriqueños)

This short story of one of Puerto Rico's foremost literary essayists and journalists contains a short biography partly based on the notes and remembrances of his sister, Paulita Canales Viuda de Platet, plus a small anthology and bibliography. A useful introduction to the author's works.

5153 **Castellanos, Rafael Ramón.** Rufino Blanco Fombona: ensayo bibliográfico. Caracas: Ediciones del Congreso de la República, 1975. 514 p., bibl.

A schematic biography accompanied by an extremely useful bibliography which portrays in minute detail the staggering diversity of Blanco Fombona's intellectual life—as creative writer, historian, political and cultural commentator, critic, translator and editor. The book's clear format and extensive documentation make it a major contribution to Blanco Fombona scholarship.

Concha, Jaime. *Martin Rivas* o la formación del burgués. See item **3211**.

5154 **Cornejo Polar, Antonio.** Glorinda Matto de Turner: para una imagen de la novela peruana del siglo XIX (UCV/E, 2:3, enero/junio 1977, p. 91–107)

A very intelligent, well-documented article which examines Matto de Turner's work in the theoretical context of her times. The author finds in Matto de Turner's narrative system a complexity sometimes overlooked due to the apparent simplicity of her plots. He also sees in her work a reflection of several literary concerns of the period.

La crítica literaria y estética en el siglo XIX cubano. See item **5017**.

5155 **Dellepaine, Angela B.** Los folletines gauchescos de Eduardo Gutiérrez (IILI/RI, 104/105, julio/dic. 1978, p. 487–506)

The author compellingly argues that Gutiérrez's novels should be considered in their own context as popular literature, and not as something they were never intended to be, namely, "literary" novels. In the process, she constructs an interesting aesthetic for popular literature, both in terms of the author's intentions and the audience's expectations. Superbly researched and documented.

Dessau, Adalbert. *Zivilisation und Barbarei* im lateinamerikanischen Roman. See item **5020**.

5156 Fray Mocho desconocido. Estudio y compilación por Pedro Luis Barcia. Buenos Aires: Ediciones del Mar de Solís, 1979. 370 p.

In recent years, José S. Alvarez, better known as Fray Mocho, has become something of a cult figure among younger Argentines, not for his novels which are universally considered mediocre, but for his lively, often humorous, vignettes of Buenos Aires life during the decades around the turn of the century—a period marked by tremendous social, economic and demographic changes, all of which Alvarez portrays from the perspective of the man in the street, often an emigrant, a *compadrito* or a *provinciano*. The present volume contains a remarkably, thorough preliminary study plus some 40 pieces taken from *Caras y Caretas*, a magazine edited for several years by Alvarez himself with each article signed by one of his several pseudonyms: Fray Mocho, Fabio Carrizo, etc. The term *desconocido* refers to the fact that the very incomplete *Obras completas* of 1961 failed to include these obvious products of Alvarez's pen. An important book.

5157 Grases, Pedro. Algunos temas de Bello. Caracas: Monte Avila Editores, 1978. 191 p.

Pedro Grases is hardly unknown to Bello scholars, and in this latest volume on Bello he again demonstrates his exceptional competence in the area. Consisting of 21 essays, articles and notes on different aspects of Bello's life and works, this book is particularly interesting for its several pieces on Bello's early and middle years spent in Venezuela and London—periods frequently neglected due to the overwhelming importance of his later years in Chile. A very useful book.

Jitrik, Noé. Las contradicciones del modernismo. See item **5862**.

5158 Lamore, Jean. *Cecilia Valdés*: realidades económicas y comportamientos sociales en la Cuba esclavista de 1830 (CDLA, 19:110, sept./oct. 1978, p. 41–53)

A solid contribution to scholarship, this article clearly outlines major social and economic themes in *Cecilia Valdés* against their historical background.

5159 Mas, José L. La huella de José Martí en *Ariel* (IJZ/H, 62:3, mayo/sept. 1979, p. 275–281)

Despite inconclusive evidence, the article argues that the commonality of themes in Martí and Rodó implies a direct influence of the former on the latter.

Merrell, Floyd. Hacia una interpretación de la novela histórica guatemalteca. See item **5292**.

5160 Oliver-Belmas, Antonio. Ultima vez con Rubén Darío. Madrid: Ediciones Cultura Hispánica del Centro Iberoamericana de Cooperación, 1978. 2 v. (901 p.) (Continuous pagination)

Collected in these two volumes are many essays of the late Oliver-Belmas, some of which have not been published previously. The essays in the first volume do indeed deal with Rubén Darío's life and works, but the second has to do with neither. Rather, it is a grab-bag collection of other essays by the same author, only a fourth of which even have to do with Spanish America. The editors have thus guaranteed that no one interested in the essays of the second volume, which deal mostly with Peninsular literature, will ever find them.

5161 Pupo-Walker, Enrique. El cuadro de costumbres, el cuento y las posibilidades de un deslinde (IILI/R, 102/103, enero/junio 1978, p. 1–15)

Although this very useful article deals with more than 19th-century Spanish American literature, the problem it explores is so central to much 19th-century prose that scholars should be aware of it.

5162 Recopilación de textos sobre la novela romántica latinoamericana. Selección y prólogo de Mirta Yañez. La Habana: Casa de las Américas, 1978. 576 p., bibl.

A fine collection of essays on the Spanish American Romantic novel by some of its foremost critics, including Pedro Henríquez Ureña, Fernando Alegría, Luis Alberto Sánchez, Alberto Zum Felde, Ezequiel Martínez Estrada and Enrique Anderson Imbert. The first essays discuss in general terms certain problems of Romantic prose fiction in Spanish America, while the later essays are devoted to particular novels, to wit, *Sab, Facundo, Amalia, María, Enriquillo* and *El Zarco*. Includes a good, basic bibliography.

5163 Rodríguez, Ileana. *Cecilia Valdés* de Villaverde: raza, clase y estructura familiar (AR, 5:18, 1979, p. 30–36, ill.)

In reality, the principle subjects of this article are sexism and racism as they relate to the three items in the title. Despite the author's ideological dogmatism, she nonetheless shows some insight into *Cecilia Valdés* as a social document, but ultimately, with 20th-century smugness, indicts all things associated with 19th-century liberalism, including abolitionism, Villaverde and the novel itself.

5164 Rodríguez Monegal, Emir. Rodó en el novecientos. Montevideo: Ediciones de la Casa del Estudiante, 1976? 56 p. (Cuadernos de literatura)

A dressed-up mimeograph pamphlet containing a brief chronology of Rodó's life plus four fine essays—published 1948–50(?)—on different aspects of his work, his literary generation, *Ariel*, his criticism and the parables. Very informative. Although not identical, much of this information may be found in Rodríguez Monegal's extensive prologue to Rodó's *Obras completas*.

5165 Sosa, Enrique. La economía en la novela cubana del siglo XIX. Prólogo de Mirta Aguirre. La Habana: Editorial Letras Cubanas, 1978. 319 p.

More about economics than about the novel, this excellent study nonetheless provides literary scholars of all political persuasions with countless insights into the socioeconomic contexts of the 19th-century Cuban novel, and could illuminate rereadings of much 19th-century prose. The prologue implies that literature, "*científicamente analizada*," can serve as a primary source for economic historians. Mr. Sosa's observations on the novel wisely coincide with the evidence of several justly acclaimed economic and historical studies, most notably Moreno Fraginals' *El ingenio* (see *HLAS 40:2985*) and Le Riverend's *Historia económica de Cuba* (see *HLAS 40:2943*). Slavery and the personal and social distortions it caused both among blacks and whites are the central concerns of the book. Particularly interesting from a literary perspective are the final two chapters which explore master/slave relationships and how these affect character development in several novels. Highly recommended.

5166 Tauro, Alberto. Clorinda Matto de Turner y la novela indigenista. Lima: Universidad Nacional Mayor de San Marcos, Dirección Univ. de Biblioteca y Publicaciones, 1976. 66 p., bibl., plate.

A short but useful study of the life and works of Matto de Turner. Divided into three sections: 1) her life, 2) her works, and 3) the relationship between *Aves sin nido* and the appearance of the *novela indianista* (the most important section). Includes a short chronological bibliography of the author's works but unfortunately says nothing about additional criticism.

5167 Toledo Sande, Luis. Algunas ideas en la narrativa de Jesús Castellanos (BNJM/R, 70[20]:1, enero/abril 1979, p. 53–84)

As the title indicates, this article identifies some of the principle ideological currents in Castellanos' short stories and novels. Flawed somewhat by incomplete documentation, the article nonetheless serves as a useful introduction to a writer who should not be forgotten.

PROSE FICTION: 20th Century: Mexico

BRUCE-NOVOA, *Assistant Professor of Spanish, Yale University*

MAJOR MEXICAN AUTHORS have not published during this biennium and their absence is reflected in this section. However, there has been an upsurge of activity in publishing and criticism as well as in other endeavors devoted to the promotion of Mexican literature.

The most important book of fiction to appear since *HLAS 40* is the revised and much improved second edition of José Emilio Pacheco's fine novel *Morirás lejos* (item **5202**), first published in 1967. A good novel which demonstrates how an artist can transform the clichés of popular literature into quality fiction is Fuentes' *Cabeza de hidra* (item **5184**), nevertheless a minor work in his opus. Two writers whose last books date from the mid 1960s won prestigious prizes: Inés Arredondo's excellent collection of stories *Río subterráneo* (item **5173**) was awarded a Villaurrutia Prize, and Fernando del Paso's Baroque tour de force *Palinuro de México* (item **5203**) won the National Prize for the novel. Books published by the founders of Onda literature, Gustavo Sainz (item **5210**) and José Agustín (items **5168–5169**), fall short of previous achievements with most of their followers lagging further behind. The bright light of the 1940s generation was *Fantasías en carrusel* (item **5174**), an anthology of René Avilés Fabila's stories, which displays the vast thematic spectrum and technical mastery of this prolific, but ignored writer. Among newcomers, the most promising novelist and short-story writer are María Luisa Puga (item **5208**) and Alberto Huerta (item **5192**), accomplished masters of their craft despite a propensity toward politicized writings common to young authors.

The theme of the Tlatelolco massacre (1968) continues to haunt the Mexican psyche and is presented in literature as a synecdoche for the suppression of political rights and the triumph of capitalism, imperialism, and one-party rule. It has become a symbol endowed with mythological connotations that reaches to all levels of society. The subject of urban revolution popular among younger authors—some of whom were not even teenagers when Tlatelolco occurred—is directly related to the frustration of a student movement which culminated in the massacre. Betancourt's *De como Guadalupe bajó a la montaña* (item **5178**) is a classic post-Tlatelolco, Onda short story. Tlatelolco's significance in Mexican literature merits detailed analysis and Luis Leal's article provides an outline of a subject worthy of further study (item **5236**).

Most critical attention continues to focus on Rulfo and Fuentes even if few new insights are offered. And although Pacheco's prose writings are being studied, most post-Fuentes fiction continues to be neglected. Women writers are receiving increasing attention and their skills are commended in books such as *Cuentistas mexicanas del siglo XX* (item **5181**). Still, most of them remain marginal. Recent studies on José Revueltas portend a vindicatory barrage of criticism which is either politically or emotionally biased. An objective, in-depth study of his complete works is needed. Several programs designed to improve Mexican criticism in Mexico—until now mostly limited to impressionistic essays—have been established. The Universidad Veracruzana at Xalapa is the country's most dynamic center of literary analysis and the publisher of two quality journals: *Texto Crítico* and *Semiosis*. The Colegio de México initiated a team study of Mexican prose and although its first title devoted to José Emilio Pacheco (item **5234**) lacks imagination, it reveals a disciplined methodology uncharacteristic of recent Mexican criticism. Insofar as models are concerned, Floyd Merril's is the more promising one (item **5237**).

Overall, the Mexican literary ambience is in great ferment. Literary prizes and writing workshops have increased dramatically, but since these developments are usually associated with presidential politics, the next election could spell a return to past indifference. While Joaquín Mortiz continues to lead in the publication of Mexican belles lettres, other houses such as Siglo Veintiuno and Editorial Era have almost eliminated literary works from their lists. Fortunately, Editorial Grijalbo, under the direction of Gustavo Sainz, has assumed the responsibility of publishing significant new titles, reissuing important out-of-print works and establishing its own literary prizes. Finally, the interest of Spanish publishers in Latin American literature which began after Franco's death continues to grow, an indication that more and more of the best Mexican fiction will be published in Spain.

PROSE FICTION

5168 Agustín, José. La mirada en el centro. México: Joaquín Mortiz, 1977. 216 p. (Nueva narrativa hispánica)

Included in the eight stories, written between 1964–76, are Agustín's autobiography and a long monologue that he later turned into *El rey se acerca a su templo* (see item **5169**). All the Onda characteristics appear: hip language, drugs, conflict between turned-on youth and traditional youth, as well as the generation gap. A good sampling of Agustín's thematics and his control of different narrative voices.

5169 ———. El rey se acerca a su templo. México: Editorial Grijalbo, 1978. 128, 105 p.

Novel in two sections. "Lux Externa" is a long monologue by Ernesto, a pseudo-hippie, drug dealer, who lost the woman who supported him. He is a pathetic figure; his monologue is typical Onda fare: hip language, drugs, the Mexico City street scene, the low life. Salvador, his friend, listens to the rambling monologue. "Lux Interna," narrated by Salvador for the most part, tells how he comes to go to bed with Raquel through the knowledge that she has been raped by Ernesto, in the latter's jail cell. The intent to elicit sympathy for Ernesto—a type representing the necessary violator of the sacred who leads the tabu-ridden, bourgeois Salvador into the profane ritual—is not convincing. Agustín triumphs in his manipulation of distinct languages, though his particular codes are losing the vitality they had 15 years ago, and his characters are now too familiar.

5170 Alvarado, José. Cuentos. Presentación, Alicia Molina. Prólogo, Ricardo Cortés Tamayo. México: Universidad Nacional Autónoma de México, 1977. 290 p., 1 leaf of plates: port.

The short stories in this collection are more interesting as social documents than literary fiction; they are set against the backdrop of Mexico City streets. The prologue is an excellent study of the late journalist.

5171 Alvarez, Miguel. Las cruzas. México: Joaquín Mortiz, 1977. 108 p. (Serie del volador)

A young boy searches for his origins, passing through fantastic experiences in several trips to the provinces. However, the *deus ex machina* of the insane asylum at the end forces a psychological reading. Alvarez writes brilliantly at times; it is a shame he ruined the novel with an unimaginative, weak ending.

5172 Arana, Federico. Enciclopedia de latinoamericana omnisciencia. México: Joaquín Mortiz, 1977. 116 p. (Nueva narrativa hispánica)

A delightful, alphabetized voyage through the history of Latin America in the late 20th, early 21st centuries, as if written even later. Encyclopedia-style entries mock contemporary issues such as feminism, Chicanos, politics, and society in general. Very funny.

5173 Arredondo, Inés. Río subterráneo. México: Joaquín Mortiz, 1979. 159 p. (Nueva narrativa hispánica)

Twelve short stories by one of the most talented women writers of Mexico. Arredondo constructs surfaces that reveal much more than what is actually said. By implying the underlying forces in human relationships, she fascinates the reader with the barely undefinable.

5174 Avilés Fabila, René. Fantasías en carrusel. Diseño de portada, Carlos Palleiro. Ilustraciones, Alberto Aguilar. México: Ediciones de Cultura Popular, 1978. 229 p.: ill. (Arte y literatura)

A collection of 75 stories, within the category of the fantastic, arranged according to topics (e.g., literature; vampires, ghosts, and witches; animals; mythology; religion; and politics). Some are new, but most were published previously. The majority tend to be humorous; often satirical of bourgeois society. Avilés' production is impressive, making this volume a must for any student of fantastic literature.

5175 ———. Pueblo en sombras. México: Editorial V Siglos, 1978. 105 p.

Consists of 15 short stories by one of the best Latin American writers of political satire. In addition to being very entertaining, they provide an excellent insight into the workings of Mexican society and the frustrations of living in a system based on bribery, corruption, and complete cynicism.

5176 Azar, Héctor. Las tres primeras personas. México: Editorial Grijalbo, 1977. 179 p., 2 leaves of plates: ill. (Best sellers Grijalbo)

Three Lebanese immigrants, father and two adolescent daughters, arrive in Mexico just before the Revolution. Story is told from multiple perspectives. In addition to the thoughts of the three characters, Azar uses letters, dialogue, fragments of poetry, and the memories of the man's grandson, a native-born Mexican. Offers interesting insights into immigrant participation in the infrahistory of Mexico.

5177 Azuela, Arturo. Manifestación de silencio. México: Joaquín Mortiz, 1979. 333 p. (Nueva narrativa hispánica)

Another novel centered around the Tlatelolco massacre. Azuela distinguishes his version by making the bloody incidents of 1968 a silent center. The events are not recounted, but exist in the space between the two halves of the narration; this is the play on words in the title. The events are well known by now. Azuela tells the story of a group of intellectuals from the mid 1960s through the late 1970s, a type of infrahistory. The structural idea is traditional; the narrative, likewise. The treatment of the massacre as an absence that informs the narrative has been used already, and more effectively, by Juan García Ponce in *La invitación*; Gustavo Sainz in *Obsesivos días circulares*; and José Agustín in *Se está haciendo tarde.* Azuela's achievement lies in the accessibility of his straightforward prose.

Azuela, Mariano. Three novels: The trials of a respectable family. The underdogs. The firefly. See item **6626**.

5178 Betancourt, Ignacio. De como Guadalupe bajó a la montaña y todo lo demás. México: Joaquín Mortiz, 1977. 107 p. (Serie del volador)

Betancourt's fanciful anecdotes, sarcasm, black humor, and political satire place these 11 stories in the line of Avilés Fabila. His language and tone derive from Onda literature. The title story, about holding the Virgin's painting for ransom, will be an Onda classic.

5179 Capetillo, Manuel. Plaza de Santo Domingo, 1: propio de la noche. México: Joaquín Mortiz, 1977. 200 p. (Nueva narrativa hispanoamericana)

In this strange novel of Gothic atmosphere, Capetillo's themes—sickness, aging, literary texts, desire, and memories—emerge and merge as if in a dream. Unusual events seem normal within the tone established and the dark, labyrinthine setting.

5180 Carrión Beltrán, Luis. El infierno de todos tan temido. México: Fondo de Cultura Económica, 1975. 173 p. (Primera novela)

Jacinto Chontal, a writer and revolutionary, is incarcerated and tortured. The novel traces his gradual path towards insanity. This is one more recent work in which the horrors of prison life serve as a mirror of Mexican society, a favorite technique since 1968 and the resurgence of a more politically committed literature.

5181 Cuentistas mexicanas siglo XX. Antología, introducción y notas de Aurora M. Ocampo. México: Universidad Nacional Autónoma de México, 1976. 319 p. (Nueva biblioteca mexicana; 45)

Anthology of 52 stories written by 22 women, many of them well-known (e.g., Rosario Castellanos, Elena Garro, Elena Poniatowska) and others who are deserving of more critical attention (e.g., Arredondo, Julieta Campos, Margarita Dalton). There are no critical commentaries, and the bibliography is limited to books of short stories.

5182 Dávila, Amparo. Arboles petrificados. México: Joaquín Mortiz, 1977. 128 p. (Nueva narrativa hispánica)

A dozen stories, mostly from the perspective of a woman protagonist and centered around the themes of frustrated love, male oppression of female family members and death. Dávila controls her prose to convey feelings of desperation, of unavoidable tragedy, of entrapment, which reflect the condition of the women in her stories.

5183 Elizondo Alcaraz, Carlos. Los ángeles llegaron a Sodoma. México: Joaquín Mortiz, 1977. 114 p. (Serie del volador)

Elizondo attempts to write a poetic novel, but fails to sustain its lyrical quality. A man fails to win the love of a woman who turns out to be a lesbian. Interesting for the probe of the lesbian psyche, but Elizondo bogs down in male-dominance clichés and a moral bias for heterogeneous love. Other writers have presented these themes more successfully (e.g., García Ponce, Inés Arredonda, Sergio Fernández, etc.).

5184 Fuentes, Carlos. La cabeza de la hidra. Barcelona: Librería Editorial Argos, 1978. 286 p.

This is a detective novel of foreign intrigue whose plot concerns the control of Mexico's oil. In this parody of the most read genre in the world, Fuentes uses every literary and film cliché. The number of tricks, commonplaces, echoes suggest the necessity of reading it as a commentary on writing as an intertextual whole in which a new book is simply a set of references to others. Fuentes' triumph and commentary are one and the same: in spite of all that has been said, a talented writer can still create a fascinating, enjoyable novel, and even manage to throw in some relevant political barbs.

5185 Gamboa, Federico. Diario de Federico Gamboa, 1892–1939. Selección, prólogo y notas de José Emilio Pacheco. México: Siglo Veintiuno Editores, 1977. 279 p., bibl., index, 1 leaf of plates: port.

Interesting reading for students of the history or literature and a must for Mexicanists. Reveals facets of Gamboa unsuspected by those who only read *Santa,* or were taught that he was a failed imitator of Zola. Pacheco's contribution is another surprise, in these days of forgettable introductions; his is excellent.

5186 García Ponce, Juan. La casa de la playa [sic]. 2. ed. Madrid: Sedmay Ediciones: Distribuidora, Maydi, 1977. 281 p. (Boom)

With the exception of the inexplicable mistake in the title, this version of *La casa en la playa* is unchanged from the 1966 edition (see *HLAS 30:3168*). However, it is likely that this re-edition will reach a wider public because Spanish distribution is much better than the Mexican one. The book is narrated by a liberated, woman lawyer. The style is highly evocative yet deceptively normal, almost traditional. Plot: a vacation love story. The merit lies in the poetic narration.

5187 ———. La presencia lejana. Barcelona: Círculo de Lectores, 1974. 198 p.

A painter, who seeks reintegration into an existence free from alienating personal consciousness, achieves reintegration within the *image* of love. The text is that image. Through constantly shifting metonymies of metaphors, the particularity of objects (the words themselves) and people are transcended and the novel is experienced as one image. A beautiful, Baroque, lyrical novel, first published in 1967 by Arca in Montevideo.

5188 ———. La vida perdurable. México: Joaquín Mortiz, 1970. 135 p. (Serie del volador)

A young couple's marriage seems ideal, except for an unknown lack between them. He searches her past, while she attempts to become part of his home. Finally, the real problem, individual personality, is overcome through accepting the presence of dogs in the relationship. A slow moving narrative creates the sense of impending encounter whose mystery lies below the surface. In the end, the poetic image of the surface is in itself the revelation.

5189 García Terrés, Jaime. Reloj de Atenas. México: Joaquín Mortiz, 1977. 294 p. (Serie confrontaciones)

A mixture of diary, travel guide, and literary essay by one of Mexico's most respected poets. The tedious first half is filled with significant observations and character sketches; the second centers more on Greece and the literati, both native and foreign, who have had something to do with the country. The author, who warns us that this is not a novel, did not take the time to rework his material into some genre that would eliminate the superfluous and order the valuable.

5190 Garibay, Ricardo. El gobierno del cuerpo. México: Joaquín Mortiz, 1977. 290 p. (Biblioteca paralela)

Collection of 30 stories written between 1951–76, most of which were published in journals. Good examples of Garibay's thematic variety, his unemotional style, and sometimes popular tendencies. An introduction for those who do not know the author would have been useful.

5191 ———. Verde Maira. Barcelona: Editorial Grijalbo, 1977. 156 p.

Extra-marital fun and games among the staff of a Mexico City newspaper. Garibay takes a trite anecdote and creates a very funny, dialogued novel. Easy, light reading.

5192 Huerta, Alberto. Ojalá estuvieras aquí. México: Joaquín Mortiz, 1978. 89 p. (Serie del volador)

This collection of nine stories won the Premio Nacional de Cuento, 1977. Huerta writes very well constructed, highly imaginative fiction, with little action and ambiguous plots. Like other young writers, he develops the theme of urban revolution, although his best story concerns an erotic encounter in a library. Huerta is the most promising of many young writers practicing the genre of short stories.

5193 Ibargüengoitia, Jorge. Estas ruinas que ves. México: Organización Editorial Novaro, 1975. 270 p.

A visiting professor in a small, provincial city, has an affair with another professor's wife and, finally, beds a beautiful student. The story is pure soap-opera and the writing traditional; the novel's merit lies in Ibargüengoitia's light touch, his satire and humor.

5194 ———. Las muertas. México: Joaquín Mortiz, 1977. 186 p. (Nueva narrativa hispánica)

This "new journalism" novel about the sensational Poquianchis case is Ibargüengoitia's best book to date. It consists of a masterful interweaving of perspectives drawn from police reports, official records, personal interviews, and the author's imagination. The novel is also a parody of sensationalist journalism, and on the whole, Ibargüengoitia's humor is as sharp as ever.

5195 Martín del Campo, David. Las rojas son las carreteras. México: Joaquín Mortiz, 1976. 249 p. (Nueva narrativa hispánica)

A group of young men from Mexico City, with no particular purpose in life, wander around the city until they die in an automobile accident. Although the author never belabors his point, it is clear that these young men represent additional victims of the 1960s repression of the Mexican student movement. The young men's lack of direction and the futility of their deaths are the consequences of the frustrated, earlier struggle. The novel moves slowly and lacks momentum.

5196 Matré, Gonzalo. Los símbolos transparentes. México: Editorial XXI Siglos, 1978. 435 p.

This is one more novel on the topic of the Tlatelolco massacre (1968), complete with evil CIA men, cold-blooded secret agents, poor but honorable common folk, and callous Mexican politicians who have forgotten their popular roots. The novel was blacklisted by several publishers who feared reprisals from the Mexican military. The book's notoriety naturally enhanced its prestige. Actually, the novel's characters are stereotypical and the narrative is burdened by extraneous material.

5197 Mendiola, Salvador. Guerra y sueño. México: Sistema Plan Joven, 1977. 488 p. (Colección Plan joven)

The narrator, a young novelist, writes about his brief love affair with a Trotskyite killed by soldiers. Their love constitutes a mixture of the hip-youth-music scene à-la-Onda and political fervor à-la-post-Tlatelolco massacre. The killing of the Trotskyite and the last dream of a workers' rebellion attest to the "anti-party elitism" of the narrator. Mendiola's stereotyping aside, the novel functions exceptionally well. The fragmentation of temporal planes is effective.

5198 Molina, Silvia. La mañana debe seguir gris. México: Joaquín Mortiz, 1977. 116 p. (Nueva narrativa hispánica)

The Mexican poet José Carlos Becerra was killed in an automobile accident in 1970. His lover, Silvia Molina, was about to move in with him when he died. Her telling of their love story turns into a "novela rosa" of scarce literary merit. This sentimental tribute to his memory is of value chiefly as a document on Becerra's life. He deserves better.

5199 Moya, Luis R. El aguacero. México: Joaquín Mortiz, 1977. 185 p. (Serie del volador)

The narrative describes several provincial lives whose common experiences are the presence of constant rainfall and an underlying sense of frustration. The rapid cutting from one life to another—a technique possibly derived from Moya's experience in writing film scripts—is very effective. This is an accomplished first novel.

5200 Muñiz, Angelina. Tierra adentro. México: Joaquín Mortiz, 1977. 177 p. (Serie del volador)

Set in 16th-century Spain, the novel is narrated by a young Sephardic who feels alienated from Spanish society and finds peace in Safed, a Sephardic village in Israel. The first person narrative fails to convey the language of the period, and the happy ending is too pat. Could be read as an allegorical panegyric to Zionism.

5201 Muñoz, Rafael Felipe. Relatos de la revolución: cuentos completos. México: Utopía, 1976. 311 p.

Complete collection of stories by one of the best writers of the Mexican Revolution. Most are typical of the literature of the period: much action, objective narration, no psychological insight. The introduction is too brief to be of service to the specialist and contains no bibliography. However, this collection is more complete than the one published by Mexico's Secretaría de Educación (1974, SepSetentas, 151).

5202 Pacheco, José Emilio. Morirás lejos. 2. ed. rev. México: Joaquín Mortiz, 1977. 159 p. (Serie del volador)

Many of the best Mexican novels of the last 20 years are almost unknown outside of Mexico; this one ranks among them and was first published in 1967. Two narratives alternate: the escape of an ex-Nazi who hides from his pursuers; and the history of the Jewish Diaspora. They combine into one image of humanity as persecuted and entrapped by hatred, vengeance, and violence. The second edition of this excellent novel is better with revisions which eliminated prosaic details, tightened up the language into a more poetic text.

5203 Paso, Fernando del. Palinuro de México. Madrid: Alfaguara, 1977. 725 p. (Literatura Alfaguara)

Del Paso has taken simple, common events and blown them up in Baroque fashion. The story of two cousins and a friend is transformed through a process of hyperbole and enumeration reminiscent of Góngora or Lezama Lima. Unfortunately, author lacks their lyric quality.

5204 Paz, Octavio. El ogro filantrópico. México: Joaquín Mortiz, 1979. 348 p. (Confrontaciones: los críticos)

Collection of cultural, political, literary essays, most of which were published in journals. Also contains an interview with Paz and his exchange with US historians on the future of Mexico. Example of Paz's wide range of interests.

5205 Perujo, Francisca. Pasar las líneas: cartas a una comandante. México: Joaquín Mortiz, 1977. 110 p. (Nueva narrativa hispánica)

A rather trite love story is told in a series of brief letters and diary entries. The mysterious Bruno becomes the center of the woman's world. This novel proves that women writers can perpetuate the language of male dominance as well.

5206 Poniatowska, Elena. Hasta no verte, Jesús mío. México: Editorial Era, 1969. 315 p. (Biblioteca Era)

The life of a poor woman—from childhood in the provinces, to adventures in the Revolution, to life in Mexico City—is told in first-person as if to a social worker or journalist. Narrates Mexican infrahistory through the eyes and language of a woman of the lower class. Fascinating.

5207 ———. Querido Diego, te abraza Quiela. México: Ediciones Era, 1978. 72 p. (Biblioteca Era)

Angelina Beloff, a Russian painter exiled in Paris, writes love letters to Diego Rivera, her lover who has returned to Mexico. He never answers her and Beloff turns their 10 years of love into the subject of a disintegrating future. As in her previous works—*La noche de Tlatelolco* (see *HLAS 40:6615*) and *Hasta no verte, Jesús mío* (see item **5206**)—Poniatowska seeks to disappear from the narration leaving only the voice of the character. Here, however, there is a discrepancy between Beloff's elegant Spanish and her repeated claims of inadequacy.

5208 Puga, María Luisa. Las posibilidades del odio. México: Siglo Veintiuno Editores, 1978. 303 p. (La creación literaria)

Puga proves a skilled creator of character through narrative tone in her first, surprisingly mature novel. Set in Kenya, it presents a cross-section of the country's society through the lives of different people from various classes, both black and white and including a Mexican tourist. Interior monologues, stream-of-consciousness, and flashbacks reveal the characters' lives up to the point when they are introduced by the narrative. Through the characters, Puga examines the hateful consequences of colonization, and Kenya is her dark mirror for Latin America. At times her own hatred overwhelms the story, distorting characters, but these instances are few. A most promising writer.

5209 Ramos, Agustín. Al cielo por asalto. México: Ediciones Era, 1979. 173 p. (Serie claves)

The novelist attempts to present a historical overview of the revolutionary rejection of capitalism by juxtaposing a narrative about the 1871 Paris Commune, another set in 1917, and yet others from contemporary times—including one on Che Guevara. The Bay of Pigs is listed as the first defeat of US imperialism. One hopes that the triumphant revolution will be less boring than this novel.

5210 Sainz, Gustavo. Compadre lobo. 4. ed. México: Editorial Grijalbo, 1978. 372 p., 8 leaves of plates: ill. (Best sellers)

The story of a painter's life, from childhood to first triumphs in art, narrated by his best friend who becomes a writer. Lobo, the artist protagonist, often takes over the narrative with typical Mexico City speech. The "writer" juxtaposes his own voice, a rather academic, pseudo-philosophical one. The novel lacks the humor characteristic of Sainz's narratives.

5211 Samperio, Guillermo. Lenín en el futbol. México: Editorial Grijalbo, 1978. 275 p. (Best sellers)

Consists of 31 stories—13 of which were published in Cuba with the title *Miedo ambiente* (La Habana, Casa de las Américas, 1977, 136 p.)—of proletarian, Marxist bent. Several treat the theme of urban revolution. Samperio is at his best when humor prevails.

5212 Solares, Ignacio. Anónimo. México: Compañía General de Ediciones, 1979. 215 p.

Raúl Estrada wakes up in Rubén Rentería's body. As the latter asks God to take his life, the former dies. After much torment, Raúl develops the synthesis of a new identity as Raúl Rentería. Two plot lines develop separately. The experimental aspects are interesting, but the novelist seems unwilling to break with a rational, psychological perspective. The ending seems weak.

5213 ———. El hombre habitad. Cuentos. México: Editorial Samo, 1975. 139 p. (Serie cuarta dimensión)

Solares' stories are Kafkaesque in their portrayal of characters caught in situations where something ambiguous has gone amiss. The reader is drawn into the character's experience, feeling his dilemma. Solares later combined the title story and one other to form the basis of his novel *Anónimo* (see item **5212**).

5214 ———. Puerta del cielo. México: Editorial Grijalbo, 1976. 165 p. (Best sellers)

This is a Bildungsroman in which an adolescent boy has visions of the Virgin Mary. She finally commands him to marry a prostitute's daughter in order to safeguard his purity and atone for his sins of the flesh. The novel is more of an extended short story and it could have used more development of the protagonist's character.

5215 Spota, Luis. El primer día. México: Editorial Grijalbo, 1977. 582 p. (Best sellers)

The last novel of the tetralogy, *La costumbre del poder* (see *HLAS 40:6587–6589*), takes place on the first day of Avila Puig's presidency. Spota draws the connection of all four works in the first novel which revolves around a business magnate's death. This last one also revolves around death, symbolized by the end of an outgoing president's term. The first day of the title is actually the ex-president's first day out of office, with numerous flashbacks of his past life interspersed with the present's bitter events. Unfortunately, much material from the three previous novels is repeated and the result is a tiresome book. Although Spota is not a great novelist and the corruption he reveals is common knowledge among educated Mexicans, the four books will be worth reading for those unfamiliar with the six-year term, oligarchic dictatorship institutionalized in Mexico.

5216 Valle-Arizpe, Artemio de. Andanzas de Hernán Cortes. 3. ed. México: Editorial Diana, 1978. 449 p.

In his carefully anachronistic style, Valle-Arizpe narrates Cortés' life. He uses the classic biographies and histories to document his text, clarifying and even refuting certain points, such as the burning of the ships that never happened, but also including invented scenes and dialogue. Between historical novel and academic essay, the book is very pleasant reading. A good beginning for those who do not know Cortés, or Valle-Arizpe.

5217 Zapata, Luis. Las aventuras, desaventuras y sueños de Adonis García, el vampiro de la Colonia Roma. México: Editorial Grijalbo, 1979. 223 p. (Best sellers)

This is the supposedly autobiographical monologue of the young homosexual hooker, recorded by a silent interviewer. Since the publication of Oscar Lewis' studies, many Mexicans believe that first-hand accounts of lower-class lives invariably make for interesting fiction. How this novel won a national prize is puzzling; it does represent a growing body of Mexican books that employ the same method, which is growing old fast. Jacket copy states that the material "no sufre ninguna transmutación literaria;" true indeed. Zapata could learn much from Rulfo about the language of the common people as art, and from John Rechy about making literature out of the homosexual experience.

LITERARY CRITICISM AND HISTORY

Agustín, José. Literature and censorship in Latin America today: dream within a dream. See item **5001**.

5218 Alvarado, José. Luces de la ciudad. Monterrey, México: Universidad Autónoma de Nuevo León, Dirección General de Investigaciones Humanísticas, 1978. 437 p.

A posthumous tribute to Alvarado, the book contains seven essays on him as well as his own journalistic writings. He was a cultural commentator, almost always superficial, but with an eye for details that sum up a period or event. Of special interest are the essays on the destruction of Mexico City in the wake of so-called progress and the few he wrote on northern Mexico and the Chicanos. This volume is more representative of Alvarado's work than his collection of short stories (see item **5170**).

5219 Aponte, Barbara Bockus. José Emilio Pacheco, cuentista (JSSTC, 7:1, Spring 1979, p. 5–21)

Brief but useful examination of the little-studied genre of one of Mexico's best writers. The author places him among others of his generation by relating and contrasting his work to other important writers. She draws special attention to his use of temporal levels, his emphasis of setting over anecdote or character, and his fantastic stories.

5220 Bastos, María Luisa. Clichés lingüísticos y ambigüedad en *Pedro Páramo* (IILI/RI, 44:102/103, enero/junio 1978, p. 31–41)

Very enlightening study of how Rulfo turns popular clichés into innovative language by utilizing them in contexts that charge them with multiple significance. Bastos is one of the most creative critics of Rulfo.

5221 Borgeson, Paul W., Jr. The turbulent flow: stream of consciousness techniques in the short stories of Juan Rulfo (UA/REH, 13:2, mayo 1979, p. 227–252)

A good review of Rulfo's use of techniques such as free association, suspended coherence, modulation, and interior monologue. Demonstrates the predominance of bridging techniques as the order which underlies the apparent chaos of Rulfo's texts.

5222 Bruce-Novoa, Juan. Juan García Ponce in context (*in* García Ponce, Juan. Entry into matter: modern literature and reality. Norman, Ill.: Applied Literature Press, 1976, p. 251–258)

García Ponce is the logical product of aesthetic concepts deriving from the Contemporáneos, reformulated by Octavio Paz, and reappearing in our time. Analyzes the structure of the book and relates it to García Ponce's fiction. The introduction will be useful for those unfamiliar with the author.

5223 Carter, Boyd G. Mexican literary periodicals since 1968 (Denver Quarterly [University of Denver, Colorado] 14:1, Spring 1979, p. 68–81)

The title is misleading; the journals studied by Carter actually cover the 1960s and the 1970s. Provides good overview of the best, if not the best-known journals. This is a good guide for libraries seeking to complete their holdings of Mexican literary journals.

De Beer, Gabriella. Pedro Henríquez Ureña en la vida intelectual mexicana. See item **7631**.

5224 Durán, Gloria. La magia y las brujas en la obra de Carlos Fuentes. México: Universidad Nacional Autónoma de México, 1976. 216 p., bibl. (Colección Opúsculos. Facultad de Filosofía y Letras; 85. Serie Ensayos)

Given the significant roles played by women with magical powers in Carlos Fuentes' fiction, it is a wonder that no full-length study has appeared before. Ms. Durán draws heavily on Jungian archetypes for an analysis which would have benefitted from a more detailed discussion. If anything, the book is altogether too short.

5225 Escalante, Evodio. José Revueltas, una literatura del "lado moridor." México: Ediciones Era, 1979. 116 p., bibl. (Biblioteca Era: Serie Claves)

After denying "literary" approaches that would read Revuletas' work metaphorically or stylistically, Escalante calls it a "writing machine" which forces one to suffer a metaphorical proletarian experience. Contradictions aside, the book is one of the better efforts to reevaluate Revueltas' literature.

5226 Fuentes, Carlos. The writer in an alien culture (Point of Contact [New York University, Ibero-American Language and Area Center, New York] 2:2, Spring 1979, p. 4–14)

Fuentes attributes the alienation of contemporary writers to the birth of individual freedom and the critical spirit, and the rise of a technological and future-oriented society. Literature no longer represents reintegration, but separation; society's reality is inhuman whereas art's bespeaks humanity. To write is to be alienated, from all contemporary societies.

5227 García de Aldridge, Adriana. La dialéctica contemporánea: "Tiempo Propio-Tiempo Total," en *Cumpleaños* (IILI/R, 45:108/109, julio/dic. 1979, p. 513–535)

Demonstrates that Celtic concepts of antihistory and continual creation are the sources of Fuentes' perception of time and man as plural. In his works, time is neither linear nor cyclical but a process of constant fragmentation in nature. The best article on *Cumpleaños* to date, this study also explains the basis for *Terra Nostra*.

5228 González Bermejo, Ernesto. Juan Rulfo: la literatura es una mentira que dice la verdad (UNAM/RUM, 34:1, sept. 1979, p. 4–8)

Interview with the laconic Rulfo in which he talks about the need to invent reality, instead of copying it. He laments the influence of Robbe-Grillet in Latin America, which he says has led to extremely personal novels. Explains that he cannot work at his job and write at the same time; hopes to get time off soon.

5229 Gordon, Donald K. Los cuentos de Juan Rulfo. Madrid: Playor, 1976. 196 p. (Colección Nova scholar)

Gordon categorizes Rulfo's stories according to the type of narration (monologue, monologue plus dialogue, dialogue, etc.) and discusses structure, style, language, and narrative technique. The analysis is rather traditional and adds little to the extant body of Rulfo criticism.

5230 Guerra-Cunningham, L.; Marta Paley Francescato; and **Inma Minoves-Myers.** Entrevista: José Agustín (HISPA, 8:22, 1979, p. 23–40)

Agustín discusses the definition of Onda literature, his career, influences on and recent changes in his writing. This would serve as a good introduction for those unfamiliar with Agustín. The specialist seeking new information should read the Trejo Fuentes interview (see item **5258**).

5231 Gyurko, Lanin A. The vindication of La Malinche in Fuentes' "Todos los Gatos son Pardos" (IAA, 3:3, 1977, p. 233–266, bibl.)

A detailed study of Fuentes' positive portrayal of La Malinche in this story which depicts her as the conscious founder of the Mexican nation.

5232 Herbst, Gerhard R. Mexican society as seen by Mariano Azuela. New York: Abra Ediciones, 1977. 100 p., bibl., index.

After dividing the warring camps into traditionalists and revolutionaries, with their own subgroups, Herbst reads Azuela's novels to glean relevant information. Although he succeeds in grouping this information under headings that reveal Azuela's attitudes, Herbst fails to elaborate why his writing is literature. The study's chief purpose is historical and as such, it provides useful background for literary studies.

5233 El Hijo pródigo: antología. Introducción, selección y notas de Francisco Caudet. México: Siglo Vientiuno Editores, 1979. 331 p., bibl., 8 leaves of plates: ill.

Important collection of the most significant and representative articles from the best Mexican literary journal of the 1940s. The lengthy, excellent introduction clearly explains why this journal was at the center of the period's literary activity.

5234 Jiménez de Báez, Yvette and others. Ficción e historia: la narrativa de José Emilio Pacheco. México: El Colegio de México, 1979. 348 p. (Proyecto la narrativa mexicana contemporánea. Literatura y sociedad)

This is the first publication of a project of team analysis being carried out at the Colegio de México. Other authors to be studied will include: Fuentes, Arreola, Elizondo, Sainz, and Agustín. The methodology is borrowed from Todorov, Barthes, Goldmann, and especially Kristeva. The team concentrates on three aspects: time-space, characters, intertextuality. Unfortunately, the often detailed discussions of the works never penetrate the surface to reach Pacheco's poetic world; the texts are the objects of cold scrutiny, but never subjects with their own life. The study lacks the artistic vision of quality criticism. Still, the book is useful and the research thorough. Perhaps the team will improve as the project develops.

Lannoy, Jean-Louis M. de. Indigenisme et littérature indianiste au Méxique et au Pérou. See item **5427**.

5235 Larson, Rosa. Fantasy and imagination in the Mexican narrative. Tempe: Arizona State University, Center for Latin American Studies, 1977. 154 p.

It is difficult to conceive how a study with this title would fail to mention Todorov or any major critic of fantasy. Larson merely offers a topical view of themes, with no stylistic analysis. Moreover, he ignores the work of Octavio Paz, René Avilés Fabila, and others.

5236 Leal, Luis. Tlatelolco, Tlatelolco (Denver Quarterly [University of Denver, Colorado] 14:1, Spring 1979, p. 3–13)

Good review of how the Tlatelolco massacre (1968) has been treated in Mexican literature, both prose and poetry. Author's discussion of books and pieces specifically devoted to the subject could mislead one into thinking that major authors (e.g., García Ponce, José Agustín, Gustavo Sainz) have not written on the topic when they have, albeit indirectly.

5237 Merrell, Floyd. A model of narrative analysis with application of Rulfo's "La Cuesta de las Comarades" (*in* Beck, Mary Ann and others. The analysis of Hispanic text: current trends in methodology. Jamaica, N.Y.: CUNY, York College, Department of Foreign Languages, Bilingual Press/Editorial Bilingue, 1976, p. 150–169)

Merrell's model involves the transformation of one paradigm (deep axiological opposition metaphorically expressed in thematic oppositions in a surface structure) to another which readjusts the factors of the first. Rulfo's story is analyzed to demonstrate the applicability of Merrell's model, one which offers promising possibilities. Highly interesting.

5238 Miller, Beth Kurti. Mujeres en la literatura. México: Fleischer Editora, 1978. 145 p.

Essays about and interviews with several women writers. Also discusses the image of women in the writing of men. Most of the material was previously published in journals, and the book lacks cohesiveness.

5239 Minc, Rose S. Lo fantástico y lo real en la narrativa de Juan Rulfo y Guadalupe Dueñas. New York: Senda Nueva de Ediciones, 1977. 175 p. (Senda de estudios y ensayos)

With a good balance of structuralist and mythological methods, Minc presents a close textual analysis of three representative stories by each author. The introduction contains an adequate discussion of fantasy and reality, in which she traces the evolution of the latter term through philosophical thought. Although the study is too sketchy for the specialist, it provides students with a better understanding of two terms often taken for granted.

5240 Monterroso. Compilador, Jorge Ruffinelli. Xalapa: Centro de Investigaciones Lingüístico-Literarias, Universidad Veracruzana, 1976. 75 p., bibl. (Cuadernos de *Texto crítico*; 1)

Collection of brief essays on Monterroso's prose, the majority of which have little critical value. Those by José Durand, Carlos Monsiváis, and Angel Rama stand out for their quality. Useful, though incomplete bibliography.

5241 Ostergaard, Ane-Grethe. Myte og bevidsthed i Elena Garros "La Culpa es de los Tlaxcaltecas." Odense, Denmark: Odense Universitet, Romansk Institut, 1976. 24 p., bibl. (NOK, Noter og kommentarer fra Romansk institut; 14)

Danish author analyzes Elena Garros' short story set in Mexico in the 1960s. The main protagonist, Laura, is torn between the mythological consciousness of her Indian ancestry and the modern world of the white man. She is haunted by a sense of having betrayed her true nature by embracing an alien culture. [R.V. Shaw]

5242 Oviedo, José Miguel. Fuentes; sinfonía del Nuevo Mundo (HISPA, 6:16, abril 1977, p. 19–32)

Demonstrates that the key to understanding the techniques, content and purpose of *Terra Nostra* is the "visión de los mitos como un sistema de unidades intercambiables y dispersas pero que tienden a la unidad, que se apoya en los últimos aportes de la antropología estructural." This vision is the source of repetitions in stories that are only superficially different and the reason for variations within the single voice of the narrative.

5243 Patout, Paulette. Alfonso Reyes et la France: 1889–1959. Paris: Klincksieck, 1978. 680 p., bibl.

The author traces French influences on Reyes from his youth, through his activities in the Ateneo de la Juventud, travels and, finally, to the writings of his adult life. Shows the interaction of Reyes with French writers and describes Latin American and Spanish writers living in France. Well documented; excellent bibliography.

5244 Pavón, Alfredo. El nivel inmanente en "La Sunamita" (Semiosis [Seminario de Semiótica, Teoría, Análisis, México] 1, julio/dic. 1978, p. 47–79)

Though heavily overburdened with semiotic jargon and diagrams, it is the first serious study of Inés Arredondo's prose, utilizing her best known story.

5245 Paz, Octavio. *Encuentros* de Juan García Ponce (Vuelta [México] 3:31, junio 1979, p. 34–35)

In García Ponce's fiction, according to Paz, a secret is slowly unveiled; but words invariably stop on the brink of revelation: "el núcleo, la verdad esencial, es lo no dicho." One example is the perverse innocence of love; García Ponce creates images in which bodies form visible signs because, as Paz says, innocence must be seen and not articulated in thought or speech. Article explains the poetic essence of García Ponce's prose.

5246 Prada Oropeza, Renato. Juan García Ponce: en busca del sitio perdido (Texto Crítico [México] 3:8, sept./dic. 1977, p. 129–154)

Semiotic study of García Ponce's first narrative works. Author offers good explanation of the temporal and structural elements but misses the author's amoral essence and the real contradictions in his language. The social perspective of the critic seems inappropriate for an author who seeks the asocial space.

5247 Revueltas, José. Conversaciones con José Revueltas. Entrevista de Gustavo Sainz. Introducción de Jorge Ruffinelli. Bibliografía de y sobre José Revueltas de Marilyn R. Frankenthaler. Xalapa: Universidad Veracruzana, Centro de Investigaciones Lingüístico-Literarias, 1977. 153 p., bibl. (Cuadernos de *Texto crítico*; 3)

Collection of 13 interviews with Revueltas, dating from 1950 to the last one he granted in 1976. Useful for the study of the late author. The bibliography of and about Revueltas, by Marilyn R. Frankenthaler, is excellent (p. 115–153).

5248 Robb, James Willis. Estilización artística de temas metafísicos en Alfonso Reyes (CM/D, 4:2, marzo/abril 1978, p. 27–31)

From the philosopher Bergson, Reyes took the concept of matter as descending movement and wrote essays about cosmic disintegration. Robb studies the images used by Reyes to express this concept.

5249 ———. El estilo de Alfonso Reyes: imagen y estructura. 2. ed. México: Fondo de Cultura Económica, 1978. 303 p., bibl. (Sección de lengua y estudios literarios)

Aside from a few cosmetic changes—the most helpful of which is a larger, more readable typeface—and some additions to the last chapters, this book is essentially the same as the 1965 ed.

5250 **Ruffinelli, Jorge.** José Revueltas, ficción, política y verdad. Veracruz, México: Universidad Veracruzana, 1977. 139 p., bibl., index.

Thematic study of Revueltas' fiction, tracing themes such as prison, scatological elements, alienation, avarice and exploitation, disguises, and the political universe. Demonstrates the author's evolution from optimism and complete loyalty to the Communist Party to existential pessimism and open disagreement with rigid, doctrinaire communism; although he never stopped being a communist. This is a good introduction to Revueltas even if it barely touches upon his rhetoric described by Ruffinelli as "más allá de la debilidad de un estilo . . . viene a ser su rasgo más definitorio" (p. 58).

5251 ———. Sainz and Agustín: literatura y contexto social (Texto Crítico [México] 3:8, sept./dic. 1977, p. 155–164)

Somewhat superficial study of the originators of Onda literature in Mexico. Attempts to determine their time and place, but does not go beyond the most obvious facts. Exemplifies the recent popularity of pseudo-Marxist literary criticism in Mexican literary circles.

5252 ———. Salvador Elizondo (HISPA, 6:16, abril 1977, p. 33–47)

Discusses the crisis of a writer who has pushed writing itself to the extreme of silence. Elizondo does not believe that "pure" writing is possible but neither does he want the alternatives of writers faced with the same problem. Ruffinelli asks questions concerning all the important works written by Elizondo.

5253 **Rulfo, Juan.** Situación actual de la novela contemporánea (UNAM/RUM, 34:1, sept. 1979, p. 9–14)

Speech given by Rulfo in Aug. 1965, in which he quickly and superficially reviewed the European and US novel. Uninteresting as criticism but important statement by Rulfo.

5254 **Russotto, Márgara.** Realismo, lenguaje y significado: reflexiones sobre un cuento de Revueltas (CAM, 210:1, enero/feb. 1977, p. 233–246, bibl., illus.)

A study of "El Lenguaje de Nadie," a story of Revueltas which explores the problem of a text postulating the impossibility of communication while communicating the impossibility. The answer is simpler than the question: between social classes there is a barrier, not in the text; realism is vindicated. Exemplifies articles that seek vanguardist concerns in Revueltas, while defending his non-vanguardist literature.

5255 **Schneider, Luis Mario.** México y el surrealismo: 1925–1950. México: Arte y Libros, 1978. 246 p., bibl.

This valuable contribution to the understanding of a major movement in Mexican literature and art by one of the best critics in the field is, unfortunately, almost impossible to find. The publisher stopped distributing the book.

5256 ———. Ruptura y continuidad: la literatura mexicana en polémica. México: Fondo de Cultura Económica, 1975. 200 p., bibl. (Colección Popular; 136)

In these five, lengthy and well documented essays on key moments in Mexican literary history (the Colony, neoclassicism, romanticism, modernism, and vanguardism), the author demonstrates the persistence of a conflict between progressive writers—who "cumplen con el designio vivificador que la historia reclama" (p. 193)—and the reactionary purists. Although the subject is trite, Schneider develops his thesis well and illustrates it with little-known events. Of special interest is the story of the journalists' debate which culminated in the founding of *Revista Moderna*, the modernist journal. It is a shame that the author did not add chapters on the same conflict in present-day Mexico.

Serna-Maytorena, M.M. Del corrido mexicano: su dimensión y proyección actual. See item **1370**.

5257 **Sommers, Joseph.** Oficio de tinieblas (Nexos [Sociedad de Ciencia y Literatura, Centro de Investigación Cultural y

Científica, México] 2, feb. 1978, p. 15–16)

A semi-Marxist analysis of Rosario Castellanos' best novel, pointing out ideological contradictions in the text. Author's criticism of Castellanos' pessimism and her lack of "fe en las posibilidades colectivas" reminds one of someone who demands realism and then deplores the lack of fantasy in the faithful depiction of reality.

5258 Trejo Fuentes, Ignacio and **Sergio Monsalvo.** Escribir como un fantasma en libertad: entrevista con José Agustín (La Semana de Bellas Artes [México] 100, 31 oct. 1979, p. 2–5)

Excellent interview in which Agustín discusses topics such as the new generation and how it is related to his work, the evolution of his style, accusations of misogyny, the role of sex in his work, the influence of oriental philosophy on his thought, his socialist ideals, and his role as a writer in Mexico. Essential for any student of Onda literature.

5259 Walker, Ronald G. Infernal paradise: Mexico and the modern English novel. Berkeley: University of California Press, 1978. 391 p., bibl., index.

In this study of "Mexican novels" by British writers Lawrence, Huxly, Greene, and Lowry, the author demonstrates that there is a conceptual and tonal coherence which unifies these works. He traces the origins of this coherence to Lawrence whose work informed the others when they read him, to the degree that they perceived what Lawrence wrote. A good companion to Drewey Wayne Gunn's *American and British Writers in Mexico, 1556–1973* (Univ. of Texas Press, 1974).

PROSE FICTION: 20th Century: Central America

LISA E. DAVIS, *Assistant Professor of Foreign Languages, York College of the City University of New York*

CERTAINLY, ONE OF THE MOST important historical events in Latin America's recent progress toward real political, economic and cultural freedom, and a measure of the determination and heroism such independence demands, comes to us from, as Neruda put it, "la dulce cintura de América." In brief, after years of guerrilla and open warfare, in July 1979, the Frente Sandinista dethroned the Somoza dynasty in Nicaragua, and began immediately to eradicate the effects of decades of dictatorship and repression. Therefore, the Sandinista victory, and the struggle preceding it, can serve as a touchstone in the analysis of much of the best fiction produced in Central America in the last few years. If this is true, it is because the paramount theme of that fiction is violence, generally in the form of conflicts between young leftists and oppressive militaristic regimes whose principal weapon is brutal torture. Nicaraguan writers like Sergio Ramírez in *¿Te dió miedo la sangre?* (item **5280**) and Lizandro Chávez Alfaro in *Trágame tierra* (item **5264**) treat the terrors of the Somoza dictatorship, while a similar preoccupation appears in the Costa Rican Fabián Dobles' recent *En el San Juan hay tiburón* (item **5267**). Similar themes of political corruption and the constant threat of violence and torture also dominate novels from neighboring republics. Works by writers of diverse ages, backgrounds and literary styles such as Argentina Díaz Lozano in *Eran las doce . . . y de noche* (item **5266**) and Manilo Argueta in *Caperucita en la zona roja* (item **5261**) reflect the same chaotic and precarious social order, and both demand, in one way or another, its immediate reform. The exploitation of workers employed in the production of exports and foreign complicity in their abuse are also themes in José León Sánchez's *La colina del buey* (item **5275**), about gold-mining, and Quince Duncan's *La paz del pueblo* (item **5268**) about a strike against the banana empire. Several excellent collections of short stories take a similar pessimistic attitude and manifest radical discontent with existing circumstances in various countries (e.g., José Antonio Córdova's Panama in *Con Irene y otros cuentos* (item **5265**); José María Méndez's El Salvador in *Espejo del tiempo* (item **5277**); Samuel Villeda Arita's Honduras in *El país de las voces* (item **5282**); Quince Duncan's Costa Rica in *La rebelión Pocomía y otros relatos* (item **5269**); and Hugo Rivas' Costa Rica in *Golpe de estado* (item **5281**).

One encouraging development in the fiction of Central America is the vigor and quality of its women writers, particularly those of Costa Rica as studied by Victoria Urbano, *Five women writers of Costa Rica* (item **5271**) and exemplified by Carmen Lyra (item **5276**), Yolando Oreamuno (item **5278**), and Claribel Alegría (item **5260**). Since the latter also received the 1978 Casa de las Américas award for her poetry, it is worth noting that most recent Cuban prizes for fiction have gone to Central American novels: to Manilo Argueta in 1977 for *Caperucita en la zona roja* (item **5261**) and to Joaquín Gutiérrez in 1978 for *Te acordás, hermano* (item **5273**), a record of one phase of the Costa Rican expatriate's long years in Chile.

Finally, one should single out two major works in the field: an invaluable reference work and a publishing landmark. The first is vol. 2 on Central America of Edna Coll's *Indice informativo de la novela hispanoamericana* (item **5285**), the second is vol. 1 of Miguel Angel Asturias' complete works, *Tres de cuatro soles* (item **5262**), a critical edition based on manuscripts deposited at the Bibliothèque Nationale in Paris and issued jointly by French and Mexican publishers.

PROSE FICTION

5260 Alegría, Claribel. El detén. Barcelona: Lumen, 1977. 76 p. (Palabra menor; 49)

Also universally admired for her poetry, the Salvadorian writer has composed here a poignant and penetrating study of an adolescent girl's disturbed psychological state as it manifests itself within the confines of a convent school. Recommended for its unusual treatment of sensuality vs. repression in a very contemporary setting.

5261 Argueta, Manlio. Caperucita en la zona roja. La Habana: Casa de las Américas, 1977. 217 p.

Recipient of the 1977 novel prize awarded by Casa de las Américas, the Salvadorian writer, with accomplished originality, takes us directly into the world of student subversives, balancing their fleeting intimate experiences against the constant threat of confrontation with police authorities—the Red Zone.

5262 Asturias, Miguel Angel. Tres de cuatro soles. Edición crítica. Homenaje, Aimé Césaire; prefacio, Marcel Bataillon; introducción y notas, Dorita Nouhaud. Madrid: Closas-Orcoyen, 1977. 124 p., bibl. (Edición crítica de las obras completas de Miguel Angel Asturias; 19)

This work, which Miguel Bataillon calls in his Preface an "*ars poética* y cosmogonía," initiates the series of *Obras completas* in a critical edition based on the manuscripts in the "Fonds Asturias" which the author left to the Bibliothèque Nationale in Paris. The 24 volumes will be issued jointly by the French and Mexican publishers, and this one (vol. 19) includes a meticulous scholarly introduction and a poem by Aimé Césaire dedicated to Asturias.

5263 Barrientos, Alfonso Enrique. Cuentos de Belice/Stories from Belize. Edición bilingüe, español-inglés. Guatemala: Editorial José de Pineda Ibarra, 1978. 173 p., ill.

This volume of six short stories by the Guatemalan writer, first published in 1961, voices traditional patriotic convictions about the evils of British imperialism in the area, and shows human concern for the mostly black citizenry of Belize, the victims of irrational prejudice and grinding poverty. The English translations of the stories, while generally accurate, are often linguistically bizarre.

5264 Chávez Alfaro, Lizandro. Trágame tierra. 2. ed. México: Editorial Diógenes, 1979. 282 p.

This novel from Nicaragua, which first appeared in 1969, focuses on the ideological conflicts between a father and son. While the former still waits for the Yankees to build a canal, the latter goes into the mountains to join the anti-Somoza guerrillas. Also, interesting insights into the little-known Atlantic Coast of Nicaragua, setting for the novel and the author's home.

5265 Córdova, José Antonio. Con Irene y otros cuentos. Panamá: INAC, 1976. 99 p.

Awarded the "Ricardo Miró" prize in 1975 for the short story, this collection reflects the violent tenor of contemporary Panamanian life. Employing a forceful prose which conveys drama and tension beyond the events described, the author chooses as persistent themes local persecution, imprisonment and torture of leftists, anti-Americanism, including references to the Vietnam War, and anti-militarism in general.

5266 Díaz Lozano, Argentina. Eran los doce . . . y de noche: un amor y una época. Novela. México: B. Costa-Amic, 1976. 181 p. (Escritores hispanoamericanos; 5)

From the privileged perspective of one with years of experience in the political and cultural life of her country, the Honduran novelist appeals for enlightenment and a reconciliation between young leftists and the establishment throughout Central America, a reconciliation necessary to bring justice and progress out of repression and near anarchy. While the conclusion of the novel verges on the melodramatic, her attacks on official "anti-communist" persecutions and torture ring all too true.

5267 Dobles, Fabián. En el San Juan hay tiburón. 2. ed. San José: Editorial Costa Rica, 1978. 135 p.

First published in 1967, the second edition of this fine novel is dedicated to the memory of Sandino and to "the heroic people of Nicaragua." Here, one of Costa Rica's most distinguished authors takes us up the San Juan River, the boundary between his country and Nicaragua, on a daring but ill-fated smuggling expedition which will bring arms to Somoza's enemies. Some excellent character portrayals and dramatic scenes.

5268 Duncan, Quince. La paz del pueblo. San José: Editorial Costa Rica, 1978. 193 p.

This novel has at its heart the history of Pedro Dull, a black laborer on the banana plantations, who helps to organize an unprecedented strike against the company bosses. Duncan traces the roots of several of his characters to 19th-century Jamaica, and these sections of the novel are highly original and provocative in their own right.

5269 ———. La rebelión Pocomía y otros relatos. San José: Editorial Costa Rica, 1976. 91 p.

In his most recent collection of short stories, the Costa Rican writer has published some of his best fiction to date. Of the 11 stories included here, several address themselves to the reality of the black population—the banana plantations, abuses, disunity, the African heritage—while others encompass more universal problems of the human condition, always in a prose of great precision and strength.

5270 Elizondo Arce, Hernán. La ciudad y la sombra. San José: Editorial Costa Rica, 1978. 104 p.

A welcome second edition of this delightful novel, first published in 1971, relates with touching irony and mild indignation the history of an imaginary Costa Rican city called San Gabriel, its peculiar inhabitants and institutions. The author has an unusual and refined talent for narrative and for character portrayal.

5271 Five women writers of Costa Rica. Short stories by Carmen Naranjo et al. Victoria Urbano, editor. Beaumont, Tex.: Asociación de Literatura Femenina Hispánica, 1978. 131 p.

A commendable attempt to provide a wider reading public and favorable publicity for creative writing by Hispanic women, notably Carmen Naranjo, Yolanda Oreamuno, Eunice Odio, Rima Vallbona, and the editor herself. Several stories in English translation by each writer, together with intelligent critical comments by a third collaborator, form the structural basis for this unusual collection. See item **6618**.

5272 Gutiérrez, Joaquín. La hoja de aire. Prólogo de Pablo Neruda. 3. ed. San José: Editorial Costa Rica, 1977. 59 p.

First published in 1968 in Chile, where the prolific Costa Rican writer lived and worked for many years, this brief autobiography chronicles his first wanderings through Mexico and Central America, and his less than triumphant return home. Humor and nostalgia in an appealing prose.

5273 ———. Te acordás, hermano. La Habana: Casa de las Américas, 1978. 218 p.

This remarkable narrative was awarded the 1978 Casa de las Américas prize for the novel in Cuba. The Chile of González Videla (1940s–50s) provides the background for the expansive lives of students, artists, and Bohemians from many Spanish American countries. The novel constitutes a profound statement on the emerging literary and historical conscience of an entire continent 30 years ago, and on the difficulties encountered and overcome.

5274 **Hurtado, Gerardo César.** Los vencidos. San José: Editorial Costa Rica, 1977. 241 p.

This most recent prize-winning novel by the Costa Rican author evokes the troubled world of his native Puerto Limón, where the misadventures of the protagonist Miguel Suárez introduce us to the violence on the Northern Railway, personal vendettas, and the murder of Communist Party leaders by the military. Strong prose and provocative plot.

5275 **León Sánchez, José.** La colina del buey. La vida en las minas de Abangares y la novela histórica *La colina del buey* de José León Sánchez por G. García Murillo. San José: Editorial Costa Rica, 1977. 264 p.

The second edition of this novel, first published as *Picahueso* in 1971, contains introductions by the author and one of his critics, together with a provocative essay by a young Costa Rican professor on the socioeconomic and historical importance of the book as a testimony to the character of the gold-mining industry, managed principally by North American capital. Like his earlier *La isla de los hombres solos*, this novel is painfully direct, honest and compassionate in the portrayal of human frailty and suffering.

5276 **Lyra, Carmen.** Relatos escogidos. Selección, prólogo, notas, y cronología de Alfonso Chase. San José: Editorial Costa Rica, 1977. 534 p., bibl., 7 leaves of plates: ill. (Colección Nuestros clásicos; 12)

This first collection selected from the works of Costa Rican educator, writer and political figure, includes both prose fiction and essays on various topics of social concern, notably her commitment to the Communist Party. A fine essay and bibliographical material by Alfonso Chase, plus unusual photographs of the writer and her circle complete this volume.

5277 **Méndez, José María.** Espejo del tiempo. San Salvador: Ministerio de Educación, Dirección de Publicaciones, 1974. 68 p.

This collection of 22 short stories, some of them very brief, by the distinguished Salvadorian writer, known in literary and social circles as "Chemita," generally treats with bitter humor the dark side of the human condition. Here, flashes of science fiction alternate with stark social realism.

5278 **Oreamuno, Yolanda.** Relatos escogidos. Selección, prólogo y notas de Alfonso Chase. San José: Editorial Costa Rica, 1977. 283 p., bibl. (Colección Nuestros clásicos; 13)

This fine selection from the works of the Costa Rican writer includes short stories and fragments of her only published novel, and covers a period from 1936 to 1951, five years before her tragic death. An excellent introduction, bibliography and biography by the author and scholar Alfonso Chase accompany this volume.

5279 **Pinto, Julieta.** El sermón de lo cotidiano. San José: Editorial Costa Rica, 1977. 105 p.

This new novel by the Costa Rican writer explores skillfully the relationship between two mature adults—one, a dancer, wife, and mother, and the other, a priest—who have suffered greatly and come to doubt themselves and the meaning of their lives. Faith and confidence are restored in this sensitive narrative.

5280 **Ramírez, Sergio.** ¿Te dió miedo la sangre? Novela. Caracas: Monte Avila Editores, 1977. 281 p. (Colección Continentes)

The Sandinista victory enhances the intrinsic literary value of this most recent novel by the Nicaraguan writer, who has created a kaleidoscopic vision of the world of the Somoza dictatorship over a period of several decades. The unlikely heroes, political exiles languishing in a neighboring republic, introduce us to corruption, torture, exploitation, and the pursuit of Sandino against a background of North American complicity and military intervention, denouncing the absurdity and inhumanity of the social order perpetuated by the notorious "GN" (Guardia Nacional).

5281 Rivas, Hugo and **Oscar Alvarez Araya.** Golpe de estado de Hugo Rivas. Herejía para topos de Oscar Alvarez Araya. San José: Editorial Costa Rica, 1977. 94 p. (Colección Joven creación; 1)

The first two in a series of prize-winning stories from contemporary Costa Rica by two very young writers, very different in style and content, but both of superior quality. Rivas treats more directly social and political issues, while Alvarez Araya creates his own mythological world.

5282 Villeda Arita, Samuel. El país de las voces. Cuentos premiados. Tegucigalpa: Impr. Cultura, 1976. 75 p. (Colección Claudio Barrera)

Recipient of the "Marcos Carias Reyes" prize, this collection of 11 short stories by a young Honduran intellectual speaks positively and eloquently to the problems of underdevelopment that beset this small dependent nation. Whimsical and yet profound, several of these stories denounce the ideological confusion and repression that make life difficult for all, and particularly for the thinking person.

LITERARY CRITICISM AND HISTORY

5283 Asturias, Miguel Angel. Sociología guatemalteca: el problema social del indio (Guatemalan sociology: the social problem of the Indian). The original Spanish text, followed by an English translation by Maureen Ahern. Introduction by Richard J. Callan. Tempe: Arizona State University, Center for Latin American Studies, 1977. 106 p.

This thesis was submitted by Asturias in 1923 to the Sociology Dept. of the Univ. of Guatemala. The volume includes the Spanish original, English translation and an introduction by Richard J. Callan. Of interest to those concerned with the development of Asturias' ideas. Much of what is proposed in the thesis (e.g., that European immigration be encouraged "to better" the Indian race, etc.) has been disavowed by Asturias. [Pedro F. Hernández]

5284 Bernu, Michèle. Mythe et société dans *Hombres de maíz* de M.A. Asturias (UTIEH/C, 29, 1977, p. 45–64)

The provocative question raised here is the relationship of myth to rationalism, and to real practical issues in modern Guatemala. As a complement to the magical world of the *Popol Vuh*, the characters are analyzed according to social class, and the conflict between the Indians and the ladinos becomes a struggle between diverse economic systems, problems recalling Agrarian Reform measures undertaken in Guatemala by Arbenz.

5285 Coll, Edna. Indice informativo de la novela hispanoamericana. t. 2, Centroamérica. Río Piedras: Editorial Universitaria, Universidad de Puerto Rico, 1977. 343 p., bibl., index.

This is vol. 2 in a series of invaluable guides to the literature of Spanish America for professors and students (vol. 1, *Las Antillas*, was published in 1974). It includes clear and abundant biographical and bibliographical data for a vast number of individual writers of prose fiction, who appear by countrics, plus extensive bibliographies for each republic and the area in general. A fine series highly recommended for libraries.

5286 Corvalán, Octavio. *Hombres de maíz*: una novela-mito (JSSTC, 7:1, Spring 1979, p. 33–40)

Following Lévi-Strauss and comments by Asturias himself, the author identifies the novel as a new American myth based on the conflict "*naturaleza* versus *cultura*" and on the myth-maker's (here, Asturias) capacity for "pensamiento mágico."

5287 Fonseca, Virginia Sandoval de. El presbítero Don Juan Garita. San José, Costa Rica: Ministerio de Cultura, Juventud y Deportes, Departamento de Publicaciones, 1977. 217 p., bibl. (Serie del creador analizado; 5)

This volume by the Costa Rican scholar and educator divides itself into 1) a lengthy critical exegesis of the life and literary works of the 19th-century "Fray Juan;" and 2) a useful anthology of his writings—fiction, social and political essays, and poetry. Given the paucity of material on the origins of Costa Rican literature, this type of investigation seems both valuable and essential.

5288 Guillén, Pedro. Con Miguel Angel Asturias (CAM, 212:3, mayo/junio 1977, p. 41–51)

This is an anecdotal article which records touching and great moments in the life of the Nobel prize-winner, his many close ties with Mexico, his repeated repudiation of dictatorships in Guatemala, and his profound attachment to France. All this is seen through the eyes of the author, who initiates his study with Asturias in the Canary Islands in 1974, organizing an *Homenaje* to León Felipe. Informative, warm and sympathetic.

5289 Himelblau, Jack. The sociopolitical views of Miguel Angel Asturias, 1920–1930 (HISP, 61, sept. 1977, p. 61–80)

Here, the author traces the young Asturias' intellectual progression from active political involvement toward an aesthetic solution to the social ills of Guatemala. Quoting from early works, it details his open political attacks against Estrada Cabrera, his anti-Americanism, his vision of Central America from Paris, and his adoption of Mayan culture as a motif that unifies the nation at its profoundest roots.

5290 Lagmanovich, David. Estructura y límites del cuento en "Ocelotle 33" de Miguel Angel Asturias (Nueva Narrativa Hispanoamericana [Adelphi University, Latin American Studies Program, Garden City, N.Y.] 4, enero/sept. 1974, p. 269–274)

Taking as his subject what he considers the best story of the collection *Week-end en Guatemala*, the author attributes its deficiencies not to the intrusion of a political message, the more common weakness of the volume, but to structural miscalculations. While the story possesses some stylistic merits typical of Asturias, it extends beyond an aesthetically satisfying conclusion (the discovery that Prinani and Najarro are part of the same conspiracy) in order to fulfill extraliterary exigencies.

5291 Marín Cañas, José. Coto: La Guerra del 21 con Panamá. 2. ed. San José: Editorial Costa Rica, 1976. 105 p.

A re-edition, after some 40 years, of the story of a Costa Rican expeditionary force massacred by Panamanian troops during the 1921 conflict. The narrative, in the same vein as the author's well-known *El infierno verde* (1935), is valuable for its sensitive recreation of the horrors of war and the terrible destructive potential of modern arms.

5292 Merrell, Floyd. Hacia una interpretación de la novela histórica guatemalteca (HISP, 64, 1978, p. 71–84)

This article takes as a point of departure the prolongation of "Romantic" tendencies in Guatemalan letters, which explains, in part, the long career of the historical novel as explored here: from José Milla y Vidaurre (*Los nazarenos*, 1867) to Elisa Hall (*Mostaza*, 1939). Several common characteristics allow for the formulation of a structural model for the genre, and help to interpret its relevance to contemporary social and political events.

Rodríguez Masís, René and **Antonio Acevedo E.** Indice selectivo de la prensa literaria: mayo 1972–agosto 1978. See *HLAS 41:136*.

5293 Sáenz, Jimena. Genio y figura de Miguel Angel Asturias. Buenos Aires: Editorial Universitaria de Buenos Aires, 1974. 263 p.: ill., bibl. (Genio y figura; 29)

In a straightforward but very engaging style, the author recounts the events of Asturias' life with critiques of all his works. A helpful bibliography accompanies this fine tribute from an objective but sympathetic scholar.

PROSE FICTION: 20th Century: Hispanic Caribbean

CARLOS R. HORTAS, *Associate Professor of Spanish, Hunter College*
CARLOS J. CANO, *Associate Professor of Spanish, University of South Florida*

ALEJO CARPENTIER CONTINUED to dominate the Caribbean literary scene during the past two years. Two new novels, *La consagración de la primavera* and *El arpa y la sombra*, and numerous articles about his works were published. Many more honors were bestowed upon him, notably the Miguel de Cervantes Saavedra Prize, Spain's most important literary award. Public recognition of these honors, particularly in the Cuban press, emphasized Carpentier's attainment of classical stature while still alive, thus somewhat foreshadowing his recent death. His literary legacy promises to be an enduring one.

José Lezama Lima's growing and recent popularity is exemplified by the posthumous publication of two of his works: *Oppiano Licario* (item **5306**) and his poetry, *Fragmentos a su imán* (item **5774**). Although critical attention to his works is increasing, the quality of these published studies is uneven. One exception is Enrico Santí's article on the Oedipus theme in *Paradiso* (item **5329**). The attention recently accorded Lezama augurs well for the appearance of a proper evaluation of his literary worth.

In Cuba, the government has implemented its plan of publishing new editions of works long out of print. As noted on p. 000 of this *HLAS*, 19th-century writers such as José de Armas y Céspedes, Ramón Meza, Pedro José Morillas, Francisco Calcagno, Ramón de Palma, Esteban Borrero Echeverría and 20th-century writers like Enrique Serpa, Luis Felipe Rodríguez and Carlos Loveira have reappeared in popular but professional editions. Since these works, written before the Cuban Revolution, are critical of Cuban society, the official cultural and literary policy is to regard them as revolutionary. Fernández Retamar's essay on the cultural policy of the Revolution defines the criteria for acceptable literary creations.

These developments as well as the publication of several Cuban literary histories suggest that Cuban letters have entered a period of self-analysis, designed to ascertain accomplishments, take stock of failures and identify new objectives. This concentration on evaluation, partly explains the lack of more vigorous works by young writers who must eventually replace Carpentier and Lezama Lima.

As usual, Puerto Rico offers a number of interesting short story writers, among whom Marigloria Palma and Magali García Ramis are especially recommended. A number of novelists are producing well-crafted and at times innovative works; however the *Great Puerto Rican Novel* is still not at hand. Emilio Díaz Valcárcel's experiments with language and structure fall short of our expectations of him, and Enrique Laguerre contributes nothing new stylistically, in spite of his invaluable contributions to Puerto Rican narrative over the years. Of particular note is José Luis González's *Balada de otro tiempo* (item **5303**), exceptional for its clear style and precise use of language. González is to be especially commended for his mastery of the writer's craft. For those readers interested in the life of the legendary Puerto Rican pirate, Roberto Cofresí, and in works inspired by him, a new thorough and well-written study is highly recommended (item **5299**).

Overshadowed by Cuba and Puerto Rico, the Dominican Republic receives less notice and is known by comparatively few readers of Latin American literature. Nonetheless, Dominican authors continue writing works of interest and value. For those who wish to learn about Dominican literature, one recommends *Lecturas dominicanas* (item **5305**), a well-designed and representative anthology, including short introductions to all authors represented, many of them contemporary. *Tablero* (item **5297**), a collection of short stories by Aída Cartagena Portalatín, makes interesting reading. Most editions, collections or anthologies include the almost obligatory preface by Juan Bosch, the best-known of Dominican narrators. Those unfamiliar with his short stories might pick up *Cuentos escritos en el exilio* (item **5295**), a good introduction to Dominican narrative.

Some important differences: Carmela's character grows and adapts to changing conditions (learning that she is not white, rejection in love, etc.). This is one of the first Cuban novels to introduce a Chinese character and a Chinese home setting. Meza's style is interesting as it varies from expressionistic to caricaturesque.

5311 Palma, Marigloria. Cuentos de la abeja encinta. San Juan: Universidad de Puerto Rico, Editorial Universitaria, 1975. 356 p. (Colección Uprex 48. Serie Ficción)

Brief incidents of daily life, at times absurd, at times indicative of the effect of the 20th century on Puerto Rican daily life. Characters are well-sketched and come from all groups and social classes. Humorous and satirical, these short stories make interesting and worthwhile reading. This is Ms. Palma's first published collection of short stories and they are a valuable contribution to contemporary Puerto Rican narrative.

5312 Pérez Cabral, Pedro Andrés. Jengibre. Introducción de Diógenes Céspedes. Santo Domingo: Editora Alfa y Omega, 1978. 199 p., bibl.

A new edition of a novel first published in 1940, preceded by a thorough, critical and historical study by Diógenes Céspedes. *Jengibre* is particularly notable for its conscious use of Dominican Spanish and its criticism of political oppression. The novel is both an interesting reflection of its time and a good example of Antillean literary realism, though as a novel it lacks well-defined characters and structure.

5313 Rodríguez, Luis Felipe. El negro que se bebió la luna. Prólogo de Pilar Ferreiro. La Habana: Editorial Arte y Literatura, 1978. 424 p. (Biblioteca básica de literatura cubana)

Although published in monthly installments in 1953, this is the first actual publication of the author's last novel. Set in 1868, against the background of the start of the Ten Year's War, it deals with the tragic relationship of two slaves. The novel is also an attempt to analyze Cuba's first war of independence according to economic factors.

5314 Rodríguez Demorizi, Emilio. Cuentos de política criolla. Prólogo de Juan Bosch, editor. 2. ed. Santo Domingo: Librería Dominicana, 1977. 240 p.: port. (Colección Pensamiento dominicano; 28)

A good anthology of short stories with political themes. The authors perceive Dominican politics as an activity pursued by dishonest men, crooks and thieves. Some of the stories are of very good quality; others are mere anecdotes or caricatures. Eleven authors are represented in this edition which includes a good introduction by Juan Bosch.

5315 Sarduy, Severo. Maitreya. Barcelona: Seix Barral, 1978. 187 p. (Nueva narrativa hispánica)

The simultaneous references to oriental (Buda) and tropical (Cuba) elements create a surrealistic setting for this novel. The transvestite theme and the Baroque verbal decorations make it very erotic.

5316 Serpa, Enrique. Contrabando. Prólogo de Denia García. La Habana: Editorial de Arte y Literatura, 1977. 294 p. (Ediciones Huracán)

Serpa's first novel, originally published in 1938 and written five years earlier, deals with a shipment of contraband alcohol from Cuba to the US during Prohibition. It portrays the economic ruin of Cuban fishermen by American refrigerated ships, and how the former are forced to survive by engaging in contraband. Other themes include human contraband into the US, prostitution, adultery, and various socioeconomic ills. Maritime language is used but often lacks versimilitude in the dialogues.

5317 Tapia y Rivera, Alejandro. La palma del cacique y La leyenda de los veinte años. Barcelona: Vosgos, 1975. 135 p. (Colección Grandes maestros; 79)

An inexpensive student edition, without introduction, critical commentary or bibliography.

5318 Zeno Gandía, Manuel. La charca. Novela. Barcelona: Vosgos, 1978. 249 p. (Colección Grandes maestros; 43)

An inexpensive student edition of Zeno Gandía's best novel. No critical introduction or bibliography provided. The best edition of *La charca* is still the 1966 one by the Instituto de Cultura Puertorriqueña.

LITERARY CRITICISM AND HISTORY

5319 Arana de Love, Francisca. La novela de Puerto Rico durante la primera década del Estado Libre Asociado: 1952–1962. 2. ed. Barcelona: Vosgos, 1976. 1 leaf, 93 p., 4 leaves, bibl.

This brief catalogue of novels written during 1952–62 offers little more than plot summaries and brief commentary on the literary styles and political ideology of individual authors. Its thesis is that the importance of the political status of Puerto Rico is such that commitment to one political solution or another is apparent in all the novels discussed. No other conclusions are reached.

5320 Arias, Salvador. Literatura cubana: 1959–1975 (CDLA, 19:113, marzo/abril 1979, p. 14–26)

A fine study chronologically divided into three parts: 1) the formative period leading up to the 1959 Cuban Revolution; 2) the period 1959–66 in which the intellectuals try to incorporate their work to the revolutionary process; and 3) the period 1966–75, when literary activity matched the growth and maturity of the socioeconomic environment. Includes a detailed explanation of the cultural policy of the Cuban Revolution.

5321 Barnet, Miguel. Conversación con Adriana Méndez (AR, 5:18, 1979, p. 37–43, plates)

In this interview, Barnet reveals some aspects of his childhood in an American school, his gradual integration into the revolutionary process, his early attempts to write poetry, and his discovery of ethnography. On this subject he explains many of his investigative techniques.

5322 Carpentier, Alejo. No tuvo España mejor embajador, a lo largo de los siglos, que Don Quijote de la Mancha (CDLA, 29:109, julio/agosto 1978, p. 82–85)

Carpentier's acceptance speech of the Miguel de Cervantes Prize. He defends the thesis of a Spanish origin (Cervantes and the Picaresque) of the novel. Recalling erroneous predictions of the genre's doom, he affirms his belief in its future.

5323 Feijóo, Samuel. Influencia africana en Latinoamérica: literatura oral y escrita (*in* Africa en América Latina [see *HLAS 41:9035*] p. 185–214)

A general presentation of the oral and written manifestations of the African influence in Latin American literature. Starting with the colonial period, Feijóo analizes the oral traditions, both black and white, in musical folklore. As he moves into modern times, the author examines specific areas, such as the Caribbean. He offers a list of proverbs in Spanish with a possible African origin. He ends by pointing to some cross-fertilization between the black and the white social elements.

5324 Fernández Retamar, Roberto. Formación de la cultura socialista: sus orígenes y peculiaridades (URSS/AL, 1, 1979, p. 153–161)

Essay which places the cultural policy of the Cuban Revolution in perspective. Author's discussion encompasses Castro's 1961 address "Words to the Intellectuals" and the 1975 statement entitled "Thesis on the Artistic and Literary Culture" approved by the First Congress of the Cuban Communist Party. According to the author, the challenge comes from the need to construct a universal, humanist and socialist culture over the foundations of Cuba's authentic historical roots.

5325 González, Eduardo. Alejo Carpentier: el tiempo del hombre. Caracas: Monte Avila Editores, 1978. 220 p., bibl. (Colección Estudios)

A successful attempt to explain Carpentier's literary output by means of a structuralist methodology. The author is able to "translate" many of Carpentier's archetypes into meaningful interpretations, using textual contrastive techniques.

5326 Lazo, Raimundo. Historia de la literatura cubana. 2. ed. México: UNAM, Dirección General de Publicaciones, 1974. 313 p., bibl., index (Textos universitarios)

Literary history divided into four parts: 1) offers some important general notions about Cuban society; 2) discusses the basic characteristics of the settlement of the island and the early colonial period; 3) traces the development of a native culture during the late colonial period; and 4) during the Republican period leading up to the Revolution of 1959. The author devotes sufficient space to some neglected genres such as the theater and the essay. Well written, clear and concise. Short, but selective bibliography.

5327 Méndez y Soto, E. Panorama de la novela cubana de la revolución, 1959–1970. Miami, Fla.: Ediciones Universal, 1977. 262 p., bibl., index (Colección Polymita)

PROSE FICTION

5294 Belaval, Emilio S. Cuentos de la plaza fuerte. Rio Piedras, P.R.: Editorial Cultural, 1977. 83 p.

A new edition of stories written between 1954–60. Stories are of old San Juan. This new edition is inexpensive and its large print makes for easy reading. It offers, however, no biographical or critical introduction of any kind.

5295 Bosch, Juan. Cuentos escritos en el exilio. Santo Domingo: Talleres de Amigo del Hogar, 1976. 297 p. (Colección Santo Domingo; 74/75)

Another edition of Juan Bosch's excellent short stories, preceded by Bosch's "Apuntes sobre el Arte de Escribir Cuentos." No introduction or critical study provided. An inexpensive, paperback edition.

5296 Carpentier, Alejo. Crónicas. Prólogo de José Antonio Portuondo. La Habana: Editorial Arte y Literatura, 1976. 1 v., index (Arte y sociedad)

José Antonio Portuondo's prologue is a good introduction to this selection of previously published newspaper articles by Alejo Carpentier. These articles span Carpentier's 11-year stay in Paris (1938–49), and are very important to understand the author's often-stated desire to relate Latin American and Cuban literary activity to European and Parisian cultural life.

———. Explosion in a cathedral. See item **6627**.

5297 Cartagena Portalatín, Aída. Tablero: doce cuentos de lo popular a lo culto. Santo Domingo: Editora Taller, 1978. 150 p. (Biblioteca Taller; 109)

These 12 short stories are particularly notable for their use of popular language and for their seemingly informal tone. They are fast paced and depend on interior monologue for the revelation of character. Very interesting and original writing technique, definitely worthwhile reading.

Cuentos: an anthology of short stories from Puerto Rico. See item **6616**.

5298 Díaz Valcárcel, Emilio. Harlem todos los días. Novela. San Juan, P.R.: Ediciones Huracán, 1978. 229 p.

This latest novel by Díaz Valcárcel contains some insights into the lives of Puerto Ricans in New York. The narrative is so dense it fails to hold the reader's interest despite some excellent but unsustained linguistic touches and observations. The novel is flawed and would have benefitted from more careful editing by the author.

5299 Fernández Valledor, Roberto. El mito de Cofresí en la narrativa antillana. Río Piedras, P.R.: Editorial Universitaria, Universidad de Puerto Rico, 1978. 149 p., bibl. (Colección Mente y palabra)

An excellent historical and literary approximation to the now legendary figure of the Puerto Rican pirate, Roberto Cofresí. The author has consulted all pertinent documents and historical records and has interviewed many of the older inhabitants of the southern coast of Puerto Rico and the northern coast of the Dominican Republic, which Cofresí frequently visited. Literary allusions to Cofresí are cited and novels, stories and poetry written about him are studied briefly. For anyone who would like to know more about the pirate Cofresí, this is a very good study indeed.

5300 Figueroa Berrios, Edwin. Seis veces la muerte. Prólogo, Angel Luis Morales. Río Piedras, P.R.: Editorial Cultural, 1978. 59 p.

A collection of six short stories which previously appeared in magazines and periodicals, preceded by a good introduction to the author and a critical evaluation of the stories. The narratives are interesting, well constructed and all treat the theme of death. There are no stylistic surprises here. Stories are well-crafted, though unspectacular.

5301 García Godoy, Federico. El derrumbe. Prólogo de Juan Bosch. Santo Domingo: Editora de la Universidad Autónoma de Santo Domingo, 1975. 177 p. (Publicaciones de la Universidad Autónoma de Santo Domingo; 170. Colección Historia y sociedad; 16)

This is an important novel in the history of Dominican narrative in that it was impounded in 1916 by American occupation forces. The novel's criticism of American imperialism made it "subversive" and most copies of the first edition were destroyed. Juan Bosch's excellent prologue provides the reader with a historical background and an account of the way in which the novel was saved from complete destruction.

5302 **García Ramis, Magalí.** La familia de todos nosotros. San Juan: Instituto de Cultura Puertorriqueña, 1976. 100 p. (Serie Literatura hoy; 3)

A few excellent short stories by a promising young writer. Realistic narratives of daily life often graced by a poetic, lyrical tone. Ms. García Ramis is able to create a sense of intimacy between reader and characters.

5303 **González, José Luis.** Balada de otro tiempo. Ilustraciones de Antonio Mortorell. México: Editorial Nueva Imagen, 1978. 152 p.: ill.

The love triangle, the theme of honor, and the differences between life in the mountains and in the lowlands of Puerto Rico provide a background for a rich and subtle exploration of the psychological lives of three characters. Plot and structure are very well woven. An excellent first novel by an excellent short story writer.

5304 **Laguerre, Enrique A.** Los amos benévolos. Novela. Río Piedras: Editorial Universitaria, Universidad de Puerto Rico, 1976. 275 p.

Enrique Laguerre's 10th novel, both in style and narrative structure, very much resembles his earlier works. Mr. Laguerre's themes are interesting; his investigations of the contradictions and complexities of human psychology are to be commended. Nonetheless, his style is plodding and tiresome, his narrative structure tense and overly self-conscious. One would welcome a lighter touch, some narrative relief, a certain change of pace from time to time, so as to keep the reader alert and interested.

5305 **Lecturas dominicanas.** Edición de Carlos Fernández-Rocha y Danilo de los Santos. Madrid: Playor, 1977. 372 p., bibl., ill.

Excellent sampling of Dominican literature from 1821 to the present. This collection includes all genres and reproduces works in their entirety where possible. The volume is well printed and provides short introductions for each of the authors included.

5306 **Lezama Lima, José.** Oppiano Licario. México: Ediciones Era, 1977. 232 p. (Biblioteca Era. Serie Claves)

Lezama's last work of fiction, published posthumously and probably incomplete, continues the narrative of *Paradiso*'s characters like Cemí, Fronesis, Foción, Licario, etc. The homosexual theme is also present. The style is just as Baroque as ever, combining extremely erudite language next to colloquial Cuban words.

5307 **Lloréns, Washington.** Diez pecados de humor. Trabajos de arte de Luis G. Cajiga Lugo. San Juan de Puerto Rico: Instituto de Cultura Puertorriqueña, 1977. 119 p.: ill. (Serie Literatura hoy; año 2, no. 6)

Brief and picturesque scenes by a writer who has been plying his trade for some time. The short stories have an anecdotal character to them and resemble "cuadros de costumbres." The author works toward an unexpected or "snappy" ending to tie up each story and to give it the strength it sometimes lacks in the telling. The narrations, interesting at times, offer nothing new in the way of style or technique.

5308 **Loveira y Chirino, Carlos.** Los inmorales. Prólogo de Cira Romero. La Habana: Editorial de Arte y Literatura, 1976. 305 p. (Ediciones Huracán)

Loveira's first novel, originally published in 1919, resulted from the author's support of the legalization of divorce, then a Cuban political issue. Through the experiences of a loving but unmarried couple, Loveira attacks conventional middle class morality and defends the right to follow one's conscience.

5309 **Matilla Rivas, Alfredo.** Catálogo de locos. Fotos, Francisco Pabón. San Juan de Puerto Rico: Instituto de Cultural Puertorriqueña, 1978. 64 p.: ill. (Serie Literatura hoy; 17)

A mix of free verse and free prose, this *Catálogo* is written in a labored impressionistic manner. Matilla Rivas tries to use the stream of consciousness technique and to put aside punctuation and other conventions, but the effect is very unimpressive. There is no internal structure here, no coherent meaning.

5310 **Meza, Ramón.** Carmela. Prólogo de Salvador Bueno. La Habana: Editorial Arte y Literatura, 1978. 166 p. (Biblioteca básica de literatura cubana)

Meza's novel has been compared to *Cecilia Valdés* because of the thematic similarities: forbidden love between the rich, white young man and the beautiful "mulata."

Although somewhat superficial, this study lists most of the writers and titles required for a complete picture of the Cuban novel of the Revolution. Its thematic classification (insurrection, social testimony, socialist revolution, exile, etc.) is useful too. Includes a good bibliography.

5328 Rodríguez-Puértolas, Julio. Manuel Cofiño o la superación de lo real maravilloso (IL, 1:3, May/June 1977, p. 73–80, bibl.)

A good study of Cofiño's technique (three letter types to match a changing point of view), plus his treatment of the Revolution is imbued with magical-realism (e.g., electric lights viewed as magic by the peasants). Some parallels with Carpentier, including the use of time.

5329 Santí, Enrico Mario. *Paradiso* (MLN, 94:2, March 1979, p. 343–365)

An excellent study of the Oedipus theme in *Paradiso*. According to Santí, the protagonist José Cemi is a deformed copy of the original—his father. The results are his father's death and his own homosexual tendencies. By looking at the text through a structuralist lens, this critic is able to shed light on Lezama's deliberate use of apparent errors.

5330 Schulman, Ivan A. The portrait of the slave: ideology and aesthetics in the Cuban antislavery novel (*in* Comparative perspectives on slavery in New World societies. Edited by Vera Rubin and Arthur Tuben [see item **1768**] p. 356–367)

This study links the origins of the Cuban novel to internal contradictions within the institution of slavery, repressive policies and the literary climate; especially, the influence of Domingo del Monte's literary circle. As a result, Schulman maintains that these anti-slavery novels were on the vanguard of social reform and not merely a reaction to it. An excellent study.

5331 Seminario José Martí, *Universidad de Puerto Rico, Río Piedras, 1971.* Estudios martianos: memoria del Seminario José Martí, celebrado bajo los auspicios de la Fundación José Martí y el Departamento de Estudios Hispánicos, Facultad de Humanidades, de la Universidad de Puerto Rico, Recinto de Río Piedras, Febrero, 1971. San Juan: Editorial Universitaria, Universidad de Puerto Rico, 1974. 197 p., bibl.

These memoirs include a stylistic study of Martí's prose by Manuel Pedro González, a textual comparison of the *Versos libres* by Ivan A. Schulman, the theme of freedom in poem XLV of the *Versos sencillos* by Margot Arce de Vásquez, a comparative study of Martí and Heredia by Manuel de la Puebla, a study of Puerto Rican influences on Martí by María Mercedes Solá, the inspiration of Martí for the Puerto Rico Independentists by F. Manrique Guerra, the Black man in Martí by José Ferrer Canales, Martí's warning of American imperialism by José R. de la Torre, and a lengthy article on Martí's modernity by Angel Rama.

Sosa, Enrique. La economía en la novela cubana del siglo XIX. See item **5165**.

5332 Tittler, Jonathan. Intratextual distance in *Tres tristes tigres* (MLN, 93:2, March 1978, p. 285–296)

Wayne C. Booth's *The rhetoric of fiction* serves as a theoretical basis for this study of Cabrera Infante's novel. It describes Cabrera Infante's main aim as a kind of "disarming honesty," related to Cervantes' brand of realism: to create an illusion through words while simultaneously revealing the illusion.

5333 Weiss, Judith A. On the trail of the (un)holy serpent: Cobra by Severo Sarduy (JSSTC, 5:1, Spring 1977, p. 59–69)

By means of a structuralist approach, and despite the many textual and thematic challenges posed by Sarduy, Weiss is able to explain Sarduy's methodical erasure of definitions. A case for the interpretation of *Cobra* as a "playground for one protagonist: Language."

5334 Williams, Lorna V. "El mundo alucinante:" la historia como posibilidad (*in* Simposio Internacional de Estudios Hispánicos, Budapest, 1976. Actas [see item **5067**] p. 501–504)

Although short—obviously written for an oral presentation—this article shows Arena's distrust of history as an irreversible process. The structure of the novel is proof of that: history is a cycle, and a source of fantastic adventure.

PROSE FICTION: 20th Century: Andean Countries (Bolivia, Colombia, Ecuador, Peru and Venezuela)

JOSE MIGUEL OVIEDO, *Professor of Spanish, University of California, Los Angeles*
DJELAL KADIR, *Associate Professor of Spanish and Comparative Literature, Purdue University*

CRITICA LITERARIA: La producción crítica más reciente en esta área parece haber desarrollado dos grandes polos de interés: por un lado, la crítica textual y a veces de planteamiento teórico, sobre ciertos autores, etapas y tendencias; por otro, la crítica sociológica, con marcada preocupación ideológica, de algunos procesos de nuestra literatura, el del indigenismo por ejemplo, que ha contado en el período con numerosos estudios de diversa calidad e intención. El enfoque estructuralista no ha desaparecido, por cierto, pero ha sido menos abundante (o significativo) que en los años inmediatamente anteriores. Sin embargo, los mejores ejemplos de crítica literaria no pertenecen ni a uno ni otro campo, sino al modelo más clásico del ensayo interpretativo que equilibra el examen de la obra de un autor y el de su contexto cultural. En este sentido los diversos trabajos de investigación y de recopilación realizados por Juan Gustavo Cobo Borda (items **5386–5387** y **5446**) especialmente para las publicaciones del Instituto Colombiano de Cultura, han sido de sustancial importancia por su percepción crítica, su independencia de criterio y su justa reactualización de ciertos nombres del pasado. A él se debe principalmente la reaparición ante el público lector de un ensayista de la talla de Baldomero Sanín Cano, que estaba olvidado entre los clásicos de América que nadie lee.

Los autores más estudiados siguen siendo García Márquez y Vargas Llosa, cuyas obras son examinadas con los más recientes instrumentos críticos. Un volumen que cabe destacar es el dedicado a Vargas Llosa por varios autores y compilado por Charles Rossman y Alan Warren Friedman (item **5433**). Aparte de los numerosos artículos consagrados a García Márquez hay que mencionar la exhumación de algunos viejos textos periodísticos suyos, valiosos por sus tomas de posición, que han sido también rescatados por Cobo Borda (item **5387**). Otros temas que han merecido interés de los críticos son: la novela contemporánea y novísima de Colombia, la problemática del indigenismo principalmente en Ecuador y Perú, las revalorizaciones de Mariátegui como crítico literario, la narrativa del venezolano Salvador Garmendia.

Entre los ensayistas del Perú, dos deben ser mencionados por diversas razones: el veterano Luis Alberto Sánchez, que publicó un repertorio de algunas de sus más clásicas páginas de crítica y de meditación sobre la problemática de la literatura peruana, además de un libro definitivo sobre Manuel González Prada (item **5426**); y Julio Ramón Ribeyro, notable cuentista que presentó un volumen de sus *Prosas apátridas,* hermoso libro de reflexiones sobre él mismo y su ejercicio literario que puede considerarse una pequeña obra maestra (item **5438**).

Los aportes críticos de Bolivia, Ecuador y Venezuela son menos importantes y más aislados. Mientras los dos primeros países parecen todavía atados a un viejo y poco operativo concepto de crítica social, el tercero no halla todavía los patrones interpretativos adecuados a su particular proceso. Un par de excepciones en este país son los aportes del bibliógrafo argentino Horacio Jorge Becco (item **5445**) para ordenar las fuentes literarias nacionales, y el esfuerzo histórico-literario del poeta y crítico venezolano Juan Liscano para presentar una imagen coherente de las letras en el siglo XX (item **5451**). En Bolivia ha habido un intento de difundir las obras de algunos de sus más representativos autores en este siglo tales como Jesús Lara, Guillermo Francovich, etc. (items **5380–5381**) mientras los ecuatorianos J. Icaza y Demetrio Aguilera-Malta (items **5416** y **5418**) han sido estudiados por críticos extranjeros; en ambos casos, desgraciadamente, el resultado ha dejado que desear, ya sea por la falta de rigor en las recopilaciones o en los enfoques críticos. [JMO]

NOVELS AND SHORT STORIES: Unabated is the term that best describes the production of prose fiction in this area during the biennium of 1976–1978. The prolific quantity in no way hinders the high quality of fiction being published. While Venezuela and Colombia lead the Andean pack in output, Peru, in a difficult political period, is not far behind. Actually, some of the most interesting and varied work has come out of Peru during these two years. Ecuador remains constant, with the notable exception of a poet, Jorge Enrique Adoum, turned prose writer. Bolivia, predictably enough, given its resources, lags behind.

The works' range and diversity in thematic and formal terms makes the task of covering this particular region exciting. Traditional preoccupations and socio-historical realities persist in all five countries, with national variations, of course. Bolivia still bemoans a human condition of unmitigated tragedy with a narrative voice which is predominantly a voice of *agon* (items **5335–5336**). The nativist strain continues strong in Ecuador with Dávila (item **5353**). Peru still harkens to the lyrical voice of Arguedas (item **5356**) and Colombia is still trying to exorcise the demons of its tumultuous "violencia" of this century (item **5342**). The European conquest of the New World still finds echoes in the Colombian Gómez Valderrama (item **5345**) and the archetypal figure of the *caudillo* reverberates imaginatively in Venezuela's Uslar Pietri (item **5378**).

The political novel as genre continues to receive innovative treatment with varying degrees of success—from the lyrical dream sequences of the Bolivian Vargas (item **5338**) to the revolutionary underground suspense of the Venezuelan Otero Silva (item **5376**); from the political prisons of the Peruvian Bendezú (item **5357**) to the biting satire of the Colombian Gardeazábal (item **5339**). In a related trend, the newly found mineral wealth of Venezuela, and to some extent of Colombia, sees the rise of a new narrative mode: *the novel*. Oil becomes thematically central to the Venezuelans Croce (item **5372**) and Carrera (item **5371**), as well as to the Colombian Araujo (item **5340**).

A concomitant preoccupation, one which the Uruguayan Rodó descried and whose dangers he lamented at the turn of the century as the greatest danger to Latin America—i.e., the de-Latinization of Latin America—emerges as a central issue in these writers. Causes related to this phenomenon—e.g., modernization, urbanization, a wealthier middle class, the problems of cultural homogeneity and a resultant sense of the loss of uniqueness and pluralism—occupy most authors and writers such as the Peruvian Bouroncle (item **5358**) and the Colombian Santamaría (item **5350**) who treat the problem more explicitly. The search for an autocthonous authenticity in fact remains intense and its narrative spin-offs become quite diversified. Of these derivatives, marginality could be considered as the most prevalent and most significant. In its narrative coordinates this marginality becomes variously configured as: 1) linguistic structure, as in the Venezuelan Carrera (item **5371**); 2) psychological crises—the Colombians Collazos (item **5341**) and Sánchez (item **5348**); and 3) social insecurity—the Ecuadorian Velasco Mackenzie (item **5355**) and the Peruvian Riesco (item **5365**).

Two instances of this exploration and pursuit of authenticity are particularly noteworthy for their novelty. Both come from Peru and delve into ethnic identities other than the indigenous. The first of these is Goldemberg (item **5361**) and his novel about the Jewish community and its vicissitudes in Peru during the 1920s and 1930s. The second is the fascinating novelization of the black experience in the southern desert region of Peru by Gregorio Martínez (item **5363**).

A more venerable mode of cultural self-searching, one that dates back to Peru's Ricardo Palma, consists of the compilation of Potosí's "tradiciones" by the Bolivian Ochoa (item **5337**). The Colombian Niño (item **5346**) takes us back even further in his retelling of Amerindian myths of the Amazon. In differing but related efforts Peru's Bravo (item **5359**) explores the European connection in Old World capitals, particularly Madrid, and Thorndike (item **5366**) successfully ventures into the novelization of the War of the Pacific and its calamitous consequences for Peru.

Of old masters and new lights: The Kafkaesque world of the venerable Ecuadorian Carrión (item **5352**) haunts the pages of his new collection of stories. The Peruvian Ribeyro's tales (item **5364**) have acquired an even greater intensity and greater refinement than ever before. Vargas Llosa (item **5367**) has discovered the melodramatic hilarity of popular culture, the *radio novela*, and the portentous bathos of its language. Speaking of this language, Vargas Llosa's countrywoman Riesco (item **5356**) offers an undiluted dosage of it in its everyday setting and naturally spoken form.

The media, written, spoken, and seen, receive wide coverage. In the Venezuelan Balza (item **5369**) we are indirectly treated to a history of the development of radio and television in that country and in the Colombians Erazo and Gómez (item **5344**) we witness the emergence of a new type of novel—one founded on journalism and newspaper coverage, born of the collaborative efforts of a novelist and a reporter. The genre of the cinema constitutes a significant cross-genre modulation in an experimental work by the young Venezuelan Graterol (item **5374**).

The most convincing experimental work, however, has to be the novel of the Ecuadorian poet turned novelist, Jorge Enrique Adoum (item **5351**), an avant-garde work by any standards, especially Ecuadorian. Overall, the most accomplished and exciting young writers in the region are two very different Peruvians: Alfredo Bryce Echenique (item **5360**) and Gregorio Martínez (item **5363**), as well as the two Colombians Gustavo Alvarez Gardeazábal (item **5339**) and Héctor Sánchez (item **5348**).

Finally, I should indicate three significant anthologies from Colombia which are useful and edited by Luque Muñoz (item **5144**), Collazos (item **5343**), and the Federación de Loterías de Colombia and entitled *Crónica imaginaria de la violencia colombiana* (item **5342**). [DjK]

PROSE FICTION
BOLIVIA

5335 Bascopé Aspiazu, René. Primer fragmento de noche y otros cuentos. La Paz: Editorial Casa Municipal de la Cultura Franz Tamayo, 1978. 58 p. (Biblioteca paceña: Nueva serie)

A collection of seven short stories which won the 1977 "Premio en Cuento—XI Concurso Anual de Literatura Franz Tamayo." A collection of unmitigated violence, tragedy, and death—collective-social violence, sexual and psychological torment not always well controlled by the author whose narrative falls into the bathos of melodrama. [DjK]

5336 Cáceres Romero, Adolfo. Las víctimas. Novela. Cochabamba, Bolivia: Editorial Los Amigos del Libro, 1978. 105 p.

A novelization of agony. A focus on illness and old age, impending death, and the human drama in coping with the inevitable.

A social allegory based on the individual vicissitudes of human suffering and its verbalization. [DjK]

Francovich, Guillermo. Alcides Arguedas y otros ensayos sobre la historia. See item **7850**.

5337 **Ochoa, Rubén.** Potosí de antaño. Leyendas y cuentos. La Paz: Ultima Hora, 1976. 222 p. (Biblioteca popular boliviana de Ultima Hora)

A collection of "tradiciones" in the manner of Ricardo Palma from Potosí's rich and violent history, legend, and Indian lore. A useful ethnographic document as well as revealing popular literature. A good specimen of Indigenista literatura and folklore. [DjK]

5338 **Vargas, Manuel.** Los signos de la lluvia. Novela. La Paz: Difusión, 1978. 170 p. (Colección Vereda)

A novel of run-on dream sequences, shuttling between reverie and profane sociopolitical realities—contemporary and historical—of Bolivia's history. A deliberate assault on the boundaries between life and death, death-in-life and life-in-death which sees the continuation of the same social realities and injustices. Not always successful, but a highly lyrical work of intense poetic language. [DjK]

COLOMBIA

5339 **Alvarez Gardeazábal, Gustavo.** El titiritero. Bogotá: Plaza y Janés, 1977. 269 p. (Manantial; 60)

Gardeazábal at his satirical and iconoclastic best. The novel is a sharp cutting edge which dissects the sociopolitical realities of Colombia with an irreverent focus on intellectuals, the university, political figures, and counter-culture luminaries. Delightful reading of perennially sad, social realities. [DjK]

5340 **Araújo, Roberto.** Escalera del orden. Novela. Bogotá: Pliego Editores, 1977. 159 p.

A short novel of international intrigue and suspense. Well constructed and executed as mystery novel, it pits the petrol interests of the US State Department and the CIA against the agro interests of local economy. First novel of the young author, the technical finesse it evinces promises great things to come. Acute insight into US policy for Latin America in general. [DjK]

5341 **Collazos, Oscar.** Disociaciones y despojos. Bogotá: Editorial Pluma, 1977. 122 p.

Of the younger Colombian writers Collazos is perhaps the most able in handling the adolescent psyche and narrative of coming of age. In this short, lyrical novel the young protagonist comes to terms with the strong and yet socially victimized father figure in his life upon the death of the father. A fascinating linguistic collage of the remains of Colombia's recent violent past and the modernizing cultural elements which have infused the traditionally pluralistic culture of underdevelopment. [DjK]

5342 **Crónica imaginaria** de la violencia colombiana. Selección y notas de Roberto Ruiz y César Valencia Solanilla. Bogotá: Federación de Loterías de Colombia, 1977. 240 p.

A collection of 20 short stories, preceded by an introduction and followed by brief bio-bibliographical sketch of each contributor, which documents in fiction the most violent period of Colombia's history in this century. The selections are good and broadly inclusive of political ideology, ranging from the conservative right, i.e., Hernando Tellez, to the left—García Márquez. The collection is not exhaustive by any means, but it does furnish a good cross-section of contemporary Colombian writers. [DjK]

5343 **Diez narradores** colombianos. Selección de Oscar Collazos. Barcelona: Bruguera, 1977. 186 p. (Libro amigo; 528)

A useful collection, chronologically arranged, all living authors with the exception of the first. Includes a brief introduction by the editor Oscar Collazos and a bio-bibliographical sketch of each author. Good selections by a sensitive editor who is himself a writer and included here. Each author is represented by one story. [DjK]

5344 **Erazo, Luis Ernesto** and **Jairo Gómez.** Enigma en las cenizas. Bogotá: Distribución Nacional, Librería Mundial, 1976. 237 p. (Colección Ergo; 1)

A roman-à-clef based on one of Colombia's most celebrated criminal cases of the 1970s. The authors, a novelist and a journalist, compare themselves in their introduction to Washington reporters Woodward and Bernstein, authors of the Watergate book, *All the President's Men*. Their account is interesting insofar as it allows the reader a good look at the newly wealthy society of Colombia and at the machinations of the system of justice and law enforcement in that country. Gorey, melodramatic, but true to life. [DjK]

García Márquez, Gabriel. Innocent Enréndira, and other stories. See item **6656**.

5345 Gómez Valderrama, Pedro A. La otra raya del tigre. Bogotá: Siglo Veintiuno Editores, 1977. 277 p. (La Creación literaria)

A novel of 19th-century romance, adventure, and conquest. An allegorical work which renders the European conquest of America as recurrent motif. Not particularly original, nor narratively innovative. Enjoyable reading nonetheless. Another saga of the building of an empire by foreign interests on the foundations of betrayed political and social idealism. [DjK]

Narradores colombianos del siglo XIX. See item **5144**.

5346 Niño, Hugo. Primitivos relatos contados otra vez: héroes y mitos amazónicos. Bogotá: Instituto Colombiano de Cultura, Subdirección de Comunicaciones Culturales, División de Publicaciones, 1977. 173 p., maps (Biblioteca colombiana de cultura. Colección popular; 23)

An ethnographically interesting collection of Indian tales, legends, and fables retold in a lyrical language which manages to capture the rich Amerindian tradition of oral literature. A good anthropological preface precedes the eight pieces of varying lengths included here. The author, an anthropologist by training, has rendered a good service in making these precolumbian myths and tales available to the modern reader. [DjK]

5347 Rocha Ochoa, Cesáreo. Tierra buena: cuentos y relatos. Ibagué, Colombia: Fondo de Cultura de la Beneficencia del Tolima, 1976. 133 p.

An unconvincing collection of 18 short pieces. The pieces are set in the Colombian province of Tolima which the author manages to romanticize to the point of sentimentality. As the title indicates, this is an elegy to rural innocence and the return to the land. [DjK]

5348 Sánchez, Héctor. Se acabó la casa. Relatos. Bogotá: Instituto Colombiana de Cultura, Subdirección de Comunicaciones Culturales, División de Publicaciones, 1978. 155 p. (Colección Autores nacionales; 31. Biblioteca colombiana de cultura)

The nine stories included here are actually a collection of portraits—character portraits of subjects who are the marginal elements of society, from retirees, to young vagabonds, from soldiers to refugees. Some of the pieces are more successful than others. Sánchez is at his best when he becomes satirical and sardonic. Minimal action but some delightful descriptions. [DjK]

5349 ———. Sin nada entre las manos. Novela. Barcelona: Editorial Planeta, 1976. 329 p. (Latinoamericana. Serie mayor)

Of the younger Colombian writers (since García Márquez), Héctor Sánchez is one of the most distinguished. The present work recounts the pleasures of triumph—the protagonist is a champion cyclist—and the discovery of the ambiguous and ambivalent world of professional sports, the not so sporting aspects of the world's entrepreneurs, hangers-on, and others who prey on the vicarious pleasures of success. Ably narrated, intricately interwoven, this is the author's fourth successful novel. [DjK]

5350 Santamaría, Germán. Morir último. Bogotá: C. Valencia Editores, 1978. 117 p.

A collection of six stories in which the author demonstrates great dexterity as narrator with a consistent command of the narrative voice and language of his characters. The latter are, for the most part the dispossessed of society, victims of modernization and the encroachment of 20th-century values upon the simpler life of rural society. [DjK]

ECUADOR

5351 Adoum, Jorge Enrique. Entre Marx y una mujer desnuda. Texto con personajes. 2. ed., corregida. México: Siglo Veintiuno, 1978. 311 p., ill. (Creación literaria)

The Ecuatorian Adoum is known primarily as a poet. This novel, not properly called a novel but a "texto con personajes," demonstrates the poet's acute understanding of narrative modes, textual semiotics, and intertextual strategies. A self-conscious, constantly self-referential "composition mis en abîme" which engages the perennial problem of art and social "value" in an original manner. Experimentally far beyond anything produced in Ecuador. [DjK]

Aguilera Malta, Demetrio. Seven serpents and seven moons. See item **6623**.

5352 **Carrión, Alejandro.** Mala procesión de hormigas. Cuentos. Quito: Editorial Casa de la Cultura Ecuatoriana, 1978. 243 p.

Carrión is an old hand in Ecuadorian letters and his experience shows in this collection of Kafkaesque long short stories—nine in all. Delightfully entertaining depiction of exasperating circumstances beyond man's control or anticipation. The settings range from political prisons to family situations which victimize for the most part middle class, professional men too meek or "civil" to effectively counter with meaningful action. [DjK]

5353 **Dávila Vázquez, Jorge.** El círculo vicioso. Cuentos. Cuenca, Ecuador: Departamento de Difusión Cultural, Universidad de Cuenca, 1977. 104 p. (Publicaciones de la Universidad de Cuenca; 3)

A collection of 15 short pieces, some barely more than a page with an acute sense of irony and biting satire. Centered on human situations and relationships all too fragile and susceptible to the happenstance. This young promising author published a prize-winning novel in 1976. This is his first collection of stories. [DjK]

5354 ———. Los tiempos del olvido. Cuentos 1974. Cuenca, Ecuador: Casa de la Cultura Ecuatoriana, Núcleo del Azuay, 1977. 106 p.

A tightly knit collection of 10 stories focused on the decline and disintegration of a provincial family. The stories are of uneven quality. The technical stratagems of simultaneous narration, fragmented perspective, temporal splicing while interesting do not always prove successful. [DjK]

5355 **Velasco Mackenzie, Jorge.** Como gato en tempestad. Guayaquil: Casa de la Cultura Ecuatoriana, Núcleo del Guayas, 1977. 111 p. (Colección Letras del Ecuador; 52)

A tripartite collection, eight stories in all, by one of Ecuador's more convincing young writers. Velasco Mackenzie is an intense narrator with a good command of interior monologue and lyrical psychological states. He demonstrates a good ability to handle ambiguity and express intense circumstances through allusion. His best stories deal with marginal elements of society and social victims, from young, pubescent prostitutes to uselessly old generals. [DjK]

PERU

5356 **Arguedas, José María.** Amormundo. Buenos Aires: Calicanto Editorial, 1977, 133 p.

A compilation of the Peruvian master's best short stories. Includes "Amormundo" in its four parts, as well as three other pieces. The poetic nativism of the late Arguedas comes through, as always, in the lyrical tragedy of Andean life. [DjK]

———. Deep rivers. See item **6624**.

5357 **Bendezú, Edmundo.** Niebla en la isla. Lima: Fanal, 1978. 222 p.

An interesting political novel which reveals the all too common and tragic realities of Latin America. A chronicle of the imprisonment (political) and subsequent escape of a group of young men. The novel traces the career of each and in the process discloses the harsh and sad circumstances of Peruvian politics. An intense work of tightly interwoven narrative threads. [DjK]

5358 **Bouroncle Carreón, Alfonso.** Espejismos. Novela. Lima: Editorial Arequipa, 1977. 250 p.

Fictional account of the making of a drug addict. A novel of coming of age and of desperate disintegration of a life progressively drawn to the futility of escapism through artificial means. A sad social commentary on the new middle class and the desperate disorientation of its youth, the dislocation of values, and the *espejismos* (mirages) of promise in alien (US) cultural contexts. [DjK]

5359 **Bravo, José Antonio.** A la hora del tiempo. Barcelona: Seix Barral, 1977. 237 p. (Nueva narrativa hispánicos)

Last of a quartet of novels loosely structured around the bohemian life and intellectual self-discovery of the same writer-protagonist. The second of these, *Barrio de broncas* (1971), won the author Peru's "Premio Nacional de Novela" in 1973. The present work is set, for the most part, in European capitals, primarily Madrid, and comprises the protagonist's search for meaningful links of culture and identity between Peru and the Old World. An interesting gallery of characters, particularly in Madrid. Bravo is making an impact on the Peruvian literary scene. [DjK]

5360 Bryce Echenique, Alfredo. La pasión según San Pedro Balbuena que fue tantas veces Pedro, y que nunca pudo negar a nadie. Lima: Libre 1, 1977. 277 p.

By its thematics and stratagems clearly a post 1960s novel. The work consists of the ever-multiplying fantasies and refractions of imagination of a mythomaniac, Pedro, the writer to be, whose attempts to that end comprise the present text. A refreshingly brilliant work with an acute perspective on the post 1960s intellectual mind-set. Bryce Echenique emerges as a splendid narrator whose career should be watched closely. The author's previous and first novel, *Un mundo para Julius* was a best seller. [DjK]

5361 Goldemberg, Isaac. La vida a plazos de don Jacobo Lerner. 1. ed. en español. Lima: Libre 1, 1978. 234 p.

The Spanish original of a novel that first became famous in English, it focuses on the life and social predicament of Peruvian Jewry between 1923 and 1935. The events are focused through the life of a Russian emigré (Jacobo Lerner) and the contemporaneous annals of *Alma Hebrea*, a chronicle of the Jewish community in Peru. Stylistically interesting and thematically innovative. One of the few fictional accounts of an interesting ethnic component of Spanish American society, it can be read as a cultural-historical document on the Jew in Peru. [DjK]

5362 Higa Oshiro, Augusto. Que te coma el tigre. Ilustraciones, Nobuko Tadokoro. Lima: Lámpara de Papel Editores, 1977. 113 p., ill.

A collection of six pieces focusing on the teenage scene, teenybopper "cool," and after school hangouts. An interesting perspective on secondary school in a big Latin American metropolis and the particular laws of the jungle which govern survival within that setting. This is the author's first work and is ably narrated. [DjK]

5363 Martínez, Gregorio. Canto de sirena. Lima: Mosca Azul Editores, 1977. 164 p.

Martínez is a young writer who published a collection of stories (see *HLAS 40: 6781*) and this is his first novel. The present work comprises the delightful ravings of a colorful, picaresque black man who has lived on the margins of Peruvian society with the wits and folk wisdom of his ethnic background. The narrative consists of the spicy observations of the colorful octogenarian hero which range from "scientific" speculations, culinary arts, sexual proclivities of all species, political injustices, and archaeological history. A very original and significant work, as was the author's previous book, which does for the coastal population of Afro-American ethnic pockets what Arguedas and Ciro Alegría have done for the Andean highlands and Amazonic regions. [DjK]

Ortega, Julio. The land in the day. See item **6632**.

5364 Ribeyro, Julio Ramón. La palabra del mudo. Cuentos 52/72. Lima: Milla Batres Editorial, 1977. 1 v. (220 p.)

This is vol. 3 of the author's collected short stories, the first two having been reviewed in *HLAS 40:6782*. While the title indicates that the contents include stories up to 1972, most of the stories in this volume, as the subtitle avers, have been written since, with the exception of three. In this volume which includes the author's collection *Silvio en el rosedal* (1977), the Peruvian master of the present short story in that country demonstrates that even for a master there are no limits to refinement. The pieces included here are more bookish than previous works, the urban parameters that have always defined Ribeyro's narratives seem to have shrunk even further into the library or erudition of his narrators. A brief prologue by the author posits, cursorily, his views on the genre. [DjK]

5365 Riesco, Laura. El truco de los ojos. Lima: Editorial Milla Batres, 1978. 188 p.

A run-on narrative from beginning to end through the voice and perspective of a young girl. Her eyes and utterance become the reader's window on the petit bourgeois of Lima, its pettiness, pretensions, prejudices, and senseless routine. An x-ray of middle-class values and the inner life of a city. The language is authentically that of Lima and may prove inaccessible to non-Peruvian readers at times. Nonetheless, the flavor of the portrayal, subtlely ironic, mercilessly genuine, comes through quite effectively. A valuable social document. [DjK]

5366 Throndike, Guillermo. El viaje de Prado. Lima: Libre 1, 1977. 455 p.

A good historical novel based on the War of the Pacific between Chile and Peru (1879–83) in which the latter lost a third of its richest territory in a matter of three months. Thorndike's analysis is biting, the armies and military hierarchy of both countries fare poorly; the greed of politicians for the mineral rich terraine is sharply scrutinized. A timely work with reverberations for our epoch and its panic over oil and the Persian Gulf. This is the author's second novel on this period. The first one entitled *1879* (Lima, Libre 1, 1977, 435 p., ill.) includes many historical photographs of the war. [DjK]

Vargas Llosa, Mário. Captain Pantoja and the special service. See item **6634**.

5367 ———. La tía Julia y el escribidor. Novela. Barcelona: Seix Barral, 1977. 447 p. (Biblioteca breve; 424)

A hilarious exercise of self-conscious intra-textuality in which the author exorcizes the demons of the writer. A study in the making of a writer and the unmaking of a hack. Biographers may consider the work as the author's sentimental education and rites of passage into the career of writer. A fascinating document, as well, of camp art and popular soaps or radio novels. An exercise in the constitution of a text through the entropy of popular pabulum. Fascinating also as satire and social commentary. [DjK]

VENEZUELA

5368 Antología personal del cuento venezolano, 1933–1968. Compiled by José Fabbiani Ruiz. Caracas: Ediciones de la Facultad de Humanidades y Educación, Instituto de Investigaciones Literarias, Universidad Central de Venezuela, 1977. 489 p., ill.

A fairly representative collection from the period indicated in the title, yet it remains a "personal anthology" dominated by the editor's preferences. Fifteen authors are represented with three short stories from each. A short bio-bibliographical sketch and a photograph of each author accompany the contributions included. Some notable omissions (e.g., Uslar Pietri, et al.) but a useful anthology nonetheless. [DjK]

5369 Balza, José. D: ejercicio narrativo. Caracas: Monte Avila Editores, 1977. 265 p. (Colección Continentes)

An experimentally interesting work—the narrative is the type script of a cassette recording which speaks the textually juxtaposed memoires of the narrator—a drop-out who has withdrawn to the delta of the Orinoco River, hence the title (*D*), a radio personality through whose narrative the reader acquires a fascinating account of the genesis and development of the media—radio and television—in Venezuela from the early 1930s to the 1970s. A valuable documentary and linguistic exercise. [DjK]

5370 Caracas. Universidad Católica Andrés Bello. Centro de Investigaciones Literarias. Contribución a la bibliografía de Arturo Uslar Pietri, 1906. Realizado por María Zoraída Lange de Cabrera et al.; bajo la dirección del profesor Efraín Subero. Caracas: Ediciones de la Gobernación del Distrito Federal, 1973 or 1974. 396 p. (Colección Bibliografías; 10)

An extremely useful and nearly complete bibliography, it includes a biographical chronology of Uslar Pietri, primary works of literature, journalistic essays, uncollected works, secondary studies on the author, and a short appendix of works discovered after the compilation. The primary works are divided by genre. The bibliography is fairly exhaustive and goes through 1972. A welcome tool for Uslar Pietri scholars. [DjK]

5371 Carrera, Gustavo Luis. Viaje inverso. Novela. Barcelona: Seix Barral, 1977. 311 p. (Biblioteca breve; 422)

As the title implies, this is a quest in search of authenticity; not a search in the past necessarily, but a search in a cultural context of language, a language that might authenticate the cultural and social history of a modern Venezuelan society contaminated by foreign elements and inauthenticated by the contagion of economic wealth (oil) and the invasion of its foreign trappings. Linguistically interesting in the variety of modes of utterance which range from hip to backwoods peasant lingo. [DjK]

5372 Croce, Arturo. Petróleo, mi General. Caracas: Monte Avila Editores, 1977. 509 p. (Colección Continentes)

An interesting specimen of Venezuela's socially committed literature. The work actually consists of two novels (*Ojo de agua* and *Grama Club*) and chronicles the decade of the 1950s, the death of the dictator Gómez and the advent of a new form of socioeconomic and political tyranny: oil and the international oil interest in Venezuela. The two works are interwoven into one by a set of characters which span the socioeconomic spectrum—from the impoverished marauders of Caracas' large dump to the all-powerful of the Grama Club. A brief introduction by the author precedes the volume. A fascinating social commentary, albeit a partisan point of view. [DjK]

5373 Daviú, Matilde. Maithuna. Caracas: Monte Avila Editores, 1978. 148 p. (Colección Donaire)

An uneven collection of 14 stories is the author's first book. The first two and the title story are by far the most accomplished. These are tales of violence, psychological, physical, lyrical violence which permeates all of the stories. The author is most successful when working with concrete detail. Otherwise, her lyricism becomes too hermetic, too involuted. Promising first book. [DjK]

5374 Graterol, Norbith. Texto de memoria para un corto sobre ella. Caracas: Monte Avila Editores, 1978. 112 p. (Colección Donaire)

An experimental work which weds cinematic technique and "narratology." The short novel consists primarily of narrative description and dialogue. An ironic, at times sardonic and humorous work primarily focused on the youthful world of contemporary society, this is the second novel of the young and promising Venezuelan writer. [DjK]

5375 Oropeza, José Napoleón. Las redes de siempre. Caracas: Monte Avila Editores, 1976. 226 p. (Colección Continentes)

An existential novel, narrated in the second person singular; an interior dialogue, self-conscious narrative on life, death, human relationships, solitude, and lyrical epiphany. An optimistic work, nonetheless, which emanates from the ambivalent experiences of youth and discovery, this is the author's first novel. An auspicious beginning. [DjK]

5376 Otero Silva, Miguel. Fiebre. 1. ed. en Nueva narrativa hispánica, Reimpresión. Barcelona: Seix Barral, 1930 [i.e. 1977]. 313 p., 2 leaves (Nueva narrativa hispánica)

A very important work for critics and historians, this is the author's first novel, written in 1930 and based on his firsthand experiences as a rebel fighting against the dictatorship of Gómez in the late 1920s. The novel was re-written in 1936 and again in 1971. It describes the disintegration of the Gómez regime from the insight and perspectives of one of its young victims, the autobiographical protagonist, Vidal. An interesting prologue by the author on the "Generation of 1928" in Venezuela precedes the novel. [DjK]

5377 Palacios, Inocente. Más arriba de la roca que se hunde en el mar. Cuentos. Caracas: E. Armitano, 1977. 95 p.

A tripartite collection, seven stories in all. The first three stories are by far the more convincingly executed. These are linked by the theme of the man-hunt, a controlled violence about to erupt. The narrative maintains the intensity of the theme and the suspense accentuates the imminent violence of the narrative's world. [DjK]

5378 Uslar Pietri, Arturo. Oficio de difuntos. Novela. Barcelona: Seix Barral, 1976. 351 p. (Biblioteca breve; 419)

An intriguing work by Venezuela's venerable man of letters. The haunting presence of that fascinating Latin American figure, the *caudillo,* dominates the narrative of the novel. Uslar Pietri's evocation of this archetypal figure could be considered Venezuela's version of García Márquez's patriarch (*El otoño del patriarca*) and Paraguay's *Yo el supremo* (Roa Bastos). The author's insight into the figure of the *caudillo* is extremely acute and original. [DjK]

LITERARY CRITICISM AND HISTORY
BOLIVIA

5379 **Arancibia Herrera, Mario.** Figuras de la cultura boliviana actual. La Paz: Instituto Boliviano de Cultura, Ministerio de Educación y Cultura, 1976. 411 p.

Conjunto de entrevistas hechas por el autor a unos 45 representantes de la cultura boliviana de hoy, en los campos de la poesía, la novela, el ensayo, la crítica, la filosofía, la historia, la política y el periodismo. Cada uno de los reportajes, de valor diverso, está precedido por notas generalmente ditirámbicas. [JMO]

5380 **Francovich, Guillermo.** Tito Yupanqui: escultor indio. La Paz: Librería Editorial Juventud, 1978. 144 p. (Colección ayer y hoy)

Nueve artículos y trabajos críticos del ensayista boliviano, que van desde 1945 hasta el presente y que cubren temas literarios, filosóficos y artísticos. Como se trata, por lo general, de visiones muy generales de autores y obras, difundidas primero como conferencias, la penetración crítica no es muy grande, pero al menos la información y la claridad de la prosa son dignas de hacerse notar. [JMO]

5381 **Lara, Jesús.** Chajma: obra dispera. Recopilación y edición de Josep M. Barnadas. La Paz: Librería Editorial Juventud, 1978. 304 p.

El volumen recoge páginas periodísticas y de crítica literaria, publicadas en diarios y revistas bolivianos, tanto en años juveniles del autor como en épocas muy recientes. Su intención es servir de homenaje a Lara al cumplir sus 80 años de vida. Lo que más valor testimonial puede tener es el conjunto de artículos escritos para comentar o justificar la propia obra. El resto está invariablemente teñido por su consabida y simplista defensa del comunismo en la política y el realismo social en literatura. [JMO]

5382 **Ortega, José.** La visión del hombre en la cuentística de Renato Prada (Nueva Narrativa Hispanoamericana [Adelphi University, Latin American Studies Program, Garden City, N.Y.] 4, enero/sept. 1974, p. 283–289)

Se analizan varios cuentos pertenecientes a los tres primeros libros de cuentos de Prada, con el fin de mostrar que en su obra "se plantean problemas pertenecientes a la metafísica de la existencia y, en particular, a la angustia de la condición humana ante el vacío que el ser humano no puede o no sabe llenar." El análisis destaca los aspectos de inmovilismo, decadencia y desolación que sus tramas reiteran. [JMO]

5383 ——— and **Adolfo Cáceres Romero.** Diccionario de la literatura boliviana. La Paz: Editorial Los Amigos del Libro, 1977. 337 p., bibl. (Enciclopedia boliviana)

El material biobibliográfico que esta obra recoge es sin duda útil, pero resulta dudoso que un total aproximado de 280 autores sea un número que guarde proporción con la realidad de la literatura boliviana. [JMO]

COLOMBIA

5384 **Aproximaciones** a Gustavo Alvarez Gardeazábal. Editor, Raymond L. Williams. Bogotá: Plaza y Janés, 1977. 244 p., bibl. (Manantial; 65)

Considerando que Alvarez Gardeazábal es un representante de "esa nueva narrativa que supera el regionalismo tradicional," ligado por lo tanto a García Márquez, Vargas Llosa y Rulfo, Williams recopila y presenta un repertorio de trabajos críticos, de origen más bien académico, que abarca toda la obra del joven novelista colombiano. Volumen indispensable para valorar el aporte de este discutido escritor. [JMO]

5385 **Camacho Guizado, Eduardo.** Sobre literatura colombiana e hispanoamericana. Bogotá: Instituto Colombiano de Cultura, Subdirección de Comunicaciones Culturales, División de Publicaciones, 1978. 407 p., bibl. (Colección Autores nacionales; 27. Biblioteca colombiana de cultura)

El libro contiene varios trabajos sobre literatura colombiana colonial y contemporánea, y otros dedicados a temas peninsulares e hispanoamericanos (Valle Inclán, generación de 1927, Miguel Hernández, García Lorca, Neruda). El enfoque historiográfico, el método estilístico y la preocupación por los aspectos sociales del fenómeno literario, se dejan notar en el conjunto. El ensayo sobre José Asunción Silva es de lo más valioso del volumen. [JMO]

5386 Cobo Borda, Juan Gustavo. Notas sobre la literatura colombiana (*in* Colombia hoy. Bogotá: Siglo XXI Editores de Colombia, 1978, p. 331–403)

Muy valiosa revisión crítica de varias figuras literarias de Colombia en la primera mitad del siglo XX: éstas son el crítico Sanín Cano (véase items **5389** y **5408**), el cronista Luis Tejada y los novelistas Osorio Lizarazo y Uribe Piedrahita, según declara el autor al comienzo, pero las últimas páginas están dedicadas a un quinto escritor: el joven y desconcertante Andrés Caicedo, que se suicidó en 1977 a los 25 años. Estas notas, dice Cobo Borda, son parte de "un proyecto más amplio, de rescatar algunos aportes significativos a la literatura colombiana del presente siglo." [JMO]

5387 ———. Rescate de textos: Gabriel García Márquez y J.A. Osorio Lizarazo (ECO, 34:5, marzo 1979, p. 485–487)

Excelente nota de presentación que acompaña a dos de cinco textos tempranos del primer autor, rescatados de revistas y periódicos colombianos y publicados en la revista *Eco* (véase item **5391**). [JMO]

5388 *Eco*, 1960–1975: ensayistas colombianos. Recopilación e índice de Alvaro Rodríguez. Bogotá: Instituto Colombiano de Cultura, Subdirección de Comunicaciones Culturales, División de Publicaciones, 1976. 478 p., bibl. (Serie Las Revistas. Colección Autores nacionales; 9. Biblioteca colombiana de cultura)

Esta recopilación de la revista *Eco* no sólo recoge a un buen conjunto de ensayistas colombianos, sobre temas de la más amplia variedad, sino que prueba el criterio y el rigor que, en cuanto a calidad, han sido distantivos de la revista desde su fundación. [JMO]

5389 Ensayistas colombianos del siglo XX. Selección de Jorge Eliécer Ruiz y Juan Gustavo Cobo-Borda. Bogotá: Instituto Colombiano de Cultura, Subdirección de Comunicaciones Culturales, 1976. 294 p. (Biblioteca básica colombiana; 10)

Dieciocho ensayistas, de Sanín Cano (véase item **5408**) a Valencia Goelkel (véase item **5410**), incluye esta antología que no quiere serlo. Como explica uno de sus compiladores, Jorge Eliécer Ruiz: "Si éste hubiera sido el criterio probablemente figurarían otros ensayos y algunos ensayistas adicionales de tantos méritos como los incluidos aquí." Material importante para entender las preocupaciones intelectuales y estéticas de los cultores del géneros. [JMO]

5390 García, Samuel. Tres mil años de literatura en *Cien años de soledad*: intertextualidad en la obra de García Márquez. Medellín: Ediciones Paragrama, 1977. 257 p. (Serie Crítica literaria)

El autor extiende la progenie de la novela de García Márquez desde Homero, Cervantes, Rabelais, Bruno y Vico (véase item **5397**), hasta el *Ulises* y *Finnegan's wake* de Joyce. Al margen de que algunas analogías pueden resultar forzadas o apresuradas, el indudable dominio y conocimiento que el autor tiene de esos grandes libros y antecedentes, le permiten observaciones atendibles. El problema es que el libro es tan desordenado que confunde sus pripios hallazgos. [JMO]

5391 García Márquez, Gabriel. La literatura colombiana: un fraude a la nación; Dos o tres cosas sobre "La Novela de la Violencia;" Autocrítica [and] Bogotá: la calle; Desventuras de un escritor de libros (ECO, 33[5]:203, sept. 1978, p. 1201–1206; 34[1]: 205, nov. 1978, p. 104–108; 34[5]:209, marzo 1979, p. 488–490 [and] p. 491–492; 35[2]: 212, junio 1979, p. 113–115)

Estos cinco textos tempranos de García Márquez (publicados en cuatro números de *Eco*) han sido rescatados de revistas y periódicos colombianos poco accesibles a los lectores interesados en esos años formativos de un gran escritor. De todos, los más importantes son los dos primeros por la sagacidad crítica con que enfoca la tradición literaria nacional. La nota de presentación de Cobo-Borda que acompaña a dos de ellos es excelente (véase item **5387**). [JMO]

———. Operación Carlota. See *HLAS 41: 8731.*

5392 Gariano, Carmelo. El humor numérico en *Cien años de soledad* (IJZ/H, 61:3, Sept. 1978, p. 443–450)

El valor de este trabajo, que quiere mostrar el efecto humorístico que García Márquez sabre crear a partir de los números, está limitado por la forma un poco casual con que el autor presenta sus observaciones y, especialmente, por el innecesario tono informal de su estilo. [JMO]

5393 Gilard, Jacques. En torno a las fábulas de Sánchez Juliao (ECO, 33[5]:203, sept. 1978, p. 1207–1215) adecuado comenzar consultando la opinión de 50 personas interesadas en el tema, sobre la base de un cuestionario poco riguroso. La discusión final tampoco añade mucho en esa dirección. [JMO]

PERU

Berger, Víctor. Luis Alberto Sánchez y la novela hispanoamericana: entrevista. See item **5006**.

5420 **Boivin, Monique.** El mundo narrativo de José María Arguedas: un proceso cognitivo visual y auditivo (NS, 2:3/4, 1977, p. 250–258)

Reconociendo la importancia de la percepción sensorial en la obra de Arguedas, la autora trata de mostrar cómo la visión y el oído funcionan como elementos cognitivos, así como la "integración estética" lograda a través del lenguaje y el tratamiento del tiempo y el espacio. El análisis es bastante somero y apenas si se rozan (salvo en el primer aspecto) las cuestiones planteadas. [JMO]

5421 **Bueno Chávez, Raúl.** "Mama Galla:" las figuras del mal en un relato andino (RCLL, 4:7/8, 1./2. semestres 1978, p. 93–103)

Aplicando las teorías de Propp y Bremond sobre los relatos maravillosos y populares, el autor analiza detenidamente las leyes compensatorias (degradación/evaluación, castigo/recompensa, etc.) que rigen las dos historias básicas de este hermoso relato indígena según la versión recogida por José María Arguedas hacia 1945, en la región de Canta. Las notas finales sobre la "enunciación" del relato son particularmente acertadas. [JMO]

5422 **Campos, Jorge.** Vargas Llosa y el escribidor (INSULA, 32:373, 1977, p. 11)

Reseña de la reciente obra del novelista peruano, en la que se llama la atención sobre las conexiones entre el relato y las ideas críticas expuestas por Vargas Llosa en *La orgía perpetua*, así como las relaciones entre Flaubert y el personaje Camacho. [JMO]

5423 **Castro-Klarén, Sara.** Humor y clase en *Pantaleón y las visitadoras* (RCLL, 5:9, 1. semestre 1979, p. 105–118)

Examina tres aspectos distintos pero vinculados entre sí: las connotaciones sociales encerradas en la particular onomástica del relato; las relaciones entre los tópicos naturalistas y la concepción melodramática de los personajes; y finalmente la perspectiva narrativa desde la cual se satirizan los acontecimientos y actores de la novela, y su posible conexión con situaciones históricas específicas. Lo más valioso del estudio reside en el examen del segundo punto, pues las generalizaciones y las inferencias discutibles resienten el primero y el último, respectivamente. [JMO]

Cornejo Polar, Antonio. El indigenismo y las literaturas heterogéneas: su doble estatuto socio-cultural. See item **5016**.

5424 **Díez, Luys A.** Another chapter of Peru's *comédie grotesque* (REVIEW, 23, 1978, p. 54–61)

Nota en la que se destacan los puntos de contacto que guarda *Pantaleón . . .*con Balzac, Dos Passos y "the existential picaresque trend of current fiction." Se señala también que la novela vuelve a desarrollar, irónicamente esta vez, un tema favorito del autor: el del "failing success." [JMO]

5425 **Fernández, Casto Manuel.** Aproximación formal a la novelística de Vargas Llosa. Madrid: Editora Nacional, 1977. 162 p., bibl. (Libros de bolsillo)

El título no lo dice pero el libro es, en su mayor parte, un análisis de la estructura y la sintaxis narrativa de una sola novela: *Conversación en la Catedral*. Al final, fuera de orden, se añaden un par de breves capítulos sobre *La ciudad y los perros*. Siguiendo básicamente las ideas de Todorov y Barthes, el autor hace una aplicación bastante provechosa del método estructuralista, dejando de lado todo intento de seguir los "criterios psicológicos o psicoanalíticos" que se han utilizado para entender la obra del novelista. [JMO]

5426 **González Prada, Manuel.** Selected works: 1977. Prólogo, selección y notas de Juan Velit Granda. San José, Costa Rica: Ministerio de Cultura, Juventud y Deportes, Departamento de Publicaciones, 1977. 436 p., bibl. (Serie Pensamiento de América; 10)

Amplia selección de textos poéticos y ensayos, de intención divulgadora. Los apéndices bibliográfico y cronológico son útiles, pero lo son mucho menos las páginas introductorias del antólogo. [JMO]

5427 **Lannoy, Jean-Jouise M. de.** Indigenismo et littérature indianiste au Méxique et au Pérou (NS, 3:5/6, 1978, p. 138–156)

Revisión del proceso seguido por la preocupación indigenista en esos países, y su relación con los acontecimientos sociopolíticos. El autor concluye que la cuestión indígena cobra una importancia especial en momentos de crisis nacional y que la literatura indianista es el síntoma de "un changement des rapports existant entre la classe moyenne et les populations indiennes." [JMO]

5428 **Lauer, Mirko.** Luis Alberto Sánchez: notas sobre el pensamiento burgués en la crítica literaria peruana (UCV/E, 2:4, julio/dic. 1977, p. 245–254)

Desde un punto de vista con inflexiones marxistas, el autor discute el concepto de "literatura nacional" planteado por Luis Alberto Sánchez en sus numerosos libros a lo largo de 60 años. El trabajo contiene observaciones inteligentes y agudas, pero incurre en ciertos esquemas ideológicos elevados a categoría de dogmas (los conflictos de clase, por ejemplo) y en un cierto tono revanchista que invalida gran parte de su intención crítica. [JMO]

5429 **Lipski, John M.** Narrative textures in *Conversación en la Catedral* (UA/REH, 13:1, enero 1979, p. 65–79)

El trabajo se concentra en ciertos aspectos técnicos de la estructura narrativa de la novela y destaca las relaciones entre lenguaje, sistema estructural y los motivos de incomunicación y fracaso. Lipski usa los conceptos de *paradigm, syntagm* y otros desarrollados por Barthes y Jakobson, pero su análisis no lo lleva demasiado lejos ni le impide repetir lo que ya ha sido observado por otros críticos y con otros métodos. [JMO]

Losada, Alejandro. Estructura social y producción cultural en América Latina: las literaturas dependientes, 1780–1920. See item **5041**.

5430 **Luchting, Wolfgang Alexander.** Escritores peruanos: que piensan, que dicen. Lima: Editorial Ecoma, 1977. 375 p.

Colección de entrevistas hechas a 19 escritores peruanos, que van desde Luis Alberto Sánchez hasta Enrique Verástegui, sobre sus ideas, sus trabajos y sus opiniones literarias y personales. El conjunto tiene valor limitado a los que quieran conocer más de cerca a los escritores activos o nuevos hoy en el Perú. Ciertas anotaciones del entrevistador son demasiado anecdóticas o impertinentes. [JMO]

5431 ———. La novela peruana después de Vargas Llosa (RIB, 28:3, 1978, p. 275–281)

Apretado panorama de la novela escrita en el Perú después de *La ciudad y los perros* (1963). Luchting menciona y describe brevemente las obras de Luis Urtega Cabrera, Guillermo Thorndike, José B. Adolph, Edmundo de los Ríos, José Antonio Bravo, Alfredo Bryce Echenique y otros. Se refiere también a Manuel Scorza pero sólo para denigrarlo como ejemplo de "aprovechamiento internacional." El tono personal resiente otras partes del artículo. [JMO]

5432 **Luraschi, Ilse Adriana.** Ambigüedad estructural e ideología en *La ciudad y los perros* de M. Vargas Llosa (*in* Simposio Internacional de Estudios Hispánicos, Budapest, 1976. Actas [see item **5067**] p. 459–462, bibl.)

Trata de demostrar la existencia de una contradicción entre la actitud de rebelión contra la "realidad referencial representada" y la ideología que confirma la estabilidad del sistema. La ambigüedad de la novela en los niveles del montaje, sintáctico y semántico está bien indicada, pero las conclusiones "ideológicas" a las que la autora llega parecen apresuradas o no totalmente fundadas. [JMO]

5433 **Mario Vargas Llosa:** a collection of critical essays. Edited by Charles Rossman and Alan Warren Friedman. Illustrations by Barbara Whitehead. Austin: University of Texas Press, 1978.

Se reúnen aquí un conjunto de 14 textos críticos, escritos en su mayoría por estudiosos norte-americanos, dedicados a la obra del escritor peruano, con gran variedad de enfoques y métodos. Tiene la virtud adicional de cubrir no sólo todas las novelas del autor, sino también su obra crítica y sus ideas literarias. [JMO]

Mitchell, Fergus, Jr. The foxes in José María Arguedas' last novel. See item **1410**.

5434 **Núñez, Estuardo.** José Carlos Mariátegui y la recepción del surrealismo en el Perú (RCLL, 3:5, 1. semestre 1977, p. 57–66)

Aunque la obra de este nuevo autor colombiano es breve y heterogénea (cuento, testimonio y fábula), Gilard observa en ella cualidades y rasgos que comenta entusiastamente en esta primera aproximación crítica. Su mundo imaginario tiene contactos y semejanzas, según Gilard, con el de Roa Bastos, Rulfo y José María Arguedas, y representa un "eslabón no desdeñable" dentro de la literatura costeña de Colombia. [JMO]

5394 Gutiérrez Girardot, Rafael. La literatura colombiana: 1925–1950 (ECO, 35[4]:214, agosto 1979, p. 390–424)

Visión de conjunto, muy bien organizada y con afinada percepción crítica, de un cuarto de siglo de literatura colombiana, en la que encontramos páginas dedicadas a ensayistas como Sanín Cano (véase items **5386** y **5389**) y Germán Arciniegas; poetas como Rafael Maya, Luis Carlos López y Jorge Zalamea; narradores como Uribe Piedrahita y Osoro Lizarazo; los grupos "Piedras y Cielo" y "Cántico;" la revista "Mito," etc. Destaca el severo juicio que dedica a Arciniegas. [JMO]

5395 Heise, Hans-Jürgen. Episch mündiges Lateinamerika: Zu Büchern von Gabriel García Márquez und Mario Vargas Llosa (NR, 85:4, 1974, p. 684–689)

States that during the recent decades Europe has not produced a novelist comparable to either Vargas Llosa or García Márquez, both of whom he considers the most important representative Latin American writers of the 1970s. Succinct but incisive overview of these novelists' art. [G.M. Dorn]

5396 Joset, Jacques. Un sofocante aleteo de mariposas amarillas: un episodio de *Cien años de soledad* (RIB, 28:2, abril/junio 1978, p. 149–155)

Estudio de un detalle simbólico que había sido interpretado de varios modos. Joset halla que el símbolo está relacionado tanto con las ideas de la sofocación, la calamidad y la muerte, como con los altibajos de la pasión entre Meme y Mauricio Babilonia, dentro de la cual ella es la "mariposa" y él la "lumbre." [JMO]

5397 Kadir, Djelal. The architectonic principle of *Cien años de soledad* and the Vichian theory of history (UK/KRQ, 24:3, 1977, p. 251–261)

De manera convincente, el autor presenta un análisis de ciertos aspectos de *Cien años* . . . que hacen de ella "an ontogenetic pattern which evolves into a cycle and whose genesis and demise converge to form an enclosed unit," y cuyos principios arquitectónicos y gnoseológicos tienen una fascinante semejanza con la teoría de los ciclos históricos de Vico. Hacia el final de la novela, el lector, junto con el penúltimo Areliano, "becomes aware of an architectonic principle, a system of knowledge, situated beyond the events of the novel," lo que apunta a un ciclo afin al delineado por Vico en *Scienza nuova.* [JMO]

5398 Kilmer-Tchalekian, Mary A. Nabo, el negro a quien García Márquez hizo volar (JSSTC, 6:1, Spring 1978, p. 29–37)

Comentario de un temprano texto narrativo, en cuyo personaje la autora ve "un primer esbozo de José Arcadio Buendía" por su enajenación del tiempo objetivo y su humorístico delirio. El trabajo no pasa de ser una atenta aplicación del comentario de textos para clases. [JMO]

5399 Lewis, Marvin A. *En Chimá naca un santo*: myth and violence (UK/KRQ, 25:2, 1978, p. 145–153)

Este trabajo quiere mostrar los méritos literarios de un autor colombiano muy poco leído y estudiado. El análisis de la novela intenta operar en tres planos principales (el surgimiento del "santo," la creación del mito y la rebelión), pero lo hace muy apegado al mero recuento argumental. El autor concluye que "Zapata Olivella's message is that when the rural poor realize that they can wield power too, perhaps they can control their own destinies." [JMO]

5400 Maldonado-Denis, Manuel. La violencia en la obra de García Márquez. Bogotá: Ediciones Suramérica, 1977. 41 p., bibl. (Colección Armadillo popular; 4)

Desde su enfoque de especialista de las ciencias sociales y el pensamiento marxista, Maldonado-Denis ve la novela de García Márquez como "una obra producto del subdesarrollo," y estudia algunos de sus temas: dominación extranjera, corrupción, entreguismo, etc. [JMO]

5401 Mallett, Brian J. Imagen y fantasía en la obra de García Márquez (UK/KRQ, 24:3, 1977, p. 289–299)

Interesante deslinde sobre la naturaleza y la función de la imagen en la obra del colombiano. El autor reduce su radio de observación a la imagen relacionada al "campo de la metáfora y del símil," y muestra cómo, a lo largo de toda su obra, la imagen ha cumplido una función que, apoyada en la realidad, dispara los relatos al nivel de la pura fantasía, lo que es una observación válida para entender su estética de "realista mágico." [JMO]

5402 Mena, Lucila Inés. Bibliografía anotada sobre el ciclo de la violencia en la literatura colombiana (LARR, 8:3, 1978, p. 950–1107)

Precedida por unas breves notas en las que la autora llama la atención sobre los valores, exponentes y características de esta notoria tendencia narrativa colombiana, se nos presenta una lista de 74 novelas y 35 trabajos críticos sobre el tema, lo que significa un útil esfuerzo de recopilación. El material crítico está anotado, pero lamentablemente no las novelas mismas. Otra reseña de esta bibliografía aparece en *HLAS 41:7298*. [JMO]

5403 Menton, Seymour. La novela colombiana: planetas y satélites. Bogotá: Plaza y Janés, 1978. 394 p., bibl. (Crítica literaria)

El título se explica porque el libro contiene trabajos dedicados a las novelas que el autor considera los grandes "planetas" del género en Colombia (*María, Frutos de mi tierra, La vorágine* y *Cien años de soledad*), y otros dedicados a los "satélites" u obras menores, como las de Mejía Vallejo, Héctor Rojas Herazo y Alvarez Gardeazábal (véase item **5384**). El libro tiene cierta intención polémica porque "obedece precisamente a mi repudio del concepto elaborado por Mario Vargas Llosa, Carlos Fuentes y otros muchos . . . encaminado a mostrar que la 'novela de creación,' comienza con ellos." El lenguaje del libro tiene un tono algo informal, a lo que se suma una tendencia al enfoque preceptivo del hecho literario, como se nota sobre todo en el "Manual Imperfecto del Novelista," que cierra el volumen. [JMO]

5404 Ortega, Julio. *El otoño del patriarca*: texto y cultura (HR, 46:4, Autumn 1978, p. 421–446)

Estudio desde el punto de vista de la semiología de la cultura que trata de demostrar que *El otoño del patriarca* "es, en efecto, una novela sobre un dictador latinoamericano, pero es, asimismo, la novela de pueblo latinoamericano que padece a ese dictador paradigmático." El autor analiza los distintos códigos de la obra: el político, el de la cultura popular, el mitológico, el del narrador colectivo y el de la escritura. El texto aparece así como un "programa condensado" de la cultura hispanoamericana. El trabajo es penetrante y provocativo, aunque a veces su lenguaje crítico incurre en oscuridades o adherencias retóricas, como "esta novela es la construcción desconstruida del poder" (p. 419). [JMO]

5405 Rama, Angel. Un patriarca en la remozada galería de dictadores (ECO, 29:178, agosto 1975, p. 408–443)

Extenso ensayo en el que, a propósito de *El otoño . . .*, el autor hace consideraciones sobre la literatura hispanoamericana, la figura del "dictador" en la novela, las formas estéticas que ha adoptado su presentación, etc. Su visión de la novela misma es penetrante y generalmente muy acertada en el señalamiento de los grandes temas, técnicas y virtudes de lenguaje en la obra. Su lectura se complementa muy bien con la de E. Volkening (véase item **5411**). [JMO]

5406 Rodríguez, Ilcana. Principios estructurales y visión circular en *Cien años de soledad* (RCLL, 5:9, 1. semestre 1979, p. 79–97)

Análisis marxista de los "núcleos narrativos significativos" y sus funciones estructurales y caracterizadoras, realizado para demostrar que García Márquez tiene una "visión circular de la historia," que le impide entender el papel de las "fuerzas progresistas" en América Latina. El resultado es francamente inconvincente por la crudeza metodológica de la autora y el dogmatismo con que encara el problema de la ideología de un texto. [JMO]

5407 Ruffinelli, Jorge. Gabriel García Márquez y el grupo de Barranquilla (UV/PH, 10, abril/junio 1974, p. 23–29, plates)

Valioso trabajo sobre la relación entre García Márquez, Alvaro Cepeda Samudio, Germán Vargas y Alfonso Fuenmayor, los "cuatro discutidores" recordados en *Cien años de soledad*. Según Ruffinelli, el estímulo mutuo entre estos escritores fue profundo y marcó al más famoso novelista colombiano, con una conciencia muy viva de la temática de la violencia y la necesidad de expresarla con un lenguaje liberador, ajeno a los "mediocres esquemas nacionalistas" que habían echado a perder tantas novelas de esa época. [JMO]

5408 Sanín Cano, Baldomero. Escritos. Selección y prólogo de Juan Gustavo Cobo Borda. Bogotá: Instituto Colombiano de Cultura, Subdirección de Comunicaciones Culturales, 1977. 789 p., port. (Biblioteca básica colombiana; 23)

Hecha con tanto criterio como admiración, esta voluminosa selección, precedida por un notable prólogo, muestra la importancia que, para toda Hispanoamérica, tiene la obra, muy citada pero poco leída, de Sanín Cano, gran lector de su tiempo, espíritu curioso y gran difusor de cultura. [JMO]

5409 Sims, Robert. The creation of myth in García Márquez' "Los Funerales de la Mamá Grande" (AATSP/H, 16:1, March 1978, p. 14–23)

El cuento mencionado en el título es visto como un antecedente inmediato e importante de *Cien años de soledad*, en cuanto es el primer texto en el que el narrador logra la elusiva "cohesive unity" que andaba buscando. El estudio se concentra en dos aspectos esenciales del texto: "1) the use of the *voz callejera* viewpoint, and 2) the *bricolage* construction of the short story," lo que se analiza exhaustivamente. El autor concluye que "'Los Funerales' . . . represents freedom and discovery: freedom to create the myth of Macondo and discovery of the techniques to achieve it." [JMO]

5410 Valencia Goelkel, Hernando. Crónicas de líbros. Bogotá: Instituto Colombiano de Cultura, Subdirección de Comunicaciones Culturales, División de Publicaciones, 1976. 321 p., bibl. (Biblioteca colombiana de cultura: Colección popular; 9)

Recopilación de un amplio conjunto de notas de libros escritas por el crítico colombiano sobre los más diversos autores, tema y lenguas. La mayor parte del material no supera su carácter periodístico, pero algunos pocos textos dan testimonio de la finura crítica y la sagacidad de Valencia Goelkel (véase item **5389**). [JMO]

5411 Volkening, Ernesto. El patriarca no tiene quien lo mate (ECO, 29:178, agosto 1975, p. 337–387)

Estas notas de lectura de la novela de García Márquez constituyen una meditación sobre una variedad de aspectos estéticos, literarios y sociopolíticos, algunos de los cuales parecen tener poco que ver con la obra. Lo que observa Volkening en la obra supone una actitud vigilante y atenta, pero el texto sería más eficaz si se le ahorrasen al lector las digresiones y el tono solemne del lenguaje. [JMO]

5412 Wilkie, James W.; Edna Monzón de Wilkie; and **María Herrera-Sobek.** Elitelore and folklore: theory and a test case in *One hundred years of solitude* (UCLA/JLAL, 4:2, 1978, p. 183–223, table)

La primera parte del trabajo establece las diferencias entre "elitelore" y "folklore" en un plano teórico; en la segunda aplica el primer concepto a la novela de García Márquez. Lo que esa aplicación a un caso literario concreto demuestra, no es del todo claro, porque los autores parecen criticar al novelista por haber sobreimpuesto a su visión del pueblo su propio "elitelore," que—según ellos—tiene menos que ver con la realidad colombiana que con la experiencia cultural y políticamente cosmopolita del creador, lo que es muy discutible. Por otro lado, al comparar a Macondo con una comunidad real (Aritama) que se le parece mucho, afirman que "the novel may reflect an exaggerated view of idealized people," olvidando el carácter específico del fenómeno literario, que no puede confundirse con el que estudian las ciencias sociales. En cambio, es muy ilustrativa la relación de elementos folklórico-fantásticos que los autores encuentran en la novela. En la sección Folklore de este volumen aparece otra reseña de este estudio (véase item **1009**). [JMO]

5413 Williams, Raymond L. La novela colombiana contemporánea. Bogotá: Plaza y Janés Editores Colombia, 1976. 93 p.: ports., bibl. (Enciclopedia popular ilustrada; 10)

Brevísimo recuento crítico, dirigido a un público no iniciado, sobre la novela colombiana a partir de la aparición de *Cien años de soledad*. Además de García Márquez, Williams estudia las obras de Héctor Rojas Herazo, Héctor Sánchez, Albalucía Angel y Gustavo Alvarez Gardeazábal (véase item **5384**). El aporte es valioso porque no existe otro libro dedicado a ese específico período. [JMO]

ECUADOR

5414 **Corrales, Manuel.** Las raíces del relato indigenista ecuatoriano (RCLL, 4:7/8, 1./2. semestres 1978, p. 39–52)

Esfuerzo por justificar el carácter de "novela indigenista" de *Cumandá*, de Juan León Mera. Para probar "*qué modo de presencia* tiene ese indigenismo," Corrales examina cuatro de sus rasgos: carácter documental, presencia comentadora del autor, evocación del ancestro y la justicia al servicio del poderoso. Al final, sin embargo, el autor reconoce que, teniendo en cuenta la realidad social concreta, la crítica de la estructura de dominación que hace Mera "es aún una crítica delicada, tenue, incluso a ratos velada" y que "lo mismo ocurre si nos preguntamos por cómo se define la problematicidad del indio," lo que demostraría más bien la validez de su aceptada clasificación como "novela" indianista." [JMO]

5415 **Cueva, Agustín.** En pos de la historicidad perdida: contribución al debate sobre la literatura indigenista del Ecuador (RCLL, 4:7/8, 1./2. semestres 1978, p. 23–38)

El trabajo tiene dos partes: un planteamiento teórico sobre la naturaleza y el desarrollo de la literatura indigenista ecuatoriana; y un examen de la obra de Icaza. Más interesante es esta última parte que la primera, donde las observaciones acertadas (hechas generalmente sobre enfoques marxistas) se confunden con otras propuestas inciertamente planteadas o adaptadas de otros vocabularios críticos. Por ejemplo, Cueva afirma que *Huasipungo* es una "novela universal" y quiere probarlo haciendo referencia a sus numerosas ediciones y traducciones, lo que es una confusión de términos. Pero no le falta razón cuando señala la carencia de "color local" en *Huasipungo*. [JMO]

5416 **Fama, Antonio.** Realismo mágico en la narrativa de Aguilera-Malta. Madrid: Playor, 1977. 169 p., bibl. (Colección Nova scholar)

Fama trata de probar que Aguilera-Malta no sólo es importante dentro del desarrollo de la tendencia mágico-realista, sino que cabe considerarlo "como iniciador de la misma," y por eso comienza su trabajo con una revisión de las distintas modalidades de aquella tendencia en otros autores. Sin embargo, el estudio mismo de la obra del ecuatoriano (especialmente en sus capítulos 3 y 4) no parece siempre deslindar entre los elementos mágico-realistas y los legendarios o simplemente telúricos. [JMO]

5417 **Handelsman, Michael H.** Amazonas y artistas: un estudio de la prosa de la mujer ecuatoriana. Guayaquil: Casa de la Cultura Ecuatoriana, Núcleo del Guayas, 1978. 2 v. (125, 120 p.) bibl. (Colección Letras del Ecuador; 70–71)

Estudio histórico-literario sobre la prosa escrita por mujeres ecuatorianas especialmente en este siglo. El tema es de trascendencia limitada, porque como el mismo autor reconoce, la presencia femenina en las letras de ese país no es ni muy abundante ni muy significativa. El estudio es básicamente descriptivo y de escaso valor crítico, pero tiene el mérito secundario de presentar capítulos como el dedicado a las revistas feministas, y una amplia bibliografía sobre el tema que pueden ser útiles para futuras investigaciones. [JMO]

5418 **Sackett, Theodore Alan.** El arte en la novelística de Jorge Icaza. Quito, Editorial Casa de la Cultura Ecuatoriana, 1974. 542 p., bibl.

Sackett inicia su obra con muy severas opiniones sobre la pobreza de la crítica dedicada a la obra de Icaza, especialmente por haber olvidado sus aspectos propiamente estéticos. El método que utiliza le permite realizar, en efecto, un examen detallado y amplio del tema, pero su incierto "equilibrio entre lo particular y lo general" lo lleva a dividir el estudio de modo extraño y poco operativo. Eso, y la decisión de resumir una por una las secciones de los capítulos previos como única conclusión de libro, hace tediosa la lectura. Incluye un glosario, un censo de personajes y una estadística de estos, en la que bajo el rubro "Oficios Comunes en la Novela Icaziana" inadvertidamente se registran "Parturientas." [JMO]

5419 **Situación del relato ecuatoriano:** cincuenta opiniones y una discusión. Edición e introducción de Manuel Corrales Pascual. Quito: Centro de Publicaciones de la Pontificia Universidad Católica del Ecuador, 1977. 357 p., indexes.

La intención del compilador era contribuir a un "replanteamiento" de la narración ecuatoriana. No parece el método más

Tras su experiencia europea (1919–23), el conocimiento profundo y la simpatía intelectual de Mariátegui por el surrealismo se deja notar a través de las páginas de *Amauta*, que no sólo analiza, difunde y exalta las conquistas del grupo surrealista francés (principalmente Bréton, Aragon y Eluard), sino que estimula el surgimiento de un grupo surrealista peruano, entre los que destacan Moro, Oquendo de Amat, Westphalen y sobre todo Xavier Abril, el más agresivo de todos. El artículo pone de relieve la cabal comprensión que Mariátegui tenía del surrealismo y de su trascendencia en la renovación espiritual del mundo contemporáneo, al revés de lo que sostuvo Vallejo. [JMO]

5435 Oelker, Dieter. La estructura del poder en la última novela de Mario Vargas Llosa: conversación en la catedral (Nueva Narrativa Hispanoamericana [Adelphi University, Latin American Studies Program, Garden City, N.Y.] 4, enero/sept. 1974, p. 179–192)

Análisis, bastante minucioso, de la forma como la dictadura genera una estructura de relaciones entre las diversas clases sociales representadas en esta novela (los militares, la alta y pequeña burguesía, los intelectuales, el proletariado). Esas relaciones son vistas a través de "centros de interés" que son como cortes a lo ancho del cuerpo social y que muestran su corrupción y degradación. [JMO]

5436 Ortega, Julio. La cultura peruana: experiencia y conciencia (UCV/E, 2:3, enero/junio 1977, p. 77–90)

Páginas de un ensayo sobre el pasado y el presente de la cultura peruana. Aunque fundamentalmente se ocupan de las crónicas del Inca Garcilaso y Guaman Poma, el autor las usa más bien como pretextos para reflexionar sobre las posibilidades de articular una cultura peruana. En el recurrente lenguaje del autor hay una idea clave, la del "cambio," que hay que entender como cambio revolucionario, aunque no se aclare de qué signo. [JMO]

5437 Pages Larraya, Antonio. Mariátegui y el realismo mágico (CH, 325, julio 1977, p. 149–154)

Señala la virtud precursora y actual del pensamiento crítico de Mariátegui, quien desdeñó la concepción fotográfica del realismo y propuso una estética, más adecuada a la naturaleza de la cultura hispanoamericana, que hoy conocemos con el nombre de realismo mágico. El autor invoca artículos del autor publicados entre 1925 y 1930, y afirma el influjo decisivo de las ideas de Bontempelli en la elección que Mariátegui hizo de ese término entre otros parecidos. El artículo glosa esos textos pero no los cita con la debida extensión (véase item **5434**). [JMO]

5438 Ribeyro, Julio Ramón. Prosas apátridas aumentadas. Prólogo: Abelardo Oquendo. Lima: Editorial Milla Batres, 1978. 155 p.

Segunda edición, ampliada en 40 nuevos textos, de breves anotaciones, reflexiones literarias y confesiones íntimas en las que el narrador peruano ofrece su autorretrato de artista agobiado por la conciencia de sus límites y de los valores de la sociedad en que vive. Espléndido ejercicio de prosa aparentemente muy menor y marginal dentro de su obra narrativa, pero en realidad uno de sus libros más hermosos y profundos. [JMO]

5439 Sánchez, Luis Alberto. Escafandra, lupa y atalaya: ensayos, 1923–1976. Madrid: Ediciones Cultura Hispánica, 1977. 357 p.

El interés del volumen reside en reunir viejos y clásicos trabajos de historia y literatura escritos por Luis Alberto Sánchez a comienzos de su producción crítica (antes de 1937), junto con otros correspondientes a estos últimos años. Entre aquéllos figura *Se han sublevado los indios: esta novela peruana* (1928), en el que Sánchez intentaba hacer una crítica chispeante, antiacadémica y "artística," muy influido por el tono irreverente de la época: "No atino a escribir con parsimonio y me encanta un poco la improvisación," y al final: "He escrito a medida que se me ocurrían las observaciones, pensando en voz alta." Eso bien puede definir la mayor parte de su esfuerzo crítico. [JMO]

5440 ———. Nuestras vidas son los ríos . . . : historia y leyenda de los González Prada. Lima: Universidad Nacional Mayor de San Marcos, Dirección Universitaria de Biblioteca y Publicaciones, 1977. 405 p., bibl.

Vasto estudio de la figura intelectual de Manuel González Prada, de su obra y aún de las andanzas literarias de su hijo Alfredo. Como es habitual en los ensayos del autor, la tendencia del estilo es la de amenizar y novelizar un poco la biografía del personaje, a veces con más imaginación que exactitud. Pero no cabe duda de que el conocimiento de Sánchez sobre la familia González Prada es enciclopédico. El presente libro es una versión definitiva de anteriores trabajos y biografías dedicadas al mismo tema, e incluye importantes correcciones de datos y fechas, entre ellas las del nacimiento del escritor, que queda fijada en 1844, y no en 1848 como se creía. [JMO]

5441 Tamayo Vargas, Augusto. Apuntes para un estudio de la literatura peruana. 4. ed. Lima: Librería Studium, 1977. 2 v. (510, 712 p.)

Nueva edición de esta historia literaria peruana, que cubre en dos volúmenes desde la época pre-colombiana hasta el presente. Tiene la ventaja de ser más compendiosa que la conocida *La literatura peruana* de Luis Alberto Sánchez, el trabajo clásico del género al que Tamayo Vargas sigue en líneas generales, agregando variantes de tono y gusto pero no de estructura. [JMO]

Tauro, Alberto. Clorinda Matto de Turner y la novela indigenista. See item **5166**.

5442 Valle, Miguel. Ironía e identidad en Mario Vargas Llosa (IAA, 4:3, 1978, p. 237–242, bibl.)

Análisis, un poco sucinto, de las distintas funciones que la ironía cumple en las novelas de Vargas Llosa, especialmente en relación con la identidad de los personajes. [JMO]

5443 Vargas Llosa, Mario. José María Arguedas, entre sapos y halcones. Madrid: Ediciones Cultura Hispánica del Centro Iberoamericano de Cooperación, 1978. 46 p., bibl. (Colección Plural)

Este es el texto del discurso pronunciado por el novelista a su ingreso a la Academia Peruana de la Lengua, el 24 de agosto de 1977, y es una muestra de su renovado interés por la obra de Arguedas, que él ve, en discrepancia con la mayor parte de la crítica, no como un testigo objectivo de la realidad social, sino como un creador de vivencias subjetivas muy complejas y de sutiles imágenes narrativas que transforman su obra "en algo sustancialmente distinto del modelo." [JMO]

5444 Zavaleta, Carlos E. El ensayo en el Perú, 1950–1975 (CH, 347, mayo 1979, p. 428–435)

Texto de una conferencia que hace una rápida revisión de las tendencias y nombres más importantes de este género en los últimos 25 años. [JMO]

VENEZUELA

5445 Becco, Horacio Jorge. Funetes para el estudio de la literatura venezolana. Prólogo, Pedro Grases. Caracas: Ediciones Centauro, 1978. 2 v. (303, 316 p.) (Colección Manuel Segundo Sánchez)

Excelente trabajo en dos volúmenes, que confirma la calidad de Becco como bibliógrafo, donde se recogen unas 1900 entradas que abarcan bibliografías, historias, antologías, fuentes periodísticas, etc., debidamente clasificadas y ordenadas. La obra se complementa con un amplio índice onomástico. [JMO]

5446 Borda, Juan Gustavo Cobo. Salvador Garmendia (Nueva Narrativa Hispanoamericana [Adelphi University, Latin American Studies Program, Garden City, N.Y.] 4, enero/sept. 1974, p. 291–297)

Repaso crítico de cuatro novelas y dos libros de cuentos pertenecientes a la primera etapa creadora de Garmendia. El autor destaca el "censo pausado y atento de esa ciudad neurótica menor que fija en forma microscópica . . . seres anodinos y tercamente banales." [JMO]

5447 Caracas. Universidad Católica Andrés Bello. Escuela de Letras. Centro de Investigaciones Literarias. Contribución a la bibliografía de Teresa de la Parra, 1895–1936. Realizado por Raquel Berlín . . . et al.; bajo la dirección del profesor Efraín Subero. Caracas: Gobernación del Distrito Federal, 1970. 133 p.: port. (Colección Bibliografías; 7)

Quienes realizaron o supervisaron esta compilación no se dieron el trabajo de revisarla y organizarla adecuadamente: las entradas 7, 8 y 9 remiten al *HLAS*, pero no indican los respectivos volúmenes; la 15 aparece redactada en inglés; las *Obras completas* de la autora figuran en la sección "Miscelánea" junto con textos periodísticos; buena cantidad de entradas tienen datos incompletos o están mal ordenadas, etc. La ficha biobibliográfica de la autora es totalmente confusa. [JMO]

5448 Carrera, Gustavo Luis. Proposiciones para una periodificación de la literatura venezolana (*in* Simposio Internacional de Estudios Hispánicos, Budapest, 1976. Actas [see item **5067**] p. 117–123)

El autor critica, con razón, los criterios que generalmente se aplican para periodificar la historia literaria venezolana (y, por extensión, hispanoamericana), y llama la atención sobre la necesidad de tener en cuenta "las peculiaridades regionales en lo social y en lo cultural." Pero la periodificación que propone, con designaciones como "Período de Fusión y Debate" o "Período de Crisis" no mejora mucho la cuestión, sobre todo porque, al caracterizarlos, Carrera reintroduce las mismas referencias a ciertos episodios históricos (como la dictadura pérez-jimenista), en nada distintos a otros (como el "Gomecismo") que antes ha rechazado por inadecuados. [JMO]

5449 Giménez Resano, Gaudioso. De estructuralismo y literatura. Caracas: Universidad Católica Andrés Bello, Centro de Investigaciones Literarias, 1975. 80 p., bibl.

Síntesis de divulgación del método estructuralista y de algunos de sus grandes cuestiones: lenguaje y literatura, estructuralismo y estilística, estructura y género literarios, con un comentario textual de Fray Luis de León a modo de ejemplo. El esfuerzo del autor está considerablemente limitado por cierta oscuridad expositiva y una organización no del todo coherente. [JMO]

5450 J.M. Siso Martínez, Juan Oropesa, Mariano Picón Salas: apostilla prologal de Rómulo Betancourt; correspondencia cruzada entre Rómulo Betancourt y Mariano Picón Salas, 1931–1965. Caracas: Fundación Diego Cisneros, 1977. 253 p., bibl., 17 leaves of plates: ill.

De todos los textos de amigos políticos y literarios de Picón Salas, el único que tiene relativo interés puede ser el "ensayo inacabado" de Siso Martínez, a pesar de sus largas digresiones. El resto está compuesto de documentos y semblanzas nada relevantes. [JMO]

5451 Liscano Velutini, Juan. Panorama de la literatura venezolana actual. Caracas: Publicaciones Españolas; Washington: Secretaría General de la Organización de los Estados Americanos, 1973. 414 p., bibl. (Pensamiento de América)

Esfuerzo de ordenación histórica de las letras venezolanas en este siglo. Liscano ha dividido su *Panorama* en dos grandes partes (una dedicada a la narración, otra a la poesía), reservando capítulos adicionales para otros géneros; el criterio seguido es algo discutible porque fracciona en dos series distintas de tiempo, lo que en el fondo es parte de un solo proceso. Pero el enfoque crítico es valioso y comprensivo, especialmente en el capítulo dedicado al ensayo filosófico marxista. Razonablemente, el autor incluye en su trabajo el aporte de humanistas extranjeros integrados a Venezuela, y agrega un práctico índice de obras, personajes y autores. [JMO]

5452 Lovera De-Sola, R.J. Quince años de vida venezolana a través de la obra de sus escritores: 1960–1975. Caracas, Editorial Arte, n.d. 19 p.

Texto de una informal conferencia que destaca los nombres de algunas autoras de mérito en el panorama nacional: Elisa Lerner, Miyó Vestrini, Lupe Rumazo, Antonieta Madrid, entre otras. [JMO]

5453 Peña, Alfredo. Conversaciones con Uslar Pietri. Caracas: Editorial Ateneo de Caracas, 1978. 209 p. (Colección Actualidad político. Grandes reportajes)

Unas 20 horas de diálogo con el escritor venezolano se resumen en este libro-entrevista que tiene valor para quien quiera conocer las opiniones de Uslar Pietri, especialmente las relativas a su actividad política y pública, pues el libro intenta contribuir al debate político electoral del país. [JMO]

5454 Rodríguez Ortíz, Oscar. Seis proposiciones en torno a Salvador Garmendia. Caracas: Síntesis Dosmil, 1976. 235 p., bibl. (Colección Manos libres)

Estudio de seis "categorías" del mundo narrativo del escritor venezolano, que abarcan la gama que va desde una realidad apariencial en la que "no pasa nada," hasta las situaciones u ocurrencias en las que "pasa mucho." La discriminación y el análisis de las "categorías" son básicamente correctos, pero el trabajo se resiente por un lenguaje crítico excesivamente difuso. [JMO]

5455 Subero, Efraín. Cercanía de Miguel Otero Silva. Caracas: Oficina Central de Información, 1975. 85 p., bibl., index, plates.

Páginas, de intención sobre todo laudatorias (lo que se advierte hasta en las leyendas de las fotos que acompañan el texto), sobre la persona y la obra del escritor venezolano. Lo más valioso es la cronología y la bibliografía que se incluyen al final. [JMO]

5456 Tenreiro, Salvador. Aproximaciones a el falso cuaderno de Narciso Espejo (CONAC/RNC, 40:239, nov./dic. 1978, p. 132–140)

Comentario algo desordenado e impreciso sobre la estructura, los narradores y las "isotopías" básicas (la identidad y el pecado) de la interesante y poco conocida novela de Meneses. [JMO]

Uslar Pietri, Arturo. Breve historia de la novela hispanoamericana. See item **5070**.

5457 ———. Vista desde un punto. Ensayos. Caracas: Monte Avila Editores, 1971. 347 p. (Colección Prisma)

Más páginas periodísticas y prosa de ocasión del venezolano que se suman a su antología *Veinticinco ensayos* (véase *HLAS 40:6853*) y que prueban la amplitud de sus intereses culturales y su moderada línea política. [JMO]

PROSE FICTION: 20th Century: Chile

CEDOMIL GOIC, *Professor of Spanish American Literature, The University of Michigan, Ann Arbor*

DURANTE LOS ANOS 1977 y 1978 la producción literaria de este género ha sido cuantiosa. Se ordena como es normal en niveles de distinta calidad e interés variado. En todos ellos se percibe una disminución en la preferencia por los asuntos vinculados a la caída de Allende, en comparación con los años anteriores. Sin embargo las novelas de mayor importancia, que presentan un mundo ficticio y situaciones de variada irrealidad, introducen claros indicios de aproximación a la realidad en su contexto político o social. La novela más importante del bienio es *Casa de campo* de José Donoso, una obra maestra de la novelística hispanoamericana (item **5462**). Al lado de ella destacan dos obras de novelistas de la generación de Donoso. Ellos son, *Los convidados de piedra* de Jorge Edwards (item **5463**) y *Dulce chilenos* (Santiago: Pomaire, 1977, 226 p.) de Guillermo Blanco. Entre los más nuevos novelistas ha sido reveladora la publicación de *La Beatriz Ovalle* de Jorge Marchant Lazcano (item **5466**) joven novelista nacido en 1950.

Pero lo más notable de estos años ha resultado ser sin duda la publicación de prosas de Gabriela Mistral y de Pablo Neruda. Las *Cartas de amor* de Gabriela Mistral (item **5482**) constituyen un acontecimiento excepcional por su revelador contenido y su notable expresión. A esta publicación siguió la edición de dos distintas compilaciones de artículos, ensayos poéticos y críticos, de la Mistral: *Gabriela piensa en . . .* (item **5483**) y *Materias* (item **5484**). En el volumen *Para nacer he nacido* (item **5486**) se recogen importantes artículos, discursos y otras piezas de Pablo Neruda, no recogidas antes en libro. La prosa de ambos poetas se muestra en páginas de excepcional calidad tanto por el asunto, como por el punto dc vista y las peculiaridades en su estilo.

En la crítica e historia literaria destacan, por una parte, *La novela chilena actual* de José Promis (item **5489**) y, por otra, la serie de libros dedicados al estudio de la obra de José Donoso, por Hugo Achugar (item **5469**), George McMurray (item **5478**), Isis Quinteros (item **5490**) y Jorge Medina Vidal (item **5481**). En general, la obra de José Donoso es la que ha concertado el mayor interés de la crítica.

Unas Jornadas del Libro y la Cultura se destinaron a la discusión de lo que se ha dado en llamar en el país el "apagón cultural," fenómeno que ha afectado especialmente al consumo y a la producción del libro, que aparecen extraordinariamente deprimidos.

PROSE FICTION

5458 Aldunate, Elena. Del cosmos las quieren vírgenes. Santiago: Zig-Zag, 1977. 91 p.

Cuentos fantásticos que narran el nacimiento de una humanidad provista de aptitudes cognoscitivas y poderes sobre-humanos. Continúan una línea que va siendo característica de la autora.

5459 Así escriben los chilenos. Selección y prólogo de Jorge Marchant Lazcano. Buenos Aires: Ediciones Orión, 1977. 225 p. (Colección Así escriben)

Antología de cuentos de Baldomero Lillo, Joaquín Edwards Bello, Manuel Rojas, María Luisa Bombal, Carlos Droguett, Fernando Alegría, José Donoso, Miguel Arteche, Luis Alberto Heiremans, Jorge Edwards, Marta Blanco, Antonio Skármeta, Francisco Javier Muñoz—joven narrador inédito, n. 1948—y el propio autor de la selección. La selección es novedosa. Sus criterios violan algunas normas convencionales referentes al género.

5460 Bahamonde Silva, Mario. Derroteros y cangalla. Cuentos. Santiago: Editorial Nascimento, 1978. 312 p.

Reune los cuentos completos del autor. Bahamonde es el más importante escritor regionalista del norte del país. Su obra trasciende literariamente más allá de sus determinantes e intereses locales.

5461 Barrenechea, Julio. El compadre Mucho Gasto. Santiago: Editorial Nascimento, 1978. 122 p.

Primera y única novela del destacado poeta, recientemente fallecido. Humor e ironía caracterizan la presentación de un personaje insólito, que sirve de pretexto para hacer la crónica de una época.

5462 Donoso, José. Casa de campo. Novela. Barcelona: Seix Barral, 1978. 498 p. (Biblioteca breve; 439)

Sin exageración puede decirse que esta es la obra maestra de José Donoso y una de las obras maestras de la novela hispanoamericana contemporánea, cumbre del irrealismo vigente. La casa de campo veraniega, en la irreal Marulanda, es el centro de actividad de los grandes—un vasto clan familiar—, los niños—35 primos de ambos sexos—, los lacayos y los nativos que sirven a la producción del oro y son a la vez—los antropófagos—el objeto del miedo. Un paseo de fin de semana de los grandes—un año para los niños—es la condición de posibilidad de la exploración de lo prohibido. La partida y el regreso conforman las dos partes de la novela con sus movimientos de expansión y de represión. El mundo de la novela provoca la alegoría general del poder y de la subversión y llega a la cita que alegoriza al personaje disidente entre los grandes. El narrador es una construcción notable. Tiene la estructura del narrador decimonónico en la variedad caracterizada por la ironía de los comentarios o digresiones sobre la conducción del relato, con un ascendiente total sobre su carácter irreal y artificioso.

5463 Edwards, Jorge. Los convidados de piedra. Novela. Barcelona: Seix Barral, 1978. 364 p. (Biblioteca breve; 436)

Esta es la segunda novela del autor y, sin duda su obra más importante. La narración es presentada por una suerte de cronista generacional, pero de un grupo restringido tanto por la experiencia como por el marco social del narrador. Esto es determinante para la visión histórica del país que aparece reducida a las fluctuaciones entre tendencias propias de la aristocracia, con cierta aparente cercanía a la comprensión de *La fronda aristocrática* (2. ed. Santiago: Editorial del Pacífico, 1945, 312 p.), de Alberto Edwards. La interpretación es, sin embargo, fragmentaria, aforística, y recurre extensamente al folklore cristalizado de dichos y humoradas criollas. Evocaciones y actualizaciones se ordenan en función de la celebración del cumpleaños de un miembro del grupo. Los convidados de piedra son los ausentes, discrepantes o exiliados, en un mundo petrificado en sus posiciones políticas.

5464 Garay, Roberto M. Catalán de Puntarenas. Santiago: Editorial Nascimento, 1977. 303 p.

Novela que narra la historia del misterioso asesinato del Profesor Catalán. La obra resulta innovadora en el contexto de la literatura regional, agregando un nombre significativo al lado de Francisco Coloane y Osvaldo Wegmann.

5465 Lavín Cerda, Hernán. Los tormentos del hijo. México: Joaquín Mortiz, 1977. 120 p. (Nueva narrativa hispánica)

Narraciones largas y breves, fragmentarias, inconsecuentes, más bien textos o escrituras—neoescrituras—en las que el don del lenguaje, que arrastra citas, trasformaciones y glosas literarias—Neruda, Macedonio, Cortázar entre muchos otros—y consagra la inconexión, el absurdo, lo fantástico, y para en el esperpento o el tango con humor negro, destaca por encima de todo.

5466 Marchant Lazcano, Jorge. La Beatriz Ovalle: o, Cómo mató usted en mí toda aspiración arribista. Buenos Aires: Ediciones Orión, 1977. 158 p. (Colección Alfa de Orión. Narrativa contemporánea)

Con ésta, su primera novela, Jorge Marchant Lazcano (n. 1950) salta al primer plano de la nueva generación de narradores. Recortes de periódico, cartas, diarios de vida, citas de variado orden forman el texto de esta novela. En ellos se recoge un lenguaje coloquial marcado socialmente que tiene su momento más destacado en la configuración del personaje principal.

5467 Mujeres chilenas cuentan. Selección de Chela Reyes. Santiago de Chile: Zig-Zag, 1978. 92 p. (Libros de bolsillo Zig-Zag)

Buena muestra antológica del cuento femenino. Incluye relatos de: Eliana Cerda, Elena Aldunate, Chela Reyes, Olga Arratia, Gabriela Lezaeta, Virginia Cruzat, Marcela Paz, Maité Allamand, Elisa Serrana, Alicia Morel y Luz de Viana. No sin desigualdades ni omisiones.

5468 Ruiz-Tagle Gandarillas, Carlos. Cuentos de Santiago. Santiago, Chile: Editorial Nascimento, 1978. 179 p.

Cuentos de humor e ironía en que se presenta un mundo de vidas mínimas en las que la simplicidad, la ternura, la cotidianidad se ven alteradas por la irrupción de lo irreal, extraño o fantástico. Ruiz-Tagle tiene, desde hace tiempo, un lugar bien ganado en el cuento chileno.

LITERARY CRITICISM AND HISTORY

5469 Achugar, Hugo. Ideología y estructuras narrativas en José Donoso: 1950–1970. Caracas: Centro de Estudios Latinoamericanos Rómulo Gallegos, 1979. 330 p., bibl. (Colección Enrique Bernardo Núñez)

El joven autor uruguayo presenta una visión de las novelas de Donoso, comprendidas en las fechas del epígrafe, como un solo todo caracterizado por lo que llama "la ambivalencia ética de la libertad imaginativa." En este rasgo determinante ve un rechazo de la sociedad alienada y a la vez un modelo ideológico.

5470 Caviglia, John. Tradition and monstrosity in *El Obsceno pájara de la noche* (PMLA, 93:1, Jan. 1978, p. 33–44)

La máscara, el monstruo, la vieja, el imbunche son aspectos de la novela de Donoso analizados que contribuyen a la comprensión del equilibrio inestable de la novela entre norma y rechazo de la norma. Esta relación define el género monstruoso de la obra y fija sus posibilidades e imposibilidades.

5471 Costa, René de. El cubismo literario y la novela fílmica: *Cagliostro* de Vicente Huidobro (RCLL, 3:6, 2. semestre 1977, p. 67–79)

Excelente artículo sobre la novela-film de Huidobro, las condiciones originarias de su publicación, sus características narrativas y la recepción de las versiones inglesa y española.

Donoso, José. The boom in Spanish American literature: a personal history. See item **5023**.

Foster, David William. Chilean literature: a working bibliography of secondary sources. See *HLAS 41:28*.

5472 Fraysse, Maurice. La campagne chilenne et le *huaso* dans les romans de Blest Gana (UTIEH/C, 28, 1977, p. 91–103)

Artículo que analiza la presencia restringida del huaso en la novela de Blest Gana y las razones de ello.

5473 Housková, Anna. La narrativa chilena de resistencia antifascista (ASB/PP, 20:3, 1977, p. 157–171)

Artículo que hace un recuento de

la literatura testimonial relacionada con el golpe militar de 1973 con un énfasis partidista.

5474 Jornadas del Libro y la Cultural, *1st, Antofagasta, Chile, 1977.* Jornadas del libro y la cultura. Santiago: Editorial Universitaria, 1978. 284 p., bibl., ill. (Ediciones nueva universidad)

Dos de las principales editoriales universitarias del país se unen para presentar ponencias y resultado de unas jornadas de discusión sobre lo que se ha dado en llamar el "apagón cultural," es decir una depresión en el interés por la lectura, en el consumo y producción del libro y en el clima cultural, comprobable en la década del setenta y acentuada en los últimos años. Entre las causas, aparte la universal consideración de la crisis del libro y de la era de Gutenberg, la principal es sin duda la crisis de la industria editorial chilena, reducida a un mercado exiguo. La segunda es posiblemente el gravamen de la importación de estos que hace imposible o ha reducido drásticamente el consumo de libros. Se mencionan muchas otras causas debatibles que incluyen el sistema educacional, los métodos de enseñanza, la política universitaria y cultural del país. En excelentes ponencias se discuten diversas dimensiones y aspectos del problema.

5475 Lastra, Pedro. Conversaciones con Enrique Lihn: las novelas (Dispositio [University of Michigan, Department of Romance Languages, Ann Arbor] 3:9, otoño 1978, p. 393–407)

Interesante entrevista, anticipo de un libro de próxima publicación, en la cual Lihn elabora extensamente sobre la novela. Especiales referencias a sus obras *Batman en Chile* (see *HLAS 38:6791*), *La orquesta de cristal* (see *HLAS 40:6868*) y *El arte de la palabra*, su próxima novela.

5476 Libertella, Héctor. A literary hybrid. Translated by Edith Grossman (REVIEW, 23, 1978, p. 31–32)

Estudio de *La orquesta de cristal* (see *HLAS 40:6868*) traducido del libro de Héctor Libertella, *Nueva escritura en Latinoamérica* (Caracas: Monte Avila, 1977, p. 93–96). Review 23 dedica el Focus a Enrique Lihn, páginas 5 a 37, con textos del poeta y novelista, y con artículos sobre su obra.

5477 Lipski, John M. Donoso's obscene bird: novel and anti-novel (LALR, 4:9, Fall/Winter 1976, p. 39–47)

Como consecuencia de las ambigüedades textuales que surgen de una variada serie de oposiciones en que todo es definido en términos de su opuesto o su contrario, el autor ve en *El obsceno pájaro de la noche* no una sino dos novelas, la novela y su contrario, una anti-novela.

5478 McMurray, George R. José Donoso. Boston: Twayne Publishers, 1979. 178 p., bibl., index (Twayne's world authors series; TWAS 517)

Analiza la narrativa de Donoso hasta *Tres novelista burguesas* poniendo el acento sobre aspectos surrealistas y existenciales y el generalizado pesimismo de su obra.

5479 Martínez, Z. Nelly. José Donoso (HISP, 7:21, 1978, p. 53–74)

Entrevista anterior a la publicación de Casa de Campo en la que Donoso define polémicamente sus puntos de vista sobre la novela, la crítica, la interpretación de su obra y la gestación de su última novela.

5480 Martínez Dacosta, Silvia. Dos ensayos literarios sobre Eduardo Barrios y José Donoso. Miami: Ediciones Universal, 1976, i.e. 1977. 84 p., bibl. (Colección Polymita)

Estos ensayos plantean enfoques psicológicos que se muestran plausibles en el análisis de los personajes, Fray Rufino y Fray Lázaro, de *El hermano Asno*, pero no así en el análisis de los personajes de *El obsceno pájaro de la noche.*

5481 Medina Vidal, Jorge and others. Estudios sobre la novela *Este Domingo* de José Donoso. Montevideo: Universidad de la República, Facultad de Humanidades y Ciencias, Departamento de Lingüística, 1978. 153 p.

Once estudios reunidos como resultado de un semestre de trabajo en el curso de Estilística del profesor Jorge Medina Vidal. La mayor parte de ellos está dedicada al estudio de los personajes con criterios metodológicos diversos que incluyen desde el análisis del discurso hasta la retórica y la psicocrítica.

5482 Mistral, Gabriela. Cartas de amor de Gabriela Mistral. Introducción, recopilación, iconografía y notas de Sergio Fernández Larraín. Santiago: Editorial Andrés Bello, 1978. 243 p., bibl., ill.

Esta publicación modifica sustancialmente el estado de los estudios biográficos sobre Gabriela Mistral. Repite infortunadamente las confusiones entre vida y obra a pesar de los datos que las cartas mismas proporcionan. Así ocurre en las referencias al poema *Balada*, de *Desolación*, cuyo texto es remitido en la carta xxxviii y última de este recolección. El volumen recoge cartas a Alfredo Videla Pineda (1905–1906), cartas de los dieciseis años, y cartas de incomparable mayor interés a Manuel Magallanes Moure (1914–1921). Estas últimas revelan una pasión singular por su vehemencia y los contradictorios movimientos del ánimo de la Mistral que alteran sus fórmulas de tratamiento, desde el íntimo tú hasta el distanciador usted. Surge con claridad lo que ella misma define "soy la más desconcertante y triste (lamentable) mezcla de dulzura y dureza, de ternura y de grosería" o "soy salvajemente sincera" frente a la finura y discreción de Magallanes. Cartas sorprendentes que se leen con interés.

5483 ———. Gabriela piensa en . . . Selección de prosas y prólogo, Roque Esteban Scarpa. Santiago: Editorial Andrés Bello, 1978. 435 p.

Más de setenta artículos de Gabriela Mistral reune en este volumen Roque E. Scarpa. Están orientados por el asunto, el tratamiento de una figura, femenina o masculina de Chile, América, España y Europa y otros mundos. La Mistral muestra en ellos una rara penetración psicológica y crítica y una constante vocación americanista.

5484 ———. Materias: prosa inédita. Selección y prólogo de Alfonso Calderón. Santiago: Editorial Universitaria, 1978. 412 p. (Colección Letras de América)

Prosa no recogida en libro, no propiamente inédita, es la que se recoge aquí ordenada en cuatro secciones. Parte de su contenido coincide en la sección iii, "Personas con la selección de Roque E. Scarpa," *Gabriel piensa en . . .* (véase item **5483**). Las otras secciónes, "Lugares," "Materias," "Variedad," recogen textos de gran valor e interés.

5485 **Morand, Carlos.** Visión de Santiago en la novela chilena. Prólogo de René Jara C. Santiago: Ediciones Aconcagua, 1977. 196 p., bibl. (Colección Bello)

Estudio sobre la presentación del espacio urbano en doce novelas que tienen como escenario la capital de Chile. El análisis considera especialmente la variedad de los modos de representación y la interpretación social. Las variaciones desde *El Mendigo*, de Lastarria, y *Martín Rivas*, de Alberto Blest Gana, se extienden hasta *El obsceno pájaro de la noche*, de José Donoso, siguiendo la serie de cambios generacionales.

5486 **Neruda, Pablo.** Para nacer he nacido. Barcelona: Editorial Seiz Barral, 1978. 451 p. (Biblioteca Breve; 465)

Matilde Neruda y Miguel Otero Silva han reunido en este volumen una parte importante de la producción en prosa de Neruda. Divididos en siete "cuadernos" se ordenan artículos literarios, políticos, de viaje, prosas poéticas, discursos y manifiestos. Entre estas piezas están reunidas las dispersas crónicas de la revista *Ercilla*, los discursos de incorporación a la Facultad de Filosofía y Letras de la Universidad de Chile y de recepción del Premio Nobel de Literatura. Varias de las páginas recogidas son documentos indispensables para su biografía. En general, la prosa nerudiana se revela como una dimensión nada desdeñable del gran poeta. Poética, periodística, polémica, argumentativa, su prosa resulta original y notable. Sus rasgos gramaticales, retóricos y literarios revelan una notable maestría.

5487 **Ostria González, Mauricio.** Emelina: un folletín de Rubén Darío, a pesar de Rubén Darío (Acta Literaria, Publicación Anual [Universidad de Concepción, Instituto de Lenguas, Concepción, Chile] 2, 1977, p. 13–34)

Pormenorizado análisis del estado de la crítica de la novela de Eduardo Poirier y Rubén Darío, publicada por primera vez en Valparaíso (Imprenta y Litografía Universal, de Chaigneau y Castro, 1887, viii, 204 p.) y análisis de su estructura. Sostiene que la escritura artista constituye un factor antifolletinesco.

5488 **Parent, Georges A.** El modo narrativo en Eloy de Carlos Droguett (NS, 3:5/6, 1978, p. 157–178)

Excelente análisis del modo narrativo de Eloy y sus variedades y procedimientos. Hay interesantes contribuciones a la comprensión de la obra y al análisis de sus variaciones textuales, reconocibles entre la primera edición de Seix Barral, 1960, y la de Buenos Aires, Sudamericana, 1969, que se maneja en este análisis.

5489 Promis Ojeda, José. La novela chilena actual: orígenes y desarrollo. Buenos Aires: F. García Cambeiro, 1977. 188 p., bibl. (Colección Estudios latinoamericanos; 25)

Estudio de la novela chilena que alcanza a tres de las generaciones contemporáneas y al enfoque contrastivo de éstas frente al naturalismo. Incluye el análisis de la "teoría" de la literatura en los momentos polémicos de las generaciones y el de un número considerable de obras en sus rasgos gregarios.

5490 Quinteros, Isis. José Donoso: una insurrección contra la realidad. Madrid: Hispanova, 1978. 286 p., bibl. (Colección Véspero)

Este libro estudia la vida y la narrativa, cuentística y novelística, de José Donoso hasta *El obsceno pájaro de la noche.* El enfoque dominante considera diversos estratos simbólicos tanto en su comprensión arquetípica como en su explicación social.

5491 Schopf, Federico. La narrativa de Jorge Edwards (Studi di letteratura Ispanoamericana [Milano] 9, 1979, p. 9–43)

Excelente estudio de la obra narrativa de Jorge Edwards anterior a su novela *Los convidados de piedra.*

5492 Testimonios y documentos de la literatura chilena: 1842–1975. José Promis, compilador. Santiago, Chile: Editorial Nascimento, 1977. 386 p., bibl.

Compilacón de artículos, discursos, manifiestos, artes poéticas, en que los escritores chilenos, poetas, novelistas y ensayistas, han expresado su concepción de la literatura. La ordenación de estos materiales se hace por épocas, períodos y generaciones. Se trata de un dominio poco estudiado pero de gran importancia para el conocimiento de la literatura y de la conciencia de la literatura en los escritores chilenos.

5493 Urbistondo, Vicente. Los convidados de piedra, novela épica, épica-burguesa, y artefacto semiótico (Revista Chilena de Literatura [Editorial Univeritaria, Santiago] 12, Oct. 1978, p. 105–124)

Artículo que propone, con cierta afectación, una relación entre las concepciones expresas del novelista y su creación novelística más reciente. Cierta falta de medida se hace perceptible en la comprensión y en la valoración de la obra.

PROSE FICTION: 20th Century: River Plate Countries (Argentina, Paraguay and Uruguay)

EARL M. ALDRICH, JR., *Professor of Spanish, University of Wisconsin, Madison*
SAUL SOSNOWSKI, *Professor and Chairman, Department of Spanish and Portuguese, University of Maryland*

MOST OF THE SHORT NARRATIVES and novels reviewed in this section were published between 1976–79. These fictional works of the late 1970s are much like those produced earlier in the decade: A significant number of them are characterized by their complex narrative strategies, high level of abstraction, and distaste for obvious objective referents. They draw attention to themselves as artifice, self-consciously flaunting their linguistic opacity. A sort of existential anguish is the dominant factor in other novels and stories in which the authors confront a world where nature is perceived as process rather than substance, as continual change rather than permanence, where political and social institutions are typified by confusion and injustice, and where man cannot even know himself let alone another in an absolute sense. Fantasy; that is, the exploration of the extraordinary and the inexplicable, continues to inspire many authors. A slow yet steady trickle of conventional fiction which conveys a common sense view of reality is also apparent.

Although some meritorious works were published in Argentina during the period in question, the quality and quantity of the fiction has declined somewhat. The political realities which have so deeply affected Uruguayan literary production throughout the 1970s are now taking their toll in Argentine literature as well. Corregidor is the most active publishing house and it has afforded special opportunities for promising young writers. Two of them are Carlos Arcidiácono and Hugo Corra whose novels (items **5497** and **5515**) are notable for their complexity and abstraction without the exaggerations common to beginners. Among the established authors, Eduardo Gudiño Kieffer deserves particular note for his novel *Medias negras, peluca rubia* (item **5524**). The calculated pretentiousness of this novel mocks the pretentions of the artistic and literary world. Other established authors whose recent works should be mentioned are: Julio Cortázar, Haroldo Conti, Beatriz Guido, and Enrique Medina. Cortázar's *Territorios* (item **5517**) is a fascinating work somewhat reminiscent of his earlier *Ultima round* and *La vuelta al día en ochenta mundos*. Conti's short story collection *La balada del álamo carolina* (item **5514**) demonstrates his unique ability to evoke the special qualities of rural people. Guido's *¿Quién le teme a mis temas?* (item **5525**) shows that although each work of fiction may have, in some sense, a life of its own, at the same time it is a reflection of its creator. In his latest novel *Perros de la noche* (item **5531**), Enrique Medina continues his obsessive but arresting exploration of personal and societal degradation.

The quality and quantity of Uruguayan fiction is again disappointingly low. Jorge Musto's political novel *El pasajero* (item **5554**) won a Casa de las Américas award but objectively speaking there is little to recommend the work. It is noteworthy primarily because it is part of a rapidly growing list of fictional works published in the 1970s depicting guerrilla activity in the River Plate region. [EMA]

LITERARY CRITICISM: The initial screening of current Argentine literary criticism shows that interest in Borges continues unabated. Shelves strain and bibliographies bulge with the endless output of works on every conceivable aspect of his works. Interviews print every one of his utterances and fame seekers trail in his wake as if the writer were an object to be followed, photographed, questioned, and probed. These excesses notwithstanding, serious scholarship on Borges' profound contributions to literature is exemplified by the book-length studies by Rest and Molloy (items **5599** and **5606**). Rodríguez Monegal's literary biography has also evoked interest (item **5611**), Orgambide's polemical essay on Borges' politics is destined to provoke controversy and to provide a good basis for future discussions of the subject (item **5604**). Briefer studies of academic scholarship encompass a wide spectrum of themes and great variation in quality. Borges himself adds to his growing list of publications, including works written in collaboration with others—a companion work to his *Obras completas* (item **5503**).

Interest in Cortázar remains constant and his recent and past texts are closely followed. Arlt, Macedonio, Puig, and others are studied via multiple and varied methodologies.

Two welcome developments are the growing interest in authors who are not in standard reading lists (e.g., Girondo, Rozenmacher, Conti, Viñas, DiBenedetto, etc.) and concern with literary production.

Onetti continues to command the attention of those interested in Uruguayan literature. The publication of his articles constitutes an important addition to his bibliography (item **5637**). Fortunately, Felisberto Hernández has been (re)discovered and is the subject of several excellent studies (item **5628**). Aínsa's essays, a collection of texts on Benedetti in the Cuban *Valoración múltiple* series, and entries on Martínez Moreno and Galeano, are topics worthy of additional scholarship.

The increasing number of studies on Roa Bastos since the publication of *Yo el supremo* have not exhausted the multiple levels of this text. It is expected that available theoretical tools will enable scholars to develop further readings of this novel.

Unfortunately, there are very few studies of younger and lesser known authors (e.g., Peri Rossi, Costantini, Gambaro, Saer, Walsh, etc.) to complete the view of contemporary literary production in this region. [SS]

PROSE FICTION
ARGENTINA

5494 Aguinis, Marcos. Operativo siesta. Buenos Aires: Editorial Planeta Argentina, 1977. 127 p. (Biblioteca universal Planeta)

Careful attention to plot, economy, and the impact of a surprise ending characterize this collection of 10 stories written in a traditional vein. Humor free of ironic overtones abounds in the stories.

5495 Anderson Imbert, Enrique. Cuentos en miniatura. Antología. Caracas: Equinoccio, 1976. 183 p. (Colección Garúa)

A collection of the author's very brief narratives—ranging in length from a paragraph to a couple of pages—taken from his following works: *El mentir de las estrellas* (1940, item **5496**), *Las pruebas del caos* (1946), *El Grimorio* (1961), *El gato de Chesire* (1965), *La sandía y otros cuentos* (1969), *La locura juega al ajedrez* (1971), *La botella de Klein* (1975). The collection is prefaced by a few interesting authorial observations. His solution (as expressed in these selections) to the implications of a purely material universe and the intellectual difficulty of living as if such a universe had meaning and significance is humor.

5496 ———. El mentir de las estrellas. Buenos Aires: Emecé Editores, 1979. 245 p. (Escritores argentinos)

A collection of stories previously published in 1940 and 1946. The editors promise two more volumes, *El gato de Chesire* and *Vigilia*, at a later date.

5497 Arcidiácono, Carlos. La niña bonita. Buenos Aires: Ediciones Corregidor, 1977. 223 p. (Serie popular; 1234)

The principal characters in this novel are women: Three of them set out on vacations to escape their problems and gain perspective; the fourth, an old woman, sits in her apartment trying to reconstruct images of her past. All fail: The three who try to escape are further submerged in their problems and failures; the old woman cannot construct a coherent past which would give meaning to life. This structure provides the author with an opportunity to expose and confront the tragedy of life which lacks significance—a life in which apparent successes are really failures, in which experience provides no insight or identity. The work is a disturbing mixture of melancholy, rage, and irony.

5498 Barone, Orlando. Los lugares secretos. Buenos Aires: Macondo Ediciones, 1976. 147 p. (Los Narradores)

La soledad is the major theme and melancholy is the tone of the 25 short narratives contained in this collection. The author indicates in a prefatory interview that this work should be approached as an extended metaphor, as a symbol that suggests rather than defines. Indeed, the selections, which vary in length from five or six pages to one short paragraph, hint in a veiled manner at the failure and alienation of the protagonists without ever becoming specific.

5499 Beilin, Armando. Elfride. Buenos Aires: R. Alonso Editor, 1976. 246 p. (Colección Contemporáneos)

Black humor dominates in this novel which mocks the pretentions of contemporary society. Practitioners and gurus of psychoanalysis, the occult, self-introspection, and self-improvement are exposed as exploiters and ultimately as blind leaders of the blind.

5500 Bioy Casares, Adolfo. El héroe de las mujeres. Buenos Aires: Emecé Editores, 1978. 191 p. (Escritores argentinos)

This book brings together all the short novels and stories written by the author since *El gran serafín* (1967).

5501 Borges, Jorge Luis. Laberintos. Ilustraciones de Ducmelic. Prólogo de José Edmundo Clemente. Buenos Aires: Editorial Joraci, 1977. 65 p.: ill. (some col.)

Three of Borges' well-known narratives are accompanied by 20 beautiful reproductions of Ducmelic's paintings which are inspired by the stories.

5502 ———. Obras completas: 1923–1972. Edición dirigida y realizada por Carlos V. Frías. Madrid: Ultramar, 1977. 1161 p., 1 leaf of plates: port., bibl.

Includes prose and poetry arranged in chronological order.

5503 ———. Obras completas en colaboración. Buenos Aires: Emecé Editores, 1979. 989 p.: port., ill., bibl.

Frente al tomo en que recogía sus *Obras completas* (sic), dice Borges, en éste está "la alegría de la amistad y los hallazgos compartidos" (p. 977). Con variada fortuna, en estos textos se logró que a través de la colaboración literaria surgieran "nuevos" escritores, entre ellos el notable H. Bustos Domecq. Además de las colaboraciones con Adolfo Bioy Casares, este tomo incluye "Leopoldo Lugones" (con Betina Edelberg); El *'Martín Fierro'* y "El Libro de los Seres Imaginarios" (con Margarita Guerrero); "Qué es el Budismo" (con Alicia Jurado); "Breve Antología Anglosajona" (con María Kodama); e "Introducción a la Literatura Inglesa y Literaturas Germánicas Medievales" (con María Esther Vásquez). Complemento imprescindible para el que desea agotar los aportes de Borges. [S. Sosnowski]

5504 ———. Rosa y azul. Ilustraciones de Alfredo González. Madrid: Sedmay, 1977. 34 leaves: ill.

A beautifully produced edition of two previously unpublished narratives: "La Rosa de Paracelso" and "Tigres Azules." The book is lavishly illustrated with drawings by Alfonso González.

5505 Bosco, María Angélica. En la estela de un secuestro. Buenos Aires: Emecé Editores, 1977. 203 p. (Escritores argentinos)

The delta provides the setting, and a kidnapping provides the plot for a novel in which the prime concern is to explore ethical choices and ideological possibilities which face men. The psychology of the main character is developed with great subtlety and sensitivity.

5506 ———. Retorno a "La Ilusión." Buenos Aires: Macondo Ediciones, 1976. 173 p. (Los Narradores)

This novel, originally formulated as a drama, has as the narrator a man whose spirit has come back to inhabit his estate in order to observe the pitiful, agonizing wrangling of those to whom he has left his properties. The novel offers opportunity to speculate about the futility of clinging to past illusions, prolonging empty, deceitful traditions, and seeking satisfaction from false values.

5507 Bullrich Palenque, Sylvina. Calles de Buenos Aires. Buenos Aires: Emecé Editores, 1979. 237 p. (Escritores argentinos)

This novel is primarily interesting because it is one of Bullrich's first, written, according to her, when she was about 22 or 23 years old. It is an ironic, critical picture of Buenos Aires at the time, with a special focus on the hypocrisies inherent in the social structure.

5508 ———. Los despiadados. Buenos Aires: Emecé Editores, 1978. 228 p. (Escritores argentinos)

In Bullrich's newest novel the narrator-protagonist, a married woman, makes a journey back into her past by returning to the family house where she grew up. She is moved by an inner need to recapture the sights and smells of childhood, to evoke pleasant memories, and to consider the values associated with that period of life. At this point the conventional psychological approach which typifies most of the author's previous work is suddenly fused with the fantastic, the inexplicable, as outside forces lay siege to the house. The narrative structure, while not particularly original, is both interesting and effective: The narrator's sensitive, sensual evocation of the past as she reacts to her natural surroundings is interspersed with tension-filled accounts of the siege. The suspense is built in masterful fashion.

5509 Bustos Domecq, Honorio [*pseud. for* **Jorge Luis Borges** and **Adolfo Bioy Casares**]. Nuevos cuentos de Bustos Domecq. Ilustraciones de Fernández Chelo. Buenos

Aires: Ediciones Librería La Ciudad, 1977. 152 p., ill.

The nine stories in this edition are beautifully illustrated by Fernández Chelo.

5510 Canto, Estela. El jazmín negro. Buenos Aires: Emecé Editores, 1978. 214 p. (Escritores argentinos)

In this novel, Canto presents in a straightforward, convincing manner the misery of people who have been deprived materially and emotionally. Very effective is the author's depiction of a young girl's sense of rejection which society on all levels reinforces.

Carpentier, Alejo. A manual for Manuel. See item **6629**.

5511 Catania, Carlos. Las varonesas. Barcelona: Seix Barral, 1978. 514 p. (Nueva narrativa hispánica)

An ambitious, intricate, complex, dense, enigmatic, and tiresome novel which inevitably reminds the reader of a number of other such Argentine works which have been published in the last decade—replete with multiple narrative perspectives, insertions of documentary literature, and self-conscious manipulation of language. Readers who still admire such works will find the novel a monumental achievement.

5512 Codina de Giannoni, Iverna. Los días y la sangre. La Habana: Casa de Las Américas, 1977. 212 p. (Colección La Honda)

This novel depicts in an idealized way guerrilla activities in Buenos Aires during the regimes of Onganía and Lanusse. It adds to a growing list of fiction which is forming a genre around the "lucha guerrillera" in the River Plate region.

5513 Constante, Susana. La educación sentimental de la Señorita Sonia. Barcelona: Tusquets Editores, 1979. 129 p. (La Sonrisa vertical; 13)

This evocative novel, which belongs to the genre of intellectualized, genteel erotic fiction, was the winner of a literary prize given by Tusquets Editores in 1978. The setting is central Europe in the last years of the 19th century. The main characters are preoccupied with their sexual fantasies.

5514 Conti, Haroldo. La balada del álamo carolina. La Habana: Casa de las Américas, 1978. 162 p.

In this collection of 11 short narratives, Conti continues to demonstrate his extraordinary ability to evoke the special qualities of small-town people, to capture with poignancy a fleeting feeling of remorse, guilt, failure, rejection, or simple pleasure. The author's style is simple, deceptively simple, but with it he captures a wide range of emotions from humor to nostalgia, to sadness.

5515 Corra, Hugo. Frontera sin retorno. Buenos Aires: Ediciones Corregidor, 1978. 238 p. (Serie popular; P-1263)

A novel which is especially interesting because of its narrative structure. At the center of the work is a diary, composed of short, independent texts, in which the narrator deals with the major 20th-century theme of the possible meaning of life in an indifferent world. The diary is given special significance by another narrator who is intensely involved in interpreting its meaning and discovering more about its author.

5516 Cortázar, Julio. Las armas secretas. Edición de Susana Jakfalvi. Madrid: Cátedra, D.L., 1978. 233 p., bibl. (Letras hispánicas; 69)

This annotated edition of Cortázar's stories contains some useful commentary and analyses plus a brief bibliography. Particularly helpful as an introduction to the author's fiction.

———. End of the game, and other stories. See item **6655**.

———. A manual for Manuel. See item **6629**.

5517 ———. Territorios. México: Siglo Veintiuno, 1978. 143 p., ill.

In a work reminiscent of his *Ultimo round* and *La vuelta al día en ochenta mundos*, Cortázar gives full rein to his fertile imagination, his knowledge of art, and his impish sense of humor. In addition to his fascinating analyses of the works of a variety of artists, Cortázar also includes some unusual, complementary autobiographical evocations.

5518 El cuento argentino contemporáneo. Selección y notas, Beatriz Sarlo. Buenos Aires: Centro Editor de América Latina, 1976. 154 p. (Panoramas de la literatura; 2. Biblioteca total; 7)

An anthology of selections by 12 major Argentine writers which includes Borges, Cortázar, Ocampo, Moyano, and Conti.

5519 Cuentos de sol a sol. Selección, Néstor J. Montenegro. Buenos Aires: Nemont Ediciones, 1976. 157 p.

An anthology of stories by 14 well-known Argentine authors. Includes selections by Bioy Casares, Gudiño Kieffer, and Poletti.

5520 Cuentos fantásticos argentinos: segunda serie. Selección de Nicolás Cócaro y Antonio E. Serrano Redonnet. Buenos Aires: Emecé Editores, 1976. 274 p.

An anthology which contains stories by 26 established Argentine writers, including Borges, Bioy Casares, Gudiño Kieffer, and Ocampo. Cócaro and Serrano Redonnet have provided a concise, helpful introduction which outlines the major characteristics of the *cuento fantástico.*

5521 Diaconu, Alina. Buenas noches, profesor. Buenos Aires: Ediciones Corregidor, 1978. 229 p. (Serie popular; P-1242)

The theme of this novel is an old one: the love relationship between an adolescent girl and an older man. In this case, the protagonist is a public school teacher of 55 years of age who is without any claim to distinction. The narrative technique for developing the theme is interesting and effective: alternating between omniscient author and a dialogue between the teacher who rationalizes and an unidentified interlocutor who challenges and criticizes, the reader receives a number of extraordinary insights into the professor, his past and his present.

5522 Diez narradores argentinos. Selección de Luis de Paola. Barcelona: Bruguera, 1977. 212 p. (Libro amigo; 484)

An anthology of short stories by prominent writers including Conti, Di Benedetto, and Moyano. Brief bio-bibliographical sketch of each author.

5523 Gallardo, Sara. El país del humo. Buenos Aires: Editorial Sudamericana, 1977. 230 p. (Colección El espejo)

A collection of 46 short narratives which vary in length from several pages to a few paragraphs. The setting for most of the stories is rural Argentina but the experiences of the characters are beyond the range of common sense reality. It should be noted that the author does not try to achieve special effects through the imposition of fantasy on a regional ambient. The extraordinary atmosphere and events seem, rather, to be associated appropriately with the characters and the setting.

5524 Gudiño Kieffer, Eduardo. Medias negras, peluca rubia. Buenos Aires: Emecé Editores, 1979. 381 p., bibl. (Escritores argentinos)

This, the author's most ambitious, significant novel to date, is constructed on the basis of a confessional first-person narrative by Victor Kreisler and his complete works followed by the first person opposing account of Alterio Kreisler, a twin brother, and his complete works. A critical commentary of one of the works by T.H. Berket Jones is included along with acknowledgements and a bibliography. In one sense, this is an altogether pretentious and outrageous work—calculatedly, so, to be sure—as the author parodies the pretensions and hypocrisies of the literary-artistic world. In another sense, the work makes a serious statement, in highly original fashion, regarding the elusiveness of truth, the problematical nature of human identity, and man's propensity to delude and torment himself.

5525 Guido, Beatriz. ¿Quién le teme a mis temas? Buenos Aires: Editorial Fraterna, 1977. 386 p., 6 leaves of plates: ill.

An unusual book in which the author intersperses lengthy selections from her previously published novels and short stories with quotations from personal correspondence, interviews, and book reviews which make observations about her life and works. Also included are several photographs of Guido, her family, and her friends. The material is arranged in 16 sections entitled "Los Niños," "Los Adolescentes," "Los Padres," "Los Hermanos," "El Amor," "La Religión," etc. The selections in each section complement one another in such a way as to underscore the theme suggested by the title of the section. Guido has demonstrated with this book that although each work of fiction may have a life of its own it is, at the same time and in some profound sense, a reflection of its creator.

5526 Heker, Liliana. Un resplandor que se apagó en el mundo. Buenos Aires: Editorial Sudamericana, 1977. 143 p. (Colección El Espejo)

The three stories in this collection are connected by a common theme, the loss of an illusion. The final selection, which depicts the initiation of a young boy into the realities of life, is superior.

5527 Hernández, Juan José. La favorita. Caracas: Monte Avila Editores, 1977. 138 p. (Colección Continentes)

The perversity of man in its various forms—revenge, selfishness, greed, hypocrisy, cruelty—is depicted with great skill and restraint in the 12 stories of this collection. The sudden initiation of provincial children into the human frailties of the adult world, the shocking act of cruelty by a young child, or the cynicism of an ancient culture where men exploited and were exploited are examples of the type of narrative found in this book.

5528 Kordon, Bernardo. Adiós pampa mía. Caracas: Monte Avila Editores, 1978. 138 p. (Colección Continentes)

Kordon, who is at his best when depicting *porteño* customs and reproducing the *jerga porteña*, develops interesting psychological insights and a sustained and effective irony in the 11 stories of this collection.

5529 Levinson, Luisa Mercedes. El estigma del tiempo. Barcelona: Seix Barral, 1977. 145 p.

The characters in the 18 stories of this collection all have in common their sense of apartness and of meaninglessness in a universe which seems to resist all their efforts to understand. The anguished search for significance and personal identity is never completely masked by the humorous, ironic poses of the characters.

5530 Matamoro, Blas. Viaje prohibido. Buenos Aires: Editorial Sudamericana, 1978. 299 p. (Colección El espejo)

A detailed, intimate evocation divided into nine stories which could stand as autonomous narratives but at the same time link together in complementary fashion. The narrator recalls vividly the elements of everyday life in a Buenos Aires middle class neighborhood during the Perón era: childhood initiations into the realities of life, the secret desires, ambitions, and the discoveries of youth, even the sights, smells, and sounds of the environment. The memories are recalled with sensitivity and detail as the narrator seeks to establish his identity through evocation.

5531 Medina, Enrique. Perros de la noche. Buenos Aires: Ediciones Corregidor, 1977. 217 p.

In this novel (the plot is of little concern) Medina continues his obsession—so obvious in his previous fiction—to expose the evil of Argentine society. Personal and societal degradation are explored with a relentless fury which is calculated to produce a sense of revulsion in the reader. Medina is determined to show how far man has fallen.

5532 Mujica Láinez, Manuel. El brazalete y otros cuentos. Buenos Aires: Editorial Sudamericana, 1978. 117 p. (Colección El espejo)

A collection of six stories which had previously been published between 1965 and 1970. Each story presents the eruption of the unexpected and the inexplicable in the midst of common sense reality.

5533 ———. El gran teatro. Buenos Aires: Editorial Sudamericana, 1979. 204 p.

In this his latest novel—the title of which refers to the Teatro Colón—Mujica captures the essence of a crucial period in Argentine history—the early 1940s, a time in which old, seemingly eternal traditions were beginning to crumble. The author again blends fiction and life in his own inimitable way.

5534 ———. Obras completas. v. 1, Glosas castellanas; Don Galaz de Buenos Aires; Miguel Cané (padre); Canto a Buenos Aires; Estampas de Buenos Aires. Buenos Aires: Editorial Sudamericana, 1978. 1 v. (553 p.) bibl., plate.

This first volume contains five of his earliest works published originally between 1936 and 1946. The selections are prefaced by a relatively brief but helpful introduction which gives some historical background for them.

5535 Murena, H.A. Filosofía. Caracas: Monte Avila Editores, 1976. 129 p. (Colección Continente)

This novel belongs to a cycle called "El Sueño de la Razón." Previous novels of the cycle are: *Epitalámica, Polispuercon,* and *Caína muerte.* Like the novels which precede it, *Filosofía* is a bitter lament about the human condition which has steadily lost all value and meaning. And in the final analysis, language itself—the word—the fond hope, the last resort of the intellectual is found devoid of meaning as well.

5536 O'Donnell, Pacho. Las hormigas de Carlitos Chaplin. Buenos Aires: Editorial Sudamericana, 1978. 168 p. (Colección El espejo)

This pretentious work is structured on the basis of two alternating texts, one of them the story of a man with a passionate interest in ants and an uncanny ability to spout meaningless but influential phrases, and the other a recounting of an old Charlie Chaplin movie. The author earnestly explains that he is trying to demonstrate through his work the inefficacy of our common-sense view of reality by suggesting, presumably, a more sophisticated, more satisfying, more "truthful" view.

5537 Orphée, Elvira. *La última conquista de El Angel.* Caracas: Monte Avila, 1977. 142 p.

A series of intricately related narratives, skillfully presided over by Winkey, the torturer *par excellence.* At first almost hidden but revealed more and more as the book unfolds, this character emerges as a diabolical executioner who approaches political torture with a sort of religious and artistic fervor. In her prologue Orphée denies that the book is meant to denounce any particular government or political regime. Indeed, its chilling exposition of human cruelty, depravity, guilt, and evil transcends mere political intentions.

5538 Perés, Joan Manoel. Querida mamá. Buenos Aires: Ediciones Corregidor, 1977. 300 p. (Colección Letras del Cid; C-1202)

In this novel the narrator traces in intricate, detailed fashion the decline of an aristocratic family, recounting its tensions, conflicts, and dislocations from the last years of the 19th century into the middle of the 20th. On one level the novel may be interpreted and appreciated as the depiction of one family, and on another, one can perceive the ultimate decadence of a whole social class.

5539 Perrone, Eduardo. Días de reír, días de llorar. Buenos Aires: Ediciones de la Flor, 1976. 201 p.

The narrator of this novel evokes the experiences of his past in an environment where poverty and injustice seem to shape the lives of many people. The narrative point of view is carelessly developed but some of the scenes, especially those involving a child's initiation to the harsh realities of life, are effective.

5540 Posse, Abel. Damión. Barcelona: Argos, 1978. 270 p.

In this his third novel, Posse contrasts in an extraordinary way modern and precolumbian life. By a number of ingenious devices, including excerpts from Columbus' letters, interpolated stanzas of Maya and Nahuatl poetry, and the metamorphosis of the conquistador López de Aguirre, Posse maintains an exquisitely ironic contrast between the categorizing mentality of the European conquerors and the subtle, ever changing reality of the world they seek to understand and on which they seek to impose their order.

5541 Roffé, Reina. Monte de Venus. Buenos Aires: Ediciones Corregidor, 1976. 270 p. (Serie popular; 154)

The main concern of this somber novel is the problem of women finding meaning, self-identity, and dignity within their society. Much of the work takes place within a girl's school. Interspersed is the first-person narration of a confused, bitter woman whose life has been filled with rejection and misunderstanding.

5542 Schneider, Luis Mario. La resurrección de Clotilde Goñi. México: Joaquín Mortiz, 1977. 130 p. (Nueva narrativa hispánica)

A first novel by this Argentine author who has taken up residence in Mexico. It is a fascinating but disturbing presentation of the collision and intermingling of two worlds: the world of innocence represented by a young boy and the world of perversion as represented by the nurse of a religious order. The use of two first person points of view provides an unusual narrative structure.

5543 Stilman, Eduardo. Febo asoma. Buenos Aires: Ediciones Corregidor, 1976. 100 p. (Serie popular; 127)

The first story of this collection of 12 establishes the basic theme for all the rest: the meaning of life and its relationship to the obvious reality of death. The selections are tinged with irony, ambiguity, mystery but cannot readily be classified as fantastic.

5544 Torre Nilsson, Leopoldo. Jorge, el nadador. Buenos Aires: Ediciones Torreón, 1978 or 1979. 112 p.

This latest and brief novel about life, literature, and loneliness by Torre Nilsson is primarily interesting for the insights it gives into the extraordinary personality of its author.

5545 36 [Treinta y seis] cuentos argentinos con humor: siglo XX. Selección y notas bibliográficas por Fernando Sorrentino. Buenos Aires: Plus Ultra, 1977. 236 p.

As the title indicates, humor is the common demoninator for the stories of this anthology. Cortázar, Ocampo, Denevi, Arlt, and Bioy Casares are included. Brief bio-bibliographical notes for each author.

5546 Verbitsky, Bernardo. Octubre maduro. Buenos Aires: Macondo Edicones, 1976. 200 p. (Los Narradores)

A collection of 14 short stories in which the author presents characters who sense their own loneliness, insecurity, lost opportunities, or failures, as well as those who are seeking to define themselves within their circumstances. Subtle humor and hope always lurk below the formulations of regret and frustrations.

URUGUAY

5547 Benedetti, Mario. Con y sin nostalgia. México: Siglo Veintiuno, 1977. 156 p.

A collection of nine short stories, written from exile, in which the author bitterly denounces the political repression and social decadence of his native country.

5548 Castillo, Alvaro. El calor del enero. Barcelona: Plaza & Janés, 1977. 239 p. (Novelista del día)

The author, in a brief, ironic preface to his collection of 10 short narratives, says that one of his friends has suggested that the book should be titled *Delirium tremens*. Indeed, drunkenness and alcohol are prominent elements in several of the selections. However, the author has primarily and effectively been interested in presenting characters who are involved in meaningless but slavish ritual or who have reached a point of deep anguish, apartness, or cynicism. A disturbing, provocative work.

5549 El cuento uruguayo contemporáneo. Selección y notas, Heber Cardoso. Buenos Aires: Centro Editor de América Latina, 1978. 173 p. (Panoramas de la literatura; 15. Biblioteca total; 59)

An anthology of stories by 17 representative writers, including Onetti, Benedetti, Martínez Moreno, and Arregui. A brief bio-bibliographical note is included for each author.

5550 Galmés, Héctor. Las calandrias griegas. Novela. Montevideo: Ediciones de la Banda Oriental, 1977. 108 p. (Colección Acuarimántima; 7)

This novel is an evocation of Montevideo during the late 1950s. The characters find their dreams, hopes, and goals somehow frustrated or beyond their reach.

5551 Hernández, Felisberto. El caballo perdido y otros cuentos. Buenos Aires: Calicanto Editorial, 1976. 230 p.

A collection of 10 of Hernández' narratives which includes a few selections with autobiographical content, some of his best known stories, and his posthumous work "El Caballo Perdido." The selections are preceded by a short but informative prologue by José Pedro Díaz and an interesting commentary by Hernández himself about the writing process.

5552 Jorge. El libro de Jorge. Montevideo?: Club del Libro, 1976. 117 p.

A collection of 33 humorous sketches in which a definition of an object provides the starting point. The humor is based on incongruity and irony.

5553 Montserrat, María de. El país secreto. Caracas: Monte Avila, 1977. 223 p.

In this novel the gradual psychological disintegration of a family which has been forced by social upheavals and prejudice to move about, finally settling in abject poverty in Montevideo, is captured through the alternating point of view. Shifting between the first and second person of the protagonist, the daughter of the family, and the "we" of the family itself, the reader comes to an ironic knowledge of the conflicts and misunderstandings within the family situation.

5554 Musto, Jorge. El pasajero. La Habana: Casa de las Américas, 1977. 168 p.

A trivial political novel which won a Casa de las Américas prize in 1977. The aimless, uncommitted narrator returns to Uruguay, his native country, to join a rebel organization where through a series of incompetent militant activities he begins to establish a sense of purpose and belonging. The work is confused in parts and dangerously close to maudlin in others. Although the intent of the work is serious, it is hard to keep from laughing.

5555 Nueva antología del cuento uruguayo. Selección de Arturo Sergio Visca. Montevideo: Ediciones de la Banda Oriental, 1976. 411 p. (Biblioteca mayor; 1)

This anthology of short stories contains selections by 28 authors. The works cover the period from the last decade of the 19th century to the 1960s, providing an evolution of the Uruguayan short story from its origins. The selections are prefaced by a brief historical account of the short narrative in Uruguay.

5556 Somers, Armonía. Muerte por alacrán. Buenos Aires: Calicanto Editorial, 1979. 186 p.

In the 12 narratives of this collection, the author creates an atmosphere of fear, mystery, and oppression. The dream-like, or more accurately, nightmarish quality of the selections is achieved through a purposeful, relentless obscuring of logic, of familiar points of reference, of meaning.

5557 Trobo, Claudio. El trabajo del gato. Caracas: Ediciones Centauro, 1977. 311 p.

This political novel, written almost completely in dialogue form, captures the frustrations, tensions, and fears of present-day life in Montevideo. The problems of inflation and poverty, the uncertainty of family life and social institutions, and most of all the sense of political repression are presented effectively.

LITERARY CRITICISM AND HISTORY
ARGENTINA

5558 Aizenberg, Edna. Alberto Gerchunoff: ¿gaucho judío o antigaucho europeizante? (UNAM/AL, 15, 1977, p. 197–215)

Trabajo que postula a fondo las aparentes contradicciones en los textos y la conducta política de Gerchunoff. Responde adecuadamente a las variantes frente a las oscilaciones de la política liberal y conservadora de las élites dominantes. Desde *Los gauchos judíos* (1910), Gerchunoff debió ajustar el optimismo de una Argentina aparentemente abierta que se cerraba sobre sus dominios.

5559 Alazraki, Jaime. Lectura estructuralista de "El Sur" de Borges (UCV/E, 2:3, enero/junio 1977, p. 109–119)

Se asienta en citas de Barthes y Genette para leer las versiones de las dos muertes de Dahlmann. Sugiere apuestas diferentes al valor del coraje: acatado como mito de la sangre; rechazado como acto de lucidez. Aprecia este cuento por haberle dado expresión literaria a esta visión ambivalente.

5560 Antezana J., Luis H. Algebra y fuego: lectura de Borges. Louvain, Belgium: Bureau du Recueil, Bibliothèque de L'Université Catholique, 1978. 163 p., bibl., index (Recueil de travaux d'histoire et de philologie; 6:13)

Intento de establecer un modelo de las relaciones entre el discurso ficticio y el discurso poético para luego estudiar cómo la organización de la expresión (Hjelmslev) condiciona la organización del "contenido." La prosa de Borges es objeto de análisis, de excusa casi, para formular ese posible modelo. A partir de esta lectura importaría examinar las propuestas que surgen de sus enunciados. Estudio serio que debe inscribirse en la bibliografía que se regocija en el pálido fuego de la fórmula algebraica.

5561 Bacarisse, Pamela. The first four novels of Manuel Puig: parts of a whole? (IAA, 4:4, 1978, p. 253–264, bibl.)

Traza la trayectoria de Puig a partir de una escueta presentación de estudios y realizados. Intenta formular una cronología del desarrollo de las actitudes ya la ideología de Puig basándose primordialmente en *The Buenos Aires affair* y *El beso de la mujer araña*.

5562 Barnatán, Marcos Ricardo. Conocer Borges y su obra. Barcelona: DOPESA, 1978. 125 p.: bibl., ill. (Colección Conocer; 10)

Pequeño album de fotos, textos y entrevistas. Recorrido basado en las simpatías de un conocedor de su obra.

5563 Biagini, Hugo E. Macedonio Fernández: pensador político (HISPA, 7:25, 1978, p. 11–20)

Expone un aspecto que había sido soslayado en aras de reiterados estudios sobre "lo novedoso" e "inclasificable" de Macedonio (MF). Documenta sus intereses por la cosa pública, los contactos políticos y la vasta influencia que ejerció Spencer sobre él y, en menor grado, los hombres del 90. También son de sumo interés los rechazos de MF a toda intervención estatal, los ataques al poder sindical y los correlatos entre el nivel de civilización y la coerción del gobierno. Se elabora así el sentido de su apoyo a un "gobierno aristocrático."

5564 Borello, Rodolfo A. Autores, situación del libro y entorno material de la literatura en la Argentina del siglo XX (CH, 108: 322/323, abril/mayo 1977, p. 35–52, tables)

Describe hechos específicos del mercado literario y la lastimosa relación entre el ejercicio de la literatura y su remuneración. Anunciado como prólogo de un panorama de la literatura argentina entre 1930 y 1970. Util planteo de aproximaciones evitadas en muchos estudios "académicos."

5565 Borges. Buenos Aires: Editorial El Mangrullo, 1976. 94 p.: ill. (Colección Letra abierta; 1)

Buen *dossier* que recoge entrevistas hechas por María Esther Gilio y otros, testimonios de su madre, Bioy Casares, Hernández Arregui, Bianco y Raúl Scalabrini Ortiz, datos de colaboraciones en revistas, una breve antología de textos, fotos y una cronología. Nada nuevo; espacio festivo, sin embargo, para el que recorre toda mención de Borges.

5566 Borges: obra y personaje. Montevideo: Acali Editorial, 1978. 119 p., bibl. (Colección Estudios críticos; 2)

Ensayos de Sucre, Canfield, de Espada, y Benavides sobre diversos aspectos de la obra de Borges y una breve conversación de Fornaro con Borges. Nivel desparejo. Poco agrega a lo ya repetido.

5567 Borges, Jorge Luis. Borges para millones. Buenos Aires: Ediciones Corregidor, 1978. 111 p.: ill. (Colección Especial; M-1256)

Texto del film del mismo título en que Borges vuelve a dialogar sobre su vasto repertorio de gustos, preferencias y las variantes de sus textos. Las imágenes sugeridas se suman a lo conocido. El íntimo Borges "para muy pocos lectores" prevalece a pesar de la transformación en objeto de consumo.

5568 Carroll, Robert C. Borges and Bruno: The geometry of infinity in *La muerte y la brújula* (MLN, 94:2, March 1979, p. 321–342, ill.)

Trabajo erudito que postula una estrecha relación entre el cuento de Borges, y *De la causa, principio e uno,* de Giordano Bruno. Se considera que la lógica geométrica del Renacimiento determina la estructura y lógica de esta narración detectivesca.

5569 Cohen, Howard R. Eduardo Mallea: a selective annotated bibliography of criticism (AATSP/H, 62, Oct. 1979, p. 444–467)

Utilísima labor para los lectores de Mallea. Cubre los materiales publicados hasta 1978.

5570 Coulson, Graciela. *Fantomas* o la nueva estética de Cortázar (UCLA/JLAL, 4:2, Winter 1978, p. 225–229)

Sigue las propuestas de Cortázar en torno a la unión de planos literarios y políticos. Inserta a *Fantomas* en la "nueva estética" ya anunciada con *Libro de Manuel* y algunos cuentos de *Alguien que anda por ahí*. Las conformaciones gráficas del texto suscitan la pregunta "¿no será quizá la historieta la novela proletaria del futuro?"

5571 Cruz, Jorge. Genio y figura de Manuel Mujica Láinez. Buenos Aires: Editorial Universitaria de Buenos Aires, 1978. 225 p.: ill.

Siguiendo el formato tradicional de esta serie, Jorge Cruz logra una útil presentación de este autor. Para una primera lectura.

5572 D'Lugo, Marvin. "Las Babas del Diablo:" in pursuit of Cortázar's "reel" world (UA/REH, 11:3, oct. 1977, p. 395–409)

Abarca la complejidad de la experiencia individual y su transmisión a través del lenguaje (una entidad colectiva). Analiza especialmente el proceso de la relación y la búsqueda de medios mecánicos expresivos (cámara, máquina de escribir) que resultan en el alejamiento del protagonista ante un encuentro con sus propias experiencias. Observa el problema en dos niveles: Michel se transforma en "voyeur" de sus propios actos visto por la dicotomía narrador/partícipe y el deseo de actuar frente a la pasividad inherente a los que transcriben/viven una realidad mediatizada a través de la escritura o la fotografía.

5573 Doyle, Raymond H. La huella española en la obra de Jorge Luis Borges. Madrid: Playor, 1976. 186 p., bibl. (Colección Nova scholar)

Texto basado en un sistema de asociaciones, semejanzas, coincidencias . . . huella inevitable no siempre útil para la búsqueda del rastreador.

5574 Dufour, Marie-Cecile and **Guy Bourdé.** Las lettres françaises dans la revue argentine *Sur,* 1931–1964 (CDAL, 16, 1977, p. 153–188)

Excelente trabajo descriptivo de la presencia de la literatura francesa en la revista fundada por Victoria Ocampo. Cubre dicho material bajo las rúbricas "La Poésie Hermétique," "Le Surréalisme," "L'Engagement Politique," "L'Inspiration Chrétienne," "L'Existentialisme," "Le Nouveau Roman," a la vez que indica brevemente las ausencias que también definieron a *Sur.* Faltaría una secuela que analizara a fondo las proyecciones de estas opciones.

5575 Echavarren, Roberto. *El beso de la mujer araña* y las metáforas del sujeto (IILI/RI, 44:102/103, enero/junio 1978, p. 65–75)

Estudia conflictos y censura gubernamental y religiosa mediante los recursos cinematográficos de la narración. Examina los planos narrativos dentro del contexto de las nociones de Lévi-Strauss sobre el "bricoleur."

5576 Engelbert, Jo Anne. Macedonio Fernández and the Spanish American new novel. New York: New York University Press,1978. 216 p.; bibl., index (A Center for Inter-American Relations book)

Estudio informativo sobre las propuestas de la obra de Macedonio. Los cuestionamientos de Macedonio de la tradición literaria occidental están bien planteados. No se elabora a fondo, sin embargo, el empalme con la llamada "nueva novela hispanoamericana." Contribución sólida a la bibliografía de Macedonio.

5577 Epple, Juan Armando. Bibliografía de Manuel Puig y sobre él (RIB, 28:2, abril/junio 1978, p. 165–168)

Util recopilación que exige constantes revisiones debido a la popularidad de Puig en ciertos círculos publicitarios. Cita 44 referencias.

5578 ———. *The Buenos Aires affair* y la estructura de la novela policíaca (UV/PH, 18, abril/junio 1976, p. 43–59, ill.)

Uno de los trabajos más serios sobre la tercera novela de Puig a partir de una clara elucidación de los presupuestos de la novela policial. Un análisis claro de las claves que sugiere toda obra de este género y que, en otro nivel, permite una lectura conjunta del proyecto de Puig.

5579 Espejo, Miguel and **Carlos Dámaso Martínez.** Jorge Luis Borges: "Soy un escritor y quizás un poeta" (UV/PH, 18, abril/junio 1976, p. 14–22, plates)

Entrevista llevada a cabo en Buenos Aires en 1976. Entre las múltiples variantes de toda charla con Borges, también se afirma: "Yo creí en un tiempo que la crítica era el análisis de los textos, idea bastante corriente en Francia. Ahora creo que no, creo que lo importante es ubicar al crítico como creador y a la crítica como un hecho creativo."

5580 Flint, J.M. The prose style of Roberto Arlt: towards a reappraisal (IAA, 5:2, 1979, p. 161–177)

Defensa (¿es aún necesaria?) de la prosa de Arlt y del uso del lunfardo en sus obras. Parecería justificar su valor mediante la apelación a Quevedo y a expresionistas alemanes (ver los argumentos de Borges que intentan incorporar a Carriego a la tradición para rescatarlo de la visión que le ha sido asignada).

5581 García Núñez, Fernando. Cristianismo y escolástica en *Adán Buenosayres* (A, 43:1, 1979, p. 24–44)

Reiteradamente el autor parece más preocupado por deslindes dentro del cristianismo (y lo que su título sugiere) que por su relación con la novela de Marechal. Una vez establecida la presencia de dichos aspectos, se omite *la proyección*—que justificaría esta lectura—de su sentido para una mejor comprensión de la novela.

5582 Goštautas, Stasys. Buenos Aires y Arlt: Dostoievsky, Martínez Estrada y Scalabrini Ortiz. Madrid: Insula, 1977. 328 p.; bibl., index.

Lectura que se centra en "el problema urbano" por considerarlo "la idea clave" de Arlt. No dejan de sorprender las referencias del subtítulo como elementos integrales del análisis ni la intención inicial de una "crítica fenomenológica." Son conflictivas las declaraciones en torno a la ideología que sustentan (o no) los textos de Arlt. Es adecuado el marco descriptivo en el que se estudia a Arlt y muy positivo el intento de divulgar su obra.

5583 Gregorich, Luis. Dos décadas de narrativa argentina de 1955 a hoy (CONAC/RNC, 39:236, mayo/junio 1978, p. 45–70)

Descripción de la narrativa argentina actual a partir de una somera presentación de su contexto histórico. Los breves enunciados sobre autores de la generación del 55 dan paso a las preferencias por los más recientes (generación del 66?) Moyano, Puig, Blaistein y Tizón. Hay una nómina de 30 autores y obras preferidas de la generación del 55 y de las promociones más recientes. Información útil.

5584 Hughes, Psiche. The concept of suicide in Borges' stories in relation to the themes of destiny and aggression (HISP, 67, sept. 1979, p. 61–71)

Ante la ausencia (¿notoria?) de suicidios en la obra de Borges—una escasa media docena—se estudia su aparente discrepancia con la aceptación del destino y la agresión (?). El Obispo Wilkins procedería, sin duda, a catalogar los tipos de suicidio según el instrumento vengador.

5585 Hulme, Peter. Macedonio Fernández's "técnica del mareo:" the analysis of a literary device (IAA, 3:4, 1977, p. 351–364, bibl.)

Relaciona las nociones de Macedonio sobre "belarte" con los enunciados de Jakobson sobre "literaturidad" y Shklovsky sobre "priëm" y "ostraneye" para pasar luego al estudio del "mareo" como recurso literario y la insistencia de Macedonio en el problema de la escritura como único problema del arte. Se aplican sus teorías a una lectura de *Museo de la novela de la eterna.*

5586 Interpretaciones y claves de *Adán Buenosayres.* 2. ed. Montevideo: Alcaldi Editorial, 1977. 159 p.; bibl. (Colección Estudios críticos; 1)

Reproduce la conocida reseña de Cortázar (*Sur,* 1948), el excelente estudio de Adolfo Prieto (1959) y un ensayo de Graciela de Sola (1960). Se suma la lectura-índice-sonrisa amistosa (¿elegíaca?) de Washington Benavídez que al cerrar este pequeño libro vuelve a entablar un diálogo abierto con las claves de *Adán Buenosayres* enunciadás por el propio Marechal para inaugurar otro cenáculo.

5587 Jitrik, Noé. La novela futura de Macedonio Fernández: con un retrato discontinuo, una antología y una bibliografía. Caracas: Universidad Central de Venezuela, Ediciones de la Biblioteca, 1973. 144 p.; bibl. (Nuevos planteamientos; 11)

El retrato discontinuo de MF—compuesto por citas de múltiples fuentes—cede a un estudio que analiza el proyecto que surge de la obra de Macedonio. La breve antología y la noticia bio-bibliográfica preparada por Horacio Jorge Becco (p. 125–144) hacen de este pequeño tomo una introducción de bolsillo a futuras lecturas.

5588 Jorge Luis Borges. Buenos Aires: Editorial Freeland, 1978. 157 p.; bibl.

Recopilación de varios ensayos que exploran la obra de Borges desde diferentes perspectivas. Contiene los conocidos textos de Macherey y Genette, entre otros. La traducción al castellano de textos publicados antes en otros idiomas es útil si bien como antología carece de unidad formal más allá de la "mirada analítica externa."

5589 Justo, Liborio. Literatura argentina y expresión americana. Buenos Aires: Editorial Rescate, 1977. 190 p.; bibl.

Notas redactadas a lo largo de varias décadas. Las referencias testimoniales y polémicas constituyen valiosos aportes a la bibliografía sobre los des(encuentros) de Boedo y Florida y las lecturas de Lugones y Borges frente a las propuestas de Arlt y Castelnuovo. Son discutibles las sugerencias de la vía hacia la expresión nacional pero constituyen una lectura necesaria para la redacción de la vida literaria argentina.

5590 Kaminsky, Amy. The real circle of iron: mothers and children, children and mothers, in four Argentine novels (LALR, 4:9, Fall/Winter 1976, p. 77–86)

Las variantes de estas relaciones en una interesante presentación de *Mañana digo basta* y *La tercera versión,* de Silvina Bullrich, y *La señora Ordóñez* y *El cruce del río,* de Marta Lynch.

5591 León, Pedro R. *Fiesta en noviembre* de Eduardo Mallea; contrapunto estilístico y preocupación ética (IAA, 3:4, 1977, p. 331–350)

Estudia las relaciones de la novela de Mallea con *Point counter point* de Huxley y establece las modificaciones hechas para *Fiesta* . . . León sostiene que los contrastes le permiten a Mallea subrayar su preocupación existencial y su responsabilidad ética. Convendría preguntarse con qué armoniza esa concordancia de voces contrastantes que definiría el uso del contrapunto en Mallea.

5592 Levine, Suzanne Jill. La tendencia pastoril en dos obras de Adolfo Bioy Casares (ECO, 34[4]:208, feb. 1979, p. 377–402)

Estudio basado en *La invención de Morel* y *Plan de evasión*. Intenta describir el desarrollo histórico de lo pastoril ligándolo a los "pretextos" de la ciencia ficción en las novelas de Bioy. Lo propuesto sobre los mitos y la parodia de lo pastoril merece ser estudiado por separado.

5593 Lihn, Enrique. Borges y Borges (CONAC/RNC, 228/231, enero/junio 1977, p. 43–54, plate)

A propósito de una variante del "Borges y yo" que se articula entre el Borges que escribe y lega a la literatura y el Borges que lamentablemente (a veces) polemiza contra la historia. Texto éste que no solo revela múltiples instancias contradictorias de Borges (por demás conocidas) sino las opciones de uno de los mejores poetas chilenos de su generación.

5594 Maharg, James. A call to authenticity: the essays of Ezequiel Martínez Estrada. University, Miss.: Romance Monographs, 1977. 203 p.; bibl. (Romance monographs; 26)

Se estudian en líneas paralelas las manifestaciones temperamentales del autor y las preocupaciones temáticas desarrolladas en sus ensayos. La sobriedad de la lectura no oculta la carencia de un profundo análisis ideológico que permitiría una mayor comprensión de su impacto sobre las generaciones posteriores. Bibliografía útil.

5595 Marani, Alma Novella. Tonos y motivos italianos en la literatura argentina. La Plata: Universidad Nacional de la Plata, Facultad de Humanidades y Ciencias de la Educación, Centro de Estudios Italianos, 1977. 219 p.; bibl. (Monografías y tesis; 11)

Sólido conjunto de notas sobre la influencia italiana en varios autores argentinos. Se destacan los textos sobre Manzoni, Lugones y Banchs. El recorte tradicional de "tesis" no dificulta el futuro desarrollo de estos estudios bibliográficos.

5596 Masiello, Francine. Oliverio Girondo: el carnaval del lenguaje (HISPA, 6:16, abril 1977, p. 3–17)

Importante trabajo sobre los proyectos de la vanguardia argentina a través de la obra de Girondo. Analiza los recursos poéticos y su cuestionamiento de la referencialidad mimética. A través de apelaciones a lo lúdico, el texto se enfrenta al predominio de lo racional y a sus representaciones literarias. Las búsquedas invi/inci/tan a las innovaciones textuales y a las que se extienden fuera de la página literaria.

5597 Memorias de la vida literaria argentina. Selección, estudio preliminar y notas de María Angélica Scotti. Buenos Aires: Editorial Kapelusz, 1977. 282 p. (Grandes obras de la literatura universal; 134)

Si bien la literatura autobiográfica argentina ya ha sido estudiada ampliamente, la introducción de Scotti sirve de marco apropiado para una selección de textos y recuerdos de Manuel Gálvez, E. García Velloso, V. Martínez Cuitiño (valiosos apuntes sobre "El Café de los Inmortales"), Mastronardi y Victoria Ocampo. Suma de versiones que se inclinan hacia una lectura "oficial," "tradicional," de ciertas memorias de cierta vida literaria argentina.

5598 Meyer, Doris. Victoria Ocampo: against the wind and the tide. With a selection of essays by Victoria Ocampo, translated by Doris Meyer. New York: G. Braziller, 1979. 314 p.; bibl., 8 leaves of plates: ill., index.

Util para el público de habla inglesa. La admiración por ciertas facetas de V. Ocampo parece obstruir un estudio a fondo de sus actividades y producción literaria que en ambos planos no siempre estuvo "contra viento y marea."

5599 Molloy, Silvia. Las letras de Borges. Buenos Aires: Editorial Sudamericana, 1979. 220 p.

Excelente aporte a la inagotable crítica sobre Borges. Molloy apela a una sólida formación teórica desde la cual lee los enunciados de Borges en torno a sus propuestas específicas y a los "topoi" que se han transformado en rúbrica del autor. (Cabría ampliar la lectura para abarcar los textos más recientes de Borges.)

5600 Montecchia, M.P. Reportaje a Borges. Buenos Aires: Ediciones Crisol, 1977. 123 p.

Resultado de una serie de entrevistas realizadas entre los últimos meses de 1975 y los primeros de 1976. La lectura permite el reconocimiento del placer frecuentado en tantas charlas pasadas. La reiteración y la variada entonación de ciertas respuestas distan de toda monotonía.

5601 Morello-Frosch, Marta. La ficción se historifica: Cortázar y Rozenmacher (RCLL, 3:5, 1. semestre 1977, p. 75–86)

Sólida lectura de las modificaciones que van desde "Casa Tomada" a "Cabecita Negra" a través de su inscripción en las transformaciones histórico-sociales de sus respectivos contextos. Los escenarios seleccionados por estos autores subrayan el afincamiento en modos de producción divergentes que modifican su transcripción literaria. Parte de un importante proyecto de investigación.

5602 Neghme Echeverría, Lidia. La complejidad fantástica en *La invención de Morel* (ECO, 33[6]:204, oct. 1978, p. 1222–1240)

Estudia "lo fantasmagórico" y "lo fantasmático" en la novela de Bioy Casares. Se centra en las técnicas narrativas que crean una distancia entre lo relatado y lo verosímil. Señala con acierto y precisión la problemática de la representación y la reproducción simultánea de un texto intercalado en otro.

5603 Ocampo, Victoria. Testimonios: décima serie, 1975–1977. Buenos Aires: Editorial Sudamericana, 1977. 290 p.; bibl.

Breves textos sobre mujeres, lecturas-reseñas de varios libros (es necesario subrayar la atención prestada a Malraux), reflexiones sobre varias obras teatrales y cinematográficas, una contestación sobre la UNESCO y cartas dirigidas a varios periódicos bonaerenses, constituyen esta entrega de una labor tardía y quizá ya no tan reveladora como textos anteriores.

5604 Orgambide, Pedro G. Borges y su pensamiento político. México: Comité de Solidaridad con el Pueblo Argentino, Casa Argentina, 1978. 93 p.

Texto necesariamente polémico en el que se analizan las relaciones de los textos de Borges con su conducta política dejando de lado la ponderada noción de una incoherencia entre las propuestas literarias y los pronunciamientos personales. Presentación que se quiere "juicio de Borges ante el pueblo."

5605 Pokalchuk, Yuri. El hombre y el tiempo en la obra de Cortázar (URSS/AL, 20:4, 1978, p. 161–178)

Divide la prosa de Cortázar en dos tendencias: 1) predominio del elemento fantástico; 2) "prosa filosófica realista" con énfasis en "la composición." Propone un "héroe colectivo" para la "narrativa urbana." Hay referencias útiles a otros autores aunque contiene errores de información. Organización, tipología y conclusiones cuestionables.

Prático de Fernández, Aída. Guía bibliográfica de la literatura de Mendoza. See *HLAS 41:43*.

5606 Rest, Jaime. El laberinto del universo: Borges y el pensamiento nominalista. Buenos Aires: Ediciones Librerías Fausto, 1976. 201 p.; bibl. (Textos de apoyo)

Uno de los libros más importantes de la vasta bibliografía sobre Borges. El corpus del libro—tres capítulos publicados inicialmente en la revista *Hispamérica*—es seguido por un valioso epílogo, "El 'silencio privilegiado'," en el que se recuperan los sentidos literarios y filosóficos del pensamiento nominalista en Borges, pensamiento que se ramifica hacia las relaciones con "una realidad empírica."

5607 Ricci, Graciela. Los circúitos interiores: Zama, en la obra de Antonio diBenedetto. Buenos Aires: F. García Cambeiro, 1974. 109 p.; bibl. (Colección Estudios latinoamericanos)

Jung, Suzuki, Fromm sirven de base para un análisis de *Zama* con referencias al resto de la obra de diBenedetto. Buen ejemplo de esta línea crítica que subraya la imperiosa necesidad de estudios adicionales desde otros enfoques.

5608 Rodríguez, Ana María de. La creación corregida: estudio comparativo de la obra de Ernesto Sábato y Alain Robbe-Grillet.

Caracas: Universidad Católica Andrés Bello, Instituto de Historia, Centro de Lenguas Indígenas, 1976. 89 p.; bibl.

Seria aproximación al tema a partir de consideraciones generales sobre la novela contemporánea. Los presupuestos narrativos de ambos autores son analizados con especial atención a *El túnel* y *La Jalousie*. Importante para los estudiosos de Sábato.

5609 Rodríguez Alcalá, Hugo. Críticos españoles de *Don Segundo Sombra* (RIB, 29:1, 1979, p. 53–64)

Interesante recopilación de las reacciones de Maeztu, A. Alonso, Da Cal y Ayala ante la novela de Güiraldes. Los comentarios de estos críticos apuntan la distancia de las lecturas que merecía el texto y aportan datos para plantear los esquemas críticos de estos lectores.

5610 ———. La primera reacción crítica en torno a *Don Segundo Sombra* (IAA, 5:1, 1979, p. 19–37, bibl.)

Al cumplirse medio siglo desde la publicación de la novela de Güiraldes, el autor registra los comentarios iniciales hechos por Lugones (que la ubicó junto a *Facundo* y *Martín Fierro*), Giusti, Juan B. González y Korn.

5611 Rodríguez Monegal, Emir. Jorge Luis Borges: a literary biography. New York: Dutton, 1978. 502 p.; bibl., 4 leaves of plates: ill.; index.

Ninguna biografía podrá superar la que emerge de los múltiples encuentros a los que se ha sometido Borges. De esa conjunción cabrá destacar la composición de este texto que lo recorre por las vías de la amistad, la admiración y las inevitables preferencias por ciertos rincones y enunciados.

5612 Santibáñez, Carlos. La incomunicación en dos obras hispanoamericanos (CAM, 36[213]:4, julio/agosto 1977, p. 119–132, bibl.)

Breves referencias a "La Autopista del Sur" (Cortázar) ceden paso a la detallada descripción de la trayectoria y el fracaso de Castel (*El túnel*, de Sábato). Intenta asir proyecciones "universales" mediante dos escuetas referencias a Marx.

5613 Scholz, Lāszló. Todos los viajes el viaje (*in* Simposio Internacional de Estudios Hispánicos, Budapest, 1976. Actas [see item **5067**] p. 413–419)

Menciona medios de transporte concretos y pasos al "viaje interior" para señalar que los personajes de Cortázar están en perpetua búsqueda de sí mismos, de otros seres humanos y del punto en el que la realidad cuaja en un orden. Lamentablemente no encara el problema crucial al que alude: los límites impuestos por la visión del mundo de Cortázar al logro de sus objetivos.

5414 Sosnowski, Saúl. Contemporary Jewish-Argentine writers: tradition and politics (LALR, 6:12, 1978, p. 1–14)

Analiza los cambios radicales desde las propuestas ilusorias (¿ilusas?) de Gerchunoff hasta las miradas críticas que ejercen autores más recientes: Rozenmacher, Szichman, Steimberg, Goloboff.

5615 ———. *Jauría*, de David Viñas: continuación de un proyecto desmitificador (RCLL, 4:7/8, 1978, p. 165–172)

Viñas continúa su desmitificación de la versión oficial de la historia a través de la dinámica entre las provincias y el Puerto y sus correlatos de violencia en las relaciones sexo-arma, el desarme de los caudillos, los abusos y distorsiones ya presentes en *Los hombres de a caballo* y en *Los dueños de la tierra*.

5616 Valdés Gutiérrez, Gilberto. Haroldo Conti: alias Mascaró, alias La Vida (CDLA, 18:107, marzo/abril 1978, p. 58–71)

Extensa reseña de *Mascaró, el cazador americano* (1975). Subraya la politización del autor y sus desfases en su trayectoria narrativa. Es útil revisar las modificaciones de "Oreste" desde *En vida* hasta *Mascaró*.

5617 Verbitsky, Bernardo. Conciencia subdesarrollada y literatura nacional (*in* Cultural nacional. Buenos Aires: Ediciones Crisol, 1976, p. 299–320)

Una entusiasta presentación de la obra de Lucio V. Mansilla, seguida por una breve exaltación de *Juan Moreira* (Eduardo Gutiérrez) y *Martín Fierro* (Hernández). Se postula la permanencia de estos aportes de raigambre popular como integrantes fundamentales de la tradición literaria argentina.

5618 Victoria Ocampo: la viajera y una de sus sombras (Pájaro de Fuego [Sequals Editora, Buenos Aires] 1:1, sept. 1977, p. 13–22, plates)

Testimonios con motivo de su ingreso a la Academia Argentina de Letras que se inician con una visión panorámica y amistosa de Ernesto Schóo. Se suman textos de Syria Poletti, Angel J. Battistessa y José Bianco sobre su extensa labor intelectual. Frida Schultz de Mantovani coordina una "entrevista a sí misma" en que V.O. comenta la vasta galería que frecuentó: Caillois, Camus, Huxley, Nehru . . .

PARAGUAY

5619 Díaz-Pérez, Viriato. Espronceda en la *Revue Hispanique*: misceláneas paraguayas. Edición de Rodrigo Díaz-Pérez. Palma de Mallorca: L. Ripoll, 1976. 127 p.; bibl., 1 leaf of plates: facsim.

Nuevo tomo de las obras recogidas por su hijo, Rodrigo Díaz-Pérez. Además del texto sobre Espronceda, son de interés para un estudio de las percepciones locales sus lecturas de Whitman y Herder. Las misceláneas paraguayas continúan las pinceladas ya presentes en tomos anteriores y refuerzan el buen ojo del costumbrista.

5620 Feito, Francisco E. Paraguay en la obra de Gabriel Casaccia. Buenos Aires: Fernando García Cambeiro, 1977. 185 p. (Colección Estudios latinoamericanos; 23)

Importante aporte al conocimiento de una de las mayores figuras de la literatura paraguaya. Constituye una lectura sólida e informada de los motivos centrales de su obra. Está elaborada desde un bien planteado enfoque crítico.

5621 Foster, David William. Augusto Roa Bastos. Boston: Twayne, 1978. 133 p.; bibl., index (Twayne's world authors series: TWAS 507)

Sigue el formato tradicional de esta serie informativa. Los análisis de la obra siguen los intereses estructuralistas del crítico con un desplazamiento del contexto histórico como referencia de orden secundario. Sugiere áreas de interés que desarrolla en otros textos.

5622 Leinhard, Martin. Apuntes sobre los desdoblamientos, la mitología y la escritura en *Yo el Supremo* (HISPA, 8:19, 1978, p. 3–12)

En breves y escuetas anotaciones el autor logra elucidar algunos de los aspectos más trajinados de la novela de Roa Bastos. Son de especial importancia las relaciones señaladas entre el ejercicio del poder y la escritura y sus múltiples incorporaciones a lecturas que exigen la presencia de la mitología guaraní.

5623 Najt, Myriam and **María Victoria Reyzabal.** El significado de la vida en *Higo de hombre* de Roa Bastos (CH, 350, agosto 1979, p. 265–280, bibl.)

Lectura metódica que elabora las ideologías que se manifiestan a través de varias voces narrativas y las modificaciones de los mitos tradicionales alterados en ese contexto. La afirmación de la vida por sobre toda imposición cede a la intención ideológica que explicita la Dra. Monzón al final del texto: la concientización del pueblo llevará a un proceso revolucionario.

URUGUAY

5624 Aínsa Amigues, Fernando. Onetti's devices (LALR, 3:5, Fall/Winter 1974, p. 79–96)

Ubica a Onetti en un contexto de transición constante. Señala las correspondencias entre un mundo cuyos valores tradicionales fueron abolidos y que no ha logrado reemplazarlos por otros que respondieran a las crisis del mundo contemporáneo, con las búsquedas y falta de fe en los hombres que delinea a los personajes de Onetti. Siguiendo las ideas de Colin Wilson, estudia el motivo del rechazo de una realidad para optar por otra y el consiguiente "descenso al yo." Otro tema de interés es la elaboración del problema de la identidad y la fragmentación del personaje.

5625 ———. Tiempo reconquistado: siete ensayos sobre literatura uruguaya. Montevideo: Ediciones Geminis, 1977. 193 p.; bibl. (Colección Novus orbis)

La página ligera alterna con ensayos sobrios en los que se manifiesta la importancia del crítico uruguayo. Merecen una lectura especial sus trabajos sobre *Los tres gauchos orientales*, de A. Lussich, la Generación del 17 y las revisiones generales sobre la novela del 45 y los nuevos narradores. Las páginas dedicadas a Martínez Moreno constituyen una buena introducción a su obra.

Benedetti, Mario. El escritor y la crítica en el contexto del subdesarrollo. See item **5005**.

5626 Bojorge, Horacio. José Luis Dimas Antuña, 1894–1968: vida y obra de un autor poco conocido (UBN/R, 18, mayo 1978, p. 159–175, plate)

Labor de rescate con datos bío-bibliográficos del autor uruguayo de *Israel contra el ángel* (1921), *El cántico* (1926), etc.

5627 Díaz, José Pedro. Felisberto Hernández: una conciencia que se rehúsa a la existencia (Nueva Narrativa Hispanoamericana [Adelphi University, Latin American Studies Program, Garden City, N.Y.] 4, enero/sept. 1974, p. 117–144)

Uno de los mejores estudios panorámicos del autor (1902–63). Se destacan la transición de Felisberto a la literatura fantástica y las páginas dedicadas a "los objetos," suma de una relación angustiosa y desdichada con su espacio.

5628 Felisberto Hernández ante la crítica actual. Edición de Alain Sicard. Caracas: Monte Avila Editores, 1977. 431 p.; bibl., 16 leaves of plates: ill. (Colección estudios)

Resultado de las investigaciones llevadas a cabo en el Centro de Investigaciones Latinoamericanas de la Universidad de Poitiers en 1973–74. Incluye análisis de Andreu, Concha, Fell, Goloboff, Mignolo, Moreno Turner, Perera San Martín, Renaud, Saad, Saer, Wilson, Yurkievich. Las discusiones en torno a las ponencias, los apéndices (bibliografía e ilustraciones), y el excelente nivel de las presentaciones transforman a este volumen colectivo en uno de los productos más serios y coherentes sobre Felisberto.

5629 Kadir, Djelal. Juan Carlos Onetti. Boston: Twayne Publishers, 1977. 160 p.; bibl., index (Twayne's world authors series; TWAS 469)

Dadas las restricciones de la serie, esta presentación formula una lectura adecuada de la obra de Onetti. Kadir apunta aspectos importantes de sus novelas y las engarza con desarrollos novelísticos posteriores.

5630 Lasarte, Francisco. Función de "misterio" y "memoria" en la obra de Felisberto Hernández (CM/NRFH, 37:1, 1978, p. 57–79)

"Explicación falsa de mis cuentos" hubiera sido un buen punto de partida para este estudio (aparece al final). El autor postula que mediante el análisis de los conceptos "misterio" y "memoria"—que Felisberto Hernández (FL) propone—se puede plantear una definición de su mundo ficticio tan ajeno a todo ajuste convencional. Se utilizan los términos para las dos primeras etapas de su producción: 1) *Fulano de tal, Libro sin tapas, La cara de Ana, La envenenada*; 2) *Por los tiempos de Clemente Colling, El caballo perdido* y *Tierras de la memoria*, según la clasificación adoptada por FL. Se sugiere la búsqueda del "misterio deseable" como presencia constante en su obra (en un sentido amplio). *El caballo perdido* recibe una atención especial.

5631 Ludmer, Josefina. Onetti: los procesos de construcción del relato. Buenos Aires: Sudamericana, 1977. 211 p.

Consta de tres ensayos: "Homenaje a *La vida breve*: 25 años," "Contar el Cuento" y "La Novia (Carta) Robada (a Fáulkner)." Obligada lectura para todo estudioso de la obra de Onetti. Las bases que aportan el formalismo ruso, un bien elaborado y asimilado estructuralismo en variadas facetas se sustentan en el marxismo para ofrecer páginas que sirven como modelo de integración crítica.

5632 Mathieu-Higginbotham, Corina. Fáulkner y Onetti: una visión de la realidad a través de Jefferson y Santa María (HISP, 61, sept. 1977, p. 51–60)

Estudia las relaciones entre "Una Rosa para Emily" y "La Novia Robada" (véase item **5631**) a partir de un análisis de las circunstancias en las que se inscriben los personajes. Desarrolla el papel que cumplen el lugar de nacimiento y la comunidad en el proceso de alienación y acercamientos a la locura de los protagonistas de cada uno de estos textos.

5633 Méndez, Mabel. Indice analítico de *Pégaso* (UBN/R, 17, 1977, p. 123–213)

Indice alfabético (más que analítico) de esta importante revista publicada entre 1918 y 1924. Constó de 72 entregas bajo la dirección de César Miranda (seudónimo usado: Pablo de Grecia) y José María Delgado. Incluye interesantes textos de Quiroga, Reyles, Rodó, Amorim, Herrera y Reissig, Juana de Ibarbourou, Sabat Ercasty, Storni, Vargas Vila, M.E. Vaz Ferreira y otros.

5634 Morán, Carlos Roberto. Los pensamientos descalzos de Felisberto Hernández (CH, 324, junio 1977, p. 547–558, bibl.)

Trabajo panorámico introductorio sobre el cada vez menos desconocido uruguayo. Elabora acertadamente—y siguiendo a Díaz—la relación con los objetos y los desplazamientos del cuerpo ante "el Personaje" y su espíritu. Las presencias siniestras y la neurosis urbana asoman a sus textos y de allí ocasionalmente ceden a la per/versidad/versión.

5635 Morello-Frosch, Marta. *Con las primeras luces* de Martínez Moreno: la decadencia sin historia (RCLL, 4:7/8, 1978, p. 153–163)

Estudia la novela a partir de la ausencia de un *verdadero* pasado histórico identificable como vector que organiza el texto. La decadencia de una familia patricia uruguaya es vista desde un contexto que detalla la ausencia de ciertas ideologías y del afincamiento local.

5636 Mose, K.E.A. The fire next time?: three visions of violence in Uruguayan literature (NS, 2:3/4, 1977, p. 207–222)

Describe la destrucción del status quo en *Sombras sobre la tierra*, de Francisco Espínola; *Corral abierto*, de Enrique Amorim; y *Gracias por el fuego*, de Mario Benedetti. Se intenta demostrar que los hechos planteados en un "segundo nivel de realidad ficticia" responden a elementos similares y que en cada caso se puede detectar la peculiaridad de sus respectivos momentos de producción. Para lograrlo es necesaria una elaboración teórica y contextual mas detallada.

5637 Onetti, Juan Carlos. Réquiem por Faulkner. Montevideo: Arca, 1975. 235 p. (Calicanto; 8)

Recopilación de artículos y notas periodísticas publicadas por Onetti desde 1939 recogidas cronológicamente: 1) "La Piedra en el Charco" (1939–41) firmado por Periquito el Aguador; 2) "Cartas y Notas Humorísticas" (1940–41) firmado por Groucho Marx; y 3) "Requiem por Faulkner" y otros artículos (1953–71) entre los que hay destacar los dedicados a Arlt y Faulkner. Las declaraciones hechas en entrevistas (1966–75) completan un cuadro fundamental para la lectura que reitera motivos ya detectables en *El pozo*.

5638 Recopilación de textos sobre Mario Benedetti. Compilación y prólogo de Ambrosio Fornet. La Habana: Casa de las Américas, 1976. 299 p.; bibl. (Serie Valoración múltiple)

Al útil prólogo de Ambrosio Fornet se suman artículos que cubren la multifacética producción de este ensayista, novelista, cuentista y poeta uruguayo. Los estudios pertenecen a Ruffinelli, Baeza, Nils Castro, Fernández Retamar, F. Alvarez, G.D. Carrillo, Guyot, M.E. Bermúdez, J. Ludmer, Beberfall, J. Díaz, Seiguerman, Arias, Rein, Osnajansky y Mercier. El carácter introductorio de algunos textos es seguido por elaboraciones más detalladas sobre aspectos y obras específicas. La acostumbrada sección de "Otras Opiniones" cierra este valioso tomo.

5639 Saad, Gabriel. Eduardo Galeano: la literatura como una pasión latinoamericana (CH, 324, junio 1977, p. 454–469)

Presentación amistosa que reseña la carrera de Galeano desde la publicación de *Los días siguientes* (1963) hasta *La canción de nosotros* (Premio Casa de las Américas, 1975). Alterna las circunstancias que dieron lugar a la publicación de *Guatemala, clave de Latinoamérica* y *Las venas abiertas de América Latina* con lecturas más detalladas de sus cuentos, especialmente de *Vagamundo*. Buen trabajo introductorio.

5640 Visca, Arturo Sergio *comp.* Cartas inéditas de Horacio Quiroga (UBN/R, 18, mayo 1978, p. 9–39, plate)

Fascinante agregado de 38 cartas dirigidas a Luis Pardo que se suman a las 256 publicadas anteriormente. Son cartas cotidianas a las que no son ajenas las referencias literarias intercaladas con su labor agrícola y las preocupaciones familiares. Escritas entre 1907 y 1920(?). Son de especial interés algunos versos que acompañan a las misivas y las referencias específicas a su sentido de la profesión.

POETRY

HUMBERTO M. RASI, *Chief Editor, Inter-American Publications, Pacific Press*
RUBEN A. GAMBOA, *Assistant Professor of Spanish, Mills College*
OSCAR HAHN, *Associate Professor of Spanish, University of Iowa*
DAVID LAGMANOVICH, *Professor of Argentine Literature, Universidad Nacional de La Plata, Argentina*
PEDRO LASTRA, *Professor of Spanish, State University of New York at Stony Brook*
CAROLYN MORROW, *Associate Professor of Spanish, University of Utah*
BETTY TYREE OSIEK, *Professor of Spanish, Southern Illinois University at Edwardsville*
ELIANA RIVERO, *Professor of Spanish, The University of Arizona*

ANTOLOGIAS Y ESTUDIOS GENERALES

Los trabajos de índole general que nos ha correspondido reseñar para este volumen no ofrecen novedades sorprendentes. Se advierte, eso sí, una intención de abarcar en las antologías zonas más amplias de la producción poética—rescatando figuras olvidadas o marginales—y, en la crítica, la voluntad de utilizar esquemas innovadores de investigación y análisis.

Entre las antologías internacionales recibidas, se destaca la dedicada a la poesía negrista en las Américas (item **5666**) y una minuciosa recopilación de poemas sobre las plantas (item **5653**).

En el ámbito de la crítica merecen mencionarse tres intentos de periodización de la poesía hispanoamericana (items **5651**, **5864** y **5874**), un sugestivo análisis de la "negritud" en la América hispana (item **5860**), y una valiosa colección de trabajos sobre el surrealismo latinoamericano (item **5872**). El modernismo—sus orígenes, contactos y proyecciones—sigue concitando nuevos enfoques y animadas polémicas (items **5651**, **5858** y **5862**).

Desiderata: un estudio crítico del ciclo último de la poesía rebelde y solidaria hispanoamericana, en su trayectoria desde la Guerra Civil Española (item **5847**) hasta su cultivo quizá declinante en la década de los 1970 (item **5667**). [HMR]

ARGENTINA, URUGUAY Y PARAGUAY

Antologías: Merecen mención la útil antología de la poesía argentina, especialmente representativa en lo contemporáneo, de Martini Real (item **5656**) y la colección de textos gauchescos prologada por Angel Rama (item **5665**).
Libros de Poesía: Entre los libros que, o bien son colecciones de obras completas o representan una parte sustancial de la producción de un autor, deben mencionarse especialmente los de dos poetas actuales de máxima importancia en la Argentina: Edgar Bayley (item **5684**) y Roberto Juarroz (item **5770**). También es de interés, entre los autores de otras generaciones, la recopilación de la obra poética completa del escritor judeoargentino César Tiempo (item **5841**). En la escasa producción poética válida del Paraguay se destaca la abarcadora muestra de la dilatada labor poética de Josefina Plá (item **5814**).
Estudios: Valioso el de Julieta Gómez Paz sobre cuatro mujeres que ejercen influencia en la poesía contemporánea argentina (item **5857**).

Balance: *Paraguay*: Escasísima actividad poética de valor; uno de los más prometedores entre los numerosos rimadores aún no conocidos fuera del país parece ser Jorge Canese (item **5697**). *Uruguay*: La figura mayor de la poesía uruguaya contemporánea sigue siendo Mario Benedetti, aun desde el destierro (items **5685** y **5686**); Rolando Faget y Enrique Estrázulas son dos de las voces más interesantes entre los jóvenes que publicaron libros de poesía durante el período considerado. *Argentina*: Como si se estuviera en una etapa de recapacitación y balance, antes que de importantes avances en nuevas direcciones, los últimos años se caracterizaron por la aparición de una nutrida serie de volúmenes que presentan en forma total o parcial recopilaciones de la producción de poetas importantes: Bayley, Juarroz, González Tuñón, Petit de Murat, Granata, Fernández Moreno, Radaelli, Brughetti (items **5684**, **5692**, **5739**, **5755–5756**, **5770**, **5811–5812** y **5816**). Entre los libros nuevos, se asiste a una constante reiteración de las modalidades expresivas de Jorge Luis Borges (item **5687**); a la sostenida profundización en la mente como elemento generador de vivencias poéticas que caracteriza a Alberto Girri (item **5750**); y, en los más jóvenes, a una diversificación de tendencias y actitudes. En este último sentido, resulta de interés mencionar el contorno social que define la poesía de algunos (como Diz, item **5727**), el uso del "lunfardo" (item **5718**) y la presencia cada vez más importante de poesía valiosa producida en el interior del país, ya sea en lugares remotos como Salta (item **5706**) o en la zona metropolitana, como La Plata (item **5824**). Dos figuras relativamente poco conocidas pero que hay que tener en cuenta son Darío Cantón (item **5698**) y Cristina Piña (item **5813**). [DL]

CHILE

Considerando que la actividad editorial alcanza en Chile uno de los puntos más bajos en la historia del país, cabe reconocer que en 1978–79 se logró un leve repunte, gracias a la iniciativa personal de los propios poetas. Las editoriales ligadas al gobierno se dedicaron principalmente a la difusión de escritos relacionados con la historia militar de Chile. Uno de los hechos sobresalientes fue la publicación—a cargo de diversos recopiladores—, de las cartas y otras prosas de Gabriela Mistral, inéditas o extraídas de viejos diarios y revistas. Otros sucesos significativos: la aparición de las revistas culturales *La Bicicleta* y *Cal y Canto* que acogieron a los poetas noveles; el concurso "Poesía Joven 79," organizado por los centros de estudiantes de la Universidad de Chile; la celebración del cincuentenario de Enrique Lihn y la muerte del poeta Juan Guzmán Cruchaga. Entre los libros publicados en Chile destacan: *A partir de Manhattan*, de Lihn (item **5775**); *Mester de Bastardía*, de Manuel Silva Acevedo (item **5834**); y *Purgatorio*, de Raúl Zurita. En el exterior continuó la avalancha de antologías sobre el golpe militar y sobre el tema del exilio; aumentó la ya excesiva bibliografía sobre Pablo Neruda, y se notó un creciente interés en la obra de Vicente Huidobro. Pero lamentablemente hay una notable e injusta ausencia de trabajos críticos sobre otros poetas chilenos significativos. La excepción la constituyó Enrique Lihn. Sus poemas fueron publicados en inglés por New Directions, de New York, y *Review* le dedicó una de sus ediciones. Entre los libros impresos fuera de Chile destaca también *Noticias del extranjero*, de Pedro Lastra (item **5773**). Tres tendencias predominan en la actual poesía chilena: la corriente "lárica," bajo el magisterio de J. Teillier; una segunda dirección que se ciñe a las ideas estéticas de Lihn; y una tercera que entronca con Parra pero que ha conseguido liberarse y que propende al "objetivismo" poético. [OH]

BOLIVIA, PERU Y ECUADOR

Se empiezan a advertir en el área la presencia y la gravitación de algunos poetas jóvenes, en cuyas variadas manifestaciones pueden señalarse las notas caracterizadoras de una nueva tendencia generacional: Se trata, en los casos más significativos, de una poesía a muy controlada y consciente del orden productivo de las relaciones con la tradición, que opta por una lenguaje poético vigilado y renuncia a las amplificaciones frecuentes en ciertos sectores de la poesía a anterior. Mitre y Nicomedes Suárez, en Bolivia; Eduardo Muñoz, en Ecuador, y el grupo de poetas que publicaron bajo el sello de *La Sagrada Familia* y que ahora se constituye como ediciones Ruray/Poesía en el Perú—López Degregori, O'Hara, Rebaza y Sánchez Hernani (items **5778**, **5798**, **5817** y **5826**), son nombres promisores que se inscriben decididamente en esta línea o se aproximan a sus exigencias.

El interés por la obra de César Vallejo se ha mantenido e incluso intensificado en el período: varios artículos importantes (items **5879**, **5910** y **5923**), libros individuales y colectivos (items **5877** y **5912**) y nuevas ediciones de sus trabajos en prosa y en verso, son contribuciones valiosas en lo que ya puede considerarse como un campo específico de estudio. Otros autores que merecieron también atención de la crítica fueron José María Eguren, César Dávila Andrade y Emilio Adolfo Westphalen. Este último fue objeto de un homenaje, digno de la mayor difusión (item **5892**).

En este punto tienen particular importancia la compilación de trabajos críticos sobre José María Eguren, y la edición de la *Poesía completa de Vallejo* preparada por Juan Larrea (item **5839**).

Entre los poetas de promociones próximas sobresale de Antonio Cisneros (item **5712**), y—en un plano algo más reducido—Jorge Suárez (item **5837**).

La actividad editorial en el Perú ha seguido respondiendo al intenso y productivo quehacer de los poetas y de los estudiosos del género, especialmente a través de organismos universitarios, de instituciones privadas o de empresas de grupos particulares. Es sensible la declinación del índice de publicaciones realizadas hasta hace poco tiempo por el Instituto Nacional de Cultura. En Ecuador, esta actividad ha experimentado un desarrollo extraordinario: las numerosas ediciones de la Casa de la Cultura Ecuatoriana, sobre todo en sus núcleos de Quito y Guayaquil, constituyen un excelente estímulo para la creación y la crítica. Aunque en un grado muchísimo menor, algo parecido puede señalarse sin embargo con respecto a Bolivia, donde estas tareas han empezado a preocupar a la dirección de la Casa Municipal de la Cultura Franz Tamayo, de La Paz.

La singularidad de la obra de Alfredo Gangotena (1904–1945) merece una activa consideración crítica. La publicación reciente (item **5745**) es una buena prueba de interés revalorativo. Es muy estimable que se le incluyera en una colección popular, pero hace falta también un texto mayor—cuidadoso, informativo y anotado—que permita situar a este poeta casi desconocido en el sitio relevante que le corresponde en el proceso de la poesía hispanoamericana llamada de vanguardia. [PL]

COLOMBIA Y VENEZUELA

La poesía joven de Colombia y Venezuela es hermética pero absolutamente espontánea consistiendo en su mayoría de poemas antipoéticos, simbólicos y lapidarios sobre la muerte y lo absurdo de esta era tecnológica y dictatorial y, en su minoría, de poemas sugestivos e íntimos de tipo sensual y lírico.

Entre recopilaciones importantes, deben mencionarse las dedicadas a poetas colombianos de reconocido talento como León de Greiff (item **5757**) y Eduardo Carranza (item **5701**) y a venezolanos como el modernista Alfredo Arvelo Larriva (item **5681**). Al definir qué criterios aplican en la recopilación de antologías, varios críticos colombianos nos ofrecen una visión panorámica de la poesía del país (items **5851–5852**, **5861** y **5863**).

Entre las obras críticas y antologías dedicadas a poetas consagrados, cabe destacar una sobre Rubén Darío (item **5719**) y las excelentes aportaciones de Héctor H. Orjuela al estudio de José Asunción Silva (items **5830**, **5832** y **5900**). En cuanto a trabajos sobre poetas posteriores, deben mencionarse uno sobre Eduardo Carranza (item **5913**) y otro dedicado a Luis Carlos López (item **5880**). En general, los estudios críticos son sumamente heterogéneos, abarcando temas que van desde la ecología (item **5890**) hasta la metafísica (item **5917**).

Para concluir, debe señalarse que a pesar de la notable mejora en la calidad de obras editadas en Venezuela, faltan aún buenas antologías de la nueva poesía venezolana así como estudios serios y recientes sobre el tema. Por lo contrario, en Colombia ya se han publicado buenas antologías tales como una de poemas predilectos de 23 autores con notas autobiográficas (item **5663**) y una recopilación de las obras de poetisas colombianas (item **5658**). [BTO]

CENTROAMERICA Y PANAMA

La poesía centroamericana y de Panamá continúa desarrollándose a grandes pasos. Es constante la aparición de jóvenes de gran talento y madurez poética, con lo cual el nivel artístico de la producción lírica es cada vez superior.

Los libros de poesía reseñados en este volumen fueron publicados, en su mayoría, entre 1976 y 1978, aunque se incluyen algunos publicados entre 1966 y 1975. La dirección fundamental que se aprecia es la persistencia de poesía abiertamente comprometida, lo que es de esperarse dada la coyuntura histórica de la región; y dentro de este terreno el conflicto, más o menos urgente dentro de la obra individual, sobre la manera de darle forma poética a la preocupación social: ¿exteriorismo o transcendentalismo?, ¿lenguaje directo o lenguaje figurado? Es característica, en este respecto, la aparición en Costa Rica del *Manifiesto transcendentalista* (item **5935**), como ejemplo de una polémica incesante.

En el plano de la crítica, cabe destacar el trabajo de Raymond Skyrme sobre Rubén Darío (item **5916**), una definición de la poética de Darío que descuella por la lucidez de su enfoque. [RG]

ANTILLAS HISPANAS

El perfil poético del Caribe arroja una continua búsqueda y reflexión en sus raíces de identidad, al igual que la crítica relacionada. La poesía de los albores románticos e independentistas (los siboneístas cubanos, los indianistas puertorriqueños, Rafael María de Mendive) y de los clásicos (José Martí, Julián del Casal) es objeto de estudios y reediciones (items **5662**, **5782**, **5843**, **5883** y **5926**). El interés en lo intrínsecamente antillano se destaca asimismo en una serie de valoraciones, revisiones, análisis y compilaciones de la poesía del siglo XIX; figuras más históricas que poéticas, como la puertorriqueña Lola Rodríguez de Tió y el cubano Domingo del Monte reciben atención por su obra cultural, civil y docente (items **5654** y **5889**), como también la merecen ya en el siglo XX la dominicana Camila Henríquez Ureña y su legado familiar (item **5934**). Prosigue el enfoque en un verso de entraña popular con publicaciones de y sobre Nicolás Guillén, Luis Palés Matos y Manuel del Cabral (items **5693–5694**, **5761**, **5908** y **5928**). Los poetas del grupo de *Orígenes* aún se dejan oir: Lezama Lima póstumamente (item **5774**) y Eliseo Diego en *Los días de tu vida* (1977). La nueva poesía y su dedicación a un lenguaje y visión coloquialmente actuales florece en Puerto Rico sobre todo en las mujeres jóvenes (item **5660**), en Cuba en una rica tercera promoción revolucionaria (items **5652** y **5659**) y en la República Dominicana con la muestra de *Meridiano* 70 (item **5844**). [ER]

MEXICO

Obras importantes de poesía son *Pasado en claro* y *Poemas*, ambas de Octavio Paz (items **5803** y **5804**). Esta última consiste de nuevas versiones y reincorporaciones de poemas que se omitieron en la edición de 1968. Asimismo, cabe destacar: *En honor de las palabras* de Montes de Oca (item **5789**); *Vivir para ver* de Aridjis (item **5679**); *Gatuperio* de Deniz (item **5726**); *Poemas en el regazo de la muerte* de Fraire (item **5741**); y finalmente, las obras de dos hijos de poetas: *Versión* de D. Huerta (item **5766**) y *Plagio* de González de León (item **5753**). En cuanto a estudios críticos, deben mencionarse tres excelentes trabajos sobre Octavio Paz (items **5875**, **5898** y **5924**).

En breve, cabe señalar la disminución de la poesía comprometida y la ascendencia de temas personales y metafísicos que manifiestan, entre otros, los poemas de Montes de Oca. [CM]

ANTHOLOGIES

5641 Alma y corazón: antología de las poetisas hispanoamericanas. Selecciones y crítica por Catherine R. Perricone. Miami, Fla.: Ediciones Universal, 1977. 199 p.; bibl. (Colección Antologías)

Antología de intención escolar, con selecciones de 26 poetisas hispanoamericanas desde Sor Juana hasta las contemporáneas, incluyendo cinco cubanas en el exilio. Contiene notas biobibliográficas. [HMR]

Anthology of Mexican poetry. See item **6614**.

5642 Antología de la poesía boliviana. Selección de Yolanda Bedregal. La Paz, Bolivia: Editorial Los Amigos del Libro, 1977. 625 p.; index (Enciclopedia boliviana)

La autora declara que el extenso volumen no pretende el análisis ni la valoración sino que expone un "conjunto de muestras." Estas son numerosas y dispares: algunas piezas de las épocas prehispánica y colonial, y 205 autores de la época republicana. Lo contrario de una antología: su designio acumulativo es abrumador y no acrecienta su utilidad. [PL]

5643 Antología de la poesía en Arequipa en el siglo XX. Selección e introducción de Jorge Cornejo Polar. Arequipa: Instituto Nacional de Cultura, Filial en Arequipa, 1976. 320 p.; bibl.

Valiosa recopilación, dispuesta con amplitud que no excluye la exigencia valorativa. El excelente estudio preliminar de Jorge Cornejo es rico en informaciones y juicios sobre la actividad poética en una zona influyente dentro del mapa cultural del Perú. Textos de 41 autores, desde Percy Gibson (1885–1960) a Duilio Ayala Macedo (n. 1949). [PL]

5644 Antología de la poesía mexicana moderna. Selección, introducción, comentarios y notas de Andrew P. Debicki. London: Támesis, D.L., 1976. 305 p.; bibl. (Colección Támesis: Serie B., Textos; 20)

Well-done anthology that includes between seven and 18 poems from each of the following: Gutiérrez Nájera, Díaz Mirón, Nervo, González Martínez, Tablada, López Velarde, Reyes, Maples Arce, Pellicer, Gorostiza, Torres Bodet, Villaurrutia, Novo, Owen, E. Huerta, Paz, Chumacero, Bonifaz Nuño, García Terrés, Sabines, Castellanos, Montes de Oca, Bañuelos, Zaid, Pacheco, Aridjis. Includes a brief biography and bibliography of the writers together with a short list of critical works on each. There is as well a concise, helpful introduction to Mexican poetry of 1890–1970 by Debicki. A valuable text. [CM]

5645 Antología del soneto hispanoamericano. Edición de Hugo Emilio Pedemonte. San Salvador, El Salvador: Dirección de Cultura, Ministerio de Educación, 1972. 407 p.; index.

Muestras del arte de 144 poetas hispanoamericanos de todos los tiempos que cultivaron el soneto. La antología, organizada cronológicamente, refleja la evolución estética y la tenaz vitalidad de esta forma poética que sigue gozando de diestros cultores. [HMR]

5646 Antología poética hispanoamericana. Buenos Aires: Fondo Editorial Bonaerense, 1978. 583 p.

Muestras de 190 poetas contemporáneos de Hispanoamérica y España, precedidas de breves notas biobibliográficas. Los poetas ya establecidos conviven en esta antología con una mayoría de escritores menores. [HMR]

5647 Chile: poesía de la resistencia y el exilio. Selección de Omar Lara y Juan Armando Epple. n.p.: n.p., n.d. 130 p.

Antología de poemas que incorporan diferentes vivencias y reacciones motivadas por el golpe militar chileno. La primera sección incluye textos escritos en Chile y que ahora se publican en forma anónima, con excepción del poema "Somos 5000," de Víctor Jara, redactado durante su confinamiento en un campo de prisioneros políticos. La segunda sección recoge poemas creados en el exilio. Algunos de los autores seleccionados son: Fernando Alegría, Efraín Barquero, Hernán Lavín, Gonzalo Rojas, Waldo Rojas, Armando Uribe y David Valjalo, entre otros. [OH]

5648 Las cien mejores poesías líricas venezolanas. Selección y prólogo de Pedro P. Barnola. 5. ed. Barcelona, España: Publicaciones Reunidas; Caracas: Distribuidora Estudios, 1976. 361 p.

Anthology compiled for the general reader rather than toward showing the development of Venezuelan poetry. Fifth revised edition of first anthology of 100 best poems of the country. [BTO]

5649 El corazón del fuego. Antología del Movimiento Hora Zero. Selección de textos y notas de Manuel Velázquez Rojas. La Cantuta, Perú: Ediciones Universidad Nacional de Educación, 1971. 52 p.: ill. (Artes y letras)

Antología del Movimiento Hora Zero, que debe considerarse como una de las publicaciones centrales de ese grupo. Además de las muestras poéticas—entre las que se destacan los textos de Enrique Verástegui y Jorge Nájar—incluye algunos manifiestos que provienen de la revista que los poetas de la promoción editaron en 1970 y 1971. El libro de José Miguel Oviedo, *Estos 13* (1973), reconoce la oportunidad y la importancia de los materiales reunidos en esta antología (véase *HLAS 40:7030*). [PL]

5650 Cuatro poetas jóvenes. Selección de Bernardo Callejas. La Habana: Universidad de La Habana, Departamento de Actividades Culturales, 1978. 70 p. (Serie Literatura y arte)

La presente edición ilustra la obra de cuatro Menciones de Poesía del Concurso "13 de Marzo:" Marilyn Bobes León (*Alguien está escribiendo su ternura*) y Luis Beiro Alvarez (*Jornada*) en 1977, Francisco Mir Mulet (*Proyecto de olvido y esperanza*) y Nelson Herrera Ysla (*Poesía sin límites*) en 1978. Poesía de calidad, antologada también por Randall y por Peña Gutiérrez (véase items **5652** y **5659**), incluye a una singular poeta feminista que había recibido el Primer Premio de Poesía en el Concurso "La Mujer en la Revolución" (1977), a los 22 años de edad. [ER]

5651 Del modernismo al compromiso político: antología temática de la poesía hispanoamericana. Selección de Hellén Ferro. Buenos Aires: Editorial Cuarto Poder, 1975. 249 p.

A diez años de su *Antología comentada de la poesía hispanoamericana* (New York: Las Américas Publishing Co., 1965), Ferro ofrece aquí una antología organizada en torno a temas e ilustrada con poesías representativas. Arbitraria a veces, pero sugestiva, su selección y clasificación propone tres etapas cronológicas sucesivas: 1) el modernismo, 2) la poesía de la nación, y 3) del mundonovismo al compromiso político. [HMR]

5652 Estos cantos habitados/These living songs: fifteen new Cuban poets. Edited by Margaret Randall. Fort Collins: Colorado State University, Department of English, 1978. 143 p. (Colorado State Review new series; 6:1)

Esta antología incluye una selección de 15 poetas de la última promoción revolucionaria: Raúl Rivero (n. 1945), Alex Fleites (n. 1954), Norberto Codina (n. 1951), Soleida Ríos (n. 1950), Alex Pausides (n. 1951), Francisco Garzón Céspedes (n. 1947), Víctor Rodríguez Núñez, Milagros González, Osvaldo Sánchez Crespo (n. 1958), Angel Pena, Francisco Mir Mulet (n. 1954), Osvaldo Navarro (n. 1946), Waldo Leyva (n. 1943), Nelson Herrera Ysla (n. 1947) y Ramón Fernández Larrea (n. 1958). La obra de todos ilustra el papel de la poesía en un proceso social como el cubano, la expresión creadora desde una experiencia revolucionaria. Los textos están presentados en forma bilingüe, y la introducción de Randall aporta información sobre la evolución histórica y el carácter único de esta joven poesía. [ER]

A fist and the letter: revolutionary poems of Latin America. See item **6617**.

5653 La flora en la poesía: mil y más poemas sobre las plantas. Antología. Selección, normas, prólogos, notas e introducciones de Víctor Manuel Patiño. Cali, Colombia: Imprenta Departamental del Valle del Cauca, 1976. 929 p.; bibl. (Poetas ibéricos y panamericanos; 1)

Vasta y curiosa antología temática en la que el compilador conjuga botánica y poesía. Los 1019 poemas, clasificados prolijamente, giran en torno a la vida vegetal—semilla, hierba, árbol, flor, fruta—y provienen de autores americanos y peninsulares. Se incluye la traducción de las composiciones escritas en otros idiomas y varios índices. Aunque se echan de menos algunos poemas conocidos, la amplitud de la selección es admirable. [HMR]

León, Julio Antonio. Afro-Cuban poetry: an unpublished treasure. See item **1282**.

5654 Lola Rodríguez de Tió. Compilador, Carlos F. Mendoza Tió. San Juan, Puerto Rico: Mendoza Tió, 1978. 387 p.; bibl., index (Investigaciones literarias; 3)

Vol. 3 de una continuada obra de compilación histórica, que interesa al estudioso de nuestro siglo XIX en el Caribe. Los homenajes en prosa y verso que se rinden a esta "musa de Cuba y Puerto Rico" incluyen, entre otras, las firmas de Juana Borrero, Dulce María Borrero, Rubén Darío, José de Diego, Manuel Fernández Juncos, Eugenio Florit, Federico Henríquez Carvajal, Conde Kostia, Luis Lloréns Torres, Ricardo Palma, J.A. Pérez Bonalde, Luisa Pérez de Zambrana, Gustavo Sánchez Galarraga, José Santos Chocano, Diego Vicente Tejera, Luis G. Urbina y Enrique José Varona. Ellos son muestra del fervor patriótico que marcó la vida y obra de esta mujer insular, a través de cuya producción de poesía menor se avalora el surgir de un sentimiento nacionalista específicamente antillano, desarrollado después en las obras mayores de José Martí y Eugenio María de Hostos. [ER]

5655 Marcos, Juan Manuel. El ciclo romántico modernista en el Paraguay. Asunción: Ediciones Criterio, 1977. 147 p.; bibl.

Antología de poetas paraguayos en el período 1860–1935. No deja de sorprender la referencia de "Los Fundadores del Patriotismo" asignada a la llamada generación del 900. También incluye una breve sección sobre el modernismo. [S. Sosnowski]

5656 Los mejores poemas de la poesía argentina. Selección de Juan Carlos Martini Real. 3. ed. aumentada y corregida. Buenos Aires: Ediciones Corregidor, 1977. 384 p.

Abundante en el número de poetas y en los poemas seleccionados: colección útil como panorama general debido a la amplitud de criterio del compilador. Cronológicamente, abarca desde Olegario Víctor Andrade (1839–82) hasta Eduardo D'Anna (n. 1948). Estéticamente, además de las corrientes generalmente reconocidas, se anota la presencia de poetas infrecuentemente representados pero valiosos, tales como Alfredo Brandán Caraffa (vanguardia); Juan Pedro Calou (posmodernismo); Homero Expósito, Enrique Santos Discépolo y Homero Manzi (letras de tango); Ariel Ferraro, Raúl Galán y Manuel J. Castilla (poesía de las provincias); Mario Satz y Marcelo Pichon Rivière (últimas promociones), etc.: amplitud que convierte a este libro en un índice actual y actualizado de nombres, tendencias y autores. [DL]

The newest Peruvian poetry in translation. See item **6621**.

Now the volcano: an anthology of Latin American gay literature. See item **6622**.

5657 La nueva poesía amorosa latinoamericana. Compiladores: Saúl Ibargoyen Islas y Jorge Boccanera. México: Editores Mexicanos Unidos, 1978. 347 p., bibl.

Antología temática que recoge muestras de 110 poetas latinoamericanos de este siglo, con buena representación de los contemporáneos. Superadas las convenciones del modernismo y los hermetismos de la vanguardia, la lírica de hoy tiende a expresar con más llaneza el sentimiento amoroso y la pasión erótica. [HMR]

5658 Oficio de poeta: poesía en Bogotá. Compilación de Rosa Jaramillo. Bogotá: Universidad de San Buenaventura, 1978. 298 p.

Publication of poems read at Buenaventura University by 23 Bogotá poets, ranging in age from 21–83. The poems of each are preceded by a short autobiography and answers to seven questions about the art of poetry. [BTO]

5659 Peña Gutiérrez, Isaías. Ocho nuevos poetas cubanos (HU, 1:4, junio 1976, p. 121–134, illus.)

Breve muestra de jóvenes talentos, que presenta al lector colombiano algunos valores de los "novísimos:" Omar González, Efraín Morciego Reyes, Luis Beiro Alvarez, Mercedes Rodríguez García, Víctor Rodríguez, Bladimir Zamora, Pedro de la Hoz, Arturo Arango. [ER]

5660 Poemario de la mujer puertorriqueña. Edición al cuidado de Lydia Zoraida Barreto. San Juan de Puerto Rico: Instituto de Cultura Puertorriqueña, 1976. 2 v.: ill. (Serie Literatura hoy; 10)

Jugosa colección de talentos jóvenes, que incluye cortas muestras de las poetas Marina Arzola, Iris M. Landrón, Luz Raquel Avila, Olga Nolla, María Arrillaga, Angela María Dávila, Magaly Quiñones, Dalia Nieves, Isabel López (vol. 1) y Etnairis Rivera, Maritza Pérez Otero, Luz Ivonne Ochart, Leida Santiago, Vanessa Droz, Marisol Villamil, Dinorah Marzán, Ana I. Rivera Lassén, Gina Delucca Juncos (vol. 2). Esta nueva poesía puertorriqueña femenina se inscribe de lleno en la contemporaneidad, y revela una expresión madura que hasta ahora no resonaba en otras voces poéticas de la isla; su temática se engarza en la experiencia cultural de la mujer y en una socialización híbrida que pugna por lograr su identidad. La más prometedoras son: Etnairis Rivera, Olga Nolla, Angela María Dávila y Luz Ivonne Ochart, de textura lírica y técnica comparable a la mejor poesía escrita por las últimas promociones de mujeres cubanas, mexicanas y uruguayas. [ER]

5661 Poesía contemporánea: 11 [i.e. once] poetas hondureños. Ilustraciones de Adriana Bonisconti. v. 1, Clementina Suárez; v. 2, Jorge Federico Travieso; v. 3, Jaime Fontana; v. 4, Antonio José Rivas; v. 5, Pompeyo del Valle; v. 6, Roberto Sosa; v. 7, Oscar Acosta; v. 8, José Adán Castelar; v. 9, Edilberto Cardona Bulnes; v. 10, Rigoberto Paredes; v. 11, José Luis Quesada. San José, Costa Rica: Editorial Universitaria Centroamericana (EDUCA), 1978. 11 v. (Unpaged): ill.

Con motivo del cuarto centenario de la fundación de Tegucigalpa se publican estos volúmenes. Cada uno de ellos contiene una pequeña muestra de la obra de los poetas hondureños contemporáneos más destacados. [RG]

5662 Poesía criollista y siboneísta. Antología. Compilación, prólogo y notas, Jesús Orta Ruiz. La Habana: Editorial Arte y Literatura, 1976. 400 p. (Biblioteca básica de literatura cubana)

Muestra panorámica de una poesía de tradición popular, que comprende desde los albores del siglo XVII a fines del XIX; el editor es un conocido cultivador de la décima campesina cubana. Los poetas incluidos van desde los famosos (José María Heredia) a los prácticamente desconocidos (Ursula de Céspedes). De interés histórico. [ER]

5663 Poesía de autoras colombianas. Selección y notas de Eddy Torres. Prólogo de Eduardo Carranza. Bogotá: Caja Agraria, 1975. 333 p.; bibl. (Colección de publicaciones históricas; 7)

Thirteen-page prologue by poet Eduardo Carranza briefly surveys poetry and literary history from Spanish Middle Ages until today. Judges that although not first rank, the women poets represented in the collection of 91 poems by 37 authors deserve a highly creative second place. Editor, Eddy Torres, gives a short biographical introduction to each poetess who has been published in book form. Selections span colonial times until 1975, International Women's Year. [BTO]

5664 Poesía ecuatoriana del siglo XX: ganadores del concurso Ismael Pérez Pazmiño mantenido por diario *El Universo*. v. 1, Años 1959, 1960, 1961, 1962, 1963; v. 2, Años 1964, 1965, 1966, 1967, 1968, 1969; v. 3, Años 1970, 1971, 1972, 1973, 1974, 1975. Guayaquil: Casa de la Cultura Ecuatoriana,

Núcleo del Guayas, 1976. 3 v. (Colección Letras del Ecuador; 11, 13, 15)

Laboriosa tarea de recopilación de los poemas seleccionados en los certámenes anuales del diario *El Universo*, de Guayaquil, entre 1959 y 1975. Una suma considerable de trabajos (51 envíos fueron distinguidos con diversas menciones), que vista desde una perspectiva crítica ajena al contexto en que se generó—y en el que fue un estímulo valioso—no deja muchas notas memorables: "Boletín y Elegía de las Mitas," de C. Dávila Andrade (Segundo Premio en 1959) e "Itinerante entre los Muertos," de C.E. Jaramillo (premiado en 1970), son los poemas que sobresalen en un conjunto de escasos o muy fragmentarios relieves. [PL]

5665 Poesía gauchesca: B. Hidalgo, L. Pérez, M. de Araúcho, H. Ascasubi, E. del Campo, J. Hernández. Prólogo de Angel Rama. Selección, notas y cronología de Jorge B. Rivera. Caracas: Biblioteca Ayacucho, 1977. 484 p.

La utilidad principal de esta edición de textos gauchescos se encuentra en el informativo prólogo de Angel Rama, así como en hacer accesibles composiciones de Luis Pérez y de Manuel de Araúcho, escasamente representados en otras compilaciones de este tipo de poesía. [DL]

5666 Poesía negra de América. Edición de José Luis González y Mónica Mansour. México: Ediciones Era, 1976. 484 p.; indexes.

Util antología de la poesía negrista de las Américas, que reúne composiciones de autores destacados que escribieron en castellano, francés, inglés o portugués. Mónica Mansour, que ya publicó un estudio sobre el tema (*La poesía negrista*, México: Ediciones Era, 1973), ofrece en la introducción una síntesis comparativa de la poesía de tema negro en estas cuatro regiones lingüísticas y culturales. Notas biobibliográficas, traducciones e índices. [HMR]

5667 Poesía rebelde en Latinoamérica. Editores: Saúl Ibargoyen y Jorge Boccanera. México: Editores Mexicanos Unidos, 1978. 348 p.

La poesía de denuncia y protesta—testimonio de una actitud ante la realidad y de una etapa histórica—alcanza su apogeo hacia la década del 60 en Latinoamérica. Esta antología reúne poemas de 129 autores, algunos anónimos y otros inéditos, que escribieron en castellano, francés, inglés y portugués su mensaje de rebeldía, militancia y solidaridad. [HMR]

5668 Poetisas mexicanas: siglos XVI, XVII, XVIII y XIX. Antología y prólogo de José María Vigil. Estudio preliminar de Ana Elena Díaz Alejo y Ernesto Prado Velázquez. 2. ed. México: Universidad Nacional Autónoma de México, Dirección General de Publicaciones, 1977. lxxviii, xxxiii, 362 p., 14 leaves of plates: ill. (Nueva biblioteca mexicana; 43)

Reedition of an anthology, originally prepared in 1893, which contains works from 95 poetesses. While many of the poems are of marginal quality, others are important literary contributions. Valuable as a survey of women writers of Mexico over the centuries. [CM]

5669 Rosenbaum, Sidonia Carmen. Modern women poets of Spanish America: the precursors, Delmira Agustini, Gabriela Mistral, Alfonsina Storni, Juana de Ibarbourou. Westport, Conn.: Greenwood Press, 1978 [i.e. 1945]. 273 p.; bibl., index.

Reimpresión de un trabajo precursor publicado en 1945. Aunque la bibliografía sobre Delmira Agustini, Gabriela Mistral, Alfonsina Storni y Juana de Ibarbourou ha crecido sustancialmente desde entonces, estos cuatro estudios en inglés conservan—especialmente en su detallado análisis estilístico—buena parte de su validez original. [HMR]

BOOKS OF VERSE

5670 Aguilar Mora, Jorge. No hay otro cuerpo. México: Joaquín Mortiz, 1977. 123 p. (Las dos orillas)

The poet-critic Aguilar Mora (b. 1946) is one of Mexico's outstanding young authors. A few of his subjects here are the writer's craft, the other, love, passion, identity, the city and Roland Barthes. An important book. [CM]

5671 Albán Rivas, Laureano Alberto. Chile de pie en la sangre. San José: Editorial Costa Rica, 1975. 115 p.: ill.

Lamento, imprecación, elegía, denuncia: Laureano Albán erige su canto al pueblo chileno y profiere, con su lirismo esencial, una plegaria de esperanza para el porvenir. [RG]

5672 ———. Solamérica, 1969/1972. 2. ed. San José: Editorial Costa Rica, 1977. 115 p.: ill.

Canto a la esencia de América. El poeta le da preferencia al endecasílabo y con gran voluntad de estilo va hilvanando imágenes que hacen aflorar la vivencia del hombre latinoamericano. Esta segunda edición recoge *Vocear la luz*, grupo de poemas escritos en la misma época que *Solamérica* (1969–72). [RG]

5673 ———. Sonetos cotidianos. Dibujos de Carlos Barboza. San José: Editorial Costa Rica, 1978. 80 p.: ill.

Albán se entrega a la búsqueda de la esencia inmanente de las cosas, para lo cual hace pasar la realidad por el alambique del verso, que recoge la esencia y la ilumina. "Sonetos Corporales," "Sonetos Conyugales," "Sonetos Minerales," la corporeidad mortal del hombre, el poder transcendente del amor y la belleza virtual de la materia dan configuración a los poemas. [RG]

5674 ———. Sonetos laborales. San José: Editorial Costa Rica, 1977. 93 p.: ill.

Era de esperarse que el uso asiduo del endecasílabo en la lírica de Albán habría de desembocar en el soneto. En estos poemas, el autor aprisiona certeramente la esencia de las herramientas humildes—la pala, el martillo, la aguja, la plomada—; y en la loa a la herramienta va implícito no sólo el elogio al obrero sino la defensa de su derecho al trabajo que lo honra y lo dignifica. [RG]

5675 **Alegría, Claribel.** Sobrevivo. La Habana: Casa de las Américas, 1978. 62 p.

Claribel Alegría ha pasado a llenar el vacío creado por la muerte de Claudia Lars. En lenguaje sencillo, Alegría esboza la reminiscencia, la angustia, la visión del mundo contemporáneo. Recibió el Premio Casa de las Américas 1978. [RG]

5676 **Alvarez, Rosa Elvira.** El alba perdurable. Panamá: Ediciones INAC 1977. 257 p.; bibl. (Colección Múltiple; 7. Sección Poesía)

Rosa Elvira Alvarez, poeta del posvanguardismo panameño, ha hecho del romance su mejor vehículo de expresión lírica. Este libro recoge su obra completa: *Nostalgia* (1941), *El alba perdurable* (1968), *Romance de la montuna* (1969) y *Siete sonetos al Escorial* (1970). [RG]

5677 **Aridjis, Homero.** Antología poética. Introducción de Guillermo Sucre. Madrid: Akal Editor, 1977. 152 p.

Welcome anthology of the poetry of one of Mexico's most talented writers. Contains selected works from *Vivir para ver* (see item **5679**), *Quemar las naves* (1975), *El poeta niño* (1971), *Ajedrez-navegaciones* (1969), *Los espacios azules* (see item **5678**), *Antes del reino* (1963), *Los ojos desdoblados* (1960). Includes as well a brief, perceptive introduction to Aridjis' poetry by Guillermo Sucre. [CM]

5678 ———. Los espacios azules. México: Joaquín Mortiz, 1968. 107 p. (Las dos orillas)

Short descriptive poems of great force. Aridjis in simple language creates a poetic world of charm and beauty. [CM]

5679 ———. Vivir para ver. México: Joaquín Mortiz, 1977. 125 p. (Las dos orillas)

Collection of verse of various styles, including two sections of prose poems ("Desfiguros" and "Fuego Nuevo"). Aridjis is inspired by a variety of people and situations. The result is poetry that is moving, often humorous (as in "Putas en el Templo"). Impressive addition to the work of an important author. [CM]

5680 **Arturo, Aurelio.** Obra e imagen. Bogotá: Instituto Colombiano de Cultura, Subdirección de Comunicaciones Culturales, 1977. 156 p. (Biblioteca básica colombiana; 21)

This collection of poetry of intimate suggestiveness and originality was prepared by the author before his death. The poetry is followed by six translations and reproductions of short critical studies by nine well-known Colombian authors. [BTO]

5681 **Arvelo Larriva, Alfredo.** Obras completas. v. 1, Verso y prosa. Prólogo y notas de Alejandro Angulo Arvelo. Caracas?: Biblioteca de Temas y Autores Barineses, 1977. 1 v.; bibl., indexes.

Volume of annotated verse by the well-known Modernist was written during the movement's second Venezuelan epoch. It includes good critical prologue and notes by Alejandro Angulo Arvelo, nephew of the poet. [BTO]

5682 **Aymará, Dionisio.** Aprendizaje de la muerte. Poemas. Caracas: Editorial

Contemporánea, 1978. 98 p. (Colección Poesía; 1)

Poems express varied approaches to the theme of death, the author's first and last obsession. Some reflect the author's agonized acceptance of it; others his hatred of its finality. [BTO]

5683 Balza Donatti, Camilo. Sonetos del campo y del amor: 1957–1972. Maracaibo: Asociación de Escritores Venezolanos, Seccional Zulia, 1975. 59 p. (Cuadernos literarios de la Asociación de Escritores Venezolanos, Seccional Zulia; 1)

Popular edition of 40 sonnets, about half of which are on "el campo." Reflects mastery of the sonnet form and an unusually original talent in expressing universal emotions in new and different, yet deeply-felt images. [BTO]

5684 Bayley, Edgar. Obra poética. Edición al cuidado de Francisco Squeo Acuña. Buenos Aires: Ediciones Corregidor, 1976. 198 p. (Biblioteca de poesía; 1152)

La figura mayor del invencionismo argentino en una recopilación de la totalidad de su obra en verso, publicada en varios libros y parcialmente en revistas literarias de gran significación tales como *Arturo*, *Poesía Buenos Aires*, *Invención II* y *Zona*. Experimental y lírico a un tiempo, alcanza sus poemas más logrados en los que, previamente inéditos, ingresan directamente en este volumen: los titulados *Celebraciones* (1968–76). Un poeta importante y una colección sumamente valiosa para seguir el desarrollo de la moderna poesía argentina. [DL]

5685 Benedetti, Mario. La casa y el ladrillo. Dibujos de Anhelo Hernández. México: Siglo Veintiuno, 1976. 138 p.: ill. (La Creación literaria)

Poemas del exilio, escritos con dolor en patrias "interinas" y "suplentes," en el tono coloquial característico de los versos de Benedetti. "La Casa y el Ladrillo," sobre la vida de los exiliados, y "Bodas de Perlas," evocación de una vida matrimonial en común y también de una época, son los mejores de la colección, quizá porque son también los más personales y aquellos en donde la consigna política no se siente como obligación panfletaria, sino como actitud libremente asumida y consustanciada con la propia vida. [DL]

5686 ———. Poemas de otros. México: Editorial Nueva Imagen, 1979. 125 p.

Diversas modalidades quedan representadas en estos poemas: la intimista, la testimonial y también de la voz de seres novelescos creados por el propio Benedetti. La colección no tiene la unidad de otros libros del autor, pero sirve como un muestrario de varios aspectos de su tarea. [DL]

5687 Bollo, Sarah. Mundo secreto. Montevideo: Talleres Gráficos La Paz, 1977. 44 p.

Dos series de poemas, en general apegados a modalidades expresivas tradicionales, que atestiguan la continuidad—50 años desde el primer libro—de una vocación poética. [DL]

5688 Borges, Jorge Luis. Adrogué. Ilustraciones de Norah Borges. Adrogué, Argentina: Ediciones Adrogué, 1977. 75 p.: ill.

La ciudad bonaerense de Adrogué está íntimamente ligada a los recuerdos juveniles de Borges y los suyos; esta compilación (que según el buen prólogo de Roy Bartholomew "es, hasta ahora, su más depurado intento de antología poética personal") reúne trece composiciones de distintos años, ilutradas por Norah Borges y, como dice el colofón, "debe ser considerada un homenaje de Jorge Luis Borges y Norah Borges de Torre a Adrogué y un homenaje de Adrogué a Jorge Luis Borges y Norah Borges de Torre." [DL]

5689 ———. Historia de la noche. Buenos Aires: Emecé, 1977. 148 p. (Obra poética de Borges)

Libro desparejo por la acumulación un tanto mecánica de poemas dispares, mantiene sin embargo un nivel de calidad debida al oficio y a la repetición de algunos característicos temas borgianos. Quizá el más personal de estos poemas sea "The Thing I Am" ("Soy el que sabe que no es más que un eco, / El que quiere morir enteramente. / Soy acaso el que eres en el sueño"); el menos interesante, "Milonga del Forastero," de tono aburridamente repetitivo. [DL]

5690 Branly, Roberto. Siempre la vida. La Habana: Editorial Letras Cubanas, 1978. 44 p. (Colección Mínima poesía; 8)

Breviario poético de un autor de la primera promoción revolucionara (véase item **5799**). La poesía de Branly tiene cierto carácter de obsesiva alucinación, casi surrealista a veces. [ER]

5691 **Brannon de Samayo, Carmen.** Obras escogidas. v. 1/2. Selección, prólogo y notas de Matilde Elena López. San Salvador: Editorial Universitaria, 1973–1974. 2 v. (311, 458 p.): ill.

Excelente edición de la obra de Claudia Lars (seudónimo de la autora) punto culminante de la poesía femenina salvadoreña e hispanoamericana. [RG]

5692 **Brughetti, Romualdo.** Antología en tres movimientos. Selección y prólogo de Alberto Coronato. Buenos Aires: Emecé Editores, 1977. 131 p.

La estructura "musical" de este libro se presta singularmente para presentar una selección de los poemas de Brughetti, correspondientes a siete libros que se extienden entre 1962 y 1976. Oportuna recolección, pues el autor es más conocido como ensayista y crítico de arte que como poeta, actividad en la que tiene sobrados méritos para ser considerado por la crítica. [DL]

5693 **Cabral, Manuel del.** Obra poética completa. Santo Domingo: Editora Alfa y Omega, 1976. 609 p.

Recopilación de textos del mayor poeta dominicano, cuya labor en verso corre a veces paralela a la vena popularísima del cubano Guillén o al lirismo de la más conocida poesía antillana y centroamericana de la posvanguardia. Este volumen compendia, además de los significativos *Compadre Mon* (1940), *Trópico negro* (1942), *Sangre mayor* (1945), *De este lado del mar* (1948) y *Los huéspedes secretos* (1951), los libros de la madurez: *Pedrada planetaria* y *14 mundos de amor* (1962), *La isla ofendida* (1965), *Egloga del 2,000* y *Sexo no solitario* (1970), así como las prosas poéticas de *Chinchina busca el tiempo* (1945). En esta variedad puede apreciarse una obra diversa, de corte social y rebelde o íntimamente sexual, que revive a veces ecos del chileno Neruda y que confirma a Cabral como el primer poeta de su país. [ER]

5694 **———.** Palabra. Santo Domingo: Editora Alfa y Omega, 1977. 137 p.: ill.

Pequeño de tamaño y amplio en la experimentación, este libro último y singular del mayor poeta dominicano ilustra su uso de un lenguaje sabrosamente antipoético, prosificado a ratos, y concentrado al máximo en ocasiones definitorias: "Más que el fuego, su sonrisa/desinfectaba a los conquistadores. / Con su inocencia estoy lavando dientes." (Guatemoc). [ER]

5695 **Cabrales, Julio.** Omnibus. León: Universidad Nacional Autónoma de Nicaragua, 1975. 78 p. (Colección Poesía; 9)

Colección heterogénea sin ningún intento de clasificación. Si, por ejemplo, todos los poemas religiosos que aparecen dispersos por el libro hubieran sido presentados en grupo, el resultado habría sido mucho más efectivo. Pese a esto, el talento poético de Cabrales se revela en muchas de sus poesías. [RG]

5696 **Cajina-Vega, Mario.** El hijo. León: Universidad Nacional Autónoma de Nicaragua, 1976. 84 p. (Colección Teatro, novela, cuento; 6)

Poemas en prosa que recogen reminiscencias—sensaciones, acontecimientos—de la niñez. [RG]

5697 **Canese, Jorge.** Más poesía. Asunción?: Ediciones Criterio, 1977. 88 p.

Desde poemas eróticos ("Soñarte Desnuda") hasta declaraciones políticas ("Carta en Clave a un Compañero Preso"), con muchos momentos prosaicos pero también algunos de verdadera poesía, apoyada en estructuras rítmicas que suelen recordar la pulsación de los versos de Nicolás Guillén. [DL]

5698 **Cantón, Darío.** Abecedario médico Cantón: vademedicumnemotecnicusabreviatus. Buenos Aires: Archivo Gráfico Editorial, 1977. 33 p.

Recreación poético-humorística a partir de un catálogo de especialidades medicinales; original contribución de un poeta y sociólogo argentino cuya labor merece la atención de la crítica. [DL]

5699 **Cárcamo, Jacobo V.** Preludio continental. Antología. v. 1, Brasas azules. Laurel de Anáhuac. Pino y sangre. Selección y prólogo de Pompeyo del Valle. Tegucigalpa: Secretaría de Cultura, Turismo e Información, 1977. 69 p. (Colección El Pez volador)

Este primer volumen de la antología incluye selecciones de *Brasas azules* (1938), *Laurel de Anáhuac* (1954) y *Pino y sangre* (1955). Es poesía de corte americanista con algunos toques de protesta social. [RG]

5700 Caro, José Eusebio. Poesías completas. Edición preparada por Lucio Pabón Núñez. Bogotá: Editorial Kelly [and] Ministerio de Educación Nacional, Instituto Colombiano de Cultura Hispánica, 1973. 277 p.; bibl.

Laudable publication gathers the complete works of the Romantic Colombian poet, father of Miguel Antonio Caro, from various editions and from scattered periodicals. [BTO]

5701 Carranza, Eduardo. Los pasos cantados: el corazón escrito. Antología-creación, 1935–1975. Bogotá: Instituto Colombiano de Cultura, Subdirección de Comunicaciones Culturales, División de Publicaciones, 1975. 403 p. (Colección Autores nacionales; 8. Biblioteca colombiana de cultura)

Popular edition of poems from various books published 1936–74 by this prolific poet. Chronological order shows that some of his earlier poems and poems-in-prose often are marred by "piedracielista" excesses in rhetoric, sentimentality and self-plagiarism. Poems written in his maturity show superior craftsmanship (see *HLAS 40:7055*). [BTO]

5702 Carrera, Margarita. Del noveno círculo y Antología mínima. Poemario. Guatemala: Editorial Universitaria, 1977. 154 p.: ill. (Colección Creación literaria; 8)

De la sencillez y tranquilidad que se transparentan en la *Antología mínima* (1951–69), Margarita Carrera pasa a la expresión desgarrada de *Del noveno círculo* (1975), poema largo y denso en el que se vuelca toda la angustia del vivir. [RG]

5703 Castelar, José Adán. Entretanto. Tegucigalpa: Editorial de la Universidad Autónoma de Honduras, 1979. 76 p.

La infancia y la protesta social constituyen la médula de este poemario. J.A. Castelar representa uno de los más jóvenes contribuyentes a la lírica hondureña. [RG]

5704 Castellano Girón, Hernán. El automóvil celestial. Bari, Italy: Gea Editrice, 1977. 94 p.

La mayor parte de la poesía conversacional y narrativa que se escribe actualmente en Hispanoamérica adolece de los mismos defectos, notorios sobre todo en los poemas largos: superabundancia verbal, carencia de tensión y de intensidad, y cierre gratuito de los poemas. La conclusión de un poema debe obedecer a una necesidad interna, puesto que incluso un final abierto es, paradojalmente, una forma eficaz de cierre, si el ritmo interior así lo solicita. El libro de Hernán Castellano se inscribe en dicho tipo de poesía, sin superar las limitaciones señaladas. Aspectos positivos: cierta actitud desenfadada, cierto humor corrosivo; y en lo formal, la impecable factura de los versículos. Edición bilingüe en español e italiano. [OH]

5705 Castellanos, Dora. Año dosmil contigo. Caracas: Editorial Arte, 1977. 168 p., 1 leaf of plates: ill.

High quality, symbolically sensual and lyrical poems on love. Without excessive sentimentality. [BTO]

5706 Castilla, Manuel J. Triste de la lluvia. Poemas. Jujuy, Argentina: B. Salas, 1977. 120 p.

Una voz importante de la poesía argentina del interior del país. Desde su provincia natal, Salta, Castilla cultiva un decir poético que transmuta los elementos localistas en una suerte de suprarregionalismo. "La Tierra es Mía," uno de los poemas más bellos del volumen, sintetiza líneas temáticas que no son solamente paisajísticas, sino también hondamente reveladoras del drama humano. [DL]

5707 Cea, José Roberto. Mester de picardía. Portada e ilustraciones de Carlos Gonzalo Cañas. Buenos Aires: Ediciones Bermejo, 1977. 73 p.: ill. (Colección La Payana)

Manual del amor erótico con fines revolucionarios: Cea hace elogio del erotismo como ejemplo puro de libertad y como arma para atacar las caducas estructuras de El Salvador. [RG]

5708 Cerruto, Oscar. Cántico traspasado. Obra poética. La Paz: Biblioteca del Sesquicentenario de la República, 1976. 250 p. (Biblioteca del Sesquicentenario de la República; 19)

Antología que incluye una muestra representativa de los libros de Cerruto, desde *Cifra de las rosas* (1957) hasta *Reverso de la transparencia* (1975). El prólogo de Oscar Rivera-Rodas informa sobre el proceso de esta poesía, en la cual las aproximaciones a una realidad concreta o imaginada significan una empresa de búsqueda y reconocimiento de la identidad. [PL]

5709 **Charpentier, Jorge.** Poemas de la respuesta. San José: Editorial Costa Rica, 1977. 59 p.

La respuesta del amante, del hombre, de un niño, de Dios: cuatro facetas del pensamiento que se nos dan impregnadas con todos los matices del dolor humano. [RG]

5710 **Chase, Alfonso.** El libro de la patria. Poesía, 1970–1972. San José: Editorial Costa Rica, 1976. 171 p.: ill.

En "El Libro de la Patria," la voz lírica dialoga con presidentes, poetas, artistas y escritores costarricenses y del elogio que les traza—detalle íntimo, imagen sencilla—va surgiendo la tela de la patria, un tapiz en el que quedan delineados un pueblo y un poeta. En "Celebración de Memorias," Chase complementa el diseño y, con la madurez de su palabra, logra transmutar el acervo cultural en rasgo personal, esencial. [RG]

5711 ———. Los pies sobre la tierra. San José, Costa Rica: Mesén Editores, 1978. 115 p.

Incisivo a veces, a veces lírico, Alfonso Chase traza los contornos de su alma: resonancias de la niñez, preocupaciones sociales, solidaridad con el pueblo, erotismo, ironía, furia política; y, por encima de todo, el dolor de la patria, el amor a la patria. Uno de los valores de la nueva poesía costarricense. [RG]

5712 **Cisneros, Antonio.** El libro de Dios y de los húngaros. Dibujos de David Herskovitz. Lima: Libre-1, 1978. 146 p.: ill.

El título sintetiza con felicidad el variado escenario por el que discurre el hablante de este notable libro de Cisneros: Poesía situada, que da cuenta de una suma de experiencias concretas, que son lugares, encuentros y lecturas; pero también interiorización problematizadora que vincula así "lo humano y lo divino" en un espacio constituido por una rica intertextualidad de base: vital y literaria a un mismo tiempo. [PL]

5713 **Contreras, Raúl.** En la otra orilla. Poemas. San Salvador, El Salvador: Ministerio de Educación, Dirección de Publicaciones, 1974. 65 p.

Ya en *Presencia de humo* (1959), Raúl Contreras había dado muestra de su dominio del soneto. En esta colección—57 sonetos—el poeta se adentra en el sentido de la vida y en el forzoso paso a la "otra orilla." [RG]

5714 **Coronil Hartmann, Alfredo.** El mundo poético de Alfredo Coronil Hartmann. Estudio crítico y selección de textos de Ludovico Silva. Ilustraciones de Alirio Palacios. Caracas: Banco Nacional de Descuento, 1977. 213 p.: ill.

Ludovico Silva has selected poems from four books published by the author since 1967. Although obviously skilled, the symbolist poet is anachronistic. [BTO]

5715 **Corretjer, Juan Antonio.** Poesías. Ilustraciones de Antonio Maldonado. San Juan: Instituto de Cultura Puertorriqueña, 1976. 45 p.: ill. (Cuadernos de poesía; 11)

Colección de textos representativos de un poeta de neta raíz antillana, cantor del suelo borinqueño y sus figuras. Su obra lírica, de sincero compromiso social, había aparecido en libros de corte neocriollista, entre los cuales se destacan *Agüeybana* (1932), *Amor de Puerto Rico* (1937), *Tierra nativa* (1951), *Alabanza en la torre de Ciales* (1953), *Yerba bruja* (1957), *Genio y figura* (1961), *Canciones de consuelo que son canciones de protesta* (1971), *Construcción del sur* (1972) y *Aguinaldo escarlata* (1974). Aquí se recoge una muestra que lo hermana al cubano Nicolás Guillén y al dominicano Manuel del Cabral. [ER]

5716 **Cross, Elsa.** La dama de la torre. México: Joaquín Mortiz, 1972. 93 p. (Las dos orillas)

Talented works from a young writer of great promise. The inspiration for some of the poems is medieval and European; others are delicately personal. [CM]

Cuadra, Pablo Antonio. Songs of Cifar and the sweet sea. See item **6637**.

5717 **Cuesta, Jorge.** Poemas y ensayos. v. 1, Poemas; v. 4, Ensayos 3. 2. ed. Prólogo de Luis Mario Schneider. Recopilación y notas de Miguel Capistrán y Luis Mario Schneider. México: UNAM, 1978. 667 p. (Colección Poemas y ensayo)

Second edition (first one 1964) of the complete poetry and selected sociopolitical essays of a writer-critic active from the mid 1920s until his death in 1942. While not a major author of the period, Cuesta wrote poetry that still has literary value. [CM]

5718 **Cuniberti, Nyda.** Debute Buenos Aires. Buenos Aires: Editorial Quetzal, 1977. 110 p.

El interés especial de esta colección de poemas reside en el uso del "lunfardo"—jerga de los bajos fondos de Buenos Aires—dentro de la forma del soneto y, en ocasiones, en el tratamiento de temas de la antigüedad grecolatina: conflicto de temas y medios expresivos que da por resultado un seguro efecto humorístico. El mejor autor "lunfardista" dentro del marco de una poesía nacional que a veces se caracteriza por su engolamiento: refrescante y grata. [DL]

5719 Darío, Rubén. Poesía. Introducción y selección de Jorge Campos. Madrid: Alianza Editorial, 1977. 143 p.; bibl. (El Libro de bolsillo; 66. Sección Literatura)

Consists of distinctive and subjective poems intelligently selected by the editor from Darío's major works, preceded by an introduction (11 p.) to the poet's life and works. [BTO]

5720 Dávalos, Jaime. Cantos rodados; poemas para cantar, 1960–1972. Buenos Aires: Ediciones La Verde Rama, 1974. 65 p.

Poesía destinada al canto, generalmente de inspiración folklórica, sobre motivos de la vida rural en el norte de la Argentina; ocasionalmente ("Canto al Sueño Americano"), de tono político. [DL]

5721 Dávila, Roberto. Poemas. México: UNAM, 1978. 95 p. (Colección Poemas y ensayos)

Dávila's first book of poetry, *El cuerpo de la tierra*, was published in 1969. This work continues to explore many of the earlier concerns: love, youth, nature and the earth. A writer of marked talent, Dávila here experiments with various poetic forms, including the prose poem, with great success. [CM]

5722 Débole, Carlos Alberto. Mirar por dentro. Buenos Aires: Editorial Losada, 1977. 80 p.

A partir de los primeros años de la década de 1950 (su primer libro, *La soledad repleta*, es de 1951), un continuo fluir de libros atestigua la sostenida vocación poética de Débole. Estas páginas cultivan una modalidad poco frecuente en otros libros suyos: la expresión concisa, sintética ("En el silencio está todo el canto"), que deriva su valor poético de lo penetrante de una intuición y de la economía con que se entrega al lector. El tema general del espejo ("A veces, / como una memoria, / hace irreal el presente," p. 33) unifica las cuatro series de esquicios que constituyen el libro: "Mirar por Dentro," "Siempre Amor," "Reflets sur l'Eau" y "El Antes y el Después." [DL]

5723 Debravo, Jorge. Canciones cotidianas. San José: Editorial Costa Rica, 1977. 63 p.

La conciencia—y el dolor—de la propia soledad se yergue en algunos de estos poemas; pero Debravo, con el optimismo vital que lo caracteriza, transciende la angustia con la expresión de un amor esencial. En este respecto, "El Canto de Amor a las Cosas" que cierra la colección constituye un verdadero logro. Publicado por primera vez en 1967. [RG]

5724 ———. Los despiertos. San José: Editorial Costa Rica, 1977. 53 p.

La voz de Debravo adquiere mejor definición: la imagen se acrisola, los ritmos se adecúan a las necesidades expresivas y el pensamiento revela mayor precisión y madurcz. Obra póstuma que pone de manifiesto el humanismo del autor. La primera edición es de 1972. [RG]

5725 ———. Nosotros los hombres. San José: Editorial Costa Rica, 1977. 108 p.

La protesta social como vivencia pura es el pulso que da vida a estos poemas; de ahí que el lenguaje directo que Debravo utiliza esté tan cargado de emoción lírica. El valor artístico de los poemas no es consistente, pero por momentos—como en el caso de "Torturado" o "Caminando"—la conjugación de palabra, tono y ritmo alcanza la exactitud poética. Fue publicado originalmente en 1966. [RG]

5726 Deniz, Gerardo. Gatuperio. México: Fondo de Cultura Económica, 1978. 115 p. (Letras mexicanas; 116)

Hermetic verse that demands much of its reader, but worth the effort. It exhibits stunning use of language, with metaphors as dense as those in his earlier book, *Adrede*. [CM]

5727 Diz, Hugo. Manual de utilidades; poemas, 1972/74. Rosario, Argentina: Ediciones La Ventana, 1976. 90 p.

Uno de los poetas jóvenes de tendencia social, Diz entrega un poemario que puede ejemplificar algunas de las preocupaciones ideológicas de nuestros días: la lucha de clases, Vietnam, el derrocamiento de Allende en Chile y los conflictos sociales no resueltos en la Argentina y los Estados Unidos. Valioso a pesar de frecuentes recaídas en el prosaísmo. [DL]

5728 **Dobles Yzaguirre, Julieta.** Los pasos terrestres. Dibujos de Sonia Romero. San José: Editorial Costa Rica, 1976. 75 p., 10 leaves of plates: ill.

El ámbito de la familia—padres, hijos, la infancia—sirven de marco para la expresión poética de una metafísica de la esperanza. [RG]

5729 **———.** El peso vivo. 2. ed. San José: Editorial Costa Rica, 1976. 65 p.

Amor y muerte se conjugan por medio de un estilo sencillo, cargado de emoción. Junto con la segunda edición de *El peso vivo* (1968), la colección recoge *Reloj de siempre*, publicado originalmente en 1965. [RG]

5730 **Durán, Manuel.** El lago de los signos. México: Joaquín Mortiz, 1978. 62 p. (Las dos orillas)

This volume has wonderfully witty poems ("Cuarteto para Instrumentos de Mal Aliento"), others on the serious questions of man's existence and some of a sociopolitical nature ("El Presidente Allende Atraviesa un Espejo"). The work gives evidence of significant talent. Earlier books by Durán are *La paloma azul* (1959, see *HLAS 23:5130*) and *El lugar del hombre* (see *HLAS 28:2120*). [CM]

5731 **Echavarría, Rogelio.** El transeúnte. Bogotá: Instituto Colombiano de Cultura, Subdirección de Comunicaciones Culturales, División de Publicaciones, 1977. 115 p.; bibl. (Colección Autores nacionales; 23. Biblioteca colombiana de cultura)

The poet infuses themes of everyday life with universality by the strength and audacity of his imagery and metaphor. Popular edition of limited interest to serious students of Colombian poetry. [BTO]

5732 **Echeverría, Juan Martín.** Un sentimiento de urgencia. Poemas. Caracas: Editorial Contemporánea, 1978. 99 p. (Colección Poesía; 2)

Concise poems of a profound symbolic depth mirror the absurdity of modern life in its tragic and at times humorous aspects. Promising poet. [BTO]

5733 **Eguren, José María.** Antología de José María Eguren. Nota y selección por Manuel Mejía Valera. México: Comunidad Latinoamericana de Escritores, 1974. 123 p.; bibl. (Minilibros CLE; 6)

Aunque no se trata expresamente de un homenaje, esta breve antología aparece en el centenario del nacimiento del poeta y es un buen indicio del interés que su obra empieza a suscitar fuera de su país. La edición es modesta, pero resultará útil para un público poco familiarizado con la singular y perdurable poesía del autor (véase *HLAS 38:6938–6939*). [PL]

5734 **Eielson, Jorge Eduardo.** Poesía escrita. Prólogo de Ricardo Silva Santisteban. Lima: Instituto Nacional de Cultura, 1976. 319 p.: facsims.; bibl.

Edición cuidadosa y casi completa de la obra poética de Eielson, en la que se ha incorporado abundante material inédito o sólo publicado en revistas y periódicos. Poesía escrita, pero también—en una zona extensa—textualidad desescrita. El conjunto muestra los méritos y los límites de la experimentación, sus aciertos y riesgos más graves, sobre todo cuando esta palabra se niega a sí misma y desemboca literalmente en el vacío. Libro como espacio suscitador y polémico. [PL]

5735 **Escobar Galindo, David.** El país de las alas oscuras. Barcelona: Vosgos, 1977. 60 p. (Nudo al alba; 59)

En doce poemas densos, de ritmo lentos y períodos largos, Escobar Galindo nos presenta el cuadro alucinante de la realidad salvadoreña. Obtuvo el Premio de Poesía Carabela 1976. [RG]

5736 **Escobar Velado, Oswaldo.** Patria exacta y otros poemas. Poesía. Selección, prólogo y notas de Italo López Vallecillos. San Salvador, El Salvador: UCA Editores, 1978. 196 p. (Colección Gavidia; 14)

Además de los libros publicados en vida del autor, esta antología recoge una serie de poemas dispersos, agrupados en la sección "Patria Exacta." Constituye, por lo tanto, una colección mucho más completa que la publicada en 1967. Es un testimonio al valor artístico de este poeta vanguardista salvadoreño. [RG]

5737 **Estrázulas, Enrique.** Confesión de los perros. Montevideo: Ediciones de la

Banda Oriental, 1975 or 1976. 75 p. (Colección Acuarimántima)

Antología de los primeros libros de poemas de este joven autor (n. 1942). La sección que responde al título, compuesta por poemas no incluidos en libros anteriores, supera en gran medida el tono entre romántico y nerudiano de muchas páginas (por ejemplo: "Yo huelo tierra floja y almacenes / huelo ese fondo oscuro de grillos y de zanjas / y llego yo / navío de maderas podridas / olvidado en río que arrastra cielo y cáscaras") y va encaminando su búsqueda hacia un lenguaje más contemporáneo. [DL]

5738 Faget, Rolando. No hay luz sin consecuencias. Montevideo: Ediciones de la Balanza, 1976/77 [i.e. 1977]. 57 p. (Serie Poesía)

Una de las voces más interesantes de la joven poesía uruguaya. Poesía de tono conversacional, que no excluye ni las influencias de los grandes poetas del siglo (Vallejo, Neruda) ni las incitaciones de la cotidianeidad. Una dichosa libertad expresiva ("Me enseñaron el olor del amor / es sur y rojo") aleja a estos poemas del empaque retórico; la búsqueda de la identidad poemática moviliza recursos de monólogo y diálogo: "Tengo que deshacer mi nombre / grano a grano / no sé qué arena soy / no sé si es jueves / tengo que descubrir mi nombre hoy / (tango del viudo) / tengo que deshacer y que inventar / saber como me llamo / ahora / para siempre." El poema incluye la reedición de *Poemas de río marrón* (1971), con un perspicaz prólogo de Enrique Estrázulas. [DL]

5739 Fernández Moreno, César. Buenos Aires me vas a matar: 15 poemas largos dispuestos a modo de autobiografía. México: Siglo Veintiuno Editores, 1977. 169 p. (La Creación literaria)

"La Tierra se ha quedado Negra y Sola" (1950)—una de las más bellas elegías de la poesía argentina—, "Argentino hasta la Muerte" (1954) y las dos composiciones "Un Argentino en Europa," son los poemas más valiosos de esta colección de Fernández Moreno (n. 1919), poeta y teórico de la posvanguardia argentina. [DL]

5740 Florián, Mario. Obra poética escogida, 1940–1976. Lima: Librería Studium, 1977 or 1978. 321 p.

Oportuna antología de un autor preocupado por las expresiones nativistas en la poesía peruana, que evidencia las cualidades de una escritura generalmente diáfana, en la que se resuelve con acierto la conflictiva asimilación de lo popular y lo culto. La muestra abarca la obra de Florián desde 1940, y permite apreciar su fidelidad a una temática arraigada en la circunstancia histórica y social. [PL]

5741 Fraire, Isabel. Poemas en el regazo de la muerte. México: Joaquín Mortiz, 1977. 85 p. (Las dos orillas)

Impressive pieces from an outstanding woman poet. Influenced by E.E. Cummings and Wallace Stevens among others, Fraire writes intellectually demanding works with here and there a touch of humor. This book gives further development to some of the themes of *Sólo esta luz* (see *HLAS 34:3817*) and is somewhat easier to understand than the earlier book. [CM]

5742 Franco, José. Horas testimoniales. Poesía. Panamá: INAC, 1976. 69 p.

Poemas en torno a Susuna, guerrillera uruguaya. José Franco depura el verso corto para deslindar los contornos poéticos de la protesta social. [RG]

5743 Frisch, Uwe. Contracantos. México: Joaquín Mortiz, 1971. 107 p. (Las dos orillas)

Winner of the Premio Nacional de Poesía 1970, this volume collects Frisch's poetry of 1958–65. While announced as "Canciones contra la Epoca," the works in their varied personal and existential statements are in harmony with a good part of Mexican poetry of the 1960s. [CM]

5744 Gallegos Mancera, Eduardo. Ancho río, alto fuego: 1964–1974. Caracas: n.p., 1975. 214 p.: ill.

Usually obvious Communist commitment, yet poet reflects views with surprising poetic genius. Striking images, rhythmic and sonorous free verse and profound emotion expressed without pathos. [BTO]

5745 Gangotena, Alfredo. Poesía completa. Traducciones de Gonzalo Escudero y Filoteo Samaniego. Mensaje de Jules Supervielle. Prólogo de Juan David García Bacca. 2. ed. Guayaquil: Casa de la Cultura Ecuatoriana, Núcleo del Guayas, 1978. 224 p. (Colección Letras del Ecuador; 58)

Este libro es una verdadera tarea de rescate de una obra casi desconocida en Hispanoamérica, a pesar de la primera edición de 1956. La sugerente poesía de Gangotena (n. 1904), escrita principalmente en francés, se aproxima en muchos aspectos a las preferencias superrealistas, sobre todo por el carácter de abierta aventura imaginaria que proponen sus textos y por la libertad de las asociaciones que los constituyen. La presente publicación permitirá reinscribir el nombre de su autor en el sitio que le corresponde. [PL]

5746 García Saraví, Gustavo. Salón para familias. Buenos Aires: Compañía Impresora Argentina, 1977. 73 p.

Composiciones de tono conversacional y a la vez intensamente poético, en donde la vida cotidiana aparece transfigurada y entrega al lector, a pesar de su aparente simplicidad, una visión renovada de la realidad. [DL]

5747 Garnier, Leonor. De las ocultas memorias. Poesía. San José: Editorial Costa Rica, 1974. 100 p.

En verso áspero, cortante, Leonor Garnier esquematiza la angustia ante lo rutinario, lo mediocre, lo convencional, lo falso. [RG]

5748 Gavidia, Francisco Antonio. Recopilación de José Mata Gavidia. Obras completas. v. 1/2. San Salvador: Ministerio de Educación, Dirección de Publicaciones, 1974. 2 v. (592, 455 p.)

Excelente edición de la obra poética de este insigne poeta salvadoreño, uno de los primeros consejeros poéticos de Rubén Darío. [RG]

5749 Gerbasi, Vicente. Retumba como un sótano del cielo. Caracas: Monte Avila Editores, 1977. 100 p. (Colección Altazor)

Deep, often inarticulate emotion underlies the poet's metaphor. Maturity concomitant with knowledge of and capacity to express the depths of these "underground" vibrations. [BTO]

5750 Girri, Alberto. Arbol de la estirpe humana. Buenos Aires: Editorial Sudamericana, 1978. 140 p. (Poesía)

Un libro más de uno de los mayores poetas argentinos, lleno de las agudas—y mentales—observaciones que constituyen su modalidad fundamental. Poesía en que la lógica o se rebela o canta pero no se somete al sentimiento, como si estuviera representada por la composición que ambiguamente se titula "¿En el Idioma de Hegel?," que comienza así: "Una lógica / de afirmaciones y negaciones, / y en el que toda / afirmación, negación, / se trasciende, / y con la cual, / con su perfecto armado, / se produce, atrae, / un vacío distante lo mismo / de la nada que de la existencia." Con sus manerismos y exageraciones, con sus subtextos alquímicos y filosóficos, con el armado riguroso de poemas que se aproximan a silogismos o que se desbarrancan súbitamente hacia palabras presuntamente antipoéticas, Girri construye una gran poesía y ocupa un territorio en el que reina de manera absoluta, al margen de toda debilidad sentimental tanto como de toda experimentación desaforada, y siempre en el dominio absoluto de su voz. [DL]

5751 Goded, Jaime. Poemas. México: Dirección General de Publicaciones, Universidad Nacional Autónoma de México, 1977. 87 p. (Colección Poemas y ensayos)

Interesting second collection of poetry by a promising writer. His first, *Poesía*, was published in 1969. [CM]

5752 González, Otto Raúl. La siesta del gorila y otros poemas. San José, Costa Rica: Editorial Universitaria Centroamericana (EDUCA), 1972. 122 p. (Colección Septimo día)

Poesía de honda preocupación social. Viet Nam, el negro estadounidense, la situación política de Guatemala, entre otras inquietudes, quedan presentados a través de imágenes fuertes en un lirismo conciso y calcinante. [RG]

5753 González de León, Ulalume. Plagio. México: Joaquín Mortiz, 1973. 131 p. (Las dos orillas)

Verse by an important figure on the Mexican literary scene. The daughter of Sara de Ibáñez in one section, "Plagios," creates poems by taking lines from other authors (Shakespeare, Proust, Pascal). Dazzling throughout. [CM]

5754 González Rincones, Salustio. Antología poética. Caracas: Monte Avila Editores, 1977. 207 p.; bibl. (Colección Altazor)

Long and erudite introduction to the poet and Venezuelan poetry by a contemporary poet-editor. Includes 58 poems from three different unpublished works and other published and unpublished poems written during González Rincones' European exile. He is a 20th-century Modernist who writes cryptogrammatic anti-poetry. Prematurely deceased, the poet reveals his needs in a desire to escape, to hide or in a wish for metamorphosis. [BTO]

5755 **González Tuñón, Raúl.** Poesías. Selección y prólogo de Félix Pita Rodríguez. La Habana: Casa de las Américas, 1977. 286 p. (Colección Literatura latinoamericana; 82)

Buena selección de las poesías del mejor de los "poetas sociales" de la Argentina, en cuyas páginas lo derivativo (por ejemplo, de Neruda) no llega a obliterar totalmente la expresión individual. Las figuras de "Juancito Caminador"—el poeta—y "la rosa blindada"—la poesía—son parte indeleble de la poesía argentina contemporánea. Es superficial el prólogo de Félix Pita Rodríguez, y arbitraria la cronología final. [DL]

5756 **Granata, María.** Antología poética. Buenos Aires: Emecé Editores, 1978. 152 p.

Selecciones de cuatro libros de poesía: *Umbral de tierra* (1942), *Muerte del adolescente* (1946), *Corazón cavado* (1952) y *Color humano* (1966), en general apegados a formas tradicionales que denotan su filiación neorromántica y su pertenencia a lo que en la Argentina se ha intentado definir como "generación de 1940." [DL]

5757 **Greiff, León de.** Antología de León de Greiff. Selección y prólogo de Germán Arciniegas. Notas de Abel Farina, Eduardo Castillo y Juan Lozano y Lozano. Lexicon incompleto por Alvaro Villar G. Bogotá: Instituto Colombiano de Cultura, Subdirección de Comunicaciones Culturales, División de Publicaciones, 1976 or 1977. 336 p.; bibl. (Biblioteca colombiana de cultura. Colección popular; 18)

Consists of poems selected by Germán Arciniegas who introduces this popular edition with a short prologue. The poems chosen are the least hermetic and most accessible to the public. The edition also includes a useful if somewhat incomplete Lexicon of De Greiff's poetic vocabulary (p. 205–312) and three articles by Colombian writers dated 1918, 1920 and 1956. [BTO]

5758 **Grütter, Virginia.** Poesía de este mundo. San José: Editorial Costa Rica, 1973. 99 p.

Virginia Grütter crea un lenguaje sencillo, coloquial, cargado de humor e ironía; en él vierte el sentimiento amoroso, el recuerdo de la infancia, la preocupación política. [RG]

5759 **Guardia, Miguel.** Tema y variaciones con otros poemas, 1952–1977. México: UNAM, 1978. 324 p. (Colección Poemas y ensayos)

Complete poetry of the Mexican poet and journalist. Contains *Tema y variaciones* (1952), *El retorno y otros poemas* (1956), *Palabra de amor* (1966), *Trece cuartillas* (1967), *Sólo vine a despedirme* (1968) and an unpublished book, "Atentamente." Guardia's subjects are personal and social matters and existential concerns. [CM]

5760 **Güiraldes, Ricardo.** Poemas místicos. 2. ed. Buenos Aires: Editorial Ricardo Güiraldes, 1977. 26 p.

Aunque disponibles en otros libros, estos siete poemas—publicados por primera vez en 1928, es decir póstumamente—aparecen aquí en una edición de notable decoro visual. El texto será de interés para los lectores del autor de *Don Segundo Sombra*, pues muestra su frecuentación del tema religioso y su familiaridad con el pensamiento oriental. [DL]

5761 **Guillén, Nicolás.** Obra poética. v. 1, 1920–1958; v. 2, 1958–1972. Ilustraciones del autor. La Habana: Instituto Cubano del Libro, 1972. 2 v.: ill. (Letras cubanas; 5)

Colección de obras del mayor poeta cubano, que comprende en el tomo 1 los poemas jóvenes inéditos (*Cerebro y corazón*, 1922) y los de transición (escritos entre 1927 y 1930), además de los libros significativos aparecidos a lo largo de 27 años: *Motivos de son* (1930), *Sóngoro cosongo* (1931), *West Indies, Ltd.* (1934), *Cantos para soldados y sones para turistas* (1937), *España* (1937), *El son entero* (1947) y *Elegías* (1948–1957), así como la poesía de sátira política escrita entre 1949–1953 y el poema en décimas "El Soldado Miguel Paz y el Sargento José Inés" (1952), no aparecidos antes en libro. El segundo tomo incluye *La paloma de vuelo popular* (1958), *Tengo* (1964), *Poemas de amor* (1964) y *El gran zoo* (1967), además de los hasta entonces inéditos *La rueda dentada* y *El diario que a diario* (1972, véase *HLAS 38:6955–6958*). También se incluyen en el primer volumen un importante prólogo de Angel Augier ("La Poesía de Nicolás

Guillén," que sitúa al cantor cubano en la línea histórica evolutiva que le llega desde José María Heredia y José Martí, forjadores de la poesía en el siglo XIX), y una detallada cronología. El segundo volumen se completa con una bibliografía activa y pasiva (que se aumentará en años posteriores con la publicada en 1975 por el Instituto Cubano del Libro, véase *HLAS 40:7196*, y el suplemento a la misma en 1977, véase item **5928**); y con un glosario de términos y frases cubanos útiles al lector no familiarizado con el lenguaje afroantillano. Es ésta una importante colección, que junto con las prosas (véase *HLAS 40:7232*) y sus más recientes colecciones y libros—*El corazón con que vivo* y *Poemas manuables*, 1975 (véase *HLAS 40:7084–7085*) y *Por el mar de las Antillas anda un barco de papel* (1977)—proporciona al estudioso un panorama cabal de la rica obra guilleniana, que crece cuantitativa y cualitativamente en sus casi 60 años de producción. [ER]

5762 Guzmán Cruchaga, Juan. Sed. Valparaíso: Ediciones Universitarias de Valparaíso, 1978. 79 p. (Colección Cruz del sur)

El último libro escrito por el autor de "Canción," poco antes de su muerte, acaecida en 1979. Poemas de corte clásico, dueños de un temple de ánimo sereno, tranparente, con algo de ese misterio infaltable en los poetas auténticos. [OH]

5763 Hahn, Oscar. Arte de morir. 2. ed. Santiago: Editorial Nascimento, 1979. 102 p.

Se publica en Chile el importante libro de Hahn (véase *HLAS 40:7088*), suceso del que se ha hecho cargo la crítica hispanoamericana con unánime interés. La nueva edición agrega cuatro textos que muestran el adensamiento de la expresión visionaria que define y sitúa a esta poesía renovadora y singular. [PL]

5764 Holguín, Andrés. Nueva aventura y otros poemas. Bogotá: Ediciones Tercer Mundo, 1977. 77 p.

Diplomat, literary critic, university professor and founder of *Razón y Fábula*, the poet selects, in reverse chronological order, poems he considers representative of his various books. Adds some previously unpublished compositions. His lyricism purifies as he develops and matures. [BTO]

5765 Huerta, David. Cuaderno de noviembre. México: Alacena/Era, 1976. 105 p.

Thoughtful verse on the nature and limits of memory by the son of Efraín Huerta. Although difficult, it is rewarding for the determined reader. [CM]

5766 ———. Versión. México: Fondo de Cultura Económica, 1978. 79 p. (Letras mexicanas)

Talented and sensitive poems on love, human existence, memory, the other, Oct. 1968 and a number of other subjects. Form and content are more complex than in his first book, *El jardín de la luz* (1972, see *HLAS 40:7093*). Huerta is one of the best of Mexico's young writers. [CM]

5767 Huerta, Efraín. Antología poética: homenaje. Prólogo de Rafael Solana. Guanajuato, México: Ediciones del Gobierno del Estado de Guanajuato, 1977. 223 p.

A collection of works from one of the best known of Mexico's *poetas comprometidos*. Concerned not only with political and social issues, Huerta writes also poetry with existential and erotic content. Included are selected poems from *Absoluto amor* (1935), *Línea del alba* (1936), *Poemas de guerra y esperanza* (1943), *Los hombres del alba* (1944), *La rosa primitiva* (1950), *Los poemas de viaje* (1956), *Estrella en alto* (1956), *El Tajín* (1963), *Otros poemas*, *Poemas prohibidos y de amor* (see item **5768**), *Los poemínimos* (1974), *Los eróticos y otros poemas* (1974) and *Circuito interior* (1977). This is an especially valuable anthology since it often contains selections that are different from those in the Mortiz anthology of 1968 as well as Huerta's more recent poetry. [CM]

5768 ———. Poemas prohibidos y de amor. México: Siglo Veintiuno Editores, 1973. 150 p. (Colección mínima)

A selection of poems from four decades. The themes are political and personal. [CM]

5769 Illescas, Carlos. Manual de simios y otros poemas. México: UNAM, Dirección General de Publicaciones, 1977. 148 p. (Colección Poemas y ensayos)

En Carlos Illescas—aunque exiliado—tiene Guatemala un poeta mayor. La riqueza del léxico, la amplitud y sonoridad de los ritmos y la sólida textura del poema le imparten a su obra un lirismo hondo, cargado de la esencia vital de los elementos terrestres. [RG]

5770 **Juarroz, Roberto.** Poesía vertical. Antología mayor. Introducción de Roger Munier. Buenos Aires: Ediciones C. Lohlé, 1978. 219 p.

Un gran poeta, de lenguaje propio extraordinariamente exigente y depurado, donde la profundidad más contemporánea de los planteamientos poéticos se une a cierto carácter clásico de la enunciación en armonioso equilibrio. Juarroz (n. 1925) se dedica desde hace más de 20 años a la teoría y la práctica de la "poesía vertical," concepto este último que recibe una exégesis brillante en la notable introducción de Roger Munier. Desde los primeros poemas (1958) hasta la *Sexta poesía vertical* (1975) y los poemas adicionales de *Nueva poesía vertical* (1977), aparece aquí una selección nutrida, que presenta lo mejor y lo más permanente, si así puede decirse, de un poeta que jamás decae en su nivel de calidad. Indispensable para el especialista en literatura argentina y de sumo interés para el lector de poesía de cualquier país. [DL]

5771 **Kamenszain, Tamara.** Los no. Buenos Aires: Editorial Sudamericana, 1977. 67 p. (Poesía)

La referencia inicial es al teatro *No* japonés; los poemas finales tienen que ver con el circo criollo; todos ellos se articulan alrededor de los símbolos de estas y otras representaciones, es decir, de los elementos fundamentales de irrealidad en la vida humana. Una inquisición que no es sólo estética sino también metafísica otorga unidad a estos notables poemas de una joven autora cuya producción debe ser seguida por los especialistas. [DL]

5772 **Kovadloff, Santiago.** Zonas e indagaciones. Buenos Aires: Botella al Mar, 1978. 47 p.

Kovadloff (n. 1942) es uno de los jóvenes poetas argentinos cuya obra está aún en pleno desarrollo. Este libro ofrece una buena muestra de su calidad poética y de la seriedad de su búsqueda, frecuentemente centrada en el lenguaje: "Oscuros, súbitos signos; pronombres, nombres, giros de tu sintaxis;/ el deleite de describir y contar imprimiéndole al vaso,/ a episodios céntricos, ánimos variables, tu sello" (p. 16). Un poeta cuya producción futura hay que seguir con atención. [DL]

5773 **Lastra, Pedro.** Noticias del extranjero. México: Premiá Editora, 1979. 101 p.

La poesía de Pedro Lastra provoca en el lector un temple de ánimo que puede ser descrito como un sentimiento resignado de la fugacidad de las cosas y de las relaciones humanas. Dicho sentimiento no surge de una constatación meramente positivista que se agota en su formulación: el hablante queda a la vez conmovido existencialmente por ella. Pero su reacción no se manifiesta en el nivel de los significantes; se produce más bien la enajenación del hablante, y lo que queda en primer plano es el temple de ánimo que hemos señalado. Poesía fina—sin connotaciones artepuristas—, en el sentido de que no emplea elementos estilísticos decorativos. El lenguaje aparece en su desnudez y son los signos ceros los que funcionan como significantes. *Noticias del extranjero* instala a Pedro Lastra en la primera línea de la poesía chilena actual. [OH]

5774 **Lezama Lima, José.** Fragmentos a su imán. Prólogos de Cintio Vitier y José Agustín Goytisolo. Barcelona: Lumen, 1978. 187 p. (El Bardo; 131)

Segunda edición póstuma del desaparecido poeta cubano, que recoge poemas escritos entre 1970 y 1976. Esta edición de *Fragmentos* añade un prólogo de José Agustín Goytisolo, "La Espiral Milagrosa," que complementa el de Cintio Vitier ("Nueva Lectura de Lezama") a la edición cubana (La Habana: Arte y Literatura, 1977). Junto a su novela póstuma, *Oppiano Licario* (véase *HLAS 40:6690*), este último libro poético culmina una obra rica y profunda, comenzada en 1937 con *Muerte de Narciso* y desarrollada en *Enemigo rumor* (1941), *Aventuras sigilosas* (1945), *La fijeza* (1949), *Dador* (1960) y *Orbita de Lezama Lima* (1966). En ella, según Vitier, el poeta dejaba el objeto en su "místico exterior" y lo reducía a "sustancia paladeable de lo desconocido;" pero *Fragmentos*, a diferencia de sus textos más herméticos, es poesía casi clara y medular, expresiva de una fina angustia que ejecuta el supremo inventario de ese gran "animal mitológico" que fue Lezama, y lo humaniza hacia el fin, lo hace mayor y más completo en su iridescente arborescencia. [ER]

Lihn, Enrique. The dark room and other poems. See item **6640**.

5775 ———. A partir de Manhattan. Valparaíso, Chile: Ediciones Ganymedes, 1979. 70 p.

En una línea ya característica dentro de la poesía de Lihn—la de la "poesía de paso," inaugurada por el libro homónimo—se inscribe el núcleo de esta nueva obra del poeta chileno. El hablante se configura como el residente pasajero de algún lugar del mundo, bajo el estímulo de la alienante realidad que lo rodea. Esta vez el fundamento referencial es la ciudad de New York. Su visión de la gran urbe le provoca una mezcla de náusea y espanto, y en este aspecto es afín a la de García Lorca en *Poeta en Nueva York*. Pero más allá de esta compartida repulsión, el tratamiento verbal es absolutamente distinto en ambos poetas. García Lorca establece un sistema de connotaciones cuya clave es difícil de develar y que redunda frecuentemente en un buscado hermetismo de cuño surrealista. Enrique Lihn, en cambio, ejercita un suerte de realismo fenomenológico, que le permite sondear el referente mismo y hacerlo emitir signos acerca de la condición humana, en un lenguaje cercano al de las notas de viaje. Sólo que en esta ocasión se trata de un viaje—no excento de horror, pero sí de grandeza—, al infierno impersonal de la monstruosa cosmópolis. [OH]

5776 **Liscano Velutini, Juan.** Rayo que al alcanzarme . . . 1974–1976. Caracas: Monte Avila Editores, 1978. 95 p. (Colección Altazor)

The poet reveals his mastery of words chosen to express his profound feelings about life, fleeting time and inevitable death. [BTO]

5777 **Llerena, Edith.** La piel de la memoria. Madrid: Playor, 1976. 108 p. (Nueva poesía)

Libro sorprendente, tal vez la poesía de más alto perfil estético entre las mujeres que escriben fuera de Cuba. De tono levemente nostálgico, se salva en su firmeza de recuerdo concreto y plástico. Esta poeta, que según declaración propia empezó a escribir versos en 1968, fue lamentablemente excluida (u omitida) de un libro donde hubiera brillado con luz singular, *La última poesía cubana* (véase *HLAS 38:6911*). [ER]

5778 **López Degregori, Carlos.** Un buen día: 1975–1977. Portada y diagramación de Luis Rebaza. Lima: Ediciones La Sagrada Familia, 1978. 1 v. (Unpaged)

Texto dividido en 12 secciones o estancias, que conforman los momentos de una reflexión cuya materia es la incertidumbre y la extrañeza de lo real. El libro sugiere dos lecturas, según se consideren las partes aisladas o se atienda al sentido del conjunto. Un acierto constructivo de López Degregori (1953), que resuelve las exigencias de su escritura mediante cortes y variaciones, y el empleo oportuno y vigilado de recursos dialógicos e interrogativos. [PL]

5779 **Luque Muñoz, Henry.** Lo que puede la mirada, 1974–1976. Bogotá: Editorial Andes, 1977. 89 p. (Colección de poesía música del bosque)

Poems with innumerable images and metaphors affirm that the imagination is absolute liberty. They also indicate an effort to impart feeling to the intellectual and to make his emotions understandable. [BTO]

5780 **McKay, Roberto.** Producción Tobango. Panamá: Ediciones INAC, 1977. 197 p. (Colección múltiple; 10. Sección Poesía)

El erotismo es la vena más sobresaliente en la poesía de McKay. El libro, que recoge obra escrita entre 1965 y 1976, registra un paulatino desbroce de los procedimientos expresivos hasta desembocar en los lúcidos aciertos de "Tejado sobre Paredes apenas Levantadas" (1974). [RG]

5781 **Mallman, Arturo.** Tentativas. Buenos Aires: Editorial Tres Tiempos, 1977. 1 v. (Unpaged)

Breve colección—probablemente la primera—de un poeta de tono meditativo y grave, que alcanza su mejor tono en la expresión que bucea en la propia identidad: "Ya entregué todas mis armas./ Nadie apunta hacia mí./ Ahora, el enemigo que tengo/ soy yo." [DL]

5782 **Martí, José.** Ismaelillo. Edición facsimilar, introducción y notas de Angel Augier. La Habana: Editorial Arte y Literatura, 1976 [i.e. 1977]. 173 p.: ill.

Hermosa edición facsimilar (de la de 1882) de un libro clave en la poesía hispanoamericana. En la introducción, Angel Augier resume los antecedentes históricos del texto, importantes a todo estudioso de Martí, hace un esbozo analítico del libro en cuanto primicia del modernismo (simbolismo titular, recursos estilísticos, rasgos del lenguaje) y complementa su ensayo sobre el proceso de creación poética del maestro cubano con una rica serie de fotografías, zincografías y reproducciones de cartas y originales en verso. Es un valioso libro, hecho con esmero y exquisitez en la tipografía, el formato y la calidad artística de la impresión: digno homenaje a la obra "más hermosa que padre alguno haya escrito al hijo de su sangre." Se completa con un apéndice de concordancias que coteja las variantes en el texto de 1882 con los manuscritos martianos. [ER]

5783 Martínez Ocaranza, Ramón. Elegía de los triángulos. México: Editorial Diógenes, 1974. 156 p.

A resident of Morelia, Martínez Ocaranza writes poetry heavily imbued with the Indian past. Often this is a framework for social and political comments on the events of 1968. [CM]

5784 Méndez, Concha. Antología poética. Surtidor; Canciones de mar y tierra; Vida a vida; Niño y sombras; Lluvias enlazadas; Sombras y sueños. México: Joaquín Mortiz, 1976. 123 p. (Las dos orillas)

The accomplished poetry of Concha Méndez (b. 1898) is usually delicately personal, occasionally anguished. Included here are selections from works published between 1928 and 1944. Méndez was married to the Spanish poet Manuel Altolaguirre. [CM]

5785 Michelena, Alejandro. Formas y fórmulas. Montevideo: Libros de Granaldea, 1978. 23 p.

Trece poemas, algunos de los cuales bordean el prosaísmo; en los mejores, sin embargo, la falta de tensión expresiva no impide la aparición de modestos trazos iluminadores, como cuando habla de "gente que camina / por el mismo rincón años y años / y luego se retira / a sentarse en la plaza con palomas / y cree que fue importante / ese papel tocado por sus manos." Esta atención a lo humano alrededor suyo parece una característica de los versos de Michelena y le ofrece ocasión para un cierto tipo de testimonio. [DL]

5786 Millán, Gonzalo. La ciudad. Québec, Canada: Les Editions Maison Culturelle Québec-Amérique Latine, 1979. 120 p.

Este extenso poema representa una muestra del "objetivismo" poético preconizado por Gonzalo Millán, que consiste en la mención llana de sucesos y cosas, sin agregados de ninguna naturaleza que contribuyan a dibujar alguna imagen del hablante. Una serie de frases construidas con la estructura de la oración gramatical simple se suceden entonces, intentando fundar "la ciudad," en cuyo seno coexisten diversos elementos relacionados con el golpe militar chileno. Esta tentativa del bien dotado poeta que es Millán resulta a la postre más interesante que eficaz. Porque si bien es laudable su propósito renovador, no lo es en cambio el resultado. La larga enumeración del mismo esquema sintáctico durante 119 p. redunda en una monotonía fatigante. Millán parece no haber vislumbrado que un poema largo debe someterse a ciertas leyes estructurales (entre ellas las relativas a los juegos de clímax y anticlímax), y que no consiste en una mera adición vegetativa de frases petrificadas, que se acumulan en una ilusión de crecimiento, pero que en realidad no avanzan hacia ninguna parte. [OH]

5787 Mitre, Eduardo. Ferviente humo: 1966–1968. Ilustraciones de Mario Vargas Cuéllar. Cochabamba, Bolivia: Ediciones Portales, 1976. 39 p.: ill.

Los textos recogidos aquí pertenecen a un plazo intermedio entre los dos libros publicados por Mitre (1943): *Elegía a una muchacha* (1965) y *Morada* (1975). Estos poemas completan el curso de un pausado proceso de desarrollo y permiten evaluar la trayectoria de un autor que merece atención. Palabra nítida y controlada, que opera con sabiduría en el nivel connotativo. [PL]

5788 Montes de Oca, Marco Antonio. Las constelaciones secretas. Buenos Aires: Fondo de Cultura Económica, 1976. 68 p. (Letras mexicanas)

Witty and moving at the same time, Montes de Oca explores the serious issues of man's existence with a light touch. While the form and language of these poems are unlike those of his early works (see *HLAS 34:3831–3834*), the talent and originality are the same. [CM]

5789 ———. En honor de las palabras. México: Joaquín Mortiz, 1979. 67 p. (Las dos orillas)

Brilliant collection composed of seven long poems. In their metaphorical and linguistic inventiveness, these works resemble Montes de Oca's early poetry more than do the poems of *Lugares donde el espacio cicatriza* and *Las constelaciones secretas* (see items **5788** and **5790**). The writer's metaphysical concerns have perhaps their most impressive development in "Entre las Dos y las Tres," "A Primera Sangre" and "El Santo Sepulcro." [CM]

———. The heart of the flute. See item **6641**.

5790 ———. Lugares donde el espacio cicatriza. México: Joaquín Mortiz, 1974. 1 v. (Unpaged): ill. (Las dos orillas)

In a book that unites experimentally the visual and the conceptual, Montes de Oca gives further development to some of his familiar preoccupations—fate, existence, poetry, identity, to name a few. Although the form (prose poems here) differs from that of *Se llama como quieras* (1974, see *HLAS 38:6980*), the concerns and the sense of humor are similar. Unusual in this book is the inclusion of some political commentary. Rewarding, as always is the case with Montes de Oca. [CM]

5791 Morales, Beltrán. Juicio final, Andante. León: Universidad Nacional Autónoma de Nicaragua, 1976. 132 p. (Colección Poesía; 11)

Poemas cortos, cortantes; predominio del *collage* en la forma y de la sátira en el tono; uso de la invectiva y de la palabrota: Beltrán Morales es poeta violento, iconoclasta. Los poemas de *Juicio final* son del período 1966–69, en tanto que los de *Andante* fueron escritos entre 1970–75. [RG]

Moro, César. The scandalous life of César Moro: in his own words. See item **6642**.

5792 Muñoz Salazar, Eduardo. Las canciones iluminadas. Quito: Casa de la Cultura Ecuatoriana, 1974. 85 p.: ill. (Colección Poetas del Ecuador; 7)

Una voluntad de precisión y de control preside la escritura de estos poemas. Las imágenes de la naturaleza o las situaciones emocionales suelen definirse con una parquedad cercana a la del *hai-kai*, y también con parecido poder de sugerencia. Libro de interés en la joven poesía ecuatoriana, por lo que contiene y por lo que anuncia: una conducta poética que se orienta hacia el rigor. [PL]

5793 Nadereau, Efraín. Y fue el pasado ardiendo. La Habana: Ediciones Unión, 1978. 99 p. (Colección Manjuarí/Poesía)

Interesante libro de corte épico, que testimonia hechos de la historia de Cuba en una vena hermana a Neruda y Cardenal. Los libros anteriores del poeta habían recibido premios y menciones: *Tránsito por la naturaleza* (1969), *A final de la palabra* (1971) y *La isla que habitamos* (1972). [ER]

5794 Nájar, Jorge. Patio de peregrinos. Lima: Proceso, 1976. 70 p.: ill.

Esta poesía revela la presencia de un hablante obsedido por el conflicto entre lo ensoñado y lo vivido. Su exploración "en busca de una verdad oculta," vislumbrada y desmentida al mismo tiempo, ocurre en un espacio que se establece siempre entre esos polos conflictivos: ley estructural que confiere unidad y dinamismo dramático al conjunto. Invención, sueño, dibujo, grabado (de escenarios y situaciones) son aquí signos de un mismo campo semántico, fuertemente valorizado. Esos signos, y la cercanía de sus contrarios entregan la clave de esta nueva aventura poética de Nájar. [PL]

5795 Navarrete, Raúl. Memoria de la especie. México: Joaquín Mortiz, 1978. 86 p.

Winner of the Premio Nacional de Poesía 1977, this book presents sensitive verse on many topics. Navarrete is a writer of definite talent. [CM]

5796 Nogales Guzmán, Eduardo; Eddy Quintana Lanza; and **Nicomedes Suárez.** Poemas. La Paz, Bolivia: Casa Municipal de la Cultura Franz Tamayo, 1978. 266 p. (Biblioteca paceña. Nueva serie)

Los tres libros incluidos (*Raíces de ceniza viva* de Nogales, *Con los cinco sentidos* de Quintana y *Caballo al anochecer* de Suárez) merecieron el premio Mención en el XI Concurso Anual de Literatura Franz Tamayo, de 1977. Sobresale entre ellos el conjunto de Nicomedes Suárez—*Caballo al anochecer*—, cuya singularidad reside en la sugestiva irrealización de la materia natural que simula ser su referente. Poesía que puede desconcertar por su apariencia de ingenuidad, que no es sino sutileza en el empleo de recursos e indicios irrealizadores. [PL]

5797 Núñez, Rafael. Poesías. Prólogo de Ramón de Zubiría. Estudios de Carlos Valderrama Andrade y Nicolás del Castillo Mathieu. Bogotá: Instituto Caro y Cuervo, 1977. 402 p.: ill.; bibl. (Biblioteca colombiana; 13)

This volume reproduces a 1914 edition, adds 34 unpublished poems selected from a notebook, single sheets published in Cartagena, and two albums of unpublished poems dedicated to María Gregoria de Haro. The poems are arranged according to date of publication not date of composition. Regrettably, the edition is not critical but it provides an admirable selection of Núñez's complete poems and the introductions to each section discuss valuable information and offer, where possible, the poems' dates of composition. [BTO]

5798 O'Hara, Edgar. Mientras una tórtola canta en el techo de enfrente. Portada y diagramación de Luis Rebaza. Lima: Ruray/ Poesía, 1979. 46 p.

Breve antología de un sector de la obra de O'Hara (1954), que incluye textos escritos entre 1973 y 1977, publicados en *Situaciones de riesgo* (1974), *Orígenes y finalidades* (1976) y *La mujer de luna llena* (1978). Los poemas seleccionados ilustran una empresa fervorosa y lúcida de fundación de una poética, que el autor denomina "de la conciencia." El término define con propiedad el carácter de esta poesía variada y precisa, que sitúa a O'Hara en un lugar de importancia en la literatura actual de su país. [PL]

5799 Oraá, Francisco de. Bodegón de las llamas. La Habana: Editorial Letras Cubanas, 1978. 42 p. (Colección Mínima poesía, 12)

Muestrario de textos de uno de los poetas de la primera promoción revolucionaria (que publicaron obra ya madura en los 60). Estilo diferente al conversacional, con concienzudas metáforas. [ER]

Pacheco, José Emilio. Don't ask me how the time goes by. Poems, 1964–1968. See item **6645**.

5800 ———. Islas a la deriva. México: Siglo Veintiuno Editores, 1976. 159 p. (Creación literaria)

A collection of poems on many different subjects by one of Mexico's leading authors. It includes, among others, meditations on time, the mysteries of nature, Mexico's past and present and memories of Canada. There are two sections of poetry translated and reworked from other sources, one from Constantine Cavafy and the other from a Greek anthology. [CM]

5801 Parra, Nicanor. Sermones y prédicas del Cristo de Elqui. Santiago: Universidad de Chile, Facultad de Ciencias Físicas y Matemáticas, Estudios Humanísticos, 1977. 21 leaves: ill.

La idea motriz del libro es interesante: el empleo de un personaje casi legendario, de profunda raigambre popular, como hablante de los poemas. La elección de Parra es acertada: Domingo Zárate Vega, charlatán religioso chileno, conocido también como "el Cristo de Elqui." Pero a pesar de cierto trabajo intertextual con los escritos de Zárate, todo termina por convertirse en un acto de fonomímica, en el que la única voz que se escucha es la del antipoeta de los "artefactos," con su rebuscada audacia, con sus chistes supuestamente desacralizadores, con su iconoclastia que ya no asusta ni convence a nadie y con sus seudo ingeniosidades, entre las que brillan perlas como las siguientes: "En Chile no se respetan los derechos humanos . . . Claro que yo les voy a pedir que me digan / en qué país se respetan los derechos humanos." [OH]

5802 Parra del Riego, Juan. Poesía. Huancayo, Perú: Casa de la Cultura de Junín, n.d. 204 p.

Se edita por primera vez en el Perú la obra poética completa de Parra del Riego (1894–1925), reunida y publicada en Montevideo por Esther de Cáceres en 1943. Rescate justo de una poesía influyente en su tiempo, por la singularidad de los temas—la exaltación del dinamismo de la vida contemporánea—y por su audacia formal: la recurrencia a versificaciones provocativas, como el polirritmo. [PL]

5803 Paz, Octavio. Pasado en claro. México: Fondo de Cultura Económica, 1975. 44 p.

A long poem containing many of the writer's favorite themes, among them meditations on the nature of identity, memory, language, artistic creation, ancient Mexico, youth, time and death. In its choice of subjects, the work seems in many ways a companion piece to *Vuelta* (1976, see *HLAS 40:7133*). [CM]

5804 ———. Poemas: 1935–1975. Barcelona: Seix Barral, 1979. 719 p., 8 leaves of plates: ill.

Handsome, well-done edition of most of the poetry of a leading Spanish-American writer. Includes *Libertad bajo palabra* (1935–57, see *HLAS 24:5443*); *Días hábiles* (1958–61); *Homenaje y profanaciones* (1960); *Salamandra* (1958–61, see *HLAS 28:2161*); *Sólo a dos voces* (1961); *Ladera este* (1962–68, see *HLAS 36:6587*); *Hacia el comienzo* (1964–68); *Blanco* (1966, see *HLAS 32:4220*); *Topoemas* (1968, see *HLAS 36:6588*); *Vuelta* (1969–75, see *HLAS 40:7133*); *Pasado en claro* (1974). Also contains three prose works—*¿Aguila o sol?* (1949–50); *La hija de Rappaccini* (1956); *El mono gramático* (1974)—which the author believes overlap the boundaries of poetry. Eleven poems suppressed in the 1968 edition of *Libertad bajo palabra* have been reinstated, others have been revised and some works reordered in accordance with Paz's affirmation that "los poemas son objetos verbales inacabados e inacabables." [CM]

5805 Paz Paredes, Margarita. Litoral del tiempo. Antología poética. Presentación de Efraín Huerta. Prólogo de Roberto Oropeza Martínez. Guanajuato, México: Ediciones del Gobierno del Estado de Guanajuato, 1978. 252 p.: ill.

Welcome selection of works from one of Mexico's most important poets. Contains verse from *Sonaja* (1942); *Voz de la tierra* (1946); *El anhelo plural* (1948); *Andamios de sombra* (1949); *Dimensión del silencio* (1953); *Presagio en el viento* (1955); *Casa en la niebla* (1956); *Rebelión de ceniza* (1960); *La imagen y su espejo* (1962); *El rostro imposible* (1963); *Adán en sombra* (1964); *Lumbre cautiva* (1968); *Señales* (1972); *El crimen fue en Santiago* (1973); *Otra vez la muerte* (1976); *Puerta de luz líquida* (1978) and two unpublished poems, "El Ser Imaginario con Quien la Soledad Quisiera Conversar" and "Carta desde un Lugar Cualquiera." Paz Paredes' subject matter is both personal and social. [CM]

5806 Paz Soldán y Unanue, Pedro. Poesías completas. v. 2. Lima: Academia Peruana de la Lengua, 1975. 1 v. (Clásicos peruanos; 2)

Según el plan anunciado por Estuardo Núñez en el vol. 1 (véase *HLAS 40:7134*), se incluyen en este vol. 2 los ocho "Poemas Mayores" del autor y otros textos no recogidos anteriormente en libro, como "Rimas del Rímac y Chispazos" y "Nuevos Chispazos." Valioso aporte para el estudio de la poesía del siglo XIX en el Perú y en Hispanoamérica. [PL]

5807 Pedroso, Regino. Obra poética. La Habana: Editorial Arte y Literatura, 1975. 352 p. (Colección Letras cubanas)

Colección de libros del poeta proletario. Contiene un interesante prólogo de Félix Pita Rodríguez, donde se traza el itinerario de la llamada poesía social en los años anteriores a 1959, "Regino Pedroso y la Nueva Poesía Cubana" (véase item **5808**). [ER]

5808 ———. Regino Pedroso. Selección y prólogo de Osvaldo Navarro, con la colaboración del autor y de su esposa, Petra Ballagas. La Habana: Unión de Escritores y Artistas de Cuba, 1975. 481 p., bibl., 8 leaves of plates: ill. (Colección Orbita)

Antología crítica de la obra en prosa y verso de uno de los autores de raigambre popular que más se destacaron en la Cuba prerrevolucionaria, señalado también por sus luchas políticas (los otros dos serían los poetas Manuel Navarro Luna y Nicolás Guillén). De valor a los estudiosos de la poesía social en el Caribe. [ER]

5809 Pereira, Gustavo. Segundo libro de los somaris. Caracas: Monte Avila Editores, 1979. 67 p. (Colección Los espacios cálidos)

Concise "somaris," a form invented by the gifted, young poet inspired by Oriental styles such as the *haiku*. [BTO]

5810 Pérez, Hildebrando. Aguardiente y otros cantares. La Habana: Casa de las Américas, 1978. 77 p.

Este libro mereció el Primer Premio en el Concurso Casa de las Américas (1978). Dos partes lo constituyen—"Aguardiente" y "Cantar de Hildebrando"—y en ellas se cruzan diversas exploraciones poéticas del mundo propio, como naturaleza e historia cercanas. El grado de elaboración no es siempre sostenido y a veces condesciende con la monotonía discursiva, pero adquiere relieve en la condensación expresiva y en la recurrencia a ciertas formas características del cancionero nativo. [PL]

5811 Petit de Murat, Ulyses. Agonías de la memoria. Buenos Aires: Emecé, 1977. 84 p.

Como en otros libros del autor, el tono elegíaco—aquí representado por composiciones dedicadas a Leonor Acevedo de Borges, a Eugene O'Neill y al músico popular Aníbal Troilo, entros otros—es el predominante: poesía torturada, con algunas lejanas deudas con el surrealismo y otras más claras con el existencialismo, y testimonio valioso de un quehacer poético incesante. [DL]

5812 ———. Marea de lágrimas y otros poemas: 1929–1977. Buenos Aires: Ediciones Botella al Mar, 1978. 89 p.

A pesar de la brevedad del volumen, una importante compilación que recoge poemas de casi medio siglo. Entre ellos, el espléndido "Marea de Lágrimas" (de *Conmemoraciones*, 1929) y el conversacional "Elegía Menor a Horacio Quiroga" (de *Marea de lágrimas*, 1937) son dos notables composiciones elegíacas. Esta antología, inteligentemente organizada, concluye con "Afirmación," un texto en prosa sobre la poesía, datado en 1976: "una y otra vez poesía, esa invasión, esa marea, esa dicha de poder tenerle fe a la suprema irrealidad, a la constante vacilación de las palabras." Poeta insuficientemente conocido y que hay que estudiar. [DL]

5813 **Piña, Cristina.** Oficio de máscaras. Buenos Aires: Botella al Mar, 1979. 83 p.

Profunda poesía aparentemente organizada sobre la búsqueda del lenguaje, pero que supera ese nivel para constituir una serie de entradas en la reflexión metafísica; poesía, en consecuencia, que tiene en el silencio su destino último, tal como está, indicado en uno de los poemas, el titulado "Todo Jardín Prohibido" en donde se lee: "pájaro ciego / trazando alucinados / itinerarios truncos / en la caja de cristal / de la palabra / el nombre se suicida / en blancas estructuras de vocales / y la flor del silencio / martillea las manos." Una gran poeta. [DL]

5814 **Plá, Josefina.** Antología poética: 1927–1977. Asunción?: Ediciones Cabildo, 1977. 97 p.: ill.

La distinguida poeta (n. 1909) pero incorporada a la vida intelectual del Paraguay desde 1927—data de los poemas iniciales recogidos en su primer libro, *El precio de los sueños* (1934)—, entrega aquí una buena selección (aunque modestamente impresa) de su poesía hasta la fecha, incluyendo algunos poemas no publicados en libro. Interesante testimonio de una valiosa personalidad femenina. [DL]

5815 **Quirós, Rodrigo.** En defensa del tiempo. Poemas. San José: Editorial Costa Rica, 1977. 44 p.

En estos poemas, Quirós se enfrenta al amor vivencial para dilucidarlo y, al transformarlo en materia lírica, descubre que el amor es temporalidad y el tiempo, puro impulso amoroso. [RG]

5816 **Radaelli, Sigfrido Augusto.** Poesía total, 1965–1975. Prólogo de Guillermo Ara. Buenos Aires: Plus Ultra, 1978. 189 p.

Poesía reflexiva, meditativa, profunda, sin novedades formales pero de alta dignidad expresiva, que frecuentemente asume el tema mismo de la poesía: "Lo que ocurre / es que detrás de tu silencio, / para quien sepa acercarse a tu corazón y escucharlo, / hay un canto," dice en *Hombre callado* (1965), el primero de los cuatro libros aquí compilados. [DL]

5817 **Rebaza, Luis.** Población activa: 1976–1977. Lima: Ediciones La Sagrada Familia, 1978. 28 p.: ill. (Poesía; 2)

Primera entrega poética de Rebaza (n. 1958), que cuenta entre sus méritos una apreciable destreza para configurar, en breves trazos verbales, situaciones provocativas y sugerentes. Poesía que procede por fusión y condensación de imágenes; que a menudo dibuja actitudes o gestos y los valoriza por medio de alusiones y de alianzas insólitas. [PL]

5818 **Rivero, Raúl.** Poesía sobre la tierra. La Habana: Ediciones Unión, 1973. 63 p. (Premio UNEAC de Poesía 1972 Julián del Casal)

Aunque tardíamente, esta anotación destaca la obra de un buen poeta de la segunda promoción revolucionaria. Su primer libro, *Papel de hombre*, había recibido el Premio David en 1969; en ambos sobresale un genuino lirismo, y dentro de la experiencia contemporánea en Cuba, una amorosa sensualidad hacia las cosas. [ER]

5819 **Robleto, Octavio.** El día y sus laberintos. León: Universidad Nacional Autónoma de Nicaragua, 1976. 144 p. (Colección Poesía; 10)

Octavio Robleto ha hecho del epigrama su forma favorita. La rutina cotidiana, el amor y la muerte están plasmados en poemas de sutil ironía y gran soltura. Cuando ensaya el soneto, sin embargo, se le contrae la mano y el poema sale tenso, falto de naturalidad. [RG]

5820 Rocasolano, Alberto. Es de humanos. La Habana: Unión de Escritores y Artistas de Cuba, 1976. 144 p. (Manjuarí: Poesía)

Tercer libro publicado por el poeta, donde continúa una trayectoria de testigo cotidiano del suceder. En Rocasolano se ilustra bien el estilo conversacional de la nueva poesía cubana (antes evidenciado en sus poemarios *Diestro en soledades y esperanzas,* (1967) y *A cara y cruz* (1970). [ER]

5821 Rossler, Osvaldo. El cuerpo escrito, 1950–1977. Buenos Aires: Losada, n.d. 78 p. (Poetas de ayer y de hoy).

En las páginas preliminares, Rossler dice que algunos de sus poemas "pueden ser juzgados en una línea intermedia entre lo tradicional y la expresión de vanguardia." También afirma: "nunca he dejado de pensar que la poesía antes que nada es imagen." Ambas afirmaciones son correctas y sirven para entender mejor una poesía que frecuentemente (como en los poemas de *Hombre interior,* 1963) adquiere una notable tensión metafísica. [DL]

5822 Sabat Ercasty, Carlos. Sonetos de las agonías y los éxtasis. Montevideo: Academia Nacional de Letras, 1977. 196 p. (Biblioteca de la Academia Nacional de Letras. Serie III, Escritos)

Este nutrido sonetario, escrito al filo de los 90 años, no aporta nuevas perspectivas a la distinguida carrera poética de Sabat Ercasty, pero ofrece la constancia de una admirable fidelidad a la poesía. A los 60 años de la publicación de su primer libro—*Pantheos* (1917)—es notable verificar la persistencia de temas e imágenes fundamentales del modernismo. [DL]

5823 Sabines, Jaime. Nuevo recuento de poemas. México: Joaquín Mortiz, 1977. 291 p. (Biblioteca paralela)

Welcome edition of the complete poetry up to the moment of a writer who has been a significant figure in Mexican literature since 1950. Contains the following works: *Horal* (1950); *La señal* (1951); *Adán y Eva* (1952); *Tarumba* (1956); *Diario seminario y poemas en prosa* (1961); *Poemas sueltos* (1962); *Yuria* (1967); *Algo sobre la muerte del mayor Sabines* (1973); and *Maltiempo* (1972, see *HLAS 36:6594*). [CM]

5824 Sajón de Cuello, Raquel. Columpiaba el alto cielo una alondra . . . La Plata, Argentina, n.p., 1976. 114 p.

Acentos neorrománticos perviven, tenuemente modificados, en este libro—tercero de la autora, después de *En la alta noche* (1959) y *Tiempo de cenizas* (1965)—de profundo intimismo, gran dignidad expresiva y constante buceo en los temas fundamentales del hombre: el tiempo, la muerte, el amor. La figura materna ilumina y unifica el discurso poético. De especial interés para la crítica que sigue el desarrollo de la literatura escrita por mujeres. Importante también para quienes se interesan por la poesía en La Plata, ciudad que, aunque próxima a Buenos Aires, tiene rasgos propios ejemplificados en una larga serie de poetas. [DL]

5825 Salado, Minerva. Tema sobre un paseo. La Habana: Ediciones Unión, 1978. 61 p. (Premio UNEAC de Poesía 1977 Julián del Casal)

Segundo libro de una joven poeta cubana, quien con su *Al cierre* (1972) había ganado el Premio "David" de la Unión de Escritores y Artistas de Cuba. En el primero la distinguía una original concreción de lenguaje testimonial, dialogado ("poemas radiofónicos"), de temas y personajes revolucionarios. En éste, la celebración de una ciudad y de una vida se concentra en un lirismo sutil y hondo, que prescinde de artificios y hasta de puntuación, y que convoca al amor para cantarlo. Todo ello, en una poesía que es cabal cifra de su época y de las nuevas promociones cubanas, las cuales han depurado el habla lírica hasta su expresión más certera. [ER]

5826 Sánchez Hernani, Enrique. Por la bocacalle de la locura. Lima: Ediciones La Sagrada Familia, 1978. 44 p.: ill. (Poesía; 4)

Epígrafes reveladores de Mariátegui y de Pound insinúan el propósito de la poesía de Sánchez Hernani (n. 1953), y contribuyen a definirla como una búsqueda de "la realidad por los caminos de la fantasía." Las tres breves e intensas secciones del libro responden a ese designio fundador: manifiestan una vocación atenta a las lecciones poéticas recibidas y capaz de conjugarlas con acierto en un ámbito imaginativo personal. [PL]

5827 Sánchez León, Abelardo. Rastro de caracol. Lima: Industrial Gráfica, 1977. 108 p. (Ediciones de la clepsidra; 7)

Poesía exasperada y vuelta sobre sí misma, en un autocuestionamiento continuo acerca de su validez. Su tema es la pregunta sobre el sentido—o sinsentido—de lo real, cuya precariedad convierte el acto de la escritura en "penoso ejercicio de las palabras." De ahí el tono reiterativo, la disonancia buscada, la ruptura de las convenciones genéricas: prosaísmo literal que apenas disimula la presencia de un hablante muy reconocible en su dimensión concreta. El talento verbal de este hablante es indudable, y aunque su abrumada biografía suele imponerse con algún exceso en el recuento de las variadas experiencias que fija en el texto, el libro tiene verdadero interés como poética del escepticismo. [PL]

5828 Segovia, Francisco. Dos extremos. México: El Taller Martín Pescador, 1977. 24 p. (Colección La hojarasca)

Segovia's first book of poems includes his excellent "Lavandera," published in *Plural* earlier. Highly evocative, subtle, erotic imagery based on concrete reality. This is a young poet of great promise. [J. Bruce-Novoa]

5829 Selva, Salomón de la. Versos y versiones nobles y sentimentales. Managua: Fondo de Promoción Cultural, Banco de América, 1975. 181 p. (Serie literaria; 2. Colección Cultural Banco de América)

Conjunto de poemas originales inspirados en sugerencias clásicas. Esta colección, inédita hasta la fecha, amplía considerablemente la obra poética del autor. [RG]

5830 Silva, José Asunción. Intimidades. Introducción de Germán Arciniegas. Edición, prólogo y estudio preliminar de Héctor H. Orjuela. Bogotá: Instituto Caro y Cuervo, 1977. 171 p.; bibl., index, 8 leaves of plates: 8 ill. (Serie La Granada entreabierta; 18)

Excellent critical study precedes the initial publication of 27 original poems and six translations from a manuscript copy of an album of adolescent poems by Silva. Orjuela, the editor, documents how he obtained these translations in the handwriting of a woman who was a friend of Silva. Orjuela also explains his inclusion of 26 first versions of poems published earlier, but not widely-known, from that same manuscript, including some from recondite periodicals, most of which were examined earlier by other investigators. Analyzes all of these early poems and concludes that although they are unimportant artistically, they should be published in order to complete Silva's works. A brilliant discovery on the part of one of the finest students of Colombian poetry. Contains a newly-discovered childhood photograph of Silva and several facsimiles of poems and other documents. [BTO]

5831 ———. Obra completa. Prólogo de Eduardo Camacho Guizado. Notas y cronología de Eduardo Camacho Guizado y Gustavo Mejía. Caracas: Biblioteca Ayacucho, 1977. 325 p., bibl.

Although Camacho Guizado includes a few discoveries of Silva's poems found in previously unknown publications, this edition is neither critical nor definitive. A far more complete, critical and scholarly compilation of Silva's works is the one edited by Héctor Orjuela (see item **5832**). [BTO]

5832 ———. Poesías. Edición crítica de Héctor H. Orjuela. Bogotá: Instituto Caro y Cuervo, 1979. 352 p.: ill., plates (Biblioteca colombiana; 18)

This volume is the result of years of investigation and perusal of bibliographic sources in Colombia. Orjuela, a scholar well known for his rigor and diligence, has published one of the most needed critical editions in all Hispanic poetry. His assiduous research uncovered the lost manuscript of "Intimidades" (see item **5830**) included in the edition. His introduction describes the careful scholarship which produced an edition with variants from several manuscripts and sources. Contains photographs. [BTO]

5833 Silva, Ludovico. In vino veritas. Caracas: Contexto, 1977. 146 p.: ill.

This is the third book of poetry by a prolific prose writer. Main themes are death and the desolation of life in the era of the atomic bomb. [BTO]

5834 Silva Acevedo, Manuel. Mester de Bastardía. Santiago de Chile: Ediciones El Viento en la Llama, 1977. 50 leaves (Colección Poemas y relatos del país más largo del mundo)

A veces en la línea de la antipoesía, a veces con un acento más personal, los poemas de este libro consiguen dar en el blanco, sobre todo cuando rebasan las barreras del ingenio fácil y calan hondo en ciertas miserias de la condición humana. Dada la actual situación política de Chile, en ocasiones es preciso leer entre líneas. Pero siempre la crítica y la denuncia valientes están allí, en la simple mención del referente o en el sistema de connotaciones abierto por los textos. [OH]

5835 **Suardíaz, Luis.** Como quien vuelve de un largo viaje. La Habana: Unión de Escritores y Artistas de Cuba, 1975. 231 p. (Contemporáneos)

Segundo libro de un poeta que ha publicado poco, pero que es una de las voces notables de la primera promoción cubana *post*-1959. Su poesía no soslaya el detalle anecdótico, pero lo transforma en limpia imagen permanente, de impacto cristalino; su lenguaje es certero, feliz y líricamente preciso (véase item **5836**). [ER]

5836 ———. Leyenda de la justa belleza. La Habana: Editorial Letras Cubanas, 1978. 47 p. (Colección Mínima poesía; 20)

Muestra de una serie de breviarios poéticos de alta calidad. El presente encapsula algo de lo mejor de Suardíaz en cuatro momentos de su producción: composiciones de *Haber vivido* (1966) y de *Como quien vuelve de un largo viaje* (1975), y varios poemas publicados sólo en revistas (véase item **5835**). [ER]

5837 **Suárez, Jorge.** Sonetos con infinito. Cochabamba, Bolivia: Talleres Gráficos Rocabado, 1976. 61 p.

Obra transgresora, que suele impugnar la norma preceptiva desde ella misma, después de haber probado con eficacia su dominio. Un libro de interés en la poesía boliviana actual, que inscribe también en los textos la reflexión sobre la escritura. En el grupo final—"Sonetos del Pájaro Diablo"—el temple irónico, desenfadado y escéptico del hablante intensifica la dimensión crítica en la medida en que ella se da en un marco restrictivo, burlado en el acto que aparenta seguirlo. [PL]

5838 **Teillier, Jorge.** Para un pueblo fantasma. Prólogo de Enrique Lafourcade. Valparaíso: Ediciones Univeritarias de Valparaíso, 1978. 138 p. (Colección Cruz del Sur)

El Jorge Teillier de siempre. Invariable desde su primer libro *Para ángeles y gorriones* (1956). Nostalgia del pasado y nostalgia del futuro. La niñez añorada como una edad de oro, ya perdida, y su presencia fantasmal en el espacio de la memoria. También, homenajes a escritores afines y a amigos desaparecidos. Pero lo que en sus primeros libros era fresco y atractivo ha terminado por codificarse, transformándose en una retórica. Sin embargo, una de sus mayores virtudes—la formación de atmósferas maravillosas—reaparece en varios de los textos actuales. El prólogo de Enrique Lafourcade es perfectamente prescindible. [OH]

Vallejo, César Abraham. César Vallejo: the complete posthumous poetry. See item **6648**.

5839 ———. Poesía completa. Edición crítica y exegética de Juan Larrea. Barcelona: Seix Barral, 1978. 932 p.; bibl., index. (Biblioteca crítica)

Un extenso prólogo y otras páginas informativas anteceden al corpus poético, redispuesto aquí con un nuevo criterio. Las diferencias mayores corresponden a la ordenación del conjunto que el editor denomina *Poemas póstumos*: "Nómina de Huesos," "Sermón dela Barbarie" y "España, Aparta de mí esteCáliz." Prolijas y polémicas notas puntualizan los fundamentos del criterio adoptado (véase item **5879**). Más aspectos novedosos: la inclusión de "Poemas Juveniles" y de otros no recogidos antes en volumen: primeras versiones de algunos textos de *Los heraldos negros*, *Trilce* y *España, aparta . . .* ; un "Vocabulario" vallejiano y, como apéndice, la tesis de 1915: "El Romanticismo en la Poesía Castellana." Edición que sin duda suscitará exámenes pormenorizados. [PL]

5840 **Villanueva Chinchilla, Arnaldo.** El tercer ojo. Poesías sociales. Tegucigalpa: Villanueva Chinchilla, 1975. 51 leaves: ill.

Villanueva inscribe en su poesía el dolor que le inspira la privación y pobreza que sufre su pueblo. [RG]

5841 **Zeitlin, Israel.** Poesías completas. Introducción de Eduardo Stilman. Buenos Aires: Stilman Editores, 1979. 223 p.

Cinco libros y dos poemas extensos de César Tiempo (seudónimo de Israel Zeitlin) que reúnen su poesía publicada entre 1926 y 1978. Apoyado en una actitud inicial posmodernista (en *Versos de una . . .* , firmado "Clara Beter"), Tiempo desarrolla una temática judeoargentina a partir de su *Libro para la pausa del sábado* (1930), que presenta una nota nueva en la literatura rioplatense. El libro tiene una nota introductoria de Eduardo Stilman. [DL]

5842 **Zito Lema, Vicente.** La paz de los asesinos. Buenos Aires: Editorial Papeles de Buenos Aires, 1976? 8 leaves (Colección La pluma y la palabra; 17)

Larga composición de tono combativo. No es buena poesía y posiblemente no es poesía (aunque va precedida por una breve "Arte Poética"), pero el autor (n. 1939) deberá ser tenido en cuenta para quienes busquen constancias, en la producción literaria, del proceso de radicalización ocurrido en la Argentina que culminó en el período 1973–76. [DL]

GENERAL STUDIES

5843 **Acevedo, Ramón Luis.** La poesía indianista puertorriqueña en el siglo XIX (ICP/R, 17:65, oct./dic. 1974, p. 24–36, bibl.)

Interesante estudio que examina los rasgos del indianismo en las Antillas en comparación al resto de Hispanoamérica, y destaca a los poetas más significativos de este americanismo literario en Puerto Rico como exponentes de un intento de afirmación nacional. [ER]

5844 **Alvarez, Soledad.** A propósito de *Meridiano 70*: sobre poesía social dominicana (CDLA, 19:114, mayo/junio 1979, p. 134–140)

Corta visión histórica de la poesía dominicana, que enfatiza su vena combativa y social bajo los 30 años de la dictadura trujillista. Se basa en una muestra de poetas recogida por Casa de las Américas en 1978, pero el lector no llega a captar claramente la nómina incluida en *Meridiano 70*. [ER]

5845 **Beltrán Guerrero, Luis.** Modernismo y modernistas. Caracas: Academia Nacional de la Historia, 1978. 162 p.; bibl. (El Libro menor; 4)

Reedición conjunta de seis conferencias en las que el autor evoca a cuatro destacados escritores venezolanos—Manuel Díaz Rodríguez, Pedro-Emilio Coll, Rufino Blanco-Fombona y Andrés Mata—y analiza los contactos literarios de Rubén Darío y José Enrique Rodó con Venezuela. [HMR]

5846 ———. Poetas actuales de Venezuela (CONAC/RNC, 234, enero/feb. 1978, p. 71–81, bibl., ill.)

Reproduction of a "Prologue," written for an anthology of living poets (b. between 1890 and 1930) translated into the Serbo-Croatian language. Rapid overview of past literary history and of poets who are popular today. [BTO]

5847 **Bertrand de Muñoz, Maryse.** Les poètes hispano-americains et la Guerre Civile Espagnole (*in* Simposio Internacional de Estudios Hispánicos, Budapest, 1976. Actas [see item **5067**] p. 265–276)

La delegación de poetas hispanoamericanos que asistió en 1937 al Segundo Congreso Internacional de Escritores para la Defensa de la Cultura, celebrado en Madrid y Valencia, sintió el fuerte impacto de la Guerra Civil Española. La obra de César Vallejo, Pablo Neruda, Nicolás Guillén y otros escritores registra vívidamente esa experiencia, y a la vez constituye el antecedente de la poesía comprometida, rebelde y solidaria cuyos temas alcanzarían amplia difusión en Hispanoamérica un cuarto de siglo más tarde. [HMR]

5848 **Bollo, Sarah.** El modernismo en el Uruguay: ensayo estilístico. 2. ed. corregida y aumentada. Montevideo: Universidad de la República, División Publicaciones y Ediciones, 1976. 116 p.; bibl.

Buen resumen, de valor principalmente didáctico, con abundancia de citas de los autores uruguayos de la época considerada. La falta de un índice de nombres limita su utilidad como elemento de consulta. [DL]

5849 **Camurati, Mireya.** Una ojeada a la poesía concreta en Hispanoamérica: dos precursores y escasos epígonos (CH, 103:308, feb. 1976, p. 134–146)

Reseña de la escasa poesía concreta latinoamericana, con referencia a algunos escritores que la cultivaron: Eugen Gomringer (n. Bolivia, 1925), Edgardo Antonio Vigo (n. Argentina, 1928), y los integrantes del Grupo Noigandres, organizado hacia 1952 en São Paulo, Brasil. Poetas hispanoamericanos como Vicente Huidobro, Juan José Tablada y Octavio Paz experimentaron en ciertas etapas de su obra con técnicas afines. [HMR]

5850 **Cartier de Hamann, Marta.** La Brasa: una expresión generacional santiagueña. Santa Fe, Argentina: Librería y Editorial Colmegna, 1977. 212 p.: ill.

En la línea de trabajos recientes (de David Lagmanovich y de Edelweis Serra) sobre literaturas regionales argentinas—es decir, sobre ámbitos literarios ajenos a Buenos Aires—, este libro aporta datos sobre las letras en la provincia de Santiago del Estero en la década de 1920, inaccesibles en otras fuentes. [DL]

5851 **Charry Lara, Fernando.** Poesía colombiana del siglo XX (ECO, 35[4]:214, agosto 1979, p. 337–370)

Beginning with Silva, whom the author feels belongs in the 20th century, Charry Lara analyzes poets whom he considers representative of the epoch. His judgment is perceptive if, on occasion, excessively generous when evaluating certain poets. Still, he rightly praises lesser-known ones who deserve further recognition such as Aurelio Arturo, Juan Gustavo Cobo Borda and Rogelio Echevarría. The final part of his study consists of a list of names, dates and works. [BTO]

5852 **Cobo Borda, Juan Gustavo.** La tradición de la pobreza (ECO, 35[4]:214, agosto 1979, p. 371–389)

Although as the title indicates, the poet-critic believes Colombian poetry is "poor," the content of his article belies this impression. He indicates that there are some good poems written by 20th-century authors and justly notes that Colombian anthologies are not discriminating enough and should exclude many minor poets. The distinctions drawn by Cobo Borda identify valuable poems from the bulk of Colombian poetry which he aptly characterizes as "poesía pueblerina." In contrast, he offers revealing insights into Colombian poets who have compositions of lasting value, such as Jorge Gaitán Durán, Eduardo Cote Lamus, Fernando Arbeláez, Rogelio Echevarría and others. In fact, Cobo Borda would prefer that Colombian poetry be recognized as consisting of a few poems by great writers rather than by the many poems of minor ones. [BTO]

5853 **Davis, Lisa E.** *Revista de las Antillas*: el modernismo como resistencia cultural en Puerto Rico (*in* Simposio Internacional de Estudios Hispánicos, Budapest, 1976. Actas [see item *5067*] p. 133–140)

Esquema ideológico del origen y desarrollo modernistas en Puerto Rico, a partir de la teoría literaria y acontecimientos políticos subyacentes a la fundación y carácter de la *Revista de las Antillas* (1913–14); ella sirvió de portavoz y de núcleo intelectual a la primera generación bajo la dominación norteamericana (Luis Lloréns Torres y sus contemporáneos). [ER]

5854 **Fernández Moreno, César.** Entrevista con Roberto Fernández Retamar: sobre la poesía conversacional en la América Latina (UNION, 1, enero/marzo 1979, p. 110–135)

Interesantes juicios críticos sobre periodización y vertientes de la poesía hispanoamericana, en especial acerca de poesía conversacional y antipoesía. Ampliación de conceptos claves que Fernández Retamar ha venido elaborando en sus medulares ensayos sobre el tema. [ER]

5855 **Finlayson E., Clarence.** Tres poetas colombianos: ensayos. Medellín, Colombia: Universidad Pontificia Bolivariana, 1974. 58 p. (Colección Rojo y negro; 77)

Reprints three profound studies of José Asunción Silva, Guillermo Valencia and Porfirio Barba-Jacob by Finlayson, a Catholic writer of philosophical essays and literary criticism. The essays were reprinted on the 20th anniversary of Finlayson's death. [BTO]

5856 **Florit, Eugenio.** Poesía en José Martí, Juan Ramón Jiménez, Alfonso Reyes, Federico García Lorca y Pablo Neruda: cinco ensayos. Miami, Fla.: Ediciones Universal, 1978. 153 p. (Colección Polymita)

Publicación conjunta de cinco ensayos que, con excepción del dedicado a Pablo Neruda, habían aparecido separadamente entre 1952 y 1965. Florit—poeta y crítico—analiza con fina sensibilidad, y en el caso de la obra poética de José Martí y Alfonso Reyes, ofrece una cuidadosa visión de conjunto. [HMR]

5857 **Gómez Paz, Julieta.** Cuatro actitudes poéticas: Alejandra Pizarnik, Olga Orozco, Amelia Biagicni, María Elena Walsh. Buenos Aires: Conjunta Editores, 1977. 109 p.; bibl.

Muy útil para el conocimiento de una zona poco transitada de la poesía argentina contemporánea. Especialmente destacable es el minucioso estudio sobre la poesía de Alejandra Pizarnik. La línea de "poesía como destino" es seguida por la autora en una indagación del sentido de la poesía argentina escrita por mujeres. [DL]

Gonzáles, Norma and **Luis Zelkowics.** Breves notas en torno a la funcionalidad de la décima en la poesía venezolana. See item **1426**.

5858 Gutiérrez Girardot, Rafael. Sobre el modernismo (UCV/E, 2:4, julio/dic. 1977, p. 207–234)

Ensayo polémico pero sugestivo sobre los factores que determinaron la aparición del modernismo literario hispanoamericano, y sobre las relaciones de éste con la Generación del 98 en España. Ambos movimientos fueron respuestas contradictorias a la creciente racionalización de la vida y al predominio de las formas de vida urbanas. En este sentido el modernismo sería una reacción autónoma y auténtica de Hispanoamérica ante la modernización, con respuestas paralelas en otras zonas de la cultura occidental. [HMR]

5859 Hernández Rueda, Lupo. La generación del 48 en la poesía dominicana (EME, 6:32, sept./oct. 1977, p. 45–56, bibl.)

Bosquejo histórico de un grupo transicional en la poesía quisqueyana, que se desarrolla a partir de una fructífera vanguardia anterior (véase *HLAS 40:7166* y *7170*). Los poetas de esa generación (entre ellos el autor del artículo) aportan una poesía testimonial, enraizada en lo dominicano pero también transcendente. [ER]

5860 Jackson, Richard L. Black song without color: the black experience and the négritude of synthesis in Afro-Spanish American literature (RIB, 26:2, abril/junio 1976, p. 143–161)

Rasgos peculiares de la poesía negra hispanoamericana, en contraste con la "negritud" de otras regiones. Debido al mestizaje y a otros factores culturales, el poeta negro de Hispanoamérica—Uruguay, Ecuador, Perú, Panamá, Colombia, Cuba—siente apego a la patria, defiende la reivindicación de todos los oprimidos y tiende hacia la fraternidad humana más allá de las razas. [HMR]

5861 Jaramillo Agudelo, Darío. Notas introductorias para una (im)posible antología de la poesía colombiana (ECO, 35[4]: 214, agosto 1979, p. 425–441)

Considers that a good anthology should choose the most popular poets; 10 is sufficient in his opinion from among all those writing in the 20th century. Not generous in his criticism, the author believes that Germán Pardo García has nothing to do with literature; that Eduardo Carranza is a good minor poet; that León de Greiff has written some well-known popular poems. Nevertheless, Jaramillo Agudelo's selection criteria and analysis of the 10 best Colombian poets whom he would choose for his anthology are excellent. [BTO]

5862 Jitrik, Noé. Las contradicciones del modernismo: productividad poética y situación sociológica. México: El Colegio de México, Centro de Estudios Lingüísticos y Literarios, 1978. 128 p. (Jornadas; 85)

Agudo análisis de las tensiones ideológicas y estéticas que reflejó y propuso el modernismo hispanoamericano. Partiendo de los esquemas de la crítica francesa reciente—Jacques Derrida, Grupo Tel Quel—y concentrándose en la figura de Rubén Darío, el autor explora los vaivenes y antinomias de este movimiento: localismo/universalismo, resistencia/avance, cultura pobre/estética rica, autonomía/dependencia, etc. Significativamente, varias de estas contradicciones siguen caracterizando a la sociedad y a la literatura latinoamericana de hoy. [HMR]

León, Julio A. Los cabildos afro-cubanos y su poesía. See item **5133**.

5863 Madrid-Malo, Néstor. La poesía colombiana hasta fines del siglo XIX (CONAC/RNC, 40:240, enero/feb. 1979, p. 70–86, bibl.)

Critic shows much literary perspicacity in a well-focused analysis of the principal Colombian poets from colonial times to the last generation of Romantic writers, as well as poets of various other literary tendencies, excluding José Asunción Silva. Stresses the importance of some early poets who are often neglected and underrated. [BTO]

5864 Mansour, Mónica. Otra dimensión de nuestra poesía (UV/PH, 2, abril/junio 1972, p. 33–39, ill.)

La autora sostiene que hacia fines del siglo pasado la poesía mexicana evolucionó, en sus temas, de lo circunstancial e inmediato a lo general y absoluto. Esta reflexión sobre el destino del hombre, el sentido de la vida, Dios, la soledad y la muerte, iniciada con los "Contemporáneos," se ha mantenido hasta los poetas mexicanos de hoy. [HMR]

5865 Pérez Blanco, Lucrecio. Los conceptos de vida, Dios y muerte en tres poetas hispanoamericanos del siglo XIX (UA/REH, 12:2, mayo 1978, p. 163–198)

Catalogación de la actitud literaria de José Joaquín Olmedo, Andrés Bello y José María Heredia ante los conceptos de vida, amor, Dios y muerte. La poesía de estos tres escritores, rastreada a través de estos temas básicos, marca la evolución del neoclasicismo al naciente romanticismo hispanoamericano. [HMR]

5866 ———. La poesía vanguardista hispanoamericana ante los temas universales (UCNSA/EP, 6:1, sept. 1978, p. 9–30, bibl.)

La postura literatura de César Vallejo, Vicente Huidobro y Jorge Luis Borges frente a Dios, la vida, el amor y la muerte. Con este trabajo el autor completa una serie de 10 artículos dedicados a catalogar la actitud de poetas hispanoamericanos destacados—desde los precolombinos hasta los vanguardistas—ante estos temas universales. La suya ha sido una tarea de acopio, más que de análisis. Se incluye bibliografía. [HMR]

Perus, Françoise. Literatura y sociedad en América Latina. See item **5051**.

5867 Prats Sariol, José. La más reciente poesía cubana (UH/U, 209, julio/dic. 1978, p. 87–117)

Importante estudio que delimita seis rasgos esenciales a la poesía cubana de las nuevas promociones (plena identificación revolucionaria, temática absolutamente abierta a cualquier aspecto de la realidad, humildad del "yo" poético, sencillez expresiva, intensificación de lo explícito, lo anecdótico y lo irónico, apertura estilística a formas tropológicas y métricas) y que analiza textos de 13 poetas. Complementario a la antología de Margaret Randall (item **5652**). [ER]

5868 Rivera Rodas, Oscar. Cinco momentos de la lírica hispanoamericana: historia literaria de un género. La Paz: Instituto Boliviano de Cultura, 1978. 360 p.; bibl.; index.

Ensayo sustancioso—ganador del Premio Centenario de la Academia Mexicana (1976)—que analiza la trayectoria de la lírica hispanoamericana desde 1880, tomando en cuenta la cosmovisión y el lenguaje de los poetas. Rivera Rodas—poeta y crítico boliviano—distingue convincentemente cinco momentos sucesivos: enunciación, revelación, sugestión, disociación e identificación. [HMR]

5869 Rivero, Eliana. Las nuevas poetas cubanas (AR, 5:17, nov. 1978, p. 31–37)

Sucinto estudio que aborda el problema de la periodización en las nuevas generaciones poéticas cubanas, y analiza la obra de tres mujeres poetas (Belkis Cuza Malé, Nancy Morejón y Lina de Feria). [ER]

5870 Rodríguez Rivera, Guillermo. En torno a la joven poesía cubana (UNION, 17:2, junio 1978, p. 63–80)

Estudio panorámico que vale por su intento de delimitar grupos y promociones dentro de la creciente producción poética en Cuba; menos profundizador que el de Prats Sariol (véase item **5867**) pero complementario al mismo. [ER]

5871 Sambrano Urdaneta, Oscar. Contribución a una bibliografía general de la poesía venezolana en el siglo XX. Caracas: Universidad Central de Venezuela, Facultad de Humanidades y Educación, Escuela de Letras, 1979. 367 p.

Lists 747 authors and 2,068 works and includes information on anthologies, selected works, and critical evaluations. This useful compilation is further enhanced by an alphabetical list of authors, a chronology of contemporary Venezuelan poetry, and a listing of the recipients of the Premio Municipal de Literatura in Caracas. An important contribution. [G.M. Dorn]

5872 Surrealismo/Surrealismos: Latinoamérica y España. Edición de Peter G. Earle y Germán Gullón. Philadelphia: University of Pennsylvania, Department of Romance Languages, n.d. 161 p., bibl.

Importante colección de trabajos leídos en el XVII Congreso del Instituto Internacional de Literatura Iberoamericana (1975): Anna Balakian "Latin-American Poets and the Surrealist Heritage;" Jaime Alazraki "Surrealism: the Sacred Disease of Our Time;" Emir Rodríguez Monegal "Surrealism, Magical Realism, Magical Fiction;" Mario E. Ruiz "Mestizaje, Mitología y Alquimia: Ingredientes del Surrealismo Centroamericano;" Estuardo Núñez "La Recepción del Surrealismo en el Perú;" José Emilio Pacheco "La Batalla del Surrealismo: Octavio Paz y la Revista *Estaciones*;" Afranio Coutinho "O Surrealismo no Brasil;" Keith A. McDuffie "César Vallejo y el Humanismo Socialista vs. Surrealismo;" René de Costa "Huidobro y el Surrealismo;" Alfredo A. Roggiano "El Surrealismo en Argentina y Enrique Molina;" Erdmute Wenzel White "The Folklorization of Surrealism in Two Brazilian Masterpieces: *Macunaíma* and *Cobra norato*;" Alberto Gutiérrez de la Solana "Huellas Surrealistas en el Teatro de Roberto Arlt;" Paul Ilie "El Surrealismo Español como Modalidad;" Ricardo Gullón "¿Hubo un Surrealismo Español?;" Gonzalo Sobejano "El Surrealismo en la España de Postguerra: Camilo José Cela;" José María Capote Benot "Comentario a un Poema Surrealista Inédito de Luis Cernuda." Se incluye además una bibliografía selecta. [HMR]

5873 Trayectoria de la poesía gauchesca. Buenos Aires: Plus Ultra, 1977. 165 p.; bibl. (Ensayos; 17)

Contiene: Horacio Jorge Becco "La Primitiva Poesía Gauchesca y Bartolomé Hidalgo;" Rodolfo A. Borello "Introducción a la Poesía Gauchesca;" Adolfo Prieto "La Culminación de la Poesía Gauchesca;" Félix Weinberg "La Poesía Gauchesca de Hidalgo a Ascasubi;" trabajos de pareja calidad, entre los cuales se destaca el de Borello por su claridad y sentido de síntesis. [DL]

5874 Yurkievich, Saúl. Poesía hispanoamericana: curso y transcurso (UTIEH/C, 27, 1976, p. 271–279)

Intento de esquematizar y caracterizar a grandes trazos la trayectoria de la poesía hispanoamericana de este siglo. Yurkievich admite las dificultades de toda periodización estricta, pero propone cuatro períodos; 1) el modernista; 2) el vanguardista; 3) el de la poesía pura, existencial y surrealista; y 4) el neorrealista. [HMR]

SPECIAL STUDIES

5875 Aguilar Mora, Jorge. La divina pareja: historia y mito; valoración e interpretación de la obra ensayística de Octavio Paz. México: Ediciones Era, 1978. 226 p.

Though an analysis of Paz's essays, the poet-critic Aguilar Mora's 1976 doctoral dissertation provides important background material for understanding the leading Mexican writer's verse. Aguilar Mora presents a literary and philosophical examination that clarifies some of the central concepts in Paz: *soledad, otredad, poema, tiempo*, to name a few. [CM]

5876 Alstrum, James J. Las *Gotas amargas* de José Asunción Silva y la poesía de Luis Carlos López (ICC/T, 33:2, mayo/agosto 1978, p. 280–303)

Compares and contrasts form and theme in some of Silva's 13 *Gotas amargas* with selected poems by López. Concludes that both were antipoets before Nicanor Parra invented the term. Believes that both used satire to censure social evils, one of the post-vanguardist characteristics of Spanish American poetry deserving further study. [BTO]

5877 Arévalo, Guillermo Alberto. César Vallejo: poesía en la historia. n.p.: C. Valencia Editores, 1977. 185 p.; bibl., index.

Los principios metodológicos que orientan la investigación son "los postulados fundamentales de las escuelas historicistas, y especialmente del marxismo, sin que por ello se dejen de lado los aportes que en sus análisis han hecho algunos críticos 'a-históricos'" (p. 3). Aunque resulta algo reiterativa y a veces enfática, esta lectura contiene notas y precisiones estimables. [PL]

5878 Arreola Cortés, Raúl. Miguel N. Lira: el poeta y el hombre. México: Editorial Jus, 1977. 308 p.; bibl. (Colección Crítica literaria; 1)

Valuable study of the life and works of a member of the Mexican generation of 1929. In addition to analyzing the poetry, Arreola Cortés examines the influence of Bécquer, Lorca and popular verse on Lira. [CM]

5879 Bary, David. Vallejo's *Obras poéticas completas* and the technical critique of Juan Larrea (HR, 47:4, Autumn 1979, p. 425–440)

Examen puntual y razonado de una proposición para el reordenamiento de la poesía de Vallejo (véase item **5839**), según el ensayo previamente publicado por Larrea con el título "Los Poemas Póstumos de César Vallejo a la Luz de su Edición Facsimilar" (en *Aula Vallejo*, 11/13, 1974). Estudio que invita y contribuye a resolver un confuso problema de diferencias textuales. Interesante y útil para el especialista. [PL]

5880 Bazik, Martha S. The life and works of Luis Carlos López. Chapel Hill: University of North Carolina Press, 1977. 147 p.; bibl. (North Carolina studies in the Romance languages and literatures; 182)

This book fills the need for an extensive and informative study of Luis Carlos López' life and works. Includes a five-page bibliography and appendixes with miscellaneous correspondence, some from well-known writers and literary figures, and three previously unpublished poems. [BTO]

Blanco Fombona, Rufino. Rufino Blanco Fombona íntimo. See item **5146**.

5881 Blengio Brito, Raúl. Herrera y Reissig: del romanticismo a la vanguardia. Montevideo: Universidad de la República, División Publicaciones y Ediciones, 1978. 172 p.

Estudio minuciosamente documentado de la vida y la obra de Herrera y Reissig, destinada a convertirse en indispensable para quienes se interesen por el proceso del modernismo poético en el Uruguay. No aparece en el índice el capítulo noveno, "Valoración" (p. 153–168), quizá el más valioso del volumen por su ponderado juicio crítico. [DL]

5882 Cárdenas de Monner Sans, María Inés. Martín Fierro y la conciencia nacional. Buenos Aires: Editorial La Pléyade, 1977. 111 p.; bibl.

Interesantes estudios sobre aspectos específicos del texto de José Hernández, que agregan información al contexto histórico y contribuyen a la tarea permanente de reinterpretar la obra máxima de la poesía gauchesca argentina. [DL]

5883 Casal, Julián del. The poetry of Julián del Casal. v. 2. Edited by Robert Jay Glickman. Gainesville: University Presses of Florida, 1976. 1 v.; bibl., ill., indexes (A University of Florida book)

Este admirable volumen complementa al primero de la serie de tres (véase *HLAS 40:7057*), funcionando a manera de glosario y de comentario histórico-analítico. Se da aquí información minuciosa sobre cada uno de los textos de Casal reunidos en el vol. 1, ofreciendo un cúmulo de documentos bio-bibliográficos que impresionan por lo exhaustivo de su detalle y lo comprensivo de su trazo. El examen de las variantes textuales y de las circunstancias de escritura y publicación es definitivo; la explicación histórica se enriquece con grabados, reproducciones facsimilares, gráficas y tablas de concordancia. Obra imprescindible al estudioso de Casal y de la poesía modernista. [ER]

5884 Cobo Borda, Juan Gustavo. Jorge Zalamea: notas críticas (ECO, 34:5, marzo 1979, p. 550–556)

Characterizes Jorge Zalamea as a man of letters rather than novelist or poet. Erudite and candid notes by *Eco*'s editor document Zalamea's profound desire to become a great poet but rank his best poems as third-rank. [BTO]

5885 Costa, René de. The poetry of Pablo Neruda. Cambridge, Mass.: Harvard University Press, 1979. 213 p., bibl., index, 6 leaves of plates: ill.

Consciente de que la mayoría de los trabajos críticos que existen sobre Neruda adolecen de un cierto "partidismo," por razones políticas o estéticas, de Costa se propone estudiar la obra del poeta chileno, realizando una labor integradora de sus facetas políticas y no políticas, a través del examen de sus libros claves. Para ello de Costa se refiere a los distintos estilos poéticos de Neruda, concentrándose cada vez en una sola obra maestra, como ejemplo privilegiado de un estilo particular. Las direcciones que de Costa visualiza y los libros que las representan son: la poesía amorosa (*Veinte poemas de amor y una canción desesperada*); el experimento de la Vanguardia (*Tentativa del hombre infinito*); el hermetismo (ciclo de las *Residencias*); la poesía épica (*Canto general*); el lirismo pleno (las *Odas*) y la poesía conversacional (*Estravagario*). Excelente trabajo de carácter introductorio, para el ámbito de habla inglesa. [OH]

5886 *Cuadernos Hispanoamericanos.* Revista mensual de cultura hispánica. Centro Iberoamericano de Cooperación. Nos. 343/345, enero/marzo 1979– . Madrid.

Entire issue (800 p.) devoted to Octavio Paz. About 80 articles discuss all aspects of Paz's work: his poetry, essays, esthetics, philosophy, world-view, etc. Contributors include: Manuel Benavides, Jaime Alazraki, Raúl Chavarri, Blas Matamoros, José Emilio Pacheco, Carlos García Osuna, Alicia Borinsky, and Alberto Blasi. A major tribute to one of Latin America's greatest poets and essayists. [Ed.]

5887 Fernández Latour de Botas, Olga. Prehistoria de Martín Fierro. Buenos Aires: Librería Editorial Platero, 1977. 151 p.; bibl., index.

Intenta "la aproximación al poema de Hernández a partir de lo que pudo ser el pasado no escrito de los individuos que lo inspiraron" (p. 14); estudia "el macrocosmos del hombre *folk*" (la clase gaucha, los caracteres de su cultura) y "el microcosmos del cantor en la realidad y en el poema" (aspectos de la lírica y la narrativa); relaciona también, como en trabajos anteriores de la misma autora, el poema de Hernández y los romances matonescos. Exposición erudita, competente manejo de fuentes, inteligente aprovechamiento de la teoría folklórica. Indispensable sobre el tema. [DL]

5888 Fernández Sosa, Luis F. Northrop Frye y unos poemas anagógicos de Lezama Lima (AATSP/H, 61:4, Dec. 1978, p. 877–887)

Ambicioso proyecto que aplica conceptos arquetípicos (Jung, Auerbach) y del New Criticism. Exposición un tanto verbosa, de interés al especialista. [ER]

5889 García Marruz, Fina. De estudios delmontinos (BNJM/R, 19[68]:3, sept./dic. 1977, p. 17–40)

Estudio histórico de las relaciones amistosas y literarias entre Domingo del Monte y José María Heredia. Abundantemente ilustrado con el epistolario. [ER]

5890 Glickman, Robert J. José Asunción Silva ante los avances tecnológicos de su época (NS, 1:1/2, 1976, p. 180–190)

Author discusses an unusual facet of Silva as an ecology-minded writer who would spare nature from the period's technological advances in communication and travel. The article analyzes how these technological innovations both repelled and attracted the poet. [BTO]

5891 Gottlieb, Marlene. No se termina nunca de nacer: la poesía de Nicanor Parra. Madrid: Playor, 1977. 165 p., bibl. (Colección Nova scholar)

Después de trazar el desarrollo de la poesía de Parra, desde *Cancionero sin nombre* hasta los "artefactos," la autora estudia algunos de los motivos recurrentes en la antipoesía y algunos de sus procedimientos estilísticos, mostrando su función desacralizadora. Este trabajo se limita a repetir y reorganizar conceptos ya manidos sobre la obra de Nicanor Parra, y en consecuencia no representa un aporte significativo. Puede ser útil, en cambio, para lectores no especializados. [OH]

5892 Homenaje a Emilio Adolfo Westphalen (Creación & Crítica [Lima] 20, agosto 1977, p. 1–81)

Páginas fervorosas (81 p.) admirativas y justas dedicadas a un escritor ejemplar en la literatura peruana por su rigurosa producción poética y ensayística, y por su conducta intelectual, definida en la presentación de este homenaje como "un caso de moral literaria sin concesiones." Notas y textos críticos de M. Vargas Llosa, E. Peña, M. Moreno Jimeno, J.M. Oviedo, S. Baciu, C.G. Belli, J. Ortega, A. Cueto, J. Sologuren, R. Silva-Santisteban, R. González Vigil, A. Ferrari, E. Verástegui, E. Rivera Martínez y B. Podestá. Poemas de C. Moro, J.E. Eielson, A. Cisneros y A. Rojas. [PL]

5893 Hoover, Judith Myers. The urban nightmare: alienation imagery in the poetry of T.S. Eliot and Octavio Paz (JSSTC, 6:1, Spring 1978, p. 13–28)

Interesting study of correspondences between Eliot's *The waste land* and some of the poems in *Libertad bajo palabra* and *Salamandra*. [CM]

5894 Jones, Sonia. Alfonsina Storni. Boston: Twayne Publishers, 1979. 149 p.; bibl., index (Twayne's world authors series; TWAS 519)

Excelente estudio biográfico y crítico, que ocupará su lugar—sin sustituirlo—junto al ya clásico trabajo de Julieta Gómez Paz, *Leyendo a Alfonsina Storni* (Buenos Aires: Losada, 1966). Completo, equilibrado y objetivo; sin duda lo mejor que se ha escrito hasta ahora en inglés sobre la notable poeta argentina. [DL]

5895 Lázaro, Felipe. José Lezama Lima: fundador de poesía (CH, 318, dic. 1976, p. 713–719, table)

Breve descripción histórica de la obra y la personalidad del poeta cubano, elaborada ante su muerte; contiene un cuadro cronológico de su vida, actividades literarias y editoriales, y publicaciones. De interés al novicio. [ER]

5896 El Lenguaje poético de César Dávila Andrade. Estudios de Jaime Romo N., E. Vásquez López, L. Montoya Andrade y E. Wolfsohn. Quito: Ediciones de la Universidad Católica, 1977. 179 p.; bibl.

La poesía de Dávila Andrade es estudiada aquí mediante la aplicación de un método técnico de análisis, que en este caso se ciñe al modelo establecido por Jean Cohen en su libro *Estructura del lenguaje póetico*. Los autores siguen puntualmente las formulaciones de Cohen, a partir de la base teórica que procura el concepto de *desviación*. Las descripciones de los rasgos principales advertidos en los niveles semántico y fónico se ordenan en minuciosos cuadros estadísticos, en los que se apoyan para determinar la propiedad y el sentido de la división en dos épocas de la poesía de Dávila Andrade. Un esfuerzo entusiasta y una sana reacción contra los excesos del impresionismo interpretativo; pero que tampoco logra superar con eficacia otras precariedades: el mecanicismo y la reiteración simplificadora. [PL]

5897 MacAdam, Alfred J. *Et in Arcadia ego*: Borges' elegiac poetry (HIUS/R, 38:1/2, 1974/1975, p. 53–61)

La preferencia de Borges por epitafios y elegías en su poesía temprana (1923–30) apunta a un intento de sobrevivir en los lectores que acudan a su obra literaria. Lectura lúcida de dos poemas de *Fervor de Buenos Aires* desde la perspectiva de su producción posterior. [HMR]

5898 Magis, Carlos Horacio. La poesía hermética de Octavio Paz. México: El Colegio de México, 1978. 352 p.; bibl. (Serie Estudios de lingüística y literatura; 7)

Valuable work of criticism that concentrates on Paz's work up to 1957 and especially on *La estación violenta* (1948–57), nine of his most famous poems, including "Himno entre Ruinas" and "Piedra de Sol." Magis analyzes major themes (solitude, identity, *otredad*, linguistic creation, love, death, time, the dream, the nature of reality) as well as the rhythm, structure and symbols of Paz's poetry. [CM]

5899 Meneses, Carlos. Poesía juvenil de Jorge Luis Borges. Barcelona: Olañeta Editor, 1978. 76 p. (Pequeña Biblioteca Calamvs Scriptorivs; 18)

Importante trabajo sobre el período menos conocido de la poesía de Borges; la sección "Poemas 1919–1922" trae 18 composiciones, algunas de las cuales aparecen en libro por primera vez (las restantes habían aparecido en trabajos de Guillermo de Torre, Gloria Videla, Marcos Ricardo Barnatán y el propio Carlos Meneses, no siempre en publicaciones de fácil acceso). [DL]

5900 Orjuela, Héctor H. *De sobremesa* y otros estudios sobre José Asunción Silva. Bogotá: Instituto Caro y Cuervo, 1976. 124 p. (Serie la Granada entreabierta; 14)

Four essays on Silva's prose works: 1) on the poet's novel *De sobremesa*; 2) on the influence of Joris-Karl Huysman; 3) of Maria Baskirtseff on Silva's life and novel; and 4) on the theme of "anguish" in his prose and poems. Indispensable study of Silva's prose. [BTO]

5901 Osiek, Betty Tyree. Las *Gotas amargas* de José Asunción Silva: antecedentes de la antipoesía (*in* Congreso del Instituto Internacional de Literatura Iberoamericana, XVII, Madrid, 1978. Actas. Madrid: Ediciones de Cultura Hispánica del Centro Iberoamericano de Cooperación, 1978, v. 2, p. 745–757)

Análisis de 13 poemas de Silva que reflejan una visión desengañada de la vida. Se percibe en ellos una perspectiva semejante a la que expresaría Nicanor Parra en su poesía—desilusión, ironía, tragedia—, como resultado de una actitud parecida ante el materialismo y la indiferencia de la sociedad contemporánea. [HMR]

5902 ———. José Asunción Silva. Boston: Twayne Publishers, 1978. 186 p.; bibl., index (Twayne's world authors series; TWAS 505)

Having already published in Spanish a useful monograph on Silva's poetry: *José Asunción Silva: estudio estilístico de su poesía* (México: De Andrea, 1968), the author makes this Colombian writer now more accessible to English readers through a methodical life-and-works study. The book offers a brief background chapter on Spanish American Modernism, followed by others devoted to Silva's biography, poetry and prose works, including his uneven novel *De sobremesa*. A selected, annotated bibliography completes the volume. [HMR]

5903 Paz, Octavio. Xavier Villaurrutia en persona y en obra. Con 10 dibujos de

Juan Soriano y una iconografía. México: Fondo de Cultura Económica, 1978. 85 p.; bibl., 8 leaves of plates.

An account of Paz's friendship with Villaurrutia together with critical comments on the latter's poetry. Important for its remarks on Mexican poetry of the 1930s and the period of the Contemporáneos. [CM]

Pucciarelli, Eugenio. Motivos filosóficos en la poesía de Martínez Estrada. See item **7522**.

5904 **Rangel Frías, Raúl.** Evocación de Alfonso Reyes. Monterrey: Gobierno del Estado de Nuevo León, 1978. 47 p., 1 leaf of plates.

Eulogy of the life and works of Reyes. [CM]

5905 *Review.* Center for Inter-American Relations. No. 23, 1978– . New York.

Esta edición de *Review*, centrada en la figura del escritor chileno Enrique Lihn, constituye en justo homenaje a su importante labor en el campo de la poesía, la narrativa y el ensayo. Además de las colaboraciones del propio poeta, cabe destacar los excelentes trabajos críticos sobre la obra de Lihn, preparados especialmente para esta publicación: Waldo Rojas "A Generation's Response to *The Dark Room*;" Héctor Libertella "A Literary Hybrid" sobre *La orquesta de cristal*; y George Yúdice "The Poetics of Breakdown." [OH]

5906 *Revista Iberoamericana.* Instituto Internacional de Literatura Iberoamericana. Universidad de Pittsburgh. Vol. 45, Nos. 106/107, enero/junio 1979– . Pittsburgh, Pa.

Número de esta revista dedicado por entero al tema "Vicente Huidobro y la Vanguardia" (398 p.). Reúne los trabajos del Simposio auspiciado y organizado por la Universidad de Chicago entre el 5 y 8 de Abril de 1978. Incluye 40 artículos divididos en las siguientes seis secciones: 1) Las Primeras Obras de Huidobro; 2) Otros Vanguardistas; 3) "Altazor;" 4) Otros Aspectos de Huidobro y la Vanguardia; 5) Las Ultimas Obras de Huidobro; 6) Otros Aspectos de la Vanguardia; Ultraísmo, Surrealismo, Gonzalo Rojas. [OH]

5907 **Rodríguez Monegal, Emir.** Neruda, el viajero inmóvil. Nueva versión ampliada. Caracas: Monte Avila Editores, 1977. 487 p.; bibl. (Colección Estudios)

Reedición del conocido ensayo de Monegal sobre la poesía de Pablo Neruda. Incluye dos capítulos nuevos "Retrato en el Tiempo," que se cierra con la muerte del poeta, y "La Unica Residencia," sobre los últimos libros de Neruda, y agrega una cuarta parte titulada "El Sistema del Poeta," donde se demuestra que la estética del *don profético* es el principio unificador y totalizador que rige la poesía nerudiana, por encima de las diferentes "máscaras" adoptadas por el poeta a través de su extensa producción literaria. [OH]

5908 **Romero García, Luz Virginia.** El aldeanismo en la poesía de Luis Palés Matos. Río Piedras: Editorial Universitaria, Universidad de Puerto Rico, 1977. 119 p.; bibl. (Colección Uprez; 42. Serie Estudios literarios)

De visión ingenua y estilo muy poco maduro (proyecto de tesis), este libro tiene sin embargo el interés de tratar un aspecto poco glosado del autor puertorriqueño de poemas negristas (*Tuntún de pasa y grifería*, 1937). [ER]

5909 **Rosales, Luis.** La poesía de Neruda. Madrid: Editora Nacional, 1978. 276 p.; bibl. (Alfar; 34)

A pesar del título, menos de la mitad del volumen está dedicado a estudiar la poesía de Neruda. El libro incluye además un extenso ensayo sobre las *Soledades* de Góngora y otro sobre el tema "Simbolismo y Significación." Aunque el artículo sobre Neruda peca ocasionalmente de impresionismo y repite conceptos ya conocidos, resulta interesante cuando Rosales adopta la perspectiva del memorialista y combina el recuerdo de su experiencia personal ante el fenómeno Neruda, con su análisis de los poemas y con el efecto de esa experiencia en el Luis Rosales poeta. [OH]

5910 **Salvia, Anthony J.** La tradición ironizada: el uso del número en *Poemas humanos* de César Vallejo (UA/REH, 12:1, enero 1978, p. 93–111)

Análisis de un aspecto significativo de la poesía de Vallejo. El examen realizado por Salvia se caracteriza por la coherencia de su punto de vista y por sus precisas observaciones acerca del sentido de esos símbolos, según la particular manera en que la "tradición numerológica" es asumida en *Poemas humanos*. Trabajo bien fundado, no sólo en la investigación vallejiana anterior, sino también en formulaciones teóricas solventes. Su consulta será útil para el especialista. [PL]

5911 Santí, Enrico Mario. The politics of poetics (CU/D, 8:4, Winter 1978, p. 28–40)

Lengthy, detailed review of Rachel Phillips' *The poetic modes of Octavio Paz* (see *HLAS 36:6672*) and Monique J. Lemaître's *Octavio Paz: poesía y poética* (see *HLAS 40:7200*). Contains important comments on the difficulties in relating Paz's poetry and his essays. [CM]

5912 Séminaire César Vallejo, *Poitiers, France, 1971–1972*. Séminaire César Vallejo. v. 2, Travaux de synthèse. Poitiers, France: Université de Poitiers, Centre de Recherches Latino-Américaines, 1972/1973. 1 v., bibl. (Travaux de l'année universitaire 1970; 72)

Vol. 2 del importante *Séminaire César Vallejo* (see *HLAS 38:7137* sobre el vol. 1, *Analyses* de textes). El vol. 2 contiene las ponencias leídas en esa ocasión y las discusiones a que cada una de ellas dio lugar: Rubén Bareiro Saguier "César Vallejo y el Mestizaje Cultural;" Michèle Bernu "L'Ecriture sur l'Ecriture dans la Poésie de César Vallejo;" Enric Miret "Conflicto y Contradicción en la Obra de César Vallejo;" Alain Sicard "Contradiction et Renversement Matérialiste dans la Poésie de César Vallejo, avant *Poemas humanos*;" y Saúl Yurkievich "El Salto por el Ojo de la Aguja: Conocimiento de y por la Poesía." [PL]

5913 Serpa de Francisco, Gloria. Gran reportaje a Eduardo Carranza. Bogotá: Instituto Caro y Cuervo, 1978. 458 p.; bibl.; 1 leaf of plates (Serie La Granada entreabierta; 21)

Author-editor's comments on the life and works of Eduardo Carranza are included with a collection of documents, speeches, eulogies, periodical articles, literary criticism and personal comment by friends and acquaintances. Of value because of the documents rather than the editor's narrative of a life already well known and with little critical evaluation of Carranza's uneven though brilliant poetry. [BTO]

5914 Serra, Edelweis. El cosmos de la palabra: mensaje poético y estilo de Juan L. Ortiz. Buenos Aires: Ediciones Noé, 1976. 129 p.; bibl., 3 leaves of plates: ill. (Colección Los Lanzallamas)

Excelente aplicación de modernos criterios de análisis literario a una obra poética —la del argentino Juan L. Ortiz (1896–197?) —poco conocida, que resulta así iluminada y explicada con desusada profundidad. La seriedad del enfoque crítico se une a una expresión cuidadosa y clara. Este trabajo debe ser tenido en cuenta por quienes se interesan en las aplicaciones de la "nueva crítica" en América Latina. [DL]

5915 Silva-Santisteban, Ricardo. José María Eguren, aproximaciones y perspectivas: estudios seleccionados. Lima: Universidad del Pacífico, Departamento de Humanidades, 1977. 281 p.; bibl. (Serie Departamentos académicos; 4)

Excelente suma de trabajos críticos, que atestigua el interés revalorativo por la obra del autor. El volumen se divide en tres partes: 1) Biografía; 2) Reseñas, Estudios Generales y Exégesis Particulares de la Poesía; y 3) Reseñas y Estudios sobre la Prosa. La selección de los textos es rigurosa y amplia. Con muy buen criterio, el compilador empieza por incluir todas las notas contemporáneas a los libros de Eguren, facilitando así el conocimiento diacrónico de la crítica. [PL]

5916 Skyrme, Raymond. Rubén Darío and the Pythagorean tradition. Gainesville: University of Florida Presses, 1975. 108 p.; bibl. (Latin American monographs. 2d series; 15)

Excelente análisis de la poética de Rubén Darío. Partiendo de la visión mística del mundo del poeta nicaragüense, Skyrme establece relaciones con poetas franceses del siglo XIX que postulan una visión similar, o sea, una actitud esencialmente religiosa ante el arte. Es uno de los aportes recientes más valiosos a la bibliografía sobre Darío. [RG]

5917 Subero, Efraín. El sentido espiritual metafísico en la poesía de Fernando Paz Castillo. Caracas: Universidad Católica Andrés Bello, Centro de Investigaciones Literarias, 1975. 28 p.; bibl.

Admirable study of the ideas of various philosophers and of four themes in the poetry of Fernando Paz Castillo: metaphysics, man, God and death. [BTO]

5918 Taylor, Martín C. Sensibilidad religiosa de Gabriela Mistral. Versión española de Pilar García Noreña. Preliminar de Juan Loveluck. Madrid: Gredos, 1975. 332 p.; bibl., indexes; 4 leaves of plates: ill. (Biblioteca románica hispánica; 2. Estudios y ensayos; 233)

Iluminador examen de los componentes religiosos en la obra de Gabriela Mistral. Analiza el papel de la tradición hebraica—particularmente del Antiguo Testamento—y la búsqueda de la armonía trascendente, a través del catolicismo, de la teosofía y del pensamiento de Tagore, Nervo y Bergson. El capítulo medular del libro se titula "La Poética del Sacrificio." En él se estudian los diversos elementos que configuran dicho sistema estético fundado en el calvario de Jesucristo. [OH]

5919 Torres Roggero, Jorge. La cara oculta de Lugones. Buenos Aires: Ediciones Castañeda, 1977. 117 p.; bibl., ill. (Colección perspectiva nacional; 4)

La tesis de este trabajo es que "tanto la poesía como la narrativa lugoniana se desarrollan bajo el signo de un simbolismo mítico" (p. 54): el desarrollo de esta premisa conduce a una interesante relectura, la que aceptada o no por el lector, destaca sin embargo la validez de nuevos enfoques críticos. [DL]

5920 Valdés, Mario J. En busca de la realidad poética: un estudio de *Piedra de sol* (NS, 2:3/4, 1977, p. 259–269)

Structuralist study of the poem. Points out the significant role of the number five in the work and that of Venus and its orbit; suggests as the poem's central meaning "el encuentro de la unidad en la coexistencia del ser como el yo y el otro enlazados en un destino común." [CM]

5921 Vargas Llosa, Mario. El tordo fugitivo (VIA, 2, enero 1977, p. 10–15)

Nota sobre la poesía de Juan Gonzalo Rose (véase *HLAS 40:7147*), a propósito del libro *Las nuevas comarcas* (1976). Vincula esta poesía con el designio modernista, en cuanto el mundo plasmado por Rose es también un mundo mental, que "no expresa una realidad sino un deseo:" función creadora compensatoria que levanta otra realidad ideal frente a los agobios de la realidad empírica. Descripción sugestiva, cordial y exigente. [PL]

5922 Vidales, Luis. Nueve poetas en uno: el polifacético León de Greiff (CDLA, 19:110, sept./oct. 1978, p. 68–73)

Poet-critic gives exceptional interpretation of León de Greiff's complex and contradictory universe. Characterizes the poet as an egocentric in retreat from harsh reality, as a supporter of causes, as one brutally frank toward persons he disliked, and as incommunicative except in poetry. Favors his simpler poems. Concludes that many others served as veiled social protest. [BTO]

5923 Westphalen, Emilio Adolfo. Eguren y Vallejo: dos casos ejemplares (CM/D, 14:6[84], nov./dic. 1978, p. 3–7, ill.)

Con su acostumbrado rigor, Westphalen se refiere a algunas cuestiones graves y fundamentales en la obra de Eguren y Vallejo: concepto de la poesía y del poema, actitud ante la palabra, relaciones con la tradición. Ensayo lúcido, preciso y cortés ("glosas," según Westphalen), que ilustra cómo las reflexiones sobre poética realizadas por un practicante consciente de las posibilidades de su discurso teórico, pueden convertirse en una recreación memorable. Páginas imprescindibles, ejemplares ellas mismas. [PL]

5924 Wilson, Jason. Octavio Paz, a study of his poetics. New York: Cambridge University Press, 1979. 192 p.; bibl., index.

Important examination of the relationship between Paz and the surrealists. Wilson considers surrealism the basic influence of Paz's verse, even in *Ladera este*, but one that is not revealed in his poetic style. Instead, the influence can be traced to the poet's attitude to life based on categories like the overcoming of opposites and the timeless moment, among others. Completed before the publication of *Pasado en claro* (1975) and *Vuelta* (1976), the book is a collection of recent and earlier essays and therefore not as unified as it might be. [CM]

5925 Wood, Cecil G. The creacionismo of Vicente Huidobro. Fredericton, Canada: York Press, 1978. 300 p.; bibl.

Libro que tiene la desventaja de presentar ante el público de habla inglesa a un autor de estatura mundial, cuya obra poética (hay traducciones de su narrativa) prácticamente no ha sido vertida al inglés. Cecil Wood examina la teoría creacionista de Vicente Huidobro y su incidencia en sus poemarios, desde *Adán* hasta sus publicaciones postreras, empleando a *Altazor* como eje irradiador de significados. [OH]

5926 Yero, Luis R. Mendive: poeta y forjador de conciencias (UCLV/I, 54, mayo/agosto 1976, p. 149–156, bibl.)

Sucinta valoración histórica del maestro de Martí, quien también propició la publicación de poetas como Joaquín Lorenzo Luaces, Juan Clemente Zenea, José Jacinto Milanés y "Plácido" en su *Revista de la Habana* (1853–1857). Se le confirma como romántico de transición y como mentor de la generación posterior. [ER]

5927 Yúdice, George. Vicente Huidobro y la motivación del lenguaje. Buenos Aires: Editorial Galerna, 1978. 311 p.; bibl.

Con las herramientas que le proporcionan el estructuralismo y el post-estructuralismo, Yúdice se aboca al estudio de la poesía de Huidobro, empleando tres tipos de enfoque: 1) el análisis componencial (Hjelmslev) para *Horizon Carre, Poemas árticos*, etc.; 2) el análisis semiótico cuyo centro es el lenguaje autorreferencial de *Altazor*; y 3) los análisis de la subjetividad (Benveniste, Lacan) que examinan *Ver y palpar, El ciudadano del olvido* y *Ultimos poemas*. Sin duda uno de los trabajos más acuciosos y penetrantes sobre la poesía de Vicente Huidobro. [OH]

MISCELLANEOUS

5928 Antuña, María Luisa and **Josefina García-Carranza.** Bibliografía de Nicolás Guillén: suplemento 1972–1977 (BNJM/R, 19[68]: 3, sept./dic. 1977, p. 61–123)

Continuación de la bibliografía que sobre el Poeta Nacional de Cuba siguen compilando las autoras (la primera parte había aparecido sin sus nombres, sin embargo, bajo "Instituto Cubano del Libro;" véase *HLAS 40:7196*). Contiene, además de la obra poética, artículos periodísticos, discursos, y diversas colaboraciones en publicaciones seriadas. El fichero pasivo recoge interesantes contribuciones al estudio de Guillén publicadas a partir de 1972, y un apéndice de asientos bibliográficos rezagados que abarca desde 1933 hasta 1971. [ER]

5929 Becco, Horacio Jorge. Leopoldo Lugones, bibliografía en su centenario: 1874–1974. Buenos Aires: Ediciones Culturales Argentinas, Ministerio de Cultura y Educación, Secretaría de Estado de Cultura, 1978. 169 p.; indexes.

A pesar de la demora en su publicación (cuatro años después de la fecha límite), y a despecho de la abundancia de erratas, es la mejor bibliografía existente sobre Lugones y la fuente potencial de nuevas investigaciones lugonianas. Los 851 asientos cubren la totalidad de la obra en libros y buena parte de la crítica. Indispensable elemento de referencia para el lugonista; conveniente para toda persona interesada en el modernismo literario hispanoamericano. [DL]

5930 Benedetti, Mario. Letras de emergencia. México: Editorial Nueva Imagen, 1977. 156 p.

Reedición de un libro publicado en Buenos Aires: Editorial Alfa, 1974. Contiene un detallado prólogo del autor; un texto titulado "Canto Libre y Arte de Emergencia;" poemas destinados a ser cantados, casi todos los cuales han sido en efecto musicalizados; un cuento ("Relevo de Pruebas"), un grupo de fábulas (en prosa) y otras composiciones: materiales, todos ellos, de decidida intención política revolucionaria. [DL]

5931 Dorn, Georgette M. Luso-Hispanic Recordings at the Library of Congress (LARR, 14:2, Summer 1979, p. 174–179)

Reseña histórica del Archivo de Grabaciones que posee la División Hispánica de la Biblioteca del Congreso. Iniciada en 1942, esta importante colección—de valor documental y humano—contaba a mediados de 1978 con la voz de 376 autores destacados de América Latina, España y Portugal que habían grabado en castellano, portugués, francés, catalán y varias lenguas indígenas. Entre estos poetas, narradores, ensayistas e historiadores se contaban cinco Premios Nobel. [HMR]

5932 Fernández Retamar, Roberto. Introducción a José Martí. La Habana: Casa de las Américas, 1978. 216 p. (Colección de estudios martianos)

Recopilación de ensayos críticos que el poeta y ensayista cubano había publicado entre 1965 y 1977; recogidos antes parcialmente en *Lectura de Martí* (1972), aparecen ahora en "forma más homogénea" y con la adición de trabajos nuevos. Se titulan: "Introducción a José Martí;" "Martí, Lenin y la Revolución Anticolonial;" "Martí y Ho Chi Minh: Dirigentes Anticolonialistas;" "La Revolución de *Nuestra América*;" "Desatar a América y Desuncir el Hombre;" "Martí en Marinello;" "El 26 de Julio y los Compañeros Desconocidos de José Martí." De valor medular a una actualización ideológico-estética del pensamiento de Martí, son de interés sobre todo literario el ensayo titular y el penúltimo, que elucidan la tarea creadora martiana, su filiación como escritor y revolucionario americano, y la ubicación poética y modernista del Maestro de Cuba. [ER]

5933 Handelsman, Michael H. Amazonas y artistas: un estudio de la prosa de la mujer ecuatoriana. Guayaquil: Casa de la Cultura Ecuatoriana, Núcleo de Guayas, 1978. 2 v.; bibl. (Colección Letras del Ecuador; 70/71)

Trabajo que puede interesar a los estudiosos del tema. Contiene abundante información bibliográfica, y en este aspecto sobresale el Capítulo 3 dedicado a "Las Revistas Feministas," desde fines del siglo XIX. La escritura, el texto y la interpretación de las obras son irrelevantes. [PL]

5934 Henríquez Ureña, Camila. Invitación a la lectura: notas sobre apreciación literaria. 3. ed. La Habana: Editorial Pueblo y Educación, 1975. 181 p.

Enjundioso volumen que recoge conferencias sobre crítica y teoría de los géneros. Su autora, hermana de los reconocidos Pedro y Max Henríquez Ureña, nació en la República Dominicana pero hizo de Cuba su patria adoptiva. En estas páginas, en sendos prólogo y epílogo, le rinden homenaje el poeta y alumno suyo Luis Rogelio Nogueras y la crítica Mirta Aguirre. [ER]

5935 Manifiesto trascendentalista y poesía de sus autores. San José: Editorial Costa Rica, 1977. 191 p.

Oponiéndose a poesía elaborada, al uso de lenguaje directo en el verso y a poemas que obedecen servilmente a determinadas ideologías políticas, los autores—Laureano Albán Ronald Bonilla, Julieta Dobles y Carlos Francisco Monge, poetas por destino y vocación—definen la poesía: expresión de intuiciones trascendentales por medio de imágenes creadas con lenguaje figurado. No les anima el propósito de formular definiciones originales sino más bien el de aclarar el origen, la historia y la responsabilidad del quehacer poético. [RG]

5936 María Eugenia Vaz Ferreira, 1875–1975: bibliografía. Montevideo: Biblioteca Nacional, 1975. 48 p.

Bibliografía preparada por personal técnico de la Biblioteca Nacional del Uruguay. El repertorio, cuyos ítems no están numerados, contiene "Testimonios Personales" (entre ellos, 32 manuscritos), "Obra" (en libros, diarios y revistas, y traducciones), "Crítica" e "Iconografía." De interés para el investigador. [DL]

5937 Mistral, Gabriela. Gabriela piensa en . . . Selección de prosas y prólogo, Roque Esteban Scarpa. Santiago, Chile: Editorial A. Bello, 1978. 435 p.

Nuevas muestras de un aspecto de la producción de Gabriela Mistral que ha sido poco estudiado: su personalísima y trabajada prosa. Ordenados en seis secciones, estos textos de la poetisa chilena dibujan una suerte de galería de personajes de diversa índole: 1) Mujeres representativas; 2) Figuras de nuestro Chile; 3) Figuras de América; 4) Figuras de España; 5) Figuras de Europa; y 6) Figuras de la Aventura. Lamentablemente, el compilador no señala el origen de los prosas antologadas. See also item **5482**. [OH]

———. Gabriela piensa en . . . See item **5483**.

———. Materias: prosa inédita. See item **5484**.

5938 Nalé Roxlo, Conrado. Borrador de memorias. Buenos Aires: Plus Ultra, 1978. 222 p. (Nuestros novelistas)

Interesantísimas memorias de la vida literaria en Buenos Aires, especialmente durante la década de 1920, con datos sobre figuras mayores y menores así como jugosas anécdotas, en un tono de humor muy personal. [DL]

5939 Rokha, Pablo de. Pablo de Rokha contra Neruda. Selección de textos y prólogo de Diego Arenas. Buenos Aires: Editorial Galerna, 1978. 159 p. (Colección Pólemos)

Selección de textos de Pablo de Rokha que ilustran uno de los episodios más lamentables de la vida literaria chilena: su obsesiva animadversión contra Pablo Neruda. Según el prologista y recopilador, los escritos rokhianos—varios de ellos inhallables—representan un caso límite de esa enfermedad profesional que aqueja a muchos creadores latinoamericanos, transformándolos en personajes egocéntricos, llenos de envidias y de celos literarios. [OH]

5940 Vallejo, César Abraham. Enunciados de la guerra española. Selección, prólogo y notas de Armando Zárate. Buenos Aires: R. Alonso Editor, 1976. 67 p.; bibl., ill. (Colección Argumentos)

Buen trabajo de recopilación de los artículos escritos por Vallejo en 1937. Incluye el discurso en el II Congreso Internacional de Escritores para la Defensa de la Cultura: "La Responsibilidad del Escritor." Aunque algunos de los cinco textos eran conocidos, este es el primer volumen que los reúne en forma independiente y orgánica. [PL]

5941 ———. Obras completas. t. 2, El arte y la revolución. Lima: Mosca Azul Editores, 1973. 167 p.

Util reedición de un conjunto de artículos y textos breves escritos por Vallejo después de sus viajes a la Unión Soviética (1928, 1929 y 1931). Incluye como "Apéndices" varias notas afines a la temática del volumen, datadas entre 1926 y 1937–38. Las reflexiones registradas en este libro "de pensamiento y acción revolucionaria" iluminan aspectos significativos de la práctica creadora del autor. [PL]

Drama

GEORGE WOODYARD, *Professor of Spanish, University of Kansas*

ONCE AGAIN, THIS IS A fertile period both for plays and for serious criticism. The established writers continue writing, and new plays by Azar, Cañas, Chocrón, Halac, Pla and Rovinski show their considerable ability to manipulate human relationships with dexterity in creating good drama. Jorge Díaz returns with his old strength and vigor; José de Jesús Martínez continues his strong protest with an effective self-referential technique within the *creación colectiva*. Benedetti's new play echoes a familiar theme—torture—with a powerful technique. There are promising young writers with solid first plays, such as Romero and Torres Molina, both of whom use the idiom of the game to create tension. Reprintings of previous works, some of which were virtually inaccessible, include plays by Buenaventura, Carballido, Chocrón, Carlos Felipe, Gambaro, Julio Ortega, César Rengifo and Egon Wolff. Also in this category is a new anthology by Dauster, Lyday, and Woodyard that makes nine plays available for classroom use.

This period is notable for the critical attention to the theatre history, as seen in the studies on Venezuelan theatre (items **6022**, **6043**, **6049** and **6056**), Colombia (item **6077**), Peru (item **6058**), plus invaluable collections that give panoramic views of popular theatre (item **6061**), radical theatre (item **6057**), and the *creación colectiva* (item **6039**). In individual studies, the range of critical method spans Aristotle, Brecht, Artaud and, myth, as well as newer systems of metatheatre (item **6036**) and semiotics (items **6059** and **6060**). *Texto Crítico* (item **6070**) devoted a complete issue to new Spanish American theatre, and a special issue of *Revista Chicano-Riqueña* focused on Hispanic theatre in the US, an area which is receiving greater critical attention than ever (item **6076**). New studies focus on the theatre of Aub, Carlos Fuentes and Pavlovsky; an item of particular interest is Kaiser-Lenoir's study on the *grotesco criollo* (item **6045**). Sadly lacking still are good histories of the contemporary theatre in Argentina, Chile, Colombia and Mexico which would provide a thorough analytical view of these vital movements.

PLAYS

5942 Aliber, Alicia and **Bernardo Aliber.** Mis abuelos campesinos. Obra teatral en dos partes. Buenos Aires: Ediciones del Carro de Tespis, 1974. 77 p. (Colección Nuestro teatro, 40)

Nostalgic recreation of grandparents and youth by a first-person narrator/participant. Sentimental, poignant fluff.

5943 Azar, Héctor. Los muros vacíos. Drama en tres actos. México: Textos CADAC, 1978. 63 p.

In a more realistic vein than his previous works, Azar deals once again with the limits of human love. Through a circular structure and flashbacks, Azar portrays a middle-aged woman's futile attempt to find love in a world of meaningless objects.

5944 Benedetti, Mario. Pedro y el capitán. Pieza en cuatro partes. México: Editorial Nueva Imagen, 1979. 91 p. (Serie Literatura)

The game is torture, the prize is death. Spell-binding play between torturer and tortured with the anticipated results, but getting there is both intense and convincing.

5945 Buenaventura, Enrique. Teatro. Bogotá: Instituto Colombiano de Cultura, 1977. 272 p. (Colección Popular; 21)

Los papeles del infierno, five short bitter forms of violence; *El menú*, grotesque vision of successful politician; *La orgía*, social class deformation; *Soldados*, the banana massacre of 1928; and the classic *A la diestra de Dios Padre.* Dynamic, scathing, highly theatrical pieces.

Cabrera y Quintero, Cayetano Javier de. Obra dramática. Teatro novohispano del siglo XVIII. See item **5114a**.

5946 Calveyra, Arnaldo. Teatro. Latin American trip. Caracas: Monte Avila Editores, 1978. 78 p. (Colección Teatro)

A curiously stylized and documentary anti-US political play with supposedly mythical overtones of Orpheus' descent into hell, leading to personal encounters with individual mortality. Short on subtlety, long on hyperbole, with a weak plot.

5947 Cañas, Alberto. Una bruja en el río. Premio Aquileo J. Echeverría de Teatro, 1977. San José: Editorial Costa Rica, 1978. 112 p., plates.

Love story of one girl with many pretenders, with a note of magic intended into the criteria for selection. Pleasant but conventional.

5948 Carballido, Emilio. Tres obras. México: Editorial Extemporáneos, 1978. 254 p.

This reprinting of *Silencio, pollos pelones . . .* (1963), *Un pequeño día de ira* (1966), and the previously unpublished *Acapulco, los lunes* (1970) provides easy access to three plays by the ever-popular Mexican playwright. The first two have been enduring successes; *Acapulco, los lunes* is not one of his best efforts.

5949 Castellanos de Ríos, Ada; Zenobio Calizaya Velásquez; and **Luis Llanos Aparicio.** Teatro boliviano. Jugando a soñar [de] Ada Castellanos de Ríos. Dad al César lo que es del César y a Dios lo que es de Dios [de] Zenobio Calizaya Velásquez. La leyenda de Supay Calle [de] Luis Llanos Aparicio. Premios del Concurso de Obras Teatrales en un Acto del Instituto Boliviano de Cultura, 1976. Introducción de Andrés Canedo. La Paz: Instituto Boliviano de Cultura, 1977. 80 p.

Jugando a soñar: a young university student has lapsed into a coma, ostensibly as a result of a student riot, but probably because of her inability to resolve conflicts between social classes. *Dad al César lo que es del César y a Dios lo que es de Dios*: Manuel, a miner, stands before San Pedro to be judged, after having died in a mine accident while stealing minerals. Poverty and hunger are insufficient defense pleas to escape damnation. *La leyenda de Supay Calle*: a 17th-century setting in colonial La Paz and the least viable of these three plays which all together reveal a higher level of dramatic interest than has customarily been found in the Bolivian theatre.

5950 Centeno Güell, Fernando. Las danzas de Job. Poema coreográfico, en un prólogo, tres movimientos y un epílogo. San José: Editorial Costa Rica, 1977. 83 p.

An ambitious symbolic dance/poem that attempts to capture Job's suffering with a stylized, elevated language. It fails.

5951 Chocrón, Isaac E. El acompañante. Pieza en dos partes. Caracas: Monte

Avila Editores, 1978. 85 p. (Colección Teatro)

In the modern idiom of the two-character play, *El acompañante* is entertaining but a bit too precious. Operatic background provides a natural lead into the audition for accompanist, but results in melodramatic attempts to create tension. Not up to Chocrón's usual standards.

5952 ———. Teatro. El quinto infierno. Animales feroces. Asia y el Lejano Oriente. Selección y prólogo de Francisco Rivera. Caracas: Monte Avila Editores, 1974. 277 p.

A recompilation of three early Chocrón favorites, selected by Francisco Rivera for their representative quality.

5953 **Comedias y sainetes** argentinos. v. 1, Antología. Selección, introducción, notas y propuestas de trabajo: Nora Mazziotti. Buenos Aires: Ediciones Colihue, 1979. 282 p.; bibl. (Colección Literaria LYC [Leer y crear])

Anthology of Argentine plays prepared as school edition. Includes: Nicolás Granada *Al campo!*; Enrique Buttaro *Los distraídos o La torta de la novia*; Roberto Lino Cayol *Pompas de jabón o El veraneo de don Ponciano*; Federico Mertens *La carabina de Ambrosio*; Roberto J. Payró *Mientraiga*; Alejandro Berrutti *Ciudado con los bonitas*. Typical urban comedies of the period 1900–40.

5954 **Cuadra, Fernando.** La familia de Marta Mardones. Obra en tres actos (EC/M, 24, 1977, p. 103–166)

A determined lady struggles to maintain the family unity in spite of problems presented by a pregnant unmarried daughter, a philandering son, and a useless husband. Good human interest, although technique is unsophisticated, typical of Cuadra.

5955 **Cuchi Coll, Isabel.** La familia de Justo Malgenio: puertorriqueños en Nueva York. Comedia en tres actos. Madrid: Gráfica Internacional, 1974. 121 p.

Puerto Rican family in New York exemplifies the normal acculturation problems, but without the dramatic intensity or vigor of *La carreta*.

5956 **Díaz, Francisco.** Tragedia en verso, escrita por el poeta salvadoreño Francisco Díaz, en el año de 1842, con motivo de la muerte del General Francisco Morazán. Tegucigalpa: Instituto Morazánico, 1976. 77 p.

A reprinting of an 1842 romantic tribute to the Central American hero, General don Francisco Morazán, to make it available as a school text. Heroic but very dated.

5957 **Díaz, Jorge** and **José González Torices.** Teatro. El locutorio [de] Jorge Díaz. Premio Valladolid de Teatro Breve 1976, Caja de Ahorros Provincial de Valladolid. El cerco de la peste [de] José González Torices. Finalista del Premio Valladolid de teatro breve 1976. Valladolid, Spain: Caja de Ahorros Provincial de Valladolid, 1976. 67 p.

El locutorio shows Díaz at his intrinsic best: a couple in a closed space, wrestling with existential and metaphysical issues of life, love, truth, and death. Obvious touches of his *Cepillo de dientes* period, but with a new flavor. (González Torices is a Spaniard.)

5958 **Díaz Vargas, Henry.** El puño contra la roca: pieza corta de un acto (UA/U, 51:197, abril/junio 1976, p. 109–115)

Monologue of a torturer unsuccessful in breaking his victim. Clichéd techniques.

5959 **Diego, Celia de.** Bajo el poncho azul. Comedia dramática en tres actos y un epílogo sobre la vida del General Juan Lavalle, 1828–1841. Buenos Aires: Casa Pardo, 1977. 79 p., bibl.

Yet another example of the constant interest in historical drama, on the life of Gen. Juan Lavalle from 1828 till 1841 during the *federal/unitario* conflict in Argentina. Feminist perspective of women behind the men in battle lends more than usual interest.

5960 **Elizalde, Fernando de.** El sombrero de Guindas. Un acto en dos pasos. Buenos Aires: Casa Impresora Francisco A. Colombo, 1977. 44 p.

Two characters, one dominant in each *paso*, search for meaning and identity in their jaded lives. Heavy symbolism with touches of the absurd and a happy resolution.

5961 **Endara, Ernesto.** Una bandera (LNB/L, 262, dic. 1977, p. 111–122)

A father recalls proudly the memory of his son, killed in the Panamanian resistance against US domination. Monologue interrupted by choruses, documentary techniques. Sincere message, but lacks dramatic tension.

5962 **Enríquez Gamón, Efraín.** La agonía del héroe. Asunción: Editorial el Gráfico, 1977. 143 p.

An ill-fated effort to dramatize the memory of Paraguay's 19th-century boy wonder, Francisco Solano López. Useful as a historical re-examination, but too cumbersome to be theatrical.

5963 **Estevanell, Justo Esteban.** El impacto. Teatro. La Habana: Editorial Arte y Literatura, 1976. 75 p.; ill. (Mínima teatro; 1)

Hapless and hungry street vendor struggles for survival in pre-revolutionary Cuba. Unadulterated propaganda.

5964 **Felipe, Carlos.** Requiem por Yarini. Drama trágico en tres actos. Miami, Fla.: Ediciones Calesa, 1978. 66 p.; plate.

Re-edition (in exile) of Felipe's best play about love inside the Havana brothels of 1910. Syncretism and magic create ambiance and good theatrical effects.

5965 **Galich, Manuel.** Puedelotodo vencido. La Habana: Editorial Gente Nueva, 1978. 44 p.

Interesting adaptation of an indigenous *quiché story* from the *Popol Vuh*, in which the pretentious figure who tries to dominate the others is vanquished. Obviously didactic.

5966 **———.** El tren amarillo y otras obras. La Habana: Editorial Letras Cubanas, 1979. 459 p.

Reprinting of six of Galich's best plays. Strong social protest within Aristotelian framework. Besides the title play, includes *El pescado indigesto*; *Pascual Abah*; and the trilogy *Los Natas* (*Papá Natas*, *La mugre*, and *El último cargo*).

5967 **Gambaro, Griselda.** Teatro. Las paredes. El desatino. Los siameses. Buenos Aires: Editorial Argonauta, 1979. 165 p.

With this new edition of old plays by one of Argentina's most important and original contemporary playwrights, *Las paredes* finally becomes available to the reading public.

5968 **Gandara, Enrique** [*pseud. for* **Oscar Rius**]. El teatro de las tres carátulas. Ensayo de farsa. Buenos Aires: Editorial Central, 1977. 125 p.; bibl.

Man/woman relationships in a technique that tries to outdo Brecht through elaborate distancing. In final analysis, not very satisfying.

5969 **Garibay, Ricardo.** Mujeres en un acto. Juegos de odio. La guerra. Crema Chantilly. La prisionera. Gap. México: Editorial Posada, 1978. 143 p.

Five one-acts on feminist problems ranging from masculine violence to sexual eroticism and liberation. In this first incursion into theatre, the prolific Garibay reveals a good perception of feminine sensibilities and concerns.

5970 **Gaviria, José Enrique.** Caminos en la niebla y otras piezas teatrales. Bogotá: Instituto Caro y Cuervo, 1978. 149 p. (Serie La Granada entreabierta; 23)

Collection of five plays of little theatrical interest except *Kaiyou* (1942), whose setting in exotic Haiti with emphasis on African legends and conflict between blacks and mulattos is suggestive of *Emperor Jones*.

5971 **Ghiano, Juan Carlos.** Tres tragicomedias porteñas. Narcisa Garay, mujer para llorar. Antiyer. Corazón de tango. Prólogo de Atilio Betti. Buenos Aires: Goyanarte Editor, 1977. 189 p.

A new edition of three classical Argentine sainetes attests to the continuing dramatic viability of these urban tragicomedies.

5972 **González, Juan.** Doce paredes negras. Experimento inconcluso en tres actos. Río Piedras, P.R.: Editorial Cultural, 1978. 149 p.

A compassionate view of the frustrations and disappointments in finding love and happiness in the gay world. Provocative and insightful.

5973 **González González, Sergio.** Las provisiones. Premio Teatro, Consurso 26 de Julio de la Dirección Política de las Fuerzas Armadas Revolucionarias. La Habana: Editorial Arte y Literatura, 1976. 77 p.

A mother's anguish over the death of her child brings into focus the conflict between strong religious beliefs (Testigos de Jehová) and revolutionary goals in contemporary Cuba (see Flora Lauten's *Los hermanos*, *HLAS 40:7279*).

5974 **Halac, Ricardo.** Segundo tiempo. Buenos Aires: Editorial Galerna, 1978. 159 p.; ill.

An unsophisticated but convincing look at a young housewife's attempt to establish her own identity. The husband's desperate and sometimes pathetic efforts to deal with women's lib are played off against the mother's conventional views of woman's role. Argentores' best play for 1976.

5975 **Herrera, Larry.** Canario de la mala noche. Prólogo de Carlos Giménez. Caracas: Editorial Ateneo de Caracas, 1979. 97 p.

Regard for esthetics dominates the political compromise of this view of liberty and justice in 19th-century Venezuela. Herrera, a young writer, has promise.

5976 **López Pérez, Heriberto.** Teatro. Bogotá: Ediciones Alcaraván, 1977. 152 p.

Four plays, each with its historical background, which succeeds as political invective but not as theatre. *La última batalla de los vencidos en un día de terror y de miseria*, for example, incorporates documentary segments from the Vietnam War into a hyperbolic statement against North American imperialism.

5977 **Luaces, Joaquín Lorenzo.** *A tigre, zorra y bulldog*: presentación de Magaly Pérez Machado (UCLV/I, 58, 1978, p. 73–185)

Havana comedy of 1863 involves a Molière-type miser against a pair of fortune hunters. Verse dialogue is simple and natural, the characters typical of developing *bufo* style.

5978 **Martínez, José de Jesús.** La guerra del banano. Teatro. Premio Ricardo Miro, 1975. Panamá: Instituto Nacional de Cultura, 1976. 95 p.; plates.

By Panama's best-known playwright, this documentary piece about the 1974 banana strike is vitriolic in denouncing US imperialism, but effective theatre for the self-referential role-playing within its *creación colectiva* structure.

5979 **Medina, Roberto Nicolás.** Erase un viejo pirata: un pirata y un loro, en dos travesías y un hundimiento. Buenos Aires: Editorial Plus Ultra, 1977. 95 p.; ill. (Colección El escenario)

Good full-length children's play of which too few find their way into print.

5980 **Mendes, Alejandro Samuel.** En el Valle de Oronqota. La Paz: Casa Municipal de la Cultura Franz Tamayo, 1978. 103 p. (Biblioteca paceña. Nueva serie)

Non-traditional theatre with Incan "chromatic" style and structure, recreating a famous conquest by the Inca Tupac Yupanqui.

5981 **Mendive, Rafael Maria de.** *La nube negra*: drama en cuatro actos y en versos (UCLV/I, 54, mayo/agosto 1976, p. 157–180)

Fragments of an 1863 Cuban play which show good understanding of dramatic structure and lively dialogue in a love story.

5982 **Montalvo, Juan.** El libro de las pasiones. Ambato, Ecuador: Ediciones de la Casa de la Cultura, Núcleo Provincial de Tungurahua, 1976. 456 p. (Colección Popular de la bibliografía ambatena; 3)

Five plays from the 1870s by Ecuador's famous essayist and patriot: *La leprosa*; *Jara* (vengeance); *El descomulgado* (love); *Granja* (jealousy); and *El dictador* (ambition?). Sentimental pieces edited for patriotic, not dramatic, reasons.

5983 **Mora, Juan Miguel de.** Plaza de las Tres Culturas, Tlatelolco. Obra en tres actos. México: Editores Asociados Mexicanos, 1978. 101 p.

The massacre of Tlatelolco is potentially good material for a modern day tragedy, but in Mora's hands it becomes another conventional diatribe filled with demagoguery, unbelievable characters and strained dialogue.

5984 **Morales, Jacobo.** Cinco sueños en blanco y negro. Río Piedras, P.R.: Editorial Antillana, 1977. 69 p.; ill.

Five "dreams" (or perhaps nightmares)—virtually monologues—whose central themes reflect despair, anguish, and death in an oppressive, mechanistic society. Aggressive, biting, convincing.

5985 **Muello, Juan Carlos.** Que lindo es estar casado . . . y tener la suegra al lado. Guerra a las polleras. Buenos Aires: Editorial Kiek, 1977. 172 p. (Teatro familiar y popular)

Two popular comedies without transcendental value, written in typical language of Buenos Aires.

5986 9 [i.e. **Nueve**] **dramaturgos** hispanoamericanos. Antología del teatro hispanoamericano del siglo XX. v. 1/3. Ottawa: GIROL Books, 1979. 3 v. (273, 226, 181 p.) bibl.

This anthology, published in three volumes, is designed to make available important works of contemporary Spanish American theatre. Editors Dauster, Lyday, and Woodyard have supplied each play with a brief critical introduction and a bibliography on each individual author. Plays included: Vol. 1, Usigli, *Corona de sombra*; Triana, *La noche de los asesinos*; Dragún, *El amasijo*; Vol. 2, Villaurrutia, *Invitación a la muerte*; Gambaro, *Los siameses*; Wolff, *Flores de papel*; Vol. 3, Marqués, *Los soles truncos*; Díaz, *El cepillo de dientes*; Carballido, *Yo también hablo de la rosa*.

5987 **Oliva, Felipe** and **Roberto Orihuela.** Un pelo en plena juventud [de] Felipe Oliva. Ramona [de] Roberto Orihuela. La Habana: Unión de Escritores y Artistas de Cuba, 1978. 142 p. (Manjuarí. Teatro)

Two plays that make a strong statement about women's rights to work and to sexual equality. Didactic theatre lacking subtlety with express purpose of satisfying revolutionary goals.

5988 **Ortega, Julio.** Ceremonia y otros actos. Lima: Libros de Postdata, 1974. 194 p.

Ten of Ortega's one-act plays, plus the poetic-documentary *Mesa Pelada*, show a range of concerns with political, social, and existential issues. The clean-cut style and black humor emphasize an anti-establishment posture, and put Ortega squarely in the vanguard of contemporary theatre.

5989 **Pla, Josefina.** La creación literaria. Teatro. Fiesta en el río. Pieza en tres actos. Primer premio: Cuarto Concurso de Obras Teatrales de Radio Charitas, 1976. Asunción: Editorial Siglo XXI, 1977. 112 p.

Free-spirited girl defies community standards of love and marriage with nearly fatal consequences, as demanded by folk traditions. Poetic, semi-verse form, good conflict and dramatic tension.

5990 **Premios Protea, 1976.** México: Editorial Extemporáneos, 1977. 1 v. (Unpaged)

Contains three new Mexican plays. *Dentro de estos ocho muros* by Rafael Ramírez Heredia, is a play of political and sexual intrigue presented in alternating scenes on a divided stage. *Santa Catarina* by Oscar Villegas realistically portrays the pressures and the homosexuality at a military school. Agustín Bandrich's *Réquiem para Lecumberri* is a lengthy, realistic exposé of the conditions in the infamous Mexican prison.

5991 **Rabinovich, José.** Con pecado concebida. Obra teatral en cuatro actos. Buenos Aires: Ediciones del Carro de Tespis, 1975. 72 p. (Colección Nuestro teatro; 41)

A dying woman relives her past as a rich Catholic married to a Jewish taxi driver. The interaction touches on fundamental aspects of Jewish and Christian life styles and attitudes, but the exaggerated character and the absence of dramatic tension make the play ineffective.

5992 *Revista Chicano-Riqueña.* Año 7, No. 1, Invierno 1979– . Gary, Indiana.

This special issue, subtitled "Nuevos Pasos," is dedicated entirely to Chicano and Puerto Rican drama. Prefaced with an introduction by Nicolás Kanellos and Jorge A. Huerta, the issue offers recent works by R. Arias, R. Duarte-Clarke, E. Portillo-Trambley, C. Morton, R. Sierra, J. Carrero, M. Algarín and T. Laviera, and M. Piñero.

5993 **Reyes García, Ismael.** El envés del teatro. Trabajos de arte de Augusto Marin. San Juan, P.R.: Instituto de Cultura Puertorriqueño, 1977. 84 p. (Serie Literatura hoy; 2:4)

A Rosencrantz and Guildenstern approach, applied to the support crew backstage, interacting with the action. Original, clever idea developed in two short plays: *Los tramoyistas* and *¡Ella o yo!*

5994 **Reyes Ortiz, Félix.** Teatro. Las lanzas. Plan de una representación. Prólogo de Julio de la Vega. La Paz: Instituto Boliviano de Cultura, 1976. 101 p. (Clásicos bolivianos; 4)

Two plays by the first recognized Bolivian playwright (1828–82): *Plan de una representación*, a school farce with a commedia dell'arte flavor; *Las lanzas*, an historical version of independence. Surprisingly fresh verse.

5995 **Rivas, Ana.** 30 [i.e. Treinta] dineros. Premio IX Festival Internacional de

Teatro del Brasil. Buenos Aires: Ediciones Dintel, 1972. 61 p.

Twelve old friends from Buenos Aires reunite for dinner in a Last Supper setting. With the "master" absent, they recant their weaknesses and treasons. Contemporary problems, but overt symbolism is distracting.

5996 **Rodríguez, Jorge Mario.** El derrumbe. Los otros. Buenos Aires: Nuevas Ediciones Argentinas, 1977. 102 p. (Producciones teatrales scena)

Rodríguez (b. 1931) writes self-reflexive plays reminiscent of the game techniques of *La noche de los asesinos*. *El derrumbe* is the desperate struggle of weak children against the omnipotent fiction of the Family. *Los otros* shares the same characteristics, but with a more contrived ending.

5997 **Romero, Mariela.** El juego. Caracas: Monte Avila Editores, 1977. 66 p. (Colección Teatro)

Two women (girls?) involved in a love/hate relationship of mutual dependency is suggestive of Gambaro's *Los siameses*. Cruel, highly theatrical, role-playing. Romero is both talented and promising.

5998 **Rovinski, Samuel.** Un modelo para Rosaura o la manera de acomodar una historia a nuestro gusto. Tragicomedia burguesa en dos actos. Premio de Teatro, Editorial Costa Rica, 1974. San José: Editorial Costa Rica, 1975. 126 p.

A suggestion of incest colors this trivial story of two siblings; he is the bon-vivant, she has doubts about her impending marriage. The Pirandellian twist of continuing the play during the supposed intermission makes this one of Rovinski's better efforts.

5999 **Ruiz Cano y Sáenz Galiano, Francisco Antonio,** *marqués de* Soto Florido. Drama de los palanganas Veterano y Bisoño. Documentos inéditos sobre: Micaela Villegas, (la Perricholi); la quinta de Copacabana; y el hijo del Virrey Amat. Publicado, prologado y anotado por Luis Alberto Sánchez. Lima: Editorial Jurídica, 1977. 142 p.

Cumbersome dialogue performed on the steps of the Lima cathedral the nights of 17, 18 and 19 July 1776 as a long and acerbic satire against the Viceroy Amat for his scandalous love affair with Micaela Villegas (la Perricholi), and other sins of commission and omission. In his introduction, Sánchez states that the authorship of this work cannot be attributed definitely to Ruiz Cano. Thoroughly researched, interesting to theatre historians.

6000 **Saldarriaga Sanín, Rodrigo.** Diles que no me maten: versión teatral del cuento del mismo nombre de Juan Rulfo (UA/U, 50:196, enero/marzo 1976, p. 39–41)

This dramatized version of Rulfo's famous story of a murderer apprehended and executed after years of flight unfortunately lacks the theatrical power of the original.

6001 **Sánchez, Florencio.** Barranca abajo. Prólogo de Alcides Abella. Montevideo: Ediciones de la Banda Oriental, 1978. 59 p.

New edition of this River Plate classic has a psychological analysis of the play with an explanation of the realism/naturalism of the period.

6002 **Schinca, Milton A.** Delmira y otras rupturas. Chau, todo. Delmira. Las raíces. Teatro. Montevideo: Ediciones de la Banda Oriental, 1977. 105 p.

In *Delmira*, the identity issue is emphasized by having both faces of the schizophrenic on stage simultaneously. *Chau todo* also explores identity problems in a trite matrimonial conflict. *Las raíces* departs from the *Blancos* vs. *Colorados* conflict of the Uruguayan civil wars. The plays attempt to compensate for deficiencies in structure and dialogue through elaborate technical effects—rapid flashbacks, simultaneity, black-outs, etc.

6003 **Serulle, Haffe.** La danza de Mingo. Santo Domingo: Ediciones de Taller, 1977. 73 p. (Biblioteca Taller; 77)

Within a black Caribbean setting, a woman defends her man who has defied local authority. A poetic play with all the rhythmic quality of a Guillén poem, filled with superstition, sensuality and telluric qualities. Makes a successful political statement.

6004 **Shand, William.** Teatro. Farsa con rebelde. Secuestros, perros y otras yerbas. La elección de José. Adobe para los mansos. El sastre. Estudio preliminar de Raúl H. Castagnino. Buenos Aires: Ediciones Corregidor, 1976. 283 p. (Serie Mayor; 153)

Five plays by the prolific English writer long established in Argentina. Sympathetic, inoffensive characters who suffer the cruel instincts of others: *Farsa con rebelde, La elección de José* and *El sastre* all share the theme of sadism. Satiric theatre, very playable.

6005 Silva, Jaime. La fantástica isla de los casianimales: teatro (EC/M, 25, 1977, p. 145–171)

An allegory of love and liberty over tyranny in a Doolittle-type fantasy island "peopled" with a "*perroglífico, elefángel, librélula, abuelostra*" and others. Clever and effective theatre.

6006 ——— and **Gabriel Rojo.** Apocalipsis: vodevil de ciencia-ficción en dos partes (EC/M, 25, 1977, p. 173–195)

A socio-economic play disguised in a futuristic 29th century with elements of farce, slap-stick humor, and allegory. Innovative, potentially funny and theatrical.

6007 Soberón Torchia, Edgar and **Alfredo Arango.** Pepita de Marañón: es mas, el día de la lata (LNB/L, 274, dic. 1978, p. 55–92)

Cross-section of Panamanian lower-class ambiance that portrays multiple cultural infusion through music, language, politics, etc. Lively, colorful, varied, poignant picture of massive problems.

6008 Tapia y Rivera, Alejandro. Bernardo de Palissy. Barcelona: Editorial Vosgos, 1977. 175 p. (Colección Grandes maestros; 89)

A 16th-century French historical figure sets an example of Christian purity and nobility for the working class. This four-act verse play suffers melodramatic patterns of its time (1857), but is better than most.

6009 Teatro César Rengifo. Selección de Francisco Garzón Céspedes. La Habana: Casa de las Américas, 1977. 419 p.

Six plays (no new ones) by Venezuela's most prolific dramatist in two cycles: 1) *Mural de la guerra federal: los hombres de los cantos amargos, Un tal Ezequiel Zamora, Lo que dejó la tempestad*; and 2) *Mural del petróleo: el vendaval amarillo, El raudal de los muertos cansados, Las torres y el viento.* Marxist values dominate the historical and political issues.

6010 Teatro cubano del siglo XIX. v. 1, Antología. Edición de Natividad González Freire. La Habana: Editorial Arte y Literatura, 1975. 438 p. (Biblioteca básica de literatura cubana)

Five representative plays from 19th-century Cuba, ranging from the neoclassic to naturalistic: José María Heredia's *Los últimos romanos,* heroism of self-sacrifice before surrender; José Jacinto Milanés' *El conde Alarcos,* romanticized version of popular Hispanic theme of love and loyalty; Joaquín Lorenzo Luaces' *Aristodemo,* classical legend; Alfredo Torroella's *El mulato,* racial injustice; José de Armas y Cárdenas' *Los triunfadores,* corruption in Madrid society at end of 19th century (for v. 2 of this *Antología,* see *HLAS 40:7268*).

Teatro en Honduras. See item **5120a**.

6011 Teatro latinoamericano. Dos obras de creación colectiva. Selección del Departamento de Teatro de la Casa de las Américas. La Habana: Casa de las Américas, 1978. 229 p. (Col. La honda)

Closing of sugar mills in Tucumán in 1966 triggered *El fin del camino* by Libre Teatro Libre de Córboda—heavily documented Argentine sociopolitical protest. *I took Panamá* by Bogotá's TPB is a political documentary on US aggression and internal Colombian politics. Both are dated issues which have lost their fire.

6012 Torres Molina, Susana. Extraño juguete. Buenos Aires: Editorial Apex, 1978. 76 p.; plate (Colección Círculo mágico)

Two women admit a traveling salesman to their hermetic world with cruel and humiliating results. The sudden revelation of the ritual and game elements evaluates the theatricality. Entertaining, cruel, excellent.

Tres piezas teatrales del Virreinato. See item **5122**.

6013 Trujillo, Manuel and others. Teatro. Los siete pecados capitales. Caracas: Monte Avile Editores, 1974. 130 p. (Colección Teatro)

Brief vignettes commissioned by Antonio Costante for El Nuevo Grupo of Venezuela: Manuel Trujillo, *Avaricia*; Luis Britto García, *Gula*; Rubén Monasterios, *Lujuria*; Isaac Chocrón, *Pereza*; Luisa Lerner, *Envidia*; José Ignacio Cabrujas, *Soberbia*; Román Chalbaud, *Ira.* Individual styles and techniques, clever idea for light fare.

6014 Urquizo Huici, Carlos Fernando. Paranoia. La Paz: Comité Cívico Paceño, 1978. 49 p.

Simplistic view of false value systems that lead to generational problems and drug addiction in youth.

6015 Uslar Braun, Arturo. Teatro selecto. El silencio del señor. El otro Cristo. El zorro de seda Talleyrand. Caracas: Publicaciones Españolas, 1976. 221 p.

El silencio del señor, sex intrigue leading to prostitution; *El otro Cristo,* a verbose and skewed version of the passion, crucifixion and resurrection; *El zorro de seda Talleyrand,* Talleyrand holds the final trump card in his pact with the Devil. Satiric pieces with good features but weak structure.

6016 Vadell, Jaime; José Manuel Salcedo; and **David Benavente.** Bienaventurados los pobres. Presentación de Beltrán Villegas. Santiago: Ediciones Aconcagua, 1978. 73 p. (Colección Bello)

Departs from *La Araucana* and the relationship of the Church and the Indian in colonial society to offer analogies about contemporary times. Documentary based on Padres Camilo Henríquez and Alberto Hurtado is one of Chile's best in this vein.

6017 Valdés Vivó, Raúl. Naranjas en Saigón. La Habana: Editorial Arte y Literatura, 1977. 73 p. (Mínima teatro; 3)

Parallel action between market vendors and American headquarters justifies popular resistance to American intervention in Vietnam. Better than most plays of its kind.

6018 Vallejo, César Abraham. Teatro completo. t. 1, Lock-out. Entre las dos orillas corre el río; t. 2, Colacho hermanos o Presidentes de Américas. La piedra cansada. Prólogo, traducciones y notas de Enrique Ballón Aguirre. Lima: Pontificia Universidad Católica del Perú, Fondo Editorial, 1979. 2 v. (177, 217 p.)

Lock-out, class struggle in a metallurgical factory; *Entre las dos orillas corre el río,* post-revolutionary Russian exploration of exploitation; *Colacho hermanos o presidentes de América,* political satire; *La piedra cansada,* escapist theatre into precolumbian Incan times. The Marxist political and ideological militancy of Vallejo dominates these works which examine class struggle and advocate active resistance against class exploitation. Clearly not of the caliber of his poetry.

6019 Vilalta, Maruxa. Historia de él. Obra en 17 cuadros. Premio Nacional Juan Ruiz de Alarcón de la Asociación Mexicana de Críticos de Teatro a la Mejor Obra de 1978. México: Universidad Nacional Autónoma de México, Difusión Cultural, Departamento de Teatro, 1979. 59 p.; plates (Textos de teatro; 12)

A man's unscrupulous rise to economic and political power brings out the inevitable sycophants and love intrigues. Vilalta ambitiously manipulates 87 characters through 17 scenes with Brechtian skill, but the mosaic of scenes creates an undesirable fragmentation.

6020 Wolff, Egon. Niñamadre. Flores de papel. Kindergarten. Prólogo de Juan Andrés Piña. Santiago: Editorial Nascimento, 1978. 1 v. (Unpaged)

A collection consisting of one of Wolff's earlier plays and two more recent dramas. In *Niñamadre,* the title character wrestles with the conflict between her extreme need for love and her last opportunity to bear a child. *Flores de papel* is a powerful drama that traces the step-by-step domination of a street ruffian over a lonely woman. *Kindergarten* revolves around the tensions and game-playing between two brothers, a situation compounded when their sister moves in with them.

CRITICAL WORKS

6021 Azar, Héctor. Zoon theatrykon: análisis, reflexiones y proposiciones para integrar la Teoría Cadac como un nuevo método de enseñanza artística, 1954–1973. México: UNAM, Comisión de Nuevos Métodos de Enseñanza, 1977. 106 p.

Pt. 1 postulates the use of film, TV and theatre for propagation of culture on a national scale, following principles adopted by Azar's CADAC; pt. 2 is a panoramic view of world (especially Mexican) theatre today, showing dehumanization of the form and insisting on government support. Helpful in understanding Azar's own approach to theatre.

6022 Azparren, Leonardo. El teatro venezolano y otros teatros. Caracas: Monte Avila, 1979. 247 p.

The core of this book deals with the development of Venezuelan theatre during the post World War II period. Azparren, director and critic, wrote some of the essays in the 1960s, updated them for this volume. Especially good treatment of Chocrón, Lerner and Santana, sandwiched between views of European theatre and theoretical essays in the sociology of the theatre.

6023 Berenguer Carisomo, Arturo. Pautas de la cultura nacional: el teatro (*in* Cultura Nacional. Buenos Aires: Ediciones Crisol, 1976, p. 321–332)

In the roots of Argentine theatre, Berenguer points to the agrarian character and the circus for their fundamental importance in leading to the Golden Decade (1900–10).

6024 Bruce-Novoa, Juan and **David Valentín.** Violating the image of violence: Ibarguengoitia's *El atentado* (UK/LATR, 12:2, Spring 1979, p. 13–21)

Ibarguengoitia's play demythifies the positive aspects of the violence essential for political change through burlesque, farce, and Brechtian distancing, according to this perceptive study.

6025 Callan, Richard J. *Juicio final*: a definition of human existence (UK/LATR, 12:1, Fall 1978, p. 17–20)

Shows how Martínez successfully dramatizes the problem of commitment, not to deeds, but to the mysterious essence of life.

Carvalho-Neto, Paulo de. Concepto y realidad del teatro folklórico latinoamericano. See item **959**.

6026 Castagnino, Raúl Héctor. Crónicas del pasado teatral argentino, siglo XIX. Buenos Aires: Editorial Huemul, 1977. 265 p. (Colección Temas del hombre)

Disparate essays with an anecdotal flavor on various facets of 19th-century Argentine theatre. Fascinating for their historical interest, if not analytical.

6027 ———. Revaloración del género chico criollo. Buenos Aires: Universidad de Buenos Aires, Facultad de Filosofía y Letras, Instituto de Teatro, 1977. (Serie Cuadernos)

A reprinting of Castagnino's study (first published in *El teatro en Iberoamérica* in 1965) which provides a useful working definition with descriptive examples of *género chico* and *teatro breve* in Argentina.

6028 Chrzanowski, Joseph. Theme, characterization and structure in *Los invasores* (UK/LATR, 11:2, Spring 1978, p. 5–10)

Shows that the dream and Christian motifs are the principal unifying elements that give structural intelligibility to this psychological play.

6029 *Conjunto.* Casa de las Américas. No. 35, enero/marzo 1978 [through] No. 41, julio/sept. 1979– . La Habana.

This Cuban quarterly is devoted to the theatre, both in Cuba and in other parts of Latin America. Each issue normally focuses on the theatre of a particular country or playwright. The journal's Marxist orientation explains the emphasis on the most revolutionary of contemporary Latin American and international theatre. Besides interviews and critical studies, the journal frequently includes texts of plays.

6030 Cruz Díaz, Rigoberto. Muy buenas noches, señoras y señores. 2. ed. Santiago de Cuba: Editorial Oriente, 1978. 216 p.; facsims., plates.

Adventures of a circus/theatre company operating in Cuba from 1923–59, as told by the principal participants. Anecdotal, entertaining.

6031 Cruz-Luis, Adolfo. El movimiento teatral cubano en la Revolución (CDLA, 19:113, marzo/abril 1979, p. 40–50)

Panoramic view of Cuban theatre since the Revolution, presented in three periods: 1) 1959–64: an initial period of organization and establishment; 2) 1965–70: an intense period of searching for new methods consonant with sociopolitical goals, which led to the formation of many new groups; and 3) 1971 to present: a period of maturation that coincides with constitutional processes. Good resumé of objectives; little reference to specific works.

6032 Dauster, Frank. *La hija de Rappaccini*: dos visiones de la fantasía (RIB, 28:2, abril/junio 1978, p. 157–163)

Gives a strong second to Carballido's motion in favor of Paz's originality in "adapting" the Hawthorne story to the stage. The use of a Messenger with mythic qualities who links the lovers to figures of Tarot cards provides the right touch, a technique used by Carballido in his own plays. Perceptive article.

6033 Dembo, Samuel. El Nuevo Grupo: un nuevo teatro para Caracas. Fotografías de Samuel Dembo. Caracas: El Grupo, 1977. 93 p.: ill.

Handsomely illustrated history of Caracas' El Nuevo Grupo on their 10th anniversary. Limited text gives a flavor of the group's aspirations and achievements.

6034 Eidelberg, Nora. La ritualización de la violencia en cuatro obras teatrales hispanoamericanas (UK/LATR, 13:1, Fall 1979, p. 29–37)

Examines *Infierno negro, El menú, Hablemos a calzón quitado* and *El señor Galíndez* with Artaudian concepts of ritual and violence to comment on Latin American sociopolitical systems.

6035 Fernández, Guido. Los caminos del teatro en Costa Rica. San José: Editorial Universitaria Centroamericana, 1977. 186 p.; plates.

Recompilation of reviews published in *La Nación* between 1970–76 on various national and international plays performed in San José. Of only limited value as a Costa Rican theatre history.

6036 Foster, David William. Una aproximación a la escritura metateatral de *Ida y Vuelta* de Mario Benedetti (HISPA, 8:19, 1978, p. 13–25)

Analyzes the principal themes and technique of variations, asides and retardations that make this Benedetti play a classic example of metatheatre. Illuminating study of a solid play.

6037 ———. Elements of audience participation in Gentile's *Hablemos a calzón quitado* (UK/LATR, 12:2, Spring 1979, p. 23–35)

Studies the effectiveness of an experimental structure in achieving a sociopolitical statement.

6038 Garrido, Lenín. La imagen teatral. San José: Editorial Costa Rica, 1972. 175 p.; bibl.

Aristotelian approach to theoretical speculations on the essential principles of theatre (poetry, action, presence, etc.) followed by an analysis of the concepts of "active image" and "synthesis of the arts." Erudite and useful explication of dramatic functions, based on various theoreticians and texts.

6039 Garzón Céspedes, Francisco. El teatro de participación popular y el teatro de la comunidad: un teatro de sus protagonistas. La Habana: Unión de Escritores y Artistas de Cuba, 1977. 146 p.; plates.

Personal testimonies by Garzón Céspedes, Herminia Sánchez, Manuel Terraza and others regarding the importance of community theatre in fostering the goals of the Cuban Revolution.

6040 Gerdes, Dick. Recent Argentine vanguard theatre: Gambaro's *Información para extranjeros* (UK/LATR, 11:2, Spring 1978, p. 11–16)

A recent Gambaro play, studied in light of theories on space and author-actor relationships, as well as the parallel technique of violence and children's games, finds Gambaro effective at creating psychological cruelty.

6041 González Bosque, Hernán. Teatro inca: la escena enraizada (CH, 328, oct. 1977, p. 116–130)

Reevaluation of precolumbian Incan theatre includes descriptive background on Incan rituals, dances, language, religion; gives helpful nod toward Artaud and the use of masks. See also item **5130**.

———. Teatro ritual americano: El cautivo cristiano. See item **5131**.

6042 Grossman, Lois. *The children of Sánchez* on stage (UK/LATR, 11:2, Spring 1978, p. 33–39)

Sees in the English translation of Leñero's adaptation of Oscar Lewis' anthropological study an art form that is a tragedy of the human condition and not merely a social document.

6043 Hernández, Gleider. Tres dramaturgos venezolanos de hoy: R. Chalbaud, J. I. Cabrujas, I. Chocrón. Caracas: Ediciones El Nuevo Grupo, 1979. 142 p. (El Nuevo Grupo; 3)

Hernández uses an eclectic methodology in studying three major plays by each of the three writers (also actors and directors) of El Nuevo Grupo, who also happen to be the principal Venezuelan dramatists today. This critical study of Venezuelan theatre is most welcome.

6044 Hernández, Helmo. Notas acerca de una experiencia teatral en Lota (UH/U, 200, 1973, p. 93–113)

A Cuban examines Víctor Torres' *Una casa en Lota Alto* (as well as the theatre history of the Chilean mines which led up to it) and concludes that the Brechtian structure is an effective medium in the dialectical process, important for developing solidarity.

6045 Kaiser-Lenoir, Claudia. El grotesco criollo: estilo teatral de una época. La Habana: Casa de las Américas, 1977. 208 p.; bibl.

Carefully researched study of the development of the Argentine *grotesco criollo* as seen in Discépolo, Ghiano and others. Sees the subgenre as an esthetic reaction to social conflict between European immigrants and ruling class. Complex and sensitive treatment of a complex set of issues.

6046 Karavellas, Panos D. La dramaturgía de Samuel Eichelbaum. Montevideo, Uruguay: Ediciones Geminis, 1976. 188 p.; bibl. (Colección Novus orbis)

This study of character and technique in Eichelbaum's plays extolls his merits, but the absence of a critical method leads to some invalid conclusions, in the opinion of this editor.

6047 Kerr, R.A. La función de la Intermediaria en *Yo también hablo de la rosa* (UK/LATR, 12:1, Fall 1978, p. 51–60)

Demonstrates how the complex function of the Intermediaria reflects the basic principles of art embedded in this delightful play.

6048 Korn, Guillermo. Unos pasos por el teatro. Caracas: Ediciones Casuz, 1977. 158 p.

A curious collection of periodical reviews and other commentaries, mostly concentrating on Korn's period as a collaborator in the Teatro Universitario of Caracas, but with earlier material (from the 1920s) from Argentina.

6049 ———. Teatro en Caracas: de febrero de 1978 a abril de 1979. Caracas: Ediciones Casuz, 1979. 141 p.

Journalist reporting on about 50 plays presented in Caracas during 1978–79.

6050 *Latin American Theatre Review.* University of Kansas, Center for Latin American Studies. Vol. 11, No. 2, 1977; Vol. 12, No. 1, 1978; Vol. 12, No. 2, 1978; Vol. 13, No. 1, 1979– . Lawrence, Kansas.

In addition to separate articles listed, these issues contain reports on theatre activities and festivals in Argentina, Chile, Colombia, Cuba, Ecuador, Peru, Venezuela, and the US. Other articles focus on plays by: José Martí, René Marqués, Egon Wolff, Max Aub, Roberto Arlt, Osvaldo Dragún, and Celestino Gorostiza, as well as articles and reports on absurdist theatre in Cuba, theatre in Allende's Chile and interviews with Ricardo Monti, Alejandro Sieveking and Wilberto Cantón.

6051 Leal, Rine. Mendive dramaturgo (UCLV/I, 54, mayo/agosto 1976, p. 143–148)

Makes a case for Martí's teacher as a neglected dramatist on the basis of his love play, *La nube negra.* A fairly convincing case.

6052 Lomelí, Francisco A. Los mitos de la mexicanidad en la trilogía de Rodolfo Usigli (CH, 333, marzo 1978, p. 466–477)

A brief commentary on Usigli's three "antihistorical" *Corona* plays, concentrating on the importance of Maximiliano and Carlota, Cuauhtémoc and Cortés, and the Virgin of Guadalupe as elements in the creation of a Mexican mythology. Stresses interplay of historical characters; most attention to *Corona de fuego*, least to *Corona de luz.*

6053 López, Estela R. El teatro de Max Aub. Barcelona: Artes Gráficas Medinaceli, 1977. 200 p.; bibl. (Colección Uprex)

Thematic approach to the 48 plays of this exiled Spanish author (1903–72) concludes that Aub was the true proponent of Spanish theatre during the 1940s, although his influence has been minimal because his theatre of ideas is largely unknown.

6054 Luna Arroyo, Antonio. Julio Prieto y la escenografía (UIA/C, 12:59, feb. 1977, p. 128–143, ill., plates)

Laudatory review of Prieto's skill as an extremely versatile and successful painter and set designer, responsible for more than 500 works since 1942. Includes brief introduction to the history of scenography.

6055 Martínez Arango, Gilberto. Hacia un teatro dialéctico: ensayo de teoría y práctica del hecho teatral. Medellín, Colombia: Revista Teatro, 1979. 95 p.; bibl.

Marxist dialectics applied to Aristotle and Brecht to develop a theory of revolutionary theatre, which is itself applied to a production of Boal's *Revolución en América del Sur*. Neither new nor helpful.

6056 Monasterios, Rubén. Un enfoque crítica del teatro venezolano. Caracas: Monte Avila Editores, 1975. 128 p.

Without pretending to be a complete history of Venezuelan theatre, this study provides some background before the 1950s, from which the present movement dates, followed by panoramic sketches of a score of contemporary authors, which, although brief, contain interesting insights and conclusions about the way the current theatre has evolved.

6057 Monleón, José. América Latina: teatro y revolución. Caracas: Editorial Ateneo de Caracas, 1978. 234 p.

Monleón, director of Primer Acto, postulates some leftist theories about the relationship of politics, social conditions, and theatre in the introduction to this series of interviews conducted over a period of several years with the major playwrights, directors and critics of Latin American theatre. Invaluable collection of personal and professional commentaries by Jaime Kogan, Jorge Díaz, Atahualpa del Cioppo, Augusto Boal, and many other politically committed artists in Latin America.

6058 Morris, Robert J. The contemporary Peruvian theatre. Lubbock: Texas Tech Press, 1977. 98 p. (Graduate studies. Texas Tech University; 15)

Panoramic coverage of Peruvian theatre from 1946 to present. Thorough analytical studies of all works by 14 contemporary playwrights are well-balanced. The only comprehensive study available on present-day Peru.

6059 Negri, Orbit E. and **Ana María Lorenzo.** Aproximación semiótica a un texto dramático. Buenos Aires: Editorial Plus Ultra, 1978. 155 p.

Semiotic study of Ghiano's *Narcisa Garay: mujer para llorar* departs from Tadeusz Kowzan's principles; provides an excellent model for semiological approaches to drama. Portion of semiotics of scenography published earlier (see *HLAS 40:7332*).

6060 Peñuela Cañizal, Eduardo. Myth and language in a play by Carlos Fuentes (UK/LATR, 13:1, Fall 1979, p. 15–27)

Uses a semiotic approach to study myth and language in *Todos los gatos son pardos*; posits relationships with Asturias.

6061 Popular theatre for social change in Latin America: essays in Spanish and English. Edited by Gerardo Luzuriaga. Los Angeles: UCLA Latin American Center Publications, 1978. 432 p.; bibl., plates (UCLA Latin American studies; 41)

These 26 essays (in Spanish, with five in English), plus prologue and bibliography, explore the multi-faceted relationships of educational and political theatre to popular theatre. Under the categories of: 1) Theory and Methods; 2) National Panoramas; 3) Folkloric and Children's Theatre; 4) Festivals; and 5) Theatre Groups and Experiences; the volume stresses the importance of the popular theatre movement in Latin America. Invaluable item.

6062 Rapoport, Iosif Matveevich. El trabajo del actor. La Habana: Universidad de La Habana, Departamento de Cultura, 1978? 64 p.; ill. (Serie Literatura y arte)

A Cuban student manual designed for basic training in acting, with a general orientation to the theatre.

6063 Recopilación de textos sobre el teatro latinoamericano de creación colectiva. Compiled by Francisco Garzón Céspedes. La Habana: Casa de las Américas, Centro de Investigaciones Literarias, 1978. 564 p.; bibl. (Serie Valoración multiple)

A compilation of ca. 20 articles on the origins and objectives of the *creación colectiva* movement in Latin America since the mid-1960s. Ranges from theoretical essays by Carlos José Reyes, Enrique Buenaventura and others to specific group experiences and play productions (Libre Teatro Libre, TEC, Cuatrotablas, etc.). Strong Cuban imprint with Marxist orientation to revolutionary theatre techniques to be applied in emerging countries. An indispensable item for a comprehensive view of the movement.

6064 Richards, Katherine C. The Mexican existentialism of Solórzano's *Los fan-*

toches (LALR, 4:9, Fall/Winter 1976, p. 63–69)

Sees in *Los fantoches* a combination of Mexican folklore and existentialism, a point which has been made earlier.

6065 Rodríguez Suro, Joaquín. Religión e historia en *Todos los gatos son pardos* de Carlos Fuentes (PUC/V, 24:93, março 1979, p. 45–51, bibl.)

The play attempts to demythify history and to unmask religious bonds by using Cortés as a symbol of individual liberty, but correctly suggest that Fuentes' expression is deeper and richer in his novels.

6066 Rubio, Isaac. La Argentina de Osvaldo Dragún: entre Ionesco y Brecht (NS, 3:5/6, 1978, p. 179–198)

Shows how two plays by Dragún (*Milagro en el Mercado Viejo* and *Heroica de Buenos Aires*) intent on presenting Argentine reality fail because of the author's ambivalence over two esthetics: Brechtian commitment and the essential pessimism of theatre of the absurd.

6067 Schanzer, George O. El teatro vanguardista de Eduardo Pavlovsky (UK/LATR, 13:1, Fall 1979, p. 5–13)

The first panoramic study of this important Argentine playwright's corpus generally available.

6068 Skirius, A. John. Mexican introspection in the theater: Carlos Fuentes (UA/REH, 12:1, enero 1978, p. 25–40)

Examines the problems Fuentes faced in dramatizing cosmological and political paradoxes in *Todos los gatos son pardos*, and concludes that the job was too ambitious for one play. Faithful to the text, recognizes Paz's influence, but ignores existing criticism.

6069 Sosa Cordero, Osvaldo. Historia de las Varietés en Buenos Aires: 1900–1925. Buenos Aires: Ediciones Corregidor, 1978. 433 p.: plates.

Faithful reconstruction, carefully documented and indexed, of the personalities, theatres, and myriad forms—varieties, music-hall, circus, reviews, mimes, magicians, etc.—that dominated this escapist tendency in Buenos Aires. A labor of love to recapture past traditions.

6070 *Texto Crítico.* Universidad Veracruzana, Centro de Investigaciones Lingüístico-Literarias. Año 4, No. 10, mayo/agosto 1978– . Xalapa, México.

For the first time, editor Jorge Ruffinelli has put together an issue dedicated entirely to Latin American theatre. Critics from both the US and Latin America offer interviews with leading Mexican playwrights as well as numerous articles on general dramatic trends and specific dramatists.

6071 *Tramoya.* Universidad Veracruzana. No. 10, enero/marzo 1978– . Xalapa, México.

Dedicated to children's theatre. Contains several articles as well as play texts by M.A. Tenorio (*El día que Javier se puso águila*); E. Hernández, H. Dávalos, M. Mendoza, and J. Jiménez (*Barrionetas*); E. Carballido (*Dos obras y un modelo*).

6072 ———. ———. No. 11, abril/junio 1978– . Xalapa, México.

In addition to several articles of a critical nature and a short story by the Mexican dramatist Oscar Villegas, this issue includes the texts of two plays: *Los papeles del infierno*, a collection of three one-acts by the Colombian Enrique Buenaventura, and *La fábrica de los juguetes*, an existential, symbolic work with an element of social protest by the Mexican Jesús González Dávila.

6073 Vanossi, Jorge; Patricio Esteve; and **Julio Mauricio.** El teatro (*in* Arte y cultura en la Argentina. Buenos Aires: Editorial de Belgrano, 1977, p. 151–178)

Reflections by Esteve and Mauricio on the state of the art, and their relationship to contemporary Argentine theatre. As useful as public interviews of this kind ever are.

6074 Villacrés Stanton, Helena. El almanaque de Juárez de Emilio Carballido y México en 1968 (UK/LATR, 12:2, Spring 1979, p. 3–12)

Points out the way Carballido uses an epic structure and a 19th-century historical setting to reflect on Mexico's past vis-á-vis her present dangers after the Tlatelolco massacre.

6075 Villegas, Guillermo Antonio. Mecanismo de dramatización de un mito: *El tigre* de Aguilera-Malta (ICC/T, 33:2, mayo/agosto 1978, p. 247–253)

Brief, insightful article shows how linguistic and symbolic (fire/water) elements fuse magic and reality into *realismo mágico.*

6076 Watson-Espener, Maida Isabel. Observaciones sobre el teatro chicano, nuyorriqueño y cubano en los Estados Unidos (CONAC/RNC, 40:239, nov./dic. 1978, p. 81–95)

The first study which attempts a comprehensive view of Hispanic theatre in the US, finds more differences than similarities in objectives, themes, and use of language. Helpful in laying the groundwork for further study.

6077 ——— and **Carlos José Reyes**. Materiales para una historia del teatro en Colombia. Bogotá: Instituto Colombiano de Cultura, 1978. 718 p.

This collection of essays contains an immense treasure of data and interpretive analysis of the Colombian theatre, past and present. In addition to prologue by Carlos José Reyes and a four-part appendix, the core of the collection consists of 40 essays: eight on colonial, eight on 19th century, five on the first half of the 20th century, and 19 on the contemporary theatre. Although many of the essays had been published previously, their appearance in this volume greatly facilitates access to information about Colombia, where the current theatre movement is one of the most vital in all of Latin America.

BRAZIL: Novels

ALEXANDRINO SEVERINO, *Chairman, Department of Spanish and Portuguese, Vanderbilt University*

THE PREMATURE DEATHS OF Clarice Lispector (d. 1977) and Osman Lins (d. 1978) have impoverished Brazilian literature. Both of these novelists shared a metaphysical longing for the absolute and used language and fictional techniques to probe man's existential condition and to examine the forces which have confined him to it. Lispector's presence continues to influence the Brazilian literary scene as is evident from the impact of her last novel *Um sopro de vida* (see item **6096**) published posthumously and widely acclaimed. For example, the noted dancer Marilena Ansaldi has adapted the novel to the stage in an extraordinary performance which transmutes thoughts and language into bodily rhythms.

Like Lispector, Osman Lins was also at the peak of his artistic potential when he died. His best-known and most successful work, *Avalovara* (item **6665**) was recently translated into English by Gregory Rabassa with the customary precision and elegance of style. At the December 1978 meeting of the Modern Language Association, American professors of Luso-Brazilian literature paid homage to Lins in a panel organized and presided by Professor Regina Igel of the University of Maryland.

The most notable novels of the biennium are the work of well-established writers who can be divided into two distinct groups: the older ones, who write traditional novels concentrating on content, character portrayal, plot, and overlooking matters of technique; and the younger ones who focus on craftsmanship, paying less attention to *what* is said than to *how* it is said. Nélida Piñón, for instance, delves into the nature of narrative by examining and transforming an old, standard text—the libretto from Verdi's famous opera (item **6104**). Autran Dourado, an accomplished theoretician, describes eccentric human behavior and events bordering on the fantastic in a manner reminiscent of Guimarães Rosa but lacking his metaphysical overtones. In Ariano Suassuna's fictionalized account of his life and that of his family, the prose has a quality that can best be described as "armorial," a term which approximates the nature of myths and folkways of his native Northeast. Luis

Vilela, in a most successful second attempt at a novel (his first, *Os novos*, was not well received), depicts the urban madness of a city such as São Paulo where the people have become as impervious and calloused as its concrete buildings. Though restricted in scope Vilela's novel blends form and content harmoniously in an interesting plot, superb character delineation and excellent dialogue (item **6110**).

Other authors write entertaining and suspenseful novels that are traditional in structure and varied in content. Jorge Amado, a storyteller of magical gifts, responsible for creating unforgettable characters such as Gabriela and Dona Flor, abandons his usual Bahian setting for Rio de Janeiro in his new novel *Farda Fardão, camisola de dormir* (item **6079**) and focuses on political intrigues associated with membership in Brazil's prestigious Academy of Letters.

The influence of old masters such as Proust and Eça de Queiroz is reflected in Josué Montello's masterful evocation of things past in his novel about the dying days of Alcântara, a city in his native state of Maranhão (item **6097**). Departing from his usual themes of blood and revenge set in the Bahian cacao country, Adonias Filho takes time out to write a delightful tale of adventure and young love dedicated to his grandchildren (item **6078**). After a 25-year lapse, Fernando Sabino has published a second novel depicting the picaresque wanderings of Viramundo, a character who participates in social events and encounters notable personalities, thinly disguised as fictional (item **6105**). Jorge Andrade, well known playwright, has written an ambitious novel in which he seeks to unravel the labyrinth of his life by juxtaposing it against the historical trajectory of his country (item **6081**).

The novelistic events of the last two years were written by Raduan Nassar and Paulo Francis, two professionals of great promise. In biblical terms, Nassar writes about the conflict between a father and son who are set apart by two differing civilizations, an older one and a new one which belongs to the adopted land (item **6099**). In contrast, Paulo Francis' very contemporary language describes the self-indulgent behavior of the Brazilian well-to-do (item **6088**).

Contrary to what was noted in the last two volumes, *HLAS 38* and *HLAS 40*, sociopolitical and allegorical novels which decry the evils of the oncoming technological age have declined. A few examples are Plínio Cabral's *Umbra* (item **6083**) and *Direita, esquerda, volver* (item **6082**); Roberto Drummond's *O dia em que Ernest Hemingway morreu crucificado* (item **6086**); and Paulo Francis' *Cabeça de negro* (item **6088**).

An important literary event has been the appointment of Eduardo Portela, a well known critic, as Minister of Education in the João Figueiredo government. Moacyr Scliar's *Doutor Miragem* (item **6107**) won the coveted Guimarães Rosa Prize for best novel in 1978–79. An important translation worthy of mention is Ivan Angelo's *A festa* translated by Thomas Colchie and published in the US by Pilguin Press. José Americo de Almeida, the venerable author of *A bagaceira* (1928), died in February 1980 at the age of 93.

6078 Aguiar Filho, Adonias. Fora da pista. Rio: Editora Civilização Brasileira, 1978. 100 p. (Coleção Vera Cruz; 263)

The novel's dedication to the author's grandchildren reveals its intent. It is an excellent, fast moving, detective story, which will appeal to adolescents for its plot and adults for its artistry. Adonias Filho's novelistic traits such as the portrayal of barbaric brutality in bare-knuckled, hard-hitting language are absent but present are the southern Bahian setting and the inclusion of genuinely Brazilian elements—in this case, the portrayal of Indians and their customs. Should be read.

6079 Amado, Jorge. Farda Fardão, camisola de dormir. Rio: Editora Record, 1979. 1 v. 239 p.

Quite a departure for the author, this novel does not take place in Bahia nor does it have beautiful sensual mulatto girls. Instead, *Farda Fardão* is a satirical description of the political inner strengths which involve the acceptance of a writer by the Brazilian Academy of Letters. A delightful story, fun to read, impossible to put down.

6080 ———. Tieta no agreste. Romance. Rio: Editora Record, 1977? 590 p.; ill.

Another addition to Amado's gallery of strong-minded, sexually liberated women protagonists. From shepherdess to prostitute to respected wealthy woman, Tieta (Dona Antonieta) exposes the idiosyncrasies of small-town life and the foolishness of male chauvinism. More sexually subdued than Tereza Batista, Tieta has none of the mystique, "the clove and cinnamon," that characterized Gabriela. Interesting and pleasant reading.

6081 Andrade, Jorge. Labirinto. Prefácio de Sábato Magaldi. Rio: Paz e Terra, 1978. 224 p. (Coleção Literatura e teoria literária; 19)

Autobiography disguised as fiction. Well-known playwright searches for life's meaning through the labyrinth of his country's past as well as his own. He meanders through the patriarchal, rural society which came to an end as he was growing up; he faces anew the difficult relationship with his father, marred by the artistic sensitivity which set them apart. Distinguished prose, vivid dialogue. Outstanding.

6082 Cabral, Plínio. Direita, esquerda, volver. São Paulo:Editorial Nórdica, 1978. 141 p.

The author of an excellent novel *Ticonderoga* (see *HLAS 40:7408*), Plínio Cabral does it again in this novel which depicts the foibles of inmates in a mental hospital, all of them victims of a very specific political situation—modern day Brazil—or of the inhuman quality of modern life. Intelligent writing; superb dialogues. Recommended.

6083 ———. Umbra. São Paulo: Summus Editorial, 1977. 97 p.

This novel belongs to a group referred to in *HLAS 40* (p. 472) as "post 1984." It portrays allegorically the consequences of excessive mechanization and technology. Life in the Dead City becomes an organized struggle for survival, after pollution dries up rivers and destroys cities. Recommended.

6084 Costa, Flávio Moreira da and **Roberto Grey.** As margens plácidas. Romance. São Paulo: Editora Atica, 1978. 118 p.; facsims., plates (Coleção de autores brasileiros; 19)

Donga's alienation stems from existential as well as sociopolitical causes. Neither his psychiatrist nor the twice-his-age Helga can alleviate his extreme despondency. The extremely intimate quality of the novel is parodied by the technical device of having the editor, the author, and the protagonist write footnotes, poking fun at the sentimentality and fictional exaggerations of the text. Interesting but undistinguished.

6085 Dourado, Waldomiro Autran. Armas e corações. Rio: Difel, 1978. 186 p.

Four narratives contained in one novel with no apparent link among them. They unravel one "thread" of the cosmic "embroidery" to refer to a title the author gave one of his books. The four novelettes, especially the last one, "The Extraordinary Lady from the Land of Dreams," depict the real and the unreal, fantasy arising from the commonplace, in a manner reminiscent of Guimarães Rosa's *Primeiras estórias.* A superb novel by an accomplished writer.

6086 Drummond, Roberto. O dia em que Ernest Hemingway morreu crucificado. Romance. São Paulo: Editora Atica, 1978. 176 p.; ill., plate (Coleção de autores brasileiros; 29)

Characters in this novel, by a prizewinning (Paraná Prize for the Short Story) prose-fiction writer, include American Brazilianists as well as American public figures of the political and entertainment world together with their Brazilian counterparts. A collage of contemporary political events, the novel depicts the nightmarish contemporary world dominated by US cultural exports. In a most fitting representation, the cover portrays the crucified Hemingway tied to an upside down Coca-Cola bottle watched by Marilyn Monroe. Will not appeal to those who prefer a minimum of plot and unity in a work of art. Recommended.

6087 França, Oswaldo. As lembranças de Eliana. Rio: Editora CODECRI, 1978. 103 p. (Coleção Edição do Pasquim; 44)

Psychological study of a passive and lonely woman who recollects her past life consisting of seemingly insignificant events. Her quiet and calm descriptions heighten the pathos. Pleasant reading.

6088 Francis, Paulo. Cabeça de negro. Rio: Editora Nova Fronteira, 1979. 207 p.

Very dynamic contemporary language describes the fast, degenerate life of the upper crust in the city of Rio de Janeiro. Author contrasts the futility of an indulgent society, preoccupied with sex and drugs, with the political struggle, the torturers, the murderers, and the martyrs. Because of the subject matter, fast pace and topicality, this novel is assured success. On his way to becoming the Harold Robbins of Brazil, Paulo Francis is an accomplished writer, knowledgeable of his metier and with many years of experience as a journalist. Recommended.

6089 Freyre, Gilberto. O outro amor do Dr. Paulo. Seminovela, continuação de *Dona Sinhá e o Filho Padre*. Rio: Livraria José Olympio Editora, 1977. 242 p.; plate.

A sequel to a former novel, *Dona Sinhá e o Filho Padre*. The renowned sociologist Gilberto Freyre (*The masters and the slaves*) has been criticized for the literary quality of his writings in sociology. The reverse is true of his fiction in which sociological and historical considerations overshadow character and plot. Undistinguished.

6090 Gomes, Paulo Emilio Salles. Três mulheres de três PPPês. São Paulo: Editora Perspectiva, 1977. 101 p. (Coleção Paralelos)

Three love stories concerning three women and their relationships with a common protagonist, Mr. Polydoro. Female frailty and sham are traits which bind the three stories. Excellent writing by a distinguished film critic who died recently. Recommended.

6091 Guimarães, Josué. E tarde para saber. Porto Alegre, Brazil: L&PM Editores, 1977. 160 p.

Tender love story of rich girl and poor boy who are "star crossed" by the sociopolitical situation. Linear story with technical surprises, it provides good reading for a spring afternoon, no more.

6092 ———. Os tambores silenciosos. Romance. Porto Alegre, Brazil: Editora Globo, 1977. 213 p. (Coleção Sagitário)

Zealous censors spreading terror among the people in a small, southern Brazilian city receive their just deserts. The book is flawed by an altogether too obvious poetic-justice twist, but enhanced by symbolic devices (e.g., red-breasted, black birds hover surrealistically over the city announcing impending doom). Recommended.

6093 Hilst, Hilda. Ficções. São Paulo: Edições Quirón, 1977. 332 p. (Coleção Jorgral; 6)

Endless and confusing word arrangements make reading difficult. Author's work has commanded high praise from critics, but remains inaccessible to the general reader. The book includes previously published *Fluxofloema* and *Quado's*. Challenging.

6094 José, Elias. Inventário do inútil. Romance. Rio: Editora Civilização Brasileira, 1978. 166 p. (Coleção Vera Cruz; 258)

Aldo, the protagonist, attempts to come to terms with a weighty rural heritage and the legacy of his ancestors, as well as with his own tarnished past. He makes an "inventory of the useless," discovering, in the end, how to live with his "dethroned" self, his scanty possessions and his loneliness. Told in the first person, this novel shows technical skill and mature craftsmanship. Recommended.

6095 Lins, Osman. O visitante. Romance. 3. ed. São Paulo: Summus, 1979. 184 p.

Third edition of a novel which marked Osman Lins' first serious effort in prose fiction. It won the Fabio Prado Prize when it first came out. This edition includes several invaluable study aids: bibliographies, critics' opinions regarding this and other works by the author, as well as the latter's statements in interviews concerning his work.

6096 Lispector, Clarice. Um sopro de vida. Pulsações. 2. ed. Rio: Editora Nova Fronteira, 1978. 162 p.

Posthumous narrative by one of the two outstanding Brazilian novelists (Guimarães Rosa being the other) of the post-modernist generation. This "novel," like so many of Clarice's works, is plotless but written with unusual depth of feeling. It consists of a dialogue between the author and "the wrinkles of eternity" (p. 88). As usual, the language is innovative, poetic and filled with startling associations. Excellent.

6097 Montello, Josué. A noite sobre Alcântara. Rio: Libraria José Olympio Editora, 1978. 1 v.

This is the thirteenth novel depicting the Maranhão saga the author began in 1940 with *Janelas Fechadas* ("Closed Windows"). It is an evocative account of a beautifully majestic, opulent city grown to seed. Natalino, the protagonist, lives Alcântara's last days, his own personal life as barren and unfulfilled as the dying city. Montello's fictional guides are the 19th century masters, Proust and Eça de Queiroz. Traditional though it is in form and content, it is a highly satisfying work. Highly recommended.

6098 ———. Os tambores de São Luís. Romance. Ilustrações de Poty. 2. ed. Rio: Libraria José Olympio Editora, 1976. 487 p.; ill.

A well conceived novel dealing with slavery in the state of Maranhão. The author builds a Tolstoian panorama of slave life while at the same time portraying well known political and intellectual figures. The Negro Damião, a champion of freedom for his race, finds understanding among enlightened intellectuals. Of these, Sousândrade's portrayal is one of the most interesting. One of the few fictionalized accounts of Brazilian slavery. Recommended.

6099 Nassar, Raduan. Um copo de cólera. Novela. São Paulo: Livraria Cultura Editora, 1978. 86 p.

Written several years before *Lavoura arcaica* (see item **6100**), this novel reads now like an embryonic version of the former. The same rich, convoluted language is expressed in the extensive monologue of two protagonists in conflict and in love. Recommended.

6100 ———. Lavoura arcaica. Romance. Rio: Livraria José Olympio Editora, 1975. 193 p.

Widely acclaimed by critics when first published, this novel tells the story of a father/son conflict, ironically reminiscent of the "Prodigal Son" theme. The return of this son, however, is physical not spiritual. Impressive first novel, told in an extensive monologue. The rich and complex language befits a modern parable. Highly recommended.

6101 Paiva, Mário Garcia de. O suor no rosto. Novela. 2. ed. rev. São Paulo: Editora Moderna, 1978. 158 p. (Série ficção brasileira; 3)

Several short-story traits are present in this first novel by Paiva. Characters are few, the plot simple, conflict minimal, and the language taut. These features are more suited for the short story than for a novel which is, therefore, sluggish and uninteresting. Author is a far more effective short-story writer than novelist.

6102 Penna, Cornelio. Fronteira. Biografia, introdução e notas de Afrânio Coutinho. n.p.: Edições de Ouro, n.d. 175 p. (Estrela; 675. Coleção Prestigio)

This popular edition of an old classic is being reissued at a more receptive time than when it was first published in 1935. Then, Brazilian prose fiction was dominated by sociopolitical writers of the Northeast. Penna's successful portrayal of a psychological state of mind straddling the "frontier" between dream and reality, sanity and madness, deserves greater recognition. Excellent.

6103 Pereira, Antônio Olavo. Contramão. Novela. 2. ed. rev. Rio: Livraria José Olympio Editora em convênio com a Ministério da Educação e Cultura, Instituto Nacional do Livro, 1975. 79 p. (Coleção Agarana; 113)

Eighth ed. of a novel first published in 1949, when the regionalist novel of the Northeast reigned supreme, smothering all other fictional endeavors. A psychological novel, *Contramão* portrays the loneliness of man amid the impersonality of the urban milieu. The title is an apt description for the wanderings of the protagonist who travels in directions that run counter to the norm. Well written work which deserves a better reception and greater recognition. Recommended.

6104 Piñon, Nélida. A força do destino. Rio: Editora Record, 1977. 127 p.

After the deaths of Clarice Lispector and Osman Lins, Piñon is one of Brazil's foremost writers. The novel examines and gently mocks an old and well known text:

the libretto of Verdi's famous opera. The author-become-protagonist questions the protagonists' behavior and offers new possibilities for unraveling the story. Ingenious quest into the art of narrative fiction. Highly recommended.

6105 Sabino, Fernando. O grande mentecapto. Rio: Editora Record, 1979. 225 p.

Twenty-three years after his first novel, Sabino has brought forth the much awaited story of Viramundo. A mixture of poet and saint as well as madman and rogue, Viramundo's hilarious and sarcastic encounters with Minas' high and low society, place him alongside famous Brazilian literary figures such as Macunaíma, Vitorino Papa-Rabo, and Ponciano de Azevedo Furtado. Every great writer must sooner or later create his Viramundo. Sabino has succeeded in creating his. Excellent.

6106 Scliar, Moacyr. O ciclo das águas. Porto Alegre, Brazil: Editora Globo, 1977. 133 p. (Coleção Sagitário)

This novel, like many others written by the author, narrates the saga of Jewish immigrants in the south of Brazil. Esther is a Polish Jew brought to Brazil as a white slave. Her life as a prostitute, told in short, cinematographic chapters, is juxtaposed to the description of scientific research on polluted water organisms undertaken by her son. In "the cycle of waters," as in the cycle of life, pure water may originate in pollution. Recommended.

6107 ———. Doutor Miragem. Romance. Porto Alegre, Brazil: L&PM Editores, 1978. 181 p.; bibl.

Disconnected episodes in the life of a young doctor are narrated from multiple points of view and through manipulations of time and space. The novelist, himself a medical doctor, presents the modern physician as anti-hero. Recommended.

6108 Suassuna, Ariano. História d'o rei degolado nas caatingas do sertão: ao sol da onça caetana. Romance armorial e novela romançal brasileira. Estudo de Idelette Muzart Fonseca dos Santos. Rio: Livraria José Olympio Editora, 1977. 135 p.; ill., plate.

The author, a member of the Recife School, attempts to revive folk themes of *literatura de cordel,* folk dances and the popular music of the Northeast. Incidents from the author's childhood and the lives of his relatives are interspersed with mythic episodes of fabulous animals and battles determined by the course of stars. Excellent.

6109 Teixeira, Maria de Lourdes. A ilha da Salamandra. São Paulo: Global Editora, 1976. 141 p. (Autores brasileiros contemporâneos)

The novel takes place on a desert island in which isolation as well as prolonged close contact with rugged nature trigger irrepressible passions in the protagonist. Base evil slowly takes over a complacent, subdued personality which like the salamander, silently burns in its cavern habitat. Good psychological treatment contributes effectively to setting and plot. Interesting and quite different from other novels by Teixeira.

6110 Vilela, Luiz. O inferno é aqui mesmo. Romance. Ilustrações, Celso Imperatrice. São Paulo: Editora Ática, 1979. 224 p.; ill. (Coleção de autores brasileiros; 32)

"Hell is São Paulo," a city of concrete and of people equally insensitive, a place where personal ambition prevails over human fellowship. The novel has some vivid portrayals: the homosexual Marcelo; Heloisa, the frustrated wife of a dedicated reporter. Edgar, the narrator, is a Nick Carroway without a Gatsby, for there is no innocence left. Superb dialogue. Highly recommended.

Short Stories

MARIA ANGELICA GUIMARAES LOPES DEAN, *Lecturer in the Humanities, University of Wisconsin, Parkside*

IN THE LAST FEW YEARS, there has been a change in the direction of the Brazilian short story which is becoming more eclectic both thematically and stylistically. Until recently, the regional tale was dominant and the psychological narrative, a separate subgenre, was subordinate to the former. Now, psychological themes prevail and gone is the arduous and ardorous emulation of Guimarães Rosa. Even subordinate trends of the genre, exemplified by stories about "minorities" follow the prevalent trend towards psychological introspection. Writers who live in different states or who practice different professions, women, or homosexuals, have produced collections focusing on their condition. The perspectives of these stories vary ranging from the private to the social, the modes run from the naturalistic to the fantastic, and the narrative from limpid to elliptic.

The transformation of the Brazilian story becomes apparent when examining three aspects: theme, style, and language and structure. In the first case, it is not surprising that storytellers regard the human being as their chief theme or preoccupation. He is examined as individual, as world in itself, and, more often, as cell or constituent element of family or working group. Among instrospective writers, the more notable are Telles, José, Ramos, Bezerra and Ferraz, who still focus on classical themes of love and death as well as on the ages of man. Pellegrini, for example, shows a whole segment of society through his "meninos" (item **6154**). Stories about aging prevail not only among established writers such as Trevisam, Telles, Ferraz and Campos but also among more recent ones such as Jardim, José and J.C. Martins. Another notable development has been the relaxation of censorship which has permitted the reappearance of *homo politicus* as a literary subject in Brazil. A recurrent theme of this new political fiction—most of which is "committed" or *engagé* in the Sartrian sense—is condemnation of the repressive tactics of past governments.

Styles, like themes, span a wide scale ranging from the naturalistic through the realistic to the fantastic. Practitioners of naturalism such as Silveira, J.C. Martins, Carbonieri, Rey, and their forerunner, Trevisam, portray social deviants by dwelling on the accumulation of sordid and eschatological detail. Such presentation of minutiae conveys realism and symbolism at once and marks the existential limitations of a doomed universe, exemplified by the feudalistic society of Latin America. These stories tend to stress *homo sexualis,* until recently the province of the novel in Brazil.

In addition to this intensely graphic style, there is a more balanced realism exemplified by old and new authors such as Telles, Ferraz, Bezerra, Jardim, A.M. Martins, and Campos who succeed in depicting reality on a broader scale. Another strong stylistic trend further removed or even opposed to naturalism, is fantasy which can be rooted in historical reality as in the case of Christo (see item **6115**) or emanate from worlds not subject to natural laws as in the case of Colasanti, Rubião, Gesteira and I. Teixeira (see items **6124**, **6133**, **6161** and **6164**). Their fiction, akin to both science fiction and surrealism, has a poetic quality when describing introspective characters freed from daily contingencies. Loose and evanescent, the metamorphoses described in stories by these writers are often witty and thus more amusing than frightening. When themes become political, however, the grotesque overwhelms the fanciful and the fantasy turns into nightmare. Allegory is a favorite device for transmuting political situations into battles of good and evil played out by mythical gods, angels and monsters. Emediato's stories are outstanding in this regard because of the interaction of private symbols with pagan or biblical allusions. In contrast, there is the frightening verisimilitude of Christo's tales in which persecution takes place in factual rather than allegorical Belo Horizonte.

The third and last aspect of the stories under consideration is their use of language and structure. As in other aspects, diversity prevails and language ranges from the colloquial and accessible to the complex, tortuous and abstruse. Structures are equally varied and run from simple, straightforward narratives exemplified by Vilela's tales (item **6172**) and Konder's journalistic accounts (item **6139**) to the more complex interior monologues of Alves and José (items **6113** and **6137**) and the puzzles, tropes and schemes more characteristic of poetry but present in Teixeira's stories (see item **6165**).

The recognition extended to this elaborate style is evident in the granting of First Prize to Sérgio Martagão Gesteira in the 1976 Paraná Short Story Contest. A brilliant though hermetic practitioner of the fantastic story, Gesteira stands in sharp contrast to those who won lesser prizes, mostly realists in their use of style and structure. The weakening of Guimarães Rosa's influence signals a trend towards colloquial syntax and vocabulary and away from poetic devices. The underlying elliptical quality of this overtly simple and straightforward language generates a tautness which established the dramatic tension of these stories. Through this mimetic device less becomes more and the rapidity and incompleteness of episodes and of behavior is underscored. This characteristic has been perspicaciously noted by Wilson Martins when discussing Carbonieri, a writer representative of this trend. Other notable practitioners of elliptical writing are Trevisan, Ferraz, Daunt Neto, Bezerra, Gomes, Pellegrini, and Silveira.

To conclude, it can be said that overall, Brazilian short stories are consistently good. More than 50 years after the Modernist Revolution, the genre has attained the goals set by Mario de Andrade for Brazilian literature: the right to aesthetic inquiry; the updating of Brazilian artistic intelligence; and the forging of a national consciousness.

6111 Abreu, Caio Fernando. Pedras de Calcutá. São Paulo: Editora Alfa-Omega, 1977. 124 p. (Biblioteca Alfa-Omega de cultura universal. Série 2. Atualidade; 12)

Outstanding collection defined by its young author as "um livro de horror . . . exacerbado, do dia a dia . . . principalmente da minha geração." Powerful and imaginative treatment of anguish and alienation caused by internal conflicts, social pressure and drugs. Abreu started early, winning prestigious literary awards.

6112 Almeida, Roniwalter Jatobá de. Ciríaco Martins e outras histórias. Contos. São Paulo: Editora Alfa-Omega, 1977. 120 p. (Biblioteca Alfa-Omega de cultura universal. Série 2. Atualidade; 13)

Stories about the troubles and rare joys of migrant workers who leave the Northeast for São Paulo told in fine monologues by a perceptive and compassionate writer. "Via Sacra" describes the daily fight for survival of these workers.

6113 Alves, Henrique L. Dos pássaros perdidos. Contos. São Paulo: Edições H, 1979. 55 p.

Introspective authors says: "I write stories within daily dimensions, trying to achieve the necessary realism . . . of the 'shadows' covering S. Paulo . . . divided between reality and dream . . ." Cryptic, allusive stories have intriguing mixture of poetical mood and succinct dialogue.

6114 Araújo, Maria Lysia Corrêa de. Em silêncio. Rio de Janeiro: Livraria J. Olympio Editora *em convênio com o* Instituto Nacional do Livro, 1978. 103 p.

Stories of clear, classical style about fantastic events: man devoured by lobster, narrator visited by her dead to the sound of Bach, woman obsessed by mouse, and man by cat. High-quality collection was named *Em silêncio* because stories remained unpublished for many years. Their worth finally recognized, the collection received distinguished prizes.

6115 Betto, Frei [*pseud. for* **Carlos Alberto Libanio Christo**]. A vida suspeita do subversivo Raul Parelo. Contos. Rio de Janeiro: Civilização Brasileira, 1979. 105 p. (Coleção Vera Cruz; 275)

Talented author, famous for his political vicissitudes and version of them, skillfully exposed real events through fantasy. Frei Betto resembles fellow magic realists and "mineiros," Murilo Rubião and Roberto Drummond. A wry, poetical, humorous, and occasionally tragic book.

6116 Bezerra, Francisco Sobreira. A noite mágica. Contos. Ilustrações de Aderbal Moura. São Paulo: Editora Atica, 1979. 93 p. (Coleção de autores brasileiros; 43)

Well-drafted parables in limpid, lucid style suggest a wealth of interpretations: some are thrillers, others allegories. As in many recent Brazilian stories, these tales are strongly influenced by cinematic techniques of elision and juxtaposition—perhaps explained by author's long experience as movie connoisseur and critic. An intellectual, impressive book, with fine illustrations.

6117 Borba Filho, Hermilo. Sete dias a cavalo. Novelas. Porto Alegre: Editora Globo, 1975. 148 p. (Coleção Sagitário)

Part of a trilogy of the late author, book presents varied, popular characters in unusual and often hilarious situations. Bold syntax adds to magic realism. An amusing, distinguished collection, steeped in colorful Northeastern lore, akin to Suassuna's, to whom one of the stories is dedicated. Should be read.

6118 Campos, José Maria Moreira. Os doze parafusos. São Paulo: Editora Cultrix, 1978. 142 p.

Renowned writer offers readers a wide choice of finely wrought stories in remarkable language ranging from the tender, to the humorous, to the tragic.

6119 Carbonieri, José Fernando de Mafra. Homem esvaziando os bolsos. Contos. Rio de Janeiro: Civilização Brasileira, 1977. 149 p. (Coleção Vera Cruz; 234)

Representative of contemporary Brazilian fiction, many of these stories are challenging riddles formulated in a rich miscellany of Biblical themes, international show business idols, and blue jeans. Elliptic episodes and syntax convey the setting of nocturnal São Paulo, a jungle inhabited by muggers, dope addicts, kidnappers, transvestites and corrupt policemen. Admirable.

6120 Cardozo, Flávio José. Zélica e outros. Contos. Rio de Janeiro: Livraria F. Alves Editora, 1978. 109 p. (Ipê)

A regional author who focuses on Santa Catarina, Cardozo writes with enviable breadth and humor. His characters, a colorful lot, are depicted in bold strokes and with warmth. This southerner belongs to a literary family of illustrious eastern and northeastern picaresque writers: Amado, Borda Filho and Suassuna.

6121 Carneiro, Caio Porfírio. Chuva: os dez cavaleiros. São Paulo: Editora HUCITEC, 1977. 100 p.; ill.

All 10 sober and somber stories in this collection include a mysterious and solitary horseman who arrives in quasi-deserted towns where the atmosphere matches the rider's mood. Vengeance is a dominant theme in these curious and well-written tales (see also *HLAS 38:7346*).

6122 Carone, Modesto. As marcas do real. Rio de Janeiro: Paz e Terra, 1979. 131 p. (Coleção Literatura e teoria literária; 34)

Carone is a skillful craftsman who often excels in stories that are sparse, cerebral, and often metaphysical. Some pieces border on prose poems, others consist of meditations and a biography. Successful, unconventional fiction.

6123 Carvalho, Murilo. Raízes da morte. Ilustrações de Alderbal Moura. São

Paulo: Editora Atica, 1977. 94 p.: ill. (Coleção de autores brasileiros; 12)

In limpid language and lyrical mood, young author tells about countryside and villages in six stories of notable dramatic scope. The collection is worthy of this beautifully illustrated volume.

6124 **Colasanti, Marina.** A morada do ser. Rio de Janeiro: Livraria Francisco Alves Editora, 1978. 80 leaves (Ipê)

The title of these vignettes is a clever pun: "the house of being" signifies not only "the word" according to Heidegger but doubles as the name of a high-rise apartment building which is the setting of these stories. Irony, poetry, and fantasy connect these tales—one per apartment—which are often metamorphoses. Ingenious, well-structured, and delightful collection.

6125 **O conto da mulher** brasileira. Organização, seleção e notas de Edla van Steen. Estudo crítico de Nelly Novaes Coelho. São Paulo: Vertente Editora, 1978. 252 p. (Coleção Panorama; 1)

Women writers do not limit themselves to women as topic. This excellent collection demonstrates how women's writing can be economical, incisive, unsentimental—traits popularly regarded as "masculine."

6126 **O conto da propaganda.** Organizado por Dennis Toledo. Antônio Torres and others. São Paulo: Vertente Editora, 1978. 112 p.

The ambiguous title of the collection, *The advertising story*, indicates that while the stories are told by advertising men, they are not about advertising (except for the one by Josué Montello which deals with the theme wittily). One is gratified to know that Brazilian advertising is produced by more than competent writers. Many stories are excellent.

6127 **Corrêa, Glauco Rodrigues.** O caso da pasta preta e outros casos. Contos. Florianópolis: Governo do Estado de Santa Catarina, 1977. 58 p. (Coleção Cultura catarinense. Série Literatura, conto)

Stories set in Santa Catarina introduce large cast of characters consisting mostly of humble adults and children who narrate daily incidents from their viewpoint. Limpid style enhances poetry. Fine, harmonious collection which includes a few stories with a gentle ironic touch.

6128 **Daunt Neto, Ricardo.** Homem na prateleira. Contos. Ilustrações de Daisy Startari. São Paulo: Editora Atica, 1979. 95 p. (Coleção de autores brasileiros; 39)

Top-notch, oblique stories run gamut from gently ironic ("Manequim 42") to tragic ("Helena e os Seus," "A Almofada"). Powerful, yet malleable language. Author has progressed from hermeticism of earlier work, "Juan."

6129 **Dias, Milton.** As outras cunhãs. Estórias de domésticas. Fortaleza: Academia Cearense de Letras, 1977. 112 p. (Coleção Antônio Sales; 5)

Praised by severe critics such as W. Martins and A. Olinto, these stories have also been judged as loosely structured "crônicas." The *cunhãs* or women from Ceará are mostly spirited servants. Dias' powers of observations and lifelike dialogue are enhanced by a colorful and gentle style.

6130 **Elis, Bernardo** [*pseud. for* **Bernardo Elis Fleury de Campos Curado**]. André louco. Contos. Rio de Janeiro: Livraria J. Olympio Editora, 1978. 102 p.

From one of our finest regionalist-psychologists, something old, something new. Collection comprises title story (novela first published in 1944); two stories (1956); and two new ones. In all five, Goiás's Elis's marvelous language conveys varied cast of flesh and blood characters in all their complexity and drama.

6131 **Ferraz, Geraldo.** KM 63 [i.e. Quilômetro sessenta e três]: 9 contos desiguais. Ilustrações de Daisy Startari. São Paulo: Editora Atica, 1979. 109 p.: ill. (Coleção de autores brasileiros; 35)

Stories by a master told in tortured syntax about strong, believable characters of all ages. This is the same author who, in his teens, made his mark on Modernismo.

6132 **Fonseca, Rubem.** Os prisioneiros. Contos. 3. ed. Rio de Janeiro: Editora Codecri, 1978. 118 p. (Coleção Edições do Pasquim; 29)

Third printing of memorable collection, first published 1963. Epigraph is from Lao Tse "We are prisons of ourselves." Sparse language and firm scaffolding convey difficult or ineffable situations and passions. Style, indicative of its decade, chastises bureaucrats and psychoanalysts, who deny the inevitability of such a prison.

6133 Gesteira, Sergio Martagão. O convento das alarmadas. Contos. São Paulo: Vertente Editora, 1978. 79 p. (Coleção Prosa viva)

First book by winner of 1976 Paraná Contest offers strange world in which feelings and actions weigh less than words. Brilliant narrative about abstract, barely human characters reminiscent of masked actors in play of the absurd in the manner of Joyce, Ionesco, Lispector and Rubião. Difficult but worthwhile.

6134 Giaquinto, Antonio. Dragão de mofo. São Paulo: Vertente Editora, 1978. 71 p. (Coleção Econômica; 4)

The musty dragon (also title story) aims high and succeeds. Powerful, tender, humorous, and suspenseful, it is the auspicious start for a 24-year-old writer who combines indignation at social injustices with literary talent. One of *Escrita*'s first contest winners.

6135 Gomes, Alvaro Cardoso. A teia de aranha. São Paulo: Editora Atica, 1978. 126 p.; ill. (Coleção de autores brasileiros; 17)

Collection successfully launches new writer whose dense, oblique stories reveal universe of powerless characters, imprisoned in monstrous spider web. Motif is stressed: by women knitting or crocheting, by Pessoa's epigraph (". . . aranha enorme que nos tece . . . teia negra que nos prende?") and by numerous illustrations in handsome paperback.

6136 Grossmann, Judith. A noite estrelada. Rio de Janeiro: Francisco Alves, 1977. 253 p.

Author conveys an original literary perspective and a wry world vision by a startling yet masterful use of words, occasionally archaic or abstruse. The last stories are distinctive in that they deal with Jewish life. First rate collection written in a style reminiscent of Guimarães Rosa.

6137 José, Elias. Inquieta viagem no fundo do poço. Belo Horizonte: Imprenta Oficial Belo Horizonte, 1974. 173 p.

In this "journey to the bottom of the well" characters explore strangeness resulting from love or madness. The interior monologues are inventive and poetical. Superb dramatic stories in which language is beautifully honed.

6138 ———. Um pássaro em pânico. Ilustrações de Elifas Andreato. São Paulo: Editora Atica, 1977. 77 p.: ill. (Coleção Nosso tempo)

Superb collection by author for whom the extremes of literature are opposing roles of serving as "pasttime" or as a vehicle for "social condemnation." He observes: "Mature writers . . . see the worlds of others, not merely their own, and therefore acquire a larger consciousness." The stories combine tragedy and comedy in lucid language.

6139 Konder, Rodolfo. Cadeia para os mortos: históricas de ficção política. São Paulo: Editora Alfa-Omega, 1977. 105 p. (Biblioteca Alfa-Omega de cultura universal. Série 2. Atualidade; 11)

These pedestrian accounts are of topical rather than literary interest because they signal the reemergence of political writing in Brazilian fiction.

6140 Lago, Mário. Rabo da noite. Contos. Rio de Janeiro: Civilização Brasileira, 1977. 155 p. (Coleção Vera Cruz; 260)

Compassionate and dramatic stories mix poetry and humor. "Ursa Maior, Ursa Menor" and title novella ("Night's Tail") are unforgettable. Anecdotal endings, however, detract from others.

6141 Lessa, Orígenes. O escritor proibido: 1929–1979. Prefácio de Genolino Amado. Ilustrações de Jane Maia. Rio de Janeiro: Nórdica, 1979. 79 p.: ill.

Reprint marks 50th anniversary of collection. In delightful prose, author narrates small slices of life (e.g., tall man obsessed by short girl who does not notice him; "wicked writer," etc.). Refreshing, light-weight, good fiction. A fit tribute to a prolific writer who has entertained several generations.

6142 Lodi, Aluizio. Guacamayas. Rio de Janeiro: Livraria F. Alves Editora, 1978. 99 p. (Ipê)

Stories by anthropologist who is also accomplished writer offer marvelous blend of aboriginal folklore woven with Christian tradition, as well as rich syntax and vocabulary reminiscent of Guimarães Rosa. An exciting book.

6143 Machado, Luiz Carlos. A luz difusa do abajur lilás. Contos. Rio de Janeiro: Livraria Editora Cátedra, 1977. 122 p.

Machado has developed since his

Noitre macho (1973, see *HLAS 38:7375*). These characters transcend bohemian underground of earlier collection, with more moods, more subtlety, more variation in style.

6144 Maranhão, Haroldo. Vôo de galinha: peças de um minuto ou dois, ou nem isso: quase todas no formato de carambolas. Contos redondos. Belém: Editora Grafisa, 1978. 118 p.

Described by their author as "short short stories . . . taking one minute or two . . . as round as *carambolas* (berries);" these delightful pieces show his ingenuity, lyricism and skill. Eclectic themes range from beautiful butterflies to father concerned with daughter's honor. The tone is fantastic, poetic and sardonic.

6145 Mariotti, Humberto; Moreira da Costa; and **Idelma Faria.** Os Vencedores: 1978. Introdução de Vicente Ataide. São Paulo: McGraw-Hill, 1978. 142 p.

Consists of stories by the recipients of three writing awards granted in 1978 and listed in declining order: 1) Mariotti is a physician with a fine command of language and structure who gently mocks the absurdities of life; 2) Moreira da Costa reproduces Rio's bohemian milieu with humor (see also *HLAS 40:7432*); and 3) poet Idelma Fari is also concerned with absurdities but of the heart. Book includes a good introduction and pieces by other minor winners.

6146 Martins, Anna Maria. Sala de espera. Apresentação de Antonio Cândido. São Paulo: Edições Melhoramentos, 1978. 124 p.

Collection about the rich and powerful of São Paulo who are dehumanized by their own power and riches. Characters are depicted with severity by a moralist author. Book differs from previous, symbolic collection, *A triologia do emparedado* (see *HLAS 38:7381*).

6147 Martins, Júlio César Monteiro. Sabe quem dançou? Contos. Ilustrações de Miguel Angelo. Rio de Janeiro: Editora CODECRI, 1978. 120 p.: ill. (Coleção Edições do Pasquim; 31)

Talented, young writer uses variety of approaches and diction from different milieus in fine stories where the grotesque colors social outcasts as well as military overlords (conveniently disguised by Spanish names). Collection is more homogeneous than his earlier *Torpalium* (see item **6148**). Martins is a spiritual descendant of Rabelais.

6148 ———. Torpalium. São Paulo: Editora Atica, 1977. 78 p.: ill. (Coleção Autores brasileiros; 13)

Stories by a very young author, whose indignation at injustice, perception of nuances, and humor are worth reading. For a more homogeneous collection, see his later stories (item **6147**).

6149 "Missa do Galo" de Machado de Assis: variações sobre o mesmo tema. São Paulo: Summus, 1977. 109 p.: ill.

Six contemporary writers (Antônio Callado, Autran Dourado, Julieta de Godoy Ladeira, Lygia Fagundes Telles, Nélida Piñón and Osman Lins) pay homage to the Master's famous story. Emulating him, Piñón uses clichés to connote spiritual vulgarity; Lins compares Nogueira and Conceição to Stendhal's Julien and Madame de Rênal; Ladeira explores "bad" Conceição, as does Dourado; Callado introduces Machado as character; and Telles chooses fragmented narrative.

6150 Monteiro, Benedicto. O carro dos milagres. Ilustrações de Tumminelli. Rio de Janeiro: Novacultura Editora, 1975. 94 p.: ill.

Unusual Amazonian regional fiction, consists of title novella on vicissitudes of countryman travelling to fulfill a religious vow—a tour-de-force monologue—and of shorter stories.

6151 Moura, Antônio José de. Notícias de terra. São Paulo: Edições Símbolo, 1978. 91 p.

Stories are interrelated by an imaginary setting, the police state of Bragalto, dominated by Count von Souza and his vigilante organization of "1000 Eyes." Although some allusions are heavy-handed and certain stories overly clever, their general level is good. Representative of late 1970s Brazilian writing on political repression.

6152 Mulheres & [i.e. e] mulheres. Rio de Janeiro: Editora Nova Fronteira, 1978. 170 p.

High caliber fiction by well-known male and female writers most of which has been published before. Kaleidoscope of themes and styles are exemplified by: Callado's madwoman; Piñón's apparently submissive housewives; Telles' faithless lovers; Lispector's dreamy drunk; Pontes' unloved woman; Veiga's imaginative girl and efficient school teacher.

6153 Novos contistas: vencedores do VII Concurso Nacional de Contos do Paraná. Rio de Janeiro: Livraria F. Alves Editora, 1977. 228 p. (Ipê)

Collection presents three stories each by Paraná Contest winners. Except for first-prize author, Martagão, whose works are successful exercises in surrealism, others are realistic thematically and stylistically.

6154 Pellegrini Júnior, Domingos. Os meninos. São Paulo: Vertente Editora, 1977. 88 p.

According to author, his boys are "different people, . . . not autobiographical . . . All they have in common is their origin, the lower middle-class, which they resemble by their curiosity and perplexity." Admirable book of sensitive stories presented in various approaches and moods. Pellegrini is one of our most promising and productive young writers.

6155 Penteado, Darcy. Crescilda e os Espartanos. São Paulo: Edições Símbolo, 1977. 189 p.

Painter turned storyteller is both missionary for cause of homosexuality, and perceptive social critic of bourgeoisie. Penteado writes with ease, even if most stories are more journalistic than literary. Important writer on homosexuality, a minor theme in current Brazilian fiction.

6156 ———. Teoremambo: delito delirante para coro e orquestra. Ilustrações do autor. São Paulo: Livraria Cultura Editora, 1979. 108 p.: ill.

Collection continues homosexual themes and social criticism noted in *Crescilda e os espartanos* (item **6155**) but far more subtly developed in these tighter, less anecdotal and more literary stories. Penteado is a talent worth watching.

6157 Ramos, Ricardo. Toada para surdos. Contos. Rio de Janeiro: Editora Record, 1977. 138 p.

Fleeting impressions often captured in nervous anacoluthic yet clear and incisive syntax reveal world in which time, especially the past of memories, plays an important role. Skillful, complex satires include circular interior monologues. Outstanding collection.

6158 Rebelo, Marques [*pseud. for* **Eddy Dias da Cruz**]. Contos reunidos. Prefácio de Josué Montello. Rio de Janeiro: Livraria J. Olympio Editora *em convênio com o* Instituto Nacional do Livro, 1977. 284 p.; bibl.

An important first edition: the stories of this great modernist are collected in one volume including "Stela me Abriu a Porta," out of print for decades. Rebelo's Rio is alive as in the 1930s when "Oscarina" and "Três Caminhos" (also included here) were first published. These beloved stories set the pattern for much post-modernist fiction.

6159 Rey, Marcos. O pêndulo da noite. Contos. Rio de Janeiro: Civilização Brasileira, 1977. 180 p. (Coleção Vera Cruz; 288)

Lively language presents a frightening picture of nocturnal São Paulo (the night pendulum of the title) where characters rob, kill or scheme to kill for the sake of power or money. All of the characters are criminals in this impressive yet depressing book.

6160 Rosa, Vilma Guimarães. Carisma. Rio de Janeiro: Livraria J. Olympio Editora, 1978. 143 p.

A writer in her own right, Guimarães Rosa's daughter creates a world miles apart from her father's mythical sertão. Her characters are rich and seemingly untroubled in these well-crafted stories written in a romantic vein—a novelty in current Brazilian fiction.

6161 Rubião, Murilo. A casa do girassol vermelho. Contos. São Paulo: Editora Atica, 1978. 61 p.; bibl., ill. (Coleção de autores brasileiros; 22)

The precursor of Brazilian magic realism is at it again with his usual aplomb. His story line is straighter than in previous works and his characters are more substantial. Required reading.

6162 Silva, Aguinaldo and others. Vida cachorra. Rio de Janeiro: Civilização Brasileira, 1977. 197 p. (Coleção Vera Cruz; 244)

Four strong writers reveal dangers and sorrows in the lives of homosexuals (Silva); young revolutionists (Carbonieri); São Paulo crime lords and prostitutes (João Antônio). Only Rey's stories sustain a touch of humor.

6163 Silveira, Francisco Maciel. Esfinges. Contos. Ilustrações de Claudio Cesar Minervino. São Paulo: Editora Atica, 1978. 142 p.: ill. (Coleção de autores brasileiros; 21)

This handsomely illustrated collection was awarded some important, literary prizes and introduces a powerful writer whose paradoxical stories deal with the sordid and the poetical in varied fare: mysteries, science fiction, naturalistic stories, short poems. Recommended reading.

6164 Teixeira, Ivan. Fabulemas. São Paulo: Livraria Editora Fernando Pessoa, 1973. 33 p.

Short, short "fables" are also puzzles in which poetic devices (alliteration, asonance, inverted word order) mix with puns, jokes, and proverbs. This ludic fiction belongs to concrete poetry and makes delightful reading.

6165 Teixeira, Ubiratan. Históricas de amar e morrer. São Luiz: Edições SIOGE, 1978. 53 p.

Most of these stories concern the neglected, the poor and the persecuted in São Luiz do Maranhão. Notwithstanding the author's obvious concern for social justice, he does not turn his stories into tracts but succeeds rather in presenting characters which are admirable in their refusal of condescension.

6166 Telles, Lygia Fagundes. Seminário dos ratos. Rio de Janeiro: Livraria J. Olympio Editora, 1977. 126 p.

There are a wealth of characters in the stories of this great writer. As Wilson Martins has observed, she is "able to go beyond the autobiographic chalk circle within which so many modern short-story writers turn." She possesses the first quality for a fiction writer: a combination of the old craftsmanship and the new approaches. Splendid achievement.

6167 Trevisan, Dalton. Crimes de paixão. Rio de Janeiro: Editora Record, 1978. 118 p.

"The illicit is thrill and the thrill is life" seems to be the motto of Trevisan's characters. Crimes of passion sometimes end in death, sometimes in lifelong battles—usually conjugal. Slight variation on the theme of woman's inability to communicate with man (e.g., she can communicate with dumb animals). The terse, elliptical style, much of it dialogue, is the author's trademark.

6168 ———. Primeiro livro de contos. Antologia pessoal. Rio de Janeiro: Editora Record, 1979. 142 p.

Author's personal anthology presents some of his best stories. Despite the occasional and renowned cruelty of Trevisan's scalpel, one detects the great compassion he feels for his characters whose vicissitudes are caused by love.

6169 ———. A trombeta do anjo vingador. Ilustrações de Glauco Rodrigues. Rio de Janeiro: Editora Codecri, 1977. 141 p.: ill. (Coleção Edições do Pasquim; 19)

Trevisan presents his cast once again: hostile spouses waging battle. The theme of miniature is a constant throughout, both in the size of people and the scope of detail. These somber, occasionally grotesque stories are elliptical—even more so than previous Trevisan writings.

6170 Ubaldo, Edson. Bandeira do divino. São Paulo: Editora do Escritor, 1977. 109 p. (Coleção do escritor; 18)

This is one of the few regional collections published in the late 1970s. Well-crafted, traditional stories show a southern Brazil which is not the stereotype, industrial region of recent immigrants, but an area as picturesque as the northeast of greater regional and literary fame.

6171 Véras, Paulo. O cabeça-de-cuia. Contos. São Paulo: Editora Moderna, 1979. 135 p. (Série Ficção brasileira; 7)

Dramatic stories told in interior monologues of stream of consciousness reveal varied characters in Brazilian hinterland, mostly children and adolescents. The author writes with economy and assurance.

6172 Vilela, Luiz. Contos escolhidos. Rio de Janeiro: Livraria F. Alves Editora, 1978. 114 p. (Ipê)

In this new anthology by the well-known author (see *HLAS 40:7416*), stories are extended tableaux told by a coolly ironic narrator. Vilela's clear style transmutes the commonplace into art.

Crônicas

GERALD M. MOSER, *Professor Emeritus of Spanish and Portuguese, The Pennsylvania State University*

IN 1977 AND 1978, most Brazilian crônicas reflected everyday life as it was lived and perceived in the big cities of Rio and São Paulo, where large newspapers offer space to many talented writers. Compared to earlier years, Rio Grande do Sul and its capital, Porto Alegre, have given rise to surprisingly numerous articles, with the encouragement of the Saturday supplement of *O Correio do Povo* in particular. João Pessoa, the capital of little Paraíba, is well represented by three collections, all of them published in 1977. On the other hand, Fortaleza (Ceará), which was so prominent earlier, is absent for reasons unknown to me.

Several good authors belonging to past generations are available in new editions, foremost among them Artur Azevedo, who dominated the field around the turn of the century, Rubem Braga, now considered the living "dean" among *cronistas*, Carlos Drummond de Andrade, Guilherme Figueiredo, the late Clarice Lispector, and the *gaúcho* master of the mini-crônica, Mário Quintana. Some of these editions, such as Quintana's anthology, were prepared for students.

L.F. Veríssimo and C.E. Novais have been joined by the *paulista* Lourenço Diaféria as satirists and, as far as that is now permitted, political commentators in their popular crônicas. There are others who write well: the *gaúchos* Osvaldo Moacir Alvarez and Sérgio da Costa Franco, the brilliant social columnist Nina Chavs, the humorous *paulista* Jurandir Ferreira. Guilherme Figueiredo expanded the scope of the genre to cover gastronomy. Diaféria invented a frame story for his collection, making the circus a symbol of the crazy "run around" from which the modern city dwellers suffer, especially the poor among them. For originality, Antônio Lima from Aracaju, Sergipe, takes the prize by having used the biographical variety of the crônica to present 40 of his contemporaries in that city as an anarchic "people's academy."

It is a pity that no new collection of crônicas was published by "Drummond," i.e. Carlos Drummond de Andrade. I also would have liked to see three more works which were published in 1978: Novais' *O chá das duas: D. Corrupção e D. Subversão*, Artur da Távola's *Alguém que já não fui*, and Veríssimo's *Amor brasileiro*.

To end with a paradox, here are two new definitions of the undefinable crônica:

"A soap bubble reflecting the fleeting, volatile everyday." (Ademaro Prezia)

"The crônica offers a unique opportunity to do anything—poetry, sociology, religion and general goofing-off [*besteira*]. My preference for the crônica has no other cause than the opportunity it gives me to vary without restraint." (Ney Messias)

6173 Alvarez, Osvaldo Moacir. Sorrisos e lágrimas. Artigos e crônicas. Canoas: Editora La Salle, 1978. 69 p.

The short human-interest stories are told in a clipped, vigorous language that is easy to read and conveys its sensitive message in a straightforward manner. Originally published in the journal *O Timoneiro*.

6174 Azevedo, Artur. Teatro a vapor. Edição de Gerald M. Moser. São Paulo: Editora Cultrix *em convênio com o* Instituto Nacional do Livro, 1977. 197 p.

A series of 105 crônicas in the shape of small dramatic sketches, produced by the wittiest Brazilian of his time for *O Século* (Rio) from 1906–08 when he died. He comments on local, national and international events that engaged the attention of cariocas, whom he mimicks goodhumoredly.

6175 Blanc, Aldir. Rua dos artistas e arredores. Crônicas. Ilustrações de Mariano. Rio de Janeiro: Codecri, 1978. 195 p. (Pasquim; 37)

Such a street exists in Vila Isabel, a Rio suburb, connected with composer Noel Rosa. Like Noel, Blanc writes popular songs. He also writes crônicas, sometimes in verse, for the satirical *Pasquim*. For his humor, he relies on colloquial Rio slang, a gallery of invented characters, and a liberal dose of mockery, *gozação*.

6176 Braga, Kenny. Voa, passarinho. Crônicas. Porto Alegre: Movimento, 1977. 99 p. (Rio Grande; 30)

First published in Porto Alegre newspapers during a difficult time for a writer craving liberty and sincerity. Braga writes poems in prose, accumulating similes like a poet manqué who seeks consolation in sex and alcohol while furiously clinging to the present moment. His melancholy recalls Mário Quintana's, but humor and musicality are absent.

6177 Braga, Rubem. 200 [i.e. Duzentas] crônicas escolhidas: as melhores de Rubem Braga. Rio de Janeiro: Record, 1977. 320 p.

Anthology made by "old Braga" himself, the only Brazilian whose reputation rests entirely on crônicas. Braga's seem inspired by a greater human warmth than anyone else's, whether he writes from the perspective of Ipanema or returns to his childhood home in Espírito Santo. Except for two short pieces, the crônicas antedate 1967.

6178 Campos, Paulo Mendes. Poéticas, patéticas e patetas. Rio de Janeiro: Tecnoprint, 1975. 181 p. (Edições de Ouro; 27)

Collection of 27 crônicas and short stories by the well-known Mineiro poet transplanted to Copacabana and its bars. The humanity that appears in them is painted as pathetic or stupid. There is precious little poetry in the prose.

6179 Chavs, Nina. Paris via Varig. Prefácio de Jorge Amado. Rio de Janeiro: Francisco Alves, 1977. 192 p.

Saturday articles sent by a social columnist from Paris to *O Globo* (Rio), probably 1973–77. She is a consummate artist of light pitter-patter spiced with fancy, malice and verve. Her best reflect the life and problems of young Brazilian women of the jet set.

6180 Crispim, Luiz Augusto. O arco e a fonte. Prefácio de Nathanael Alves. João Pessoa: A. União, 1977. 246 p.

Nostalgia characterizes the better commentaries on local topics, first published in *O Norte*. They are too vague and allusive to appeal to readers unfamiliar with João Pessoa.

6181 Diaféria, Lourenço. Circo dos cavalões. Croniquinhas. São Paulo: Summus, 1978. 175 p.

Diaféria owes his popularity perhaps to a social concern that recalls Rubem Braga. Diaféria writes about the people of São Paulo. His batting average does not approach Braga's, but now and then he has clever ideas. There is a frame story about a circus which ends in identification with a poor laborer's plight.

6182 Faé, Walter José. Koisas de poeta & outras coisas. São Paulo: Nova Epoca, 1978. 140 p.

Written between 1976–78 for newspapers in Americana, S. Paulo, they are sentimental, nostalgic *jornalismo provinciano*. Some are obituaries, a good many are reviews of books of poetry. Faé himself likes to write poetry.

6183 Ferreira, Jurandir. A visita. São Paulo: Editora do Escritor, 1977. 147 p.

One of the few well made books of crônicas: a tasteful cover design, clear, large print, wide margins, and good writing. An experienced fiction writer demonstrates with humor that humanity does not change, in spite of all claims to the contrary. He uses a wealth of original imagery. The humorous articles contrast with tender obituaries, among them a gem, "Tia Afonsina."

6184 Figueiredo, Guilherme. Comes & [i.e. e] bebes: ensaios de culinária e gastronomia. Rio de Janeiro: Civilização Brasileiro *em convênio com o* Instituto Nacional do Livro, 1978. 154 p.; bibl.

The playwright, who is also a great gourmet, had already published *Comidas, meu santo* (1964). Gastronomy is an unusual theme in crônicas; his are knowledgeable, even erudite, witty and beautifully written. Some are in verse, some are series of sententious observations.

6185 ———. A pluma e o vento. Crônicas. Rio de Janeiro: Cátedra *em convênio com o* Instituto Nacional do Livro, 1977. 175 p.

An entertaining grabbag of anecdotes and reminiscences, with substantial information about certain writers and artists, seasoned by poems, including his Portuguese versions of sonnets by Shakespeare. Two special themes stand out: evocations of his native Campinas and of two happy days spent in the black ghetto of Charlotte, North Carolina.

6186 Franco, Sérgio da Costa. Ruas mortas. Crônicas. Porto Alegre: Movimento, 1977. 108 p.

Porto Alegre, its streets, inhabitants and transformations, come to life. Below local color we are led to recognize ourselves. The title misleads: nothing is dead in this book, written with great empathy and an eye for significant detail. Parable-like crônicas selected from *O Correio do Povo* (1973–77).

6187 Gióia Júnior, Rubens. O nó da gravata. Crônicas. São Paulo: Melhoramentos, 1978. 168 p.: ill.

The author used to write crônicas for radio before writing for São Paulo newspapers. The selections date from 1977 and deal engagingly with a large variety of topics in a youthful, up-to-date but correct language, conveying vaguely Christian messages. Some topics are unusual: Málaga, Jimmy Carter, a kidney stone (inspiring a poem).

6188 Gouvêa, Paulo de. O grupo. Outras figuras—outras paisagens. Prefácio de Augusto Meyer. Porto Alegre: Movimento em convênio com o Instituto Estadual do Livro, 1976. 190 p.

Crônicas first published between 1973–76 in *O Correio do Povo.* The bulk are recollections of a group of six artists and writers who used to meet during the 1920s. They are bound up with the theater, the newspapers, the countryside (Cachoeira), all of it very local, very anecdotal, very picturesque.

6189 Lima, Antônio Carlos de Vasconcelos. Academia popular: retalhos provincianos. Aracaju: n.p., 1977. 139 p.

The author conceived the original idea of composing 40 crônicas based on interviews with 40 local "immortals" of both sexes and all ages, forming an academy without statutes. A very provincial city is thus evoked. Many of the artless, vivid articles appeared first in *Diário de Aracaju* and *Gazeta de Sergipe.*

6190 Lispector, Clarice. Para não esquecer. Ilustrações de Leo Amorim. São Paulo: Atica, 1978. 103 p. (Autores brasileiros; 20)

Posthumous miscellany of jottings, unlike the ordinary crônicas. They include pearls, such as impressions of West Africa and Switzerland, an encounter with a leashed *coatimundi,* conversations with her children, thoughts on painting, daydreams, many meditations about writing, and a 17-page outpouring of feelings concerning Brasília. No sources given.

6191 Luft, Lya. Matéria do cotidiano. Prefácio de Guilhermino César. Porto Alegre: Grafosul *em convênio com o* Instituto Estadual do Livro, 1978. 82 p.

Written for *O Correio do Povo* between 1963 and 1976, some as realistic reportage, others as poetic prose. Children and young people are of particular concern to her, who is also a teacher. But her most attractive columns deal with women's changing condition.

6192 Maciel, Marcial. Candelabro II. Curitiba: Editora Litero-Técnica, 1976. 275 p.

A miscellany of stories, speeches, verses and 24 crônicas occupying about one third of the volume, which were written by an octogenarian lawyer and journalist, active in politics. His articles, many of them published in the little *Correio de Piraí,* are vehicles for suggested improvements or moral lessons.

6193 Maia, Benedito Geraldo. Quadros da vida. Crônicas e poemas. João Pessoa: União, 1977. 199 p.

The crônicas occupy the first 100 pages, the rest is poetry. Most concern public figures, institutions, events, such as an academic reception. Absent from this "daily register of the city" is the intimately human experience that can make a crônica worthwhile. First published between 1974–76 in *A União* and *O Norte*.

6194 Menezes, Holdemar [Oliveira de]. O barco naufragado. Crônicas. Florianópolis: Governo do Estado de Santa Catarina, 1976. 84 p.

The shipwrecked boat of the title symbolizes the journalist's lack of courage to be true to his convictions. The stories are odd, in an attempt to amuse the reader. They appeared first in the journal *O Estado*.

6195 Nilce [dos Santos], Maria. Crônica de uma ilha (muito) doida. Vitória: Gráfica Jóia, 1977. 128 p.

A social columnist, she feels daring and independent enough to lampoon her state, its incoherences, and its public figures, including herself. Spicy anecdotes and name dropping are her dish. This froth has little to offer anyone unfamiliar with Espírito Santo politicians and its "beautiful people."

6196 Novaes, Carlos Eduardo. A travessia da Via Crucis. Crônicas. Ilustrações de Vilmar Rodrigues. Rio de Janeiro: Nórdica, 1975. 169 p.: ill.

The success of *O caos nosso de cada dia* (1974) induced Novaes to give his new brilliant collection a similar title alluding to traffic congestion and noise pollution. He gives facts and figures, exaggerating the consequences mockingly. Events of 1974 and enduring problems are commented upon with grim humor—grim like Vilmar's illustrations.

6197 Oliveira, Alfredo de. Essas coisas (crônicas) que acontecem. Prefácio de José Gonçalves de Oliveira. Ilustrações de José Augusto de Campos Filho. Recife: Gráfica Carangá, 1976. 215 p.: ill.

A long series of misadventures, *desencontros*, told with erotic frankness and presented as character sketches or episodes of his own life, for no other purpose than to amuse. Campos Filho's caricatures serve the same purpose.

6198 Para gostar de leer. Crônicas. v. 1/3. Ilustrações de Aderbal Moura. São Paulo: Editora Atica, 1977/1978. 3 v. (77, 78, 78 p.): ill.

Three-volume set of primers consisting of 20 crônicas each by four well-known authors: Carlos Drummond de Andrade, Fernando Sabino, Paulo Mendes Campos, and Rubem Braga. Each volume is arranged according to theme: vol. 1) "Children," "Animals," "In the Consumer World," "Human Types," and "Language and Man;" vol. 2) "At Home," "At Work," "Traveling," "At School," and "In the Street;" and vol. 3) "Confusions," "Disputes and Solutions," "Understanding and Misunderstanding," "Deeds and Intentions," and "Solicitations." Vol. 1 is introduced by short biographies. Vol. 2 includes chronologies and numerous snapshots of the authors. Vol. 3 contains a collective interview of the four writers based on questions submitted by schoolchildren.

6199 Prezia, Ademaro. A dança do Papa. Crônicas. Prefácio de W. Junqueira Ferreira. Aguas da Prata: Empresa Gráfica da *Revista dos Tribunais*, 1978. 150 p.

The weekly crônicas were written for newspapers in Ribeirão Preto, Poças de Caldas and São João da Boa Vista from 1952 on. Commenting on recent events, they impart historical background in an entertaining fashion (e.g. about several popes). Most crônicas end with jokes.

6200 Queiroz, Júlio de. Umas, passageiras; outras, crônicas. Florianópolis: Governo do Estado de Santa Catarina, 1976. 86 p.

A curious potpourri of articles about the delights of good company in little Florianópolis, travels in postwar Germany, and visits with Benedictine nuns and monks. Queiroz has a sharp eye for the ridiculous and a cultivated humanistic attitude rarely found in the New World.

6201 Quintana, Mário. Prosa & verso. Porto Alegre: Editora Globo, 1978. 121 p. (Coleção Série Paradidática)

Includes poems and crônicas taken from *Sapato florido* (1947), *Caderno H* (1973) and *A vaca e o hipogrifo* (1977). The poet is a born and delightful magician who recreates the world in miniature stories, nostalgic verse, epigrams, maxims, or humorous observations. This is a first rate work.

6202 Regina, Boneca. Crônicas. Prefácio de Alfeu Lisboa de Castro. Porto Alegre: Editora Globo, 1977. 118 p.: ill.

The articles, dating from 1945 on, are poems in effusive, sensuous prose. Her warmth can become cloying; her fondness for children saves her. Two poems by Erico Veríssimo and two letters by Monteiro Lobato, friends of hers, enhance the volume, as do ingenuous pastels drawn by her grandchildren and great-grandchildren.

6203 Rodrigues, Nelson. O reacionário. Memórias e confissões. Rio de Janeiro: Editora Record, 1977. 526 p.

Crônicas (rather than memoirs or confessions) written with verve, humor, and in the case of those touching on family members deep feeling, by Brazil's best-known dramatist. [R.E. Dimmick]

6204 Silva, Aloysio Guilherme de. O livro, essa criatura . . . Crônicas. Prefácio de Nelson Vaz. Rio de Janeiro: Livraria São José, 1976. 77 p.

In a few erudite articles, the author, a book collector, writes about finds, anonymity, pseudonyms, and compiles quotations, especially of minor poets. Two pieces discuss individual authors: old João de Castro and Juan Ramón Jiménez, but without originality. About as far as one can get from the light and lively crônica.

6205 Silveira, Helena. Memórias da terra assassinada. 2. ed. São Paulo: Símbolo, 1976. 165 p.: ill.

Reedition of a book of travel sketches about Lebanon in more peaceful times, *Damasco e outros caminhos* (1957). It was written with literary pretensions as a declaration of love for Beirut, "city for the senses." A new preface expresses horror and hope. Photos of war-ravaged Beirut contrast brutally with the rhapsodic text.

6206 Tannuri, Victor. Vim passar esta noite com vocês. Crônicas. Prefácio de João Augusto Didier. Epílogo de Yvette V.P. de Almeida. Brasília: Gráfica Brasil Central, 1974? 93 p.

Many of the articles are no more than fairy tales or edifying homilies by a well meaning doctor. The collection would be interesting if more crônicas had to do with his profession or with Brasília, where he has lived since its inception.

6207 Távola, Artur da [*pseud. for* **Paulo Alberto Monteiro de Barros**]. Mevitevendo. Crônicas. Prefácio de Jorge Amado. Rio de Janeiro: Salamandra, 1977. 153 p.

Crônicas published in *O Globo* (ca. 1975) by a journalist who pioneered in television criticism. There is little of this here; the other articles, frequently in the form of chaotic enumerations, display shallow philosophy, psychology and communication theory. Távola himself calls them "somewhat silly reflections." At least, he reflects on serious matters.

6208 Tolipan, Alberto. Ontem, hoje e sempre. Crônicas. Seleção e prefácio de H. Pereira da Silva. Rio de Janeiro: Departamento Gráfico do M.A.F.C., 1978. 158 p.

Pious and posthumous homage through selections from over a thousand crônicas, "more or less forgotten" after having been broadcast between 1956 and 1958 over Radio Continental, Rio. Calling for the preservation of vestiges of the past and protesting against crime and garbage. Of small value.

6209 Trombini, Sinibaldo. Simples mensagens. v. 1, Crônicas; v. 2, Poesias. Curitiba: Editora Litero-Técnica, 1978. 84 p. (2 v. in one)

The aged author wanted his first book to bring a message of brotherly love to all readers who have trusting souls. All 10 crônicas preach charity from a spiritualist viewpoint. They are sincere, serious, and without literary merit.

6210 Veríssimo, Luís Fernando. O rei do rock. Crônicas. Porto Alegre: RBS/Editora Globo, 1978. 145 p. (Coleção RBS/Editora Globo; 1)

The relaxation of press censorship can be sensed in several of the best crônicas, such as "Novelas Eleitorais" or "A Ultima do Papagaio" (about the disappearance of parrot jokes). Unfortunately one feature is missing: Veríssimo's delightful drawings. The crônicas are taken from *Jornal do Brasil* and *Zero Hora*.

6211 Viana, Chico [*pseud. for* **Francisco José Gomes Correia**]. De mãos atadas: reflexões e desatinos de um rapaz de província. Crônicas. Prefácios de Elizabeth Marinheiro, Francisco de Assis Dantas e Chico Viana. Ilustrações de Flávio Tavares. João Pessoa: G. G. S., 1977. 111 p.: ill.

Most of the crônicas are banal dialogues between couples, their arguments or confessions, laid in João Pessoa and surroundings. Several appeared in *O Norte*.

6212 Vinagre, Belminda Stela de Faria. *Crônicas de outono.* Prefácio de Juarez da Gama Batista. João Pessoa: União, 1976. 92 p

Her first book of new crônicas and old ones published in the newspapers *O Norte* and *O Momento.* Guided by intuitive feminine sensitivity, she reflects on her experiences. Her homespun thoughts about feast-days are worth reading.

6213 Visconti, Nicolino. A rosa azul. Contos e crônicas. Juiz de Fora: Esdeva, 1977. 135 p.

Visconti's first collection is named after a pious and mendacious crônica written by the late Humberto de Campos. In homely prose, Visconti talks about the ordinary pleasures of growing up as a poor "plebeian," seeks refuge in Christian faith, and attempts to impart it to others. "Why am I so sentimental and so mystical?" he asks himself.

Poetry

RALPH E. DIMMICK, *General Secretariat, Organization of American States*

VERSE IS PRODUCED IN BRAZIL in what might be termed industrial quantities: the contributing editor reviewed about 800 items in making the selection for this volume of *HLAS.* Given the commercial possibilities of even the best of poetry, one might conclude that the vanity press is in significant factor in the country's publishing economy.

In this deluge, many currents mingle, but none is at present preponderant. Traditional veins continue to be exploited, witness innumerable collection of *trovas*—quatrains in the folk manner, generally the work of urban dwellers whose principal talent consists in finding words that rhyme. A writer such as Vitto Santos (item **6324**) would not have seemed out of place in the Romantic age, nor would ones like José Rodrigues Pinto (item **6312**) or Olney Borges Pinto de Souza (item **6335**) have been uncomfortable among the Parnassians. Early Modernism relives in the work of Evandro Barrêto (item **6224**); the Symbolist trend is prolonged in the compositions of Onestaldo de Pennafort (item **6307**) and Alphonsus de Guimaraens Filho (item **6263**). On the farthest fringes of the avant-garde are those who have all but abandoned words for "visual poetry"—diagrams, designs, photomontages, etc. Good examples are provided by Aquiles Branco (item **6228**), Hugo Mund Júnior (item **6295**), and Dailor Varela (item **6343**). Somewhat within the fringe stand the Concretists, for whom the physical disposition of words on a page is of more significance than syntax—*e.g.* Augusto de Campos (item **6232**), Helena Parente Cunha (item **6247**), and Duda Machado (item **6280**)—and the practitioners of *poesia-praxis,* of which the leading exponent is Mário Chamie (item **6237**).

Poetry of social protest is by no means a novelty in Brazil—compositions of Castro Alves are outstanding examples of the genre in the 19th century—but as the reins of censorship are gradually relaxed there appears to be a marked upsurge in reaction to the present regime and prevailing social conditions. Manifestations range from the rather primary efforts of victims (items **6217** and **6332**) to those of sympathizers possessed of greater literary endowments (items **6271**, **6281** and **6292**), including an immigrant bishop (item **6234**).

One notes a few new editions of colonial authors: Cláudio Manoel da Costa (item **6241**), Gregório de Mattos (item **6285**), Bento Teixeira (item **6339**); there are also useful reprints of later but long-unavailable works (items **6230**, **6255** and **6344**). Welcome are collected editions of verse by Amadeu Amaral (item **6219**), Sosígenes da Costa (item **6242**), Edgard Mata (item **6284**), Menotti del Picchia (item **6310**), Egas Moniz (item **6347**), Gilberto Mendonça Teles (item **6340**), Onestaldo de Pennafort (item **6307**), and Alphonsus de Guimaraens Filho (item **6263**) for the opportunity they provide to fill in the recent past and reevaluate certain figures of the present.

A number of figures of established reputation added thereto by new works: Carlos Drummond de Andrade (items **6220** and **6221**), José Paulo Moreira da Fonseca (item **6256**), Stella Leonardos (item **6274**), Waldemar Lopes (item **6278**), Carlos Nejar (items **6296** and **6297**) and Geraldo Pinto Rodrigues (item **6319**); particularly notable in this respect was Telmo Padilha, with no less than four new collections (items **6300–6303**).

New names of promise to be noted are those of Lúcia Aizim (item **6214**), Patrícia Blower (item **6226**), Ilka Brunhilde Laurito (item **6272**), Mauro Gomes Aranha de Lima (item **6275**), Jomar Morais de Souto (item **6333**), and especially Anderson Braga Horta (items **6266–6268**).

Among poets to disappear from the literary scene were Joaquim Cardozo (d. 2 Nov. 1978) and Odylo Costa Filho (d. 19 Aug. 1979). The Federal District awarded Menotti del Picchia the Brasília Prize for Literature for his collected work.

6214 Aizim, Lucia. Errância. Poesia. Rio de Janeiro: Editora Vozes Limitada, 1978. 122 p.

Concise expression, vivid imagery, and poignant sentiment are the hallmarks of these lyrics; particularly impressive are those reflecting feelings of a recent immigrant to Brazil.

6215 Almeida, J.A. Pio de. Ciclo. Porto Alegre: Lume Editora Artes Gráficas, 1977. 49 p.: ill.

Whatever his subject—from a flower to a band of rebels—Almeida seeks to convey the essence of being rather than physical reality ("Caço o canto da ave o movimento do seu vôo/a idéia e o perfume do vale").

6216 Almeida, Márcio. Previsão de haveres na terra do Puka. Ilustrações de Maria José Boaventura. Belo Horizonte: Editora Lemi, 1978. 38 p.: ill.

"Viver é um treino para o ato de ser," says Almeida, who finds that the process of growing up is as much one of loss as of gain.

6217 Alverga, Alex Polari de. Inventário de cicatrizes. São Paulo: Teatro Ruth Escobar, 1978. 58 p.

Verse by a political prisoner ("um combatente provisório/de uma causa quase eterna no homem"), more impressive for its stark depiction of police brutality than for aesthetic qualities.

6218 Alvim, Francisco. Passatempo. Rio de Janeiro: Oficinas da Companhia Editora Fon-Fon e Seleta, 1974. 80 p.: ill. (Coleção Frenesi)

Alvim's fragmented still lifes remind one of paintings by Braque.

6219 Amaral [Penteado], Amadeu. Obras. Poesias completas. São Paulo: Editora HUCITEC *em co-edição com a* Secretaria da Cultura, Ciência e Tecnologia do Estado de São Paulo, 1977. 274 p.

Characterized by careful attention to form, clarity, a preference for the sonnet and themes drawn from classic mythology, the Bible, and the Middle Ages, Amaral's verse well justifies Manuel Bandeira's classification of the poet as a "neo-Parnassian" of the generation following the appearance of the Symbolists.

6220 Andrade, Carlos Drummond de. Discurso de primavera e algumas sombras. 2. ed., aumentada. Rio de Janeiro: Livraria J. Olympio Editora, 1978. 125 p.

Even in occasional verse and protests at environmental pollution, pseudoscientific gobbledegook, and the relentlessness of modern advertising, Drummond shows himself a master poet by his subtle handling of language, his brilliant imagery, and his ability to impart universal significance to personal feeling (first edition 1977).

6221 ———. O marginal Clorindo Gato. Ilustrações de Darel. Rio de Janeiro: Avenir Editora, 1978. 54 p.: ill. (Coleção Depoimentos; 2)

Satirical fable of how in death a criminal becomes a saint.

6222 **Araújo, Henry Corrêa de.** Tempo contrário tempo. Ilustrações de Melado. Belo Horizonte: Editora Comunicação *em coedição com a* Secretaria Municipal de Cultura, Informação, Turismo e Esportes da Prefeitura Municipal de Belo Horizonte, 1976. 78 p.: ill.

Araújo's impersonal considerations on the meaning of Minas and the arts of love and literary composition are less likely to be remembered by the reader than Melado's illustrations, which have the air of a comic strip drawn by Aubrey Beardsley.

6223 **Avila, Affonso.** Discurso da difamação do poeta. Antologia. Suplemento de leitura organizado por Affonso Romano de Sant'Anna. São Paulo: Summus Editorial, 1978. 111 p. (Palavra poética; 1)

Repetition and parallelism are among the most ancient of poetic devices. Avila abuses them, constructing entire poems out of metamorphoses on a single line—in one case on the name of the author of "Por que me Ufano de meu País." Contains selections from previously published collections and new compositions.

6224 **Barrêto, Evandro.** Aedo. Salvador: Edições Cordel, 1976. 71 p.: ill. (Série Iniciação; 7)

Barrêto's verse belatedly recalls the playful aspects of early Modernism: "se é jogo ou poesia/quem sabe o que é."

6225 **Bertolino, Pedro** [*pseud. for* **Pedro Bertolino Silva**]. Trajeto. Poemas. Florianópolis: Edição do Governo do Estado de Santa Catarina, 1976. 79 p. (Coleção Cultura catarinense. Série Literatura: poesia)

The word diagrams of the second half of this book are as meaningless to the viewer as is life to the poet in the compositions of the first half.

6226 **Blower, Patrícia [Maria Costa].** Descompasso. Rio de Janeiro: Livraria Editora Cátedra, 1978. 79 p.

Blower is the poet of the "Infeliz Cidade" of poverty, drudgery, monotony, and lack of personal contact between elbow-rubbing multitudes.

6227 **Boyadjieff, Christo.** Viagens. Poemas. Rio de Janeiro: Editora Artenova, 1977. 59 p.

The compositions of this Bulgarian long resident in Brazil are pervaded with a melancholy sense of time gone by and of life's approaching end.

6228 **Branco, Aquiles.** Vôo das cinco. Fotos de Renato Wandeck. Arte final do autor. Cataguases, Brazil: J. Branco Ribeiro Filho, 1977. 55 p.: ill.

Numbers and letters combined in graphic designs rather than words. One "poem" consists solely of periods.

6229 **Brasileiro, Francisco.** Poesia. São Paulo?: n.p., 1976. 93 p.

Wisdom of the people in pretentious literary garb.

6230 **Brazil, Zeferino.** Visão do ópio. Poemas. 2. ed. Porto Alegre: Divisão Cultural, Sport Club Internacional, 1974. 95 p. (Coleção Príncipe; 2)

First published in 1906, this fantasy evokes the Romantics of an earlier era—the Alvares de Azevedo of *A noite na taberna*, for example.

6231 **Brito, Mário da Silva.** Suíte em dor maior. Rio de Janeiro: Civilização Brasileira, 1978. 141 p. (Coleção Vera Cruz; 265)

Clever but superficial reflections on life and death, often epigrammatic, the character of which is suggested by the title of the collection. Curious similarity between "Burleska" and item **6221**.

6232 **Campos, Augusto de.** Reduchamp. Iconogramas de Julio Plaza. São Paulo: Edições S.T.R.I.P, Distribuição Nacional, Livraria Editora Duas Cidades, 1976. 64 p.: ill.

Campos seeks to achieve with words the effects attained by Marcel Duchamp in painting, in which "entre o visível e o invisível" there is an "imprevisível choque."

6233 **Carneiro, Geraldo Eduardo.** Na busca do sete-estrelo: ópera de cordel. Rio de Janeiro: Companhia Editora Fon-Fon e Seleta, 1974. 49 p.: ill. (Coleção Frenesi)

The making of a lower-class criminal, told in terms of surrealist cinema.

6234 Casaldáliga, Pedro. Antologia retirante. Poemas. Rio de Janeiro: Civilização Brasileira, 1978. 240 p.

The verse of the Catalan Vicar Apostolic of São Félix do Araguaia reveals not only commitment to liberation movements ("llamo al Orden de mal,/ y al Progreso de mentira") but also genuine poetic talent (e.g. "El pez"). Includes Spanish and Catalan originals accompanied by the poet's Portuguese translations.

6235 Castro, Luiz Paiva de. O cometa é um homem a cavalo. Poemas de Diamantina e da raiz de um país. Rio de Janeiro: José Alvaro Editor, 1978. 155 p.

Poems inspired in colonial legend and the more recent past of a historic mining center.

6236 César [da Silva], Guilhermino. Sistema do imperfeito & [i.e. e] outros poemas. Porto Alegre: Editora Globo, 1977. 184 p. (Estante de poesia Henrique Bertaso; 1)

"A falta de senso é o senso do mundo." This being the poet's view of existence, it is unsurprising that he should declare: "Do absurdo a poesia/vem/se a lógica não lhe tira as asas." However, 184 pages of poetry of the absurd are a bit too much.

6237 Chamie, Mário. Objeto selvagem. São Paulo: Edições Quíron *em convênio com o* Instituto Nacional do Livro, Ministério da Educação e Cultura, 1977. 586 p. (Coleção Sélesis; 12)

Complete poetic work to date, including previously unpublished compositions, of the inventor of "poesia praxis."

6238 ———. Sábado na hora da escuta. Antologia. São Paulo: Summus Editorial, 1978. 126 p. (Palavra poética; 2)

Selection, based on texts collected in *Objeto selvagem*. The concluding "Comentários e Sugestões para um Estudo da Poesia de Mário Chamie" are useful to those seeking to arrive at an understanding of the author's technique and intentions.

6239 Claver, Ronald. As margens do corpo. Porto Alegre: Editora Movimento *em convênio com o* Instituto Estadual do Livro, Departamento de Assuntos Culturais, Secretaria de Educação e Cultura do Rio Grande do Sul, 1978. 50 p.: ill. (Coleção Poesiasul; 17)

Claver sings of Minas Gerais, his beloved, and a child symbolizing Latin America in language he describes as "signos que deslizam na/superfície do dicionário."

6240 Corrêa, José Ronaldo. União com o infinito. Ilustrações do autor. São Paulo: Editora do Escritor, 1977. 64 p.: ill. (Coleção do poeta; 17)

In copulating, Corrêa finds himself in communion with the universe.

6241 Costa, Cláudio Manoel da. Poesia. Seleção, organização e posfácio de João Etienne Filho. Belo Horizonte: Editora Itatiaia, 1976. 150 p. (Biblioteca básica brasileira; 1)

Useful selection from the poetry of a leading 18th-century Arcadian, followed by a rather naive editorial appreciation.

6242 Costa, Sosígenes da. Obra poética. 2. ed., rev. e ampliada por José Paulo Paes. São Paulo: Editora Cultrix *em convênio com o* Instituto Nacional do Livro, 1978. 317 p.

Writing in provincial obscurity, employing Parnassian vocabulary and Symbolist imagery, Costa nonetheless displayed a Modernist liking for themes and devices of folklore, humorous sallies, and nose-thumbing at bourgeois convention.

6243 Costa Filho, Odylo. Notícias de amor. Rio de Janeiro: Artenova *em convênio com o* Instituto Nacional do Livro, 1977. 136 p.: ill.

"Mais confissão do que meditação, mais sombra de amor feliz do que denúncia dos males do mundo" says the author of these generally conventional, sentimental, superficial compositions.

6244 Craveiro, Paulo Fernando. O pintor de fêmeas. Desenhos de Francisco Brennand. Recife: POOL Editorial, 1977. 29 p.: ill.

Brief lyrics of classic sobriety, heavily charged with sensuality.

6245 Cruz, Paulo Bandeira da. Itinerário do boi além do campo. Rio de Janeiro: Editora Artenova, 1976. 49 p.

A present-day apocalypse, in which contemporary images substitute for those of the Bible.

6246 Cunha, Carlos. A flauta onírica. Salvador: Nosso Tempo, 1977. 63 p. (Coleção Travessia, poesia baiana; 1)

Life as lived and life as dreamed are

grafted together in a world of symbols through Cunha's "cirurgia poética."

6247 Cunha, Helena Parente. Corpo no cerco. Rio de Janeiro: Edições Tempo Brasileiro *em convênio com o* Instituto Nacional do Livro, 1978. 123 p. (Coleção Tempoesia; 19)

Among experimenters with words—their metamorphoses and the effects produced by their physical arrangement on a page—Cunha stands out for pursuing such devices, not as ends in themselves, but as a means of truly poetic expression (e.g., "alcancei a absoluz/onde o tempo instranspõe/e a alma DEUSsolve").

6248 Danieli, Edoardo Carlo. Cores de sombras. Poemas. Capa de Elisa Setti Riedel. Desenhos de Giácomo Perroni. São Paulo: n.p., 1979. 130 p., 5 leaves of plates: ill.

Danieli describes his poems as "minha visão do mundo, em fragmentos . . . assuntos pessoais que extrapolados vão ao infinito." The vision is indeed fragmentary, but Danieli scarcely succeeds in giving universal significance to his personal experience.

6249 Diniz, Valdimir. Até o 8° [i.e. oitavo] round. Rio de Janeiro: Livraria Francisco Alves Editora, 1978. 46 p.

Wryly humorous criticism of the established order.

6250 Faria, Alvaro Alves de. Em legítima defesa. São Paulo: Edições Símbolo, 1978. 89 p.

Given the grim picture Faria paints of economic and civic reality in present-day Brazil, one can understand classification of suicide as "self-defense." Added to the title collection is the third edition of the author's *Quatro cantos de pavor e alguns poemas desesperados*, first printed in 1973.

6251 Félix, Moacyr [*pseud. for* **Moacyr Félix de Oliveira**]. Canção do exílio aqui. Rio de Janeiro: Civilização Brasileira, 1977. 113 p. (Coleção Vera Cruz; 251)

Alceu Amoroso Lima keenly observes: "este nosso poeta se sente exilado de sua época . . . exilado tanto pelo coração como pela inteligência. Não é um exílio no espaço, mas no tempo e nas instituições dominantes . . . não é uma evasão, mas uma revolta."

6252 ———. Invenção de crença e descrença. Rio de Janeiro: Civilização Brasileira, 1978. 95 p. (Coleção Vera Cruz; 266)

Selections (sometimes altered) from works published in 1944 to 1966, plus poems written in 1978. In characteristic style the author "explains" the title as "nascido . . . da existência e da história vistas como o eixo de um ser-sendo para a liberdade através de transformações gestadas como necessárias pelo movimento da vida num espaço-tempo essencialmente dialético."

6253 ———. Neste lençol. Rio de Janeiro: Civilização Brasileira, 1977. 95 p. (Coleção Vera Cruz; 252)

Consists of a 38-page rhapsodic gush in praise of sexual intercourse, followed by selections from previous publications.

6254 Figueiredo, Guilherme. Ração de abandono e outros poemas. 2. ed. Rio de Janeiro: Livraria Editora Cátedra *em convênio com o* Instituto Nacional do Livro, 1978. 127 p.; bibl.

An accomplished verse technician, with preference for the sonnet, Figueiredo is at his best in satirical expressions (e.g. when he declares "Meus inimigos são / Homenagens que presto aos meus amigos"). Extensive bio-bibliographical notes.

6255 Fioravanti, Gervásio. Horas marianas e outros poemas. Recife: Prefeitura Municipal do Recife, Secretaria de Educação e Cultura, Conselho Municipal de Cultura, 1978. 186 p.; bibl. (Coleção Recife; 2)

Reprint of works of a retarded Romantic (1870–1936), conventional in themes and technique, but not without charm. Critical notes by Mauro Mota, Luiz Delgado, Adelmar Tavares, Arthur Azevedo.

6256 Fonseca, José Paulo Moreira da. Sextante. Rio de Janeiro: Tempo Brasileiro, 1977. 90 p. (Coleção Tempoesia; 15)

Love as liberation from self—first in union with, and feeling for, others—leads ultimately to God, in whose presence the poet says "posso ser eu mesmo/imensamente."

6257 Fraga, Antônio. Moinho e. Poema dramático. Rio de Janeiro: Edições Mundo Livre, 1978. 75 p.

Described by the author as a modern version of an ancient fertility rite, these dialogues vaguely relating to pregnancy contain one notable aphorism: "a paz universal . . . é um tiro a espera de gatilhos."

6258 Franco, Georgenor [de Sousa]. Poemas escolhidos. Belém: Serviço de Imprensa Universitária, 1976. 131 p.

Tenderly sentimental verse, for which piety, filial devotion, and carnal attraction provide the principal themes.

6259 Freitas Filho, Armando. Mademoiselle Furta-Cor. Oito poemas eróticos. Ilustrações de Rubens Gerchman. Florianópolis: Editora Noa Noa, 1977. 27 p.: ill.

Celebration of sex in vivid metaphor.

6260 Garcia, Gardênia. Corpo de sal. Rio de Janeiro: Massao Ohno, 1979. 105 p.: ill.

The poet is intensely conscious of her womanhood and of its fulfillment in the act of love.

6261 Góes Sobrinho, José de Faria. Canto em silêncio. Ilustração de capa, Celita Vaccani. Rio de Janeiro: Edições Achiamé, 1978. 168 p.

Posthumously published, sententious academic verse, relieved by a few delightfully unpretentious compositions in the urban folk manner (e.g. "Elegia de Agosto," "Maria").

6262 Gomes, João Carlos Teixeira. O domador de gafanhotos. Salvador: Fundação Cultural do Estado de Bahia *sob os auspícios* do Governo do Estado da Bahia, 1976. 131 p. (Coleção Ilha de Maré; 1)

Gomes believes that poetry today has a "missão de resistência e não ceder ao delírio cerebralista que está transformando a poesia num jogo inócuo . . . de signos vazios;" his compositions—descriptive, reflective, or expressive of inner feeling—fully achieve that mission.

6263 Guimaraens Filho, Alphonsus de. Agua do tempo. Poemas escolhidos e versos inéditos. Rio de Janeiro: Editora Nova Aguilar *em convênio com o* Instituto Nacional do Livro, 1976. 240 p.; bibl. (Biblioteca Manacial; 61)

The overview (1935–75) provided by this anthology confirms Guimaraens' position as one of the finest poets of this century. Relatively untouched by Modernist and post-Modernist currents, he is best classified as a second-generation Symbolist, a mystic preoccupied with death but with firm hope in eternal life (e.g. "Quando eu Disser Adeus . . .").

6264 Gullar, Ferreira [*pseud. for* **José Ribamar Ferreira**]. Antologia poética. Rio de Janeiro: Fontana [and] Summus Editorial Ltda., São Paulo, 1976 or 1977. 102 p.

The evolution of Gullar from poetical exercises in which words are more important than meaning to lyrics expressive of real personal feeling and human solidarity is well brought out in this selection by the author.

6265 Holanda, Gastão de. O atlas do quarto. Poemas. Rio de Janeiro: Fontana, between 1972 and 1979. 184 p.

Holanda's evocations of Recife and its floods and of human misery in a Rio *favela* are brilliant, his comments on music perceptive, and his appreciation of carnal love vividly conveyed—but his compositions have the flat ring of prose.

6266 Horta, Anderson Braga. Exercícios de homem. Brasília: Senado Federal, 1978. 136 p. (Coleção Machado de Assis; 13)

The title of this collection is perhaps more apt than intended. Though many of the poems speak of concern for a better world, Horta seems oddly uninvolved; the compositions are coldly formal; the linguistic inventions ("trevalume," "vitrígneos") smack more of artifice than of art.

6267 ———. Incomunicação. Ilustrações de Tércio L. Rimoli. Belo Horizonte: Editora Comunicação *em convênio com o* Instituto Nacional do Livro, 1977. 95 p.: ill.

The search for truth, beauty, self-knowledge, and poetic expression is more important than attainment of the goal, says Horta. Be this as it may, his achievement as regards the last-mentioned is impressive. Skillfully crafted, embellished by striking imagery, strongly musical in effect, pervaded by a sense of life's mystery and a tragic consciousness of the flight of time, the compositions of this collection establish Horta as a figure to be reckoned with in contemporary Brazilian poetry.

6268 ———. Marvário. Brasília: Clube de Poesia de Brasília, 1976. 45 p. (Série Buriti; 2)

The sea and its moods, fishermen and their loves, and the creatures that move through the depths are the recurring subjects of Horta's lulling lines.

6269 Jorge, Franklin and **Leila Míccolis.** Impróprio para menores de 18 [i.e. dezoito] amores. Poemas. Desenhos internos de Rodolfo Capeto. Natal: n.p., 1976. 40 p.: ill. (Coleção Limiar; 1)

Specialists in intercourse, both authors take pride in calling a spade a spade—and their verse is more replete with spades than a well-stocked hardware store.

6270 Jorge, José Guilherme de Araújo. Antologia poética. Rio de Janeiro: Edições Nosso Tempo, 1978. 175 p.

Titles such as "Versos a meu Pai Morto," "Bandeira do Brasil," "Tão Simples este Amor," and "Bom Dia, Amigo Sol!" suggest the character of Araújo Jorge's work and perhaps the quality as well. He will never gain a place in literary history, but has won by far the greatest audience of any Brazilian poet of this century: to date over 1,500,000 copies of his works have come from the press.

6271 Klafke, Aristides. Esquina dorsal. Poemas. Capa e ilustração de Mangel. São Paulo: Edições Pindaíba, 1978. 63 p.

These verses of a rebel against the established order, living "no verso do avesso," who declares "meu ódio é quase tudo," have a fine epic sweep.

6272 Laurito, Ilka Brunhilde. Sal do lírico. Antologia poética. São Paulo: Edições Quíron, 1978. 130 p.: ill. (Coleção Sélesis; 13)

More affecting than the poet's meditations on bodily extinction is her reminiscence of a dead love ("O Anônimo"); more pungent than her evocations of carnal love are her mordantly ironic outcries against the dehumanization of modern city life.

6273 Leite, Waldimir Maia. O ofício da busca: e outros ofícios. Poemas. Ilustrações de Maria Margot. Recife: Companhia Editora de Pernambuco, 1978. 75 p., 6 leaves of plates: ill.

Leite's vision might be termed prismatic, transforming the most commonplace of objects into a rainbow of sparkling imagery.

6274 Leonardos [da Silva Cabassa], Stella. Romanceiro de Anita e Garibaldi. Florianópolis: Edição do Governo do Estado de Santa Catarina, 1977. 208 p.: ill. (Coleção Cultura Catarinense. Série Literatura: Poesia)

Ballads inspired by the participation of the Italian revolutionary Giuseppe Garibaldi in the southern Brazilian revolt of 1835 known as the War of the Ragamuffins, and his liaison with Ana Ribeiro, who became his companion in arms. Lyric passages surpass in effectiveness those of epic intent.

6275 Lima, Mauro Gomes Aranha de. Vidraça. Ilustrações de Miriam Straus. Foto de Mitsumasa Fujitsuka. São Paulo: Massao Ohno, 1979. 93 p.: ill.

Verse of a very young man, in love with love ("todas as mulheres são mulheres preferidas"), concerned for his fellow man ("Escravo/Carne que nasceu noite!"), full of hope for the future ("Há sempre um sonho que parte / A procura de um outro mundo"). Quite promising.

6276 Lívia Nádia. Um bicho de seda tecendo lembranças. Poesia. Rio de Janeiro: Livraria Editora Cátedra, 1977. 58 p.

The physical excitement of love gives life to the poet's delicate expressions of fleeting moods.

6277 Lopes, Manuel. Campo-ilha-urbs: ou, Canto puro, com muito amor, para São Luís do Maranhão. São Luís: Edições SIOGE, 1977. 50 p.

Two love letters to São Luís, described more in terms of atmosphere than of specific detail.

6278 Lopes, Waldemar. Sonetos da despedida. Brasília: Gráfica-Escola de Jornal e Artes do Sindicato dos Jornalistas Profissionais de Brasília, 1976. 13 p.

Five compositions, subtle in expression, brilliant in execution, in which the poet regretfully takes leave of Brasília.

6279 Loureiro, João de Jesus Paes. Porantim. Poemas amazônicas. Prefácio de Octávio Ianni. Rio de Janeiro: Civilização Brasileira, 1978. 139 p. (Série Novos poetas do Brasil. Coleção Poesia hoje; 24)

As the Amazon carries all in its stream, so this loosely structured rhapsody gathers elements of folklore, history, ethnology, botany, and geography in a sweeping flood of verse.

6280 Machado, Duda. Zil. Rio de Janeiro: Grupo de Planejamento Gráfico, 1977. 47 p.

Meaning is conveyed less by words than by their typographical disposition on the page, at times with highly effective results.

6281 Maia, Geraldo. Triste cantiga de alguma terra. Rio de Janeiro: Editora Tempo Literário, 1978. 107 p.

With a keen eye for telling detail, Maia conveys to the reader in brilliantly incisive language a totally disabused and utterly unforgettable vision of Brazilian social reality.

6282 Maia, João Domingues. O caderno turquesa. Rio de Janeiro: Edições Tempo Brasileiro, 1978. 91 p. (Coleção Tempoesia; 20)

Love poems, ranging from erotic enthusiasm to consciousness of the ephemeral nature of passion and regret for the "dor de não sentires no amanhã o que sentias."

6283 Marques, Saulo Mendonça. Sombras de agonia. Poesia. 2. ed. João Pessoa: A União Companhia Editora, 1976. 116 p.: ill.

The measure of Marques' vapidly introspective verse is given by the lines "com olhos colados/em mim mesmo/sem nada ver além."

6284 Mata, Edgard [*pseud. for* **Edgar de Godoi da Mata Machado**]. Obra poética. Organização de Cilene Cunha de Souza. Rio de Janeiro: Tempo Brasileiro *em convênio com o* Instituto Nacional do Livro, 1978. 119 p.; bibl.

First printing in book form of the scanty surviving work of a highly typical Symbolist who has been unjustly forgotten. Edition organized by Cilene Cunha de Souza, who also provides an introductory essay.

6285 Mattos Guerra, Gregorio de. Poemas escolhidos. Seleção, introdução e notas de José Miguel Wisnik. São Paulo: Editora Cultrix, 1976. 333 p.; bibl.

Representative selection of works by a colonial poet best known for his satires; didactically useful at the university level.

6286 Mello, Manoel Caetano Bandeira de. Uma canção à beira-mar. Introdução de Fernando Sales. Rio de Janeiro: Livraria Editora Cátedra *em convênio com o* Instituto Nacional do Livro, 1977. 46 p.

Ten-line, hendecasyllabic poems marked by a strong beat rhythm (a form of supposedly folk origin), all evoking sea and shore.

6287 Mello, Thiago de. Estatutos do homem. Ilustrações de Aldemir Martins. São Paulo: Martins Fontes, 1977. 23 p.: ill.

A proclamation of faith in man and human freedom.

6288 Melo, Helbe Oliveira de. O sono do seixo. Recife: Editora da Universidade Federal de Pernambuco, 1978. 85 p.

Particularly successful in capturing moods of nature (e.g. "Outono," "E Cai a Chuva"), the poet writes graceful verse pervaded by melancholy and a sense of loneliness.

6289 Menegale, Heli. Permanência do azul e outros poemas. Edição organizada por Alphonsus de Guimaraens Filho. Capa de Maria Waihrich Salle. Porto Alegre: Editora Globo, 1979. 175 p.; bibl. (Estante de poesia Henrique Bertaso; 3)

A provincial poet in the best sense of the term, Menegale paints the rural landscape and the small-town scene in a Minas as unaffected by the rush of present-day existence as his verse is untouched by 20th-century currents in literature.

6290 Mesquita, Luiza de. Tempo de mar, tempo de amar. Rio de Janeiro: Livraria São José, 1977. 173 p.

Mesquita has what one might call a Poseidon complex, an erotic obsession with the sea—the sole subject of her rapturous verse.

6291 Míccolis, Leila. Silêncio relativo: poemas de 1976. Ilustrações de Rodolfo Capeto. n.p.: n.p., 1977? 62 p.: ill.

Bitterly ironic views of life (childhood, love, the literary profession). "O diabo é exatamente tão feio quanto se pinta," Míccolis declares.

6292 Miranda, Luiz de. Solidão provisória. São Paulo: Editora Alfa-Omega, between 1976 and 1978. 72 p.

Condemned to silence, freedom fighters find themselves completely alone—but with the hope that their isolation will not last forever.

6293 Moura, Clóvis. Manequins corcundas. São Paulo: Editora Italo-Latino-Americana Palma, 1977. 86 p. (Poetas do Brasil de hoje)

Sadness is the dominant note of these lyrics: on the personal plane, for the ravages of time; on the more broadly human plane, for man's indifference—or contribution—to the suffering of his fellows.

6294 Mourão, Gerardo Mello. Rastro de Apolo. São Paulo: Edições GRD, 1977. 181 p.: ill. (Coleção Amereida; 1)

In the third volume of Mourão's confusing trilogy *Os peãs*, written in a mingling of Portuguese, French, Spanish, Latin, and Greek, the poet seeks Apollo (whose basic legends he recounts after the fashion of a folk poet of the Northeast) in bars from Buenos Aires to New York and Amsterdam. Includes biographical and critical sketch of the author (8 p.).

6295 Mund Júnior, Hugo. Germens: 1967/1977. Brasília: Gráfica Brasil Central Ltda., 1977. 93 p.: chiefly ill.

In a world in which images are rapidly replacing words as a means of communication, works such as Mund's collection of diagrams, photos, and typographical designs may represent the poetry of the future. May its day never come!

6296 Nejar, Carlos. O chapéu das estações. Prefácio de José Maria Cançado. Rio de Janeiro: Editora Nova Fronteira, 1978. 103 p.; bibl. (Coleção Poiesis)

In the most extended of these examples of his ear-pleasing but mind-baffling verse, Nejar's concern is with the nature of God and of love. His conclusion is that "O entendimento/não é coisa de homens/mas de anjos/Só na dor entendemos." Contains an introductory essay by José Maria Cançado and a bibliography of works by and about the poet.

6297 ———. O poço do calabouço. Rio de Janeiro: Salamandra, 1977. 105 p.; bibl.

"Liberdade vigiada é o nosso nome," says Nejar and it is to winning freedom—even if only in death—that man must bend all efforts. Work previously published in Portugal in 1974. Contains critical bibliography on Nejar (p. 99–105).

6298 Nogueira, Estephania. Tempo de busca. Poesias. Prefácio de Haroldo Bruno. Recife: CEPE (Companhia Editora de Pernambuco), 1978. 70 p.

"Me/visto na canção/que/nasce da fusão/da/pura sensação/com/o mundo da ilusão" the author declares, in lines typical of her odd verse structure.

6299 Oliveira, Sylvio Cavalcanti de. Inventário (poético) do Recife. Prefácio de Ariano Suassuna. Rio de Janeiro: Civilização Brasileira *em convênio com o* Instituto Nacional do Livro, 1979. 191 p. (Coleção Vera Cruz; 253)

The sights, sounds, folklore, and history of Recife catalogued in the style of an urban folk poet. Manuel Bandeira evoked the city far more successfully 50 years ago in 75 lines.

6300 Padilha, Telmo. Canto rouco. Rio de Janeiro: Editora Civilização Brasileira, 1977. 117 p.: ill.

With dignity and simplicity, Padilha raises again questions that have troubled man since time began: How can he distinguish reality from illusion? How can he make himself understood by his fellows? What awaits him at the end of his road? What is God's ultimate purpose in creation? The poet has no answers.

6301 ———. Pássaro noite. Rio de Janeiro: Gráfica Olímpica Editora, 1977. 64 p.

Padilha's verse here deals with "incomunhões"—outstretched hands that do not touch, messages sent but never received, vain waits, grasps at an ever-elusive essence of poetry.

6302 ———. Poesia encontrada. Prefácio de Tristão de Athayde. Rio de Janeiro: Antares, 1978. 179 p.

Restraint, reflection, and refinement are the hallmarks of this poet, whose work—as well observes the critic Alceu Amoroso Lima (whose pseudonym is Tristão de Athayde)—escapes classification on the basis of subject matter or manner. A selection by the author from previously published collections.

6303 ———. Vôo absoluto. Rio de Janeiro: Civilização Brasileira, 1977. 156 p. (Coleção Vera Cruz; 257)

Padilha's verse is as remarkable for what it suggests as for what it specifically states: "Não me peças mais que este/dizer que não diz,/senão em rota indireta./Que as palavras são armaduras/do dizer que mais diz./Atrás dela é mais clara a chama que mais brasaqueima porque não diz."

6304 Paiva, José Rodrigues de. Memórias do navegante. Rio de Janeiro: Editora Artenova, 1976. 111 p.; bibl.

In theme a voyage in time, in execution a curious pastiche of styles, motifs, and even quotes from authors ranging from Camoes to the Concretists.

6305 Peixoto, Mariza Lopez. Claustro. Desenho da capa de João P. Jacques Piraine. Arte final de Cláudio Silveira. Fotos internas de Raul Kuplich e Adroaldo Peixoto. Porto Alegre: Redacta, 1978. 63 p.: ill.

For a woman in love, the world is born anew, and the poet conveys its freshness and surprise to the reader with admirable directness.

6306 Penna, Juju Campbell. Poemas descomunicados. Rio de Janeiro: Livraria Editora Cátedra, 1978. 61 p.

Reynaldo Bayrão characterizes Penna's poetry as "fragmentária e discursiva," composed of "mosaicos e fortas dissonâncias." Many of the fragments glitter; unfortunately Penna does not assemble her mosaic into readily recognizable patterns. The title of the collection is highly appropriate.

6307 Pennafort [Caldas], Onestaldo de. Nuvens da tarde. Ilustrações de Carlos Leão. 2. ed., aumentada. Rio de Janeiro: Gráfica Olímpica Editora, 1978. 109 p., 1 leaf of plates: ill.

A Symbolist of the second generation, Pennafort practices the art of the miniaturist, capturing a scene, a mood, a passing thought in verse of exquisite brevity and grace. Collection first appeared in the volume *Poesias* (1954).

6308 Pereira, Marcus. Inconfidências. Prefácio de Paulo Duarte. São Paulo: Editora HUCITEC, 1977. 75 p.

A moving tribute to the poet's father and a brilliant evocation of his great-grandmother are the most striking of these highly personal poems.

6309 Picchia, Paulo Menotti del. Juca Mulato. Ilustrações de Emilio Di Cavalcanti, Tarsila do Amaral e Anita Malfatti. Desenho da capa de Cândido Portinari. São Paulo: Editora Cultrix *em co-edição com a* Secretaria da Cultura, Ciência e Tecnologia do Estado de São Paulo, 1978. 85 p.: ill.

The immense popularity of this work ("onde se amalgamam . . . a mestria parnasiana, a inspiração romântica e o frêmito de brasilidade") ever since its appearance in 1917 is attested by nearly 100 printings.

6310 ———. Poesias: 1907–1946. São Paulo: Martins *em co-edição com a* Secretaria da Cultura, Ciência e Tecnologia do Estado de São Paulo, 1978. 231 p.

"O que se nota . . . na sucessão dos versos que encerra êste volume, é inquietação, irreverência, pesquisa, inconformismo e anseio de constante renovação" wrote this prominent Modernist of his progress from Parnassianism to *Verdamarelismo.*

6311 Pinheiro, Paulo César. Canto brasileiro. Poemas e canções. Rio de Janeiro: Companhia Brasileira de Artes Gráficas, 1976. 193 p.

The words to some of the writer's popular-song successes are superior to his efforts at conventional composition.

6312 Pinto, José Rodrigues. Sonetos do solpôr. São Paulo: Martins, 1975. 53 p.

Pinto is a thoroughly conventional practitioner of the sonnet, but the group inspired by his wife breathes sincere affection.

6313 Pisani, Osmar. As raízes do vento. Ilustrações de Rodrigo de Haro. Florianópolis: Edição do Governo do Estado de Santa Catarina, 1976. 96 p.: ill. (Coleção Cultura catarinense. Série Literatura, poesia)

Vague in meaning ("não organizo meus sonhos aparentes"), Pisano's verse, centering on fishermen and Desterro Island, is nonetheless rich in lyrical qualities ("amor é como música ausente/transfigurado no êxtase").

6314 Piva, Roberto. Abra os olhos e diga ah. São Paulo: Massao Ohno, 1976. 24 p.: ill.

The specifically evocative eroticism of "Ganimedes 76" contrasts sharply with the *coq-à-l'âne* character of the rest of this collection.

6315 Prado, Adélia. O coração disparado. Rio de Janeiro: Editora Nova Fronteira, 1977. 111 p. (Coleção Poiesis)

Torn between the calls of religion and those of the flesh, Prado inclines toward the latter, which she treats with disarming frankness.

6316 Rezende, Sebastião. Itinerário do não. Poesia. Belo Horizonte, Imprensa Oficial, 1976. 122 p.

Handling the very short line with exceptional effectiveness, Rezende wrote of *o homem–não,* man prevented from self-realization by a world in which prohibitions are the order of the day. One regrets his untimely death.

6317 Rocha, Carlos Eduardo da. Poema de Brasília. Tradução de Ana Maria Kurchinof de Kantor. Retrato do autor e ilustrações de Manuel Kantor. Edição bilingüe. Salvador: Edições Travessia, 1977. 61 p.: ill.

The architectural drama of Brazil's new capital transformed into poetic metaphor. Bilingual edition in Portuguese and Spanish.

6318 Rocha, Martha Carvalho. Cantochão. Poesia. Rio de Janeiro: Editora Artenova, 1977. 94 p.

A "spontaneous" poet, Rocha depends more on sudden inspiration than on systematic development of thought or feeling.

6319 Rodrigues, Geraldo Pinto. O punhal do tempo. Prefácio de Carlos Burlamáqui Köpke. Posfácio de Léa Vinocur Freitag. Foto de Alvaro de Costa. São Paulo: Clube de Poesia de São Paulo, 1978. 85 p.

"Se outono existe, é só comigo,/na minha vida desfolhada" says Rodrigues as he enters into the autumn of life, conscious that "O tempo, qual punhal, jugula as glórias/dos feitos e das obras essenciais." Severely classic as always, his verse is now tinged with typically Brazilian *saudade.*

6320 Rodrigues, Jaime Luiz Leitão. Mira/miragem. São Paulo: Empresa Gráfica da *Revista dos Tribunais,* 1977. 65 p.

Enigmatic word-play, the message of which appears to be that life is but grasping at illusion.

6321 Ronald, C. [*pseud. for* **Carlos Ronald Schmidt**]. Dias da terra: 1975/1976. São Paulo: Edições Quíron *em convênio com o* Instituto Nacional do Livro, 1978. 192 p. (Coleção Sélesis; 16)

Poetry and philosophy are supposed to go "hand in hand" in this volume; unfortunately the thought is fuzzy and the expression sadly prosaic.

6322 Sant'Anna, Affonso Romano de. A grande fala do índio guarani perdido na história e outras derrotas: moderno *Popol Vuh.* São Paulo: Summus Editorial, 1978. 108 p.

Disorderly collection of random thoughts, lacking both rhyme and reason.

6323 Santos, Luís Sérgio Azevedo dos. Carta aberta. Ilustrações de José de Dome. Campos: Grupo Uni-Verso, 1976. 80 p.: ill.

Santos' poems have the quality of daguerreotypes: they give a clearly defined vision of life but not the illusion of life itself.

6324 Santos, Vitto. Poesia. Rio de Janeiro: Livraria São José, 1968. 174 p.

Santos is a 20th-century Casimiro de Abreu; in an earlier age his conventionally sentimental compositions would have served as lyrics for popular *modinhas.* Previously overlooked for inclusion in *HLAS.*

6325 ———. O verbo amar. Teresópolis: Edições Cadernos da Serra, 1978. 49 p.

A tender tribute to love as the vital principal in all ages and aspects of life.

6326 Savary, Olga. Sumidouro. Desenhos de Aldemir Martins. Prefácio de Nelly Novaes Coelho. São Paulo: Massao Ohno/ João Farkas/Editores, 1977. 61 p.: ill.

Savary's 21 brief compositions (only four of which exceed 10 lines), though distinguished by "o rigor da ordem sobre o ardor da chama," are rather overwhelmed by the 10-page critical introduction.

6327 Savino, Antônio. Invenção da aurora. Ensaio introdutório de Marcos Konder Reis. Rio de Janeiro: Emebê Editora, 1978. 114 p.: ill.

Though evoked in every aspect of nature and episode of daily life, in the end the poet's beloved seems but a "mulher de papel."

6328 Silva, Benedicto Luz e. Vento noturno. Ilustrações de B. L. Silva. São Paulo: Editora do Escritor, 1978. 57 p.: ill. (Coleção do poeta; 19)

Seeking the meaning of life, the poet comes to the conclusion that "a única realidade é a dúvida/e estamos condenados a não ter respostas."

6329 Silva, Luis Martins da. Rua de mim. Rio de Janeiro: Edições Tempo Brasileiro *em convênio com o* Instituto Nacional do Livro, 1977. 101 p. (Coleção Tempoesia; 13)

The poet provides his own "autoretr(el)ato:" "Essa vocação/para sofrer passados/e sorrir futuros/esse renegar quixotesco/do aqui e do agora/esse sentir presente/sem fronteiras/essa poesia/da noite/do dia/do amanhã."

6330 Simão, MaGrace. O sonho da maçã negra. Belo Horizonte: Gráfica Diamante, 1977. 61 leaves.

Simão is convincing in short love lyrics, in which the flesh cries out: not so, however, in longer compositions on time, newspapers, and stock raising.

6331 **Simões, Antonio Lima.** Toada de Tangerino. Poemas. n.p.: n.p., between 1974 and 1978. 51 p.

Verse of an amateur, at times merely naive, at times possessed of unpretentious charm.

6332 **Solrac, Carlos.** Funeral. Poemas. n.p.: n.p., 1978. 64 p.: ill.

This collection is well summed up in the lines "O poeta canta a dor do mundo/Com alegria submersa/No lôdo da vida."

6333 **Souto, Jomar Morais.** Itinerário lírico da cidade de João Pessoa. 3. ed., rev. e ampliada. João Pessoa: Editora Universitária/UFPb, 1977 [i.e. 1978]. 84 p.: ill. (Coleção Miramar; 2)

Extraordinarily successful atmospheric evocation of a city which has the "permanência de uns olhos sempre a esperar," in whose church towers "passeiam de par em par badalos dentro das lendas a se perderem de vista."

6334 **Souza, Claudio [Rubens de] Mello e.** O domador de cavalos. Rio de Janeiro: Editora Record, 1978. 137 p.

An excess of imagery obscures the basic structure of the longer compositions ("Poema Verde"); the short ones ("Tio Tomé") leave a clearer impression of the poet's meaning.

6335 **Souza, Olney Borges Pinto de.** Os velozes retratos. Poesias 1965/69. São José dos Campos: n.p., 1977. 87 p.

Souza exhibits a Parnassian preference for the sonnet and erudite vocabulary—and a Parnassian detachment even when dealing with such sensual subject matter as "Nus."

6336 **———.** Os vínculos da solidão: poesia 1969/1978. São Paulo: Clube de Poesia, 1979. 96 p.

"A para-quedista" is a rare example of perfection in the work of a highly uneven poet for whom genuine inspiration all too often resolves into platitude.

6337 **Tahim, Jacirema da Cunha.** Poema. Posfácio de José Paulo Moreira da Fonseca. Rio de Janeiro: Edições Tempo Brasileiro *em convênio com o* Instituto Nacional do Livro, 1977. 132 p. (Coleção Tempoesia; 10)

Just as existence is a circle, in which death is a return to the nature from which all life springs, so through meditation the poet's thought fuses with memory and past and present become one.

6338 **Tavares, Ildásio [Marques].** O canto do homem cotidiano. Rio de Janeiro: Edições Tempo Brasileiro *em convênio com o* Instituto Nacional do Livro, 1977. 85 p. (Coleção Tempoesia; 11)

Mildly amusing, mildly satirical descriptions of commonplace people and events.

6339 **Teixeira, Bento.** Prosopopéia. 9. ed. Com introdução, estabelecimento do texto e comentários por Celso Cunha e Carlos Durval. São Paulo: Edições Melhoramentos *em convênio com o* Instituto Nacional do Livro, 1977. 182 p.; bibl. (Memória literária)

Excellent critical edition, abundantly annotated, of the earliest monument of Brazilian literature.

6340 **Teles, Gilberto Mendonça.** Poemas reunidos. Prefácio de Emanuel de Moraes. Rio de Janeiro: Livraria J. Olympio Editora *em convênio com o* Instituto Nacional do Livro, 1978. 307 p.: port; bibl.

Collected verse (earliest books represented by selections) of a poet concerned with medium rather than message, who writes from the head rather than the heart. ("Eu sei/que a vida inteira eu vou ficar falando/sobre a eficácia da palavra, quando/podia gritar muito, e não gritei."). Bibliography of works by the author; critical articles by A.G. Ramos Jubé, Jayme Paviani, Cassiano Ricardo, Darcy Damasceno, Jesus Barros Boquady, and others.

6341 **Trentin, Ary Nicodemos.** Investiduras. Introdução de José Clemente Pozenato. Porto Alegre: Editora Movimento *em convênio com o* Instituto Estadual do Livro, 1976. 53 p.: ill. (Coleção Poesiasul; 14)

Death overcomes life, silence stills speech, solitude is stronger than love—yet the poet must go about his task of giving enduring meaning to words.

6342 **Varejão Filho, Lucilo.** A imagem de pedra. Poesia. Ilustrações de Ladjane. Prefácio de Marcos Vinicios Vilaça. Recife:

Companhia Editora de Pernambuco, 1973. 58 p.: ill.

Love and death are the main themes of Varejão's verse, on which the Bible has a strong influence.

6343 Varela, Dailor. Babel. Natal: Fundação José Augusto, 1974. 1 portfolio; 30 leaves: ill.

Designs or pictures illustrating the titles of compositions presumably are to be considered "visual poetry."

6344 Vargas Netto, Manoel do Nascimento. Poemas farrapos. Textos de Luiz Simões Lopes. Ilustrações de Vladimir Machado. Rio de Janeiro: Civilização Brasileira, 1978. 1 portfolio; 45 leaves: 5 ill.

Actual episodes in the War of the Ragamuffins (1835–45) proved less inspiring to the "prince of traditionalist poets of Rio Grande do Sul" than the horses, spurs, and other belongings of the participants.

6345 Veras, Everaldo Moreira. Fissuras. Poemas. Recife: Companhia Editora de Pernambuco, 1978. 151 p.

Melancholy ("Exma. Sra. Dona Tristeza") is the tutelary genius of these gentle lyrics of love and daily life.

6346 Vieira, Oldegar [Franco]. Folhas de chá. Salvador: n.p., 1976. 105 p.

One hundred and five *hokku*, some successful ("O Lago"), some grotesque ("Um Ovo").

6347 Villar, Péthion de [*pseud. for* **Egas Moniz Barreto de Aragão].** Poesia completa. Nota biográfica de Ana Moniz de Aragão do Rêgo Maciel. Ensaio crítico de Heitor P. Fróes. Brasília: Ministério de Educação e Cultura e Conselho Federal de Cultura, 1978. 505 p.; bibl.

First edition of the collected poetic works (including compositions in French) of a significant but second-rank Symbolist. Bibliography of works by Moniz.

6348 Werneck, Ronaldo. Pomba. Poema. Fotos e efeitos especiais de Adriana Monteiro. Cataguases: Prefeitura Municipal de Cataguases, 1977. 101 p.: ill.

A carnivalesque confusion of childhood recollections, scraps of conversation, and local sights and sounds constitutes the author's tribute to Cataguases upon its centennial, to be read from any point, in any order.

6349 Zanon, Artemio. A execução da lavra: da região das minas, julho/agosto, 1974. Porto Alegre: Editora Metrópole, 1978. 80 p.

For three quarters of this book Zanon insists on comparing the work of the poet with that of the miner, but gives no hint whether the labor is for gems of purest ray serene or merely the basest of lead.

Drama

BENJAMIN M. WOODBRIDGE, JR., *Professor of Portuguese, University of California, Berkeley*

OF THE CONTEMPORARY PLAYWRIGHTS under review, the most satisfying are still names familiar from past years: Jorge Andrade (items **6351** and **6366**), Dias Gomes (items **6366** and **6370**), and Gianfrancesco Guarneiri (items **6366**, **6371** and **6372**). They are, to be sure, uneven, but they continue to produce moving drama within the bounds of good taste. Younger practitioners confuse political and social propaganda with art, and they throw in such a heavy dose of vulgarity in language and in scene that the reader tends to side with the censors who ban their plays from the stage. The writers complain stridently about censorship, but refuse to take any responsibility or to attempt to deliver their message in any of the veiled forms at their command. We, as well as they, are the losers, for some of them show considerable talent, especially Plínio Marcos (items **6375–6377**). He skillfully creates atmosphere and constructs dialogue ably, but only in *Quando as máquinas param* does the reader empathize with the characters.

Continued interest in older texts brings us a welcome new edition of Anchieta's plays (item **6350**). Although it hardly replaces M. de L. de Paula Martins' 1954 text, it does serve as a useful complement. The much later Arthur Azevedo, while predictably light, is always entertaining (item **6354**). Carlos Câmara (item **6357**) reflects a period and a type of comedy rather than an individual personality; but on occasion he used the conventions of his day with such skill as to be amusing still for today's readers.

Among works related to the theater one should note the present popularity of studies of dramatic activity outside the big capitals of Rio de Janeiro and São Paulo (items **6512a–6513**). Worthy of mention also are such products of long research as Augusto Gonçalves' historical dictionary of Brazilian theater (see *HLAS 40:7655*) and Miroel Silveira's specialized essay on the contributions of Italians to the drama of their adopted country (item **6517**).

ORIGINAL PLAYS

6350 Anchieta, José de. Teatro de Anchieta. Originais acompanhados de tradução versificada, introdução e notas de Armando Cardoso. São Paulo: Edições Loyola, 1977. 372 p.; bibl.; facsims. (Obras completas; 3)

A new edition, based in part on an examination of the Rome manuscript. Introduction characterizes Anchieta's dramatic formula and studies the technical evolution of his theater. Numerous helpful footnotes. A step beyond Maria de Lourdes de Paula Martins' trailblazing 1954 edition (see *HLAS 21:4375*).

6351 Andrade, Jorge. Milagre na cela. Rio de Janeiro: Paz e Terra, 1977. 93 p. (Coleção Teatro; 1)

Through torture and violation while in prison on a charge of subversion, a nun achieves a new perception of what it means to be a human being. But in spite of some preaching, the message is obscure, for she gains her freedom by a lie: the end seems to justify the means, in flat contradiction to her earlier behavior.

6352 Araújo, Nélson Correia de. Cinco autos do Recôncavo. Salvador: Fundação Cultural do Estado da Bahia, 1977. 59 p. (Coleção Sílio Boccanera Júnior; 1)

Five historical skits from a pageant celebrating the 300th anniversary of the Archdiocese of Bahia (1976); dramatic interest slight.

6353 Assunção, Leilah. Da fala ao grito. São Paulo: Edições Símbolo, 1977. 282 p.; ill.

Through scenes at once comic and serious, individuals struggle more or less successfully against the conventions of bourgeois society.

6354 Azevedo, Arthur. Teatro a vapor. Organização, introdução e notas de Gerald M. Moser. São Paulo: Editora Cultrix *em convênio com o* Instituto Nacional do Livro, 1977. 197 p.; bibl.

Brief skits from a Rio newspaper of 1906–08. Based on ephemeral events of the time, the scenes, dealing with human foibles and weaknesses, are characterized by lively, natural dialogue. Notes explain many of the topical allusions.

6355 Bender, Ivo and **Carlos Carvalho.** Entrenós. Teatro. Porto Alegre: Editora Garatuja *em co-edição com o* Instituto Estadual do Livro, 1976. 188 p.

Two dramatists from Rio Grande do Sul start out with promising situations and develop them with varying success. Bender is intellectual and hard-edged; Carvalho is the more moving of the two. For other plays by Bender, see *HLAS 40:7609*.

6356 Bloch, Pedro. Dona Xepa. Texto integral. Rio de Janeiro: Edições Nosso Tempo, 1977. 132 p.

This edition contains a note by Gilberto Braga on his adaptation of the play (see *HLAS 34:4249*) for a soap opera, and a balanced analysis of Bloch's theater by Paulo Rónai.

6357 Câmara, Carlos. Teatro: obra completa. Pesquisa, introdução e notas de Ricardo Guilherme e Marcelo Costa. Apresentação de Octacílio Colares. Fortaleza: Academia Cearense de Letras, 1979. 695 p., 14 leaves of plates: ill. (Coleção Antônio Sales; 8)

Diffuse, light situation-comedy musicals written 1919–39 by a Ceará dramatist (1881–1939). Much of the humor is facile, but some scenes are wonderfully comic.

6358 Castro, Consuelo de. A prova de fogo. São Paulo: Editora HUCITEC, 1977. 120 p. (Coleção Teatro)

Dramatization of a student take-over of São Paulo's Faculdade de Filosofia in the late 1960s. Tense, emotional, well-constructed, but too drawn-out.

6359 Chaves, Mauro. O virulêncio. São Paulo: Departamento de Artes e Ciências Humanas, Comissão de Teatro, 1979. 70 p.: music (Coleção de textos de teatro; 2)

A hospital where the injured are tyrannically regimented and contaminated with the "virus of silence" ("o virulêncio") presumably symbolizes the police state.

6360 Chaves Neto, João Ribeiro. Patética. Rio de Janeiro: Civilização Brasileira, 1978. 99 p.

Murder, by the police, of an honest television reporter, enacted by a circus company in the name of conscience.

6361 Coelho Júnior, Hélio Gomes and **Luiz Eduardo Gunther.** Pássaro de louça. Curitiba: n.p., 1974. 31 p.

In his last hours a young idealist, condemned to be shot after the murder of a high government official, pours out long laments on the meaninglessness of life.

6362 Costa, Odir Ramos da. Sonho de uma noite de velório. Rio de Janeiro: Ministério da Educação e Cultura, Fundação Nacional de Arte, Serviço Nacional de Teatro, 1976. 86 p. (Coleção Prêmios; 6)

An undertaker, so uniformly cynical as to be unconvincing, expands his firm at the expense of his employees.

6363 Curado, Ada. Sob o tormento da espera. Goiânia: Oriente, 1976. 51 p.

A revolutionary idealist who takes to violence finally concludes that he has violated his own ideals. The handling of the situation is unconvincing.

6364 Dürst, Walter George. Rosa lúbrica. Rio de Janeiro: Paz e Terra, 1978. 117 p. (Coleção Teatro; 4)

A reworking of an earlier play, *Dez para as sete* (see *HLAS 30:4204*), with fewer characters and a tighter plot.

6365 Escobar, Carlos Henrique de. A caixa de cimento. Rio de Janeiro: Civilização Brasileira, 1978. 174 p.

Diffuse and confused play on the abuse of political authority.

6366 Feira brasileira de opinião. Prefácio de Décio de Almeida Prado. São Paulo: Global, 1978. 230 p.

Ten short plays banned from the stage by censorship, presumably for their overt championing of the oppressed underdog. Décio de Almeida Prado's preface takes the form of a play in which well-known 19th-century writers defend the right to free speech. Quality of the plays is unequal; in some, poor taste and exaggeration of woes turn the reader off. Established writers Dias Gomes, Gianfrancesco Guarneiri, and especially Jorge Andrade present the finest work.

6367 Fernandes, Millôr. Bons temps, hein?! Porto Alegre: L&PM Editores, 1979. 79 p. (Coleção Teatro de Millôr Fernandes; 6)

A mildly satirical musical covering events in Brazil from 1964 to 1979.

6368 ———. Flávia, cabeça, tronco e membros. Tragédia ou comédia em dois atos. Port Alegre: L&PM Editores, 1977. 151 p. (Coleção Teatro de Millôr Fernandes; 3)

A diffuse, melodramatic play that seems to point up the madness of 20th-century humanity.

6369 ———. O homem do princípio ao fim. Porto Alegre: L&PM Editores, 1978. 131 p. (Coleção Teatro de Millôr Fernandes; 5)

Aspects of human sensibility are presented in a string of pertinent quotations from poets, playwrights, and storytellers (e.g., the *Bible*, Shakespeare, Molière, James Thurber). The format is reminiscent of *Liber-*

dade, liberdade, 1965 (see *HLAS 30:4210*) which was co-authored by Millôr Fernandes.

6370 Gomes, Alfredo Dias. As primícias. Alegoria político-sexual em 7 quadros. Rio de Janeiro: Civilização Brasileira, 1978. 100 p. (Coleção Teator hoje; 31)

A protest against abuse of political power is expressed in the guise of a young couple's rebellion against the landowner's traditional right to spend the wedding night with the bride. The language is graphic without being vulgar.

6371 Guarnieri, Gianfrancesco. Gimba, presidente dos valentes. Peça em 1 prólogo e 2 tempos. Rio de Janeiro: Serviço Nacional de Teatro, Ministério da Educação e Cultura, 1973. 82 p. (Coleção Dramaturgia brasileira)

Tension builds up in the midst of expertly-handled popular dialogue in this 1959 drama of a *favela* hero. He is killed, but his spirit survives in a young man who idolized him.

6372 ———. Teatro. v. 2, A semente; v. 3, O filho do cão, O cimento (TV). Rio de Janeiro: Civilização Brasileira, 1978. 2 v. (149, 172 p.)

In *A semente* (1961), excess in the misfortunes of the working class takes some of the punch out of the potentially moving plot; natural, idiomatic dialogue saves the play. In *O Filho do cão* (1964) suspense builds up inexorably as cynical landowner and hypocritical saint each take advantage of superstitious tenant farmers. In *O cimento* (1962, TV play) there is loss of credibility through excess of meanness in bosses and of misfortunes among workers.

6373 Gullar, José Ribamar Ferreira. Um rubi no umbigo. Peça teatral em dois atos. Rio de Janeiro: Civilização Brasileira, 1978. 114 p.

The old theme of the curse of wealth in a rather improbable plot.

6374 Levi, Clovis and **Tânia Pacheco.** Se chovesse vocês estragavam todos. Comédia. n.p.: Europa Empresa Gráfica e Editora, 1977. 88 p.: ill.

A parable on the dangers of a society molded into conformity by a steely hand wearing a kid glove.

6375 Marcos, Plínio. Dois perdidos numa noite suja. Peça em dois atos. São Paulo: Global, 1978. 93 p.

Two bums make life miserable for each other, and one eventually shoots the other.

6376 ———. Homens de papel. Teatro. São Paulo: Global, 1978. 88 p.

Struggle of ragpickers with a mean-spirited boss; they lose in the end.

6377 ———. Navalha na carne. Quando as máquinas param. São Paulo: Global, 1978. 95 p.

The first play consists of an ugly scene between a pander and his woman. The second is a moving drama of a poor young couple faced with the realities of unemployment and pregnancy.

6378 Porfírio, Pedro. O belo burguês. Rio de Janeiro: Europa, 1978. 51 p.

Plays of social protest based, according to the author, on reality; good dialogue.

6379 Schwarz, Roberto. A lata de lixo da história. Farsa. Rio de Janeiro: Paz e Terra, 1977. 86 p. (Coleção Teatro; 2)

Machado de Assis' short story "O Alienista" serves as a framework for a satire on contemporary politics. Cinematographic rapidity often blurs meaning.

6380 Segall, Maurício. O coronel dos coronéis. A história e a lenda do "coronel" Delmiro Gouveia, Ceará-1863/Alagoas-1917. Rio de Janeiro: Civilização Brasileira, 1979. 127 p., bibl. (Coleção Teatro hoje; 32)

A play on the career of a Northeastern political boss is skillfully woven into the rather improbable plot; middle-class idealization of the downtrodden sentimentalizes their plight.

6381 Teatro Mobral/SNT. Cinco peças. Rio de Janeiro: Ministério da Educação e Cultura, Serviço Nacional de Teatro, 1975. 174 p. (Coleção Premios; 1)

Of these comedies aimed at an unsophisticated audience only Walmir Ayala's *A pobreza envergonhada*, a "lyric drama" of an encounter between a young man and an elderly lady, qualifies as literary theater.

6382 Valle Filho, Esmerino Ribeiro do. Julgamento de uma freira. Belo Horizonte: Imprensa Oficial, 1974. 47 p.

Rambling dialogue between an angel and the devil over the soul of a nun.

6383 **Wilker, José.** Em algum lugar fora deste mundo. Rio de Janeiro: Wilker, 1979. 121 p.

An elderly couple, their daughter, and grandson live under the same roof, but each is psychologically imprisoned within his own desolate world.

6384 **Xavier, Nelson.** Trivial simples. Teatro de terror. Rio de Janeiro: Gráfica Editora do Livro, 1976? 55 p.: ill.

A man and his wife repeatedly go through increasingly frenzied rituals that end in his murdering her. Meaning, if any, obscure.

6385 **Zichia, Jécia.** A corrente. Ilustrações de Gilberto Faccinelli. São Paulo: Spell Produções Editoriais, 1976. 61 p.: ill.

A character who claims that chains prevent her from realizing her potentialities seems rather a neurotic unable to adapt to life.

Literary Criticism and History

WILSON MARTINS, *Professor of Portuguese, New York University*

THE FIVE OUTSTANDING WORKS annotated in this volume are, in alphabetical order: Alfredo Wagner Berno de Almeida's *Jorge Amado: política e literatura* (item **6458**); Sônia Brayner's *Labirinto do espaço romanesco* (item **6461**); Alexandre Eulálio's *A aventura brasileira de Blaise Cendrars* (item **6406**); Raimundo de Meneses' *Dicionário literário brasileiro* (item **6427**); and Jon S. Vincent's *João Guimarães Rosa* (item **6484**). These five works confirm once again that best results in criticism and literary history are obtained in inverse proportion to the predominance of theoretical considerations (see item **6438**).

An important new development in this regard is the open reaction against the fallacy of theory, its resulting alienation, "denationalization," and other undeniable shortcomings. In most recent critical works of importance, one detects a growing realization that excessive theoretical commentaries may explain themselves, but not literature. Moreover, scholars in applied linguistics dispute the applicability of their terminology and concepts to literary criticism.

Another interesting development is the return of "historicism" which, although long neglected, is now back in vogue even among writers who use a very up-to-date critical approach such as Sônia Brayner (item **6461**). Her historical interpretations are more perceptive and rewarding than many critical works. She exemplifies the trend towards a more diversified criticism as well as the desire to use methodologies other than the dominant ones, those defined as purely and exclusively "esthetic," "structuralist," and "semiotic," and thus invariably reductionist. One reads more and more of the growing disappointment generated by these reductionist methodologies which disregard nationality and are referred to as "European" by the Yale school of criticism. The excessive theorizing characteristic of these methodologies consists of explanations formulated a *priori* of the literary work. Thus, an explanation does not issue from a work, it precedes it. All encompassing and perfect in their abstract formulation, these theoretical explanations may be universal but bear no relation to any specific literature. Brazilian critics, for example, have remarked on the lack of relevance such methodologies have for Brazilian literature.

News of the death of the New Criticism has been greatly exaggerated. After its initial extravagant claims were refuted, its essence became an integral part of all contemporary criticism regardless of schools and systems and including the "European" variety. We are nowadays at a stage which can be best defined as being "Beyond Formalism" to borrow the phrase from Geoffrey Hartman's challenging title. In a recent essay, A. Walton Litz stated that "the general trend of literary criticism since 1945 has been from consensus to diversity, from the dominance of formalistic criticism to a bewildering variety of criticisms which seek to move 'beyond' or 'against' formalism."[1] Contrary to Litz's statement, the nature of this "bewildering variety" continues to be formalistic. The oppressive "dominance of formalistic criticism" to which he refers will have come to an end when its deadening constraints have been shed and its positive aspects adopted leading to the emergence of a "*New* New Criticism." Indeed, one could say that the history of literary criticism is the history of a continual process of shedding and adopting whereby trends and schools succeed and eventually replace one another.

Nowadays, the process will consist in combining, or rather in striking a balance between, the formalistic fallacy and non-formalistic types of interpretations. That this process is already underway has been noted by observers of the literary scene in the US and in Italy who refer to it as a "ritorno al De Sanctis" or a return to De Sanctis', a turnabout in literary criticism somewhat akin to those perennial Back-to-Bach movements in the history of music.

Ever since the French realized that they were the last to arrive at the New Criticism (too late, alas!), they have been overcompensating for their tardiness by generating a frantic outpouring of formalistic criticism. In the course of doing so, however, they overwhelmed what they sought to rescue and annihilated literature by reducing it to linguistics.

Today, the last bastion of ultraformalism holds out in France. In the meantime, Brazilian literary criticism, wavering between the French and American poles of attraction, appears on the verge of taking the great leap beyond formalism. Such a liberating move, however, must be impelled by the courage of the heretic who does not hesitate to burn in public idols that have been slavishly worshipped for years.

[1] A. Walton Litz, "Literary Criticism" (*in* the *Harvard Guide to Contemporary American Writing*. Edited by Daniel Hoffman. Cambridge, Mass.: Harvard University Press, 1979, p. 51)

GENERAL

6386 Alencar, José Martiniano de. Correspondencia: cartas e documentos. Organizados por Raimundo de Menezes. 2. ed. São Paulo: Editora HUCITEC *em convênio com o* Instituto Nacional Livro, 1977. 181 p.

Useful compilation of letters and papers by Alencar or related to him, most of them previously published elsewhere.

6387 Alencar 100 [i.e. cem] anos depois: homenagem da Academia Cearense de Letras ao escritor José Martiniano de Alencar, no centenário de sua morte. Fortaleza: Academia Cearense de Letras, 1977. 453 p.; bibl.; 5 leaves of plates (Coleção Antônio Sales; 7)

Interesting, accessible but uneven, collection of essays commemorating the centenary of Alencar's death.

6388 Avila, Affonso. O poeta e a consciência crítica: uma linha de tradição; uma atitude de vanguarda. 2. ed. revista e ampliada. São Paulo: Summus Editorial, 1978. 142 p.

Since the author sees himself as a vanguard critic (all others being referred to as "naive," "incompetent" or "outdated") his book constitutes an excellent example of vanguard criticism.

6389 Azevedo, Rafael Sânzio de. O Centro Literário: 1894–1904. Pesquisa e texto de Sânzio de Azevedo. Fortaleza: Casa de José de Alencar da Universidade Federal do Ceará, 1973. 32 p.; bibl.

Includes informative and useful bio-bibliographic data.

6390 Bibliografia e crítica de Agrippino Grieco: coletânea de estudos publicados por ocasião da comemoração do octogésimo aniversário do nascimento do escritor, com transcurso em 15 de outubro de 1968 e quando de seu falecimento em 25 de agosto de 1973. Organizada por Donatello Grieco e Fernando Sales. Supervisionada por Francisco de Assis Grieco. Rio de Janeiro: Livraria Editora Cátedra *em convênio com o* Instituto Nacional do Livro, 1977. 233 p.

Very useful compilation about a reputable critic who is rapidly receding into oblivion.

6391 Boaventura, Maria Eugênia de Gama Alves. Movimento Brasileiro: contribuição ao estudo do Modernismo. São Paulo: Secretaria da Cultura, Ciência e Tecnologia, Conselho Estadual de Artes e Ciências Humanas, 1978. 217 p.; bibl., ill. (Coleção ensaio; 89)

Not brilliant, but a conscientious and informative study. The title refers to the journal established in 1928 and directed by Renato Almeida.

6392 Bolle, Adélia Bezerra de Meneses. A obra crítica de Alvaro Lins e sua função histórica. Petrópolis: Editora Vozes, 1979. 117 p.; bibl.

Alvaro Lins, in his time the "emperor of Brazilian criticism," was later submersed by the New Criticism and ensuing theories of literary analysis. He deserves a sensitive and balanced study such as this one.

6393 Bopp, Raul. Vida e morte da Antropofagia. Rio de Janeiro: Civilização Brasileira *em convênio com o* Instituto Nacional do Livro, 1977. 94 p. (Coleção Vera Cruz; 243)

An important member of the Antropofagia Group reminisces; scarce, but valuable, inside information.

6394 Bosi, Alfredo. O ser e o tempo da poesia. São Paulo: Editora Cultrix *com a colaboração da* Universidade de São Paulo, 1977. 220 p.; bibl.; 4 leaves of plates: ill.

Essays by a sensitive critic.

6395 Broca, Brito. Românticos, pré-românticos, ultra-românticos: vida literária e romantismo brasileiro. Prefácio de Alexandre Eulálio. São Paulo: Editora Polis *com a colaboração do* Instituto Nacional do Livro, 1979. 356 p.; bibl.; index (Coleção estética. Série obras reunida de Brito Broca; 1)

A good but minor critic attracted by the curiosities of literature and literary life; pleases more than he instructs.

6396 Buarque de Hollanda, Sergio. Cobra de vidro. 2. ed. São Paulo: Editora Perspectiva *em co-edição com a* Secretaria da Cultura, Ciência e Tecnologia do Estado de São Paulo, 1978. 194 p. (Coleção Debates; 156)

There are only minor differences between the original edition (1944) and this one: the essay on Manuel Bandeira, its title changed, has been expanded, and a few more articles have been included.

6397 Castro, Sílvio. Teoria e política do Modernismo brasileiro. Petrópolis: Editora Vozes, 1979. 146 p.; bibl.; index.

Written as a complement to the author's previous work (*A revolução da palavra*, see *HLAS 40:7671*), this study raises some debatable points, particularly the view that Modernismo continues to this day.

6398 Cendrars, Blaise. Etc. . . . , etc. . . . : um livro 100% brasileiro. São Paulo: Editora Perspectiva, 1976. 212 p.; facsims.; ill. (Coleção Debates; 110)

Useful compilation of Cendrars' writings about Brazil.

6399 Chamie, Mário. Casa da Epoca. São Paulo: Conselho Estadual de Artes e Ciências Humanas, 1979. 371 p. (Coleção ensaio; 94)

Memoirs, interviews, articles, prefaces, by the main theoretician and poet of *Práxis*. Indispensable.

6400 Colares, Otacílio. Lembrados e esquecidos: ensaios sobre literatura cearense. v. 4. Fortaleza: Imprensa Universitária da Universidade Federal do Ceará, 1979. 214 p.

Essays about books and authors related to Ceará (e.g., Carlos de Vasconcelos, Bias Mendes, Cordeiro de Andrade, Rodolfo Teófilo, etc.). Useful (for vols. 1/3, see *HLAS 40: 7673*).

6401 Cunha, Fausto. A leitura aberta: estudos de crítica literária. Rio de Janeiro: Livraria Editora Cátedra *em convênio com o* Instituto Nacional do Livro, 1978. 301 p.; bibl.

Good essays by a competent literary critic on various past and present writers (e.g., José Veríssimo, Martins Pena, Augusto Meyer, Aníbal Machado, Euclides da Cunha, Júlia Cortines, Da Costa e Silva, etc.).

6402 Dantas, Macedo. Cornélio Pires: criação e riso. São Paulo: Livraria Duas Cidades *em co-edição com a* Secretaria da Cultura, Ciência e Tecnologia do Estado de São Paulo, 1976. 357 p.; bibl.

Benevolent biography which does not meet the need for a study of Cornélio Pires' place in Brazilian regionalism. Nevertheless, this contribution is very useful because of its careful bibliography (the first one established with such care and accuracy).

6403 Dimas, Antonio. Manuel Bandeira no *Diário Nacional* (USP/LL, 6, 1977, p. 25–36)

Bandeira as "cronista;" includes useful bibliographic information and corrections.

6404 Ellis, Myriam. O café: literatura e história. São Paulo: Edições Melhoramentos *com a colaboração da* Universidade de São Paulo, 1977. 259 p.; bibl.

Although compiled from a historian's point of view, this collection of texts pertaining to coffee in Brazilian literature is useful.

6405 Eu, Herberto Sales. Depoimento tomado en gravação. [Gravação de] Eneida Leal. Rio de Janeiro: Livraria Editora Cátedra, 1978. 82 p.; bibl.; ill. (Série escritor ao vivo; 1)

Informative.

6406 Eulálio, Alexandre. A aventura brasileira de Blaise Cendrars: ensaio, cronologia, filme, depoimentos, antologia. São Paulo: Quíron *em convênio com o* Instituto Nacional do Livro, 1978. 301 p.; bibl.; ill.; index (Livro de figuras; 1)

In addition to Eulálio's own introduction, the book includes essays written by different authors on Cendrars and Brazil as well as a rich and invaluable photographic record and bibliography. Indispensable work on the subject.

6407 *Europe.* Revue littéraire mensuelle. Année 57, No. 599, mars 1979– . Paris.

Issue entirely dedicated to Brazilian Modernismo includes articles by Pierre Rivas, Mário da Silva Brito, Haroldo de Campos, Wilson Martins, etc. as well as modernist manifestos and an anthology (see items **6425**, **6428**, **6470**).

6408 Galvão, Walnice Nogueira. Mitológica rosiana. São Paulo: Editora Atica, 1978. 126 p.; bibl. (Ensaios; 37)

Heterogeneous and uneven compilation includes a valuable reprint of Júlio César Leal's play about Antônio Conselheiro whose date had been misprinted for about half a century.

6409 Gomes, Danilo. Escritores brasileiros ao vivo. Belo Horizonte: Comunicação *em convênio com o* Instituto Nacional do Livro, 1979. 63 p.

Consists of good interviews with 33 contemporary Brazilian writers such as Ary Quintella, Herberto Sales, Domingos Carvalho da Silva, Wander Piroli, Adonias Filho, Josué Montello, etc.

6410 Graciliano Ramos: coletânea. Organizada por Sônia Brayner. Rio de Janeiro: Civilização Brasileira *em convênio com o* Instituto Nacional do Livro, 1977. 316 p.; bibl. (Coleção Fortuna crítica; 2)

This is an excellent and invaluable collection of critical essays comparable to other volumes in the "Fortuna Crítica" series published up to 1979 (e.g., *Carlos Drummond de Andrade*, 1977; *Cassiano Ricardo* and *Cruz e Sousa*, 1979).

6411 Heyck, Denis Lynn. Coutinho's controversy: the debate over the *nova crítica* (LARR, 14:1, 1979, p. 99–113, bibl.)

Excellent appraisal of the subject is balanced, well-informed and indispensable now that Afrânio Coutinho has been surpassed by a new generation of theoreticians and the overtheorizing cycle he generated in the 1950s comes full circle again.

6412 Historiadores e críticos do romantismo. v. 1, A contribuição européia: crítica e história literária. Seleção e apresentação de Guilhermino César. Rio de Janeiro: Livros Técnicos e Científicos Editora *com a colaboração da* Universidade de São Paulo, 1978. 193 p.; bibl.; index (Biblioteca universitária de literatura brasileira. Serie A: ensaio, crítica, história literária; 5)

Consists of some very rare texts by early European historians of Brazilian literature (Bouterwek, Sismondi, Denis, etc.)

brought together for the first time and useful as a documentary record.

6413 Houaiss, Antônio. Estudos vários sobre palavras, livros, autores. Rio de Janeiro: Paz e Terra, 1979. 248 p. (Coleção Literatura e teoria literária; 33)

Sundry essays by a recognized scholar and academician cover literature and linguistics.

6414 Jofré Barroso, Haydée M. Vida y saga de José Mauro de Vasconcelos. Buenos Aires: Librería El Ateneo Editorial, 1978. 163 p.

First comprehensive book on Vasconcelos by his Argentine translator. Overenthusiastic and uncriticial.

6415 José Américo: o escritor e o homem público. João Pessoa: A União, 1977. 344 p.; bibl.; ill.

Convenient and useful collection of essays and documents pertaining to José Américo de Almeida's careers both as writer and public figure.

6416 Jubé, Antônio Geraldo Ramos. Síntese da história literária de Goiás. Goiânia: Editora Oriente, 1978. 144 p.

Only for the record.

6417 Leite, Ligia Chiappini Moraes. Regionalismo e modernismo: o caso gaúcho. São Paulo: Editora Atica, 1978. 293 p.; bibl.; ill. (Ensaios; 52)

Author admits that her work is debatable and inconclusive. After deciding to apply modernist criteria to the study of *gaúcho* regionalism, she discovered, to no one's surprise, that they are substantially different.

6418 Lopes, Hélio. A divisão das águas: contribuição ao estudo das revistas românticas *Minerva Brasiliense* (1843–1845) e *Guanabara* (1849–1856). São Paulo: Conselho Estadual de Artes e Ciências Humanas, 1978. 352 p.; bibl.; index (Coleção ensaio; 88)

Careful and perceptive, hence very valuable.

6419 Magalhães Júnior, Raymundo. José de Alencar e sua época. Edição comemorativa do centenário de morte de José de Alencar. 2. ed., corr. e aumentada. Rio de Janeiro: Civilização Brasileira *em convênio com o* Instituto Nacional do Livro, 1977. 405 p.; bibl. (Coleção Vera Cruz; 240)

Excellent biography.

6420 ———. Poesia e vida de Augusto dos Anjos. Rio de Janeiro: Civilização Brasileira *em convênio com o* Instituto Nacional do Livro, 1977. 328 p.; bibl. (Coleção Vera Cruz; 241)

Good biography but it says nothing new.

6421 ———. A vida vertiginosa de João do Rio. Rio de Janeiro: Civilização Brasileira *em convênio com o* Instituto Nacional do Livro, 1978. 386 p.; bibl. (Coleção Vera Cruz; 245)

Another good biography by a master of biographies which still does not answer the question: Was João do Rio venal?

6422 Martins, Ari. Escritores do Rio Grande do Sul. Porto Alegre: Universidade do Rio Grande do Sul, 1978. 636 p.; bibl.

This comprehensive biobibliographical dictionary is an indispensable reference.

6423 Martins, Eduardo. Coriolano de Medeiros: notícia biobibliográfica. Ed. ilustrada. João Pessoa: A União Companhia Editora, 1975. 73 p.; bibl.; ill.

Useful biobibliography of a regional historian (Paraíba).

6424 Martins, Wilson. História da inteligência brasileira. v. 7, 1933–60. São Paulo: Editora Cultrix [and] Editora da Universidade de Sao Paulo, 1979. 697 p.; bibl.; ill.; indexes.

Last volume, covering period 1933–60. For previous vols. 1/6, see *HLAS 40:3996* and *HLAS 40:7692*.

6425 ———. The modernist idea: a critical survey of Brazilian writing in the twentieth century. Translated by Jack E. Tomlins. Westport, Conn.: Greenwood Press, 1979. 345 p.; bibl.

This is the only comprehensive and critical analysis of Brazilian Modernismo in either Portuguese or English. For comment on Portuguese original, *O modernismo*, published in 1965, see *HLAS 28:2420*.

6426 Mascarenhas, Dulce. Carlos Chiacchio: homens & obras, itinerário de dezoito anos de rodapés semanais em A tarde. Salvador: Fundação Cultural do Estado da Bahia, 1979. 138 p. (Coleção Cabrália; 5)

A good introduction to an almost forgotten critic who enjoyed his moment of provincial celebrity.

6427 **Meneses, Raimundo de.** Dicionário literário brasileiro. Prefácio de Antonio Candido. Apresentação de José Aderaldo Castello. 2. edição revista, aumentada e atualizada. Rio de Janeiro: Livros Técnicos e Científicos *com a colaboração da* Universidade de São Paulo, 1978. 803 p.

Second edition issued in a single volume has been reasonably updated and corrected. This is one of the most useful and complete of all dictionaries of Brazilian literature. Provides supplements on schools, movements, academies, and terminology.

6428 **Monegal, Emir R.** Mário de Andrade/Borges: um diálogo dos anos 20. São Paulo: Perspectiva, 1978. 126 p.

Draws a parallel between two contemporary modernists and includes an interesting appendix consisting of Nicolás Olivario's articles on Brazilian literature of the 1920s and Mário de Andrade's "Literatura Modernista Argentina."

6429 **Moraes, Herculano.** Visão histórica da literatura piauiense. Rio de Janeiro: Companhia Editora Americana, 1976. 179 p.; bibl.; index.

Consists of bio-bibliographical annotations of writers and books related to Piauí, followed by a brief anthology (p. 125–173).

6430 **Moraes, Jomar.** Apontamentos de literatura maranhense. São Luís: Edições SIOGE, 1976. 187 p.; bibl.

Adheres faithfully to its title. Annotations include very useful dates and data.

6431 **Morais, Eduardo Jardim.** A brasilidade modernista: sua dimensão filosófica. Rio de Janeiro: Graal, 1978. 193 p.; bibl.

This study of Graça Aranha's philosophical ideas has a misleading title and should be read with caution.

6432 **Mota, Artur.** História da literatura brasileira. v. 3, t. 1/2. Introdução de Alcântara Silveira. São Paulo: Academia Paulista de Letras, 1978. 529 p. (Biblioteca; 7)

One may dispute the wisdom of publishing the continuation of Mota's *História*, which has never been highly regarded.

6433 **Onofrio, Salvatore d'.** Poema e narrativa: estruturas. São Paulo: Livraria Duas Cidades, 1978. 131 p.; bibl.

Study of literary theory argues that literature cannot ignore its linguistic foundations.

6434 **Orico, Osvaldo.** José de Alencar: patriarca do romance brasileiro. 2. ed., rev. Rio de Janeiro: Livraria Editora Cátedra *em convênio com o* Instituto Nacional do Livro, 1977. 218 p.; bibl.

Mere paraphrasing of Alencar's "Como e Por Que Sou Romancista."

6435 **O Partenon Literario** e sua obra. Porto Alegre: Edições Flama *co-edição com o* Instituto Estadual do Livro, Departamento de Assuntos Culturais, Secretaria da Educação e Cultura do Rio Grande do Sul, 1976. 204 p.

Good source for the history of an important literary society and its review, *Revista do Partenon Literario.*

6436 **Peixoto, Silveira** [*pseud. for* **José Benedicto Silveira Peixoto**]. Falam os escritores. v. 3. 2. ed. São Paulo: Conselho Estadual de Cultura, Comissão Estadual de Literatura, 1971. 280 p.; ill. (Coleção Textos e documentos; 30)

Like the interviews of the previous two volumes (1971), these also exhale a musty odor, having been conducted in the 1940s and on a generally shallow level—which is not to say that they are altogether lacking in interest.

6437 **Pereira, Armindo.** Julgamento de valores: a esfera iluminada II-aproximações, referênci as, interpretações e julgamentos; crítica e ensaio. Rio de Janeiro: Livraria Editora Cátedra *em convênio com o* Instituto Nacional do Livro, 1977. 287 p.; bibl.

Collected articles on literary figures such as Peregrino Júnior, Herberto Sales, Jorge de Lima and other minor ones. Routine.

6438 **Perrone-Moisés, Leyla.** Texto, crítica, escritura. São Paulo: Editora Atica, 1978. 158 p.; bibl. (Ensaios; 45)

This university dissertation with a somewhat mystifying title, and probably defended in Paris, concerns contemporary French theoretical criticism, chiefly Roland Barthes as the core influence. In this respect, it may serve as a useful introductory guide to subject.

6439 **Pinheiro, Cônego Fernandes.** Curso de literatura nacional. 3. ed. Apresentação de Mário Portugal Fernandes Pinheiro. Rio de Janeiro: Livraria Editora Cátedra *em con-*

vênio com o Instituto Nacional do Livro, 1978. 521 p.; ill.

Originally published in 1862 as a handbook for college students, one wonders at the usefulness of this new edition issued with a deceptive new title (the original being *Curso elementar de literatura nacional*). May be of use to libraries lacking the original edition.

6440 Portella, Eduardo. Dimensões, I [i.e. primeiro]: o livro e a perspectiva, crítica literária. 3. ed., rev. e diminuída. Rio de Janeiro: Edições Tempo Brasileiro *em convênio com o* Instituto Nacional do Livro, 1977. 166 p.; bibl. (Obras de Eduardo Portella; 1)

This is an indispensable work for a collection on Brazilian modern criticism.

6441 Porter, Dorothy B. Afro-Braziliana: a working bibliography. Boston: G.K. Hall, 1978. 294 p.; bibl.; ill.; indexes.

Useful work, although one may take exception to its all-inclusive concept of "African." Full of misspellings.

6442 Proença Filho, Domício. Estilos de época na literatura, através de textos comentados. 5. ed., rev. e aumentada. São Paulo: Editora Atica, 1978. 335 p.; bibl.; ill.

A modern, updated, intelligent and original handbook for college literature courses (and for the general reader as well).

6443 Queiroz Júnior, Teófilo de. Preconceito de cor e a mulata na literatura brasileira. São Paulo: Editora Atica, 1975. 123 p.; bibl. (Ensaios; 19)

Shallow and bungled study which nevertheless points to an interesting field of inquiry.

6444 *Revista Brasiliense* [sic. *Niterói*]. Ciências, letras e artes. Academia Paulista de Letras. Vol. 9, Tomo 1, No. 1, 1978– . São Paulo.

Facsimile reprint of a bibliographic rarity: the only two issues of a famous periodical of Brazil's Romantic movement published in Paris in 1836 (187 p.). Includes an introduction by Plínio Doyle and a critical evaluation by Antônio Soares Amora.

6445 Romero, Sylvio. Sílvio Romero: teoría, crítica e história literária. Seleção e apresentação de Antonio Candido. Rio de Janeiro: Livros Técnicos e Científicos Editora *com a colaboração da* Universidade de São Paulo, 1978. 233 p.; bibl.; index (Biblioteca universitária de literatura brasileira. Série A: Ensaio, crítica, história literária; 2)

Selections from Romero's work with an excellent introduction.

6446 Sampaio, Newton. Uma visão literária dos anos 30. Prefácio de Assis Brasil. Curitiba: Fundação Cultural de Curitiba, 1979. 335 p.; index.

Consists of literary articles and interviews conducted by the author and rescued from a number of newspapers. Interesting as a document of and about the 1930s in Brazilian literature.

6447 Sant'Anna, Affonso Romano de. Por um novo conceito de literatura brasileira. Rio de Janeiro: Eldorado, 1977. 237 p.; bibl.

The title promises more than the book delivers, or the book delivers other than the title promises. Nevertheless, these are high-quality critical essays.

6448 Santiago, Silviano. Uma literatura nos trópicos: ensaios sobre dependência cultural. São Paulo: Editora Perspectiva *com a colaboração da* Secretaria de Cultura, Ciência e Tecnologia do Estado de São Paulo, 1978. 207 p.

While the author proposes that Brazilian literature should be "tropical" (i.e. free from dependence on foreign influences) he still looks at it through the lens of French theories and French authors.

6449 São Paulo, Brazil (state). **Comissão de Literatura.** O movimento academicista no Brasil: 1641–1820/22. v. 2, t. 1/2; v. 3, t. 4/6. Pesquisa, planejamento e supervisão de José Aderaldo Castello. Fixação de texto de Isaac Nicolau Salum and Yêdda Dias Lima. São Paulo: Secretaria da Cultura, Ciência e Tecnologia, Conselho Estadual de Artes e Ciências Humanas, 1974/1978. 5 v. (317, 337, 278, 357, 185 p.) (Coleção Textos e documentos; 28/29, 31, 33/34)

See *HLAS 40:7670*.

6450 Schwarz, Roberto. O pai de família e outros estudos. Rio de Janeiro: Paz e Terra, 1978. 147 p.; bibl. (Coleção Literatura e teoria literária; 27)

Essays on various unrelated subjects by a disciple and protégé of Antônio Cândido (see *HLAS 40:7730*).

6451 Simon, Iumna Maria. Poetic evolution in the industrial era: the Brazilian Modernists (*in* Manchester and São Paulo: problems and rapid urban growth. Edited by John D. Wirth and Robert L. Jones [see *HLAS 41:9411*] p. 35–49)

The author examines Brazilian Modernist poetry in relation to big cities and machinery as exemplifying the "crisis of poetry." But, on the contrary, poets of this school saw themselves as the bards of a new industrial civilization.

6452 Sodré, Muniz. Teoria da literatura de massa. Rio de Janeiro: Tempo Brasileiro, 1978. 130 p.; bibl. (Biblioteca Tempo universitário; 49)

That paraliterature or mass literature aspires to be regarded as literature is nothing new. Still, certain authors including this one, wish to persuade that it is.

6453 Teles, Gilberto Mendonça. A retórica do silêncio: teoria e prática do texto literário. São Paulo: Editora Cultrix *em convênio com o* Instituto Nacional do Livro, 1979. 345 p.; bibl.

Compilation of prefaces, lectures and essays previously published elsewhere. The title implies a conceptual unity that is lacking.

6454 Val, Waldir Ribeiro do. Geografia de Machado de Assis. Rio de Janeiro: Livraria São José, 1977. 94 p.; bibl.; ill.

Meticulous survey of all references in Machado's work to the city of Rio de Janeiro and its urban mores designed to prove that the "absence of landscape" in his writings is misleading. Minor study which is useful and more of an oddity than critically stimulating.

6455 Veríssimo de Mattos, José. José Veríssimo, teoria, crítica e história literária. Seleção e apresentação de João Alexandre Barbosa. Rio de Janeiro: LTC *com a colaboração da* Editora da Universidade de São Paulo, 1978. 287 p.; bibl.; index (Biblioteca universitária de literatura brasileira)

Excellent selection of texts on a scholarly level.

6456 Viana Filho, Luiz. A vida de José de Alencar. Rio de Janeiro: J. Olympio *em convênio com o* Instituto Nacional do Livro, 1979. 311 p.; bibl.; 9 leaves of plates: ill. (Coleção Documentos brasileiros; 187)

Biography issued in commemoration of the centenary of Alencar's death emphasizes his public life.

PROSE FICTION

6457 Albergaria, Consuelo. Bruxo da linguagem no Grande sertão: leitura dos elementos esotéricos presentes na obra de Guimarães Rosa. Rio de Janeiro: Tempo Brasileiro, 1977. 154 p.; bibl.

Another occultist reading of Guimarães Rosa (see *HLAS 40:7732*).

6458 Almeida, Alfredo Wagner Berno de. Jorge Amado, política e literatura: um estudo sobre a trajetória intelectual de Jorge Amado. Rio de Janeiro: Editora Campus, 1979. 313 p.; bibl. (Contribuições em ciências sociais; 3)

Very well researched, meticulous and serious study will be indispensable for understanding Amado's ideology in relation to his works. Unfortunately, written in sociologese.

6459 Almeida, Nelly Alves de. Literatura e sentimento. Goiânia: Oriente, 1977. lxxxviii, 128 p.; bibl. (Cadeira da Academia Goiana de Letras; 14)

Despite the clearly amateurish title, this book is essentially about Hugo de Carvalho Ramos, the big man of Goiás' literature. More commemorative than scholarly.

Baden, Nancy T. Popular poetry in the novels of Jorge Amado. See item **1059**.

6460 Bourdon, Albert-Alain. Les religions afro-brésiliennes dans l'oeuvre de Jorge Amado (BEPB, 35/36, 1974/1975, p. 145–203, tables)

Somewhat excessive is the author's allegation that the undeniable pervasiveness of African religions in Jorge Amado's novels safeguarded their intrinsic "unity," after his crucial ideological split from "socialist realism" in 1955.

6461 Brayner, Sônia. Labirinto do espaço romanesco: tradição e renovação da literatura brasileira, 1880–1920. Rio de Janeiro: Civilização Brasileira *em convênio com o* Instituto Nacional do Livro, 1979. 322 p.; bibl.; indexes.

Excellent study of Brazilian fiction during the Realist period.

6462 Correia, Nereu. A tapeçaria linguística d' *Os sertões* e outros estudos. São Paulo: Quíron *em convênio com o* Instituto Nacional do Livro, 1978. 176 p. (Logos; 11)

Sundry articles of uneven interest and quality on contemporary authors, from Euclides da Cunha to Guimarães Rosa, Plínio Salgado, Santos Moraes, etc.

6463 Covizzi, Lenira Marques. O insólito em Guimarães Rosa e Borges: Crise da mímese/mímese da crise. São Paulo: Atica, 1978. 156 p.; bibl. (Ensaios; 49)

Rather than a study in comparative literature, these are two different term papers on two different writers.

6464 David-Peyre, Yvonne. Erico Veríssimo, lecteur de Flaubert (UTIEH/C, 29, 1977, p. 97–121)

Occasional similarities between Emma Bovary and a minor character in *O tempo e o vento* are presented as evidence of Flaubert's influence on Erico Veríssimo. Unconvincing.

6465 Eustis, Christopher. Time and narrative structure in *Memórias póstumas de Brás Cubas* (UW/LBR, 16:1, Summer 1979, p. 18–28)

Excellent analysis.

6466 Florentino, Teresinha Aparecida del. A produção e consumo da prosa de ficção em São Paulo: 1900–1922 (USP/RH, 56:112, out./nov. 1977, p. 499–515)

A suggestion for more systematic research.

6467 Fody, Michael. Criação e técnica no romance de Moacir C. Lopes. Tradução de Ilza Viegas e José Augusto Carvalho. Rio de Janeiro: Livraria Editora Cátedra, 1978. 262 p.; bibl.

This first comprehensive study of Lopes' work reflects the appreciation of American critics for a novelist less highly regarded by their Brazilian counterparts.

6468 Fresnot, Daniel. O pensamento político de Erico Veríssimo. Rio de Janeiro: Graal, 1977. 97 p.; bibl.

Well intentioned but weak presentation of the subject. Moreover, one wonders at the wisdom of inflating Veríssimo's "political thought."

6469 Furlan, Oswaldo Antônio. Estética e crítica social em Incidente em Antares. Florianópolis: Universidade Federal de Santa Catarina, 1977. 168 p.; bibl. (Ensaios catarinenses)

Should be read as the good Master's dissertation it originally was.

Guimarães, Reginaldo. O folclore na ficção brasileira: roteiro das *Memórias de um sargento de milícias*. See item **1080**.

6470 Jackson, Kenneth D. A prosa vanguardista na literatura brasileira: Oswaldo de Andrade. São Paulo: Perspectiva, 1978. 101 p.

Reading of yesterday's text through the concepts of today's vanguard.

6471 Jozef, Bella. Chronology: Clarice Lispector (REVIEW, 24, 1974, p. 24–26, ill.)

This useful chronology includes one serious mistake: in 1944, *Perto do coração selvagem* was almost entirely ignored rather than "enthusiastically greeted" by critics.

6472 Marinheiro, Elizabeth. A intertextualidade das formas simples, aplicada ao *Romance da Pedra do Reino* de Ariano Suassuna. Rio de Janeiro: n.p., 1977. 184 p.; bibl.

Of 174 pages of text, 64 or 37 percent consist of a laborious synopsis of André Jolle's and Julia Kristeva's ideas, the combination of which are then mechanically applied in the remaining pages to a reading of Suassuna's novel.

6473 Moog, Clodomir Vianna. Eça de Queirós e o século XIX. 6. ed. Rio de Janeiro: Editora Nova Fronteira, 1977. 352 p.; bibl. (Coleção Vidas extraordinárias)

The development of Queirosian studies has rendered this book somewhat obsolete. Nevertheless, a good biography which makes pleasant reading.

6474 Ramos, Clara. Mestre Graciliano: confirmação humana de uma obra. Rio de Janeiro: Civilização Brasileira, 1979. 272 p.; ill. (Coleção Retratos do Brasil; 134)

A psychological biography by Graciliano Ramos' daughter; sensitive, authoritative, indispensable.

6475 Reichmann, Ernani. O trágico de Octávio de Faria: livro comemorativo ao 70°. aniversario de nascimento de Octávio de Faria, 15–10–1978. Anexos de Clementino Schiavon Puppi. Curitiba: Editora Universidade Federal do Paraná, 1978. 321 p.; bibl.

Unquestionably, this is the most important work ever written about Octávio de Faria. Still, it is disappointing that the author presents his material and reflections as "notes" and marginal comments rather than integrating them into the organic structure of a book (see item **6477**).

6476 Rio de Janeiro. Biblioteca Nacional. José de Alencar, catálogo da exposição comemorativa do centenário de morte, 1877–1977. Organizado pela Seção de Promoções Culturais. Rio de Janeiro: Biblioteca Nacional, 1977. 91 p.; 10 leaves of plates: facsims.

Invaluable reference.

6477 Sadek, Maria Teresa Aina. Machiavel, Machiavéis: a tragédia octaviana, estudo sobre o pensamento político de Octávio de Faria. São Paulo: Símbolo, 1978. 205 p.; bibl.

Has Octávio de Faria ever been a fascist ideologically? Contradicting her own evidence, the author replies "no." Her book, however, points to a renewed interest in Faria's work (see item **6475**).

6478 Santos, Wendel. A construção do romance em Guimarães Rosa. São Paulo: Editora Atica, 1978. 231 p.; bibl. (Ensaios; 48)

The title is not accurate since this analysis is restricted to the "novel" *Buriti* (for unexplained reasons the author regards it as a novel). All manner of interpretations are applied, regardless of their compatibility or redundance: from psychoanalysis (Bachelard and Freud) through structuralism and myth criticism to semiotics. The author considers himself a phenomenologist and follower of R. Ingarden.

6479 Schüler, Donaldo. Plenitude perdida: uma análise das seqüências narrativas no romance *Dom Casmurro* de Machado de Assis. Porto Alegre: Editora Movimento *em convênio com o* Instituto Estadual do Livro, Departamento de Assuntos Culturais, Secretaria de Educação e Cultura do Rio Grande do Sul, 1978. 70 p.; bibl. (His Formas da narrativa; 2. Coleção Ensaios; 19)

Exactly what the subtitle states.

6480 Silverman, Malcolm. Stylistic evolution of Maria Alice Barroso's works (AATSP/H, 60:3, Sept. 1977, p. 478–485)

Good introduction to a novelist who is still insufficiently known.

6481 Souza, Ronaldes de Melo e. Ficção e verdade: diálogo e catarse em *Grande sertão: veredas*. Brasília: Clube de Poesia de Brasília, 1978. 129 p.; bibl. (Série Compromisso; 3)

Another reading of *Grande sertão: veredas* that is more psychological than critical.

6482 Vara, Teresa Pires. A mascarada sublime: estudo de Quincas Borba. São Paulo: Livraria Duas Cidades *em co-edição com a* Secretaria da Cultura, Ciência e Tecnologia do Estado de São Paulo, 1976. 99 p.; bibl.

Structuralist reading according to French theories.

6483 Viggiano, Alan. Itinerário de Riobaldo Tatarana. Rio de Janeiro: José Olympio Editora *em convênio com o* Instituto Nacional do Livro, 1978. 69 p.; bibl.

Meticulous survey of the geography of *Grande sertão: veredas*.

6484 Vincent, Jon S. João Guimarães Rosa. Boston: Twayne, 1978. 182 p.; bibl.; index (Twayne's world authors series; TWAS 506)

The first comprehensive work on the subject in English. Excellent.

POETRY

6485 Barbieri, Ivo. Oficina da palavra. Rio de Janeiro: Achiamé, 1979. 111 p.; bibl. (Crítica literária; 3)

First book on Mário Faustino's poetry and poetic theory by an admirer.

6486 Busatto, Luiz. Montagem em "Invenção de Orfeu." Prefácio de Gilberto Mendonça Teles. Rio de Janeiro: Ambito Cultural Edições, 1978. 131 p.; bibl. (Série Ambito/ensaio; 2)

In his epic "Invenção de Orfeu," Jorge de Lima applied a technique akin to cinema montage in order to introduce classical sources which are detailed in this scholarly study (see also *HLAS 40:7736*).

6487 Campos, Augusto de. Poesia, antipoesia, Antropofagia. São Paulo: Cortez & Moraes, 1978. 128 p.; bibl.

Correctly assuming (but not admitting) that the time has come to draw the balance sheet for São Paulo's Concretist

Movement, its poets have begun to produce reprints and anthologies. This volume contains articles written between 1959–76 concerning their experiments.

6488 50 [i.e. Cinqüenta] anos de Catimbó. Coordenação de Souza Barros. Rio de Janeiro: Livraria Editora Cátedra *em convênio com o* Instituto Nacional do Livro, 1977. 224 p.; plates.

Interesting selection of critical essays, articles, recollections, anecdotes, concerning Ascenso Ferreira is somewhat repetitive and heavy on personal folklore but convenient for the study of the poet.

6489 Cirne, Moacy. A poesia e o poema do Rio Grande do Norte. Natal: Fundação José Augusto, 1979. 108 p.

Critical texts and manifestoes, followed by an anthology of the so-called poetic vanguard of Rio Grande do Norte.

6490 Correia Pacheco, Armando. O simbolismo no Paraná (RIB, 28:1, enero/marzo 1978, p. 3–17)

An interesting survey of the peculiar intellectual atmosphere in which Brazilian Symbolism evolved, with special reference to Andrade Muricy's memoirs.

6491 Cruz, José Carlos de Santana. A continuidade poética em Da Costa e Silva. Teresina: Editora Nossa, 1976. 90 p.; bibl.

Well meaning but impressionistic and shallow commentary on the poet includes a large selection of his poems.

6492 Cruz e Sousa. Coletânea organizada por Afrânio Coutinho. Rio de Janeiro: Civilização Brasileira *em convênio com o* Instituto Nacional do Livro, 1979. 362 p. (Coleção Fortuna Crítica; 4)

Vol. 4 in this series consists of a most useful collection of critical essays (see also item **6410** and *HLAS 40:7734*).

6493 Dantas, Antônio Arruda. Ibrantina Cardona. São Paulo: Editora Pannartz, 1976. 114 p.; bibl.; 3 leaves of plates: ill.

Life of a minor poet and eccentric personality which is comprehensive and sympathetic but in need of heavy editing.

6494 Faustino, Mario [*pseud. for* **Mario Faustino dos Santos e Silva].** Poesia-experiência. São Paulo: Editora Perspectiva, 1977. 281 p.; bibl. (Coleção Debates; 136. Literatura)

Convenient collection of Faustino's literary page on *Jornal do Brasil* (1956–58) mainly devoted to the commenting upon modern theories of poetry.

6495 Fernandes, José de Anchieta. Por uma vanguarda nordestina. Natal: Fundação José Augusto, 1976. 128 p.; bibl.

Provides interesting information on vanguard poetry groups in the provinces (Rio Grande do Norte, in this case).

Fitz, Earl E. Two Baroque poets in colonial Portugal and Spanish America. See item **5084**

6496 Fundação Casa de Rui Barbosa. Memória literária V [i.e. cinco]: os dois mundos de Cornelio Penna. Rio de Janeiro: 1979. 57 p.

Catalogue of an exhibition of Penna's works, both as writer and painter, includes a sensitive introduction by Alexandre Eulálio (see also *HLAS 40:7719*).

6497 Garcia, Nice Seródio. A criação lexical em Carlos Drummond de Andrade. Rio de Janeiro: Editora Rio *em convênio com as* Faculdades Integradas Estácio de Sá, 1977. 131 p.; bibl.; index (Série universitária; 3)

Descriptive survey on a strict linguistic level.

6498 Gomes, Lausimar Laus. O mistério do homem na obra de Drummond. Rio de Janeiro: Edições Tempo Brasileiro *em convênio com o* Instituto Nacional do Livro, 1978. 91 p.; bibl.

Unabashed impressionism: why not?

6499 Lopes, Hélio. Franco de Sá: 1836–1856. São Luís: SIOGE, 1978. 65 p.; bibl.

Good essay about a minor and (justly) forgotten poet. Also includes an anthology.

6500 ———. Cláudio: o lírico de Nise. São Paulo: Livraria Editora Fernando Pessoa, 1975. 198 p.; bibl.

No serious student of Claudio Manoel da Costa can ignore this scholarly reading of his 12 sonnets in Portuguese, inspired by his beloved Nise.

6501 Marques, Oswaldino. O laboratório poético de Cassiano Ricardo. 2. ed. Rio de Janeiro: Civilização Brasileira *em convênio com o* Instituto Nacional do Livro, 1976. 455 p.; bibl.; index.

Reprint of the foremost critical analysis of Cassiano Ricardo's works.

6502 Moisés, Massaud. A criação poética. São Paulo: Edições Melhoramentos *com a colaboração da* Universidade de São Paulo, 1977. 156 p.; bibl.; indexes.

Excellent handbook of poetic theory, noteworthy for its didactic qualities.

6503 Ponteiro, Giovanni. Alguma poesia, 1930: Carlos Drummond de Andrade's auspicious debut (IAA, 4:2, 1978, p. 93–114, bibl.)

Another competent study of Drummond's poetry which is more comprehensive, incidentally, than implied by its awkward title.

6504 Regis, Maria Helena Camargo. Linguagem e versificação em Broquéis. Porto Alegre: Editora Movimento *em coedição com a* Editora da UDESC-Universidade para o Desenvolvimento do Estado de Santa Catarina, 1976. 91 p.; bibl. (Ensaios; 13. Coleção Santa Catarina; 9)

Designed as a reading of Cruz e Sousa according to the principles of Russian Formalism, the study reduces poetry to a level of mere craftsmanship.

6505 Sá, Alvaro de and **Moacy Cirne.** Do modernismo ao poema/processo e ao poema experimental: teoria e prática (VOZES, 72:1, jan./feb. 1978, p. 33–49, bibl.)

Excerpts of *Texto*, a dictionary of literary terms according to the meaning "Processo" theoreticians think they should have.

6506 Sayers, Raymond. The black poet in Brazil: the case of João Cruz e Sousa (UW/LBR, 15, Summer 1978, p. 75–100)

The best essay in English on Cruz e Sousa.

6507 Silva, Anazildo Vasconcelos da. Lírica modernista e percurso literário brasileiro. Rio de Janeiro: Editora Rio *em convênio com as* Faculdades Integradas Estácio de Sá, 1978. 117 p.; bibl. (Letras: Série prática)

Author perceives all Brazilian poetry as "modernista" from 1922 to present, an interpretation which is historically and esthetically erroneous. Still, the book includes useful transcriptions of the lyrics of popular songs and so-called "mimeographed poetry."

6508 Simon, Iumna Maria. Drummond: uma poética do risco. São Paulo: Editora Atica, 1978. 210 p.; bibl.; diagr. (Ensaios; 43)

Critically limited and unsatisfactory rereading of Drummond's through modern methodology.

6509 Soares, Angélica Maria Santos. O poema, construção ás avessas: uma leitura de João Cabral de Melo Neto. Rio de Janeiro: Edições Tempo Brasileiro *em convênio com o* Instituto Nacional do Livro, 1978. 86 p.; bibl.

The author proposes a reading of João Cabral from the "inside" or the "reverse" as a means of discovering or uncovering the secrets of composition.

DRAMA

6510 Brownell, Virginia A. Martyrs, victims and gods: a view of religion in contemporary Brazilian drama (UW/LBR, 15, Summer 1978, p. 129–150)

Two constant yet opposing tendencies throughout the history of Brazil have been popular religious fanaticism and anticlericalism. Contrary to what this article suggests, these trends do not necessarily reflect the present state of disarray of the Catholic Church.

6511 Kolneder, Wolfgang. Erfahrungsbericht über die Inszenierung des Theaterstücks für Kinder: *Stokkerlok und Millipilli* von Rainer Hachfeld und Volker Ludwig in Curitiba, Paraná (IA/ZK, 28:4, 1978, p. 91–93, ill.)

Frustrations of a German director in the staging in Brazil of a play for children. See also items **6512** and **6514**. [B. Woodbridge]

6512 Ludwig, Volker. Über die Schwierigkeiten, emanzipatorisches Kindertheater in Brasilien bekannt zu machen (IA/ZK, 28:4, 1978, p. 89–91)

Difficulties and triumphs in German seminars given in 15 Brazilian capitals on theater dealing with problems children experience in real life rather than fairy tales. See also items **6511** and **6514**. [B. Woodbridge]

6512a Moura, Carlos Francisco. O teatro em Mato Grosso no século XVIII. Cuiabá:

Edições UFMT, 1976. 84 p.: ill. (Coleção Olhos de recreio)

A somewhat jingoistic exposition of Mato Grosso's claims to theatrical activity ahead of other regions of Brazil. [B. Woodbridge]

6513 Muricy, [José Cândido de] Andrade. O teatro Guaíra (UFP/EB, 1:1, 1976, p. 155–161, bibl.)

Discursive report—largely personal reminiscences—on the history of the Curitiba theater in its various incarnations. [B. Woodbridge]

6514 Ott, Manfried. Zusammenarbeit mit Theatergruppen, Beispiel Brasilien (IA/ZK, 28:4, 1978, p. 83–87)

Intercultural problems in German attempts to produce German theater in Brazil. See also items **6511** and **6512**. [B. Woodbridge]

6515 Para una historia del teatro en el Brasil central del siglo XVIII (Revista de Cultura Brasileña [Embajada de Brasil en España, Madrid] 49, julio 1979, p. 69–78, ill.)

Spanish translation of a document of 1790 on dramatic activity in Mato Grosso, taken from item **6512a**. [B. Woodbridge]

6516 Paulo Pontes: a arte da resistência. Testemunhos e teatro. Depoimentos a Rui Veiga e Mário Augusto Jakobskind. Depoimentos de Bibi Ferreira . . . et al. Uma peça inédita de Paulo Pontes. Prefácio de Antônio Callado. São Paulo: Editora Versus, 1977. 78 p. (Coleção Testemunhos; 1)

Tributes to a champion (1940–1976) of socially-oriented theater precede a lecture by him, an interview, and a play written in collaboration. For one of his better-known plays, see *HLAS 40:7626*. [B. Woodbridge]

6517 Silveira, Miroel. A contribuição italiana ao teatro brasileiro, 1895–1964. São Paulo: Edições Quíron *em convênio com o* Instituto Nacional do Livro, 1976. 319 p.; bibl. (Coleção Logos; 5)

In the light of the sociological contribution of Italian immigrants and their descendants to Brazilian society, this carefully-researched study, based on a University of São Paulo dissertation, chronicles the evolution of their dramatic activity, especially in the area of comedy of manners. [B. Woodbridge]

6518 Tolman, Jon M. An allegorical interpretation of João Cabral de Mello Neto's *Morte e vida severina* (AATSP/H, 61:1, March 1978, p. 57–68)

Good reading of *Morte e vida severina*'s "philosophical dimension," which, says the author, "is important as social protest."

6519 Vieira, César [*pseud. for* **Idibal Almeida Piveta**]. Em busca de um teatro popular: Teatro União e Olho Vivo. São Paulo: Departamento Gráfico do Grupo Educacional Equipe, 1978. 196 p.: ill.

A lawyer-dramatist outlines in concrete detail the history, the methods, the goals, and the achievements of a group that regards the theater as an implement for social reform. The group's main production 1972–1976 was *Rei Momo* (see *HLAS 40:7642*), a musical doubtless more appealing on stage than on the printed page. [B. Woodbridge]

MISCELLANEOUS (Bibliographies, letters, memoirs, etc.)

6520 Arinos Filho, Afonso [*pseud. for* **Afonso Arinos de Melo Franco Filho**]. Primo canto: memórias da mocidade. Rio de Janeiro: Civilização Brasileira, 1976. 257 p.; bibl.

Like the autobiography of his father (see item **6525**), to which it forms a rewarding pendant, this book of memoirs concentrates on the author's public life, more particularly its parliamentary aspects. Of special interest to historians of the early 1960s, it may also be read with pleasure by the general public. [R.E. Dimmick]

6521 Ayala, Walmir. A fuga do arcanjo: diário III. Rio de Janeiro: Editora Brasília/Rio, 1976. 129 p.

Perceptive reflections on literature and literary figures, professions of religious faith, moving appreciations of friends and friendship, and the veiled chronicle of a strong but partly resisted attraction to a person of the same sex form the substance of an intimate journal of unusual interest and grace of expression. [R.E. Dimmick]

6522 Chaves, Mauro. Contravérbios. Ilustrações de Gustavo Rosa. Rio de

Janeiro: Civilização Brasileira, 1977. 205 p.: ill. (Coleção O homem que ri; 5)

Many of these changes rung on familiar proverbs contain wry comments on present-day Brazil (e.g., "A fé imobiliária remove as montanhas do litoral"). [R.E. Dimmick]

6523 Duarte, Paulo. Mário de Andrade por ele mesmo. Prefácio de Antônio Cândido. 2. ed., corr. e aumentada. São Paulo: Editora HUCITEC *em co-edição com a* Secretaria da Cultura, Ciência e Tecnologia do Estado de São Paulo, 1977. 370 p.; bibl.

Introductory chapters in conversational style, devoted to Andrade's activity as a writer and a promoter of cultural activities, occupy the first half of this volume; correspondence exchanged between Andrade and Duarte and Andrade's letters to Sérgio Milliet constitute the second. The frankness with which Andrade unburdened himself to friends provides insight into the thought and aesthetic of the "Pope of Modernism;" his uninhibited, highly personal treatment of Portuguese makes for delightful reading. [R.E. Dimmick]

6524 ———. Memórias. v. 5, Apagada e vil mediocridade; v. 6, Ofício de trevas; v. 7, Miséria universal, miséria nacional e minha própia miséria; v. 8, Vou-me embora pra Pasárgada. São Paulo: HUCITEC, 1977/1978. 4 v.

Continuation of author's memoirs (for vols. 1/4, see *HLAS 40:7772*). Covers on one level the years 1936–40, on another the early 1920s. Interesting picture of the life of liberals under Vargas' Estado Novo. While it contains valuable information, historians will find it difficult to mine, owing to the confused presentation and lack of any sort of index. [R.E. Dimmick]

6525 Franco, Afonso Arinos de Melo. Memórias. Poema de Carlos Drummond de Andrade. Notas de Alceu Amoroso Lima, Antônio Gontijo de Carvalho, Odilo Costa Filho, Francisco de Assis Barbosa, Péricles Madureira de Pinho, Pedro Nava. Rio de Janeiro: José Olympio *em convênio com o* Instituto Nacional do Livro, 1979. 1263 p.; ill. (Coleção Alma do tempo; 1)

A figure without parallel in Brazilian public life, Afonso Arinos has accompanied his activity as a congressman, senator, foreign minister, and diplomat by a career as a law professor and constant literary output in history, criticism, journalism, and poetry. His memoirs (three volumes here republished in one—see *HLAS 28:1359* and *HLAS 32:4910*) are as notable for their stylistic distinction and personal reflections on art, literature, and life in general as for Arinos' appreciation of public figures and events. Useful name index. [R.E. Dimmick]

6526 ———. Memórias. v. 4, Alto-mar, maralto. Rio de Janeiro: Livraria J. Olympio Editora, 1976. 155 p., 1 leaf of plates: ill.

Concerned with the years since his retirement from public life, the last volume of the author's memoirs is more personal and reflective than the first three. See item **6525**. [R.E. Dimmick]

6527 Jardim, Luís [Inácio de Miranda]. O meu pequeno mundo: algumas lembranças de mim mesmo. Rio de Janeiro: Livraria J. Olympio Editora, 1976. 187 p.

"Tentei dar uma visão do que foi a minha vida, mais precisamente a grande vida do meu íntimo," says Jardim of these recollections of childhood and early youth in Garanhuns and a nearby fazenda. Supposedly addressed to the younger generation, they will doubtless be more appreciated by the older, by reason of their nostalgic value. [R.E. Dimmick]

6528 Mendes, Murilo [Monteiro]. Retratos relâmpago. São Paulo: Conselho Estadual de Cultura, 1973. 106 p. (Coleção Textos e documentos. Secretaria de Cultura, Esportes e Turismo; 24)

Random reflections on writers, plastic artists, and composers, some of which constitute striking prose poems. [R. E. Dimmick]

6529 Menotti del Picchia, Paulo. Entardecer. Capa e ilustrações de Paulo R.W. Penteado. São Paulo: MPM Propaganda, 1978. 156 p.; ill.

Handsomely printed selection by the author of examples of his work in all genres—poetry, drama, biography, oratory, *crônicas*, novel, and short story. [R. E. Dimmick]

6530 Mota, Mauro. Modas e modos. Recife: Editora Raiz, 1977. 228 p.; bibl.; index.

Collected papers related to Pernambuco in general, and Recife in particular, contain valuable historical data, inside information, and sensitive analysis. Particularly interesting are the chapters on Gilberto Freyre, Ascenço Ferreira, journalism in Recife and the city itself.

6531 Nava, Pedro. Memórias. v. 4, Beira-mar. Poesias de Alphonsus de Guimaraens Filho e Nei Leandro de Castro. Rio de Janeiro: José Olympio, 1978. 408 p.

The title notwithstanding, this fourth volume of memoirs covers years (roughly 1922–29) Nava spent in Belo Horizonte as a medical student, and offers a kaleidoscope of street scenes, philosophic reflections on the ills to which flesh is heir, and recollections of figures prominent in the Modernist Movement (in which Nava took a modest part), all presented in his usual savorily flamboyant style. [R. E. Dimmick]

6532 Octavio, Rodrigo [*pseud. for* **Rodrigo Octavio de Langgard Meneses**]. Minhas memórias dos outros. Rio de Janeiro: Civilização Brasileira, 1978. 260 p. (Coleção Retratos de Brasil; 119)

Reprint of pedestrian work by a diplomat and supreme court judge first issued in 1934, of interest to historians of the early years of the Brazilian republic. [R. E. Dimmick]

6533 Sousa Andrade, Joaquim de. Sousândrade, prosa. Edição crítica, introdução e notas de Frederick G. Williams e Jomar Moraes. São Luís: Edições SIOGE, 1978. 186 p.; bibl., 14 leaves of plates: ill.

The editors recognize that Sousândrade was "poeta e tão somente poeta;" however, his collected prose writing, entirely topical in nature, constitutes "o *corpus* do ideário desse singular e excêntrico poeta e cidadão brasileiro." [R.E. Dimmick]

FRENCH AND ENGLISH WEST INDIES AND THE GUIANAS

NAOMI M. GARRETT, *Professor Emeritus, West Virginia State College*

A SIGNIFICANT UPSURGE has been noted recently in the literary activity of most of the regions covered in this section. There is a decrease in the literature of some areas, Martinique and Jamaica, for example, but this is counterbalanced by the greater quantity of works from Haiti and Guyana. Haiti has been particularly productive, especially in poetry and literary criticism.

Poetry leads all genres throughout the area. Edward Brathwaite's *Black and blues* (item **6590**), a new edition of Léon Laleau's complete poetic works (item **6552**), Jean Brierre's volume of verse for children (item **6546**), and a posthumously published collection of Roussan Camille's poetry (item **6547**) deserve special notice.

Literary criticism shows growth in quantity and quality. An individual article and the special journals on Aimé Césaire (items **6557** and **6560**) indicate the seriousness with which he is considered in this country and abroad. Studies on Jacques Roumain and Jacques Stéphen Alexis (items **6558**, **6568** and **6575**), Claude McKay (items **6605** and **6609**), Derek Walcott (item **6611**) and others are equally worthy of mention.

A trend observed throughout the entire region is the use of Creole or folk languages in literary works. Haiti's first novel in Creole, *Dézafi*, is the subject of a critical study (item **6569**). Poets and short-story writers of Haiti, Jamaica, Barbados, Trinidad and Guyana, in particular, are proving that their native languages are suitable vehicles to express their ideas and represent their cultures. Rudolph Muller's volume in Creole and in French (item **6554**) won the Prix Littéraire Paulette Deschamps Frisch in 1978.

The number of women creative writers in the area is increasing. Six women contributed stories to *Love and the hardware store* (item **6579**), the first publication in the Trinidadian "Island Woman Series." Jane Grell is a co-editor of the *Sea gull* (item **6582**) and author of one of the tales in the volume. Chioneso Kaur, Norma Nichols and Barbra Zencraft provide collections of poems (items **6594**, **6595** and **6601**). Alice Hippolyte, winner of the Prix Deschamps 1976 (item **6538**) and Adelina Moravia (item **6540**) produce well written novels. A woman, Mona Guérin, is the only French language dramatist included in this issue (item **6541**).

In the English-speaking Caribbean, government sponsorship has fostered an increase in literary expression, especially among young writers. Montserrat's first contribution to this section (item **6582**) results from the University Centre's Creative Workshop project. Several entries from Guyana are compiled or published under the auspices of that country's Ministry of Information and Culture. The encouragement provided by early publication should promote the budding talents of these young writers.

FRENCH WEST INDIES
PROSE FICTION

6534 Courtois, Félix. Durin Belmour. Roman ou conte fantastique. Port-au-Prince: Imprimerie des Antilles, 1977. 193 p.

The author uses the Faustian theme in his description of life in Port-au-Prince at the turn of the century. A merchant who wishes to rise in commercial and social affairs forms a pact with a worker of magic. The merchant is very successful; but his refusal to obey one of his benefactor's demands leads to tragedy. A well developed story.

6535 ———. Scènes de la vie port-au-princienne. Roman. Port-au-Prince: Imprimerie des Antilles, 1975. 255 p.

Novel presents episodes in the life and adventures of three young Haitians in Port-au-Prince in the years immediately preceding and during the American Occupation. It provides interesting views of family, social and political life in the capital city during those uneasy years. Weak in plot development.

6536 Delmas, René. Les Moeurs haitiennes. v. 1, Les aventures d'Emile. Nouvelle. Port-au-Prince: Editions Fardin, 1978. 100 p.

The first in a two-volume study of Haitian customs. Story of small town, naive young man dedicated to the priesthood by his father. When the son fails to follow the desired profession the elder man finds an equally unsophisticated bride for him. The results are amusing. An interesting, well told story of provincial life.

6537 ———. Ma fiancée des orangers. Roman. Port-au-Prince: Les Ateliers Fardin, 1978. 235 p.

A young provincial girl whose family moves to Port-au-Prince for better educational facilities is overwhelmed by city life. Determined to become a liberated woman, she leaves her family, renounces her fiancé, and eventually falls into prostitution. The story, narrated by the rejected suitor, gives glimpses of life in small towns as well as among elements of society in the capital city.

6538 Hippolyte, Alice. Ninon, ma soeur . . . Port-au-Prince: Edition Henri Deschamps, 1976. 143 p.

This novel, winner of the Prix Deschamps 1976, condemns the insincerity, infidelity, immorality and prejudice of the Haitian privileged class. The author ridicules the frivolous life of this group showing how it causes suffering for others. An interesting, well written first novel.

6539 Marcelin, Frédéric. Thémistocle-Epaminondas Labasterre. Petit récit haitien. Port-au-Prince: Editions Fardin, 1976. 323 p.

A new edition of a realistic novel criticizing Haitian political and social life at the turn of the century. The author warns idealistic youths against the false super-patriot who would use them only for his own political advancement.

6540 Moravia, Adeline. Aude et ses fantômes. Roman. Port-au-Prince: Editions Caraïbes, 1977. 245 p.

A young woman, member of an old family from Jérémie, researches her background, beginning with her first ancestors from Europe and Africa. Her findings form the basis for an interesting, well written novel, presenting the social history of a family and a community.

DRAMA

6541 **Guérin, Mona.** La pension vacher. Port-au-Prince: Editions du Soleil, 1978? 115 p.; plates.

Two short, well-written plays. The first, a comedy in two acts, describes a boarding house upheaval caused by a guest who spreads malevolent and baseless rumors. Skillful handling of the action avoids unfortunate consequences. The second play, a one-act farce, draws its action from a case of mistaken identity. A significant contribution to the author's dramatic production (see also *HLAS 40:7780*).

POETRY

6542 **Adyjeangardy.** Poèmes de mes dix-sept ans. Port-au-Prince: Imprimerie Henri Deschamps, 1977. 31 p.

Thirty poems of varied inspiration by a young writer still in his teens. His verse shows promise.

6543 **Assali, N. Donald.** Chanson boula et autres poèmes. Paris: Editions Saint-Germain-des Prés, 1978. 51 p. (Collection A l'écoute des sources)

Consists of 26 poems in verse and in prose praising Haiti, the elegance of the black girl and peasant traditions. Creole expressions heighten the native flavor. The volume takes its name from one of the Creole poems based on the peasant's idea of the soul's return to Africa after death.

6544 **Baridon, Silvio F.** and **Raymond Philoctête.** Poésie vivante d'Haiti. Paris: Les Lettres Nouvelles- Maurice Nadeau, 1978. 298 p.; bibl.; ill.; map.

The volume presents 61 poets writing between 1945–77; the majority are in exile. Selections chosen are representative of the poets' works though limited by the size of the volume, the dispersion of the writers and the relative inaccessibility of their verse. The introduction gives a good sketch of Haitian poetry from its earliest years to the present. Bibliographies, biographical sketches and a literary map add to the usefulness of the collection.

6545 **Batravil, Dominique.** Boul pik. Poèmes. Port-au-Prince: Editions Choucoune, 1978. 27 p.

Small plaquette containing 17 poems, the majority in Haitian Creole. Those in French contain occasional Creole lines or expressions.

6546 **Brierre, Jean-François.** Images d'argile et d'or. Dakar, Sénégal: Nouvelles Editions Africaines, 1977. 93 p.

A collection of 67 poems written for children and dedicated to the poet's grandchildren. Much of this entertaining and instructive verse deals with nature, animals and insects. An attractive, beautifully illustrated volume which will appeal to adults as well as children.

6547 **Camille, Roussan.** La multiple présence. Derniers poèmes. Sherbrooke, Canada: Editions Naaman [and] Editions Caraïbes, Port-au-Prince, 1978. 99 p.; plates (Collection Création; 40)

A posthumously published collection of verse by a talented poet. The majority of the lyrical, rhythmical poems, written since the publication of Camille's *Assaut à la nuit*, speak in defense of the underprivileged in his society. A long preface written by the poet in 1953 discusses the importance of tradition and indigenous culture in artistic works. Photos and biographical notes complete the volume.

6548 **Campfort, Gérard.** Poèmes (IFH/C, 134, juin/juillet 1977, p. 87–92)

Seven short, delicate poems of love by the author of *Clés* and *Eaux* (see also *HLAS 34:4308–4309*).

6549 **Charles, Christophe.** L'aventure humanine. Poésies, 1964–1974. Préface de Roger Gaillard. Port-au-Prince: Ateliers Fardin, 1975. 158 p.; ill.

Section titles in this four-part volume: "Désastre," "Malaise," "Cycle de la Parole," "Hurler," describe the poet's strong emotions and the type of poetry in each part. He goes from despair to sensitive love to a cry of suffering, but ends on a note of optimism. The talented young writer explains his verse in an interview with Marius Jean-Louis.

6550 Dauphin, Marcel. Flammeches. Poèmes. Port-au-Prince: Les Editions Fardin, 1976. 186 p.

Nostalgic lyrical verse in which the exiled poet longs for his country and its simple pleasures and sings of its beauty. He pleads for compassion for the underprivileged and for universal brotherhood. The latest in a long list of published works (see *HLAS 34:4313*).

6551 Deux jeunes poètes d'Haïti et de la Diaspora haïtienne: Christophe Charles et Josaphat Large (IFH/C, 132, dec. 1976/jan. 1977, p. 63–76)

Presentation of poems by two young Haitians who draw their inspiration from their country. Charles lives and writes in his native Port-au-Prince; Large, originally from Jérémie, has lived and worked in New York for the past 10 years. The writer of the short introduction advises poets in Haiti and abroad to become better acquainted for their mutual benefit.

6552 Laleau, Léon. Oeuvres poétiques. Port-au-Prince: Imprimerie Henri Deschamps, 1978. 311 p.

New edition of the entire poetic works of Laleau including poems appearing in print for the first time. The collection received the Prix Littéraire Henri Deschamps for 1978. One can still appreciate the delicate, elegant verse of the "prince of poets" and notice his evolution from neo-romantic to indigenous verse. Mona Guérin wrote the "Avant-Propos" for the volume.

6553 Leroy, Frantz. Poèmes en prison. Port-au-Prince: Imprimerie Les Presses Port-au-Princiennes, n.d. 32 p.

Poems of personal sentiment, reflection and nostalgic longings written while in prison. Thoughts of family, friends and the deprived masses inspire most of this verse. Good imagery.

6554 Muller, Rudolph. Paroles en pile. Parol anpil. Port-au-Prince: Imprimerie Henri Deschamps, 1978? 154 p.

Well presented volume containing poems in Haitian Creole and in French. Poet attacks bourgeois hypocrisy and shows concern for the lower classes in his society. Illustrations are scattered throughout this volume which won the Prix Littéraire Paulette Deschamps Frisch.

6555 Timal. La revolte du silence. Poèmes. Port-au-Prince: Ateliers Fardin, 1977. 60 p.; ill.

Collection of 32 poems. Among the best are those in which the young poet shows compassion for the deprived masses and reveals a nostalgic longing for Haiti.

6556 Vilfort, Lyonel. Manne cordiforme: choix de poèmes. Port-au-Prince: Les Editions Fardin, 1975. 80 p.; ill.

Small volume of 10 poems. Seven are extracts from longer lyrical works; the last three are shorter selections in Creole. First published verse of a gifted young poet.

SPECIAL STUDIES

6557 Almeida, Lilian Pestre de. Christophe: cuisinier entre nature et culture (IFH/C, 130, sept. 1976. p. 33–62)

Author bases her interpretation of Aimé Césaire's *La tragédie du Roi Christophe* on "le triangle culinaire" in Lévi-Strauss' *Mythologiques III*. She points out the frequent use of culinary terms and references to foods to support her unusual thesis. She sees Christophe as the "cuisinier" who wishes to establish a stable, powerful state built by hard work and characterized by an authentic African culture from which all indolent, mulatto traits would be banished.

6558 Auguste, Yves. Du nègre masqué de Stéphen Alexis à l'homme invisible de Ralph Ellison (IFH/C, 135, oct. 1977, p. 41–55)

Maintains that there is a close relationship between the Haitian who masks his inner being to conform to societal expectations and the black American who hides his feelings because of white domination. Each finally becomes invisible to himself and to others. The author asserts that the theme of invisibility in the novels of both Alexis and Ellison grows out of social and racial exploitation.

6559 Berrou, Raphaël and **Pradel Pompilus.** Histoire de la littérature haïtienne: illustrée par les textes. t. 1. Port-au-Prince:

Editions Caraïbes, 1975. 734 p.; plates.

This vol. 1 of a projected three-volume work covers the period fron Independence (1804) to 1898 which saw the flourishing of romanticism. (Subsequent volumes will study the literature from 1898 to the present.) The current work gives a good presentation of well chosen selections from writers of all genres. A very useful work. One awaits vols. 2/3.

6560 *Cahiers Césairiens.* Pennsylvania State University, French Department. Vols. 1, 1974 [through] 3, 1977– . University Park, Pennsylvania.

The first three issues of a proposed series of specialized journals devoted to Aimé Césaire, the Martinican poet, playwright, essayist and one of the founders of Négritude. Articles are by well known Césaire scholars, or writers interested in his works. Interviews with the poet, discussions and analyses of his verse and theatre, resumés of scholarly theses on the writer are included. The *Cahiers* are useful not only for Césaire specialists but for anyone interested in Negro-African literature.

6561 **Un centenaire:** Jean Price Mars, 1876–1976 (IFH/C, 132, déc. 1976/jan. 1977, p. 4–40, bibl., plates)

The major part of this issue is dedicated to the memory of Jean Price-Mars, internationally recognized scholar, anthropologist and statesman who died in 1969. Excerpts from his unpublished memoirs, a partial bibliography of his numerous works, tributes by well known writers and a letter from President de Gaulle are included. Photos of Price-Mars are placed throughout the issue.

6562 **Charles, Christophe.** Regards sur la jeune poésie haïtienne (IFH/C, 139, juillet 1978, p. 59–72)

Discussion of new poets writing since 1960 shows that Haiti continues to produce a large number of young writers. The majority are grouped around "Collections" to facilitate publication. Many have several volumes to their credit. A few are still writing; others, for various reasons, have not appeared in print recently. Two new trends "le spiralisme" and "le pluréalisme" and their proponents are discussed.

6563 **Davis, Thulani.** Léon-Gontran Damas: 1912–1978 (Washington Review [Washington] 3:6, April/May 1978, p. 14–15, plate)

Salient facts on the life and verse of a great poet of Négritude are made available for the general public by this article. A poem paying tribute to Damas and a note of personal recollection are included.

6564 **Feldman, Yvette Tardieu.** Frédéric Marcelin: premier romancier féministe des Caraibes (IFH/C, 130, sept. 1976, p. 65–70)

Though women were early celebrated in Haitian poetry they were rarely selected as protagonists by novelists. Marcelin's *Marilisse* (1903) which appeared 10 years before the Jamaican DeLisser's *Jane's career,* began a trend not only in Haiti but in the entire Caribbean. *Marilisse* realistically portrays a woman of the lower classes fighting for survival. The critic hails this work as one of the first classics of Caribbean feminism.

6565 **Hoffman, Léon-François.** Etat présent des études littéraires haïtiennes (*The French Review,* 49:5, April 1976, p. 750–758)

This excellent presentation on current studies of Haitian literature provides information for students and researchers. Bibliographical sources and locations of available works are given. Annotations and critical comments are helpful. Earlier bibliographies are noted.

6566 **———.** Pour une bibliographie des études littéraires haïtiennes (IFH/C, 134, juin/juillet 1977, p. 3–54)

A more up-to-date listing of Haitian works and of critical studies on the literature. Majority of items are from the present century. Works formerly unobtainable but now available in reprints are listed. Well researched study.

6567 **Lewis, Maureen Warner.** The African impact on language and literature in the English-speaking Caribbean (*in* Africa and the Caribbean: the legacies of a link. [see item **2499**] p. 101–123)

The introduction of indentured Africans into the British West Indies resulted in modified forms of African languages which are still used in that area. Former traditions provide themes and symbols for literary works which reflect the rhythms, speech and manners of Afro-Caribbean cultures. The author believes that maintaining cultural links with African traditions is important in freeing Caribbean natives from the psychological effects of the colonial/neocolonial past.

6568 Marty, Anne. Le socialisme dans l'oeuvre de Jacques Roumain et Jacques Stéphen Alexis (IFH/C, 136/137, fév. 1978, p. 29–42)

Notes significant parallels between Roumain and Alexis in background, education, life, ideas and literary works. Both attacked religion, which they saw serving the bourgeoisie, and their government's attachment to the US. Both were influenced by Marxism, drawing from it elements they believed beneficial to the peasant masses. Statements and conclusions are well documented.

6569 Médard, Michelle Lafontant. Pour une lecture de *Dézafi* (IFH/C, 140, oct./nov. 1978, p. 55–97)

An interpretation and analysis of Frankétienne's *Dézafi*, first Haitian novel written in Creole. The critic asserts that this symbolist work describes the zombification of individuals and communities by three powerful forces: politics, religion and the military. A community is rendered powerless until a liberating force frees it from stagnation and death. An important study for anyone interested in new directions in Haitian literature.

6570 Pompilus, Pradel. Louis Joseph Janvier par lui-même: le patriote et le champion de la Négritude. Port-au-Prince: Imprimerie des Antilles, 1976. 97 p. (Les Classiques de la littérature haïtienne)

Excerpts from works of Louis-Joseph Janvier project a physical and mental image of the political and social historian. Janvier's ideas on agrarian reform, education, civilian government, religion and prejudice are presented. Pompilus' commentaries provide an enlightening background for the well chosen passages. Questions for discussion and suggestions for themes at the end of the volume are useful for further research.

6571 ———. Sur quelques corrections d'Etzer Vilaire (IFH/C, 138, mai 1978, p. 83–94, ill.)

Comparison between the original version of several lines of Vilaire's poetry and the changed final edition shows the poet continually in the process of improving his verse. Most changes result in better expression in form and content. The original and the corrected lines are provided.

6572 Racine, Daniel L. Léon-Gontran Damas: 1912–1978: founder of Négritude. A memorial casebook. Washington: University Press of America, 1979. 298 p.

Collection of essays, articles, poems, eulogies, telegrams and testimonies paying homage to Léon Damas, one of the founders of Négritude and author of the first published work growing out of that movement. Several selections of the poet's verse are included. A worthy tribute to the role played by Damas in his affirmation of values of blacks and their contributions. Bibliography, photos of the poet and biographical sketches of the contributors are provided.

6573 Rey, Ghislaine. Anthologie du roman haïtien de 1859 à 1946. Préface de Thomas H. Lechaud. Sherbrook, Canada: Editions Naaman, 1978. 197 p.; bibl.; ill.; map; tables (Collection Anthologies; 2)

A two-part volume (1859–1915; 1915–1946) containing excerpts from and discussion of Haitian novels from the first to appear in 1946. Author notes the variety of subjects treated. Purpose is to publicize works of early novelists, some of whom are not well known. Biographical notes, bibliography, names of libraries containing works and a list of novels in manuscript are included. Useful for the general reader of Haitian fiction as well as for the scholar.

6574 St. Vil, Joseph D. Dans le paysage haïtien. Les origines d'une langue (thèse); Union libre au pied de l'autel (roman); La colère de Joas et L'enfant de la balle (nouvelles); Un cas de transfert du latin au langage haïtien et Vers un carnaval artistique (chroniques). Port-au-Prince: Imprimerie Centrale, n.d. 282 p.

In addition to a rather interesting essay on the origin of Haitian Creole, this volume contains a novel, two short stories and isolated philosophic thoughts. The works of fiction reveal various aspects of Haitian society.

6575 Trouillot, Hénock. Dimension et limites de Jacques Roumain. Port-au-Prince: Les Editions Fardin, 1975. 206 p.; bibl.

Author asserts that Roumain's early poetry was elegaic and, though this was a period of great political activity, he seemed principally concerned with perfecting his art. Roumain's "indigénisme" began with his peasant novel *La montagne ensorcelée* in 1932, and his poetry "de combat" appeared first in 1937 with "Madrid." The critic has high praise for *Gouverneurs de la rosée* in which Roumain captures the real life, emotions and language of the Haitian peasant in an artistic presentation. A well documented study of one of Haiti's greatest writers.

ENGLISH WEST INDIES
PROSE FICTION

6576 **Clarke, A.M.** Revolution at grass roots, and other stories. Port-of-Spain?: Educo Press, n.d. 100 p.

A collection of 17 stories portraying life among the poorer groups in Trinidadian society. Most are earthy tales which mock the results of US influence on local mores and culture. Several reveal a low opinion of women and scoff at Western religion. The title is that of the first story in the volume.

6577 **Cranmore, Frederick.** The West Indian. New York: Theo. Gaus, 1978. 122 p.

In a search for his identity, a young Guyanese in New York reflects upon life in his country and details his reasons for leaving. The political situation prior to independence and racial divisions are roundly criticized. The novel contains good descriptive passages and images.

6578 **Dumas, Frédéric.** Chimères de la mer. Paris: Editions France-Empire, 1976. 252 p.; maps, plates.

One of the three accounts of adventure included in this work describes an attempt to locate the Caravelles—la Capitana and la Santiago—of Christopher Columbus which are reported to have sunk off the coast of Jamaica. The ships are not found, but the recounting of the adventure makes an interesting story. It also provides the basis for interaction between the French underwater explorer and Jamaicans with whom he deals.

6579 **Love and the hardware store** and other stories. Edited by Lance Baptiste. Port-of-Spain: Imprint Caribbean, 1977. 128 p.; ill.

Collection of 15 stories, the first publication in the Island Woman Series. Five of the stories appeared previously in a local Caribbean review. Each one treats, in a different manner, love Caribbean style. Six of the writers are women.

6580 **Sadeek, Sheik.** Bundarie boy. Introduction by Mohamed Hamaludin. Rev. ed. Georgetown: The Author, 1976. 86 p.

The rather unusual story of a young East Indian farm boy growing up in the Guyanese interior. This revised edition of an earlier National Gold Medal award novel has been prepared especially for use in national schools.

6581 ———. Song of the sugarcanes. Georgetown: The Author, 1975. 206 p.

A grandson of indentured East Indian immigrants writes a novel about the life of these people on the sugarcane plantations. The interesting story is highly flavored with East Indian culture and traditions. The writer shows the dehumanizing effects of the indenture system but presents former British Guiana as a haven of new life for the immigrant from India.

6582 **The sea gull** and other stories. Edited by Howard A. Fergus and V. Jane Grell. Plymouth, Montserrat: Alliouagana Commune, 1976. 95 p.

Six writers contributed these 13 interesting stories based on life and folklore of Montserrat and neighboring islands. One tale, "Betrayed," recounts an abortive slave rebellion in Monteserrat in 1768. Three of the stories are in Creole. First compilation of the University Centre's creative workshop in the island.

6583 **Seyfarth, Fritz.** Tales of the Caribbean: a feast of islands. Photography by Harold Hawley. Illustrations by Dee Carstarphen. Clinton Corners, N.Y.: John de Graff, 1978. 167 p.; bibl.; ill.; maps; plates.

Adventure in the Caribbean. Stories and historical information about the Lesser Antilles and experiences in these islands.

6584 **Why, John A.** Nice and nasty. Tales. Georgetown: National Lithographic Co., 1976. 73 p.

Tales and poems about life, people and incidents in Guyana. Majority of the stories are very clever and told in an interesting manner. Several were originally broadcast on the national radio's short story series.

6585 Williams, N.D. Ikael Torass. La Habana: Casa de las Américas, 1976. 501 p.

A young student from the privileged class of a small West Indian island goes to University College in Jamaica for further study. His experiences bring him in touch with all levels of the society, including the Rastafarians, and provide the opportunity to portray people of all classes. This first novel, winner of the Casa de las Américas Award for 1976, is well written and its characters well drawn.

DRAMA

6586 Charles, Bertram. The alexin of our cure. Georgetown: n.p., n.d. 26 p.; plates.

A short three-act drama in which a young wife's guilt induces a mild form of leprosy. The theory of an interested doctor proves correct when the heroine, led to confess her transgression, is cured. The play which relates to a local situation has limited appeal.

6587 Sadeek, Sheik. Two stage sketches: based on *The declaration of Sophia.* The gap: from colonialism to socialism. The gift: from colonialism to socialism. Georgetown: The Author, 1976. 18 p.

Two short ideological skits extolling the virtues of socialism.

POETRY

6588 Anand, George Vidyah. Hungry voices cry. A collection of poems. Georgetown: Guyana National Service Publishing Centre, n.d. 15 p.; ill.

Seven poems praising the socialistic government and its concern for the people of Guyana.

6589 Blenessequi, Omartelle. Glorianna. A long poem. Demerara, Guyana: n.p., 1976. 54 p.

A narrative poem extolling the natural beauty of Guyana and the triumph of virtue, truth and love over evil.

6590 Brathwaite, Edward Kamau. Black & blues. La Habana: Casa de las Américas, 1976. 91 p.

Caribbean life and culture greatly influenced by African oral traditions are central themes in this small but important collection. Music and speech of the islands give a special flavor to the verse. It portrays the unhappy lot of the black West Indian who often finds relief by expressing himself in a blues style. The poet calls for a radical change in the conditions of the Caribbean people. A significant volume by an outstanding poet.

6591 Douglas, Allister. Thoughts in my mind. Georgetown: Labour Advocate Job Printing Department, n.d. 16 p.

Love for individuals close to the poet and compassion for mankind in general furnish themes for this small collection of poems. Verse full of optimism.

6592 Forrester, Ivan. A voice from Cuffy's grave. Introduction by Denis Williams. Georgetown?: People's National Congress, Office of the General Secretary [and] Ministry of National Development, 1976. 32 p.

The Guyanese interior with its great rivers and forests is the inspiration and source of images for the verse in this small collection. The poet's personal experiences bring a freshness to his country's poetry. A short, short story about the interior and an essay, "Hints for the Hinterland," are included.

6593 Harry, Carlyle. Life. A book of poems. Foreword by Basi Blair. Georgetown: The Dritchlow Labour College, 1976? 35 p.

These 35 poems by a young writer present daily concerns and life in Guyana. The poet criticizes forces which divide the people of his country as well as those of the islands with similar backgrounds. He sees the need for integration of forces and talents to make real progress.

6594 Kaur, Chioneso Kulwant. New moon rising. A collection of poems and poetic prose. n.p.: n.p., 1977? 59 p.

Collection of 19 poems and one story, the first publication of a young poet. Her verse reveals sensitivity and compassion for her people. A glossary of Indian terms is included in the volume.

6595 **Nichols, Norma.** Thoughts and things. A collection of poems. Foreword by Desmond Bacchus. Georgetown: Labour Advocate Job Printing Department, n.d. 45 p.

These 50 poems on a variety of themes grow out of the traditions and culture of Guyana. Poet pays tribute to her country's political leaders and expresses faith in Guyana's revolution and future.

6596 **Prasad, Krishna.** Born to die. A collection of poems. Demerara, Guyana: The Author, 1977. 24 p.

Small volume of 32 poems on biblical characters and subjects. The poet's purpose is evangelistic.

6597 **Rahaman, Ray.** Douglah. Bridgetown: Rayton Enterprises, 1976. 49 p.; ill.; plates.

The verse in this small volume reveals a young poet in search of his identity and trying to come to grips with living in a black world dominated by white cultural values. Several poems show signs of budding talent.

6598 **St. John, Bruce.** Joyce & Eros and Varia. Bridgetown: Yoruba Press, 1976. 54 p. (Benin books; 001)

Academic life, love, history and native scenery furnish themes for the poems in this collection, the first the gifted poet has published in standard English. His earlier verse is in Barbadian Creole, some of which has been translated into Spanish.

6599 **Todd, Hugh.** Window of my Mind. Poems. Georgetown: National Lithographic Co., n.d. 32 p.

Small collection of patriotic poems designed to encourage participation in the national revolution. A feeling of sincerity pervades the verse. Illustrations of Guyanese scenes.

6600 **Wong, Orlando.** Echo. Kingston?: Sangster's Book Stores, 1977. 44 p.

These 36 poems, a few in Jamaican dialect, express a cry for freedom from oppression and suffering. Many portray the underprivileged man's ability to laugh at his conditions in order to survive. The poet makes a compassionate plea for justice and human dignity.

6601 **Zencraft, Barbra.** Native soul. With notes and introduction by George B. Wallace. Kingston: Sangster's Book Stores, n.d. 270 p.; ill.

Poems and proverbs in Jamaican dialect and in standard English. All attempt to portray the tempo and philosophy of native life and thought. Proverbs have an accompanying explanation in standard English. A glossary of Creole terms used in poems is found at the end of the volume.

SPECIAL STUDIES

6602 **Baytop, Adrianne.** The emergence of Caribbean English literature (LALR, 4:9, Fall/Winter 1976, p. 29–38)

Early literary production in the West Indies was greatly influenced by British models but was indigenous in theme and imagery. With independence, the literature has passed through a period of rebellion against colonial influence and has come of age, finding its language, style and inspiration in its own society and traditions. This literature by its own merits now belongs in the "mainstream of world letters." A list of outstanding writers and distinguished awards received by them is included.

6603 **Gilkes, Michael.** Mulatta *angst* and Mittelhozer's *Sylvia* (RIB, 29:1, 1979, p. 3–14)

The writer sees Mittelhozer's novel as an exposé of the hypocrisy and intrigue in a typical 20th-century colonial West Indian society. He describes the heroine as representing the destructive disorientation which results from a mixed heritage.

6604 ———. Racial identity and individual consciousness in the Caribbean novel. Introduction by A.J. Seymour. Georgetown: Ministry of Information and Culture, National History and Arts Council, 1975. 52 p. (The Edgar Mittelholzer memorial lectures series; 5)

An incisive critical analysis of the Caribbean novel with special attention given to elements revealed by the novelists. The author sees the majority of Caribbean writers suffering from division of consciousness because of their multiracial ancestry. Some regard this heritage as a weakness while others consider it a strength and a source of new and original growth towards identity.

6605 Hensell, William H. Some themes in the Jamaican poetry of Claude McKay (AU/P, 40:2, June 1979, p. 123–139)

This study of McKay's early poems reveals that his protests against injustice and deprivation did not begin with his life in the US. The poet's Jamaican verse, while portraying love for the land and people, constantly speaks out against conditions which victimize the underprivileged. McKay's protests are more universal than racial.

6606 Independence 10: Guyanese writing, 1966–1976. Introduction by A.J. Seymour. Georgetown: Ministry of Information and Culture, National History and Arts Council, 1976? 222 p.; bibl.

Poems, short stories and essays representing Guyana's literary production during the first 10 years of independence. History, traditions, national pride, local concerns and nature provide themes for most of the works. Writers reveal considerable talent. A bibliography is included. Should be of special interest to students of Guyanese literature.

6607. *Kaie.* National History and Arts Council of Guyana. No. 12, Oct. 1975– Georgetown.

This issue of the official organ of the National History and Arts Council of Guyana presents a report of literary competitions organized by the Council. Prize-winning works and those obtaining honorable mention are included. An introduction by A.J. Seymour and photos of works by Guyanese artists add to the volume.

6608 Kairi: annual of the arts, 1976. Edited by Christopher Laird. Port-of-Spain: n.p., 1976? 62 p.; bibl.; plates.

A review of cultural and literary events of 1976. Critiques of literary works are included as well as several complete poems, short stories and a drama. An annotated bibliography, photos of art works and a calendar of events add to the value of the volume.

Midgett, Douglas. West Indian version: literature, history, and identity. See *HLAS 41: 1065.*

6609 Morris, Mervyn. Contending values: the prose fiction of Claude McKay (Jamaica Journal [Institute of Jamaica, Kingston] 9:2/3, 1975, p. 36–52, ill.)

The critic believes that McKay, though better known as a poet, deserves greater recognition for his prose fiction. His novel, *Banana bottom,* and his short stories in *Gingertown* are among the finest achievements of Jamaican literature. Characters, especially in the novel, portray values and attitudes of the Jamaican people. The article gives insight into McKay's fiction.

Nettleford, Rex M. Caribbean cultural identity: the base of Jamaica; an essay in cultural dynamics. See *HLAS 41: 1071.*

6610 Parris, D. Elliott. Perspectives of the creative writers (*in* The Commonwealth Caribbean into the seventies: proceedings of a conference held on 28–30 September, 1973, Howard University, Washington, D.C. Edited by A.W. Singham. Montreal, Canada: McGill University, Centre for Developing-Area Studies *in co-operation with* the Committee on Caribbean Studies, Howard University, Washington, D.C., 1975, p. 145–169, tables)

A survey of 20 major writers of the English-speaking Caribbean area examines their political, racial, social and cultural attitudes. Conclusions drawn are that the West Indian writer is little concerned with political militancy; his chief interest is the freedom of the artist to portray his subject, taking cognizance of the milieu out of which it grows.

6611 Thieme, John. Gnarled sour grapes: a review of St. Lucian poet Derek Walcott's most recent collection (FIU/CR, 7:4, Oct./Dec. 1978. p. 51–53)

Author sees in *Sea grapes,* Walcott's most recently published collection, the poet's disenchantment with events occurring in the Caribbean. The verse warns against the insincerity of dishonest leaders who deceive others in seeking their own aggrandizement.

TRANSLATIONS INTO ENGLISH

MARGARET SAYERS PEDEN, *Professor of Spanish, University of Missouri, Columbia*

IN THE FIRST SECTION of Latin American literature in translation (see *HLAS 40*, p. 517), an arbitrary period was chosen and only publications within those dates were considered. This second section begins the slow process of assessing those works that were published before 1966, as well as a branching out into books and articles on the theory, bibliography, and practice of translation. Some very important works fall within that new category, among them, George Steiner's *After Babel* (item **6685**), one of the most valuable studies ever published on the subject of translation, and of the related areas of writing, reading, and criticism. An entirely different sort of book, but one that is of breakthrough importance, is *Translation & translators*, edited by the late Stefan Congrat-Butlar (item **6675**). This source book offers indices of translators, programs, marketing, prizes, and other valuable information. Congrat-Butlar conceived of this volume as the first of six, and worked on the second volume—to be devoted to a bibliography of critical writings—up to the time of his death. I have no information as to whether or not his project will be carried out.

Though totally unscientific, some interesting statistics are reflected in the entries contained here. Though obviously more works than those represented were published during the two-year interval since the last publication of the *Handbook*, the ratio of works translated into English from the Portuguese is radically lower than those from Spanish-language writers. Some reasons for this discrepancy are readily apparent, but there may be a message here for aspiring translators—as well as an indication of a need for more adventurous publishing. Poetry, as I have long maintained, does seem to have more outlets for publication than prose, especially short stories. And "big names" are probably being over-published while very good writers remain as yet undiscovered by a North American audience. We are all familiar with the commercial factors in publishing which make this so.

A point regarding publishing. Nine of the entries in this section (and 11 in the first) were published under the imprint of the University of Texas Press. With the exception of Borges (who was at Texas immediately before these books were published), the authors are not among the well known names of the *Boom* who are regularly published in the eastern commercial houses. The University of Texas Press was for years a pioneer in publishing translations of Latin American literature, and we owe them an enormous debt. But recently their editorial policy has changed, and the numbers of new names under the UT Press logos has been substantially reduced. (Similarly, one is reminded by the Paz/Beckett anthology of Mexican poetry and the Nist/Leite anthology of Brazilian poetry, that Indiana University Press was also at one time a major publisher of Latin American literature in translation.) We can be extremely grateful for a number of small presses and university presses now picking up some of that slack, but one would welcome a reversal of current policy by Texas, once the leader in introducing to North America worthwhile but not commercially viable new Latin American writers.

And when one turns to the major translations of this section, the university presses will see that these ventures do not go unrewarded. In 1979, Frances Horning Barrclough won the Columbia Translation Center prize for her sensitive translation of José María Arguedas' *Deep rivers* (item **6624**) a UT Press book. The problems of Arguedas' mythic tone, his mixture of Spanish and Indian languages, are inventively met in this translation. Gregory Rabassa encountered a similar challenge in Demetrio Aguilera Malta's *Seven serpents and seven moons* (item **6623**) and met the challenge with intelligence. My own choice for the most interesting translation during this period is Barbara Stoler Miller's brilliant version of Agueda Pizarro's *Shadowinnower* (item **6647**). Pizarro's poetry is new; hers is a unique voice, and Miller has effected a remarkable recreation of that voice in English. The translation which is in my opinion the most controversial is the one that received the National Book Award for translation, Clayton Eshleman's very careful rendition of the posthumous poetry of César Vallejo. Eshleman worked closely with a respected scholar, José Rubia Barcia, to order the poems chronologically and to establish variorum texts. However, while one must respect their careful study, the translations are somehow overly academic.

In sum, a predominance of established figures, with a sprinkling of new names and feminist ventures are annotated below.

TRANSLATIONS FROM SPANISH
I. ANTHOLOGIES: POETRY AND PROSE

6612 Alvarado de Ricord, Elsie; Lucha Corpi; and **Concha Michel.** Fireflight: three Latin American poets. Translated into English by Catherine Rodríguez-Nieto. English and Spanish. Berkeley, Calif.: Oyez, 1976. 109 p.

This volume was published with the assistance of the National Endowment for the Humanities. The translator's rationale for the grouping of these three contemporary women poets is that she knows each personally and hopes the poems "will provide . . . a glimpse of work whose existence . . . might otherwise not have (been) suspected, and whose range and vigor may surprise . . ." Of the three, Lucha Corpi is the most interesting, especially her "Marina" (Malinche) cycle, written "in vindication." Translations are adequate to good.

6613 Another republic: 17 European and South American writers. Edited by Charles Simic and Mark Strand, with notes on contributors. New York: The Ecco Press, 1976. 247 p.

Four of the 17 writers contained in this very personal, and perhaps conventional, anthology are Latin American, Julio Cortázar, Octavio Paz, Carlos Drummond de Andrade, and Nicanor Parra. In the introduction, the editors touch on the place of translations in literature. The poem has the ability to "exist powerfully in a language other than the one in which it was written." How else, the editors ask, can one explain the young poets who seem to be more influenced by foreign poets than their own. And "how else are we to account for the recent increase in the exchange of literary ideas and the growth of an international style which is dominant in poetry today?" The translation process would have been better illustrated if the originals were included.

6614 Anthology of Mexican poetry. Edited by Octavio Paz. Translated by Samuel Beckett. Bloomington: Indiana University Press, 1958. 213 p.

An essay on poetry and tradition by C.M. Bowra, and an excellent introduction to the history of Mexican poetry by Octavio Paz. The anthology contains selections from most of the best-known, and occasionally the lesser, Mexican poets from the early colonial period through the years preceding World War II. An excellent representation, within those outlines. The question of the translation is an interesting one. Howard T. Young has called them "some of the best we have from Spanish verse." Translated by a world-renowned author who is obviously cognizant of the problems of translations, the poems read beautifully. There is, however, a oneness of voice that indicates the pervasive presence of the translator. Still, a landmark edition.

6615 The Borzoi anthology of Latin American literature. v. 1, From the time of Columbus to the twentieth century; v. 2, The twentieth century: from Borges and Paz to Guimaraes Rosa and Donoso. Edited by

Emir Rodríguez Monegal, with the assistance of Thomas Colchie. New York: Alfred A. Knopf, 1977. 982 p.

An enormous undertaking. Representation of authors has been made to show evidence of a literature in development: "It cannot yet be said that there is a cohesive Latin American literature . . . There is, rather, a continental literature in process . . ." The selections are limited to prose and fiction, with the exception of the chronicles, memoirs, and documents of the colonial period. There are the usual problems in excerpting longer works, but there really is no alternative to excerpting. The historical and critical orientation for each author is very helpful. The inclusion of Brazilian authors is a positive feature of this anthology. Luis Harss considers this the "best available anthology," in spite of the heavy emphasis on the moderns and contemporaries. It is impossible to address the question of the quality of the translation as it varies so widely—from very good to nearly unacceptable (see also item **5009**).

6616 Cuentos: an anthology of short stories from Puerto Rico. Edited and with a preface by Kal Wagenheim. With Spanish and English on facing pages. New York: Schocken Books, 1978. 170 p.; bibl.

That rarity, a bi-lingual edition of prose pieces, this collection makes one question the advantages of *en face* publication of prose. The editorial decision to make the Spanish and English correspond exactly, by pages, creates artificial paragraphs and white spaces in both texts. The translations are adequate to good, from those stories containing extremely difficult colloquial speech to stories written in standard, almost elegant, Spanish. Those translators struggling with the very special idiom of Puerto Rican Spanish respond in some cases by ignoring dialect and in others by attempting a re-creation in similar English. This very difficult task is more effective in the stories whose setting is New York; the cadences of English as spoken by Puerto Ricans in New York sound strange on the lips of island Puerto Ricans. Good introduction. Small bibliography for further reading in English. Various translators.

6617 A fist and the letter: revolutionary poems of Latin America. Translated by Roger Prentice and John M. Kirk. Text in English and Spanish. Vancouver: Pulp Press, 1977. 119 p.: ill.

The poems of 21 revolutionary poets are included in this very interesting collection, among them Roque Dalton, Ernesto Cardenal, Roberto Fernández Retamar, Nicolas Guillén, and René Depestre. From Cardenal's "but He who made the delicate cells of the ear/ will He not listen?/ and He who invented the camera of the eye, can He not see?" to Depestre's corroding "Poem to Howl/ Beneath the White House Windows," these poems encompass every aspect of revolutionary zeal—even love, as seen in Roberto Armijo's moving "His Will." The translations are very good, accurate, and appropriate in tone, but they are maddeningly reformed typographically. The space of a poem is an element of its essence, and the spatial arrangement of the lines of these poems is a violation of the originals. *En face.*

6618 Five women writers of Costa Rica. Short stories. Edited by Victoria Urbano. Beaumont, Tex.: Asociación de Literatura Femenina Hispánica, 1978. 131 p.

The aim of this anthology is to "help acquaint the American reader with the feminine literature of Central America." The five (Naranjo, Oreamuno, Odio, Urbano and Vallbona) have been selected because they have "contributed to enrich the contemporary literature of Costa Rica within the universal trend which distinguished their own personal style." Two are now dead. The volume also includes critical essays on the authors. Various translators.

6619 Green, Ernest S. *tr.* Mexican and South American poems: Spanish and English. Translated by Ernest S. Green and H. von Lowenfels. New York: Gordon Press, 1977. 398 p.; index.

The love and dedication lavished on this edition of Romantic 19th-century poets is evident throughout the collection. It is always painful to note that love is not enough. The poems themselves are not the greatest in the canon of that literature, and the translations are stiff and labored, but accurate.

6620 Latin-American literature today. Edited by Ann Fremantle. New York: New American Library, 1977. 342 p. (A mentor book; ME1587)

Totally eclectic: many countries, many authors, many periods, many genres, some well-known—Fuentes, García Márquez, Neruda, Paz, Rulfo, Vargas Llosa, Cortázar, Borges—others of varying degrees of national and international fame. In many ways, this makes for a very fresh anthology. The editor points out that the beginning writer in Latin America today has his own models in addition to the continental and North American models available to those writers represented here. No need to address levels of translation: take your pick.

6622 Now the volcano: an anthology of Latin American gay literature. Edited by Winston Leyland. Translated by Erskine Lane, Franklin D. Blanton, Simon Karlinsky. English, Portuguese or Spanish. San Francisco: Gay Sunshine Press, 1979. 287 p.; ill.

This volume comprises "thirteen short stories, two excerpts from novels, twenty-nine poems, one long memoir, and seven reproductions of paintings/drawings by artists from four countries." The literary contributions are largely Brazilian. The best known writers represented here are the Mexicans Salvador Novo and Xavier Villaurrutia, and the Spaniard Luis Cernuda. The selections have been chosen specifically to illustrate the sexual preferences of the writers. A much greater service for gay literature would have been to anthologize the *best* work of the authors.

NOVELS

6623 Aguilera Malta, Demetrio. Seven serpents and seven moons. Translated from the Spanish by Gregory Rabassa. Austin: University of Texas Press, 1979. 305 p.

John S. Brushwood points out that the author, like Agustín Yáñez, is fond of the unforgettable, extraordinary character. True. Very few contemporary novels feature a wooden, crucified, Christ that descends from its cross to participate in the everyday affairs of a village. To deal with the regionalisms, word play, and mythic language, of this underrated author, Rabassa has had to "invent" a new language which absorbs the Spanish into the English. Very successful.

6624 Arguedas, José María. Deep rivers. Translated by Frances Horning Barraclough. Introduction by John V. Murra. Afterword by Mario Vargas Llosa. Austin: University of Texas Press, 1978. 248 p. (The Texas Pan American series)

This translation of *Los ríos profundos* was awarded the 1978 Columbia Translation Center Award, and with good reason. Arguedas was one of those writers, like Asturias, like Aguilera Malta, who *invented* a language that was neither Spanish *nor* Indian. In his informative introduction, ethnohistorian Murra sketches some of the intricacies of this creation. And adds, parenthetically in a footnote, that "no one has yet undertaken to translate Arguedas into Spanish." Vargas Llosa's afterword offers to the reader who may not be familiar with Arguedas an illuminating discussion of the author's world: "One could say of a novel so cleverly autobiographical that Arguedas has transplanted his own trials into the narrative in a symbolic fashion." Most of the problems of translation have been ingeniously solved. One wishes it were possible to eliminate the footnotes, but as the translator's are mingled with those of the author himself, perhaps in this instance they are not as intrusive as usual.

6625 Arreola, Juan José. The fair. Translated by John Upton. Illustrations by Barbara Whitehead. Austin: University of Texas Press, 1977. 154 p.: ill. (Texas Pan American series)

Edith Grossman calls this novel a "collage composed of many voices;" the translator calls it "a gallery of voices," (a phrase often used to describe Cabrera Infante's TTT); John Brushwood, a portrait of a town, and a "kind of autobiography." As a major portion of the novel is in dialogue, what Grossman calls the translator's extreme sensitivity to language is particularly welcome. Bradley Shaw finds the notes very helpful; this reader would prefer a different solution, but, unfortunately, cannot suggest one. The glossary is, without doubt, valuable. The convention for dividing the fragments of the novel is less effective in this edition than in the original.

6626 Azuela, Mariano. Three novels: The trials of a respectable family. The underdogs. The firefly. Translated by Frances Kellam Hendricks and Beatrice Berler. San Antonio: Trinity University Press, 1979. xxv, 373 p.

This translation of three major novels

of Mariano Azuela is an admirable project. *The underdogs*, one of the truly great novels of Latin American literature, is *due* a new translation (it appeared earlier, in 1962, in a New American Library edition). In some respects there are improvements (we are not, for example, submitted to the apellation "Blondie" for the Güero Margarito), but some of the very specific and difficult problems of this text have not been resolved. The two remaining novels, *The trials of a respectable family* and *The firefly*, have fewer problems and are more comfortable in these English versions than *The underdogs*. Introduction by Hendricks. Also includes excerpts from Luis Leal's *Mariano Azuela: life and works*.

6627 Carpentier, Alejo. Explosion in a cathedral. Translated by John Sturrock. New York: Harper & Row, 1979. 351 p. (Harper colophon edition)

Baroque, magically real, *Explosion . . .* has been called Carpentier's best novel, and Victor Hughes one of his best delineated characters. The Spanish title more closely relates to the historical epoch, the Age of Enlightenment, the English refers to a symbolic painting in the home of the protagonist. Sturrock quite reasonably reproduced Carpentier's style. A reissue of his 1963 translation.

6628 Cortázar, Julio. Hopscotch. Translated from the Spanish by Gregory Rabassa. New York: Pantheon Books, 1966. 564 p.

This book, this translation must surely be considered one of the breakthrough publications in Latin American literature in the English-speaking world, setting the stage for many works to follow. Though Alfred J. MacAdam believes that the novel is dated, it has, in fact, weathered well, and will continue to be studied as "a philosophical manifesto, a revolt against literary language, and the account of an extraordinary spiritual pilgrimage," as it has been classified by Luis Harss. The translation, as indicated, is similarly a milestone in Spanish American literature.

6629 ———. A manual for Manuel. Translated from the Spanish by Gregory Rabassa. New York: Pantheon Books, 1978. 391 p.

In the opening pages the author—truthfully? fictionally?—tells the reader that "This man is dreaming something I had dreamed in a like manner during the days when I was just beginning to write . . ." The dream is crucial, if ultimately unresolved as to meaning. Difficult, disturbing, *Manuel . . .* is Cortázar's most "novelistic" work since *Hopscotch*, and if not an invitation to skip about the squares of that game, certainly a challenge demanding participation in a different one. This is one of Rabassa's finest translations—which is saying a lot. The Spanish *Postdata* to the first two pages is changed in the translation to an explanatory note for American (North American?) readers.

6630 Fuentes, Carlos. Aura. Translated by Lysander Kemp. New York: Farrar, Straus & Giroux, 1965. 74 p.

This early novel signals a direction Fuentes will explore consistently in his later work. Not receivd seriously by some critics, in fact, the theme of the passage of one consciousness through two, or many, bodies is a constant throughout Fuentes' writing. The author conceives of this novel as one of a trilogy completed by Birthday and Distant Relations. A very good translation.

6631 ———. The hydra head. Translated from the Spanish by Margaret Sayers Peden. New York: Farrar, Straus & Giroux, 1978. 292 p.

6632 Ortega, Julio. The land in the day. Translated from the Spanish by Julio Ortega and Ewing Campbell. Austin, Tex.: New Latin Quarter Editions, 1978. 95 p.

A student of utopian literature, the author suggests as a convention for his own utopian fiction an origin that departs "from itself" as well as from "its tradition." This impressionistic, experimental, and epigrammatic fiction is preceded by a Borgesian Preface whose interplay with the primary text places the work squarely within the confines of the newest writing. The translation is perhaps evidence that authors are too close to the original to achieve the most utopian translations of their own works.

6633 Scorza, Manuel. Drums for Rancas. Translated from the Spanish by Edith Grossman. New York: Harper & Row, 1977. 214 p.

These 34 18th-century titled chapters ("Concerning the Pyramid of Sheep which the People of Rancas Built Without Wishing to Emulate the Egyptians") comprise what Patricia Tobin calls, with justification, the first in a series of novels which form a "searing chronicle of injustice." This most recent—and perhaps most realistic—of a series of Peruvian Indianist novels is a powerful, and, if the introduction is to be taken literally, completely true representation of events that are "but pale reflections of reality." With very few exceptions, this is also a very true translation.

6634 Vargas Llosa, Mario. Captain Pantoja and the special service. Translated from the Spanish by Gregory Kolovakos and Ronald Christ. New York: Harper & Row, 1978. 244 p.

The New York Times called this "an uproariously slapstick novel." Vargas Llosa has acknowledged that this is the first time he employed humor in his work, but that after trying to write a more "serious" novel, this material demanded comic treatment. The style is no less complex, however, than in the similarly constructed *The green house.* The desire to create simultaneity of time among several plot lines is the hallmark of the author's work, and especially notable here. Excellent translation.

6635 ———. The time of the hero. Translated by Lysander Kemp. New York: Grove Press, 1966. 409 p.

One remembers the excitement with which *La ciudad y los perros* was received, and agrees with Alastair Reid that "Mario Vargas Llosa's book makes the majority of novels written in our day look shabby and thin by comparison . . ." An excellent translation, stumbling only on that perennial problem in translation, nicknames and epithets. And obviously something had to be done with the title; perhaps the irony of the English is the answer.

POETRY

6636 Borges, Jorge Luis. The gold of the tigers. Selected later poems. A bilingual edition in English and Spanish. Translated by Alastair Reid. New York: Dutton, 1977. 95 p.

The poems, selected from *El oro de los tigres* and *La rosa profunda*, are beautifully translated; many have been previously published in translation in North American magazines and reviews. Many are love poems, not a genre Borges is particularly well known for. Beautiful love poems. Several are poetic versions, or continuations, of his famous fragment "Borges and I": ". . . I am in a circular cell and the infinite wall is closing in./ Neither of the two deceives the other, but we both lie./ We know each other too well, inseparable brother./ You drink the water from my cup and you wolf down my bread./ The door to suicide is open, but theologians assert that, in the subsequent shadows of the kingdom, there will I be, waiting for myself." The ultimate inseparability. It would be difficult to find better translations, and in what other author are prefaces as engrossing as the poetry? "Blindness is a confinement, but it is also a liberation, a solitude propitious to invention, a key and an algebra."

6637 Caudra, Pablo Antonio. Songs of Cifar and the sweet sea. Selections in English and Spanish. Translated and edited by Grace Schulman and Ann McCarthy de Zavala. New York: Columbia University Press, 1979. 120 p. (A Center for Inter-American Relations book)

Cifar is Cuadra's Odyssean voyager of Lake Nicaragua. These simple, at times lyrical, poems combine the real world of that fresh water "sea" and the mythological echoes of the ageless Aegean. Only an infrequent error in literal meaning ("cook" for *cuque*; "pushed down" for *tumbé*) interrupts an inventive and generally felicitous translation. This translation was sponsored by the Center for Inter-American Relations. One hopes to see more. Good brief introduction by Schulman. Notes at end of book. Glossary. *En face.*

6638 Gómez-Correa, Enrique. Mother-darkness. English version by Susana Wald. Collages by Ludwig Zeller. Toronto: Oasis, 1975. 30 p.: ill.

Physically, graphically, this is a handsome volume (of a limited edition of 270 numbered copies). The surreal poem, dated Guatemala City, Aug. 1972, a love poem directed to a mother figure, "The blue thread cut/ Where I am to continue the dialogue from one room to another/ To drink again the milk that you gave me in my childhood?", is more difficult to assess. Without the original Spanish, judgments are difficult to make about the translation, but one sees signs of a lack of total familiarity with the Spanish that results in overly-literal phrases.

6639 Guillén, Nicolás. Tengo. Translated by Richard J. Carr. Prologue by José Antonio Portuondo. Detroit: Broadside Press, 1974. 142 p.

In a brief introductory note the translator identifies these poems as representing "a capsule history of the Cuban Revolution . . . meant for the people and the loudspeaker and not for the parlor." Though these are very interesting, at times, very moving poems, they are not well served in this translation. Perhaps the greatest difficulty lies in the effort to reproduce the emphatic rhythm and rhyme of the originals. Occasionally, too, over-reliance on the literal damages the sense *and* sound.

6640 Lihn, Enrique. The dark room and other poems. Edited with an introduction by Patricio Lerzundi. Translated by Jonathan Cohen, John Felstiner, and David Unger. New York: New Directions, 1978. 147 p.

Enrique Lihn is the most recent in an exemplary line of Chilean poets including Pablo de Rokha, Vicente Huidobro, Nicanor Parra, and the Nobel laureates Gabriela Mistral and Pablo Neruda. He is both a continuation and repudiation of these voices. In his brief introduction, Patricio C. Lerzundi speaks of the "antipoetry" of Lihn's form. But Lihn himself has stressed his loyalty to the Neruda of the *Residencias*. By any count, this is difficult poetry, and difficult to translate. Perhaps it is the rhythm, the music, of the original that is most missed here, for the translations are basically accurate. An important collection. *En face*.

6641 Montes de Oca, Marco Antonio. The heart of the flute. English and Spanish on opposite pages. Translated by Laura Villaseñor. Introduction by Octavio Paz. Pittsburgh: International Poetry Forum, 1978. 60 p., 1 leaf of plates: ill. (Byblos editions; 1)

This very beautiful edition was underwritten by a grant from the Westinghouse Electric fund—one would wish this were a trend. In his brief introduction, Octavio Paz characterizes this poetry as "A search for the springs of song—a pilgrimage toward the roots of the tree that speaks—the heart of the flute." Paul West refers to the poem's *thunderstructure*. Montes de Oca himself speaks of his "curling litany" of love, an apostrophe to Grace. This very richly textured poetry gives the appearance of complexity of translation, but this is not necessarily the case. The translator beautifully recreates the first two-thirds of the long poem, but inexplicably, something falls flat in the last third of her translation. Even so, the book is an important contribution to the canon of this prolific poet. *En face*.

6642 Moro, César. The scandalous life of César Moro: in his own words. Translated from the French and Spanish by Philip Ward. New York: Oleander Press, 1976. 24 p. (Oleander modern poets; 6)

One would have welcomed more information in this volume. The poems translated are undated, and unidentified as to source. The translator does make the point that "literature on Moro is still relatively sparse." With a 1973 collection translated from the French (*Love till death*), Moro seems to be enjoying more attention in English than in Peru or Spanish America in general. Almost totally ignored by Spanish American anthologists, Moro's work is perhaps most accessible through a bibliography prepared by Julio Ortega. To judge from these translations, Moro at least deserves more study. However, the difficulty of obtaining the originals makes even more lamentable their absence in the translation.

6643 Neruda, Pablo. The heights of Macchu Picchu. Translated by Nathaniel Tarn. Introduction by Robert Pring-Mill. New York: Farrar, Straus & Giroux, 1966. 71 p.

Probably Neruda's single greatest poem, combining the social and political concerns of the poet with *poetry*. Pring-Mill's comments on the poem's progression are very discerning. This translation (an old one, also published 14 years ago) is interesting. For a long time I was convinced that it was a good one but more recently, I am bothered by the strangeness of some lines, "I could not love within each man a tree/ with its remaindered autumns on its back . . ." and of some word choices, "Mother of stone and sperm (*espuma*) of condors." Nevertheless, Tarn is a sensitive poet and the translation has great moments.

6644 ———. To the women of the world. Translated from the Spanish. Illustrations by Maureen Scott. London: M. Scott, 1974. 2, 13 leaves: ill.

A frustrating edition insofar as information is concerned. The illustrator—major, it's true, in terms of the concept of the book—is listed, but not the translator. Credit is given the "Albanian artist whose design is freely used for the front cover," but the original title of the poem is nowhere to be found. The motivation for the book is clear: "Illustrated in memory of a great poet who, in company with the finest artists, gave his lifework to the cause of socialism."

6645 Pacheco, José Emilio. Don't ask me how the time goes by. Poems, 1964–1968. With parallel text in the original Spanish. Translated by Alastair Reid. New York: Columbia University Press, 1978. 155 p.

These *ably* translated poems are extremely varied, from the epistemological musings of "In These Circumstances" to the often amusing "Animals Know." Form is similarly wide-ranging, from the prose lines of "Descriptions of a Castaway in His Wanderings" to the stair-stepped single phrase of "Goethe." Through all the collection one perceives a vision of destruction and disaster, but Thomas Hoeksema has suggested that "despite the weight of negativity suggested by these dominant themes, Pacheco's poems carry a positive thrust as well." The book was cited for its "correspondence of fragmentation" (Hoeksema). Some readers may find the very diversity distracting, but the most interesting question is which directions Pacheco will follow in the future. One technical question about the translation: why were many of the epigraphs left untranslated? *En face.*

6646 Parra, Nicanor. Emergency poems. In Spanish with parallel English translations. Translated by Miller Williams. London: Boyars, 1977. 154 p.; indexes.

An English edition of the New Directions 1972 publication.

6647 Pizarro, Agueda. Sombraventadora = Shadowinnower. English and Spanish. Translated by Barbara Stoler Miller with the poet. New York: Columbia University Press, 1979. 103 p.

By any strict interpretation of the *Handbook*'s guidelines, this collection does not belong here. The author is a New Yorker born of European parents. It is her statement that she chose Spanish as the language of this collection because of her encounter with Latin America and its literature that makes this poetry an oblique offspring of the literature reviewed in these columns. But the poetry is so delightful, so new, so strong (recalling most readily the vigor of Anglo-Saxon kennings) that it deserves mention. Neruda, de Greiff, García Márquez, mentioned by the author as influences, are *not* so much influences as presences. The particular problems of translation also dictate notice here; the translator, whose previous experience lies in translating Sanskrit poetry, has met a fascinating challenge with imagination and pleasing invention.

6648 Vallejo, César Abraham. César Vallejo: the complete posthumous poetry. In English and Spanish. Translated by Clayton Eshleman and José Rubia Barcia. Berkeley: University of California Press, 1978. 339 p.: ill.

No one could dispute the importance of this volume, nor fail to appreciate the enormous effort of scholarship which has been devoted to it, based on the recent availability of Vallejo's worksheets. But Eshleman, who in the past has been criticized for being overly free in his translations, here, having decided "to work off the literal edge of what Vallejo is saying and to be as uninterpretative as possible," is too dependent on pedantic detail to produce that fusion of accuracy and creation that results in the ideal translation. Specifically, it is a mistake to have maintained the Spanish punctuation in the English; that some misspellings and typographical oddities were intentional is surely questionable; and the reliance here on latinate cognates is particularly detrimental to the *poetry* of the translation. This translation won the 1979 National Book Award for Translation.

SHORT STORIES AND OTHER PROSE WRITINGS

6649 Bioy Casares, Adolfo. The invention of Morel and other stories. Translated from *La trama celeste* by Ruth L.C. Simms. Prologue by Jorge Luis Borges. Illustrated by Norah Borges de Torre. Austin: University of Texas Press, 1964. 237 p.

Bioy Casares has recently begun to

emerge from the shadow of his co-author, and, in the volume, prologuist, Borges, who points out the rareness of "works of reasoned imagination" in Spanish. (Borges also orients the reader by informing him that the invention of Morel "alludes filially to another island inventor, Moreau.") He does not address himself to the stories, which are best described as pale Borges. Simms is usually a very good translator. Here, however, one wishes for a less formal tone.

6650 Borges, Jorge Luis. Dreamtigers. Translated by Mildred Boyer and Harold Morland. Introduction by Miguel Enguídanos. Austin: University of Texas Press, 1964. 95 p.: ill.

Ronald Christ writes that "the heterogeneous pieces in this miscellany hang together . . . because each one contributes to a portrait of a writer who, for once, is only hiding behind a paper-thin screen." Miguel Enguídanos says that Borges "loved to play with this idea," that *El hacedor* "would make his earlier works unnecessary, including his two extraordinary collections of stories, *Ficciones* and *El Aleph*." Whatever its place in the sum of his work, this collection is an extraordinary "portrait" of a man, and includes the often anthologized "Borges and I," perhaps the ultimate metaphor for a writer. Borges, in spite of his conceptual complexities, does not pose major problems of translation, so he comes through fairly well here, even though these are among the less successful of the many translations of his work.

6651 ———. Ficciones. Edited and with an introduction by Anthony Kerrigan. New York: Grove Press, 1962. 174 p.

This collection, along with *Labyrinths* (see item **6652**) represents the first major Borges assault on the North American consciousness. Since their publication, editions, studies, anthologized pieces, and disciples have multiplied, moving rapidly toward the infinite so inherent in Borges' fictions. Borges' translators are similarly numerous. In addition to Kerrigan, Alastair Reid, Helen Temple, Ruthven Todd, and Anthony Bonner have contributed to this volume. It is therefore difficult to speak of the overall quality of the translation. In general, the pieces read very well.

6652 ———. Labyrinths. Selected stories & other writings. 2. ed. rev. Edited by Donald A. Yates & James E. Irby. Preface by André Maurois. New York: New Directions, 1964. 260 p.; bibl.

The fictions contained in this edition are almost exactly those published in *Ficciones* (see item **6651**). The essays and parables do not appear in that collection. Translations, in addition to those of the editors, are by Harriet de Onís, L.A. Murillo, John M. Fein, Julian Palley, Dudley Fitts, and Anthony Kerrigan. André Maurois refers to one of Borges' own lines to describe his genius: "They seek neither truth nor likelihood; they seek astonishment. They think metaphysics is a branch of the literature of fantasy." The translations, if not definitive, are, like those of *Ficciones*, intelligent. Also, a basic chronology, bibliography, and bibliography of translations.

6653 ———. Other inquisitions, 1937–1952. Translated by Ruth L. C. Simms. Introduction by James E. Irby. Austin: University of Texas Press, 1964. 205 p.

In his introduction, Irby sees the "method" of Borges' essays as "the *activation* of thought, shared by author and reader, miraculously effected over fatal distance and time by words whose sense alters and yet lives on . . ." The subjects of these essays, many first published in Victoria Ocampo's *Sur*, reflect the catholicity of Borges' own readings (further evidenced in the helpful index). It is sometimes difficult to distinguish between a Borges essay and a Borges fiction. The same elegant prose characterizes each; the prose is nicely conveyed in the translation.

6654 Cardenal, Ernesto. The Gospel in Solentiname. Translated by Donald D. Walsh. Maryknoll, New York: Orbis Books, 1976. 265 p.

These "dialogues" that take the place of sermons were undertaken in church, in a thatched hut, and in the open air. Cardenal's custom was that "one of those who reads best (generally a boy or a girl) reads aloud the entire passage on which we are going to comment. Then we discuss it verse by verse." Cardenal felt that since the Gospel was written for the poor and the uneducated it is not unusual that their commentaries should be as profound as that of many theologians.

Since Cardenal preferred a protestant edition of the Gospel entitled *Dios llega al hombre*, the translator worked from that book: "The angel came into the place where she was and said to her: 'I congratulate you, God-favored one!'" It's very difficult to stand up against, "And the angel came in unto her, and said, Hail, thou that art highly favoured, the Lord is with thee: blessed art thou among women."

6655 **Cortázar, Julio.** End of the game, and other stories. Translated from the Spanish by Paul Blackburn. London: Collins, Harvill P., 1968. 227 p.

Cortázar perhaps thinks of himself first not as a novelist, but as a writer of brief fiction (a "sprinter," he has said, not a "long distance runner"), and this collection contains some of his best-known and most-anthologized pieces: "Axolotl" and "The Pursuer," as well as the story that served as the inspiration for Antonioni's *Blow up*. Cortázar's intellectual and controlled prose should travel without difficulty from Spanish to English, which is generally the case here. Occasionally, however, the translator has enlarged on Cortázar's spare prose or chosen a turn of phrase that shades the original. Nevertheless, the English-language reader will be generally well served. This is an English edition of the earlier Pantheon Books publication (New York: 1967).

6656 **García Márquez, Gabriel.** Innocent Eréndira, and other stories. Translated from the Spanish by Gregory Rabassa. New York: Harper & Row, 1978. 183 p.

This is, as Gene H. Bell-Villada has noted, a "curious collection." Some of the stories were written when García Márquez was 19 and not published previously even in Spanish. Vargas Llosa calls these pieces part of García Márquez's "pre-history." The English-language collection is, to alert the bilingual reader, not the same as that published in Spanish under the same title. So the variety here is what might be expected from the wide span of years covered in their writing. The title piece, more accurately a novella than a short story, was conceived of as a film script. It is a delight. In sum, the whole is less than vintage García Márquez, though predictably vintage Rabassa—though even he must be haunted by the loss of the poetry of the *Cándida Eréndira* and her *abuela desalmada*.

6657 **———.** No one writes to the Colonel and other stories. Translated from the Spanish by J.S. Bernstein. New York: Harper & Row, 1968. 170 p.

An interesting collection of the author's early writing. The title story is, of course, a novella, but otherwise this (and *Leaf storm and other stories*) is probably a better collection than the more recent *Innocent eréndira*. At the time of their publication Robert G. Mead intelligently noted (though a crystal ball wouldn't be needed) that it "and the publication next year of his novel *One hundred years of solitude*, will secure a place for García Márquez among the growing constellation of Latin American authors who are familiar to U.S. readers." Oliver T. Mayers found this "a smooth translation." Earl Shorris found the translation "clumsy." The truth is that it is both.

6658 **Guibert, Rita.** Seven voices: seven Latin American writers talk to Rita Guibert. Translated from the Spanish by Frances Partridge. Introduction by Emir Rodríguez Monegal. New York: Alfred A. Knopf, 1973. 436 p.

Interviews with Pablo Neruda, Jorge Luis Borges, Miguel Angel Asturias, Octavio Paz, Julio Cortázar, Gabriel García Márquez, and Guillermo Cabrera Infante. The format of the interviews, in contrast with the more literary-oriented *Into the mainstream*, is based primarily on questions with social or political bias. A very valuable source of information, particularly when one considers that two of these major figures are dead and we will not have these kinds of revelations from them again. Each interview is quite different from the others, developing from the personality of each subject. Well translated.

6659 **Hispanic folktales** from New Mexico. Edited with an introduction and notes by Stanley L. Robe. Foreword by Wayland D. Hand. Berkeley: University of California Press, 1977. 223 p. (Folklore studies; 30)

Although this book does not fall strictly within the guidelines of this section, it should be annotated because of the unusual process of its translation. The tales are certainly Hispanic in origin, but according to the Introduction, they were not translated for publication, but, rather, during the phase of compilation. "The choice of English seems to have been determined . . . by the . . . language competency of the young people who went out into the small communities [to gather them] . . ." The field collectors "preferred to use Spanish . . . [but] it was certainly not a written language for them. Consequently the narratives were transcribed and presented in English . . ."

6660 Marqués, René. The docile Puerto Rican. Essays translated with an introduction by Barbara Bockus Aponte. Philadelphia: Temple University Press, 1976. 137 p.

A well-translated edition of a not very well known aspect of Marqués' writing, his essays. As the translator points out in her introduction, "many of Marqués' essays purposely fuse cultural concerns with political ones and his arguments concerning their inseparability are particularly cogent." The pieces are unified by these concerns. The seminal study which gives the title to the book reveals Marqués' fears of cultural and intellectual assimilation by the US, and examines not so much "the reasons for this docility, such as weakness, or ignorance, or complexes, or any intricate combination of these three," but rather "the kind of data and analysis which can establish a rational proof of his [the Puerto Rican's] docility."

6661 Martí, José. Our America: writings on Latin America and the struggle for Cuban independence. Translated by Elinor Randall, with additional translations by Juan de Onís and Roslyn Held Foner. Edited with an introduction and notes by Philip S. Foner. New York: Monthly Review Press, 1977. 448 p.; bibl.; index.

In the history of North America we have no figure in which poet and author are joined with patriot and military leader to the extent we see in José Martí. This large volume gathers together his writings on "nuestra América" (in an earlier volume the editor compiled Martí's essays and newspaper pieces on the US) and his thoughts on the preparations for the Cuban War of Independence. Copiously footnoted, and with attribution of sources, *Our America* is of value to the scholar as well as of interest to the layman reading Martí for the first time. The translation is cogent and intelligent, revealing the deep humanity of the author.

6662 Paz, Octavio. The bow and the lyre: the poem, the poetic revelation, poetry and history. 2. ed. Translated by Ruth L.C. Simms. Austin: University of Texas Press, 1973. 281 p.

Rachel Phillips has called *The Bow and the lyre* "Paz's most systematic statement of his often vatic, always intelligently original theories on poetry and the nature of 'the poetic act.'" The second edition, on which this translation is based, differs a great deal from the earlier edition published in 1956, so one may assume that he is reading an oeuvre which benefits from the experience and reflection of many years. Paz's prose is elegant, and the translation reflects the rhetorical level well.

6663 Rulfo, Juan. The burning plain and other stories. Translated and with an introduction by George D. Schade. Austin: University of Texas Press, 1967. 175 p.

Schade, who considers Rulfo to be "perhaps the best writer of fiction in Latin America today" (1967), points out that most critics have devoted their attention to Rulfo's brilliant novel, *Pedro Páramo*, abandoning the stories to the limbo where many good stories and collections languish. But the reader may possibly recognize at least two of the pieces, which have been rather widely anthologized, "Talpa," and "Luvina." John S. Brushwood finds the language of the stories "strong, simple, even coarse." The translation works very well, with the exception of the fact that some of that "coarseness," or harshness, has been blurred.

6664 Vargas Llosa, Mario. The cubs and other stories. Translated from the Spanish by Gregory Kolovakos and Ronald Christ. New York: Harper & Row, 1979. 139 p.

The team of Kolovakos and Christ is beginning to be regularly associated with translations of Vargas Llosa's work, and these are uniformly good translations. These six stories combine the Spanish publications *Los cachorros* (1967) and *Los jefes* (1965), both of which postdate the author's first, important novel, *La ciudad y los perros*, but predate his general acceptance as a major Spanish American writer. Of interest as his only collection of short fiction, *The cubs* is equally rewarding for the insights offered in the author's preface.

TRANSLATIONS FROM PORTUGUESE

6666 Meireles, Cecília. Poemas en tradução = Poems in translation. In English and Portuguese on facing pages. Translated by Henry Hunt Keith and Raymond S. Sayers with the assistance of Francisco de Sousa Neves and Antonio Salles Filho. Washington: Brazilian-American Cultural Institute, 1977. 167 p.

In their very helpful introduction, the translators refer to Cecília Meireles as the greatest woman poet in Portuguese. A contemporary of the Brazilian Modernista movement, this poet was not really of the movement, but considered herself more spiritually allied with symbolism. This selection from the very large corpus of her poems is a good introduction to her work. The translations are accurate, and tend more toward the literal than poetic; Earl F. Fitz does not agree, mentioning, for example, that Sayers . . . with his appreciation of the subtleness at work in the Portuguese, departs from the original, giving a "more liberal interpretation" of it, and in effect "creates new poems." The translators themselves confess the difficulty of reproducing the "musicality" of this poetry. *En face.*

6667 Modern Brazilian poetry, an anthology. Translated and edited by John Nist. With the help of Yolanda Leite. Bloomington: Indiana University Press, 1962. 175 p.

The editor outlines in his introduction his understanding of the four phases of Brazilian Modernism. He begins his anthology with poets in the second phase, in the person of Manuel Bandeira, and ends with a representative of the newer poets of the post-Modernist age, Paulo Bomfim. Some of this poetry is very commited, conversational, not difficult to translate. In those poems that are more dependent on the ambiguous language of poetry, the translations are slightly flat, and overly literal. Brief notes on the poets.

6668 Padilha, Telmo. Bird/night. Poems. Bilingual ed. Translated from the Portuguese by Fernando Camacho. London: R. Collings, 1976. 61 p. (Amazon books)

This volume is a selection from two collections of Padilha's poetry. The author won, in 1975, the "National Literature Prize" of Brazil, a major honor. This not unattractive book, however, is a classic example of what a translator and printer can do to an author: ". . . deceitful, untruthful, useless and conscious-smitten;" "There go the madmen/ mounted on their bling jennets;" "Because words are amour duty (armaduras);" "So many ripes/ and none sustains/ the infinite body;" "It remains only as the wet/ of a masterly conceived drainage . . ." The simple, unimagistic, language is completely subverted in this version. A list of errata in the Portuguese is bound in; the infinitely greater list of errata in the English does not appear. *En face.*

6669 Ramos, Graciliano. Childhood. Translated from the Portuguese by Celso de Oliveira. Introduction by Ashley Brown. London: Owen, 1979. 174 p. (UNESCO collection of representatives work. Brazilian series)

Ashley Brown defines this engaging work as "a memoir written like a novel . . . Few writers have told us so acutely what it means to grow up, to find one's identity." It seems today exotic—remote in time and space—and yet universal, as such experiences are. The translation is very good at times, interrupted only occasionally with an awkward word or phrase. Minor, but pleasing.

6670 Ribeiro, João Ubaldo. Sergeant Getúlio. Introduction by Jorge Amado. Boston: Houghton Mifflin, 1978. 146 p.

This novel has been highly acclaimed by the knowledgeable José Yglesias. Jorge Amado's introduction accords unstinting praise to the author, who according to Amado, has left behind the "formal researchers" of some experimental writers to undertake a direction "in which Brazilian literature should evolve." Patricia Tobin, argues that it is the *articulateness* of Getúlio, the author's "refusal to bestow a cheap, macho dignity through silence" which is "the master stroke" that makes this novel literature and not cheap sensationalism. The question of articulateness, however, raises an interesting point. Ribeiro here is his own translator. I do not think the translation is entirely satisfactory, as normality of English language patterns has at times been sacrified for the transmission of the *violence* of language. Further fuel to the burning question (!) of whether an author is the best translator of his own work.

6671 Seljan, Zora. The story of Oxala: the feat of Bomfim. A play in the Afro-Brazilian tradition. Translation from the Portuguese. London: Collings; Rio de Janeiro: Sel Editora, 1978. 52 p.: ill.

The daughter of an explorer and ethnologist, the author has researched Negro and native Indian folklore in Brazil. In her "Explanation," she states that the Feast of Bomfim, the inspiration for this play, is "one of the best examples of religious syncretism in our times . . . a compound of Catholic saints and African orixas." One perceives the mythic tones heard in some Haitian and African writers. There is no acknowledgement of a translator; the translation is very good.

6672 Veríssimo, Luís Fernando. Bits and pieces. Translated from the Portuguese by Ana Beatriz Davi Borges Duarte. Porto Alegre: Riocell, 197– . 136 p.: ill.

An amusing collage of satiric newspaper columns and drawings published, surprisingly, by the Brazilian cellulose-producing company Riocell—an event not likely to be imitated in the sister continent to the north: "The author of this book works . . . across the river from where we have our plant . . . We thought a selection of his newspaper 'bits and pieces' would make a fitting present in this, our fifth anniversary." The writing and cartoons are deft, light, and very much in tune with the world. Not strictly "literary," but interesting for their contemporaneity. The translation is excellent.

TRANSLATION: PRACTICE, THEORY, BIBLIOGRAPHIES

6673 Acuff, Skip and **Claudia Johnson.** Literary journals and magazines publishing translations (Translation Review [Richardson, Texas] 4, 1979, p. 45–69)

An extremely valuable bibliography of periodicals that publish literary translations. The survey was taken for all languages, but applies, obviously to Latin American translations. Out of some 200, 130 replied, the "positive responses far outnumbering the few discouraging words." Even better, "to our surprise the vast majority of editors even extended a welcome to previously unpublished translators and authors." This should be good news for everyone.

6674 Adams, Robert Martin. Proteus, his lies, his truth: discussions of literary translation. New York: Norton, 1973. 192 p.; bibl.

Written by a comparatist and translator, this book takes as its major goal the desire "to make its readers conscious of the many ways in which a translation can succeed or fail, alert to the many different levels of equivalence." We see here the beginning of a realization that criticism is translation: "A good deal of modern criticism, when we think of it, takes the form of paraphrase, which is intralingual translation of a special sort." As usual, Spanish language authors and examples are at a minimum—García Lorca, Cervantes, Borges, Góngora—but the author devotes a few words to a Belitt translation of a Neruda ode. Witty and interesting study.

6675 Congrat-Butlar, Stefan. Translation & translators: an international directory and guide. New York: R.R. Bowker Co., 1979. 241 p.; index.

In the words of its editor, this volume is intended for the use of "1) editors and publishers; 2) college, university, and special libraries; 3) teachers and students of translation and interpretation; 4) the growing number of international organizations, governmental and intergovernmental agencies, and commercial and industrial enterprises that employ translators and/or interpreters on their staff, or who use their services regularly on a free-lance basis." A landmark volume listing associations, center, awards, fellowships, grants, prizes, guidelines, codes of practice, model contracts, copyright, legislation, journals, books, recent history and breakthroughs, register of translators and interpreters, training and access to the profession, translators' and interpreters' market place.

6676 Felstiner, John. Translating Pablo Neruda's "Galope Muerto" (PMLA, 93:2, March 1978, p. 185–195)

Felstiner says that "no other poem by Neruda has elicited the fascinated uncertainty" of this work. Preceding his comments on the translation process (his translation and the original are reproduced), he situates the poem in the social and poetic development of the poet. The author finds that a reading of the poem is facilitated through an analysis of its *como* (simile) and *-ando* structures: "Nouns normally serve to identify things in space, verbs to release them in time." "Galope Muerto" does both at once, "bears the brunt of things in flux, yet holds them up to be perceived." He ends with a discussion of Neruda's earlier writings as contrasted to the later socially motivated poetry, and finds them not so different.

6677 Freudenthal, Juan R. and **Patricia M. Freudenthal.** Index to anthologies of Latin American literature in English translation. Boston: G.K. Hall, 1977. 199 p.; bibl.; indexes.

The purpose of this *Index* "is to provide access to 116 anthologies of Latin American literature in translation while identifying 1122 Spanish-American and Brazilian authors representing 20 nations." The anthologies are listed alphabetically; there are, in addition, lists of authors, translators (some 415), and a geographic index. Brief introduction on Latin American literature. A bibliography of further readings on history, essay, and criticism is included. Very valuable. For another comment on this work, see *HLAS 41:110*.

6678 *Index Translationum.* UNESCO, International Institute of Intellectual Cooperation. No. 28, 1979– . Geneva.

This index is an annual bibliographical catalogue. No. 28, this issue, catalogues: "47, 232 translated books published in 1975 in 67 Member States [of the UN] and one non-member state, and includes a relatively small number of translations published in earlier years not previously listed in the *Index.*" The entries are listed by "principal author." Strangely, since the index is devoted to translated works, there is no bibliography of translators. This is still a valuable source book, especially for those works translated into languages *other than* English.

6679 Latin American fiction and poetry in translation. Compiled by Suzanne Jill Levine. New York: Center for Inter-American Relations, 1970. 72 p.

One of the first valuable resource tools for translations of Latin American literature, more recently superseded by Bradley A. Shaw's two compilations (see item **6684**).

6680 Longland, Jean R. World world vast world of poetic translation (LARR, 12:1, 1977, p. 67–86, bibl.)

Synthesis of the working procedures and tenets of an established translator of medieval and 20th-century Portuguese. A series of illustrations of boners and of problems with possible solutions, for example, the growing acceptance of assonance as a poetic convention in English-language poetry. Her description of the poet's aim, a paraphrase of Pessoa: "The translator is a feigner./ So completely should he feign/ that the pain he truly suffers/ is never seen as pain."

6681 Paris, Jean. On translation (LALR, 3:5, Fall/Winter 1974, p. 63–78)

The article begins with a convincing analysis of the difficulties inherent in translating the word "translation" itself, which the author proposes derives from the fact that the English word is based on "two incompatible interpretations—*translatio/ traductio*—corresponding to the two principles that Roman Jakobson detects as the root of any linguistic activity: *translatio* is the Latin word for "metaphor"/ *traductio* is the Latin word for "metonymy." Translation, therefore, is "ambiguous by necessity . . . because it encompasses the two basic operations of language itself." The author concludes that "it is impossible to translate into a foreign language," and illustrates his position with a brilliant reading of three translations of a Verlaine quatrain. To offset his thesis that one structure totally excludes all others (reiterating the impossibility of translation), he offers the possibility that "translation may also be the only discipline which raises the ultimate question: what *is* poetry? what *is* a work of art?"

6682 Schulte, Rainer. The act of translation: from interpretation to interdisciplinary thinking (Translation Review [Richardson, Texas] 4, 1979, p. 3–8)

This article is an explication of how the process of translation can lead to an intensified interpretation of the literary text and how it encourages interdisciplinary thinking. Schulte suggests that recent literary criticism has "increased the distance between reader and text to the extent that the scholar/critic reverses the function he was supposed to perform." He suggests that the critic might profit from approaching a text from the perspective of the translator. And as translation is a decision-making process, a problem-solving activity, he believes that the skills of translation may be applied to the interaction necessary in an interdisciplinary situation. See also the article "Translation: an Interpretive Act through Visualization" in a special translation issue of *Pacific Quarterly Moana* (5:1, Jan. 1980).

6683 A selective bibliography of bibliographies of Hispanic American literature. 2. ed. greatly expanded and rev. Edited by Shasta U. Bryant. Austin: Institute of Latin American Studies, University of Texas Press, 1976. 100 p. (Guides and bibliographies series; 8)

The major purpose in this revised edition remains the same as for the first: "To provide a useful and specific tool for students of Hispanic American literature . . . , confined primarily to lists in which literature is paramount." The bibliographical entries are alphabetized by editor. The index contains both editor and subject listings. There is a large listing under translations. Very helpful.

6684 Shaw, Bradley A. Latin American literature in English, 1975–1978. New York: Center for Inter-American Relations, 1979. 23 p.

A bibliography comprising a "comprehensive list of United States and, to some extent, British books which include Spanish American and Brazilian fiction, poetry, drama, or the literary essay in English translation." Extremely valuable source book. This is an update of the more extensive *Latin American literature in English translation: an annotated bibliography* (New York University Press, 1976). For bibliographer's comment see *HLAS 41:47*.

6685 Steiner, George. After Babel: aspects of language and translation. London: Oxford University Press, 1975. 507 p.; bibl.; index; plate: 1 col. ill.

By any accounting, one of the major studies of translation, "the first systematic investigation of the phenomenology and processes of translation inside language and between language since the eighteenth century." Modern man feels a great nostalgia for the time before Babel when "words and objects dovetailed perfectly." Babel was "a second fall," and we have been struggling with the problems of communication ever since. Hence translators are "men groping towards each other in a common mist." But the translator may tread more closely than any other writer to the original and long-for-*Ur-Sprache*. A translation "will show the lineaments of that 'pure speech' which precedes and underlies both languages. A genuine translation evokes the shadowy yet unmistakable contours of the coherent design from which, after Babel, the jagged fragments of human speech broke off." A Bible for any translator.

6686 Suárez-Murías, Marguerite C. Interdisciplinary credit in the humanities: black literature in Latin America in translation (LALR, 4:7, Fall/Winter 1975, p. 49–56)

This article examines methods for designing a course in black literature drawn from the French, Portuguese, and Spanish-speaking cultures of Latin America. Specific issues considered are: 1) the subject of ethnicity; 2) the pedagogic approach to the course; 3) the benefits derived from the course; 4) pitfalls to be avoided; and 5) the practical aspects of putting the course into effect within an academic budget. An intelligent appraisal of possibilities, but what one misses is a trial syllabus.

6687 *Sur.* Revista semestral. Nos. 338/339, enero/dic. 1976– . Buenos Aires.

Edited by Victoria Ocampo, this issue is devoted to the topic "Problemas de la Traducción" and consists of pieces originally published in *The world of translation* and reproduced here in Spanish. The most notable one is probably Borges' "Las Versiones Homéricas" (p. 110–115) the source of his often quoted statement on translation: "Ningún problema tan consustancial con las letras y con su modesto misterio como el que propone una traducción." Less known, but equally interesting, is the comment on the "superstition" of the inferiority of translations: "Presuponer que toda recombinación de elementos es obligatoriamente inferior a su original, es presuponer que el borrador 9 es obligatoriamente inferior al borrador H—ya que no puede haber sino borradores. El concepto de *texto definitivo* no corresponde sino a la religión o al cansancio." In her introductory comments, Ocampo credits Jaime Rest with the selection and translation of the pieces in this edition.

6688 Tate, Allen. The translation of poetry. Address and panel discussion presented at the International Poetry Festival held at the Library of Congress April 13–15,

1970. Washington: Library of Congress *by the* Clarke Whittall Poetry and Literature Fund, 1972. 40 p.

The panel consisted of noted poets and translators, William Jay Smith, Louis Untermeyer, Tate, Zulfikar Ghose, Gerge Gavronsky, Miller Williams, Yehuda Amichai, Donald Finkel, Harold P. Wright, and John Malcolm Brinnin. Their opinions reflect the usual span of positions—from poetry can, to poetry cannot, be translated. Interesting comments by extremely talented artists.

6689 Wilgus, Alva Curtis. Latin America, Spain and Portugal: a selected and annotated bibliographical guide to books published in the United States, 1954–1974. Metuchen, N.J.: Scarecrow Press, 1977. 910 p.; index.

A bibliography of paperback editions. Literature is not listed separately, but is extensively covered in the subject index. The bibliography is divided into three sections: 1) Latin America; 2) Spain and Portugal; and 3) Dictionaries, Grammars, Readers, and Textbooks. Translations may be found by consulting the entries for the primary author. Translators are indicated in the entries, but there is no separate bibliography of translators.

6690 Woodbridge, Hensley. C. A bibliography of Brazilian poetry in English translation: 1965–1977 (UW/LBR, 15, Summer 1978, p. 161–188)

A very useful bibliography, prepared in two parts, one in the form of a supplement added in late 1977 after the editor was able to consult the Borzoi Anthology (see item **6615**) and acquire further information through individual translators. The list of anthologies consulted is in itself a helpful source. It is not surprising to find that Carlos Drummond de Andrade is the most widely translated of contemporary Brazilian poets.

JOURNAL ABBREVIATIONS LITERATURE

A Abside. Revista de cultura mexicana. México.

AAFH/TAM The Americas. A quarterly publication of inter-American cultural history. Academy of American Franciscan History. Washington.

AATSP/H Hispania. American Association of Teachers of Spanish and Portuguese. Univ. of Cincinnati. Cincinnati, Ohio.

AFH Archivum Franciscanum Historicum. Firenze, Italy.

ANLE/G Boletín de la Academia Norteamericana de la Lengua Española. New York.

AR Areito. Areíto, Inc. New York.

ARBOR Arbor. Madrid.

ASB/PP Philologica Pragensia. Academia Scientiarum Bohemoslovenica. Praha.

AU/P Phylon. Atlanta Univ. Atlanta, Ga.

BEPB Bulletin des Études Portugaises et Bresiliennes. Institut Français de Lisbonne *avec la collaboration de* Etablissements Français d'Enseignement Supérieur, Instituto de Alta Cultura, et du Departamento Cultural do Itamarati. Lisbon.

BNJM/R Revista de la Biblioteca Nacional José Martí. La Habana.

BRP Beitrâge zur Romanischen Philologie. Rûtten & Loening. Berlin.

CAM Cuadernos Americanos. México.

CDLA Casa de las Américas. Instituto Cubano del Libro. La Habana.

CH Cuadernos Hispanoamericanos. Instituto de Cultura Hispánica. Madrid.

CM/D Diálogos. Artes/Letras/Ciencias Humanas. El Colegio de México. México.

CM/NRFH Nueva Revista de Filología Hispánica. El Colegio de México [and] the Univ. of Texas. México.

CONAC/RNC Revista Nacional de Cultura. Consejo Nacional de Cultura. Caracas.

CU/D Diacritics. A review of contemporary criticism. Cornell Univ., Dept. of Romance Studies. Ithaca, N.Y.

EC/M Mapocho. Biblioteca Nacional, Extensión Cultural. Santiago.

ECO Eco. Librería Bucholz. Bogotá.

EME Revista Eme-Eme. Estudios dominicanos. Univ. Católica Madre y Maestra. Santiago de los Caballeros, R.D.

FENIX Fénix. Biblioteca Nacional. Lima.

FIU/CR Caribbean Review. Florida International Univ., Office of Academic Affairs. Miami.

HISP Hispanófila. Univ. of North Carolina. Chapel Hill.

HISPA Hispamérica. Revista de literatura. Takoma Park, Md.

HIUS/R Revista Hispánica Moderna. Columbia Univ., Hispanic Institute in the United States. New York.

HR Hispanic Review. A quarterly devoted to research in the Hispanic languages and literatures. Univ. of Pennsylvania, Dept. of Romance Languages. Philadelphia.

HU Hojas Universitarias. Revista de la Fundación Univ. Central. Bogotá.

IA/ZK Zeitschrift für Kulturaustausch. Institut für Auslandsbeziehungen. Berlin, FRG.

IAA Ibero-Amerikanisches Archiv. Ibero-Amerikanisches Institut. Berlin, FRG.

ICC/T Thesaurus. Boletín del Instituto Caro y Cuervo. Bogotá.

ICP/R Revista del Instituto de Cultura Puertorriqueña. San Juan.

IFH/C Conjonction. Institut Français d'Haïti. Port-au-Prince.

IGFO/RI Revista de Indias. Instituto Gonzalo Fernández de Oviedo [and] Consejo Superior de Investigaciones Científicas. Madrid.

IILI/RI Revista Iberoamericana. Instituto Internacional de Literatura Iberoamericana. *Patrocinada por la* Univ. de Pittsburgh. Pittsburgh, Pa.

IJZ/H Hispania. Revista española de historia. Instituto Jerónimo Zurita, Consejo Superior de Investigaciones Científicas. Madrid.

IL Ideologies & Literature. A journal of Hispanic and Luso-Brazilian Literatures. Univ. of Minnesota, Institute for the Study of Ideologies and Literature. Minneapolis.

INDEX Index on Censorship. Writers & Scholars International. London.

INSULA Insula. Madrid.

INTI Inti. Univ. of Connecticut, Dept. of Romance Languages. Storrs.

JSSTC Journal of Spanish Studies: Twentieth Century. Kansas State Univ., Dept. of Modern Languages. Manhattan.

LALR Latin American Literary Review. Carnegie-Mellon Univ., Dept. of Modern Languages. Pittsburgh, Pa.

LAP Latin American Perspectives. Univ. of California. Riverside.

LARR Latin American Research Review. Univ. of North Carolina Press *for the* Latin American Studies Association. Chapel Hill.

LNB/L Lotería. Lotería Nacional de Beneficencia. Panamá.

MLN Modern Language Notes. Johns Hopkins Press. Baltimore, Md.

NR Die Neue Rundschau. S. Fischer Verlag. Frankfurt.

NS NS NorthSouth NordSud NorteSur NorteSul. Canadian Journal of Latin American studies. Canadian Association of Latin American Studies. Univ. of Ottawa.

PMLA Publications of the Modern Language Association of America. New York.

PUC/V Veritas. Revista. Pontifícia Univ. Católica do Rio Grande do Sul. Porto Alegre, Brazil.

QIA Quaderni Ibero-Americani. Associazione per i Rapporti Culturali con la Spagna, il Portogallo e l'America Latina. Torino, Italy.

RCLL Revista de Crítica Literaria Latinoamericana. Latinoamericana Editores. Lima.

REVIEW Review. Center for Inter-American Relations. New York.

RIB Revista Interamericana de Bibliografía [Inter-American Review of Bibliography]. Organization of American States. Washington.

UA/REH Revista de Estudios Hispánicos. Univ. of Alabama, Dept. of Romance Languages, Office of International Studies and Programs. University.

UA/U Universidad. Univ. de Antioquia. Medellín, Colombia.

UAEM/H Histórica. Univ. Autónoma del Estado de México, Instituto de Investigaciones Históricas. México.

UBN/R Revista de la Biblioteca Nacional. Ministerio de Educación y Cultura. Montevideo.

UC/A Anales de la Universidad de Cuenca. Cuenca, Ecuador.

UCLA/JLAL Journal of Latin American Lore. Univ. of California, Latin American Center. Los Angeles.

UCLV/I Islas. Univ. Central de las Villas. Santa Clara, Cuba.

UCNSA/EP Estudios Paraguayos. Univ. Católica Nuestra Señora de la Asunción. Asunción.

UCV/E Escritura. Teoría y crítica literaria. Univ. Central de Venezuela, Escuela de Letras. Caracas.

UFP/EB Estudos Brasileiros. Univ. Federal do Paraná, Setor de Ciências Humanas, Centro de Estudos Brasileiros. Curitiba, Brazil.

UH/RJ Romanistisches Jahrbuch. Univ. Hamburg, Romanisches Seminar, Ibero-Amerikanisches Forschungsinstitut. Hamburg, FRG.

UH/U Universidad de La Habana. La Habana.

UIA/C Comunidad. Revista de la U.I.A. Cuadernos de difusión cultural. Univ. Iberoamericana. México.

UK/KRQ Kentucky Romance Quarterly. Univ. of Kentucky. Lexington.

UK/LATR Latin American Theatre Review. A journal devoted to the theatre and drama of Spanish and Portuguese America. Univ. of Kansas, Center of Latin American Studies. Lawrence.

UNAM/AL Anuario de Letras. Univ. Nacional Autónoma de México, Facultad de Filosofía y Letras. México.

UNAM/RMS Revista Mexicana de Sociología. Univ. Nacional Autónoma de México, Instituto de Investigaciones Sociales. México.

UNAM/RUM Revista de la Universidad de México. México.

UNION Unión. Unión de Escritores y Artistas de Cuba. La Habana.

UNMSM/L Letras. Univ. Nacional Mayor de San Marcos. Lima.

URSS/AL América Latina. Academia de Ciencias de la URSS [Unión de Repúblicas Soviéticas Socialistas]. Moscú.

USP/LL Língua e Literatura. Univ. de São Paulo, Depto. de Letras, Faculdade de Filosofia, Letras e Ciêncas Humanas. São Paulo.

USP/RH Revista de História. Univ. de São Paulo, Faculdade de Filosofia, Ciências e Letras, Depto. de História [and] Sociedade de Estudos Históricos. São Paulo.

UTIEH/C Caravelle. Cahiers du monde hispanique et luso-brésilien. Univ. de Toulouse, Institut de'Études Hispaniques, Hispano-Americaines et Luso-Brésiliennes. Toulouse, France.

UV/PH La Palabra y el Hombre. Univ. Veracruzana. Xalapa, Mexico.

UW/LBR Luso-Brazilian Review. Univ. of Wisconsin Press. Madison.

VIA Via. A new literary magazine. Univ. of California, Office of Student Activities. Berkeley.

VOZES Vozes. Revista de Cultura. Editora Vozes. Petrópolis, Brazil.

MUSIC

ROBERT STEVENSON, *Professor of Music, University of California, Los Angeles*

IN 1979, AFTER A LAPSE OF SEVEN YEARS since volume 18 in 1972, the General Secretariat of the Organization of American States sponsored publication of volume 19, in the invaluable *Compositores de América* series (see item **7011**). So far as distribution by nation goes, the total of 322 composers covered by the series from its inception in 1955 includes: 32 Argentines, 23 Brazilians, 20 Venezuelans, 19 Chileans, 18 Uruguayans, 14 Mexicans, 13 Colombians, and 13 Peruvians. Other Latin American nations have each six or less entries. This series gives the United States 104 entries and Canada 39 against a total of 179 for all other Western Hemisphere countries combined. In order to redress the imbalance, the Brazilian Ministério das Relações Exteriores, Departamento de Cooperação Cultural, Científica e Tecnológica sponsored publication (1975–78) of a *Compositores Brasileiros* series comprising 34 printed oblong catalogs of which the one devoted to such a prolific composer as Camargo Guarnieri (item **7042**) runs 82 p. Moreover, the updated mimeographed catalog of Marlos Nobre's works, fleshed out with discography and criticisms was received at the Library of Congress in April 1979 and consists of 106 p. (item **7060**).

Brazil became the Latin American nation best covered lexicographically with the publication in 1977 of the excellent two-volume *Enciclopédia da música brasileira: erudita, folclórica e popular* (item **7048**, not in the Library of Congress holdings at press time). Outdistancing so valuable a work as Rodolfo Arizaga's *Enciclopedia de la música Argentina* (371 p., see *HLAS 36:4520*), the Brazilian lexicon (1190 p.) covers new territory by including numerous articles on reigning pop stars and some exceptionally useful appendixes. Foreigners may balk at Vila-Lobos, Novais, and Matos, not to mention the inconsistent handling of Luiz Heitor Corrêa de Azevedo's name in main-entry series (under Heitor) and at the rear of vol. 2. Occasionally, pre-1875 figures tend to pale, are inadvertently omitted or reported with errors of detail. Nonetheless, the only criticism one could raise is the lack of bibliographies following individual entries in an otherwise epoch-making encyclopedia.

The most luxurious general encyclopedia published to date in a Latin American country may well be the *Enciclopedia de México* (see *HLAS 38*, p. 544). Vols. 10 through 11, published in 1977, complete the set and contain articles of varying merit on: Aniceto Ortego (1825–75); Cenobio Paniagua Vásquez (1821–82); Angela Peralta (1845–83); Manuel M. Ponce (1886–1948); Silvestre Revueltas (1899–1940); José Rolón (1883–1945); Jesús C. Romero (1893–1958); Juventino Rosas (1868–94); Luis Sandi Meneses (1905–); Rafael J. Tello (1872–1946); and Felipe Villanueva (1862–1893). However, more precise and penetrating articles on Mexican 19th-century worthies are those by Jorge Velazco, the multifaceted Mexican Leonard Bernstein of the 1970s (see items **7148–7154** published in *Diorama*, Sunday cultural supplement to *Excelsior*).

The United States encyclopedia of the 1970s that did most handsomely by Latin Americans was Nicolas Stonimsky's revision of *Baker's Biographical Dictionary of Musicians* (6. ed., N.Y.: Schirmer Books-Macmillan, 1978). The extent of coverage is exemplified by the number of Latin Americans listed in the first letter of the alphabet: José Antonio Abreu (Venezuela, 1939); [Lan Adomian], Miguel Aguilar-Ahumada (Chile, 1931–); Pedro Humberto Allende Sarón (1885–1959); Renato Almeida, Carlos Roque Alsina (Argentina, 1941–); Luigi Alva (Peru, 1927–); Alberto Alvarado (Mexico, 1864–1939); René Amengual (Chile, 1911–54); Mário de Andrade, Rafael Aponte-Ledée (Puerto Rico, 1938–); José Ardévol (Cuba, 1911–); Rodolfo Arizaga (Argentina, 1926–); Claudio Arrau, Vicente Ascone (Uruguay, 1897–); José Vicente Asuar (Chile, 1933–); Daniel Ayala (Mexico, 1906–75); and Lauro Ayestarán (Uruguay, 1913–66).

The esteem accorded Latin American music in Germany reached a new high in the final supplementary volume to the behemoth *Die Musik in Geschichte und Gegenwart* (Kassel, Bärenreiter, 1979). The Brazilian authority, long resident in Paris, Luiz Heitor Corrêa de Azevedo, provided articles on: Luciano Gallet (1893–1931); Hans Joachim Koellreuther (1915–); José Angel Lamas (1775–1814); Leopoldo Américo Miguéz (1850–1902); Juan Manuel Olivares (1760–97); Juan Paris (1750–1845); Celestino Piaggio (1886–1931); Juan Bautista Plaza (1898–1965); Nicolas Ruiz Espadero (1832–90); Esteban Salas y Castro (1725–1803); Manuel Saumell Robredo (1817–70); and on the city of Rio de Janeiro. Malena Kuss contributed articles on Alfonso de Elías; his son Manuel Jorge de Elías; and on Julio Fonseca. Robert Stevenson wrote on Gutierre Fernández Hidalgo; Fernando = Hernando Franco; Blas Galindo Dimas; Roberto García Morillo; Celso Garrido-Lecca; Francisco López Capillas; Vicente Teodulo Mendoza; Melesio Morales; José de Orejón y Aparicio; Antonio de Salazar; Francisco Manuel da Silva; and on the musical histories of the cities of Guatemala, Lima, and Mexico.

Two welcome publications are the lavishly illustrated catalog of the Pedro Travesari instrument collection owned by the Casa de la Cultura Ecuatoriana and published in 1979 by Yale University Press and the OAS (item **7125**) and the bulky catalog of instruments (mostly aerophones) in popular use throughout Peru and published in 1978 by Peru's Instituto Nacional de Cultura (item **7156**).

The outstanding ethnomusicological volume published in the biennium is Isabel Aretz's doctoral dissertation (item **7015**). Francisco Curt Lange's first tome of a projected 10 on the mulatto composers of Minas Gerais covers their activities in the late colonial period and reveals the unique mastery of a lifetime (item **7055**). The fitting swan song of the notable Chilean historian Eugenio Pereira Salas (1904–79) is his fastidiously annotated bibliography of Chilean music and music literature from its origins to the late 19th century (item **7103**).

The best single-volume introduction to the music of any single Latin American nation yet published is Samuel Claro Valdés' *Oyendo a Chile* (item **7100**), accompanied by a cassette of illustrative excerpts. Gerard Béhague's introduction to the art-music of the whole of Latin America brilliantly synthesizes previous literature, while at the same time adding important new dimensions to the 20th-century panorama (item **7002a**).

As for magazines: Esperanza Pulido's bimonthly *Heterofonía* (quarterly after 1979) took pride of place as the most lasting and highly regarded Mexican music periodical of the decade. The Cuban serial *Música*, published by Casa de las Américas at Havana, contained considerably less information, much of it either tendentious or reprinted from prior publications. Thanks to the vigilance and vision of

Luis Merino and Magdalena Vicuña, the primacy of *Revista Musical Chilena* as a thorough and scholarly journal continued unchallenged in the biennium. *Revista INIDEF* published at Caracas is a sumptuous vehicle for field trip reports, ethnomusicological and folklore summations, and even in one isolated instance for the republication of an 18th-century Peruvian cantata composed in honor of the Virgin of Copacabana (item **7155a**). In the US, *Inter-American Music Review* (Los Angeles) began in the fall of 1978 and *Latin American Music Review* (Austin, Texas) in the spring of 1980.

To conclude one should note an encouraging development: the publication of music as such (often an Archilles heel in Latin America) took a sharp turn for the better, not only in Venezuela but also in Mexico—where for the first time the vocal score of an entire opera was issued, José Pablo Moncayo's *La Mulata de Córdoba* (item **7138a**).

GENERAL

7001 América Latina en su música. Relatora: Isabel Aretz. Paris: Unesco, 1977. 344 p. (Serie América Latina en su cultura)

Of the 16 Latin Americans who contributed chapters to this fourth volume in the series sponsored by Unesco, *América Latina en su cultura*, three were born in Brazil, three in Cuba, two in Argentina, and one each in Chile, Colombia, Mexico, Panama, Uruguay, and Venezuela. Like this wide and careful spacing, the authors' views on the four large topics into which the book divides are equally dispersed: 1) "The Present Moment in Latin American Music;" 2) "Society and the Artist;" 3) "The Artist and His Medium;" and 4) "The Work of Art and Society." Juan Orrego-Salas' overview of recent musical creation and Roque Cordero's summary of festival repertories stimulate the reader's optimism. But exaltation seems premature after reading the gloomy final chapter by Walter Guido on the mutual ignorance that causes the music of any Latin American nation to be largely disregarded beyond its borders. The careful editing of this volume reflects favorably on Isabel Aretz de Ramón y Rivera, whose task it was to coordinate the bibliography, eliminate errors, and reduce duplications.

7002 Aretz de Ramón y Rivera, Isabel. Música y danza: América Latina continental, excepto Brasil (*in* Africa en América Latina. Relator: Manuel Moreno Fraginals. México: Siglo XXI Editores, 1977, p. 238–278 [El mundo en América Latina])

As early as 1563 large crowds of frenzied blacks, dancing to incessant drums, so impeded traffic in Lima that the town council restricted their dancing to Nicolás de Ribera Square and one other public plaza. For mutual assistance, colonial blacks joined confraternities under the patronage of a saint, who was often none other than the Christian equivalent of an African deity. In 1598 the Peruvian viceroy signed a royal order prohibiting any further drum dancing by black confraternities. In 1770 the viceroy at B.A. inveighed against lascivious black singing and dancing to drums. In 1816 the Montevideo chapter restricted "the dances called tangos (candombés) to late afternoons outside city walls." Continuing with cited documents, Aretz draws a hemispheric panorama from the earliest importation of blacks to the present. She classifies instruments of possible African derivation, transcribes six black examples recorded 1947 through 1968 in humid zones of countries with large numbers of blacks on the coast (Colombia, Ecuador, Honduras, Venezuela) and discusses such other issues as *negritos* (whites made up as blacks for Carnival events) and "blacks"—made up or real—in Spanish American theater. Drawing on a profusion of previously published monographs (including her husband's), she brilliantly handles a highly complex and entangling subject.

Aretz, Isabel and **Luis Felipe Ramón y Rivera.** Areas musicales de tradición oral en América Latina. See item **953**.

7002a Béhague, Gerard. Music in Latin America: an introduction. Englewood Cliffs, N.J.: Prentice-Hall, 1979. 369 p., map, music, plates.

Worthily capping many years, this text is dedicated to Gilbert Chase—the author originally commissioned to write it for the Prentice-Hall History of Music Series. Although lacking a master bibliography at the close, each of the 10 chapters closes with Bibliographical Notes certifying the author's profuse acquaintance with the literature published since Nicolas Slonimsky's *Music of Latin America*. Art-music, not folk or tribal, occupies him. In his format, Spanish-speaking America is perceived as a chronological continuum (in contrast with Slonimsky, who proceeded country-by-country). The 20th century (chaps. 5–10) obviously engrosses Béhague, at the expense of the 19th (chap. 4). No music book presently before the public excels Béhague's in placing contemporary Latin America on a par with contemporary Europe.

7003 Bensusan, Guy and **Charles R. Carlisle.** Raíces y ritmos/roots and rhythms: our heritage of Latin American music (LARR, 8:3, 1978, p. 155–160)

Outlines of 52 bilingual radio programs presenting and discussing the Latin American musical heritage over KCLS, Flagstaff, Ariz., during 1976. The knowledgeable and wide-ranging authors (Northern Arizona Univ. and North Texas State Univ.) developed this valuable series for the Flagstaff Centennial and Arizona Bicentennial celebrations.

Cáceres, Abraham. Preliminary comments on the marimba in the Américas. See item **958.**

7005 Ellmerich, Luís. História da música. Prefácio de Francisco Mignone. 4. ed., rev. e ampliada. São Paulo: Editora fermata do Brasil, 1977. 364 p., bibl., plates.

In this omnigatherum, the chronological gives way to the topical. Brazil is well represented with annotated lists of composers, lists of operas, lists of instrument makers, and stories of operas. Other Latin American nations fare badly, especially in comparison with the fulsome treatment of the United States. Although containing a few rudimentary musical notations, the book foregoes musical analysis or any delving into stylistic problems.

7006 Festival folklórico hispanoamericano. Excmo. Ayuntamiento de Madrid, Instituto de Cultura Hispánica, Centro Cultural Villa de Madrid, 16 mayo–12 junio 1977. Madrid: Instituto de Cultura Hispánica, 1977. 20 p., illus.

Colombia, Dominican Republic, Guatemala, Panama, Philippines, Puerto Rico, US, and Venezuela sent dancers to participate in a folklore festival held May/June 1977. This handsome program booklet lists the dances, dancers, musicians, and in several instances explains the dances.

Grebe, María Ester. Objeto, métodos y técnicas de investigación en etnomusicología. See item **977.**

7007 Lange, Francisco Curt. Charles Seeger and *Americanismo Musical* (IAMR, 1:2, Spring/Summer 1979, p. 245–251)

Although not mentioned in the obituaries of *The New York Times* and *Musical Quarterly*, Charles Seeger's dozen years (1941–53) as music chief of the Pan American Union (after 1948, Organization of American States) deserves remembrance.

7008 ———. Una nueva revista: un nuevo vocero musical de las Américas (HET, 12:2, marzo/abril 1979, p. 4–6)

Background of the founding of the *Inter-American Music Review* (Fall 1978).

7009 Marco, Guy A. Information on music: a handbook of reference sources in European languages. With the assistance of Sharon Paugh Ferris and Ann M. Garfield. v. 2, The Americas. Littleton, Colo.: Libraries Unlimited, 1977. 296 p., bibl.

Latin America occupies items 839–1332 (p. 94–210) in this valuable annotated bibliography. Organized alphabetically by countries (including Spanish- and Portuguese-speaking nations as well as Barbados, Guyana, Surinam, Trinidad-and-Tobago), this 494-item listing usefully updates Gilbert Chase's 1962 *A guide to the music of Latin America*. Includes dissertations, with appropriate reference to *Dissertation Abstracts*. Garfield's selectivity omits various worthwhile titles but prevents the lists from becoming cluttered with Chase's frequently inconsequential entries. Her breakdowns under "The Language of Music," "Direct Information Sources," "Biographical Sources," "Lists of Music," and "Discographies" (with their many subheadings), run the danger of unrealistic, overly precise schematization.

7010 Merino, Luis. Una nueva Revista de Musicología Latinoamericana (UCIEM/R, 33:146/147, abril/sept. 1979, p. 126–128)

Summarizing the contents of *Inter-American Music Review* inaugural issue, Merino comments on articles about music in Caracas and San Juan, P.R., cathedrals.

7011 Organization of American States. Secretaría General. Unidad Técnica de la Música. Compositores de América: datos biográficos y catálogos de sus obras (Composers of the Americas: biographical data and catalogs of their works). v. 19. Washington: 1979. 145 p., illus., music.

No. 19 in the series inaugurated by Guillermo Espinosa in 1955, this volume catalogs the works of 16 composers, of whom four are credited to Brazil (João Souza Lima, Gilberto Mendes, Willy Corrêa de Oliveira, Olivier Toni); one to Chile (Alfonso Montecino); two to Colombia (Blas Emilio Atehortúa, Francisco Zumaque Gómez); one to Costa Rica (Benjamín Gutiérrez); two to Dominican Republic (Margarita Luna, Manuel Simó); one to Mexico (Mario Kuri-Aldana); two to Puerto Rico (Héctor Campos-Parsi, Jack Delano); two to US (William Kraft, John E. Price); and one to Uruguay (José Serebrier). Efraín Paesky, chief of the Technical Unit, wrote the introduction.

Palarea, Alvaro Fernaud. Comportamiento musical, educación musical y folklore en América Latina. See *HLAS 40:9014*.

7012 Ramón y Rivera, Luis Felipe. Para una revisión de la terminología usada en la etnomúsica (MHD/B, 7, 1976, p. 123–127)

The eminent Venezuelan ethnomusicologist eloquently argues for the use of the Spanish equivalent of Afro-American instead of terms such as Negro or Blacks. He deprecates such terms as *Música negra, blanca, mestiza, mulata*. However, *criollo* remains a valid category capable of competing with *folklórico*.

7013 Stevenson, Robert. Visión musical norteamericana de las otras Américas hacia 1900 (UCIEM/R, 31:137, enero/marzo 1977, p. 5–35, music)

Latin American musical impact in the US during the 19th century.

7014 Tekiner, Roselle. The evidence of the panpipe for prehistoric Trans-Pacific contact (MVW/AV, 31, 1977, p. 7–132, bibl., illus., maps, tables)

The outgrowth of a dissertation done at CUNY under Paul Tolstoy's direction, this definitive analysis of about 70 panpipes in 20 US and European museums concludes with such useful dicta as these: "Therefore judged on its own merit, the similarity von Hornbostel discovered between panpipes of the Solomon Islands and the western Amazon cannot be interpreted either as resulting from direct contact between the two areas or the existence of a historical relationship between the panpipes" and "As far as is known, double row panpipes that are constructed to permit the simultaneous blowing of two notes that are an octave's distance apart, occur only in South America and in Melanesia. In Melanesia its distribution is restricted primarily to the Solomon Islands. It was a common feature of prehistoric Peruvian panpipes and temporal continuity in South America is suggested by its recent popularity in the central Andean highlands. A historical relationship between double row panpipes in Melanesia and South America is supported by its co-occurrence in both areas with features that are not known to exist in panpipes elsewhere in the world."

ARGENTINA

7015 Aretz de Ramón y Rivera, Isabel. Música tradicional de La Rioja. Caracas: Edición INIDEF (Instituto Internacional de Etnomusicología y Folklore), 1978. 612 p., illus., music, plates (Biblioteca INIDEF, 2)

Exhaustive study conducted on the highest level by the unique authority recognized as early as 1946 in *HLAS 12:3374*. The present monumental companion volume, ready for the press since 1967, worthily caps a lifetime of unmatched endeavor. Reviewed in *Inter-American Music Review* (1:2, Spring/Summer 1979, p. 236–237).

7016 Barcia, José. Tangos, tangueros y tangocosas. Buenos Aires: Editorial Plus Ultra, 1976. 266 p. (Temas Contemporáneos, 3)

An anthology of 59 newspaper pieces by a veteran journalist (b. B.A., 1911) who presently writes for *La Nación*.

7017 Bayardo, Lito. Mis 50 años con la música argentina. Buenos Aires: Ediciones Radio, 1976. 212 p., illus., plates.

Born at Rosario on 3 March 1905, the author was the first son of Manuel Reyes García and Luisa Ferrari, both of whom died at the age of 33. He made his way in the theatrical world with his stage name and became a leading light in the Argentine Society of Authors and Composers writing 604 songs (usually lyrics, sometimes with music) that are listed alphabetically by title (p. 199–212). These fall under such types as: "vals, ranchera, tango, cumbia, rumba, polca, milonga, and bailecito." His acquaintance with Gardel, Libertad Lamarque, and numerous other popular music personalities, provided him with numerous anecdotes that aroused reader interest.

7018 Cantón, Darío. Gardel: ¿a quién le cantás? Buenos Aires: Ediciones de la Flor, 1972. 219 p., tables.

Listed in *HLAS 31:8163* (1969), but not annotated, the introduction to the present volume originally appeared in the *Revista Latinoamericana de Sociología* (4:3, nov. 1968). The author, after analyzing 97 (not 99) representative tango lyrics from Gardel's recorded repertory, concluded that during the initial two decades of the sung tango 1918–30/35 (before 1918 tangos were instrumentals), the narrator was almost always a man complaining of his sad fate. Abandoned or betrayed by a fickle woman, he reflects on his haunts of yore. His mother, if mentioned, is a mere passive, long-suffering servant to his household needs. He never mentions the work by which he gains a livelihood, political or social movements, nor stable emotional relationships such as those engendered by family and religion. The tango lyrics analyzed are printed on p. 57–219. *Fumando espero* and *Mi vieja viola* (p. 119–120 and 154) were not recorded, composed, nor written by Gardel, and should not have been included.

7019 Carrizo, Juan Alfonso. Cantares tradicionales del Tucumán: antología de los cancioneros de Catamarca, Salta, Jujuy, Tucumán y La Rioja recogidos y anotados. Estudio preliminar por Alberto Rougés. Prólogo para la tercera edición por Bruno C. Jacovella. Tucumán, Arg.: Imprenta de la Univ. Nacional de Tucumán, 1974. 82 p., music.

El Tucumán in the title refers to the northern region that in colonial times included Jujuy, Salta, Tucumán, Catamarca, Santiago del Estero, La Rioja, and part of Córdoba. Texts and melodies of five romances, 37 romancillos and rimas infantiles, seven Christmas villancicos. The melodies consistently imply tonic-dominant-subdominant harmonies.

7020 Gobello, José and **Jorge Alberto Bossio.** Tangos, letras y letristas. Buenos Aires: Editorial Plus Ultra, 1975. 216 p.

Texts of 99 tangos grouped under 45 authors, with their brief biographies. Composers of each tango are named, but without biographies.

7021 Goldman, Albert. Tango's macho mystique (Esquire [New York] 89:5/6, March 1978, p. 80–81, illus.)

Ken Russell's five-million "graffito," *Valentino* (as *The New Yorker* called it in the issue of 7 Nov. 1977, p. 119), starred 39-year-old Nureyev playing the role of a much younger Rudolph Valentino (1895–1926). The film begins with distance shots of Valentino trying to teach the tango to Nijinsky (played by Anthony Dowell). Using this as gambit, Goldman apostrophizes the Argentine tango as "unquestionably the finest dance music that Latin America has ever produced . . . The greatest hero of the tango is Carlos Gardel (1887–1935) . . . whose 497 records and nine films are constantly being reissued or replayed." According to Goldman, the *idée fixe* endlessly repeated in every sung tango is that "the man has been betrayed by the woman." Irene and Vernon Castle (died 1918) bowdlerized the tango when introducing it to international café society around 1915.

7022 Guibert, Fernando. Los argentinos y el tango. Dibujos del autor. Buenos Aires: Ediciones Culturales Argentinas (ECA), Ministerio de Cultura y Educación, 1973. 226 p., illus., plates.

Mixed in with poems from his *Poeta al pie de Buenos Aires* (1953) and *Tango* (1962), the author summarizes scholarly literature by Vicente Rossi, Carlos Vega, Manuel Ricardo Trelles, and others. Although pleasant reading, the poems occupy more than half the book and sorely irritate the reader searching for facts.

7023 Guny Hernán Fierro, Ramón. Recuerdos del gaucho argentino. Tucumán,

Arg.: The Author, 1973. 48 p., illus., music.

Consists of 21 of the author's poems set by Gerónimo Ledesma (No. 9), Francisco Escaño (No. 5), Miguel L. Argañaraz (No. 4), Raúl Costa (No. 2), and Carlos Paliza (No. 1). The musical language is that of "composed folklore." Numerous copying errors mar the edition, an index is needed, and the author's autobiography fails to identify his collaborators sufficiently.

7024 Hidalgo, Ginamaría. Argentino, yo también soy argentina. Buenos Aires: Editorial Albatros, 1978. 150 p., plates.

Rambling anecdotes substitute for a solidly documented life in the autobiography of this pretty but now aging TV soprano named "Woman of the Musical Year" by the Argentine Institute of Public Opinion in 1972. She does not spare herself when she quotes B.A. criticism of her Teatro Colón recital in Dec. 1973 as an "artistic error."

7025 Martínez Moirón, Jesús. El mundo de los autores. Incluye la historia de S.A.D.A.I.C. Introduction by Alberto Francisco Sampedro. Buenos Aires: Sampedro, 1971. 595 p., facsims., plates.

Consists of a history of SADAIC, the Sociedad Argentina de Autores y Compositores de Música, created by presidential decree on 31 Jan. 1937 when the Asociación Argentina de Autores y Compositores de Música merged with the Círculo de Autores y Compositores de Música. The vast accumulation of data on popular music and composers is enriched by numerous photographs and facsimiles, but the lack of any index, even of names, prevents ready access to the documentation. The Society's president in 1971 was Ariel Ramírez, born at Santa Fe in 1921, president of Jujuy and Tucumán from 1941–43, thereafter with some exceptions of B.A., and composer of the *Misa Criolla* in 1964.

7026 Pampín, Manuel *ed.* La historia del tango. v. 1, Sus orígenes; v. 2, Primera época; v. 4, Epoca de oro; v. 5, El bandoneón; v. 6, Los años veinte; v. 8, El tango en el espectáculo. Buenos Aires: Ediciones Corregidor, 1977. 6 v. (144, 140, 135, 156, 163, 162 p.) illus., music, plates.

Vols. 3, 7, 9–10 were not available for review. In vol. 1, the first four chapters by Jorge B. Rivera provide a thumbnail social history of B.A. from 1850 to 1900, a necessary background. Chap. 2 by Blas Matamoro on musical origins summarizes Carlos Vega and Lauro Ayestarán. In the last two chapters, José Gobello traces the evolution of tango lyrics and the origin of the word "tango." In vol. 2, the authors trace the tango from 1880 to 1900 and discuss places where it was danced. The biographies of early tango composers are valuable. Like early jazz, the early tango flourished in bordellos—many of which are identified. In vol. 4 of this history series, the five leaders of tango ensembles discussed are Vicente Greco, Roberto Firpo, Francisco Canaro, Agustín Bardi, and Francisco Lomuto. Each essay outlines the leader's life and lists his musical credentials. But even with Bardi, whom Sierra designates as "el compositor de los músicos," no musical examples or analysis sustain Sierra's thesis. Vol. 5 describes how the first tango ensembles comprising violin, harp, and flute gave way to violin, guitar, and concertina (*bandoneón*), an instrument of German manufacture (1864–1949). From 1922 to 1930, the Alfred Arnold firm advertised it as "the only ideal instrument of the interpretation of the Argentine tango." In the 1920s, Enrique Pollet (1901–73); Pedro Laurenz (1902–72); Pedro Maffia (1900–67); and Luis Petrucelli (1903–41) were leading virtuosos of the instrument. In vol. 6, chap. 2 traces the history of the famous tango *La Cumparsita* first recorded in 1917, revived in 1924 with new lyrics by Enrique Maroni and Pascual Contursi, and the subject of a third round of litigation in 1942. Enrique Delfino, blind composer of music for 14 films and of numerous tango successes (d. 10 Jan. 1967), is the central theme of chaps. 3 and 4; Juan de Dios Filiberto and Eduardo Donato of chaps. 5 and 6. The period 1922–28, seen as an optimum period for the Argentine economy, here supplies the background for a fascinating panorama of popular music history. Vol. 8 notes how Gardel made his cinema début in *Flor de Durazno* (1917) and Libertad Lamarque in *Adiós, Argentina* (1930). The phenomenal success of *Tango* (1933) starring Azucena Maizani, evoked *Dancing* and *Idolos de la radio* (1934). Among retrospectives of the tango, *Mi noche triste* (1952); *Homero Manzi* (1964); *Discepolín* (1967); and *Quintero* (1970), appealed to nostalgia buffs.

7027 Pellettieri, Osvaldo. Tango (2) [i.e. dos]: Enrique Santos Discépolo, obra poética: un antecedente, Celonio Flores; un contemporáneo, Enrique Cadícamo. Buenos Aires: Todo es Historia, 1976. 141 p., bibl., illus. (Todo es historia, 8)

Discépolo (b. B.A., 27 March 1901 of Italian immigrant parents) conducted an orchestra that recorded for Pathé, acted in films, toured Europe (1935–36) and Central America (1945), and at his death (B.A., 23 Dec. 1951) left a legacy of lyrics to the most popular tangos of his epoch. In this valuable and well-organized book, his poetry is treated as literature that captured his nation's pulse. In order to situate him in his epoch, Pellettieri also studies tango lyricists Celedonio Flores and Enrique Cadícamo.

7028 Pérez Llana, Carlos; Jorge Fontenla; and **Pola Suárez Urtubey.** La música (*in* Pirovano, Ignacio and others. Arte y cultura en la Argentina. Buenos Aires: Editorial de Belgrano, 1977, p. 107–128)

Cast in the form of a dialogue with two respondents to queries by the host (an official of the Univ. de Belgrano) this wide-ranging survey embraces such diverse topics as how to distinguish classic from popular music, the appeal of Renaissance and Baroque music, Argentine schools of piano playing, prerequisites for a successful career, and the future for Argentine composers. In introducing the respondents, Pérez Llano identifies Fontenla (b. 7 Dec. 1927, B.A.) as composer, pianist, conductor, director of the Univ. of Cuyo (Mendoza) Orchestra in 1968, teacher at Escuela Superior de Música, B.A. (1971) and Suárez Urtubey. She graduated from the M. Gómez Carrillo Conservatory and as Licenciada (1965) and Doctor in Musicology (1972) from the Pontificia Univ. Católica Argentina. She is the author of *La música en revistas argentinas* (1970), *Alberto Ginastera en cinco movimientos* (Premio Municipal, 1973, essay category), and essays on the musical history of the Teatro Colón.

7029 Priore, Oscar del. El tango de Villoldo a Piazzolla. Buenos Aires: Crisis, 1975. 80 p., illus., plates (Cuadernos de Crisis, 13)

This pop history of the tango contains 88 illustrations ranging from sheet music covers to intimate photos of the stars who wrote the lyrics, sang and composed them. Between 1940–49 the singers Armando Moreno, Alberto Castillo, Angel Vargas, and Carlos Roldán made 129, 115, 106, and 105, tango recordings. Libertad Lamarque and Mercedes Simone made 74 and 27. To judge by number of recordings, the leading orchestras and ensembles were those led by Francisco Canaro (345), Juan D'Arienzo (232), Aníbal Troilo (189), and 10 more with 100 to 172 recordings.

7030 Puccia, Enrique Horacio. El Buenos Aires de Angel G. Villoldo, 1860 . . . 1919. Buenos Aires: Películas Impulso, 1976. 351 p., illus.

In this profusely illustrated panorama, Villoldo's career as the leading composer and author of tangos in his epoch is integrated with current events in B.A. In the preface José Gobello defends Puccia's accuracy, despite the lack of scholarly apparatus. The only music facsimile is an atypical fox-trot, *Atlántida*, composed the year before Villoldo died.

7031 Rossler, Osvaldo. Protagonistas del tango. Buenos Aires: Emecé Editores, 1974. 157 p.

Open letters, mostly adulatory, to nine lyricists, 11 singers, and six composers of tangos. The tribute to Gardel is a 29-line poem. Lacking hard kernels of fact, the incense offered on the altars of the 26 stars of tango has sociological value but is useless to an encyclopedist.

7032 Ruiz, Irma and **Néstor R. Ceñal.** Análisis musical del tango hasta 1920: sus estructuras más representativas (Ritmo [La Plata, Arg.] 5:6, 1977, p. 3–12, 17–18, music, plates)

Valuable analyses of E. Arolas' *Derecho viejo* (1917); M. Aróztequi's *El apache argentino* (1913); A. Bardi's *Lorenzo* (1916) and *Tinta verde* (1914); A. Bevilacqua's *Venus* (1902); F. Canaro's *Nobleza de arrabal* (1919); C. Posada's *Cordón de oro* (ca. 1915); and A. Villoldo's *El choclo* (1905).

Salmon, Russell O. The tango: its origins and meaning. See item **1029**.

7033 Serrano Redonnet, Ana. Pautas de la cultura argentina (*in* Cultura Nacional. Buenos Aires: Ediciones Crisol, 1976, p. 333–346)

Thumbnail sketch of Argentine musical history, lacking footnotes or bibliography.

7034 Suárez Urtubey, Pola. Carlos Vega: 1898–1966 (Ritmo [La Plata, Arg.] 5:6, 1977, p. 20–21, plate)

Although a famous fighter, Vega did not claim to be perfect. In a letter to the Arabist Julián Ribera y Tarragó dated 4 May 1932, Vega voiced qualms concerning his transcriptions of certain 17th-century vocal excerpts in the Fray Gregorio de Zuola Codex from Cuzco (now in B.A.'s Ricardo Rojas Museum). His bibliography of about 350 entries catalogued by Carmen García Muñoz still qualifies him as the giant of his generation.

7035 Vignati, María Emilia. La música étnica argentina (Ritmo [La Plata, Arg.] 5:5, 1975, p. 8–10, plates)

Although Col. Charles Wellington Furlong made the first recordings of aboriginal music in Argentina (*Tierra del Fuego*) in 1907 (18 years after recordings of aboriginal music began in the US) colonial missionary accounts, such as the illustrated *Hin und Her* by the Jesuit Florian Paucke, often provide remarkably full data.

BOLIVIA

7036 Limpias de Parada, Asunta. Vivencias: poesía y composiciones musicales. La Paz: Editorial Casa Municipal de la Cultura "Franz Tamayo," 1977. 308 p., illus., music notations.

The poet-composer (b. 11 April 1915, Trinidad) provides an anthology of 86 sensitive poems, 41 of which are preceded by her folkloric melodies. She classes the latter under such subheadings as *taquirari* (2/4), *polka* (3/4), *carnaval* (6/8), and *cueca* (6/8). Publication of this pleasant anthology was sponsored by the Alcalde Municipal of La Paz, Mario Mercado Vaca Guzmán. Bertha Alexander de Alvéstegui, Bolivian Directora General de Cultura, wrote the commendatory preface.

7037 Vásquez Messmer, Peter. Compositores bolivianos. La Paz: Escuela de Artes Gráficas Don Bosco, 1975. 96 p., illus., music, plates.

Brief, often impressionistic biographies of 10 composers from La Paz, two from Oruro, eight from Potosí, four from Cochabamba, three from Tarija, six from Sucre, three from Beni-Santa Cruz. No composers born before 1831 enter the scheme, with the result that many of Bolivia's best creators are omitted. Jaime Laredo, virtuoso violinist (b. 1941, p. 62), hardly rates as a composer. His contemporary Atiliano Auza León is omitted. The criteria for inclusion are not clear.

BRAZIL

7038 Almirante [*pseud. for* **Henrique Foreis**]. No tempo de Noel Rosa. 2. ed. Rio: Livraria Francisco Alves Editora, 1977. 229 p., bibl., plates.

Written under the pen name of Almirante, this life-and-works survey of the hero of samba Noel Rosa (1910–37), a native of the Federal District who died of tuberculosis aged only 27, lovingly retraces the history of urban popular music in this epoch. Contains composer's discography.

7039 Alves, Henrique L. Sua excia. o samba. 2. ed. rev., ampliada e fartamente ilustrada. São Paulo: Edições Símbolo, 1976, 174 p., bibl., illus.

This revised and amplified edition of a book that won the Carlos de Laet Prize in 1968 is the work of an author (b. 2 Jan. 1931, São Paulo), son of Vitautas and Brone Losinskas. After beginning his career as a translator of Polish works, he specialized in Afro-Brazilian sociology. Not musical analysis but a parade of personalities from Donga (Ernesto dos Santos) and Sinho (José Barbosa da Silva) to Chico Buarque de Hollanda comprises the core of the book. The illustrations include the author with Donga on the 50th anniversary of *Pelo telefone* and with Clementina de Jesus and Jair Rodrigues.

7040 Andrade, Mário de. O banquete. São Paulo: Livraria Duas Cidades, 1977. 163 p., bibl.

Death surprised Andrade (25 Feb. 1945) during his third year of writing musical criticism and chronicle for the *Folha da Manhã*. Left unfinished at his death was a serialized Platonic dialogue. In it, he used fictional Sarah Light to typify the international patron who neglects the national product, Félix de Cima to epitomize a self-made immigrant magnate interested in artists only as playthings, Siomara Ponga to represent the vain singer whose only repertory is chestnuts, and Janjão to represent the Brazilian composer's points of view. Chaps. 7 through 10 of the dialogue were never completed, despite having been carefully planned.

7041 Barros, Armando de Carvalho. A música: ambientes históricos, sua história geral em quadros rápidos, artes comparadas. Brasília: Instituto Nacional do Livro, 1973. 232 p., bibl.

Chaps. 35 through 39 of this general history treat of Brazilian musical history and folkmusic. Useful as a summary of basic facts.

7042 Brazil. Ministério das Relações Exteriores. Departamento de Cooperação Cultural, Científica e Tecnológica. Compositores brasileiros: catálogos de obras. Brasília: Fundação Visconde de Cabo Frio, 1975/1978. 35 v. (Unpaged) illus., music.

Consists of 35 unpaginated booklets ranging from five to 76 p. and including introductions in English, Spanish, and German. The composers whose works are impressively catalogued in these booklets are: Ernani Aguiar (jan. 1977, 9 p.); Armando Albuquerque (julho 1976, 20 p.); Heitor Alimonda (jan. 1977, 6 p.); Carlos Almeida (nov. 1976, 8 p.); Lycia De Biase Bidart (fev. 1978, 43 p.); Brenno Blauth (out. 1976, 14 p.); Lina Pires de Campos (nov. 1977, 11 p.); Lidembergue Cardoso (jan. 1976, 12 p.); Dinorá de Carvalho (março 1977, 30 p.); Sérgio O. de Vasconcellos Corrêa (set. 1976, 21 p.); Luís Ellmerich (nov. 1977, 13 p.); Eduardo Escalante (fev. 1978, 21 p.); Mario Ficarelli (maio 1976, 9 p.); Camargo Guarnieri (nov. 1977, 76 p.); Najla Jabôr (julho 1977, 27 p.); Bruno Kiefer (1975, 14 p.); Osvaldo Lacerda (abril 1976, 33 p.); João de Souza Lima (dez. 1976, 21 p.); Ernst Mahle (março 1976, 30 p.); Gilberto Mendes (junho 1976, 17 p.); Francisco Mignone (fev. 1978, 62 p.); Henrique de Curitiba Morozowicz (dez. 1977, 14 p.); Marlos Nobre (dez. 1977, 26 p.); A. Theodoro Nogueira (dez. 1977, 24 p.); Willy Corrêa de Oliveira (1975, 9 p.); José Penalva (fev. 1978, 26 p.); José Antonio Almeida Prado (out. 1976, 22 p.); Cláudio Santoro (abril 1977, 44 p.); Yves R. Schmidt (jan. 1977, 34 p.); Kilza Setti (dez. 1976, 11 p.); Adelaide Pereira da Silva (dez. 1977, 10 p.); Ricardo Tacuchian (dez. 1977, 24 p.); Emilio Terraza (agosto 1976, 8 p.); Luiz Carlos Lessa Vinholes (out. 1976, 5 p.); Ernst Widmer (dez. 1977, 34 p.). Each catalog begins with a one-page biography and portrait. Next comes a sample page from the composer's work. The catalogs proceed chronologically. Where the size of the total oeuvre justifies it, works are broken down under sections. For example, Mignone's output is subdivided as follows: canto e piano; coro a cappella; coro e instrumentos; piano; outros instrumentos solos; duo; trio; quarteto; quinteto; outros conjuntos; orquestra de cordas; orquestra; orquestra e instrumento solista; orquestra e voz solista; and orquestra, coro e solistas. The date of composition of each work is given. Next exact instrumentation is specified, duration is given in minutes and seconds, and the publisher is listed. The author of the text of a vocal work is identified, the date of premiere is stated, and the details of any recording are specified (with exact number of the disc). The composers' birth data include year and place, but not month and day. All six women (Bidart, Campos, Carvalho, Setti, Silva) except Jabôr permitted publication of their birth year. Birth years for the 28 men range from 1897 (Mignone) to 1950 (Aguiar). Styles of the men range from Mana-Zucca type to the most arcane eye-music. Except for Carlos Chávez, Alberto Ginastera, and a few National Prize Chilean composers, nothing as refined, precise or monumental has ever been published in Latin America as this nationally-sponsored series of catalogs. Every substantial Latin American library should acquire this set for its collection.

7043 Camêu, Helza. Introdução ao estudo da música indígena brasileira. Rio: Conselho Federal de Cultura, Departamento de Assuntos Culturais, 1977. 295 p., 67 p. (Musical supplement) bibl., music, plates.

This handsome and extremely ambitious treatise is the fruit of 42 years' research beginning in 1930 at the Museu Nacional de Rio, and continuing thereafter at the Museu do Indio. In 1962, the author published *Música indígena* (see *HLAS 27:1205*), dealing *inter alia* with tribal musics of the Kadiweu, Guaikuru, Urubu, and Kayowá. In that monograph, she concluded that Brazilian tribal musics varied greatly in beauty (*beleza*). Songs of the above named tribes, and especially of the Tembé (collected by Darcy Ribeiro in 1951), merited her approbation, in comparison with the "impoverished" music of the Borôro. In the present volume she again assembles travelers' reports on indigenous Brazilian music. These run the gamut from Jean de Léry's *Histoire d'un voyage* (1585 ed.) to Terence Turner's *Northern Cayapó music* (1963). In her zeal to endow Brazilian tribal musics with esthetic significance, she stresses the European repercussions of Léry's melodic transcriptions—without however animadverting on the uses of which Gabriel Sagard and Marin Mersenne put these melodies. She does signal Rousseau and Fétis, both of whom botched Léry. When seeking harmonic implications, she seems unaware that in 1632 Sagard already published harmonizations of the same melodies that three centuries later Villa-Lobos exploited in *Trois poèmes indiens* (Paris, 1929). The implications of archaeological instruments such as those found on Marajó island, escape her purview. Any future editions should include an analytical index. The hand drawn examples are too informally copied to suffice in a volume of this scientific scope. Given the geographical area and time span covered, Camêu deserves gold stars. Even so prolific a specialist as Frances Densmore never attempted to conjure both the history and ethnography of the entire US tribal output in a single tome.

7044 Carvalho, José Jorge de. La música de origen africano en Brasil (*in* Africa en América Latina. Relator: Manuel Moreno Fraginals. México: Siglo XXI Editores, 1977, p. 279–303 [El mundo en América Latina])

Author lists instruments (11 idiophones, 17 membranophones) evincing West or Central African influences or precedents. He laments the continuing authority of Luciano Gallet (1893–1931), Mário de Andrade (1893–1945) and Oneyda Alvarenga (b. 1911), whose generation-old writings are still accepted as schematizations of Afro-Brazilian music. Calls for new authoritative overviews exploiting the *vissungos* first collected as long ago as 1928 by Ayres de Mata Machado Filho, and discussed in *Music in the Americas* (Indiana Univ. Research Center in Anthropology, Folklore, and Linguistics, 1967), p. 64–67.

7045 Colás, Francisco Libânio. Marcha Fúnebre. No. 1. Transcribed and edited with a biobibliographical introduction by Jaime C. Diniz. Recife, Brazil: Edição do Coro Guararapes do Recife, 1979. 21 p., music.

Colás (b. Maranhão, 1827 or 1833) moved to Recife in the 1850s, and after taking a leading role in that city's musical life for three decades died there 9 Feb. 1885. Useful as a testimony to local composition, the present march is a soulful 79-measure A minor work nowadays performed at all Coro Guararapes orchestral concerts. Biographical data corrects *Enciclopédia da música brasileira* (1977).

7046 Corrêa de Azevedo, Luiz Heitor. Rio de Janeiro (MGG [Supplement] 16, 1979 [columns] 1562–1565, bibl.)

Valuable survey from the visit to the Rio vicinity written up by Jean de Léry (1578, numerous later editions) to 1978.

7047 Diniz, Jaime C. Um momento de nossa história musical (Boletim da Cidade do Recife [Prefeitura Municipal do Recife, Conselho Municipal de Cultura] 1, junho 1976, p. 69–76)

Euclides Fonseca (1854–1929) wrote four works for the lyric stage, two of which qualify as operas. The one-act *Leonor*, commissioned by the Club Carlos Gomes for first performance in the Teatro Santa Isabel of Recife (7 Sept. 1883) takes for its subject matter the same events of 1643 treated in Adolfo Maersch's *Marilia de Itamaraca* (1854). Leonor Coutinho (dramatic soprano), her brother Nuno (bass), and Antonio (tenor) are the three singing characters. The composer left an autobiography, thus far unedited, that supplied Diniz with numerous important biographical details. This fine essay by the paramount Brazilian musicologist usefully explores the late 19th century—one of the most fertile epochs in national music history.

7048 Enciclopédia da música brasileira: erudita, folclórica e popular. Edited by Marco Antônio Marcondes. São Paulo: Art Editora, 1977. 2 v. (1190 p.) (Continuous pagination) bibl.

Régis Duprat (b. 11 July 1930, Rio) coordinated the art music articles; Oneyda Alvarenga (b. 6 Dec. 1911, Varginha, Minas Gerais) the folkloric; and José Eduardo Homem de Melo the popular. Marco Antônio Marcondes was general editor of this notable encyclopedia enlisting a staff of 50. In addition to name-subject entries (not always alphabetized for the convenience of foreign users), the encyclopedia is enriched with eight appendixes (members of Academia

Brasileira de Música; LPs of art composers; list of Brazilian operas; musical periodicals; theaters in Brazil; alphabetized titles of all musical selections mentioned in the composer-interpreter entries; and general bibliography). Because of the heroic size of the accomplishment any fault-finding—always possible in discussing a work of this scope—smacks of ingratitude. Jaime Diniz's hand would have improved both colonial and 19th-century reportage. However, Lange's epoch-making contributions to Brazilian musical historiography are recognized. The chief strength of the encyclopedia which deserves praise is the generous coverage of current popular recording artists. If one generalized criticism must be offered: the individual articles lack bibliographies. Nor is this lack redeemed by a final general bibliography (28 p.) which consists mostly of window-dressing while omitting substantial titles. Nonetheless, this two-volume set is so important an achievement that no Latin American collection can afford to miss it.

7049 Fonseca, Carlos Alberto da. A arte da India no Brasil (USP/LL, 6, 1977, p. 43–49)

Unless four records of George Harrison—"Tomorrow Never Knows" and "Love to You" (1966), "Within You, Without You" (1967), and "The Inner Light" (1968)—are considered pathbreakers, Brazilian contact with the music of India began with three visits by Ravi Shankar. Eight discs by him are easily obtainable in Brazil. More authentic Indian music recordings do not circulate. Sonal Mansingh, female dancer and company, appeared at the Teatro Municipal in São Paulo (19–22 Nov. 1975) and also toured Rio, Salvador, Brasília, and Belo Horizonte. At São Paulo (Teatro Galpão) the male dancer Astad Deboo choreographed various Purana and Mahabharata sacred texts in kathakali style (10/12 June 1976).

7050 França, Eurico Nogueira. A evolução de Villa-Lobos na música de câmera. Rio: Ministério de Educação e Cultura, Departamento de Assuntos Culturais, Museu Villa-Lobos, 1976. 97 p., music.

Prize-winning analysis of 19 chamber works by a leading Brazilian musicologist. This monograph belongs to a series that when completed ought to be translated and published with a proper index. Includes frontispiece.

7051 Freed, Richard. Liner notes for Orquesta Sinfónica del Brasil. Washington: Organización de los Estados Americanos, Ediciones Interamericana de Música, Unidad Técnica de Música, 1978. 1 p., plate (Stereo OEA-002)

Background information on Marlos Nobre's *In Memoriam*; Heitor Villa-Lobos's *Bachianas Brasileiras No. 4* (orchestral transcription premiered 6 June 1942, NYC); and Cláudio Santoro's *Interacciones Asintóticas* (Spanish spellings prevail in this album). Isaac Karabtchevsky conducted the Orquestra Sinfónica do Brasil.

7052 Garcia, José Maurício Nunes. *Matinas do Natal* para coro, solitas, orquestra e orgão. Edited with bilingual preface by Cleofe Person de Mattos. Rio, FUNARTE (Fundação Nacional de Arte), Instituto Nacional de Música, MEC (Ministério de Educação e Cultura), 1978. 69 p., facsim., music, plate.

Handsome edition of 1799 Christmas mattins for Rio Cathedral, preceded by an illuminating foreword. Reviewed in *Inter-American Music Review* (1:2, Spring/Summer 1979, p. 239–240).

7053 Grebe, María Ester. Ukrinmakrinkrin (UCIEM/R, 33:148, oct./dic. 1979, p. 48–57, music)

Penetrating analysis of Marlos Nobre's 1964 three-movement chamber composition (dramatic soprano, piccolo, oboe, French horn, piano) setting texts in the Xucuru dialect. Dedicated by Recife-born Brazilian to Alberto Ginastera, this frequently performed youthful work was produced during Nobre's stay in B.A. on a fellowship at the Centro Latinoamericano de Altos Estudios Musicales.

Gullar, Ferreira [*pseud. for* **José Ribamar Ferreira**]. Poema sujo. See *HLAS 40:7529*.

7054 Kubik, Gerhard. Die "Brasilianische Sanza" in Museum für Völkerkunde, Wien (MVW/AV, 31, 1977, p. 1–5, bibl., illus.)

Johann Georg Schwarz, American consul in Vienna (1827–48) bequeathed a handsome *sanza* to the Vienna Museum für Kinst und Industrie that was described in Alfred Janata's 1961 *Aussereuropäische Musikinstrumente* under catalog-number 151 as a "sanza of Brazilian blacks." Kubik identifies it as having originated in the Loango coastal region of Africa and as being mislabeled in Janata's catalog, or as having been taken to Brazil from the Loango coast.

7055 Lange, Francisco Curt. História de música nas Irmandades de Vila Rica. v. 1, Freguesia de Nossa Senhora do Pilar do Ouro Preto: pt. 1. Belo Horizonte, Brazil: Arquivo Público Mineiro, Imprensa Oficial, 1979. 458 p. (Publicação, 2)

In this first of a projected 10-volume series, Lange embarks on a monumental exposé of documentation having to do with the Minas Gerais mulatto pleiad. Reviewed in *Inter-American Music Review* (1:2, Spring/Summer 1979, p. 240–241).

7056 ———. Pater José Maurício und Arno Philipp: Deutsch-brasilianischer Kulturaustausch zwischen Porto Alegre und Wien im Jahre 1900 (IHS/SJ, 21/22, 1973/1974, p. 113–128)

Robert Eitner's *Quellen-Lexikon* misattributed five violin concertos to José Maurício Nunes Garcia. Eitner first learned of the Brazilian composer from an article entitled "Ein brasilianischer Tonsetzer" by Arno Philipp published in the *Deutschen Kunst- und Musikzeitung* (17:1/3, 1900). In 1889, Philipp (b. Saxony) emigrated to Rio Grande do Sul where he became a prominent language teacher, translator, and journalist. In 1897, he founded the Club Haydn at Porto Alegre. Two years later this club sponsored first performance in Porto Alegre of Nunes Garcia's Requiem composed in 1816 (published at Rio by I. Bevilacqua & Co. in 1897). With his usual command of detail, Lange unravels the mystery of the Eitner misattribution, the pertinent facts of Philipp's biography, and the circumstances of the Porto Alegre premiere.

Lima, Jackson da Silva. O folclore em Sergipe. See item **1088**.

7057 Lody, Raul Giovanni da Motta. O som do Adjá. Salvador, Brazil: Departamento de Cultura da SMEC, Prefeitura Municipal de Salvador, 1975. 101 p., illus., music, plates.

In this popular account of two dozen African divinities whose cults flourish in Bahia, the author (who is both a journalist and folklorist) analyzes the functions and attributes of Exú, Ogun, Oxóssi, Omulú, and 20 other personages. Lacking footnotes or bibliography, the descriptions of the orixás are sufficiently succinct and vivid to attract a wide general readership. The section on candomblé music (p. 85–88) and the transcriptions that follow may not please a rigorous ethnomusicologist but will satisfy most tourists.

7058 Marconi, Marina de Andrade. Folclore do café. São Paulo: Secretaria da Cultura, Ciência e Tecnologia, Conselho Estadual de Cultura, 1976. 134 p., bibl., illus., musical notations, plates (Col. Folclore, 4)

To unify this collection of 27 major and four minor songs—all in 2/4 or 4/4 with two exceptions—the lyrics always mention coffee. The music is frequently repetitive; for instance, the tune for "São Sebastião" on p. 90 barred in 4/4, is practically identical with the tune for "São João Batista" on p. 94 barred in 2/4. C Major is the transcriber's favorite key (eight songs) but she also transcribes five in B Major. This monograph won the Premio Sílvio Romero, Instituto pela Campanha de Defesa do Folclore Brasileiro in 1966.

7059 Muniz Júnior, José. Do batuque à escola de samba. São Paulo: Ediçoes Símbolo, 1976. 207 p., bibl., illus.

The author (b. Penedo, Alagoas, 1933) grew up in Santos where he directed public relations for the "Escola de Samba X-9" (1954–74). Beginning in 1967 he wrote for the newspaper *Cidade de Santos (Folhas)* columns on samba, its history, propagators, and financiers. The present book is a journalist's attempt to codify and update samba history for the general reader. Costumes and personalities take precedence. Musical instruments are illustrated and explained but musical analysis is in short supply.

7060 Nobre, Marlos. Catálogo classificado cronológico: discografia, críticas. Rio: Ministério das Relações Exteriores, Departamento de Cooperação Cultural, Científica e Tecnológica, 1978? 1 v. (Various pagings)

Extension of Nobre's catalog published Dec. 1977 with one newer work, *Homenagem a Villa-Lobos* for guitar (p. 46, 1977); and adding to his discography *Quinteto de sopros* (Angel No. S3ARX 41). Also includes file of critical notices in Portuguese, Spanish, German, and English. No introductory biography.

7061 Nóbrega, Adhemar. Os choros de Villa-Lobos. Rio: Museu Villa-Lobos, Ministério de Educação e Cultura (MEC), Departamento de Assuntos Culturais, 1975. 138 p., facsims., music, table.

Authoritative musical analyses of 14 choros dated 1920–29 with many musical examples. Outside the cycle of 14, Villa-Lobos wrote also *Deux choros (bis)* for violin and cello (Paris, 1929) and an orchestral *Introdução aos Choros* (1929) premiered in 1944.

7062 Oliveira, José Zula de. Trilha folclórica de Guaraqueçaba (UFP/EB, 1:1, 1976, p. 137–153, music, plates)

Founded in 1838, Guaraqueçaba (coastal Paraná) formerly boasted a 17-member band called Mãe do Mato. Directed by Antônio Fernando Lima and later by João Soares da Cruz, this band faded in the face of radio and TV. Nonetheless, such local composer-lyricists as Leonildo Silveira Xavier and Arcelino de Jesus gave the author sample creations for publication in the essay, to prove that regional music has not died entirely. Music of a batuvana (syncopated 2/4, parallel thirds, percussion interludes) played during fandangos at Guaraqueçaba and Serra Negra illustrates what folkloric survivals the author could spot.

7063 Peixoto, Daniel. Padre Chromácio, mística & música. Recife, Brazil: Companhia Editora de Pernambuco, 1976. 225 p.

With a preface by Archbishop Dom Nivaldo Monte (dated Natal, 18 sept. 1976), this biography lovingly traces the life and times of a notable priest-musician whose parish was Jaboatão—Chromácio Leão Teixeira da Silva (b. 28 June 1886, Vila da Penha, now Canguaretama, Rio Grande do Norte; d. 5 Jan. 1951, Jaboatão where he had lived since 4 Feb. 1912). Organizer of a Salvation Army-type band, he also composed three Masses, a symphony, four choros, four hymns, and much else catalogued (p. 185–196). In the preface, Archbishop Monte urges a further tribute—the publication of at least a representative body of his compositions.

7064 Pereira, Marcus. Música: está chegando a vez do povo. v. 1., A história de "O Jogral." São Paulo: HUCITEC (Editora de Humanismo, Ciência e Tecnologia), 1976. 93 p., illus.

In 1965, the author (b. São Paulo, 1930), educated for the bar at the Univ. de São Paulo, teamed with the composer Luís Carlos Paraná (d. 3 Dec. 1970) to open a nightclub in São Paulo called "O Jogral." One grand objective was the propagation of distinctively Brazilian popular music. In 1973, the author formed his company "Discos Marcus Pereira" to record and disseminate the national product. The reminiscences in this impressionist survey culminate with the author's promise to keep his campaign for national values in high voltage.

7065 Pina Filho, Braz Wilson Pompeo de. Conservatório de Música da UFGo.: 16 anhos. Fotos: Thomas Hoag. Goiânia, Brazil: Universidade Federal de Goiás, 1973. 82 p., plates.

Brief history of the conservatory (founded 15 Jan. 1956) includes lists of professors and subjects; their activities outside the conservatory (1954–72); dated achievements of graduates; festivals promoted by the conservatory (1967, 1968, 1970, 1971); extension courses; and recitals by distinguished visitors (1958–72). Valuable record, because of precise dates and names.

7066 Pinto, Luiz Alvares. Arte de solfejar. Edited and introduction by Jaime C. Diniz. Recife, Brazil: Governo do Estado de Pernambuco, Secretaria de Educação e Cultura, 1977. 51 p., facsim., music (Col. Pernambucana, 9)

This nonpareil ed. of Pinto's 1761 path-breaking treatise (reviewed in *Inter-American Music Review*, 1:2, Spring/Summer 1979, p. 242–243) again reveals the unsurpassed learning of the musicologist who, apart from Lange, has done the most to revive the Brazilian 18th century.

7067 Rangel, Lucio. Bibliografia da música popular brasileira. Rio: Livraria São José, Gráfica Olímpica Editora, 1976. 20 p.

With 228 titles organized alphabetically by first names of authors, this first attempt at a bibliography of Brazilian writings on popular music is both timely and profitable. The compiler freely acknowledges the wide disparity of value among the writings cited.

7068 Roberto Aussel y Miguel Angel Grollet: ganadores del Concurso Internacional de Guitarra en París (Ritmo [La Plata, Arg.] 5:5, 1975, p. 11, plates)

The first prize-winner of the 1975 International Guitar Contest sponsored by Radio France (attracting 91 guitarists from 24 countries) was the 21-year-old Roberto Aussel of Porto Alegre, Brazil, pupil of Jorge Martínez Zárate of B.A.

7069 Stevenson, Robert. The Brazilian Bishop who launched the first piano publication: 1732 (IAMR, 1:2, Spring/-Summer 1979, p. 211–215, bibl.)

João Seyxas da Fonseca (1691–1758), a native of Rio, consecrated Bishop (4. Oct. 1733), patronized the first publication specified for the piano, Lodovico Guistini's 12 *Sonate da Cimbalo di Piano* (Florence, Italy, 1732).

7070 ———. Francisco Manuel da Silva (MGG [Supplement] 16, 1979, columns 1706–1707, bibl.)

Biography and works list of the composer of the Brazilian national anthem.

7071 Vasconcellos, Gilberto. Música popular: de olho na fresta. Rio: Graal, 1977. 111 p., illus.

Reprinting of five newspaper and magazine articles published in São Paulo (*Cadernos Almanaque, Debate e Crítica, Movimento*) and Rio (*Opinião*) in 1975 and 1976. Primarily a study of lyrics, this collection stresses the move from protest song (1960–68) to apolitical songs (1972–76). The author credits Roberto Schwarz's "Remarques sur la Culture et la Politique au Brésil: 1964–1969" in *Les Temps Modernes* (288, 1970) for cardinal viewpoints. Questions of musical style or technique fall completely outside the author's range of interests.

7072 Vasconcelos, Ary. Raízes da música popular brasileira: 1500–1889. São Paulo: Livraria Martins Editora, 1977. 362 p., bibl., illus.

The author (b. Rio, 1926) has been prominent as critic and journalist since 1943. His definition of "música popular" includes everything secular, except opera and concert music. The bulk of this useful chronological vademecum (p. 33–349) comprises thumbnail biographies of personalities, from José de Anchieta (1534–97) to Chiquinha Gonzaga (1845–1935), "the most famous woman in Brazilian popular music history." The bibliographies at the close of each short life stress titles by Corrêa de Azevedo, Cernicchiaro, Andrade, Almeida, Melo, and other standard historians of Brazilian music.

THE CARIBBEAN (except CUBA)

7073 Aretz, Isabel and **Luis Felipe Ramón y Rivera.** Un cursillo de folklore: la música (Universo [Universidad Autónoma de Santo Domingo, Facultad de Humanidades] 4, julio/dic. 1973, p. 11–98, maps, music, plates)

Black musical expressions flourish in present-day Dominican Republic whereas folk music of Spanish-descent does not, not even in central Cibao zone or southeastern Barahona. For example, romances and old dances such as the *carabine, mangulina,* and *yuca* (notated example of the latter appears on p. 94) must be sought assiduously. The *merengue,* of mid-19th-century mulatto origin, has now become "composed music" listened to, rather than danced to, in the capital. Further journeys to relatively inaccessible outlying islets and interior locales may permit later folklorists to recover more of the now vanished past and to teach it anew to coming generations of Dominicans. Also includes prolific discussion of regional songs, musical instruments classified in the usual manner, animistic beliefs incorporated in song texts, and a large iconography (p. 95–-98).

7074 Beckett, Sibthorpe [Leopold]. History of the Jamaica Philharmonic Symphony Orchestra: rebirth and emergence (IJ/JJ, 9:4, 1975, p. 27–32)

This seminal survey filled with names and dates is a model of local history. In the 1890s, Astley Clerk managed the Lewis Winkler Music Room on King Street and in the next decade established the Cowen Music Rooms. Clerk also published original compositions by Benjamin DeCordova Reid and Granville Campbell. The Theatre Royal, dating back to 1778, was the site of a 1904 choral and orchestral concert conducted by Madame de Montagnac. The Ward Theatre which opened in 1921 on the same site (northeast of Victoria Park), succeeded the Theatre Royal as the locale for major musical events—including concerts in the late 1930s by a Jamaica Symphony Orchestra conducted by Frank Bradley and by military bandmaster Robert Jones. The author (b. Franklin Town,

Kingston, 16 Dec. 1920) was educated at Kingston College (1935–38) and Commercial College (1939) and joined the staff of the Jamaica Supreme Court in 1946. The son of Joshua Uberto Beckett, high-ranking officer of the Jamaica Constabulary, he began as a choirboy under George Davis Goode (Port Royal, 23 July 1882, longtime organist and choirmaster of St. Michael's Church). On 1 July 1940, he founded the Surrey Philharmonic Orchestra. Despite interference from the Edward Gordon String Orchestra (winner of the Musical Competition Festival in Nov. 1940), the Surrey succeeded in making its first public appearance at a Carnival on the grounds of Kingston College in Nov. 1941 and in giving its formal début concert 16 Feb. 1942 at air-cooled Ormsby Hall. In Sept. 1945, the author formed the YMCA Choral Group. In 1946, this group began appearing with the Jamaica Philharmonic Symphony—new name of the Surrey. In 1952, the Jamaica Philharmonic moved to Ward for two of its programs, one enlisting the Jamaican pianist and folklorist Olive Lewin, the other the British Guiana conductor Rudolph Dunbar. In 1955, the "Y" Choral Group and Jamaica Philharmonic presented *Elijah* in the 2000-seat Carib Cinema, in 1956 the Brahms Requiem in Ward, and on 9 April 1957 *Messiah* at the Carib. In 1961, the Jamaica School of Music was founded (89 Hope Road, Kingston) to cooperate with the training program of the Jamaica Philharmonic Symphony Orchestra. The author lists prominent Jamaican music faculty and students and concludes with a section on the financing of the Jamaica Philharmonic by private patrons and sustaining members. On its 35th anniversary, "it was the only group of its kind in the Caribbean."

7075 Burnette, Mackie. Pan and Caribbean drum rhythms: interview by Shirley Maynier Burke (IJ/JJ, 11:3/4, 1978, p. 14–20, bibl., illus., music, plates)

The Trinidadian steel-pan player Mackie Burnette emigrated to Jamaica in 1962, in which year he founded the Jamaica All Stars. After promotional tours in Mexico and Guantánamo, he visited Lagos, Nigeria, for FESTAC in 1977. According to him, Jamaicans "appreciate that strong basic rhythm, and they are not listening to the subtle polyrhythms which characterize African music. I have repeatedly failed to get complex rhythms across to an audience. You have to make it as basic as possible or they get bored, very bored and restless . . . Another thing is the electronic amplification of sound which may have reached a loudness beyond that which is normal to the human ear, and the ears are being deafened—not only here in Jamaica [but elsewhere]." This fascinating, although discursive, interview concludes with "transcriptions and notations by Gus Brathwaite" of 17 rhythmic patterns including *shango*, *umele* (*oumele*), *do-doop*, *jab-jab*, *mento*, *coromantee*, and *congo*. Mento beat "has a Spanish influence" mixed with African. On the second beat, Trinidadians dance one-step, Jamaicans tend to dance a two-step. Older Jamaicans who are inheritors of the mento tradition, easily dance the calypso, but younger Jamaicans accustomed to the heavy Ska and Reggae beat, seem content with the mere adaptation of the calypso.

7076 Clerk, Astley. Arawak musical instruments: extract from a lecture given in 1913 (IJ/JJ, 11:3/4, 1978, p. 21–24, illus.)

The Arawaks arrived in Jamaica about 200 AD, Columbus discovered the island 4 May 1494. Four months later he returned to be greeted by the cacique residing on what is now called Goats' Island (the largest and highest of the seven islands in Old Harbour Bay). With the cacique came a troupe of uniformed musicians. According to Andrés Bernáldez in *Historia de los Reyes Católicos* (Seville, 1870, vol. 2, p. 74), two painted Indians wearing green feather helmets held elaborately carved trumpets ("habia otros dos hombres así pintados en otra forma; estos traían dos trompetas de palo muy labradas de pájaros y otras sutilezas; el leño de que eran muy negro").

7077 ———. Extract from "The Music and Musical Instruments of Jamaica" (IJ/JJ, 9:2/3, 1975, p. 59–67, illus., music)

This extract from lectures delivered at Edmondson Hall (Wesley Guild, 19 Nov. 1913) and Jamaica Institute (Kingston Athenaeum, 15 Dec.) gives a running summary of Jamaica music history. Despite inept organization, ethnic bias, and shoddy citing of authorities, Clerk grasped many valuable historic and ethnic data. His authorities include Bernáldez, Sloane, Thomas Coke, Matthew Gregory "Monk" Lewis (Frank Cundall's *Bibliographia Jamaicensis*, No. 291); J. Stewart

(No. 285); William Beckford (Nos. 19, 281); Washington Irving, I.M. Belisario (No. 294); George Grove; William Harris (No. 1068); and Jekyll. From Sir Hans Sloane he garners his first three musical examples (Whydaw, Angola, and Koromanti Songs). From Walter Jekyll's collection of Port Royal mountain music, *Jamaica Song and Story* (1907, p. 71, 182, 226, 235) he takes the four airs that to him most closely resemble "American Plantation or Jubilee Songs." His next example is Samuel Coleridge-Taylor's arrangement of the same Bamboula air exploited in Louis Moreau Gottschalk's Opus 2. The author criticizes Sloane's and Beckford's data on musical instruments used by blacks and J.G. Stedman's concerning cognates used by Surinam blacks. Instruments mentioned: *gumbie = goombah = goombay = gumbay*; ngoma; dundo; bender; banja; jenkoving; abeng; cumba. Roots for some of these terms exist in Ewe, Twi, and Ga.

Davis, Stephen and **Peter Simon.** Reggae bloodlines: in search of the music and culture of Jamaica. See *HLAS 41:1017*.

Hedrick, Basil C. and **Jeannette E. Stephens.** In the days of yesterday and in the days of today: an overview of Bahamian folkmusic. See item **1274**.

7078 Jones, Anthony Mark. Steelband: a history; the Winston "Spree" Simon story. Port-of-Spain: Educo Press, 1975? 39 p., illus., tables.

In this monograph the author lists competition winners (ping-pong solo and steel orchestra for 1952–64, Panorama winners for 1963–73); devotes 10 pages to drawings of instruments; and gives a thumbnail biography of the great pioneer Winston "Spree" Simon, who grew up in the deprived area of John John. In 1939, Simon "invented" the melody pan, forerunner of the ping-pong or tenor pan. In 1950, the first steelband traveled abroad. Previously called Red Army Steelband and now renamed Merrymakers, the group was led by Leonard Morris. A year later the Trinidad All Steel Percussion Orchestra (T.A.S.P.O.) raised funds to tour England.

7079 Juste-Constant, Voegeli. Approche ethnomusicologique du vouvou [vodou] haïtien (IPGH/FA, 21, junio 1976, p. 95–140, bibl., illus., music, plates)

The author, who is Haitian, was an employee of the Bureau d'Ethnologie at Port-au-Prince in 1972. From 1973 to 1975, he studied ethnomusicology at INIDEF (Instituto Interamericano de Etnomusicología y Folklore), Caracas. In 1976, he transferred to Canada. This essay, based on the chapter on Haitian vodou ceremonial music in the author's INIDEF thesis presented Dec. 1974, includes 10 lengthy musical examples. The author transcribes only one of these in 4/4—a soloist's invocation of the Father Eternal Atibon Legba, punctuated by the congregation's *aï bobo* (= amen). Even here, however, he transcribes the widely wandering soloist's melody (ranging a 15th) in asymmetrical rhythmic patterns. The other melody transcriptions shift constantly from 2/8, 3/8, 5/8, 6/8, 9/8, to 12/8. These 10 richly divagating melodies that frequently include wide, "difficult" skips, are undergirded by drum patterns (not shown in the transcriptions) that bind the music into ecstatic wholes. Designed above all to induce spirit possession or trance states, the vodou melodies shown in this essay are pentatonic (exx. 4, 6, 7), heptatonic (3, 5, 10) or heptatonic with f♯ and f^1♮, hexatonic (2) or hexatonic with c^1♯ and c^1♮. African components are not so all-pervasive as to prevent the texts from mentioning Christian saints and the Ave Maria. The author's extensive discussion of rites is enriched with three photographs of instruments (*assotor*, the largest vodou drum; *hountor*, second drum in size; *couacoua* = kwa-kwa).

7080 Lizardo Barinas, Fradrique. Danzas y bailes folklóricos dominicanos. v. 1, Etnografía y folklore. Santo Domingo: Fundación García Arévalo, 1975. 329 p., bibl., illus., maps, music notations (Col. Investigaciones, 2. Serie Etnología)

The author (b. 4 Aug. 1930, Santo Domingo) studied medicine before turning to folklore—which he studied with Flérida de Nolasco, then Argeliers León (in Cuba, 1961), and Isabel Aretz and Luis Felipe de Ramón y Rivera. Martha Ellen Davis, anthropology student at the Univ. of Illinois, wrote the introduction (p. 19–31) stressing Lizardo's supreme services in collecting the fast disappearing traditional dances, including their music and choreography throughout the Dominican Republic. The more than 30 dances reviewed in this valuable anthology include the *tumba, carabiné, jaiba, mangulina, yuca,* and *merengue.* By diagramming dancers' positions and showing their proper dress, the author enables the interested reader to re-create the majority of the rural dances that he hopes to save from extinction. The purpose of this welcome text is therefore both didactic and scientific.

7081 Mancebo, Licinio. El Archivo Nacional de Música de la República Dominicana y su historia (HET, 13:1, enero/marzo 1980, p. 47–48)

Created by Presidential Decree of 15 Nov. 1968, the Dominican Republic Archivo Nacional de Música (ANM) counted as first director Elila Mena de Rivera. She was followed in 1970 by Gracita Senior de Pellerano and after 4 Oct. 1971 by Licinio Mancebo.

7082 Montgomery, Ruth Reynolds and **Edna McGuire.** Stories from 3 islands: Haiti, Jamaica, Puerto Rico. New York: Friendship Press, 1977. 32 p., maps, illus., music notations.

To quote the dust jacket: "As Ruth Montgomery completed work on this book she expressed her 'hope and prayer that through these pages about the Caribbean, the love, warmth and desires of children, youth and adults may be felt by the readers, as they come closer to the hearts of our Caribbean neighbors'." The tune of the Jamaican national anthem, "Jamaica: Land We Love," is given (p. 17), but not that of the Haitian.

7083 O'Gorman, Pamela. The introduction of Jamaican music into the Established Churches (IJ/JJ, 9:1, 1975, p. 40–44, bibl.)

Long before Pius XII's *Musicae sacrae disciplinae* (25 Dec. 1955) countenancing "rhythmic music," hymn tunes of American and European origin were being Africanized by Jamaican Pentecostals, Church of God, City Mission, and Salvation Army converts. "Harsh vocal timbre, percussive accompaniment, rhythmic body movement, improvisation and spontaneous harmonization transformed Western hymns into a neo-African form that is today considered part of the heritage of Jamaican folk music." However, Jamaican Established Churches resisted this Africanization and instead gingerly accepted folkish imports from Great Britain, such as Geoffrey Beaumont's Anglican *Folk Mass* (1956). Only when a young Jamaican Roman Catholic, Barry Chevannes, returned home after seven years in the US did any rhythmic music by a Jamaican-born composer start encroaching on Established domain. Beginning in 1968 at St. Patrick's, Waterhouse, then at Aquinas Centre and at various Yard Masses, Chevannes pioneered in replacing foreign imports such as *Blowin' in the Wind, Song of a Happy Man,* and the like, with Jamaican dialect verse accompanied by mento guitar. By 1975 his songs had become an interdenominational *lingua franca.* A watershed was reached in Feb. 1970 when students at the Univ. of the West Indies occupied the Creative Arts Centre as a symbol of protest against the policy of moulding them into imitation Europeans. Following the lead of Chevannes, others such as Olive Lewin, Lisa Narcisse, Noel Dexter, and Richard Ho Lung, S.J., successfully composed in a Jamaican folkish style. The author closes with a survey of congregational reactions in 1975. Her conclusion: "folk services account for only a small proportion of the total number of services held in most churches. Indeed, many churches still regard the use of indigenous music as an unfortunate encroachment of secularism, fit to be heard only at young people's socials."

Reckford, Verena. Rastafarian music: an introductory study. See *HLAS 41:1080.*

7084 Rosa-Nieves, Cesáreo. Los bailes de Puerto Rico (ICP/R, 17:65, oct./dic. 1974, p. 14–18)

In this richly footnoted historical survey of dance in Puerto Rico, the learned author begins with a reference to confraternity *bailes* in honor of saints in 1712 and a citation from Fray Iñigo Abbad declaring dancing to be by far the most popular diversion throughout the island in 1789. Dances already in vogue before 1800 included seis, garabato, matatoros, cadenas, caballo, sonduro, puntillanto or zapateo, fandanguillo, and bolanchera. In 1849 Manuel A. Alonso called the seis next to cadenas the most popular dance. Of the three theories on the origin of the Puerto Rican danza, the author prefers the opinion of Salvador Brau who called it a derivative of the merengue introduced by military bands from Cuba in 1842–43. Captain-Gen. Juan de la Pezuela prohibited the lascivious couples merengue in 1849. Composed on fast 2/4, the merengues of 1855 began with an introductory eight-bar walkaround (*paseo*), followed by the dance proper—which grew in length from only 16 bars to as many as 132 measures divided into as many as five sections. Puerto Rican composers of merengues included such standouts as Francisco Santanella, Nemesio Quiñones, Aurelio Dueño, Felipe Gutiérrez Espinosa, Ramón Girona, and Jorge Cucullu. Around 1855 appeared a rash of merengues bearing such colorful names as *La Mulata, El Yambú, Rabo de Puerco, La Charrasca,* and *Ay no quiero Comer Mondongo.* In 1870, Julian Andino (1845–1926) accompanied his danza *La Margarita* with alternating triplets and duplets in 2/4 rather than the habanera rhythm of dotted eighth and 16th followed by two 8th-notes. Among exponents of Andino's "elastic triplet" accompaniment that became typical in the Puerto Rican danza, Manuel Tavárez, Juan Morel Campos, Braulio Dueño Colón, Angel Mislán, and José Quintón gained greatest renown.

CENTRAL AMERICA

7085 Bonilla, Secundino. Cantos al Niño Dios antes de su nacimiento (BNBD, 8, nov./dic. 1975, p. 32–34)

Three versions of the Christmas carol *Ven, dulce Amado mío* collected at León, Totogalpa, and Condega, Nic. In all three versions, the triple-meter major mode melody moves in treacly parallel thirds with an accompanying voice. The compiler also publishes an older text of the same carol, running to 14 (instead of seven) quatrains, collected at Granada, Nic.

7086 Cardenal Argüello, Salvador. Apuntes sobre la música en Nicaragua (BNBD, 8, nov./dic. 1975, p. 23–31)

On p. 27, the author speaks of Luis Abraham Delgadillo (1887–1961) as having died a few months ago which indicates this essay waited 13 or 14 years for publication. Cardenal Argüello's previous publication annotated in *HLAS* appeared *HLAS 9* (1946) and *HLAS 11* (1948): two parts of *Música indígena para marimba,* a collection of airs published in Granada, Nic., in *Cuadernos del Taller San Lucas,* (3/4, 1943 and 1944). His sources for the present essay include Gilberto Vega Miranda's *Breviario del recuerdo: antología de músicos nicaragüenses* (Managua, 1945 [i.e. 1946], 212 p.); general histories of Nicaragua by Tomás Ayón and José D. Gámez; the Marqués de Lozoya's *Vida del Segoviano Rodrigo de Contreras;* and Ephraim George Squier's *Nicaragua: People, Scenery, Monuments* (1852). Lacking, however, are the key documents needed to buttress any informed survey: musical excerpts from the capitular act of León's Cathedral.

7087 Dos canciones misquitas: Tiniska No. 1, Tiniska No. 2, Luniko Waikna No. 1, Luniko Waikna No. 2 (BNBD, 26, nov./dic. 1978, p. 69–70, music)

The music for all four songs is in 3/4, D Major. Tiniskas parse in 3 + 3 + 3 + 3 bars; a held note occupies every third bar; the repeated rhythmic figure of two eighth-notes, quarter-note, eighth-note and eighth-note rest appears everywhere except in bars 3, 6, 9, 12. Luniko waiknas, parsing 3 + 3 + 3 + 3; 3 + 3 + 3 + 3, develop an equally repetitive rhythmic scheme. Skips in all four songs are prevailingly downward, with descending octaves, minor 6ths and perfect 5ths prevalent in luniko waiknas.

Fortune, Armando. Presencia africana en la música panameña. See item **1158**.

7088 Lara F., Celso A. Cuentos y cuenteros populares de Guatemala (Tradición Popular [Universidad de San Carlos de Guatemala, Centro de Estudios Folklóricos] 11, 1977, p. 2–19, bibl., illus., maps, plates)

Biographies of seven outstanding Guatemalan storytellers and thumbnail identifications of four others form the bulk of this article. At the outset comes a story told and sung by 37-year-old Oscar Alvarado, originally of Antigua but resident of the Guatemala City suburb of San José El Esfuerzo during the 33 sessions that he worked as the author's informant (26 Aug. 1975–4 Jan. 1977). Alvarado's tale concerns a king about to die if not cured by a special flower growing in the distant mountains. The youngest of the king's three sons finds the flower. His elder brothers kill him. To a D minor tune in 3/4 ranging over only a fifth, a self-speaking rustic pipe ends up disclosing the murder to the king, who thereupon executes the wicked elder brethren.

7089 Lemmon, Alfred E. Archivo General de Indias, "Guatemala 956:" un legajo musical (HET, 12:1, enero/feb. 1979, p. 20–23)

The account books of Guatemala Cathedral (1782–97) document payments to Rafael Antonio Castellanos, chapelmaster until his death in 1791, to this interim successor Miguel Pontaza, to his sister Micaela Castellanos from 1792, and to José Tomás Guzmán, organist.

7090 ———. El Archivo Musical de la Catedral de Guatemala (HET, 12:4, sept./dic. 1979, p. 9–12)

Excellent analysis of cathedral music holdings, supervision of which is vested in the historian-archivist Licenciado Agustín Estrada Monroy.

7091 ———. Dos fuentes de investigación para la música colonial guatemalteca (HET, 12:2, marzo/abril 1979, p. 30–33)

The Guatemala Cathedral Music Archive and the Archivo General de Centroamérica yield rich documentation—samples of which are here shown by the notable investigator who during the summer of 1978 held a Matilda Geddings Gray grant. The circulation of cathedral music to outlying places, not only in Guatemala, but also in Honduras, El Salvador, and Chiapas, evinces a widespread colonial music culture.

7092 O'Brien, Linda Lee. Music education and innovation in a traditional Tzutuhil-Maya community (*in* Enculturation in Latin America: an anthology. Johannes Wilbert, ed. Los Angeles: UCLA Latin American Center Publications, University of California, 1976, p. 377–393, bibl. [UCLA Latin American studies, 37])

Traditional cultural values transmitted by *cofradía* officers, shamans, midwives, and musicians were not sufficiently understood by the author (b. Rochester, N.Y., 13 Nov. 1936; B.S. Mary Rogers College, Maryknoll, N.Y., 1964) at the outset of her Guatemalan assignment to teach music in Colegio Monte María (1965–67). A music researcher at Santiago Atitlán (14,000 inhabitants of whom 13,500 are Indians); she completed fieldwork there in 1972 for her 1975 UCLA Ph.D. dissertation (284 p.) chaired by Josef M. Pacholczyk, "Songs of the Face of the Earth: Ancestor Songs of the Tzutuhil-Maya of Santiago Atitlán, Guatemala" (*Dissertation Abstracts International*, Vol. 36, No. 7, Jan. 1976, p. 4098A–4099A). Parts of the present essay repeat her dissertation (p. 377 = p. 20; p. 378 = p. 22–25; p. 382 = p. 30). Topics range from "Cofradía Musicians" and "Becoming a Musician" to "Innovation in Tzutuhil Music." Her conclusion: "The acculturation process of Tzutuhil music is one of incremental syncretism, in which the adaptation of alien forms in terms of an indigenous counterpart results in identification of the alien form with the ancestral tradition, into which it is assimilated." For anthropologist's comment, see *HLAS 41:954*.

———. La música folklórica de Guatemala. See item **1180**.

7093 Sarmientos, Jorge. Raíces y futuro de la música en Guatemala y Latinoamérica (UCIEM/R, 33:148, oct./dic. 1979, p. 58–65)

Valuable synthesis of Sarmientos' accomplishments as composer-conductor preceded by notes on the careers of Jesús Castillo (1877–1946) and his brother Ricardo Castillo (1894–1966).

7094 Schroeder, Pollyanna T. Un músico de dos mundos (OAS/AM, 31:4, abril 1979, p. 21–25, illus.)

Miguel Angel Sandoval Cabrera (b. 3 Nov. 1903, Guazacapán, Santa Rosa dept., Guatemala) made his debut as a pianist in Guatemala City at age 10. At 14, he enrolled in St. John's College, Belize, and in 1919 moved to NY. In 1925, he became a US citizen. In 1927, Beniamino Gigli contracted him as accompanist and took two of his songs on tour. In 1932 he became Nino Martini's accompanist.

From 1940–47 he was a CBS staff composer, director and accompanist. During 1947–49, he directed the national radio station TGW at Guatemala City, thereafter returning to NY where he died 24 Aug. 1953. His published output includes seven piano pieces, 20 concert songs, and 24 annotated Latin American folk-type songs arranged for piano and solo voice.

7095 Vogt, Evon Z. On the symbolic meaning of percussion in Zinacanteco ritual (UNM/JAR, 33:3, Fall 1977, p. 231–244, bibl.)

"Zinacantan is a Tzotzil-speaking *municipio* of some 12,500 contemporary Mayas located just to the west of San Cristóbal de Las Casas in the central highlands of Chiapas." Among various percussive sounds ranging from skyrockets (symbolizing lightning, thunder, and clouds) to bells (rung to mark the passage of time, arrivals, departures, deaths), the most sacred is the sound of the *t'ent'en* = slit-drum (= Aztec *teponaztli*). Played only once a year at San Sebastián feast (Jan. 25), it emits "two sounds, one higher and one lower, which are described by informants as being *bankilal* and *'its'inal*, symbolizing the senior-junior principle that pervades Zinacanteco culture . . . This small sacred drum embodies, above all, a symbol of the arrival of the New Year."

CHILE

7096 Aguirre González, Francisco Javier. Significado literario y alcance político de la Nueva Canción Chilena (CH, 328, oct. 1977, p. 5–31)

The author classifies Chilean folk music as belonging primarily to the cueca, tonada, refalosa (= resfalosa = resbalosa), trote, and vals genres. He defines as regional variants the cachimbo norteño, mapuchina, and sajuriana. The Parra family headed by Violeta were authentic pioneers of the New Song. Sergio Ortega was in 1976 the paramount figure of the New Song. He wrote the cantatas *La fragua* and *¿Qué hora puede ser en Valparaíso?* and the anthem of Unidad Popular, *Venceremos*.

7097 Cánepa Guzmán, Mario. La ópera en Chile: 1839–1930. Santiago, Editorial del Pacífico, 1976. 305 p., bibl., illus., plates.

After a long career beginning in 1940 as poet, short story writer and playwright, the author published *El teatro en Chile* in 1966, *El teatro social y obrero* in 1971, and a textbook history of Chilean theatre in 1974. The present handsome volume synthesizes information from M.L. Amunátegui, R. Hernández, E. Pereira Salas, D. Quiroga, and others. Eschewing musical analysis, the 16 chapters mostly chronicle the Chilean premieres of standard repertory operas. The few side glances at indigenous opera composers' efforts to gain a hearing (Aquinas Ried, Eliodoro Ortiz de Zárate, Próspero Bisquert, Pablo Garrido, Carlos Puelma) add up to a tale of repeated frustrations. This book needs a thorough index. Another book now needs to be written on the same subject by a musicologist.

7098 Claro Valdés, Samuel. José de Campderrós: 1742–1812; de mercader catalán a Maestro de Capilla en Santiago de Chile (Anuario Musical [Barcelona] 30, 1977, p. 123–134, bibl.)

Bound for Callao on the British-built 900-ton *Aquiles*, Campderrós departed as a trader from Cádiz on 5 Jan. 1775. Witnesses who on 14 Dec. 1774 confirmed him to be a 32-year-old bachelor (AGI, Contratación 5519 and 1777) included the painter Francisco Clapera and the merchant Juan Francisco Mascaró, residents of Cádiz who had known him 15 and 20 years, respectively. In all likelihood Campderrós, though born in Barcelona, had therefore lived in Cádiz since about 1754. The cathedral personnel at his disposal when he arrived in Santiago de Chile toward the close of 1792 consisted of a vocal quartet, paired violins, two flutes or oboes, organ and continuo. His opponent for the Chilean chapelmastership that he held from 1792 to death was Antonio Aranaz, a native of Santander, theatrical composer and manager who came from Buenos Aires to compete for the post. Aranaz remained at Santiago until 1796, then moved to Valparaíso until 1802 when he left for Montevideo from whence he returned to Spain. The 84 works by Campderrós in Santiago de Chile archive catalogued by Claro Valdés (see *HLAS 38:9095*) include 16 Masses—orchestral Mass in G published in Claro Valdés's *Antología de la música colonial en América del Sur* (see *HLAS 38:9004*)—various other Latin works such as psalms, lamentations, and offices of the dead; and 18 villancicos.

7099 ———. José Zepiola: músico de la Catedral de Santiago (ACH/B, 41:88, 1974 [i.e. 1978] p. 221–235)

Authoritative biography and works study with frequent fresh insights from cathedral documents.

7100 ———. Oyendo a Chile. Santiago: Editorial Andrés Bello, 1979. 139 p., bibl., illus.

Splendid panorama of Chilean music history, beautifully organized, and written with the distinguished author's usual acumen, flair, and impartiality. As a welcome novelty, the volume is accompanied with a 90-minute cassette containing 52 music examples. Claro's 15-p. pamphlet of liner notes elucidates the cassette. Review of text and cassette appeared in *Inter-American Music Review* (1:2, Spring/Summer 1979, p. 237–238) and in *Revista Musical Chilena* (33:146/147, abril/sept. 1979, p. 117–119).

7101 ———. La vida musical en Chile durante el gobierno de don Bernardo O'Higgins (UCIEM/R, 33:145, enero/marzo 1979, p. 5–24, bibl.)

Definitive account of the epoch 1817–23, with appropriate glances forward and backward. O'Higgins, who studied piano in London, showed educated taste. Both before his rule and in later years in Lima (1823–42) music was his consolation. With accustomed mastery, Claro marshals a wealth of evidence to show how during his rule, music and instrument imports were stimulated, how bands were favored, he describes what were the antecedents of the Manuel Robles and Ramón Carnicer national anthems, what were the reigning social diversions involving music, and who were the musical personalities at the forefront of secular and sacred compositions.

Dannemann R., Manuel. Plan Multinacional de Relevamiento Etnomusicológico y Folklórico. See item **1207**.

7102 **Grebe, María Ester.** León Schidlowsky Gaete (MGG [Supplement] 16, 1979, columns 1663–1664, bibl.)

Schidlowsky (b. Santiago, 21 July 1931) achieved front rank status in Chilean music before emigrating to Israel in 1969.

7103 **Merino, Luis.** Don Eugenio Pereira Salas: 1904–1979, fundador de la historiografía musical en Chile (UCIEM/R, 33:148, oct./dic. 1979, p. 66–87, bibl.)

Masterful survey of Pereira Salas' titanic career, accompanied by complete bibliography of his 14 books, 69 articles, and 64 reviews on music.

7104 ———. Federico Heinlein, el compositor (UCIEM/R, 33:145, enero/marzo 1979, p. 25–47, bibl., music)

With his usual finesse, meticulousness, and wide-ranging perspective, the editor of *Revista Musical Chilena* itemizes and analyzes the creative output of a resident of Chile since 1940 who like Virgil Thomson shines as both critic and composer. Includes music examples and a catalogue.

7105 ———. Presencia del creador Domingo Santa Cruz Wilson en la historia de la música chilena (UCIEM/R, 33:146/147, abril/sept. 1979, p. 15–79, bibl., music)

No South American composer has been more magisterially studied than the titanic Santa Cruz in this seminal essay. Chilean music from 1928–68 reflected his dynamism. Includes catalog.

7106 ———. Visión del compositor Juan Orrego-Salas (UCIEM/R, 32:142/144, abril/dic. 1978, p. 5–105, bibl., music)

Splendid analysis of the creative development of the eminent Chilean who from 1961 has directed the Latin American Music Center at Indiana Univ., Bloomington. The wealth of detail, the consistently sympathetic insights, and the excellent proportions make this monograph a model of its kind. Includes 34 music examples and catalog.

7107 **Orrego-Salas, Juan.** Compositor por sobre todo (UCIEM/R, 33:146/147, abril/sept. 1979, p. 5–14)

Six decades of composition mark the career of Domingo Santa Cruz, already so prominent in Chilean music as to be awarded the Premio Nacional de Arte a generation ago in a ceremony at the Teatro Municipal in Santiago on 4 Dec. 1951.

7108 **Parra, Violeta.** Toda Violeta Parra: antología de canciones y poemas. Precedida de "Violeta Entera" de Alfonso Alcade *comp.* Fotografías de Patricio Guzmán. Buenos Aires: Ediciones de la Flor, 1974. 137 p., plates.

The folkloric singer and political activist (b. San Carlos, Ñuble, southern Chile, 1917) composed boleros, tonadas, and corridos at 20, became a star of Radio Chilena in 1953, toured the Soviet Union in 1954, founded the Museo de Arte Popular at Concepción in 1957, returned to Santiago in 1958, appeared on Argentine TV in 1961 and in the same year again toured the Soviet Union. From 1961–64, she lived in Paris, wherein she published her collection *Poésie populaire des Andes* (1965). She died at Carpa de la Reina in 1971. This anthology of her poetry lacks the enhancement of musical transcriptions.

7109 **Pereira Salas, Eugenio.** Biobibliografía musical de Chile: desde los orígenes a 1886. Santiago: Ediciones de la Universidad de Chile, 1978. 136 p. (Serie de monografías. Anexas a los *Anales de la Universidad de Chile*)

Worthily crowning a lifetime of bibliographical and historical studies, this monograph ends where Ramón Arminio Laval began in his *Bibliografía musical* (89 p.) published in 1896 in the *Anuario de la Prensa Chilena*. Reviewed in *Inter-American Music Review* (1:2, Spring/Summer 1979, p. 241–242). Includes musical appendix.

Pérez Ortega, Juan. Música folklórica infantil chilena. See item **1218**.

7110 Quiroga, Daniel. Clásicos de la música chilena llegan al disco (UCIEM/R, 33:145, enero/marzo 1979, p. 129–133)

Under auspices of the Ministerio de Relaciones Exteriores, the Facultad de Ciencias y Artes Musicales y de la Representación of the Univ. de Chile in 1978 emitted two LPs under the title *Antología de la música chilena*. These pathbreaking discs include Enrique Soro's piano concerto (excellently interpreted by the Dean of Faculty, Herminia Raccagni); Alfonso Leng's *La Muerte de Alsino*; Pedro Humberto Allende's *La Voz de las Calles*; Domingo Santa Cruz's *Preludios Dramáticos*; Acario Cotapos's *Tres Movimientos Sinfónicos*; and Alfonso Letelier's *Preludios Vegetales*. Accompanied by informed liner notes, the *Antología* handsomely surveys four decades of Chilean symphonic music. The luminous quality of the Chilean creative impulse 1920–60 makes these records an indispensable testament.

7111 ———. Don Domingo, el colega (UCIEM/R, 33:146/147, abril/sept. 1979, p. 80–92)

Among Domingo Santa Cruz's fruitful enterprises, none blossomed more beautifully than Chilean music periodicals culminating in *Revista Musical Chilena*.

7112 Seeger, Charles. Saludos a Domingo Santa Cruz (UCIEM/R, 33:146/147, abril/sept. 1979, p. 93–95)

Seeger's last literary contribution, penned only a few weeks before his death (6 Feb. 1979) was this tribute to the giant of Chilean music.

7113 Temporada Internacional de Conciertos, *V, Santiago, 1976.* Temporada internacional de conciertos 1976, 12 de mayo al 1 de octubre, Teatro Oriente: 12 conciertos de abono. Santiago: Universidad Católica de Chile, Instituto de Música, 1976. 31 p., illus.

Patronized by the Banco Hipotecario de Chile, with the added sponsorship of the Goethe Institut, Consejo Británico, and *El Mercurio* newspaper, the dozen concerts showcased the chamber orchestra of Catholic Univ. and an array of international celebrities (Victoria de los Angeles, John Ogdon, John Carewe, Joerg Demus, Zagreb soloists, Hamburg New Music group). Ginastera's first string quartet and Camargo Guarnieri's string trio represented South America in the series.

7114 Van Kessel, Juan *ed.* El desierto canto a María: bailes chilenos de los santuarios marianos del Norte Grande. t. 1. Santiago: Ediciones Mundo, 1977. 304 p., bibl. (La fe de un pueblo, 4)

This collection of 1316 dance songs (texts only) is fourth in a series sponsored by the Seminario Latinoamericano de la Facultad de Teología de la Univ. Católica de Chile. The songs were gathered at the Marian sanctuaries of Las Peñas, La Tirana, and Ayquina in northern Chile (Tarapacá and Antofagasta). In the introduction (p. 7–39), the compiler-editor eloquently argues for the preservation and enhancement of popular cyclical devotions such as that of La Tirana (annually, 14–17 July).

COLOMBIA

Abadía Morales, Guillermo. Compendio general de folklore colombiano. See item **1227**.

7115 Percio García, Jenaro. El maestro Luis A. Calvo. Prólogo de Jorge Patiño Linares. Bucaramanga, Colombia: Editorial Salesiana, 1975. 252 p., plates.

Calvo (b. Gámbita, 28 Aug. 1882) went to Bogotá in 1905. In 1910, he wrote his "Intermezzo No. 1," followed by his danza "Livia." Six years later he was exiled to the leper colony of Agua de Dios. After long national and international recognition as a composer of sentimental songs and religious works, he died there 22 April 1945. Transcribed by Luis Guzmán, a Colombian who joined the US Marine Band, Calvo's rondo "Entre Naranjos" was played on tour by the US Marine Band in 1944.

7116 Piñero Corpas, Joaquín. Historia de la música colombiana: la llave del tesoro (ACH/BHA, 64:718, julio/sept. 1977, p. 507–509)

Rodolfo Pérez in Antioquia, Director of the Coltejer Choir; María Cristiana Sánchez de Vesga, soul of the "Grupo Ballestrinque;" Amalia Samper, leader of the Choir of the Univ. de Los Andes; and Luis Antonio Escobar in Bogotá have cooperated in reviving the priceless colonial repertory. But above all, José Ignacio Perdomo Escobar has given this repertory impetus by his guardianship of historic treasure and his publications.

7117 Stevenson, Robert. El Archivo Musical de la Catedral de Bogotá (ACH/BHA, 64:718, julio/sept. 1977, p. 499–502)

Overview of heretofore published catalogs of colonial music, culminating in José Ignacio Perdomo Escobar's monumental 1976 tome.

CUBA

7118 Barnet, Miguel. Entrevista a Esther Borja (AR, 5:17, 1978, p. 38–42, plates)

Originally published in *La Gaceta de Cuba* (No. 126, Aug. 1974) this interview reveals that the Cuban lyric soprano was born in Havana (Corrales 80) 5 Dec. 1913. She studied with the singer Lalo Elósegi at the Escuela Normal para Maestros where she was elected president of the Directorio Estudiantil. She made her début at the Lyceum (Feb. 1935) singing a song-cycle composed for her by Ernesto Lecuona (1896–1963) to texts by José Martí. She toured Latin America and the US, and appeared in the film *Adiós, Buenos Aires* with Lecuona (1938) and in *Flor de Yumuri* (1943). In 1961, she was a Workers' Union Delegate to the USSR and in 1964 a delegate to a Festival at Sopot (= Zoppot), Poland. Throughout her career she specialized in Cuban repertory.

Baron, Robert. Syncretism and ideology: Latin New York *salsa* musicians. See item **1256**.

7119 Corrêa de Azevedo, Luiz Heitor. Esteban Salas y Castro (MGG [Supplement] 16, 1979, columns 1629–1630, bibl.)

Biography with works of the pioneer Cuban composer (b. Havana, 25 Dec. 1725; d. Santiago de Cuba, 14 July 1803).

7120 ———. Manuel Saumell Robredo (MGG [Supplement] 16, 1979, column 1653)

Discusses the celebrated contradanza composer (b. 1817, d. 14 Aug. 1870 in Havana).

García González, José. Algunas consideraciones lingüísticas a propósito de un nuevo cuento afrocubano. See item **1268**.

Moldes, Rhyna. Música folklórica cubana: con la historia, ritmos e instrumentos de origen hispano-africano. See item **1289**.

7121 Smith, Octavio. La muchacha y la sombra (BNJM/R, 19:2, mayo/agosto 1977, p. 51–69, bibl., facsims., music)

Four Cuban revolutionaries headed by Joaquín de Agüero y Agüero were shot on 12 Aug. 1851. As a tribute to Agüero's memory, either Vicente de la Rosa Betancourt (Camagüey-born mulatto who died in the 1870s) or Nicolás González (d. 1892) composed a danza known variously as *La Sombra de Agüero* or *Los Lamentos*. This danza inspired the poem by the 20-year-old Luisa Porro y Muñoz first published in the June 1855 issue of the magazine *Brisas de Cuba* with the title "Impresiones de la Danza La Sombra." The author of this discursive article offers fascimiles of the two manuscript versions of the danza (both are the same danza, although not so recognized by the author) without attempting to decide which composer should be credited—Rosa Betancourt or González.

7122 Urfé, Odilio. La música y la danza en Cuba (*in* Africa en América Latina. Relator: Manuel Moreno Fraginals. México: Siglo XXI Editores, 1977, p. 215–237 [El mundo en América Latina])

Until 1900, the festive year culminated on Jan. 6, so far as the black-member Cuban cabildos were concerned. Eliseo Grenet (1893–1950) collected a sugar-cane estate black work song exploited by Ernesto Lecuona in *Niña Rita* (1927) as the tango congo *Mamá Inés* sung by Rita Montaner. Blacks from Nigeria, Dahomey, Zaire, and other specified areas preserved their African beliefs in Cuban *santería* and enlivened their cult and festival observances with specific

African drums and dances. The author adds a useful list of popular and art composers who profited from Cuba's unsurpassed black heritage.

ECUADOR

7123 **Coba Andrade, Carlos A.** Constantes y variantes en la etnomusicología y folklore (Sarance [Instituto Otavaleño de Antropología, Otavalo, Ecuador] 1:1, oct. 1975, p. 28–44)

This essay is based on a paper read at the First Anthropological Congress of Andean Countries (Primera Reunión de Antropología de los Países del Grupo Andino, La Paz, Sept. 1975) and comments on the bibliography for Ecuadorean ethnomusicology. Author rightly begins with Ecuadorean songs and dances collected during the 1862 South American tour of eminent naturalist Marcos Jiménez de la Espada (1831–98) published in *Actas del Congreso Internacional de Americanistas, IV Reunión, Madrid, 1881* (Madrid, Fortanet, 1883, vol. 2, p. ix–lx).

———. Estudio sobre el tumank o tsayantur: arco musical del Ecuador. See item **1244**.

7124 **Muriel, Inés.** Contribución a la cultura musical de los jívaros en el Ecuador (IPGH/FA, 21, junio 1976, p. 141–157, music)

According to the author, this is the translated résumé of her unpublished *Beitrag zur Musikkultur der Jivaro in Ekuador* presented in 1968 to the Institut für Musikwissenschaft at Leipzig, where she presently teaches in Karl-Marz-Univ. In 1974 she was a grantee of INIDEF at Caracas. Subject matter: instruments, festivals, analyses of 26 melodies collected by the missionary Raimundo M. Monteros and published at Quito in his *Música autóctona del Oriente Ecuatoriano* (1942) and of melodies recorded in 1958 by a French expedition to the Jívaro led by Philippe Luzuy. The author does not attempt to underlay the five examples transcribed by her from the latter source. Nor does she do anything with texts. "In this monograph, linguistic analysis—number of works in the verses, structure of the verses, possible grouping into strophes, and anything whatsoever having to do with verbal meanings or even with the mere words themselves—is not attempted."

7125 **Rephann, Richard.** A catalogue of the Pedro Travesari Collection of musical instruments (Catálogo de la colección de instrumentos musicales Pedro Travesari). Spanish translation: Lola Odiagal. Washington: Organization of American States, 1978. 139 p., bibl., illus.

In 1974 the director of the Yale Collection of Musical Instruments catalogued the "fewer than 900 musical instruments" in the Pedro Travesari instrument collection housed in the Casa de la Cultura Ecuatoriana, Quito. He classes item 4137 as an anonymous 17th-century clavichord (scale C/E – a^2) made in Ecuador and 4136 as an Ecuadorean virginal, tampered with, but inscribed by "Joaquín de Ovanda (Ovando) 1796 Maio 16." Items 3483–3487 are precolumbian clay conch trumpets from Tuncahuán, Ecua.; items 3269–3282 are precolumbian conch *silbatos* from Tuncahuán. Items 3071–3072 are archaeological *silbadores*; items 3076–3088 are archaeological anthropomorphic *silbatos*; items 3095–3102 are archaeological zoomorphic *silbatos*. According to Rephann, Pedro Travesari exhibited part of his collection in 1906 at Rome where he met the collector Evan Gorga. An exchange agreement dated 1 Jan. 1907 resulted in the trade of 70 instruments. On 1 May 1951 Ecuador officially acquired the collection. Rephann's classification system is the Sachs-Hornbostel, as modified by the Comité International des Musées et Collections des Instruments de Musique. Having published this catalog, Rephann puts an end to the published rumor that the collection contains "ca. 4000 instruments, mainly European."

MEXICO

7126 **Alcaraz, José Antonio.** La música de Rodolfo Halffter. México: UNAM, Difusión Cultural, Depto. de Música, 1977. 61 p., discography, plates (Cuadernos de música. Nueva serie, 4)

Succinct biography with works list and discography. Reviewed in *Inter-American Music Review* (1:2, Spring/Summer 1979, p. 235–236).

7127 **Algunos datos sobre la vida del compositor mexicano Francisco Atienza** (CENIDIM [Centro Nacional de Investigación, Documentación e Información Musical Carlos Chávez, Boletín informativo, México] enero 1980, p. 2)

In 1715 the then Puebla Cathedral Maestro de Capilla Atienza (appointed 15 Jan. 1712) competed unsuccessfully against Zumaya for the Mexico City chapelmastership. A member of the Mexico City cathedral choir from no later than 1695, he had vied with Zumaya for the post of Antonio de Salazar's substitute in Feb. 1710. He died at Puebla in March 1726.

7128 Appendini, Guadalupe. Homenajes a Manuel M. Ponce en el XXXII aniversario de su muerte (Excelsior [México] 13 marzo 1980, p. B1, B3, illus.)

Ponce's death 24 April 1948 motivates annual remembrances—those in 1980 being here listed in conjunct with a useful résumé of his life and works. His favorite pupil and adopted son Carlos Vázquez, inheritor of his manuscripts, recalls that *Estrellita* was composed in 1912 during a train trip from Mexico City to Aguascalientes. Ponce was inspired by seeing a shining star from the train window.

7129 Bellinghausen, Karl. Algunos aspectos de la enseñanza musical en México (CENIDIM [Centro Nacional de Investigación, Documentación e Información Musical Carlos Chávez, Boletín informativo, México] enero 1980, p. 3–4)

Not only in the chief population centers of New Spain but in such outposts as Mérida, Durango, and Valladolid [= Morelia], specialized music instruction was gratuitously given in the colonial period (e.g., in 1667 and 1793). Such decentralization might well be attempted nowadays.

7130 ———. Los instrumentos musicales en la Nueva España en el siglo XVI (CENIDIM [Centro Nacional de Investigación, Documentación e Información Musical Carlos Chávez, Boletín informativo, México] nov./dic. 1979, p. 4)

Bernal Díaz del Castillo (Genaro García ed., 1904, vol. 2, p. 423) reported a Lucullan banquet at Mexico City celebrating peace between Charles V and Francis I (1538). Harps, vihuelas, flutes, dolcians, shawms, and a family of trumpets played between courses.

7131 Catalyne, Alice Ray. Manuel de Zumaya (ca. 1678–1756): Mexican composer for church and theater (*in* Festival essays for Pauline Alderman: a musicological tribute. Editor: Burton L. Karson. Associate editors: Joan Meggett, Eleanor Russell, and Halsey Stevens. Provo, Utah: Brigham Young University Press, 1976. 279 p., bibl., illus., music notations)

Dr. Catalyne, whose 1953 dissertation on "The Double-Choir Music of Juan de Padilla" established her as a paramount authority, here surveys the life and works of the native-born composer of the first (1711) North American opera. She justifies transcriptions of tonos by Manuel de Villaflor and Antonio Literes, neither of whom visited the New World, because their manuscripts circulated in Mexico. Transcription errors mar measures 11 and 16 of the Villaflor and 18 of the Literes. Neither Zumaya transcription is complete.

7132 Civiera Taboada, Miguel. Sensibilidad yucateca en la canción romántica. t. 1. ca: Editorial Libros de México, 1978. 330 p., music, plates (Serie Luis Coto, 6. Col. de arte popular y folklore)

The author of this vol. 1 in a projected two-tome set (b. 3 Feb. 1916, Mérida), sometime student at the Univ. Ibero-Americana and at UNAM's Facultad de Filosofía y Letras, is an employee of the Archivo General de la Nación (as of 1 March 1961) and has published three previous works annotated in *HLAS 24:3872*, *HLAS 34:1678*, and *HLAS 35:6718*. The title and voluptuous cover-drawing embellishing the present volume forecast a frothy album of no scientific pretension. However, the three chapters in this first volume (survey of Yucatán song 1821–1900; influences on Yucatán songs 1900–40; and lyricists and composers 1940–70) provide much local data which, although diffuse and disorganized, cannot be easily located elsewhere (e.g., José Jacinto Cuevas, the first to incorporate folk-derived themes in an orchestral *Mosaico yucateco* and composer of *Himno yucateco*, b. and d. Mérida, 16 Aug. 1821–6 May 1878, dates which escaped Jesús C. Romero's "Historia de la música" in *Enciclopedia yucatanense*, vol. 4, 1944, p. 675). On the other hand, the often quoted biography of Gonzalo Roig (b. and d. Havana 20 July 1890–13 June 1970) counts as one among many digressions (p. 74–76). The author has made a valuable addition to Yucatán music bibliography marred by the informality of an illustrated scrapbook.

7133 Estrabau, Gilberto de. A batutazo limpio (Excelsior [Diorama de la cultura, México] 2 marzo 1980, p. 11)

The 18 existing orchestras in the republic employ 2,200 players—of whom 300 are foreigners whom the union leader Venus Rey promises to extirpate. When he does so, the Orquestra Filarmónica de la Ciudad de México will be threatened. These orchestras offer approximately 700 concerts annually, 300 in the Federal District, 400 outside. Prices at Bellas Artes orchestral concerts range from 200 to 60 pesos. Attendance therefore costs less than a bullfight or night club.

7134 Garrido, Juan S. Historia de la música popular en México: 1896–1973. México: Editorial Extemporáneos, 1974. 190 p., bibl., facsims., plates (Col. Ediciones especiales)

Beginning with 1930, the year that XEW (La Voz de la América Latina) was inaugurated, Garrido lists year by year through 1973 "hits," identifying each by category (ranchera, bolero, vals, corrido, pasodoble, and the like). Every annual listing is preceded by an essay on some prominent personage or happening of the year. This valuable collection of 96 numbered sections is a quarry from which future excavators will mine gems. However, snippets without an analytical index and casual music examples give no sense of flow. Printed in hard-to-read brown ink, the text is by no means as palatable as the fascinating subject matter promises. Still the volume is an indispensable purchase for anyone interested in Latin American commercial music. The 20-title bibliography arranged alphabetically by title, not author, needs expansion.

7135 Halffter, Rodolfo. Don Lindo de Almería: suite del ballet, partitura. 2. ed. México: Ediciones Mexicanas de Música, A.C., 1978. 53 p., music.

Completed at Madrid in 1935, this attractive seven-section ballet suite for double string quintet and percussion was first published in 1956. Extremely performable without choreography, it deserves widest circulation.

7136 Hinson, Maurice and **Charlotte Martin** *eds.* Piano music of Viceregal Mexico. Chapel Hill, N.C.: Hinshaw Music, 1979. 12 p., music.

José Manuel Aldana's *Minuet de Variaciones* is the *pièce de résistance* of this short anthology. The polaca testifies to Beethoven's early penetration into Mexico—since it is a simplified keyboard version of the *Allegretto alla Polacca* from his string trio *Serenade*, Opus 8.

7137 Lemmon, Alfred E. Preliminary investigation: music in the Jesuit missions of Baja California, 1698–1767 (The Journal of San Diego History [San Diego Historical Society, Calif.] 25:4, Fall 1979, p. 287–297, illus.)

Jesuits arrived at Mexico City in 1572. Their Lower California evangelization began in 1697. Among notable musicians dispatched to the peninsula, Juan María Salvatierra excelled. "His musical ability equipped him well to leave behind several descriptions of Indian dances." However, he was but one worthy musician among many. In this fine article (published in Spanish with an added section on 19th-century Baja California, see *Heterofonía*, 10:4, julio/agosto 1977, p. 13–17; and 10:5, sept./oct. 1977, p. 14–17), the learned author buttresses his precisions with 43 extensive bibliographical footnotes.

7138 ———. Research in colonial Mexican music (AAFH/TAM, 35:3, Jan. 1979, p. 391–398)

Invaluable introduction to the literature and tools for Mexican music research, especially in the capital, by a foremost investigator.

7138a Moncayo, José Pablo. La mulata de Córdoba; ópera en un acto. Partitura para canto y piano. México: FONAPAS (Fondo Nacional para Actividades Sociales) and EDIMEX (Ediciones Mexicanas de Música), 1979. 52 p., music.

The reduction of this piano-vocal score was supervised by the head of the Conservatorio Nacional, Armando Montiel Olvera. The libretto in three scenes by Agustín Lazo and Xavier Villaurrutia dramatizes the colonial legend told in Luis González Obregón's *México viejo.*

Paredes, Américo. A Texas-Mexican cancionero: folksongs of the Lower Border. See item **1358**.

7139 Rodríguez, Ignacio. El maestro José F. Velázquez es una institución en el ambiente pianístico (Excelsior [Diorama de la cultura, México] 17, nov. 1979, p. 13B, 17B, illus.)

At 80, the pianist recalls highlights of a career as piano teacher in the capital. His recital 21 Feb. 1917 in the Sala Wagner included works by Campa, Florduy, and Ponce. He has consistently favored Mexican repertory in this teaching.

7140 Stevenson, Robert. Antonio de Salazar (MGG [Supplement] 16, 1979, columns 1630–1631, bibl.)

Biography and works list of a paramount maestro at Puebla (appointed 11 July 1679) and Mexico City (25 Aug. 1688), where he died 25 March 1715.

7141 ———. Baroque music in Oaxaca Cathedral (IAMR, 1:2, Spring/Summer 1979, p. 179–203, bibl., music)

Three sections deal with music (1642–67; 1668–1740; 1741–86). Special emphasis on the Zapotec genius Juan Matías, his successor Mateo Vallados, and on the nonpareil Manuel de Zumaya (b. Mexico City, d. Oaxaca, 5 Oct. 1754).

7142 ———. Festival Mexicano-Norteamericano de las Artes en Chicago (HET, 12:4, sept./dic. 1979, p. 6–8)

On 21 April 1979, Silvestre Revueltas's student days in Chicago were honored with a one-day festival. Anna Sokolow—who went to Mexico with seven dancers in 1939 and choreographed *El Renacuajo Paseador* of Revueltas as well as ballets by Rodolfo Halffter, Blas Galindo and Rafael Elizondo—returned to Revueltas's music for ballets presented in NYC in 1974 and 1979. This article also specifies the ballets of Chávez and Moncayo offered abroad (dates and places).

7143 ———. Manuel de Zumaya en Oaxaca (HET, 12:1, enero/feb. 1979, p. 3–9)

Clarification of Zumaya's last years (1738–54) with a catalog of his works in Oaxaca Cathedral Archive. Zumaya died there 5 Oct. 1754.

7144 ———. Mexico City Cathedral: the founding century (IAMR, 1:2, Spring/Summer 1979, p. 131–178, bibl., musical facsims.)

Detailed history (1539–1622) with special emphasis on chapelmasters Lázaro del Alamo, Hernando Franco, and Juan Hernández.

7145 ———. A neglected Mexican guitar manual of 1776 (IAMR, 1:2, Spring/Summer 1979, p. 205–210)

Analysis of Case MS VMT 582 V29e at the Newberry Library, Chicago. This 1776 manuscript guitar tutor written by Juan Antonio Vargas y Guzmán at Veracruz reaches 303 pages. It rates as the bulkiest extant colonial music treatise.

7146 ———. Los sucesores de Juan Matías (HET, 12:2, marzo/abril 1979, p. 7–13)

Matías' triumphs included the training of excellent disciples. Among them his immediate successor at Oaxaca Cathedral, Chapelmaster Mateo Vallados composed music for 11 villancicos of Sor Juana Inés de la Cruz sung at Oaxaca on St. Catherine's day, 1691.

7147 El tango en México: historia interesante del tango y sus intérpretes en México, con una selección única de letras originales. Jorge Sareli: editor. México: Editorial Diana, 1977. 287 p., ill.

The editor, who has made a career since 1944 of propagating the Argentine tango in Mexico, devotes the first 54 p. to memories, photos, and newspaper clippings. The bulk of the book is an anthology of 500 tango lyrics. Although the majority are identified by author and composer, the lyrics are never documented by year or publisher. To become meaningful to strangers, these tango lyrics need the kind of program-noting that José Gobello gave 50 lyrics in *Conversando tangos.*

7148 Velazco, Jorge. Bohemio chopiniano (Excelsior [Diorama de la cultura, México] 16 dic. 1979, p. 9)

Luis Baca (1826–55), son of a govenor of Durango lived in Paris (1844–52), where he wrote two operas, *Leonora* (Carlo Bozetti) and *Giovanna di Castiglia* (Temistocle Solera).

7149 ———. Un capricho de Ricardo Castro (Excelsior [Diorama de la cultura, México] 6 enero 1980, p. 10–11, illus.)

Excellent relation of the life and works of the Durango-born composer (7 Feb. 1864) whose tours of the US (1885) and Europe (1903–06) brought him world recognition. After returning from the US, he joined the Group of the Six (including Campa and Villanueva) at Mexico City who were dedicated to shaking off the shackles of Italian opera. Nevertheless, his own *La légende de Rudel* had to be translated from French to Italian when premiered at the Teatro Arbeu the year before his premature death in Mexico City 28 Nov. 1907. Velazco eloquently appeals for resuscitation of Castro's concertos for cello and for piano—unjustly buried along with other *proezas* of the Porfirian period.

7150 ———. Carlos Chávez histórico (HET, 12:1, enero/feb. 1979, p. 10–12)

Excellent synthesis of the life and accomplishments of Chávez by an author possessed of like vitality and leadership ability.

7151 ———. El caso Beristaín (Excelsior [Diorama de la cultura, México] 30 dic. 1979, p. 9)

Joaquín Beristaín (b. 20 Aug. 1817) helped found in 1838 the short-lived Escuela Mexicana de Música. Death on 3 Oct. 1839 interrupted a pedagogic and creative career of infinite promise.

7152 ———. Claroscuro de Melesio Morales (Excelsior [Diorama de la cultura, México] 2 nov. 1979, p. 9, illus.)

Penetrating analysis of the career of Mexico's most successful composer of operas. Now all consigned to oblivion, *Romeo e Giulietta* (27 Jan. 1863) and *Ildegonda* (27 Jan. 1866) were the first of the five (librettos in Italian) mounted at the capital—the last having been *Cleopatra* (Teatro Nacional, 14 Nov. 1891).

7153 ———. Imprenta musical (Excelsior [Diorama de la cultura, México] 11 nov. 1979, p. 9)

In 1826, Elízaga pioneered in printing music in the young republic. He published two theory texts (1823, 1835). But the academies for music instruction founded by him, by Agustín Caballero and Joaquín Beristaín, and by José Antonio Gómez (15 Dec. 1839) were ephemeral institutions. Velazco queries the numerous name changes and changes of curriculum in the national conservatory (from 1970 to 1979, six radical curriculum revisions were introduced, a new one with each successive director).

7154 ———. Lástima que fue médico (Excelsior [Diorama de la cultura, México] 4 nov. 1979, p. 9, illus.)

Aniceto Ortega (b. Tulancingo, 17 April 1825) became an obstetrician. However, the talent demonstrated in his *episodio musical, Guatimotzin* (13 or 25 Sept. 1871), merited a composer's career (d. Mexico City, 17 Nov. 1875).

Vogt, Ezon Z. On the symbolic meaning of percussion in Zinacanteco ritual. See *HLAS 41:984*.

PERU

7155 Arguedas, José María. Nuestra música popular y sus intérpretes. Lima: Mosca Azul Editores, 1977. 29 p., illus.

Collected reprints of seven newspaper reviews dating from 1940 through 1968. Ima Sumac, the stage name chosen by Moisés Vivanco for his Lima-reared protégée, Emperatriz Chiavarri, grew up knowing not a word of Quechua. Her vaunted "stylizations" were deformations that betrayed Andean folk music. On the other hand, Arguedas stamps with approval Jaime Guardía, "the best player of the charango in Peru," and Rául García, a guitar virtuoso from Ayacucho. According to Arguedas, Spanish overlords denied Peruvian indigenes the guitar but encouraged them to play the harp and violin.

7155a Axel Roldán, Waldemar. La música en la Catedral de Lima (INIDEF, 3, 1977/1978, p. 36–64, music)

Author's transcription of José de Orejón y Aparicio's *A del día a de la fiesta* previously published in *Latin American Colonial Music Anthology*, 1975, p. 247–255. See *HLAS 38:9022*. Undocumented introduction precedes music transcription. Editor's note at p. 64 reads: "Due to communication difficulties it was impossible to obtain by [press] time bibliography for the present article."

Bernal, Dionicio Rodolfo. La muliza: teorías e investigaciones, origen y realidad folklórica, su técnica literaria y musical: folklore del Perú. See item **1392**.

Chaumeil, J. and **J.P. Chaumeil.** El rol de los instrumentos de música sagrados en la producción alimenticia de los yagua del noroeste peruano. See *HLAS 41:1124*.

7156 Instituto Nacional de Cultura (Peru).

Mapa de los instrumentos musicales de uso popular en el Perú: clasificación y ubicación geográfica. Diseño gráfico y dibujos, Alfonso Respaldiza. Lima: Oficina de

Música y Danza, 1978. 583 p., bibl., illus., plates (Serie mapas culturales)

This indispensable catalog of Peruvian popular-culture instruments—classified according to the Hornbostel-Sachs system as modified by Carlos Vega (1946) and Izikowitz (1935)—reflects highest credit on its compilers. Cesar Bolaños headed the team comprising Alida Salazar, Josafat Roel Pineda, and the esteemed Chilean composer and researcher resident in Peru since 1974, Fernando García. Of aerophones, which predominate in popular Peruvian organology, they list 71 scale-type syrinxes, 32 quenas. Although bibliographical references accompany each listed item, the volume lacks an alphabetized or chronological master bibliography. For Luis Merino's review, see *Revista Musical Chilena* (33:148, oct./dic. 1979, p. 97–99).

7157 Stevenson, Robert. Peru in international music encyclopedias (IAMR, 1:2, Spring/Summer 1979, p. 222–228)

Assessment of the treatment accorded Peru in the *Diccionario Oxford de la Música* (B.A., 1964) and in other international lexicons.

URUGUAY

7158 150 [i.e. **Cientocincuenta**] **años de música uruguaya:** ciclo de 22 conciertos a realizarse en el Paraninfo de la Universidad los días miércoles a las 18 y 30 horas desde el 7 de mayo hasta el 8 de octubre. Organizado por el Conservatorio Universitario de Música, Facultad de Humanidades y Ciencias. Montevideo: Comisión Nacional de Homenaje del Sesquicentenario de los Hechos Históricos de 1825, 1975. 1 v. (Unpaged) (Ediciones del sesquicentenario)

Works by 47 Montevideo composers from colonial times to the present were performed in the cycle of 22 concerts. Brief biographies (in chronological sequence) precede the programs. Except for two women, the composers permitted publication of their exact birth dates. One program was exclusively devoted to Carlos Estrada's works (in commemoration of the fifth anniversary of his death, 7 May 1970), but the other 21 programs mixed composers. Héctor Tosar Errecart was allotted only token representation with an insignificant *Danza Criolla*, whereas 10 works by Pedro Ipuche Riva were listed. This indicates who was the hero of the year.

7159 García Muñoz, Carmen. Lauro Ayestarán: 1913–1966 (Ritmo [Revista del Conservatorio de Música Juan José Castro, México] 5:6, 1977, p. 22–23)

Ayestarán's range distinguishes him from all other Montevideo-born musicologists. Equally at home in historical and ethnomusicology, his essays ranged from a tribute to Carlos Gardel (1960) to a life-and-works study of Domenico Zipoli (1962). In addition, he presided at the founding of the musicological chair in the Pontificia Univ. Católica and trained the best River Plate musicologists now active.

7160 Pulido, Esperanza. Entrevista con Francisco Curt Lange (HET, 13:1, enero/marzo 1980, p. 17–23)

Recounts history of Dr. Lange's transcendental labors in editing six stout volumes of *Boletín Latino-Americano de Música*, seven issues of *Revista de Estudios Musicales*, 12 numbers of *Archivo de Música Colonial Venezolana*; describes his activities as director of the Instituto Interamericano de Musicología created in 1940; and of his founding of the Editorial Cooperativa Interamericana. Valuable details of his personal biography conclude with his reactions to the V Conferencia Interamericana de Educación Musical held at Mexico City the second week of Oct. 1979 and to the problems of teaching historical musicology.

VENEZUELA

7161 Acuña, Guido. Apuntes para una biografía del maestro Vicente Emilio Sojo. Caracas: The Author, 1974. 47 p., illus.

Sojo (b. Guatire, 8 Dec. 1887; d. Caracas, 11 Sept. 1974) left Guatire in 1906 and settled in the capital where he made his living in the tobacco industry. He sided with Gen. José Manuel Hernández before becoming one of the founding members of the Rómulo Betancourt's Acción Democrática. In the campaign of 1973, he embraced Carlos Andrés Pérez's cause. In 1925, he married Efigenia Montero (d. 1935). Of their four sons, the first and third died young, Efren Vicente became a newspaperman and Carlos de la Trinidad entered commerce. His second marriage (Hilda Crouzet) terminated abruptly. These revelations sample this "intimate" biography, which stresses the nobility, self-sacrifice, and high artistic ideas of a leading mid-century composer.

Juárez Toledo, J. Manuel. Música tradicional de los yucpa-irapa del Estado Zulia, Venezuela. See item **1427**.

7162 Ramón y Rivera, Luis Felipe. La música popular de Venezuela. Caracas: Ernesto Armitano, 1976. 209 p., bibl., music, plates.

A superb study of Venezuelan popular music replete with valuable schematizations, factual details, and lavish illustrations. Pedro Elías Gutiérrez's joropo Alma llanera inserted in his short zarzuela of that name premiered 19 Sept. 1914, has travelled the continent—most recently in the version popularized by the Spanish singer Julio Iglesias (without composer attribution). For Luis Merino's review of this seminal publication, see *Revista Musical Chilena* (33:148, oct./dic. 1979, p. 99–103).

7163 Salazar, Rafael Henrique. Luis Mariano Rivera: alma y canción de Canchunchú. Caracas, Fondo Musical Latinoamericano, 1975. 190 p., bibl., music notations.

Luis Mariano Rivera (b. Canchunchú, 1907) was the son of landowner Antonio Font who died while he was a child—leaving him and his mother in poverty. At 25, while still an illiterate, he began versifying. In 1954, he took his musical group Alma Campesina to Caracas. From 1958–62, he interrupted his folk-singing career to work as an inspector at Güiria de la Costa. In 1963, he returned to Canchunchú, where Alfredo Armas Alfonzo, Cultural Director at the Univ. de Oriente, arranged for him to record his songs under Luis Felipe Ramón y Rivera's supervision at Caracas. Two years later a book was published in his honor, *Canchunchú Florido* (named for his song and for the folk group of that name established by him). The musical appendix to the present follow-up book contains the melodies of 10 songs by him. Although the harmonic syntax can usually be surmised, even *Canchunchú Florido* (p. 185) is incorrectly notated (measures 7–10).

7164 Stevenson, Robert. La música en la Catedral de Caracas hasta 1836 (UCIEM/R, 33:145, enero/marzo 1979, p. 48–114, bibl.)

Exhaustive history, beginning with 1580 in Coro—site of the cathedral until its removal to Caracas in 1636, and concluding with the death of Cayetano Carreño in 1836.

JOURNAL ABBREVIATIONS MUSIC

AAFH/TAM The Americas. A quarterly publication of inter-American cultural history. Academy of American Franciscan History. Washington.

ACH/B Boletín de la Academia Chilena de la Historia. Santiago.

ACH/BHA Boletín de Historia y Antigüedades. Academia Colombiana de la Historia. Bogotá.

AR Areíto. Areíto, Inc. New York.

BNBD Boletín Nicaragüense de Bibliografía y Documentación. Banco Central de Nicaragua, Biblioteca. Managua.

BNJM/R Revista de la Biblioteca Nacional José Martí. La Habana.

CH Cuadernos Hispanoamericanos. Instituto de Cultura Hispánica. Madrid.

HET Heterofonía. Revista musical bimestral. México.

IAMR Inter-American Music Review. R. Stevenson. Los Angeles, Calif.

ICP/R Revista del Instituto de Cultura Puertorriqueña. San Juan.

IHS/SJ Staden-Jahrbuch. Beiträge zur Brasilkunde. Instituto Hans Staden. São Paulo.

IJ/JJ Jamaica Journal. Institute of Jamaica. Kingston.

INIDEF Revista INIDEF. Consejo Nacional de la Cultura (CONAC) Instituto Interamericano de Etnomusicologia y Folklore. Caracas.

IPGH/FA Folklore Americano. Instituto Panamericano de Geografía e Historia, Comisión de Historia, Comité de Folklore. México.

LARR Latin American Research Review. Univ. of North Carolina Press *for the* Latin American Studies Association. Chapel Hill.

MGG Die Musik in Geschichte und Gegenwart. Kassel. Wilhelmshöhe, FRG.

MHD/B Boletín del Museo del Hombre Dominicano. Santo Domingo.

MVW/AV Archiv für Völkerkunde. Museum für Völkerkunde in Wien und von Verein Freunde der Völkerkunde. Wien.

OAS/AM Américas. Organization of American States. Washington.

UCIEM/R Revista Musical Chilena. Univ. de Chile, Instituto de Extensión Musical. Santiago.

UFP/EB Estudos Brasileiros. Univ. Federal do Paraná, Setor de Ciências Humanas, Centro de Estudos Brasileiros. Curitiba, Brazil.

UNM/JAR Journal of Anthropological Research. Univ. of New Mexico, Dept. of Anthropology. Albuquerque.

USP/LL Língua e Literatura. Univ de São Paulo, Depto. de Letras, Faculdade de Filosofia, Letras e Ciências Humanas. São Paulo.

PHILOSOPHY

JUAN CARLOS TORCHIA ESTRADA, *General Secretariat, Organization of American States*

LOS MATERIALES CORRESPONDIENTES A LA PRESENTE sección confirman lo expuesto en el *HLAS 40* (p. 557–558) sobre la distinción entre una filosofía que llamaríamos académica, profesional o tradicional, y las formas "comprometidas," que cuestionan la anterior por no representar un pensamiento autóctono o expresivo de la realidad latinoamericana (americanismo filosófico), por ser una expresión ideológica no consciente (marxismo), o por no dedicarse a una meditación liberadora de la tradicional dependencia material e intelectual (filosofía de la liberación). Aunque lo dicho supone un cierto grado de simplificación, representa las grandes líneas.

Lo que denominamos filosofía académica constituye el grueso de la producción filosófica latinoamericana, abarca una gran variedad de tendencias y se expresa en un grupo considerable de revistas (véase *HLAS 40*, p. 558), lo cual no excluye que en algunas de éstas aparezcan trabajos de las otras orientaciones.

En las influencias que recibe el pensamiento latinoamericano no se notan mayores diferencias con respecto al pasado inmediato, coincidiendo con un panorama europeo que tampoco presenta grandes variaciones. En las exposiciones o análisis críticos que se producen en América Latina están representadas todas las manifestaciones filosóficas occidentales que de un modo u otro tienen alguna vigencia.

En la presente entrega, entre las ediciones de autores "clásicos" debemos destacar la edición de escritos sobre educación del pensador positivista mexicano Gabino Barreda (item **7538**), así como la continuación de las *Obras* de Antonio Caso (item **7540**) y el tomo tercero de las *Obras* de Samuel Ramos (item **7544**). Estas dos últimas ediciones de *Obras completas* están a cargo de la Universidad de México.

La literatura historiográfica sobre el pensamiento filosófico latinoamericano sigue acrecentándose. En Brasil, por ejemplo, volvemos a encontrar varios ejemplos de ese interés. Una muestra nos parece ser la versión portuguesa del libro *Filósofos brasileños*, de Guillermo Francovich (item **7568**), publicada a más de 30 años de aparecer en castellano, y después de haberse enriquecido el tema con varias importantes obras posteriores. Además de hacer justicia al esfuerzo pionero de Francovich, revela, en una época de grandes dificultades editoriales, que existe un interés sobre ese tipo de obras.

Mayor novedad comportan los tres volúmenes de *As idéias filosóficas no Brasil* (item **7578**), preparados por un destacado grupo de especialistas. Un esfuerzo colectivo semejante sólo se había realizado anteriormente en México.

Siempre dentro de la bibliografía sobre Brasil corresponde destacar dos obras de Antonio Paim: *Problemática do culturalismo* (item **7595**), que se refiere a esa corriente brasileña, y *O estudo do pensamento filosófico brasileiro* (item **7592**), que analiza cómo han sido tratados historiográficamente los temas de ese pensamiento y trata otros problemas propios de él.

Con motivo del centenario de Andrés Bello han aparecido varios trabajos, entre los cuales destacamos uno de Arturo Ardao (item **7547**). Este autor, además, ha hecho una nueva contribución a la historia de las ideas filosóficas en América Latina con su reciente obra, *Estudios latinoamericanos* (item **7618**).

Constituye de hecho un examen casi total del pensamiento de Enrique José Varona la serie de artículos escritos por Pablo Guadarrama González sobre dicho autor (items **7571–7575**). Pensamos que el enfoque marxista que lo caracteriza no es la más apropiada hermenéutica para este caso, pero el conjunto no puede desconocerse como intento sistemático de abordar la figura del positivista cubano.

Entre los escritos de autores no latinoamericanos que se ocupan directa o indirectamente del pensamiento filosófico en la región son dignos de notar en el presente volumen la obra de Reine Guy (item **7576**); otras dos obras colectivas publicadas por la Universidad de Toulouse, en las que se reconoce la infatigable acción de Alain Guy: *Philosophes ibériques et ibéroamericains en exil* (item **7600**) y *Pensée ibérique et finitude* (item **7597**); la antología del pensamiento político latinoamericano publicada en Italia por Riccardo Campa (item **7627**); la obra de Werner Krauss (en alemán) sobre el iluminismo de habla española y portuguesa (item **7638**); y el libro de Henry C. Schmidt, *The roots of lo mexicano* (item **7654**).

Un tema que parece permanente es el de la naturaleza, sentido o autenticidad del pensamiento filosófico latinoamericano. Nuevas publicaciones sobre el asunto indican que se mantiene la preocupación de la filosofía latinoamericana por su propia identidad. El ejemplo más saliente entre los materiales del presente volumen es el primer tomo de las actas del IX Congreso Interamericano de Filosofía (item **7579**). Propósito semejante tiene la publicación de algunas de las ponencias presentadas al Coloquio de Filosofía llevado a cabo en Morelia, México, en 1975 (item **7559**). Por último, y sin agotar la lista, un volumen con una orientación temática similar, para el caso especial del Brasil, es el de Roberto Gomes, *Crítica de la razão tupiniquim* (item **7570**).

En el ámbito de la filosofía de la liberación, Enrique Dussel, uno de sus representantes más destacados, intenta una fundamentación de la misma en su *Introducción a una filosofía de la liberación* (item **7563**), en tanto Cerutti Guldberg clarifica aspectos de esa tendencia (item **7558**). Víctor Massuh, en cambio, realiza una severa crítica de esa orientación (item **7834**).

De los trabajos de mayor contenido teórico destacamos, en primer lugar, el libro de Adolfo P. Carpio sobre el sentido de la historia de la filosofía (item **7532**). Otras obras de consideración en ese sentido son las de Danilo Cruz Vélez (item **7504**), Miguel Reale (item **7853**) y Manuel Granell (item **7793**). Encontramos dignas de señalar también, cada una dentro de su orientación, obras como *Metamorfoses da liberdade*, de Ubiratan Macedo (item **7515**); *La superación de la filosofía*, de Juan Nuño (item **7519**); *Latinoamérica tercer mundo*, de Leopoldo Zea (item **7528**); y los ensayos que revelan la continuidad de la meditación de Guillermo Francovich (items **7508** y **7698**). Un artículo destacable es el de Enrique Haba sobre lo racional y lo razonable (item **7774**).

En materia de crítica, como ocurre desde hace un tiempo, junto a trabajos ocasionales o de poca profundidad hay otros de muy buena calidad y alto nivel técnico. Limitándonos solamente a libros, señalaremos el de García Bazán sobre la gnosis (item **7671**); los de Lluberes (item **7703**) y Menezes (item **7705**) sobre temas de filosofía moderna; y el de López Soria sobre Lukács (item **7742**). Somos conscientes de que cometemos injusticia por omisión en el caso de muchos buenos artículos de autores como Pucciarelli, Cappelletti, Guariglia, Presas, Miró Quesada, Maliandi, Gracia, Rosales, Li Carrillo y varios más.

Entre las revistas que aparecen por primera vez en esta entrega señalamos *Es-*

critos de Filosofía, de la Academia Nacional de Ciencias de Buenos Aires, dirigida por Eugenio Pucciarelli. Cada número se dedica a un determinado tema. Los dos primeros se han ocupado del lenguaje y de la ideología, respectivamente.

En esta bibliografía se incluyen libros y artículos de autores latinoamericanos, cualquiera sea el tema filosófico de que se ocupen, y de autores no latinoamericanos, siempre que traten asuntos relativos al pensamiento y la filosofía de América Latina.

En el presente número, la gran mayoría de las entradas corresponden a publicaciones aparecidas entre 1976 y 1978, pero hay también anteriores y posteriores a ese período.

En la subsección "Obras Generales y Didácticas" se agrupan los trabajos que responden a ese título, pero también otros que, por su número, no justificarían una subsección independiente. También se incluyen allí libros o artículos que se refieren a Latinoamérica general, como tema o problema.

Bajo la designación de "Pensamiento Latinoamericano" recogemos tres tipos de escritos: las reediciones de "clásicos" del pensamiento latinoamericano ("Fuentes"); los estudios críticos sobre la filosofía en América Latina ("Filosofía Latinoamericana"); y los estudios históricos no estrictamente filosóficos pero vinculados a la filosofía ("Historia de las Ideas").

Las divisiones de los trabajos sobre historia de la filosofía no requieren aclaraciones, excepto la imprecisa línea entre la filosofía "moderna" y la "contemporánea" en lo que se refiere a las últimas décadas del siglo XIX. Tendemos a colocar bajo "Filosofía Contemporánea" a los autores que desarrollaron su obra—o lo principal de ella—en nuestro siglo.

La división por disciplinas filosóficas se atiene a los criterios más generalizados, aunque los casos en que un trabajo puede caer bajo más de un título son inevitables.

OBRAS GENERALES Y DIDACTICAS

7501 Ardao, Arturo. Praxis y espacio exterior (*in* Homenaje al doctor Rafael Pizani. Caracas: Universidad Central de Venezuela, Facultad de Ciencias Jurídicas y Políticas, 1979, p. 31–43)

Interesantes reflexiones sobre un tema poco frecuentado por los filósofos: el efecto de la ciencia y la tecnología espaciales sobre los conceptos tradicionales de la filosofía. En parte se enlaza con el pensamiento de Teilhard.

7502 Camacho, Luis A. La investigación en filosofía (UCR/RF, 15:40, enero/junio 1977, p. 37–40)

Sobre aspectos institucionales de la investigación filosófica.

7503 Coutinho, Evaldo. O lugar de todos os lugares. São Paulo, Editora Perspectiva, 1976. 215 p.

Extensas reflexiones basadas en un radical subjetivismo extencial. La obra quiere ser una especie de introducción a otra: *A ordem fisionômica.*

7504 Cruz Vélez, Danilo. Aproximaciones a la filosofía. Bogotá: Instituto Colombiano de Cultura, Subdirección de Comunicaciones Culturales, División de Publicaciones, 1977. 252 p., bibl. (Colección Autores nacionales; 19. Biblioteca colombiana de cultura)

Se recogen trabajos aparecidos entre 1947 y 1976. Se compone de: "El Hombre y la Cultura" (1948); "La Filosofía y la Cultura" (1961); "La Metafísica y las Ciencias del Lenguaje" (1962); y otros varios artículos sobre Hegel, Nietzsche y Heidegger.

7505 Demushkina, E.V. Una contribución a la historia de la formación de la inteligencia latinoamericana (UCP/IAP, 7, 1973, p. 71–87)

Entendiendo por 'inteligencia' los sectores dedicados al pensamiento, la enseñanza, la ciencia, etc., se trata de una repaso general y esquemático de su historia, principalmente en el siglo XIX, y con juicios propios del marxismo oficial.

7506 **Fernández Pinto, Ronaldo.** Los intelectuales latinoamericanos y el proceso de cambio (UCR/RCS, 9, abril 1975, p. 95–119, bibl.)

Enfoque sociológico y "científico-político" del intelectual latinoamericano.

7507 **Fóscolo, Norma** and **Daniel Prieto.** Para abordar la cotidianidad latinoamericana (RFL, 2:3/4, enero/dic. 1976, p. 111–129)

El problema de la cotidianidad se analiza en autores europeos para aplicarlo (en la medida en que el pensamiento del "centro" es aplicable a la "periferia") a la realidad latinoamericana.

7508 **Francovich, Guillermo.** Los caminos del exceso. Sucre, Bolivia: División de Extensión Universitaria, 1977. 136 p.

Contiene tres ensayos: "Los Caminos del Exceso" es un extenso paralelo de Valéry y Kierkegaard, publicado orginalmente en 1948; "El Casuista de Pascal" continúa la meditación pascaliana del autor; y "La Existencia como Economía, como Desinterés y como Caridad" (título de la obra principal de Antonio Caso) remite a los tres órdenes distinguidos por Pascal la esencia de la posición filosófica del filósofo mexicano.

7509 **Fundação Getúlio Vargas,** *Rio de Janeiro.* **Instituto de Estudos Avançados em Educação. Centro de Documentação.** Filosofia e filosofia da educação no Brasil: bibliografia. Apresentação de Cecilia Andrade Dornelles. Rio: 1975. 114 p.

Util instrumento bibliográfico. Véase también *HLAS 40:9479*, un intento anterior, aunque de diferente estructura.

7510 **García Bazán, Francisco.** El lenguaje de la mística (Escritos de Filosofía [Academia Nacional de Ciencias, Centro de Estudios Filosóficos, Buenos Aires] 1:1, enero/junio 1978, p. 17–28)

Los temas del trabajo son: caracterización de la experiencia mística; la expresión de la experiencia mística (modalidades o "tipología" de los místicos); y la lengua de los místicos (influencia de la tradición espiritual).

7511 **Gotthelf, René.** Calibán como símbolo de la cultura latinoamericana (RFL, 2:3/4, enero/dic. 1976, p. 93–109)

Sobre la obra del ensayista cubano Roberto Rodríguez Retamar, *Calibán. Apuntes sobre la cultura en nuestra América.*

7512 **Hernández, Carmen Cecilia.** Fenomenología histórica de las religiones. México: Editorial Jus, 1975. 126 p.

Util esquema didáctico que se propone extraer los principales rasgos y componentes de las religiones en general.

Lemos, Néstor. Folklore y filosofía: la literatura paremiológica o refranesca, fuente primigenia de la filosofía. See item **987**.

7513 **Lo Mónaco, Vincenzo P.** El problema de un saber propio de nuestra América desde un punto de vista antropológico cultural (Actualidades [Centro de Estudios Latinoamericanos Rómulo Gallegos, Caracas] 1, 1976, p. 57–73)

El problema de un saber propio (o pensamiento propio) de América Latina no se resolverá si no se incorporan los elementos metodológicos que proporciona la antropología cultural. Se opone así a los enfoques puramente "filosóficos" del problema.

7514 **Lyra Filho, Roberto.** Filosofia, teologia e experiência mística (UMGFF/K, 22:69, jan./dez. 1976, p. 136–145)

El filosófo, el teólogo y el místico deben considerar sus respectivas búsquedas como interdependientes.

7515 **Macedo, Ubiratan de.** Metamorfoses da liberdade. São Paulo: Institução Brasileira de Difusão Cultural (IBRASA), 1978. 250 p.

Conjunto de trabajos filosóficos de buena calidad, agrupados en tres partes: 1) estudios de naturaleza teórica, como el problema del punto de partida de la filosofía o la teoría de los valores; 2) trabajos críticos sobre Kant, Ortega y Sciacca (muestra gran simpatía por este último autor); 3) ensayos sobre el pensamiento filosófico en Brasil, especialmente el pensamiento católico.

7516 **Maturo, Graciela.** Una filosofía del corazón para el mundo nuevo (RFL, 2:3/4, enero/dic. 1976, p. 131–137)

Sobre el tema de una "filosofía del corazón," "como representativa del pueblo latinoamericano del que ha surgido." En tanto "filosofía del pueblo," se contrasta con la filosofía de los intelectuales.

7517 **Medinacelli, Carlos.** La reivindicación de la cultura americana. Cochabamba, Bolivia: Los Amigos del Libro, 1975. 177 p.

Conjunto de ensayos, la mayoría de tema literario. En otros, al hilo de un libre comentario sobre escritos de Guillermo Francovich o José Vasconcelos, el autor expresa su opinión sobre el pensamiento latinoamericano, generalmente criticando la adopción del positivismo. Hay también un largo ensayo sobre Nietzsche.

7518 **Mendizábal Prem, Francisco.** Tesis provisionales. Para la determinación de una línea teórica y política que permitan una intervención correcta en las diferentes prácticas científicas y en la práctica política de los pueblos centroamericanos y latinoamericanos (UCR/RF, 15:41, julio/dic. 1977, p. 227–236)

Tesis como: "la filosofía es lucha de clases en la teoría;" y "solamente una posición materialista superadora de Hegel es consecuente en filosofía," son suficientemente indicativas de la posición del autor.

7519 **Nuño Montes, Juan Antonio.** La superación de la filosofía y otros ensayos. Caracas: Ediciones de la Biblioteca, Universidad Central de Venezuela, 1972. 236 p., bibl. (Colección Temas; 45)

Reúne conferencias y artículos pronunciados o publicados entre 1963–71. Contiene trabajos sobre el sentido de la filosofía contemporánea; el existencialismo (Sartre y Buber); las ideologías actuales; y sobre temas epistemológicos, de carácter más técnico que los anteriores. En general es de lectura no prescindible, por la abundancia de opiniones, independientemente de que se compartan o no. El único referente al pensamiento latinoamericano ("Germanización de la Filosofía Latinoamericana") es tal vez el menos equilibrado o críticamente bien fundado.

7520 **Paladines E., Carlos.** Presencia de Hegel en América (RFL, 2:3/4, enero/dic. 1976, p. 81–91)

Los temas del trabajo son: 1) "Hegel y su Pensamiento Explícito sobre América;" 2) "Hegel y la Filosofía Latinoamericana." El enfoque es el característico de la filosofía de la liberación.

7521 **Pérez Alcocer, Antonio.** Introducción histórica a la filosofía. Prólogo de Fernando Sodi Pallares. 2. ed. México: Editorial Tradición, 1977. 294 p., bibl., index.

Panorama de la historia de la filosofía. Lo preside la idea de que el tomismo es el sistema verdadero, siendo el pensamiento moderno negación "de los componentes sustanciales del ser concreto según los concibe Santo Tomás."

7522 **Pucciarelli, Eugenio.** Motivos filosóficos en la poesía de Martínez Estrada (CH, 326/327, agosto/sept. 1977, p. 1–20)

En la mejor tradición ensayística, se examinan las relaciones entre filosofía y poesía en general, la concepción de la poética en Martínez Estrada, los rasgos de idealismo y pesimismo en su poesía y la relación de éstos con la última fase de prédica social del autor de *Radiografía de la pampa.*

7523 **Romero, Paulino.** Distintas posiciones en la filosofía de la educación (LNB/L, 233, julio 1975, p. 22–42)

Repasa diferentes corrientes de filosofía de la educación en Latinoamérica.

7524 **Sábato, Ernesto.** Significado de Pedro Henríquez Ureña (UNPHU/A, 3:12/13, enero/junio 1975, p. 11–26)

En parte memoria y en parte apreciación de los valores del gran maestro dominicano. Lo enfoca en su pensamiento filosófico; en su enseñanza del idioma y la literatura; y en sus ideas sociales y sobre la unidad hispanoamericana.

7525 **Semana Internacional de Filosofia,** *2d, Petrópolis, Brazil, 1974.* Filosofía e realidade brasileira: atas da II Semana Internacional de Filosofía realizada na cidade de Petrópolis, RJ, de 14 a 20 de julho de 1974. Rio de Janiro: Sociedade Brasileira de Filósofos Católicos, 1976. 2 v., bibl.

Además de los discursos propios de este tipo de reuniones, el contenido de este volumen se divide en las siguientes secciones: Conmemoraciones de Sto. Tomás, San Buenaventura y Kant; Filosofía Brasileña; Filosofía Latinoamericana y Mundial; Investigación Filosofía y Enseñanza de la Filosofía; y Filosofía y Ciencias. Entre los latinoamericanos hay ponencias de Creusa Capalbo, Celina Junqueira, G. Pinheiro Machado, Fernando Arruda Campos, Alberto Caturelli y Agustín Basave.

7526 **Silva, Ludovico.** De lo uno a lo otro: ensayos filosófico-literarios. Caracas:

Ediciones de la Biblioteca, Universidad Central de Venezuela, 1975. 270 p.

Ensayos de muy variada temática. Los de mayor vinculación con la filosofía tratan de Lukács, Merleau-Ponty, San Agustín, Heidegger y temas marxistas como la ideología y la alienación.

7527 **Soto Badilla, José Alberto.** Paideia latinoamericana y filosofía de la integralidad (FH, 14:162, junio 1976, p. 425–438) 425–438)

Sobre algunas ideas del filósofo italiano Michele Federico Sciacca aplicables a la interpretación de la realidad latinoamericana.

7528 **Zea, Leopoldo.** Latinoamérica, Tercer Mundo. México: Editorial Extemporáneos, 1977. 162 p. (Colección Latinoamérica. Serie Ensayo; 1)

Reúne diversos trabajos. En ellos, dice el autor en su declaración inicial, "vuelvo a plantear mi preocupación por situar la historia de esta nuestra América con el resto de la Historia Universal." Señalamos, por sus temas, dos artículos: "La Filosofía Actual en América Latina" y "La Filosofía como Proyecto Nacional y Latinoamericano."

7529 **———.** Latinoamérica y la política de la cultura (CONAC/RNC, 34:224, abril/mayo 1976, p. 9–23, plate)

"Política de la cultura" se entiende como participación de la cultura en la vida ciudadana. La política de la cultura debe expresar "la racionalidad que haga conscientes las metas seguidas por cualquier política." El autor expresa además sus opiniones sobre la situación latinoamericana actual, en el contexto del tema del artículo.

7530 **Zilles, Urbano.** A crise da filosofia e a filosofia da crise (Convivium [Revista bimestral de investigação e cultura, Editòra Convívio, São Paulo] 21[17]:3, maio/junho 1978, p. 215–227)

En realidad, se trata de reflexiones sobre la civilización contemporánea y el lugar de la persona humana dentro de ella.

TEORIA DE LA FILOSOFIA

7531 **Bueno, Miguel.** La conciencia crítica en la evolución histórica de la filosofía (CAM, 197:6, nov./dic. 1974, p. 99–118)

Examen del grado de cientificidad de la filosofía en su historia, con el pensamiento kantiano como línea divisoria entre "filosofar" e "investigar."

7532 **Carpio, Adolfo P.** El sentido de la historia de la filosofía: ensayo ontológico sobre la "anarquía" de los sistemas y la verdad filosófica. Buenos Aires: Editorial Universitaria de Buenos Aires (EUDEBA), 1977. 446 p. (Temas)

El punto de partida de la obra es el efecto relativista del historicismo sobre la verdad filosófica o el fenómeno de la "anarquía de los sistemas." La salida para esa limitación sólo puede ser, para el autor, una especie de justificación de los términos del dilema: la verdad y la historia. Para ello, la verdad no se entenderá, a la manera tradicional, como *adequatio* o *coincidentia*, sino en la línea de "la teoría heideggeriana de la verdad como apertura y des-ocultamiento." El problema central es, por lo tanto, "cómo ha de entenderse la verdad, para que la pluralidad de las filosofías quede ontológicamente fundada." Este es el esquema de la obra, que el autor llena con consideraciones sobre la historia de la filosofía desde el punto de vista historiográfico; el ahistoricismo; el historicismo; la concepción clásica de la verdad; la estructura de la existencia y la naturaleza de la verdad; el tema de la metafísica; y el filosofar como trascender. Sobre la base del aludido concepto de la verdad, el sentido de la historia de la filosofía sería "la verdad de la filosofía," entendida no en un sentido proposicional, sino como "el proceso mismo de la filosofía, . . . su gestión, . . . su des-ocultamiento." Es una de las obras filosóficas más importantes del pensamiento argentino de los últimos 20 años.

7533 **Flury, Víctor J.** Hacia una filosofía intempestiva (UCR/RF, 15:41, julio/dic. 1977, p. 193–196)

Reflexiones sobre la situación y la posible naturaleza de la filosofía en el mundo actual, igualmente alejadas del enfoque cientificista y de la actitud ideológica.

7534 **Pérez Rojas Reyes, Antonio.** La autoconciencia: una angustia filosófica (UCR/RF, 15:41, julio/dic. 1977, p. 233–236)

Sobre ventajas e inconvenientes de ocuparse del tema de la filosofía en sí misma.

7535 Ramírez, Celedonio. La dialéctica de la filosofía: enamoramiento del ser (UCR/RF, 11:33, julio/dic. 1973, p. 247–258)

Construcción explicativa de la naturaleza del devenir filosófico, incluyendo el sentido de las tres grandes etapas de esa historia: antigua, medieval y moderna.

7536 Saco, Gustavo. La filosofía y la ciencia (UNMSM/L, 48:82/83 [1. semestre] 1976, p. 11–31)

Concepción de la filosofía muy estrechamente ligada a la ciencia.

7537 Sánchez Vásquez, Adolfo. Filosofía e ideología (UCR/RF, 15:41, julio/dic. 1977, p. 159–163)

Después de relacionar la filosofía con la sociedad, se define la ideología en términos marxistas. Luego se exponen los aspectos en que, según el autor, la ideología determina el quehacer filosófico. Excepcionalmente una filosofía puede analizar con éxito ideologías; pero para ello deberá primero ser consciente de su naturaleza ideológica.

PENSAMIENTO LATINOAMERICANO: FUENTES

7538 Barreda, Gabino. La educación positivista en México. Selección, estudio introductivo y préambulos de Edmundo Escobar. México: Editorial Porrúa, 1978. 281 p., bibl. (Sepan cuantos . . . ; 335)

Se considera propósito de la obra "reunir . . . aquellos escritos, cartas, informes y opúsculos [de Barreda] que hablan, comentan o discuten exclusivamente sobre educación." El estudio preliminar analiza la bibliografía sobre el positivismo mexicano en general y sobre Barreda en particular. Cada texto va precedido de una breve introducción por parte de quien tuvo a su cargo la edición.

7539 Barreto de Menezes, Tobias. Estudos de filosofia. Introdução de Paulo Mercadante e Antonio Paim. 2. ed. São Paulo: Editorial Grijalbo *em convênio com o* Instituto Nacional do Livro, 1977. 461 p., bibl. (Estante do pensamento brasileiro)

Reproduce, con menor aparato crítico, los tomos 1 y 2 de la edición de *Obras completas* do Tobias Barreto publicada por el Instituto Nacional do Livro, en 1966.

7540 Caso, Antonio. Obras completas. v. 9, Discursos a la nación mexicana; El problema de México y la ideología nacional; Nuevos discursos a la nación mexicana; México. Prólogo de Leopoldo Zea. Compilación de Rosa Krauze de Kolteniuk. México: Dirección General de Publicaciones, UNAM, 1976. 390 p., tables (Nueva biblioteca mexicana; 21)

Con este volumen continúa la feliz iniciativa de la Univ. de México de publicar las obras completas de Antonio Caso. En el presente se recogen sus ensayos sobre la realidad nacional mexicana, tema al que se refiere también el prólogo de Leopoldo Zea. Las diferencias de contenido entre este volumen y las obras originales están claramente indicadas. Como en otros de la misma serie, se acompaña un índice cronológico que da noticia de la publicación original y de otras posteriores de cada uno de los trabajos incluidos. Véase otros vols. en *HLAS 40:9448*.

7541 Fatone, Vicente. Extremism in oriental philosophy (Point of Contact [Ibero-American Language and Area Center, New York University, New York] 2:1, April/May 1978, p. 45–50)

Traducción de un trabajo de Fatone, de 1947, incorporado al primer volumen de sus *Obras completas* (1972).

7542 Ponce, Aníbal. La gramática de los sentimientos. Buenos Aires: Editorial Boedo, 1978. 76 p.

Se reedita esta obra del psicólogo y ensayista argentino, sin indicación crítica alguna. Hay edición reciente de las obras completas de Ponce (véase *HLAS 40:9427*).

7543 ———. Humanismo y revolución. Selección y prólogo de Jaime Labastida. Lima: Ediciones Populares Los Andes, 1970? 243 p., bibl. (Colección Fondo de cultura popular; 34)

Selección de escritos de Aníbal Ponce. Aunque publicado en Perú, la Advertencia está fechada en México. El prólogo de Labastida muestra particular simpatía por Ponce y su adhesión al marxismo. Sitúa la biografía intelectual de Ponce en el contexto de la época.

7544 Ramos, Samuel. Obras completas. v. 3, Estudios de estética. Filosofía de la vida artística. Prólogo de Cardiel Reyes. México: Universidad Nacional Autónoma de México, Dirección General de Publicaciones, 1977. 337 p., bibl. (Nueva biblioteca mexicana; 43)

Este tercer tomo de las obras completas de Ramos contiene la doctrina estética del autor, parte muy importante de su obra, aunque corrientemente es más conocido por sus escritos sobre tema mexicano. Contiene dos libros: *Filosofía de la vida artística* (1950) y *Estudio de estética* (1963). El prólogo de Cardiel Reyes proporciona una excelente orientación sobre la estética de Ramos.

PENSAMIENTO LATINOAMERICANO: FILOSOFIA LATINOAMERICANA

7545 **Abad Nebot, Francisco.** Andrés Bello en la historia social del pensamiento (IGFO/RI, 37:147/148, enero/junio 1977, p. 239–247)

Relaciona la obra lingüística de Bello con su lógica.

7546 **Andrilli, Rosa V.** Filosofía como axiología y pedagogía como axiología en acción: el intento de Alejandro Korn (UNL/U, 85, julio/dic. 1976, p. 151–173)

Destaca lo que hay de pensamiento pedagógico en Korn, como resultado de su axiología, y lo examina en el proceso de superación de la pedagogía positivista. Señala lo que considera limitaciones del intento de Korn en ese sentido.

7547 **Ardao, Arturo.** La iniciación filosófica de Bello (CONAC/RNC, 40:241, marzo/mayo 1979, p. 67–83, plate)

Es parte de un trabajo más amplio, del cual aparecen aquí sólo las dos primeras partes: una trata de la obra de Bello *Análisis ideológica de los tiempos de la conjugación castellana* y la otra sitúa la posición de Bello en la historia de la gramática filosófica.

7548 **Barceló Larraín, Joaquín.** Tradición e innovación como condiciones para una filosofía hispanoamericana (Cuadernos de Filosofía [Universidad de Concepción, Instituto Central de Filosofía, Concepción, Chile] 6, 1977, p. 167–180)

El cuerpo del artículo trata en realidad sobre el concepto de tradición. Con ese bagaje, se concluye: "la única tarea para una filosofía latinoamericana es incorporarse a la tradición filosófica de Occidente." Pero esta tarea tiene dos caras: recibir el *traditum* de esa tradición, y elaborar su propio *tradendum*, (lo que se elabora como propio con aquella base y se transmite al futuro).

7549 **Biagini, Hugo E.** La expresión "filosofía latinoamericana" (LARR, 14:2, 1979, p. 198–201)

Utiles distinciones conceptuales en torno a la expresión "filosofía latinoamericana."

7550 ———. Revistas filosóficas argentinas (Revista Nacional de Cultura [Ministerio de Educación, Secretaría de Cultura, Buenos Aires] 4, 1979, p. 139–156)

Utiles indicaciones sobre revistas filosóficas argentinas, muchas de ellas desaparecidas. El recuento comienza con la *Revista de Filosofía*, dirigida por José Ingenieros.

7551 ———. Tesis estadounidenses sobre pensamiento argentino (UBAFFL/C, 17:26/27, enero/dic. 1977, p. 201–209)

El contenido abarca más de lo que indica el título y en conjunto es un inventario útil y no realizado anteriormente.

7552 **Buljevic, Ossandon.** La concepción de una filosofía americana en Alberdi (CH, 349, julio 1979, p. 128–143)

Después de exponer la posición de Alberdi frente a la posibilidad de una filosofía americana, se extraen consecuencias de esa posición para una filosofía de la liberación.

7553 **Campos Barrantes, Eliam.** Posibilidades y límites de una filosofía latinoamericana auténtica (UCR/RF, 16:43, enero/junio 1978, p. 87–91)

Polemiza con una ponencia de Miró Quesada, defendiendo las tesis clásicas de la filosofía de la liberación.

7554 **Carvalho, Laerte Ramos de.** A formação filosófica de Farias Brito. São Paulo: Saraiva [and] Universidade de São Paulo, 1977. 208 p., bibl.

Este libro se publicó por primera vez en 1951, pero tuvo circulación restringida. Abarca el pensamiento de Farias Brito desde 1886 hasta 1895. Miguel Reale destaca las características de la obra en el Prefacio. Contiene, en apéndice, textos de Farias Brito.

7555 **Caturelli, Alberto.** La filosofía en Argentina: 1610–1976 (Cuadernos de Filosofía [Universidad de Concepción, Instituto Central de Filosofía, Concepción, Chile] 6, 1977, p. 93–109, bibl.)

Resumen del pensamiento filosófico argentino desde la Colonia hasta la actualidad. Las bases de interpretación son las mismas que el autor mostró en *La filosofía en la Argentina actual* (véase *HLAS 34:5186* y *HLAS 28:3258*). En apéndice se dan datos sobre Facultades, institutos, bibliografías, revistas, etc.

7556 ———. La lógica-metafísica del Padre José Angulo, S.J. (UCA/S, 32:126, 1977, p. 287–312, tables)

Trabajo monográfico sobre un texto manuscrito hallado en Cochabamba, ilustrativo sobre la enseñanza de la lógica en la Univ. de Córdoba en el siglo XVIII.

7557 Cerutti Guldberg, Horacio. Aproximación a la historiografía del pensamiento ecuatoriano (Pucará [Universidad de Cuenca, Facultad de Filosofía, Letras y Ciencias de la Educación, Cuenca, Ecuador] 1, enero 1977, p. 21–48)

Contiene útil información sobre antecedentes de una historiografía sobre el pensamiento en Ecuador.

7558 ———. Posibilidades y límites de una filosofía latinoamericana después de la "filosofía de la liberación" (UC/A, 33, abril 1978, p. 9–18)

Aporta útiles distinciones para abordar el sentido, la breve historia y los matices de la filosofía de la liberación. Es resumen de un libro que el autor anuncia y que se puede sospechar será una contribución a la dilucidación del concepto mismo de "filosofía de la liberación."

7559 Coloquio Nacional de Filosofía, *1st, Morelia, México, 1975.* La filosofía actual en América Latina. México: Editorial Grijalbo, 1976. 211 p., bibl. (Teoria y praxis; 25)

Como en el caso del volumen dedicado a "Filosofía y Ciencias Sociales," se recogen aquí ponencias seleccionadas de entre las presentadas al Primer Coloquio Nacional de Filosofía, Morelia, México, 4–9 agosto 1975. Sobre el tema: "Función Actual de la Filosofía en Latinoamérica" escriben: Arturo Arado (p. 9–20), intentando proyectar a la actualidad la temática de la "emancipación mental," originada en el siglo pasado; Rosa Krauze (p. 73–83), quien en realidad ensaya una defensa bien argumentada de la filosofía analítica; Francisco Miró Quesada (p. 85–98), aprobando y a la vez criticando el concepto de filosofía de la liberación, pero sobre todo destacando el valor de una "filosofía rigorista," de fundamento inequívocamente racional; y Arturo A. Roig (p. 135–152), enrolado con motivación ética y exaltado estilo en la filosofía de la liberación aunque distinguiéndose de la modalidad "populista" argentina. Cercanos al tema mencionado son los siguientes artículos: Enrique Dussel, "La Filosofía de la Liberación en Argentina: Irrupción de una Nueva Generación Filosófica (p. 55–62): breve historia del asunto; María Rosa Palazón M., "Características Reales y Posibles de la Filosofía Latinoamericana" (p. 99–114): meditación en torno a escritos de Salazar Bondy y Leopoldo Zea; y Mario Sambarino, "La Función Sociocultural de la Filosofía en América Latina" (p. 165–181, véase item **7603**). Completan el volumen los siguientes trabajos: Rolando Cordera Campos, "Notas sobre la Colaboración entre Filósofos y Científicos Sociales en México" (p. 21–32); Arnaldo Córdova, "La Filosofía de la Revolución Mexicana" (p. 33–54); José Antonio Portuondo, "Ideas Estéticas de la Revolución Cubana" (p. 115–123); María Elena Rodríguez de Magis, "Dos Interpretaciones del Pensamiento Latinoamericano: el Río de la Plata y la América Mestiza" (p. 125–133); Ricaurte Soler, "Consideraciones sobre la Historia de la Filosofía y de la Sociedad Latinoamericanas" (p. 153–163): uno de los pocos trabajos que tratan la historia de la historiografía de las ideas en América Latina, escrito desde un punto de vista materialista dialéctico; Abelardo Villegas, "Proyecto para una Filosofía Política de América Latina" (p. 183–192): superando el historicismo y la filosofía analítica, propone un programa "de una posible filosofía latinoamericana concebida como una meditación práctica de la realidad;" René Zavaleta Mercado, "El Conocimiento Social de América Latina" (p. 193–201); y Leopoldo Zea, "La Filosofía Actual en América Latina" (p. 203–211): adopta el tema de la liberación, pero en realidad propone una filosofía latinoamericana como ideología (programa de cambio) y como filosofía de la historia; y más aún, defiende su propio enfoque de ciertas críticas.

7560 **Dessau, Adalbert.** La ontología nacional en la obra de Samuel Ramos (UCLV/I, 50, enero/abril 1975, p. 155–166)

Comentarios, desde un punto de vista marxista, a *El perfil del hombre y la cultura en México*, de Samuel Ramos.

7561 **Devés Valdés, Eduardo.** El quehacer filosófico y su relación con el problema de la cultura nacional de Alejandro Korn (RFL, 2:3/4, enero/dic. 1976, p. 139–151)

Se destaca a Korn como antecedente—en la línea de Alberdi y Echeverría—de una filosofía de raíz nacional. Luego se le hacen observaciones críticas desde una posición más "avanzada" dentro de la misma línea.

7562 **Dorestal, Yves.** Tesis para el trazo de nuevas perspectivas para una nueva práctica de la filosofía en Centro América (UCR/RF, 15:41, julio/dic. 1977, p. 223–225)

La "nueva práctica" que se propugna sería un "arma teórica al servicio de la emancipación de los pueblos centroamericanos."

7563 **Dussel, Enrique D.** Introducción a una filosofía de la liberación latinoamericana. México: Extemporáneos, 1977. 149 p., bibl., illus. (Colección Latinoamérica. Serie Ensayo; 4)

No es un trabajo crítico sobre la filosofía de la liberación como corriente o tendencia, sino la exposición de la propia filosofía del autor, a la cual considera como filosofía de la liberación o fundamento de ella. Los temas básicos, sin embargo (centro-periferia, opresor-oprimido, voz del pueblo, etc.) coinciden con los de la mencionada corriente.

7564 **Echeverría, Carlos E.** and **Augusto Serrano.** La filosofía como inserción en la cotidianidad: la filosofía en América Central (UCR/RF, 15:41, julio/dic. 1977, p. 201–206)

Con base en algunas tesis de Gramsci, según los autores partir de la cotidianidad e insertarse en el sentido común "es la tarea revolucionaria de producir un filosofar auténtico." Este artículo apareció también en *Revista de la Universidad* (Tegucigalpa, 6:13, oct. 1977, p. 35–41).

7565 **Escobar, Roberto.** El sentido de lo americano en los filósofos chilenos (EC/M, 26, 1978, p. 25–33)

Contiene información útil sobre el tema.

7566 **España, Olmedo.** El positivismo en Iberoamérica. Heredia, Costa Rica: Departamento de Filosofía, Universidad Nacional, 1977. 24 p., bibl. (Colección Popular; 3)

Breve panorama basado en el caso de Argentina, México, Chile y Cuba. Cierta literatura de apoyo es marxista, pero las conclusiones son de índole muy general.

7567 **Fell, Claude.** José Vasconcelos au Chili: documents pour une controverse (UHB/EHA, 10, 1975, p. 15–31)

Resonancias polémicas del paso de Vasconcelos (como Ministro de Educación), por Chile, en 1922. Interesan los documentos periodísticos que reproduce.

7568 **Francovich, Guillermo.** Filósofos brasileiros. Prefácio de Gerardo Dantas Barreto. Adendo de Antônio Paim. Rio: Presença, 1979. 126 p.

Publicado en 1943 en Buenos Aires en la Biblioteca Filosófica dirigida por Francisco Romero, y escrito varios años antes, este libro fue uno de los pioneros de la época de gran incremento de los estudios sobre el pensamiento filosófico latinoamericano. Se presenta ahora traducido al portugués, sin cambios pero con un capítulo final a cargo de Antonio Paim y un prefacio de Gerardo Dantas Barreto.

7569 **Gallardo, Helio.** Pensamiento iberoamericano: las limitaciones de la filosofía clásica (UCR/RF, 15:40, enero/junio 1977, p. 109–149, bibl.)

Se critica a muy variados autores en lo que respecta a su posición frente al problema de si existe un pensamiento iberoamericano. Ninguno de ellos acertó porque todos están sumidos en la "filosofía clásica," es decir, no materialista-dialéctica. Además, todas esas posiciones son ideológicas. Algunas críticas son innecesariamente ofensivas.

7570 **Gomes, Roberto.** Crítica da razão tupiniquim. Porto Alegre: Editora Movimento, 1977. 104 p., bibl. (Coleção Dialética; 6)

Reflexiones sobre el modo de ser brasileño y sobre la posibilidad de una filosofía propia en Brasil. Ajeno a las orientaciones de la filosofía de cátedra o profesional, entiende un pensamiento propio como un retorno a la introspección nacional, y en tal sentido tiene puntos de contacto con algunos representantes de la filosofía de la liberación.

7571 **Guadarrama González, Pablo M.** El ateísmo y el anticlericalismo de Enrique José Varona (UCLV/I, 59, enero/abril 1978, p. 164–182)

Desde el punto de vista marxista-leninista característico del autor, reconoce en Varona "a uno de los más relevantes representantes del ateísmo y el anticlericalismo, que a pesar de su óptica burguesa encierra muchos elementos valiosos."

7572 ———. Enríque José Varona y el positivismo (UCLV/I, 54, mayo/agosto 1976, p. 3–25)

La interpretación científica de las ideas de Varona sólo puede realizarse basándose en el marxismo-leninismo. Desde este supuesto se examinan las relaciones de Varona con el positivismo europeo.

7573 ———. Las ideas éticas de E.J. Varona (UCLV/I, 55/56, sept. 1976/abril 1977, p. 171–202)

Las ideas de Varona sobre la moral son juzgadas desde un punto de vista marxista.

7574 ———. Las ideas socio-políticas de Enrique José Varona (UCLV/I, 57, 1977, p. 51–110)

Traza, desde un claro punto de vista marxista, la evolución política de Varona, que habría ido, según el autor, desde el liberalismo burgués a una cierta forma de admisión del socialismo.

7575 ———. La sociología en el pensamiento filosófico de Enrique José Varona (UCLV/I, 60, mayo/agosto 1978, p. 83–126)

En la misma línea que los trabajos anteriores, continúa la revisión marxista del pensamiento de Varona. En sus últimos años, y a pesar de la influencia de la sociología positivista, Varona no habría sido escéptico, como se ha dicho, sino que habría atisbado el advenimiento del socialismo.

7576 **Guy, Reine.** Axiologie et métaphysique selon Joaquim Xirau. Le personalisme contemporain de l'Ecole de Barcelone. Préface de Jean-Marc Gabaude. Toulouse, France: Université de Toulouse-Le Mirail, 1976. 309 p., bibl. (Publications de l'Université de Toulouse-Le Mirail. Série A; 33)

Xirau perteneció al grupo de los filósofos españoles "transterrados" a México con motivo de la Guerra Civil. El presente estudio es el más detallado que se le ha consagrado. Contiene también una útil bibliografía.

7577 **Hübner, Jorge Iván.** El pensamiento filosófico en España e Iberoamérica (Cuadernos de Filosofía [Universidad de Concepción, Instituto Central de Filosofía, Concepción, Chile] 6, 1977, p. 13–17)

Las dos principales afirmaciones son: 1) una filosofía latinoamericana "autóctona" no es posible porque la filosofía es universal; 2) se puede ser optimista en cuanto al futuro de la filosofía en América Latina.

7578 **As idéias filosóficas no Brasil.** v. 1, Séculos XVIII e XIX; v. 2, Século XX, pt. 1; v. 3, Século XX, pt. 2, Coordenador, Adolpho Crippa. São Paulo: Editora Convivio, 1978. 3 v. (238, 205, 240 p.) bibl.

Esta obra colectiva—semejante a la llevada a cabo en México (véase *HLAS 38:9503*)—es prueba del interés con que se encara en Brasil el estudio de su pasado filosófico. La mayoría de los autores son conocidos por contribuciones anteriores a sus respectivos temas. Los autores y los temas son los siguientes: Vol. 1, Fernando Arruda Campos, la filosofía colonial; Paulo Mercadante, el eclecticismo; Nelson Saldanha, la Escuela de Recife; R.S. Maciel de Barros, el positivismo durante el Imperio; D. Odilão Moura, efectos del iluminismo; U. de Macedo, el pensamiento católico en el segundo reinado; Miguel Reale, la doctrina de Kant en Brasil. Vol. 2, Antonio Paim, la corriente culturalista; Carlos Lopes de Matos, Farias Brito; Vamireh Chacon, el marxismo; Adolpho Crippa, Vicente Ferreira da Silva; Odilão Moura, el pensamiento católico en el siglo XX. Vol. 3, A.L. Machado Neto, la filosofía del derecho; Creusa Capalbo, la filosofía de la educación; Benedito Nunes, el pensamiento estético; Leonidas Hegenberg, la lógica y la filosofía de la ciencia. Los vols. 2 y 3 están dedicados al siglo XX. Algunos artículos tienen bibliografía. El coordinador ha sido Adolpho Crippa, autor de una introducción a los tres volúmenes sobre el tema de la filosofía en Brasil, a la cual enfoca como parte del pensamiento occidental. La obra se considera un primer intento y se espera reelaborarla en otras ediciones.

7579 **Inter-American Congress of Philosophy,** *9th, Caracas, 1977.* La filosofía en América: anales del IX [i.e. noveno] Congreso Interamericano de Filosofía, t. 1. Caracas: Sociedad Venezolana de Filosofía, 1979. 253 p.

Este libro recoge los trabajos presentados al IX Congreso Interamericano de Filosofía y que se refieren a la sección del Congreso titulada "La Realidad Latinoamericana como Problema del Pensar Filosófico," que a su vez se dividió en tres temas: 1) *La enseñanza de la filosofía en América Latina*: Hay aquí ponencias de dos autores que se han ocupado de este asunto anteriormente: Risieri Frondizi y Diego Domínguez Caballero. La ponencia de Frondizi es una propuesta bien fundamentada y con cierto grado de detalle. Domínguez Caballero se ocupa más bien de la didáctica de la iniciación filosófica. Manuel A. Aguirre trata también este tema y de su posición parece claro índice su consideración de la filosofía marxista como "la síntesis de lo más alto que ha producido el pensamiento humano." Carlos Mato Fernández propone planes que desarrollen el espíritu crítico y racionalista. Carlos E. Oliva se refiere a la enseñanza secundaria. Cerutti Guldberg propone un "Anteproyecto de *pensum* para la especialidad de filosofía con orientación latinoamericana." Otras contribuciones son: Joaquín Barceló, "Observaciones acerca de la Enseñanza de la Filosofía en la Educación Superior" y Joaquín Sánchez Mac Gregor, "Praxis Universitaria en México: Ideología y/o Ciencia." 2) *Historia y evolución de las ideas filosóficas en América Latina*: Tres ponencias tienen por título este segundo tema. La de Arturo Ardao es sumamente aclaradora y resulta un buen marco de referencia para profundizar la cuestión planteada. Leopoldo Zea deriva esa cuestión más bien a sus conocidas preocupaciones por una filosofía de la historia de "nuestra América" y las críticas que como historiador de las ideas le han dirigido Raat y Hale. Angel J. Cappelletti concluye que no hay una filosofía de América Latina, pero que el análisis del re-pensamiento de lo europeo por los pensadores latinoamericanos puede llevar a una filosofía de la historia sobre América Latina. Fuera de una ponencia de Manuel Claps sobre "La Historia de las Ideas como Historia de las Ideologías," todas las demás de esta segunda parte son de naturaleza crítica. Los temas y autores son los siguientes: sobre Rodolfo Mondolfo, Diego Pro y Angel J. Cappelletti; sobre Francisco Romero, William Cooper; sobre Macedonio Fernández, Hugo E. Biagini; sobre Alejandro Korn, W. Kilgore y J.C. Torchia Estrada; sobre Farias Brito, F. Gillette Sturm; sobre el positivismo en Haití, Max Wilson; sobre Deustua, Jack Himelblau; sobre el hombre colonial, G. de Mello Kujawski; sobre el culturalismo brasileño, Antonio Paim; sobre la teoría de los valores de Risieri Frondizi, Gene G. James; y sobre la utopía en América, Roberto Escobar. 3) *Posibilidad y límites de una filosofía latinoamericana*: Para la ponencia de Francisco Miró Quesada, véase *HLAS 40:9476*. Asimismo, para la de Elías Campos Barrantes, véase item **7553**. Igualmente, para la de Antonio Paim, item **7594**. Con una variante (referente a la filosofía de la liberación) también la ponencia de Horacio Cerutti Guldberg la recogemos aparte: item **7558**. Agustín Basave, en la suya, no cree que haya una "filosofía americana," sin que por ello el pensamiento latinoamericano deje de tener características propias. Este autor acentúa el tinte religioso de la filosofía latinoamericana. Francisco Larroyo retoma temas expuestos en sus libros anteriores sobre el tema y critica varias concepciones de lo americano, especialmente aquellas que él denomina de anticipación profética. No nos sería posible resumir todos las ponencias restantes. Señalamos algunas: Santiago Vidal Muñoz, "La Filosofía y la Historia de las Ideas en América;" Horacio Cerutti Guldberg, "Posibilidades y Límites de una Filosofía Latinoamericana después de la 'Filosofía de la Liberación'" (véase item **7558**); Nelson Saldanha, "Cultura y Filosofía en Latinoamérica;" Max Aguirre C., "Problemas Inherentes a la Constitución de una Filosofía Americana;" José Jara, "El Lugar Histórico del Pensar Latinoamericano;" Ramiro Pérez Reinoso, "Posibilidades de una Filosofía Latinoamericana;" Joaquín Barceló, "El Entroncamiento con la Tradición como Unica Posibilidad para un Filosofar Latinoamericano;" Manuel Granell, "Filosofía Latinoamericana y Espíritu Viajero."

7580 Ladusāns S.I., Stanislavs. A filosofia no Brasil hoje (Cuadernos de Filosofía [Universidad de Concepción, Instituto Central de Filosofía, Concepción, Chile] 6, 1977, p. 155–166)

El trabajo versa en realidad sobre los "niveles de originalidad" del pensamiento brasileño actual, según las conclusiones a que llegó el autor en una especie de "censo" de filósofos que realizó en Brasil, una parte del cual se refleja en su obra *Rumos da filosofia atual no Brasil.*

7581 Láscaris, Constantino. Algunos pensadores centroamericanos: Juan José Arévalo, José Mata Gavidia, Julio Fausto Fernández, Francisco Peccorini, José Salvador Guandique, José Coronel Urtecho, Pablo Antonio Cuadra, Diego Domínguez Caballero, la Panameñidad (UCR/RF, 15:41, julio/dic. 1977, p. 281–307, bibl.)

Trabajo muy útil para el conocimiento del pensamiento centroamericano del presente siglo.

7582 Leiva, Miguel da Costa. El pensamiento de Enrique Molina Garmendia (Cuadernos de Filosofía [Universidad de Concepción, Instituto Central de Filosofía, Concepción, Chile] 6, 1977, p. 45–82)

Abarca la época de formación de Molina, y su pensamiento hasta 1914. El trabajo es parte de una obra en preparación que, a juzgar por este fragmento, puede ser de real importancia en la bibliografía del filósofo chileno.

7583 Lockhart, Washington. Determinaciones fundamentales de la actitud filosófica de Vaz Ferreira (UBN/R, 17, 1977, p. 55–122)

La intención del trabajo, a través de una extensa exposición, es descubrir el fondo de intuiciones personales y de actitudes ante el mundo y la vida que constituirían la "actitud filosófica" de Vaz Ferreira.

7584 Maliandi, Ricardo. Die philosophische Ethik des 20. Jahrhunderts in Lateinamerika (*in* Die Wertkrise des Menschen: Philosophische Ethik in der heutigen Welt. Edited by Norbert Huppertz. Festschrift für Hans Reiner. Meisenheim am Glan, FRG: Verlag Anton Hain, 1979, p. 197–213)

De estructura semejante a su artículo "Trayectoria y Sentido de la Etica en el Pensamiento Latinoamericano," pero en el aspecto contemporáneo trata más especialmente la teoría de los valores de Risieri Frondizi.

7585 Martínez, Agustín. La filosofía en Venezuela: recopilación bibliográfica (Semestre de Filosofía [Universidad Central de Venezuela, Caracas] 1:1, julio/dic. 1977, p. 153–160, bibl.)

Contiene algo más de 120 asientos, por orden alfabético de autor.

7586 Mejía Valera, Manuel. El hombre y los valores en la filosofía latinoamericana del siglo XX (CAM, 205:2, marzo/abril 1976, p. 145–152)

Nota crítica a la antología de Frondizi y Gracia, *El hombre y los valores en la filosofía latinoamericana del siglo XX* (véase *HLAS 38:9468*).

7587 Miliani, Domingo. Leopoldo Zea: conciencia vigilante de América Latina (UCAB/M, 4, 1975, p. 523–532)

Sobre el significado de la obra latinoamericanista de Leopoldo Zea.

7588 Millán C., Enrique. Evolución filosófica en Latinoamérica (CBR/BCB, 15:1, dic. 1978, p. 92–100)

Esquema muy panorámico de las corrientes filosóficas del siglo XIX latinoamericano. Que los grandes pensadores no son estudiados en América, o que las corrientes dominantes son el "eclecticismo" y el marxismo, son conclusiones cuestionables del trabajo.

7589 Mora Rodríguez, Arnoldo. Las tareas de la filosofía latinoamericana (UCR/RF, 15:41, julio/dic. 1977, p. 211–215)

Las bondades de la filosofía latinoamericana actual serían el desarrollo de la teoría de la dependencia y la influencia del marxismo.

7590 Ortega, Hugo O. El surgimiento del pensamiento de la liberación (USMLA/LA, 5:6, mayo 1976, p. 58–73)

Encuentra el origen de la filosofía de la liberación en ciertos aspectos recientes de la obra de Leopoldo Zea; en la teología de la liberación; y en la crítica a ciertas orientaciones de las ciencias sociales. Luego expone, con un sentido de adhesión, temas de esta corriente, comentando a algunos de sus representantes.

7591 Paim, Antônio. Bibliografia filosófica brasileira: período contemporâneo, 1931–1977. São Paulo: Edições GRD [and] Instituto Nacional do Livro, 1979. 246.

La primera versión de este útil trabajo bibliográfico apareció en 1972 (véase *HLAS 40:9479*). Esta ampliación extiende la información hasta 1977. En la Introducción, Antonio Paim extrae conclusiones sobre la actividad filosófica en Brasil en base a los datos de esta bibliografía.

7592 ———. O estudo do pensamento filosófico brasileiro. Rio: Tempo Brasileiro, 1979. 157 p. (Biblioteca tempo universitário; 57)

Valiosa contribución a la historiografía sobre el pensamiento filosófico en el Brasil. Además del tema central, contiene capítulos sobre los problemas propios del pensamiento brasileño, la cuestión de la originalidad y los fundamentos morales de la cultura brasileña. La bibliografía es muy útil.

7593 ———. Momentos destacados del pensamiento filosófico brasileño (UM/R, 22, julio/sept. 1976, p. 27–62)

Sostiene que las principales figuras del pensamiento en Brasil "se inspiraron en la filosofía europea para resolver determinados problemas suscitados por . . . [la] evolución político-cultural [de Brasil]." Por eso "no hay identidad entre los grandes movimientos filosóficos de ese ciclo y las corrientes y tendencias brasileñas." Esta afirmación básica se ilustra con cuatro momentos: el pensamiento de Pinheiro Ferreira; el de Ferreira França; el de Tobias Barreto; y el culturalismo contemporáneo (Reale). Muy útil que el trabajo aparezca en una revista de lengua española.

7594 ———. Possibilidades e limites de uma filosofia latinoamericana (UCR/RF, 16:43, enero/junio 1978, p. 83–85)

Interesante enfoque del problema que, al comentar una ponencia de Miró Quesada, representa una posición propia de Brasil, no siempre tenido plenamente en cuenta cuando se habla de "filosofía latinoamericana."

7595 ———. Problemática do culturalismo. Rio: Pontificia Universidad Católica, 1977. 69 p.

Desde Tobías Barreto hasta Miguel Reale y Djazir Menezes hay, para el autor, una tradición culturalista en el pensamiento brasileño. El enfoque del libro no es histórico sino sistemático, con frecuente apelación a Reale y Menezes.

7596 **Parisí, Alberto.** Filosofía y clases sociales en América Latina (RFL, 2:3/4, enero/dic. 1976, p. 67–80)

El trabajo se subtitula: *Nota sobre cuestiones epistemológicas relativas al discurso de la filosofía de la liberación.*

7597 **Pensée ibérique et finitude:** essais sur le temps et la morte chez quelques écrivains espagnols et portugais contemporains. Ouvrage collectif de l'Equipe de Recherche associée au C.N.R.S. No. 80 sur la philosophie de langue espagnole et portugaise. Toulouse, France: Association des Publications de l'Université de Toulouse-Le Mirail, 1972. 197 p. (Serie A; t. 17)

De los temas tratados en esta oportuna publicación en francés, destacamos, por su vinculación con el pensamiento latinoamericano, el trabajo de Alain Guy, "La Temporalité et la Mort selon José Gaos."

7598 **Pérez Perazzo, Ermila Elíes de.** De la colonia a Bello (Semestre de Filosofía [Universidad Central de Venezuela, Caracas] 1:1, julio/dic. 1977, p. 21–35)

Repasa la obra de algunos filósofos coloniales en Venezuela y luego expone partes de la *Filosofía del entendimiento,* de Bello. Parece el texto de una exposición oral.

7599 **Pescador Sarget, Augusto.** La filosofía en Bolivia en el siglo XX (Cuadernos de Filosofía [Universidad de Concepción, Instituto Central de Filosofía, Concepción, Chile] 6, 1977, p. 93–109)

Trata los siguientes autores: Mamerto Oyola, Ignacio Prudencio Bustillos, Guillermo Francovich, Roberto Prudencio y Manfredo Kempff Mercado. También señala nombres más recientes.

7600 **Philosophes ibériques et ibéro-américains en exil.** Ouvrage collectif de l'Equipe de Recherche associée au C.N.R.S. No. 80 sur la philosophie de langues espagnole et portugais. Toulouse, France: Association de Publications de l'Université de Toulouse-Le Mirail, 1977. 190 p. (Série A; t. 34)

Esta obra colectiva, animada por Alain Guy, contiene dos trabajos que interesan a la crítica del pensamiento en Hispanoamérica: uno de Reine Guy sobre Ferrater Mora y otro de Zdenek Kourim sobre Octavio Paz. El primero verso sobre *El ser y el sentido,* del filósofo catalán cuya importante obra filosófica se desarrolló viviendo en Latinoamérica y en los Estados Unidos.

7601 **Pino Iturrieta, Elías.** José Gaos en nuestra historia de las ideas (CELRG/A, 1975, p. 43–48)

Apreciación y reconocimiento de la obra y la influencia de José Gaos en el desarrollo de la historiografía de las ideas en América Latina.

7602 Romanell, Patrick. Samuel Ramos on the philosophy of Mexican culture: Ortega and Unamuno in Mexico (LARR, 10:3, Fall 1975, p. 81–101)

La mayor parte del artículo se dedica a Ortega y su influencia sobre Ramos como autor de *Perfil del hombre y la cultura en México.* También hay consideraciones críticas sobre esta última obra. Apareció en castellano en *Cuadernos de Filosofía* (Univ. de Concepción, Chile, 6, 1977, p. 21–231)

7603 Sambarino, Mario. La función sociocultural de la filosofía en América Latina (Actualidades [Centro de Estudios Latinoamericanos Rómulo Gallegos, Caracas] 1, 1976, p. 23–35)

El tema es cercano al muy transitado del sentido, posibilidad o autenticidad de la filosofía latinoamericana. Sin situarse por completo en ninguno de los dos extremos habituales (el americanismo o el universalismo) el asunto es tratado con objetividad y el trabajo es de útil lectura.

7604 Sasso, Javier. Lo general y lo abstracto en Bello (CONAC/RNC, 39:238, sept./oct. 1978, p. 10–22)

Examen circunstanciado del tema en la *Filosofía del entendimiento,* de Andrés Bello, puesto en relación con la tradición filosófica (se muestra la cercanía del nominalismo de Bello con el de Berkeley) y con el pensamiento actual sobre el asunto.

7605 Schmidt, Henry C. Antecedents to Samuel Ramos: Mexicanist thought in the 1920s (UM/JIAS, 18:2, May 1976, p. 179–202, bibl.)

Se estudian los antecedentes de *El perfil del hombre y la cultura en México* (1934), de Samuel Ramos, en Vasconcelos, Caso, Alfonso Reyes y Daniel Cosío Villegas, examinando escritos de estos autores de la década de los 20.

7606 Shul'govskii, A.F. Romanticism and positivism in Latin America: a response to Leopoldo Zea (*in* Soviet historians on Latin America: recent scholarly contributions [see item **1817**] p. 188–208)

Crítica a la interpretación de Leopoldo Zea, desde un punto de vista marxista oficial. A la vez es una exposición general del tema (romanticismo y positivismo en América Latina), desde el mismo punto de vista.

7607 Simposio de Filosofía Latinoamericana, *Universidad del Salvador, 1973.* América Latina, filosofía y liberación. Buenos Aires: Editorial Bonum, 1974. 54 p. (Enfoques latinoamericanos; 7. Sección Filosofía y teología. Serie filosófica)

Reproduce las ponencias de un simposio que tuvo lugar en la Universidad del Salvador (Buenos Aires), en 1973. Las ponencias no son expresivas de la corriente denominada "filosofía de la liberación," pero tratan el tema de la filosofía latinoamericana como filosofía de la liberación y en algunos casos en realidad se ocupan de temas conexos.

7608 Tedesco, Juan Carlos. El positivismo pedagógico argentino (CPES/RPS, 10: 26, enero/abril 1973, p. 37–48)

Previa consideración del positivismo como ideología, la exposición se centra en Carlos Octavio Bunge.

7609 Torchia Estrada, Juan Carlos. Bibliografía reciente sobre el pensamiento filosófico latinoamericano: obras generales y panoramas nacionales (UBAFFL/RF, 26: 24/25, enero/dic. 1976, p. 109–114)

Trabajo de índole bibliográfica.

7610 ———. Cartas de Alejandro Korn a Francisco Romero: 1924–1927 (RIB, 29:3/4, 1979, p. 323–336)

Reproduce 12 cartas. Contiene presentación y notas aclaratorias.

7611 ———. Fuentes del pensamiento latinoamericano: nota sobre algunas ediciones recientes (CIF/RLF, 4:1, marzo 1978, p. 82–89)

Se refiere a reediciones de autores "clásicos" en el pensamiento filosófico latinoamericano. Los países considerados son México, Brasil y Argentina.

7612 Vidal Muñoz, Santiago. Filosofía en Chile (Cuadernos de Filosofía [Universidad de Concepción, Instituto Central de Filosofía, Concepción, Chile] 6, 1977, p. 19–44)

Síntesis del pensamiento filosófico en Chile en los siglos XIX y XX, que el autor presenta "en calidad de repertorio filosófico." Quien se interese por el tema puede ver este trabajo en relación con la reciente obra de R. Escobar, *La filosofía en Chile* (véase *HLAS 40:9459*).

7613 **Weinstein, Michael A.** The structure of anti-positivist philosophy in Latin America (UNL/H, 16, 1975, p. 165–183)

Lo más interesante de este trabajo es que considera que el pensamiento latinoamericano de la "edad de oro" (ejemplificado en Korn, Vasconcelos y Vaz Ferreira) tendría vigencia actual y podría constituir "a rationally defensible philosophy of life."

7614 **Zamora, Francisco.** Idealismo y materialismo dialéctico: una polémica con el doctor Antonio Caso. México: Editorial Nuestro Tiempo, 1978. 190 p. (Colección Pensamiento político de México)

Entre los años 1934 y 1935, el autor de este libro sostuvo una polémica periodística con el maestro Antonio Caso sobre el materialismo dialéctico, luego continuada por otra entre Caso y Lombardo Toledano. Aquí se reproducen los artículos de Caso y de Zamora durante la polémica, además de un grupo de artículos del segundo. Los de Caso han aparecido en la edición de sus obras completas, pero aquí se reproduce la polémica entera.

7615 **Zea, Leopoldo.** La filosofía como conciencia histórica en Latinoamérica (Tiemporeal [Simón Bolívar Universidad, Caracas] 3, enero/abril 1975, p. 4–11)

Lo que se intenta es un esquema de la "filosofía de la historia de nuestra América." "La filosofía propia de nuestra América" es "la filosofía como toma de conciencia de nuestra realidad . . . Filosofía de liberación *versus* filosofía de dominación. Pero no para nuevos enfrentamientos, sino para que éstos sean innecesarios." Este artículo apareció también en *Casa de las Américas* (La Habana, 16:95, marzo/abril 1976, p. 58–65).

PENSAMIENTO LATINOAMERICANO: HISTORIA DE LAS IDEAS

7616 **Albarracín Millán, Juan.** Orígenes del pensamiento social contemporáneo de Bolivia. La Paz: Empresa Editora Universo, 1976. 218 p., bibl., index (Sociología boliviana contemporánea; 1)

"Sociología" se entiende en términos muy amplios, como análisis de la situación del país, que incluye desde la geografía hasta la industria. La exposición comienza con la obra del naturalista francés d'Orbigny. Se trata del primer volumen de una obra que abarcará cuatro. El presente está dedicado al siglo XIX. Los autores estudiados son: J.A. Aramayo, M.V. Ballivián, P. Kramer, M. Baptista, G. René Moreno, J.C. Váldez y J.M. Pando. Obra útil por tratarse de un tema que ha trascendido muy poco.

7617 **Ardao, Arturo.** Del mito Ariel al mito anti-Ariel (Actualidades [Centro de Estudios Latinoamericanos Rómulo Gallegos, Caracas] 2:2, 1977, p. 7–27)

Se trata de una meticulosa crítica, con abundancia de citas textuales, a un juicio sobre el *Ariel* de Rodó contenido en el libro de Carlos Rangel, *Del buen salvaje al buen revolucionario.* Tal vez lo más importante del trabajo, proveniente de uno de los mejores conocedores de Rodó, reside en la tesis de que la difundida dicotomía entre América Latina como mundo de Ariel, y Estados Unidos como representación de Calibán, nunca estuvo—en esos términos simplistas por lo menos—en el pensamiento ni en el texto del autor de *Ariel.*

7618 **———.** Estudios latinoamericanos: historia de las ideas. Caracas: Monte Avila, 1978. 223 p. (Colección Estudios)

Nueva reunión de trabajos del destacado historiador de las ideas en Uruguay que, como el volumen anterior, *Filosofía de lengua española,* confirma la extensión de su obra al campo más amplio de América Latina. Contiene: "La Idea de la Magna Colombia: de Miranda a Hostos;" "Magna Colombia y Gran Colombia en la Carta de Jamaica;" "El Supuesto Positivismo de Bolívar;" "Interpretaciones de Rosas;" "Juárez en la Evolución Ideológica de México;" "Asimilación y Transformación del Positivismo en Latinoamérica;" "El Americanismo de Rodó;" "Del Calibán de Renan al Calibán de Rodó;" "Génesis de la *Lógica viva* de Vaz Ferreira;" "Ciencia y Metafísica en Vaz Ferreira."

7619 **Bagú, Sergio.** José Luis Romero: evocación y evaluación (CAM, 36[213]:4, julio/agosto 1977, p. 97–104)

Con recuerdos y evocaciones personales, presentados a poco de fallecer el gran historiador argentino, es un testimonio valioso sobre el valor y el pensamiento de José Luis Romero como historiador.

7620 Baralt, Rafael María. Obras completas. v. 7, Escritos políticos. Prólogo por Augusto Mijares. Maracaibo, Venezuela: Edición de la Universidad del Zulia, Dirección de Cultura, 1972. 710 p., illus., tables.

Contiene, entre otros escritos, *Lo pasado y lo presente* y *La libertad de imprenta*, ambos publicados en Madrid en 1849.

Barreda, Gabino. La educación positivista en México. See item **7538**.

7621 Bazán, Francisco. Eligio Ayala, el pensador. Asunción: Editorial Curupí, 1976. 186 p.

Presidente del Paraguay (1924–28), Ayala escribió sobre la "cuestión social" y el materialismo dialéctico. De orientación espiritualista y formado en el pensamiento posterior al positivismo, se interesó por la obra de Nietzsche y de Schopenhauer. Este libro es una biografía y un recuento de su pensamiento y su acción política.

7622 Becco, Horacio Jorge. La historia de las ideas en América Latina: contribución a su bibliografía (FJB/BH, 47, may 1978, p. 283–298, bibl.)

Adelanta parte de una bibliografía preparada para una obra de la UNESCO: *América Latina en sus ideas.*

7623 Besouchet, Lídia. Renan e o Imperador do Brasil: a "questão religiosa" (BMA/BB, 38, jan./junho 1977, p. 81–91)

Sobre las relaciones personales y la afinidad en ideas entre Pedro II y Renan.

7624 Biagini, Hugo E. Macedonio Fernández, pensador político (HISP, 7:21, 1978, p. 11–20)

Con abundante apelación a fuentes, reconstruye la posición política de Macedonio Fernández, cercana al liberalismo spenceriano, y descarta algunas interpretaciones "populistas" que aparecieron en Argentina al calor de ciertas modas políticas.

7625 ———. El progresismo argentino del ochenta (RIB, 28:4, 1978, p. 373–384)

Exposición de lo que podría denominarse pro y contra de la doctrina y de la realidad del "progreso" en la Argentina del ochenta en el siglo pasado.

7626 Burns, E. Bradford. Ideology in nineteenth-century Latin American historiography (HAHR, 58:3, Aug. 1978, p. 409–431)

La conclusión a que arribó esta investigación, basada en un intento de "biografía colectiva," es que los historiadores latinoamericanos del siglo XIX reflejaron, en su obra, más la visión de una clase social que un punto de vista nacional.

7627 Campa, Riccardo. Antologia del pensiero politico latino-americano: dalla colonia alla seconda guerra mondiale. Bari, Italy: Editori Laterza, 1970. 598 p.

Después de una extensa introducción sigue la antología propiamente dicha. El contenido, hasta el siglo XIX, es muy semejante al de la *Antología del pensamiento social y político de América Latina*, que Zea y Villegas prepararon para la colección Pensamiento de América de la OEA; pero incluye muchos más autores del siglo XX. La expresión "pensamiento político" está tomada con cierta latitud, porque autores como Korn, Henríquez Ureña, Alfonso Reyes, F. Romero, Samuel Ramos, etc. están representados por textos no necesariamente políticos. Libro omitido anteriormente. El único de su naturaleza que conocemos en italiano.

7628 Capalbo, Creusa. A influência de Jacques Maritain no pensamento filosófico brasileiro (Convivium [Revista bimestral de investigação e cultura, Editora Convívio, São Paulo] 21[17]:3, maio/junho 1978, p. 281–289)

Se refiere principalmente a la influencia de Maritain en el pensamiento político de ciertos grupos católicos de Brasil.

7629 Cerqueira Filho, Gisálio. A influência das idéias socialistas no pensamento político brasileiro, 1890–1922. Rio: Faculdade Cândido Mendes, Instituto Universitário de Pesquisas do Rio de Janeiro, 1975. 108 p., bibl., tables.

Investigación importante por su propósito: rastrear la formulación de ideas socialistas en los grupos obreros. Sus fuentes son, por lo tanto, periódicos y folletos y en general manifestaciones ideológicos que no fueron las de los grupos "letrados."

7630 Davis, Harold Eugene. El pensamiento social en las Américas (UNL/H, 19, 1978, p. 85–97)

Visión panorámica que abarca tanto Estados Unidos como América Latina.

7631 De Beer, Gabriella. Pedro Henríquez Ureña en la vida intelectual mexicana

(CAM, 36[215]: 6, nov./dic. 1977, p. 124–131)
Oportuno resumen de la influencia de Henríquez Ureña en México.

7632 Echeverría, Juan María. Las ideas escolásticas y el inicio de la revolución hispanoamericana (UCAB/M, 5, 1976, p. 279–338, bibl.)
En el marco de una tradicional polémica, afirma que no fueron las ideas francesas de la Ilustración, sino las escolásticas españolas las que jugaron el papel decisivo en la ideología de la Independencia. Delimita el campo al período 1808–14. El centro del trabajo es la comparación entre Suárez y Rousseau.

7633 Etcheverry Stirling, José Enrique. El americanismo de José Enrique Rodó (UBN/R, 14, marzo 1976, p. 7–13)
Se refiere principalmente al discurso pronunciado por Rodó ante el Congreso de Chile en 1910.

7634 Fell, Eve-Marie. Sources françaises du courant raciste en Amérique du Sud (UHB/EHA, 10, 1975, p. 63–77)
Se destacan textos de Le Bon y Vacher de Lapouge como fuentes de González Prada, Carlos Octavio Bunge, Ingenieros, Arguedas, etc., en relación con las ideas de dichos autores sobre el problema racial. Contribución útil.

7635 Germaná, César. Mariátegui, el marxismo y la revolución (ANA, 1, enero/marzo 1977, p. 83–87, bibl.)
Se ocupa brevemente del libro de D. Messeguer, *Mariátegui y su pensamiento revolucionario* (1974).

7636 Grases, Pedro. Del liberalismo al positivismo en Venezuela (Semestre de Filosofía [Universidad Central de Venezuela, Caracas] 1:1, julio/dic. 1977, p. 37–49)
Texto de una conferencia. Al autor no le interesa tanto llegar a conclusiones como señalar incitaciones para el estudio de la época. Sin embargo, conviene destacar una conclusión muy general: "la gran preocupación del pensamiento y la literatura en Hispanoamérica es la explicación del ser de cada pueblo, tanto como indagar las líneas del porvenir."

7637 Kossok, Manfred. La ilustración en la América Latina: ¿mito o realidad? (UCP/IAP, 7, 1973, p. 89–100)
Se refiere, con buena información, a las distintas interpretaciones de la influencia de la Ilustración en América Latina. La traducción es defectuosa y no ayuda a la intelección del artículo.

7638 Krauss, Werner. Die aufklärung in Spanien, Portugal und Lateinamerika. München, FRG: W. Fink, 1973. 251 p. (Aufklärung und Literatur; 4)
La obra está dedicada principalmente a España. Al final contiene un capítulo sobre la Ilustración en Hispanoamérica y otro sobre Portugal y Brasil.

7639 Labastié de Reinhardt, María Rosa. Una polémica poco conocida: Germán Ave-Lallemant—José Ingenieros, 1895–1896 (CEHA/NH, 8:14, abril 1975, p. 86–102)
Interesante aportación a los orígenes de las ideas socialistas en la Argentina. Se refiere a un trabajo juvenil de Ingenieros sobre el socialismo (cuyo fondo filosófico era positivista) y a una crítica que le fue hecha, desde el punto de vista marxista.

7640 Más, José L. En torno a la ideología de José Martí: su identificación con F.R. Lammennais y el romanticismo social (CAM, 34[199]: 2, marzo/abril 1975, p. 82–114, bibl.)
Muestra, en lectura casi paralela, numerosos temas de Martí relacionados con el pensamiento de Lammennais.

7641 Mejía Valera, José. Mariano H. Cornejo: el sociólogo; 1863–1942 (CAM, 34[198]: 1, enero/feb. 1975, p. 120–134)
Util trabajo sobre la sociología positivista de Cornejo, de gran influencia en Perú.

7642 Melis, Antonio. El debate sobre Mariátegui: resultados y problemas (RCLL, 2:4, 1976, p. 123–132)
Comentarios a varias obras de la abundante literatura reciente sobre José Carlos Mariátegui.

7643 Montenegro, João Alfredo de Sousa. O liberalismo radical no império (Convivium [Revista bimestral de investigação e cultura, Editora Convívio, São Paulo] 21[17]: 3, maio/junho 1978, p. 228–260)
Capítulo de un próximo libro sobre *As idéias políticas no Brasil.*

7644 Nachman, Robert G. Positivism and revolution in Brazil's First Republic:

the 1904 revolt (AAFH/TAM, 34:1, July 1977, p. 20–39)

Revisión de los objetivos políticos de la revolución de 1904 y el papel de las ideas positivistas en ella. Véase la reseña del historiador en *HLAS 40:4141.*

7645 Núñez, Estuardo. La experiencia europea de José Carlos Mariátegui y otros ensayos. Lima: Empresa Editora Amauta, 1978. 118 p., bibl.

Todos los ensayos se relacionan directamente con Mariátegui. Los de mayor interés general son los referidos a la experiencia de Mariátegui en Italia, Francia y Alemania. Otros interesan para la vida intelectual peruana de la época.

7646 Olaso, Ezequiel de. Notas sobre el catolicismo ilustrado de Manuel José de Lavardén. A doscientos años de su "Discurso" (Criterio [Buenos Aires] 51:1801/1802, dic. 1978, p. 768–773)

Muestra cómo un "Discurso" de Lavardén, de 1778, ilustra sobre la influencia de Benito Jerónimo Feijóo en Buenos Aires. Trabajo útil y bien escrito.

7647 Pacheco, César. Unamuno y Riva-Agüero: un diálogo desconocido (UP/A, 4:7, 1977, p. 101–165)

Reproduce un conjunto de cartas intercambiadas entre Unamuno y Riva-Agüero desde 1905–14. A este valor documental añade el de un extenso estudio preliminar de amplio contenido sobre esa época en el Perú.

7648 El pensamiento político nacionalista: antología. v. 3, pt. 1, El estatuto del coloniaje. Seleccionada y comentada por Julio Irazusta. Buenos Aires: Obligado Editora, 1975. 245 p.

Este volumen continúa la difusión comentada de materiales de *La Nueva República* (sobre los dos primeros volumenes véase *HLAS 40:9511*), en este caso correspondiente a 1931.

7649 Pino Iturrieta, Elías. El pensamiento de Tomás Lander (IEH/A, 1, 1974, p. 83–121, bibl.)

Contribución monográfica al estudio de los escritos políticos de Tomás Lander que el autor sitúa en la línea del pensamiento liberal.

7650 Portocarrero M., Felipe. El pensamiento político de Haya de la Torre (ANA, 1, enero/marzo 1977, p. 37–48, bibl.)

Se expone y critica la base teórica original del aprismo, contenida en la obra de Haya de la Torre, *El antiimperialismo y el Apra.* Véase el comentario del historiador en *HLAS 40:3557.*

7651 Rivara de Tuesta, María Luisa. José de Acosta: un humanista reformista. Lima: Editorial Universo, 1970. 147 p., bibls. (Historia de las ideas en el Perú)

El tema central de este útil estudio es la obra de Acosta, *De procuranda indorum salute,* la cual—se concluye—"responde a los caracteres de una obra humanista reformista cristiana, en su aspecto general, y aun tiene puntos de contacto con el pensamiento fundamental de Erasmo de Rotterdam."

7652 Rodríguez Leal, Edgard. Fray Antonio Caulín, ideología historia. Caracas: Universidad Central de Venezuela, Facultad de Humanidades y Educación, Instituto de Antropología e Historia, 1975. 202 p., bibl.

Estudio monográfico sobre la obra de Fray Antonio Caulín, *Historia de la Nueva Andalucía,* publicada originalmente en el siglo XVIII.

7653 Roig, Arturo. Importancia de la historia de las ideas para América Latina (Pucará [Universidad de Cuenca, Facultad de Filosofía, Letras y Ciencias de la Educación, Cuenca, Ecuador] 1, enero 1977, p. 49–55)

Sobre la evolución del estudio de la historia de las ideas en Latinoamérica, cuya última etapa coincidiría, en el interés por lo social, con la filosofía de la liberación. Al final reproduce recomendaciones hechas a la UNESCO en 1974 sobre el enfoque que debe darse a la historia de las ideas en la región, que en esencia preconizan abrir el tema a su contexto social, histórico, ideológico, etc.

7654 Schmidt, Henry C. The roots of lo mexicano: self and society in Mexican thought, 1900–1934. College Station: Texas A&M University Press, 1978. 195 p., bibl., index.

Obra de historia de las ideas que apela a numerosas fuentes para señalar los antecedentes de *El perfil del hombre y la cultura en México,* de Samuel Ramos, punto de arranque del movimiento de definición de *lo mexicano.* Además del precedente más claro de autores como Vasconcelos, Caso, Reyes y Cosío Villegas, se remonta al pensamiento de la Revolución y del positivismo. Contiene útil bibliografía.

7655 Schnelle, Kurt. El siglo XVIII e Hispanoamérica (BRP, 15:2, 1976, p. 267–273)

Panorama general de la Ilustración en Hispanoamérica.

Selva, Salomón de la. Ideas de la emancipación norteamericana y de la independencia de Hispanoamérica. See item **2421**.

7656 Trabulse, Elías. El erasmismo de un científico: supervivencias del humanismo cristiano en la Nueva España de la Contrarreforma (CM/HM, 28:2, oct./dic. 1978, p. 224–296, bibl.)

El tema del trabajo (parte aparentemente de un estudio preliminar a la próxima edición de obras teológicas de Francisco Hernández) es el contenido de la *Doctrina cristiana*, del mencionado autor, y la influencia recibida por él del erasmismo español de la época. El artículo se extiende a consideraciones generales sobre el erasmismo español en la historia de las ideas y es un trabajo imprescindible.

Vanden, Harry E. Mariátegui: marxismo, comunismo, and other bibliographic notes. See *HLAS 41:14*.

7657 Weinberg, Gregorio. Modelos educativos en el desarrollo histórico de América Latina. Introducción de Germán W. Rama. Buenos Aires: UNESCO, Economic Commission for Latin America [and] United Nations Development Plan, 1977. 65 p. (Publicaciones Proyecto Desarrollo y Educación en América Latina y el Caribe; DEALC, 5)

Interesante intento de combinar los sistemas de educación del pasado con las ideas filosóficas y políticas preponderantes, dentro del marco de referencia de un determinado "modelo de desarrollo." La época estudiada abarca desde la Ilustración hasta el positivismo. El enfoque promete aportes tanto a la clarificación de los esquemas educativos como a la historia de las ideas.

7658 ———. Sobre la historia de la tradición científica latinoamericana (AI/I, 3:2, marzo/abril 1978, p. 72–78)

Tiende a destacar el valor de la tradición científica latinoamericana con ejemplos significativos. El trabajo resulta también muy útil como información sintética sobre el tema.

7659 Wilhite, John F. Foreign ideas in New Granada: 1760–1830 (SECOLAS/A, 8, March 1977, p. 5–18)

Sobre la historia intelectual y política de la época. Véase reseña del historiador en *HLAS 40:3162*.

7660 Yeager, Gertrude Matyoka. Gabriel René-Moreno and the intellectual context of late nineteenth-century South America (UT/SSQ, 59:1, June 1978, p. 77–92, bibl.)

Util para mostrar las influencias ejercidas sobre René-Moreno, especialmente en Chile. Utiliza el caso también para mostrar la importancia de examinar la historiografía y la historia de las ideas en el siglo XIX latinoamericano.

HISTORIA DE LA FILOSOFIA: FILOSOFIA ANTIGUA Y MEDIEVAL

7661 Angelelli, Ignacio. En torno a la interpretación de *Analíticos Primeros I-38* (CIF/RLF, 5:1, marzo 1979, p. 71–75)

El interés en el texto analizado reside en que es "una de las pocas fuentes aristotélicas del tema de la *reduplicación*, muy desarrollado luego en la tradición escolástica."

7662 Argerami, Oscar. Metafísica y experiencia en la escolástica del siglo XIII (CIF/RLF, 5:1, marzo 1979, p. 43–52)

En el siglo XIII hubo un balance entre metafísica y empirismo, y no el solo predominio de la primera, según suele afirmarse.

7663 Bazán, Bernardo Carlos. La noética de Temistio: ca. 320–390 (USB/RVF, 5/6, 1976/1977, 51–82)

Versa sobre el *Comentario sobre el Tratado del alma*, de Temistio, en el contexto del debate sobre la naturaleza del hombre (en esencia: sobre el *De Anima* de Aristóteles) que tuvo lugar en la Universidad de París en el siglo XIII.

7664 Briancesco, Eduardo. ¿Cómo interpretar la moral de San Anselmo? (CIF/RLF, 4:2, julio 1978, p. 119–140)

Trabajo de crítica monográfica. Los problemas que plantea la doctrina moral de San Anselmo son considerados en función de la bibliografía especializada sobre el tema.

7665 Cappelletti, Angel J. Ensayos sobre los atomistas griegos. Caracas: Sociedad

Venezolana de Ciencias Humanas, 1979. 161 p.

La intención del autor es "llenar una laguna de la bibliografía filosófica hispanoamericana." El volumen contiene los siguientes trabajos: "Leucipo y los Orígenes del Atomismo Griego;" "La Etica de Demócrito," aparecido también en *Estudios Paraguayos* (Univ. Católica de Nuestra Señora de la Asunción, 6:1, 1978); "Escepticismo y Atomismo en Metrodoro de Quíos;" "Anaxarco de Abdera: la Búsqueda de la Felicidad;" y "Epicuro y la Muerte."

7666 ———. La ética de Demócrito (UCNSA/EP, 6:1, sept. 1978, p. 41–60)

Comentario detallado, con abundantes citas textuales. Se considera que la ética de Demócrito debe ser considerada a la luz de sus doctrinas ontológicas y gnoseológicas, pero no como una derivación de ellas, sino en forma paralela.

7667 ———. Familia y esclavitud en Aristóteles (USB/RVF, 7, 1977, p. 7–44)

Utiliza principalmente los textos pertinentes de la *Política* y el *Económico*, de la escuela aristotélica.

7668 ———. El sonido y el oído, según Aristóteles (USB/RVF, 5/6, 1976/1977, p. 19–49)

Exposición bien documentada. Complementa otros trabajos del autor sobre los sentidos en Aristóteles (véase *HLAS 40:9535* y *9537*).

7669 ———. Las tareas del sentido común según Aristóteles (CIF/RLF, 5:1, marzo 1979, p. 3–14)

Sobre la función del sentido común en Aristóteles, que es "la constitución en la conciencia del objeto sensible único y singular."

7670 Cordero, Néstor Luis. Lenguaje, realidad y comunicación en Gorgias (Escritos de Filosofía [Academia Nacional de Ciencias, Centro de Estudios Filosóficos, Buenos Aires] 1:1, enero/junio 1978, p. 135–142)

Exposición clara, enfocando el tema en el contexto del significado de la sofística en general.

7671 García Bazán, Francisco. Gnosis: la esencia del dualismo gnóstico. Prólogo de Armando Asti Vera. 2. ed., corr. y aumentada. San Antonio de Padua, Argentina: Ediciones Castañeda, 1978. 371 p., bibl., index (Colección Estudios filosóficos; 3)

La obra es, que sepamos, la primera introducción a la historia y el contenido de las doctrinas gnósticas, escrita originalmente en castellano y elaborada con buen conocimiento de las fuentes y utilización de una amplísima bibliografía. El enfoque es fenomenológico. Desde el punto de vista interpretativo, considera al gnosticismo como "una forma de *filosofia perennis et universalis*, porque patentiza . . . una experiencia profunda de lo Absoluto como la Unidad verdadera . . ." La segunda parte es una antología de textos gnósticos. Contiene bibliografía e índice de nombres.

7672 Gómez-Lobo, Alfonso. Las vías de Parménides (CIF/RLF, 3:3, nov. 1977, p. 269–281)

Dos versos fundamentales del poema de Parménides son examinados gramaticalmente, rechazando tres traducciones al español. Luego se pasa al problema hermenéutico propiamente dicho y se señalan puntos pendientes de dilucidación.

7673 Gracia, Jorge J.E. Philosophy in the Middle Ages: a reminder (UPR/D, 11:29/30, nov. 1977, p. 233:243)

Reelaborando una tesis de Gilson, ofrece un útil servicio de clarificación de las relaciones entre revelación, teología y filosofía en el Medioevo, concluyendo que más que de "filosofía medieval," debiera hablarse de "pensamiento medieval" o de "filosofía en la Edad Media" (aquello que de filosofía hay en un pensamiento dominado por la teología).

7674 ———. What the individual adds to the common nature according to Suárez (New Scholasticism [Catholic University of America, Catholic Philosophical Association, Washington] 53:2, Spring 1979, p. 221–233)

El tema es el tratamiento de Suárez (*Disp. Met.*, V, 2) de si el individuo agrega algo a la naturaleza común (o genérica) de que es parte. El autor sostiene que la opinión de Suárez es coherente y que los problemas que suscita son de naturaleza semántica. Una consecuencia más general sería admitir que Suárez es uno de los últimos grandes escolásticos y que tiene personalidad propia frente a sus antecesores (Santo Tomás, Ockham, Scoto, etc.) aunque los utilice.

7675 Guariglia, Osvaldo N. Dominación y legitimación en la teoría política de Aristóteles (CIF/RLF, 5:1, marzo 1979, p. 15–42)

El objetivo del trabajo es "presentar algunos temas centrales de la teoría política de Aristóteles" utilizando aclaraciones lingüísticas de ciertos conceptos, pero también el examen de la "realidad social y política en la que tales términos surgen."

7676 Interdonato, Francisco. Santo Tomás y el pensamiento contemporáneo (Estudios de Filosofía [Instituto Riva-Agüero, Lima] 1:93, 1975, p. 62–93)

La tesis del autor, que ejemplifica con varios temas contemporáneos, es que la actualidad del tomismo sólo puede consistir en la aplicación de su núcleo esencial a problemas filosóficos del presente, en lugar de mantenerse en el comentario y la repetición.

7677 López Salgado, Cesáreo. Crítica de la filosofía naciente a la religiosidad homérica (USB/RVF, 9, 1979, p. 91–107)

"Queremos estudiar la actitud o relación de la filosofía presocrática respecto a la religiosidad que encuentra en los poemas homéricos su fuente principal, y que se consideraba en aquellos siglos como religión popular y oficial entre los griegos."

7678 ———. Suficiencia y trascendencia del ser en el *Poema* de Parménides (UCA/S, 33:129, 1978, p. 167–186)

Exposición y análisis crítico del *Poema*, compulsando varias autoridades en la labor de interpretación.

7679 Lorite Mena, Jorge. Tales: la *Physis* y el simbolismo mítico del agua (ECO, 33[6]:204, oct. 1978. p. 1193–1211)

Sobre el paso de lo mítico a lo filosófico por obra de Tales.

7680 Mas Herrera, Oscar E. Transmisibilidad o intransmisibilidad del pensamiento: estudio de la cuestión XI, *De Magistro*, de las cuestiones *De Veritate* de Santo Tomás de Aquino (UCR/RF, 16:43, enero/junio 1978, p. 41–58)

Trabajo muy detallado. De los cuatro artículos que componen el *De Magistro*, se estudia especialmente el primero: "De si un hombre puede enseñar y ser llamado maestro o sólo Dios." La intención es "destacar la posición del Aquinate respecto de la enseñanza, el papel del maestro y, especialmente, la naturaleza de la iluminación de la inteligencia."

7681 Peña Cabrera, Antonio. El pensamiento de San Agustín (UNMSM/L, 48:82/83, [1. semestre] 1976, p. 32–42)

Examen del pensamiento de San Agustín en función de dos temas: la creación y la trascendencia.

7682 Souza, Eudoro de. Horizonte e complementariedade: ensaio sobre a relação entre mito e metafísica nos primeiros filósofos gregos. São Paulo, Editora Universidade de Brasília/Livraria Duas Cidades, 1975. 144 p.

Sobre la complementariedad como idea clave para comprender el mito del horizonte, de Homero a Heráclito.

7683 Vianna, Sylvio Barata de Azevedo. O estranho Heráclito de Efeso (UMGFF/K, 22:69, jan./dez. 1976, p. 1–27)

Caracterización general de la doctrina y la modalidad filosófica de Heráclito.

7684 ———. As origens do atomismo grego (UMGFF/K, 23:70, jan./dez. 1977, p. 1–26)

Sobre Leucipo y Demócrito, y sus antecedentes.

7685 Zilles, Urbano. O método escolástico medieval (PUC/V, 21:82, junho 1976, p. 93–97, bibl.)

Breve síntesis del método escolástico en filosofía, con algunas consideraciones sobre escolástica y mística.

HISTORIA DE LA FILOSOFIA: FILOSOFIA MODERNA

7686 Andrade, Sonia Maria Viegas. A crítica do direito natural na primeira filosofia do direito de Hegel (UMGFF/K, 23:70, jan./dez. 1977, p. 27–39)

Se refiere a un escrito de Hegel sobre derecho natural, de 1801, recientemente traducido al francés. El comentario es sobre la edición realizada en dicho idioma (1972).

7687 Antonietta, Eduardo. Spinoza y el antifinalismo (CIF/RLF, 3:3, nov. 1977, p. 237–249)

La crítica de Spinoza al pensar teleológico no habría impedido una cierta forma de finalidad interna en su sistema.

7688 Bernardini, Amalia. Un redescubrimiento del probabilismo ético del siglo XVII (UCR/RF, 15:40, enero/junio 1977, p. 61–72)

Util comentario al libro de D. Patine, *Juan Caramuel: probabilismo de enciclopedia* (1975).

7689 Biagini, Hugo E. Aporte a las bibliografías lockeanas de Hall y Woolhouse (UBAFFL/RF, 26:24/25, enero/dic. 1976, p. 99–108)

Contribución a la bibliografía sobre Locke, complementaria de la que vienen realizando los autores citados en el título. Abarca desde 1929 hasta 1969. Contiene, naturalmente, trabajos en español, no siempre recogidos en otros repertorios.

7690 ———. Las primeras ideas políticas de Locke (IEP/REP, 211, enero/feb. 1977, p. 247–253)

Sobre el Locke de los *Two tracts on government* y sus relaciones con la doctrina madura de ese autor.

7691 Brito, Emilio. Hegel y las estéticas (CIF/RLF, 4:3, nov. 1978, p. 213–254)

Las estéticas de Kant, Schiller, Nietzsche, Heidegger, Lukács y Adorno son examinadas en función de la estética hegeliana.

7692 Campo, Anibal del. El tiempo en la filosofía de Kant (UBN/R, 14, marzo 1976, p. 153–169)

El tiempo en las tres Críticas y otros escritos de Kant.

7693 Cappelletti, Angel J. Antropología y ética de Condillac (UCNSA/EP, 4:2, dic. 1976, p. 83–97)

Exposición bien apegada a los textos y comentada. La fortuna histórica de Condillac se debió a no haber extraído, en lo metafísico, todas las consecuencias de su doctrina.

7694 Dascal, Marcelo. Spinoza: pensamento e linguagem (CIF/RLF, 3:3, nov. 1977, p. 233–236)

Sobre la teoría del lenguaje en Spinoza, en cuyo sistema el autor no encuentra una adecuada relación entre lenguaje y pensamiento.

7695 Díaz A., Jorge A. El tiempo y las experiencias de la conciencia (USB/RVF, 7, 1977, p. 45–80)

Intento de aclarar ciertas dificultades de la *Fenomenología del espíritu,* de Hegel. El objetivo es "desentrañar cómo aparece el tiempo en la trama fenomenológica."

7696 Di Filippo, Luis. Baruch Spinoza: un clásico de la tolerancia (SHA/D, 126, Verano 1975, p. 53–60)

Consideraciones sobre el pensamiento político de Spinoza.

7697 Esperon, Arturo. La negación dialéctica de la negación. Morelia, Mexico: Universidad Michoacana de San Nicolás Hidalgo, 1976. 113 p.

Intenta ayudar a orientarse en el tema de la dialéctica. Después de situarlo en la historia de las ideas, los capítulos centrales se dedican a Hegel y Marx.

7698 Francovich, Guillermo. Ensayos pascalianos. Sucre, Bolivia: Imprenta Universitaria, 1979. 173 p.

La obra es a la vez exposición y comentario, glosa o repensamiento propio y propuesta de sistematización de los materiales fragmentarios de los *Pensamientos* de Pascal.

7699 Giglioli, Giovanna. Lo finito y lo eterno en el *Bruno* de Schelling (UCR/RF, 15:40, enero/junio 1977, p. 41–47, bibl.)

Sobre el diálogo *Bruno,* de Schelling, dentro de la evolución de este autor, y en función de las interpretaciones de Semerari y Luckács.

7700 Gutiérrez A., Carlos B. La fundamentación de la ética de Kant y la peligrosidad de la terminología de los valores (ECO, 34[4]:208, feb. 1979, p. 434–444)

Sobre el concepto y la función del valor absoluto en la ética de Kant.

7701 Hoyos Vásquez, Jaime. Presentación: Kant y el problema de la metafísica; materiales para el estudio de la obra de Martín Heidegger (UN/IV, 48/40, abril 1977, p. 67–77)

El trabajo sirve de introducción a traducciones de escritos de Heidegger y Cassirer sobre Kant.

7702 Kogan, Jacobo. Actualidad de Spinoza (CAM, 36[213]:4, julio/agosto 1977, p. 105–118)

Definiendo "la actualidad permanente de una filosofía" como "la solidez del sistema en que ha sido expuesta," aplica este criterio a la filosofía de Spinoza.

7703 Lluberes, Pedro. Ciencia y escepticismo: aproximación a Descartes. Caracas: Equinoccio, 1976. 317 p., bibl., illus.

Resultado de un seminario sobre las *Meditaciones metafísicas* de Descartes. Considerado por el autor como "libro introductorio, . . . de nivel intermedio." Antes de entrar al tema metafísico en Descartes se examina la ciencia cartesiana y sus antecedentes y el problema del escepticismo en la época. Aunque obra de intención didáctica, el grado de detalle supera lo meramente introductorio.

7704 Martins, Estevão de Rezende. Autonomia e liberdade: a influencia de Rousseau sobre a ética pré-crítica de Kant (CIF/RLF, 4:2, julio 1978, p. 101–117)

Trabajo bien elaborado, que responde al subtítulo.

7705 Menezes, Djacir. Motivos alemães: filosofia, hegelianismo, marxologia, polêmica. Rio de Janeiro: Livraria Editora Cátedra [and] Instituto Nacional do Livro, Ministério da Educação e Cultura, 1977. 195 p.

Kant, Nietzsche y sobre todo diversos aspectos de Hegel son los principales temas de este libro. Sobre el autor véase *HLAS 38:9481*.

7706 Museo Judío de Buenos Aires. Entrega del Premio Baruch Spinoza al Dr. Eugenio Pucciarelli. Buenos Aires: 1977. 30 p.

Folleto conmemorativo del otorgamiento del Premio Baruch Spinoza al destacado profesor y filósofo argentino actual. Contiene una disertación de Pucciarelli sobre Spinoza.

7707 Pérez Botero, Luis. G.W. Leibniz y el desarrollo de las ciencias del lenguaje (UA/U, 51:197, abril/junio 1976, p. 5–26, bibl.)

El tema en Leibniz es examinado en relación con Platón, Aristóteles y Hobbes, y especialmente en comparación con Locke. De todos ellos, Leibniz fue "quien más . . . se sintió en el punto límite entre la filosofía de la lengua y la ciencia de la lengua o lingüística."

7708 Pucciarelli, Eugenio. Seguridad social y libertad individual en la filosofía política de Spinoza (CIF/RLF, 3:3, nov. 1977, p. 213–221)

Los extremos de la seguridad social y la libertad individual giran en torno a la concepción del Estado. Luego, en relación con estos temas, el autor señala algunas dificultades en el sistema de Spinoza.

7709 Santos, Ely Souto dos. Hegel (PUC/V, 20:78, junho 1975, p. 137–164, bibl.)

Resumen y comentario de textos hegelianos sobre el problema de la historia.

7710 Soto Badilla, José Alberto. Antonio Rosmini y la unidad como exigencia en los sistemas del idealismo trascendental: Fichte y Schelling (UCR/RF, 15:40, enero/junio 1977, p. 85–98)

Estudia la crítica de Rosmini a Fichte y Schelling en su obra *Saggio storico-critico sulle categorie e la dialettica* (póstumo, 1883).

7711 ———. Spinoza y Schelling: sobre el problema metafísico (FH, 15:178, oct. 1977, p. 685–694)

Sobre la influencia de Spinoza en Schelling.

7712 Ursua Lezaun, Nicanor. Fichte frente a Rousseau: la polémica sobre la influencia de las artes y las ciencias sobre el bien en la humanidad (ARBOR, 97:377, mayo 1977, p. 85–90)

Esposición de la crítica dirigida por Fichte a Rousseau en su obra *Algunas lecciones sobre el destino del sabio* (1794).

7713 Vial Larraín, Juan de Dios. Cogito, ergo sum (UBAFFL/RF, 26:24/25, enero/dic. 1976, p. 17–34)

Sobre el *cogito* en Descartes y su significación en la filosofía moderna.

7714 Xirau, Ramón. Tres irreverencias verdaderas a propósito de Hegel (CM/D, 14:4, julio/agosto 1978, p. 12–18, illus.)

"Comentario-discusión," según lo denomina el autor, en el cual se profundizan, con buen ejercicio de pensamiento propio, tres temas de Hegel.

HISTORIA DE LA FILOSOFIA: FILOSOFIA CONTEMPORANEA

7715 Aguirre, Antonio. Consideraciones sobre el mundo de la vida: pts. 1/2 (USB/RVF, 9, 1979, p. 7–32; 11, 1979, p. 7–31)

Minucioso trabajo, en dos partes, sobre la forma en que Husserl entiende el concepto de *Lebenswelt*, especialmente en su última obra, *La crisis de las ciencias europeas y la fenomenología trascendental.*

7716 **Albizu, Edgardo.** El lenguaje en la hermenéutica filosófica de Gadamer (Escritos de Filosofía [Academia Nacional de Ciencias, Centro de Estudios Filosóficos, Buenos Aires] 1:1, enero/junio 1978, p. 79–102)

Util exposición de la obra de Gadamer, poco frecuentada en la literatura filosófica de habla española.

7717 **Basave Fernández del Valle, Agustín.** Análisis crítico del positivismo lógico (UNL/H, 19, 1978, p. 13–27)

Más que análisis es un severo ataque. "Positivismo lógico" se entiende en términos muy amplios, desde el Círculo de Viena hasta la filosofía analítica.

7718 **Camacho, Luis.** Las cuatro etapas de la corriente analítica (UCR/RF, 12:34, enero/junio 1974, p. 53–57)

Bosquejo del desarrollo de la filosofía analítica en nuestro siglo (orígenes, positivismo lógico, análisis del lenguaje, situación actual).

7719 **Campo, Aníbal del.** Heidegger y la experiencia del ser (UBN/R, 17, 1977, p. 7–24)

Texto de una conferencia. En gran parte trata de la evolución del pensamiento de Heidegger y las interpretaciones a que dio lugar.

7720 **Casalla, Mario Carlos.** Crisis de Europa y reconstrucción del hombre: un ensayo sobre Martin Heidegger. Buenos Aires: Castañeda, 1977. 166 p., bibl. (Colección Estudios filosóficos; 1)

Intenta primero "poner de manifiesto la comprensión heideggeriana de la tradición europea-occidental, a través de su caracterización del pensamiento metafísico." Al final, se establece un diálogo con el autor estudiado desde la propia circunstancia americana. Incluye una bibliografía sobre Heidegger en castellano (1936–70).

7721 **Castañeda, Hector-Neri.** El atomismo sintáctico en la filosofía posterior de Wittgenstein, y la naturaleza de las cuestiones filosóficas (UCR/RF, 15:41, julio/dic. 1977, p. 175–186)

La filosofía originada en las *Investigaciones filosóficas* de Wittgenstein y la filosofía del lenguaje ordinario tuvieron un predominio breve. El autor se propone explicar ese hecho desde el punto de vista de la estructura interna de esas filosofías. El método que les es común es un "atomismo sintáctico, a veces léxico, que no permite ni una visión adecuada del lenguaje ni una resolución de problemas filosóficos genuinos." Concluye con apreciaciones sobre el estado actual de la filosofía de habla inglesa, en la que ve mayor diversidad y "fertilización" entre las distintas corrientes.

7722 **Cersósimo, Emilse Beatriz.** Algunas convergencias significativas entre el pensamiento antiguo y el moderno (Megafón [Centro de Estudios Latinoamericanos, Buenos Aires] 1:1, julio 1975, p. 39–42)

Breve exposición de las ideas del pensador rumano Lucien Blaga sobre el conocimiento, en comparación con Jung.

7723 **Chong, Moisés.** El fenómeno de la evolución según Teilhard de Chardin (LNB/L, 268, junio 1978, p. 30–37)

Comentarios sobre Teilhard de Chardin en general y sobre su concepto de "evolución."

7724 **Colle, Raymundo.** Información, evolución y entropía (CPU/ES, 11, [1. semestre] 1977, p. 111–130, bibl., tables)

Pone en relación un aspecto de la doctrina filosófica de Teilhard de Chardin con el fenómeno de la entropía y la teoría matemática de la información.

7725 **D'Alessio, Juan Carlos.** Lenguaje y ontología en la falacia naturalista de G.E. Moore (Escritos de Filosofía [Academia Nacional de Ciencias, Centro de Estudios, Buenos Aires] 1:1, enero/junio 1978, p. 161–163)

Examina, en *Principia Ethica,* lo que Moore denomina "falacia naturalista."

7726 **Fernández, Rodrigo.** Marcuse: posibilidad y concreción (UCR/RF, 12:34, enero/junio 1974, p. 59–70)

Exposición general de las ideas de posibilidad, liberación y humanización dentro del pensamiento de Marcuse y de su crítica a la sociedad actual.

7727 **Florián, Víctor.** Jacques Derrida y la oposición naturaleza/cultura (UN/IV, 46/47, agosto 1976, p. 45–52)

La relación naturaleza-cultura en Lévi-Strauss, Rousseau y Derrida.

7728 **García Canclini, Néstor.** Lingüística y psicoanálisis en la filosofía de Paul Ricoeur (Escritos de Filosofía [Academia Nacional de Ciencias, Centro de Estudios Filosóficos, Buenos Aires] 1:1, enero/junio 1978, p. 103–112)

Exposición, pero también comentario, sobre el tema del lenguaje en Ricoeur.

7729 **García Isaza, Alfonso.** Interrogatorio a Louis Althusser (UPB, 33:116/118, 1973, p. 279–290, bibl.)

Es, en realidad, una crítica a las ideas de Althusser, desde lo que el autor estima una neutra "lógica elemental."

7730 **———.** ¿Marcuse, nuevo sofista? (UA/U, 50:196, enero/marzo 1976, p. 5–14)

Crítica a *Eros and civilization.*

7731 **Glossário de Derrida.** Supervisão geral de Silviano Santiago. Trabalho realizado pelo Departamento de Letras de la Pontificia Universidade Católica de Rio de Janeiro. Rio: Livraria F. Alves Editora, 1976. 95 p., bibl., indexes.

Como lo indica el título, es un glosario de los principales conceptos utilizados por Derrida. Las aclaraciones suelen sufrir la limitación de valerse de los mismos términos que se trata de aclarar.

7732 **González de León, Antonio.** Marcuse: izquierda y contrarrevolución (UNAM/RMCP, 21:79, enero/marzo 1975, p. 77–89)

Visión panorámica de Marcuse, en especial su reformismo social.

7733 **Gutiérrez Alemán, Carlos B.** El neokantianismo como punto de partida de la filosofía de Heidegger (UN/IV, 48/49, abril 1977, p. 47–65)

El tema del trabajo es el neokantismo de la primera época Heidegger y su relación con el problema del valor.

7734 **Hernández, Joaquín.** El marxismo como filosofía (UCE/A, 354, 1976, p. 59–80)

"Lectura filosófica" de *Historia y conciencia de clase,* de Lukács.

7735 **Herrera Restrepo, Daniel.** *Idea de la filosofía*: 1911 (ECO, 35[1]:211, mayo 1979, p. 67–79)

Sobre el contenido de un manuscrito de Husserl titulado *Idea de la filosofía,* que ese autor escribió en 1911, poco después de aparecer su trabajo *La filosofía como ciencia rigurosa.*

7736 **Hoyos Vásquez, Guillermo.** Fenomenología como epistemología: ruptura del sistema fenomenológico desde la materialidad histórica (CIF/RLF, 4:1, marzo 1978, p. 3–20)

Dos problemas actuales, el epistemológico y el de la historicidad del sujeto, pueden beneficiarse de "un confrontamiento crítico con la fenomenología."

7737 **Jaimes M., Fernando.** Jacques Derrida o el pensamiento de la diferencia (USB/F, 21:61, enero/abril 1979, p. 5–25)

Expone el pensamiento de Derrida y lo defiende como una vía apropiada para el filosofar futuro, especialmente en Latinoamérica. No se refiere solamente a un problema de la lingüística, sino "a lo más medular de la filosofía: el problema del ser como presencia."

7738 **Kassa, Peter.** Algunas consideraciones en torno a la filosofía de Marcuse (Polémica [Universidad de Carabobo, Dirección de Cultura, Valencia, Venezuela] 1, junio 1976, p. 81–105)

Sobre la teoría crítica de la sociedad en Marcuse y sus reflexiones en torno a la sociedad actual.

7739 **Kothe, Flávio R.** Caminhos e descaminhos da crítica: encontro marcado com Heidegger (Letras de Hoje [Pontifícia Universidade Católica do Rio Grande do Sul, Centro de Estudos da Lingua Portuguesa, Porto Alegre] 27, março 1977, p. 5–22, bibl.)

Sobre Heidegger y la teoría de la literatura.

7740 **Kries Saavedra, Rafael.** Marxismo y filosofía: Karl Korsch, 1923 (CELRG/A, 1975, p. 49–54)

Consideraciones sobre Korsch y su obra *Marxismo y filosofía.*

7741 **Leão, Emmanuel Carneiro.** O pensamento de Heidegger no silêncio do hoje (VOZES, 71:4, maio 1977, p. 5–18)

Exégesis heideggeriana. Sus principales temas son el lenguaje y el "ser-con."

7742 **López Soria, José Ignacio.** De lo trágico a lo utópico: sobre el primer Lukács.

Caracas: Monte Avila Editores, 1978. 277 p. (Colección Estudios)

Se trata de una biografía intelectual de Lukács hasta 1918. El autor trabajó en el archivo de Lukács en Budapest y la documentación es de primera mano. Con ese grado de detalle y de conocimiento directo no creemos que exista nada semejante escrito originalmente en castellano.

7743 ———. Evolución filosófica del primer Lukács (CDLA, 19:113, marzo/abril 1979, p. 114–118)

Sobre los orígenes del pensamiento de Lukács y la primera época del filósofo húngaro, hasta su afiliación al Partido Comunista en 1918 (véase item **7742**).

7744 Mainetti, José Alberto. El problema del cuerpo en Unamuno (UBAFFL/RF, 26:24/25, enero/dic. 1976, p. 35–49)

Sobre la filosofía del cuerpo que resulta en Unamuno de su temática de la muerte y la inmortalidad.

7745 Marquínez, Germán. Zubiri visto desde Latinoamérica (USB/F, 19:55, enero/abril 1977, p. 129–145)

El objetivo del trabajo es mostrar cómo el filósofo español contemporáneo Javier Zubiri puede servir al proyecto de al filosofía de la liberación y cómo, de hecho, ha sido utilizado por representantes de esa tendencia.

7746 Martínez A., Agustín. Nietzsche: sentido de una crítica (CAM, 209:6, nov./dic. 1976, p. 101–124)

La crítica referida es la de Nietzsche a la religión y la moralidad, comenzando con sus opiniones en *El origen de la tragedia*.

7747 Mayz Vallenilla, Ernesto. Fenomenología del conocimiento: el problema de la constitución del objeto en la filosofía de Husserl. 2. ed. Caracas: Equinoccio, 1976. 366 p.

La obra se publicó originalmente en 1956 y fue reconocida como una exégesis rigurosa de la parte acotada del pensamiento de Husserl.

7748 Mora R., Arnoldo. Federico Nietzsche: las grandes etapas de su pensamiento (UCR/RF, 9:33, julio/dic. 1973, p. 201–214)

Ensayo de apreciación del pensamiento de Nietzsche en su conjunto.

7749 Munita R., Enrique. Josiah Royce y el pensamiento americano (UC/AT, 433, 1976, p. 71–81, plate)

Artículo panorámico sobre Royce, autor escasamente representado en la literatura filosófica de habla española.

7750 Nadal, Tarcísio de. Tarefa da filosofia (PUC/V, 3:90, junho 1978, p. 89–109)

Exposición de la obra de Ortega y Gasset, *¿Qué es filosofía?*

7751 Neves, Flávio. O inatismo em visão contemporânea (UMGFF/K, 23:70, jan./dez. 1977, p. 124–133, bibl.)

La vuelta al innatismo, especialmente en Jung y Chomsky.

7752 Nogueira A., Humberto. Proyecciones del pensamiento de Pierre Teilhard de Chardin (CPES/PE, 30:350, mayo/junio 1974, p. 14–23)

Búsqueda de los elementos de una actitud política en los escritos de Teilhard.

7753 Núñez Tenorio, J.R. Humanismo, estructuralismo y marxismo: Sartre, Althusser, Marx. Caracas: Ediciones de la Facultad de Humanidades y Educación, Universidad Central de Venezuela, 1976. 213 p., bibl.

Desde una posición marxista se analiza la obra de Althusser y el segundo Sartre. A este último se lo considera todavía demasiado adherido a las consecuencias del "sistema categorial" de su primera etapa.

Nuño Montes, Juan Antonio. La superación de la filosofía y otros ensayos. See item **7519**.

7754 Orellana Rodríguez, Mario. El pensamiento teilhardiano: ejemplo de superación del conflicto ciencia-religión (CPU/ES, 9, sept. 1976, p. 120–151)

La afirmación—ejemplificada en la obra de Teilhard—de que ciencia y religión "son partes de una realidad cognoscitiva mayor," se basa en el supuesto de que es la religión lo que da sentido a la búsqueda científica.

7755 Patrício, Jaciro Campante. A rebelião das massas: testemunho significativo de passados inacabados (FFCLM/EH, 13/14, 1975, p. 113–141)

Análisis de la obra de Ortega. *La rebelión de las masas*, desde un punto de vista lexicológico, tras el antecedente de Jean Dubois, *Le vocabulaire politique et social en France de 1869 a 1872*. El examen intenta, por ejemplo, percibir la estructura político-social del momento y la visión del mundo del autor.

7756 Pecorrini, Francisco L. El "Ser" heideggeriano, como fundamento último del "Nous" aristotélico (UCR/RF, 15:41, julio/dic. 1977, p. 255–260)

El pensamiento de Heidegger utilizado para interpretar a Aristóteles.

7757 Presas, Mario A. En torno a las meditaciones cartesianas de Husserl (CIF/RLF, 4:3, nov. 1978, p. 269–280)

Introducción a una edición de las Meditaciones cartesianas, de Husserl, traducidas por el autor. Las Meditaciones son situadas en la biografía filosófica de Husserl y en la evolución de su obra. Trabajo de muy buena factura.

7758 Romero, Francisco. Nietzsche (CAM, 36[214]:5, sept./oct. 1977, p. 101–117)

Como homenaje al ilustre filósofo argentino, se reproduce un artículo de 1946.

7759 Rosales, Alberto. Una aproximación a *Ser y tiempo* (USB/RVF, 5/6, 1976/1977, p. 119–144)

Extensa nota sobre la obra de Heidegger, *Die Grundprobleme der Phänomenologie* (1975; publicación de un curso de 1927) en su relación con Sein und Zeit.

7760 ———. Observaciones críticas a la idea de temporalidad propia en *Ser y tiempo* de Heidegger (USB/RVF, 8, 1978, p. 83–96)

El concepto de "temporalidad propia" en *Ser y tiempo* es examinado y luego criticado de modo de quedar disuelto "en un haz de problemas" o interrogantes que el autor resume al final del trabajo.

7761 Sanabria, José Rubén. Wittgenstein y la filosofía (UNL/H, 16, 1975, p. 23–44)

Repaso general de la obra de Wittgenstein y en especial de su concepción de la filosofía.

7762 Silva, Juan-Manuel. Aproximación a Gabriel Marcel (ISTMO, 92, mayo/junio 1974, p. 18–38, plates)

Artículo panorámico, con numerosas transcripciones textuales, inclusive del teatro de Marcel.

Silva, Ludovico. De lo uno a lo otro: ensayos filosófico-literarios. See item **7526**.

7763 Simon, Paul Albert. O que está em jogo na racionalidade, Segundo Jean Ladrière (Presença Filosófica [Sociedade Brasileira de Filósofos Católicos, São Paulo] 5:2, avril/junio 1979, p. 33–59, plate)

Análisis de la obra de Jean Ladrière, *Les enjeux de la rationalité: le défi de la science et de la technologie aux cultures* (1977).

7764 Sologuren López, Jaime. Fin de la filosofía-comienzo del pensar (USB/RVF, 8, 1978, p. 97–133)

Examen de la cuestión del pensar en Heidegger.

7765 Uranga, Emilio. Martin Heidegger y la filosofía de la cultura (UY/R, 18:107, sept./oct. 1976, p. 39–67)

Reproduce un artículo publicado originariamente en 1949, en el cual se intenta extraer materiales para la sociología y la filosofía de la cultura, de la obra de Heidegger, *La esencia del fundamento.*

7766 Vélez Sáenz, Jaime. La estructura ontológica del ser-ahí en Heidegger (UN/IV, 48/49, abril 1977, p. 21–46)

Exposición de la doctrina del Dasein en Heidegger y clarificación de la misma por comparación con otras posiciones.

7767 Zilles, Urbano. O personalismo na filosofia e a filosofia do personalismo (PUC/V, 21:83, set. 1976. p. 204–243)

Exposición basada en *El personalismo*, de Mounier.

7768 Zurcher Blen de Carrillo, Joyce M. Lenguaje y realidad en la filosofía del atomismo lógico de Bertrand Russell (UCR/RF, 15:40, enero/junio 1977, p. 1–21, bibl.)

Se examina *The philosophy of logical atomism*, de Russell.

LOGICA, GNOSEOLOGIA Y TEORIA DE LA CIENCIA

Angelelli, Ignacio. En torno a la interpretación de Analíticos Primeros I-38. See item **7661**.

7769 Battistella, Ernesto H. Reflexiones sobre la enseñanza de la lógica deóntica (Semestre de Filosofía [Universidad Central de Venezuela, Caracas] 1:1, julio/dic. 1977, p. 133–149, tables)

Es en realidad una introducción didáctica a la lógica deóntica, utilizando lo elaborado por G.H. von Wright.

7770 Brunelli, Marilene Rodrigues de Mello. A compreensão filosófica da natureza (UMGFF/K, 22:69, jan./dez. 1976, p. 117–135)

Sobre el concepto de naturaleza (entendida como "conjunto de fenómenos exteriores") en Platón, Aristóteles, Kant y Hegel.

7771 Domínguez, Javier. Heisenberg: abstracción y unificación (Universidad Nacional de Colombia [Revista de extensión cultural, Medellín] 2/3, mayo/dic. 1976, p. 84–88, plates)

Comentario al trabajo de Heisenberg, "La Abstracción en la Ciencia Moderna de la Naturaleza," en su libro *Más allá de la física.*

7772 Gómez, Ricardo. Categorialismo y error en la filosofía de la ciencia (CIF/RLF, 4:3, nov. 1978, p. 255–268)

Las epistemologías de Kant y T.S. Kuhn (*The structure of scientific revolutions*) son analizadas críticamente, en relación con el problema del error.

7773 González Asenjo, Florencio. El lenguage de la ciencia (Escritos de Filosofía [Academia Nacional de Ciencias, Centro de Estudios Filosóficos, Buenos Aires] 1:1, enero/junio 1978, p. 29–35)

Estimando que la ciencia no es unitaria y que en consecuencia hay tantos lenguajes científicos como ciencias, examina en particular el lenguaje de la física y el de la psicología. La posición es más amplia de lo que es frecuente en autores provenientes de la filosofía de las matemáticas o de la ciencia natural.

7774 Haba, Enrique P. Lo racional y lo razonable (UCR/RF, 16:43, enero/junio 1978, p. 1–32, bibl., tables)

Destaca la distinción entre lo racional y lo razonable en la epistemología actual. Frente a la preferencia absoluta de ciertos autores por lo razonable como "método" de las ciencias sociales humanas, cree que en éstas se debe intentar, hasta donde sea posible, introducir la mayor rigurosidad de lo racional. Buen trabajo teórico.

7775 Iglesias, Severo. Principios del método científico. México: Verum Factum Editores, 1976. 286 p., bibl. (Temas básicos; 1)

Tras consideraciones de índole general se exponen los métodos inductivo, analítico-sintético, experimental, explicativo, axiomático, estructuralista, dialéctico, fenomenológico y "comprensional."

7776 Miró Quesada, Francisco. Los mecanismos de ideologización de las teorías (Escritos de Filosofía [Academia Nacional de Ciencias, Centro de Estudios Filosóficos, Buenos Aires] 1:2, julio/dic. 1978, p. 11–26)

Expone la existencia y funcionamiento de varios mecanismos (fallas o errores) connaturales a la constitución de teorías científicas, mediante los cuales esas teorías pueden "ideologizarse." La mayoría de los ejemplos se refieren a la economía. En sus términos más generales, el problema reside en la dificultad de verificar teorías que no son matemáticas ni lógicas.

7777 Monteiro, João Monteiro. Filosofia e biologia (SBPC/CC, 27:10, out. 1975, p. 1082–1091, bibl.)

Sobre la importancia de la biología para la concepción filosófica del hombre y la sociedad. Se utilizan las obras de Popper, Lorenz, Quine, etc., pero sobre todo la de Moscovici, *La societé contre nature* (1972).

Nuño Montes, Juan Antonio. La superación de la filosofía y otros ensayos. See item **7519**.

7778 Ortiz Amiel, Rodolfo. Sobre la validez de la ciencia (UCR/RF, 16:43, enero/junio 1978, p. 59–62)

De hecho abarca dos temas: 1) La influencia de la realidad socio-económica sobre el desarrollo de la ciencia (aunque no sobre su contenido); y 2) la función de la experiencia sensible en la física.

7779 Pereira, Oswaldo Porchat. Contra o historicismo em teoria da ciência (USP/RH, 50[2]:100, 1974, p. 483–514)

Análisis y crítica (esto último desde una "postura epistemológica crítica") del historicismo como "orientación teórica y metodológica que . . . se propone elucidar la naturaleza de la ciencia . . . por su historia." No hay, sin embargo, alusión a autores específicos que representan esa orientación, la cual es discutida como un paradigma teórico.

7780 Piza, A.F.R. de Toledo. Sobre a natureza do pensamento científico (SBPC/CC, 29:1, jan. 1977, p. 36–69)

Sobre la distinción entre pensamiento científico y pre-científico.

7781 Pucciarelli, Eugenio. Ideología y ciencia (Escritos de Filosofía [Academia

Nacional de Ciencias, Centro de Estudios Filosóficos, Buenos Aires] 1:2, julio/dic. 1978, p. 3–10)

La ideología infiltra la labor científica (teórica, racionalmente fundada) por numerosos canales. Sin embargo, la conciencia de que así ocurre, facilita la crítica y disminuye el inconveniente efecto de la ideología.

7782 **Roetti, Jorge Alfredo.** Lenguaje natural y lógica (Escritos de Filosofía [Academia Nacional de Ciencias, Centro de Estudios Filosóficos, Buenos Aires] 1:1, enero/junio 1978, p. 113–133)

Intenta mostrar "algunas vías para evitar el relativismo lingüístico absoluto y posibilitar la construcción de la lógica . . . como teoría necesariamente fundada . . ."

7783 **Silva, Maria Beatriz Nizza da.** Ciências e artes: as formas do saber (SBPC/CC, 27:8, agôsto 1975, p. 859–863)

Para mostrar—siguiendo a Foucault—cómo las unidades de saber que hoy se usan (ciencia, literatura, filosofía, etc.) no se han presentado de la misma manera en la historia, persigue la distinción entre ciencias y artes en publicaciones que circulaban en Brasil en la época colonial. Estos datos resultan de interés histórico por sí mismos.

7784 **Stahl, Gerold.** La ambigüedad de los indicadores (Escritos de Filosofía [Academia Nacional de Ciencias, Centro de Estudios Filosóficos, Buenos Aires] 1:1, enero/junio 1978, p. 157–160)

Los indicadores referidos son, en el lenguaje común, términos como "yo," "él," "esa casa," etc.

7785 **Walton, Roberto J.** Perspectivo y relacionismo en el pensamiento de Florencio González Asenjo (UBAFFL/RF, 26:24/25, enero/dic. 1976, p. 81–86)

La exposición se refiere a la gnoseología de González Asenjo y está basada en su obra principal, *El todo y las partes* (1962), y en un libro posterior: *Antiplatitudes* (1976).

7786 **Yánez Cortes, Roberto.** La ideología pre-científica en el contexto de descubrimiento de la epistemología (Escritos de Filosofía [Academia Nacional de Ciencias, Centro de Estudios Filosóficos, Buenos Aires] 1:2, julio/dic. 1978, p. 129–137)

Sobre mecanismos que operan en casos de crisis científicas. Bachelard y Althusser constituyen apoyos a estas consideraciones.

AXIOLOGIA Y ETICA

Bernardini, Amalia. Un redescubrimiento del probabilismo ético del siglo XVII. See item **7688**.

Briancesco, Eduardo. ¿Cómo interpretar la moral de San Agustín? See item **7664**.

Cappelletti, Angel J. Antropología y ética de Condillac. See item **7693**.

———. La ética de Demócrito. See item **7666**.

Gutiérrez A., Carlos B. La fundamentación de la ética de Kant y la peligrosidad de la terminología de los valores. See item **7700**.

7787 **Maliandi, Ricardo.** Un conflicto básico de la vida moral (UNAM/D, 22, 1976, p. 159–188)

Después de establecer el conflicto básico entre casuística y ética situacional, Simmel, Hartmann, Bergson y otros filósofos son utilizados para profundizar en la naturaleza de ese conflicto y el de universalidad e individualidad en la ética.

Martins, Estevão de Rezende. Autonomia e liberdade: a influencia de Rousseau sobre a ética précrítica de Kant. See item **7704**.

7788 **Pasquali, Antonio.** Etica y comunicaciones (CONAC/RNC, 39:232, julio/agosto 1977, p. 14–31)

El tema es el poco transitado de lo que la ética puede contribuir a la ordenación y regulación de las comunicaciones. Esa contribución no estaría tanto e una función moralista como práctica, formulando un derecho de las comunicaciones y políticas de la comunicación.

7789 **Rabossi, Eduardo A.** Acerca de una prueba posible de los primeros principios éticos (CIF/RLF, 4:1, marzo 1978, p. 21–38, bibl.)

El tema se trata tomando como guía para la discusión el contenido del capítulo IV de *Utilitarianism*, the John Stuart Mill ("On what sort of proof the principle of utility is susceptible"). Una de las principales conclusiones del trabajo es que los principios éticos son en efecto susceptibles de prueba.

ANTROPOLOGIA FILOSOFICA Y CIENCIAS HUMANAS

7790 **Agulla, Juan Carlos.** Análisis ideológico y sociología del conocimiento (Escritos de Filosofía [Academia Nacional de Ciencias, Centro de Estudios Filosóficas, Buenos Aires] 1:2, julio/dic. 1978, p. 65–70)

Sobre los planteos de Mannheim en *Ideología y utopía.*

7791 **Carpio, Adolfo P.** Sensibilidad y disposicionalidad (UBAFFL/RF, 26: 24/25, enero/dic. 1976, p. 7–15)

Partiendo de la doctrina kantiana de la afección, el artículo se propone continuarla, desde bases ontológico-existenciarias, "a manera de consideraciones preliminares para una teoría general de la sensibilidad."

7792 **Coloquio Nacional de Filosofía,** *1st, Morelia, Mexico, 1975.* La filosofía y las ciencias sociales. México: Editorial Grijalbo, 1976. 332 p., bibl. (Teoría y praxis; 24)

Selección de ponencias presentadas a la Sec. 2, "La Filosofía y las Ciencias Sociales" del Primer Coloquio Nacional de Filosofía, Morelia, México, 1975. Contribuciones de autores latinoamericanos o que actúan en Hispanoamérica: José Luis Balcárcel, "Fundamentación Científica de la Estética" (p. 9–23): defiende una estética marxista; Mario Bunge, "La Posible Utilidad del Filósofo en la Ciencia Social" (p. 43–69): señala los campos en que el filósofo puede ayudar al científico social y preconiza ese acercamiento; Agustín Cueva, "Sobre el Concepto de 'Enajenación'" (p. 71–93): examen del tema dentro de la "lógica interna" de la doctrina marxista; Silvia Durán Payán, "Lingüística y Filosofía" (p. 95–110): crítica al estructuralismo y sus bases en la lingüística, con alguna simpatía marxista; Javier Esquivel, "Estructura y Función de la Ideología" (p. 111–125): en qué consisten y por qué son eficaces las ideologías; Ricardo Guerra Tejada, "Autodestrucción y Comunidad Concreta" (p. 155–159): meditación sobre la esencia humana y la superación del nihilismo; Alberto Híjar, "Posibilidad de la Estética como Ciencia" (p. 160–172): fundamentación de la estética en función de la economía política marxista; Cesáreo Morales García, "La Sociología y la Forma de su Cientificidad" (p. 173–186): la cientificidad sociológica no es la que concibe la sociología empírica, sino la que resulta de ciertas tesis marxistas; Mario H. Otero, "Tres Modalidades de Inmanentismo" (p. 187–204): sobre Kuhn, Habermas y Althusser; José I. Palencia Gómez, "El Proceso de la Religión como Hecho Histórico" (p. 205–220): sobre la religión como hecho histórico-social; Carlos Pereda, "Sobre el Concepto de Prueba" (p. 221–239): uno de los trabajos de mayor densidad teórica en el volumen; Carlos Pereyra Boldrini, "Sobre la Relación entre Filosofía y Ciencias Sociales" (p. 241–256); Santiago Ramírez Ruiz, "Historia y Psicoanálisis" (p. 275–285): una de las afirmaciones es: la "ciencia freudiana" tiene la misma estructura que la "ciencia marxista;" Adolfo Sánchez Vázquez, "La Ideología de la Neutralidad Ideológica en las Ciencias Sociales" (p. 287–313).

7793 **Granell Muñiz, Manuel.** Ethología y existencia: fundamentaciones ethológicas. Caracas: Equinoccio, 1977. 206 p., bibl. (Colección Parámetros)

En una extensa Introducción, el autor indica que, a pesar de la diversidad de temas, los trabajos recogidos tienen la unidad que le otorga ser complemento de lo expuesto en su obra principal: *La vecindad humana. Fundamentación de la ethología* (1969). Esa misma Introducción es importante como biografía filosófica del autor.

7794 **Guariglia, Osvaldo N.** Ideologías: argumentación y finalidad en la lógica de las ciencias sociales (CIF/RLF, 4:1, marzo 1978, p. 39–74)

Definiendo la ideología como "una concepción *errónea* de la realidad social," bien por mezclar lo descriptivo con la "valoración político-moral," bien por encubrir un interés, examina el fenómeno dentro de la lógica de las ciencias sociales, especialmente en relación con el tipo de argumentación que para el autor es propia de esas ciencias. Trabajo de muy buena calidad.

7795 **Japiassu, Hilton.** Interdisciplinaridade e patologia do saber. Rio: Imago Editora, 1976. 221 p. (Série Logoteca)

El tema del libro es la epistemología de las ciencias humanas. El enfoque interdisciplinario se considera una exigencia interna de esas ciencias, con consecuencias para la interpretación de la naturaleza humana. La investigación es parte de una tesis defendida en Francia y lleva en prefacio de Georges Gusdorf.

7796 **Jara, José.** El hombre y su diferencia histórica (USB/RVF, 9, 1979, p. 53–90)

El tema es examinado en la obra de Foucault, *Las palabras y las cosas.*

7797 **Jarauta Marión, Francisco.** Epistemología e historia de las ciencias (UN/IV, 46/47, agosto 1976, p. 3–9)

Enfoque de la relación filosofía-historia de la ciencia desde un punto de vista marxista.

7798 **Li Carrillo, Víctor.** La "Gestaltpsychologie" y el concepto de estructura (USB/RVF, 8, 1978, p. 7–81)

"La presente disertación forma parte de un trabajo más amplio cuyo propósito consiste en estudiar la génesis y la evolución del concepto de estructura en la ciencia contemporánea." El trabajo total será también un análisis del estructuralismo contemporáneo y su relación con el desarrollo del pensamiento filosófico y la evolución del pensar científico. Trabajo de muy buena calidad.

7799 **Maliandi, Ricardo.** Conciencia de la muerte y reflexión tanatológico (USB/RVF, 7, 1977, p. 81–97)

Interesantes reflexiones sobre la *meditatio mortis* en la historia de la filosofía, pero sobre todo en su relación con el filosofar humano y su origen.

7800 **Mas Herrera, Oscar E.** La libertad interior (UCR/RF, 9:33, julio/dic. 1973, p. 225–230)

Ensayo reflexivo sobre la libertad humana, a la cual se le señalan, entre otros rasgos, el ser un misterio y un proyecto.

7801 **Mendonça, Eduardo Prado de.** A construção da liberdade. São Paulo: Editora Convívio, 1977. 116 p.

El problema de la libertad es enfocado desde diversos ángulos, entre ellos el psicológico, el socio-político, el metafísico y el moral.

7802 **Miguelez, Roberto.** Ciencia y valores (CIF/RLF, 4:3, nov. 1978, p. 195–211)

El problema de las presuposiciones de valor es examinado en el caso particular de la sociología.

7803 **Moreno, Fernando.** Problemas epistemológicos de la sociología crítica: elementos de teoría y crítica social (CPU/ES, 9, sept. 1976, p. 59–95)

Análisis de los reclamos de la sociología crítica (en concreto, de la Escuela de Frankfurt), en relación con los problemas epistemológicos del conocimiento sociológico. Dichos reclamos serían más aplicables a la ciencia política que a la sociología. Utiliza abundante bibliografía.

7804 **Nudler, Oscar.** Notas para una epistemología de las ciencias humanas (CLAEH, 20, dic. 1978, p. 55–64)

Se propone una integración de métodos que se utilizan en las ciencias humanas y que se denomina "holismo refinado."

7805 **Otero Bello, Edison.** La distinción "ciencias de la naturaleza — ciencias de la sociedad" (CPU/ES, 9, sept. 1976, p. 96–119)

Examen de varias manifestaciones del problema, cuyo eje quiere ser el reconocimiento de que en la distinción estudiada obran diferentes concepciones del hombre y de la naturaleza.

7806 **Palerm, Angel.** Modos de producción y formaciones socioeconómicas. México: Editorial Edicol, 1976. 214 p., bibl. (Colección Sociológica conceptos)

El concepto de "modo de producción" constituye, según el autor, la contribución más importante de Marx a la teoría y la métodología histórico-social. "El volumen está organizado con la intención de facilitar al estudioso una colección introductoria de textos fundamentales sobre el proceso de elaboración de la teoría de los modos de producción, desde Marx a los autores contemporáneos . . ." Los autores incluidos son: Marx, Rosa Luxemburgo; Wittfogel; Chayanov, Kula, Polanyi, Preobrayenski. Los textos de cada autor van precedidos de introducciones aclaratorias. Al final, se esbozan consideraciones sobre la relación ciencia social/praxis social.

7807 **Parfait, Blanca H.** El destino como categoría de la vida (UBAFFL/RF, 26:24/25, enero/dic. 1976, p. 73–79)

Reflexiones en torno al concepto de destino en Simmel, como categoría de la vida.

7808 **Pró, Diego F.** Entre la ontología y la antropología filosóficas (UCA/S, 33:127, enero/marzo 1978, p. 39–54)

Meditación de fondo aristotélico que

se propone "ver cómo funcionan los atributos del Ente y el Ser en el ser del hombre" o "ligar la antropología filosófica con la ontología general."

7809 Pucciarelli, Eugenio. La controversia de los humanismos (UBAFFL/RF, 26:24/25, enero/dic. 1976, p. 51–72)

Inteligente análisis de cuatro formas actuales de humanismo: "el evolutivo (o científico), el integral (o cristiano), el existencialista (o filosófico) y el socialista (o marxista)." El humanismo, en la actualidad, está amenazado desde tres ángulos: el etnocentrismo, el totalitarismo y la masificación.

7810 Quiles, Ismael. El hombre y la evolución según Aurobindo y Teilhard. Buenos Aires: Ediciones Depalma, 1976. 154 p., bibl. (Colección Oriente-occidente; 1)

Estudio comparativo de los dos autores, en lo que se refiere al evolucionismo y la concepción del hombre, tomando en cuenta las diferentes tradiciones de ambos autores, las fuentes comunes (el evolucionismo científico) y una compartida visión mística de la unidad cósmica.

7811 Ríu, Federico. La alienación como concepto sociológico (USB/RVF, 7, 1977, p. 99–117)

El concepto de alienación es considerado en la sociología "empirista" y en la sociología "dialéctica." Merton y Marcuse sirven de sendos ejemplos.

7812 Santos, Ely Souto dos. O homen como factor de cultura (PUC/V, 21:82, junho 1976, p. 98–107, bibl.)

Artículo panorámico sobre antropología cultural.

7813 Sazbón, José. Mito e historia en la antropología estructural. Buenos Aires: Nueva Visión, 1975. 94 p.

Contiene tres trabajos: "El Pensamiento Mítico" (inédito); "Sartre y la Razón Estructuralista" (1968); y "El 'Nuevo Humanismo' de la Antropología Estructural" (1971).

7814 Vidal Muñoz, Santiago. Epistemología antropológica (UNL/H, 16, 1975, p. 185–214)

Intento de fundamentación de una antropología interdisciplinaria.

FILOSOFIA DEL DERECHO Y FILOSOFIA POLITICA

7815 Alcántara Salazar, Gerardo. ¿Ciencia marxista o fetichismo burges?: unidad de teoría y método en la ciencia social. Lima: Editorial Pedagógica Asencios, 1977. 106 p.

La verdadera ciencia social es el marxismo. La ciencia social burguesa es fetichismo. Estas tesis ilustran sobre la orientación y el tono del libro.

Andrade, Sonia Margia Viegas. A crítica do direito natural na primeira filosofia do direito de Hegel. See item **7686**.

7816 Arnáiz Armigó, Aurora. Ciencia política. 2. ed. México: Editorial Paz, 1976. 602 p.

Texto universitario de teoría del Estado. Reedición ampliada. La primera edición es de 1961.

7817 ———. Etica y estado. 2. ed. México: UNAM, 1975. 318 p., bibl. (Textos universitarios)

Algunas definiciones básicas que estructuran el libro son: "El ser del Derecho es la justicia. El ser del estado es la ética. El ser de la norma jurídica, lo justo. El ser del acto político, el bien común." Más que un libro de texto es una obra en la que se toma posición, con gran preocupación por la situación éticopolítica contemporánea.

7818 Biagini, Hugo E. Bibliografías sobre ideología (Escritos de Filosofía [Academia Nacional de Ciencias, Centro de Estudios Filosóficos, Buenos Aires] 1:2, julio/dic. 1978, p. 175–177)

Complemento bibliográfico al volumen de la revista *Escritos de Filosofía* dedicado al tema de la ideología.

7819 ———. La ideología liberal (Escritos de Filosofía [Academia Nacional de Ciencias, Centro de Estudios Filosóficos, Buenos Aires] 1:2, julio/dic. 1978, p. 107–114)

Intento de clarificar diversos conceptos, enfoques y modalidades del liberalismo.

———. Las primeras ideas políticas de Locke. See item **7690**.

7820 Brauer, Daniel. Hermenéutica y crítica de la ideología (Escritos de Filosofía [Academia Nacional de Ciencias, Centro de

Estudios Filosóficas, Buenos Aires] 1:2, julio/dic. 1978, p. 145–149)

Se refiere a la obra *Hermeneutik und Ideologiekritik* (1971), en la que colaboran von Apel, Borman, Bubner, Gadamer, Giegel y Habermas.

7821 **Busto, Jorge del.** Violencia y derecho (Estudios de Filosofía [Instituto Riva-Aguero, Lima] 1:93, 1975, p. 94–105)

El tema principal es, en realidad, el de la coacción jurídica. El pensamiento de Santo Tomás es el eje de las consideraciones del autor.

7822 **Capestany, Edward J.** Filosofía política. Buenos Aires: Ediciones Depalma, 1975. 259 p. (Serie Conducta y comunicación; 5)

Con la estructura de un texto o manual, es sin embargo una obra de opinión. La orientación es la que hoy se denominaría cristiana tradicional.

7823 **Cappelletti, Angel J.** Etapas del pensamiento socialista. Madrid: Las Ediciones de la Piqueta, 1978. 120 p.

Se ocupa de cuatro pensadores socialistas, considerados como "cuatro modelos ideológicos del socialismo moderno, escalonados a través de un siglo de historia." Las trabajos son los siguientes: "Babeuf y el Supremo Valor de la Igualdad;" "Saint-Simon: Tecnocracia y Cristianismo;" "Luis Blanc y el Socialismo Democrático;" y "Blanqui o la Pasión Revolucionaria."

7824 **Caturelli, Alberto.** La política de Maurras y la filosofía cristiana (UNL/H, 16, 1975, p. 129–164)

En el mismo año el autor publicó un breve libro con el mismo título (véase *HLAS 40:9690*).

7825 **Cueva, Mario de la.** La idea del Estado. México: UNAM, 1975. 414 p.

Historia de la idea del Estado desde la Antigüedad hasta el siglo XX. La mitad del libro está destinada a "tres doctrinas que han hecho historia:" el pensamiento político de la Iglesia católica; Hegel; y Marx.

7826 **Cullen, Carlos A.** Jurgen Habermas o la astucia de la razón imperial (EC/RFL, 2:3/4, enero/dic. 1976, p. 3–65)

El tema es la obra de Habermas, conocida en sus fuentes originales, expuesta con relativo detalle y vista desde el ángulo de la teoría de la dependencia (como expresión del "centro" que no comprende los problemas de la "periferia").

7827 **Escobar, Carlos Henriquez de.** Discursos, instituções e história. Rio: Editora Rio, 1975. 156 p. (Semeion; 3)

Como lo indica el propio autor, se trata de estudios sobre los discursos ideológicos, la necesidad de una ciencia sobre ellos y el lugar del psicoanálisis y la lingüística en esa tarea.

7828 **Flores Olea, Víctor.** Política y dialéctica: introducción a una metodología de las ciencias sociales. México: UNAM, Facultad de Ciencias Políticas y Sociales, 1975. 171 p., bibl.

Reúne conferencias dictadas a alumnos universitarios, con intención introductoria. Es, en realidad, una introducción al marxismo como único método viable "para abordar científicamente el mundo de lo histórico-social." La última conferencia, sin embargo, se refiere al futuro del marxismo en función de las circunstancias del mundo actual y los cambios ocurridos desde las previsiones de Marx hasta hoy.

7829 **Galvão, Luís Alfredo.** Marx & Marx: a teoria e prática do marxismo no tempo da revolução alemã de 1848. São Paulo: Editora Atica, 1977. 174 p., bibl. (Coleção Ensaios; 25)

Estudio del desarrollo del marxismo a través de la acción de Marx y Engels durante la revolución de 1848, y sus consecuencias para la concepción de la práctica política. Obra interesante.

González de León, Antonio. Marcuse: izquierda y contrarrevolución. See item **7732**.

Guariglia, Osvaldo N. Dominación y legitimación en la teoría política de Aristóteles. See item **7675**.

7830 **———.** Ideología como instrumento de análisis sociopolítico (Escritos de Filosofía [Academia Nacional de Ciencias, Centro de Estudios Filosóficos, Buenos Aires] 1:2, julio/dic. 1978, p. 39–48)

El tema es el análisis de la siguiente proposición: "'Ideología' es un conjunto de creencias . . . asumido por un determinado grupo o élite revolucionaria, que sirve para cohesionar al grupo y justificar sus actos violentos." Se analiza en la ideología de Sorel y en la sociología de Pareto.

Kassa, Peter. Algunas consideraciones en torno a la filosofía de Marcuse. See item **7738**.

7831 López, Mario Justo. Ideología y derecho (Escritos de Filosofía [Academia Nacional de Ciencias, Centro de Estudios Filosóficos, Buenos Aires] 1:2, julio/dic. 1978, p. 85–95)

La relación entre ambos conceptos se analiza en algunas doctrinas jurídicas (como las de Kelsen y Cossio) y en la teoría política de Burdeau. La ideología (entendida como "ideario") podría ser la "piedra angular" para la vigencia del derecho.

7832 Martínez Paz, Fernando. La ética en el jusnaturalismo contemporáneo (Boletín de la Facultad de Derecho y Ciencias Sociales [Universidad Nacional de Córdoba, Argentina] 39:1/3, enero/julio 1975, p. 11–56)

Apoyándose principalmente en fuentes de orientación cristiana, considera "la ética contemporánea del derecho natural en sus relaciones con el derecho." Son temas del trabajo el hombre como ser moral, la relación entre ética y derecho y entre derecho natural y derecho positivo.

7833 Massini, Carlos Ignacio. Ensayo crítico acerca del pensamiento filosófico-jurídico de Carlos Marx. Estudio preliminar de Bernardino Montejano, h. Buenos Aires: Editorial Abeledo-Perrot, 1976. 128 p., bibl.

Tesis doctoral. Crítica a la concepción del Derecho de Marx. El análisis de los textos de Marx ocupa la mayor extensión, pero también se examinan la interpretación estructuralista (especialmente Poulantzas) y la interpretación "voluntarista," vigente en la Unión Soviética.

7834 Massuh, Víctor. Filosofía y ciencias sociales: a propósito de la ideología de la liberación (Escritos de Filosofía [Academia Nacional de Ciencias, Centro de Estudios Filosóficos, Buenos Aires] 1:2, julio/dic. 1978, p. 27–38)

Trata, por un lado, de la relación entre la filosofía y las ciencias humanas (la primera no debiera diluirse en las segundas); además, es una crítica frontal—la más directa que conocemos—al concepto de "liberación" y su significado dentro de la corriente filosófica que lo utiliza como su concepto central.

7835 Miró Quesada, Francisco. El lenguaje de la política (Escritos de Filosofía [Academia Nacional de Ciencias, Centro de Estudios Filosóficos, Buenos Aires] 1:1, enero/junio 1978, p. 37–41)

Lo más importante del artículo es el señalamiento del carácter performativo del lenguaje del político cuando éste expresa su compromiso ante sus oyentes.

7836 Moreira, Vital. Marcuse e a teoria de revolução (UMG/RBEP, 48, jan. 1978, p. 155–191)

Análisis detallado de la teoría de la revolución en Marcuse, que para el autor es una teoría de la no-revolución. Señala cuánto difiere de la posición marxista.

7837 Nino, Carlos Santiago. Las concepciones fundamentales del liberalismo (CIF/RLF, 4:2, julio 1978, p. 141–150)

Por debajo de las interpretaciones político-económicas del liberalismo, el autor identifica dos concepciones básicas que definen esa corriente de pensamiento: el individualismo y el antiperfeccionismo. Trabajo útil, de naturaleza analítica.

7838 ———. Some confusions around Kelsen's concept of validity (ARSP, 64:3, 1978, p. 357–377)

Varios autores habrían malinterpretado el concepto de validez legal en Kelsen, especialmente en lo relacionado con su carácter normativo, lo cual tiene importantes consecuencias para la apreciación general de la teoría.

7839 Orozco S., Luis Enrique. La dialéctica en los fundadores del materialismo histórico (PUJ/UH, 7, junio 1974, p. 111–171)

Extensa exposición. El tema es analizado en Marx, Engels y Lenin.

7840 Pucciarelli, Eugenio. Derroteros recientes de la teoría de la ideología (Escritos de Filosofía [Academia Nacional de Ciencias, Centro de Estudios Filosóficos, Buenos Aires] 1:2, julio/dic. 1978, p. 151–168)

Panorama temático reciente (con indicación de fuentes) del problema, de gran utilidad informativa.

———. Seguridad social y libertad individual en la filosofía política de Spinoza. See item **7708**.

7841 Ramos Alva, Alfonso. 7 [i.e. Siete] tesis equivocadas del marxismo-leninismo sobre Indoamérica. Lima: Instituto de

Estudios Antiimperialistas, 1977. 57 p., illus. (Publicaciones del IDEA,; 2)

Con resonancias, en el título, de los *Siete ensayos* de Mariátegui, es una crítica a ciertas tesis del marxismo-leninismo latinoamericano y de los defensores de la teoría de la dependencia, basándose en el pensamiento político de Haya de la Torre.

7842 **Salazar, Diego Renato.** Teoría del estado. Bogotá: Librería Jurídicas Wilches, 1979. 241 p., bibl.

Se trata de un manual cuyo principal tema es el desarrollo del Estado—y su concepción—en la historia.

7843 **Sazbón, José.** Ideología como contenido e ideología como forma (Escritos de Filosofía [Academia Nacional de Ciencias, Centro de Estudios Filosóficos, Buenos Aires] 1:2, julio/dic. 1978, p. 49–55)

El concepto de ideología desde el ángulo de los recientes desarrollos del estructuralismo y la semiología.

7844 **Stéfano, Victoria.** La dialéctica revolucionaria (Semestre de Filosofía [Universidad Central de Venezuela, Caracas] 1:1, julio/dic. 1977, p. 107–131)

El tema principal es *Historia y conciencia de clase*, de Lukács, pero colocando ese pensamiento en el contexto de las discusiones internas del marxismo desde fines del siglo XIX hasta 1924.

7845 **Tobón Sanin, Gilberto.** Carácter ideológico de la filosofía del derecho (UM/R, 21, enero/marzo 1976, p. 59–86)

Escrito desde un punto de vista marxista. El derecho entra en el terreno de lo ideológico. El iusnaturalismo y el positivismo jurídico son ideologías. El derecho se conoce científicamente como expresión de un modo de producción.

7846 **Vásquez, Eduardo.** Derecho y libertad (USB/RVF, 9, 1979, p. 109–129)

Examen de la crítica de Hegel a la moralidad de Kant.

7847 **Vélez Correa, Jaime.** El análisis marxista: ensayo crítico. Bogotá: Ediciones Theológica Xaveriana, 1977. 57 p., bibl.

El llamado análisis marxista es descompuesto y criticado en sus componentes. Se concluye dudando de su carácter científico y se afirma que se basa en una cosmovisión no demostrada.

FILOSOFIA DE LA HISTORIA Y DE LA CULTURA

7848 **Crippa, Adolfo.** Mito e cultura. São Paulo: Editora Convivio, 1975. 214 p.

Se intenta aprovechar la aportación que los mitos, como explicación de los orígenes, pueden hacer a la comprensión de la cultura y de la diversidad de culturas.

Cruz Vélez, Danilo. Aproximaciones a la filosofía. See item **7504**.

7849 **Derisi, Octavio Nicolás.** Esencia y ámbito de la cultura. Buenos Aires: Editorial Columba, 1975. 72 p. (Colección Esquemas; 117)

Obra introductoria, desde un punto de vista espiritualista y cristiano.

7850 **Francovich, Guillermo.** Alcides Arguedas y otros ensayos sobre la historia. La Paz: Librería Editorial Juventud, 1979. 187 p.

Contiene dos trabajos de tema boliviano: el primer ensayo, sobre Alcides Arguedas, autor de *Pueblo enfermo*, y otro sobre historiografía boliviana. Los restantes continúan la meditación del autor sobre filosofía de la historia.

7851 **Hernández de Alba, Gonzalo.** Notas sobre la epistemología analítica de la historia (UN/IV, 46/47, agosto 1976, p. 69–77)

Señala características de lo que en la literatura filosófica de habla inglesa se denomina "filosofía crítica de la historia," frente a la filosofía de la historia y la historiografía tradicionales.

7852 **Mata Gavidia, José.** Historiografía (UCR/RF, 15:41, julio/dic. 1977, p. 165–174, bibl.)

Según el autor, el título de estas consideraciones debió ser "Historiarquía." Bajo él se propone tratar de "los principios del ser de lo histórico."

7853 **Reale, Miguel.** Experiência e cultura. Para a fundação de uma teoria geral da experiência. São Paulo: Editora de Universidade de São Paulo [and] Editora Grijalbo, 1977. 284 p.

Intento de una teoría general de la experiencia que tienda a recuperar la unidad de naturaleza y cultura, o de una teoría del conocimiento que abarque todos los aspectos de la realidad. En ese contexto, la cultura sería "lo que emerge históricamente de la experiencia, a través de un continuo proceso de objetivaciones cognoscitivas y prácticas."

7854 **Weinberg, Gregorio.** Hacia una "planetarización" de la historia (CAM, 210:1, enero/feb. 1977, p. 123–128)

Es estudio de la historia, hasta ahora, ha dejado fuera grandes sectores de población y pueblos enteros. La corrección de ese error es la "planetarización" de la historia, que no lo es sólo en extensión sino también en la ampliación de las categorías de interpretación.

ESTETICA Y FILOSOFIA DEL ARTE

Brito, Emilio. Hegel y las estéticas. See item **7691**.

7855 **Estrada, José María de.** La esencia de lo estético (UCA/S, 33:127, enero/marzo 1978, p. 9–16)

Reflexiones de fondo aristotélico sobre el arte como imitación.

7856 **Kogan, Jacobo.** El arte como conocimiento y como lenguaje (CAM, 33[195]:4, julio/agosto 1974, p. 95–105)

Si bien el arte no es conocimiento, como algunos filósofos sostienen, "contiene un mensaje, el cual, si bien resulta inanalizable, no deja de ser una 'idea'." Estas consideraciones se realizan al hilo de un análisis de las ideas de Kant y Whitehead.

7857 **Lida, Raimundo.** Santayana y la autonomía de lo estético (CAM, 35[204]:1, enero/feb. 1976, p. 55–66)

Sobre la negación de la independencia de lo estético en Santayana.

7858 **Losa, Margarida.** A desumanização da arte e da crítica: extrapolações a partir de Ortega, Lukács, Barthes e Marcuse (COLOQ, 46, nov. 1978, p. 11–19)

"Formalismo" y "realismo" en la interpretación del arte, vistos a través de los autores estudiados.

7859 **Marta Sosa, Joaquín.** Sociopolítica del arte. Caracas: Equinoccio, 1975. 224 p.

La intención es "hacer un estudio socio-político-histórico del arte, dentro del capitalismo, e investigar la posibilidad de que el arte sea un factor social."

Ramos, Samuel. Obras completas. See item **7544**.

7860 **Ranea, Alberto Guillermo.** Las ideas estéticas de José Ortega y Gasset (CIF/RLF, 4:2, julio 1978, p. 151–165)

Trabajo bien elaborado y bien escrito. Desentraña, de la obra diversa de Ortega, una estética y examina cómo ella es aplicada al análisis del hecho literario. Ortega habría estado menos alejado del romanticismo de lo que él pensaba.

7861 **Ravera, Rosa María.** El arte como lenguaje (Escritos de Filosofía [Academia Nacional de Ciencias, Centro de Estudios Filosóficos, Buenos Aires] 1:1, enero/junio 1978, p. 143–155)

Repasa la problemática de la relación entre arte y lenguaje. Tiende a destacar lo privativo del arte.

7862 ———. La especifidad del signo pictórico (UBAFFL/RF, 26:24/25, enero/dic. 1976, p. 87–91)

El signo pictórico englobado en la problemática de la semiótica.

7863 ———. Plástica e ideología (Escritos de Filosofía [Academia Nacional de Ciencias, Centro de Estudios Filosóficos, Buenos Aires] 1:2, julio/dic. 1978, p. 115–128)

Enfoque semiológico—bien que no lingüístico—del tema.

FILOSOFIA DEL LENGUAJE

Albizu, Edgardo. El lenguaje en la hermenéutica filosófica de Gadamer. See item **7716**.

7864 **Capalbo, Creusa.** A linguagem como mediação necessária para o pensamento filosófico e científico (UC/V, 31:2, 1975, p. 45–50)

Sobre el campo y las tareas de la filosofía del lenguaje.

D'Alessio, Juan Carlos. Lenguaje y ontología en la falacia naturalista de G.E. Moore. See item **7725**.

Dascal, Marcelo. Spinoza: pensamento e linguagem. See item **7694**.

7865 **Freiberger, Mário João.** Linguagem e mito (PUC/V, 20:78, junho 1975, p. 165–177, bibl.)

Consideraciones generales sobre las relaciones entre mito y lenguaje, y especialmente sobre el lenguaje de la mitología. La dimensión mítica del hombre persiste aún y no fue remplazada por lo racional.

García Canclini, Néstor. Lingüística y psicoanálisis en la filosofía de Paul Ricoeur. See item **7728**.

7866 **Gutiérrez, Claudio.** Ambigüedad y comunicación (CIF/RLF, 3:3, nov. 1977, p. 251–267)

El trabajo se propone: "un intento de aclarar el tema de la comunicación desde un punto de vista lógico." La ambigüedad se incorpora al análisis por considerarla inherente a toda lenguaje "excepto en casos límites."

7867 **Martín, José Pablo.** El análisis del lenguaje en Aristóteles (CIF/RLF, 5:1, marzo 1979, p. 53–70, bibl.)

Intenta "aportar elementos para la explicitación de una teoría aristotélica sobre el lenguaje."

7868 **Pochtar, Ricardo.** Sobre el aspecto creativo del uso del lenguaje (Escritos de Filosofía [Academia Nacional de Ciencias, Centro de Estudios Filosóficos, Buenos Aires] 1:1, enero/junio 1978, p. 43–51)

El propósito del trabajo es presentar "una discusión de ciertas dificultades planteadas por . . . la idea de 'creatividad lingüística' dentro . . . de la teoría del lenguaje elaborada por la gramática generativo-transformacional."

7869 **Pucciarelli, Eugenio.** Tiempo y lenguaje (Escritos de Filosofía [Academia Nacional de Ciencias, Centro de Estudios Filosóficos, Buenos Aires] 1:1, enero/junio 1978, p. 165–189)

En este trabajo que es a la vez panorámico y analítico, el autor continúa sus investigaciones sobre el tiempo. Se examinan, entre varios otros, los análisis de Benveniste y André Jacob, así como los estudios sobre el tiempo y la lógica. En términos generales, el tema es el lenguaje como expresión del tiempo ("el lenguaje del tiempo"), pero, sobre todo, el tiempo como ínsito en el lenguage ("el tiempo del lenguaje").

7870 **Rabossi, Eduardo A.** Meaning, force and explicit performatives (Philosophica [Rijksuniversiteit, Gent, The Netherlands] 19:1, 1977, p. 89–109)

El tema, que el autor elabora con consideraciones propias, es la doctrina de Austin sobre "explicit performative sentences." Después de examinar varias críticas, concluye que la posición de Austin es, en lo básico, correcta.

7871 **Sazbón, José.** Lenguaje y escritura (Escritos de Filosofía [Academia Nacional de Ciencias, Centro de Estudios Filosóficos, Buenos Aires] 1:1, enero/junio 1978, p. 7–16)

El tema es examinado en la obra de Derrida.

METAFISICA

Argerami, Oscar. Metafísica y experiencia en la escolástica del siglo XIII. See item **7662**.

7872 **Chong M., Moisés.** Actualidad de la metafísica (LNB/L, 270/271, agosto/sept. 1978, p. 46–58)

La metafísica que se estima renovada no es la tradicional sino la prolongación del saber científico sobre la naturaleza y sobre el hombre.

Cruz Vélez, Danilo. Aproximaciones a la filosofía. See item **7504**.

Hoyos Vásquez, Jaime. Presentación: Kant y el problema de la metafísica; materiales para el estudio de la obra de Martín Heidegger. See item **7701**.

7873 **Marimón Batlló, Ricardo.** Ontología, gnoseología y teología: tres estadios de la metafísica (UCA/S, 33:129, 1978, p. 187–200)

El tema es tratado "siempre de acuerdo con la doctrina filosófica y teológica de Santo Tomás de Aquino en su *Suma Teológica*, la. q. 13 . . .".

7874 **Nuño, Juan.** Contra las metafísicas (Semestre de Filosofía [Universidad Central de Venezuela, Caracas] 1:1, julio/dic. 1977, p. 7–20)

Defensa de la filosofía crítica o analítica que hace del examen del lenguaje su tarea, escrita en estilo animado y escasamente técnico.

Soto B., J.A. Spinoza y Schelling: sobre el problema metafísico. See item **7711**.

JOURNAL ABBREVIATIONS PHILOSOPHY

AAFH/TAM The Americas. A quarterly publication of inter-American cultural history. Academy of American Franciscan History. Washington.

AI/I Interciencia. Asociación Interciencia. Caracas.

ANA Análisis. Cuadernos de investigación. Apartado 11093. Correo Santa Beatriz. Lima.

ARBOR Arbor. Madrid.

ARSP Archiv für Rechts- und Sozialhilosophie. Franz Steiner Verlag. Wiesbaden, FRG.

BMA/BB Boletim Bibliográfico. Biblioteca Mário de Andrade. São Paulo.

BRP Beiträge zur Romanischen Philologie. Rütten & Loening. Berlin.

CAM Cuadernos Americanos. México.

CBR/BCB Boletín Cultural y Bibliográfico. Banco de la República, Biblioteca Luis-Angel Arango. Bogotá.

CDLA Casa de las Américas. Instituto Cubano del Libro. La Habana.

CEHA/NH Nuestra Historia. Centro de Estudios de Historia Argentina. Buenos Aires.

CELRG/A Araisa. Anuario del Centro de Estudios Latinoamericanos Rómulo Gallegos. Caracas.

CH Cuadernos Hispanoamericanos. Instituto de Cultura Hispánica. Madrid.

CIF/RLF Revista Latinoamericana de Filosofía. Centro de Investigaciones Filosóficas. Buenos Aires.

CLAEH Centro Latinoamericano de Economía Humana. Montevideo.

CM/D Diálogos. Artes/Letras/Ciencias Humanas. El Colegio de México. México.

CM/HM Historia Mexicana. El Colegio de México. México.

COLOQ Colóquio. Revista de artes e letras. Fundação Calouste Gulbenkian. Lisboa.

CONAC/RNC Revista Nacional de Cultura. Consejo Nacional de Cultura. Caracas.

CPES/PE Política y Espíritu. Cuadernos de cultura política, económica y social. Santiago.

CPES/RPS Revista Paraguaya de Sociología. Centro Paraguayo de Estudios de Sociológicos. Asunción.

CPU/ES Estudios Sociales. Corporación de Promoción Universitaria. Santiago.

EC/M Mapocho. Biblioteca Nacional, Extensión Cultural. Santiago.

EC/RFL *See* RFL.

ECO Eco. Librería Bucholz. Bogotá.

FFCLM/EH Estudos Históricos. Faculdade de Filosofia, Ciências e Letras, Depto. de História. Marília, Brazil.

FH Folia Humanistica. Ciencias, artes, letras. Editorial Glarma. Barcelona.

FJB/BH Boletín Histórico. Fundación John Boulton. Caracas.

HAHR Hispanic American Historical Review. Duke Univ. Press *for the* Conference on Latin American History of the American Historical Association. Durham, N.C.

HISP Hispanófila. Univ. of North Carolina. Chapel Hill.

IEH/A Anuario. Univ. Central de Venezuela, Instituto de Estudios Hispanoamericanos. .Caracas?

IEP/REP Revista de Estudios Políticos. Instituto de Estudios Políticos. Madrid.

IGFO/RI Revista de Indias. Instituto Gonzalo Fernández de Oviedo [and] Consejo Superior de Investigaciones Científicas. Madrid.

ISTMO Istmo. Revista del pensamiento actual. México.

LARR Latin American Research Review. Univ. of North Carolina Press *for the* Latin American Studies Association. Chapel Hill.

LNB/L Lotería. Lotería Nacional de Beneficencia. Panamá.

PUC/V Veritas. Revista. Pontificia Univ. Católica do Rio Grande do Sul. Porto Alegre, Brazil.

PUJ/UH Universitas Humanistica. Pontificia Univ. Javeriana, Facultad de Filosofía y Letras. Bogotá.

RCLL Revista de Crítica Literaria Latinoamericana. Latinoamericana Editores. Lima.

RFL Revista de Filosofía Latinoamericana. Ediciones Castañeda. San Antonio de Padua, Arg.

RIB Revista Interamericana de Bibliografía [Inter-American Review of Bibliography]. Organization of American States. Washington.

SBPC/CC Ciência e Cultura. Sociedade Brasileira para o Progresso da Ciência. São Paulo.

SECOLAS/A Annals of the Southeastern Conference on Latin American Studies. West Georgia College. Carrollton.

SHA/D Davar. Revista literaria. Sociedad Hebraica Argentina. Buenos Aires.

UA/U Universidad. Univ. de Antioquia. Medellín, Colombia.

UBAFFL/C Cuadernos de Filosofía. Univ. de Buenos Aires, Facultad de Filosofía y Letras. Buenos Aires.

UBAFFL/RF Revista de Filosofia. Univ. de Buenos Aires, Facultad de Filosofia y Letras. Buenos Aires.

UBN/R Revista de la Biblioteca Nacional. Ministerio de Educación y Cultura. Montevideo.

UC/A Anales de la Universidad de Cuenca. Cuenca, Ecuador.

UC/AT Atenea. Revista de ciencias, letras y artes. Univ. de Concepción, Chile.

UCA/S Sapientia. Organo de la Facultad de Filosofía. Univ. Católica Argentina Santa María de los Buenos Aires. Buenos Aires.

UCAB/M Montalbán. Univ. Católica Andrés Bello, Facultad de Humanidades y Educación, Institutos Humanísticos de Investigación. Caracas.

UCE/A Anales de la Universidad Central del Ecuador. Quito.

UCLV/I Islas. Univ. Central de las Villas. Santa Clara, Cuba.

UCNSA/EP Estudios Paraguayos. Univ. Católica Nuestra Señora de la Asunción. Asunción.

UCP/IAP Ibero-Americana Pragensia. Univ. Carolina de Praga, Centro de Estudios Ibero-Americanos. Prague.

UCR/RCS Revista de Ciencias Sociales. Univ. de Costa Rica. San José.

UCR/RF Revista de Filosofía de la Universidad de Costa Rica. San José.

UHB/EHA Etudes Hispano-Américaines. Univ. de Haute Bretagne, Centre d'Etudes Hispaniques, Hispano-Américaines et Luso-Brésiliennes. Rennes, France.

UM/JIAS Journal of Inter-American Studies and World Affairs. Univ. of Miami Press *for the* Center for Advanced International Studies. Coral Gables, Fla.

UM/R Revista Universidad de Medellín. Centro de Estudios de Posgrado. Medellín, Colombia.

UMG/RBEP Revista Brasileira de Estudos Politicos. Univ. de Minas Gerais. Belo Horizonte, Brazil.

UMGFF/K Kriterion. Revista da Faculdade de Filosofia da Univ. de Minas Gerais. Belo Horizonte, Brazil.

UN/IV Ideas y Valores. Revista del Instituto de Filosofía y Letras. Univ. Nacional. Bogotá.

UNAM/D Diánoia. Univ. Nacional Autónoma de México, Centro de Estudios Filosóficos. México.

UNAM/RMCP Revista Mexicana de Ciencias Políticas. Univ. Nacional Autónoma de México, Facultad de Ciencias Políticas y Sociales. México.

UNL/H Humanitas. Univ. de Nuevo León, Centro de Estudios Humanísticos. Monterrey, Mex.

UNMSM/L Letras. Univ. Nacional Mayor de San Marcos. Lima.

UNPHU/A Aula. Univ. Nacional Pedro Henríquez Ureña. Santo Domingo.

UP/A Apuntes. Univ. del Pacífico, Centro de Investigación. Lima.

UPB Universidad Pontificia Bolivariana. Medellín, Colombia.

UPR/D Diálogos. Univ. de Puerto Rico. Rio Piedras.

USB/F Franciscanum. Revista de las ciencias del espíritu. Univ. de San Buenaventura. Bogotá.

USB/RVF Revista Venezolana de Filosofía. Univ. Simón Bolívar [and] Sociedad Venezolana de Filosofía. Caracas.

USMLA/LA La Antigua. Univ. de Santa María La Antigua, Oficina de Humanidades. Panamá.

UT/SSQ Social Science Quarterly. Univ. of Texas, Dept. of Government. Austin.

UY/R Revista de la Universidad de Yucatán. Mérida, Mex.

VOZES Vozes. Revista de cultura. Editora Vozes. Petrópolis, Brazil.

INDEXES

ABBREVIATIONS AND ACRONYMS

Except for journal acronyms which are listed at a) the end of each major disciplinary section, (e.g., Art, History, etc.); and b) after each serial title in the *Title List of Journals Indexed*, p. 781.

a	annual
ABC	Argentina, Brazil, Chile
A.C.	antes de Cristo
ACAR	Associação de Crédito e Assistência Rural, Brazil
AD	Anno Domini
A.D.	Acción Democrática, Venezuela
ADESG	Associação dos Diplomados de Escola Superior de Guerra, Brazil
AGI	Archivo General de Indias, Sevilla
AGN	Archivo General de la Nación
AID	Agency for International Development
Ala.	Alabama
ALALC	Asociación Latinoamericana de Libre Comercio
ANAPO	Alianza Nacional Popular, Colombia
ANCARSE	Associação Nordestina de Crédito e Assistência Rural de Sergipe, Brazil
ANCOM	Andean Common Market
ANDI	Asociación Nacional de Industriales, Colombia
AP	Acción Popular
APRA	Alianza Popular Revolucionaria Americana
Arg.	Argentina
Ariz.	Arizona
Ark.	Arkansas
ASA	Association of Social Anthropologists of the Commonwealth, London
ASSEPLAN	Assessoria de Planejamente e Acompanhamento, Recife, Brazil
Assn.	Association
Aufl.	Auflage (edition, edición)
AUFS	American Universities Field Staff Reports, Hanover, N.H.
Aug.	August, Augustan
b.	born (nacido)
B.A.	Buenos Aires
Bar.	Barbados
BBE	Bibliografia Brasileira de Educação
b.c.	indicates dates obtained by radio-carbon methods
BC	Before Christ
bibl.	bibliography
BID	Banco Interamericano de Desarrollo
BNDE	Banco Nacional de Desenvolvimento Econômico, Brazil
BNH	Banco Nacional de Habitação, Brazil
Bol.	Bolivia
BP	before present
b/w	black-and-white
C14	Carbon 14
ca.	circa
C.A.	Centro América, Central America

CACM	Central American Common Market
CADE	Conferencia Anual de Ejecutivos de Empresas, Peru
CAEM	Centro de Altos Estudios Militares, Peru
Calif.	California
CARC	Centro de Arte y Comunicación
CARICOM	Caribbean Common Market
CARIFTA	Caribbean Free Trade Association
CBD	central business district
CD	Christian Democrats, Chile
CDI	Conselho de Desenvolvimento Industrial
CEBRAP	Centro Brasileiro de Análise e Planejamento, São Paulo
CECORA	Central de Cooperativas de la Reforma Agraria, Colombia
CEDAL	Centro de Estudios Democráticos de América Latina, Costa Rica
CEDE	Centro de Estudios sobre Desarrollo Económico, Univ. de los Andes, Bogotá
CEDEPLAR	Centro de Desenvolvimento e Planejamento Region, Belo Horizonte, Brazil
CEDES	Centro de Estudios de Estado y Sociedad, Buenos Aires
CELADE	Centro Latinoamericano de Demografía
CEMLA	Centro de Estudios Monetarios Latinoamericanos, México
CENDES	Centro de Estudios del Desarrollo, Venezuela
CENIDIM	Centro Nacional de Información, Documentación e Investigación Musicales, Mexico
CEPADE	Centro Paraguayo de Estudios de Desarrollo Económico y Social
CEPA-SE	Comissão Estadual de Planejamento Agrícola, Sergipe, Brazil
CEPAL	*See* ECLA.
CES	constant elasticity of substitution
cf.	compare
CFI	Consejo Federal de Inversiones, B.A.
CGE	Confederación General Económica, Argentina
CGTP	Confederación General de Trabajadores del Perú
ch., chap.	chapter
CHEAR	Council on Higher Education in the American Republics
Cía.	compañía
CIA	Central Intelligence Agency
CIDA	Comité Interamericano de Desarrollo Agrícola
CIE	Centro de Investigaciones Económicas, Buenos Aires
CIP	Conselho Interministerial de Preços
CLACSO	Consejo Latinoamericano de Ciencias Sociales, Secretaría Ejecutiva, Buenos Aires
CLASC	Confederación Latinoamericana Sindical Cristiana
CLE	Comunidad Latinoamericana de Escritores, México
cm	centimeter
CNI	Confederação Nacional da Industria, Brazil
Co.	company
COBAL	Companhia Brasileira de Alimentos
Col.	collection, colección, coleção
Colo.	Colorado
COMCORDE	Comisión Coordinadora para el Desarrollo Económico, Uruguay
comp.	compiler
CONDESE	Conselho de Desenvolvimento Econômico de Sergipe, Brazil
Conn.	Connecticut
COPEI	Comité Organizador Pro-Elecciones Independientes, Venezuela
CORFO	Corporación de Fomento de la Producción, Chile
CORP	Corporación para el Fomento de Investigaciones Económicas, Colombia
Corp.	Corporation
C.R.	Costa Rica

CUNY	City University of New York
CVG	Corporación Venezolana de Guayana
d.	died
DANE	Departamento Nacional de Estadística, Colombia
DC	developed country; Demócratas Cristianos, Chile
d.C.	después de Cristo
Dec.	December, décembre
Del.	Delaware
dept.	department
depto.	departamento
dez.	dezembro
dic.	diciembre
DNOCS	Departamento Nacional de Obras Contra as Sêcas, Brazil
D.R.	Dominican Republic
Dra.	Doctora
ECLA	Economic Comission for Latin America
ECOSOC	UN Dept. of Economic and Social Affairs
Ecua.	Ecuador
ed(s).	edition(s), edición(es), editor(s), redactor(es)
EDEME	Editora Emprendimentos Educacionais Florianópolis, Brazil
Edo.	Estado
EEC	European Economic Community
EFTA	European Free Trade Association
e.g.	exempio gratia [for example]
El Sal.	El Salvador
ELN	Ejército de Liberación Nacional, Colombia
estr.	estrenado
et al	et alia [and others]
ETENE	Escritório Técnico de Estudios Econômicos do Nordeste, Brazil
ETEPE	Escritório Técnico de Planejamento, Brazil
EUDEBA	Editorial Universitaria de Buenos Aires
EWG	Europaische Wirtschaftsgemeinschaft. *See* EEC.
facsim.	facsimile
FAO	Food and Agriculture Organization of the United Nations
feb.	February, febrero
FEDECAFE	Federación Nacional de Cafeteros, Colombia
fev.	fevreiro, février
ff.	following
FGTS	Fundo do Garantia do Tempo de Serviço, Brazil
FGV	Fundação Getúlio Vargas
FIEL	Fundación de Investigaciones Económicas Latinoamericanas, Argentina
film.	filmography
fl.	flourished, floresció
Fla.	Florida
FLACSO	Facultad Latinoamericana de Ciencias Sociales, Buenos Aires
fold. map	folded map
fold. table	folded table
fols.	folios
FRG	Federal Republic of Germany
ft.	foot, feet
FUAR	Frente Unido de Acción Revolucionaria, Colombia
Ga.	Georgia
GAO	General Accounting Office, Washington
GATT	General Agreement on Tariffs and Trade
GDP	gross domestic product

GDR	German Democratic Republic
Gen.	General
GMT	Greenwich Meridian Time
GPA	grade point average
GPO	Government Printing Office
Guat.	Guatemala
h.	hijo
ha.	hectares, hectáreas
HLAS	*Handbook of Latin American Studies*
HMAI	*Handbook of Middle American Indians*
Hnos.	Hermanos
Hond.	Honduras
IBBD	Instituto Brasileiro de Bibliografia e Documentação
IBRD	International Bank of Reconstruction and Development
ICA	Instituto Colombiano Agropecuario
ICAIC	Instituto Cubano de Arte e Industria Cinematográficas
ICCE	Instituto Colombiano de Construcción Escolar
ICSS	Instituto Colombiano de Seguridad Social
ICT	Instituto de Crédito Territorial, Colombia
IDB	Inter-American Development Bank
i.e.	id est [that is]
IEL	Instituto Euvaldo Lodi, Brazil
IEP	Instituto de Estudios Peruanos
IERAC	Instituto Ecuatoriano de Reforma Agraria y Colonización
III	Instituto Indigenista Interamericano, Mexico
IIN	Instituto Indigenista Nacional, Guatemala
Ill.	Illinois
illus.	illustration(s)
ILO	International Labour Organization, Geneva
IMES	Instituto Mexicano de Estudios Sociales
in.	inches
INAH	Instituto Nacional de Antropología e Historia, México
INBA	Instituto Nacional de Bellas Artes, México
Inc.	incorporated
INCORA	Instituto Colombiano de Reforma Agraria
Ind.	Indiana
INEP	Instituto Nacional de Estudios Pedagógicos, Brazil
INI	Instituto Nacional Indigenista, Mexico
INIT	Instituto Nacional de Industria Turística, Cuba
INPES/IPEA	Instituto de Planejamento Econômico e Social, Instituto de Pesquisas, Brazil
IPA	Instituto de Pastoral Andina, Univ. de San Antonio de Abad, Seminario de Antropología, Cuzco, Peru
IPEA	Instituto de Pesquisa Econômico-Social Aplicada, Brazil
IPES/GB	Instituto de Pesquisas e Estudos Sociais, Guanabara, Brazil
IPHAN	Instituto de Patrimônio Histórico e Artístico Nacional, Brazil
ir.	irregular
ITT	International Telephone and Telegraph
Jam.	Jamaica
jan.	January, janeiro, Janvier
JLP	Jamaican Labour Party
JUCEPLAN	Junta Central de Planificación, Cuba
Jul.	juli
Jun.	Juni
Kans.	Kansas
km	kilometers, kilómetros

Ky.	Kentucky
l.	leaves, hojas (páginas impresas por una sola cara)
La.	Louisiana
LASA	Latin American Studies Association
LDC	less developed country
Ltda.	Limitada
m	meters, metros, monthly
M	mille, mil, thousand
MAPU	Movimiento de Acción Popular Unitario, Chile
MARI	Middle American Research Institute, Tulane University, New Orleans
Mass.	Massachusetts
MCC	Mercado Común Centro-Americano
MCN	multinational corporation
Md.	Maryland
MDB	Movimento Democrático Brasileiro
MDC	more developed countries
MEC	Ministério de Educação e Cultura, Brazil
Mex.	Mexico
Mich.	Michigan
mimeo	mimeographed, mimeografiado
min.	minutes, minutos
Minn.	Minnesota
MIR	Movimiento de Izquierda Revolucionaria, Chile
Miss.	Mississippi
MIT	Massachusetts Institute of Technology
MLN	Movimiento de Liberación Nacional
mm.	millimeter
MNR	Movimiento Nacionalista Revolucionario, Bolivia
Mo.	Missouri
MOIR	Movimiento Obrero Independiente y Revolucionario, Colombia
MRL	Movimiento Revolucionario Liberal, Colombia
ms.	manuscript
msl	mean sea level
n.	nacido (born)
N.C.	North Carolina
n.d.	no date
N. Dak.	North Dakota
Nebr.	Nebraska
neubearb.	neurbearbeitet (revised, corregida)
Nev.	Nevada
n.f.	neue Folge
N.H.	New Hampshire
Nic.	Nicaragua
NIEO	new international economic order
NIH	National Institutes of Health, Washington
N.J.	New Jersey
N. Mex.	New Mexico
no(s).	number(s), número(s)
NOSALF	Scandinavian Committee for Research in Latin America
Nov.	noviembre, November, novembre, novembro
n.p.	no place, no publisher
NSF	National Science Foundation
NY	New York
NYC	New York City
OAS	Organization of American States

oct.	October, octubre
ODEPLAN	Oficina de Planificación Nacional, Chile
OEA	Organización de los Estados Americanos
OIT	*See* ILO.
Okla.	Oklahoma
Okt.	Oktober
op.	opus
OPANAL	Organismo para la Proscripción de las Armas Nucleares en América Latina
OPEC	Organization of Petroleum Exporting Countries
OPEP	Organización de Países Exportadores de Petróleo
OPIC	Overseas Investment Corporation
Oreg.	Oregon
ORIT	Organización Regional Interamericana del Trabajo
out.	outubro
p.	page
Pa.	Pennsylvania
Pan.	Panama
PAN	Partido Acción Nacional, Mexico
Par.	Paraguay
PC	partido comunista
PCR	Partido Comunista Revolucionario, Chile and Argentina
PCV	Partido Comunista de Venezuela
PDC	Partido Demócrata Cristiano, Chile
PEMEX	Petróleos Mexicanos
PETROBRAS	Petróleo Brasileiro
PIP	Partido Independiente de Puerto Rico
PLANAVE	Engenharia e Planejamento Limitada, Brazil
PLANO	Planejamento e Assesoria Limitada, Brazil
PLN	Partido Liberación Nacional, Costa Rica
PNM	People's National Movement, Trinidad and Tobago
PNP	People's National Party, Jamaica
pop.	population
port., ports.	portrait/s
PPP	purchasing power parities
P.R.	Puerto Rico
PRD	Partido Revolucionario Dominicano
PRI	Partido Revolucionario Institucional, Mexico
PROABRIL	Centro de Projetos Industriais, Brazil
Prof.	Professor
PRONAPA	Programa Nacional de Pesquisas Arqueológicas, Brazil
prov.	province, provincia
PS	Partido Socialista, Chile
pseud.	pseudonym, pseudónimo
pt(s).	part(s), parte(s)
PUC	Pontificia Universidade Católica, Rio
PURSC	Partido Unido de la Revolución Socialista de Cuba
q.	quarterly
R.D.	República Dominicana
rev.	revisada, revista, revised
R.I.	Rhode Island
Rio	Rio de Janeiro
S.a.	semiannual
SALALM	Seminar on the Acquisition of Latin American Library Materials
S.C.	South Carolina
sd.	sound

S. Dak.	South Dakota
SDR	special drawing rights
Sec.	section, sección
SELA	Sistema Económico Latinoamericano
SENAC	Serviço Nacional de Aprendizagem Comerical, Rio
SENAI	Serviço Nacional de Aprendizagem Industrial, São Paulo
Sept.	September, septiembre, septembre
SES	socio-economic status
SESI	Serviço Social de Industria, Brazil
set.	setembre
SIECA	Secretaría Permanente del Tratado General de Integración Centroamericana
SIL	Summer Institute of Linguistics
SINAMOS	Sistema Nacional de Apoyo a la Movilización Social, Peru
S.J.	Society of Jesus
s.n.	sine nomine
SNA	Sociedad Nacional de Agricultura, Chile
SPVEA	Superintendência do Plano de Valorização Econômica de Amazônia, Brazil
sq.	square
SUDAM	Superintendência do Desenvolvimento da Amazônia, Brazil
SUDENE	Superintendência do Desenvolvimento do Nordeste, Brazil
SUFRAMA	Superintendência da Zona Franca de Manaus, Brazil
SUNY	State Universities of New York
t.	tomo, tome
T. and T.	Trinidad & Tobago
TAT	Thematic Apperception Test
TB	tuberculosis
Tenn.	Tennessee
Tex.	Texas
TG	transformational generative
TL	Thermoluminescent
TNP	Tratado de No Proliferación
trans.	translator
U.K.	United Kingdom
UN	United Nations
UNAM	Universidad Nacional Autónoma de México
UNCTAD	United Nations Conference on Trade and Development
UNDP	UN Development Programme
UNEAC	Unión de Escritores y Artistas de Cuba
UNESCO	United Nations Educational, Scientific and Cultural Organization
univ.	university, universidad, universidade, université, universität
uniw.	uniwersytet
UP	Unidad Popular, Chile
URD	Unidad Revolucionaria Democrática
URSS	Unión de Repúblicas Soviéticas Socialistas
Uru.	Uruguay
US	United States of America
USIA	United States Information Agency, Washington
USSR	Union of Soviet Socialist Republics
UTM	Universal Transverse Mercator
v.; vol.	volume, volumen
Va.	Virginia
Ven.	Venezuela
V.I.	Virgin Islands
viz.	videlicet, that is, namely
vs.	versus

Vt.	Vermont
W.I.	West Indies
Wis.	Wisconsin
Wyo.	Wyoming
yr.	the younger, el joven, year

TITLE LIST OF JOURNALS INDEXED *

* Journals that have been included in the *Handbook* as individual items are listed alphabetically by title in the Author Index.

Abside. Revista de cultura mexicana. México. (A)

Actualidades. Centro de Estudios Latinoamericanos Rómulo Gallegos. Caracas.

Agricultural History. Agricultural History Society. Univ. of California Press. Berkeley. (AHS/AH)

Alfa. Univ. de São Paulo, Faculdade de Filosofia, Ciências e Letras. Marília, Brazil (FFCLM/A)

Allpanchis. Instituto de Pastoral Andina. Cuzco, Perú. (IPA/A)

Amazonia Peruana. Centro Amazónica de Antropología y Aplicación Práctica. Lima.

América Indígena. Instituto Indigenista Interamericano. México. (III/AI)

América Latina. Academia de Ciencias de la URSS [Unión de Repúblicas Soviéticas Socialistas]. Moscú. (URSS/AL)

América Latina. Centro Latino-Americano de Pesquisas em Ciências Sociais. Rio. (CLAPCS/AL)

American Anthropologist. American Anthropological Association. Washington. (AAA/AA)

American Antiquity. The Society for America Archaeology. Menasha, Wis. (SAA/AA)

American Ethnologist. American Anthropological Association. Washington. (AAA/AE)

American Historical Review. American Historical Association. Washington. (AHA/R)

American Journal of Public Health and the Nation's Health. The American Public Health Association. Albany, N.Y. (APHA/J)

Américas. Organization of American States. Washington. (OAS/AM)

The Americas. A quarterly publication of inter-American cultural history. Academy of American Franciscan History. Washington. (AAFH/TAM)

Anais. Arquivo Histórico do Rio Grande do Sul. Porto Alegre, Brazil.

Anais do Museu Paulista. São Paulo. (MP/AN)

Anales de Arqueología y Etnología. Univ. Nacional de Cuyo, Facultad de Filosofía y Letras. Mendoza, Arg. (UNC/AAE)

Anales de la Universidad Central del Ecuador. Quito. (UCE/A)

Anales de la Universidad de Cuenca. Cuenca, Ecuador. (UC/A)

Anales del Instituto de Investigaciones Estéticas. Univ. Nacional Autónoma de México. México. (IIE/A)

Anales del Instituto Nacional de Antropología e Historia. Secretaría de Educación Pública. México. (INAH/A)

Anales del Museo Nacional David J. Guzmán. San Salvador. (MNDJG/A)

Análisis. Cuadernos de investigación. Apartado 11093. Correo Santa Beatriz. Lima. (ANA)

Annales: Économies, Sociétés, Civilisations. Centre National de la Recherche Scientifique *avec le concours de la* VIe Section de la'École Pratique des Hautes Études. Paris. (AESC)

Annales de Démographie Historique. Société Demographie Historique. Paris.

Annals. Organization of American States. Washington. (OAS/A)

Annals of the Southeastern Conference on Latin American Studies. West Georgia College. Carrollton. (SECOLAS/A)

Anthropological Linguistics. A publication of the Archives of the Languages of the World. Indiana Univ., Anthropology Dept. Bloomington. (IU/AL)

La Antigua. Univ. de Santa María La Antigua, Oficina de Humanidades. Panamá. (USMLA/LA)

Antropología. La Paz.

Antropología Andina. Cuzco, Peru.

Anuario. Instituto de Investigaciones Históricos Dr. José Gaspar Rodríguez de Francia. Asunción.

Anuario. Univ. Central de Venezuela, Instituto de Estudios Hispanoamericanos. Caracas. (IEH/A)

Anuario. Univ. Michoacán de San Nicolás de Hidalgo, Escuela de Historia. Morelia, México.
Anuario Bibliográfico Ecuatoriano 1976 y 1977 y Bibliografía Ecuatoriana. Univ. Central del Ecuador, Biblioteca General, Editorial Universitaria. Quito.
Anuario Bibliográfico Uruguayo de 1978. Biblioteca Nacional. Montevideo.
Anuario Colombiano de Historia Social y de la Cultura. Univ. Nacional de Colombia, Facultad de Ciencias Humanas, Depto. de Historia. Bogotá. (UNC/ACHSC)

B.B.A.A. Boletín Bibliografíco de Antropología Americana. Instituto Panamericano de Geografía e Historia, Comisión de Historia. México. (BBAA)
Beiträge zur Romanischen Philologie. Rütten & Loening. Berlin. (BRP)
Belizean Studies. Belize Institute of Social Research and Action. Belize City.
Berichte zur Entwicklung in Spanien, Portugal, Lateinamerika. München, FRG. (BESPL)
Bibliografía Histórica Mexicana: 1976–1978. El Colegio de México, Centro de Estudios Históricos. México.
Bibliographie d'Articles des Revues: Novembre 1979–Juillet 1980. Institut des Hautes Études de l'Amérique Latine. Centre de Documentation. Paris.
Bibliography of the English-Speaking Caribbean. Books, articles and review in English from the arts, humanities, and social sciences. Iowa City, Iowa.
Boletim Bibliográfico. Biblioteca Mário de Andrade. São Paulo. (BMA/BB)
Boletim Bibliográfico da Biblioteca Nacional. Biblioteca Nacional. Rio de Janeiro.
Boletim da Cidade do Recife. Prefeitura Municipal do Recife, Conselho Municipal de Cultura. Recife, Brazil.
Boletim Informativo e Bibliográfico de Ciências Sociais. Associação Nacional de Pós-Graduação e Pesquisa em Ciências Sociais. Rio de Janeiro.
Boletín. Academia de Historia del Cauca. Popayán, Colombia.
Boletín. Museo Arqueológico de la Serena, Chile.
Boletín. Provincia de Santa Fe. Ministerio de Gobierno. Archivo General de la Provincia. Santa Fe, Argentina.
Boletín Americanista. Univ. de Barcelona, Facultad de Geografía e Historia, Depto. de Historia de América. Barcelona. (UB/BA)
Boletín Bibliográfico. Banco Central de Nicaragua. Managua.
Boletín Bibliográfico. Biblioteca del Congreso Nacional. Sección Procesamiento. Santiago.
Boletín Cultural y Bibliográfico. Banco de la República, Biblioteca Luis-Angel Arango. Bogotá. (CBR/BCB)
Boletín de Antropología Americana. Instituto Panamericano de Geografía e Historia. México.
Boletín de Artes Visuales. Anuario. Organización de los Estados Americanos, Secretaría General. Washington.
Boletín de Ciencias Económicas y Sociales. Univ. Centroamericana José Simeón Cañas, Depto. de Economía. San Salvador.
Boletín de Coyuntura Socioeconómica. Univ. del Valle, División de Ciencias Sociales y Económicas, Centro de Investigación, y Documentación Socioeconómica. Cali, Colombia.
Boletín de Estudios Latinoamericanos. Centro de Estudios y Documentación Latinoamericanos. Amsterdam. (CEDLA/B)
Boletín de Filología. Univ. de Chile, Instituto de Filología. Santiago. (UC/BF)
Boletín de Historia y Antigüedades. Academia Colombiana de Historia. Bogotá. (ACH/BHA)
Boletín de Información. Centro Interamericano de Artesanía y Artes Populares (CIDAP). Cuenca, Ecuador.
Boletín de la Academia Chilena de la Historia. Santiago. (ACH/B)
Boletín de Academia Colombiana. Bogotá. (ACO/B)
Boletín de la Nacional de Historia. Buenos Aires. (ANH/B)
Boletín de la Academia Nacional de la Historia. Caracas. (VANH/B)
Boletín de la Academia Norteamericana de la Lengua Española. New York. (ANLE/B)
Boletín de la Biblioteca Nacional. Lima. (PEBN/B)
Boletín de la Facultad de Derecho y Ciencias Sociales. Univ. Nacional de Córdoba, Argentina.
Boletín de la Real Sociedad Geográfica. Madrid. (RSG/B)
Boletín del Archivo General de la Nación. Managua.

Boletín del Archivo General de la Nación. Secretaría de Gobernación. México. (MAGN/B)
Boletín del Archivo Histórico. Congreso de la República. Caracas.
Boletín del Archivo Histórico de Jalisco. Guadalajara, México.
Boletín del Archivo Histórico de Miraflores. Caracas.
Boletín del Departamento de Investigación de las Tradiciones Populares. México.
Boletín del Instituto Riva-Agüero. Pontifica Univ. Católica del Perú. Lima. (IRA/B)
Boletín del Museo del Hombre Dominicano. Santo Domingo. (MHD/B)
Boletín del Sistema Bibliotecario de la UNAH. Univ. Nacional Autónoma de Honduras. Tegucigalpa.
Boletín Histórico. Fundación John Boulton. Caracas. (FJB/BH)
Boletín Informativo para Asuntos Migratorios y Fronterizos. Comité de Servicio de Los Amigos, Centro de Información para Migración y Desarrollo. México.
Boletín Informativo Trotskysta. Tendencia Cuartainternacionalista. Organización Trotskysta Revolucionaria. Lima.
Boletín Nicaragüense de Bibliografía y Documentación. Banco Central de Nicaragua, Biblioteca. Managua. (BNBD)
Britain and Latin America. An annual review of British-Latin American relations. Latin American Bureau. London.
Bulletin. Société Suisse des Américanistes. Geneva. (SSA/B)
Bulletin de l'Académie des Sciences Humaines et Sociales d'Haiti. Port-au-Prince. (ASHSH/B)
Bulletin de l'Institut Français d'Études Andines. Lima. (IFEA/B)
Bulletin des Études Portugaises et Bresiliennes. Institut Français de Lisbonne *avec la collaboration de* Etablissements Français d'Enseignement Supérieur, Instituto de Alta Cultura, et du Depto. Cultural do Itamarati. Lisbon. (BEPB)
Bulletin d'Information. Association des Archivistes, Bibliothecaires, Documentalistes Francophones de la Caraïbe, Section Haiti. Port-au-Prince.

CCS Current Awareness Service. Caribbean Community Secretariat. Information and Documentation Section. Georgetown, Guyana.
CENIDIM. Boletín informativo. Centro Nacional de Investigación e Información Musical Carlos Chávez. México.
Cadernos DCP. Univ. Federal de Minas Gerais, Faculdade de Filosofia e Ciências Humanas, Depto. de Ciência Política. Belo Horizonte, Brazil. (UFMG/DCP)
Cahiers Césairiens. Pennsylvania State Univ., French Dept. University Park.
Cahiers des Amériques Latines. Paris. (CDAL)
Canadian Psychiatric Association Journal. Ottawa.
Canadian Review of Studies in Nationalism/Revue Canadienne des Études sur le Nationalisme. Univ. of Prince Edward Island. Charlottetown.
Caravelle. Cahiers du monde hispanique et luso-brésilien. Univ. de Toulouse, Institut d'Études Hispaniques, Hispano-Americaines et Luso-Brésiliennes. Toulouse France. (UTIEH/C)
Caribbean Quarterly. Univ. of the West Indies. Mona, Jam. (UWI/CQ)
Caribbean Review. Florida International Univ., Office of Academic Affairs. Miami. (FIU/CR)
Caribbean Studies. Univ. of Puerto Rico, Institute of Caribbean Studies. Río Piedras. (UPR/CS)
Caribbean Studies. Univ. of the West Indies. Mona, Jamaica. (UWI/CS)
Caribe. Univ. of Hawaii, Dept. of European Languages and Literatures. Honolulu.
El Caribe Contemporáneo. Univ. Nacional Autónoma de México, Facultad de Ciencias Políticas y Sociales, Centro de Estudios Latinoamericanos. México.
Caricom Perspective. Caribbean Community Secretariat. Georgetown, Guyana.
Casa de las Américas. Instituto Cubano del Libro. La Habana. (CDLA)
Casa del Tiempo. Univ. Autónoma Metropolitana. Dirección de Difusión Cultural. México.
Casas Reales. Museo de las Casas Reales. Santo Domingo.
Centro Latinoamericano de Economía Humana. Montevideo. (CLAEH)
Church History. American Society of Church History, Univ. of Chicago. Chicago, Ill. (ASCH/CH)
Ciência e Cultura. Sociedade Brasileira para o Progresso da Ciência. São Paulo. (SBPC/CC)

Ciencia y Sociedad. Instituto Tecnológica. Santo Domingo.
Ciencia y Tecnología. Editorial Universidad de Costa Rica. San José.
Cladindex. Resúmen de documentos CEPAL/ILPES. Organización de las Naciones Unidas. Comisión Económica para América Latina (CEPAL). Centro Latinoamericano de Documentación Económica y Social (CLADES). Santiago.
Clio. Academia Dominicana de la Historia. Santo Domingo. (ADH/C)
Colección Documental de la Independencia del Perú. Comisión Nacional del Sesquicentenario de la Independencia. Lima.
Colóquio. Fundação Calouste Gulbenkian. Lisboa.
Communications. École des Hautes Études en Sciences Sociales, Centre d'Études Transdisciplinaires. Paris. (EHESS/C)
Comunidad. Revista de la U.I.A. Cuadernos de difusión cultural. Univ. Iberoamericana. México. (UIA/C)
Conjonction. Institut Français d'Haïti. Port-au-Prince. (IFH/C)
Conjunto. Casa de las Américas. La Habana.
Controversia: Para el Exámen de la Realidad Argentina. México.
Convivium. Revista bimestral de investigação e cultura. Editora Convívio. São Paulo.
Creación & Crítica. Lima.
Criterio. Buenos Aires.
Critica d'Arte. Studio Italiano de Storia dell'Arte. Vallecchi Editore. Firenze, Italy. (CA)
Cuadernos Americanos. México. (CAM)
Cuadernos de Filosofía. Univ. de Buenos Aires. Facultad de Filosofía y Letras. Buenos Aires. (UBAFFL/C)
Cuadernos de Filosofía. Univ. de Concepción, Instituto Central de Filosofía. Concepción.
Cuadernos del Consejo Nacional de la Universidad Peruana. Lima.
Cuadernos del Seminario de Historia. Pontificia Univ. Católica del Perú, Instituto Riva-Agüero. Lima. (PUCP/CSH)
Cuadernos Hispanoamericanos. Instituto de Cultura Hispánica. Madrid. (CH)
Cuadernos Hispanoamericanos. Revista mensual de cultura hispánica. Centro Iberoamericano de Cooperación. Madrid.
Cuadrante. Centro de Estudios Regionales. Tucumán, Arg. (CER/C)
Cultura. Ministério da Educação e Cultura, Diretoria de Documentação e Divulgação e Divulgação. Brasília. (MEC/C)
Cultures. United Nations Educational, Scientific and Cultural Organization. Paris. (UNESCO/CU)
Current Anthopology. Univ. of Chicago, Ill. (UC/CA)

Dados. Instituto Universitário de Pesquisas. Rio de Janeiro. (DADOS)
Davar. Revista literaria. Sociedad Hebraica Argentina. Buenos Aires. (SHA/D)
Denver Quarterly. Univ. of Denver. Denver, Colo.
The Developing Economies. Institute of Developing Economies. Tokyo. (IDES/DE)
Diacritics. A review of contemporary criticism. Cornell Univ., Dept. of Romance Studies. Ithaca, N.Y. (CU/D)
Diálogos. Artes/Letras/Ciencias Humanas. El Colegio de México. México. (CM/D)
Diánoia. Univ. Nacional Autónoma de México, Centro de Estudios Filosóficos. México. (UNAM/D)
Dispositio. Univ. of Michigan, Dept. of Romance Languages. Ann Arbor.
El Dorado. Univ. of Northern Colorado, Museum of Anthropology. Greeley.

Eco. Librería Bucholz. Bogotá. (ECO)
Económico. Ministerio de Economía y Finanzas. Montevideo.
Ecuador, Bibliografía Analítica. Banco Central del Ecuador. Centro de Investigación y Cultura. Cuenca.
La Educación. Organization of American States, Dept. of Educational Affairs. Washington. (OAS/LE)
Encuentro: Selecciones para Latinoamérica. Centro de Proyección Cristiana. Lima.
English Journal. East Lansing, Mich.
Escritos de Filosofía. Academia Nacional de Ciencias, Centro de Estudios Filosóficos. Buenos Aires.
Escritura. Teoría y crítica literaria. Univ. Central de Venezuela, Escuela de Letras. Caracas. (UCV/E)
Esquire. New York.
Estudios Andinos. Univ. of Pittsburgh, Latin American Studies Center. Pittsburgh, Pa. (UP/EA)
Estudios Atacameños. San Pedro de Atacama, Chile.

Estudios Contemporáneos. Univ. Autónoma de Puebla, Instituto de Ciencias, Centro de Estudios Contemporáneos. Puebla, México.
Estudios de Cultura Náhuatl. Univ. Nacional Autónoma de México, Instituto de Historia, Seminario de Cultura Náhuatl. México. (UNAM/ECN)
Estudios de Historia Moderna y Contemporánea de México. Univ. Nacional Autónoma de México. México. (UNAM/E)
Estudios de Historia Novohispana. Univ. Nacional Autónoma de México, Instituto de Investigaciones Históricas. México. (UNAM/EHN)
Estudios Fiscales. México.
Estudios Latinoamericanos. Polska Akademia Nauk [Academia de Ciencias de Polonia], Instytut Historii [Instituto de Historia]. Warszawa. (PAN/ES)
Estudios Paraguayos. Univ. Católica Nuestra Señora de la Asunción. (UCNSA/EP)
Estudios Sociales. Corporación de Promoción Universitaria. Santiago. (CPU/ES)
Estudos Brasileiros. Univ. Federal do Paraná, Setor de Ciências Humanas, Centro de Estudos Brasileiros. Curitiba, Brazil. (UFP/EB)
Estudos e Pesquisas em Administração. Univ. Federal de Paraíba, Curso Mestrado em Administração. João Pessoa, Brazil.
Estudos Históricos. Faculdade de Filosofia, Ciências e Letras, Depto. de História. Marília, Brazil. (FFCLM/EH)
Ethnicity. New York.
Ethnohistory. Journal of the American Society for Ethnohistory. Buffalo, N.Y. (ASE/E)
Ethnology. Univ. of Pittsburgh, Pa. (UP/E)
Ethnomusicology. Ann Arbor, Mich.
Ethnohistoria y Antropología Andina. Museo Nacional de Historia. Lima.
Etnologia Polona. Warsaw.
Étdes Hispano-Américaines. Univ. de Haute Bretagne, Centre d'Études Hispaniques, Hispano-Américaines et Luso-Brésiliennes. Rennes, France. (UHB/EHA)
Europe. Revue littéraire mensuelle. Paris.
Excelsior. Diorama de la cultura. México.
Explicación de Textos Literarios. California State Univ., Dept. of Spanish and Portuguese. Sacramento.

FEM. Publicación femenina. Nueva Cultura Feminista. México.
Fénix. Biblioteca Nacional. Lima. (FENIX)
The Florida Historical Quarterly. The Florida Historical Society. Jacksonville. (FHS/FHQ)
Folia Humanistica. Ciencias, artes, letras. Editorial Glarma. Barcelona. (FH)
Folklore Americano. Instituto Panamericano de Geografía e Historia, Comisión de Historia, Comité de Folklore. México. (IPGH/FA)
Folklore Annual. Austin, Tex.
Foreign Language Index. Public Affairs Information Service. New York.
Franciscanum. Revista de las ciencias del espíritu. Univ. de San Buenaventura. Bogotá. (USB/F)
Fund og Forskning i det kongelige samlinger. Copenhagen.
Futurable. Fundación Argentina Año 2000. Buenos Aires.

The Geographical Mazagine. London. (GM)
Geosur. Asociación Sudamericana de Estudios Geopolíticos e Internacionales. Montevideo.
Geschichte und Gesellschaft. Zeitschrift für Historische Sozialwissenschaft. Univ. Bielefeld, Fakultät für Geschichtswissenschaft. Bielefeld, FRG. (UB/GG)
Guatemala. Unión de Guatemaltecos. La Habana.
Guías y Catálogos. Archivo General de la Nación. México.

Heterofonía. Revista musical bimestral. México. (HET)
Hispamérica. Revista de literatura. Takoma Park, Md. (HISPA)
Hispania. American Association of Teachers of Spanish and Portuguese. Univ. of Cincinnati, Ohio. (AATSP/H)
Hispania. Revista española de historia. Instituto Jerónimo Zurita, Consejo Superior de Investigaciones Científicas. Madrid. (IJZ/H)
Hispanic American Historical Review. Duke Univ. Press *for the* Conference on Latin American History of the American Historical Association. Durham, N.C. (HAHR)
Hispanic Review. A quarterly devoted to research in the Hispanic languages and literatures. Univ. of Pennsylvania, Dept. of Romance Languages. Philadelphia. (HR)
Hispanófila. Univ. of North Carolina. Chapel Hill. (HISP)

Historia. Univ. Católica de Chile, Instituto de Historia. Santiago. (UCCIH/H)
Historia Crítica. Revista de la Carrera de Historia. Univ. Nacional Autónoma de Honduras. Tegucigalpa.
Historia Mexicana. El Colegio de México. México. (CM/HM)
Historia Obrera. Centro de Estudios Históricos del Movimiento Obrero Mexicano. México. (CEHSMO)
Historia Paraguaya. Anuario de la Academia Paraguaya de la Historia. Asunción. (APH/HP)
Historia y Cultura. Museo Nacional de Historia. Lima. (PMNH/HC)
The Historian. A journal of history. Phi Alpha Theta, National Honor Society in History. Univ. of Pennsylvania. University Park. (PAT/TH)
Histórica. Pontificia Univ. Católica del Perú, Depto. de Humanidades. Lima. (PUCP/H)
Histórica. Univ. Autónoma del Estado de México, Instituto de Investigaciones Históricas. México. (UAEM/H)
Historical Reflections/Reflexions Historiques. Univ. of Waterloo, Dept. of History. Waterloo, Canada.
Históricas. Univ. Nacional Autónoma de México, Instituto de Investigaciones Históricas. México.
Hojas Universitarias. Revista de la Fundación Univ. Central. Bogotá. (HU)
L'Homme. Revue française d'anthropologie. La Sorbonne, l'École Pratique des Hautes Études. Paris. (EPHE/H)
Humanitas. Boletín ecuatoriano de antropología. Univ. Central del Ecuador, Instituto de Antropología. Quito. (UCEIA/H)
Humanitas. Univ. de Nuevo León, Centro de Estudios Humanísticos. Monterrey, Mex. (UNL/H)
Humboldt. Revista para o mundo ibérico. Ubersee-Verlag. Hamburg, FRG. (HUMB)

Ibero-Americana Pragensia. Univ. Carolina de Praga, Centro de Estudios Ibero-Americanos. Prague. (UCP/IAP)
Ibero-Amerikanisches Archiv. Ibero-Amerikanisches Institut. Berlin, FRG. (IAA)
Ideas y Valores. Revista del Instituto de Filosofía y Letras. Univ. Nacional. Bogotá. (UN/IV)
Ideologies & Literature. A journal of Hispanic and Luso-Brazilian literatures. Univ. of Minnesota, Institute for the Study of Ideologies and Literature. Minneapolis. (IL)
Inca. Centro de Estudiantes de Arqueología. Lima.
Index on Censorship. Writers & Scholars International. London. (INDEX)
Index Translationum. UNESCO, International Institute of Intellectual Cooperation. Geneva.
The Indian Historian. American Indian Historical Society. San Francisco, Calif.
Indiana. Beiträge zur Volker-und Sprachenkunde, Archäologie und Anthropologie des Indianischen Amerika. Ibero-Amerikanisches Institut. Berlin, FRG. (IAI/I)
Indiana Folklore. Bloomington.
Indice de Artículos de Publicaciones Periódicas en el Area de Ciencias Sociales y Humanidades. Instituto Colombiano para el Fomento de la Educación Superior (ICFES). División de Documentación e Información. Bogotá.
Indice de Ciências Sociais. Instituto Universitário de Pesquisas do Rio de Janeiro (IUPERJ). Rio de Janeiro.
Información Documental Costarricense y Centroamericana. Univ. of Costa Rica. Instituto de Investigaciones Sociales. San José.
Informaciones. Univ. Nacional de Asunción, Escuela de Bibliotecología. Asunción.
Insula. Madrid. (INSULA)
Inter-American Economic Affairs. Washington. (IAMEA)
Inter-American Music Review. R. Stevenson. Los Angeles, Calif. (IAMR)
Interciencia. Asociación Interciencia. Caracas. (AI/I)
Inti. Univ. of Connecticut, Dept. of Romance Languages. Storrs. (INTI)
Investigaciones y Ensayos. Academia Nacional de la Historia. Buenos Aires. (ANH/IE)
Islas. Univ. Central de las Villas. Santa Clara, Cuba. (UCLV/I)
Istmo. Revista del pensamiento actual. México. (ISTMO)

Jahrbuch für Geschichte von Staat, Wirtschaft und Gesellschaft Lateinamerikas. Köln, FRG. (JGSWGL)
Jamaica Journal. Institute of Jamaica. Kingston. (IJ/JJ)
Jamaican Historical Review. The Jamaican Historical Society. Kingston. (JHS/R)
Journal de la Société des Américanistes. Paris. (SA/J)
Journal of American Folklore. American Folklore Society. Austin, Tex. (AFS/JAF)

Journal of Anthropological Research. Univ. of New Mexico, Dept. of Anthropology. Albuquerque. (UNM/JAR)
Journal of Belizean Affairs. Belize City. (JBA)
Journal of Caribbean History. Univ. of the West Indies, Dept. of History [and] Caribbean Universities Press. St. Lawrence, Barbados. (UWI/JCH)
A Journal of Church and State. Baylor Univ., J.M. Dawson Studies in Church and State. Waco, Tex. (BU/JCS)
Journal of Commonwealth & Comparative Politics. Univ. of London, Institute of Commonwealth Studies. London. (ICS/JCCP)
Journal of Developing Areas. Western Illinois Univ. Press. Macomb. (JDA)
Journal of Economic History. New York Univ., Graduate School of Business Administration *for the* Economic History Association. Rensselaer. (EHA/J)
Journal of Ethnic Studies. Bellingham, Wash.
Journal of European Economic History. Banco de Roma. Roma.
Journal of Family History. Studies in family, kinship and demography. National Council on Family Relations. Minneapolis, Minn. (NCFR/JFH)
Journal of Historical Geography. Academic Press. London.
Journal of Information Science, Librarianship and Archives Administration. United Nations Educational, Scientific and Cultural Organization. Paris. (UNESCO/JIS)
Journal of Inter-American Studies and World Affairs. Sage Publication *for the* Center for Advanced International Studies, Univ. of Miami. Coral Gables, Fla. (SAGE/JIAS. *See also* UM/JIAS)
Journal of Interdisciplinary History. The MIT Press. Cambridge, Mass. (JIH)
Journal of Latin American Lore. Univ. of California, Latin American Center. Los Angeles. (UCLA/JLAL)
Journal of Latin American Studies. Centers or institutes of Latin American studies at the universities of Cambridge, Glasgow, Liverpool, London and Oxford. Cambridge Univ. Press. London. (JLAS)
Journal of Negro History. Association for the Study of Negro Life and History. Washington. (ASNLH/J)
Journal of Peasant Studies. Frank Cass & Co. London. (JPS)
Journal of Popular Culture. Bowling Green, Ohio.
The Journal of San Diego History. San Diego Historical Society. San Diego, Calif. (SDHS/J)
Journal of Social and Political Studies. Council on American Affairs. Washington.
Journal of Social History. Univ. of California Press. Berkeley. (UCP/JSH)
Journal of Spanish Studies: Twentieth Century. Kansas State Univ., Dept. of Modern Languages. Manhattan. (JSSTC)
Journal of the Folklore Institute. Indiana Univ. Bloomington. (IU/JFI)
Journal of the History of Ideas. City College. New York. (JHI)
Journal of the West. Los Angeles, Calif. (JW)
Journalism Quarterly. Association for Education in Journalism *with the cooperation of the* American Association of Schools, Depts. of Journalism [and] Kappa Tau Alpha Society. Univ. of Minnesota. Minneapolis. (AEJ/JQ)

Kaie. National History and Arts Council of Guyana. Georgetown. (NHAC/K)
Karukinka. Instituto de Investigaciones Históricas de Tierra del Fuego. Buenos Aires.
Kentucky Romance Quarterly. Univ. of Kentucky. Lexington. (UK/KRQ)
Kriterion. Revista da Faculdade de Filosofia da Univ. de Minas Gerais. Belo Horizonte, Brazil. (UMGFF/K)

Labor Information Bulletin. Organization of American States. Inter-American Commission of Women. Washington.
Latin American Literary Review. Carnegie-Mellon Univ., Dept. of Modern Languages. Pittsburgh, Pa. (LALR)
Latin American Perspectives. Univ. of California. Riverside. (LAP)
Latin American Research Review. Univ. of North Carolina Press *for the* Latin American Studies Association. Chapel Hill. (LARR)
Latin American Theatre Review. A journal devoted to the theatre and drama of Spanish and Portuguese America. Univ. of Kansas, Center of Latin American Studies. Lawrence. (UK/LATR)
Letras. Univ. Nacional Mayor de San Marcos. Lima. (UNMSM/L)
Letras de Hoje. Pontifícia Univ. Católica do Rio Grande do Sul, Centro de Estudos da Lingua Portuguesa. Porto Alegre, Brazil.

Les Lettres Romances. Univ. Catholique de Louvain, Fondation Universitaire de Belgique. Louvain, Belgium. (UCL/LR)
Lexis. Revista de lingüística y literatura. Pontificia Univ. Católica del Perú. Lima. (PUC/L)
Libros al Día. Caracas.
Lingua. North-Holland Publishing Co. Amsterdam. (LINGUA)
Língua e Literatura. Univ. de São Paulo, Depto. de Letras, Faculdade de Filosofia, Letras e Ciências Humanas. São Paulo. (USP/LL)
Logos. Revista de la Facultad de Filosofía y Letras, Univ. de Buenos Aires.
Lotería. Lotería Nacional de Beneficencia. Panamá. (LNB/L)
Louisiana History. Univ. of Southwestern Louisiana, Louisiana Historical Association. Lafayette.
Luso-Brazilian Review. Univ. of Wisconsin Press. Madison. (UW/LBR)

Man. A monthly record of anthropological science. The Royal Anthropological Institute. London. (RAI/M)
Mapocho. Biblioteca Nacional, Extensión Cultural. Santiago. (EC/M)
Mariner's Mirror. Society for Nautical Research. Sussex, United Kingdom.
Marxist Perspectives. Transaction Periodicals Consortium. Rutgers Univ. New Brunswick, N.J. (RU/MP)
Megafón. Centro de Estudios Latinoamericanos. Buenos Aires.
Mélanges de la Casa de Velázquez. Paris.
Mensário do Arquivo Nacional. Rio de Janeiro.
México: Artículos Clasificados. Univ. Nacional Autónoma de México. Facultad de Ciencias Políticas y Sociales. Centro de Documentación. México.
Meyibó. Univ. Nacional Autónoma de México, Centro de Investigaciones Históricas [and] Univ. Autónoma de Baja, Centro de Investigaciones Históricas. México.
Military History of Texas and the Southwest. Military History Press. Austin.
Missionalia Hispanica. Instituto Santo Toribio de Mogrovejo [and] Consejo Superior de Investigaciones Científicas. Madrid. (ISTH/MH)
Modern Language Journal. The National Federation of Modern Language Teachers Association [and] Univ. of Pittsburgh. Pittsburgh, Pa. (MLTA/MLJ)
Modern Language Notes. Johns Hopkins Univ. Press. Baltimore, Md. (MLN)
Modern Language Review. Univ. of Guyana, Dept. of Modern Languages. Georgetown.
Montalbán. Univ. Católica Andrés Bello, Facultad de Humanidades y Educación, Institutos Humanísticos de Investigación. Caracas. (UCAB/M)
Die Musik in Geschichte und Gegenwart. Kassel. Wilhelmshöhe, FRG. (MGG)

NS NorthSouth NordSud NorteSur NorteSul. Canadian journal of Latin American studies. Canadian Association of Latin American Studies. Univ. of Ottawa. (NS)
The National Bibliography of Barbados. Public Library. Bridgetown.
National Geographic Magazine. National Geographic Society. Washington. (NGS/NGM)
Natural History. American Museum of Natural History. New York. (AMNH/NH)
Ñawpa Pacha. Institute of Andean Studies. Berkeley, Calif. (IAS/ÑP)
Die Neue Rundschau. S. Fischer Verlag. Frankfurt. (NR)
New Mexico Historical Review. Univ. of New Mexico [and] Historical Society of New Mexico. Albuquerque. (UNM/NMHR)
The New Scholar. Univ. of California, Center for Iberian and Latin American Studies [and] Institute of Chicano Urban Affairs. San Diego. (UCSD/NS)
New Scholasticism. Catholic Univ. of America, Catholic Philosophical Association. Washington.
Nexos. Sociedad de Ciencia y Literatura, Centro de Investigación Cultural y Científica. México.
Nicaráuac. Revista bimestral del Ministerio de Cultura. Managua.
Niterói. Revista brasiliense. Ciências, letras e artes. Academia Paulista de Letras. São Paulo.
Norte Grande. Revista de estudios integrados referentes a comunidades humanas del Norte Grande de Chile, en una perspectiva geográfica e histórico-cultural. Univ. Católica de Chile, Instituto de Geografía, Depto. de Geografía de Chile, Taller Norte Grande. Santiago. (UCC/NG)
North Dakota Quarterly. Univ. of North Dakota. Grand Forks.

Notes et Études Documentaires. France—Direction de la Documentation. Paris. (FDD/NED)
Nova Americana. Giulio Einaudi Editora. Torino, Italy.
Nuestra Historia. Centro de Estudios de Historia Argentina. Buenos Aires. (CEHA/NH)
Nueva Narrativa Hispanoamericana. Adelphi Univ., Latin American Studies Program. Garden City, N.Y.
Nueva Revista de Filología Hispánica. El Colegio de México [and] the Univ. of Texas. México. (CM/NRFH)

L'Oeil. Revue d'art mensuelle. Nouvelle Sedo. Lausanne, Switzerland. (OEIL)
Orbis. Bulletin international de documentation linguistique. Centre International de Dialectologie Générale. Louvain, Belgium. (CIDG/O)
Orbis. A journal of world affairs. Foreign Policy Research Institute, Philadelphia, Pa. *in association with the* Fletcher School of Law and Diplomacy, Tufts Univ., Medford, Mass. (FPRI/O)

The Pacific Historical Review. Univ. of California Press. Los Angeles. (UC/PHR)
Pájaro de Fuego. Sequals Editora. Buenos Aires.
La Palabra y el Hombre. Univ. Veracruzana. Xalapa, México. (UV/PH)
El Palacio. School of American Research, Museum of New Mexico [and] Archaeological Society of New Mexico. Santa Fe. (SAR/P)
Past and Present. London. (PP)
Patrimonio Histórico. Instituto Nacional de Cultura, Dirección del Patrimonio Histórico. Panamá. (INC/PH)
Pensamiento Económico. Organo oficial de divulgación. Colegio Hondureño de Economistas. Tegucigalpa. (CHE/PE)
Pesquisas: História. Univ. do Vale do Rio dos Sinos, Instituto Anchietano de Pesquisas. São Leopoldo, Brazil.
Philologica Pragensia. Academia Scientiarum Bohemoslovenica. Praha. (ASB/PP)
Philosophica. Rijksuniversiteit. Gent, The Netherlands.
Phylon. Atlanta Univ. Atlanta, Ga. (AU/P)
Planindex. Resúmen de documentos sobre planificación. Organización de las Naciones Unidas. Comisión Económica para América Latina (CEPAL). Centro Latinoamericano de Documentación Económica y Social (CLADES). Santiago.
Plantation Society. Univ. of New Orleans. New Orleans, La.
Ploughshares. A journal of the arts. Massachusetts Council on the Arts. Cambridge.
Point of Contact. New York Univ., Ibero-American Language and Area Center. New York.
Polémica. Univ. de Carabobo, Dirección de Cultura. Valencia, Venezuela.
Política y Espíritu. Cuadernos de cultura política, económica y social. Santiago. (CPES/PE)
Presença Filosófica. Sociedade Brasileira de Filósofos Católicos. São Paulo.
Proceedings of the American Philosophical Society. Philadelphia, Pa. (APS/P)
Proceedings of the Pacific Coast Council on Latin American Studies. Univ. of California. Los Angeles. (PCCLAS/P)
Proceso. Huancayo, Peru.
Publicaciones. Univ. de San Juan, Instituto de Investigaciones Arqueológicas. San Juan, Argentina.
Publications of the Modern Language Association of America. New York. (PMLA)
Pucará. Univ. de Cuenca, Facultad de Filosofía, Letras y Ciencias de la Educación. Cuenca, Ecuador.

Quaderni Ibero-Americani. Associazione per i Rapporti Culturali con la Spagna, il Portogallo e l'America Latina. Torino, Italy. (QIA)

Red River Valley Historical Journal. Red River Valley Historical Association. Durant, Okla.
Relaciones. Estudios de historia y sociedad. El Colegio de Michoacán. Zamora, México.
Relaciones de la Sociedad Argentina de Antropología. Buenos Aires. (SAA/R)
Research in African Literatures. Univ. of Texas Press. Austin.
Review. Center for Inter-American Relations. New York. (REVIEW)
Revista Argentina de Administración Pública. Instituto Nacional de la Administración Pública. Buenos Aires.
Revista Brasileira de Biblioteconomia e Documentação. Federação Brasileira de Associações de Bibliotecários. São Paulo.

Revista Brasileira de Cultura. Ministério da Educação e Cultura, Conselho Federal de Cultura. Rio. (CFC/RBC)

Revista Brasileira de Estudios Políticos. Univ de Minas Gerais. Belo Horizonte, Brazil. (UMG/RBEP)

Revista Brasileira de Folclore. Ministério da Educação e Cultura, Companha de Defesa do Folclore Brasileiro. Rio. (CDFB/RBF)

Revista Brasileira de Lingüística. Sociedade Brasileira para Professores de Lingüística. São Paulo. (SBPL/RBL)

Revista Canadiense de Estudios Hispánicos. Univ. of Toronto. Toronto.

Revista Centroamericana de Economía. Univ. Nacional Autónoma de Honduras, Programa de Postgrado Centroamericano en Economía y Planificación del Desarrollo. Tegucigalpa.

Revista Chicano-Riqueña. Gary, Ind.

Revista Chilena de Antropología. Santiago.

Revista Chilena de Historia y Geografía. Sociedad Chilena de Historia y Geografía. Santiago. (SCHG/R)

Revista Chilena de Literatura. Editorial Universitaria. Santiago.

Revista Coahuilense de Historia. Colegio Coahuilense de Investigaciones Históricas. Saltillo, México.

Revista Colombiana de Antropología. Ministerio de Educación Nacional, Instituto Colombiano de Antropología. Bogotá.

Revista de Biblioteconomia de Brasília. Univ. de Brasília, Associação dos Bibliotecários do Distrito Federal e Departamento Biblioteconomia. Brasília.

Revista de Ciencias Sociales. Univ. de Costa Rica. San José. (UCR/RCS)

Revista de Comunicação Social. Ceará, Brazil.

Revista de Crítica Literaria Latinoamericana. Latinoamericana Editores. Lima. (RCLL)

Revista de Cultura Brasileña. Embajada del Brasil en España. Madrid.

Revista de Dialectología y Tradiciones Populares. Centro de Estudios de Etnología Peninsular, Depto. de Dialectología y Tradiciones Populares, Consejo Superior de Investigaciones Científicas. Madrid. (CEEP/RD)

Revista de Economía Latinoamericana. Banco Central de Venezuela. Caracas. (BCV/REL)

Revista de Estadística y Geografía. Secretaría de Programación y Presupuesto, Coordinación General de los Servicios Nacionales de Estadística, Geografía e Informática, Dirección General de Estadística. México.

Revista de Estudios Hispánicos. Univ. of Alabama, Dept. of Romance Languages, Office of International Studies and Programs. University. (UA/REH)

Revista de Estudios Políticos. Instituto de Estudios Políticos. Madrid. (IEP/REP)

Revista de Filosofía de la Universidad de Costa Rica. San José. (UCR/RF)

Revista de Filosofía Latinoamericana. Ediciones Castañeda. San Antonio de Padua, Argentina. (RFL)

Revista de Historia. Univ. de Concepción, Instituto de Antropología, Historia y Geografía. Concepción, Chile.

Revista de História. Univ. de São Paulo, Faculdade de Filosofia, Ciências e Letras, Depto. de História [and] Sociedade de Estudos Históricos. São Paulo. (USP/RH)

Revista de Historia. Univ. Nacional de Costa Rica, Escuela de Historia. Heredia. (UNCR/R)

Revista de Historia Americana y Argentina. Univ. Nacional de Cuyo, Facultad de Filosofía y Letras, Instituto de Historia. Mendoza. (UNC/RHAA)

Revista de Historia de América. Instituto Panamericano de Geografía e Historia, Comisión de Historia. México. (PAIGH/H)

Revista de Historia del Derecho. Buenos Aires.

Revista de Historia Militar. Servicio Histórico Militar. Madrid. (SHM/RHM)

Revista de Indias. Instituto Gonzalo Fernández de Oviedo [and] Consejo Superior de Investigaciones Científicas. Madrid. (IGFO/RI)

Revista de Información Científica y Técnica Cubana. Academia de Ciencias de Cuba. Instituto de Documentación e Información Científica y Técnica. La Habana.

Revista de la Academia Boliviana de Ciencias Económicas. Cochabamba, Bolivia.

Revista de la Biblioteca Nacional. Ministerio de Educación y Cultura. Montevideo. (UBN/R)

Revista de la Biblioteca Nacional José Martí. La Habana. (BNJM/R)

Revista de la Facultad de Derecho. Univ. Autónoma de México. México. (UNAM/RFD)

Revista de la Junta Provincial de Historia de Córdoba. Archivo Histórico Monseñor P. Cabrera. Córdoba, Argentina. (JPHC/R)

Revista de la Sociedad Bolivariana de Venezuela. Caracas. (SBV/R)
Revista de la Universidad. Univ. Nacional Autónoma de Honduras. Tegucigalpa. (HUN/RU)
Revista de la Universidad Complutense. Madrid. (RUC)
Revista de la Universidad de Costa Rica. San José. (UCR/R)
Revista de la Universidad de México. Univ. Nacional Autónoma de México. México. (UNAM/RUM)
Revista de la Universidad de Yucatán. Mérida, Mex. (UY/R)
Revista de la Universidad del Zulia. Maracaibo, Venezuela. (UZ/R)
Revista de la Universidad Nacional de Córdoba. Córdoba, Argentina. (UNC/R)
Revista de Letras. Univ. de Puerto Rico en Mayagüez, Facultad de Artes y Ciencias. Mayagüez. (UPRM/RL)
Revista de Oriente. Univ. de Puerto Rico, Colegio Universitario de Humacao. Humacao. (UPR/RO)
Revista de Política Internacional. Instituto de Estudios Políticos. Madrid. (IEP/RPI)
Revista de SINASBI. Información Científica y Tecnológica de Archivos y de Estadística e Informática, Comisión Coordinador del Sistema Nacional de Servicios de Bibliotecas e Información. Caracas.
Revista del Archivo General de la Nación. Buenos Aires.
Revista del Archivo General de la Nación. Instituto Nacional de Cultura. Lima. (PEAGN/R)
Revista del Archivo Histórico del Guayas. Guayaquil, Ecuador. (AHG/R)
Revista del Instituto de Antropología. Univ. Nacional de Tucumán. San Miguel de Tucumán, Arg. (UNTIA/R)
Revista del Instituto de Cultura Puertorriqueña. San Juan. (ICP/R)
Revista del México Agrario. Confederación Nacional Campesina. México. (CNC/RMA)
Revista del Museo Nacional. Casa de la Cultura del Perú, Museo Nacional de la Cultura Peruana. Lima. (PEMN/R)
Revista del Pensamiento Centroamericano. Centro de Investigaciones y Actividades Culturales. Managua. (RCPC)
Revista del Arquivo Municipal. Prefeitura do Município de São Paulo, Depto. Municipal de Cultura. São Paulo. (AM/R)
Revista do Instituto de Estudos Brasileiros. Univ. de São Paulo, Instituto de Estudos Brasileiros. São Paulo. (USP/RIEB)
Revista do Instituto do Ceará. Fortaleza, Brazil.
Revista do Instituto Histórico e Geográfico Brasileiro. Rio. (IHGB/R)
Revista do Instituto Histórico e Geográfico de São Paulo. São Paulo. (IHGSP/R)
Revista do Instituto Histórico e Geográfico Guarujá/Bertioga. São Paulo. (IHGGB/R)
Revista do Museu Paulista. São Paulo. (MP/R)
Revista dos Tribunais. São Paulo.
Revista Eme-Eme. Estudios dominicanos. Univ. Católica Madre y Maestra. Santiago de los Caballeros, República Dominicana. (EME)
Revista Española de Lingüística. Madrid.
Revista Hispánica Moderna. Columbia Univ., Hispanic Institute in the United States. New York. (HIUS/R)
Revista Histórica. Museo Histórico Nacional. Montevideo. (UMHN/RH)
Revista Iberoamericana. Instituto Internacional de Literatura Iberoamericana *patrocinada por la* Univ. de Pittsburgh, Pa. (IILI/RI)
Revista Interamericana de Bibliografía [Inter-American Review of Bibliography]. Organization of American States. Washington. (RIB)
Revista Latinoamericana de Filosofía. Centro de Investigaciones Filosóficas. Buenos Aires. (CIF/RLF)
Revista Letras. Univ. Federal do Paraná, Setor de Ciências Humanas, Letras e Artes. Curitiba, Brazil. (UFP/RL)
Revista Lotería. Lotería Nacional de Beneficencia. Panamá. (LNB/L)
Revista Mexicana de Ciencias Políticas y Sociales. Univ. Nacional Autónoma de México, Facultad de Ciencias Políticas y Sociales. México. (UNAM/RMCPS)
Revista Mexicana de Sociología. Univ. Nacional Autónoma de México, Instituto de Investigaciones Sociales. México. (UNAM/RMS)
Revista Musical Chilena. Univ. de Chile, Instituto de Extensión Musical. Santiago. (UCIEM/R)
Revista Nacional de Cultura. Consejo Nacional de Cultura. Caracas. (CONAC/RNC)

Revista Nacional de Cultura. Ministerio de Cultura y Educación, Secretaría de Estado de Cultura. Buenos Aires.

Revista Paraguaya de Sociología. Centro Paraguayo de Estudios Sociológicos. Asunción. (CPES/RPS)

Revista Universidad de Medellín. Centro de Estudios de Posgrado. Medellín, Colombia. (UM/R)

Revista Venezolana de Filosofía. Univ. Simón Bolívar [and] Sociedad Venezolana de Filosofía. Caracas. (USB/RVF)

Revue d'Histoire Economique et Sociale. Editions Marcel Rivière *avec le concours du* Centre National de la Recherche Scientifique. Paris.

Ritmo. La Plata, Argentina.

Ritmo. Revista del Conservatorio de Música Juan José Castro. México.

Romanistisches Jahrbuch. Univ. Hamburg, Romanisches Seminar, Ibero-Amerikanisches Forschungsinstitut. Hamburg, FRG. (UH/RJ)

SECOLAS Annals. Kennesaw College, Southeastern Conference on Latin American Studies. Marietta, Georgia.

SELA en Acción. Secretaría Permanente del Sistema Económico Latinoamericano, Oficina de Información. Caracas.

San Marcos. Lima.

Santiago. Univ. de Oriente. Santiago de Cuba.

Sapientia. Organo de la Facultad de Filosofía. Univ. Católica Argentina Santa María de los Buenos Aires. Buenos Aires. (UCA/S)

Sarance. Instituto Otavaleño de Antropología. Otavalo, Ecuador.

Savacou. Caribbean Artists Movement. Kingston.

Science and Society. New York. (SS)

Scientific American. Scientific American, Inc. New York. (SA)

La Semana de Bellas Artes. México.

Semestre de Filosofía. Univ. Central de Venezuela. Caracas.

Semiosis. Seminario de Semiótica, Teoría, Análisis. México.

Série de História. Coleçao Museu Paulista, Univ. de São Paulo, Brazil.

Signos. Estudios de lengua y literatura. Univ. Católica de Valparaíso, Instituto de Literatura y Ciencia del Lenguaje. Valparaíso, Chile. (UCV/S)

Signs. Journal of women in culture and society. The Univ. of Chicago Press. Chicago, Ill. (UC/S)

Síntesis Informativa Iberoamericana. Instituto de Cultura Hispánica. Centro de Documentación Iberoamericana. Madrid.

Smithsonian. Smithsonian Institution. Washington.

Social and Economic Studies. Univ. of the West Indies, Institute of Social and Economic Research. Mona, Jamaica. (UWI/SES)

Social Science Quarterly. Univ. of Texas, Dept. of Government. Austin. (UT/SSQ)

South Atlantic Bulletin. South Atlantic Modern Language Association. Chapel Hill, N.C.

Southern California Quarterly. Historical Society of Southern California. Los Angeles. (HSSC/SCQ)

Southwestern Historical Quarterly. Texas State Historical Association. Austin. (TSHA/SHQ)

Staden-Jahrbuch. Beiträge zur Brasilkunde. Instituto Hans Staden. São Paulo. (IHS/SJ)

Statistical Bulletin of the OAS. Organization of American States. General Secretariat. Washington.

Studi di Letteratura Ispanoamericana. Milano.

Studies in Comparative International Development. Rutgers Univ. New Brunswick, N.J. (RU/SCID)

Studies in the Anthropology of Visual Communication. Society for the Anthropology of Visual Communication. Washington.

Studies in the Social Sciences. West Georgia College. Carrollton.

Suplemento Antropológico. Univ. Católica de Nuestra Señora de la Asunción, Centro de Estudios Antropológicos. Asunción. (UCNSA/SA)

Sur. Revista semestral. Buenos Aires.

Temas Económicos. Univ. de Antioquia, Facultad de Ciencias Económicas, Dept. de Economía. Medellín, Colombia.

Texto Crítico. Univ. Veracruzana, Centro de Investigaciones Lingüístico-Literarias. Xalapa, México.

Thesaurus. Boletín del Instituto Caro y Cuervo. Bogotá. (ICC/T)

Thesis. Nueva revista de filosofía y letras. Univ. Nacional Autónoma de México, Facultad de Filosofía y Letras. México.

Tiemporeal. Simón Bolívar Univ. Caracas.
Tiers Monde. Problèmes des pays sous-développés. Univ. de Paris, Institut d'Étude du Dévellopement Économique et Social. Paris. (UP/TM)
Tradición Popular. Univ. de San Carlos de Guatemala, Centro de Estudios Folklóricos. San Carlos. (USCG/TP)
Tradiciones de Guatemala. Guatemala.
Tramoya. Univ. Veracruzana. Xalapa, México.
Transactions of the Institute of British Geographers. London.
Trans/Form/Ação. Faculdade de Filosofia, Ciência e Letras de Assis. Assis, Brazil.
Translation Review. Richardson, Tex.
Trimestre Económico. Fondo de Cultura Económica. México. (FCE/TE)
Trinidad and Tobago National Bibliography. Central Library of Trinidad and Tobago [and] The Univ. of the West Indies Library. Port of Spain.

Unesco Journal of Information Science, Librarianship and Archives Administration. United Nations Educational, Scientific and Cultural Organization. Paris. (UNESCO/JIS)
Unión. Unión de Escritores y Artistas de Cuba. La Habana. (UNION)
Universidad. Univ. de Antioquia. Medellín, Colombia. (UA/U)
Universidad. Univ. Nacional del Litoral. Santa Fe, Argentina. (UNL/U)
Universidad de La Habana. La Habana. (UH/U)
Universidad Nacional de Colombia. Revista de extensión cultural. Medellín.
Universidad Pontificia Bolivariana. Medellín, Colombia. (UPB)
Universo. Univ. Autónoma de Santo Domingo, Facultad de Humanidades. Santo Domingo. (UASD/U)

Urban Anthropology. State Univ. of New York, Dept. of Anthropology. Brockport. (UA)

Veritas. Revista. Pontifícia Univ. Católica do Rio Grande do Sul. Porto Alegre, Brazil. (PUC/V)
Via. A new literary magazine. Univ. of California, Office of Student Activities. Berkeley. (VIA)
Vozes. Revista de cultura. Editora Vozes. Petrópolis, Brazil. (VOZES)
Vuelta. México.

Wari. Ayacucho, Peru.
Washington Review. Washington.
Western Folklore. Univ. of California Press *for the* California Folklore Society. Berkeley. (CFS/WF)
The Western Historical Quarterly. Western History Association, Utah State Univ. Logan. (WHQ)

YaxKin. Instituto Hondureño de Antropología e Historia. Tegucigalpa. (YAXKIN)
Yucatán: Historia y Economía. Revista de análisis socioeconómico regional. Univ. de Yucatán, Centro de Investigaciones Regionales, Depto. de Estudios Económicos y Sociales. Mérida, México.

Zacatecas. Anuario de historia. Univ. Autónoma de Zacatecas, Depto. de Investigaciones Históricas. Zacatecas, México.
Zeitschrift für Kulturaustausch. Institut für Auslandsbeziehungen. Berlin, FRG. (IA/ZK)
Zeitschrift für Missionswissenschaft und Religionswissenschaft. Lucerne, Switzerland. (ZMR)
Zona Franca. Editorial Trazón. Caracas.

SUBJECT INDEX

Bibliography and General Works (1–250)
Art (251–950)
Folklore (951–1500)
History (1501–4500)
Language (4501–5000)
Literature (5001–7000)
Music (7001–7500)
Philosophy (7501–8000)

AUTHOR INDEX

Bibliography and General Works (1–250)
Art (251–950)
Folklore (951–1500)
History (1501–4500)
Language (4501–5000)
Literature (5001–7000)
Music (7001–7500)
Philosophy (7501–8000)